PSYCHOLOGY
A First Encounter

CONSULTANTS

Vito Modigliani, Simon Fraser University (Chapters 2, 5, and 9)
Christine J. Storm, Mount Allison University (Chapters 2, 9, and 10)
Barry L. Beyerstein, Simon Fraser University (Chapters 3 and 7)
William Turnbull, Simon Fraser University (Chapters 6 and 11)
Jocelyn Calvert, Open Learning Institute, Vancouver, British Columbia (Chapter 7)
Helen Boritch, University of Western Ontario (Chapter 8)
Janet N. Strayer, Simon Fraser University (Chapter 10)
Sheldon Ksionzky, City of Los Angeles Personnel Department (Chapter 12)
Marilyn L. Bowman, Simon Fraser University (Chapters 13 and 14)

PSYCHOLOGY
A First Encounter

Dennis Krebs
Simon Fraser University

Roger Blackman
Simon Fraser University

HBJ Harcourt Brace Jovanovich, Publishers

San Diego   New York   Chicago   Austin   Washington, D.C.
London   Sydney   Tokyo   Toronto

To Danielle and Lamour; Pam, Christopher, and Nicholas—
who had to share us with this endeavor for the past five years.

PREFACE

Our goal in writing this book was to provide the most engaging, unambiguous, and highly integrated introduction to psychology available today. As there is no shortage of psychology textbooks, we set ourselves an ambitious task. How well we have succeeded will be determined by psychology instructors who compare this work with others and by psychology students who evaluate what they learn from it. Although instructors and students must set their own criteria for making these judgments, we outline here the standards we set for ourselves and the methods we employed to meet them.

Teaching methodology should follow from philosophy of education. We are no different from most teachers in believing that knowledge is the fundamental currency of education. However, true knowledge is elusive: it is difficult to acquire and even more difficult to convey. In our view, the responsibility of teachers of psychology—and a central objective of textbooks—extends beyond the presentation of factual information to the obligation of encouraging students to question the information they receive by stimulating critical thinking. In turn, the responsibility of students extends beyond passive memorization of factual information. To acquire a real understanding of psychology, students must challenge and question the information presented to them. In this sense, a proper introduction to psychology stimulates an *encounter* between the student and the field.

This book is for students committed to understanding the fundamentals of psychology. If commitment is expected, commitment should be given in return. Before writing each chapter, we asked students what they hoped to learn—what questions they brought to the field. Whenever possible, we started from these questions, disclosing honestly how far the discipline has come.

For example, many students wonder whether intelligence and mental disorder are inherited. In the text, we invite the reader to accompany us on a brief journey through the history of thinking on the topic (beginning with the early research of Charles Darwin's cousin, Francis Galton). We describe the tools of the trade, the methods psychologists employ to probe beyond common sense (in this case, studies of twins, research on brain function, and so forth); we acknowledge the limitations of such methods (biases in intelligence tests, problems diagnosing mental disorders, the shared environment of twins, and the like); and we summarize the results of research, showing how they support or fail to support competing conclusions. True, we indicate which conclusion seems most reasonable to us (intelligence and mental disorder result from an interaction between inherited dispositions and various kinds of experience), but we actively discourage passive acceptance of pat answers. Rather, we encourage active and ongoing consideration of relevant evidence and exploration of its implications. Psychology is a rapidly changing field: today's "facts" may become tomorrow's misconceptions.

The central challenges in writing this text were to capure the significance of theory and research in psychology without oversimplifying it and stripping away its vitality, and to guide students through the rich array of topics in the field without boring, overwhelming, or losing them. Few, if any, psychologists have a thorough and contemporary command of every aspect of psychology; certainly, we frequently sought advice and information from specialists in particular areas of the discipline. Specifically, ten colleagues—all expert in their areas—have made important contributions to the text (see the list of consultants preceding this Preface). Integrating their input with our work took longer than anticipated; a project we believed would require two years stretched over half a decade. Yet, we are convinced the final product demonstrates the value of this tactic: the textbook combines coherence of breadth with uniformity of depth.

This text differs from others in several important ways. First, as a comparison of references should verify, it contains more information: we explore most topics in greater depth than the typical introductory text, and we are more up-to-date. The obvious danger in an in-depth approach is that students will feel overwhelmed by argument and become buried in detail. However, oversimplifications are usually more difficult to understand and less interesting than more detailed discussions: they make less sense and their significance is unclear. We took the time we believed necessary to guide our readers through the history and logic of crucial issues, emphasizing important implications and trusting that their significance would make the journey exciting. We also resisted the temptation to color the discipline black and white. Where there are competing claims on the truth, as there are in most areas of psychology, we did not select a winner and banish the rest. Instead, we analyzed the competition and provided readers with the means to evaluate their own decision. This means entrusting readers with the responsibility

for critically appraising arguments—an exercise we believe fosters understanding.

Second, the text is divided into fewer chapters than most. There are two reasons for this: to maintain the continuity of major discussions that explore essential crossroads and intersections, and to construct units that fit the weekly needs of the typical semester-length course offered by most colleges and universities. Because the assignment of material to specific chapters is always somewhat arbitrary, the sequence we recommend is not absolute. All chapters have clearly delineated sections and most divide quite neatly in half (for example: Brain and Behavior, Memory and Thinking, Motivation and Emotion, Physical and Cognitive Development). Thus, instructors may be selective in the assignment of sections, omitting those that do not fit with their course design.

Third, consistent with the continuity within chapters, the text is highly integrated. Although psychology is a diverse field, there are many intersections among its areas. We integrate many such intersecting areas by viewing them from multiple theoretical perspectives. For example, in the opening chapter we view the field of psychology in *historical* perspective—a perspective employed throughout the text to understand the growth of ideas in other areas. In Chapter 1 we also introduce the evolutionary, cognitive-developmental, social learning, psychoanalytic, and humanistic perspectives, applying them, when appropriate, to subject matter throughout the remaining chapters.

Although we emphasize the evolutionary and cognitive-developmental perspectives more than other texts do, we give all theoretical approaches their due—for each has its domain of competence. *Evolutionary theory* offers ways of thinking about such ultimate questions as "Why are humans among the most social of all species?" and "Why do humans reproduce sexually instead of asexually?" *Cognitive-developmental theory* outlines the growth of rational thought. *Social learning theory* explains how social behavior is shaped by the influence of others. *Psychoanalysis* offers insights about the irrational aspects of our nature. The *humanistic approach* provides insights about our nobler side. Theoretical perspectives are valuable tools: They enable us to view things from different angles, tie them together in systematic ways, and examine new issues with greater sophistication.

Fourth, the text features many learning aids. Every chapter contains several boxes on interesting issues on the periphery of mainstream areas and in-depth examinations of critical topics. For example, Chapter 1 contains a box on the profession of psychology; Chapter 2 has a box on teaching language to apes; Chapter 3 includes a box on the effect of drugs on the brain and behavior; Chapter 4 features a box on ESP, telepathy, and other paranormal phenomena; Chapter 10 presents a box on moral development from a feminine perspective; and Chapter 12 has a box on self-actualization.

Because we believe that many ideas are most clearly conveyed graphically, textual material is well-illustrated with figures and tables. Two functions of tables are to integrate ideas and to compare and contrast positions. For example, in Chapter 1 we compare and contrast the five basic research methods used by psychologists, and in Chapter 10 we compare the four theoretical perspectives on attachment, play, sex-typing, and moral development. Key terms are **boldface** in the text, listed at the end of each chapter, and defined in the Glossary at the end of the book. Each chapter contains a list of recommended readings to guide those who wish to pursue a particular topic.

Ancillaries include: Study Guide, Instructor's Manual, and Test Book (available in printed and computerized formats).

Special Acknowledgments

We are especially grateful to: Kathy Denton and Pam Blackman, who saw us through the ups and downs of authorship and helped us with countless aspects of the task; our children, Danielle and Lamour Krebs and Christopher and Nicholas Blackman, who sometimes were helpful (and sometimes were not); university staff members Marietta Hay and Anita Turner, whose calmness and competence balanced our lack of same; colleagues and students such as Terry Creighton, Chuck Crawford, Marianne Schroeder, Carla Zaskow, and Ross Powell, who helped us when we stumbled off the path; the team at Harcourt Brace Jovanovich — Marcus Boggs (acquisitions editor), Robert C. Miller (manuscript editor), Dean N. Reed and Cheryl Solheid (designers), Karen E. Lenardi (production editor), Rebecca Lytle (art editor), Eleanor Garner (permissions editor), Sharon Weldy (production manager) and all the others — whose thoroughgoing professionalism and unrelenting good humor made this text possible.

Reviewers

We are also grateful to the following reviewers for their sound appraisals and helpful suggestions: Mary Kay Biaggio, Indiana State University; Rex Bierley, University of North Dakota; Jay Braun, Arizona State University; Thomas S. Brown, University of Health Sciences-Chicago Medical School; William Buskist, Auburn University; Arnold Buss, University of Texas at Austin; Roger D. Jennings, Portland State University; Michael Levine, University of Illinois at Chicago; Roger N. Moss, California State University-Northridge; Robert Ochsman, University of Arkansas at Little Rock; Steven Prentice-Dunn, University of Alabama; Paul G. Shinkman, University of North Carolina; Sandra M. Singer, University of Southern Indiana; and Jean Volckmann, Pasadena City College.

Dennis Krebs
Roger Blackman

CONTENTS

3
BRAIN AND BEHAVIOR / 96

6
MEMORY AND THINKING / 246

7
MOTIVATION AND EMOTION / 296

8
HUMAN SEXUALITY / 348

9

PHYSICAL AND COGNITIVE DEVELOPMENT / 412

10

SOCIAL DEVELOPMENT / 468

11

SOCIAL PSYCHOLOGY / 522

12

PERSONALITY, INTELLIGENCE, AND PSYCHOLOGICAL TESTS / 584

13

ABNORMAL PSYCHOLOGY / 656

14

THE TREATMENT OF
PSYCHOLOGICAL
DISORDERS / 728

PSYCHOLOGY
A First Encounter

1

Ψ

THE FIELD OF PSYCHOLOGY

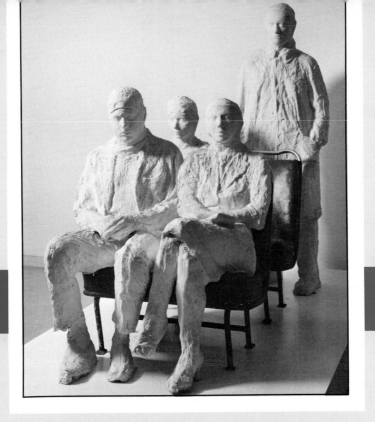

During 1976 and 1977, a brutal killer terrorized the people of New York. Calling himself "Son of Sam," David Berkowitz shot six people to death and seriously injured seven others. Son of Sam appeared to select his victims at random. He wrote taunting poems with rhymes such as

> AND HUGE DROPS OF LEAD
> POURED DOWN UPON HER HEAD
> UNTIL SHE WAS DEAD.
>   YET, THE CATS STILL CAME OUT
> AT NIGHT TO MATE
>   AND THE SPARROWS STILL
> SING IN THE MORNING.

When he was finally captured, Berkowitz, a postal clerk, was arming himself for a mass murder at a discotheque. Asked why he had murdered innocent people, he said that he had been commanded to do so by a 6,000-year-old man who communicated to him through a dog owned by his neighbor, Sam Carr. When first brought to court, Berkowitz pleaded not guilty to charges of murder by reason of insanity.

On February 4, 1974, the 19-year-old granddaughter of newspaper magnate William Randolph Hearst was carried kicking and screaming from her apartment by several members of a small group of radicals who called themselves the Symbionese Liberation Army. They held Patty Hearst as a "prisoner of war" in a small, dark closet, indoctrinating her with their radical political views. Within a short time, Patty sent a shocking statement to the press in which she claimed that she had renounced her parents, her friends, and the American political system, changed her name to "Tania," and joined the Symbionese Liberation Army. Most people doubted the sincerity of Patty Hearst's statement until she was recorded on a security camera participating in a bank robbery with her captors. She eluded the FBI for some 20 months but was finally caught and convicted of armed robbery. Supporters of Patty Hearst claimed that she had been brainwashed.

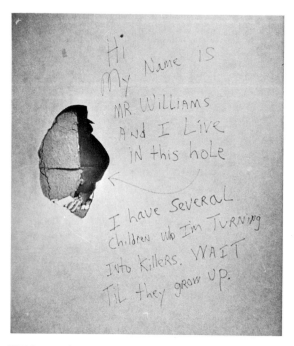

Writing on the wall of the apartment occupied by David Berkowitz, the "Son of Sam" killer

"Tania" (Patty Hearst) in front of a Symbionese Liberation Army insignia

THE SCOPE OF PSYCHOLOGY

The behavior of David Berkowitz and Patty Hearst raises interesting questions about human nature. Did Berkowitz really think he was being commanded by a 6,000-year-old man? Was he insane, or was he feigning insanity in an attempt to escape a charge of first-degree murder? Was Patty Hearst actually brainwashed? What is insanity? What is brainwashing? Many people turn to the field of psychology expecting to learn how to answer such questions.

The Depth of Psychology

The field of psychology is a natural place to search for answers to questions about human nature, but there are limits to the answers that can be found. In this text, for example, we describe the techniques that psychologists use to assess personality and to diagnose mental disorders, but these techniques are far from perfect. Berkowitz would probably be diagnosed as a schizophrenic, but the symptoms of schizophrenia overlap with the symptoms of many other mental disorders. Psychologists have not yet discovered what causes schizophrenia; they do not know whether it is one disorder or many. Indeed, there are at least two dozen competing theories of schizophrenia.

Similarly, the results of research on group pressure, attitude change, techniques of persuasion, conformity, intense states of arousal, self-perception, social development, and other social and emotional phenomena (examined in Chapters 10 and 11) can help explain what happened to Patty Hearst. But they will not supply a complete explanation. The information contained in psychology is valuable for those who seek to improve their understanding of themselves and others, but it must be sifted, processed, digested, integrated, and applied before it can supply useable insights into complex human behaviors.

An introduction to the field of psychology is, in certain respects, like making a new acquaintance. Typically, we form preliminary impressions of people; then, as we get to know them better, we revise and refine these impressions. Not infrequently, we discover that our first impressions were overly simple and inexact. The same is true of psychology. When students initially approach the field — and, indeed, when psychologists initially attack a problem — their questions are often simple and the answers seem within grasp. However, as they become familiar with the field, they acquire an increasing appreciation for its complexity and depth (see Box 1-1).

The Breadth of Psychology

Although the field of psychology is often unable to supply final answers to common questions about human nature, it encompasses a much broader range of topics than most people expect. Although psychology is most often associated with understanding abnormal behavior and the behavior of people in their everyday lives, the field contains many other areas (as examples, the areas concerned with basic aspects of human nature such as seeing, hearing, touching, perceiving, feeling, and thinking). Figure 1-1 depicts the many branches of psychology.

Many people, when they first approach psychology, are motivated to acquire knowledge that will enable them to help troubled people and to understand themselves. Research on such matters as how people perceive visual displays, how neural impulses are transmitted in the brain, and how rats learn to press a bar for food seem irrelevant to their concerns. Many students take courses in the basic areas of psychology only because they are required to do so, yet often they acquire a great deal of valuable information. Assume, for example, that your goal is to understand mental disorders. As we show in Chapter 13, many theories of disorder are based on fundamental principles of sensation, perception, learning, and motivation; some of the most interesting insights into mental disorders to date have arisen from research on the physiology of the brain.

Psychology: A Definition

Examining the diverse array of areas in psychology, you might wonder how to characterize the

Box 1-1

Changing Assumptions About the Nature of Knowledge

In a study that spanned almost a decade, William Perry, Jr., Director of the Bureau of Study Counsel at Harvard University, and his associates interviewed a sample of students at several points during their college careers. They found that first-year students typically view events in *right – good* versus *wrong – bad* terms. Young students tend to believe that their task is to learn the right answers to academic questions and that the task of teachers (and textbooks) is to convey these answers. To such students, right answers mean concrete facts. In the words of one student, "Theory might be good for the teachers, but . . . the facts are what's there. And I think . . . that should be the main thing" (Perry, 1968, p. 67).

As they got older, most of the students interviewed by Perry and his colleagues underwent a significant change. Rather than assuming that there is one, ultimate, correct answer to significant questions, they began to examine issues from a variety of points of view. As one student put it, "You find yourself thinking in complex terms: weighing more than one factor in trying to develop your own opinion. . . . Somehow what I think about things now seems to be more — ah, it's hard to say right or wrong . . . but it seems [pause] more sensible" (p. 100).

According to Perry and his associates, most students ultimately develop a sense of commitment to their best ideas, even though they recognize that these ideas are not the only or last word. One student said

> You never decide . . . on one . . . set answer. . . you add and detract as you go along. You never really make a single decision as to what is best and what is worst . . . [but] you can't hang in the air, leave your answer suspended all the time. You've got to make some sort of decision, but this decision isn't final" (p. 146 – 47).

The following partial list of positions describes the main assumptions held by the college students Perry interviewed. As the students became older, they typically displayed attitudes consistent with the higher-numbered positions.

Position 1   The student's views of the world tend to be polarized along such lines as *we – other, right – wrong, good – bad,* and so on. The student believes that there are right answers for everything, that Authority knows these answers, and that it is Authority's job to teach them.

Position 3   The student accepts uncertainty as a realistic but temporary possibility in areas in which Authority hasn't found the answers yet.

Position 4   The student accepts that uncertainty (and, therefore, diversity of opinion) is actually widespread and decides that everyone has a right to their own opinion.

Position 6   The student realizes the necessity of finding a place in a world of uncertainty through some form of personal commitment (which is not the same as the unquestioned commitment to a single belief in Authority).

Position 7   The student makes an initial commitment in some area.

Position 9   The student realizes that commitment is an ongoing, unfolding activity.

field as a whole. Psychology has been defined in many ways over the years. At its inception, it tended to be defined as the study of the *mind*. One of the founders of psychology, William James (1890), wrote that "Psychology is the Science of Mental Life, both of its phenomena and of their conditions. . . . The phenomena are such things as we call feelings, desires, cognitions, reasoning, decisions, and the like." Later, psychology was defined as the study of *behavior*. John B. Watson (1919) insisted that "psychology is that division of natural science which takes human behavior—the doings and sayings, both learned and unlearned—as its subject matter."

The emphasis on behavior has tended to prevail. Most texts define psychology as the sci-entific study of behavior. However, in these defi-nitions, behavior is broadly defined. For exam-ple, Clark and Miller (1970) define behavior as "processes that are observable, such as gestures, speech, and physiological changes, and processes that can only be inferred such as thoughts and dreams."

Psychology is the scientific study of the mind and of behavior. It is also the study of the body and the emotions: the study of thoughts, perceptions, feelings, sensations, motivations, and actions. The field of psychology is as large, dynamic, and diverse as its central subject matter —people.

It is informative to view psychology as a branch on the tree of knowledge. We can see

FIGURE 1-1
The Branches of Psychology

separate branches on a tree and therefore easily discern their distinctiveness, but all of the branches are an integral part of the tree, each contributing to the growth of other branches and to the growth of the tree as a whole. That is the relationship between psychology and such other disciplines as biology, zoology, chemistry, anthropology, and sociology. Although psychology is a distinct discipline, it is an integral part of the tree of knowledge. As such, it contributes to the ideas that are the lifeblood of other fields of study and benefits from their products. As we shall see, many major psychological theories were developed by scholars from other fields. Most psychologists make no attempt to fence out other disciplines, feeling that the more that psychology can draw from related disciplines, the more useful a crop of knowledge it will produce.

PSYCHOLOGY IN HISTORICAL PERSPECTIVE

"Who knows only his own generation remains always a child," wrote Cicero. One way to enhance our understanding of events is to trace their origins — to discover what led up to them and how they changed as they developed. Let us view the discipline of psychology in historical context. When did psychology originate? What was it like in the beginning? How has it changed over the years? The answers to these questions depend, of course, on what we mean by psychology. If we mean knowledge about people, then the field of psychology has existed from the time people began to achieve insights about themselves. If we mean a branch of knowledge, however, then the origin of psychology is typically marked at the time that it became a formally recognized scientific discipline.

There is disagreement among historians about when psychology emerged as an independent science, but it generally is accepted that the formal science of psychology began sometime between 1860 and 1879. The first experimental laboratory for studying psychological phenomena was established in Leipzig, Germany, sometime between 1875 and 1879. Its founder, who is commonly considered to be the father of psychology, was Wilhelm Wundt (1832–1920). William James (1842–1910), one of the first American psychologists, also established a small laboratory at Harvard University in 1875. Although the exact date on which psychology became a formal science is not known, the relative youth of the discipline stands in marked contrast to many other disciplines. The first person to hold an eminent university position in psychology was one of Wundt's students, James McKeen Cattell, who died in 1944. Interestingly, more than 90% of all the psychologists who ever existed are believed to be alive today.

By and large, this late-developing branch of knowledge — psychology — is an outgrowth of 3 major disciplines: philosophy, physics, and physiology. Early psychologists tended to pursue philosophical questions, using methods borrowed from physics. The first individuals to call themselves "psychologists," Wundt and James, were trained as physicians but held positions in philosophy at their respective universities. In its early years, psychology also was influenced by the biological ideas of Charles Darwin and by research in physiology.

The issue that captured the attention of the first psychologists involved the relationship between events in the real world and people's "psychological" experiences of them. The major event that set the stage for the development of the science of psychology was the publication of *Elements of Psychophysics* (1860) by physicist Gustav Theodor Fechner (1801–1887). Fechner created a formula, now called **Fechner's Law,** to outline the relationship between physical qualities and psychological events. The formula indicates that such psychological experiences as the perceptions of tallness, heaviness, or loudness increase with the logarithm of the height, weight, or volume of the objects that produce them. Fechner's early work was significant because, in demonstrating that psychological experiences such as heaviness and loudness could be measured reliably and objectively, it paved the way for the founding of psychology as an experimental science.

As is often true of new sciences, several competing schools of thought developed in psychology during the early years. These schools reflected the views held by prominent figures in the discipline. We will briefly examine each of these early schools and the main issues on which they differed.

Structuralism

The first school of thought in psychology, **structuralism,** was headed by Wilhelm Wundt. As far as Wundt was concerned, structuralism was not a school—it *was* psychology. Edward Bradford Titchener (1867–1927), an Englishman who studied at Oxford and Leipzig, was Wundt's most distinguished and devoted student. Titchener, who established a laboratory at Cornell University, brought structuralism to the United States.

Wilhelm Wundt

The goal of structuralism was to discover the most basic elements of people's immediate conscious mental experiences in much the same way that chemists were discovering the basic elements of physical matter. Structuralists employed the method of **introspection**—training people to reflect on and to analyze their own mental experiences. It became centrally important to structuralists to distinguish between the elements of people's mental experiences and the physical stimuli that cause them. If you look at the sky, what do you see? If you say "the sky," you are committing

what Titchener called the "stimulus error" (describing a psychological experience in terms of the external physical stimulus that gave rise to it). Your psychological experience might be "vast blueness" or "depressing gray." Structuralists believed that such mental experiences should be the basis of psychological study.

Although all of this may hardly seem like psychology to you, it is interesting to speculate about the conclusions that structuralists reached concerning the elements of the mind. Titchener identified three main types of mental elements: *sensations,* such as sounds and smells that originate from external stimuli; *images,* such as those in our memories; and *affections* or *feelings,* such as pain and pleasure. In *An Outline of Psychology* (1896), Titchener supplied a list of the elements of sensation that contained over 44,000 qualities! As the distinguished psychological historian E. G. Boring noted, "As against the 64 then known elements of chemistry, the mind seemed pretty well provided for" (Boring, 1942, p. 10).

Today, structuralism is mainly of historical interest. The school more or less died with Titchener in 1927. Although you may hear the word "structuralism" today in reference to the theories of such scholars as Jean Piaget, Lawrence Kohlberg, and Claude Levi-Strauss, the modern term refers to a theoretical orientation quite different from that of Wundt and Titchener. In fact, the theories of these modern "structuralists" are closer to those of the early school of thought that became the main opponent of structuralism— **functionalism.**

Functionalism

In his attempt to establish the superiority of structuralism, Titchener published a paper in 1890 in which he contrasted the structural and functional views. According to Harrison (1963, p. 395), "What Titchener was attacking was in fact nameless until he named it; hence he . . . did more than anyone else to get the term functionalism into psychological currency." Functionalism was more a way of thinking than a clearly articulated school. It was primarily concerned with the functions or processes of the mind, rather than with its structure.

The principles of functionalism owed a great deal to the ideas of Charles Darwin (1809 – 1882). To quote one historian, ''American psychology owes its form and substance as much to the influence of evolutionary theory as to any other idea or individual'' (Schultz, 1987, p. 109). We consider Darwin's theory of evolution in Chapter 2, and we explore its application in many other chapters of this text.

In the early years of psychology, the ideas of Darwin influenced this new branch of science in three major ways:

1. They suggested that humans are related to other animals and therefore that insights about human functioning and behavior could be obtained by studying nonhuman animals.

2. They emphasized that humans (and other organisms) adapt to their environment, which suggested to psychologists that adaptation might also help to account for the nature of mental events.

3. They stressed that there is a good deal of variation among individuals of the same species, which laid the groundwork for the study of individual differences in psychology.

The contributions of Sir Francis Galton on the differences in the mental capacities of individuals and the inheritance of intelligence (especially as outlined in his book *Hereditary Genius,* 1869) were strongly influenced by the work of his cousin, Darwin.

It has been suggested that William James was the first functionalist. Although opposed to

William James

Wundt's structuralism, James was not motivated to assume leadership of any school. In fact, functionalism became most clearly defined as a school under the influence of James Rowland Angell (1869 – 1949) from the University of Chicago. In 1906, Angell became the fifteenth president of the American Psychological Association and, in his presidential address, supplied the first clear statement of the main themes of functionalism. Allowing that functionalism was ''little more than a point of view, a program, an ambition,'' Angell set forth its three main themes:

1. Functionalism is not concerned with determining the elements of conscious experience (sensations, images, affections); rather it is concerned with studying how the mind works.

2. The most general function of the mind is to mediate between the external events that occur in the environment and the internal events that people experience. A major goal of psychology is to determine how and why various mental operations help people adapt to their environment.

3. Functionalism is concerned with the relationship between mind and body.

If structuralism reflected the rigor and precision of life in Germany during the early part of the twentieth century, then functionalism reflected the early American spirit of progress, accomplishment, and purpose. Functionalism was dynamic and practical, and based on the study of how things change, adapt, and survive. In contrast to structuralism, functionalism related to both human and nonhuman animals, and was ideally suited to the investigation of real-life events. As a result, it set the stage for applications of psychological knowledge to such fields as psychiatry, education, and industry.

Behaviorism

Functionalism was a bridge to the most influential of all early schools of psychology — **behaviorism.** Although some of the experimental findings on which the school of behaviorism was built were published in the late nineteenth and early twentieth centuries (in particular, Ivan Pavlov's discovery of **conditioned reflexes** in 1902 and

E. L. Thorndike's **law of effect** in 1911; see Chapter 5), behaviorism did not emerge as a major school of thought until 1913 with the publication of John B. Watson's (1878–1958) article "Psychology as the Behaviorist Views It."

The keynote of behaviorism was objectivity. Watson sought to make psychology an objective branch of the natural sciences. He argued forcefully against the structuralist viewpoint, which he believed was unscientific in both content and method. In his view, a true science cannot study things such as "consciousness," "mind," and "image" because they are not observable phenomena. Zoologists don't ask animals what is on their minds. To Watson, introspection was not a suitable method of scientific study. (Observations based on introspection cannot be verified, and no scientist can observe the contents of his or her own mind and report objectively on the results.) Watson believed that the only legitimate object of psychological study was observable behavior. In his view, the task of psychology was to discover the laws that govern the relationship between events in the environment that impinge on people (stimuli) and their reactions to the events (responses).

Watson placed tremendous emphasis on the role of learning in shaping people's behavior. This is reflected in his most widely quoted statement:

> Give me a dozen healthy infants, well-formed, and my own specified world to bring them up in and I'll guarantee to take any one at random and train him to become any type of specialist I might select — doctor, lawyer, artist, merchant-chief, and, yes, even beggarman and thief, regardless of his talents, penchants, tendencies, abilities, vocations, and race of his ancestors. (1930, p. 104)

It is clear from Watson's statement that he took an extreme stand on one of the oldest controversies in psychology — heredity versus environment, or nature versus nurture (see Chapter 2).

The central goal of behaviorism was to foster the *prediction* and *control of behavior*. This largely entailed discovering the laws of learning, which, according to behaviorists, were the laws that explained the connection between observable stimuli and observable responses. Behaviorists sought to start with the most elementary connections between stimulus and response and,

after these elementary relationships were understood, to go on to explore the ways in which they were combined into more complex connections. The use of nonhuman animals for research seemed ideal for this purpose, since animals such as rats operate on a relatively simple and predictable level. As Watson explained, "I never wanted to use human subjects. I didn't like the shabby, artificial instructions given to subjects. With animals, I was at home. I was keeping close to biology with my feet on the ground" (Watson, 1936, p. 276). (Interestingly, both Watson and E. L. Thorndike had to conduct research on animals in the basement of the home of their advisor, William James, because Harvard did not wish to encourage the presence of odorous animals in its hallowed halls.)

John B. Watson

Like structuralists, behaviorists assumed that they could explain complex sequences of behavior in terms of combinations of smaller elements. However, unlike structuralists, behaviorists defined these elements in terms of observable behaviors rather than subjective internal experiences. Like functionalists, behaviorists believed in the relatedness of humans and nonhumans, the value of applying psychology to real-life problems (the value of controlling behavior), and the importance of adaptation in explanations of human functioning. However, while functionalists attended to the influence of both heredity and environment in adaptation, behaviorists focused almost exclusively on the effect of the environment in adaptation.

Behaviorism caught on in America with a

fervor unmatched by any other school of psychological thought. A review of Watson's book *Behaviorism* in the *New York Times* (August 2, 1925) went so far as to suggest that "it marks an epoch in the intellectual history of man." The *New York Herald Tribune* speculated that it might be "the most important book ever written." The behavioristic emphasis on the role of the environment supplied a scientific basis for the assumption that all people were free from the shackles of instinct and were masters of their own fates. What better underpinning for the "rags to riches" story so characteristic in America; anyone — no matter how lowly born — could become president! Within a few years after the publication of Watson's book, most textbooks were defining psychology as the science that seeks to predict and control behavior — a definition that prevails in many psychology texts today. According to one analyst, the impact of behaviorism in America was so great that "virtually every American psychologist, whether he knows it or not, is now a methodological behaviorist" (Bergmann, 1956, p. 270).

Although most psychologists would not go quite as far as Bergmann, the influence of behaviorism on contemporary psychology cannot be denied. Its most ardent modern advocate is B. F. Skinner, whose ideas we consider in Chapter 5 on learning. The author of one book on the history of psychology (Schultz, 1987) asserts that "B. F. Skinner has become the most important and influential individual in psychology today" (p. 243). Again, not everyone would agree with this assessment; for example, one study shows that the works of seven other scholars were cited more frequently in psychological studies published in 1975 than the works of Skinner (see Table 1-1). However, Skinner's ideas clearly have had tremendous impact. Consistent with the traditional value that behaviorists attach to the practical applications of their research, Skinner has long advocated the transformation of society through a "technology of behavior," which is based on his belief that all significant behaviors can be controlled through the efficient use of rewards and punishments. In 1948, Skinner published *Walden Two,* a novel of a fictional utopian community based on his principles of learning. Another book, *Beyond Freedom and Dignity* (1971) outlines the more philosophical implications of Skinner's position.

Gestalt Psychology

Like functionalists and behaviorists, psychologists associated with **Gestalt psychology** opposed structuralism. However, as interest in structuralism waned, behaviorists and Gestalt theorists began to direct their attacks at one another.

Gestalt psychology was founded by Max Wertheimer (1880–1943) and two of his students, Kurt Koffka (1886–1941) and Wolfgang

TABLE 1-1

The 15 Social Scientists Most Frequently Cited by Psychologists in 1975

Scholar	Citations*
S. Freud	1,426
J. Piaget	1,071
B. J. Winer (book on statistics)	749
A. Bandura	650
H. J. Eysenck	537
D. T. Campbell	515
E. Goffman	514
B. F. Skinner	501
E. H. Erikson	494
S. Siegel (book on statistics)	466
R. B. Cattell	428
J. P. Guilford	392
C. R. Rogers	387
J. B. Rotter	386
A. H. Maslow	367

* Number of times the 15 most-cited social scientists were referenced in the social science literature in 1975.
Source: Adapted from Endler, N. S., Rushton, J. P., & Roediger, H. L., III. (1978). Productivity and scholarly impact (citations) of British, Canadian, and U.S. departments of psychology (1975). *American Psychologist,* Table 2, p. 1064.

B. F. Skinner

Köhler (1887–1967), who were subjects in Wertheimer's early experiments. Wertheimer, Koffka, and Köhler all earned their academic degrees in Germany, but each eventually came to America. Wertheimer, a close friend of Albert Einstein, taught at the New School for Social Re-

Gestalt Psychologists

Max Wertheimer

Kurt Koffka

Wolfgang Köhler

search in New York; Koffka, at Smith College; and Köhler, first at Harvard and then at Swarthmore.

Gestalt psychologists disagreed with the idea espoused by both structuralists and behaviorists that complex forms of behavior are composed of combinations of more simple forms — an idea Gestalt psychologists called the "bricks-and-mortar" approach. By contrast, the defining doctrine of Gestalt psychology was "the whole is more than the sum of its parts." The German word *Gestalt,* which lent the school its name, means, roughly translated, configuration, form, structure, or pattern. Gestalt theorists looked at the organized whole of the behavior rather than at its more elementary components.

One way to obtain a sense of the difference between viewing experience as the sum of individual elements and viewing it as an overall pattern is to consider a piece of music. Does a musical composition consist simply of the sum of the particular notes that comprise it, or does the pattern or organization of notes determine its nature? Gestalt psychologists would argue for the latter view. They would insist that even if you changed all of the individual notes in a symphony by changing its key, the essential nature of the piece would remain the same.

Much of the often bitter controversy between structuralism and Gestalt psychology centered around explanations of perception. Later, as behaviorists began to attack Gestalt theorists, the controversy shifted to laws of learning. Köhler, who studied a colony of chimpanzees on Tenerife in the Canary Islands during World War I, attempted to disprove the behaviorist assumption that learning develops one step at a time. Köhler showed that chimpanzees learn by insight, which involves viewing the elements of a problem as a pattern, organized whole, or *Gestalt* (Chapter 6).

In the final accounting, the ideas of the Gestalt theorists have had the greatest impact on the areas of perception and thinking (see Chapters 4 and 6). Compared to the ideas of behaviorists, however, they have exerted little influence on the field of learning. Interestingly, the Gestalt school has also had a relatively major impact on social psychology — primarily through the work of another German immigrant, Kurt Lewin (1890–1947), who viewed the behavior of individuals and the behavior of groups as a function of the whole situation. Lewin organized the first sensitivity training groups (T-groups) at the National Training Laboratories in Bethel, Maine, laying the foundation for what was to become the sensitivity-training and encounter-group movements.

Psychoanalysis

The *psychoanalytic* school of psychology was founded by an Austrian physician who spent most of his life in Vienna. As far as international renown is concerned, he became the most famous of all psychologists. Even today his works are referred to more frequently than those of any other psychologist (see Table 1-1). We speak, of course, of the founder of **psychoanalysis,** Sigmund Freud (1856–1939).

To many people, psychology is nearly equivalent to psychoanalysis. All this business of quantifying mental experiences and figuring out how animals learn seems irrelevant to understanding human nature. For this reason, it is somewhat misleading to call psychoanalysis a "school" of psychology. Psychoanalysis had little in common with the other schools; it developed independently and was concerned with entirely different issues. Whereas structuralism, functionalism, behaviorism, and Gestalt psychology focused on conscious experience or observable behavior in normal organisms, psychoanalysis concentrated on the study of unconscious mental processes and abnormal behavior. Whereas the other schools emphasized the importance of experimental research, psychoanalysis mainly employed the case-study approach and

Sigmund Freud

was much more theoretical in nature than the traditional schools of psychology.

During the last half of the nineteenth century, there were two competing views on the causes of what we now call mental disorders. The prevailing view attributed mental disorders to physical causes, particularly to abnormalities in the brain. The opposing view, entertained by a minority of physicians, held that they were caused by psychological factors. Late in the nineteenth century, a number of physicians (Sigmund Freud among them) began to employ **hypnosis**—a psychological treatment that induces an altered state of consciousness—as a means of curing the disorder they called **hysteria.** (Hysteria involves physical symptoms such as paralysis that were believed to stem from psychological problems; see Chapter 13.) It is interesting to note that although the form Freud's research took was quite different from that of members of the early schools of psychology, he too was interested in the general issue of the relationship between physical and mental experiences.

Freud found that when some of his patients were under the influence of hypnosis, they were able to recall traumatic, early-childhood events that they could not remember when they were in a normal state. Typically, these events were sexual in nature. Freud's first book, written with another physician, Josef Breuer (1842–1925), and published in 1895, was called *Studies on Hysteria.* Together with a number of theoretical chapters, it contained five case studies. The most influential was that of "Anna O," an attractive young woman who was being treated by Breuer for hysteria. ("Anna O's" real name was Bertha Pappenheim. She later became a noted Jewish feminist who founded the Federation of Jewish Women and helped establish educational seminaries for young women.) In one instance, Breuer reported that Anna could not bring herself to drink water. Under hypnosis, she remembered that during her childhood she had felt extreme disgust on seeing a dog she disliked drink water from a glass. After recounting the incident, she felt relieved and was able to drink water. On the basis of such observations, Freud made two profound inferences. The first was that the mind consists of conscious and unconscious components and that the unconscious exerts a powerful influence on behavior; this inference became the

Abraham Maslow

cornerstone of his theory of personality. The second was that the act of remembering repressed events and desires has therapeutic effects; this inference became the cornerstone of **psychoanalytic psychotherapy.**

As Freud's theory evolved, he abandoned hypnosis as a means of delving into the unconscious in favor of the technique of **free association** (saying whatever comes to mind), the interpretation of ''slips of the tongue'' (which have come to be called ''Freudian slips''), and the analysis of dreams (in which Freud believed that unconscious memories and urges reveal themselves in disguised forms). By the time that Freud died in 1939, he had written more than 30 volumes and his theory, which was treated with disdain in its early years, had begun to have profound influence on psychology, psychiatry, and other social sciences (especially sociology and anthropology), as well as on philosophy, religion, art, and literature.

Although the ideas of the behaviorists Watson and Skinner have greatly affected the direction of modern experimental psychology, Freud's theory has succeeded more than any other in capturing the popular imagination and in influencing other branches of intellectual endeavor. Freud's greatness was recognized by E. G. Boring, author of the classic history of psychology. In the 1929 edition of *The History of Experimental Psychol-*

ogy, Boring laments that psychology has not produced as great a figure as Charles Darwin. In the second edition of his book in 1950, however, Boring characterizes Freud as ''the greatest originator of all.'' We discuss Freud's theory of psychosexual development in Chapter 10, his psychoanalytic theory of personality in Chapter 12, and psychoanalytic therapy in Chapter 14.

Humanistic Psychology

Until the 1950s, psychoanalysis and behaviorism constituted the major theories in psychology. During the 1950s, however, a revolt of sorts against these dominant viewpoints was generated by two sources: **humanistic psychology** and **cognitive–developmental theory.** Calling themselves the ''third force'' in psychology, humanistic psychologists objected to the model of humans that is intrinsic to the behavioristic and psychoanalytic perspectives. Humanistic psychologists characterized behaviorism as mechanistic, dehumanizing, superficial, and empty; they viewed psychoanalysis as overly concerned with abnormal behavior, pessimistic, and base. A noted humanistic psychologist, Abraham Maslow (1908–1970) allowed that the study of ''stunted, immature, and unhealthy specimens'' could yield only a stunted and unhealthy psychology (Maslow, 1954, p. 234).

The "third force" in psychology consists of a rather diverse array of ideas and attitudes. One statement, authored by Bugental (1967), identifies six points of difference between humanistic psychology and the traditional behavioristic orientation:

1. Adequate understanding of human nature cannot be based exclusively (or even in large part) on research findings from animal studies. Again, man is not "a larger white rat," and a psychology based on animal data obviously excludes distinctly human processes and experience.

2. The research topics chosen for investigation must be meaningful in terms of human existence and not selected solely on the basis of their suitability for laboratory investigation and quantification. Currently, topics not amenable to experimental treatment tend to be ignored.

3. Primary attention should be focused on man's subjective, internal experiences, not on elements of overt behavior. This is not to suggest that overt behavior be discarded as a subject of study, but rather that it should not be the only subject of investigation.

4. The continuing mutual influence of the so-called pure psychology and applied psychology should be recognized. The attempt to sharply divorce them is detrimental to both.

5. Psychology should be concerned with the unique, individual case instead of the average performance of groups. The current group emphasis ignores the atypical, the exception, the person who deviates from the average.

6. Psychology should seek "that which may expand or enrich man's experience." (Bugental, 1967, p. 9)

Philosophical and often antiexperimental in orientation, humanistic psychologists have decried the inhuman ways in which they believe individuals have come to be treated in western society—as cogs in the industrial wheel, as pawns in games played by giant bureaucracies, as statistics and numbers. They view modern people as alienated, alone, oppressed, and conforming. As antidotes to these problems, humanists encourage openness, honesty between people, self-disclosure, and authenticity. According to the humanistic view, the ultimate responsibility of every individual is the pursuit of **self-actualization**—the attempt to achieve one's full potential. We consider the humanistic theory of motivation developed by Abraham Maslow in Chapter 7 and the humanistic theory of personality developed by Carl Rogers in Chapter 12. We also describe humanistic forms of psychotherapy in Chapter 14.

Although it is embraced by many psychologists who work with troubled people and by some theorists, the humanistic school of psychology has been criticized by some experimentally oriented researchers. In an invited address to the 81st Annual Convention of the American Psychological Association in 1973, Canadian psychologist D. O. Hebb suggested that humanistic psychology "confuses two very different ways of knowing," which could be called scientific and philosophical. According to Hebb, scientific psychology "has little to tell us about how to live wisely and well." Science proceeds slowly, attacking problems that can be solved with existing methods. Hebb argues that the problems addressed by humanistic psychology are broad and philosophical in nature and, as such, fall outside the science of psychology.

Cognitive–Developmental Theory

The second assault on the dominance of behaviorism and psychoanalysis originated in the ideas of Swiss child psychologist Jean Piaget (1896–1980). Although Piaget began publishing in the late 1920s, his ideas did not become popular in North America until almost half a century later. In a way, Piaget's cognitive–developmental theory is similar in the history of its development to Freud's psychoanalysis. Although Piaget was familiar with the work of Gestalt and behavioristic theorists, he developed his theory quite independently from mainstream psychology. And although Piaget's theory supplies competing explanations for many of the events explained by the Gestalt view of perception and the behavioristic view of learning, it is mainly concerned with quite different issues. As the name implies, cognitive–developmental theory is concerned with the *growth* of *thinking*. The main method Piaget used to study the origin of knowledge was to observe children, especially his own, in their natural environments, from birth through their childhood years. Piaget came to believe that children's knowledge about the world develops in a number of distinct stages, and he spent more than 50 years attempting to discover how these stages of development are structured.

For many years, North American psychologists made little of Piaget's work. Indeed, the lack of control in Piaget's methods of observation, his disdain for statistics, and his tendency to study his own children seemed quite unscientific to many experimental psychologists. Piaget's theory caught on during the 1950s, however, and at present it is one of the major theoretical approaches in psychology. Piaget published more than 30 books and was active in the field until his death in 1980 at age 84. We consider Piaget's theory in detail in Chapter 9, and we consider the cognitive–developmental approach to social development in Chapter 10.

The subject matter, goals, and research methods of the early schools of psychology are summarized in Table 1-2.

Jean Piaget

TABLE 1-2

Summary of the Seven Early Schools of Psychology

School	Subject Matter	Goals	Research Methods
Structuralism	Immediate conscious experience	To discover the basic elements of immediate conscious experience and the laws governing their connections	Introspection
Functionalism	Function of mental processes; ways in which the mind works	To determine the ways in which mental processes help people adapt to their environments	Objective measures, informal observation, and correlational studies
Behaviorism	Behavior and the principles of learning	To predict and control behavior	Objective measures of behavior; formal experiments
Gestalt Psychology	Patterns of experience, with emphases on perception, memory, and thinking	To understand patterns of conscious experience as wholes	Subjective reports, behavioral measures; demonstrations
Psychoanalysis	Unconscious mind and abnormal behavior	To develop a theory of personality that explains unconscious motives and abnormal behavior	Case studies
Humanism	Human experience	To foster psychological growth and self-actualization	Theoretical in orientation; case studies
Cognitive-Developmental Theory	Structure of knowledge	To describe and explain the development of knowledge in children	Observations of children, interviews, and experiments

PSYCHOLOGY TODAY

If you asked a sample of present-day psychologists to which school of psychology they subscribe, most would be puzzled by the question. Few contemporary psychologists identify with schools. Although there are still psychologists who call themselves behaviorists, psychoanalysts, cognitive developmentalists, humanists, and so on, most psychologists are *eclectic*—taking what they consider to be the best from all approaches.

In an important sense, psychology outgrew its early schools; it became too big to be encompassed by a handful of theoretical orientations. The growth of membership in the major professional organization of psychologists, the American Psychological Association (APA), supplies a good index of the growth of the field (see Figure 1-2). When the APA was founded in 1892, it contained only 31 charter members (including such dignitaries as William James, James Mark Baldwin, and James McKeen Cattell). By 1985 the number had mushroomed to over 60,000. The dramatic growth in the number of psychologists has led some observers to remark that if the

present trend were to continue at the projected rate, there would eventually be more psychologists than people in the world!

Most psychologists identify more with an area of specialization than with a theoretical approach. If you ask a psychologist what kind of psychologist he or she is, you are much more likely to be told a clinical psychologist, a developmental psychologist, a social psychologist, or a physiological psychologist than a psychoanalyst, a behaviorist, or a humanist. The major fields of specialization of contemporary psychologists are outlined in Figure 1-3. Let us briefly consider the nature of these fields in roughly the order in which we discuss them in this text.

Evolution, Heredity, and Environment

Human beings are the product of millions of years of evolution. Although the theory of evolution is commonly considered the province of biology, it supplies a valuable perspective on human na-

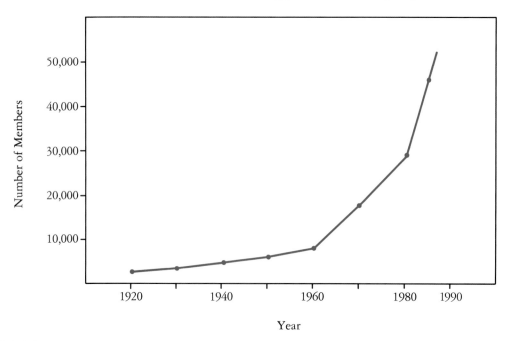

FIGURE 1-2
Growth in Membership of the American Psychological Association (1930–1985)
Source: American Psychological Association, 1985.

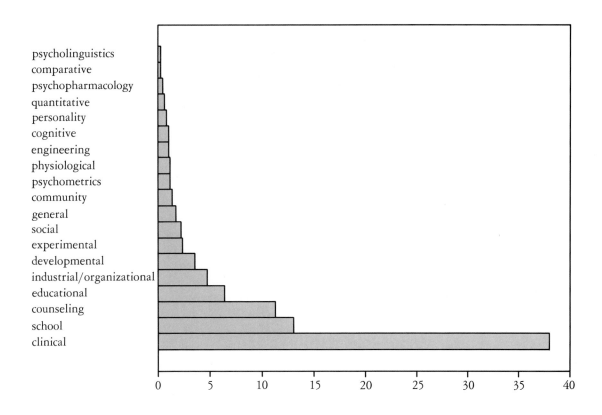

Percent of Psychologists in Specialization

FIGURE 1-3

Contemporary Areas of Specialization in Psychology *Source:* After Stapp, J., Tucker, A. M., & VandenBos, G. R. (1985). Census of psychological personnel: 1983. *American Psychologist, 40,* 1317–51.

ture. Humans are unique among species in their ability to profit from experience; however, they are still primates and, as such, share many of the characteristics or other primates. Indeed, the degree or amount of DNA shared by humans and chimpanzees is over 99%.

William James made frequent reference to Darwin in his classic work *Principles of Psychology.* During the past decade, revisions in Darwin's theory of evolution have sparked the development of a new field of inquiry called **sociobiology** — the study of the biological evolution of social behavior. Some psychologists affiliate themselves with this specialization. Among the topics studied by sociobiologically oriented psychologists are the evolution of helping behavior and altruism, morality, parent–child relations, relations among peers, human sexuality, and sex differences in behavior.

The process of evolution gives rise to inher-ited dispositions possessed to a greater or lesser degree by all members of a species. Early functionalists such as Galton were interested in inherited characteristics, but they were mainly interested in the role of heredity in producing differences between people, especially differences in intelligence. The study of individual differences is called **differential psychology.**

We have seen that behaviorists attribute virtually all of the variation in the way people behave to differences in their experiences. One of the classic controversies in psychology relates to the relative influence of heredity and environment (nature and nurture) on various human characteristics. In Chapter 2, we examine the evolution of the human species and the role of heredity in human behavior. In addition, we examine the ways in which nature and nurture interact to produce such characteristics as intelligence, language, and sex-role identity.

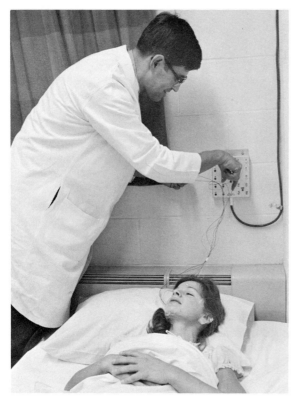

A psychologist conducting research on the brain
Source: Sleep Disorders Center, Dartmouth Medical School. Hanover, NH.

Brain and Behavior

One of the primary specializations within experimental psychology used to be known as **physiological psychology** but is now more popularly called *brain and behavior*. Although psychologists typically do not study the brain for its own sake (that is the job of physiologists and neurologists), one could hardly hope to understand mental experiences, emotional reactions, and human behavior without understanding how the brain works.

The main parts of the brain and their functions are described in Chapter 3, but the focus of our concern is how brain activity affects psychological experiences. Some of the interesting questions we address in this chapter are: What happens when a brain is stimulated electrically or chemically? In what ways does the human brain compare to and differ from the brains of other animals, and what is the significance of these similarities and differences for an understanding of human nature? What happens to the brains of humans and other animals who are deprived of adequate nutrition and experiences when they are young? Do individuals who grow up in enriched environments develop larger brains than those who do not? How are memories stored? What happens to the electrical activity in the brain when people sleep, dream, meditate, or undergo hypnosis?

Sensation and Perception

In Chapter 4 we describe the structure of our sensory systems, especially the eye and ear, and we outline how they work. However, as with the discussion of the brain, the focus of our attention lies in the psychological experiences of sensation and perception. As was true of early structuralists and Gestalt psychologists, experimental psychologists who study sensation and perception attempt to explain the contents of consciousness. However, their methods differ in that they discard the questionable method of introspection in favor of more objective ways of inferring what is going on in people's minds.

The basic goal of researchers in this field is to explain how physical stimuli, such as light waves, are transformed into psychological experiences such as the perception of an image. In the common-sense view of the average person, the eye is much like a camera — it simply snaps pictures of the external world. This view is limited, however, as a comparison of the following two sets of stimuli shows:

(a) 13579
(b) ßCDEF

Although the first two characters in each series are identical, they are perceived as a pair of numbers in the first instance and as a single letter in the second. This example shows that perception involves much more than taking snapshots of objects in the environment; it involves the active interpretation of the output of the sensory systems. This interpretation is remarkably accurate but not perfectly reliable, as impossible figures like the ones shown in Figure 1-4 demonstrate.

Learning

For decades, largely due to the influence of behaviorism, the dominant concern in psychology was

The Trident

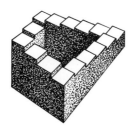

The never-ending staircase

FIGURE 1-4

Two Impossible Figures   *Source:* Penrose, L. S., & Penrose, R. (1958). Impossible objects: A special type of visual illusion. *British Journal of Psychology, 49,* 31–33 (The Trident only).

to discover the laws of learning.   In the same way that the brain and the central nervous system form the core of our physical being, learning lies at the core of our psychological nature.   Humans are unique among species in their capacity to learn and in the extent to which learning shapes their behavior.

Psychologists interested in learning attempt to discover the basic laws that govern how our behavior changes with experience (see Chapter 5).   Many psychologists believe that these laws are essentially the same for human and nonhuman animals, and they conduct experiments on cats, rats, pigeons, and even worms.   If you have ever attempted to train a dog, you have engaged in the type of activity characteristic of many learning researchers.   (Incidentally, do you think an animal would learn better if you gave it a reward every time it performed a trick or only some of the times?   The answer in Chapter 5 may surprise you.)

Motivation and Emotion

What causes you to feel hungry?   Is it because your stomach is empty?   Although the amount of food in your stomach may affect how hungry you feel, it is by no means the only factor.   Psychological researchers have found that people differ in their tendency to feel hungry when their stomachs are empty.   Some people eat only when their stomachs are empty and stop eating when they are full.   Other people tend to eat whenever appealing food is placed in front of them.   What might cause this difference?   Whatever your answer, we should point out that exactly the same phenomena have been found in rats!   Obese rats eat when tempted by appealing food; normal rats eat when their stomachs are empty.

In Chapter 7 we discuss basic physiological needs such as hunger and thirst and other, more purely psychological needs such as those for achievement and self-actualization.   A similar range is found in our treatment of emotion.   We consider the role of the brain and the nervous system in mediating emotions and, in addition, we consider the relationship between thoughts and feelings and the effect of emotional experiences on our social behavior.   In view of the significance of sex to so many aspects of human behavior, we devote an entire chapter to this special motive and its accompanying emotional states.

Cognitive Psychology

Psychologists engaged in **cognitive psychology** study thought processes: how people remember and forget things, how they reason, and how they solve problems.   During the heyday of behaviorism, relatively little research was conducted on mental processes.   The mind was treated as a black box, and theorists focused almost exclusively on the relation between inputs to the box (stimuli) and outputs from it (responses).   Some 35 years ago, cognitive psychologists peeked into the box and have been enthusiastically exploring its contents ever since.

We review the work of cognitive psychologists in several chapters of this text.   At the end of Chapter 5, we present evidence that learning is better viewed as an internal change in mental processes than as a change in overt behavior.   Particularly interesting is the research of early Gestalt psychologist Wolfgang Köhler on insight in chimpanzees.   Chapter 6 is devoted to a discussion of memory, reasoning, problem solving, and creativity.   How many types of memory do you think you have? The evidence suggests that humans possess at least two quite different systems for remembering. Can you improve your memory? The answer to this question is a clear yes, if you use the right strategy. We examine these strategies, as well as strategies for improving your ability to solve problems, in Chapter 6.

Piaget and other psychologists have investigated the ways in which infants acquire knowledge about the world and the ways in which that knowledge develops from infancy to adulthood. Closely associated with the development of thought is the development of language. As we demonstrate in Chapter 9, the common-sense view that children acquire language by copying adults and being corrected is, at best, only partially correct. Careful studies of the way in which children learn to talk reveal that their language is not a simple reflection of the language of their parents. Do you hear many parents say "She goed home"? Then why do so many children talk that way?

Developmental Psychology

Psychologists who specialize in the study of children used to be called *child psychologists,* but over the past decade, they have come to be referred to as *developmental psychologists.* The change in name is significant. Studying how individuals change from birth to death is significantly different from simply studying children. Individuals engaged in **developmental psychology** investigate the same sorts of phenomena that other psychologists study—but from a different perspective. While evolutionary psychologists attend to the evolution of characteristics in species over millions of years, developmental psychologists attend to the growth of characteristics in individuals during their lifetimes. This is a valuable perspective because the end products of adulthood are often extremely complex; observing the development of individuals from more simple forms places them in a more understandable context.

We devote two chapters to topics of special interest to developmental psychologists, and we view issues from a developmental perspective in many other chapters of the text. In Chapter 9 we describe the main strands in physical, perceptual, and cognitive development from birth to matu-

rity. In Chapter 10 we describe the main strands of social development, focusing on such questions as: How do infants and nonhuman animals form emotional bonds with their parents and other members of their species? What are the most effective ways of raising children? How do children develop a sense of morality? How do children learn to behave in ways appropriate to their gender?

Social Psychology

People influence other people in a variety of ways. Some ways are direct and very obvious; others are quite subtle. In Chapter 11 we describe several types of social influence, ranging from the most subtle (the effect of the mere presence of others) to the most blatant (obedience to authority). In one study, for example, social psychologist Stanley Milgram found that he could induce most people to deliver what they believed to be dangerous electric shocks to an innocent victim simply by insisting that they follow his instructions. In addition, we discuss two types of social cognition—*attitudes* and *attributions.* The study of attribution focuses on the ways in which people make inferences about the causes of other people's behavior. An important question in the study of attribution relates to how well the average person plays the role of social scientist—someone who seeks to explain the causes of social behavior.

Personality and Assessment

The area in psychology dealing with *personality* is covered by two quite different types of psychologist: psychologists who have developed grand, overriding theories of personality (or, more exactly, theories of human nature) and psychologists who are interested primarily in the measurement of individual differences.

Although philosophers as far back as the Golden Age of Greece speculated about the development of personality and the distinction between different types of people, it was not until the advent of Freud's grand theory of psychoanalysis that the creation of psychological theories of personality began in earnest. In addition to psychoanalytic and neopsychoanalytic theories, there are at least three other types of theory: humanistic theories, learning theories, and cognitive theories. Each theory focuses on the aspects of human nature that it deems most significant. For example, psychoanalytic theories focus on sexual and aggressive instincts, humanistic theories focus on the capacity for self-actualization, learning theories focus on learning experiences, and cognitive theories focus on the role of thinking. We evaluate the major theories of personality and attempt to identify the strengths and limitations of each in Chapter 12.

In part, the instruments developed by psychologists to assess aspects of personality are derived from their general, theoretical orientations. You have probably heard of the inkblot test (see Figure 1-5), designed by Hermann Rorschach in the late 1920s. A psychoanalyist might use this test to assess unconscious processes, but a learning theorist would be more likely to employ a behavior rating scale (see Chapter 12). Similarly, cognitive personality theorists employ tests that measure the ways in which people think about themselves and others. Many psychological tests are atheoretical, however; they have been developed to assess such important attributes of people as extroversion, anxiety, and intelligence.

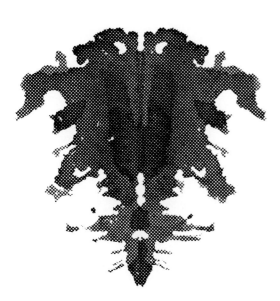

FIGURE 1-5
A Rorschach Inkblot

Abnormal Psychology

Since the beginning of recorded history, some individuals have behaved in ways that others consider abnormal. Incidents of abnormal behavior and, indeed, the very nature of abnormality have been explained in different ways during different eras. In the eighteenth century, individuals we would now consider insane were treated as if they were criminals. In the nineteenth century, with the advent of modern medicine, the afflictions of such people were attributed to medical problems. Perhaps the single greatest contribution of psychoanalysis was to stimulate a revision of the medical model of mental illness. Freud argued strongly that a great deal of abnormal behavior originates from psychological, not physical, sources.

In Chapter 13 we consider three main issues: (1) the nature and definition of abnormal behavior and psychological disorder, (2) the description and classification of various disorders, and (3) the causes of psychopathology. The American Psychiatric Association has prepared a classification of mental disorders to aid clinicians in diagnosing various forms of abnormal behavior. But even with the use of such aids, psychiatric diagnosis is, at best, an imperfect enterprise. The type of distinction that medical doctors are able to make between such physical maladies as the measles and chickenpox simply cannot be made between most psychological disorders — suggesting, among other things, that it may be inappropriate to view some psychological disorders as mental "illnesses."

The key that ultimately will unlock the mysteries of mental disorders lies in the discovery of their causes. The evidence suggests that most psychological disorders are caused by a complex combination of factors — some mental, some emotional, and some physical. Researchers from a variety of fields are working diligently to discover the causes of various disorders.

Psychotherapy

The stereotype of psychotherapy portrays a patient lying on a couch recounting his or her dreams to a bearded psychoanalyst. In actuality, however, relatively few psychologists engaged in psychotherapy are psychoanalysts. Many psychotherapists affiliate themselves with theoretical

BOX 1-2
THE PROFESSION OF PSYCHOLOGY

Imagine that you meet a woman and learn that she is a psychologist. Knowing her profession in itself will not tell you what she does for a living. She might treat troubled people in the privacy of her office; she might work at an industrial plant, attempting to determine how satisfied various employees are with their jobs; she might conduct experiments on the brains of rats at a research institute; or she might teach at a university or college. Psychologists perform a wide range of services; however, some are more common than others.

Many people think that psychologists are private practitioners who work in their own offices and treat people with psychological problems. But if you have to guess where a randomly picked psychologist works, don't guess that the person administers psychotherapy in a private office. Guess that the person works in an educational setting. Only about 16% of the members of the American Psychological Association surveyed by Joy Stapp and Robert Fulcher in 1983 were employed in private practice, whereas about 43% were employed in schools, colleges, and universities. However, you would be making a fairly

educated guess if you said that a psychologist was a psychotherapist. Many psychologists who work in hospitals and clinics administer psychotherapy, and hospitals and clinics are the second most prevalent job setting for psychologists —with about 25% of the psychologists surveyed finding employment in this setting (see illustration).

Where psychologists work gives only a general idea of what they do. Psychologists do three main things: 1. Conduct research on psychological issues, 2. Teach psychology, 3. Apply the findings of psychological research to practical problems. Many psychologists engage in all three activities; some, in two; and some, almost exclusively in one. A brief examination of the main jobs held by psychologists exemplifies the services they perform.

Many students assume that the only job of a *university professor* is to teach. This is an understandable assumption; teaching is often the only task that a student sees a professor perform. Although teaching psychology is the major part of the job of the typical psychologist who works at most two-year colleges, it is only about one-third of the job of the

average psychologist who works at most four-year colleges and universities. Someone has to generate the ideas, conduct the research, and publish the information that constitutes the growing body of knowledge that we call psychology. The average university professor is expected to devote from one-third to one-half of his or her time conducting research, writing articles and books, giving professional talks, and engaging in other scholarly activities. Because psychology is a relatively new and rapidly growing discipline, at the same time that psychologists are teaching what is already known (or what is believed), they and others are refining the old ideas, casting out some, and introducing others.

Psychologists who work in the psychology departments of universities and colleges typically have Ph.D. degrees and specialize in particular areas of research. Psychologists who work in the education departments of universities and colleges typically possess Ed.D. degrees. **Educational psychologists,** as they are called, conduct basic research on learning, develop new methods of teaching and assessing learning, train teachers, construct educational tests, and design educational programs.

School psychologists work in elementary and high schools. They usually do not teach or conduct research; rather, they spend their time testing and counseling students on academic, vocational, and personal matters. They give students tests to determine their intellectual potential, areas of strength and weakness, and possible emotional difficulties, and they counsel students with learning disabilities and other psychological problems. School psychologists also consult with teachers, often helping them set up special programs to deal with such problems as low morale, excessive aggressiveness, and drug abuse.

Counseling psychologists work in schools and universities. In addition, many psychologists with degrees in counseling psychology work in other settings, such as rehabilitation centers, where they administer psychological tests, give vocational guidance, and counsel people with minor personal problems. For example, a counseling psychologist might work with a student who has a study block or who feels socially isolated.

More psychologists obtain a degree in clinical psychology than in any other area. (This statistic is not inconsistent with the assertion that most psychologists work at universities, because many **clinical psychologists** hold university positions.) Almost 30% of all psychologists hold Ph.D.s in clinical psychology, and an additional 10% hold degrees in counseling and guidance. Of the psychologists who receive degrees in clinical psychology, approximately 25% work in *applied* settings — especially in hospitals and clinics.

Clinical psychologists often are confused with three other types of therapist: counseling psychologists, psychiatrists, and psychoanalysts. Clinical psychologists have degrees in psychology. They specialize in the assessment of psychological disorders, the diagnosis of psychopathology, and the treatment of psychological problems. They typically work for a year in an institutional setting before receiving their degrees. Counseling psychologists typically have degrees in education. **Psychiatrists** are medical doctors with M.D. degrees who have completed residency programs in the diagnosis and treatment of mental disorders. Psychiatrists may conduct physical examinations of patients and prescribe drugs; clinical psychologists may not.

Although many psychiatrists subscribe to Freud's psychoanalytic theory of abnormal behavior, the term **psychoanalyst** applies only to those who have been trained in a psychoanalytic institute and who themselves have been psychoanalyzed. In most parts of the United States, only physicians are permitted to become practicing psychoanalysts. In Canada, Europe, and some states, however, any suitable, well-educated person can apply for analytic "lay" training and eventually become a fully accredited psychoanalyst. Freud's daughter Anna is a famous example of an exceptional psychoanalyst who did not have an M.D. degree.

Industrial psychologists are to industry what school psychologists are to schools. As a general goal, industrial psychologists attempt to maximize the job satisfaction and productivity of workers. They test workers to determine their areas of interest and their strengths and weaknesses, counsel individual workers, and set up special training programs. In addition, many industrial psychologists consult with personnel managers concerning the qualities that identify successful job applicants and conduct organization-wide efficiency analyses.

Two specialized areas within industrial psychology involve quite different types of tasks. Psychologists in

Continued on p. 26

consumer research design questionnaires and surveys to assess consumers' attitudes toward products, pretest various sales devices, and may also help design advertisements. Psychologists who specialize in *engineering psychology* are concerned with maximizing the efficiency and safety of relationships between people and machines. Typically this involves testing the effect of variations in parts of, for example, automobiles, airplanes, or spacecraft. The color of a dial, the type of lettering on a set of instructions, and the shape of an instrument may affect the efficiency of their use and, in some cases, save lives.

Environmental psychology is concerned with the effect of the environment on people. **Environmental psychologists** work on such problems as pollution, overpopulation and crowding, the control of cancer-producing agents, the effective use of energy, and the design of buildings. It is becoming more and more apparent that small differences in the arrangement of a room, the color of an office, the location of a door, and the amount of space available can have profound effects on people's emotional state and social behavior.

Community psychologists work with community organizations to help prevent mental-health problems and to supply treatment for psychological disorders. They may, for example, develop programs to minimize family violence, poverty, unemployment, and prejudice. Community psychologists generally believe that it is better to work with troubled people in the community than to lock them up in institutions.

The American Psychological Association has published a book (1976) on career opportunities. The author describes opportunities for employment, techniques for enhancing the chances of obtaining a job, and a number of nontraditional areas to which psychologists have begun to contribute. As Woods points out, psychologists are employed in a wide range of nontraditional settings, including research organizations, private consulting firms, architectural companies, religious institutions, drug and alcohol rehabilitation programs, military establishments, law-enforcement agencies, recreational institutions, judicial systems, and correctional facilities. In addition to the jobs we have considered, psychologists may program computers, develop birth-control programs, help television channels prepare programming, edit textbooks, work at day-care centers, or conduct research on drugs for pharmacological firms. Just as people are complex and multifaceted, so too is the profession of psychology.

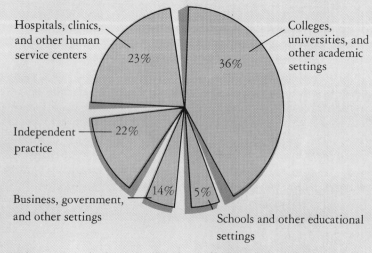

Hospitals, clinics, and other human service centers **23%**

Independent practice **22%**

Business, government, and other settings **14%**

5% Schools and other educational settings

Colleges, universities, and other academic settings **36%**

Where Psychologists Work: Full-time Employment Settings of American Ph.D.s in Psychology (1983) *Source:* Adapted from Stapp, J., Tucker, A. M., & VandenBos, G. R. (1985). Census of psychological personnel: 1983. *American Psychologist, 40,* 1317–51.

Freud's couch

approaches other than psychoanalysis and employ other types of psychotherapy; most are eclectic, drawing from the insights and techiques of all major theories and types of therapy. Indeed, in the treatment of some disorders, *clinical psychologists* may not even attempt psychotherapy. They may refer a patient for a physical form

of treatment, such as electroconvulsive shock therapy, psychosurgery, or drugs. (Clinical psychologists are not qualified to give these forms of treatment themselves; psychiatrists are.)

We describe the major types of physical and psychological treatment in Chapter 14. In addition, we explore a difficult question: How well do the treatments work? In the 1950s, psychologist Hans Eysenck reviewed the evidence on the effectiveness of the major types of psychotherapy and concluded that troubled individuals who do not receive psychotherapy improve as much as those who do (without the financial hardship). Eysenck's analysis has been severely attacked. More recent and thorough reviews have reached more favorable conclusions. However, even in these reviews some serious questions are raised about the effectiveness of some kinds of psychotherapy. How would you determine whether or not psychotherapy works? Like so many other psychological issues, what might appear on first glance to be a fairly straightforward matter proves on examination to be exceedingly complex.

THE SCIENCE OF PSYCHOLOGY AND THE PSYCHOLOGY OF COMMON SENSE

It has been said that all people consider themselves to be psychologists. Certainly we all accumulate a vast store of psychological information in our day-to-day lives, develop ideas about human nature, and test these ideas against our own experience. The term we use for knowledge acquired in this way is *common sense*. Before we consider the science of psychology, it is appropriate to address the question: What does psychology offer that cannot be acquired through common sense?

In some cases, experiments in psychology produce the same conclusions that people reach using common sense. "The average person can think up twice as many ideas when working with a group than when working alone," concluded psychologist Alexander Osborn in a study conducted in 1957. But doesn't everybody know that "two heads are better than one"? In 1969 William

Berkowitz found that, other things being equal, the attractiveness of people to each other depends on their similarity. That sounds like another way of saying, "birds of a feather flock together." So why study psychology? Or, perhaps more pointedly, why invest taxpayers' money in psychological research (see Box 1-3)?

It shouldn't be surprising to discover that some results of psychological research are matters of common sense. After all, both types of conclusion stem from a common goal—to understand people. Furthermore, many psychologists (particularly social psychologists) study "everyday" behavior—the same behavior that supplies the basis of common-sense conclusions. However, as demonstrated in Box 1-4 (page 30), the results of psychological research often differ from common-sense. Psychology and common sense differ in at least three ways:

Box 1-3
Social Science—Mistrusted and Misunderstood

During the 1970s, Senator William Proxmire, in his capacity as chairman of the Senate committee that oversees the National Science Foundation (NSF), began issuing "Golden Fleece" awards. These awards were intended to draw attention to certain grants awarded by NSF that represented, in Senator Proxmire's words, "outrageous wastes" of the taxpayers' money. For example, a March 1975 award went to a project proposed by Ellen Berscheid of the University of Minnesota. Senator Proxmire characterized this grant in a press release:

The biggest waste has to be $84,000 to find out why or how or if or how long people fall in love. I object to this because no one—not even the NSF—can argue that falling in love is a science: not only because I'm sure that even if they spend $84

million or $84 billion they won't get an answer that anyone would believe. I'm against it because I don't want the answer.

In an essay on anti-intellectualism and social science, Shaffer (1977, p. 821) notes two reasons for Senator Proxmire's objection to the study. The first is disagreement between intellectuals and the public over the value of knowledge. Senator Proxmire does not want the answer, Shaffer writes, because "love is better celebrated than studied, and ignorance is bliss because the mysteriousness of the process of falling in love adds to one's appreciation." The second reason is the public's misunderstanding of the nature of knowledge. In stating that falling in love is not a science, Senator Proxmire dismisses the basic assumption held by social scientists that behavior

obeys certain laws and that these laws can be revealed by scientific research.

Berscheid has provided a spirited defense of the research proposed in her grant application (Berscheid and Walster, 1978) and others have risen to the defense of social scientists. For example, in 1975 *New York Times* columnist James Reston wrote: "If the sociologists and psychologists can get even a suggestion of the answer to our patterns of romantic love, marriage, disillusion, divorce—and the children left behind—it could be the best investment of federal money since the Louisiana Purchase." But social scientists should take warning. If they are not to be mistrusted and misunderstood, they must make a greater effort to inform the public of the value and nature of scientific knowledge about behavior.

1. Common-sense accounts of behavior typically are based on casual observation; psychological researchers employ more carefully controlled and systematic methods when collecting evidence.
2. Psychological researchers are usually more cautious in drawing conclusions about the causes of behavior than people who employ only common sense.
3. Common-sense accounts of behavior generally are cast in language that is effi-

cient but imprecise; psychological research is described in much more exact terms.

Let us examine these points of contrast in more detail.

Collecting Evidence: Casual versus Systematic Approaches

One way in which the average person is handicapped in his or her role as psychologist is related to the tools of the trade. Most people do not possess the tests and instruments necessary to measure such characteristics as brain waves, intelligence, unconscious urges, moral development, attitudes, or personality traits. In addition, even when appropriate measures are available, many people do not have the opportunity to make the controlled, repeated, and systematic observations that are the essence of psychological research.

Presumably, the proverb "two heads are better than one" developed because team effort often works better than individual performance. However, there are situations in which the opposite holds true; then it is said that "too many cooks spoil the broth." Like common sense, psychological research often produces contradictory findings. For example, six years after Osborn (1957) reported that "the average person can think up twice as many ideas when working with a group than when working alone," another group of researchers reached essentially the opposite conclusion: "Four persons attacking a problem individually and pooling their efforts will, on the average, produce about 30 percent more ideas than if they attempted to solve the problem in a group session" (Dunnett, Campbell, and Jaastad, 1963).

Whereas contradictory principles may exist side by side in the minds of the average person, contradictory results constitute a challenge to psychological researchers and serve as an impetus for further research. Subsequent research on this particular issue, summarized by Davis, Laughlin, and Komorita (1976), has established some of the conditions under which "two heads are better than one" and some of the conditions under which "too many cooks spoil the broth." The systematic collection of evidence under controlled conditions allows psychologists to go beyond the single-factor explanations exemplified by proverbs to develop and test theories that recognize the complexity of human behavior.

The Weight of the Evidence

Confirmation versus Proof Some people believe that young children need their mothers at home and, therefore, that mothers with jobs that take them away from home are more likely than mothers without such jobs to have poorly behaved children. Suppose that a psychologist carries out a careful survey of children of mothers in the labor force and finds that they are more poorly behaved than the children of mothers who do not work away from home. You may accept this evidence as *proof* that young children need their mothers at home (especially if you already hold this view). But a psychologist would (or should) be more cautious and claim only confirmation. The distinction between proof and confirmation is subtle but important. **Proof** establishes a proposition as correct or true; a mathematical theorem can be proved. Confirmation is weaker than proof. **Confirmation** of a prediction in psychological research means only that the evidence is *consistent with* the prediction; a confirmed prediction is probably—but not certainly—correct.

Predictions are often derived from theories. For example, the prediction regarding the behavior of the children of mothers in the labor force might be derived from a theory containing the assumption that children whose mothers are not at home to care for them will develop behavior problems. As with the confirmation of predictions, the fact that the evidence supports a theory does not guarantee that the theory is correct. Suppose that the group of mothers who are in the labor force in our example contained more single parents than the group of mothers who are not in this category. In that case, the results of the survey would also support a theory containing the assumption that children with single parents are more poorly behaved than children with two parents. Thus, even though a prediction may be confirmed, the theory that led to the prediction may be incorrect. It is possible to be right for the wrong reason. One of the hallmarks of sound research is the use of procedures that permit not only the confirmation of predictions (and therefore of the theories from which they were derived) but also the disconfirmation of alternative explanations.

Positive versus Negative Evidence Researchers are also more cautious than common-sense decision makers in the weight they give to positive versus negative evidence. Most of us have heard arguments about issues such as

Box 1-4
PSYCHOLOGICAL KNOWLEDGE AND COMMON SENSE

Once you know the answer to a question, it may seem like a common-sense conclusion. But would you think the conclusion obvious if you didn't know it in advance? Vaughan (1977) gave students in her introductory psychology courses at the University of Pittsburgh a true–false quiz during the first class. Here are some of the questions on Vaughan's test; supply your own answers before reading further.

___ 1. Biologists study the body; psychologists study the mind.

___ 2. The best way to ensure that a desired behavior will persist after training is completed is to reward the behavior every single time it occurs (rather than intermittently) throughout training.

___ 3. The more highly motivated you are, the better you will do at solving a complex problem.

___ 4. Memory can be likened to a storage chest in the brain into which we deposit material and from which we can withdraw it later if needed. Occasionally, something gets lost from the "chest," and then we say we have forgotten it.

___ 5. The basis of a baby's love for its mother is the fact that the mother fulfills the baby's physiological needs for food, and so forth.

___ 6. Children's IQ scores have very little relationship to how well they do in school.

___ 7. A schizophrenic is someone with a split personality.

___ 8. Psychiatrists are defined as medical people who use psychoanalysis.

___ 9. To change people's behavior toward members of ethnic minority groups, we must first change their attitudes.

If you think that the best

---

whether women are worse drivers than men. Those who believe that women are worse drivers seem to require only a slim diet of examples of poor female driving (positive evidence) to nourish their belief. At the same time, they are likely to ignore or discount negative evidence (good female driving or poor male driving). Although most of us realize that a single positive example is insufficient evidence, there seems to be a natural tendency for people to emphasize positive rather than negative results.

In psychological research, on the other hand, negative evidence actually is regarded as more powerful than positive evidence. The reason is that if careful research disconfirms a prediction, then the theory that generated that prediction must also be incorrect. But if careful research confirms a prediction, psychologists cannot claim with certainty that the theory from which the prediction is derived is correct. They can say only that there is an increased probability that the theory is correct.

The Language of Science: Efficiency versus Precision

There are over 20 different dictionary definitions of the term "anxiety." When the word is used in conversation, how do you know what is meant? The same question can be asked about such concepts as mental illness and intelligence. Recall the conclusion reached by Dunnett and his co-workers (1963) on individual versus group prob-

answer to each question is "true," you are wrong, but you are in good company. Most of Vaughan's students did also. In fact, over 80% of these students thought that questions 4, 5, and 9 were true. However, psychological research has indicated that the best answer to each of these questions is "false." A full discussion of why the statements are not true is provided in the relevant chapters of this text. Briefly, the reasons are as follows:

1. Psychologists study the body and the mind, especially as they interact with one another and produce observable behavior (Chapter 1).

2. It is well-established that behaviors that are partially reinforced are more resistant to extinction than behaviors that are continually reinforced (Chapter 5).

3. People are most efficient at solving problems when they are moderately aroused and least efficient when either unaroused or extremely aroused (Chapter 7).

4. People actively construct and reconstruct the information that they store in memory, and forgetting often involves a failure in retrieval (Chapter 6).

5. Infants (and animals) become attached to caretakers who satisfy emotional needs, such as the need for security and "contact comfort" (Chapter 10).

6. IQ scores have a significantly positive correlation with academic performance in children (Chapter 12).

7. Split personality refers to the dissociative disorder called *multiple personality.* Schizophrenia refers to a severe thought disorder involving loss of contact with reality (Chapter 13).

8. Psychiatrists are medical doctors who specialize in treating psychological disorders. Most psychiatrists draw from many forms of treatment, including psychoanalysis (Chapter 14 and Box 1-2).

9. Social psychologists have found that inducing people to change their behavior toward members of minority groups causes them to change their attitudes toward them, but that direct attempts to change peoples' attitudes generally are not very successful (Chapter 11).

lem solving, and compare it with its corresponding proverb ("too many cooks spoil the broth"). The researchers' statement, although general in form, is more explicit and unambiguous and is stated in a manner that makes clear what is meant. The proverb is more pithy but leaves certain questions unanswered. How many is "too many"? Does the metaphor apply to all types of "cooks" and to all types of "broth"? How do we know at precisely what point the "broth" is "spoiled"?

One way in which scientists gain precision in communication is by using operational definitions rather than dictionary definitions. An **operational definition** cites the procedures or set of operations used to measure the concept that it defines. The operational definition of a dish is its recipe. The recipe identifies the ingredients of the dish and gives their measurements, enabling cooks to recreate the dish themselves. Similarly, readers of a research report dealing with "anxiety" should be told whether the concept was measured by a paper-and-pencil test, by physiological recording, or by some other means. Operational definitions supply this information, allowing readers to repeat the essential details of the research.

In summary, although the methods psychologists use are far from infallible, they are a significant improvement over common sense. Let us turn to a more detailed consideration of these methods, starting with those that are most similar to common-sense methods and going on to those that are more controlled and rigorous.

THE METHODS OF PSYCHOLOGICAL RESEARCH

Psychological research spans a wide range — not only in content but also in method. To consider three of many possible examples, a psychologist might unobtrusively observe children in a playground, examine the effects of biofeedback on the voluntary control of blood pressure, or compare the educational achievement of socioeconomically disadvantaged and advantaged children.

It is obvious that the conclusions that can be drawn from a research study depend on the particular results that are obtained. It may be less obvious, but it is equally true, that research conclusions also depend on the method used to collect the evidence. In their continuing quest to develop and refine their understanding of people, psychologists employ five main methods: naturalistic observation, the case study, the sample survey, the correlational approach, and the experiment. Each method gives rise to a different type of conclusion — some general and tentative, some specific and firm. When interpreting the results of psychological research, it is important to remain sensitive to the strengths and limitations of the methods employed to produce the results.

Naturalistic Observation

Of the various methods used by psychologists, *naturalistic observation* comes closest to the common-sense approach. As the term implies, **naturalistic observation** involves the observation of behavior in its natural context. There are two main differences between naturalistic observation and common sense. First, common-sense observations are generally casual; naturalistic observations are typically more careful and systematic, often involving extensive written or filmed records. Second, researchers are usually much more cautious in interpreting the results of naturalistic observation than common-sense decision makers are in interpreting the results of everyday experience. Researchers are concerned less with proving a point than with obtaining an objective description of patterns of behavior.

Some fields of psychological investigation, such as physiological and sensory psychology, make little use of naturalistic observation. Naturalistic observation is most extensively employed in the study of animal behavior, in developmental psychology, and in social psychology. Observation of the behavior of animals in their natural habitat is called **ethology.** One of the founding fathers of this field, Konrad Lorenz, won a share of the Nobel Prize in 1973 for his penetrating insights into a wide range of animal behavior.

A study by F. Strayer (1981), in which he filmed three- to six-year-old children as they engaged in free play activities, supplies a good example of how psychologists employ naturalistic observation to study human behavior. Strayer created an inventory of the various types of prosocial behavior displayed by the children and coded the films accordingly. The inventory described such behaviors as offering, giving, sharing, cooperating, helping, and approaching an upset peer (see Figure 1-6). Careful analyses of the prosocial behavior of the children yielded two conclusions: (1) preschool children tend to adopt different styles of prosocial behavior and (2) certain children receive much more help than others.

As we have seen, Jean Piaget also employed naturalistic observation in his early studies. Piaget supplemented his naturalistic observations with small experiments — a practice quite common in ethology.

The major advantage of naturalistic observation is that it provides an investigator with the opportunity to see how particular actions fit into the overall flow of behavior. In the same way as it can be misleading for a remark to be quoted out of context, it may be misleading to interpret the results of laboratory research out of the context in which the behaviors in question naturally occur. This principle has been clearly demonstrated in research on captive animals. In recent years, long and careful observations of primates in their natural environments have established that a great deal of the aggressive, apathetic, and sexual behavior of caged primates is no more representative of their natural habits than the behavior of people in concentration camps and prisons is representative of normal human activity.

Naturalistic observation is a descriptive, as opposed to an explanatory, approach to research. It supplies a rough sketch of the overall picture, but it provides a weak basis for drawing conclusions about why the observed behavior patterns occurred. Naturalistic observation is better suited for inspiring questions than for providing answers.

The Case Study

A **case study** is an in-depth investigation of a single unit. Although the subject is generally a person, the unit could be a single school, a single community, or a single event. The case-study method is often used by psychologists who assess personality and treat psychological disorders. Because Sigmund Freud developed the theory of psychoanalysis almost entirely on the basis of his case studies, it is appropriate to consider a classic case reported by Freud, one to which he devoted some 140 pages in his *Collected Papers,* as an example.

A problem experienced by a four-year-old Austrian boy named Hans was brought to Freud's attention. Hans' parents were concerned about their son's intense fear of horses. Hans would go out only when very few horses were in the street, and he was afraid that a horse would come into his bedroom and bite him. Freud agreed to take on the case and proceeded to inquire about Hans' background. Freud's immediate goal was to cure Hans' problem, but he also had a long-term goal —to gather evidence that would enable him to develop and refine a general theory of abnormal behavior.

Freud discovered that Hans had recently witnessed a horse having a seizure. That information, of course, seems relevant to Hans' problem, but Freud collected other information as well. He discovered that Hans had an unusual

(a) Giving

(b) Sharing

FIGURE 1-6

Types of Prosocial Behavior   *Source:* Adapted from Rushton, J., & Sorrentino, M. (1981). *Altruism and helping behavior* (pp. 334 and 335). Hillsdale, NJ; Lawrence Erlbaum Associates.

interest in the part of his body he called his "widler" and that he had spent the summer receiving the undivided attention of his mother while his father was away on business. Indeed, Hans had been sleeping with his mother in her bed and, it was reported, had made sexual overtures to her. At summer's end, Hans moved to a new neighborhood and his father returned to claim much of his mother's attention (in particular, by barring Hans from his mother's bed). On the basis of this information, Freud concluded that Hans' anxiety was caused by an unconscious fear that his father would punish him for his unconscious desire to possess his mother but that this association had been repressed and redirected to a fear of horses. (For an elaboration of the basis of such conclusions in psychoanalytic theory, see Chapters 12 and 14).

Freud's conclusions may seem a little far-fetched, and some psychologists think they are (see Wolpe & Rachman, 1960). In any event, they demonstrate the limitations of the case-study approach. The possible causes of an individual's behavior are virtually infinite. There is no way of knowing with certainty which of the many possible causes gave rise to Hans' fear of horses. To narrow down the possibilities, an analyst must draw on a theory that directs attention to particular candidates. Freud's theory led him to attend to background information about Hans' relationships with his mother and father. Different theories would direct investigators' attention to other areas, such as Hans' more recent experience with the horse. Although the information supplied by the case study is often a rich source of illumination, this method cannot convincingly establish a causal connection between different events (in this case study, between Hans' fear of horses and his fear of his father).

The case-study method of psychological research is quite similar to common-sense methods. It becomes a more valuable tool, however, in the hands of individuals who have repeated experiences with the same types of people in similar situations. Psychologists who specialize in the treatment of phobias, for example, may conduct a large number of case studies and build theories of what causes phobias by attending to commonalities among the cases. In part, that is how Freud developed his theory of psychoanaly-

sis. Each new case supplies an uncontrolled test of the theory and a basis for refining it. Once developed, aspects of the theory may be evaluated by more rigorous methods.

The Sample Survey

Whereas the case-study method enables an investigator to obtain a great deal of information about one person or case, the **sample survey** provides a researcher with a limited amount of information about various groups of people. If you have ever received a questionnaire in the mail or been contacted by telephone regarding where you shop, what television programs you watch, or for whom you intend to vote, you have participated in a sample survey. The goal of sample surveys is not to find out about you per se but to find out about people like you in general.

Alfred Kinsey's classic study of sexual behavior is a good example of the sample survey method of research (see Chapter 8). Kinsey and his assistants knocked on thousands of doors to interview men and women about their sexual habits, asking them about the types of sexual behaviors in which they had engaged, the frequency with which they practiced them, the number of partners they had had, and other related questions. Kinsey alone interviewed over 7,000 people.

The purpose of survey research, such as Kinsey's study, is to obtain an indication of the behavior of a **population** of people by collecting information from a **representative sample.** Here, the term "representative" refers to the degree to which the people in the sample group possess the same characteristics as the people in the population from which the sample has been drawn. As the titles of the books in which Kinsey published his findings — *Sexual Behavior in the Human Male* and *Sexual Behavior in the Human Female* — indicate, the population with which Kinsey was concerned was large. The population of concern to other survey researchers may be smaller (as examples, all college students, all employees of a company, all females who have had children before they turned 21).

One key to good survey research lies in the

representativeness of the sample. Although common sense might guide a researcher to sample as many people as possible, the number of people in a sample is not the most important aspect of the survey. This point was well demonstrated when the magazine *Literary Digest* attempted to predict the outcome of the 1936 presidential election. The magazine sent questionnaires to over 10 million potential voters and obtained responses from over 2 million of them. On the basis of this sample, the magazine predicted a landslide victory for Alfred Landon. Who was Landon? You have probably never heard of him. In fact, there was a landslide victory — but it was for Franklin Roosevelt. *Literary Digest* ceased publication shortly thereafter.

The error made by *Literary Digest* is a common one; the magazine failed to obtain a representative sample. In the 1936 election, Democratic and Republican voters split along socioeconomic lines. Because *Literary Digest* obtained its mailing list from telephone directories and driver-license records, its sample was biased in favor of people who drove cars and owned telephones in 1936. These people were mainly from the middle and upper classes, which were predominantly Republican; the voters, however, were predominantly Democrat.

How many people do you need to sample in order to predict an event? Surprisingly few, if the sample is representative of the population as a whole. Each week the Nielsen organization asks some 1,500 Americans to indicate which television programs they watched during the previous week. On the basis of this sample, Nielsen is able to supply a reasonably accurate representation of the viewing habits of over 200 million Americans. Kinsey's sample, on the other hand, was not representative of all individuals, as the titles of his books contend. In addition to sampling only American males and females, Kinsey underrepresented the lower socioeconomic classes and rural segments of the population and his sample contained no black Americans. What Kinsey actually described was sexual behavior in middle-class, urban, white American people. The sexual behavior of members of the population who don't fit this description may be quite different.

In addition to problems associated with the representativeness of samples, surveys may fail to obtain valid information because people are reluctant to tell the truth about themselves. For example, we might expect people who were asked by Kinsey about sexual involvements with animals to be reluctant to admit to any, especially where such behaviors are treated as serious crimes. To be fair to Kinsey, we should point out that he was a skilled interviewer and that he attempted to check the accuracy of his subjects' reports of their sexual behavior by interviewing a sample of their spouses.

We all conduct surveys in our everyday lives, especially when we find ourselves in disagreement with someone over an issue about which others have an opinion. We might contact several of our friends to see if they also think that their psychology teacher is hopelessly inept. A group of friends is, of course, not a representative sample, and such "survey" questions are often not worded in a very objective way. It is therefore not surprising that people tend to assume that many more people share their opinions than actually do. We discuss this phenomenon, the **false consensus effect,** in Chapter 11.

Despite its limitations, the sample survey is a valuable research tool when it is used properly. Like the conclusions reached through naturalistic observations and case studies, the conclusions that can be drawn from sample surveys are primarily descriptive. Surveys describe the behaviors that are characteristic of a particular population of people; they do not explain the behavior that they describe.

The Correlational Approach

The next two methods we will consider — the correlational and experimental methods — lie at the heart of psychological research. They are the most rigorous and therefore the most different from the common-sense approach. Both methods are designed to provide precise statements of the relationship between operationally defined variables. The *correlational approach* allows a researcher to draw conclusions about what *goes with* what; the *experimental approach* allows a researcher to draw conclusions about what *causes* what.

Consider the following two statements from Anderson (1971, p. 14):

1. If differences on variable A are *produced,* then differences on variable B are observed.

2. If differences on variable A are *observed,* then differences on variable B are observed.

For a more concrete example, substitute "level of anxiety" for "variable A" and "final-exam performance" for "variable B."

Although slight, the difference between "produced" and "observed" at the end of the first phrase of each statement (authors' emphasis) is important. When an investigator systematically *produces* differences on one variable and then observes the resulting differences on a second variable, he or she is using an **experimental approach** and the relationship uncovered is a *causal* one. When an investigator simply *observes* the relationship between values on two variables, he or she is using a **correlational approach** and the relationship uncovered is a *predictive* one. The following example should clarify the distinction between predictive and causal relationships and, by extension, between correlation and experimental research.

Anxiety and Performance   Will you do better on a test if you are anxious or if you are not? Common sense may suggest that being highly anxious interferes with the clear thinking needed to perform well, but anxiety could also have the opposite effect. People who are anxious may be more energetic and alert and therefore do better on a test than those who are not anxious. How could you determine which, if either, relationship prevails? One way to attack the problem is to determine the correlation between level of anxiety and level of performance by giving students a test of anxiety and a test of performance (an exam perhaps) and then determining if those who scored high on the anxiety test scored high or low on the performance test. Assume you found that the students who scored highest on the anxiety test generally scored lowest on the performance test. Could you conclude that anxiety impairs exam performance? The answer is no.

The statement "anxiety impairs performance" implies that high anxiety *produces* an impairment of performance, which describes a causal relationship. Although the results of the correlational study are consistent with the conclusion that high anxiety causes poor performance, they are also consistent with the opposite relationship — that poor performance causes high anxiety. All that a correlational study can establish is that the values on two variables go together. Correlational information is sufficient if your purpose is to predict values on one variable from knowledge of values on another variable. But when the object of the research is to determine what *causes* what, rather than what *goes with* what, an experiment is needed.

In some cases, of course, the direction of causal connection between two correlated variables appears to be obvious. The well-established correlation between smoking and cancer, for example, would hardly be regarded as evidence that cancer causes smoking! Nonetheless, it is improper to infer causal connections even in such cases. Although it is implausible for cancer to cause smoking, it is quite possible that something related to smoking (other than smoking itself) — called in research, a **third factor** — is responsible for the correlation. For example, imagine that cancer is caused by a biochemical agent that also has the property of making smoking more pleasurable. In that case, people who have the agent would be more likely both to get cancer and to smoke than people in whom the agent is missing, producing a correlation between smoking and cancer.

Returning to the study of anxiety and exam performance, there are several third factors that could be responsible for the correlation between these two variables. The number of hours spent studying for the exam is one candidate; a student who spends a considerable amount of time studying for an exam may be less anxious and perform better than a student who is not as well prepared. Another third factor could be confidence; more confident students may be more likely to feel less anxious about the exam and to score higher than less confident students.

Correlational studies are not powerless to deal with the problem of third factors. If these factors can be identified before the research is conducted, steps can be taken to control them. For example, you might attempt to hold constant the number of hours that students spend studying for the exam. If you were successful and a corre-

BOX 1-5
A FINDING THAT DID NOT BEAR FRUIT

Some years ago, Scandinavian scientist S. Akerfeldt (1957) announced a simple test for the diagnosis of schizophrenia. Since there are no simple procedures available for reliably diagnosing this severe disorder, confirmation of his findings would have had enormous benefits. Unfortunately, researchers in other countries were unable to confirm his results.

Investigation showed that Ackerfeldt had given his test to a group of hospitalized schizophrenics and compared their test performances with those of a group of mentally stable individuals who were not hospitalized. He found a correlation between the outcome of the test and the presence or absence of schizophrenia. He matched the two groups on a number of third factors, such as age and sex, thereby eliminating them as possible causes of the correlation. However, he did not match the two groups on diet.

The schizophrenic patients received hospital food, whereas the members of the comparison group ate their meals at home. Examination of the hospital diet showed that it was deficient in citrus fruits. Ackerfeldt had developed an excellent diagnostic test to detect vitamin C deficiency! When a group of normal people with the same diet as the schizophrenics was given the test, the difference in average scores disappeared.

Identifying and eliminating third factors, one by one, is a laborious and complicated business. Correlational researchers can never be completely sure that they have dealt with all possible third factors. Variation in the one factor that is overlooked may create the correlation between two otherwise unrelated variables.

---

lation between level of anxiety and exam performance were still obtained, then you could rule out study time as a third factor. An alternative approach would be to allow study time to vary but to measure its value by asking students to report how many hours they studied to prepare for the exam. The effect of study time on the correlation between anxiety and exam performance could then be extracted by statistical means. In many cases, a correlational result first interpreted as evidence of a direct causal relationship has later been found to be due to the influence of an overlooked third factor. The importance of controlling factors is described in Box 1-5.

Although in principle correlational research is not sufficient to establish cause–effect relationships, in practice the evidence can be quite compelling. For example, several possible third-factor explanations of the smoking–cancer link have been investigated, but none has proved sufficient to account for the correlation. Those who are willing to risk smoking may feel that they can beat the odds of getting cancer, but they would be foolish to dismiss the strong possibility that smoking causes cancer, even though the evidence is correlational.

Applications of Correlational Research The correlational method is preferable to other research approaches in three situations. The first is exploratory research. For example, people who suffer from a particular psychological disorder can be given a variety of tests by researchers to determine other characteristics that distinguish them from people who do not suffer from the disorder. Any differences that emerge may then be investigated more systematically. The second circumstance is when the principal objective of research is to predict (rather than to change or to explain) a particular behavior. Prime examples are the use of scores on a personnel selection test to predict job performance and the use of IQ scores to predict academic success. Thirdly, the correlational method is used when it is impractical, impossible, or unethical to conduct an experiment on an issue. For example, it is not feasible to manipulate such variables as sex, marital status, height, or social class to assess their effects on other variables. Similarly, because no one would deliberately isolate, deprive, or harm infants to study the effects of these experiences on their development, investigators observe the characteristics of infants who have been unfortunate enough to undergo such adverse experiences.

Interpreted correctly (in terms of predictive relationships), correlational research has provided much of the evidence on which we base our understanding of behavior. This is particularly true in such fields as educational psychology and personality research, in which manipulation of variables is often impractical or impossible.

The Experimental Approach

The final method we consider — the experimental approach — is used most frequently by psychologists and is the most highly controlled of all methods. The basic idea behind the **experimental method** is to manipulate one variable while controlling all others and to observe its effect on the behavior in question. To obtain the control necessary to conduct a successful experiment, most investigators set up experiments in laboratories. The experimental approach is the only method that permits a researcher to conclude that a change in one variable causes a change in another.

If you have ever changed your diet in order to lose weight, tried listening more attentively in order to get along better with a friend, or, more generally, changed something in order to see whether it produces a change in something else, you have attempted to conduct an experiment. It is exceedingly difficult to conduct a good experiment. To see why, let us consider an example.

Imagine that you have a friend who thinks that he has happened on a cure for the common cold. He had a cold, took a particular combination of pills, and his cold got better. Realizing that one case is hardly enough to establish a discovery, he has been trying his "cure" on his friends ever since. To date he has given it to six

people, and each one of them has recovered within two days.

Your friend has conducted an experiment. He has produced a change in one condition (the presence or absence of his "cure") and has observed a change (or a set of changes) in another (the presence or absence of a cold). We call the condition your friend has manipulated (giving the pills) the **independent variable** of the experiment and the outcome (recovery from the cold) the **dependent variable.** The second variable is dependent because it is hypothesized to be contingent on the first variable. The first variable is manipulated independently of all other variables that might affect the subject's behavior. As we shall see, the manipulation of pill-giving (the *intended* independent variable) did not live up to this definition.

Although your friend has conducted an experiment, he has not conducted a very good one. First, consider the causal relationship he claims he has discovered. Although a change in the independent variable is associated with a change in the dependent variable, we cannot be sure that it was the independent variable that caused this change (in other words, that the medication produced the improvement). Your friend has permitted factors other than the independent variable to vary, and these factors may have affected the outcome of the experiment. Before he can establish that his medication caused the change, he must rule out other plausible causes of the observed effect.

Consider the variable *time,* for example. If your friend had given the cold sufferers his combination of pills and waited a full month before checking their health, you would not be at all surprised to find that everyone recovered. Time is a great healer. The cold sufferers could have recovered spontaneously (regardless of the drugs) in a month, a week, or even two days. Your friend should test his cure in a different way — by determining whether a group of people who took his cure recovered faster than a group of people who did not.

Thinking of the problem this way implies making a comparison between a group of cold sufferers who take the pills and a group of cold sufferers who do not. The hypothesis is that the former group will show more change (or more

rapid change) than the latter group. Most psychological experiments are structured in this way. We call groups such as those taking the pills **experimental groups** and groups that continue as usual **control groups.**

The basic idea underlying an experiment is simple but powerful. Because it is impossible to anticipate and to measure all of the possible forces or variables that can affect an outcome such as recovery from a cold, researchers do not even try. Rather, they permit these forces to affect two different groups of people. Researchers isolate the effect of the variable in which they are interested by ensuring that it is the only variable that differs systematically (in every case) between the two groups. For example, your friend could give his pills to the experimental group but not to the control group. If this were the only systematic difference between the two groups, then he could conclude that the pills caused any observed differences in outcome.

Assume that your friend now attempts to conduct a proper experiment. He finds eight people with colds and puts four in an experimental group and four in a control group. To remember which subjects he has assigned to each group, he puts four females in one group and four males in the other. He gives the subjects in the experimental group the pills that he believes will cure their colds but doesn't give the subjects in the control group any medication. He finds that three of four subjects in the experimental group recover after three days, compared to only one in the control group.

Certainly the evidence is becoming more compelling, but three important questions should be asked before the conclusions of this or any experiment are accepted:

1. Were *enough* subjects compared to permit a reliable conclusion about whatever differences were observed between the two groups?
2. Were there any *systematic differences* between the two groups other than the one under investigation?
3. Were subjects assigned to groups *randomly*?

Box 1-6
STACKING THE DECK

In 1958, J. V. Brady and his colleagues published the results of an experiment on reactions to stress in monkeys. Two groups of monkeys were established, with *four* animals in each group. A pair of animals, one from each group, was placed in a restraining apparatus; at intervals, both monkeys were threatened with an electric shock. One group of monkeys had previously been trained to press a switch to prevent the shock from occurring. Each monkey from this group was put within reach of the switch, thus giving him control of the shock. The other monkey in the pair was helpless; he was totally dependent on the actions of the monkey in charge of the switch to prevent the shock. This was clearly a stressful situation for both animals, but one member of the pair showed a much greater response to the stress than the other. Can you guess which one it was—the

monkey in control or his helpless partner?

The researchers were surprised to find that the monkeys in control responded worse to the stress: they developed ulcers, and some of them died. Their helpless partners apparently suffered no ill-effects. This finding led the researchers to label the trained monkeys the *executive* group and to compare these monkeys to human executives whose decisions have serious consequences for those who work for them. The helpless group of monkeys was compared to the humans whose fate is determined by executive action. The results of the experiment seemed to indicate that the burden of decision making gives executives ulcers, while their powerless subordinates feel little stress. Although plausible, this conclusion began to be doubted when subsequent research consistently failed to confirm Brady's finding

(see Seligman, 1975).

A closer look at Brady's method showed that there were two problems with his experiment. First, four monkeys are not enough to constitute a proper group. Second, the monkeys were not randomly placed in groups. Brady chose the first four monkeys who learned to press the switch for the executive group, assigning the slowest four to the helpless group. Because speed of learning is related to emotionality, Brady unwittingly stacked the deck by putting the four monkeys who were likely to be the most emotional animals into the executive group. The introduction of this bias probably led to the observed difference in response to stress. In fact, a similar experiment by Weiss (1968), in which monkeys were randomly assigned to groups, showed that it is *less* stressful to be in control than to be helpless.

Your friend fails all three tests implicit in these questions. First, four subjects per group is not enough to permit a reliable conclusion about the differences he observed for a very basic reason: the pattern of recovery times could have occurred by chance. We consider how to decide the number of subjects to assign to groups and whether observed differences are significant in the statistical discussion in the Appendix.

Second, assigning all males to one group and all females to the second group is a critical mistake; it creates a systematic difference between the two groups other than the one in question. Given the results, we don't know whether people who take your friend's "cure" tend to recover from colds faster than people who do not or whether females tend to recover from colds at different rates than males. For an experimenter to conclude that the differences between groups being compared were caused by the differences in

"FIND OUT WHO SET UP THIS EXPERIMENT. IT SEEMS THAT HALF OF THE PATIENTS WERE GIVEN A PLACEBO, AND THE OTHER HALF WERE GIVEN A DIFFERENT PLACEBO."

the independent variable, the experimenter must ensure that all other systematic differences between the two groups have been controlled. This is usually accomplished by randomly assigning subjects to groups.

Third, if you take a large sample of people, randomly divide them into two equal-sized groups, measure any of their various characteristics, and then compare the average values for the two groups, these values should be approximately equal. By making the groups equal on average before exposing them to a difference in the independent variable, an investigator can ensure that the observed differences in outcome were caused by the differences in the ways in which the groups were treated. The dangers of drawing conclusions about differences between groups that have *not* been created randomly are exemplified in Box 1-6.

If your friend obtained a large sample of subjects, randomly assigned them to two groups, gave the pills to subjects in the experimental group and gave nothing to the subjects in the control group, then observed a clear difference in the rate of recovery of the subjects in the two groups, could he conclude that he had found a cure for the

common cold? No. In giving the subjects in the experimental group pills but not giving those in the control group any pills, he has introduced a subtle — but systematic — difference between the two groups other than whether or not they ingested the medication in the pills. Pill-taking, as distinct from the taking of medication, could have caused the different recovery rates of the two groups.

You may have heard the term **placebo effect.** (*Placebo* is Latin for "I shall be pleasing.") An example of the placebo effect occurs when a patient takes a medication that is actually ineffective but experiences improvement because he or she expects to get better. For years physicians have recognized the placebo power of new drugs ("hurry up and prescribe it while it still works"), and a large number of studies have documented it. As we show in Chapter 4, this is especially the case for drugs that purport to ease pain. The standard procedure for dealing with the placebo effect in research is to "blind" the subjects to the difference in treatments by not telling them whether they are in the experimental group or the control group. When the treatment is a drug (to relieve pain, for example), *both* groups are given pills that are identical in appearance. The pill for the experimental group contains the substance being tested; the pill for the control group contains an ineffective filler, such as cornstarch. The ineffective pill is called a placebo. When the drug is disguised in this way, the subjects in the two groups have no basis for developing different expectations about the effect of the treatment.

Not only do subjects have expectations that might influence their behavior, but researchers are keenly interested in the effects of the variables that they themselves manipulate. Researchers' expectations could also influence the outcome of a drug test, particularly when they must make such subjective decisions as determining the level of pain experienced by a subject. If the subject is "blinded," shouldn't the researcher also be "blinded" to the identity of the subjects who are actually receiving the drug? It is, in fact, standard research practice to do just this; it is called the **double-blind procedure.** A coded label is used to distinguish the drug and the placebo pills, so that both researcher and subject are prevented

Box 1-7
Ethical Guidelines for Research with Human Subjects

The value of contributing to knowledge must be weighed against the rights, dignity, and welfare of the participants in psychological research. All universities require that psychologists clear proposed studies involving human subjects with an ethics committee before conducting them. The principles listed below are advanced by the American Psychological Association to guide investigators in dealing with the ethical concerns that arise in the course of planning and conducting research with human subjects.

a. In planning a study, the investigator has the responsibility to make a careful evaluation of its ethical acceptability. To the extent that the weighing of scientific and human values suggests a compromise of any principle, the investigator incurs a correspondingly serious obligation to seek ethical advice and to observe stringent safeguards to protect the rights of human participants.

b. Considering whether a participant in a planned study will be a "subject at risk" or a "subject at minimal risk," according to recognized standards, is of primary ethical concern to the investigator.

c. The investigator always retains the responsibility for ensuring ethical practice in research. The investigator is also responsible for the ethical treatment of research participants by collaborators, assistants, students, and employees, all of whom, however, incur similar obligations.

d. Except in minimal-risk research, the investigator establishes a clear and fair agreement with research participants, prior to their participation, that clarifies the obligations and responsibilities of each. The investigator has the obligation to honor all promises and commitments included in that agreement. The investigator informs the participants of all aspects of the research that might reasonably be expected to influence willingness to participate and explains all other aspects of the research about which the participants inquire. Failure to make full disclosure prior to obtaining informed consent requires additional safeguards to protect the welfare and dignity of the research participants. Research with children or with participants who have impairments that would limit understanding and/or communication requires special safeguarding procedures.

e. Methodological requirements of a study may make the use of concealment

from developing expectations that could bias the outcome of the experiment.

Keeping these considerations in mind, it is clear that the difference between the two groups in the common-cold example could be due to the placebo effect and/or to what is called the **experimenter expectancy effect.** Assuming that the pills are not the long sought-after cold cure, we can safely expect that the introduction of double-blinding will eliminate the remaining difference between the two groups in their average rate of recovery from a cold.

It remains only to add that it is important in psychological research to be clear and precise about exactly what effects are being sought. Your friend would not be justified in concluding that he had cured the common cold if the sole measure he used was the self-report of his patients. This measure of outcome might indicate only that he had discovered a way to make people

or deception necessary. Before conducting such a study, the investigator has a special responsibility to (i) determine whether the use of such techniques is justified by the study's prospective scientific, educational, or applied value; (ii) determine whether alternative procedures are available that do not use concealment or deception; and (iii) ensure that the participants are provided with sufficient explanation as soon as possible.

f. The investigator respects the individual's freedom to decline to participate in or to withdraw from the research at any time. The obligation to protect this freedom requires careful thought and consideration when the investigator is in a position of authority or influence over the participant. Such positions of authority include, but are not limited to, situations in which research participation in required as part of employment or in which the participant is a student, client, or employee of the investigator.

g. The investigator protects the participant from physical and mental discomfort, harm, and danger that may arise from research procedures. If risks of such consequences exist, the investigator informs the participant of that fact. Research procedures likely to cause serious or lasting harm to a participant are not used unless the failure to use these procedures might expose the participant to risk of greater harm, or unless the research has great potential benefit and fully informed and voluntary consent is obtained from each participant. The participant should be informed of procedures for contacting the investigator within a reasonable time period following participation should stress, potential harm, or related questions or concerns arise.

h. After the data are collected, the investigator provides the participant with information about the nature of the study and attempts to remove any misconceptions that may have arisen. Where

scientific or humane values justify delaying or withholding this information, the investigator incurs a special responsibility to monitor the research and to ensure that there are no damaging consequences for the participant.

i. Where research procedures result in undesirable consequences for the individual participant, the investigator has the responsibility to detect and remove or correct these consequences, including long-term effects.

j. Information obtained about a research participant during the course of an investigation is confidential unless otherwise agreed upon in advance. When the possibility exists that others may obtain access to such information, this possibility, together with the plans for protecting confidentiality, is explained to the participant as part of the procedure for obtaining informed consent.

say that their colds were cured and perhaps even to *believe* that they were cured; but more objective evidence would be required before the conclusion that they were actually cured could be reached.

Let us summarize the points we have been exemplifying. An experiment requires the manipulation of one variable (the independent variable) and the observation of its effect on another variable (the dependent variable). To conclude

that the change in the independent variable caused the difference in the dependent variable, the experimenter must ensure that the difference is not caused by a systematic change in some other variable. Usually the experimenter assigns different subjects randomly to two groups, the experimental group and the control group, and compares the average values of the dependent variables for each group. Sometimes the experimenter arranges for the same subjects to serve first

TABLE 1-3
Summary of Major Strengths and Weaknesses of the Five Approaches to Research

Approach	Strengths	Weaknesses
Naturalistic Observation	Observation of behavior in its natural context; seeing the whole picture; fertile source of hypotheses	Little opportunity to control variables; difficult to distinguish cause from coincidence; potential for bias in selection and interpretation of observations
Case Study	Study of rare events and instances; extensive evidence gathered on object of study; often compelling means of illustrating theory or argument	Lack of generalizability of findings; unconvincing basis for establishing relationships between variables
Sample Survey	Description of character of representative sample of population; effective means of measuring actions, attitudes, opinions, preferences, and intentions	Lack of explanatory power; validity of findings may be limited by unrepresentativeness of sample; reliability of responses difficult to determine; self-report may be inaccurate as measure of actual behavior
Correlational Study	Measurement of nature and degree of association among variables; sound basis for prediction; applicable to a wide variety of hypotheses and situations	Limited opportunity to control third factors; insufficient basis for drawing conclusions about causal relationships
Experiment	Manipulation of variables to control extraneous influences; best method for identifying causal relationships among variables	Artificiality of laboratory environment; limited generalizability of findings; manipulation of certain variables unethical or impractical

in the experimental group and then in the control group, or vice versa. The comparison is then made between the average values of the dependent variable under the experimental and control *conditions.* The principle is the same whether groups or conditions are the basis for comparison.

One of the most common and serious criticisms that can be leveled at an experiment is that it failed to control the influence of a **confounding variable**—a variable that, if left uncontrolled by the experimenter, could cause systematic differences between the performance of subjects in the experimental and control groups (or conditions). This variable is labeled *confounding* because its effect on the dependent variable is indistinguishable from that of the independent variable, thus confounding or confusing the interpretation of experimental findings. The influence of potential confounding variables is controlled in three ways: (1) by ensuring that they vary between groups randomly, (2) by holding them constant, and (3) by statistical means. The availability of procedures to deal with confounding variables is the principle source of the power of the experiment in psychological research. That is why most experiments are conducted in the laboratory under highly controlled conditions and why the method is the furthest

removed from the common-sense approach.

The procedures of experimental research allow an investigator to isolate specific causes of behavior, but the rigor of an experiment may be offset by a lack of **ecological validity.** The conclusions drawn from experiments—particularly those carried out in the highly artificial environment of the psychological laboratory—sometimes have limited generality and add little to our understanding of naturally occurring behavior.

In closing, we must make two important points. First, although we have taken pains to distinguish the approaches to psychological research we have described (see Table 1-3), they are not mutually exclusive. All empirical research involves some observation, and it is not uncommon to find experimental and correlational methods mixed within a single study. Our reason for distinguishing these approaches is to emphasize that the interpretation of the results of research—the type of conclusion reached—must take into account the way in which the evidence was obtained. Second, when conducting an experiment, and indeed when engaging in any type of psychological research, it is extremely important to respect the rights of participants. The ethical principles that guide psychologists in conducting research are outlined in Box 1-7.

SUMMARY

1. Psychology is the scientific study of mental processes, emotional reactions, and behavior. Now an independent discipline, psychology has roots in physics, philosophy, and physiology. The first psychological investigations, conducted a little more than 100 years ago, examined philosophical questions with methods borrowed from physics.

2. Early psychological thinking was dominated by structuralism, which sought to identify the primary elements of immediate conscious experience, and by functionalism, which examined the processes through which organisms adapt to their environment. These two schools of thought were followed by behaviorism, which attempted to categorize the basic elements of learned behavior, and by Gestalt psychology, which concentrated on the ways in which perceptual events are organized ("the whole is greater than the sum of the parts" being the central maxim of the Gestalt school).

3. Later schools include psychoanalysis, humanistic psychology, and cognitive-developmental theory. Following their founder, Sigmund Freud, psychoanalysts use dream analysis and free association to reveal their patients' unconscious impulses, which are often sexual in origin. Humanistic psychologists study the unique ways in which individuals fulfill their potential in everyday life. Cognitive–developmental theorists, such as Jean Piaget, focus on the growth of knowledge in children.

4. Most modern psychologists identify with areas of specialization rather than with schools or theories. The principal areas of psychological specialization are sociobiology and differential psychology, brain and behavior, sensation and perception, learning, motivation and emotion, cognitive psychology, developmental psychology, social psychology, personality and assessment, abnormal psychology, and psychotherapy.

5. Research in psychology sometimes produces the same conclusions that people reach using common sense. However, psychological research differs from common sense in three important ways:
   (a) Common-sense accounts of behavior typically are based on casual observation; psychological researchers employ more carefully controlled and systematic methods when collecting evidence.
   (b) Psychological researchers are usually more cautious in drawing conclusions about the causes of behavior than people who employ only common sense.
   (c) Common-sense accounts of behavior generally are cast in language that is efficient but imprecise; psychological research is described in much more exact terms.

6. The research method closest to the common-sense approach is naturalistic observation, which involves the observation of behavior in its natural context. A major advantage of this method is that it provides an investigator with the opportunity to see how particular actions fit into the overall flow of behavior. It is a descriptive, rather than an explanatory, approach to research.

7. The case-study approach to research is an in-depth investigation of a single unit. Often used in the assessment of personality and in the study of psychological disorders, this method is also a more descriptive than explanatory approach to research.

8. Investigations of the characteristics of groups of people are often carried out through sample surveys. This descriptive approach to research is widely used to reveal people's opinions, attitudes, preferences, and intentions.

9. The two most rigorous approaches to research are the correlational study and the experiment. The correlational approach studies "what goes with what"; the experimental approach is designed to reveal "what causes what."

10. Because it provides the investigator with the opportunity to control variables that might otherwise obscure the specific cause of the behavior being studied, the experiment is the most effective approach for establishing causal relationships in psychological research.

KEY TERMS

Psychology
Fechner's Law
Structuralism
Introspection
Functionalism
Behaviorism
Conditioned Reflex
Law of Effect
Gestalt Psychology
Psychoanalysis
Hypnosis
Hysteria
Psychoanalytic Psychotherapy
Free Association
Humanistic Psychology
Cognitive – Developmental
  Theory
Self-actualization
Sociobiology

Differential Psychology
Physiological Psychology
Cognitive Psychology
Developmental Psychology
Educational Psychologist
School Psychologist
Counseling Psychologist
Clinical Psychologist
Psychiatrist
Psychoanalyst
Industrial Psychologist
Environmental Psychologist
Community Psychologist
Proof
Confirmation
Operational Definition
Naturalistic Observation
Ethology
Case Study

Sample Survey
Population
Representative Sample
False Consensus Effect
Experimental Approach
Correlational Approach
Third Factor
Experimental Method
Independent Variable
Dependent Variable
Experimental Group
Control Group
Placebo Effect
Double-blind Procedure
Experimenter Expectancy
  Effect
Confounding Variable
Ecological Validity

RECOMMENDED READINGS

American Psychological Association. (1985). *Careers in psychology.* Washington, D.C.: American Psychological Association. A thorough and up-to-date description of employment opportunities for psychologists. This book describes the types of jobs that psychologists do, the proportions of psychologists that are employed in different jobs, and the problems that psychologists encounter in obtaining employment.

Cozby, P. C. (1985). *Methods in behavioral research,* (3rd ed.). Palo Alto, CA: Mayfield. A

clearly written account of research methodology with well-chosen examples.

Nordby, V. J., & Hall, C. S. (1974). *A guide to psychologists and their concepts.* San Francisco: W. H. Freeman. A paperback that gives brief biographies of 42 prominent psychologists and outlines their ideas.

Reynolds, P. D. (1982). *Ethics of social science research.* Englewoods Cliffs, NJ: Prentice-Hall. A paperback that helps researchers develop their own strategies for solving the ethical problems encountered while conducting research.

Schultz, D. P., & Schultz, S. E. (1987). *A history of modern psychology,* (4th ed.). New York: Academic Press. An excellently written introduction to the history of psychology.

Siegel, M. H., & Zeigler, H. P. (1976). *Psychological research: The inside story.* New York: Harper & Row. Behind-the-scenes accounts of the trials and tribulations of research by 19 prominent psychologists.

2

EVOLUTION, NATURE AND NURTURE

HEREDITY AND ENVIRONMENT

Genetic Transmission
Genes and Biological Characteristics
Genes and Behavior
Assessing Heredity and Environment
    Twin Studies ▪ Adoption Studies
Intelligence
    Racial Differences in IQ

GENETICS AND GENDER

The Conflict between Heredity and
    Environment
        Genetic Females Reared as Males ▪
        Genetic Males Reared as Females ▪
        Masculinized Females

ENRICHMENT AND DEPRIVATION

Early Deprivation
    The Effects of Social Isolation on
    Monkeys ▪ The Effects of Early
    Institutionalization
Early Enrichment
    The Effects of Enrichment on Rats ▪
    The Effects of Enrichment on Children

MATURATION AND EXPERIENCE

Critical Periods in Physical
    Development
        Imprinting ▪ Attachment
Sensitive Periods in Human
    Development

It necessarily follows . . . from what has been acknowledged, that the best men should as often as possible form alliances with the best women, and the most depraved men, on the contrary, with the most depraved women; and the offspring of the former is to be educated, but not of the latter, if the flock is to be of the most perfect kind . . . As for those youths who distinguish themselves, either in war or other pursuits, they ought to have rewards and prizes given them, and the most ample liberty of lying with women, that so, under this pretext, the greatest number of children may spring from such parentage. . . . ''

By whom was this written? If you guess Adolph Hitler or some other demagogue, you are wrong. It was written by the philosopher Plato during the fourth century B.C. (Davis, 1849, p. 144). The idea of breeding humans as we do animals is repugnant to most people today, but it has had many advocates throughout history. The concept is based on a belief in **genetic determinism** — the doctrine that certain characteristics are inherited rather than acquired through learning. This idea has always been shrouded in controversy. Consider, for example, the following statement, written more than 100 years ago by British philosopher John Stuart Mill:

I have long felt that the prevailing tendency to regard all the marked distinctions of human character as innate, and in the main indelible, and to ignore the irresistible proofs that by far the greater part of those differences, whether between individuals, races, or sexes, are such as not only might but naturally would be *produced by differences in circumstances,* is one of the chief hindrances to the rational treatment of great social questions, and one of the greatest stumbling blocks to human improvement. (1869, p. 162, *emphasis added*)

Mills advocated a position based on **environmental determinism** — the belief that certain characteristics are acquired through experience, not through inheritance. An obvious corollary of this point of view is that if the circumstances of an individual are changed, he or she will change accordingly.

Is our psychological makeup affected more by the characteristics we inherit from our parents **(heredity)** or more by the way in which we are brought up, the physical world in which we live, and the people with whom we interact **(environment)?** Are we born with a certain nature, or are we born as a *blank slate* ready to be shaped by our environment? In what ways do heredity and environment interact to produce human behavior? These fundamental questions in psychology have been hotly debated throughout the history of the discipline. In this chapter, we discuss the influence of heredity and environment on human behavior.

EVOLUTION

It is appropriate to launch a discussion of heredity and environment by reviewing one of the most influential theories of all time — the theory of evolution. The theory of evolution deals with far-reaching questions concerning the origin of species, the reasons why there are different species on the planet, the ways in which different species are related, and the forces that lead to the creation of new species.

Darwin and the Theory of Evolution

The originator of the theory of evolution was Charles Darwin. Let us relive Darwin's visit to the Galapagos Islands in 1831. The Galapagos are an archipelago (a group of small islands in relatively close proximity). Darwin made an important observation concerning the wildlife on these islands — different islands contained animals that were similar in many respects but were sufficiently different to justify classifying them as different species. For example, 14 species of finch inhabited the Galapagos at that time. The species that inhabited certain islands had blunt beaks, but species of finch on other islands, although similar in most other respects, had sharp beaks. In Darwin's day, most people believed that all species had been created by God in the forms in which they existed. However, it seemed implausible to Darwin that all of the species he

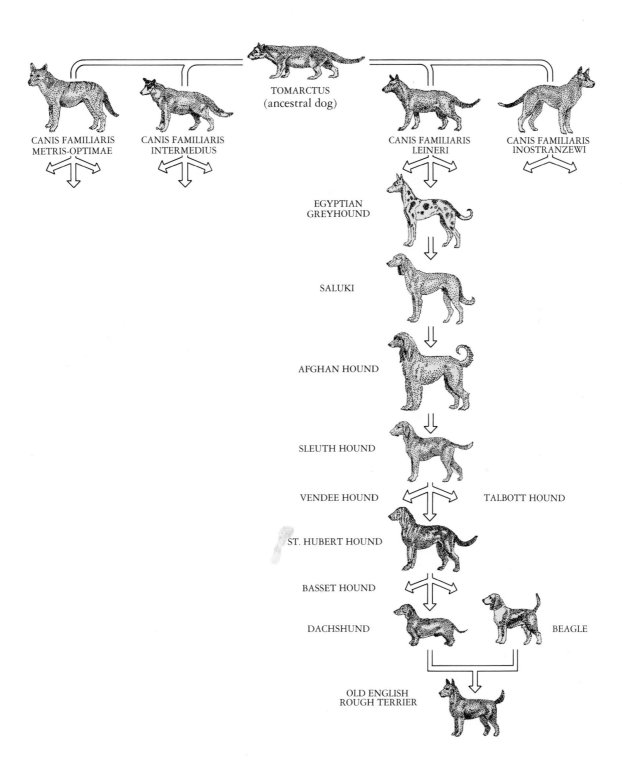

FIGURE 2-1
Evolution of the Old English Rough Terrier Through selective breeding (artificial selection), many types of dog have been created. This "family tree" shows how the Old English Rough Terrier evolved from the ancestral dog. *Source:* After Moore, R., & the Editors of LIFE. New York: TIME Incorporated, 1962, pp. 86–87.

observed on the Galapagos Islands could have been created independently. They were similar in too many respects. Darwin considered the alternative that the various species he observed stemmed from a common ancestor, perhaps one that lived centuries ago when the islands may have been joined by land. But if this were the case, how did they acquire the features that caused them to become different species?

Selective Breeding and Natural Selection
Darwin was familiar with the ways in which breeders since the Neolithic age had developed new strains of cereal, new breeds of dog, new types of cattle, and other living things. They selected a pair of plants or animals that possessed certain desirable characteristics and bred them with one another; then they bred the offspring of this union, then the offspring's offspring, and so on. The characteristics the breeders wanted to foster might be physical (for example, the size, shape, and flavor of corn), temperamental (aggressiveness in cocks), or behavioral (pointing behavior in hunting dogs). The offspring of inbred animals tended to possess more of the desired characteristics than other animals. When bred with one another, or with other animals who possess these characteristics, such animals tended to produce offspring with even more of the desired characteristics. Figure 2-1 shows the steps leading from an ancestral dog, *Tomarctus,* to an Old English Rough Terrier. The question that puzzled Darwin was how such selection could occur under natural conditions without the intervention of humans?

A close examination of the characteristics that differentiated one species of finch from another in the Galapagos Islands supplied a clue. Darwin noted that different islands contained different types of food and that the beaks of the finches that inhabited them were adapted to the type of food available (see Figure 2-2). For example, finches on islands with lots of seeds had stout, conical beaks; finches on islands with lots of insects had long, slender beaks. Darwin concluded that finches born with the types of beak that enabled them to adapt to their environment and to survive until sexual maturity must have mated with other finches born with this adaptive characteristic until, over the centuries, all surviv-

ing members of the species acquired the appropriate type of beak. Darwin surmised that finches with beaks that did not enable them to survive failed to produce other finches with nonadaptive beaks; therefore, nonadaptive beaks failed to evolve. Over many generations, the process of **natural selection** transformed the species that were adapting to new environments into new species. Note that in artificial breeding, humans select the characteristics that evolve; in Darwin's theory, the environment or nature selects the characteristics (hence, the term *natural* selection).

In summary, Darwin's theory of evolution contained the following assumptions:

1. More individuals are born in each species than survive to sexual maturity.

2. There is variation among the individuals of all species; indeed, no two individuals are identical.

3. Certain differences among individuals are *adaptive.* The individuals who possess the adaptive characteristics are more likely to survive and reproduce in the environment into which they are born.

4. Some adaptive differences among individuals are inherited.

5. The environment does not contain enough resources to support all individuals.

6. A struggle for existence occurs among individuals; those who possess the most adaptive characteristics, by definition, win the struggle.

7. Individuals who survive and reproduce pass on their adaptive characteristics to their offspring, who are more inclined to inherit these adaptive traits than the offspring of parents who do not possess them.

8. Over many generations, this process may result in the creation of new species.

Interestingly, Darwin was not the only one to develop this explanation for evolution. While he was working on a book presenting his theory and documenting it with masses of evidence, he received a letter from a young scholar named Alfred Russell Wallace outlining essentially the same theory that Darwin had been working on for decades. In a quandary, Darwin wrote to a close friend: "Wallace says nothing about publication, but as I had not intended to publish any sketch, can I do so honourably . . . ? I would far rather burn my whole book, than he or any other man should think that I had behaved in a paltry spirit" (Darwin, 1856, p. 117). Darwin's colleagues resolved his dilemma for him, arranging for both men to offer their ideas together on July 1, 1858, before the Linnean Society of London — an official presentation of the theory of evolution. Darwin then began writing up the evidence he had been collecting for almost 30 years. *On the Origin of Species by means of Natural Selection or the Preservation of Favoured Races in the Struggle for Life* appeared in print in 1858.

FIGURE 2-2

Species of Galapagos Finch Many species of finch have evolved from a single ancestral form. Depending on their feeding habits, Galapagos finch have developed beaks of a shape and size adapted to (a) the removal of tree bark in search of insects; (b) and (c) the collection of small seeds on the ground; (d) the crushing of large, thickly coated seeds; or (e) the manipulation of cactus spines to probe for small insects. *Source:* Adapted from Bernstein, R. A., & Bernstein, S. (1982). *Biology: The study of life* (p. 141). San Diego, CA: Harcourt Brace Jovanovich.

The Evolution of Behavior

Today, virtually everyone accepts the idea that physical structures evolve through natural selection. However, some people are reluctant to apply the principles of evolution to such psychological characteristics as mental ability, temperament, and behavior. Darwin was not reluctant, however; he believed strongly that behavior, intelligence, and temperament evolve in the same way that physical characteristics evolve. The Galapagos finches he observed differed not only in physical characteristics but in behaviors as well. For example, finches from one species displayed the ability to use a tool; they dislodged insects from tree-bark crevices by using a cactus spine (see illustration (e) of Figure 2-2).

Consider another example: the evolution of aggression. If aggression were adaptive in a species, then individuals who inherited aggressive traits would be more likely to survive and reproduce aggressive individuals like themselves, and the species would become more aggressive in nature. But would this process not lead to disaster? It is important to note that the theory of evolution does not dictate that evolution must proceed in one consistent direction (for example, toward increasing aggressiveness). Nor does the theory in any way imply that species become increasingly perfect. New characteristics evolve only to enable individuals to adapt to their environments. If an environment changes, then characteristics that were adaptive in the old environment may become maladaptive and no longer be selected, or the species may become extinct. If there are sufficient tough guys in the environment, it may be most adaptive to be nonaggressive; if there are sufficient "wimps" in the environment, it may be most adaptive to be aggressive. In fact, high degrees of aggression are maladaptive in virtually all species (Lorenz, 1966), and most conflicts are settled through such ritualistic encounters as that shown in Figure 2-3.

FIGURE 2-3

Adaptive Responses to Aggression Aggressive behavior by a higher-status female wolf elicits a submissive response from a lower-status female.

It is interesting to note that when Darwin first formulated his theory, the idea that characteristics could be inherited was a bold inference that had no known direct experimental support. Although the basic principles of **genetic transmission,** or heredity, had been outlined in 1866 by Austrian monk Gregor Mendel (1822–1884), they went unnoticed until 1900 and were unknown to Darwin. Mendel's *factors* are now known as **genes**—the basic units of heredity. We will discuss the relationship between genes and behavior shortly. For now, it is important to note that for Darwin's purpose—and for evolutionary theory in general—it is not necessary to understand the mechanisms that produce various behaviors; it is necessary only to establish that the differences in behavior are inherited (for example, that the offspring of aggressive parents are more aggressive than the offspring of less aggressive parents). For the purpose of evolution, it makes no difference whether the differences are caused by hormones, physical size, the hypothalamus, or a hangnail—as long as they are inherited.

Proximate and Ultimate Causes Psychologists seek to understand why people behave in particular ways; they attempt to determine the *causes* of behavior. So do evolutionary biologists. But psychologists and evolutionary biologists tend to focus on different levels of explanation. The causes with which the theory of evolution is concerned are **ultimate** (or **distal**) **causes;** evolutionary biologists explain behaviors in terms of their evolutionary origins. Psychologists, in contrast, tend to explain behaviors in terms of their more **immediate** (or **proximate**) **causes.**

Consider an example. An evolutionary biologist who is asked "Why do humans behave aggressively?" might answer that "Aggression was adaptive in the early history of the species; fighting enabled people to defeat competitors, survive, and reproduce" (see Barash, 1982). A psychologist who is asked the same question would probably give a different answer, attributing aggression to such factors as personality characteristics, learning experiences, or observation of aggressive models (see Baron, 1977). A neurophysiologist would supply an even more proximate explanation, attributing aggression to certain electrical and chemical activities in the brain (see Chapters 3 and 14).

To fully understand a behavior, we must view it from different perspectives, attending to both ultimate and proximate causes. When we look at human behavior, we can imagine viewing it through a special kind of telescope. The evolutionary perspective supplies the broadest focus (see Figure 2-4). From the evolutionary perspective, we ask such questions as: What adaptive functions did the behavior serve in the past? What environmental factors caused it to evolve? Why do individuals in other species perform or fail to perform the behavior? When we look at the behavior from the perspective of psychology, we sharpen our focus considerably, asking such questions as: What genetic, environmental, and physiological factors influence the behavior? How does it develop in individuals? What stimuli evoke it? How is it shaped by learning? The evolutionary perspective supplies the ultimate answer to the question "Why?" It explains why the proximate mechanisms that determine behavior exist (as examples, why sex is pleasurable; why humans have large brains, why they feel bad when they are socially isolated, why they feel protective toward their offspring, and why they learn through experience).

Sociobiology and the Evolution of Altruism

When we think of evolved behaviors, the selfish, aggressive, and competitive behaviors that enable people to prevail in the struggle for survival come most readily to mind. Many people assume the theory of evolution dictates that all species, including humans, must be selfish by nature because, by definition, only dispositions that enhance their fitness are selected. But there is quite unequivocal evidence that individuals in some species sacrifice their lives for the sake of others and engage in other fitness-reducing or **altruistic** behaviors. For example, some species of soldier-class bees in effect commit suicide when they sting intruders, thus sacrificing their lives for the benefit of the other bees. Worker-class bees spend their entire lives tending the queen bee, often without producing any offspring of their own.

How could such altruistic behavior evolve if the individuals who behave altruistically are less likely to win the struggle for existence and to pass on their altruistic dispositions to succeeding generations? Darwin was aware of the problem that

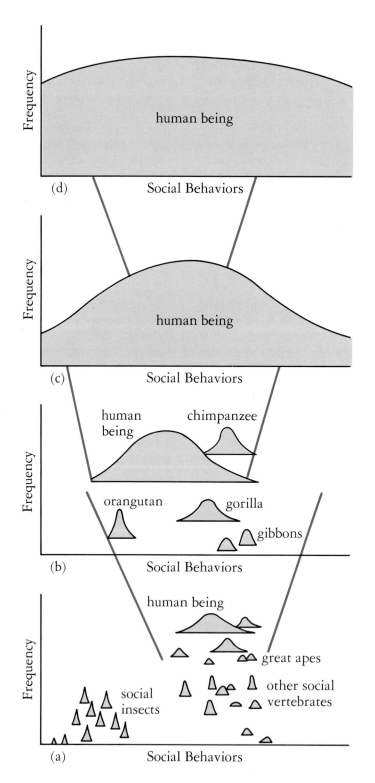

FIGURE 2-4
Perspectives on Social Behavior   (a) Biologists view behaviors across all animal species.   (b and c) Prima-
tologists/anthropologists study behaviors of fewer animal species. (d) Psychologists focus on social behaviors of
living humans.   *Source:* After Barash, D. P. (1982). *Sociobiology and behavior* (2nd ed., p. 149).   New York: Elsevier.

evidence of altruism in social insects created for his theory; in his words, "It at first appeared to me insuperable and actually fatal to the whole theory" (Darwin, 1859, p. 203). Attempting to resolve this paradox was the major impetus for the development in the early 1970s of a new branch of evolutionary theory called **sociobiology** — "the systematic study of the biological basis of all social behavior" (Wilson, 1975, p. 595).

The explanation offered by sociobiologists for the evolution of altruism is based on the idea that the unit of evolution — what is selected — is genes, not individuals. In most cases, the best way for individuals to propagate their genes is to ensure their own survival and to reproduce, thus maximizing their **individual fitness.** However, in some species, the most efficient way for certain individuals to propagate their genes is to help those who share replicas of their genes to survive and reproduce (to help their relatives). In the case of some social insects, sisters share 75% of their genes, rather than 50% as humans and most animals do. The extreme altruism shown to sisters in certain species of bees, ants, and termites is explained as a means of maximizing what sociobiologists call **inclusive fitness** — an individual's net genetic representation in succeeding generations. To quote the founder of sociobiology, E. O. Wilson (1975), "If the genes causing altruism are shared by two organisms because of common descent, and if the altruistic act by one organism increases the joint contribution of these genes to the next generation, the propensity to altruism will spread through the gene pool" (pp. 3–4).

Sociobiology focuses on behaviors that are characteristic of members of various species as a whole — on differences between species, not on differences between individuals. Most sociobiological theory and research relates to nonhuman animals. However, sociobiologists have not been hesitant to apply their principles to human behavior: "Unless we elect to deny evolution and claim that some qualitative, unbridgeable chasm separates us from the rest of life, we must be compelled to look for evolution's imprint on our own behavior just as we seek — and find — it in other species" (Barash, 1982, p. 144).

Sociobiologists insist that to obtain a full understanding of human nature, we must understand the characteristics that were adaptive in the environments of our ancestors and that were therefore propagated. Barash (1982) gives an example, noting that sugar is sweet to humans. The tendency to find sugar sweet is part of our nature; it is an evolved disposition, as are dispositions to find other activities pleasurable. Anteaters do not find sugar sweet; ants are sweet to them. Barash speculates that humans were selected for responding positively to the chemicals contained in ripe fruit. Those who inherited the tendency to like sugars obtained valuable nutrition and survived to reproduce more of their kind. Today, of course, sugar is much more readily available than it was to our ancestors; moreover, humans tend to be less active physically, so they need less sugar. As a result of the changes in the environment that have made sugar so available, the disposition to find sugar sweet has become *maladaptive.* In fact, if natural selection were free to exert its influence, the tendency to find sugar as sweet as some people seem to find it might be selected out of human nature.

Sociobiologists have provided fresh and often provocative perspectives on many behaviors that we discuss in other chapters. The behavior that gives rise to the most intense physical pleasure in humans (and probably other animals as well) is sexual intercourse. Given the importance of sexual activity to the propagation of people's genes, it is easy to understand why the disposition to find sex pleasurable would evolve (see Chapter 8). Learning theory explains how rewards and punishments control human behavior (Chapter 5); evolutionary theory explains why some things are rewarding and others are punishing.

Sociobiological theory also has inspired psychologists from several areas to conduct research on issues hitherto neglected in psychology (see Crawford, Smith, & Krebs, 1987). Sociobiology directs attention to the implications of genetic relatedness for social behavior. For example, such psychologists as Krebs and Miller (1985) and Rushton (1982) have suggested that the disposition has evolved in humans to behave altruistically toward kin and people who resemble kin (people who are similar, familiar, and members of one's in-group). Humans possess the capacity to behave altruistically, but only in certain circumstances. Sociobiologists have adduced evidence that dispositions to cooperate and to reciprocate also have evolved in humans, as have dispositions to cheat and to deceive (Trivers, 1984). Sociobiology also offers an explanation for why people tend to favor some individuals over others. It predicts, for example, that parents who are no longer able to propagate their genes (due to such factors as age, infirmity, or unavailable mates) will be most willing to sacrifice themselves for their offspring.

The most controversial claims of sociobiologists probably center around sex differences in behavior. Sociobiologists note that there is a very important difference between the sexes: females are capable of producing many fewer offspring than males. In humans, females can produce only one offspring every nine months under ordinary circumstances, whereas males are physically capable of producing thousands of offspring. In addition, females know with certainty that their babies are their own; the father's identity may be much less certain. According to sociobiologists, these differences give rise to significant differences in the social and sexual behavior of males and females. In general, a female propagates her genes by producing a small number of high-quality offspring (offspring who possess the characteristics that will enable them to survive, reproduce, and ensure the survival of their offspring) and heavily invests in them. Males, on the other hand, are more disposed to use a high-quantity strategy — propagating their genes by impregnating several females and investing less heavily in their offspring. Due to the differences in orientation between the two sexes, sociobiologists suggest that males of most species compete for females and that females tend to be more selective than males.

Sociobiologists ask why males are different physically, behaviorally, and temperamentally from females in some species but not in others, and why most species are polygamous (males mate with many females) but some, such as eagles, form "marriages" for life. In general, sociobiologists answer that individuals in a species inherit dispositions to behave in ways that have enabled them to propagate their genes (enhance their inclusive fitness) most effectively in the past. Different strategies work in different environments; for example, different mating strategies would be adaptive in environments that contain differing proportions of males and females.

Compared to other species, human males and females tend to be quite similar, both physically and behaviorally. Although sociobiologists suggest that human males tend to be more promiscuous than human females, they grant that human males invest more heavily in their offspring than the males of most other species. Indeed, in some cultures, males are highly paternal and females compete intensely for a small number of high-quality males (Dickeman, 1979).

Does the genetically based position of sociobiology imply genetic determinism and a rejection of the impact of culture and learning on human behavior? Do sociobiologists believe that all human behavior is controlled by genes? Definitely not. Barash makes the position of sociobiologists clear:

> We are the products of biological evolution: a slow, natural process that proceeds by the differential reproduction of individuals and, hence, the gradual replacement of genes in a population [but] we also are experiencing cultural evolution, an incredibly rapid progression of events that occurs even within the lifespan of a single individual. (p. 318)

Sociobiologists grant that most human behavior is shaped by learning and culture, but stress the point that the ability to learn (for example, as it is determined by brain size or by the experience of pleasure) is, in itself, a product of evolution.

In closing, we should mention that, in addition to the impact of learning, there is another related problem in using evolutionary theory to explain human behavior. The environment that selected the characteristics that caused the evolution of the human species has changed radically during the last 10,000 years and continues to change, largely due to changes in culture. According to such evolutionary theorists as Noonen (1987): "These changes, facilitated by our capacity for culture, have happened so quickly that they most likely have outpaced the evolution of reproductively appropriate behaviors in many cases" (p. 47). In an important sense, we are adapted to an environment in which we no longer live.

Human Evolution

Box 2-1 outlines the process of evolution, starting from the fundamental division between plants and animals. According to the fossil record, the line leading to *Homo sapiens* began to diverge from the other primate groups a relatively long time ago. Indeed, a recent estimate indicates that it might have been as long as 5–10 million years ago (Washburn, 1978), or even longer. Although we do not know what circumstances were responsible for such branching, we do know that these circumstances led to a pattern of life that eventually resulted in bipedal (two-footed) gait, erect posture, use of hands as instruments for tool-making, and, later, in a much larger brain.

We know that our early ancestors were hunters and gatherers and that they lived together in relatively small social groups, probably of extended families. We know that some of our ancestors hunted large game (such as mammoths) —an activity that would have required a highly sophisticated ability to cooperate and to communicate. Such communities could not have functioned well unless there was a division of labor in obtaining food (for example, men doing the hunting and women gathering vegetation), in child rearing (women probably assumed the major responsibility for this task), and in such other activities as domesticating animals (the dog was domesticated about 100,000 years ago).

The mysteries of human evolution are far from resolved. We know how we differ from other primates and we know the characteristics that distinguish us must have evolved because they were adaptive—but we don't know exactly how or why. It is commonly assumed that such

physical adaptations as brain size give rise to such behavioral adaptations as use of language. However, some scholars suggest that the reverse may supply a better account of the process. According to Mayer (1978, p. 54), "Behavior often—perhaps invariably—serves as a pacemaker in evolution."

Consider how cooperation in hunting, for example, was enhanced by the ability to communicate. The adaptiveness of these behaviors may have led to the selection of individuals who possessed the physical characteristics (for example, a large brain) that gave rise to such behaviors. According to Washburn and Lancaster (1968, p. 293), it is possible that "our intellect, interest, emotions, and basic social life. . .are evolutionary products of the success of the hunting adaptation." We provide a somewhat speculative account of how the capacity for language may have evolved in early humans shortly. The point to be made here is that the adaptiveness of such behaviors as hunting, dependent on such abilities as language, may have given rise to the evolution of the brain, rather than vice versa.

As the process of evolution is becoming more fully understood, the significance of such social behaviors as pair-bonding, group living, care of young, cooperation, and reciprocity are becoming more fully appreciated (see Axelrod & Hamilton, 1981; Lovejoy, 1981). We are a social species by nature; cooperative group living is one of our most important adaptations (more on this in Chapter 10).

Dryopithecus Australopithecus Neanderthal man Modern man

Ramapithecus Homo erectus Cro-Magnon man

BOX 2-1

THE TREE OF LIFE

It is difficult to relate to changes that occurred over thousands, millions, and sometimes billions of years. Yet, according to the theory of evolution, the endless variations produced by combinations of genes in conjunction with the selective pressures exerted by different environments have produced, over the eons, an extraordinarily large number of species, a great many of which have become extinct.

Traditionally, the relationships among animals have been organized in terms of a **phylogenetic** (evolutionary) **tree**. The figure contains a simplified version of the phylogenetic tree, with special focus on the primate branch.

The earliest and most basic step in evolution was the separation of living cells into cells that could manufacture their own food from raw materials (giving rise to the plant kingdom) and cells that depended on other organisms for their food (giving rise to the animal kingdom). The first animals were the single-celled **protozoa**. The second animals to develop were the multicellular **metazoa**. At first, all metazoa were **invertebrates** (animals that lack a backbone or spinal column).

The emergence of **vertebrates** (animals that possess a spinal column) occurred about 450 million years ago. Exactly how vertebrate animals evolved is not well known; for this reason, the connection between the vetebrate line and the invertebrate line in the phylogenetic tree is broken, as shown in the fig-

ure. The first vertebrates to evolve were fishes. From the point of view of the human species, the next important evolutionary steps were the emergence of amphibians from fishes, of reptiles from amphibians, and, finally, of mammals from reptiles. Birds also evolved from reptiles, but independently from mammals.

As the figure indicates, the first mammals emerged about 200 million years ago. They were small and shy and lived in the shadow of the reptiles that then predominated. About 65 million years ago, for reasons that are not yet clear, most reptilian species underwent rapid extinction; at the same time, many mammalian groups (or **orders**) began rapidly evolving. The order of mammals to which humans belong is the

Biological and Cultural Evolution   Human behavior is affected by both biological and cultural evolution. Because most aspects of culture are behavioral, they are not directly traceable in the fossil record. Accordingly, the reconstruction of cultural evolution must be based on indirect evidence. Tools are one major way to assess the level of cultural development because, as a culture develops, its tools become more varied and sophisticated. The existence of dwellings arranged in a certain way (for example, camps or several caves inhabited at the same time) indicate a communal life and are also evidence of culture.

Figure 2-5 shows a comparative analysis of the development of three aspects of evolution—upright posture and locomotion, brain size, and culture (as indicated by tool evolution).

With regard to cultural evolution [Figure 2-5(a)], we can presume that our earliest ancestors could make use of such tools as sticks or stones at least at the level displayed by modern chimpanzees. About three million years ago, *Australopithecus* made very simple pebble tools by striking a few flakes off of the round stones found in river beds (Weaver, 1985). Tools of this primitive kind were made continuously for

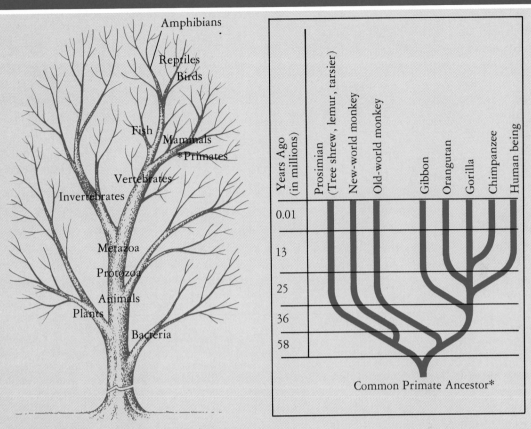

Origin of Life—3.5 Billion Years Ago

The Phylogenetic Tree The first vertebrates appeared about 450 million years ago, the first mammals about 200 million years ago, and the first primates about 65 million years ago. The graph to the right shows the evolution of the primates.

primate order. The main relationships between humans and other primates are also shown in the figure.

Among the primates, the great apes (chimpanzees, gorillas, and orangutans) are most closely related to humans and the prosimians are least related.

one million years—a relatively slow evolutionary pace. By 1.5 million years ago, *Homo erectus* was making considerably more sophisticated tools than those of *Australopithecus.*

The earliest evidence of *Homo sapiens,* our species, is about 300,000 years old. One member of this species, the *Neanderthal* people, emerged about 100,000 years ago. The physical characteristics of the Neanderthals were strikingly similar to those of modern people and their tools (made from flint flakes) were relatively sophisticated. About 35,000 years ago, the *Cro-Magnon* people emerged. They were physically

indistinguishable from humans today and made all sorts of tools, not only from stones but also from bones and other materials. Some Cro-Magnon artifacts appear to have been ceremonial, rather than utilitarian, and some seem to have had purely aesthetic value. The evidence suggests that Cro-Magnon people lived in communities, engaged in extensive hunting, decorated their caves with paintings, and conducted elaborate burial ceremonies. Finally, about 10,000 years ago, *Homo sapiens* began to make the transition from hunting and gathering to farming. This led to the formation of permanent settlements: the

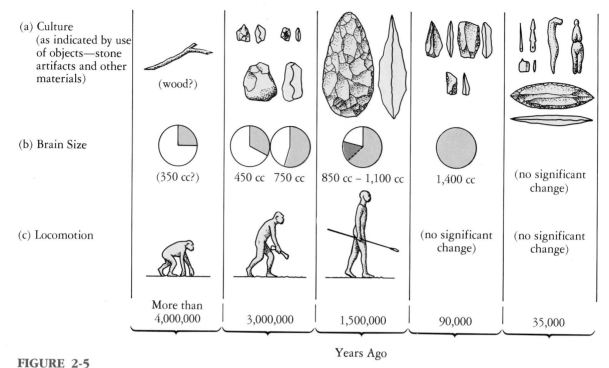

FIGURE 2-5

Biological and Cultural Evolution Successive columns show the comparative evolution of culture (indicated by increasing sophistication of tools), brain size, and upright bipedal locomotion. *Source:* Adapted from Washburn, S. L. (1978, September). The evolution of man. *Scientific American,* 196–97.

building of villages, towns, and cities; and the development of civilization. (The root of this last word, the Latin word *civis,* means citizen or city dweller.)

Referring to Figure 2-5, we can see that humankind has not changed much physically since the time of *Homo erectus.* Although most brain development had occurred by then, the human brain was not completely developed until about 100,000 years ago. Cultural development, on the other hand, proceeded at a relatively slow pace until about 100,000 years ago and then accelerated. So, physical evolution seems to have ceased about 100,000 years ago—at the same time that cultural evolution began to increase.

Cultural evolution continues to progress at an ever-accelerating pace; where it will lead cannot be foreseen. Many scholars believe the capacity to learn and to generate culture, made possible by the evolution of the human brain, has superseded physical evolution in our species. We are a species that has acquired the capacity to flexibly adapt to the environment on a minute-to-minute and day-to-day basis, leaving little oppor-

tunity for natural selection to work. Finches with the strongest beaks may prevail over other members of their species in an environment full of tough-skinned seeds, but would not prevail if other finches could develop nutcrackers. The capacity to develop nutcrackers and other forms of culture has become the defining characteristic of the human species.

Although no serious scholars deny that learning and culture exert a tremendous influence on human behavior, the human species is still heir to the physical characteristics that have evolved over millions of years. The challenge is to understand the roles played by these two forces—heredity and environment. How do the two interact? Are some behaviors primarily determined by biological evolution, as part of our *nature,* and other behaviors primarily determined by cultural evolution, as shaped by *nurture?* How powerful are the forces of heredity—the products of biological evolution? Can they be overridden by what we learn—the products of cultural evolution? We examine *communication* as a case in point to demonstrate the process of evolution and the ways in which genetic and environmental factors interact to produce this complex ability.

The Evolution of Communication

When a male dog urinates on a tree at the corner of the yard, the dog is communicating; chemical traces tell other dogs that the area is his territory. When a male stickleback fish develops a red underbelly in the spring, it also is communicating; the red underbelly tells the female of the species that the male is ready to mate. A monkey's shriek warns other monkeys that a predator is near. A young child in need of assistance while dressing says "Mommy, sock." A professor delivers a lecture. These are also acts of communication. All communications have three essential components: a sender, a message, and a receiver. Why do communication systems evolve in a species? Why do these systems differ between species? In this section, we examine how evolutionary forces have shaped the development of communication — from the simple but effective signaling systems of lower animals to the complex and rich language used by humans.

Communication in Lower Animals
We open by supplying a general answer to the first of the two questions just posed — why do communication systems evolve: the ability to communicate is adaptive because the individuals in most species are dependent on one another for survival and for the propagation of their genes. Communication is helpful in ensuring reproduction, raising young, competing for territory, defending against predators, and in many other ways. For example, consider the mating behavior of a small fish, the three-spined stickleback.

Sticklebacks mate only once a year, always in the spring. The male prepares to mate by selecting a territory, driving away strangers (particularly other sticklebacks), and building a nest. After completing the nest, the male develops a conspicuous red underbelly. He courts passing females, whose readiness to mate is shown by their shining and bulky bodies, each containing 50–100 eggs. When females in this condition enter his territory, the male performs a zigzag dance that continues until a female begins to follow him in a head-up posture (see Figure 2-6). The male then turns toward the nest, and the fe-

male follows. With thrusting movements, the male prompts the female to lay her eggs in the nest, where he fertilizes them. The male then chases the female away and swims off to court another mate.

The proximal stimuli that regulate the mating behavior of the stickleback consist of a synchronized chain of actions in which a particular *signal* from one partner elicits a *response* in the other partner. This response, in turn, becomes the signal for the next behavioral act by the first partner, and so on. These sequences of behavior are controlled by both internal and external stimuli. The internal stimuli are generally hormonal in nature. The external stimuli are primarily of two types: conspicuous body features (the male's red underbelly) and movements (the zigzag dance). The system of communication used by sticklebacks is stereotypic and ritualistic. It is evoked automatically by specific cues, and responses always take the same form. This is characteristic of the communication systems of simple animals low on the phylogenetic scale. Another example is provided in Box 2-2 (page 66).

In summarizing many years of work on communication systems in several species of fish, insects, and birds, Tinbergen (1965) reached three primary conclusions:

1. A unique, ritualistic, species-specific communication system has developed in all species investigated.

2. Communication among members of the species has clear survival value. In the case of mating, for example, the ritual actions peculiar to each species prevent mating with other species, even those that are closely related. Communication also enhances the survival of individuals during food-gathering.

3. Although the communicative behavior of simple species may appear to reflect a deliberate and purposeful plan, it is purely automatic. According to Tinbergen, "Except perhaps in the highest animals, all signaling behavior is immediate reaction to internal and external stimuli" (1965, p. 74).

The automatic nature of communication in simple species became apparent in a series of studies that Tinbergen conducted on sticklebacks. The male's red belly not only serves to

FIGURE 2-6
Stickleback Mating Ritual Sticklebacks engage in a stereotypic series of actions and reactions leading to the female spawning in the nest and the male inseminating her eggs.   The pattern is unlearned and varies slightly from fish to fish.   *Source:* Adapted from Tinbergen, N. (1951).   *The study of instinct.*   New York: Oxford University Press.

attract females, it also evokes attacks from other males who are defending their territory. Tinbergen found that wooden models elicited attacks even if they looked nothing like a male stickleback, as long as the model had a prominent red area. A dramatic example of a misdirected attack occurred when a mail van passing along the road outside Tinbergen's laboratory cast a red reflection on the side of a male stickleback's glass tank; the male immediately lunged at the glass in an attack on the "intruder!" The female stickleback's behavior is similarly stereotypic and therefore occasionally inappropriate. A pregnant female will go through the full mating ritual when she sees a crude, red, wooden model—even to the extent of laying her eggs in a nonexistent nest.

Much the same sort of rigidity is found in the communication system used by birds. For example, female turkeys will brood another young animal (even a skunk) if it is fitted with a device that produces the call of a newborn turkey. Conversely, if prevented from hearing the call of their own offspring, female turkeys will attack and kill them. Such is the nature of communication among fish, insects, and birds. Let us move up the evolutionary scale to consider communication among primates.

Communication in Primates If you have ever watched monkeys in a zoo, you must have appreciated their similarity to humans in terms of communicative behavior (see Figure 2-7). Careful

and lengthy observations of communication among monkeys and apes has shown that "All signals appear to be clearly related to the immediate emotional states of the signaling individuals and their level of arousal. The information transmitted to the receiver refers primarily to the current emotional disposition of the signaler" (Bastian, 1965, p. 598).

The communication systems of primates differ from those of fish, birds, and insects in three primary ways:

1. Primates emit and respond to a broader array of signals.
2. Primates make fine distinctions among apparently similar stimuli.
3. Primates adjust their signaling and responding in accordance with the social context of the communication.

For example, two displays (the swagger and the glare) often presented by male chimpanzees signal different messages in different circumstances (Jensen, 1973). In combative situations involving other adults, the two displays signal aggression; in sexual situations, the two displays typically induce females to present themselves for

FIGURE 2-7

Nonverbal Communication in Primates Humans share with other primates characteristic expressive forms of nonverbal communication. Both show a tense mouth and face when adopting a threatening stance.

BOX 2-2
COMMUNICATION AMONG HONEY BEES

Bees, together with the other social insects, are considered to be at the peak of invertebrate evolution because they possess an elaborate social structure, because they have a strict division of labor according to different *castes,* and because they have complex communication systems. Karl von Frisch deciphered the language of bees during a series of experiments that spanned several decades (see von Frisch, 1974). He observed that when a foraging bee returns from a field of flowers, it engages in what appears to be a dance. At first von Frisch thought the dance was related to pollen-carrying, because the bees that engaged in dancing were always laden with pollen. However, in experiments with artificial feeding stations in which bees were fed sugar solutions at different locations and distances from the hive, he discovered that bees fed sugar solutions would still dance vigorously on their return to the hive.

Further observations demonstrated to von Frisch

(a)

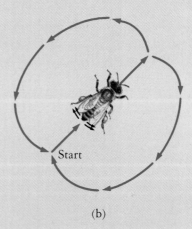

Start

(b)

The *waggle dance* is performed when the source of food is more distant, and indicates the direction of the source.

The *round dance* is performed in the hive by a returning forager when she has found pollen close to the hive.

Dances of the Honeybee *Source:* Bernstein, R. A., & Bernstein, S. (1982). *Biology: The study of life.* San Diego, CA: Harcourt Brace Jovanovich.

copulation. To the human eye, these signals appear to be the same; chimpanzees, fortunately, can tell the difference.

We now consider communication in the species with which we are most familiar—*Homo sapiens.*

Human Communication—Nonverbal Human infants communicate in much the same way that chimpanzees do. For the first few months of life, human infants communicate by coos, cries, smiles, frowns, and later, grasping and eye contact (see Chapter 9). Typically, the messages reflect the infant's current emotional state and evoke appropriate responses in adult caretakers. By the second year of life, the coos and babbles of infants

that the bees had two quite different dances. The "round dance" was performed when the food was nearby and appeared to communicate to the bees in the hive the presence of a food source but not its location. The "waggle dance" communicated information about both the presence *and* location of the food source. The direction of movement while waggling, the number of waggles, the vigorousness of the dance — each carried some meaning about the direction, distance, or amount of food. For one type of bee studied, the round dance signaled food within a radius of about 150 feet from the hive, whereas the waggle dance told about a more distant food source. For another type of bee, the cutoff was at about 300 feet. It seemed that different *dialects* of dance had evolved in different varieties of the bee species. Of particular interest was the finding that bees of one type did not understand the dance signals produced by bees of a different type.

As is typical of the ritualistic behavior of lower animals, the communication system of bees is automatic and stereotypic. The bee's dance on returning to the hive after finding food is triggered by biological mechanisms that have evolved over the ages.

Top of hive

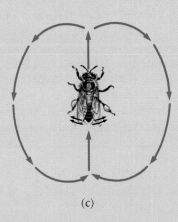

(c)

In this dance, the forager moves up the wall of the hive to indicate the bees should fly toward the sun to reach the food.

Top of hive

(d)

Here, the message is that the bees should fly on a path at a 45 degree angle to the left of the sun.

have changed to language, but that does not mean they have stopped communicating nonverbally. Humans employ two methods of communication: a nonverbal (emotional) system and a verbal (symbolic) system (Harper et al., 1978). Looking first at the nonverbal system, we can distinguish three primary forms: kinesics, proxemics, and paralanguage.

Kinesics include "gestures, movements of the body, limbs, hands, head, feet, and legs, facial expressions (smiles), eye behavior (blinking, direction and length of gaze, and pupil dilation), and posture" (Knapp, 1972, p. 5). The next time you interact with someone, watch for their kinesic signals and see if you can determine what they are communicating. Embarrassment generally shows itself in fidgeting and reduced eye contact; affection is typically reflected in frequent smiling and long periods of eye contact. Anger or rejection may be signaled by crossed arms or legs. Such gestures and expressions do not always carry these messages, of course, but Knapp reviews much research that demonstrates kinesic signals may transmit important information that helps us determine the attitudes and feelings of those with whom we communicate.

Proxemics, a term introduced by Hall (1963), concerns the distance between sender and receiver in nonverbal communication. Each of us is surrounded by a *personal space,* an area in which intrusions by others are unwelcome. The size of this personal space depends on one's relationship to the other person and on the social situation. Strangers who stand less than two to three feet away when communicating with you will almost certainly make you feel uneasy, except at a crowded gathering or in a packed elevator. Your personal space shrinks for acquaintances and friends, and may be nonexistent for loved ones. You can experience the significance of personal space by standing a foot or so away from the next stranger to whom you speak. Your action will probably cause the stranger to be noticeably uneasy and to restore his or her space by moving away from you. Indeed, you may be able to back the stranger across the room in this manner.

The term **paralanguage** (Trager, 1958) refers to the informative aspects of speech that do not involve the meanings of words and sentences. For example, the pitch of speech is a reliable clue to the sex of the speaker, at least in adults. Such other voice qualities as loudness, resonance, and tempo also carry information about the speaker, as do such vocalizations as laughing, sighing, and grunting. These signals often reflect the emotional state of the speaker. The spoken word may carry the same message, of course; sometimes, however, the verbal and nonverbal channels convey quite different signals. The polite but bored conversationalist feigning interest in someone else's ideas; the child unconvincingly denying responsibility for his or her mishap; the disappointed recipient expressing delight at the present that is "Just what I wanted" — in all these cases, videotapes of the actions of these people would probably catch them clearly conveying their true feelings through paralanguage and kinesics.

Human Communication — Verbal Although human infants communicate exclusively in nonverbal terms, they soon develop an entirely different means of communication — spoken language. A fundamental property of language is that it is *symbolic.* A *symbol* stands for or refers to objects, events, properties, and relationships; it is a code for the phenomenon it represents. In **symbolic communication,** senders must first translate the message into an appropriate sequence of symbols and then transmit the symbols to a receiver; the receiver in turn must decode the symbols to understand the meaning of the message. All this occurs so rapidly in normal adult communication that the component processes are seldom noticeable. They become very salient, however, if you try to hold a conversation with a person who is unfamiliar with your language.

A minute's reflection will show that many human activities cannot be accomplished without symbolic communication: completing a tax return, delivering a lecture, reading a newspaper, calling a friend on the telephone, discovering the genetic code, flying a plane, teaching a child to ride a bicycle — all these activities involve symbolic communication. It is important to appreciate that symbols are separate from their referents and therefore can be manipulated independently from the things they represent. Symbols allow us to bridge enormous gaps in time and space, making possible the accumulation of knowledge over countless generations. Symbolic communication is a critical ingredient in the development of the complex society in which we live. We explain how children acquire language in Chapter 9; here we speculate on a different matter — how the capacity to acquire language evolved in the human species.

The Evolution of Human Language

Imagine a party of Stone-age humans on a hunting expedition. It is reasonable to assume that the hunters shared a great deal of knowledge. They probably knew what animals were being hunted, the approximate location of the prey, the terrain, and the basic pattern of chase and kill. For them, hunting was a common enterprise that required communication. So far, this description could just as easily fit a pack of wolves or a group of chimpanzees as a band of humans. Unlike the wolves and the chimpanzees, however, the humans probably engaged in planning a *strategy* before the hunt.

How might the communication necessary for planning have taken place in a pre-language society? Pointing was probably important. One hunter might have pointed to another and then to a particular location, communicating "You go over there." Similar instructions, all made by pointing, could have been given to other members of the group, who would then be positioned at strategically appropriate points for the hunt. The simple pointing gesture could therefore have been used to organize a hunt according to the particular terrain, the animals being hunted, the weather, the skills of the individual hunters, and many other factors. The ability to communicate effectively in this way would have increased tremendously the flexibility of hunting groups, thereby increasing their probability of surviving and propagating the genes that enabled them to communicate in this manner.

Although nonverbal, the pointing gesture exhibits four central features of human language:

1. Pointing is not an automatic response to a specific signal, as are so many of the behaviors of fish, birds, and insects.
2. Pointing typically does not signal the sender's emotional state, as is the case with nonhuman primates. Instead, humans deliberately use the pointing gesture to direct and to specify another individual's behavior.
3. For pointing to serve a coordinative function, the sender and the receiver must agree on the meaning of the gesture and the appropriate response to it.
4. Pointing is an instruction that selects or abstracts a particular person or place for special consideration. *Abstraction* is sometimes viewed as the hallmark of human language.

Even today, humans sometimes communicate by pointing and by other nonverbal gestures. Consider, for example, orchestra conductors, traffic policemen, football coaches, and people who give directions to lost tourists. Indeed, our language echoes this device when we "point out" something. Although humans still use pointing,

they communicate primarily with words. The question arises as to why a nonverbal system of communication was supplemented with a verbal system in the human species.

No one knows the answer to this question with certainty, but we can safely assume there must have been some adaptive advantage to employing verbal signals rather than using pointing gestures to communicate, and we can infer that the advantage must have applied to our ancestors but not to the ancestors of other primate species. When you think about it, the advantages of language are obvious. Pointing depends on close visual contact; verbal signals are effective at greater distances and without visual contact (for example, in a dense jungle or at night). Language also leaves the hands free to perform other important tasks. Our hands are tremendously important tools; it makes sense not to shackle them with a task that may interfere with their normal functions. If it were not for language our vocal chords would be of little use, except for communicating emotion and singing.

We can speculate our ancestors encountered changes in their environment that enhanced the adaptiveness of effective communication. We know they started to hunt big game and live in bands sometime between 500,000 and 2 million years ago. The success of big-game hunting, a cooperative activity, would be significantly enhanced by the development of language, as would the success of such other cooperative activities as moving a trap, arranging a meeting place, and negotiating a division of labor. Whatever the selective forces, it is reasonable to infer they were unique to early humans, because humans are the only species that have acquired the ability to use language in its fullest sense. Social scientists have taught gorillas and chimpanzees a primitive form of sign language but, as documented in Box 2-3, it is less similar to human language than researchers originally assumed.

The essence of language does not lie in its verbal features but in its ability to employ symbols to represent things that are not immediately present. A primitive human who drew a picture of an elephant and then threw a stick representing a spear at it would be *talking* to anyone who understood the message. The role of symbolic language in communication is very important, and so too is the role of language in thought. Once you

Box 2-3
Teaching Symbolic Language to Apes

The possibility that nonhuman animals might be capable of learning a form of human language has long intrigued researchers. One of the earliest studies was undertaken by Yerkes and Learned (1925). These researchers tried and failed to teach a chimpanzee to speak. Relating the failure, they offered the following:

> If the imitative tendency of the parrot were combined with the caliber of intellect of the chimpanzee, the latter undoubtedly would possess speech, since he has a voice mechanism comparable to man's as well as an intellect of the type and level to enable him to use sounds for the purpose of real speech. (p. 53)

This statement provides an important clue to the reason for the failure. As Vygotsky (1962) later pointed out, Yerkes and Learned confused human language with human speech. We now know that nonhuman primates lack the brain mechanisms used by humans to control vocal apparatus, and without which control of vocal language is impossible.

Speech, as the vocal expression of language, is only one means of symbolic communication. Many profoundly deaf people communicate through American Sign Language, a gestural system that makes considerable use of hand signals.

Vygotsky suggested it makes more sense to use such a system in teaching symbolic language to a chimpanzee, inasmuch as the necessary actions are well within the animal's competence. Some years later, Gardner and Gardner (1969, 1975) took up this suggestion and taught American Sign Language to a female chimpanzee named Washoe. After some trial and error, the Gardners found the most efficient method of instruction was to place Washoe's hands and fingers in the desired shape and repeatedly guide her through the sign. The Gardners also used sign language when talking to one another in Washoe's presence.

At four, Washoe had learned to produce more than 130 signs and to understand many more. The signs included numerous common nouns (baby, car, pencil, woman), some modifiers (mine, yours), and some verbs (bite, catch, tickle). Washoe also produced and apparently understood some simple sentences. Asked "Who good?" she replied "Good me." Asked "What want?" her reply was "You me out."

Premack (1971; Premack & Premack, 1972) also had reasonable success in teaching human-like language to a chimpanzee — but with plastic symbols. Sarah, Premack's first subject, quickly learned symbols for her favorite fruits, as well as symbols for the humans who tended and trained her. She also learned symbols for such relationships as *on*. Premack showed that Sarah responded to the plastic token as if it were its referent. For example, she responded to a blue triangle, representing an apple, as if it were round and red rather than blue and angular.

A chimpanzee named Lana was taught to communicate with her experimenters by operating a computer-controlled keyboard (Rumbaugh & Gill, 1976). Each key, roughly equivalent to a word, had embossed on its surface a distinguishing geometric pattern. Some of the keys stood for individuals familiar to Lana; others denoted foods and drinks; another signaled a request to look out the window. By pressing sequences of keys, Lana learned to form sentences, a skill she convincingly demonstrated in a game of her own invention. To Beverly, one of her handlers, she once operated the keys to form the sequence "Beverly move behind room," apparently indicating Beverly should go into the small room behind Lana's cage. That done, Lana proceeded to type "Please machine make window open." As soon as

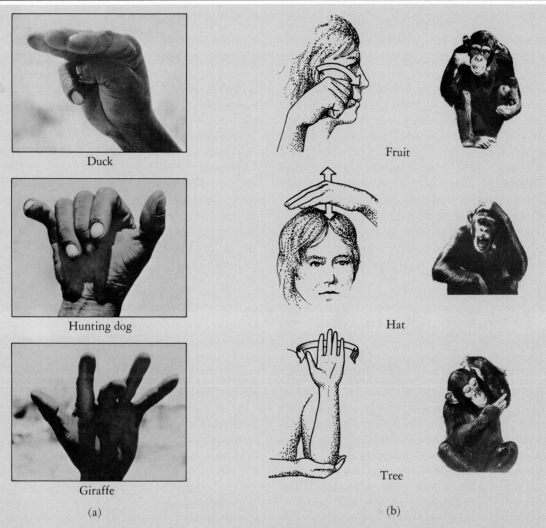

(a) Hand signs used by African Bushmen in the Kalahari Desert during hunting expeditions. (b) Chimpanzee using symbols from the American Sign Language.

Beverly opened the window, there was Lana peeking out.

Chimpanzees are not the only apes that can be taught a form of human language. Patterson and Linden (1981) trained a gorilla named Koko to use sign language. By the age of seven, Koko had mastered some 375 signs she could combine into longer utterances. For example, when asked "Are you an animal or a person?" Koko replied "Fine animal gorilla."

While impressive, these demonstrations have failed to convince at least some psychologists that apes can use language in a similar fashion to humans (Ristau, 1983; Terrace et al., 1979). Two of the concerns critics express are that the ape's intentions in communicating seem to be quite different and much more limited than those of the human child and that learning sign language is a laboriously slow and deliberate process for the ape, unlike the spontaneous and seemingly effortless learning of language by the child. Recent research has focused on whether chimpanzees are capable of symbolic communication under conditions more rigorously controlled than in earlier studies (Savage-Rumbaugh et al., 1983, 1986).

have created symbols for things, you can *discuss* them with yourself—you can think about them (see Chapter 6). Some scholars have suggested the reason why the human brain evolved into the elaborate structure that it is today is a result of the selective advantage of language to early humans, followed by the obvious selective advantages of symbolic thought. According to this view, the adaptive gains of the ability to communicate symbolically were pivotal in the evolution of the human species.

In summary, two systems of communication have evolved in humans: (1) a system of nonverbal communication similar to that employed by other primates and (2) a system of symbolic communication unique to humans. Both systems are more flexible than the stereotypic communication systems of fish, birds, and insects. To understand human nature, we must address both the ways in which humans are similar to related species (for example, nonverbal communication) and the ways in which humans are unique (for example, symbolic language and thought). Although learning and culture exert powerful effects on human behavior, the abilities to learn and to create culture have evolved in the same way as the abilities inherited by stickleback fish, honey bees, turkeys, and chimpanzees.

It is now appropriate to change focus and to turn from the broad perspective offered by the theory of evolution to the related but narrower perspective offered by behavioral geneticists. In the next section, we examine some of the important ways in which individuals differ and consider the causes of the variation within species so important in Darwin's theory.

HEREDITY AND ENVIRONMENT

At the same time that Charles Darwin was developing the theory of evolution, Sir Francis Galton, one of the founders of psychology, was conducting a related but more psychological investigation of the tendency for eminence to run in families. Galton used biographical sources to identify 977 eminent men—each one judged to be so outstanding as to have achieved a position attained "by one person in each 4,000" (Galton, 1892)—and to determine how many of the relatives of these men were also prominent. The number of prominent relatives of these eminent men was well above average. Galton concluded that such concentrations of talent and ability in families are produced by heredity and that mental, physical, and moral abilities are inherited. Adding weight to this view was the observation that the proportion of eminent men in the population varied little between England and the United States, despite the fact that education was much more widespread among American middle and lower classes of that day. Futhermore, Galton compared the success of adopted sons of Roman Catholic popes with the success of sons of the eminent men in his sample. Members of the latter group were clearly more successful, even though they lacked the social advantages of being related to a pope.

Armed with the conclusion that ability is inherited, Galton advocated improvement of the human strain by *artificial selection* (a procedure known as **eugenics**), in much the same way that Plato did in the quotation opening this chapter. According to Galton, we should decide which human characteristics are important, measure the extent to which individuals possess them, and propagate them through selective breeding. Galton founded the human eugenics movement in the hope it would lead to the realization of his dream of producing, by careful selection and mating, an extraordinarily gifted race.

Galton was right about one thing—talent often runs in families. But that does not mean that talent is inherited. Relatives not only possess similar genetic endowments, they also tend to grow up in similar environments. The talented family may be the product of shared genetic makeup or of shared experience, or both. How can we determine the relative influence of each of these factors? Before we answer this question, it is useful to review the laws of heredity and to demonstrate how our genetic makeup shapes both our physical characteristics and our behavior.

Genetic Transmission

The key prerequisite of evolution is **genetic variability** in offspring. Only if individuals show a considerable range of genetic variation in their characteristics is it possible for environmental influences to selectively enhance the survival of the best-adapted individuals. But what produces genetic variability among people? The most important factor is **sexual recombination.** All the cells in our body, except our sex cells (the sperm and the eggs), contain 46 chromosomes, each composed of thousands of complex protein structures called genes. Our sex cells contain random combinations of 23 of the 46 chromosomes. When a sperm fertilizes an egg, 23 randomly selected chromosomes from the male unite with 23 randomly selected chromosomes from the female to produce a 46-cell chromosome. With the exception of identical twins, each offspring produced by this process is unique; he or she has a genetic makeup like no other person.

Variations in offspring that foster the evolution of new characteristics also can be produced by **mutations,** which are changes in the chemical composition of the genes themselves. However, mutations that survive are exceedingly rare; most result in miscarriages during the embryo stage.

The genes contained in chromosomes determine the **genotype,** or internal genetic makeup of the person. The external, observable characteristics of a person (including his or her behavior) are called the **phenotype.** For example, a person is male, has blue eyes, is six feet tall, was first in his class throughout school, gets drunk very easily, and is a firm disciplinarian with his children — these are all characteristics of his phenotype. An important question is whether genes influence these characteristics; and if so, in what way? In other words, what is the relationship between genotype and phenotype?

Genes and Biological Characteristics

Genes are "blueprints for the assembly and regulation of proteins, which are the building blocks of our bodies, including the nervous system"

(Plomin, DeFries, & McClearn, 1980, p. 7). In some instances, these "blueprints" provide quite a precise specification and the biological characteristic is little influenced by such nongenetic factors as learning and experience (Figure 2-8). In other cases, genetic determination is much less powerful and individual variation is largely a result of environmental influences. The relative importance of genes and environment varies with the evolutionary development of a species. The route from genotype to phenotype in animals with simple nervous systems living in relatively unchanging environments is tightly specified. In contrast, the phenotype of animals with more complex brains living in unpredictable environments is less determined by their genetic makeup. As Barash has noted: "The need to interact with a variety of environments and the physical capacity to do so in complex ways also select for flexibility — that is, susceptibility to modification by experience" (1982, p. 30).

In our earlier discussion of the evolution of communication, we described the communication systems of lower animals as automatic and stereotypic — characteristics of behavior that are highly specified by the genetic blueprint and hardly influenced by environmental (nongenetic) factors. With evolution, animals' communication systems became increasingly flexible and responsive to such factors as the context of communication. In other words, the relative influence of heredity declined while the importance of environmental factors increased. This development is shown schematically in Figure 2-9.

It is important to realize that long, complex chains of events connect genes to phenotypic characteristics. The final, genetic expression of even such uncomplicated human features as eye color, blood type, or height may be affected by many nongenetic factors. For example, the potential height of a person is specified by his or her genes. However, whether or not a person attains the height programmed by his or her genes depends on a variety of environmental factors, including adequate nutrition and the absence of any childhood or adolescent diseases that affect growth. In the presence of poor nutrition or disease, people will be shorter than their genetic blueprint indicates. However, it does not follow

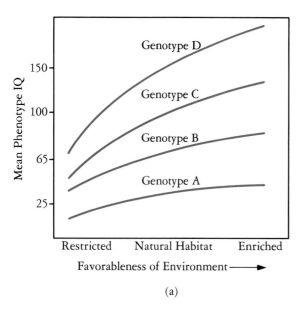

(a)

The expression of behavior (phenotype) varies with both heredity (genotype) and environment. In this example, IQ is successively higher for genotypes A, B, C and D; and for each genotype IQ increases with favorableness of the environment.

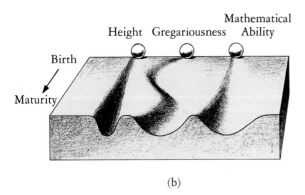

(b)

This model, based on Waddington's (1957) "epigenetic landscape," shows height as being under relatively strict genetic control while gregariousness depends more on environmental factors. The genetic control of mathematical ability is initially strong but weakens with maturity.

FIGURE 2-8

Hereditary and Environmental Contributions to Physical and Behavioral Development *Sources:* Gottesman, I. I. (1963). Heritability of personality: A demonstration. *Psychology Monographs, 77* (No. 572). Waddington, C. H. (1957). *The strategy of the genes.* London: Allen and Unwin.

that, given even better nutrition, people will grow taller than their genetically programmed height. Genetic factors set the upper limit for height; environmental factors determine whether or not that limit is reached.

Genes and Behavior

In quite rare instances, we can identify the influence of a single gene on behavior (see Box 2-4). Genes are not "magical elements that somehow blossom into behavior patterns, as when the puppeteer pulls a puppet's strings" (Plomin, DeFries, & McClearn, 1980, p. 114). All behavior results from the joint influence of many genetic and environmental factors. Consider the example of the alcoholic given by Plomin and his colleagues:

> There is no gene or protein, for example, that repeatedly causes a person to lift shot glasses and perhaps become an alcoholic. Proteins interact with other physiological intermediaries . . . which may be proteins . . . or may be structural properties of the nervous system. Environmental factors (such as . . . nutrition) may also be involved. These influences can ultimately and indirectly influence behavior in a certain direction. For example, differences in neural sensitivity to ethanol may tip the scale in the direction of alcoholism for an individual who imbibes frequently. Various genes, chemical and structural brain differences, and environmental factors may be at the root of such differences in neural sensitivity. (p. 8)

Let us now return to an issue raised earlier: how can the contributions of genetic and environmental influences to behavior be assessed? In our discussion, note that this issue involves the relative contributions of heredity *and* environment, not of heredity *or* environment.

Assessing Heredity and Environment

It is difficult to separate the influence of nature and nurture because genetically similar people (for example, mother and child, brother and sister) also tend to share the same environment. One way is to hold the environment constant and determine if similarity in behavior is correlated with similarity in genetic makeup; this is the goal of *twin studies.* Another approach is to hold the

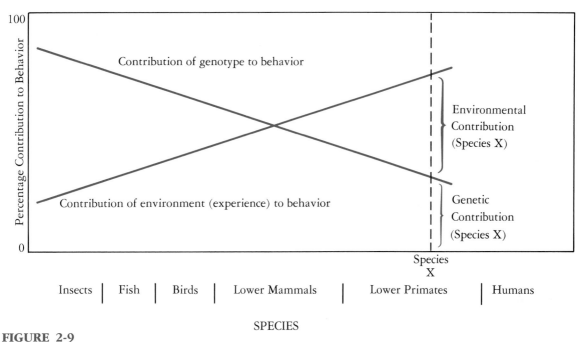

SPECIES

FIGURE 2-9

Effects of Genetic and Environmental Factors on Increasingly Complex Species The contribution of genetic factors decreases while the contribution of environmental factors increases in determining the physical and behavioral characteristics of increasingly complex species. *Source:* Adapted from Barash, D. P. (1982). *Sociobiology and behavior* (2nd ed., p. 30). New York: Elsevier.

genetic relationship constant across different environments; this is the goal of *adoption studies*.

Table 2-1 shows comparisons that can be made in these two types of study. **Twin studies** involve a horizontal comparison between the two conditions (varying in genetic relatedness) in the same row (environment). The study of identical twins raised together versus fraternal twins raised together is an example of a twin study. **Adoption studies** involve a vertical comparison between conditions in the same column. The study of identical twins raised together (birth family) versus identical twins raised apart (adoption families) is an example of an adoption study.

Twin Studies Twins occur in approximately one of every 83 births in the United States (Rao, 1978). About one-third of all twin pairs born are identical; the remainder are fraternal. Because they come from a single fertilized egg, identical twins have exactly the same complement of genes. Fraternal twins come from two different eggs and are no more alike genetically than ordinary brothers and sisters, sharing, on average, about 50% of their genes. When twins are raised together — as they almost always are — they grow up in essentially the same environments. It therefore follows that if the behavioral similarity of identical twins is greater than that of fraternal

TABLE 2-1

Comparing Conditions in Twin and Adoption Studies

		Genetic Relationship	
		Identical	Similar
Family Environment	Same	(a) Identical twins (raised together)	(b) Fraternal twins, or siblings, or parent-child (raised together)
	Different	(c) Identical twins (raised apart)	(d) Fraternal twins, or siblings, or parent-child (raised apart)

Box 2-4
Genetic Influence on Behavior — PKU

Although the blueprint for all human structures and behaviors is laid down in our genes, only rarely do we get a clear view of the operation of this genetic influence. One such instance is the genetic disorder *phenylketonuria,* or PKU as it is commonly known. Sufferers from this disease are unable to break down a chemical commonly found in our diet called phenylalanine. Before an effective treatment was found, this led to a buildup of phenylalanine to poisonous levels in the blood. The result was serious brain damage and profound mental retardation.

The cause of this disease is a defect in a single gene. Although there is nothing we can do to correct that defect, the serious consequences it once had can now usually be avoided by genetic screening and dietary treatment. Genetic screening for PKU is carried out widely as a routine hospital procedure and is estimated to reveal over 90% of infants suffering from PKU. The dietary provision is simple — no phenylalanine. This may not cure the problem entirely because some of the retardation effect is believed to occur prenatally (Bessman et al., 1978). However, the prognosis is reasonably good for this group of PKU sufferers who once accounted for about one percent of the profoundly retarded population.

Advances in our understanding of such genetic defects as PKU have led to the introduction of genetic counseling, in which prospective parents are educated in the risks of genetic problems. The need for this counseling is underlined by the fact that some 20% of infant deaths are attributable to genetic defects (Porter, 1977), whereas approximately 3% of all newborn infants have some genetic birth defect (Epstein & Golbus, 1977). In some cases, such as PKU, environmental factors that greatly ameliorate the condition can be changed. In others, such as color blindness, the condition is quite tolerable. Certain genetic defects are incurable given the state of our current knowledge, however, which has led some people to question the ethics of screening for them (Omenn, 1978).

twins, it must be because of the difference in the proportion of genes they share (100% for identical twins; 50% for fraternal twins).

The assumption of equal environments is obviously crucial to a comparison of identical and fraternal twins and merits consideration here. Certainly, twins have the same prenatal environments, are born at the same time, and generally experience events at the same age. We will limit out consideration to fraternal twins of the same sex and to twin pairs reared in the same family. Even then, however, it may not be reasonable to assume that identical and fraternal twins experience the same environments. For example, identical twins may be treated more similarly than fra-

ternal twins, thereby providing the former with more similar environments than the latter. An opposite effect is also possible: identical twins may go out of their way to establish separate identities thereby creating *less* similar environments than those experienced by fraternal twins.

One way to test for these effects is to look at the behavior of twins who have been mislabeled (identical twins who mistakenly believe themselves to be fraternal and fraternal twins who mistakenly believe themselves to be identical). Over 100 twin pairs fitting these descriptions and a larger number of correctly labeled twin pairs were studied by Scarr and Carter-Saltzman (1979). On both cognitive and personality tests,

COLOR PLATES

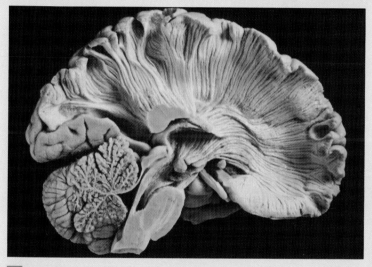

I *(top)* Cross-section of the left hemisphere of a human brain (most corpus callosum removed) showing the fibers that connect central brain structures with the cerebral cortex.

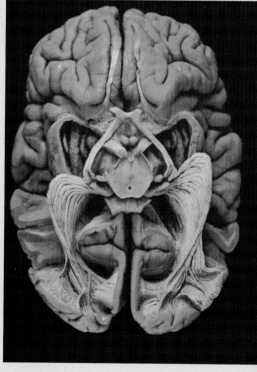

(bottom) View of the underside of the human brain showing the principal visual pathways (see Figure 4-6). The optic nerve (severed just before the optic chiasma) passes via the lateral geniculate nuclei to the visual cortex of each hemisphere.

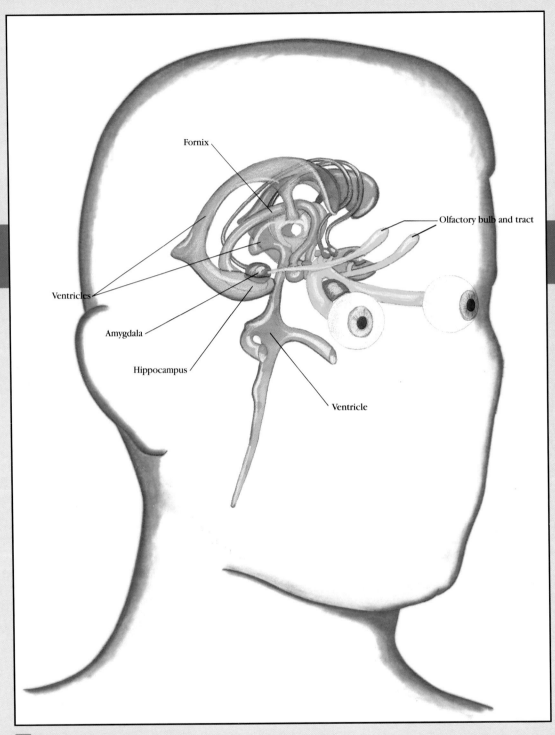

Limbic system and associated structures of the human brain (ventricles are fluid-filled hollow chambers within the brain).

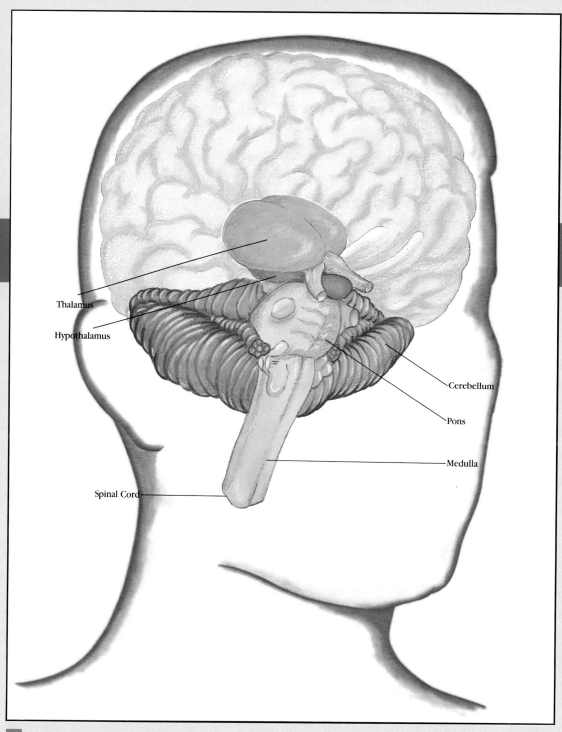

III Representation of the human brain emphasizing its core structures.

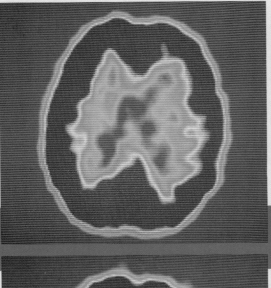

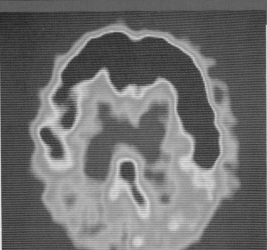

II A ring of detectors surrounds the patient's head during a PET (Positron Emission Tomography) scan. The images produced display a range of colors reflecting the amount of neural activity in different areas of the brain. The top image is normal; the bottom image reveals Alzheimer's disease.

CAT (Computerized Axial Tomography) scan produces images of brain structures. The left scan reveals a brain tumor; the right scan shows evidence of an optic nerve lesion.

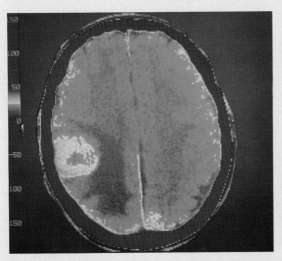

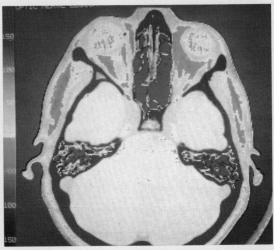

TABLE 2-2
Correlation between Differences for Identical Twins on Similarity. of Appearance and Behavioral Measures

Measure	Correlation[*]	Number of Twin Pairs
Stanford-Binet IQ test	0.05	47
WISC IQ test	−0.19	74
Personality test (average of 16 PF[†])	0.00	51

[*] A positive correlation means that identical twins who were more similar physically were more similar behaviorally.
[†] 16 PF is Raymond Cattell's 16 Personality Factors test.
Source: Matheny, A. P., Wilson, R. S., & Dolan, A. B. (1976). Relations between twins' similarity of appearance and behavioral similarity: Testing an assumption. *Behavioral Genetics, 6,* 343–52.

the twins behaved primarily according to their true genotype. If mislabeling did lead to environmental differences, they had little effect on the twins' test performance.

Another way of testing the equal-environments assumption is to determine whether the differences in behavior that do exist between identical twins are correlated with differences in their similarity of appearance. Matheny, Wilson, and Dolan (1976) measured several aspects of intelligence and personality in pairs of identical twins. They correlated differences on these measures with the degree of physical similarity between the members of each pair. Their findings, shown in Table 2-2, provide no evidence of an association between physical and behavioral similarity. Again, to the extent that variation in physical similarity led to different environments, at least for identical twins, this had no observable effect on their behavior. This support for the equal-environments assumption allows us to view the results of twin studies with some confidence.

Shields (1962) conducted a study in which he compared 44 pairs of identical twins reared together and 32 pairs of fraternal twins reared together (conditions (a) and (b) in Table 2-1). Shields gave all his twins a battery of tests that measured a large number of physical characteris-

tics and behaviors. The general conclusion from the study was that heredity exerted a clear influence on several physical and psychological characteristics. With environmental factors held constant, identical twins were more similar to one another than fraternal twins were on the following characteristics: weight, smoking habits, intelligence, and measures of temperament.

In another study, Gottesman (1966) obtained an estimate of the influence of genotype on personality characteristics by administering a personality test to 147 pairs of adolescent twins of the same sex who were reared together, 79 of which were identical and 68 of which were fraternal. Gottesman found that seven personality characteristics showed a significantly higher correlation for identical twins than for fraternal twins. Four of these characteristics were related to *extroversion* versus *introversion*—the personality dimension that describes how outgoing and other-directed versus ingoing and self-directed a person is. Dworkin and his associates (1977) managed to give a follow-up test to 42 pairs of the original twins when they were about 28 years old and again found significant, genetically based similarities in the organization of personality. Even as adults who had experienced varied environments, identical twins exhibited more similar personality characteristics than fraternal twins.

Adoption Studies The most powerful type of adoption study involves comparison of identical twins raised together with identical twins raised apart (conditions (a) and (c) in Table 2-1). Unfortunately, because the latter cases are extremely rare, few studies have been based on this comparison. What evidence does exist, however, seems clear. For example, the Shields (1962) study (described in the previous section) also included a group of 44 pairs of identical twins raised apart. The similarity between their behavioral and personality characteristics almost matched that of the identical twins reared together. And in the comparison that pitted genes against environment, Shields found the identical twins reared apart were more similar than the fraternal twins reared together.

A more frequent comparison in adoption studies is between children and birth parents and

TABLE 2-3
Parent – Child IQ Correlations for Adoptive Parents and Birth Parents

	Adoptive Parents		Birth Parents	
	Correlation	Sample Size	Correlation	Sample Size
Father – Child	0.16	175	0.40	270
Mother – Child	0.09	184	0.41	270

Source: Scarr, S., & Weinberg, R. A. (1978). The influence of "family background" on intellectual attainment. *American Sociological Review, 43,* 674 – 92.

children and adoptive parents (conditions (b) and (d) in Table 2-1). To the extent a particular behavior is influenced strongly by genotype, the children should be like their birth parents in that regard. On the contrary, if environmental factors are the dominant forces, then adopted children should be similar to their adoptive parents. Scarr and Weinberg's (1978) study yielded the data shown in Table 2-3, where we see that the correlation of IQ between children and their adoptive parents is low (but not zero) and is clearly less than the correlation of IQ between children and their birth parents. The influence of genetic and environmental factors can be seen in these data.

Adoptive studies also have been used to determine whether genetic makeup plays a role in such mental disorders as schizophrenia (see Chapter 13). We know that schizophrenia runs in families. Table 2-4 shows the risk estimates for the general population and for relatives of schizophrenics. There is about a 1% probability of a randomly chosen person becoming schizophrenic. That figure rises to 2.1% for second-degree relatives (for example, grandchildren) of a schizophrenic and to almost 10% for the children of a schizophrenic.

TABLE 2-4
Estimates for Risk of Schizophrenia

Category	Risk (Percent)
General Population	0.9
First-degree relatives:	
parents of schizophrenics	4.2
siblings of schizophrenics	7.5
children of schizophrenics	9.7
Second-degree relatives	2.1
Third-degree relatives	1.7

Source: After Rosenthal, D. (1970). *Genetic theory and abnormal behavior.* New York: McGraw-Hill.

What these data do not tell us is the relative contribution of hereditary and environmental factors to this pattern. Adoptive studies have helped psychologists separate a child's genetic influence (birth parents) and his or her environmental influence (adoptive parents). To summarize briefly, several adoptive studies of schizophrenia have revealed that children of nonschizophrenic parents raised by schizophrenic adoptive parents showed no increased risk of suffering from the disorder. These and other supportive data indicate the family pattern for schizophrenia is due to hereditary factors. Although environmental influences may well be important in triggering the disorder, the disposition for schizophrenia is, at least in part, genetically determined.

Much progress has been made, primarily due to twin and adoption studies, in estimating the relative contributions of heredity and environment to some human behaviors. We now look more closely at the results of such research as it applies to that most human attribute — intelligence.

Intelligence

Several recent studies have obtained estimates of similarities of IQ scores for pairs of people with varying degrees of genetic relatedness and raised in the same or different environments. The results are summarized in Table 2-5. The nature of the family relationship — from unrelated individuals reared in different families to identical twins reared in the same family — is shown in the first column. The correlations expected if genetic differences were the *only* source of variation in IQ are shown in the second column. The median size of the actual correlations found for each type of family relationship is shown in the third column.

TABLE 2-5
Correlation of IQ

Genetic Relatedness	Expected Correlation (genetic influence only)	Obtained Correlation
Genetically identical:		
same individual tested twice	1.00	0.87
identical twins (raised together)	1.00	0.86
identical twins (raised apart)	1.00	0.75
Genetically related:		
fraternal twins (raised together):		
same sex	0.50	0.62
opposite sex	0.50	0.62
siblings (raised together)	0.50	0.34
parent–child (birth family)	0.50	0.35
Genetically unrelated:		
Unrelated children (raised together)	0.00	0.25
Parent–child (adopt. family)	0.00	0.15

Source: After Plomin, R., & DeFries, J. C. (1980). Genetics and intelligence: Recent data. *Intelligence, 4,* 15–24.

The observed correlation in IQ for identical twins reared together (0.86), although lower than the theoretical maximum (1.00), is almost the same as the practical maximum (0.87 for the same individual tested twice). The correlation is lower for fraternal twins, which is not surprising given their weaker genetic bond. Note, however, that the observed correlation of 0.62 is higher than that expected (0.50) if the only determinant of intelligence were genetic. The difference reflects environmental influences, which are also responsible for the weak correlations (0.25, 0.15) for genetically unrelated members of adoptive families. Correlations of intermediate size

(0.34 – 0.35) are found for parents and children and for siblings who have the same genetic bonding as twins but less similar environments.

According to the findings summarized in Table 2-5 and the results of several adoptive studies, genetic factors are responsible for roughly 50% of the variation in IQ scores; the other 50% is due to environmental factors. This statement applies to variation of IQ scores *between individuals* within a population. A related issue, but one that is different in certain important respects, is the question of whether average IQ differences *between groups* of people are caused by differences in their genetic potential or by differences in their upbringing.

We now turn to a consideration of racial differences in IQ — an issue that has fueled one of the most acrimonious debates in the history of psychology. Before you read the following section, it is important to remember two things. First, *between-group* differences in IQ are generally very small compared to *within-group* differences. Second, knowing the origin of within-group differences in IQ tells us nothing about the cause of between-group differences. Even if within-group differences are shown to be 100% attributable to genetic factors, between-group differences could nevertheless be 100% due to environmental influences.

Racial Differences in IQ   Jensen (1969, 1978, 1981) has argued that the observed difference in the United States of about 15 points between the average IQ scores of blacks and whites reflects a genetic difference between the races. Jensen does not claim the difference is wholly genetic in origin; rather, he argues the difference in racial heredity is responsible for at least part of the observed difference in average IQ.

Jensen offers three primary arguments in support of his position. First, he suggests that the black – white difference in measured IQ is much larger than the difference that would be predicted from social, economic, and cultural (environmental) differences between the two groups. Therefore, Jensen concludes, it is reasonable to suppose that genetic differences between the groups must be contributing to the observed differences in measured intelligence. Although Jensen has developed methods of estimating the

degree of social, economic, and cultural differences between American blacks and whites, his methods and the results they have produced have been disputed strongly (Kamin, 1974; Mackenzie, 1984).

Second, Jensen argues that the pattern of black – white variances in abilities is dissimilar from the one that would be expected if environmental differences were the major source of the divergence between the groups. Intelligence consists of a number of abilities, including verbal reasoning, number ability, and abstract reasoning. Most psychologists believe tests that emphasize nonverbal problem-solving, perceptual ability, and abstract reasoning are less influenced by environmental training, or culture, than tests that emphasize vocabulary, verbal reasoning, and acquired information. The latter tests are sometimes referred to as culturally biased measures. Jensen (1978) has produced evidence that blacks perform relatively more poorly on nonverbal items than they do on verbal items, suggesting that cultural background or environment is not the main source of the difference. Critics of this position have been quick to point out that such nonintellectual factors as pace of life, comfort in the testing situation, and motivation may affect test performance (Kamin, 1974).

Jensen's third argument is based on a comparison of the average IQ scores for siblings of black and white children. According to genetic theory, the most probable IQ score for a full sibling lies halfway between the IQ score of his or her brother or sister and the IQ score of the general population. Thus, if one sister has an IQ of 120 and if, as intelligence testers purport, the average IQ for the population is 100, then the second sister would be most likely to have an IQ of 110. Several studies measuring the IQ scores of black and white siblings typically have found the average difference between the IQ scores of black siblings is 7 – 10 points lower than the average difference between the IQ scores of white siblings. Jensen interprets this result as an indication that the average IQ for the black population is lower than the average IQ for the white population and that IQ is determined genetically. The problem with this argument, as Mackenzie (1984) and others have pointed out, is that a similar prediction of sibling IQ can be made from an environmental point of view.

Two studies by Scarr and Weinberg (1976) present quite a different picture of racial differences in IQ from the one painted by Jensen. Scarr and Weinberg compared the average IQ scores of white and black children adopted into white families to the IQ scores of their adopted parents and to the IQ scores of their matched biological parents. Some of the black children had one black parent; some, two. The homes of all adopted children were intellectually enriched (the parents had high IQs, good jobs, good educations, and so forth). Scarr and Weinberg noted that "The biological children in our two studies had the benefits of both genes and environment; the adopted children were born to intellectually average parents but raised in intellectually enriched homes" (p. 31).

The results of these studies revealed the following patterns of data:

1. The average IQ score of adopted black children (110) was at least 15 points higher than the national average for black children and higher than the IQs of their biological parents.

2. The average IQ score of adopted black children (110) was lower than both the IQ scores of their adoptive parents (119) and the IQ scores of the biological children of their adoptive parents (117).

3. The adopted black children's school achievement followed the same pattern as their IQ scores.

4. The same pattern of results held for adopted white children. Their IQ scores were about 6 points higher than the IQ scores of their biological parents but 6 points lower than the IQ scores of the biological children of their adoptive parents.

Scarr and Weinberg (1976) concluded that because the IQ scores of white and black adopted children were comparable, "It is unlikely that the heralded differences between blacks and whites are genetically based" (p. 31). They arrived at a similar conclusion based on their measurements (from the frequencies of certain blood groups and serum protein) of African versus European ancestry in their black subjects. Contrary to predictions from the genetic-differences hypothesis,

this measure of "blackness" was found to be unrelated to IQ.

That brings us back to the original question. In the words of Scarr and Weinberg, "Given similar home environments, why does one child turn out to be brighter than another?" (p. 32). The answer, they suggest, is that although differences *between* blacks and whites are caused by environmental factors, differences *within* these groups "are largely due to genetic programming" (p. 32). The central basis for their conclusion is the finding of a consistent, positive correlation between the IQ scores of children and their biological but not adoptive parents. Similarly, the IQ scores of adopted children were much more similar to the IQ scores of their biological brothers and sisters (with whom they did not grow up) than to the IQ scores of their siblings in their adoptive families.

We can do no more than scratch the surface of this topic here. Obviously, its political and social implications are highly controversial. Readers interested in pursuing this issue may consult Mackenzie (1984), who provides a dispassionate and convincing analysis of the various claims and counterclaims of those who have investigated the relationship between race and IQ score.

The goal of the research we have been discussing is to determine the relative contribution of heredity and environment to a particular psychological characteristic — intelligence. Although it is possible to obtain estimates of the contribution of each, we must remember that hereditary and environmental influences work together to produce their results. All psychological characteristics result from the joint influence of genetically determined potentials and individual experiences. In twin and adoption studies, heredity and environment are treated as very general forces. These studies are structured to obtain estimates of the similarities in and differences between people's overall genetic relatedness and overall experience. They do not determine the ways in which heredity and environment interact (the ways in which innate potentials are shaped by environmental events). We now examine the ways in which heredity and environment interact to produce a very special characteristic — our sex or **gender identity.**

GENETICS AND GENDER

Genetic, or chromosomal, sex is determined at conception. If a Y (male) chromosome is present, it activates genes on the X (female) chromosome that cause previously undifferentiated tissue (gonads) to develop into testes rather than ovaries. All subsequent internal and external bodily changes characteristic of the male are activated by the secretion of hormones from the testes. If the father contributes an X chromosome, rather than a Y chromosome, the gonads develop into ovaries, and the course is set for the development of a female. The female pattern (internally and externally) is the prescribed route of development unless a specific change in the male direction occurs. The hormone testosterone, when present during fetal development, suppresses further development of internal female organs and promotes the development of external male organs.

Of course, the appearance of the external organs determines the assigning of sex, which leads to the child being reared as female or male and, later on, to the child's self-identification as female or male. The sequence from conception to adult gender identity is outlined in Figure 2-10. From birth on, females and males are characterized in different terms. It has been reported that newborns wrapped in pink blankets are more likely to be described as "cute," "little," and "like their mothers" (Rubin et al., 1974) than are newborns wrapped in blue blankets. Children begin calling themselves "girls" or "boys" soon after they learn to speak, at about age two. At first, however, they probably confuse the meanings of these concepts. Children do not acquire **gender permanence** — the concept that being a girl or a boy is a permanent state — until about age five or six.

The Conflict between Heredity and Environment

From the very beginning, our environment is arranged to reinforce the sex assigned to us at birth. This typically corresponds to the genetic sex of the individual. But what would happen if the wrong sex were assigned to a child at birth and a boy were brought up as a girl or a girl were

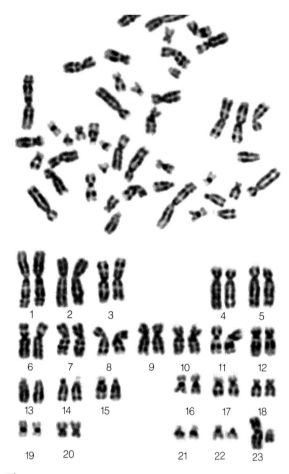

Chromosomes

Upper photo (enlarged approximately 1,500 times) of the 46 chromosomes of the normal human male. Lower photo of chromosomes arranged in appropriate pairs. (The normal human female also has pairs 1 through 22 — but pair 23 is XX rather than XY.) The chromosomes are shown undergoing mitosis (thus appear double), the stage when each chromosome duplicates itself and splits apart. *Source:* Photo by Dr. J. H. Tijo, National Institute of Health.

brought up as a boy? Would the influence of the environment overcome the influence of the genes, or vice versa? Under ordinary circumstances, these questions could never be answered. However, abnormal occurrences provide psychological researchers with unique opportunities to test significant theoretical questions. So-called sex-errors of the body—

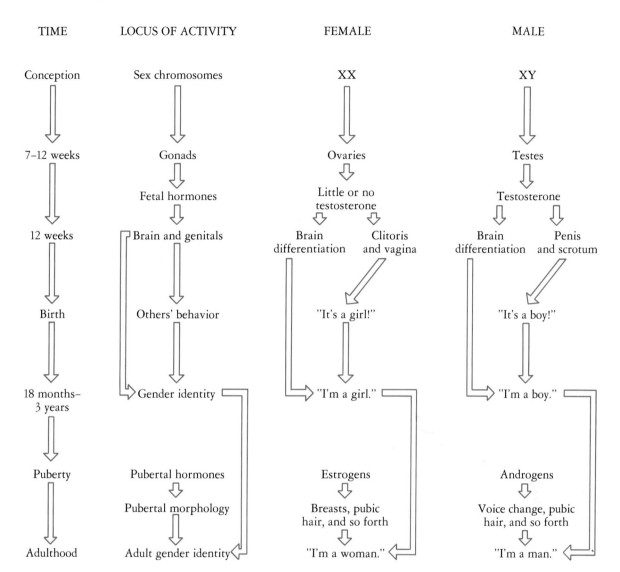

FIGURE 2-10

Development of Gender Identity The columns show how heredity and environment interact to produce a male or female identity.

accidental aberrations at one or more of the steps in gender development outlined in Figure 2-10 — give us an answer to this important question.

Due to an accident of nature, a fetus may develop tissues that are insensitive to testosterone, or a fetus with X and Y chromosomes (which would normally lead to the characteristics of a male) may fail to develop testes. These fetuses lack the necessary testosterone to continue to develop as males. In both instances, the baby is born with the appearance of a female, even though it is genetically male. The child is usually reared as a girl. Often the mistake is not discovered until as late as puberty, when the "girl" fails to menstruate or to develop a typical female body shape. Similarly, some genetic females are born with the external characteristics of males, having accidentally received an excessive amount of testosterone during fetal development as the result of a tumor on an adrenal gland or of hormonal injections given to mothers with a high risk of miscarriage.

Genetic Females Reared as Males John Money and Anke Ehrhardt (Money, 1971, 1976; Money & Ehrhardt, 1972) have extensively studied sex errors in an attempt to assess the relative influence of heredity and environment on gender identity. Money investigated two cases of children who seemed to be males at birth (appearing to possess a penis and scrotum) but who were genetically female. In the first case, the person was reared as a male. He developed normally as a boy, and was diagnosed as genetically female only when he reached puberty and started to develop breasts. Medical doctors considered it wise to reassign his sex and to allow him to develop as a girl. However, this solution was totally unacceptable to the boy himself and to his parents. Eventually, he was given surgery and hormonal treatment that permitted him to continue to live as a boy.

In the second case, the child developed medical problems shortly after birth; during examination, it was discovered that "he" was a she. Her external genitalia were surgically feminized, and she was reared as a female. She developed a firm and normal feminine gender identity. So despite identical genetic sex (female) and genital appearance at birth (male), the first child became a male and the second child became a female, depending on the sex of assignment and rearing.

On the basis of such cases, Money concluded there is an optimal period for gender assignment and for the formation of gender identity. If a mistaken gender assignment is discovered and changed before about four or five years of age, the child will accept the assignment and develop normally. Beyond this age, when gender permanence is achieved, reassignment is likely to cause severe conflicts and problems and to disrupt normal development.

Genetic Males Reared as Females It may seem amazing that something as basic and biologically determined as our sex could be changed by the way in which we are brought up. Does this imply we could take any newborn female and turn her into a male through environmental input, and vice versa? Certainly not. Although Money stresses the importance of environment in the formation of gender identity, his cases of sexual reassignment are always supplemented by corrective surgery and/or hormonal treatment to ensure that the child's biological characteristics are reformed to correspond to those of the assigned sex.

In addition, certain work by Imperato-McGinley (1974) implies that gender identity may be more flexible than John Money's case studies suggest. In a remote village in the Dominican Republic, 24 children — looking more like girls at birth — were raised as females. It turned out the children had a form of androgen insensitivity and were genetically male. At puberty their voices deepened, their genitals masculinized, and beards appeared. They subsequently changed their gender identities and were accepted as males by their society.

Clearly these results conflict with Money's contention that sex of assignment and rearing are of primary importance in determining gender identity. Of course, the parents of the Dominican Republic children may have known from the beginning that the sex of their children was ambiguous; they could have suspected the "girls" would change into boys and have raised them accordingly. Yet the results of this study raise the possibilities that adolescent hormones are of great importance in gender identity and that a new sex-role assignment can override the effects of an earlier one.

Masculinized Females Money and his associates (Ehrhardt & Baker, 1974; Money, 1971, 1976; Money & Ehrhardt, 1972) have also examined the development of genetic females prenatally masculinized by testosterone (an androgen) but surgically and hormonally treated and raised as females. Do such females behave any differently than females not exposed to this abnormal event prior to birth? A series of related studies suggests they display some characteristics later in life that stereotypically are considered masculine.

Females exposed to excessive testosterone differed from their mothers and sisters (Ehrhardt & Baker, 1974) and from a group of unrelated females (Money, 1971, 1976; Money & Ehrhardt, 1972) in the following ways. The females exposed to excessive testosterone had a greater fondness for vigorous, athletic activities and preferred boys as playmates. (However, they were no more likely to initiate fights and otherwise act aggressively than females in the comparison groups). Such females also tended to choose functional rather than pretty clothing, hairstyles, and adornments. Their activities during childhood were notably devoid of doll play or other preparations for future motherhood. These females were significantly more likely to call themselves "tomboys," although they were quite satisfied with their female gender identity. This complex of characteristics has been called the *tomboy syndrome.*

Did early exposure to testosterone affect the sex lives of the females? The answer, according to Money's findings, is "not much." Although the average age for onset of sexual dating activity was later in the prenatally testosteronized females, Money found no lack of erotic response in later life and no indication of greater-than-average likelihood of lesbianism. Many of these women married and successfully bore children.

The studies on masculinized females by Money and Ehrhardt have been criticized by Frieze and her colleagues (1978) because the comparison group of females in the Money–Ehrhardt study may have been more stereotypically feminine than would be expected in a ran-

dom sample. In addition, critics have suggested that the girls' abnormality may have affected their expectations about how masculine they would be. Despite the necessity of taking these and other qualifications into account, the possibility that prenatal testosterone produces a masculizing effect on certain brain circuits cannot be dismissed.

In summary, studies on the conflict between heredity and environment in sexual development suggest that even such a basically biological aspect of human nature as gender identity is determined by the interaction between heredity and environment.

Obtaining an estimate of the role that heredity and environment play in the development of various characteristics is primarily of interest to scholars. What most people want to know is what they can do to maximize whatever innate potential people possess. Although little can be done to modify people's genetic endowment, a great deal can be done to modify people's environment. We turn now to an examination of the ways in which favorable or unfavorable environments affect development.

ENRICHMENT AND DEPRIVATION

Environments can be extreme or atypical in several ways. One type of extreme environment occurs when a member of one species is raised in an environment that is typical of another species. Although there have been stories of humans raised by apes, wolves, and other animals, there is no firm evidence to support these claims; it is more likely that retarded or otherwise abnormal children were abandoned by their parents only briefly before being discovered living with animals. An environment also can be extreme because the developing child is deprived of normal stimulation, social contact, and other experiences to which most children are exposed or because the environment provides more stimulation and experience than usual. Psychologists have investigated the effects of both early deprivation and early enrichment.

Early Deprivation
The Effects of Social Isolation on Monkeys
Experimental studies on the effects of deprivation necessarily have involved nonhuman animals. In a number of classic studies, Harry Harlow and his colleagues (1959, 1962) raised monkeys under conditions of extreme social deprivation. The monkeys did not see another monkey or human being for the first two years of life. The isolated animals showed abnormal social reactions at four years of age, even after spending two years with other monkeys. The isolates made no attempt to defend themselves against other monkeys, did not engage in sexual activity, and interacted only minimally. The investigators concluded that during early years of development the presence of other monkeys is critical for normal development.

Harlow was interested in how the socially deprived female monkeys would behave if they had offspring. They had not known their own mothers; would they know how to act if they became mothers themselves? Harlow had considerable difficulty answering this question because the deprived females showed no interest in sexual behavior. They usually treated sexual advances from male monkeys as attacks, either running away or fighting; they apparently had no idea how to respond. Even when placed with the most attractive, gentle, and persevering males, they never achieved sexual intercourse. Harlow had to develop a machine to inseminate the females artificially, and eventually several deprived females were impregnated. When they gave birth, their behavior toward their newborn infants was extremely abnormal. Some mothers were completely apathetic; others were very aggressive. Some of the apathetic mothers slowly learned to interact with their infants if the infants were especially persevering in their attempts to nurse. But aggressive mothers remained incorrigible; some tried to kill their infants, so the re-

maining infants had to be removed to survive.

Harlow's early research suggested quite strongly that early isolation creates irreversible damage to the normal behavior of monkeys. However, in a later study, Suomi and Harlow (1978) found that monkeys who were raised in isolation for six months and who developed abnormal symptoms managed to regain normalcy after being housed for seven months with normal female monkeys three months younger in age. This suggests the maladaptive effects of social isolation can be reversed after six months but not after a period as long as two years.

Harlow's studies showed that such activities as sexual and maternal behaviors can be affected greatly or even eliminated by environmental intervention. Would these effects occur in humans? In an attempt to answer this question, several psychologists have examined children who have undergone natural types of deprivation.

The Effects of Early Institutionalization
Children in institutions suffer varying degrees of deprivation. Investigators have compared insti-

tutionalized and noninstitutionalized children as to social, emotional, physical, and intellectual functioning. Institutionalized children typically perform more poorly in all these areas than noninstitutionalized children. When the deprivation is extreme and prolonged, children often lapse into resignation, withdrawal, and apathy (Bowlby, 1969). However, the effects can be reversed if the child is placed in a different environment before he or she is too old. Skeels (1966) found that children who remain in minimum-care institutions beyond the first year of life continue to be dependent on others; about one-third died before reaching the age of 30. By contrast, children placed in a more stimulating environment (although still in an institution) for the second year of life and then placed in adoptive homes grow up to be completely normal. This study suggests that deprivation must continue beyond a year in humans to have irreversible effects.

Kagan and Klein (1973) observed a group of primitive Indians in an isolated Guatemalan village who kept their children isolated in dark, windowless rooms for the first year of life. These Indians believe that dust, air, sunlight, and the gazes of certain types of people cause infants to become ill. The infants were loved and cared for (fed on demand and held close to their mothers' body), but not spoken to, played with, or given toys. When Kagan and his colleagues studied them at one and one-half years of age, they were passive, fearful, and intellectually retarded. In Kagan's (1973) words, "If I had seen infants like the Guatemalans in America prior to my experience, I would have gotten upset, called the police, had the children removed, and begun to make gloomy statements about the fact that it was all over for these children" (p. 41). However, much to Kagan's surprise, the older children in the village were entirely normal — performing even better at eleven years of age than their American age mates on culture-fair intelligence tests.

Kagan concluded that human infants are more capable of recovering from the adverse effects of physical isolation than he previously had believed. At least this seems true of children who receive maternal affection, even if deprived of normal amounts of social and sensory stimulation until age two. These studies (including

Harlow's) are consistent in suggesting that deprivation — whether social, physical, or a combination of both — does not have irreversible effects unless it is extremely prolonged. Recovery from severe deprivation is entirely possible.

The studies we have outlined here are not especially helpful in determining what environmental inputs may be most important for later normal development. Kagan's study suggests that recovery from the effects of limited sensory stimulation is possible, given the presence of maternal affection during the period of deprivation. Although Bowlby and others have suggested that deprivation of maternal love is responsible for the debilitating effects of institutionalization, institutionalized children usually are deprived of more than their mothers. They often suffer nutritional and physical deprivation. Their environment is generally dull, unchanging, and unstimulating. As infants, institutionalized children are not jostled and not exercised to develop muscle tone. Whenever social contact is withdrawn from a child, physical neglect typically occurs as well. It is extremely difficult to separate these environmental effects.

Early Enrichment

The Effects of Enrichment on Rats If deprived environments tend to have adverse effects on development, perhaps enriched environments have beneficial effects. On the other hand, maybe a certain level of stimulation is necessary for optimal development and any additional environmental enrichment beyond this level makes little difference. A series of studies examined the effects of enriched environments on animals (Wallace, 1974). Infant rats reared in groups in large cages and given new playthings daily developed heavier cerebral cortexes (the area of the brain associated with intellectual functioning) and thicker cortical tissue than rats raised in deprived environments (living alone in standard laboratory cages). The enriched rats also behaved less emotionally and less aggressively, adapted to testing situations faster, and generally performed better on learning tasks. We discuss some of these studies in greater detail in Chapter 3.

Once again, it is not precisely clear what aspects of enrichment were responsible for these physical and behavioral advantages — the social stimulation of living in a group or the physical stimulation provided by the supply of playthings. However, both social and physical enrichment seemed to lead to greater changes than either type of enrichment by itself. Rats reared in groups without toys or rats reared with toys but without social interaction failed to make as large gains as rats reared with both.

The Effects of Enrichment on Children

Although the studies by Wallace involve rats, the possibility of such effects occurring in children must be considered. In doing so, it should be remembered that whatever effects social and physical enrichment may have on brain development, these factors combine with such other factors as nutrition, genetic makeup, and the child's sex to produce the ultimate effect.

Parents and educators, among others, are clearly interested in the effects of early experiences on development, in the possibility of accelerating development, and in the qualities of the environment that foster optimal development. Burton White (1971) has stressed that we should proceed with caution in generalizing about the effects of enriched environments. Very few carefully controlled studies with human infants provide clear information about environmental enrichment. White showed that infants in enriched visual surroundings (a highly colorful mobile suspended over each infant's crib from day 37 through day 124) were advanced in some respects but delayed in others. Cratty (1970), who has studied perceptual and motor development in children, has suggested that acceleration in one area of development can have a blunting effect on development in another area.

In 1965, the U.S. government assumed that intelligence could be increased through special training, and initiated one of the most ambitious compensatory education programs ever mounted — Project Head Start, designed to help economically and culturally disadvantaged preschool children adjust to their school system. In addition to the educational programs aimed at children, an attempt also was made to involve parents and members of the community. In 1967, two additional *Follow Through* Programs were begun on a limited, experimental basis to extend the enriched experiences of the Head Start children in kindergarten and higher grades. Parent and child centers were set up to provide services for disadvantaged families with children under age three.

Although these projects were begun with great enthusiasm and hope of success, the results were disappointing. Researers found that these enrichment programs did produce modest improvements in IQ and academic success but that most of these gains disappeared within a couple of years. What is at fault — the idea that intelligence can be enhanced through special training or the effectiveness of the enrichment programs? Psychologists have attempted to answer this question by designing controlled studies on the effects of enrichment.

In one study, Garber and Heber (1973) set up a program to give special training to black children in a Milwaukee slum. These children were considered to be "at high risk for mental retardation" (Garber, 1984) and, without intervention, were expected to show a decline in IQ test performance over the preschool years. The researchers arranged to give a group of these disadvantaged children intensive training to develop sensorimotor, language, and thinking skills. Starting at three months of age, they attended the University of Milwaukee Training Center for the Mentally Retarded for seven hours a day, five days a week. Adequate nutrition and medical care were provided. The mothers were exposed to an educational program that emphasized homemaking, childrearing, and vocational training. The children were assessed every three weeks, and the program was continued until the children entered the first grade.

Garber and Heber found that IQ scores of children in the enriched program began to climb above IQ scores of children in a contrl group after 18 months of age. By age six, the average IQ score of the enriched group was between 110 and 120, compared to 85 for the control group. At ages eight to nine, the average IQ of the enriched group had dropped to 104, but the average IQ for the control group had fallen to 80 — representing a difference of 24 IQ points between the two groups two years following termination of the intervention program.

This study has been criticized because Garber and Heber failed to provide detailed descriptions of their training procedures (Sommer & Sommer, 1983) and because they did not ensure that children were assigned randomly to the experimental and control groups (Page, 1975). Even so, the observed effects of enrichment were strikingly large. If they could be replicated, such results would supply promising support for the idea that special learning environments can enhance the growth of intelligence. The results of the Milwaukee study suggest that environmental intervention must be extreme if it is to be effective. Firkowska and others (1978) concluded that pronounced, but less intense, changes in the environment may be ineffective. These researchers based their conclusion on evidence that post-World War II reconstitution of Warsaw, Poland, along strongly egalitarian lines failed to reduce the traditional association between IQ test performance, social class, and parental occupation.

When intellectually advanced children begin their formal education, should they be allowed to progress through grades at a faster rate than the average child? One school of thought regarding formal education maintains that the practice of accelerating gifted children is unwise. Children who are much younger than other children in their grade may develop emotional and social problems. A case study of a child prodigy who was accelerated educationally is presented in Box 2-5. The unhappy life of this person has been used to support the position that age and grade should be precisely coordinated.

Clearly the relationship between nature and nurture is complex. One very important aspect of this complexity is the timing of environmental influences. We close our discussion of nature and nurture by considering the varying effects of experience at different points in development.

MATURATION AND EXPERIENCE

Critical Periods in Physical Development

The developmental process from conception to birth is usually quite regular and predictable. The genotype carries instructions that systematically guide the maturational process; by and large, it is difficult to disrupt this developmental sequence. However, some environmental events can cause severe and permanent damage to the prenatal organism in particular periods. When a particular time in development is the *only* time at which the presence or absence of an environmental event can have an effect, that time is called a **critical period** (Colombo, 1982). Critical periods are relatively brief periods during which environmental events can produce irreversible effects.

In the 1960s, many pregnant women took the tranquilizer thalidomide. The drug caused deformities in the children of the mothers who ingested it between day 34 and day 50 of pregnancy. Mothers who took the drug before day 34 or after day 50 of pregnancy did not produce children with deformities. Apparently, there is a

critical period of fetal vulnerability to the drug thalidomide.

During the winter of 1964–1965, an epidemic of German measles *(rubella)* swept the United States, causing 30,000 fetal and newborn deaths and 20,000 children to be born with handicaps. The effects of German measles on the developing organism may be devastating in the first four months of pregnancy. Any woman who contracts rubella at this time has a one in three chance of producing a child with a birth defect, which can include visual and hearing deficiencies, mental retardation, damage to the central nervous system or to the heart, and retarded physical growth.

The period when environmental intrusions can have the most damaging effect usually occurs when a particular system is in the process of development. For example, we know that insufficient protein and calories disrupt the growth of the brain and the nervous system. Because major developments do not occur in these systems until

Box 2-5
William James Sidis (1898–1944)

Few children have achieved so prodigiously or received so much popular attention as William James Sidis. He could spell and read by age three; write and type by age four; read Russian, French, and German and understand numbers, time, and the calendar by age five. At six years, Sidis was reading Hebrew and studying anatomy; later, he learned Latin and Greek.

Sidis finished elementary school in six months and was ready to attend university at age nine, after passing the entrance examination for the Massachusetts Institute of Technology and the anatomy examination for Harvard Medical School. Sidis was permitted to enroll at Harvard at age eleven; shortly afterward, he delivered a lecture on the fourth dimension before the Harvard Mathematical Club.

Sidis graduated from Harvard at 16, withdrew from academic life over the next few years, repeatedly tried to escape public attention, and died an obscure clerk at age 46.

Sidis' sad decline has been cited as an argument against the educational acceleration of intellectually gifted children. His story has served as an example to support the view that unusually talented children rarely become productive adults — that education should keep age and grade in step.

Kathleen Montour (1977) has reviewed Sidis' case, comparing him with other child prodigies who also entered college very early but succeeded in later life. Montour concludes that Sidis' decline resulted not from the intellectual acceleration to which he was subjected but from the ex-

ploitation he received at the hands of his parents.

Sidis' father was an educational extremist who believed any child could be molded into a genius if properly educated. Both parents concentrated all their efforts on Sidis' intellectual achievements from infancy onward and felt personally responsible for his prodigious learning ability, discounting any contribution of hereditary factors. Harsh in their methods and failing to provide the affection and emotional support necessary for adequate parenting, Sidis' parents exploited their child's ability and allowed him to excite undue public interest. Montour claims that Sidis failed to fulfill his childhood promise not for any reasons related to academic acceleration but because he rebelled against his parents' attempts to turn

---

the last three months of pregnancy, maternal malnutrition at this time produces the most damaging effects on the brain and the nervous system.

We have cited only some of the many instances that show the presence (for example, thalidomide) or the absence (for example, adequate nutrition) of environmental events at critical periods can influence physical development. Is this also the case for social development?

Imprinting   Under normal conditions, newly hatched ducks, chickens, and geese begin to follow their mothers soon after birth. However, if

the mother is absent from the environment at this time, they will follow a wide variety of moving objects (even though they bear little resemblance to the mother), including — as children who live on a farm usually discover — humans. After the animal has begun to follow one of these objects, the infant may develop a preference for it and objects resembling it and eventually may reject dissimilar objects, including its own mother. This process is called **imprinting.**

Attention was originally drawn to imprinting by Konrad Lorenz (1937), who contended that there is a critical period for imprinting

him into the ideal man.
However, several educators
do not support Montour's
position.

It is certainly possible to
cite many examples of
accelerated children who
have led productive and
satisfying adult lives. There
have been attempts in recent
years to design innovative
educational programs to
meet the needs of intellectually advanced children.
For example, Julian Stanley at
Johns Hopkins University
started a program in 1971 for
mathematically precocious
youths. In 1977 three
members of this group graduated from the university at
age 17. Stanley points out
that his gifted students
appear to be well-adjusted,
with few emotional prob-
lems. The study suggests
that intellectual acceleration
per se is not associated with
emotional and social mal-
adjustment.

shortly after birth (see Figure 2-11). Lorenz believed this to be an all-or-nothing phenomenon
that had a sudden onset and an equally abrupt
termination. However, this description has not
been supported by subsequent tests of the process. There seems to be a gradual rise in sensitivity to the critical stimulus, which builds up to a
peak that lasts for some days before beginning to
decline (Hinde, 1962). Therefore, it is more appropriate to say that a **sensitive** or **optimal period** exists for imprinting (Moltz, 1973). During a sensitive or optimal period, certain
behaviors can be learned more easily than at other

times, and specific environmental inputs will
allow certain behaviors to develop most successfully. If those specific environmental inputs do
not occur during the sensitive period but do
occur at some other time, the behavior may still
develop, but may take longer to develop and may
never develop as fully.

Attachment If imprinting involved only an animal following its mother (or some less-suitable
object), the phenomenon would not be especially interesting to psychologists. In fact, although animals typically abandon the response

FIGURE 2-11

Konrad Lorenz with Imprinted Ducklings
The ducklings' *following* response was imprinted on
Lorenz, rather than on their mother, because Lorenz
was the first moving object the ducklings saw in the
sensitive period for the development of this response.
Source: McAvoy, I. (1955). *Life.*

after a month or so, the *following response* appears to indicate something more — that the animal has formed an **attachment** to the object on
which it has imprinted. Moreover, this attachment paves the way for later attachments to objects similar to the one first followed. When animals reach sexual maturity and are faced with the
choice of a sexual object, they often prefer an
object similar to the one they originally imprinted
on over a member of their own species. Drakes
who imprint on a box dangling from a string at
birth make amorous advances to such a box when
they reach sexual maturity, even in the presence
of receptive and available female ducks.

Behavior similar to imprinting has been
demonstrated in a number of species. Lambs
raised by humans become social isolates among
sheep in adulthood; dogs and cats must be exposed to humans during an early period (optimally, three to eight weeks) if they are to be do-

mesticated. Thus, in some nonhuman animals at
least, early attachments formed during a sensitive
period are essential to the subsequent formation
of normal adult social behavior. Can the same be
said for humans?

Sensitive Periods in Human Development

Human infants do not develop as quickly as ducks,
geese, and goats. They do not walk until almost a
year old and they do not exhibit the types of *following behavior* characteristic of other species.
But following is not essential for imprinting to
occur (see Moltz, Rosenblum, & Stettner,
1960). Some psychologists (see Brody & Axelrod, 1971; Reed & Lederman, 1983) have suggested that the attachment process in humans is
like imprinting and that it must occur during a
specific time period after birth. However, most
authorities consider attachment to be a much
more complex process that has some similarities
to imprinting but is not directly comparable.

Although it has not been demonstrated that
the physical presence of a specific object (for instance, the mother) during one particular time is
essential for normal development (see Myers,
1984), researchers believe that the reciprocal
interaction between caretakers and children during the early years is important in shaping the
course of a child's social development (see Chapter 10). As a general statement, most psychologists believe that although there are no clear-cut
critical periods in human postnatal development,
there are sensitive or optimal periods in the development of many psychological characteristics
(Rutter, 1979).

The existence of critical periods in physical
development and sensitive periods in social development demonstrate two ways in which maturational processes programmed by genetic factors interact with environmental events. As we
mature, we become optimally ready to receive
certain environmental inputs that result in the
development of specific characteristics. In the
vast majority of human and nonhuman cases, environmental and hereditary factors interact to foster
normal development. Even when conditions are
detrimental to normal development, the plasticity and resilience of humans and, to a lesser de-

gree, of nonhumans permits a remarkable degree of recovery when the environment is improved. One of the most significant characteristics evolu-tion has fostered in humans is the capacity to mod-ify their behavior in ways that make the most of environmental opportunities.

SUMMARY

1. Genetic determinism emphasizes the inheri-tance of characteristics; environmental de-terminism stresses the role played by experi-ence and learning in the acquisition of characteristics.

2. According to Darwin's theory of evolution, new species arise because natural environ-ments select from existing species the indi-viduals that are most fit to live in those envi-ronments. The fittest individuals are those most likely to survive, reproduce, and trans-mit their adaptive characteristics to succes-sive generations. Over many generations, this process of natural selection transforms a species that is adapting to a new environment into a new species.

3. To understand behavior fully, we must know its ultimate and proximate causes. Ultimate (distal) causes, typically investigated by bi-ologists, concern the evolutionary origins of behavior. Immediate (proximate) causes, usually of more interest to psychologists, are the events that trigger behavior.

4. Sociobiologists recently have revised and ex-tended Darwin's ideas on evolution. Socio-biologists have developed the concept of in-clusive fitness, which they define as an individual's genetic representation in suc-ceeding generations. This concept has pro-vided the theoretical basis for an explanation of altruism.

5. The line of evolution that led to modern peo-ple (Homo sapiens) began to diverge from the other apes perhaps 10 million years ago. The first known hominid, Australopithecus, lived between 4 and 1.5 million years ago. Homo erectus lived between 1.5 million and 100,000 years ago; Neanderthal people lived between 100,000 and 35,000 years ago. Cro-Magnon people, our direct ancestors, emerged about 35,000 years ago. Cro-Mag-non people lived in communities, engaged in extensive hunting, decorated their caves with paintings, and conducted elaborate bur-ial ceremonies.

6. The biological characteristics of humans rather dramatically changed from 4 million to 1.5 million years ago, but cultural devel-opment (as determined, for example, by the manufacture of tools) was rather slow. By contrast, in the last 1.5 million years, the human physique has changed little whereas cultural evolution has been dramatic.

7. Communication in such primitive species as fish, insects, and birds is stereotypic and ritu-alistic; fixed responses are evoked by speci-fic stimuli. Communication in primates is more flexible and generally reflects the so-cial context. The evolution of language has enabled humans to develop a system of sym-bolic communication. By allowing us to refer to things indirectly, language frees us from the restriction of previous forms of communication to things immediately present.

8. Eminence often seems to run in families. Galton concluded that such concentrations of ability must reflect superior hereditary en-dowment. However, the similarity of such ability between kin also could be caused by similarities in environment.

9. A phenotype is an individual's set of external, observable characteristics; a genotype is a person's internal, genetic makeup. In some cases (for example, height) the relationship between genotype and phenotype is fairly straightforward. In most cases, however, the relationship between genotype and pheno-type is less direct and involves a complex set

of mediating factors, including many non-gentic influences.

10. Twin and adoption studies allow psychologists to assess the relative contributions of nature (heredity) and nurture (environment) to differences in our physical and behavioral characteristics. In some cases, such as schizophrenia, genetic factors appear to dominate. In other cases, such as intelligence, nature and nurture seem to be about equally influential in determining individual differences; however, there is no convincing evidence that observed racial differences in IQ are of genetic origin.

11. Chromosomal (genetic) sex is determined at conception and, a few weeks later, leads to the development of gonads. The female pattern is the prescribed route of development internally and externally unless a sufficient amount of the hormone testosterone is present to initiate a change in the male direction.

12. Cases in which the prenatal hormonal environment has been anomalous provide information on the relative importance of biological and social factors in the development of gender characteristics. The genders of assignment and of subsequent rearing are very important influences on gender identity, regardless of an individual's prenatal history. Gender permanence is typically achieved by age four or five.

13. Monkeys raised in isolation for the first two years of life subsequently show abnormal social reactions. However, irreversible damage appears to occur only if the period of isolation is lengthy. A group of Guatemalan Indian children who had little social and physical stimulation during their first two years showed no adverse effects on intelligence tests at age eleven. Studies of institutionalized children indicate that only if deprivation is extended and extreme do the effects become irreversible.

14. Rats that are reared in environments rich in playthings and social contacts show greater cortical development, behave less emotionally and aggressively, and perform better on learning tasks than rats that are reared in neutral or impoverished environments. The intellectual development of children and adolescents also may be accelerated. However, some psychologists warn that gains from acceleration in one area of development may be offset by losses in other areas.

15. During a critical period of development, an organism is particularly sensitive to input from appropriate environmental events; the developmental changes that occur during critical periods are irreversible. During a sensitive period, an individual's sensitivity to relevant environmental events is much less clearly limited; imprinting in some species of bird occurs during a sensitive period.

KEY TERMS

Genetic Determinism	Phylogenetic Tree	Sexual Recombination
Environmental Determinism	Protozoa	Mutation
Heredity	Metazoa	Genotype
Environment	Invertebrate	Phenotype
Natural Selection	Vertebrate	Twin Study
Genetic Transmission	Order	Adoption Study
Gene	Primate Order	Gender Identity
Ultimate (distal) Cause	Kinesics	Gender Permanence
Immediate (proximate) Cause	Proxemics	Critical Period
Altruistic	Paralanguage	Imprinting
Sociobiology	Symbolic Communication	Sensitive/Optimal Period
Individual Fitness	Eugenics	Attachment
Inclusive Fitness	Genetic Variability	

RECOMMENDED READINGS

Evolution. (1978, September). *Scientific American, 239,* entire issue. Provides an overview of many aspects of evolutionary investigation and thinking.

Hinde, R. A. (1983). Ethology and child development. In P. H. Mussen (Ed.), *Handbook of child psychology, Vol. II Infancy and developmental psychobiology.* New York: Wiley. Good coverage of critical and sensitive periods, and of the effects of early experience.

Money, J., & Ehrhardt, A. A. (1972). *Man and woman, boy and girl.* Baltimore: Johns Hopkins University Press. Presents important case-study material relevant to the issue of gender-identity development.

Pilbeam, D. (1982). *The ascent of man: An introduction to human evolution.* New York: Macmillan. An excellent survey of the factors that have shaped human form and function.

Plomin, R., DeFries, J. C., & McClearn, G. E. (1980). *Behavioral genetics: A primer.* San Francisco: Freeman. Describes genetic studies of such diverse behaviors as shyness, stuttering, alcoholism, dyslexia, and juvenile violence.

Unger, R. K. (1979). *Female and male.* New York: Harper and Row. A readable examination of issues involving sex and gender. Theoretical and empirical work on sex roles is treated in depth.

Wilson, E. O. (1975). *Sociobiology: The new synthesis.* Cambridge, MA: Harvard University Press. This book established the field of sociobiology.

3

BRAIN AND BEHAVIOR

BRAIN AND MIND

METHODS OF STUDYING THE RELATIONSHIP BETWEEN BRAIN AND BEHAVIOR

Physical Injuries and Ablations
Disease and Toxic Injury
Mind-altering Drugs
Electrical and Chemical Stimulation of the Brain
Electrical Activity Produced by the Brain
Imaging the Living Brain
The Role of Experience

EVOLUTION OF THE NERVOUS SYSTEM

Primitive Nervous Systems
Evolution of the Human Brain

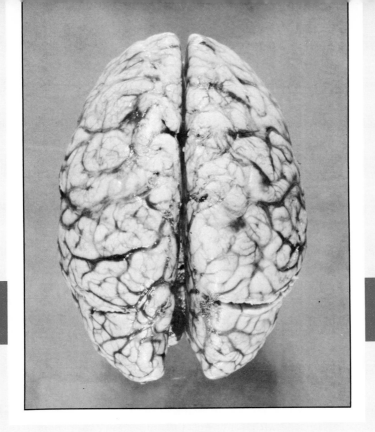

BRAIN STRUCTURE AND FUNCTION

Central Core Structures
Medulla ▪ Pons ▪ Cerebellum ▪
Reticular Formation ▪
Hypothalamus ▪ Thalamus
Limbic System and Associated
Structures
Basal Ganglia
Cerebral Cortex
Cerebral Hemispheres

COMMUNICATION IN THE NERVOUS SYSTEM

Glial Cells
Neurons
Neural Signals

MODIFIABILITY OF BRAIN CIRCUITRY

Malnutrition

Visual Deprivation
Quality of Environmental Stimulation
Implications for Treatment

THE NEURAL BASIS OF LEARNING AND MEMORY

Electrophysiological Studies of
Learning and Memory
Biochemical Studies of Learning and
Memory
Localization of Memory

CONSCIOUSNESS

States of Consciousness
Normal Consciousness ▪ Meditation
▪ Hypnosis
Sleep
The Evolution of sleep
Neural Control of Sleeping and Waking

Karen Ann Quinlan died on June 11, 1985, closing the final chapter on a poignant story that had begun a decade earlier. In April 1975, Karen became seriously ill and was taken to the hospital, where she slipped into a deep coma — the result of some undiagnosed but severe disturbance in her brain. When it became clear to her doctors that Karen would never regain consciousness, her parents were faced with an agonizing decision. Karen previously had expressed to them her wish not to be kept alive through extraordinary means. After much soul-searching, the Quinlans sued in the courts for removal of the life-support system that maintained Karen's breathing and provided her with nutrition. In a landmark decision, their plea was granted and Karen was taken off the system. Confounding medical expectations, Karen existed in what her doctor called a "chronic vegetative state" but never regained consciousness.

During the ten years that Karen Ann Quinlan maintained this "chronic vegetative state," was she alive? We might say parts of her body were alive but her mind was dead. Although many people believe that death occurs when the heart stops beating, in modern medicine the criterion for death does not involve the heart. All deaths have one ultimate cause — cerebral anoxia, or lack of oxygen in the brain. A heart that stops beating is a *sign* of death; it indicates that the blood is no longer supplying oxygen to the brain.

Of course, we cannot live without the functions of several parts of our bodies (as examples, our heart, liver, kidneys, and lungs), but these functions can be served by organ transplants or by mechanical aids. In this sense, these organs are not essential to our existence. Although we consider our various organs to be parts of ourselves, most of us believe the real *us* (our essence) lies not in our bodies but in our minds — and in the organ associated with our minds, the brain. Several respected medical specialists concluded that the extensive damage to Karen Ann Quinlin's brain meant her brain could never again sustain the mental functions most of us consider essential to a definition of human life.

Compared to other organs, the fundamental importance of the brain becomes apparent when considering transplant recipients. People who receive corneal, heart, or kidney transplants may feel a bit different, but they do not acquire any of the essential characteristics of the person who donated the organ. Imagine, however, a case in which one person receives another person's brain. Who is the recipient: the person who supplies the body or the person who supplies the brain? Most of us would say the latter.

Locating the sense of self in the brain is consistent with the fact that we have, at birth, all the brain cells we will ever possess. Unlike cells in all other parts of the body, nerve cells in the brain and in the spinal cord of mammals are unable to replenish themselves. Although brain cells grow and form new connections with each other throughout life and although they may make limited repairs to their damaged parts, they do not undergo cell division and duplicate themselves like cells of the skin, muscles, lungs, and other organs.

The reason brain cells do not duplicate themselves probably is related to their role in information processing and storage. Cells of the heart can make replicas of themselves because that organ remains essentially unchanged throughout your life. It grows bigger, of course, and may eventually show structural changes with advancing age; but it is the same heart. This is not the case with our minds, which are developing and expanding all the time. Most psychologists relate this growth of the mind to growth of the brain.

BRAIN AND MIND

It seems obvious to almost everyone today that there is a close relationship between the brain and the mind — between the physical structure that operates in accordance with physical laws and the mental events that people experience when the brain functions. However, this relationship has not always seemed self-evident. Indeed, the nature of the relationship between mind and brain, the so-called **mind–body problem,** has been argued by philosophers for centuries. There are two main positions in the controversy: the *monist* and *dualist* viewpoints. **Monists** believe brain function and mind are essentially one, and the same natural laws that determine all physical events apply to both. **Dualists** believe brain and mind are two separate entities, each functioning in terms of its own set of laws. Dualists accept that physical principles govern the operation of the brain but find no way to account for the activities of the mind in those terms.

Early monists disagreed about where the source of mental activities was located in the body. The ancient Greek philosopher Aristotle, a monist, believed that consciousness originated in the heart; this followed from his observation that the heart was the first organ to develop in chick embryos. To ''know something in your heart,'' to ''learn something by heart,'' or to suffer from a ''broken heart'' are linguistic holdovers from early monist beliefs. Plato, another Greek philosopher, disagreed; to him the brain was the seat of reason.

Nearly all modern neuroscientists (scientists who study the nervous system) are monists. They believe mental events can be explained in terms of electrical and chemical activities in the brain. Most neuroscientists who hold the monist position also accept the concept of **determinism**— the doctrine that mental and behavioral acts are produced by physical causes and, therefore, obey natural laws. This is not a denial of *free will* (the capacity to decide our future actions). The determinist position simply asserts that all of our behavior, including the capacity to make choices, is caused by potentially identifiable events in accordance with the laws of physics and chemistry.

Although a monistic and deterministic outlook is the most commonly accepted basis for the scientific investigation of brain and behavior, even the most sophisticated researchers readily admit it is only a working assumption—not an absolute fact. A Canadian pioneer in this field, D. O. Hebb, spelled out the creed under which most neuroscientists operate.

> Modern psychology takes completely for granted that behavior and neural function are perfectly correlated, that one is completely caused by the other. There is no separate soul or life force to stick a finger into the brain now and then and make neural cells do what they would not do otherwise. Actually, of course, this is a working assumption only as long as there are unexplained aspects of behavior. It is quite conceivable that some day the assumption will have to be rejected. But it is important also to see that we have not reached that day yet: the working assumption is a necessary one, and there is no real evidence opposed to it. Our failure to solve a problem so far does not make it insoluble. One cannot logically be a determinist in physics and chemistry and biology, and a mystic in psychology. (Hebb, 1949, p. xiv)

We now turn to a consideration of theory and research on the brain and its relationship to behavior. We must admit at the outset that these issues are exceedingly complex and that we do not explore them in detail. First, we examine the methods scientists use to study the brain; then we describe the main structures of the nervous system and discuss some of the functions they perform. We consider how the brain has evolved and how it develops from birth, and then turn to the issue of how the brain may be affected by such environmental influences as early experience and malnutrition, and the nature of the changes in the brain responsible for learning and memory. Finally, we look at how brain activity is related to different states of consciousness, including meditation, hypnosis, and sleep.

METHODS OF STUDYING THE RELATIONSHIP BETWEEN BRAIN AND BEHAVIOR

People were probably curious about the brain long before any written records existed, and we know that some remarkably modern insights were achieved by ancient scholars. Greek physician Galen, who lived in the second century A.D., noted that damage to the right side of the head affected movement and feeling on the left side of the body and that damage to the left side of the head affected functioning on the right side of the body. Galen also believed, as did Hippocrates (the "father of medicine") before him, that epilepsy was a physical disease of the brain rather than a result of demonic possession (see Chapter 13).

Nevertheless, the most significant advances in understanding the brain were not made until the late nineteenth century. Just as the invention of the telescope has enabled major discoveries to be made in astronomy, the methods we discuss in this section have permitted scientific study of the brain and its relationship to behavior. Some of these methods involve interventions that are accidental (for example, physical disease and injury), some deliberate (as examples, ablation, electrical and chemical stimulation, drugs). Other methods, such as recording the brain's electrical activity and forming images of the brain's structure, are noninvasive.

Physical Injuries and Ablations

It is conceivable that our earliest ancestors formed some ideas about the brain–behavior relationship after observing the effects of a well-aimed rock on the head of a foe or the behavioral or emotional changes in a member of the tribe who suffered a head injury. Serious physical damage to the brain affects behavior and conscious processes. However, no reputable scientist would ever intentionally damage a human brain simply to observe the effects, regardless of the potential scientific value of the information. Most information about the effects of damage at particular sites in the human brain on specific mental or behavioral capacities is obtained from studying the effects of severe head wounds sustained in accidents or battles and the effects of such natural calamities as strokes (the death of a group of brain cells caused by the rupture or clogging of blood vessels in that region of the brain).

A famous example is the case of the man called Tan, a Frenchman whose language difficulties were studied by eminent French surgeon Pierre Broca in 1861. The man's nickname derived from his longstanding inability to utter anything other than the syllable "tan." Broca was interested in the relationship between language and the brain, and had developed the radical notion that the capacity for language was localized in the brain. An opportunity to test this theory was afforded when Tan died a short time later. An autopsy was performed, and Broca found an area of tissue about the size of an egg was missing from the left side of Tan's brain. It has since been clearly demonstrated that this part of the brain, now called **Broca's area,** is critical for speech production.

Most early observations provided only rough guidelines for localization of the brain's functions. Some clues to where visual information is analyzed in the brain were provided when wounds to the back of the head produced areas of blindness in the patient's visual field. Later, with the introduction of firearms, the wounds (or **lesions**) from bullets more precisely localized this type of function. Today, neurosurgeons occasionally must make brain lesions in order to remove tumors or to treat severe cases of epilepsy. On these occasions, the extent and location of the tissue damage is known more precisely and patients can be tested before and after surgery.

Because opportunities for research on the human brain are limited, extensive information about the effects of brain damage has come from studies of nonhuman brains. Pierre Flourens, a nineteenth-century French neurologist, removed different parts of the brains of pigeons, rabbits, and dogs and noted the changes in their behavior. Refinements of this technique of surgical removal, or **ablation,** are still employed by brain researchers today. Examples are the experiments on brain mechanisms and learning described later in this chapter and the studies of the brain structures involved in eating described in Chapter 7.

Disease and Toxic Injury

It is not difficult to imagine our ancient ancestors also noted that bizarre behavior sometimes occurred under other circumstances (after eating certain plants, for example). Some curious early human may even have performed a primitive autopsy, discovered diseased brain cells, and related them to the behavior of the unfortunate victim. Skeletons found in some very old archeological digs show evidence that skulls were opened with extreme care. Over the last 100 years, researchers have begun an intensive investigation of the effects of disease and toxic injury to the brain and other parts of the nervous system. The results of some early studies have found their way into figures of speech. The expression "mad as a hatter," for example, entered the English language because mercury, formerly used to cure pelts in the making of hats, is highly toxic to the nervous system.

Several infectious diseases affect the nervous system. You probably remember how you felt the last time you had a high fever. The disordered thought, weird associations, and perhaps even hallucinations you may have experienced demonstrate how diseases can cause changes in the brain that affect the mind. More virulent diseases may destroy areas of the brain and produce drastic and permanent changes in behavior. The unorthodox behavior associated with rabies and the paralysis caused by polio are examples of behavioral effects of viral infections in the nervous system.

Ironically, syphilis, one of the great scourges of humankind, has contributed a great deal to our understanding of the brain. In its most advanced stage, syphilis causes severe mental aberrations, including thought disorder and mood changes. Before the introduction of modern antibiotics, sufferers in the terminal stage of syphilitic infection (then called *general paresis of the insane;* see Chapter 13) were housed in special hospitals where their mental and behavioral deterioration could be carefully recorded. After the patient's death, investigators examined the brain for signs of damage. It was discovered that various behavioral symptoms were related to specific sites of brain damage. However, although such tragic "experiments" of nature can provide valuable direction in the pursuit of scientific knowledge, the ravages of disease and injury in the nervous system are generally too widespread to allow a precise understanding.

Mind-altering Drugs

Another method of obtaining information about the relationship between brain activity and mental events has been to observe the temporary effects of mind-altering drugs. The mind-altering properties of fermented fruits and grains, the leaves and blossoms of the hemp plant, coca leaves, and the resin of the poppy have been known for centuries. Primitive cultures typically attributed these effects to supernatural causes. We now know the chemicals contained in these substances exert effects on brain cells that produce radical changes in conscious experience. The study of the effects of drugs on consciousness and behavior is called **psychopharmacology;** a classification of such drugs is provided in Box 3-1.

Electrical and Chemical Stimulation of the Brain

During the Franco–Prussian War, Carl Fritsch and Eduard Hitzig, two German physicians, applied a weak electrical current to the exposed surface of the brain of a wounded German soldier. They noted that when they stimulated different areas, different muscular movements occurred. Later they conducted a series of similar experiments on dogs, which further added to understanding the role played by particular areas of the brain. The pioneering work of Fritsch and Hitzig has developed into one of the most important modern experimental techniques for studying the brain — the electrical stimulation of nervous tissue.

Depending on which area of the brain is stimulated, people may experience particular sensations, emotions, or muscular movements. The electrical currents artificially activate cells in the brain that then respond as if they had been activated normally. Wilder Penfield — a Canadian neurosurgeon and pioneer in this field of research in the 1940s and 1950s — reported that when stimulating the exposed brain of one patient, she promptly reported hearing a song she had often sung as a child (see Figure 3-1, page 104). Today, neurosurgeons occasionally employ electrical stimulation of the brain as a means of differentiating healthy from diseased brain cells during brain surgery. With the permission of patients, a limited amount of experimental stimulation has also been conducted during these procedures. Because there are no pain receptors in the brain, patients can remain conscious during brain surgery and supply useful information about their experiences when their brains are electrically stimulated.

Box 3-1
Drugs, the Brain, and Behavior

There are many systems for classifying **psychoactive drugs** (substances that affect the brain and mind). We assign the following categories:

1. drugs that stimulate the brain
2. drugs that depress the brain
3. drugs that primarily affect perceptions and moods

Drugs used in the treatment of psychological disorders are discussed in Chapter 14.

BRAIN STIMULANTS

The best known **brain stimulants** are amphetamines, cocaine, caffeine, and nicotine. A common characteristic of stimulants is that they increase the activity of cells in certain parts of the brain (hence, the street term "speed" for amphetamines).

Amphetamines are manufactured synthetically; *cocaine,* which produces very similar physical and psychological effects, is refined from the leaves of the South American coca plant. *Caffeine,* the "pick-me-up" ingredient found in coffee, tea, coca, cola drinks and nonprescription wake-up pills, is also a strong stimulant—although we usually consume it in a very dilute form. *Nicotine* is the active ingredient in tobacco and is probably the most addictive of all drugs.

Amphetamine is sold under the registered trademarks Benzedrine® and Dexedrine®. It is used most frequently by people who wish to avoid sleeping when fatigued, but also is used to treat narcolepsy, a disease characterized by a sudden and uncontrollable urge to fall asleep during the day. Within limits, amphetamines temporarily bolster performance on sensory and motor tasks. Weak solutions of cocaine sometimes are employed as a local anaesthetic for minor surgical procedures and dental work.

Amphetamines and cocaine are both used as "social" drugs and are subject to abuse. Cocaine, smoked as "crack" or "rock," is currently experiencing wide popularity. Although most experts agree these two stimulants are unlikely to result in physical dependence and severe withdrawal symptoms, the euphoria and feeling of self-confidence they produce can lead to psychological dependence (the feeling that one must take the drug to lead a happy, trouble-free life). The medical dangers of *infrequent* cocaine use are relatively small (except for persons with certain rare allergies or heart conditions).

Prolonged use of high doses of amphetamines or cocaine presents quite a different picture. A common result is severe personality change, ranging from irritability and suspiciousness to a state indistinguishable from paranoid schizophrenia (Snyder, 1974). Marked depression follows prolonged periods of use. Ronald Siegel (1984) offers a balanced review of changing patterns of cocaine use.

BRAIN DEPRESSANTS

Increased dosages of drugs that depress brain activities lead to relaxation, clouding of consciousness, reduced sensory–motor performance, unconsciousness, deep anesthesia, and finally death. **Brain depressants** include opiates, such as morphine and heroin, barbiturates (the drug in most sleeping pills), tranquilizers, and alcohol.

The ability of *brain-depressant drugs* to relieve anxiety makes them very useful in therapy and is also a major factor that leads to their abuse. *Morphine* is still the most effective pain-relieving drug that is widely available. The discovery that the brain produces a morphine-like substance of its own (Kosterlitz & Hughes, 1975) that may regulate neural activity in parts of the brain has suggested several possible explanations for the effects of the drug. Further research in this area may also partially explain why some people develop dependence after using heroin or morphine. However, a complete explanation of the phenomenon of drug dependence requires an understanding of several complex psychological and social factors as well.

Drugs used primarily for their calming and relaxing properties are called *hypnosedatives*. Beverage alcohol, barbiturates (for example, Seconal®), and tranquilizers (as examples, Valium® and Librium®) are members of this class. Valium® is the most widely prescribed drug in the world. Although the problems of alcoholism and alcohol abuse have been known for many years, recent studies have uncovered a high incidence of abuse of other hypnosedatives.

Hypnosedatives also are used as sleeping pills; however, these drugs produce a form of unconsciousness that is quite different from normal sleep. Paradox-ically, continuous use can result in several sleep disorders, only exacerbating the difficulties that led to their use in the first place (Dement 1972, p. 81). Therefore, hypnosedatives are not recommended for more than occasional use; several effective nondrug remedies for sleep disorders do not produce these ill effects (Paupst, 1975).

The major tranquilizers (for example, Chlorpromazine®) used to treat severely psychotic individuals are also brain-depressant drugs. A description of their effects is provided in Chapter 14.

HALLUCINOGENS OR PSYCHEDELICS

The past three decades have seen a rapid increase followed by a waning in popularity of drugs that dramatically alter moods, thought processes, and perceptions. These drugs have sometimes been called **hallucinogens** or **psychedelics** (mind-expanding) because many people have felt their use helped open new mental vistas. Some of the better-known psychedelic substances are marijuana and hashish (from the hemp plant, *cannabis sativa*), peyote and mescaline (from the peyotl cactus), psilocybin and fly agaric (from different species of mushroom), jimson weed, and morning-glory seeds.

Isolating the psychoactive ingredients from these plants has allowed chemists to synthesize even more potent compounds than the naturally occurring ones. Their long chemical names are usually abbreviated or slang ones substituted by the time they are available for use.

Although the exact ways in which psychedelic drugs produce their effects on consciousness is unknown, researchers are beginning to learn how these drugs affect the chemistry of the brain. For example, some psychedelic drugs alter the concentration of neurotransmitters — chemical messengers in the brain. THC (tetrahydrocannabinol) — the active substance in marijuana and hashish — has been shown to increase concentrations of the neurotransmitter serotonin in the brain and to lower concentrations of the neurotransmitter norepinephrine (Nahas, 1975). The chemical structure of LSD ("acid") resembles that of serotonin; mescaline has certain structural similarities to norepinephrine. It is known that these neurotransmitters are involved in parts of the brain concerned with motivation, emotion, and the regulation of sleep and dreaming. Different psychedelic drugs mimic or block the normal transmission of information in the brain.

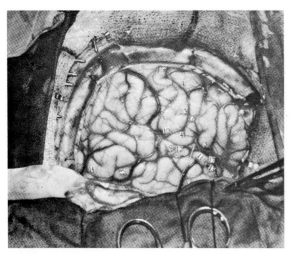

FIGURE 3-1
Penfield's "Brain Mapping" Photograph taken during brain surgery performed by Wilder Penfield, M.D. The electrical stimulating probe is poised above the exposed cerebral cortex of the patient. The small letters and numbers in the photo were placed on the surface of the brain to mark points where stimulation produced certain percepts or movements. *Source:* Penfield, W., & Boldrey E. (1937). Somatic motor and sensory representation in the cerebral cortex of man as studied by electrical stimulation. *Brain, 60,* 389–443. Oxford University Press.

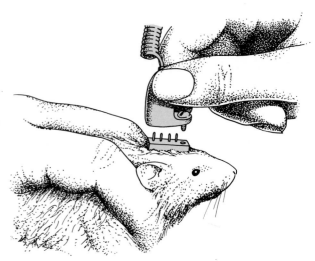

FIGURE 3-2
Permanent Electrodes Implanted in a Rat's Brain A connector is cemented to the animal's skull so that the electrodes can be hooked up to stimulation or recording equipment. *Source:* Hart, B. L. (1969). *Experimental neuropsychology: A laboratory manual.* New York: W. H. Freeman.

The information that neurosurgeons have gained from experiments on humans during brain surgery is small compared to the information produced by research on other animals. Animals like the rat shown in Figure 3-2 have had electrodes implanted in various parts of their brains for as long as several years. For some research purposes, the electrodes are replaced with tiny tubes through which chemicals can be injected. We describe some of the findings from this research later in this chapter and in our discussion of motivational mechanisms in Chapter 7.

Electrical Activity Produced by the Brain

In addition to studying the brain by stimulating it electrically, investigators have also explored the brain by measuring the electrical activity naturally generated by brain cells. Nerve cells in the brain transmit information by releasing minute chemical messengers (a process described later in Box 3-4). One of the most important discoveries in brain research — made by Richard Caton, an

English physician, in 1875 — was that these chemical changes also produce electrical discharges that can be recorded. In 1929, Hans Berger, a German researcher, invented a method of recording the brain's electrical output from *outside* the skull. Berger's method was the forerunner of the modern **electroencephalograph,** a device that measures electrical activity in the brain (see Figure 3-3). The record of electrical activity produced by this device is called an **electroencephalogram,** or **EEG.** In everyday language, this activity is often referred to as "brain waves."

The EEG permits investigators to examine brain responses to specific experiences as they occur. Changes in the brain's electrical activity occur in response to sights, sounds, and other sensory information as well as during learning, relaxation, meditation, and sleep. Computer techniques for analyzing EEG records indicate when the brain is processing information (Hillyard & Kutas, 1983). Later in this chapter, we present an example of how electrical discharges from the brain can be used to study learning.

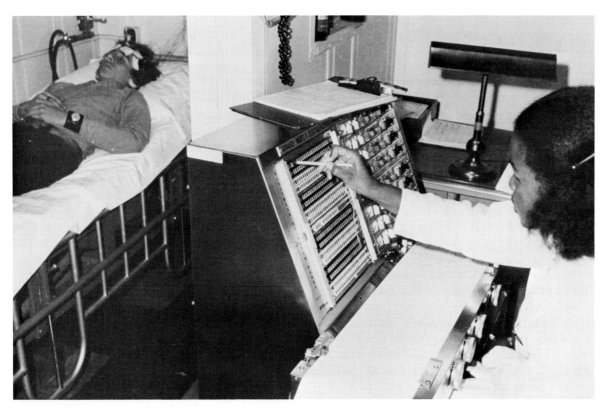

FIGURE 3-3
Electroencephalography (EEG)   While asleep, this boy's brain activity is being recorded, amplified, and printed on an electroencephalograph.

In addition to being an invaluable research device, the EEG also has become a standard clinical tool.   EEGs are routinely used in neurological examinations to detect abnormal brain activity; EEG patterns for damaged brain tissues, tumors, and epilepsy are quite distinctive.   A flat, unchanging EEG record — indicating no communication within the brain — was a primary influence in the Quinlans' decision to have their daughter's life-support equipment removed.

If you have taken a physics course, you know the passage of electricity generates magnetic fields.   The brain's electrical activity is no exception; the electrical pulses traveling through the brain create magnetic fields that can be detected outside the skull.   The EEG thus generates an **MEG,** or **magnetoencephalogram.**   These magnetic fields are very weak (measuring only about one-billionth of the earth's magnetic field) and are easily disrupted, making their measurement an extremely challenging task.   Nevertheless, the MEG may in time come to rival the EEG as a method of measuring the brain's activity.   The MEG already shows promise as a means for the early detection of such diseases as epilepsy, multiple sclerosis, and Alzheimer's disease (Weinberg, Stroink, & Katila, 1985).

Imaging the Living Brain

Much has been learned about the brain's anatomy from the examination of successive slices or sections of brains removed after death.   Now, after several recent technical breakthroughs, we can form images of the structures and activities of the living brain.   A technique called **computerized axial tomography (CAT)** provides detailed images of cross-sections of the living human brain.   A source of X rays is moved in an arc around the patient's head; at each position, sensors record X ray absorption by the brain structures in the X ray's path.   This information is analyzed by a computer that creates an image of the brain's structures—a CAT scan, shown in Figure 3-4(a)—that is displayed on a television screen. As the apparatus is rotated, successive images are collected and stored by the computer, so that a three-dimensional representation of the brain's structures is created within a matter of minutes (see color section).

A different technique **Positron Emission Tomography (PET),** provides a PET scan—a picture of the brain's function rather than its structure. A small amount of harmless radioactive material is bonded to a substance such as glucose that is metabolized in the body and then injected into the bloodstream. Brain activity breaks down the glucose, releasing particles (positrons) that are detected by sensors arranged about the head, as illustrated in Figure 3-4(b). Emission is most concentrated from areas of the brain that are most active. This information is fed to a computer that translates it into colored maps showing brain areas with differing activity levels. The PET scan is used to locate tumorous growths and abnormal areas of brain activity before surgery (Phelps & Mazziotta, 1985). Obviously, it is extremely important to know in advance if and/or how a brain tumor can be surgically reached without damaging essential structures.

A third technique developed for viewing the intact brain is **Magnetic Resonance Imaging (MRI),** formerly called **Nuclear Magnetic Resonance (NMR).** An MRI Scan involves placing the subject's head in a weak magnetic field and using sensors to detect the varying degrees to which different parts of the soft tissue in the brain become magnetized, as shown in Figure 3-4(c). From this information, a computer generates a representation of the brain's structures (see color section). Recent advances in MRI technology have produced a clearer and more detailed image than that produced in a PET Scan (Budinger & Lauterbur, 1984).

The great value of these imaging techniques is that they allow us to view the activity of the entire brain in an alert patient. This not only simplifies diagnosis of structural disorders of the brain but also provides a richer, more dynamic picture of the brain's activities to aid researchers who study basic psychological processes in areas such as perception, learning, and memory.

The Role of Experience

Most methods of studying the brain we have discussed until now rely on physical inputs—injury, disease, drugs, electrical and chemical stimulation, and surgical removal of tissue. But what about psychological inputs? Do the experiences people have in their lives affect the physical state of their brains? We know that experiences affect behavior; that is the fundamental law of learning. When we touch a hot stove, we learn to avoid it. When the sensory stimulation we receive from environmental events alters our behavior in a fairly permanent way, we intuitively sense that a physical change must have occurred somewhere inside us where this "lesson" is stored. Most of us assume that such changes occur in the brain. Modern research in biological psychology is devoted to understanding how sensory stimulation (input) changes the brain (intervening process) and modifies our behavior (outcome).

The idea that environmental experiences can change the structure and chemical composition of the brain is a very old one. In the eighteenth century, Italian researcher Malacarne attempted to determine whether the brains of animals and birds that were reared differently (underwent different experiences) showed corresponding anatomical differences. Malacarne raised pairs of dogs, parrots, goldfinches, and blackbirds, gave one member of each pair special training, and compared its brain with the brain of the untrained member of the pair. Malacarne noted greater infolding in part of the brains of his trained subjects than he did in the brains of his untrained subjects. This study was remarkably modern in its approach. Indeed, it was so forward-looking that it was ignored by Malacarne's contemporaries and by virtually everyone else until it was unearthed by psychologist Mark Rosenzweig and his colleagues in 1972. We discuss modern research that demonstrates how experience affects the structure of the brain later in this chapter.

We have described briefly the techniques and methods used by researchers to shed light on the very complex relationship between the brain and behavior. In the following sections, we describe the basic structures of the brain and indicate how they function to control behavior. We

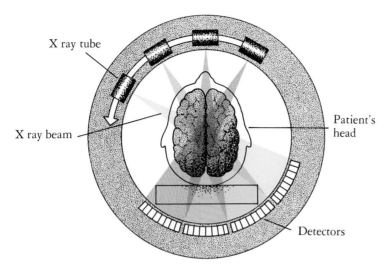

(a) Schematic Representation of a CAT Scan (computerized axial tomography)

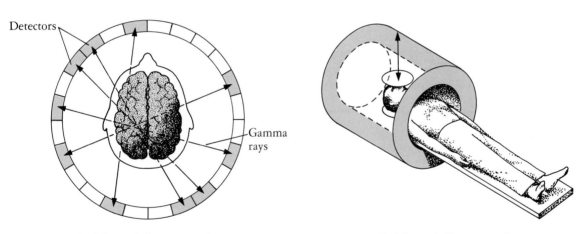

(b) Schematic Representation
of a PET Scan (positron emission tomography)

(c) Schematic Representation
of the MRI Technique (magnetic resonance imaging)

FIGURE 3-4

Computerized Diagnostic Imaging Techniques   (a) The X ray source and detectors are rotated gradually around the head.   (b) Detectors (ringing the head) record gamma rays produced when brain tissue absorbs a radioactive substance that has been injected into the bloodstream.   (c) The head is surrounded by a coil that produces a weak electrical field.   A second coil detects the degree to which different brain structures become magnetized.   *Source:* (a) and (b) Adapted from *The brain: Mystery of matter and mind.* (pp. 138, 140). New York: Torstar Books. (c) Adapted from Budinger, T. F., & Lauterbur, P. C. (1984). Nuclear magnetic resonance technology for medical science, *Science, 226,* 288–98.

begin by considering the evolution of the **nervous system** — the organism's machinery for collecting, processing, and responding to information about its environment.

EVOLUTION OF THE NERVOUS SYSTEM

As some creatures evolved from single cells to larger and more complex organisms, their needs for processing environmental information and for sequencing appropriate responses gave rise to the development of increasingly elaborate and specialized nervous systems. This is evident if we compare the nervous systems of the simple and complex organisms shown in Figure 3-5.

Primitive Nervous Systems

Throughout evolution the trend has been for **neural processing** (the analysis of sensory input and the organization of motor responses) to shift toward the head of the organism. Nerve cells of very primitive organisms, such as the hydra shown in Figure 3-5(a), are not segregated into a distinct system but instead form a random lattice or *nerve net* that is distributed throughout the body. Although this very simple nervous system cannot support anything more complex than a small set of reflexive actions, it is adequate for an organism like the hydra, which has existed for many millions of years with simple needs.

Evolutionary pressures on some organisms led to the formation of distinct heads and tails. An example is the freshwater flatworm, the planarian, in which the nerve cells are grouped into a primitive, elongated nervous system, as shown in Figure 3-5(b). Here we see the first signs of hierarchical specialization. The slightly enlarged clump of nerve cells at one end, the **head ganglion,** assumes a small degree of executive authority over the rest of the nervous system.

The pressures of evolution subsequently led to the selection of segmented bodies in such invertebrates as the honeybee. The nervous system of such invertebrates consists of a chain of semi-independent "little brains," or **ganglia,** distributed throughout each of several segments, as shown in Figure 3-5(c). (The term *ganglion* refers to clusters of nerve cells in the peripheral nervous system; *nucleus* is the corresponding term for clusters of nerve cells in the brain.) The ganglia handle input and output within their own

segments, and the head ganglion is essentially the first among equals. Unlike the brains of higher organisms, the head ganglion does not send complex commands down to muscles to spur them into action. Rather, the head ganglion coordinates the ongoing activities of the largely self-contained ganglia, ensuring that they contribute appropriately to more complex behaviors.

This kind of control is adequate for an organism that relies on a relatively small number of stereotypic reactions to its environment. However, stereotypic reactions were not adaptive for some organisms, which (for reasons not well understood) required greater flexibility to prevail in their environments. The individuals that prevailed inherited nervous systems that enabled them to make finer sensory discriminations and coordinate complex actions. These individuals, in turn, propagated increasingly elaborate nervous systems in their offspring. Through this process, the human nervous system evolved [see Figure 3-5(d)].

The human nervous system is really a collection of systems (see Figure 3-6). A primary distinction is made between the *central nervous system* and the *peripheral nervous system.* The **central nervous system** consists of the brain and the spinal cord. The **peripheral nervous system** has two divisions: the *somatic system* and the *autonomic system.* The **somatic system** is the network of nerves that relays information from the senses to the brain and the network of nerves that controls our skeletal muscles (see Chapter 4). The **autonomic system** regulates the activities of such internal organs as the heart, lungs, and glands (see Chapter 7).

Evolution of the Human Brain

Neurophysiologist Paul MacLean has proposed that the human brain is really composed of three distinct sets of structures that correspond to three major stages in the brain's evolution. As we can see in the schematic representation in Figure 3-7, the central structures of MacLean's *triune brain*

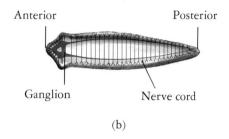

The Nerve Net of a Hydra

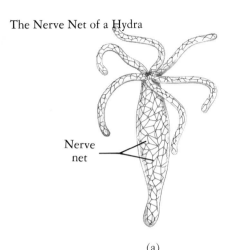

Nerve net

(a)

The Nerve Cords of a Planarian

Anterior   Posterior

Ganglion   Nerve cord

(b)

The Nervous System of a Bee

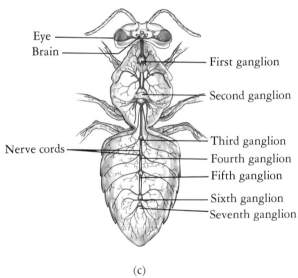

Eye
Brain

First ganglion

Second ganglion

Third ganglion
Fourth ganglion
Fifth ganglion

Nerve cords

Sixth ganglion
Seventh ganglion

(c)

The Nervous System of a Human

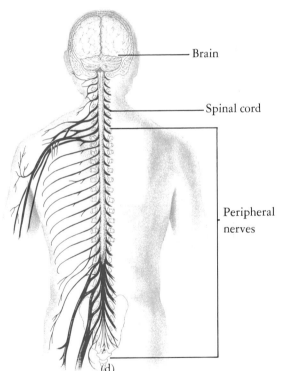

Brain

Spinal cord

Peripheral
nerves

(d)

FIGURE 3-5

Simple and Complex Nervous Systems (a) The primitive nervous system structure of the hydra consists of an unorganized network of nerve cells spread throughout the body. (b) The simple nervous system of the planarian consists of a head ganglion and two nerve cords that pass down the sides of the body to the tail. (c) The more complex nervous system of the honeybee consists of two primary nerve cords that connect several ganglia, each of which relays information between the animal's brain and nerves in all parts of the body. (d) The central nervous system of the human consists of the brain and spinal cord. The peripheral nervous system has two divisions: the somatic system (detects the external environment and controls our responses to it) and the autonomic system (performs a similar function for our internal environment). *Source:* (a) Adapted from Weinberg, S. L. (1974). *Biology: An inquiry into the nature of life* (p. 295). Newton, MA: Allyn and Bacon. (b) Adapted from Keeton, W. (1973). *Elements of biological science* (2nd ed., p. 203). New York: W. W. Norton. (c) Adapted from Snodgrass, R. E. (1965). *Anatomy of the honey bee.* Ithaca, NY: Cornell University Press. (d) Adapted from Vander, A. J., et al. (1970). *Human physiology: The mechanisms of body function.* New York: McGraw-Hill.

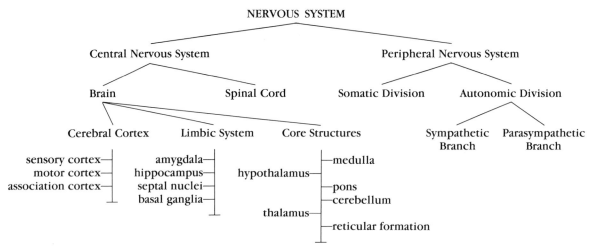

FIGURE 3-6
Organization of Human Nervous System

are outgrowths from the upper spinal cord. Mac-Lean (1973, 1982) suggested that these "old brain" or **central core** structures were the first to evolve. He called these structures the *reptilian brain* because they are virtually identical to the structures found in the brains of existing reptiles. Figure 3-8 shows the structural development of the brain in fish, reptiles, and mammals.

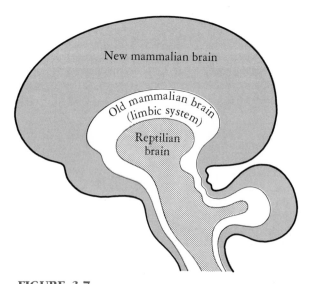

FIGURE 3-7
Triune Brain The diagram illustrates the three stages of evolution of the brain proposed by Paul MacLean.

MacLean and other researchers have demonstrated that structures in the reptilian brain control such basic processes essential to survival as respiration, temperature regulation, and the functioning of the heart, as well as such "cold-blooded" activities as killing prey.

The next major stage in the evolution of the brain occurred about 100 million years ago with the development of the **limbic system** in early mammals. Stated very simply, the limbic structures are important for the sense of smell (a vital channel of communication for primitive animals) and for the experience of emotion. It should be noted that brain evolution has been a matter of the addition rather than the replacement of structures. The human brain still has structures that correspond to the reptilian brain; the structures of the limbic system, added in the early mammalian brain, surround the reptilian brain. In the last two million years, the third component of Mac-Lean's triune brain — the **cerebral cortex** — has developed in some mammals. Although the earlier brain structures primarily serve the basic needs of survival, MacLean argues, the cerebral cortex enables individuals to think, to talk, to plan, and to create culture.

MacLean's views on the evolution of the brain are theory, not fact. However, this theory is supported by facts from other areas of research. For example, we know the brain size of our ances-

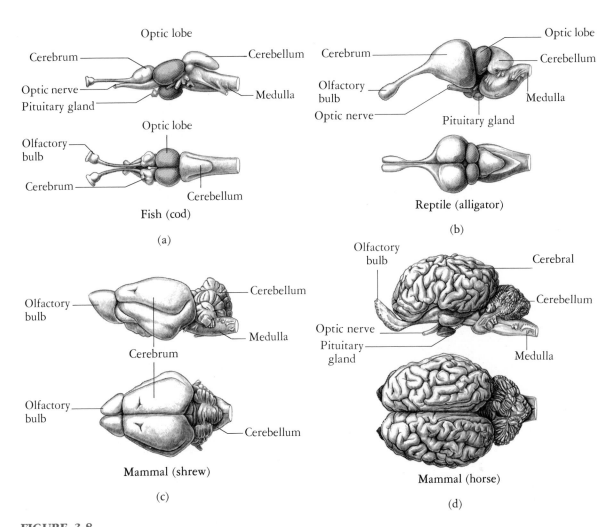

FIGURE 3-8

Evolution of Brain Structures   The brains of vertebrate animals reflect major stages in the evolutionary sequence.   Each type of brain is viewed from the left side in the upper drawing and from above in the lower drawing.   The midbrain area, shaded blue in the fish and reptile brains shown in (a) and (b), has progressively decreased in relative size during vertebrate evolution; in mammal brains, shown in (c) and (d), the midbrain has become completely covered by the greatly expanded cerebrum or cerebral cortex.   Although the brains shown here appear to be roughly the same size, they actually differ greatly in size.   (The horse brain is much larger than the others.)   *Source:* Adapted from Simpson, G. G., & Beck, W. S. (1975).   *Life: An introduction to biology* (2nd ed.).   New York: Harcourt Brace Jovanovich.

tors increased as they evolved to the point at which *Homo sapiens* became a distinct species (see Figure 3-9).   We also know the brain of the human fetus develops from the inside out and that the earliest structures are very similar to the brains of reptiles (see Figure 3-10).   Although it is reasonable to conclude the human brain

evolved in roughly the manner outlined by Mac-Lean, other views are possible.   For example, Vilensky and others (1982) believe that continuing evolution of the limbic system, more than development of the cortex, is responsible for the social and sexual characteristics that distinguish humans from non-human animals.

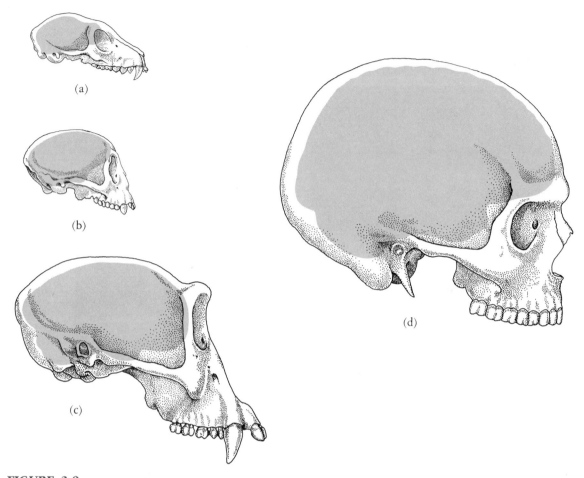

FIGURE 3-9

Increase of Brain Size with Evolution   The increase in brain size that occurred during primate evolution can be seen in this comparison of the brains (blue areas inside skulls) of (a) a prosimian, (b) a monkey, (c) an ape, and (d) a modern human.   The skulls shown here are approximately one-third their normal size.   *Source:* Adapted from Holloway, R. L. (1974, July).   The casts of fossil hominid brains. *Scientific American.*

An important aspect of the human brain is that it contains the same basic structures as the brains of sharks, crocodiles, rabbits, wolves, and chimpanzees.   The structure that makes the human brain unique (the enlarged cerebral cortex) grew on top of and in addition to these earlier structures; it did not replace them.   Thus, we can expect humans to engage in cold-blooded reptilian behavior and primitive emotional behavior when the early and lower brain structures dominate the later and higher structure.   The primitive structures remain active in more highly developed brains, but their control over behavior is strongly influenced by the later structure.   For example, humans continue to engage in repro-

ductive behavior (an activity associated with the reptilian brain), but usually act in ways deemed appropriate to their culture (an influence stemming from the cerebral cortex; see Chapter 8).   When humans behave in cold-blooded ways, such as during bizarre crimes, it is possible that their lower brain structures somehow overpowered the higher structure.

Another example of the influence of lower brain structures concerns a more "hot-blooded" response — anxiety, a significant factor in many psychological disorders.   Highly anxious individuals sometimes feel fearful in situations that, rationally, they know are not threatening.   Researcher Robert Malmo (1975) has suggested that

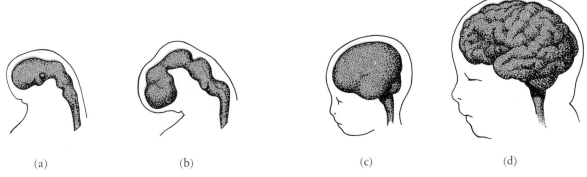

(a)   (b)   (c)   (d)

FIGURE 3-10
Development of the Human Fetal Brain (a) After three weeks of gestation, (b) after seven weeks, (c) after four months, and (d) in a newborn infant — (a) and (b) brain development strongly resembles brain development in fish and amphibians. *Source:* Adapted from Cowan, W. M. (1979). The development of the brain. *The brain: A Scientific American book.* San Francisco, CA: W. H. Freeman.

an excessive responsiveness of the limbic system may be the reason. Research has demonstrated clearly that electrical stimulation of the limbic system can evoke rage and sexual behavior in both nonhumans and humans. However, it is important to note that learning and abnormal experiences during development can produce quite similar behavioral pathologies. For this reason,

considerable controversy surrounds attempts to "cure" these disorders by treating the brain chemically or surgically (see Chapter 14). In practice, it is very difficult to separate disturbed behaviors, such as extreme violence, that are environmentally determined from disturbed behaviors that result from brain pathologies.

BRAIN STRUCTURE AND FUNCTION

Although there are various ways of grouping the brain's structures, we will follow MacLean's suggestion for organization. Consider the brain's structures in terms of three broad divisions: the central core, the limbic system and associated structures, and the cerebral cortex.

Imagine a human brain split vertically in two to form right and left halves. A side view of the exposed brain would show the structures represented schematically in Figure 3-11. At the top of the spinal cord, you would see a widening of the cord and, behind it, a ball-shaped outgrowth. These structures, which comprise the central core, correspond to MacLean's reptilian brain. Lying above the central core are several distinct structures; most of these comprise the limbic system, MacLean's second stage of brain evolution. Covering the limbic system and associated structures is the latest structure to evolve, the cerebral

cortex. (See Color Plate III, where the anatomy of the human brain is represented in a series of diagrams.) Structures that correspond to the three basic divisions we have described are added to each successive drawing. You may refer to these drawings as you read the following sections in which we describe the most important brain structures and outline their function.

Central Core Structures

Six principal structures make up the central core: the *medulla,* the *pons,* the *cerebellum,* the *reticular formation,* the *hypothalamus,* and the *thalamus.* We examine each structure in turn.

Medulla The outer portion of the spinal cord consists of neural pathways; the inner, butterfly-

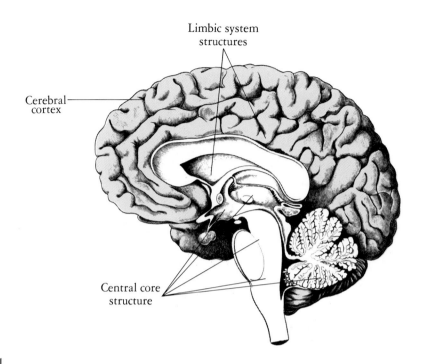

FIGURE 3-11

Cross-sectional Representation of Human Brain A section through the center of the brain. The three components of MacLean's triune brain are identifiable, although many of the limbic system structures are hidden from view. *Source:* Adapted from Stephens & North. (1974) *Biology.* New York: John Wiley and Sons.

shaped portion contains cell bodies and neural interconnections (see Figure 3-12). The brain's central core begins where the top of the spinal cord increases in diameter to form the **medulla.** Neural pathways continue through the outer portion of the medulla. The interior of the medulla is comprised of nerve nuclei — dense collections of neurons that are in close communication with each other but that also link remote areas of the nervous system. The functions of the medulla include regulation of heart rate, respiration rate, blood pressure, and body temperature. The medulla is also important in the maintenance of balance through control over skeletal muscle tone.

Pons Above the medulla is a further enlargement of brain cells, the **pons** (Latin for *bridge*), which serves as the link between the central core and higher brain structure. Several nerve centers within the pons have been implicated in the control of the sleeping–waking cycle.

Cerebellum Also classified as part of the central core, a mammalian structure — the **cerebellum** ("little brain") — lies immediately behind the medulla and the pons. The outer covering of the

cerebellum is composed of cells, arranged in layers, which are connected to nerve centers deep inside the structure. The cerebellum plays an important role in the regulation and coordination of muscular activity referred to as the **motor system.** As part of the motor system, the cerebellum is involved in creating smooth body movements and redressing small deviations from the intended path. It is also involved in the learning of skilled movements, especially those that must be executed too quickly to be guided by moment-to-moment feedback, such as playing a violin or piano. The cerebellum receives input from the sensory fibers of the spinal cord and information from the inner ear related to balance. People who have damaged cerebellums move in a jerky, spastic fashion and their speech, one of the most complex muscular acts, usually is affected severely.

Reticular Formation The **reticular formation** is a diffuse system of nerves that extends from the spinal cord, through the center of the medulla and pons, and terminates in the structures just above. Nerves extending upward from

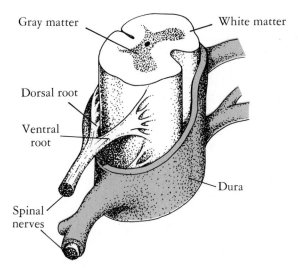

Gray matter

White matter

Dorsal root

Ventral root

Dura

Spinal nerves

FIGURE 3-12
Cross-sectional Representation of Human Spinal Cord Protected by a *dura,* or sheath, afferent nerves in the spinal cord transmit signals from body to brain (via the dorsal root) and efferent nerves carry signals from brain to body (via the ventral root). Concentration of cell bodies makes the inner, butterfly-shaped area appear gray, while the fatty covering of nerve axons makes the surrounding tissue appear white. *Source:* Adapted from Wittig, A. (1984). *Psychology: An introduction* (p. 61). New York: McGraw-Hill.

the reticular formation serve to alert the cortex to the arrival of sensory input—which explains why a loud noise, a sudden flash of light, or a poke in your side is arousing. Nerves descending from the reticular formation are important in maintaining muscle tone and in controlling various vital reflexes.

Hypothalamus The **hypothalamus,** a small structure that lies in front of the central core structures just described, is critically involved in the regulation of eating, drinking, and sexual behaviors. The hypothalamus also serves as an essential link between the nervous system and the *hormonal system*, responding to hormones secreted by glands throughout the body and, in turn, regulating them by controlling the secretions of the **pituitary gland.** The hypothalamus receives information about the nutritional status of the body and about its balance of fluids.

Thalamus The **thalamus,** situated near the center of the brain, contains nerve nuclei that relay information from the various sense organs

(except the nose) to the cortex of the brain. One function of the thalamus in primates is to receive input from the eyes and organize it into a color code before sending it to the cortex. The thalamus is also involved in memory formation, and part of it has been shown to be essential for certain kinds of learning.

We have included the hypothalamus and the thalamus as part of the central core because they are involved in the control of basic bodily functions. Both structures, however, are linked closely to the limbic system. For example, acting in concert with the limbic system, the hypothalamus is concerned with the regulation of emotional behaviors. A tumor in this region typically leads to radical change in body weight, severe emotional disturbance, and atrophy of the genital organs.

Limbic System and Associated Structures

The limbic system is composed of a number of interconnected structures, including the *amygdala*, the *hippocampus*, and the *septal nuclei*. This system formerly was called the "nose brain" because it includes the *olfactory bulbs*, which receive direct connections from the sensory receptors in the nose and have projections to the cortex. After it was shown that many of the limbic structures in humans play little or no direct role in smell (although they probably did in earlier evolutionary stages), attention turned to the suggestion that the limbic system was responsible for emotion and motivated behavior. Subsequent investigation has indicated that some but not all of these structures may serve this type of role.

The **amygdala,** for example, has been implicated in the control of defensive and aggressive behavior and, through its connections with the hypothalamus, in food selection. The **hippocampus** appears to be involved in memory; damage to it severely impairs the formation of new memories. Nevertheless, from an evolutionary perspective, it seems probable that the limbic system initially developed to serve olfactory functions. Animals benefit from basing behaviors on odor: they can smell a predator before it sees them and follow prey that is no longer present. Therefore, it might have proved adaptive for these newer regions of the brain to regulate both motivation and the formation of new memories on the basis of smell cues.

A dramatic demonstration of the limbic system's role in regulating emotion was the discovery of *pleasure centers* (Olds & Milner, 1954). Electrical stimulation of parts of a rat's limbic system, particularly the **septal nuclei,** seemed to give the animal intense pleasure. The rat would press a bar repeatedly for many hours, often totally ignoring other bodily needs, to receive occasional bursts of stimulation. However, James Olds and Peter Milner found that electrical stimulation was not always pleasurable. In some areas of the limbic system, particularly in and near the hypothalamus, stimulation seemed painful to the animal and it would work hard to avoid or terminate it. A few limbic stimulation studies have been conducted with human subjects, who reported a range of emotional responses (Heath, 1963).

Basal Ganglia   The **basal ganglia** are a group of nerve centers lying above the limbic system and below the cortex, with intimate connections to both. Like the cerebellum, the basal ganglia appear to be involved in the organization of motor behavior. However, the cerebellum controls rapid movements; the basal ganglia appear to play an important role in controlling slower movements and in mediating the starting and stopping of movements. Damage to the basal ganglia typically produces changes in posture and muscle tone and leads to such abnormal movements as tremors, jerks, and twitches. For example, Parkinson's disease, which can result from a chemical imbalance in this region, has the effect of generating muscle tremors when the person tries to relax. The tremors disappear as soon as movement is initiated, although the person may experience difficulty in achieving movement as well. As the disease progresses, a peculiar mask-like facial expression and lilting, singsong quality of the voice ensue. Gradually, all muscle tone is lost.

A curious property of the basal ganglia is that they are misnamed. The term *ganglia* normally is used to describe collections of cell bodies *outside* the central nervous system. For a cluster of cell bodies within the central nervous system, it is customary to use the term *nucleus*. Because the basal ganglia are in the central nervous system, they should, for the sake of consistency, have been called the *basal nuclei.*

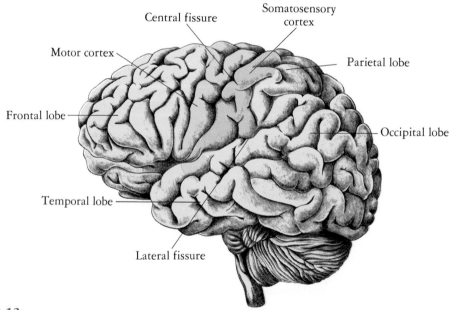

FIGURE 3-13
The Four Lobes of the Cerebral Cortex   The frontal lobe is separated from the parietal lobe by the *central fissure* and both these lobes are separated from the temporal and occipital lobes by the *lateral fissure*. Also shown are the *somatosensory* and *motor* areas of the cortex that are involved in neural input from, and output to, the body. *Source:* After Lassen, N. A., Ingvar, D. H., & Shinhoj, E. (1978, October). Brain function and blood flow. *Scientific American, 239,* 62–71.

Cerebral Cortex

From an anatomical perspective, the enlargement of the cerebral cortex distinguishes the human brain from all others. Although it appears to be a single great mass, the human cortex is actually a sheet only 1.5 – 3.0 millimeters thick with a surface area approaching 2,400 square centimeters, or about four times the size of this page. The folded or wrinkled character of the cortex was nature's solution to the problem of confining this expanding sheet into a skull that had to be small enough to pass through the birth canal. The folding also facilitates the intricate interconnections between different parts of the cortex that are needed to control complex behaviors.

The folds of the cortex divide it into four distinct areas or **lobes** (see Figure 3-13): the **frontal, parietal, temporal,** and **occipital** lobes. These lobes serve as valuable geographical landmarks, but there is a better way to map the *functional* arrangement of the cortex. During the course of the brain's evolution, different regions of the cortex have become specialized in the tasks they perform. Three types of mammalian cortex have been identified in terms of the general functions served: *sensory, motor,* and *association* cortex (see Figure 3-14).

Sensory information is relayed by the thalamus to the **sensory cortex** in a precise, orderly manner. For example, consider the projection of information from receptors in the skin to the cortex, shown in Figure 3-14. Also shown is the way the **motor cortex** projects to the motor systems. In both cases, larger cortical areas are involved for those regions of the body that are highly sensitive or dextrous.

The **association cortex** has neither direct sensory nor direct motor connections. In primates, this area shows a large increase as a proportion of total cortex, compared with older

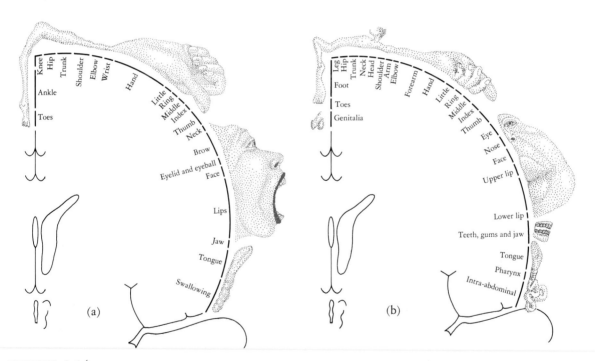

FIGURE 3-14

Somatosensory and Motor Projections in the Cortex (a) A cross section through the cerebral cortex just anterior to the central fissure. The surface of this area is the *motor cortex.* Each region of the motor cortex controls the muscular activities of a particular part of the body; the regions for some body parts are much larger than the regions for others. (b) A cross section through the cerebral cortex just posterior to the central fissure. The surface of this area is the *somatosensory cortex.* Each region receives sensory information from specific muscles, joints, and areas of the skin. Again, the regions for some body parts are much larger than the regions for others. The motor cortex and the somatosensory cortex are present in both hemispheres of the brain, although only one hemisphere is shown here for each cortex. *Source:* Adapted from Penfield, W., & Rasmussen, T. (1950). *The cerebral cortex of man.* New York: Macmillan.

Box 3-2
On Being of Two Minds

In a normal person, the fibers of the corpus callosum make information transmitted to either hemisphere of the brain equally accessible to the other hemisphere. In order to receive information in both sides of the brain, however, split-brain patients, whose corpus callosum has been cut, must scan across the scene they observe so both halves of each eye receive the same information sequentially. To study the functions of each half of the brain, researchers prevent this scanning. They ask split-brain patients to fixate on the center of a screen and then flash pictures or words very briefly to the left or to the right of the fixation point. This results in the information reaching only one of the two hemispheres (see illustration).

Visual information that reaches only one hemisphere cannot guide an action of the hand controlled by the opposite hemisphere. Thus, if the visual image of a ball reaches only the left hemisphere of a split-brain patient, the right hemisphere will not be aware of the input. If asked to select a ball from a number of alternative objects, the split-brain patient could do so with the right hand (controlled by the left hemisphere) but not with the left hand (controlled by the right hemisphere). Similarly, research on split-brain patients has shown that if an object is placed in one hand, and they are prevented from seeing their hands, they cannot use their opposite hand to select a similar

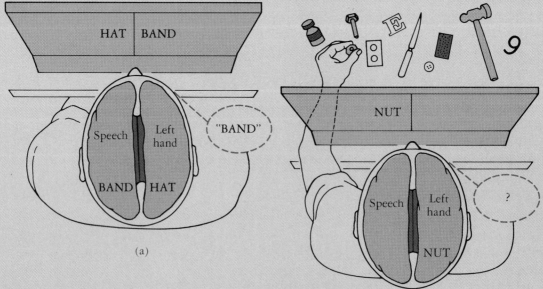

(a)

(b)

Reactions of a Split-brain Patient Researchers created these experiments to test the ability of a split-brain patient to select by touch alone an object flashed to the left or right hemisphere. *Source:* (a) After Nebes, R. D., & Sperry, C. (1971). *Neuropsychologia* (Vol. 9, pp. 247–59). Elmsford, NY: Pergamon. (b) After Restak, R. M. (1979). *The brain: The last frontier.* New York: Doubleday.

object from a group of alternative objects placed behind a screen.

One of the most important ways in which the hemispheres of the brain are specialized is in the perception and production of language. Because the left hemisphere controls speech in most people, we assume left-hemispheric dominance of language in the examples that follow.

The right hemisphere is essentially mute in split-brain patients. It is unable to verbalize the knowledge it contains in anything but the most elementary way because it cannot transmit this knowledge to the left hemisphere. However, the right hemisphere can still communicate by making gestures with the left side of the body, which it controls. If you place an object in the left hand of a split-brain patient behind a screen, the information is transmitted primarily to the right hemisphere. If you ask the patient to identify the object, the patient will be unable to say the word. However, he or she may start generating a random stream of names. If the name of the object accidentally comes up in this random sequence, the right hemisphere will hear it and may cause the head to nod or make some other gesture to indicate the correct verbal response has been made.

By means of such tests as

Specializations of the Left and Right Cerebral Hemispheres

Left Hemisphere	Right Hemisphere
Speaking, writing, and understanding language, abstract and symbolic patterns, and their manipulation Mathematical abilities Sequential, logical, analytical, time-locked thinking	Very rudimentary linguistic skills Apprehension of spatial relations and transformations Holistic thinking versus analytical and verbal processing Musical, artistic expression Emotional perception and expression

these, researchers have learned that each hemisphere of the brain in split-brain patients can have its own private sensations, memories, and ideas. Through this work, they have gained considerable insight into the special functions of each hemisphere. The left hemisphere is dominant for linguistic tasks in most people; the right hemisphere dominates in most other tasks. In recent experiments, investigators have improved the testing procedures for the right hemisphere, introducing new nonverbal modes of expression to tap its abilities. Some researchers have assumed that the disconnected right hemisphere is not conscious when isolated from its verbal neighbor. Roger Sperry (1974) argues that, on the contrary, it is " . . . a conscious system in its own right, perceiving, thinking, remembering, reasoning, willing and emoting, all at a characteristically human level." Although decidedly inferior in tasks requiring linguistic

or symbolic capabilities, the right hemisphere appears to be superior in other forms of mental processing. The table presents a somewhat speculative summary of the capacities of the two hemispheres of the brain.

To illustrate his contention that the left and right hemispheres may be simultaneously conscious in different ways that, at times, may even be at cross purposes, Sperry relates the following story about one of his split-brain patients. This woman was in the process of dressing for an appointment she considered a necessary but unpleasant obligation. She was observed buttoning up her coat with her right hand, totally oblivious to the fact her left hand was following in step, undoing each button! Obviously, her logical left hemisphere was resigned to keeping the appointment, but her right hemisphere appeared to be expressing its own contrary feelings on the matter — suggesting each hemisphere may have a "mind of its own."

types of mammal. This difference is greatest in the human brain, especially in the frontal lobes. Although some of the functions that might be served by the association cortex in the human brain are still in doubt, some regions of specialization have been identifed. These include such regions as Broca's area, which governs speech and language comprehension. Damage to these areas may result in poor comprehension of spoken and written language and may produce speech that, although phonetically and grammatically normal, consists of word sequences that often are inappropriate or even meaningless. One researcher reports that a patient asked to describe a picture of two boys stealing cookies behind a woman's back said: "Mother is away here working her work to get her better, but when she's looking the two boys looking in the other part. She's working another time." (Geschwind, 1979).

Although there is general agreement regarding the distribution of the cortical functions described here, it is important to realize that virtually all areas of the cortex are in constant communication with each other. Sensory cells have been found in areas primarily concerned with motor responses, and vice versa. At the same time, the activities in which we engage rarely require the operation of only one of these types of function. Whether we are driving a car, attending a concert, or talking to a friend, successful performance of these behaviors depends on the coordination of most of these brain regions. Discovering how this is achieved is one of the most exciting tasks facing today's brain researchers.

Cerebral Hemispheres

Figure 3-11 shows the inside of only half the brain — the left hemisphere. Missing from the figure is an almost identical set of brain structures — the right hemisphere. These two hemispheres are connected by a prominent band of nerve fibers called the **corpus callosum** (see color foldout). The fibers of the corpus callosum make it possible for the activities of the two hemispheres to blend into a unitary, conscious experience. As long as the corpus callosum is intact, each hemisphere receives information about the other's activities almost instantaneously, so it is difficult to distinguish between their separate contributions.

"EVERY ONCE IN A WHILE MY RIGHT BRAIN THROWS SOMETHING IN."

In some cases of intractable epilepsy, it has been necessary to sever the corpus callosum to effectively isolate the two hemispheres. **Split-brain patients,** persons who have undergone this operation, have been studied extensively by Roger Sperry and a number of collaborators (Sperry, 1974; Springer & Deutsch, 1985). Sperry's investigations (for which he shared the 1981 Nobel prize for physiology and medicine) have revealed a number of intriguing facts which, taken together, suggest that normal consciousness is the result of the deft interplay of contributions from two semi-independent brains in one head — the left and right **cerebral hemispheres.** Despite their superficial similarity, Sperry found that each hemisphere contributes special qualities to our unified sense of conscious awareness.

If you observed the day-to-day behavior of split-brain patients, it would be difficult to detect anything unusual (Bogen, 1979). When split-brain patients are free to move about, sufficient information for normal functioning reaches both hemispheres. However, when researchers construct special laboratory tests that direct information to one hemisphere and prevent it from reaching the other, split-brain patients behave in ways that force us to conclude that each hemisphere is unaware of the other's experiences and deliberations. Box 3-2 describes some of the techniques split-brain researchers have used to discover the special capacities of the two hemispheres and highlights some of their findings. As you read about the fascinating divisions of function between the hemispheres, remember that in the normal brain the corpus callosum keeps the hemispheres so fully interconnected that particular mental functions are unlikely to be localized as distinctly as they are when the corpus callosum is severed.

COMMUNICATION IN THE NERVOUS SYSTEM

The brain has been compared to a telephone switchboard. The idea underlying this metaphor is that the brain receives messages from distant sites and routes them to the appropriate destinations. In a very general sense, that is what happens. But the brain differs from a switchboard in too many important ways for this to be a useful model. This should become evident in the following sections as we describe the elements of the nervous system and consider how signals are transmitted through the system.

The two main types of cells in the nervous system are *glial cells* and *neurons;* the former outnumber the latter by about ten to one. The glial cells have a support function; the task of communication falls to the neurons.

Glial cells

The word *glial* is derived from the same root as the word *glue.* Early students of nervous structure believed the primary function of *glial* cells was to hold neurons together. We now know that although they do provide physical support for neurons, **glial cells** also accomplish the following:

1. They store nutrients and waste products and transport these products between neurons and the blood vessels that serve the brain.

2. Glial cells clean up the debris when neurons die and fill in the space that is left.

3. Glial cells act as insulators by forming the **myelin sheath** that surrounds neurons (see Figure 3-15).

In much the same way that plastic insulation on electrical wire prevents interference between

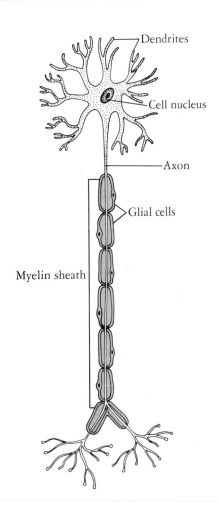

FIGURE 3-15
Neuron and Glial Cells Glial cells form the myelin sheath that surrounds the axon of the neurons. *Source:* Adapted from Goldsby, R. A. (1979). *Biology* (p. 506). New York: Harper & Row.

BOX 3-3
SYNAPTIC TRANSMISSION

How is it possible for a living cell to analyze, store, and transmit information? The answer lies in the specialized function of the different parts of the neuron. The dendrites and cell body, the *receiving* part of the neuron, operate differently from the axon, the *transmitting* portion. The cell wall, or membrane, of the dendrite and cell-body portions of the neuron has the capacity to compare the strengths of many simultaneous inputs. The response of this portion of the membrane is proportional to the relative amounts of the two opposing messages it can receive — excitation and inhibition. For this reason, we say that the membrane responds in a *graded* manner.

The axon is specialized to transmit this graded response to other neurons; in doing so, it uses an on–off code to signal its state. Such a code, similar to that used by computers, consists of "all-or-none" impulses called **action potentials.** An impulse of this kind is ideally suited for transmitting messages over long distances. Although some axons are only a fraction of a millimeter long, others — such as those that convey touch information from the soles of your feet to the

spinal cord — are more than a meter long.

Neurons communicate among themselves by releasing neurotransmitters, complex chemicals that diffuse across synaptic junctions (like the one shown in Figure 3-15) and interact with the membrane of the next neuron. We refer to the neurotransmitter's source as the **presynaptic neuron** and to its destination as the **postsynaptic neuron.** Researchers believe that neurotransmitters fit into receptor sites on the postsynaptic membrane much like a key fits into a lock. Just as not all keys will open a given lock, not all neurotransmitters will fit into a given postsynaptic receptor site. If the transmitter does fit, however, it makes the postsynaptic neuron more or less likely to respond, depending on whether its action is excitatory or inhibitory.

Reducing the probability of firing of a postsynaptic cell might seem to be an odd effect, but inhibition is a vital process in neural transmission. If one group of cells is temporarily quieted, the effects of another group of active cells will be more potent. You could not flex your arm if the message from your brain

did not inhibit the neurons controlling the triceps muscle at the same time that it excites the neurons controlling the biceps muscle. The membrane of the dendrites and the cell body of a neuron is dotted in a mosaic of connections with thousands of presynaptic cells, some of which are excitatory and some of which are inhibitory. Figure (a) diagrams this web of inputs; figure (b) illustrates how the membrane compares the relative amounts of excitation and inhibition.

The neuron analyzes and transmits information by concentrating certain chemicals within and excluding others from its cell wall. The neural membrane acts somewhat like a dam. Just as a dam first stores water and then releases it selectively, so the neuron generates signals by first preventing and then allowing chemical elements to pass through its membrane barrier. The decision to open or close the "dam gates" is controlled by the neurotransmitters. The chemicals involved at this stage are the elements sodium, potassium, and chlorine; in solution, these elements are ionized and have small electrical charges associated with them. While the neuron is resting, sodium ions are being transported out of the cell and potassium and chlorine ions are being concentrated in the cell. In a neuron's resting state, the result of this segregation of ions is a charge of about 70 millivolts (thousandths of a volt) across the cell membrane. This electrical charge across the neural membrane creates a pressure for sodium to flow in and for potassium to escape.

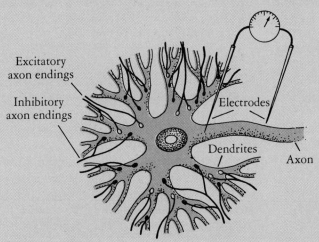

Excitatory axon endings

Inhibitory axon endings

Electrodes

Dendrites

Axon

(a) Representation of neuron—showing cell body, axon, and dendrites synapsing with adjacent neurons. Electrodes register the voltage difference across the cell membrane at the axon.

As long as the membrane remains intact, this pressure is resisted and the flow of ions is prevented. The arrival of a synaptic transmitter alters this situation. If the transmitter is excitatory, its arrival causes a local breakdown in the membrane and allows sodium ions to flow in and potassium ions to flow out. An inhibitory neurotransmitter has the opposite effect, making the interior of the cell even more negatively charged. Both effects quickly fade if they are not soon followed by more of their respective transmitters. In the excitatory case, if enough of these graded responses come together they will eventually trigger an action potential that travels down the axon of the postsynaptic neuron.

You may wonder how the strength of a stimulus that starts the neural transmission can be coded if neurons can only signal by using on–off messages. The answer is that the rate or frequency of neural impulses increases with stronger stimulation. Different neurons have maximum firing rates, ranging from a few times per second to over 1,000 times per second.

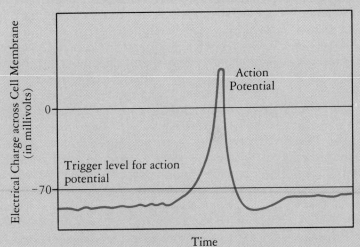

Electrical Charge across Cell Membrane (in millivolts)

Action Potential

0

Trigger level for action potential

−70

Time

(b) Change in electrical charge across cell membrane during action potential.

Synapses and Graded Postsynaptic Potentials

conversations on adjacent telephone lines, glial cells ensure separation of the information transmitted by individual neurons. Unlike the insulation that passively surrounds electrical wire, however, glial cells speed up the rate of neural transmission. Such diseases as multiple sclerosis, which attack the myelin sheath surrounding neurons, result in severe disorders of movement and perception and, ultimately, in death.

There is also evidence that some glial cells play a role in maintaining the integrity of the **blood–brain barrier**. This barrier was discovered when it was found that some substances that pass easily between the blood and the rest of the body do not do so in the brain. Glial cells attach themselves to the small blood vessels in the brain and are very selective in the chemicals they allow to pass in or out of the vessels. This or a similar mechanism protects the brain from the possibly harmful effects of certain drugs and other substances sometimes carried in the blood (Goldstein & Betz, 1986).

Neurons

The basic functional unit of the nervous system is the nerve cell, or **neuron** — a specialized cell for the analysis, storage, and transmission of information. In the past, textbooks have stated confidently that the human brain contains between 10 billion and 100 billion neurons. More recent work has indicated the cerebellum alone may contain nearly that many neurons! Suffice it to say that the brain contains an immense number of neurons. Moreover, it is possible for any one neuron to have direct connections with tens of thousands of other neurons. It has been calculated that if one million nerve cells were connected two at a time in every possible way, the number of possible combinations would total ten multiplied by itself 2,783,000 times! In view of the fact the brain contains many more than one million neurons, each with the possibility of far more extensive interconnections, the numbers become astronomical. These figures offer another indication of the complexity of the brain and the difficulty of trying to understand it.

Although there are many types, most neurons exhibit the features shown in Figure 3-15. Like other cells in the body, a neuron has a

cell body containing a **nucleus.** In addition, the neuron has a receptive end, the **dendrite,** which receives input from other neurons, and a transmitting end, the **axon,** which transmits information to other neurons. Both dendrites and axons branch extensively, permitting a single neuron to connect with a large number of other neurons. The point of functional connection between two neurons is called a **synapse.** Generally, neurons do not quite touch one another, so that synapses are actually very small spaces between adjacent neurons.

Neural Signals

Input from the environment is one source of messages in the brain. As you read these words, receptor cells in the back of your eyes are initiating the process of neural communication that results in the experience of perception. Now close your eyes and try to recall what this page looks like. The image you conjure up is probably less vivid and detailed, but the process that produces it also involves the transmission of information within your brain. In both cases, complex chemical changes are causing electrical signals to be passed through intricate networks of neurons in various locations of your nervous system.

The endings of axons contain chemicals known as **transmitter substances,** or **neurotransmitters.** When a neuron is activated, it causes these substances to be released into the **synaptic gap;** there, these neurotransmitters attach themselves to receptor sites on the receiving cell, which are usually located on its dendrites. This chemical stimulation changes the neuron's electrical state and may result in signals being sent along its axon that cause the release of neurotransmitters at the next synapse. Thus, information in the nervous system is transferred from one neuron to the next in a series of steps. For example, information from touch receptors in the skin of your hand might pass through five synaptic junctions on the way to its final destination in your cerebral cortex. The transmission of information in the nervous system is more comparable to a series of individual runners in a relay race than to a telephone wire directly connecting two instruments. When the axons of many hundreds or thousands of neurons bunch together to traverse a long distance in the body, they are referred to as **nerves.**

Not all neurons communicate exclusively with other neurons. Some neurons make synapses with glands and muscles. The release of neurotransmitters from these neurons initiates glandular or muscular activity, rather than further neural activity.

We have discussed the general process of transmitting information from cell to cell without being specific as to the changes within individual neurons that make synaptic transmission possible. Box 3-3 (page 122) summarizes the complex series of chemical events set into motion by neurotransmitters. You will see that some neurotransmitters inhibit rather than excite electrical activity in the receiving neuron. This means each nerve cell must act as a tiny decision maker, constantly evaluating opposing inputs from the neurons to which it is connected.

MODIFIABILITY OF BRAIN CIRCUITRY

We have described the structure and function of the brain and how information is transmitted within it. Now we turn our attention to certain important issues concerning the development of the brain. Specifically, we address the question of the degree to which certain general features of the environment can affect growth of the brain. The brain is composed of living tissue and must have nourishment to grow. Does malnutrition interfere with development of the brain? If so, are the effects reversible? What happens to a brain deprived of sensory input? Can an unstimulating environment slow the growth of the brain? Conversely, does an enriched environment accelerate brain growth?

In Chapter 2, we discussed conflicting viewpoints on the relative importance of environmental and genetic factors as determinants of behavior; here, we consider the *nature–nurture* controversy as it applies to the development of the brain. The *nature* position holds that neural connections become established according to a genetic plan specifying a developmental process largely unaffected by the particular environment in which growth occurs. The *nurture,* or environmentalist, position holds that the particular connections formed in the brain depend at least in part on environmental factors.

The question of how much the course of neural development can be modified by environmental factors is an old one, but the answer is still hotly debated. Like many "either/or" conflicts, this one almost certainly is wrong at both extremes. We know, for example, that babies are born with the neural apparatus for several behaviors, such as the sucking reflex, that require little or no prior experience (see Chapter 9). However, the fact that such behaviors are modified through learning implies that at least some parts of our brain must retain the potential for change throughout life.

One theory that offers a way to accommodate both genetic and environmental influences on brain development has been proposed by brain researcher Marcus Jacobson (Jacobson, 1970; Hirsch & Jacobson, 1975). Jacobson notes two main classes of neurons: **macroneurons,** which have long axons and dendrites and are concerned primarily with conveying information over long distances, and smaller **microneurons,** which are particularly prominent in such areas of the brain as the cerebral cortex. According to Jacobson, the macroneurons originate and develop while the organism is still in the embryonic stage, protected from most outside influences. Macroneurons seem to develop predominantly in accordance with genetic guidelines. Microneurons, which form many of the short interconnections between macroneurons, mature later (many not until after birth) and appear to be more responsive to environmental influences. If Jacobson's hypothesis is shown to be correct, it will help to explain how both genetic plans and environmental experiences shape the final architecture of the nervous system. It makes sense to preprogram the reflex that withdraws your hand from a hot object, but not the neural connections that allow you to type or play Bach fugues.

Until recently, the traditional view of the relative importance of nature and nurture in brain development has tended to stress genetic factors. Although researchers have always recognized that enduring changes of some form must underlie the processes of learning and memory, they have generally assumed that brain structure is largely unaffected by qualitative and quantitative differences in the environment. In the last two or three decades, however, some intriguing research has suggested the environment may play a more dramatic role in brain development than previously believed. Let's look at some of this research.

Malnutrition

Researchers have found that children who were malnourished prior to birth and/or as infants suffered a permanent reduction in head circumference, suggesting that the growth of their brains has been stunted (Winick & Rosso, 1969). Other investigators have found intellectual deficits in children who were malnourished prenatally or shortly after birth (Kaplan, 1972; Brozek, 1978). Because malnourished children typically fail to receive normal sensory and intellectual stimulation, it is difficult to determine the precise causes of their deficiencies. However, experiments on animals have helped identify the deficits specifically attributable to malnutrition.

Animal researchers have found that poor nutrition during periods of rapid brain growth can result in arrested development of the myelin sheath that surrounds axons, in stunted development of dendrites, and in an overall reduction in the number of nerve cells. Inadequate protein consumption early in life also is associated with long-term reduction of the genetic material (DNA and RNA) in the brain and with reduced concentrations of certain neurotransmitters (Wurtman & Fernstrom, 1974). The implications of these findings are enormous. When we realize that malnutrition affects a huge proportion of the population of the Third World, not to mention a shocking number of citizens in the industrialized nations, we can see that the waste in human brain potential is truly immense. Several studies have found that a good diet imposed later in childhood does not fully reverse early brain damage, although vigorous intervention before the age of two does help considerably, especially when accompanied by environmental enrichment (Meyer & Winjok, 1977).

Visual Deprivation

A **cataract** is a clouding of the lens of the eye. Some people are born with this problem; others develop it later in life. Cataracts admit light to the eyes but prevent the transmission of visual patterns. In recent years, scientists have developed surgical procedures to remove cataracts, thereby restoring the ability of the eyes to transmit patterned images. Do patients regain the ability to recognize visual stimuli after their cataracts are removed? It depends on whether the patients suffered from the condition at birth or had normal vision for a time before the problem developed.

People who develop cataracts later in life are very likely to regain good pattern vision after surgery; people who have had cataracts since birth are not. Even after much training and experience with their newly restored eyes, most patients born with cataracts report limited improvement (Gregory, 1978), suggesting that the brain mechanisms responsible for processing and interpreting patterned visual information were irreversibly impaired. Many studies on animals confirm the importance of early stimulation for the normal development of the areas of the brain involved in vision (Movshon & Van Sluyters, 1981).

Quality of Environmental Stimulation

In Chapter 2, we discussed the effects of enriched and impoverished environments on behavior. Here, we describe a classic study of the ways in which these influences affect the development of the brain. A group of psychologists, biochemists, and neuroanatomists at the University of California at Berkeley raised rats under conditions similar to those represented in Figure 3-16 (Rosenzweig, 1971, 1984). At weaning, the researchers assigned littermates randomly to enriched, normal, or impoverished rearing conditions. By assigning rats to groups in this way, the researchers could equalize genetic, prenatal, and early postnatal factors among the groups, thereby ensuring that any differences found between the groups' brains would be the result of differences

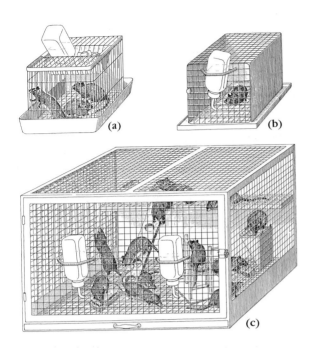

FIGURE 3-16
Enriched and Impoverished Environments
(a) Standard colony environment with three rats per cage. (b) Impoverished environment with an isolated rat. (c) Enriched laboratory environment with ten–twelve rats per cage and a variety of stimulus objects.
Source: Adapted from Rosenzweig, M. R., Bennett, E. L., & Diamond, M. C. (1972). Brain changes in response to experience. *Scientific American.*

in the quality of the environment in which they were to spend the next 30–100 days. The experimenters used a *single blind rating procedure* (the research assistant who made the anatomical or biochemical measurements was unaware of the particular environment in which each animal had been raised) in order to eliminate any bias that might result from prior knowledge of each animal's experience.

At the end of the experiment, the researchers found that, compared to normal rats, the rats reared in the enriched environment had:

1. a heavier and thicker cerebral cortex
2. more protein in their brains
3. neurons that were larger but not more numerous
4. proportionately more glial cells
5. synapses in certain parts of their brains that were larger and more robust, although reduced in number

6. elevated levels of several chemicals known to regulate neural transmission at synapses
7. a richer blood supply in the cerebral cortex
8. changes in the relative amounts of genetic material (RNA and DNA) in the brain

Of particular interest is the finding that enriched experience produced fewer but larger synaptic connections in some parts of the cerebral cortex. Does experience selectively weed out less useful synaptic connections and nurture those that are more appropriate to the animal's needs? As we demonstrate later, a change in the number and strength of synaptic connections may be one way in which new information is stored in the brain.

You may wonder just how rich the environment of a laboratory animal could be, compared with life in the wild. Rosenzweig and his colleagues also compared the brains of squirrels who had been reared in the laboratory with the brains of squirrels who had lived only in the wild (Rosenzweig et al., 1982). The laboratory animals had lived in either an impoverished or an enriched environment. As expected, the brains of the impoverished group showed significantly less development than either the enriched or the wild squirrels. There were few differences between the latter two groups, although the brains of wild squirrels did show a higher density of RNA than the brains of the laboratory squirrels reared in an enriched environment.

In summary, the results of studies on malnutrition, visual deprivation, and impoverished versus enriched environments demonstrate that the growing brain is dependent on environmental stimulation for normal development. Although many findings were obtained using animal subjects, even cautious generalization to humans leads to conclusions that emphasize the importance of nutrition and environmental enrichment for children. It is known that malnutrition and impoverished environments tend to make people lethargic and less responsive to external events. It would seem that the brains of malnourished and understimulated people therefore receive a double blow: they not only start with less, but they gain less as they go through life because they undergo fewer novel experiences.

Implications for Treatment

Information about the extent to which the nervous system can be modified has some important implications for the treatment of individuals who have suffered brain injuries. The amenability of the developing brain to modification by environmental influence becomes a virtue when it enables the brain to compensate for partial loss of function due to injury or disease. Two compensatory changes have been observed: new axon growth and increased cellular sensitivity (Marshall, 1984). New axon growth has long been known to be responsible for the regaining of skin sensitivity after damage to the underlying nerves (Weddell, 1941). The greater challenge of demonstrating new axon growth in the injured brain is a more recent accomplishment (Kerr, 1975). Neurons that lose input due to injury or disease also typically respond by increasing their sensitiv-

ity to neurotransmitter substances (Berge et al., 1983).

The capacity of the brain to compensate for injury in these ways appears to diminish greatly with development. This was clearly documented in a study by Thomas Reh and Katherine Kalil (1982) on the loss of paw dexterity in the hamster. Adult hamsters use their paws to hold and manipulate sunflower seeds while they shell the seeds with their teeth. A strategically placed lesion in the hamster's brain will impair the dexterity of one of its forepaws so that it can be used to hold but not to manipulate the seed. The time taken to shell seeds provides a simple measure of the severity of the impairment. Figure 3-17 shows the average shelling time found by Reh and Kalil for hamsters operated on at different stages of brain development. Animals operated on four to eight days from birth showed little deficit in shelling ability. Animals operated on three

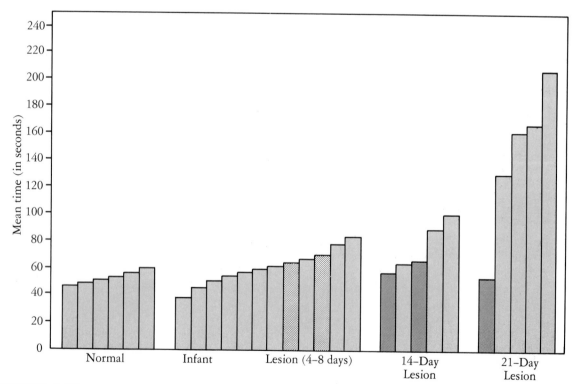

FIGURE 3-17
Reh & Kalil's Hamster Study Histogram comparing the average time required for animals with pyramidal tract lesions at three postnatal ages to shell and eat sunflower seeds. Lightly colored bars represent scores of hamsters with unilateral lesions; gray bars represent scores of animals with bilateral lesions; darkly colored bars represent the scores of sham-operated animals. *Source:* Adapted from Reh, T., & Kalil, K. (1982). Functional role of regrowing pyramidal tract fibers. *Journal of Comparative Neurology, 211,* 276–83.

weeks after birth, however, continued to take two to three times as long to shell seeds as normal adults.

Evidence from animal and human studies supports the view that the prospects for recovery from brain damage are generally much better for children than for adults. For example, it is not unusual for young children who suffer damage to the language areas of their brains to recover almost completely from the resulting language impairment. However, after the teenage years, similar damage is likely to produce permanent language impairment, as many stroke victims have found. The results of one provocative line of research contradict this general proposition. When fetal neurons were transplanted into the injured brains of adult rats, new axon growth led to improvements in motor functions (Dunnett et al., 1981) and in performance on a spatial task (Low et al., 1982).

THE NEURAL BASIS OF LEARNING AND MEMORY

Every day we learn countless new things: we are exposed to new sights and sounds; we learn information about the people we meet; we acquire new facts and skills. And although we remember a great deal of what we learn, we by no means remember all of it. While some psychologists devote their efforts to studying the environmental conditions that promote or hinder learning and remembering (see Chapters 5 and 6), others attempt to discover how new information is processed and stored in the body. Not surprisingly, psychologists in the latter group focus their attention on the brain. Computers remember data by electronic switching, by punching cards, or by magnetically rearranging molecules of iron oxide on plastic tapes. How does the brain accomplish this task? As yet we have no clear answer to this question, but a number of theories are being pursued.

One possibility is that a single memory is stored as some physical change in a particular location of the brain. There is, in this view, a "memory molecule." Dramatic support for this proposition would come from a demonstration that a memory could be moved from one brain to another by transfer of the brain tissue that contained the memory molecule. Much the same sort of idea was behind the practice in some primitive tribes of eating the brain of a slain enemy chief in the hope of acquiring his wisdom and bravery. Such brain transfer experiments have been performed by psychologists — although they used worms or rats, rather than humans, both as donors and recipients. Surprisingly, the early results were positive (for example, McConnell,

1962); after ingesting brain cells from a donor animal, the receiving animal appeared to exhibit responses immediately that had been learned by the donor. However, many failures to repeat this finding followed (Byrne et al., 1966), and the early studies were discredited on methodological grounds (Bennett, 1977). A good deal of wasted effort might have been saved had the early investigators paid more attention to the results of a classic series of experiments in memory research by Karl Lashley (1929, 1950).

Lashley's experiments showed that any particular memory is stored not in a single place in the brain but by a large collection of individual neurons. Rats were taught to find their way through a maze; subsequently, various parts and amounts of their cortex were removed. To his surprise, Lashley found that when the rats were tested as to their ability to negotiate the maze after their operations, the number of errors they made was unrelated to *which* cortical areas were removed but was related to *how much* cortex was missing. The more cortex the rats lost, the more errors they made on the maze. Similarly, the rats were able to learn new, simple tasks as long as a small amount of cortex was left in the areas required to process the necessary information. It appeared to Lashley that all areas of cortex were important for storing and retrieving the memories responsible for this type of learning.

From the results of these and many similar experiments conducted since Lashley's work, psychologists have tried to understand how neural processes can mediate memory storage and learning. The following list (adapted from Leiman & Christian, 1973) summarizes several processes various scientists have proposed as the mechanism responsible for the storage of information in our brains when we remember and learn:

1. changes in the structure or chemistry of synapses when they are activated repeatedly during the practice of a task
2. growth of new nerve endings and new synaptic connections
3. destruction of existing *inappropriate* nerve endings
4. residual excitation in nerve cells after repeated activation
5. prolonged continuation of electrical activity in networks of nerve cells
6. production of new molecules (proteins, DNA, RNA) within nerve cells

We emphasize that the foregoing processes are not mutually exclusive; it is quite possible that each process contributes at some level to the formation of a memory and to the establishment of a learned response. It also is conceivable that different processes occur in different parts of the brain or for different kinds of memory and learning.

Electrophysiological Studies of Learning and Memory

Much attention has been devoted to the study of how the electrochemical transmission of information between neurons is affected by learning. One approach is the direct observation and manipulation of neurons and their synapses in such relatively simple organisms as snails and cockroaches. Changes in the responses of individual cells are measured over time as the animal learns a simple behavior. The neurons in such animals are large enough to be seen under the microscope and identified individually. Eric Kandel and his colleagues performed a series of experiments on the sea snail, aplysia, to determine the "wiring diagram" for a simple type of learning called *habituation* (Kandel, 1976; Klein & Kandel, 1980). As the snail habituated by ceasing to respond to the repeated touching of its feeding tube, Kandel recorded the biochemical and biophysical changes that occurred in the neurons in-

volved in this behavior (see Figure 3-18). He found relatively long-lasting changes in the properties of the cell membranes and in the chemical balance at the synapses that were active during habituation.

It is more difficult to study the neural basis of learning in vertebrate animals than in invertebrates due to the greater complexity of the vertebrate nervous system. However, impressive advances have been made in identifying some of the vertebrate brain structures and processes involved in simple learned behaviors. If a puff of air is directed toward your eyes, you will blink. If that puff is paired repeatedly with the sound of a tone, you will learn to blink when the tone is presented alone; this is an example of **classical conditioning** (see Chapter 5). Although it is virtually impossible to study the neural basis of the conditioned eye-blink response in humans, such research has been conducted on rabbits and cats (see Farley & Alkon, 1985, for a review). It was found that conditioning of the eye-blink response is mediated by neurons in the central core of the brain, particularly the pons (Desmond & Moore, 1982) and the cerebellum (Glickstein, Hardiman, & Yeo, 1983). Areas of the limbic system may also be involved. For example, in studies that employed a time delay between the tone and the air puff, the hippocampus was shown to play a critical role in conditioning (Weisz, Soloman, & Thompson, 1980).

Research on the role of the hippocampus in learning and memory led to the discovery of a phenomenon called **long-term potentiation.** Bliss and Lomo (1973) found that a short burst of a high-frequency electrical stimulation of neurons entering the hippocampus of a rabbit's brain could increase neural sensitivity for up to a week or more. Subsequent studies showed that the site of these changes was the synapse. Considerable research in the last decade has been devoted to uncovering the specific mechanisms that produce long-term potentiation (see Lynch et al., 1984). Lynch has a theory which must still be regarded as speculative, suggesting that electrical stimulation triggers the following events: high-frequency neuronal activity increases calcium levels in the dendrites of the cells; increased calcium concentration activates a chemical, **calpain,** in the cells; calpain attacks the cell mem-

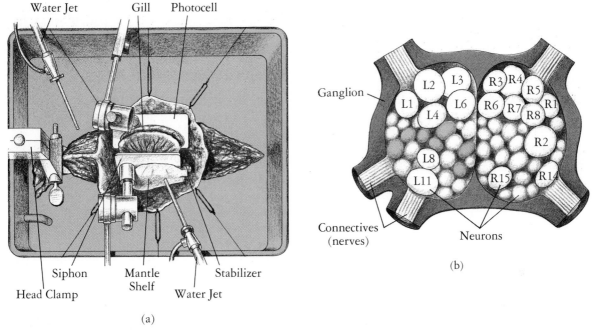

FIGURE 3-18
Kandel's Study of Habituation in *Aplysia* (a) Gill-withdrawal reflex was studied by clamping the animal in a small aquarium and recording the extent of gill contraction with a photocell. When the siphon or shelf was stimulated by a jet of water, the gill contracted, exposing the photocell to light from above. After many such stimulations, the reflex habituates — that is, the response declines.
(b) When the ganglion controlling gill contraction was exposed surgically, electrodes could be inserted into various neurons. The changes in synaptic activity that accompanied habituation of the response could then be determined. Individual neurons were labeled ant those involved in the habituation response were identified (see color coding). *Source:* Adapted from Kandel, E. R. (1970). Nerve cells and behavior. *Scientific American, 41,* pp. 57–70.

brane, creating new synaptic connections and uncovering new receptor sites. Although the calcium is pumped out of the cell quickly, the structural changes created represent a continuing "memory" of the very brief event that triggered the sequence.

Biochemical Studies of Learning and Memory

Although we do not understand fully the mechanisms responsible for registering and storing new information in the brain, scientists are reasonably confident that chemical changes within and between brain cells are involved. Moreover, they believe the synthesis of proteins (complex combinations of amino acids) plays some role in the process, because proteins are essential for neural transmission. Research has shown that learning is accompanied by changes in the protein content of the brain and in the amounts and structures of the nucleic acids DNA and RNA, two substances that direct the synthesis of new proteins (Entingh et al., 1975).

The work of Holger Hydén and his colleagues (see Hyden & Lange, 1972) in Sweden has shown that unique protein molecules are formed at particular brain sites when an animal is learning a new response. Their research also has shown that specific changes in DNA and RNA, in both neurons and glial cells, accompany learning. Although scientists agree these biochemical changes occur during the learning process, it is still unclear whether or not they are involved in the *storage* of information. It is possible the observed changes are related to communication links between neurons. According to this view, new input is stored by means of fairly permanent changes in the strength or patterns of synaptic transmission in large networks of nerve cells and new proteins are formed to produce changes in synaptic activation (rather than being, in themselves, the stored information).

Research has demonstrated that certain drugs can affect memory. For example, experiments on humans and animals have shown that **vasopressin** — a hormone produced by the hypothalamus to regulate the body's retention of water — can improve learning and retention in a wide variety of tasks (Alliot & Alexinsky, 1982; Bohus et al., 1982). Another hormone, **oxytocin,** also produced by the hypothalamus, has the opposite effect; it impairs performance on tasks that require memory (Bohus et al., 1982). An imbalance in the levels of these hormones has been found in the spinal fluid of depressed patients.

Inhalation of vasopressin improved the memory of both depressed patients and a control group of normal subjects. The injection of several other natural hormones has also been demonstrated to influence memory and learning (McGaugh, 1983). The reason for these effects is presently a matter of speculation. It is possible that such improvements in performance are not caused by direct action of the drug in the brain but are the result of drug-induced increases in alertness. Moreover, note that memory in these studies is tested in the laboratory by using standardized tasks. A leading researcher in this field has cautioned that "In no case has it been possible to demonstrate that an improvement in a test score presages improvement in the patient's real-life memory functions" (Wurtman, 1982, p. 57).

Localization of Memory

When recently asked to comment on our current knowledge regarding localization of memory, leading neuroscientist Mortimer Mishkin said: "Memory itself must be conceived of as involving rather widespread neuronal connections laid down by experiences involving widely separated structures, all of which are important in memory formation" (Restak, 1984). Although we have learned a lot about the neural basis of memory since Lashley's pioneering study, his conclusion that memory is *not* localized remains largely intact.

Nevertheless, certain structures, particularly the hippocampus, are critically involved in the establishment and maintenance of memories. Mishkin's own work with monkeys also implicates the amygdala, but for a different type of memory. The hippocampus is important for spatial memory; the amygdala appears to be involved more with memories that have a strong emotional component (Mishkin, 1978). It also is apparent that different neural mechanisms play critical roles at different stages of memory formation (Frieder & Allweis, 1982; Rosenzweig & Bennett, 1984).

CONSCIOUSNESS

In this final section, we examine what surely is the most obvious but least understood capacity of the brain — consciousness. Consciousness could be viewed as the product of evolutionary processes. This line of speculation dates back to the work of William James who, in the early 1900s, urged us to consider consciousness as a "selecting agency" that allows us to cope with situations that require us to make choices. In an elaboration of this concept, George Mandler (1975) has suggested that **consciousness** serves at least five adaptive functions:

1. Consciousness enables us to choose a course of action in terms of what we consider to be the most likely or desirable outcome.

2. It allows us to combine many different possibilities and considerations to formulate long-term plans.

3. Consciousness uses information retrieved from memory to evaluate and guide our plans and the actions based on them.

4. It plays a role in organizing new information to facilitate learning and recall, communication with others, and problem-solving.

5. Consciousness acts to maintain goal-directed behavior in the face of unexpected obstacles.

Mandler describes this last purpose of consciousness as a kind of "troubleshooting" function and cites the example of being at the wheel of your car when the brakes suddenly fail. Prior to that point, your consciousness may have been directed to a quite different activity such as planning your day's work or listening to the car radio. The routine task of driving does not require consciousness control until the brake failure demands your attention. Your consciousness is then directed to the problem, and you take appropriate action.

Each of Mandler's five functions shows that consciousness allows us to respond flexibly and deliberately to changes in our environment, rather than in a stereotypic and perhaps dangerously rigid manner. At the same time, consciousness permits us to attend selectively to features of the situation that have proved most relevant to our goals in the past and, at the same time, to monitor the environment for new and useful information. The adaptive function of consciousness would appear to provide us with a general ability to function adaptively.

States of Consciousness

Thus far we have considered consciousness as a singular state, yet it clearly is not an all-or-nothing condition. There seem to be varying degrees of consciousness, or alertness. At times, the way in which we perceive and interact with our environment may be altered so radically that we appear to be in a separate state of consciousness. In the following sections, we briefly consider three of these states: *meditation, hypnosis,* and *sleep.* The distinctiveness of each state usually is considered in terms of *conscious experience* — the thoughts and feelings we are or are not having. Here, however, we focus on the contrast between brain activity during normal consciousness and brain activities observed during these other states of consciousness. In recognition of the difference in time spent by the average person in each of these states, a more extensive consideration is given to sleep.

Normal Consciousness We use the term **normal consciousness** here to refer to the state of mind each of us typically occupies between waking in the morning and falling asleep at night. The method of recording the brain's electrical activity (the electroencephalogram, or EEG) has been used to correlate the activities of brain and mind — to provide what Hillyard and Kutas (1983) call a "second window into the information-processing activities of the human brain" (the first window being behavioral measurement).

Your brain's electrical activity would characteristically be recorded as a low-amplitude, high-frequency pattern called **beta rhythm** as you went about your daily business of perceiving environmental stimuli, recalling old memories and recording new ones, solving problems, and so on. These active periods would undoubtedly be interspersed with more relaxing periods, during which your EEG rhythm would tend to be of higher amplitude and lower frequency. This change in EEG rhythm is particularly noticeable when you shut your eyes and try to avoid attending to visual images from memory, thus eliminating a sizable proportion of the brain's visual activity. On these occasions, your EEG is likely to show an **alpha rhythm** (see Figure 3-19 for examples of EEG records). Although it has been suggested that alpha waves are beneficial to mental health, this claim generally has been overstated (Beyerstein, 1985). The relaxation procedures often used in an attempt to produce alpha waves may be of some benefit, but it is misleading to conclude the alpha rhythm itself has some health-promoting property.

Meditation **Meditation** typically involves the progressive relaxation of both mind and body. Muscular activity usually is minimized and the mind is cleared of extraneous thoughts, often by focusing on a particular object or repeating a word or phrase over and over again. EEGs taken during meditation show the effect of such procedures is generally to slow the frequency of the brain's activity (Woolfolk, 1975). It requires little practice to reach the alpha-rhythm stage; sometimes, but not always, the meditator's EEG shows the even slower **theta rhythm** (Hebert & Lehmann, 1977).

As we shall see later, this description of brain activity during meditation also characterizes the brain activity of a person falling asleep. This has led several investigators to suggest that meditation is basically an intermediate state between waking and sleeping (Elson et al., 1977). Notwithstanding the unique cognitive and exper-

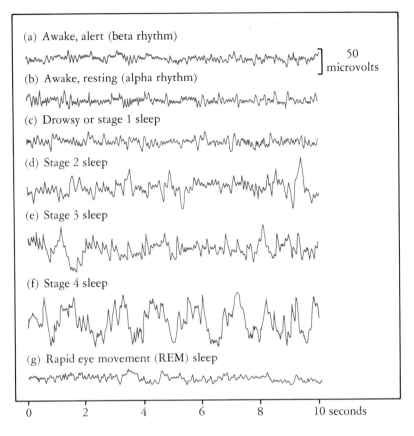

FIGURE 3-19

Electroencephalography (EEG) Before and During Sleep   In passing from alertness to Stage 4 sleep, the amplitude of the EEG increases and its frequency decreases.   This trend is reversed in REM sleep, where the EEG pattern is similar to that in an awake, alert state.   *Source:* Adapted from Mussen, P., & Rosenzweig, M. (1979).   *Psychology: An introduction* (3rd ed., p. 67).   Lexington, MA: D. C. Heath.

iential characteristics of meditation, there is little consistent evidence from EEG studies to support the view that meditation is an altered state of consciousness (Schuman, 1980).

Hypnosis   **Hypnosis** has a long history in psychology, first having been used by Sigmund Freud in his practice of psychoanalysis.   Although hypnosis is also often considered to be an altered state of consciousness (Hilgard et al., 1978), the issue remains a matter of debate (Kihlstrom, 1985). Certainly, *amnesia* (memory failure) and *analgesia* (indifference to pain) can be demonstrated to result from hypnotic suggestion, but not in all subjects.   More dramatic hypnotic effects, including those reported by Ernest Hilgard and others (1978) and discussed in Box 3-4, are found in fewer than half the subjects deemed to be highly susceptible to hypnosis (who are, in them-

selves, a minority).   Furthermore, the brain's activity during hypnosis does not differ noticeably from its activity in the normal conscious state. Nevertheless, the phenomenon of hypnosis presents an interesting challenge to consciousness theorists and is also useful as a tool in minimizing pain.

Sleep

Studies of the electrical activity in the brains of sleeping subjects have revealed that this state involves several distinct types of brain activity and experience.   Figure 3-19 shows the seven characteristic patterns of brain activity recorded by the EEG during sleep.

As we fall asleep, the EEG pattern slows in frequency and increases in amplitude.   During Stages 1–4, sometimes called **slow-wave sleep,** the brain's activity is said to reflect **neural synchrony**—a high degree of similarity in the pattern of activity in a large number of neurons. The beta activity of normal consciousness, by contrast, is referred to as **neural desynchrony.**

About 90 minutes after we fall asleep, the synchronized pattern of brain activity begins to break up. When we reach Stage 1, the EEG suddenly shows large bursts of beta rhythm, and it appears as though we have awakened. In fact, we are harder to awaken at this time than at any other period of sleep. Stage 1 sleep is characterized by irregular breathing, many small muscle jerks, and **rapid eye movements (REMs).** Sleepers roused at this time are likely to report they have been dreaming.

At the end of this short period of activity, called **REM sleep,** the cycle repeats itself, showing a progressive change in synchronous activity (see Figure 3-20). During a typical night, an adult will complete this cycle four or fives times, exhibiting a decreasing amount of slow-wave sleep and an increasing amount of REM sleep. The first REM period may last only 5 – 10 minutes; the last REM period may be as long as 40 minutes and often ends when the sleeper awakens.

Sleepers who are awakened during slow-wave sleep at other times during the night occasionally report a dreamlike experience but more

often say they were "just thinking," often about ordinary daytime concerns. These reports usually differ sufficiently from the highly visual, emotionally involving episodes of REM sleep to enable researchers to discriminate between reports from these two periods of sleep with 90% accuracy (Cartwright, 1978). Slow-wave sleep is also the period during which sleepwalking, sleeptalking, and *night terrors* occur. Although you might expect sleeptalking and sleepwalking to occur during dreaming, this is not the case. During REM periods, the brain actively inhibits the firing of the neurons that control muscle tone, thereby effectively blocking organized muscular activity by the sleeper during the dreaming stage of sleep.

Night terrors are said to occur when sleepers (usually children) awaken suddenly in a state of great fear. The mechanism that normally moves brain activity out of the deep-sleep stage seems to break down. The result is a person who is part asleep and part awake. The phenomenon of night terrors is especially puzzling because, although children often cry out and wake up trembling, with a rapid pulse, they have no recollection of what woke them. Therefore, these episodes often are more traumatic for the parents than for the children, who usually outgrow the problem. Sleepers who experience night terrors

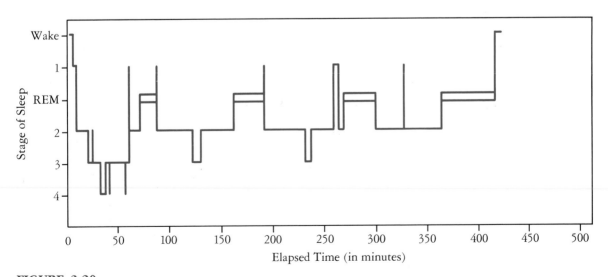

FIGURE 3-20

A Typical Night's Sleep Each night we pass through a complicated and irregular pattern of shifts from one stage of sleep to another. The three patterns exhibited by one subject during three nights of sleep are shown here. *Source:* Adapted from Lahey, B. (1983). *Psychology: An Introduction* (p. 143). Iowa: Wm. C. Brown.

Box 3-4
The Hypnotic State of Consciousness

For many people, hypnosis is the state into which stage illusionists place audience volunteers to make them behave in strange ways. Certainly *stage hypnosis* does occur, and hypnotized volunteers can be induced to act in ways that appear highly improbable and perhaps even impossible as normal behaviors. However, stage hypnosis bears only a passing relationship to the phenomenon employed by clinical psychologists to control pain *(hypnotic analgesia)* and to treat phobias *(hypnotherapy)* and by experimental psychologists to study the processes of memory and perception.

Various procedures are used to induce the hypnotic state. Some have subjects fixate on an object, such as the swinging watch on a chain that is so much a part of the stereotype of hypnotic induction. This prop is not necessary, however; the soft, slow voice of the hypnotist encouraging subjects to relax is all that is necessary. In expert hands, this procedure may lead subjects to enter a hypnotic state, where they typically report a pleasant feeling of relaxation, are less inclined to initiate action, and usually are receptive to suggestions made by the hypnotist. Differences from the normal state are generally matters of degree; contrary to popular belief, hypnotized subjects cannot be completely controlled by the hypnotist. For example, subjects cannot be made to injure themselves or others and can voluntarily start or stop an action. Nevertheless, there is considerable evidence that some hypnotized subjects are in a state of consciousness quite different from normal. Much of this evidence comes from the pioneering work on hypnosis by Ernest and Josephine Hilgard (see Hilgard, 1977, 1986).

One of Ernest Hilgard's contributions is the concept of the *hidden observer* (Hilgard, 1977, chapter 9). His report on the discovery of the hidden observer makes fascinating reading that we can only summarize here. A student (who happened to be blind) was participating in a classroom demonstration of hypnotically induced deafness. After hypnosis was induced, it was suggested to the student that he would be completely deaf to all sounds. When loud noises were made close to the subject's head, no reaction occurred; neither did the subject respond to any questions asked of him. Was the student *really* deaf or was he simply *playing* the game? The instructor probed this question by asking the hypnotically deaf student to raise a finger "if there is some part of you that

---

usually do not recall anything the next morning. Night terrors are one of several related disturbances of the brain's arousal system that result in sleep disorders (Broughton, 1982).

From the variety of experiences and patterns of brain activity that occur during sleep, we can see it is a complex and generally active state of the organism; sleep is not merely the absence of waking. In particular, humans clearly demonstrate a cyclical pattern during sleep in which the brain's activity varies from the fast rhythms of REM sleep to the slower rhythms of slow-wave sleep. We turn now to a consideration of the evolution of sleep, placing particular focus on the REM – slow-wave sleep cycle.

The Evolution of Sleep As far as we know, fish, amphibians, and reptiles do not engage in either REM or slow-wave sleep; instead, these organisms alternate between periods of deep rest and activ-

is hearing my voice and processing the information" (p. 186). The student's finger rose! The student immediately requested that his hearing be restored, saying "I felt my finger rise in a way that was not a spontaneous twitch, so you must have done something to make it rise, and I want to know what you did" (p. 186). When brought out of the hypnotic state, the student said he remembered the suggestion of hypnotic deafness being made, after which it was quiet for a while. He then remembered feeling his finger rise and asking to have his hearing restored.

At this point in the demonstration, the student was hypnotized again. The instructor then asked to speak to that part of the subject's mind that "could hear and knew what was going on when you were hypnotically deaf" (p. 187). Responses to the instructor's questions now showed this part of the hypnotized student's mind — the hidden observer — was indeed fully aware of the loud noises that had previously caused no response and of the questions from the audience. Several other demonstrations of a hidden observer in hypnotized subjects are reported in the latest edition of Hilgard's book *Divided Consciousness* (1986). In one study, subjects were given a hypnotic suggestion that they would feel no pain when they immersed one hand in a bucket of ice water. Although after 30 seconds in such a condition people normally find the discomfort intolerable, the hypnotized subjects said they felt very little pain (which was consistent with their outward appearance of calm).

It has been known for many years that in some persons hypnotic suggestion is an effective method of pain-reduction. The novel aspect of Hilgard's study was his demonstration that although hypnotized subjects were not aware of pain, the stressful nature of their experience was being registered by the hidden observer in their minds. Hil-gard showed this by employing hypnotic suggestion to remove their free hand from awareness so it could write what they were feeling. This *automatic writing,* as it is called, revealed the hidden observer did indeed register the ice-water experience as extremely painful.

Hilgard does not think of the hidden observer as a "secondary personality . . . working in the shadows of the conscious person" (1977, p. 188). That is, the hidden observer should not be regarded as equivalent to the Freudian concept of the unconscious mind. The evidence from hypnosis, Hilgard believes, "clearly favors the idea of a vertical division (split consciousness) rather than a horizontal division, in which the material would come from more primitive depths" (p. 193–94). There is still much to learn about hypnosis, but such investigations as those of the Hilgards are beginning to illuminate this remarkable state.

ity. Some researchers have suggested the REM–slow-wave sleep cycle is a development of this primitive rest–activity cycle (Kleitman, 1969) and, as evidence, point to other physiological and psychological cycles containing a 90–110 minute period. For example, daydreaming seems to occur approximately every 100 minutes during waking hours (Lavie & Kripke, 1981). If this is correct, then the REM–slow-wave cycle may be of very ancient origin indeed.

Unlike species that exhibit waking consciousness, species that do not sleep exhibit no behavioral flexibility in adapting to the environment. Rather, their behavior is highly stereotypic; the responses of these organisms to such events in their habitats as the appearance of a predator or a potential mate take the same form on every occasion. Thus, sleep may serve some function associated with the evolution of consciousness. When normal subjects are deprived of REM sleep by awaking them each time their EEG indicates they have begun this type of activity, their waking behavior is characterized by an increased frequency of difficulty in concentrating, episodes of disorientation, irritability, and, in a few cases, occasional hallucinations. These changes are not found in control subjects who are awakened during non-REM sleep. Clearly, all of these effects would tend to interfere with the adaptive functions of consciousness suggested by Mandler.

With the exception of the spiny anteater, every mammal studied to date has shown the human pattern of alternating cycles of REM and slow-wave activity during sleep. However, the amount of sleep per day, the duration of the cycle,

Box 3-5
THE PURPOSE OF SLEEP

One prominent sleep researcher (Morruzzi, 1974) has argued that the special restorative needs of some brain neurons may be met through sleep. However, the wide variety of sleep patterns exhibited among different species seems to contradict this opinion; for example, horses sleep only 2 hours per day, whereas cats sleep as much as 18 hours.

Another view emphasizes the importance of sleep as a way of conserving the organism's energy by reducing its metabolic requirements. There is support for this view in the evidence that animals with a high-waking metabolic rate (especially small animals) sleep more hours per day than animals with a lower-working metabolic rate. The intense metabolic expenditure associated with REM sleep seems to run counter to this suggestion. However, as we have already noted, slow-wave sleep seems to have evolved earlier than REM sleep, so this view may still have some merit.

A third suggestion, which includes a possible explanation for the later evolution of REM activity, is that the immobility enforced through sleep lessens the chance of encountering potential predators or other accidents that might befall a species not adapted for night mobility. From this perspective, REM sleep might partially serve to arouse an animal so it can assess possible dangers. Although there is little evidence to support this view, we know that small animals, which are frequently preyed upon, do have relatively short sleep cycles.

Studies of the development of the sleep cycle in the individual suggest REM activity is most important in infancy. Adults of almost every mammalian species sleep less than infants and spend less of their sleep in REM activity. The first figure shows that human infants spend half their first two weeks of sleep in REM activity and that most of the decline in time spent asleep represents a reduction in REM sleep. Unlike normal adults, human infants change from REM sleep to slow-wave sleep frequently and can move directly from an awake state to REM sleep. Although a distinct 24-hour rhythm of sleeping and waking is apparent by 16 weeks of age, most children do not establish a single sleep period for several years, and many people continue to take an occasional afternoon nap for the rest of their lives.

It has been suggested that the preponderance of REM sleep during the early part of life reflects stimulation essential to the maturation of the nervous system and that the decline in REM activity reflects a decrease in the rate of development of the brain's information-processing capabilities. An interesting suggestion is that

and the amount of time spent in REM activity varies from species to species. The anteater is a member of an early branch of mammals, almost totally extinct today, that still retains some reptilian features. Although it sleeps up to twelve hours a day, its brain shows no signs of REM activity; only slow-wave activity appears in the anteater's EEG. On the other hand, the opossum, a very early member of our surviving mammalian group, does follow the REM–slow-wave sleep cycle. Comparison of these two ancient mammals suggests that slow-wave sleep evolved some 180 million years ago and that REM sleep first appeared about 50 million years later (Allison & Van Twyver, 1970). The purpose of sleep is considered in Box 3-5.

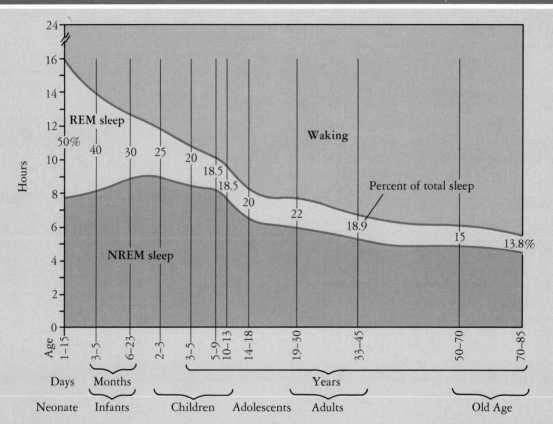

Stages of Sleep during Development The major changes with age in sleep patterns of humans are an early reduction from 50% to about 15% in the proportion of REM sleep and a continuing decrease in the total time spent sleeping. *Source:* Adapted from Roffwarg, H. P., Muzio, J. N., & Dement, W. C. (1966). Ontogenetic development of human sleep-dream cycle. *Science, 152,* 604–19.

because much important learning occurs during infancy, REM sleep may be a contributing factor in the formation of long-term memories. In fact, it has been shown repeatedly that depriving animals of REM sleep results in impaired learning (McGrath & Cohen 1978). Other experiments have shown that REM sleep increases in animals when they are given training on a new task, and if learning is extended over several days, the increase in REM sleep is greatest during the steepest part of the learning curve (Bloch, 1976).

Neural Control of Sleeping and Waking

Study of the neural mechanisms that control sleeping and waking is an active area of research. The basic questions being addressed include: How and why does sleep start? What produces the daily sleep–arousal cycle and the timing of the REM–slow-wave cycle? How and why does sleep end?

We know that several areas of the brain stem are critically involved in controlling sleeping and arousal. Perhaps most important for wakefulness is the diffuse network of neurons in the brain stem that comprise the reticular formation. Lesions in the reticular formation have been shown to produce persistent sleep in laboratory animals; electrical stimulation of this area results in the rapid arousal of sleeping animals. A part of the reticular formation called the **ascending reticular activating system** stimulates cortical activity by sending impulses to the cortex through the thalamus. At the same time, descending pathways from the cortex to the reticular system allow cognitive control over the arousal system. This picture is complicated, however, by the discovery that other areas of the brain must be intact for wakefulness to occur. For example, stimulation of portions of the thalamus can induce sleep, and ablation of other parts of this structure has been found to prevent waking.

Current thinking on the cyclical characteristics of sleep focuses on two regions in and near the pons. The destruction of one area has been shown to prevent slow-wave sleep. Neurons in this area produce the brain's supply of **serotonin,** a synaptic neurotransmitter that has been shown to be important in generating slow-wave sleep. Injections of a substance that reduces the level of serotonin can produce insomnia in cats; if the same animals are then given a drug that stimulates the production of serotonin, slow-wave sleep returns. The second area produces the neurotransmitter **norepinephrine.** The destruction of this area or the injection of substances that interfere with norepinephrine production eliminates REM activity but does not affect slow-wave sleep.

One sleep researcher has hypothesized that the mechanisms in these two areas have an antagonistic relationship (Jouvet, 1975, 1983). One structure initiates slow-wave sleep. Thereafter, interactions between the two mechanisms generate the REM–slow-wave sleep cycle. Finally, waking occurs when one mechanism overcomes the action of the other. Clearly, the concept of sleep as a passive phenomenon has been abandoned by modern researchers, who consider both sleeping and waking to be phases of complex interaction among a variety of brain structures.

SUMMARY

1. The brain is our most important organ because it is the source of our perceptions, thoughts, feelings, and actions; it provides our identity. Irreversible breakdown of communication in the brain is the principal criterion of death.

2. Most brain researchers are monists and determinists; they believe the same laws that determine all physical events apply to both brain and mind and that all mental and physical acts are caused by potentially identifiable events in accordance with such laws.

3. Evidence regarding the relationship between brain and behavior comes from a variety of sources:
   a. Damage to specific brain structures in people and animals impairs mental and motor activities in a predictable way.
   b. Drugs that alter mental experience or behavior cause chemical changes within and between brain cells.
   c. Electrical and chemical stimulation of the nervous system elicits changes in conscious experience and/or behavior.
   d. Patterns of electrical activity in the brain

correlate with psychological processes in perception, learning, memory and other mental functions.

   e. The anatomy and ongoing activity of the human brain can be imaged in the intact, alert patient.

   f. Experiencing environmental events leads to structural and functional changes in the brain.

4. In the process of evolution, the addition of new brain structures to existing ones gives more advanced species greater behavioral flexibility. Evolutionarily newer structures in the brain partially control the activities of older structures that the human brain has in common with the brains of lower species.

5. The human brain is conventionally divided into three structural groupings. The central core consists of the medulla, pons, cerebellum, reticular formation, hypothalamus, and thalamus. Surrounding the central core are the interconnected structures of the limbic system (including the amygdala, hippocampus, and septal nuclei) and the basal ganglia. The outer covering of the brain is the cerebral cortex.

6. The cerebral cortex, which is shaped into the frontal, parietal, temporal, and occipital lobes, contains specialized areas to process sensory input (the sensory cortex), to organize and control muscular activity (the motor cortex), and to support such higher mental processes as language reception and production (the association cortex).

7. The brain's two, almost symmetrical, halves (cerebral hemispheres) are joined by a thick band of nerve fibers called the corpus callosum. The testing of split–brain patients, whose corpus callosa have been severed surgically, has revealed that the left and right hemispheres of the brain have somewhat different specializations.

8. Nerve cells, or neurons, communicate electrochemically. The firing of a neuron causes the release of chemical substances (neurotransmitters) that cross the synaptic gap to an adjacent neuron, where they excite or inhibit that cell's electrical activity. Glial cells carry nutrients to and waste from neurons, clean up the debris when neurons die, and form the myelin sheath that insulates neurons.

9. Malnutrition can impede the normal growth of the brain in a manner that is difficult to reverse. Impoverished environmental stimulation can impair the development of brain structures; enriched environmental stimulation may promote this development.

10. The prospects for recovery from brain damage are greater when the damage occurs earlier in development. The brain's methods of compensating for damaged tissue include growth of new cell endings and increased sensitivity of undamaged cells.

11. New chemical substances are formed in the brain when we establish memories in the learning of new knowledge and skills. Rather than being ''memory molecules,'' these substances probably are constituents of cellular processes that allow new patterns of communication to develop in the brain.

12. Although most brain structures seem to be involved in learning and memory in some way, the hippocampus and the amygdala in the limbic system are of particular importance in transferring memory from short-term to long-term storage.

13. Consciousness seems to have evolved to provide us with a general ability to function adaptively — to take control of our actions when our ''automatic pilot'' runs into unexpected difficulties.

14. The brain's electrical activity during normal waking consciousness is recorded on an electroencephalogram (EEG) as a low-amplitude, high-frequency pattern called beta rhythm. Relaxation, particularly when it reduces visual perception and imagery, typically is accompanied by a slower EEG pattern, the alpha rhythm. The even slower theta rhythm may occur during some stages of sleep.

15. Meditation and hypnosis are states in which radically different conscious experiences

may occur but in which the EEG is similar to that observed during the transition between waking and sleeping.

16. The EEG during sleep cycles between a slow-wave stage and a rapid eye movement (REM) stage characterized by beta-rhythm activity. Dreaming occurs principally during REM sleep. Compared with people deprived of slow-wave sleep, people deprived of REM sleep show impaired functioning. The thalamus and areas in the pons appear to be involved in determining the onset, depth, and termination of sleep; the reticular system plays an important role in regulating our level of arousal.

KEY TERMS

Mind – Body Problem
Monist
Dualist
Determinism
Broca's Area
Ablation
Psychopharmacology
Psychoactive Drug
Brain Stimulant
Brain Depressant
Hallucinogen/Psychedelic
Electroencephalograph
Electroencephalogram (EEG)
Magnetoencephalogram (MEG)
Computerized Axial Tomography (CAT)
Positron Emission Tomography (PET)
Magnetic Resonance Imaging (MRI)/Nuclear Magnetic Resonance (NMR)
Nervous System
Neural Processing
Head Ganglion
Ganglia
Central Nervous System
Peripheral Nervous System
Somatic System
Autonomic System
Central Core
Limbic System

Cerebral Cortex
Medulla
Pons
Cerebellum
Motor System
Reticular Formation
Hypothalamus
Pituitary Gland
Thalamus
Amygdala
Hippocampus
Septal Nuclei
Basal Ganglia
Lobes (frontal, parietal, temporal, and occipital)
Sensory Cortex
Motor Cortex
Association Cortex
Corpus Callosum
Split-brain Patient
Cerebral Hemispheres
Glial Cell
Myelin Sheath
Action Potential
Presynaptic Neuron
Postsynaptic Neuron
Blood – Brain Barrier
Neuron
Cell Body
Nucleus
Dendrite
Axon

Synapse
Transmitter Substance
Neurotransmitter
Synaptic Gap
Nerve
Macroneuron
Microneuron
Cataract
Classical Conditioning
Long-term Potentiation
Calpain
Vasopressin
Oxytocin
Consciousness
Normal Consciousness
Beta Rhythm
Alpha Rhythm
Meditation
Theta Rhythm
Hypnosis
Slow-wave Sleep
Neural Synchrony
Neural Desynchrony
Rapid Eye Movement (REM)
REM Sleep
Night Terrors
Ascending Reticular Activating System
Serotonin
Norepinephrine

RECOMMENDED READINGS

Carlson, N. R. (1986). *Physiology of behavior* (3rd ed.). Boston, MA: Allyn and Bacon. Widely recognized as the standard reference work in this area.

Cohen, D. B. (1979). *Sleep and dreaming*. New York: Pergamon. A study of the origins, nature, and functions of sleep.

Hilgard, E. R. (1986). *Divided consciousness* (2nd ed.). New York: Wiley and Sons. A personal and persuasive view of the hypnotic state by one of the field's pioneer researchers.

Julien, R. (1981). *A primer of drug action*. New York: W. H. Freeman. Still a useful guide to the physical and psychological effects of most drugs likely to be encountered.

Kolb, B., & Wishaw, I. Q. (1986). *Fundamentals of human neuropsychology* (2nd ed.). New York: W. H. Freeman. A well-written and authoritative survey of contemporary neuropsychology.

Restak, R. M. (1984). *The brain*. New York: Bantam. A lively and well-informed popular treatment of the topic that provided the script for the critically acclaimed public television series of the same name.

Segalowitz, S. J. (1983). *Two sides of the brain*. Englewood Cliffs, NJ: Prentice-Hall. Clinical and experimental evidence are considered in this exploration of lateralization in the human brain.

Wallace, B., & Fisher, L. J. (1983). *Consciousness and behavior*. Boston, MA: Allyn and Bacon. A brief but broad survey of physiological, pharmacological, and psychological aspects of consciousness.

4

SENSATION AND PERCEPTION

O ne of the founders of the early Gestalt school of psychology, Kurt Koffka (1935), posed the question "Why do things appear as they do?" The obvious answer is "Because things are what they are." But, argued Koffka, this answer is wrong. Appearances do not always mirror reality, as the following examples show.

Have you observed that the moon appears to be much dimmer during the day than it does at night? Or have you noticed that the moon often appears to be much larger when it is on the horizon than when it is overhead? Even if you are not an avid moonwatcher, you have probably seen the moon appear to move across a gap in the clouds. What these three observations have in common (apart from the fact that they all concern the moon) is that they are all *illusions*. The facts of the matter are that the moon receives and reflects the same amount of sunlight by day as by night; the moon is always the same size; and the moon's passage across the sky is too slow for you to see it as moving. The existence of such illusions demonstrates the difference between *appearance* and *reality* — between the way things seem to be and the way things are. Most scientists are interested only in the way things are. A unique characteristic of psychologists who study sensation, perception, and awareness is that they are primarily interested in the way things appear.

The central task facing these psychologists is to trace the chain of events that links the **physical world** (the world of reality) and the **perceptual world** (the world of appearance). As we will see, the perceptual world is a representation, but not a copy, of the physical world. Investigators in this area have broken down Koffka's deceptively simple query into the following questions, each of which relates to one of the links in the chain that connects the physical and perceptual worlds:

1. How is information about the physical world transmitted to an observer?
2. How is this information detected by an observer and relayed to the brain?
3. How are these messages integrated into the typically clear and meaningful experience that we call the perceptual world?

Question 1 concerns the physical world. It is important to have an appreciation of the physical world — of its nature and its sources of information — before tackling question 2, which deals with the *sensory systems*. Question 2, in turn, supplies the necessary basis for considering question 3, which deals with the process of *perception*.

THE NATURE OF THE PHYSICAL WORLD

W hen we distinguished the physical world from the perceptual world, it probably never occurred to you to question the reality of the physical world. Everyone accepts that there is a world out there, but how can we be sure? To take a concrete example, how do you know that this book exists? You may answer that you can feel it and touch it, but the sight and feel of this book are aspects of your *perceptual* world. Your answer is a report of the events that are occurring in your mind. The challenge is to demonstrate the existence of the physical world without appealing to your perceptual world.

Don't worry if the problem seems insoluble; it has defied the best efforts of philosophers for centuries. Most psychologists simply *assume* the existence of a world consisting of objects, surfaces, and events. *Objects* are characterized by such qualities as shape, size, location, color, sound, feel, smell, and taste. The backdrop for these objects is usually a *surface,* such as the top of a table, a wall, the ground, or the sky. When the qualities of an object change, an *event* occurs: a fabric fades, a boy cries, a car moves.

Information about objects, surfaces, and events is carried to an observer by various messengers, the most important of which are *light* and *sound waves*. In reading the following discussion of these two forms of energy, keep in mind that we are describing the physical stimulus, rather than the effect that the stimulus has on an observer.

Light

What is the nature of **light** — the messenger that tells us about the color, size, shape, location, and texture of objects and surfaces? The basic answer is that light consists of particles of energy called **photons,** which travel in waves. We do not mean the type of wave you see on the surface of water. Rather, light travels in waves of moving particles that oscillate up and down as well as move forward, like a pulsating stream. A **light wave** has two important characteristics. The first, the number of photons in the stream, determines the **intensity** of the light wave. The second characteristic, **wavelength,** is the distance between successive peaks of a light wave. Inten-

sity is responsible for our experience of brightness; wavelength accounts for our experience of color.

Because photons have electrical and magnetic properties, light is called **electromagnetic radiation.** Visible light actually occupies a narrow band in a much broader spectrum of electromagnetic radiation, as you can see from Figure 4-1. Only when its wavelength lies between approximately 400 and 700 nanometers (a **nanometer** is one-billionth of a meter) is radiation of this type visible. Within this range, the longer wavelengths produce the experience of red and the shorter wavelengths produce the experience of blue. The other colors of the rainbow come from light of intermediate wavelengths. Radiation that includes all wavelengths within the visible range is seen as **white light.**

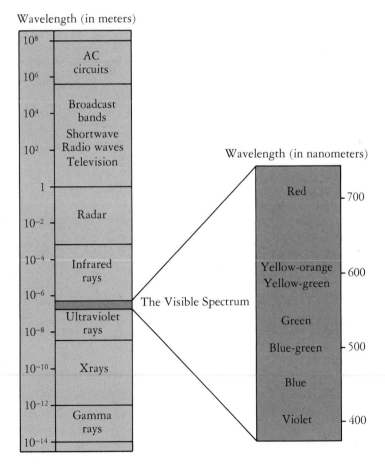

FIGURE 4-1
The Electromagnetic Spectrum The visible portion of the spectrum is enlarged in the right part of the figure. *Source:* Carlson, N. R. (1986). *Physiology of behavior* (3rd ed., p. 161). Newton, MA: Allyn and Bacon.

The first person to demonstrate that white light is composed of a mixture of wavelengths corresponding to all the colors in the visible spectrum (see Color Plate VI) was Isaac Newton. When a beam of light was passed through a prism, Newton found that the longer wavelengths of light were bent or *refracted* least by the dense material of the prism, while the shorter wavelengths suffered the most refraction. When the light coming from the prism was cast on a screen, the full spectrum of colors was revealed.

Using opaque screens with small holes to isolate the different colors, Newton investigated the effect of mixing various components of the spectrum. He found a totally unexpected result. Not only was white light a mixture of all the colors of the spectrum, but a white light could also be produced by adding together just *two* of the component colors (red and blue-green, for example, or yellow and violet). Further examination showed that white light was obtained only when the two colors were quite far apart in the spectrum. A mixture of two colors closer together produced a light of intermediate color.

In searching for a model that would describe these findings, Newton had the imaginative idea of laying out the colors of the spectrum in a circle (see Color Plate VI) instead of in a straight line. Color pairs that produced a white (or neutral gray) when mixed were placed at opposite ends of the diameters of the circle (red opposite blue-green, yellow opposite violet-blue, and so on). The two ends of the spectrum (red and violet) could not be connected in this model, but the gap could be "filled" with purple. Although it is not in the visible spectrum, purple can be produced by mixing red and blue lights.

Newton's color-circle model described the most important features of color mixing (although it provided no place for the metallic colors, silver and gold). We now call the pure colors arrayed around the rim of Newton's circle **hues** and the colors on opposite ends of the diameters of the circle **complementary hues.** As white light is added to a pure hue, the resulting color becomes increasingly washed out or *desaturated.* Such changes in **saturation** can be represented by locations on a line connecting the pure hue on the rim to the center of the circle. Finally, the outcome of mixing equal amounts of

any two pure hues is represented by the midpoint of a line connecting the hues. Thus, mixing equal amounts of pure red and pure green light produces a desaturated yellow.

We have just been describing the principles of **additive color mixture,** which apply when colored lights are combined. The rules are different when colored *paints* are mixed; the outcome is then described by the principles of **subtractive color mixture.** Blue paint appears blue because the light it reflects is predominantly of short–medium wavelength (the blue-green portion of the spectrum); long-wavelength light is absorbed by blue paint. Similarly, yellow paint mostly reflects light of long–medium wavelength (the yellow-green portion of the spectrum) and absorbs short-wavelength light. When blue and yellow paints are mixed, *both* short- and long-wavelength light rays are absorbed, leaving only medium-wavelength (green) light to be reflected and seen. Answers to most of the questions you might have about colors in the world and the way in which we perceive them can be found in a very readable account by Rossotti (1985).

Variation in time and space of the intensity and length of light waves provides us with information that is our most important source of knowledge about the physical world. But this knowledge is greatly enriched by another source —also a form of wave energy—that allows us to *listen* to events in the world.

Sound

Although the analogy of a wave on the surface of water is misleading when applied to light, it is helpful when applied to **sound.** When you toss a stone into a pond, it causes "shock" waves that ripple across the surface. Similarly, when an object in the physical world vibrates, it causes **sound waves** to ripple through the surrounding air. Consider what happens when a note is sounded on a piano. When a piano key is pressed, a hammer strikes a tightly stretched wire, making it vibrate. As the wire moves in one direction, it causes the molecules of air in its path to crowd together. This crowding, in turn, increases the pressure on adjacent molecules, causing a pressure wave to spread through the air. As the piano wire moves back in the opposite direction, the air pressure is released. The successive increases and decreases in air pressure, which continue to be generated as long as the piano wire vibrates, are represented in Figure 4-2. Sound waves are thus propagated *by* the air. In contrast, light waves are particles moving *through* the air.

The two most obvious qualities of our experience of a musical sound are its loudness and pitch. The **loudness** of a musical sound produced by a stringed instrument depends on the **amplitude** (the extent of vibration) of the strings. The **pitch** of a musical sound is determined by the **frequency** of the sound wave — the number of wave peaks to pass a point in space in one second. The higher the frequency, the higher the pitch. The correspondence of a sound's loudness and pitch to the sound wave's amplitude and frequency, respectively, can be seen by referring to Figure 4-2. Amplitude is the height of the wave; frequency is related to the distance between successive wave peaks (one *cycle* of the wave).

The notes sounded on musical instruments are complex combinations of many different tones, a mixture that is essential to an instrument's characteristic **timbre,** or sound quality. Timbre, which is also dependent on the material from which the instrument is constructed and the

technique with which it is played, is what makes a note on a guitar sound quite different from the same note played on a trumpet.

Some of the most complex sounds we hear are nonmusical, including perhaps the most important of all sounds — those produced by the human voice. Even a simple utterance, such as saying the word "yes," produces sound waves with a large range of frequency and amplitude. The frequency characteristics of an utterance can be represented by a **speech spectogram,** an example of which is shown in Figure 4-3.

Finally, we should note that sounds that have no linguistic or musical meaning are usually referred to as **noise.** Noise is composed of sound waves of many frequencies and intensities that do not exhibit the systematic pattern that characterizes musical sounds or the features we have learned to identify as spoken language.

In discussing light and sound, we have taken care to distinguish the characteristics of the physical world from the dimensions of sensory experience. The labels used to describe the physical messengers and the sensory messages are summarized in Table 4-1. It is important to use the correct term to avoid confusing the physical and perceptual worlds. Although we often speak of "colored lights," for example, you should realize

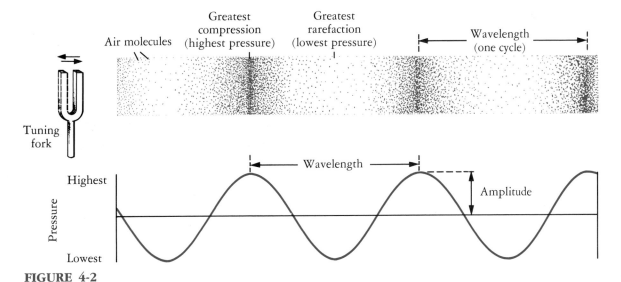

FIGURE 4-2

Diagram of Air Molecules When Nearby Sound Source Vibrates The lower part of the figure represents varying air pressure as a sound wave; the upper part shows the corresponding variation in density of air molecules. *Source:* After Yost, W. A., & Nielsen, D. W. (1977). *Fundamentals of hearing* (p. 15). New York: Holt, Rinehart & Winston.

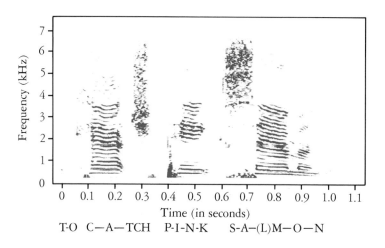

FIGURE 4-3

Speech Spectrogram Sound-wave frequencies produced by utterance "to catch pink salmon" are shown distributed over time. *Source:* Modified from Liberman, A. M., Delattre, P. C., & Cooper, F. S. (1952). *American Journal of Psychology, 65,* 497–516.

TABLE 4-1

The Physical Information Carried by Light and Sound Waves and the Corresponding Sensory Qualities

Physical Messenger	Physical Information	Sensory Quality
Light Wave	Intensity Wavelength	Brightness Color
Sound Wave	Intensity Frequency	Loudness Pitch

that light waves are not colored. The wavelength of light carries information about a particular property of the physical world, but this property cannot be called color until the light waves are intercepted by the eye and translated by the viewer's brain into a dimension of perceptual experience.

Light and sound waves are not the only carriers of information about the physical world. Such object qualities as rigidity, texture, size, shape, and temperature can be detected by touch, and chemical messengers convey information that we experience as tastes and smells. In the following sections, we consider the systems that have evolved in humans to detect and decode information transmitted from the environment—the **sensory systems.**

Our sensory systems act as translators. They receive information from the physical world and translate it into patterns of nerve impulses—a language that the brain can understand. The mechanisms that pick up this information from the physical world are called **receptors.** We first describe the structure of the sensory receptors and then show how they provide us with the raw data from which we create the perceptual world.

THE VISUAL SYSTEM

The mechanism that is specialized to detect and translate light waves is the **eye**—an intricate and complex organ that represents the culmination of millions of years of development. We begin our examination of the visual system by looking at the way in which the eye has evolved.

Evolution of the Eye

All organisms, even bacteria, are sensitive to light; yet primitive creatures have nothing resembling a visual system. The light that they absorb is not a source of visual information but a source of energy for the conversion of chemicals into nutriment. The earliest rudimentary visual system to evolve consisted of light-sensitive cells scattered over the surface of the organism's body, a system found today in the lowly earthworm. The first hint of an eye appeared when these cells clustered together in a pitlike depression of the body surface. The depression was usually located at the "head" of the body, an arrangement seen in the limpet (a rock-dwelling shellfish).

These primitive visual systems do little more than detect changes in light intensity, but this ability is adaptive because abrupt changes in the intensity of light often signal the presence of predators. Eventually, more complex eyes evolved that were capable of detecting much more of the information available in light, such as the form, texture, direction, and movement of objects. The receptor that vertebrate animals developed is the **single-lens eye.** Box 4-1 provides additional details of the evolution of the eye and describes how the single-lens eye forms an image.

Structure and Function of the Eye

The main components of the human eye are shown in Figure 4-4. We describe the role played by these structures as we trace the path followed by light waves that pass through the eye.

A tough, white outer coat called the **sclera** encloses the eyeball. The sclera is opaque except at the front of the eye, where it bulges out to form a transparent membrane called the **cornea.** Unlike most structures in the eye, the cornea receives no blood supply, because blood vessels — which are almost opaque — would scatter too much light. Behind the cornea is a circular muscle, the **iris,** that contracts and expands to vary the size of the aperture, or **pupil,** through which light waves pass. The iris is heavily pigmented, which gives eyes their characteristic color.

Many people think that the only function of the iris is to control the amount of light that enters the eye by regulating pupil size. The pupils do contract in response to increases in intensity of illumination. But they also contract when we look from a distant object to a nearer object, probably in order to "limit the rays of light to the central and optically best part of the lens except when the full aperture is needed for maximum sensitivity" (Gregory, 1977, p. 53).

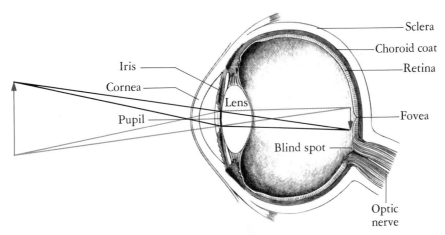

FIGURE 4-4

Cross-section of the Human Eye The functions of the labeled parts are described in the text. Note that the region of the retina in which nerve fibers leave the eye to form the optic nerve is called the *blind spot.* Although the blind spot contains no receptor cells, the visual system bridges the gap and no loss of detail is apparent to the viewer under normal conditions. *Source:* Goldsby, R. A. (1979). *Biology* (2nd ed.). New York: Harper and Row.

Box 4-1
How the Eye Forms an Image

In the nautilus, a snail, the visual pit housing the light-sensitive cells is almost fully enclosed by an opaque, protective covering. Only a pinhole opening permits light to enter this primitive eye. The first illustration indicates how this arrangement allows an image to be cast on the retina of receptor cells lining the back of the eye cavity. If the pinhole is small, any point on the retina will receive light from only one direction. The sheaf of light waves passing through the pinhole provides a retinal image of the visual scene. One problem with this arrangement is that the image is weak; the pinhole is so small that the intensity of the light entering the eye is very low.

A more efficient system evolved when the pinhole closed and the central area of the protective covering enlarged to form a translucent lens. The lens allows more light to enter the eye, so that a strong image is formed on the retina. But the image is in focus only for objects located at an appropriate distance from the eye. The light coming from nearer and farther objects is

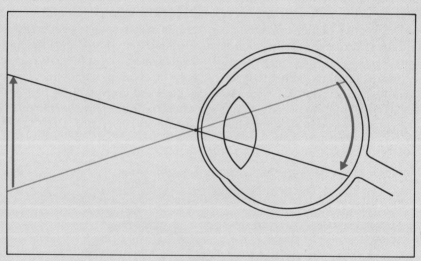

Image Formation by the Pinhole Eye

After passing through the cornea and the pupil, the light rays strike the **lens,** a crystalline structure that serves to focus light rays. The lens is held in place by muscles that control its shape. As these muscles contract or relax, the surfaces of the lens become more or less curved to bring into focus the image of objects at various distances from the eye—a process called **accommodation.** The lens, like the cornea, is free of blood vessels and takes its nutriment from the fluids in the eye's chambers. The first cells of the lens are laid down before birth, and more layers of cells are added throughout life. In fact, the thickness of the lens can quadruple over a lifetime (Paterson, 1979). In adulthood, as the cells in the center of the lens become further removed from the surrounding fluid, they die and the lens begins to harden. This progressively reduces the range over which accommodation can operate; by middle age, many people require corrective lenses

bent, or **refracted,** by the lens to focus images behind or in front of the retina, as shown in the second illustration.

In fish, the limitation of the fixed-focus lens is partially overcome by an adjustable lens. Moving backward and forward within the eye, the lens provides a range of distance over which the images of objects can be brought into focus on the retina. A better solution, found in the human eye, is a lens of variable shape. The contraction of muscles attached to the rim of the lens changes the curvature of its surfaces, providing an almost infinite range of distance over which a clearly focused image can be achieved.

It should be noted that all single-lens eyes provide a retinal image that is upside down and left–right reversed. If this strikes you as odd, you are in good company. Leonardo da Vinci, who had the creative vision to conceive of helicopters and submarines, thought that upright vision demanded an upright retinal image. In his drawings, rays of light are refracted *twice* within the eye to achieve this result. In fact, the relationships between the parts of the visual scene, preserved in the inverted retinal image, determine our visual perception of the orientation of the physical world.

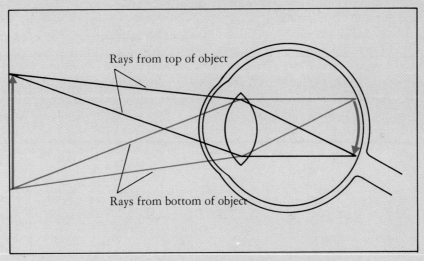

Rays from top of object

Rays from bottom of object

Image Formation by the Single-lens Eye

(eyeglasses) to help them focus, particularly on such near objects as books and newspapers.

After refraction by the lens, the light waves pass through another fluid-filled chamber before striking the **retina,** which lines the back of the eye. The retina is made up of several layers of cells; one layer contains the specialized receptor cells that convert light energy into neural impulses. It is reasonable to think that the receptor cells would be located at the *front* of the retina, where they would be in the best position to intercept the light rays. However, they are situated in the back, which means that incoming light waves must pass through several layers of retinal nerve cells (and the blood vessels that serve them) before reaching their target. One reason for this curious back-to-front arrangement is that the work done by the receptor cells requires a relatively large amount of energy — too much for the eye's fluid to supply. Therefore, nature has placed the receptor cells next to the **choroid coat** (see Figure 4-4), which is rich in blood vessels. The oxygen and other nutrients carried by the blood passing through the choroid coat provide the energy required by the receptor cells.

We have traced the path of light waves through the eye to the receptor cells. Now let us see how the receptor cells decode the messages carried by the light.

Decoding Light Waves

By *decoding,* we mean the translation of information from one form to another. This is what receptor cells do when they convert light energy into neural impulses. There are two different types of receptor cell in the human retina: *rods* and *cones.* Not only are these receptors shaped differently, as their names imply, but they also have different functions. **Rods** serve vision in conditions of dim illumination, providing information about light intensity but not about wavelength. Thus, rods contribute to our perception of brightness, but not to our perception of color. If rods were the only type of receptor cell in our retina, we would see the world in black, gray, and white. **Cones** serve vision in conditions of bright illumination. Cones are sensitive to both wavelength and intensity, and are therefore essential for the perception of color as well as the determination of brightness.

Rods and cones also differ in the way they are distributed over the retina. As Figure 4-5 demonstrates, almost all cones are packed into a roughly circular area at the center of the retina. This area, called the **fovea,** receives light from the *fixation point* — the part of the visual scene on which the eyes are focusing. The cones transmit the detailed information about the physical world that we get when we fix our gaze on it. We are also aware of more vague forms in the periphery of our vision. The rods, which populate the outer regions of the retina, provide these less detailed impressions. The outlying regions of the retina are sensitive to movement — even when it occurs quite far out in the periphery of the visual field — but they supply little specific information about the object that is moving. Typically, when rods detect movement, the eyes turn reflexively in the direction of the movement. This brings the source of movement to the center of the visual field, where the cones in the fovea can provide more detailed information.

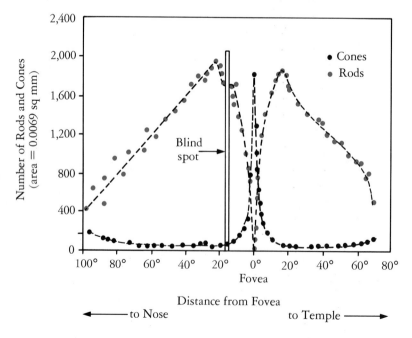

FIGURE 4-5

Density of Rods and Cones in the Human Retina Most of the cones are centrally located on the favea, while the rods are broadly distributed across the retina. *Source:* Adapted from Chapanis, A. (1949). How we see: A summary of basic principles. In *Human factors in undersea warfare.* Washington, D.C.: National Research Council, p. 7.

Box 4-2
Dark Adaptation

When you pass from a well-lit room into a dimly lit room (from a bright lobby into a dark movie theater, for example), you are able to see very little at first. Obviously, the transition from cone-based vision to rod-based vision is not immediate. In the bright lobby, your eyes are light-adapted. If you are then placed in the dark for 30 minutes and someone measures the minimum intensity of light that you can detect (your **visual threshold**), the values obtained would fall on one of the two curves shown in the illustration.

The curve in (a) would be found if the test light were shone on the cones in the fovea; the curve in (b) would be obtained if it were shone on rods in the periphery. As you can see, only a small reduction in the visual threshold is found for the cones during dark adaptation. To put it another way, after entering the dark, there is only a marginal increase in your ability to see dimly illuminated objects when you look directly at them, and what improvement does occur ceases after only two or three minutes. Foveal or cone vision, in short, is quite ineffective in dim light. For this reason, astronomers who want to detect a very faint star look off to one side of it, so that its image falls on an area of the retina populated by rods rather than cones. This improves their vision in dim light because rods, given time to become dark-adapted, are much more sensitive than cones.

The times required for dark adaptation of rods and of cones are quite different as you can see by comparing the two curves in the illustration. Put someone in the dark, and he or she will be able to see little or nothing for the first seven or eight minutes. If a light is not too dim, it can be detected by the cones if its image falls on the fovea. But during this initial period of darkness, the person will be effectively blind to visual events occurring in the periphery of the visual field. Peripheral vision will gradually return as dark adaptation occurs, although it takes an additional 20–25 minutes for the rods to reach maximum sensitivity.

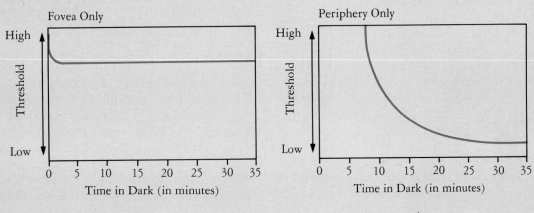

(a)   (b)

Dark Adaptation of the Eye Both graphs chart the course of time necessary for the dark adaptation of retinal receptor cells in the fovea (a) and in the periphery (b). Threshold is a measure of the minimum detectable light intensity. *Source:* After Ludel, J. (1978). *Introduction to sensory processes* (p. 157). San Francisco, CA: W. H. Freeman.

It is not intuitively obvious that we have different mechanisms for seeing in bright and dim conditions, but this feature of our visual system accounts for several of its properties, including **dark adaptation,** a phenomenon discussed in Box 4-2.

We now turn to a critical stage of the decoding process, during which light waves are translated into neural impulses.

From Light Waves to Nerve Impulses When a photon strikes a receptor cell, it causes a **photochemical reaction.** In rods, the absorption of photons from light waves changes the chemical nature of **rhodopsin,** a purple-colored pigment produced by this type of receptor cell. Because the resulting form of the pigment is lighter in color, this process is called **bleaching.** The bleaching reaction causes the rods to generate electrical impulses that are then transmitted through the network of neurons in the retina to the **optic nerve** (see Figure 4-4). Rods continuously manufacture new rhodopsin to replenish the stock that has been bleached. A necessary ingredient in this process is Vitamin A. So when parents urge their children to eat their carrots because "it will help you see better," their advice is soundly based (at least for seeing in dim light); carrots, like liver and spinach, are a good source of Vitamin A.

The chemical response of cones to light is generally similar to that of rods, except that cones contain different pigments.   In fact, a cone contains one of three pigments, which differ in their sensitivity to various wavelengths of light. The combined output of these three types of cone determines our experience of color. Many people who are colorblind are missing one or more of these three types of cone, which limits the range of colors they can detect.

There are approximately 7 million cones and 120 million rods in a typical human retina, but there are only about 1 million separate fibers in the optic nerve that transmit visual information to the cortex. This disparity means that much of the information picked up by the rods and the cones must be condensed in the layers of interconnected neurons in the retina before being passed up the optic nerve. We now discuss some of the research that has examined this process.

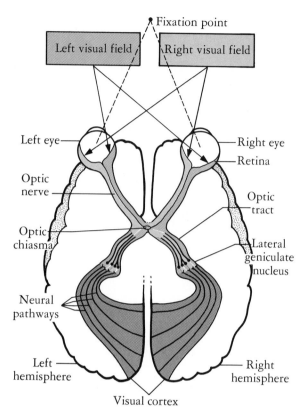

FIGURE 4-6

Major Pathways in the Human System Information from the *left* visual field falls on the *right* side of the retina of each eye, and is carried by the optic nerve via the optic chiasma and lateral geniculate nucleus to the *right* visual cortex. The opposite path is followed by information from the right visual field. *Source:* Adapted from Bootzin, R. R., Bower, G. H., Loftus, E. L., & Hall, E. (1986). *Psychology today: An introduction* (6th ed., p. 113). New York: Random House.

From Eyes to Cortex In the early 1960s, Harvard researchers David Hubel and Torsten Wiesel were investigating the visual system of cats (Hubel, 1963). By inserting tiny electrodes into the optic nerve and visual cortex of an anaesthetized cat, they were able to determine the type of visual stimulus to which individual retinal and cortical cells were most responsive. By "tapping into" an optic-nerve fiber, Hubel and Wiesel were able to measure the output of a *ganglion* cell lying in the retina. (The optic-nerve fibers are the axons of ganglion cells.) They found that for some ganglion cells, the maximum response occurred when a spot of light fell on one particular area of the retina. Moving the spot so that it fell on the surrounding area generally reduced the firing rate of the ganglion cell. They called these areas of the retina the cell's **receptive field** and concluded that the ganglion cell was connected to all or most of the rods or cones that lay within the receptive field. Some of the ganglion cells that Hubel and Wiesel studied had a receptive field with an *on* (excitatory) *center* and an *off* (inhibitory) *surround;* other ganglion cells were found to have the reverse pattern (an *off* center and an *on* surround).

Most ganglion cells had circular receptive fields, as did those in the **lateral geniculate nucleus (LGN)** — the first neural way station in the pathway between the retina and the visual cortex (see Figure 4-6). When Hubel and Wiesel investigated cells in the visual cortex, however, a different picture emerged. Not only did the receptive fields of cortical cells vary greatly in size, they also differed in shape from those of ganglion and LGN cells. In general, a cortical cell responded only to a light patch of a particular shape, orientation, and retinal location. Often the shape that activated a cell was long and thin, suggesting that the cell was functioning as an **edge detector.** Other cells were observed to respond only when a lighted edge moved across the retina in a particular direction. Although Hubel and Wiesel's work was done on cats, there is evidence that the human visual system operates in a similar manner. Goldstein (1984) has summarized the characteristics of the stimuli that maximally excite cells at different levels of the visual system, from the retina to the visual cortex (see Table 4-2). A fuller account of this complex process is provided by Robert Sekuler and Randolph Blake (1985).

The research of Hubel and Wiesel and others has shown that the information available in the pattern of rod and cone activity is condensed in a highly organized and meaningful way as it passes up the visual pathway. You might be tempted to conclude that these findings explain pattern perception (that is, that perception of a triangle, for example, results from the firing of a particular set of cortical edge-detector cells). As you will see later, however, pattern perception is not that simply explained. This should become apparent if you consider the "simple" process of recognizing a friend's face. The fact that you can do this whether the face is near or far, moving or stationary, in full view or profile, expressing laughter or anger, and so on, means that the identification of visual patterns is much more than just the ability to detect and locate edges.

The final aspect of visual decoding that we discuss is the route taken by the nerves linking the eyes to the visual cortex. The pathways in the human visual system are shown schematically in Figure 4-6. You will see that information coming from the left half of the visual field (to the left of the fixation point) falls on the right half of each retina and is "seen" by the right hemisphere. Similarly, information from the right visual field is processed by the left half of each retina and is "seen" by the left hemisphere.

TABLE 4-2
Receptive Field Characteristics of Cells at Different Levels of the Visual System

Cell	Characteristic
Optic nerve fiber (ganglion cell)	Center-surround receptive field. Responds best to small spots, but will also respond to other stimuli.
Lateral geniculate	Center-surround receptive field. Very similar to the receptive field of an optic-nerve fiber.
Simple cortical	"On" and "off" areas arranged side-by-side. Responds best to bars of a particular orientation.
Complex cortical	Will not respond to small spots. Responds best to movement of a correctly oriented bar across the receptive field. Many cells respond best to a particular direction of movement.
Hypercomplex cortical	Will not respond to small spots. Responds to corners, angles, or bars of a particular length moving in a particular direction.

Source: From Goldstein, E. B. (1984). *Sensation and perception* (2nd ed., p. 52, Table 2.1). Belmont, CA: Wadsworth.

Walls (1963) has noted an interesting aspect of the evolutionary development of these visual pathways. Animals such as birds, fish, and reptiles generally have eyes situated on the sides of their head, so that each eye predominantly sees a different part of the visual scene. Because there is little overlap or common information in the field of view of the two eyes in these animals, there is no need for the output of the two eyes to go to the same place in the brain. Thus *all* the fibers in the optic nerves from the two eyes cross over to the other side of the brain. However, as mammals evolved eyes that pointed more to the front and had increasingly overlapping visual fields, it became useful to have cells in the visual cortex that received information from *both* eyes about features in the overlapping area. This overlapping information is a very important cue to *depth* and *distance*. The direction in which the eyes point — to the side or to the front — has been related to whether an animal is a hunter or is among the hunted. Most predatory animals have eyes at the front, giving them good depth perception for judging the distance of the animals they stalk. Animals that serve as prey, on the other hand, typically have eyes at the side of the head. For them, having a wide field of view for the detection of predators is more important than depth perception.

THE AUDITORY SYSTEM

What the eye is to vision, the ear is to hearing. Vibrating objects create changes in the pressure of air molecules. Our ears detect these changes and translate them into patterns of nerve impulses that, when transmitted to the cortex, create the experience of sound.

Structure and Function of the Ear

We have just described the route traveled by light waves in the eye. Here we trace the path of sound waves as they carry information from the physical world into the ear. The major components of the human ear are shown in Figure 4-7. The fleshy **outer ear** channels sound waves into the **auditory canal.** At the end of the auditory canal lies the **eardrum,** a thin flexible sheet of tissue that vibrates in synchrony with the pulsating pressure changes of sound waves.

Beyond the eardrum, the **middle ear** contains three bones called **ossicles.** The function of the ossicles, which are the smallest bones in the

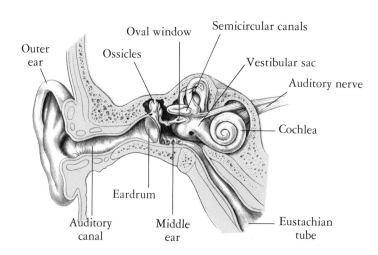

FIGURE 4-7

Cross-section of the Human Ear The functions of the labeled parts are described in text. Note that the semicircular canals, although located in the inner ear, play no role in audition; they serve the vestibular system, which is discussed later in the chapter. *Source:* Kogan, B. A. (1974). *Health* (2nd ed.). Harcourt Brace Jovanovich.

body, is to amplify and transmit vibrations of the eardrum to the **inner ear.** Attached to the middle ear is a safety device called the **eustachian tube**, which connects the middle-ear cavity to the throat; its function is to keep air pressure on each side of the eardrum at about the same level.

The inner ear contains the **cochlea**. Named after the Latin word for snail, which it resembles in outward appearance, the cochlea is a coiled tube of varying diameter securely seated in a bony recess in the skull. Figure 4-8, which shows a cross-section of the cochlear tube, reveals that it is really three tubes in one. The two larger tubes are filled with fluid. The wide end of the upper tube is covered by a flexible membrane called the **oval window.** The last of the three ossicles is attached to the outside of the oval window and passes on to it the vibrations of the eardrum. Motion of the oval window causes a wave action in the fluid that fills the larger cochlear tubes. The way in which this wave action in the cochlear fluid is translated into nerve impulses is complex and not fully understood. We describe the process briefly and discuss the information that is extracted from sound waves in the following section.

Decoding Sound Waves

The auditory receptor cells are housed in the middle tube of the cochlea (see Figure 4-8). The receptors are called **hair cells,** after the short hair which protrudes from the top of each cell. These hair cells are seated on a band of tough, fibrous material called the **basilar membrane.** Resting on the tips of the hair cells is a flap of tissue called the **tectorial membrane.** The wave action in the cochlear fluid causes the basilar and tectorial membranes to bend the hair cells one way and then the other, causing corresponding increases and decreases in the rate of firing of the neurons attached to the hair cells. This pattern of electrical activity is transmitted along the auditory nerve and ultimately is carried to the auditory cortex of the brain. The mechanism for detecting sound waves is incredibly sensitive. If sufficient care is taken to eliminate noise, a healthy, young adult can detect a sound wave that causes the basilar membrane to move a distance less than one-tenth the diameter of a hydrogen atom (von Bekesy, 1957).

The basic functions of the auditory sensory system are to translate the *amplitude* and *frequency* of sound waves into the experiences of *loudness* and *pitch,* respectively, and to enable an organism to determine the source of a sound, or to *localize* it. We now examine how these processes work.

Loudness The loudness of a sound depends on the intensity, or amplitude, of the sound wave. When you hear a loud sound, it is the result of large amplitude vibrations of the eardrum causing large waves in the cochlear fluid, which in turn

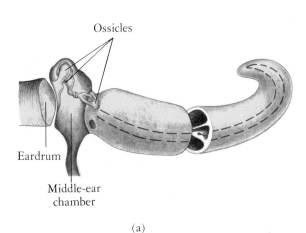

(a)

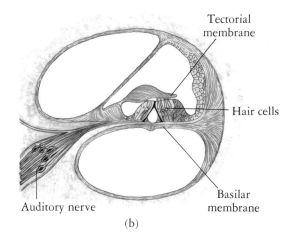

(b)

FIGURE 4-8
Structures of the Human Ear (a) Section of an uncoiled cochlea. (b) Enlargement shows the hair cells located between the basilar and tectorial membranes. *Source:* (a) Keeton, W. T., & McFadden, C. H. (1973). *Elements of biological science* (2nd ed., p. 226). New York: W. W. Norton. (b) Vander, A. J. (1970). *Human physiology* (p. 521). New York: McGraw-Hill.

lead to substantial bending of the hair cells. The greater the change in air pressure in a sound wave, the greater the corresponding change in the pattern of auditory nerve impulses. It has also been suggested that the number of neurons firing increases as sound waves become more intense (Wever, 1970). If the intensity of a sound wave is too great, the auditory system can be damaged, causing the listener to suffer hearing loss.

Pitch There are two theories about how differences in the frequency of sound waves are translated into differences in pitch: *frequency theory* and *place theory.*

The **frequency theory** asserts that the movement of the basilar membrane is essentially a copy of the sound wave that triggered the movement. According to this theory, the rate of oscillation of the hair cells — and, consequently, the rate of firing of the auditory nerves — corresponds directly to the frequency of the sound wave that triggers the motion. Noting that neurons need time to recover between firings, Wever (1970) modified the frequency theory by proposing a **volley principle** to describe how sound-wave frequency is translated into neural activity. For frequencies below about 400 Hz, the neurons keep pace by firing with every wave peak. Above 400 Hz, however, groups of neurons fire with every other peak, or every third, fourth, fifth, or any other numbered peak.

The **place theory** of how high-frequency sounds are decoded is more complex. In essence, it suggests that the wave motion in the cochlea in response to sound waves is not evenly distributed along the length of the basilar membrane. Specifically, the pitch of a high-frequency sound depends on the location of maximum wave action along the membrane (see Figure 4-9). Although this principle was proposed by Helmholtz last century, it took much painstaking and imaginative research by George von Bekesy (for which he was awarded the Nobel Prize) to provide some support for the place theory (von Bekesy, 1957). To do this, von Bekesy created mechanical devices to model cochlear action and then confirmed his ideas by microscopically observing the basilar membrane in motion through tiny windows cut in the side of a cochlea recovered from a human autopsy.

Which theory provides a correct account of pitch perception? As often happens, it seems that

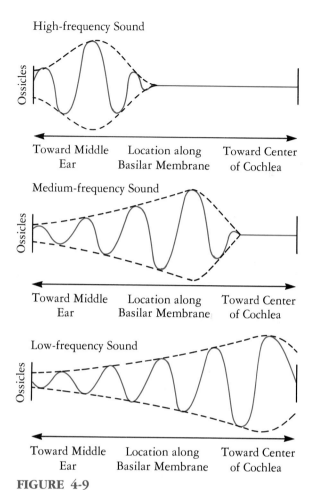

FIGURE 4-9
Place Theory of Sound-wave Decoding As frequency reduces, the location of maximum wave action on the basilar membrane (indicated by the broken-line envelope) moves toward the center of the cochlea from the end attached to the ossicles. *Source:* After Ludel, J. (1978). *Introduction to sensory processes* (p. 226). San Francisco, CA: W. H. Freeman.

the answer is both (Goldstein, 1984). The frequency theory is probably an accurate representation of pitch perception at low frequencies (below 500 – 1,000 Hz); the place theory applies to high frequencies (above 4,500 – 5,000 Hz). In between, both mechanisms operate.

Sound Localization The decoding of the intensity and frequency of sound waves requires input into only one ear, but input into both ears is required to determine where a sound is coming from. Imagine that your head is stationary and a noise occurs to your right. What information in the combined input to your ears permits you to localize the source of the noise? One cue is provided by the difference in the times of arrival of the first sound waves at the two ears, or the **interaural time.** A sound wave from the right travels directly to the right ear but takes longer to reach the more distant left ear. The difference in time depends on the location of the sound source with respect to the head, making interaural time a basis for **sound localization.** It has been shown that we can detect interaural time differences as small as one-hundredth of a second (Durlach & Colburn, 1978).

A second cue for sound localization is the difference in the intensities of the first sound waves reaching the two ears, or **interaural intensity.** A small part of this difference is due to the greater distance traveled by the sound waves reaching the ear farther from the source, but the greater part of the interaural-intensity effect is due to the *sound shadow* created by the head.

Thus, the sound waves that travel directly to one ear are more intense than the sound waves that reach the shadowed ear by a longer, indirect path. There is no difference in interaural time or intensity when the sound source is equidistant from the two ears, which means that you cannot localize sounds coming from directly in front of, above, or behind your head. You typically solve the problem by cocking your head to one side, which reinstates the two cues.

From Ears to Cortex The pathways followed by the nerve fibers connecting the auditory receptors to the auditory cortex are shown schematically in Figure 4-10. This arrangement has many more individual steps than those connecting the retinal receptors to the visual cortex. In addition, although crossover of nerve fibers does occur in the auditory system, it does not appear to result in the routing of qualitatively different in-

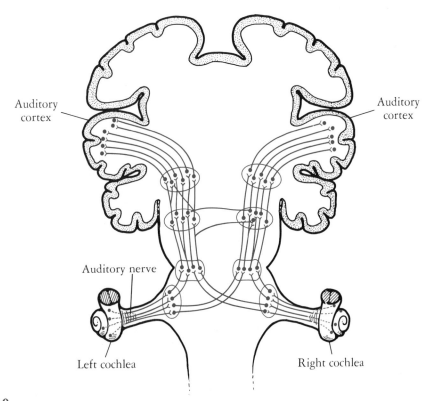

FIGURE 4-10
Major Pathways of Auditory Nerve Fibers Although a majority of nerve fibers from one cochlea crosses over to transmit auditory information to the opposite auditory cortex, there are sufficient interconnections to provide both sides of the brain with similar input. *Source:* Schiffman, H. R. (1976). *Sensation and perception: An integrated approach* (p. 74). New York: Wiley & Sons.

formation to the two hemispheres, as it does in the visual system. Most of the auditory nerve fibers from one cochlea cross over and travel to the opposite side of the auditory cortex; the remainder travel to the cortex on the same side. There is a great deal of interconnection between the left and right sides of the auditory system, so that by the time auditory input reaches the cortex, each hemisphere receives an almost equal share of the information provided by the two ears.

Vision and hearing are by far the most informative senses, but they are not the only means through which we gain knowledge of the physical world. Helen Keller, who was blind and deaf from early infancy, could not have functioned as an author, lecturer, and educator without creating a perceptual world. Lacking both visual and auditory contact with her environment, the means through which she communicated was *touch*— the topic we turn to next.

THE CUTANEOUS SENSES

Some 2,000 years ago, Aristotle suggested that there are five distinct human senses: vision, hearing, touch, taste, and smell. This idea has proved to be remarkably durable; most people today would probably use the same classification scheme. It works well for four of the senses: vision, hearing, taste, and smell have distinctive receptor mechanisms (eyes, ears, tongue, and nose) that are specialized to pick up information about the physical world carried by different messengers (light waves, sound waves, and chemical substances).

This neat and simple system begins to break down when we examine *touch*. Consider the sensory qualities that are usually given this label. Contact between our skin and the physical world may be felt as hard or soft, warm or cold, wet or dry, rough or smooth; it may tickle, itch, or cause pain. We might still want to treat *touch* as a unitary sensory system if each of these sensory qualities could be attributed to a particular pattern of stimulation in an identifiable receptor mechanism. But this is not the case. So, rather than treating touch as a single sense, we group the sensory qualities associated with touch into three categories—*pressure, pain,* and *warmth and cold*—and refer to them as the **cutaneous** (skin-based) **sensory systems.**

Pressure

Buried in a deep layer of our skin is a receptor that responds only to changes in *pressure*. The **Pacinian corpuscle** consists of the dendritic end of a neuron embedded in a ball of connective tissue. When the pressure on this ball of tissue changes, the neuron responds by altering its rate of firing. Such a pressure change is typically the result of contact between the surface of the skin and an object in the physical world.

It should be emphasized that the Pacinian corpuscle responds only to *changes* in pressure and is quite insensitive to the difference in constant level of pressure before and after any such change (see Figure 4-11). Thus, you may feel your shoes pressing on your feet when you first put them on, but this sensation soon wears off. The wearing-off process is referred to as **adaptation.** Receptors in all sensory systems show

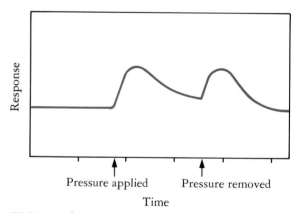

FIGURE 4-11

Response of a Pacinian Corpuscle The receptor responds to a change in pressure but adapts to any level of steady pressure. *Source:* After Ludel, J. (1978). *Introduction to sensory processes* (p. 298). San Francisco, CA: W. H. Freeman.

adaptation to continued, constant stimulation, although the time required for adaptation varies markedly for different receptors. Adaptation contributes to the efficiency of sensory functioning. Instead of overloading the perceptual system with repetitious information about constant stimuli, it is more efficient for the sensory systems to emphasize the changes that occur in stimuli. Adaptation provides such an emphasis. You might reasonably argue that one exception to this general rule of sensory adaptation must be the receptors that signal pain. But this is not the case.

Pain

Pain is a sensory signal of vital importance for survival. Those rare people who are born without sensitivity to pain lead very difficult lives (Sternbach, 1968); some have suffered serious injuries and even death due to their inability to detect and to immediately respond to a painful stimulus. People who can feel pain, of course, usually respond to a painful contact with the environment by withdrawing from the source of stimulation. The sensation you feel soon after you immerse your hand in icy water is certainly painful, and you would normally respond by withdrawing your hand. But if you persisted for about five minutes, complete adaptation to the pain would occur. Adaptation occurs because only the first few moments of painful stimulation are informative, at least in the case of contact with the skin. Pain that originates from inside the body is a different matter. You cannot simply withdraw from the cause of a toothache, a headache, or from heart pains, and as we all know, these types of pain show little or no adaptation.

For a long time, the **free nerve endings** found in the skin were thought to be the sensory receptors responsible for pain. Then it was discovered that the cornea of the eye, which contains only free nerve endings, was responsive to pressure and temperature, as well as to painful stimuli (Lele & Weddell, 1956). Thus, although free nerve endings may be involved in the sensation of pain, they are not specialized to serve *only* this function.

A different view of pain suggests that sufficiently intense stimulation of any set of sensory receptors will be painful. This seems reasonable if you think about the effects of extremely bright lights, very loud sounds, or intense cutaneous stimulation, such as a burn that results in tissue damage, although this is a less plausible account of pain that originates internally. However, the view that pain results from intense stimulation is contradicted by the evidence. Under certain conditions, very weak stimulation may cause great pain; in other cases, very intense stimulation is not felt at all (as when soldiers do not notice injuries sustained in the heat of combat).

A widely held theory of pain (Melzack & Wall, 1965, 1982; Melzack, 1973) draws from these ideas about the basis of pain, but goes beyond them to include the *state of the brain* as a critical determinant of whether a particular pattern of sensory nerve impulses results in the feeling of pain. This theory is described in Box 4-3.

Warmth and Cold

Most of the receptors for warmth and cold are buried in deep layers of the skin and are usually close to a blood supply, which tends to keep the temperature of the receptor cells stable. Nevertheless, we can detect changes in temperature at the skin's surface. To examine this process, areas of skin have been mapped to determine the temperature sensitivity of points within them (Kenshalo, 1980). Mapping is accomplished by touching points of an area of skin with a small metal probe, which is first cold and then warm. The resulting map of cold spots and warm spots has shown that a few points respond to both cold and warm probes but that the great majority of temperature-sensitive points respond only to the cold probe or only to the warm probe.

This evidence appears to suggest that the skin contains one receptor mechanism for detecting cold stimuli and one for detecting warm stimuli. We saw that the visual system has such an arrangement (rods serve vision in dim light; cones detect bright lights). But the cutaneous system for warmth and cold does not seem to work in this way. Some of the investigators who mapped the warm and cold spots on areas of their own skin also cut out small patches of skin from these areas to find the receptor cells responsible for warmth and cold. Although they were able to identify a number of anatomically distinct types of receptor

BOX 4-3
PAIN

It is natural to think of pain as a biological warning signal, but there are two distinct problems with this view. First, pain is often experienced when there is no need for warning; second, pain is sometimes absent when the body sustains serious damage. Here we examine some of the evidence to support these statements and briefly describe a theory of pain that attempts to accommodate the evidence.

Leriche (1939) questioned the biological value of pain when he wrote:

> Defense reaction? Fortunate warning? But as a matter of fact the majority of diseases, even the most serious, attack us without warning. When pain develops . . . it is too late . . . . The pain has only made more distressing and more sad a situation already long lost . . . . In fact, pain . . . makes him [the victim] more ill than he would be without it. (p. 23)

In most cases, the pain that accompanies a disease or a wound wears off as physical recovery takes place. But a few unfortunate individuals develop a condition known as *neuralgia,* or *causalgia,* in which severe pain is experienced many months or even years after the damaged tissue and nerves have healed. This pain can be triggered by a variety of stimuli, such as sudden noise, warmth, a light touch on the skin, or an increase in level of anxiety. Attempts are often made to relieve such pain through surgery, but they are frequently unsuccessful. In some cases, cutting the nerves leading from the site of the original injury to the brain actually makes the pain worse.

Equally challenging findings for any theory of pain come from studies of soldiers severely wounded in battle. Beecher (1959) found that when wounded

men were carried into combat hospitals, only one of three complained of enough pain to require morphine. You might think that wounded soldiers would be numbed by the shock of injury, yet they complained just as loudly as healthy people to pain caused by a heavy-handed injection! By contrast, Beecher found that four of five civilian patients with equally severe wounds did experience sufficient pain to warrant use of morphine.

Clearly, the amount of pain experienced from a wound depends on situational factors as well as on the severity of the injury. As Beecher concludes, the response to injury of the wounded soldier "was relief, thankfulness at his escape alive from the battlefield, even euphoria; to the civilian, his major surgery was a depressing, calamitous event" (p. 165).

In an attempt to deal

---

cell, they could find no simple relationship between cell type and the location of warm and cold spots. As with pain, it appears that there is no single type of cutaneous receptor cell specialized to detect only warmth or only cold.

It may strike you as odd that nature would give us a variety of receptor cells in the skin (at least seven different types of cell have been identified), but not pair them up in an orderly way with the different sensory experiences we have

when the skin is stimulated. We cannot offer a solution to this paradox. Except for the Pacinian corpuscle, which responds only to changes in pressure, most receptor cells in the skin appear to play some role in each of the cutaneous sensory systems. It seems to be the *pattern* of the stimulation that is important, not simply its location or intensity. The characteristics of this pattern that are responsible for the various qualities of cutaneous experience have yet to be identified.

with the diverse factors related to the experience of pain, Melzack and Wall (1965) proposed a **gate-control theory** of pain. They suggested that a mechanism in the spinal cord acts as a gate to control the flow of nerve impulses from the various parts of the body to the brain. The wider open the gate is, the more likely a person is to experience the flow of neural activity through the gate as painful. The position of the gate is determined both by ascending sensory input and by descending influences from the brain that reflect the person's motivational, emotional, and cognitive state.

Consider *acupuncture,* which is used widely in China in place of general anesthesia as a method of eliminating pain in surgery. Westerners have found it difficult to understand how the continuous twirling of needles stuck into remote parts of the body can affect the level of pain felt by a patient undergoing major surgery. It would be wrong to say that the gate-control theory explains acupuncture, but the theory is at least consistent with much of what we know about this Oriental method for controlling pain. Melzack (1973) suspects that the twirling needles may produce the exact pattern of intense, continuous stimulation necessary to close the gate in the spinal cord. In addition, it may be necessary for the patient to believe that the method will work. In suggesting that the pain elimination achieved in acupuncture is partly a placebo effect, we are generalizing from what we know about Western pain-reduction techniques. Melzack (1973, p. 33) calculated in almost half the cases he studied that the effectiveness of morphine in relieving post-surgical pain was really a placebo effect.

More recently, the attention of pain researchers has been captured by the discovery of **endorphins,** short for *endogenous* (naturally occurring in the body) *morphine-like substances* (Mayer, 1979; Akil et al, 1984). These chemicals are produced in the brain and act as powerful analgesics (painkillers). They appear to operate at sites in the midbrain that also produce analgesia when stimulated electrically. The injection into the brain of **naloxone** — a drug that counteracts the effects of opiate drugs, such as morphine — reduces the analgesia produced by stimulation, probably by inhibiting the action of endorphins. Injections of naloxone also diminish the analgesic effects of acupuncture and placebos, suggesting that the pain reduction produced in these ways also involves the production of endorphins.

Neuroscientists appear to have uncovered a common mechanism for analgesia due to opiates, brain stimulation, endorphins, stress, and placebos (Kelly, 1985). However, the complex phenomenon of pain remains a considerable challenge to our understanding (Melzack & Wall, 1982).

THE BODY SENSES

When you close your eyes, you can still keep your balance and touch the tip of your nose; you know where your limbs are. The sensory information on which these abilities depend is quite different from the impressions provided by any of Aristotle's five senses, which yield knowledge about objects and events in the world at large. Two other sensory systems tell you about one very special object — your own body. The first, the **vestibular sense,** detects the force of gravity, enabling you to maintain balance, and also responds to changes in the orientation of the body as a whole. The second body sense, the **kinesthetic sense,** employs receptors located in the muscles, tendons, and joints that detect the relationship of body parts to one another — vital information that enables you to control such coordinated movements as walking, climbing, reaching, and grasping.

The Vestibular Sense

Films of astronauts moving about in space serve as a striking reminder of the powerful influence that the force of gravity exerts on our lives. We need to be reminded of this because we are seldom aware of the considerable amount of muscular effort we put into keeping our balance and posture. Simply put, the force of gravity tells us which way is down.

The receptor system that detects gravity and informs us of changes in the body's position in space is the **vestibular mechanism** (see Figure 4-12), located close to the cochlea in the inner ear. The vestibular mechanism is comprised of three **semicircular canals,** each oriented at right

angles to the other two, filled with fluid. When the motion of your head changes, corresponding shifts in the fluid activate the hair cells found at the base of each semicircular canal. These signals cause messages to be transmitted to the muscles to adjust your posture and, more importantly, to move your eyes so that your gaze tends to remain fixed even if your head moves.

Changes in head or body motion that are regular, like the ones that occur when you jog, cause a lot of activity in the vestibular sacs — but your brain has little difficulty interpreting this information. It is a different matter when the motion is irregular and unpredictable; then vestibular activity may lead to dizziness and nausea, as you well know if you suffer from sea-, air-, or carsickness. Fortunately for persons who are repeatedly subjected to irregular body motion, such as sailors, pilots, dancers, and figure skaters, these symptoms do habituate. After a few days at sea, for example, sailors get their sea legs. **Habituation** is a wearing-off process similar to adaptation, in which the brain learns to ignore the information in the sensory input. (Habituation is also an important concept in learning, as we discuss in Chapter 5.) If you are prone to carsickness, you

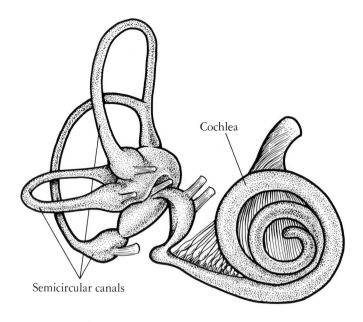

Cochlea

Semicircular canals

FIGURE 4-12

Diagram of the Vestibular Organ — the Receptor Mechanism of the Vestibular Body Sense
Three fluid-filled semicircular canals, oriented in the three dimensions of space, register the directions of gravity and changes in the head's position through action of the fluid on hair cells at the base of the canals. *Source:* Gibson, J. J. (1966). *The senses considered as perceptual systems* (p. 64). Boston, MA: Houghton-Mifflin.

may wish to note the results of a study by Schiffman (1976), who observed that motion sickness is less likely to occur in people who are in control of their motion than in people who are not in control of their motion. Schiffman concluded that the driver of a car is not as likely to become sick as a passenger.

The Kinesthetic Sense

Shut your eyes for a moment and let your arms hang by your sides. Then raise one arm until it is at a right angle with your body. When you open your eyes, you will not be surprised to see that you were successful in carrying out this simple action. But consider what it involved. First, it was necessary for your muscles to contract and relax in a coordinated fashion. Second, it was neces-

sary for you to know the position of your arm with respect to your body.

Muscular coordination is made possible by information provided by receptor cells in the muscles and in the tendons that connect muscles to bones. These receptors are responsible for the feeling of effort or strain that you experience when you use your muscles to raise an arm or lift a weight.

Knowledge of body relationships is provided by receptors in the joints — the *hinges* of your body. When you were raising your arm with your eyes shut, you knew when the shoulder *hinge* was at a right angle because the receptor cells in your shoulder joint sent messages to your brain. These signals also informed you whether your arm was pointing to your front or to your side.

THE CHEMICAL SENSES

The senses of *taste* and *smell* are often referred to as the **chemical senses** in acknowledgment of their sensitivity to the chemical composition of foods, liquids, and odors.

Taste

Four pure tastes have been identified: **sweet, bitter, salty,** and **sour.** Normally, of course, we experience some complex combination of these four tastes. The receptors for this sensory system, the **taste buds,** are found clustered in the bumps on the upper surface of the tongue. Some taste buds are sensitive only to one pure taste; others respond to two or more tastes. Salty and sour tastes can be detected with almost equal sensitivity on most parts of the tongue's surface (except the middle of the tongue, which has few taste buds). As you can see from Figure 4-13, however, the tip of the tongue is much less sensitive than the back of the tongue to bitter-tasting substances. This makes it difficult to avoid the bitter taste that characterizes some medicines, even if you toss them right to the back of your mouth. In such instances, however, you might make use of another determinant of taste sensitivity — temperature. The warmer a bitter substance is, the less noticeable its taste is.

Smell

The receptors for smell are specialized nerve endings that poke through the bony ceiling covering the upper nasal cavity. It has been estimated that this relatively inaccessible location is reached by only two percent of the particles entering the nostrils in an odor (Ludel, 1978, p. 359). Most of the air carrying the odor bypasses the smell recep-

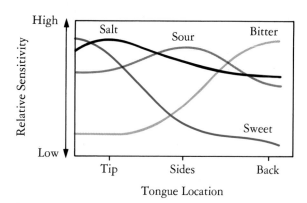

FIGURE 4-13
Relative Sensitivity of the Tongue The diagram shows the different parts of the tongue and their relative sensitivity to the four, pure tastes. *Source:* Adapted from Ludel, J. (1978). *Introduction to sensory processes* (p. 349). San Francisco, CA: W. H. Freeman.

tors and travels directly to the windpipe; in addition, many of the odor-carrying molecules are caught by the mucous lining of the nostrils. As if to compensate for this inefficiency, the smell receptors are exceptionally sensitive. Ludel (1978) has computed that we can detect an odor when as few as 40 molecules reach the smell receptors.

The task of classifying smells has proved to be extremely difficult. German scientist Hans Henning suggested a **smell prism** in 1916 (much as Newton ranged colors around a circle); violets, hydrogen sulphide, lemon, nutmeg, tar, and balsam marked the six points of the prism. Some of Henning's contemporaries criticized his use of a small number of highly trained observers to iden-

tify these categories. Henning's rebuttal clearly shows his disdain for the modern methods of research:

> The critical introspection of trained psychologists is more valuable than statistics taken on all the students in the University, and the statistical procedure, about which science in America has raved so much, has by no means the precision of a *qualitative* analysis. (Henning, 1916; from a translation by Gamble, 1921)

Other attempts to classify smells (see Amoore, 1970) have not been much more convincing. Amoore offered a seven-category system, arguing that substances that smell alike have similarly shaped molecules. However, such a

---

Box 4-4
Psi and Science

The various parapsychological phenomena involving extrasensory perception, such as telepathy, precognition, and psychokinesis, have been collectively labeled *psi*. Our purpose here is not to pass judgment on the existence of psi. That would require a detailed examination of the evidence — a task attempted in a handbook of parapsychology (Wolman, 1977). Rather, we note the particular difficulties that psi presents to the scientist.

In Chapter 1, we learned that scientists have adopted certain procedures or rules to help them draw conclusions from observations. The object of these rules is to allow only well-established conclusions to be incorpo-

rated into the body of knowledge we call science. Let us see how the evidence for psi fares in this regard.

One major problem is the questionable reliability of this evidence. More than in almost any other area, the evidence for parapsychological phenomena is widely regarded with suspicion. Revelations of various forms of deceit have naturally, if unfairly, caused many scientists to doubt the credibility of all evidence for psi. An obvious way around this problem is to arrange for the phenomena to be demonstrated under the watchful eye of scientists in the carefully controlled laboratory environment. Unfortunately, such demonstrations have not proved convincing

(see Marks & Kammann, 1980; Randi, 1983a, 1983b). Only a relatively small number of individuals appear to possess psychic abilities under such circumstances, and even their performance typically varies unpredictably from impressively accurate to no better than guessing.

Another problem is that some psi experiences do not lend themselves to controlled laboratory demonstration. An example is *precognition,* believed by some to explain such instances as a person thinking or dreaming about a relative and only later learning that the relative died at that precise moment. The difficulty here is that this pairing of events may be entirely coinciden-

correspondence has not been confirmed by further research into this system. Also, most people feel that they need more than six or seven categories to classify all the odors they can smell (Cain, 1978).

In one promising approach to smell classification, Schiffman (1974) asked subjects to make similarity judgments between many pairs of smells and then used a sophisticated statistical technique called *multidimensional scaling* to tease out the number of dimensions that the subjects appeared to be using. Schiffman found that two dimensions were sufficient to account for most of the pattern of similarity judgments. From the adjectives used by subjects to describe the smells, one was clearly a pleasant – unpleasant dimension. However, Schiffman was unable to give the other dimension a simple label, either in terms of the subjects' experiences or in terms of the physical and chemical properties of the stimulants. The classification of smells remains a challenge. As John Levine and Donald McBurney (1983) recently put it: "Of the many systems of classifying odors that have been proposed over the centuries, none has ever done much for the field except decorate textbooks."

Before completing our examination of the sensory systems, a brief comment is warranted on the so-called sixth sense. There is no known receptor for this sense, but we describe the way in which evidence about such a sense should be evaluated in Box 4-4.

tal. It has been estimated that perhaps 100 such *coincidental* pairings may occur in the adult U.S. population each year. Such a figure is only a crude estimate, but there appears to be no way to rule out a chance explanation of this type of phenomenon.

However, unreliability of evidence is not a sufficient reason for dismissing the case for psi. Many scientific conclusions are at least tentatively accepted on the basis of evidence that is just as unreliable. The differentiating factor is the existence of a theoretical framework within which to accommodate the evidence. Consider *déjà vu,* the feeling of having experienced some situation before that you believe you are encountering for the first time. The experience is just as fleeting and unpredictable — and resistant to controlled demonstration — as precognition. But *déjà vu* is generally accepted by the scientific community, because it can be explained in terms of well-established theories of memory and perception. (The elements of the new situation are sufficiently similar to those in a memory of a past situation to evoke an illusory feeling of familiarity.) Almost by definition, no such explanations are available to account for most psi experiences.

It is common to think of science as a collection of facts, but it is more correctly viewed as a set of *conclusions* (theories) drawn from observations. Scientists do not find it helpful to classify observations as true or false; rather, they try to make sense of observations by explaining them. The trouble with psi is that the observations do not make sense from a scientific point of view. They resist explanation in terms of current knowledge of physics and psychology.

Because the problem may lie either in the lack of reliability and validity of our observations or in the limited scope of our knowledge, little is gained by simply rejecting or accepting the evidence for psi. Advances in understanding — the goal of science — are achieved only when the limits of scientific knowledge are extended to incorporate reliable and valid observations. Until we can think of a way to demonstrate the reliability and validity of the evidence for psi — and to explain it — the scientist's position should remain one of suspended judgment.

THE PROCESS OF PERCEPTION

Before starting our examination of perception, a comment is warranted on the contrast between perception as you know it and perception as we describe it here. Perception appears as an immediate, direct, and generally faithful record of the objects, surfaces, and events that surround us. But psychologists have found it necessary to distinguish between perception as a *product* and perception as a *process.* It is the product — the contents of our awareness — that is familiar to us.

We are unaware of the process that creates this product because perceptual processing is typically an unconscious (or preconscious) activity. We spend much of this chapter describing *perceptual processing.* Do not expect to recognize these descriptions as reports of events that you "see" occurring in your own mind. They are descriptions of mental events that occur mostly outside your normal awareness. You will appreciate this distinction between unconscious process and conscious product when you read the following section, in which we examine the perception of *distance* and *depth.*

PERCEPTION OF DISTANCE AND DEPTH

We have shown that sensory activity, the foundation for visual perception, is the firing of receptor cells in the retina of the eye. The pattern of firing is referred to as a **retinal image.** A problem arises when you realize that the retinal image is only two-dimensional; it carries information about only those dimensions conventionally referred to as *up–down* and *left–right.*

The retinal image is an ambiguous indicator of *distance* or *depth* (we use these terms interchangeably). As demonstrated in Figure 4-14, a given retinal image can be caused by a small nearby object, by a large distant object, or by an infinite range of intermediate objects. Then how can we explain the perception of distance?

One explanation is that, in the absence of direct information, the perceptual system resolves the ambiguity by judging or inferring the

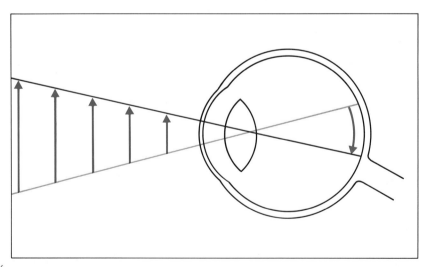

FIGURE 4-14
The Ambiguous Representation of Distance in the Retinal Image The distance of an object is not directly represented in the two dimensional retinal image; a given image could be cast by a small, near object or by a large, distant object.

distance of an object. Most psychologists believe that these judgments are made swiftly and unconsciously on the basis of **depth** or **distance cues.** Let us see what cues are available in the perception of pictures. Although pictures are flat, two-dimensional objects, they typically give rise to an impression of depth. Explaining how this works will help us understand the perception of distance in viewing the three-dimensional world.

Pictorial Cues for Distance

The two pictures in Figures 4-15 and 4-16 differ markedly in the degree to which they give the impression of depth. The picture in Figure 4-15 offers few cues for depth. Can you identify the cues that enhance the impression of depth in Figure 4-16? Psychologists have identified five **pictorial cues:** *perspective, texture gradient, interposition, shadow,* and *familiar size.*

Perspective If you look along railroad tracks running over flat land, the two rails appear to converge at the horizon even though you know that they are parallel. The apparent convergence of parallel lines toward the distance provides the cue to depth called **perspective.** Note that perspective is always present in the retinal images of real scenes that contain parallel lines. It is the

FIGURE 4-16
Crivelli, *Altarpiece: The Annunciation, with S. Emidius* A picture that provides abundant pictorial cues for depth. Reproduced by courtesy of the Trustees, The National Gallery, London.

FIGURE 4-15
Georges Braque, *Still Life: Le Jour* A picture that provides few pictorial cues for depth. *Source:* STILL LIFE: LE JOUR, Georges Braque; National Gallery of Art, Washington, Chester Dale Collection.

artist's choice, however, whether or not to create this perspective in drawing a representation of that scene.

Leonardo da Vinci was one of the first artists to appreciate the importance of perspective in creating a realistic appearance of depth in paintings and drawings. Leonardo wrote that an artist should think of the scene to be represented as if it were being viewed through a pane of glass. The light waves from the edges of objects in the scene are then imagined to etch the glass. Like the image on the retina, the resulting pattern on the glass would preserve the information carried by the pictorial cue of perspective. Earlier artists failed to provide this information. They would, for example, draw rectangular objects, such as

FIGURE 4-17

Egyptian Drawing The flat appearance of elements in Greek and Egyptian drawings results from the absence of pictorial cues, which create perspective. *Source: Psychostasis* ("soul-raising") *of Hu-Nefer, Thebes.* British Museum, London. Reprduced by courtesy of the Trustees of the British Museum.

tables, with parallel sides or would avoid the problem by showing them "edge on." This is the principal reason for the flat appearance characteristic of Greek and Egyptian paintings (see Figure 4-17).

Texture Gradient Another cue to distance is **texture gradient,** in which nearer parts of an evenly textured surface appear coarser than farther parts. In the simple dot patterns shown in Figure 4-18, only the size and spacing of the dots vary. The regularity of this variation provides a gradient in the density of texture that gives rise to the impression of a surface receding from the observer. Abrupt changes in texture gradient, as in Figure 4-18(d), are perceived as changes in the slope of the surface.

Now look at Figure 4-19. It gives rise to little or no impression of depth, despite the texture gradient evident in the coarser detail on the right of the picture and the finer grain on the left. However, if you turn the picture so that its right side is now at the bottom, you should see a familiar scene — a field of stubble receding into the distance. As we typically see the ground in only one orientation (receding from the bottom up in

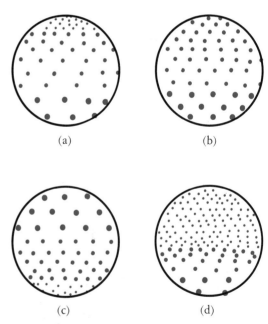

(a) (b)

(c) (d)

FIGURE 4-18

Texture Gradient as a Pictorial Depth Cue Items (a) and (b) show "floors" of different slope. Item (c) shows a "ceiling." Item (d) shows a "floor" with an abrupt change of slope. *Source:* Rock, I. (1975). *An introduction to perception* (p. 90). New York: Macmillan.

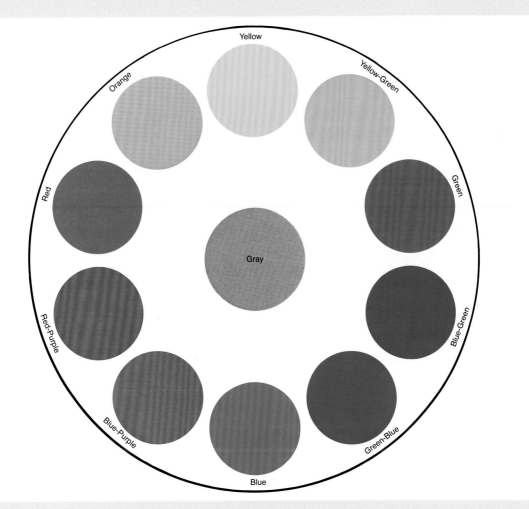

VI *(top)* The color circle displays spectral colors arrayed around the periphery (the gap between blue and red is filled with nonspectral purple). The two colors on opposite ends of a diameter are complementary; their mixture in appropriate proportions produces white. The colors on the periphery are pure.

(bottom) The visible spectrum contains the colors of the rainbow. The wavelength of light is given in nanometers (nm): one-billionth of a meter. Labels identify the wavelengths corresponding to common color names.

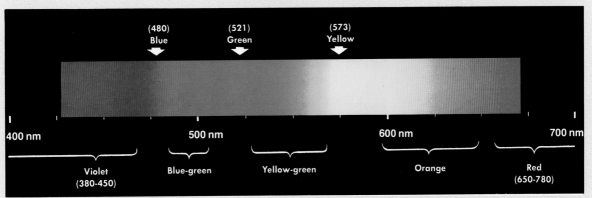

VII *(top)* As increasing amounts of white are added to the three pure hues shown at the left of each sequence, the colors become washed out (desaturated). Saturation, hue, and lightness are the primary determinants of the experience of color.

(bottom) Cover half the blue rectangle and stare at the central cross for a minute or so. When you uncover the rectangle (but keep looking at the cross), the newly visible blue will seem much more vivid than the previously exposed area. This desaturation that occurs with prolonged exposure results from selective adaptation of the retinal receptors. Give your receptors a minute or two to recover, then stare again at the cross in the (uncovered) blue rectangle. After a minute or so, look at the yellow rectangle; an area the size of the blue rectangle will appear supersaturated. Adaptation of the receptors responsible for the experience of blue intensifies the experience of the complementary color—yellow.

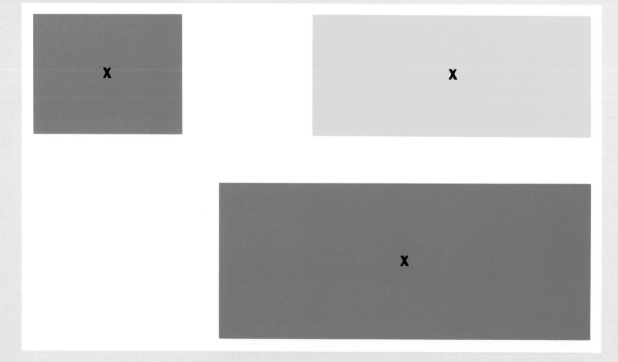

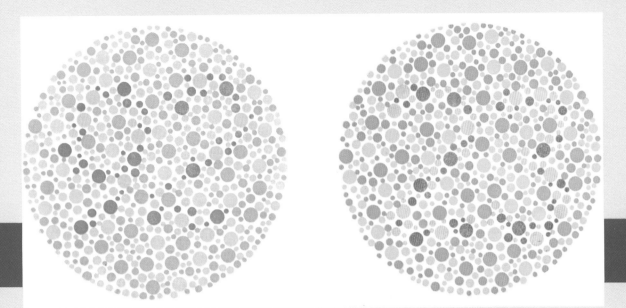

■ **VIII** *(top)* Test the possibility that you are color-blind by examining the patterns. People with *normal vision see the number 92 in the left circle and 23 in the right.* People with various forms of color blindness see only partial numerals or none at all.

■ *(bottom)* When lights of different color are combined, the result follows the principle of *additive* color mixture that underlies the color circle: red and green lights combine to give yellow; green and purple appear blue; complementary color pairs are white. When paints are combined, the result follows the principle of *subtractive* color mixture: the light reflected from the mixture has subtracted from it the wavelengths absorbed by the component paints. This is evident from the filters shown in the illustration that, like paints, also absorb light of a particular wavelength—for example, white light seen through yellow and blue filters appears green.

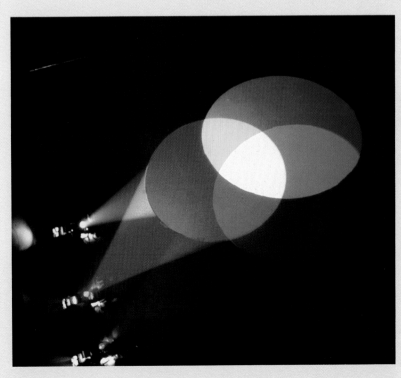

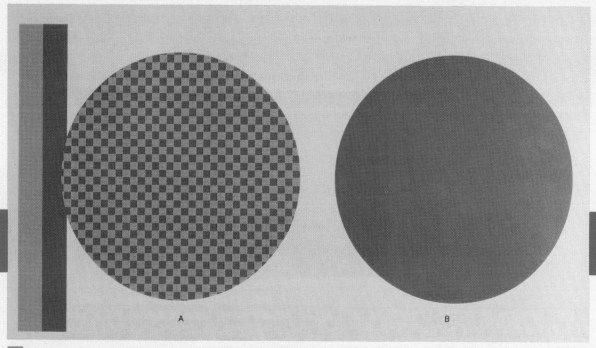

A   B

IX The principle of additive color mixture can be demonstrated without projected beams of light. Stand the book up and view the figure above from across the room. The red and green dots in the left circle will merge to produce a yellow of the same hue as the right circle. This principle is exemplified by the work of Georges Seurat (see below), whose paintings were produced by small dots of paint rather than brushstrokes (as is more evident in the enlarged detail). This technique—called *pointillism*—allows the colors to be mixed in the viewer's eye rather than on the artist's palette. You experience a similar effect when you watch color television. Georges Pierre Seurat, *Invitation to the Sideshow/La Parade*, The Metropolitan Museum of Art, bequest of Stephen C. Clark, 1960.

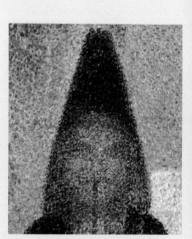

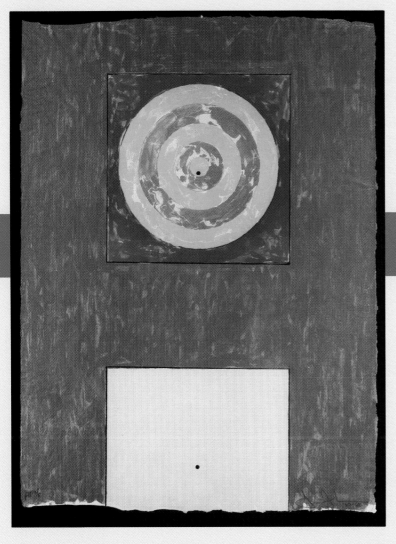

X *(top)* Stare at the center of the target in the upper square of this Jasper Johns lithograph for about two minutes; then look at the dot in the middle of the square below it. You should see more familiar colors—red, white, and blue. Selective adaptation of color receptors caused a negative afterimage to be seen in complementary colors. Jasper Johns, *Target*, Universal Limited Art Editions.

(bottom) Look alternately for about 15 seconds at the green and red stripes. Continue to do this for about 2 minutes, then look at the black and white stripes. You should see faint negative afterimages in complementary colors that are orientation-specific. Adaptation to the vertical green lines should produce red vertical afterimages; similarly for the horizontal lines. Turn your head to one side to demonstrate that the color of the afterimages is dependent on line orientation.

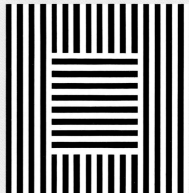

XI *(top)* Simultaneous color contrast is seen in this painting by Joseph Albers. The stripes are the same color in both halves of the painting, as is apparent when you check where they join. However, the stripes appear yellow against the gray background and gray against the yellow background. Josef Albers, *Interaction of Color*, plate VI-3.

(bottom) Although the same shade of blue is used in all parts of this figure, the spreading effect makes the blue background appear lighter where the pattern is white than where it is black.

XII The mountains of North Carolina. The blueness and fuzziness of the hills is caused by atmospheric perspective.

XIII On viewing this Op Art work by Bridget Riley, the most striking impression is movement: the lines seem to shimmer ceaselessly. Many people also see subjective colors—irregular pastel streaks typically running at right angles to the lines. Bridget Riley, *Current*, 1964. Collection, The Museum of Modern Art, New York. Philip Johnson Fund.

FIGURE 4-19
Importance of Orientation to the Depth Cue of Texture Gradient Oriented in this manner, the impression of depth in the picture is weak. Turn the book so that the right side of the picture is at bottom. Now you see a field of stubble receding into the distance.

our visual world), our perceptual system is prepared to accept texture gradient as a cue for distance along the ground only if the gradient changes in the familiar direction.

It should be noted that texture gradient can be a reliable cue to distance only if the elements of the texture are equally sized and equally spaced. If you think about the textured surfaces in your environment, you will find that almost all of them are characterized by this sort of regularity. Even if the surface is only *generally* equal in size and spacing, as in Figure 4-19, the cue of texture gradient is still effective.

Interposition A third pictorial cue that contributes to the difference in depth apparent in Figures 4-15 and 4-16 is **interposition,** in which one object partially obscures another so that the partially obscured object appears to be farther away. When this occurs in a three-dimensional scene, the partially obscured object lies behind the interposing object.

Although interposition is uninformative about the *absolute* distance of objects, it does provide a cue to the *relative* distance of objects. The fact that there are fewer instances of interpo-

sition in Figure 4-15 than in Figure 4-16 reduces the information that your perceptual system can use to locate the various objects in Figure 4-15 in the third dimension of space.

Shadow and Shading Our environment is normally illuminated from single sources of light that create differences in the brightness of surfaces **(shadow)** when objects interrupt the light rays. In addition, the varying amount of light reflected to the eyes from a surface provides information about the varying slant of the surface — a feature that can be represented in drawing by appropriate **shading.**

Because scenes are almost always lit from above, certain patterns of shadow and shading carry information about whether irregularities in surfaces are bumps or hollows. You probably see Figure 4-20 as a picture of a crater illuminated at an angle by the sun (which it is). Your perceptual system is using shadow as a cue to the lay of the land. This becomes evident when you turn the picture upside down. You assume that the sun is still shining from above and to the side, so that shadow now makes the crater look like a mound.

FIGURE 4-20
Patterns of Shadow and Shading Shadow gives this landmark the appearances of a crater—but when viewed upside down, the same shadow makes the crater look like a mound.

Familiar size One final feature of pictures often classified as a pictorial distance cue is **familiar size.** Your knowledge of the average height of people allows you to judge the distance of the people depicted in Figure 4-16. The smaller the retinal image cast by the figures, the farther away you judge them to be.

We have neglected to mention a singularly important fact about the perception of pictures and photographs: all parts of a picture are in reality at the *same* distance from a viewer. Moreover, the perceptual system is informed of this fact. (The cues that provide information about the distance of the surface of the picture itself are discussed in the next section.)

Why, then, do pictures on a flat surface give rise to the impression of depth? The answer is that pictures include some of the same distance cues present in a real-world scene. The power of these pictorial cues to evoke the impression of depth in pictures is reduced, however, by contra-

dictory cues that are simultaneously informing the perceptual system that the picture lies on a flat, two-dimensional surface. This is why the impression of depth in pictures is weak, compared to the perception of a three-dimensional scene. If the contradictory cues are eliminated, the impression of depth provided by pictorial cues is enhanced. Try looking with one eye at a picture of a three-dimensional scene through a tube or through cupped hands (to mask the surrounding frame and background) to see whether you experience a greater impression of depth.

Perspective, texture gradient, interposition, shadow, and familiar size are called pictorial cues because they are the *only* cues to depth in pictures. Cues in pictures derive their effectiveness from their role as distance cues in three-dimensional scenes. Four additional cues may provide information about distance when viewing three-dimensional scenes. The retinal images are the source of two of these cues: *binocular disparity* and *motion parallax;* the remaining two, *con-*

vergence and *accommodation,* are provided by information from the muscles that control the eyes.

Binocular Disparity

Keeping your head and eyes stationary, compare the impressions you get when you view a distant scene with one eye and with two eyes. For most people, the impression of distance is noticeably stronger when they use both eyes. The reason for this is that each eye sees a different view of the world. This phenomenon, in which a slightly different image is projected onto the retina of each eye, is termed **binocular disparity.**

For a simple demonstration of binocular disparity, look at an object about ten feet away and raise a finger at arm's length, so that it is almost in line with the object. Keeping your gaze fixed on the object, attend to the visual impression of your finger. You will see a double image of the finger. By alternately winking your eyes, you will see that each eye is providing one component of the double image. Now change your gaze and look directly at your finger. The two images of the finger should fuse into a single, clear impression. If you switch your attention (but not your gaze) back to the more distant object, that object will now be seen as a double image.

This demonstration shows that only those parts of the visual scene at or very near the distance at which you are looking give rise to a single image. Parts of the scene that are either closer or farther away give rise to double images, although we are seldom aware of this. What makes binocular disparity a distance cue is that the degree of separation of the two components of a double image depends on the distance of the viewed object from the fixation point.

It should now be apparent why, when we view a picture, binocular disparity provides evidence about distance that contradicts the evidence given by pictorial cues. The way in which objects and surfaces line up in a picture is fixed, regardless of the point from which the picture is viewed. The two eyes therefore receive the *same* view of a scene when it is represented on a two-dimensional surface. Interestingly, it *is* possible for binocular disparity to be an effective distance cue in picture viewing by using a device called a

stereoscope. The principle on which the stereoscope works is explained in Box 4-5.

Motion Parallax

Imagine yourself a passenger in a moving car, looking out a side window across a field at a house in the middle distance. Because you are moving, the images of the utility poles lining the road are moving rapidly across the retina of your eyes. The image of the more distant field will be displaced more slowly across the retina; the image of the house you are looking at will remain stationary. The rate these images of objects and surfaces displace across the retina provides information about their distance — a cue called **motion parallax.**

Similar information is available to a moving observer about the distance of objects that lie *beyond* the fixation point, although the displacement of images across the retina is then in the opposite direction. You can see this for yourself. Pick an object in the middle distance from where you are now sitting and fix your gaze on it. Now move your head from side to side. If you attend to (but don't look at) objects nearer and farther than your fixation point, you should see the nearer ones displaced in the opposite direction to your head movement and the farther ones moving in the same direction. Also notice that the rate of displacement varies with the distance from the fixation point.

Motion parallax is also present in the changing retinal image that results when you move toward the point on which your eyes are fixed. In such a case, we describe the flow of the retinal image as an **expansion pattern.** As in Figure 4-21 (page 178), your approach to a fixation point causes the image of the surrounding scene to expand outward across the retina. The rate of flow is greater for nearer than for farther parts of the scene, and this provides a cue to their distance.

We have seen that binocular disparity provides a cue to the flatness of pictures, thereby contradicting the pictorial cues that give rise to the impression of depth in the pictured scene. If you move while viewing a picture, the parts of the scene that appear to be at different distances do not show motion parallax; this is also a contradic-

Box 4-5
Binocular Disparity in Viewing Pictures and Drawings

Find a piece of cardboard measuring about 8″ × 12″; the backing from a pad of notepaper (or the pad itself) will do. Stand it upright on this page so that one of its short sides falls on the dashed line between the two squares in the first illustration. Place your head directly over and just above the cardboard screen. Alternately shut your right eye and your left eye to make sure that each eye is seeing only *one* of the squares. Now keep both eyes open and look at the pair of squares. Because you are fixating at the distance of the page, you will see separate

images of the squares. Now try to relax your gaze so that you are looking *through* the page, not at it. The two images will begin to drift together. They will probably spring apart again as you unwittingly shift your fixation back to the page. If you persevere for a minute or two, however, you should eventually be able to fuse the images of the two squares. Fusion should bring a sudden and compelling impression of depth; the squares will seem to stand out from the page as though they were solid. Since there are no pictorial cues to depth in either of the squares in the

illustration, the difference you see in the relative depth of the two squares when the images are fused is due solely to binocular disparity.

Now try the same procedure with the second illustration (the photographs of the football players).

An even more impressive demonstration of the power of binocular disparity to create the impression of depth is seen when the two parts of the third illustration are fused. These patterns were developed by Bela Julesz (1971), who called them **stereograms.** The left pattern is made up of randomly arranged dots. The right pattern is identical, except that the dots in a T-shaped area in the center of the pattern have been moved slightly to the right. The white space uncovered by this shift has been filled with a continuation of the random dot pattern and the dots overlapped by the shift have been deleted, so no change is noticeable and the T is invisible. The result is a pair of stereograms that are indistinguishable to the naked eye. Now try to fuse the two patterns by presenting one to each eye (using

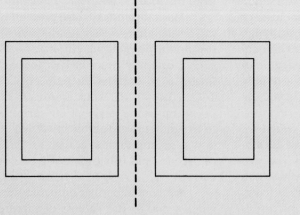

Stereogram *Source:* Rock, I. (1975). *An introduction to perception* (p. 103). New York: Macmillan.

Stereoscopic Photograph   This photograph shows Terry Bradshaw (right) of the Pittsburgh Steelers talking to Joe Ferguson of the Buffalo Bills.

the procedure described earlier).

When the patterns are superimposed, all parts of the two patterns *except the T area* fall on corresponding retinal areas and thus are fused. The systematic disparity in location of dots in the T area is interpreted by the perceptual system as a T shape floating an inch or so above a background of dots. This is the same process your perceptual system used when it interpreted the double image of your finger as representing a finger located nearer than the fixation point. If the dots in the right pattern had been shifted in the opposite direction, the T shape would appear *more distant* than the background pattern.

Julesz has referred to the viewing of stereograms as a *Cyclopean perception,* after the mythical beast called Cyclops that had a single eye in the center of its forehead. Because the pattern of shifted dots can be detected only *after* fusion of the two images by the perceptual system, the pattern is seen as if it were viewed by a single, Cyclopean eye.

Stereogram   *Source:* Julesz, B. (1971). *Formation of cyclopean perception.*   Chicago, IL: University of Chicago-Press.

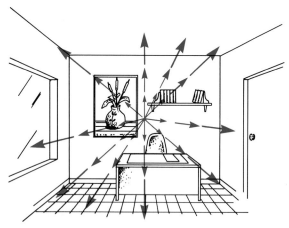

FIGURE 4-21

Motion Parallax and an Expansion Pattern
Arrows show the expansion pattern of the retinal image
as you move toward the point at which you are looking. The rate of expansion is greater for nearer than for
farther parts of the scene — providing the cue of motion parallax. *Source:* Rock, I. (1975). *An introduction
to perception* (p. 116). New York: Macmillan.

tory cue to depth in picture perception. A third
source of information that pictures are really flat
is provided by your eye muscles.

Muscular Cues for Distance

When you switch your gaze from a farther to a
nearer object, the degree of contraction of the

muscles attached to your eyeballs is altered. If
we refer to the line connecting the center of your
retina to the object you are looking at as the *line of
sight,* then we can describe this muscular change
as **convergence** of the lines of sight of the two
eyes. Since the least convergence occurs when
you look at the horizon and the greatest convergence occurs when you try to fixate the tip of your
nose, the degree of contraction of the eye muscles
could serve as a cue to the distance of the fixation
point.

As you switch your gaze to objects at different distances, the retinal images of these objects
remain in focus. This occurs because the muscles inside the eye alter the curvature of the lens,
bending the light rays from the fixation point in a
manner that keeps them focused on the retina.
This process, called *accommodation,* could also
serve as a cue to distance.

However, the muscular changes involved in
convergence and accommodation are minute
when the fixation point moves beyond about six
to eight feet from the observer. It is likely, then,
that if muscular cues do play a role in determining
distance perception, their influence is limited to
providing information about the distance of
points close to an observer.

In all, we have described nine cues for distance. They are listed in Figure 4-22, which you
may find helpful as an aid in organizing this information.

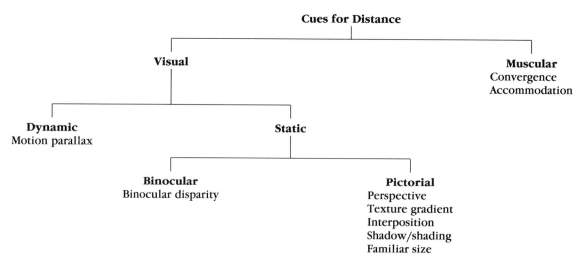

FIGURE 4-22
A Classification of Cues for the Perception of Distance

We have argued that distance must be inferred or judged because it cannot be determined directly from retinal images. This act of judgment is a perceptual process—a process of which the observer is typically unaware. Only the conclusion of this process is made available to consciousness—in the form of a three-dimensional, perceptual world. The same principle holds for the perception of *size*.

PERCEPTION OF SIZE

Size Constancy

Consider the changes that occur in your retinal images as you move about in the world. As you walk toward a friend who is standing still, the image she casts on your retina will expand. If she decides to meet you halfway, the image will expand at twice the rate. But your friend does not appear to grow larger. In general, we tend to perceive an object as maintaining a constant size, despite variations in the size of its retinal image that result from viewing the object at different distances. This tendency is referred to as **size constancy.**

You might be skeptical about characterizing perception in this way. After all, if you think about it, your friend *does* look larger as she gets closer to you in that she covers more of the background than she does when she is farther away. Note, however, that achieving the perception that your friend looks larger requires an effort of attention; you have to think about it. Your spontaneous perception is much more likely to be that your friend is of constant size.

In order to achieve size constancy, the perceptual system must take into account the distance of the object from the observer. The principle underlying size constancy can therefore be represented by the equation

$$\text{Perceived size} = \text{Retinal image size} \times \text{Distance}$$

Do not take the multiplication sign too literally; it is shorthand for "taking into account." A good way to understand size constancy is to see how this equation allows us to predict the perceptual consequences of varying retinal image size or distance, or both.

First, consider the changes that occur as you watch your friend walk toward you. The size of the image she casts on your retina increases as her distance from you decreases. Your perceptual system interprets these offsetting changes as resulting from the change in location of an object of *constant* size.

Next, consider a situation in which distance can be varied without changing the size of the retinal image. The perception of an *afterimage* provides an example. If you stare at a bright patch (the lighted bulb of a desk lamp, for example) for 20–30 seconds and then look away, you will continue to see the patch, only now it will appear darker than the surrounding visual field. The dark patch is an **afterimage,** caused by a temporary reduction in the sensitivity of the retinal receptor cells that were overstimulated by the light. The afterimage is, in effect, painted on the retina and thereby provides a retinal image of constant size.

You can simulate a change in the distance of the object represented by an afterimage by look-

Excuse me for shouting,
I thought you were further away.

Source: Reproduced by Special Permission of PLAYBOY Magazine: Copyright 1971 by PLAYBOY.

ing at near and far surfaces. If you do this, you will perceive the afterimage to be larger as the distance of the surface onto which it is "projected" becomes greater. This result is just what the equation predicts: increased distance, with retinal image size held constant, leads to increased perceived size.

Another perceptual phenomenon that can be explained by this equation is the **moon illusion** — the tendency to perceive the moon as larger when you see it on the horizon than when you see it above you.

The Moon Illusion

It is useful to think of size constancy as the outcome of a perceptual mechanism that interprets or scales the retinal image size of an object according to its distance from the observer. Ob-

viously, this can be achieved only if distance information is available. Normally, the visual input contains abundant cues for distance, but no such cues are available to tell you the distance of the moon when it is high in a cloudless sky. You may know that the moon is almost a quarter million miles away, but this knowledge does not serve as a *perceptual* distance cue. You may know that the diameter of the moon is 2,160 miles, but you cannot claim to *perceive* it as being that size. The absence of distance cues means that you perceive the size of the moon above you solely on the basis of its retinal image size.

The situation is different when you look at the moon on the horizon. In this case, you are looking over a surface that is typically rich in distance cues, such as perspective and texture gradient. From the equation for perceived size, we can predict that these cues will allow your

FIGURE 4-23
The Constancy Scaling Mechanism Pictorial cues to depth trigger the viewer's constancy scaling mechanism. This process scales up the retinal image cast by the farther girl so that she is not perceived as being abnormally small. *Source:* After Rock, I. (1975). *An introduction to perception* (p. 48). New York: Macmillan.

FIGURE 4-24
Depth Cues Depth cues indicate that the two girls are located at the same distance from the viewer; no scaling is triggered. The difference in perceived size of the two girls corresponds to the difference in their retinal image size. *Source:* After Rock, I. (1975). *An introduction to perception* (p. 49). New York: Macmillan.

perceptual mechanism to take distance into account in scaling the moon's retinal image. Because the cues indicate that the moon's distance is great, its retinal image size should be scaled up correspondingly so that a larger size is perceived. This is precisely what occurs. Depending on the strength of the distance cues available, the size of the horizon moon can be perceived to be up to 40% greater than the size of the overhead moon (Kaufman & Rock, 1962).

You can demonstrate for yourself the role played by distance cues in the moon illusion. The next time you see the moon on the horizon, note how large it looks. Then eliminate distance cues from the scene by viewing the moon through cupped hands or reduce the effectiveness of these cues by turning around and looking at the moon between your legs (as Figure 4-19 shows, the effectiveness of texture gradient depends on orientation). In both cases, the moon should appear to be smaller. As its retinal image size is always the same, you should see the horizon moon as roughly equal in size to the overhead moon on this second viewing.

The moon illusion can be understood as the result of inappropriately applied size-constancy scaling (Gregory, 1968). Such perceptual errors provide important evidence of the normal operations of the perceptual system. Similar evidence comes from a consideration of the perception of the sizes of objects seen in pictures.

Perception of Size in Pictures

The two teenagers shown in Figure 4-23 typically are seen as being of normal and roughly equal size. Yet the retinal image of the lower girl is more than twice the size of the retinal image of the upper girl. Clearly, your perceptual system is using the pictorial distance cues in the drawing to scale up the perception of the more distant girl to preserve size constancy.

A quite different impression results from viewing Figure 4-24. In a move possible only in a drawing, the two teenagers have been placed at the same apparent distance without altering their retinal image sizes. Now the difference in image size does intrude on your perception. The girl providing the smaller image *is* perceived as smaller. The pictorial cues for distance in this drawing are informing your perceptual system that the two girls are equally far away, so that the smaller image is not scaled up and size constancy is not achieved.

PERCEPTION OF FORM

Your retinal images can be described as mosaic patchworks of varying brightness and color. What you perceive, however, is a world of objects against a background of surfaces. Perception, in short, is organized or structured. Here we examine the principles underlying perceptual organization in order to provide a basis for subsequent discussion of the perception of particular shapes.

Perceptual Organization

The pioneer work on perceptual organization was done by the Gestalt psychologists. They identified two basic characteristics of **form perception:** the *grouping of elements* and *figure–ground separation*.

Gestalt psychologists' studies of the tendency in perception to group elements in certain ways led to the identification of several principles of organization. The pattern in Figure 4-25(a) is perceived as four rows of circles. This perceptual organization results from the principle of **proximity**—the tendency to group elements that are close together. In Figure 4-25(b), rows (rather than columns) are perceived; the determining principle in this case is **similarity.** Figure 4-25(c) demonstrates **closure**—the tendency to perceive disconnected elements as complete. The units of this figure are actually lines with unconnected ends, but the figure typically is perceived as an array of circles. A fourth principle of perceptual organization is **continuation.** Gestalt psychologists characterized

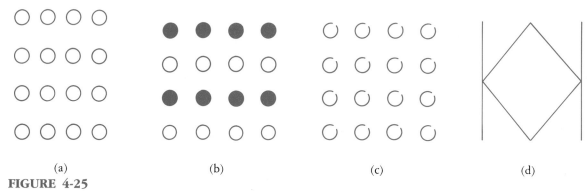

(a)   (b)   (c)   (d)

FIGURE 4-25

Gestalt Organizational Principles   These patterns demonstrate the Gestalt organizational principles of (a) Proximity, (b) Similarity, (c) Closure, and (d) Continuation.

smooth transitions between line segments as having *good continuation* and abrupt transitions as showing *bad continuation*.   The perceptual system, they believed, spontaneously organizes the pattern of lines shown in Figure 4-25(d) into a diamond between two vertical bars because such an arrangement has good continuation.   The equally possible arrangement of the letter Ʌ on top of the letter M is not perceived spontaneously due to bad continuation.

   Figure–ground separation refers to the tendency to perceive certain regions of a visual scene as *foreground* (the "figure") and adjacent regions of a visual scene as *background*.   When you look at Figure 4-26, you probably see a white vase on a black background.   Perhaps the strongest determinant of which regions are perceived as figure and which regions are perceived as background is **surroundedness.**   An area enclosed by a contour is generally seen as *figure;* the surrounding area is generally perceived as *ground.*   Other factors that have been shown to play a role in figure–ground separation are *size, orientation,* and *symmetry.*

   If you look at Figure 4-26 for more than a few seconds, you will probably see the area of figure and ground spontaneously reverse to show two dark faces silhouetted against a white background.   Continued inspection will result in the alternating perception of the two arrangements. This change in what the viewer perceives is called **figure–ground reversal.**   Some psychologists believe that such reversals provide strong evi-

FIGURE 4-26

Figure–Ground Organization   The principle of surroundedness is a strong determinant of how the viewer organizes this picture.   When first looking at this pattern, most people see a primarily white vase on a black background.   Continued inspection generally leads to a figure–ground reversal, revealing two quite different objects (profiles of Queen Elizabeth and her husband; the vase was made for the Queen's Silver Jubilee in 1977).

dence of the way in which the perceptual system operates.

Reversible Figures

There are three types of **reversible figure** and we already have seen one of these (Figure 4-26). Swiss naturalist L. A. Necker (1832) was the first to describe a second type, in which the figure undergoes a **depth reversal.** The Necker cube shown in Figure 4-27(a) can be perceived either as a cube observed from below and to the left, as illustrated in Figure 4-27(c), or as a cube seen from above and to the right, as illustrated in Figure 4-27(b). If you look at the Necker cube in Figure 4-27(a) for 30 seconds, you should see it spontaneously reverse in depth orientation. Although your perceptual system interprets this two-dimensional line pattern as representing a three-dimensional object, your perceptual system seems undecided about which of the two possible orientations of the cube should be perceived.

Figures 4-28 and 4-29 provide examples of a third type of figure that is ambiguous and therefore reversible. Figure 4-28, popularized by E. G. Boring (1930), shows the profile of a young woman's face with the tip of her nose just visible; alternatively, the young woman's chin can be perceived as the nose on the face of a much older woman. Figure 4-29, created by Joseph Jastrow (1900), shows the head of either a rabbit or a duck. The change in perception that occurs on continued inspection of these two figures can be described as **object reversal.**

Richard Gregory (1968, 1970) has suggested a psychological theory to account for reversible figures that stresses the creative nature of perception. According to Gregory, the perceptual system generates hypotheses related to which object is most likely to be represented by the sensory evidence. When viewing a three-dimensional scene with many distance cues, the perceptual system can quickly select the hypothesis that

FIGURE 4-28
Boring's Reversible Figure of an Old/Young Woman

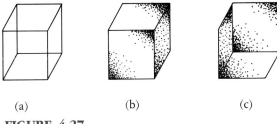

(a) (b) (c)

FIGURE 4-27
The Reversible Necker Cube Item (a) can be seen as a cube in either of the orientations represented in (b) and (c). Because (b) and (c) are equally plausible cubes, perception of cubes (a) spontaneously alternates between them.

FIGURE 4-29
Jastrow's Reversible Figure of the Head of a Rabbit/Duck

correctly interprets the sensory data. But drawings of reversible figures supply few distance cues to guide the perceptual system. In the Necker cube drawing (Figure 4-27), for example, the sensory evidence fits the hypothesis of either orientation equally well. The reversal of the cube, Gregory has suggested, is the perceptual system testing two equally plausible hypotheses as to the nature of the object represented in the drawing.

Gregory (1970) obtained further evidence that the perceptual system generates hypotheses when he examined the perception of **improbable objects.** If you closely examined the *inside* of a hollow mask of a face in good light, you would have no problem correctly perceiving the way in which the nose, chin, and other facial features bulge away from you. But if you limited the depth cues available to your perceptual system by stepping back and closing one eye, you would

perceive the mask as facing you — even though its features continue to protrude *away* from you. Apparently, the perceptual system rejects as too improbable the hypothesis that the object is an inside-out face. In this case, the hypothesis selected for perception is strongly influenced by past experience with faces. Some additional examples of the perception of improbable and **impossible figures** are described in Box 4-6.

Reversible figures and improbable objects are not the only types of stimulus that are misperceived. The perceptual system also comes to the wrong conclusion when presented with *geometric illusions.*

Geometric Illusions

Geometric illusions are geometric patterns that result in inaccurate perception. Two examples

Box 4-6
Improbable and Impossible Figures

When the shape, size, distance, or orientation of an object is made ambiguous by a reduction or conflict of depth cues, past experience may guide the way in which the perceptual system solves the problem. In the real world, the solution is usually correct. But psychologists have devised many geometric patterns and *improbable objects* that trick the perceptual system into false or illusory solutions.

No doubt, you perceive the object represented in the first illustration as a window. You probably presume that it is rectangular (like most of the windows you

have seen in the past) and that the image of the left side is shorter than the image of the right side because you

Axis of rotation
Ames' Trapezoidal Window

are viewing the window from an angle. But this could be a representation of a *trapezoidal* window, which would have a physically shorter side. Ames (1951) made such a trapezoidal window. When it was stationary, his subjects perceived it as a rectangular window seen at a slant. But when it was rotated and viewed with one eye (to reduce depth cues), the subjects saw it as oscillating back and forth, with the shorter side always appearing to be more distant than the longer side. This illusion was not dispelled even when a rod was attached so that it poked through a hole in the

of misperception of the length of a line are presented in Figure 4-30. In the Müller-Lyer illusion, shown in Figure 4-30(a), the line joining the outgoing arrowheads appears to be longer than the line joining the ingoing arrowheads, but the lines are actually of equal length (check for yourself with a ruler). In an illusion discovered by Mario Ponzo, horizontal lines of equal length are perceived as being of different lengths; in the presence of the adjacent angled lines, most people judge the upper horizontal line to be longer than the lower horizontal line.

A different type of illusory effect occurs when the direction or curvature of lines is misperceived. In the Poggendorf illusion, shown in Figure 4-31(a), you probably see the two angled lines as offset, with the lower angled line being displaced downward. However, if you sight along the angled lines with a ruler, you will see

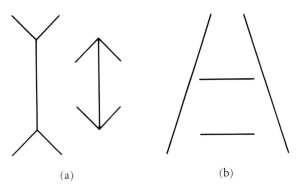

(a)   (b)

FIGURE 4-30

The Illusion of Line Depth These geometric patterns devised by Müller-Lyer (a) and Ponzo (b) create the illusion of differing line length. Most people see the vertical line joining the outgoing arrowheads as longer than the line joining the ingoing arrowheads, and see the upper horizontal line as longer than the lower horizontal line. In reality, these lines are of equal length.

window. The rod was correctly perceived as rotating—and therefore as cutting through the oscillating window!

The second and third illustrations show *impossible objects*. The representation in the second illustration is clearly possible as a two-dimensional drawing but obviously impossible as a three-dimensional object. The representation in the third illustration, however, is an untouched photograph of an object actually constructed by Gregory (1970). The secret of Gregory's *impossible-but-true* object is revealed in Figure 4-38 at the end of this chapter. As with Ames' trapezoidal window, the illusion arises because your perceptual system makes reasonable—but incorrect—judgments about the distance of different parts of the object.

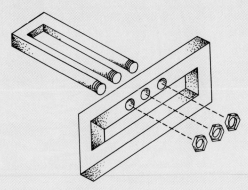

Trident, an Impossible Construction *Source:* North American Aviation's *Skywriter,* February 18, 1966, Braun & Co.

Gregory's *Impossible-but-True* **Object**

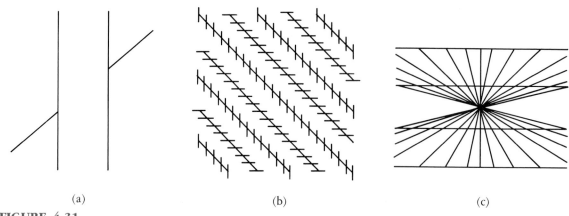

(a)　　　　　　　　　(b)　　　　　　　　　(c)

FIGURE 4-31

Illusions of Line Direction and Curvature Poggendorf's illusion (a) makes it appear that the two angled lines are not aligned. This misperception of alignment continues in Zöllner's diagram (b) where it seems that the alternating diagonal lines are not parallel. Lastly, Hering's drawing (c) creates an illusion that the inner horizontal straight lines are curved..

that they are precisely aligned. You can see an example of the Poggendorf illusion in Figure 4-16, where the sunbeam passes behind a pillar. In the Zöllner illusion, shown in Figure 4-31(b), parallel lines are misperceived; the Hering illusion, shown in Figure 4-31(c), demonstrates that straight lines sometimes appear to be curved. Another compelling misperception is the twisted cord (Cowan, 1973). Although close inspection shows that the twisted cords in Figure 4-32 form circles, it is almost impossible not to perceive them as a spiral pattern.

We have shown only a small sample of the dozens of illusory geometric patterns that have been discovered. For the interested reader, Coren and Girgus (1978) provide a useful review of illusions and of the theories that have been proposed to explain them. Gregory (1968, 1970) has attempted to account for at least some of these illusions as examples of misapplied constancy scaling. Figures 4-33 and 4-34 show how the slanted lines in the Müller-Lyer and Ponzo patterns can be viewed as elementary perspective cues. Gregory has argued that these cues are sufficient to trigger the mechanism that the perceptual system uses to scale retinal images (the operation that normally results in size constancy). Thus, the apparently more distant line is perceptually scaled up (made longer) than the appar-

ently nearer line. Put another way, if the horizontal lines in the Ponzo illusion were located where the two logs appear to be on the path in Figure 4-34, their physical sizes would have to be different for their retinal image sizes to be the same.

FIGURE 4-32

Twisted-Cord Illusion The background pattern in this drawing makes the concentric circles appear to spiral.

An important characteristic of illusions is that simply becoming aware that a misperception is occurring will not enable you to correct the error. The circles in the twisted-cord illusion (Figure 4-32) will continue to look like a spiral even after you have assured yourself that the pattern contains only circles. In such instances, knowledge available to your cognitive system is not sufficient to correct an error in the operation of your perceptual system.

We have discussed how visual input is organized. The resulting pattern is often an object with a specific shape. We now turn our attention to how this perceptual achievement occurs.

Perception of Shape

How do we perceive that objects possess specific shapes? The common-sense explanation is that the perceptual system detects the lines or boundaries that identify the contours of a figure and define its shape. We saw earlier that the visual system contains edge-detector cells. It would seem reasonable, then, to explain shape perception in terms of the stimulation of a set of these cells by the contours that outline the shape. As with many aspects of perception, however, the simple answer is inadequate.

The traditional idea that physical contours determine shape perception has been challenged by the discovery of **subjective contours**—the boundaries of a shape perceived in the absence of physical contours (Kanizsa, 1976). If you examine the pattern in Figure 4-35, you will see a white triangle with its corners resting on three black

FIGURE 4-33
The Müller-Lyer Illusion Pattern Embedded in a Realistic Setting Several pictorial cues indicate that the thick black vertical line to the left of the further man is more distant than the similar line to the left of the closer man. Perceptual scaling makes the more distant line seem longer; in reality, the two lines are the same length. *Source:* Rubertis, Roberto de. (1971). *Progetta percezione.* Officina Edizione.

FIGURE 4-34
Expansion on Ponzo The drawing shows how the two angled lines in the Ponzo illusion suggest that the upper log of the two equal-sized logs is farther away than the lower log—and thus appears longer. *Source:* Rock, I. (1975). *An introduction to perception* (p. 411). New York: Macmillan.

FIGURE 4-35
Subjective Contour The white triangle resting on the black discs is bounded by a subjective contour rather than by a continuous physical contour. *Source:* Kanizsa, G. (1976, April). *Scientific American,* p. 48.

discs. No continuous triangular contour is physically present, but you can clearly perceive the shape of a white triangle.

It is difficult to dismiss subjective contours simply as products of the imagination. Note, for example, that the triangle appears to be opaque and lighter than the white background. It could be argued that the partial contours that are physically present (where the triangle overlaps the discs) activate a sufficient number of edge-detector cells to account for the perception of a complete triangle. But this would not explain instances in which partial physical contours that are straight give rise to curved subjective contours, as in Figure 4-36(a), or cases in which the subjective contour is marked by lines of a totally different orientation, as in Figure 4-36(b).

How, then, can we explain the perception of shape? Irvin Rock (1975, 1984) has suggested that the defining characteristic of a shape is not its physical contours but the *relationship between its parts*. The location of these parts is usually indicated by physical contours but can be defined by other parts of a pattern, as in the case of subjective contours. Emphasizing the relationship between parts of a shape acknowledges that shape perception involves more than simply detecting the elements of a pattern. Consider the example of auditory input that has "shape" in the form of a melody. Even though all of the notes of a melody change when it is transposed to a different key, the relationship between the notes is preserved, leaving its "shape" unchanged.

An obvious characteristic of shape perception is that an object is perceived to keep the same form despite changes in the retinal image that occur when you view the object from different angles. This perceptual achievement is called **shape constancy.** For example, a circular dinner plate seen from an angle gives rise to an elliptical (not a round) retinal image. But we do not perceive our retinal images, so the dominant perception of the dinner plate's shape is that it is round. It might seem that this occurs because you know what the object should look like. However, an unfamiliar object also elicits shape constancy, provided that information about its slant is available. Texture gradient often provides information about slant, although perspective and shadow also may give cues to differences in distance of parts of the object. As with size constancy, the achievement of shape constancy can be represented by an equation:

$$\text{Perceived shape} = \text{Retinal image shape} \times \text{Slant}$$

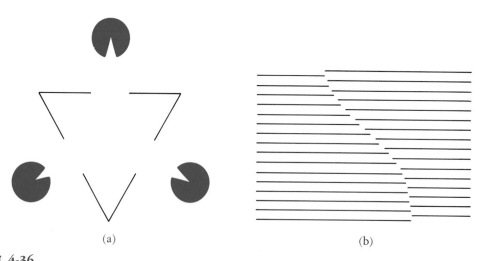

(a)　　　　　　　　(b)

FIGURE 4-36

Mixed Contours (a) A shape bounded by curved subjective contours. (b) A subjective contour created by lines of different orientation. *Source:* Kanizsa, G. (1976, April). *Scientific American*, pp. 49–50.

The fragmented pattern shown in Figure 4-37 provides little shape information, but is a recognizable object. Can you identify it? When you do finally realize that the object represents a knight on horseback, you perceive the pattern quite differently. And if you were to see the same pattern at a later time, recognition would occur more quickly, perhaps even without a noticeable lag.

Because they present such limited information, fragmented figures slow down shape perception, typically a rapid accomplishment. This reveals the otherwise unconscious process of matching the two-dimensional evidence with various hypotheses about the three-dimensional object being represented. Past experience usually leads us quickly to the correct hypothesis. But when the information is fragmentary and past experience is of little help, we may test several hypotheses before selecting one. And when the information is ambiguous, as in the case of reversible figures, the perceptual system continues to test alternative hypotheses.

FIGURE 4-37
Fragmented Picture Can you recognize the object represented in this fragmented picture (see text for identity)?

PERCEPTION OF MOVEMENT

How do you detect the movement of an object in your field of view? The answer, you might think, is that movement is detected when an image moves across the retina. Already we have seen that the retinal image does not provide sufficient information to account directly for perceptions of distance, size, and shape. Is retinal-image information sufficient to directly account for the perception of motion? Some simple observations will show that the answer, once again, is no.

Raise your eyes, and look around you. As you scan the environment, scenes pass in front of your eyes. Your retinal images move, but the world does not. This perceived stability of the environment during eye movement, called **position constancy,** demonstrates that when the perceptual system makes judgments about whether objects in the environment move, it must take into account the movement of the observer (particularly the observer's eye movement).

Now fix your gaze on a moving target in a stationary environment. In this case, the stationary part of the retinal image is perceived to represent a moving object, and the remainder of the image (which is continuously moving across the retina) is perceived to represent a stationary environment.

As in the perception of size and shape, we can state the principle on which the perceptual system operates when detecting movement in the environment as an equation:

Perceived movement =
　　Retinal-image displacement
　　　　　× Eye movement

If changes in retinal-image displacement and eye movement exactly offset each other, then perceived movement is zero and position constancy is maintained. If either factor varies alone (or both factors vary to different extents), then movement is perceived. If neither factor changes (or

BOX 4-7
MOTION AFTEREFFECTS

Have your ever stared at a waterfall and then switched your gaze to the ground surrounding it? If you have, then you have probably experienced the *waterfall illusion,* in which the ground appears to be moving in the opposite direction. Workers at conveyor belts have noticed a similar phenomenon; when the belt is stopped after a lengthy running period, they may see it moving backward. It is generally accepted that such *motion aftereffects* are due to overstimulation of movement-detector cells in the visual system, and thus fall in the same category as the afterimage that results from staring at a brightly lit surface.

A related effect that you probably have not experienced is the *spiral aftereffect.* If you watch a rotating spiral pattern for a minute or so and then stop its movement, you will see the spiral either contract or expand (depending on the direction of the spiral and the direction of its initial rotation). This aftereffect is a peculiar perceptual experience; the stationary spiral is seen to contract or expand and yet to remain the same size.

If you photocopy the spiral shown in the illustration, punch a hole in its center, and place the spiral on a record-player turntable, you can see this motion aftereffect for yourself. Use a slow speed of rotation (16 rpm, if available). Although the motor will not rotate your turntable counterclockwise, you can spin it gently backward (with the motor off) to demonstrate that the direction of the spiral's rotation determines whether the aftereffect is one of contraction or expansion.

You will also find that the spiral aftereffect transfers to other stationary objects, as does the waterfall illusion. Watch the rotating spiral for a minute and then look at a picture of a person's face. You should see the face expand or contract without changing size.

both factors change to the same extent), then no movement is perceived.

In our discussion of movement perception, we have assumed that the observer's head and body remain still. If we consider the more general case of a moving observer, then "eye movement" becomes "eye–head–body movement" in the preceding equation. The principle is unchanged, although the complexity of the perceptual system's task is increased enormously.

Most experimental studies of movement perception have employed simple stimuli (dots and lines) moving across a screen. A different approach has been taken by Johansson and his colleagues (1977, 1985), who argue that to understand the perception of movement in a three-dimensional world, we should study motion in depth rather than movement over a flat surface. For one experiment, Johansson attached lights to the shoulders, elbows, knees, and other joints of a person and filmed the person as he walked in the dark. Johansson then showed the film to subjects who were not told what it represented. All subjects spontaneously identified the pattern of moving lights as representing a person walking. Incredibly, this perception was achieved when they were limited to a glimpse of the film as short as one-fifth of a second (Johansson, von Hofsten, & Jansson, 1980)!

Until now we have considered perceived movement that is caused by the motion of objects in the environment. Next we examine four con-

Spiral Aftereffect

ditions under which movement is perceived though the object perceived to be moving is actually stationary.

Apparent Movement

During the discussion of binocular disparity, you created a double image by looking at a distant object, raising a finger near your line of sight, and alternately winking each eye. Attending to (but not looking at) your finger made its double image apparent. What you may also have noticed is that when you wink alternate eyes very quickly, your finger appears to move from side to side.

This phenomenon, in which the illusion of motion is created when nonmoving stimuli are presented in rapid succession in such a way as to imitate real movement, is variously called **apparent movement, stroboscopic movement,** or the **phi phenomenon.** Apparent movement can be perceived in some neon signs when adjacent bulbs are turned on and off in sequence to create the impression of movement. Motion pictures operate on the same general principle. The film provides a rapid succession of stationary pictures. The images of these pictures are not displaced over the retina continuously, as they are when you observe real movement, yet the impression of motion is just as vivid.

In order to study apparent movement, psychologists have devised an experimental situation to reduce movement to its simplest form. A pair of adjacent lights is turned on and off out of phase, so that only one is illuminated at a time. If the rate of alternation is too slow, then two separate blinking lights are seen. If the rate of alternation is too fast, then two continuously illuminated lights are seen. At intermediate rates, a single light is seen moving back and forth between the two locations.

The Autokinetic Effect

If you fix your gaze on a single, stationary spot of light in an otherwise dark room, the spot will appear to move after a while. This apparent movement of a stationary light, called the **auto-kinetic effect,** is a puzzling phenomenon that resists a convincing explanation. The pattern of movement reported by observers is erratic and unpredictable — just what you would expect if the effect were due to the subjects' inability to keep their eyes still. Although an early study using infrared photography of subjects' eyes found no eye movements occurring when motion of the spot is being reported (Guilford & Dallenbach, 1928), more recent studies suggest that eye movements are associated with the occurrence and direction of autokinetic movement (Matin & MacKinnon, 1964; Pola & Matin, 1977).

It has been suggested that the critical condition responsible for the autokinetic effect may be the absence of a visual frame of reference (Rock, 1984). Even though you keep looking directly at the spot of light, the lack of any other visual reference may lead you to feel that your gaze is beginning to wander. These imagined eye movements would be taken into account by your perceptual system. However, the light would continue to stimulate the same area of the retina and your perceptual system would incorrectly signal the presence of a moving light. Two pieces of evidence support this speculation. First, the size of the autokinetic effect is highly susceptible to suggestion and group pressure (Levy, 1972). Second, a similar type of effect occurs when an observer perceives an object to be moving although, in reality, the object is stationary and its surroundings are moving. This phenomenon is know as *induced movement.*

Induced Movement

We have been describing the perception of movement in terms of a change in the position of an object *relative to the observer.* But an observer typically has another frame of reference (other than himself or herself) against which to judge movement — the normally stationary scene surrounding the object. Sometimes, particularly when the positions of distant objects are not well defined relative to an observer, a change in the position of an object *relative to its surroundings* determines the perception of movement. If an object is seen moving against a stationary background, its motion will generally be perceived correctly. But if a stationary object is seen against a moving background, movement of the surrounding scene may be perceived as movement of the object **(induced movement).**

Two examples should clarify this point. When we see the moon in a gap between swiftly moving clouds, we often perceive the moon as moving and the clouds as stationary. (The moon is always moving, of course, but its change in location in space is too slow ever to be perceived as movement.) The movement we perceive in this case is induced by the moon's change in position relative to the clouds that surround it.

Induced movement can also be transferred to ourselves. You may have had the following experience. While sitting in a car at a traffic light next to a large truck, you look to your side and notice that you are rolling backward. After slamming on the brakes, you discover that you were not moving backward; instead, the truck was moving forward. Because the truck essentially filled your field of view, its movement was interpreted by your perceptual system to be the result of *your* movement.

These examples of induced movement have been classified as *intelligent errors,* because they result from perceptual strategies that work very effectively most of the time (Rock, 1983). When relative movement between an object and its surrounding or background occurs, it is almost always the object alone that is moving. When the whole of your retinal image displaces at a single rate, it is almost always because you are moving (Howard, 1982).

This description of the perception of movement as a *strategy* is disputed by psychologists who believe that physiological mechanisms—specifically, edge-detector cells sensitive to displacement of the retinal image—account for movement perception. Yet it is difficult to see how such a physiological explanation can accommodate evidence that clearly shows that retinal-image displacement is not a necessary or sufficient condition for the perception of movement. However, one type of movement perception—**motion aftereffect**—probably *is* explained by the activity of such cells (Box 4-7, page 190).

An illusion of motion that you can demonstrate for yourself was discovered by Austrian physicist Ernst Mach. Take a white index card, crease it lengthwise, and place it on an empty table so that it is in the shape of a tent. View it from above and at an angle so that you can see both

sides at once. If you look at the card from about three feet *with one eye closed* (to eliminate the depth cue of binocular disparity), the depth orientation of the card should eventually reverse. The crease will then appear to be more distant than the edges of the card, and the card will seem to stand upright on the table. While the card is reversed in depth, move your head from side to side. The card will appear to move with you, even though you know that it is stationary. When the card is seen in correct depth orientation, of course, head movement is taken into account by the perceptual system and you see the card as stationary. But when the card appears to be reversed in depth, the same correction for head movement by the perceptual system leads to the illusory perception of movement.

THE CHARACTER OF PERCEPTION

In discussing the perception of distance, size, shape, and motion, we have characterized perception as a process that responds to activity in the sensory systems and that infers (figures out) what objects or events in the physical world are causing that activity. Such a theory seems necessary because, although sensory evidence is often variable and ambiguous, the perceptual world is typically stable and precise. This view, called the **theory of indirect perception,** has received widespread support among psychologists. However, it is possible to characterize perception quite differently.

Certainly, the notion that you must figure out the appearance of the world contradicts common sense. There is little or no evidence of such a process when you introspect, or examine, your own perceptual activity. Perhaps the need to study perception in the laboratory in order to conduct experiments scientifically has led some psychologists to conclude that perception is indirect. In many studies of perception, motionless subjects view very simple, briefly presented patterns with one eye closed. Little wonder, you may feel, that perception under such circum-

stances is a judgmental or inferential process! Precisely this criticism of perceptual research and theory has been advanced by James J. Gibson (1979). Such research may be relevant to "laboratory perception," Gibson has stated, but tells us little or nothing about the ways in which mobile observers perceive their normal environment. Perception, for Gibson, is normally just what it appears to be—a process that is both direct and immediate. Gibson's **theory of direct perception** cannot be described easily in a few words, but his principal argument, as applied to visual perception, is outlined here.

When light is reflected from surfaces and objects in our environment, it takes on a structure that specifies the characteristics of the visual world. This structure constitutes information that can be picked up by any perceiver who intercepts it. According to Gibson, sufficient information is carried by this reflected light to fully account for the richness of our visual perception of the world. If this is so, then no judgmental or inferential process need be hypothesized. Rather, the perceptual system can be considered to have been shaped by evolution for the *direct*

FIGURE 4-38
Gregory's Impossible Triangle

detection of the information that specifies important properties of the environment. Although recognizing that the retina is physiologically necessary for vision, Gibson has rejected *retinal image* in the belief that this concept has led us to investigate "frozen" slices of the perceptual world and largely to ignore the information picked up in the dynamic act of looking. The retina, Gibson states, is "transparent" to the three-dimensional information that flows through it.

For more than 30 years, until his death in 1981, Gibson (1950, 1966, 1979) swam against the tide of traditional thinking about perception, but recently his views have been receiving increased support (see Michaels and Carello, 1981; Shaw & Bransford, 1977; Turvey, 1977). Although theorists who subscribe to indirect perception are not ready to yield to Gibson (see Ullman, 1980), the cogency with which Gibson argued his position is forcing perception theorists to reexamine their assumptions. In a major review of the field of perception (Haber, 1978), Gibson's views won quite favorable treatment. Although noting the relative lack of empirical evidence for a theory of direct perception, Haber agrees that "one of the most potent, though misguided, metaphors in psychology . . . [is] that the retinal image is like a snapshot" (p. 32).

The theory that perception is accomplished directly is a provocative challenge to the more orthodox view provided in this chapter, and will remain so until psychologists develop rigorous but sensitive methods of studying perception in observers as they move about in their natural environments.

SUMMARY

1. Our sensory systems serve as translators. They detect information about objects and events in the physical world and translate this information into a language that the brain can understand — patterns of nerve impulses. We have four unitary sensory systems (vision, hearing, smell, and taste), each with its own distinctive receptor mechanism (eye, ear, nose, and tongue). Two more complex sensory systems are touch, including the cutaneous (skin-based) senses of pressure, temperature (warmth and cold), and pain, and the body senses, including the vestibular and kinesthetic senses.

2. Visual information about the environment is carried by light waves, which are a form of electromagnetic radiation. Light entering the eye is focused by a lens to form an image on the retina. When light waves strike the cells of the retina, chemical changes generate electrical impulses that are relayed to the cortex of the brain along the optic nerve. Central vision is served principally by cone cells in the retina, which detect light intensity and are also essential for the perception of color. Peripheral vision is largely the result of activity in rod cells, which are sensitive only to light intensity and serve vision in dim illumination.

3. Auditory information is carried by sound waves, which are rhythmic changes in air pressure. When sound waves reach the

outer ear, they cause the eardrum to vibrate. The ossicles in the middle ear transmit these vibrations to the fluid-filled cochlea in the inner ear. Wave motion in the cochlear fluid is detected by hair cells that translate mechanical movement into electrical impulses. The loudness of a sound is determined by the amplitude (the extent of vibration) of the sound wave. The pitch of a sound is determined by the complex coding of sound-wave frequencies (frequency theory) and by the location of maximum wave action in the cochlea (place theory).

4. The receptor cells for the cutaneous senses are buried in the skin. Deformation of these cells is responsible for the sense of pressure; temperature is detected by these cells as warmth or cold.

5. The body senses are the vestibular sense and the kinesthetic sense. The vestibular system is sensitive to the direction of gravity and enables us to maintain balance. The kinesthetic system informs us of the relationship of our body parts to one another.

6. The chemical senses of taste (sweet, bitter, salty, sour) and smell operate by detecting the chemical properties of molecules that are carried in the air or dissolved in saliva, allowing us to savor our environment.

7. The term perception refers to both a process and a product. The product is an individual's perceptual world—an organized, meaningful representation of the environment. Although we are consciously aware of the perceptual world, the process of perception that creates this world is largely hidden from view.

8. Two dimensions of space (up–down and left–right) are directly represented in our retinal images. The layout of objects and surfaces in the third dimension—depth, or distance—is perceived indirectly, on the basis of depth or distance cues. Perspective, texture gradient, interposition, shadow, and familiar size are pictorial cues; each can give rise to the impression of depth in pictures as well as in three-dimensional scenes. Other depth cues result from binocular disparity and retinal-image displacement (motion parallax) and muscular cues (accommodation and convergence).

9. When we approach a distant object, the retinal image it casts grows larger, even though the perceived size of the object does not change. Size constancy (constancy of perceived size) is maintained because the perceptual system takes distance into account when interpreting retinal-image size.

10. The Gestalt psychologists demonstrated several basic principles of form perception that appear to determine the initial organization of elements into a pattern. These principles of perceptual organization include figure–ground separation, proximity, similarity, closure, and continuation. Certain ambiguous patterns (reversible figures) are spontaneously perceived to reverse in depth orientation, thereby demonstrating figure–ground, depth, or object reversal. Such effects may be the results of attempts by the perceptual system to test different hypotheses regarding the nature of the form represented by the pattern.

11. The defining characteristic of a specific shape is not its contour but the relationship between its parts. The perceptual system achieves shape constancy by taking the slant of a surface into account when an object is viewed from different angles.

12. When we move our eyes, the world remains stationary. This phenomenon is known as position constancy. In general, the perceptual system must account for changes in eye, head, and body positions in order to make the correct determination as to whether retinal-image displacement is due to movement in the environment or due to movement of the observer.

13. James J. Gibson has offered a theory of direct perception that fundamentally differs from the theory of indirect perception described in this chapter. Gibson's theory lacks strong supportive evidence but is attracting increasing attention from psychologists.

KEY TERMS

Physical World
Perceptual World
Light
Photon
Light Wave
Intensity
Wavelength
Electromagnetic Radiation
Nanometer
White Light
Hue
Complementary Hue
Saturation
Additive Color Mixture
Subtractive Color Mixture
Sound
Sound Wave
Loudness
Amplitude
Pitch
Frequency
Timbre
Speech Spectogram
Noise
Sensory System
Receptor
Eye
Single-lens Eye
Sclera
Cornea
Iris
Pupil
Refraction
Lens
Accommodation
Retina
Choroid Coat
Rod
Cone
Fovea
Visual Threshold
Dark Adaptation
Photochemical Reaction

Rhodopsin
Bleaching
Optic Nerve
Receptive Field
Lateral Geniculate Nucleus
    (LGN)
Edge Detector
Outer Ear
Auditory Canal
Eardrum
Middle Ear
Ossicle
Inner Ear
Eustachian Tube
Cochlea
Oval Window
Hair Cell
Basilar Membrane
Tectorial Membrane
Frequency Theory
Volley Principle
Place Theory
Interaural Time
Sound Localization
Interaural Intensity
Cutaneous Sensory System
Pacinian Corpuscle
Adaptation
Free Nerve Ending
Gate-control Theory
Endorphin
Naloxone
Vestibular Sense
Kinesthetic Sense
Vestibular Mechanism
Semicircular Canals
Habituation
Chemical Sense
Sweet, Bitter, Salty, and Sour
Taste Bud
Smell Prism
Retinal Image
Distance/Depth Cue

Pictorial Cue
Perspective
Texture Gradient
Interposition
Shadow
Shading
Familiar Size
Binocular Disparity
Stereoscope
Motion Parallax
Stereogram
Expansion Pattern
Convergence
Size Constancy
Afterimage
Moon Illusion
Form Perception
Proximity
Similarity
Closure
Continuation
Figure – Ground Separation
Surroundedness
Figure – Ground Reversal
Reversible Figure
Depth Reversal
Object Reversal
Improbable Object
Impossible Figure
Geometric Illusion
Subjective Contour
Shape Constancy
Position Constancy
Apparent Movement
Stroboscopic Movement
Phi Phenomenon
Autokinetic Effect
Induced Movement
Motion Aftereffect
Indirect Perception Theory
Direct Perception Theory

RECOMMENDED READINGS

Coren, S., C. Porac, & Ward, L. M. (1984). *Sensation and perception* (2nd ed.). New York: Academic Press. An excellent book with relevant illustrations and many demonstrations that challenge and involve the reader.

Gibson, James J. (1979). *The ecological approach to visual perception.* Boston, MA: Houghton Mifflin. This skillfully argued statement of a revolutionary theory is required reading for anyone who is curious about the nature of perception.

Goldstein, E. B. (1984). *Sensation and perception* (2nd ed.). Belmont, CA: Wadsworth. A well-illustrated and up-to-date textbook that conveys a lot of information in a straightforward manner.

Ludel, J. (1978). *Introduction to sensory processes.* San Francisco, CA: W. H. Freeman. By writing in a deliberately conversational tone, but without sacrificing accuracy, Ludel works hard to help the reader understand the structure and function of our sensory systems.

Rock, I. (1983). *The intelligence of perception.* Boston, MA: MIT Press. The best presentation of the taking-into-account approach to perception by one of the field's foremost theorists.

5

LEARNING

S oon after hatching, herring gull chicks peck at a red spot on their parent's bill, inducing the parent to regurgitate food that the chicks then eat. As the chicks grow older their aim improves, but on the whole they continue to peck — first at their parent's bill and later at food — in more or less the same way for the rest of their lives. Compare this eating behavior of herring gull chicks to that of human infants. At birth human infants suck reflexively, exhibiting a built-in behavior similar to the pecking of herring gull chicks. However, the sucking behavior of human infants changes almost immediately. It increases in efficiency until it is replaced by other, even more efficient methods of obtaining nutrition. Within a few months babies are able to grasp food in their hands, put it into their mouths, and chew it. Later they use spoons, and still later, other eating utensils. So the development of eating behavior in herring gulls and humans is quite different. The gulls continue to peck in more or less the same way they did at birth; human eating behavior changes radically with development.

Consider another contrast. As noted in Chapter 2, honey bees engage in "dances" to inform one another of the type and location of nectar fields. They are born with the ability to perform and understand these dances, which are ritualistic in the sense that they always follow rigidly defined forms. Compare the communication system of bees with that of humans. Human infants do not inherit a fixed set of communication skills, but are born with the capacity to learn any of the human languages in the world and to express them through speech, writing, Morse code, semaphore, and signing.

The fundamental way in which human feeding and communication behaviors differ from those of birds and bees is that human behaviors are influenced far more by learning or experience than by inheritance or instinct. This does not mean that heredity plays no role in the behaviors of animals such

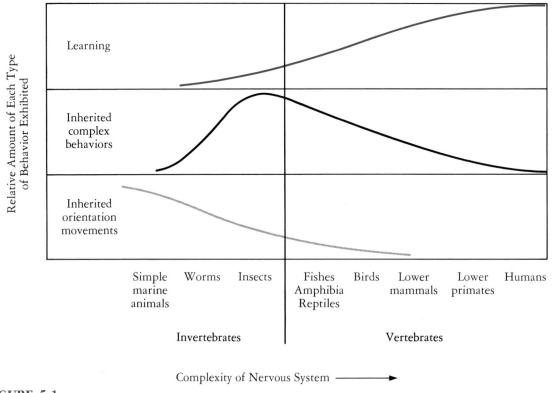

FIGURE 5-1

The Evolutionary Rise of Learning Animals with more complex nervous systems acquire proportionately more of their behavior through learning. More primitive animals exhibit a greater dependence upon inherited behavior patterns. *Source:* Adapted from Dethier, V. G., & Stellar, E. (1970). *Animal behavior* (3rd ed., p. 91). Englewood Cliffs, NJ: Prentice-Hall.

as humans or that learning plays no role in the behaviors of birds or insects. Rather, it means that one of the defining characteristics of mammals is the predominance of learning over instinct as forces that shape behavior (see Figure 5-1). Learning is the means by which such animals cope with the demands of a changing environment. Garcia has expressed this idea well.

> In a broad sense, learning is a form of adaptation of the organism to its environment. . . . Natural selection has tailored the organism to the ecological niche. Behavior provides a fine tuning, and learning is a mechanism by which the organism utilizes experience to modify behavior in this fine tuning process of adaptation to the changes in its particular niche. (Garcia, in Crider, Goethals, Kavanaugh, and Solomon, 1985, p. 180)

WHAT IS LEARNING?

In our everyday lives, we use the word *learning* in a variety of ways to represent a variety of experiences. You might say "I've learned to live with his snoring" or "I've learned to keep my eye on the ball." In these cases, learning refers to increases and decreases in one's responsivity to various stimuli. Or, after burning your hand, you might say to yourself "That will teach me not to touch a hot stove!" In this case, learning refers to the forming of a simple association between an action and a consequence. We also use the word learning to refer to motor skills ("I learned to drive a car") and to the storage of spatial information ("I learned my way around the campus"). In some situations, the term refers to the acquisition of factual knowledge ("I learned that *Methode Champenoise* is the process by which expensive champagne is fermented individually within each bottle"), and to the mastering of logical abilities ("I learned calculus"). Why do we use the same word to refer to such a wide array of experiences? What do these experiences have in common?

We can define **learning** as *a relatively enduring change in behavior potential as a result of experience or practice.* In some cases the change involves a modification of an existing response; in others it involves the acquisition of a new response. In some cases observable physical behavior is changed; in others the change occurs in internal thoughts and feelings. Sometimes the experience is externally imposed; sometimes it has an internal origin. Yet in all cases, when animals or people learn something they gain the capacity to behave differently in some respect from the way they behaved previously. Moreover, this new behavior potential is relatively lasting. Finally, the change in behavior or behavior potential stems from experience rather than innate or hereditary influences.

In our definition of learning, the term *behavior potential* is important because it emphasizes the fact that what is learned may not necessarily result in a change in behavior. Consider a rat that has learned to run through a maze to obtain food. After learning has taken place and if it is hungry, the rat will run the maze quickly and without error. However, if the animal is full, it will probably be more interested in exploring all the corners of the maze, showing no evidence that it has learned to solve the maze. This example indicates that learning is an internal change that may or may not result in an external, overt behavioral change. Whether or not behavior changes depends on other factors, such as whether the animal is motivated to perform. In the absence of such factors, the learning is a *potential* behavioral change. We discuss this topic further in the section on latent learning (p. 236).

An Evolutionary Perspective

We have suggested that as we climb the evolutionary tree, increasingly large segments of behavior are controlled by learning rather than by built-in mechanisms; indeed, the capacity to learn may well be the most essential aspect of human nature. It might seem to follow that it would be of little use to attempt to understand human learning by studying learning in nonhuman animals. Yet the major theories of learning—those of Ivan Pavlov, E. L. Thorndike, and B. F. Skinner—were developed on the basis of research on dogs, cats, and pigeons. This was possible because of the similarity of basic structure and function between humans and these animals.

In Chapter 3, we noted that the human brain contains all of the structures that the brains of other animals contain, and more. Structures responsible for higher thought processes have developed in addition to, rather than in place of, structures responsible for more basic functions. Therefore, it is reasonable to assume that humans and nonhumans possess essentially the same basic capacities to learn, but that humans possess additional higher-order capacities. The primary goal of learning theorists has been to discover the basic processes of learning. It is easier to investigate these processes in nonhuman animals than in humans because the processes are less complex,

there are fewer ethical problems involved, and most importantly, nonhuman animals can be observed under rigorously controlled conditions for virtually any length of time (often an entire life span or even several generations). However, it is important to remember that although the basic processes of learning may be essentially the same in human and nonhuman animals, the human capacity for higher forms of learning may modify the basic processes in significant ways.

In this chapter we limit our discussion to the types of learning that can be demonstrated in simple animals, from such primitive forms of learning as habituation and sensitization to such complex forms as classical and instrumental conditioning. While the evidence often will be from animal studies, the implications for understanding human experience will be emphasized.

PRIMITIVE TYPES OF LEARNING

An unconditioned reflex is an association between an **unconditioned stimulus** and an **unconditioned response.** It is called *unconditioned* because it exists without any prior learning; it is an *association* because when the (unconditioned) stimulus is presented to an animal, the stimulus automatically elicits the (unconditioned) response. The instinctive behaviors in gulls, bees, and fish that we considered earlier consist of sequences of unconditioned reflexes. Humans also possess unconditioned reflexes. The infant's sucking reflex, the knee-jerk reflex, and the startle reflex that occurs in response to a loud noise are examples of unconditioned reflexes in humans.

Given that learning involves a change in behavior as the result of experience, the most basic type of learning involves a change in an unconditioned reflex as the result of experience. The most primitive changes occur either in the *strength* of the unconditioned response or in the *readiness* with which an animal or person emits the response. A decrease in response strength (and/or readiness) to repeated stimulation is known as *habituation;* an increase in response

strength (and/or readiness) to repeated stimulation is known as *sensitization.*

Habituation

Imagine yourself in a noisy classroom. Someone is coughing; someone else is whispering; the heating system is buzzing; your neighbour is tapping her toe, and there is faint aroma of perfume. You are being bombarded with all sorts of irrelevant stimulation. If you were to pay attention to these stimuli, you would soon be unable to concentrate on the task at hand. Fortunately, you usually are able to tune out the irrelevant stimuli (see Figure 5-2). We call this phenomenon **habituation,** which means learning *not* to respond to an irrelevant stimulus. This is the most common type of learning, and has been demonstrated in every animal in which it has been studied, from protozoa to people (see Box 5-1).

Not all unconditioned reflexes are equally subject to habituation, inasmuch as it usually occurs when stimuli are unnecessary for survival. Strong stimuli, such as loud noises and intense bright flashes, elicit defensive reactions

FIGURE 5-2
Habituation to Irrelevant Stimuli Even quite strong auditory, visual, and tactile stimuli may be ignored if they are of no consequence.

that do not habituate. Biologically important re-actions, such as salivation to food and reactions to potentially harmful stimuli, not only fail to habit-uate but grow *more* sensitive with repetitions of the same or similar stimuli.

Sensitization

An example offered by Flaherty (1985) provides a helpful contrast between the processes of habitu-ation and sensitization. Imagine yourself walk-ing your dog on a dark night and on an unfamiliar route through a wooded area. At first you are alert to the noises of nature and turn to listen when the wind rustles the leaves or an animal moves through the grass. Soon, however, as nothing follows from these sounds, your response to them habituates — you begin to ignore them. Then your dog suddenly growls and barks in the direction of one such sound. You immediately

become alert and responsive again, sensitized now to these previously irrelevant stimuli that may be signals of some ominous event. **Sensiti-zation** consists of an increased readiness to re-spond, and thus is the opposite of habituation. Sensitization is very common in the animal king-dom (see Box 5-2) and occurs most frequently after encounters with noxious stimuli.

An important aspect of sensitization is that once an organism has responded to a biologically important stimulus such as a potential danger, it may become more responsive to many *other* stim-uli. Returning to the earlier example of a walk through the woods, immediately following such an experience you would probably "jump" more strongly at the unexpected sight of another person.

Habituation to biologically irrelevant stim-uli and sensitization to biologically important stimuli are important ways of coping with envi-

BOX 5-1
HABITUATION IN FIDDLER CRABS AND PEOPLE

Habituation is the reduction in frequency or strength of response to repeated applications of the same stimulus. This universal phenomenon was demonstrated in a study by Walker (1972) of the reaction of crabs to disruption of their feeding. The repeated stimulus was a standard arm movement made by a nearby human observer. The first disturbance caused 77% of the crabs to retreat to their burrows. By the tenth such disturbance, only 24% of the crabs responded by retreating.

Badia and Defran (1970) studied habituation of the orienting response in humans. The **orienting response** is an attentional reaction to any unexpected change in the environment. In humans the reaction is measured conveniently by the electrodermal response (EDR), a change in the electrical resistance of the

skin. In the experiment, female college students were seated alone in a soundproof room and informed that their physiological responses to a tone–light stimulus would be measured. Fifteen spaced presentations of the stimulus pair were given. All subjects showed a strong EDR to the first presentation, but by the fifteenth trial the EDR had diminished almost to zero. Our ability to habituate to stimuli that are repetitious and uninformative, as demonstrated in this experiment, is highly adaptive. It allows us to conserve our energy for those occasions when we must attend to — and perhaps respond to — unexpected stimuli.

This property of habituation is illustrated well by the way we adapt to city life (Glass & Singer, 1972). The modern urban environment is noisy, crowded, littered, and polluted; it appears the

urban dweller faces an endless round of obstacles, conflicts, and inconveniences. Many believe this is a highly stressful environment that leads to a variety of physiological, behavioral, and emotional problems. Yet people continue to live in cities. Urban dwellers work, raise families, and entertain themselves, seemingly with no more evidence of stress than country dwellers.

Glass and Singer believe that habituation is the key to understanding modern urban life. They feel that the most significant aspect of life in the city is not the stress but rather the city dweller's ability to ignore situations that people normally would find stressful. It is difficult to imagine what life would be like without the powerful protection of habituation.

ronmental changes. An animal is able to conserve energy (through habituation) and to increase its chances of survival (by overreacting defensively through sensitization). It has been suggested (Razran, 1971) that very simple organisms adapt to their environment *only* by means of habituation and sensitization; they are either incapable of or rarely use other forms of learning. Although not all psychologists are convinced of Razran's proposition, most would agree that for the sim-

plest forms of life, habituation and sensitization are the typical ways of adapting to environmental changes.

Although more complex animals are capable of habituation and sensitization, these modes represent only a relatively small portion of what they can learn. The next form of learning we consider, classical conditioning, permits a much greater adaptability than either habituation or sensitization.

BOX 5-2
SENSITIZATION IN SNAILS

Reactions to a repeated harmless stimulus habituate quickly. If the stimulus is clearly harmful, however, the opposite will occur: an increased tendency to respond to any stimulus. Wells and Wells (1971) conducted an experiment with snails that illustrates sensitization. The experiment consisted of three phases. In the first phase, Wells and Wells measured the snails' reaction to two stimuli, each of which was given in ten presentations.

One was a "light-off" stimulus, which consisted of briefly turning off the lamp illuminating the dish where the animals were kept. The other was a "thump" stimulus, which consisted of a brief and weak mechanical shaking of the dish. In all, ten snails responded to the stimuli by giving a total of 35 withdrawal reactions (a quick jerk of the shell over the head and withdrawal of the tentacles). In the second phase, the snails received 40 electric shocks

at one-minute intervals. Finally, the third phase of the experiment repeated the first phase. This time, the ten snails gave a total of 63 responses to the light-off and thump stimuli. There was a large and significant increase in the number of withdrawal responses in the final test compared to the initial test. The results illustrate that the withdrawal response to harmless stimuli was sensitized by experience with the electric shock.

CLASSICAL CONDITIONING

Most people have heard of Ivan Pavlov and many know that he received the Nobel prize (in 1904) for his pioneering work on dogs (see Figure 5-3). They typically assume that Pavlov was rewarded for his discovery of some basic principles of learning; but that assumption is incorrect. The Nobel prize was awarded for his research on the physiology of digestion; only some incidental observations later pursued by a curious Pavlov led him to discover **classical conditioning.**

While conducting experiments on the digestive system of dogs, Pavlov and his associates noted that the dogs would sometimes salivate before they were given food. Pavlov became intrigued by this phenomenon and began to observe the dogs carefully, using the apparatus depicted in Figure 5-4. He noted that an animal who had been fed several times by an experimenter would

salivate "spontaneously" when the experimenter approached. On further observation he discovered that the dogs also would salivate at the sight of food, whether the food was actually delivered or not. Pavlov inferred that the footsteps of the experimenter and the sight of food were *signals* for what was to follow, namely the delivery of food, and that the dogs reacted to these signals as if they were in fact the food. Pavlov used a large variety of devices such as tuning forks, bells, metronomes, buzzers, lights, geometrical figures, and tactile stimulation of the animals' bodies, to stimulate dogs before he gave them food. Each of these stimuli proved sufficient to elicit salivation once it had been paired with the delivery of food (Pavlov, 1927).

Subsequent studies of this phenomenon have shown that there are three basic elements necessary for classical conditioning—an uncon-

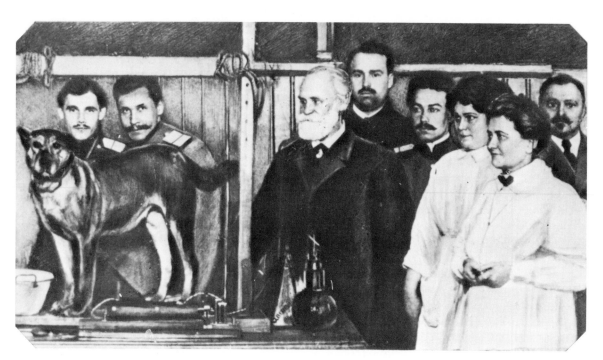

FIGURE 5-3
Ivan Pavlov in His Laboratory

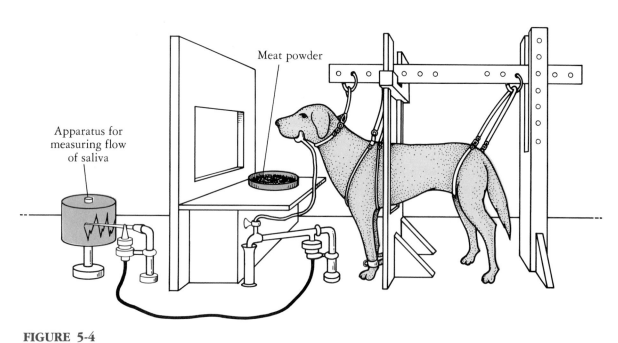

Meat powder

Apparatus for
measuring flow
of saliva

FIGURE 5-4
Pavlov's Conditioning Apparatus Saliva was collected from a tube connected to the dog's salivary gland.
The rate of flow of saliva was recorded on a rotating drum. *Source:* Yerkes, R. M., & Morgulis, S. (1909). The method of
Pavlov in animal psychology. *Psychological Bulletin, 6,* 257–73.

ditioned stimulus, a neutral stimulus, and the pairing of the two. The unconditioned stimulus automatically elicits an unconditioned response. The unconditioned stimulus in Pavlov's early work with dogs usually was food (meat powder). The unconditioned response to food was, of course, salivation. Thus, when Pavlov provided the dog with a plate of meat powder, it salivated automatically. A **neutral stimulus** is simply a stimulus that has no initial tendency to elicit the unconditioned response. The footsteps of the experimenter were neutral with respect to the salivary reflex because, by themselves, they had no power to elicit salivation. The same was true for the ticking of a metronome or the ringing of a bell. No stimulus is neutral in an absolute sense. For example, while the sound of a bell is neutral for the salivary response, it is not neutral for the startle response. When a neutral stimulus, such as a bell, is employed in conditioning, it is called a **conditioned stimulus.** More correctly, the bell is a neutral stimulus *before* conditioning has taken place and becomes a conditioned stimulus *after* conditioning (see Figure 5-5).

The third and defining characteristic of classical conditioning is the *pairing of the conditioned stimulus and the unconditioned stimulus.* Each such pairing is called a "trial." Following several trials, a "new" **conditioned response** is then elicited by the conditioned stimulus. Basically, the conditioned response is similar to the unconditioned one, although often differing from it in some details. Pavlov called the unconditioned stimulus a **reinforcer** because it strengthened the conditioned response to the conditioned stimulus. The procedure of pairing the conditioned and unconditioned stimuli is called **reinforcement.**

Although Pavlov was the first to demonstrate classical conditioning in the controlled environment of a laboratory, many instances of the phenomenon are found in older writings. Bousfield (1955, p. 828) draws attention to the following example that appears in the play "The Chaplain of the Virgin" by seventeenth-century Spanish playwright, Lope de Vega. The speaker is a monk who explains how he outwitted the monastery cats.

> Saint Ildefonso used to scold me and punish me lots of times. He would sit me on the bare floor and make me eat with the cats of the monastery. These cats were such rascals that they took advantage of my penitence. They drove me mad stealing my choicest morsels. It did no good to chase them away. But I found a way of coping with the beasts in order to enjoy my meals when I was being punished. I put them all in a sack, and on a pitch black night took them under an arch. First, I would cough and then immediately whale the daylight out of the cats. They whined and shrieked like an infernal pipe organ. I would pause for a while and repeat the operation—first a cough, and then a thrashing. I finally noticed that without beating them, the beasts moaned and yelped like the very devil whenever I coughed. I then let them loose. Thereafter, whenever I had to eat off the floor, I would cast a look around. If an animal approached my food, all I had to do was cough, and how that cat did scat!

Can you identify the key elements in this classical conditioning procedure? In particular, what were the unconditioned stimulus and response and the conditioned stimulus and response? The cough, of course, was initially a neutral stimulus. When it was paired with a thrashing (the unconditioned stimulus) that made the cats struggle to escape the sack (the unconditioned response), the cough (now the conditioned stimulus) caused the animals to "scat" (the conditioned response).

The Significance of Classical Conditioning

The discovery of classical conditioning in Russia had an enormous impact on the development of American psychology in the early 1900s. As we noted in Chapter 1, the school of behaviorism was then rapidly becoming popular, its adherents welcoming any account of behavior cast solely in terms of observable stimuli and observable responses. Moreover, classical conditioning was not limited to explaining learning in nonhuman animals. It also provided a basis for understanding such complex human conditions as phobias, empathy, and sexual perversions.

In an experiment that has become almost as famous as Pavlov's, Watson and Rayner (1920) demonstrated how Pavlov's research could account for the development of a condition of considerable significance in everyday life. These researchers showed a rat to an eleven-month-old

(a) Classical Conditioning Sequence

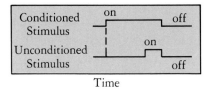

Time

(b) Before Conditioning

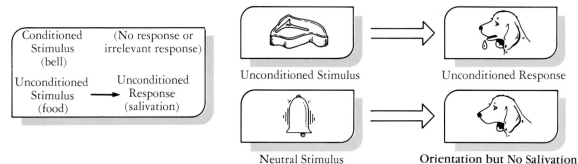

Unconditioned Stimulus

Unconditioned Response

Neutral Stimulus

Orientation but No Salivation

The Unconditioned Stimulus automatically produces the Unconditioned Response; the Neutral Stimulus does not produce salivation.

(c) During Conditioning

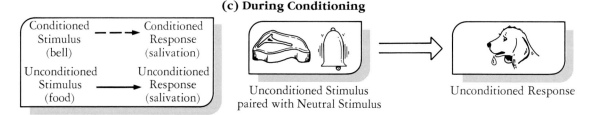

Unconditioned Stimulus paired with Neutral Stimulus

Unconditioned Response

The Unconditioned Stimulus is paired with the Neutral Stimulus; the Unconditioned Stimulus produces the Unconditioned Response.

(d) After Conditioning

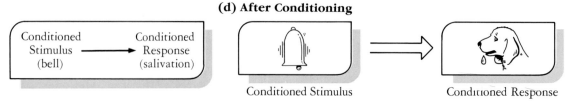

Conditioned Stimulus

Conditioned Response

The Neutral Stimulus is now the Conditioned Stimulus; it produces a Conditioned Response, salivation, which is similar to the Unconditioned Response produced by the meat.

FIGURE 5-5

Phases of Classical Conditioning   (a) The normal timing of presentation for conditioned stimulus and unconditioned stimulus.   (b) Before conditioning, the alarm is a neutral stimulus, whereas the sight of food leads to salivation.   (c) During conditioning, the neutral and conditioned stimuli are paired.   (d) After conditioning, the once-neutral stimulus now elicits the conditioned response of salivation.   *Source:* Papalia, D. E., & Olds, S. W. (1985). *Psychology* (p. 162).   New York: McGraw-Hill (picture-arrow-picture sequences only).

infant named Albert. Albert was a rather placid infant who showed no fear of the rat at all and, in fact, was mildly curious about it. However, Watson and Rayner took care of that; they paired the following presentation of the rat with a loud noise. The result was that Albert developed a fear of the rat. At first he whimpered and withdrew when it was presented; then he cried. Ultimately he cried even when the experimenters presented objects that in some way resembled the rat—a rabbit, a dog, a piece of fur, and a hairy Santa Claus mask (Figure 5-6 is a frame from a film made of the two investigators testing Albert's responses, in this case to the mask).

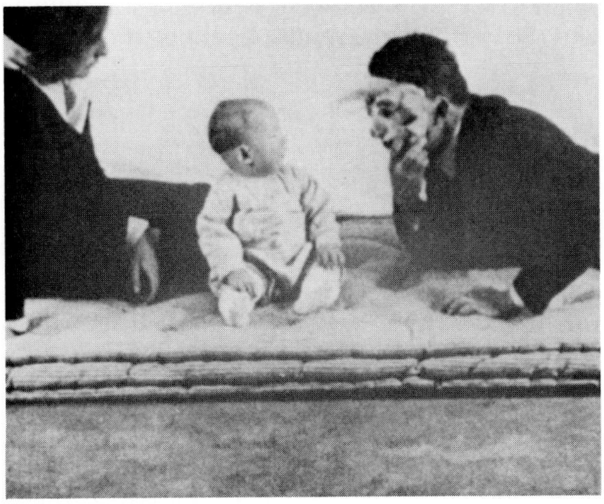

How the principles of classical conditioning explain Albert's behavior is shown in Figure 5-7. Pairing the sight of the rat (originally a neutral stimulus) with a loud noise (unconditioned stimulus) that made Albert afraid (unconditioned response) led the rat (now the conditioned stimulus) also to elicit fear (the conditioned response). Furthermore, the sight of objects that had many of the characteristics of a rat also elicited the conditioned response. You would be justified in criticizing Watson and Rayner's experiment on ethical grounds; certainly no psychologist would perform it today. Nevertheless, it does provide a dramatic demonstration of how people can develop phobias through the generalization of a classically conditioned response.

Classical Conditioning and Fear of Snakes

Pavlov did more than discover classical conditioning; he also discovered many of the conditions that affect it. Let us consider some of these conditions by examining the learning process that underlies the fear of snakes. The personal experience of a colleague and his son and daughter is instructive.

I was walking in the woods with my two children when we suddenly encountered a rattlesnake. I jumped back and yelled, scaring my children. From that moment on, they feared snakes. Pavlov would have no difficulty accounting for the development of this fear. The snake was the conditioned stimulus. My display of fear, especially

FIGURE 5-6
Watson, Rayner, and Albert Baby Albert shows signs of distress when shown a Santa Claus mask because it has hair like the rat that he learned to fear through conditioning. *Source:* Courtesy of Professor Benjamin Harris. From Watson's 1919 film.

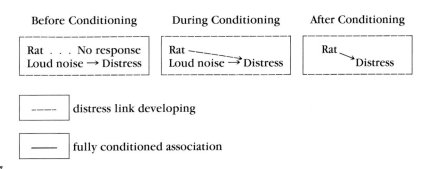

FIGURE 5-7
The Conditioning of a Fear Response By being paired with a loud noise that startled Albert, the sight of the rat became a conditioned stimulus that produced a fear response in him. Thereafter, Albert showed fear of rats or anything that shared their obvious characteristics.

yelling, was the unconditioned stimulus that elicited an unconditioned fear response in my children. Conditioning took place because the conditioned and unconditioned stimuli were paired.

Using this example, let us ask four basic questions regarding the laws of classical conditioning.

1. Our colleague saw the snake first, then yelled. What would have happened if he had screamed first (unlikely as this may seem), and then a few seconds later a snake had appeared? That is, what would have happened if the unconditioned stimulus occurred before the conditioned one?

2. Can a fear of snakes be unlearned? That is, can we extinguish a conditioned response?

3. If a person has learned to fear a particular snake, will he or she generalize this fear to other snakes?

4. If generalization does occur, could he or she learn to respond differently to different snakes—for example, to fear harmful snakes but not harmless ones?

In the following sections we describe some of the research that has provided a basis for answering such questions as these. We simplify our account by using the following abbreviations:

US — Unconditioned Stimulus
UR — Unconditioned Response
CS — Conditioned Stimulus
CR — Conditioned Response

Timing in Classical Conditioning

The timing of the CS and US presentation is an important factor in determining the effectiveness of conditioning. Four time relations have been extensively studied by psychologists: **delayed, trace, simultaneous,** and **backward conditioning.**

The CS occurs first in the delayed mode and, while it takes place, the US is presented. In the trace mode, the CS is presented and is terminated, and then the US is presented. In the simultaneous mode, both the CS and the US are presented and terminated together. Finally, in the backward conditioning mode, the US is presented and terminated before the CS is presented. These four patterns are shown schematically in Figure 5-8. Can you identify the type of conditioning that occurred in the encounter with the snake? Since the snake (CS) appeared first and was still in sight when the display of fear (US) occurred, it was an example of the delayed mode. The delayed mode is the most effective, followed by the trace and simultaneous modes. Practically no conditioning occurs in the backward mode. For many stimuli, the optimal interval between the onset of the CS and the onset of the US has been shown to be about a half second. Recent research, however, has shown that the optimal interval varies depending on such factors as the species of animal and the particular response being conditioned.

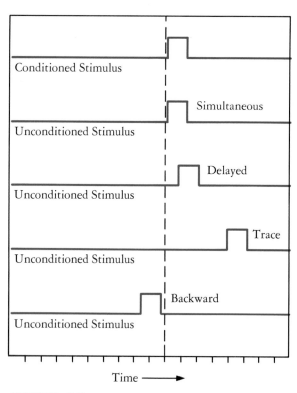

FIGURE 5-8

Four Types of Classical Conditioning The US is presented in different temporal relationship to the CS: simultaneous, delayed, trace, and backward conditioning. *Source:* Adapted from Hulse, S. H., Egeth, H., & Deese, J. (1980). *Psychology of learning.* New York: McGraw-Hill.

Extinction

What do you think Pavlov's dogs would have done if, after conditioning had taken place, he repeatedly presented the CS without the US; that is, buzzer but no food? The answer, as Pavlov found, is that the dogs eventually stop salivating. The UR grows weaker with repeated presentations of the buzzer unaccompanied by food and finally disappears, an operation we call **extinction.** Figure 5-9(b) shows that with increased presentations of the CS without the US, the strength of the CR decreases—until finally the CR is extinguished fully.

Returning to our snake example, if you wanted to eliminate fear of snakes in a child, you might show the snake to a child repeatedly, making sure that nothing occurred to reinforce the fear response. Although a child might feel fear at first, the fear would diminish with repeated encounters and then extinguish altogether. In es-

sence, this is how some behavioral psychologists cure phobias. Of course, it may be difficult to get a child who is afraid of snakes to observe one closely enough to verify that it is, in fact, harmless. Without such verification, however, the child's fear would not extinguish. Thus, many fear responses don't ever have a chance to extinguish—a phenomenon that may help explain how neurotic behavior is maintained (see Chapter 14).

Spontaneous Recovery

Suppose you extinguished a child's fear of snakes in one session. Can you assume you have eliminated the conditioned fear response permanently? What would happen if, a month after extinction had taken place, the child encountered a harmless snake in the garden? The answer is that the child would probably have a weak fear response. **Spontaneous recovery** is the name

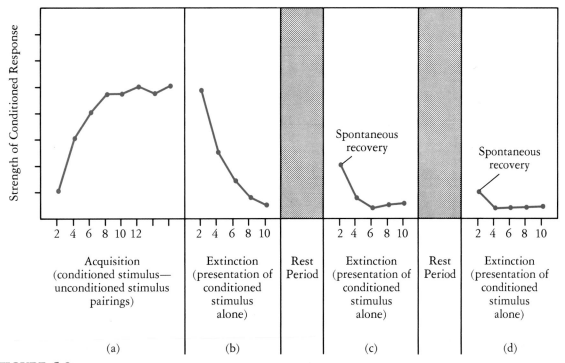

FIGURE 5-9

Acquisition, Extinction, and Spontaneous Recovery in Classical Conditioning (a) During the acquisition phase (CS–US pairing), strength of the CR increases. (b) During extinction (CS alone), strength of the CR decreases. (c, d) After a rest period (no CS or US), some spontaneous recovery of CR strength is shown. *Source:* After Crider, A. B., Goethals, G. R., Kavanaugh, R. D., & Solomon, P. R. (1986). *Psychology* (2nd ed., p. 188). Glenview, IL: Scott, Foresman.

given to the increase in strength of a conditioned response after a rest following extinction [see Figure 5-9(c)]. The point indicated by the arrow in (c) shows that the CR is stronger than it was at the end of the previous extinction phase. If you extinguish the spontaneously recovered response again (by presenting the CS alone), it will still be followed by some spontaneous recovery, though less than before [see Figure 5-9(d)]. The weaker response can then be reextinguished by the same process, and so on. After several such extinctions there will be practically no spontaneous recovery. Thus, to eliminate fear of snakes in a child permanently, you must give several series of extinction trials separated by periods of rest.

Generalization

The tendency of an organism to respond in the same way to stimuli similar to the original conditioned stimulus is called **stimulus generalization.** Baby Albert, Watson and Rayner's subject, demonstrated this phenomenon when he cried at the sight of a rabbit and a piece of fur. Dogs conditioned to salivate to a high-pitched tone will also salivate to tones of a slightly lower or higher pitch. The nearer the tone is in pitch to the original tone, the greater is the similarity in strength of the salivary response. (A typical stimulus generalization curve is presented in Figure 5-10.) Consequently, the degree of generalization (the

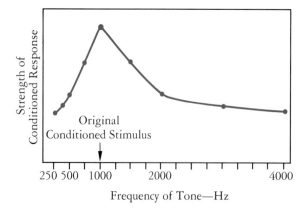

FIGURE 5-10

Stimulus Generalization The strongest CR is elicited by the CS itself, with increasingly weak CRs being elicited by stimuli that are increasingly different from the CS. In this case, the stimuli are tones of differing frequency.

strength of a CR to a test stimulus different from the original CS) is a direct function of the degree of similarity between the CS and the test stimulus. In the rattlesnake example, we would expect the fear response to be strongest to snakes that resemble rattlesnakes. Weaker responses would occur to different looking snakes and perhaps even to snake-like creatures, such as large worms.

In the examples we have considered previously, the basis of similarity is physical—similarity in sound and in the appearance of objects. Stimulus generalization in nonhuman animals occurs almost exclusively along physical dimensions. Humans, however, also respond to numerous other similarities. Imagine that you conditioned a person to respond to the visually presented word *surf* and wanted to test for stimulus generalization. You might use the word *serf,* which is similar in sound and written appearance but not in meaning. Or you might use the word *wave,* which is similar in meaning but not in sound or written appearance. Would *wave* elicit stimulus generalization? Research has shown that visual presentation of wave would elicit a stronger response than *serf.* Generalization of words based on similarity in meaning is called **semantic generalization,** and it appears to occur in all languages. Razran (1971) reports experiments showing that there is stronger generalization between the Russian words *doktor* and *vrach* (physician) than between *doctor* and *diktor* (announcer) or between *skripka* (violin) and *arfa* (harp) than between *skripka* and *skrepka* (paper clip). These examples illustrate not only semantic generalization, they also indicate the influence of higher cognitive processes in human learning.

Discrimination

Generalization occurs when an organism responds in similar ways to similar stimuli. **Discrimination** occurs when an organism responds in different ways to similar stimuli. The children in the rattlesnake story have a friend called Mark who has absolutely no fear of snakes (or, it sometimes seems, of anything else). Mark's favorite pastime is to go into the woods to hunt snakes. Quite often he is successful and returns with a "pet" garter snake wrapped around his arm.

Shortly after the rattlesnake incident, the children were quite wary of Mark. They would not approach him when he was holding a garter snake —a typical case of generalization. However, by the end of the summer they had learned to play with Mark's snakes and, in fact, were helping him hunt them. Although they were still afraid of rattlesnakes, they had extinguished their fear of garter snakes. They had learned to discriminate. Discrimination is brought about by systematic reinforcement of one stimulus, called the CS+, and nonreinforcement of another stimulus, called the CS−. Typical results of a conditioning study of discrimination are shown in Figure 5-11.

Theoretical Perspectives on Classical Conditioning

Having described the main characteristics of classical conditioning, we should consider the nature of the underlying change that occurs when an organism learns a conditioned response. An early theoretical view on this question, stemming largely from the work of Pavlov, was based on the idea of **stimulus substitution.** Current theoretical notions, however, appeal to the idea of **expectancy.**

According to the stimulus substitution theory, a bond or association between the CS and the US develops during the conditioning trials such that the CS becomes a substitute for the US. This substitution is assumed to develop automatically as a consequence of CS–US contiguity (closeness in time). After conditioning has taken place, the bond between the CS and the US is considered so strong that presentation of the CS is essentially equivalent to presentation of the US. At that point, the CS can act as a substitute for the US in eliciting the conditioned response.

In contrast, the expectancy view stresses that a conditioned organism has learned a thought, cognition, or idea—usually called an expectancy—that enables it to "know" that the CS precedes the US (Rescorla and Wagner, 1972).

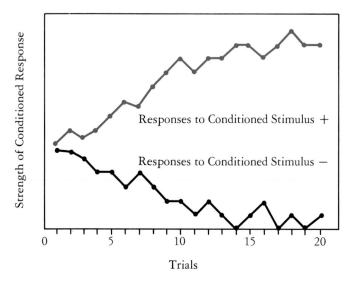

FIGURE 5-11

Stimulus Discrimination   Initially, the CR is of equal strength to the CS whether it is a tone of 1000 Hz or 2000 Hz.   When one tone is reinforced but the other is not, the strength of the CR to the former (CS+) increases while the CR to the latter (CS−) decreases.

How might we choose between these two views?   One of the implications of the substitution view is that the CR should be identical with the UR because the CS merely acts as a substitute for the US.   In contrast, the expectancy view considers the CR to be a response that prepares the animal for the reception of the US.   Therefore, depending on the circumstances, the CR may or may not be identical with the UR.   In Pavlov's experiment, only a salivary response was measured; so the CR was very similar to the UR.   On the other hand, imagine a free-ranging animal — for example, a pet dog about to be fed.   At feeding time, the food preparation activity (taking a can, opening it, and so forth) is a CS for food-in-the-mouth (the US).   If the substitution view were correct, the dog should behave the same way during eating as it does during food preparation — that is, it should sit still and salivate copiously.   But, of course, this is not the case.   Although dogs do indeed salivate during food preparation, they may also whine, wag their tails, jump up and down, rush to the place where the food is going to be served, and so on.   In short, their learned behavior (the CR) is not identical with their unlearned behavior (the UR).

The substitution view cannot account for the differences between the CR and the UR, but the expectancy view can.   The idea that one learns expectancies in classical conditioning was strongly advocated many years ago by the learning theorist Charles Tolman (Tolman, 1948).   Only recently, however, has this view become more generally accepted (Grossberg, 1982; Mackintosh, 1975; Pearce & Hall, 1980).   It should be emphasized that the expectancy is not necessarily conscious.   This is clear when you consider that classical conditioning occurs in very primitive animals, and is confirmed by such experiments as those of Weinberger, Gold, and Sternberg (1984).   These experimenters paired a soft sound (CS) with electric shock (US) in a successful attempt to condition a fear response in anesthetized rats.   Even humans, who are clearly capable of forming conscious expectancies, need not be aware of the relationship between the CS and CR for conditioning to occur.

Classical Conditioning in Humans

Classical conditioning seems to be a universal type of learning in animals; Farley and his colleagues (1983) have even demonstrated this form of learning in a single photoreceptor cell!   The principles of classical conditioning can also account for certain instances of learning in humans, as the rattlesnake example reflects. Other human behaviors that have been interpreted in terms of classical conditioning include the treatment of bed-wetting, anticipatory nausea in cancer patients, and the development of tolerance toward drugs.

Nocturnal enuresis, or bed-wetting, is a frequent problem of children who fail to respond to normal toilet-training procedures. Mowrer and Mowrer (1938) developed a treatment for this problem based on conditioning principles. A moisture-detection device is placed beneath the bed sheet and rigged to sound a buzzer when activated by urine. Before going to bed, the child is instructed to wake and turn off the buzzer when it is activated, go to the toilet and urinate, and then to go back to sleep.

The buzzer is a US that elicits two unconditioned responses in the child. First, the child is awakened. Second, the muscles that prevent further urination are tightened (bed wetters typically have no problem containing themselves when awake). The treatment is intended to pair one or both URs to the bodily sensations that accompany a full bladder. Repeated pairing of the buzzer with these sensations make the latter a CS that eventually, by itself, elicits the CR of waking and/or muscle control. Several nights of this treatment cure the problem of nocturnal enuresis in about 75% of cases (Doleys et al., 1977).

A similar principle may underlie a quite different experience, one that often distresses people undergoing chemotherapy. Chemotherapeutic treatment for cancer typically causes the patient to feel nauseous. This side effect is regarded by most patients as an undesirable but unavoidable cost of the treatment. Borysenko (1982) has suggested that for many people the nausea may be worsened by the effects of classical conditioning. A stimulus that is regularly paired with the treatment (which is the US), such as entering the hospital or receiving a telephone call confirming the appointment, can become a CS that triggers the onset of nausea (CR) well before the chemotherapeutic session has begun.

For our final example of the role of classical conditioning in human behavior, we turn to the work of Siegel and his colleagues, who have presented considerable evidence that this form of learning is responsible for the development of tolerance toward such drugs as morphine and heroin (Siegel, 1975) and may be responsible for some deaths due to heroin overdose (Siegel, Hinson, Krank, & McCully, 1982). Injection of an opiate such as heroin stimulates the body to produce antiopiates, a natural reaction aimed at protection of the body against the foreign substance (Snyder, 1984). With subsequent injections, the body produces increasingly large amounts of antiopiates. Consequently, more heroin is required for the same psychopharmacological effect; in other words, the user develops a tolerance to the drug.

Paired with the response to heroin (UR) are a range of environmental stimuli (CS), such as the room where the injection takes place, friends who are present, and so on. After many such pairings, merely the presence of the CS tends to elicit the CR of antiopiate production. Without a heroin injection, Siegel reports that the CS may actually lead to the experience of withdrawal symptoms. More seriously, when the injection occurs in a new environment that lacks the normal CS, the body's failure to produce the normal level of antiopiates may cause what had previously been a standard dose of heroin suddenly to become a fatal overdose. While evidence for involvement of classical conditioning in the development of tolerance to drugs is well accepted, Siegel's extension of his work to provide a broader theory of drug addiction has its critics (Alexander & Hadaway, 1982).

INSTRUMENTAL CONDITIONING

Most of the responses that have been classically conditioned—such as salivation, fear, sexual arousal, and pupil dilation—are involuntary and closely associated with functions controlled by the autonomic nervous system. Yet animals also can learn voluntary, nonreflexive responses. A dog learns to bark in order to get a biscuit. A cat learns to push against a small door in order to get outside. How did the dog and cat learn that making these responses would trigger these particular outcomes? How do children learn that crying brings attention? The first step toward an answer is to note that when the dog learned to bark, the cat to push against the door, and the child to cry, they were solving a problem.

During the time that Pavlov was studying salivary conditioning in dogs, E. L. Thorndike (1898, 1911) was studying problem-solving in cats. Thorndike constructed a box, similar to the one in Figure 5-12, that had a door operated by a latch that could be opened from the inside. He placed a cat inside the box and put some of its favorite food outside. Thorndike found that almost all cats that were put in the puzzle box learned to operate the latch and reach the food outside. More importantly, he found that it took less and less time for cats to escape each time they were put back in the box (see graph in Figure 5-12). The processes involved in learning to escape from a puzzle box demonstrate principles of learning that apply equally well to other situations that involve solving a problem, such as learning a maze (Figure 5-13).

The type of learning involved in solving a puzzle box or a maze is quite different than classical conditioning. Let us examine this process, called **instrumental conditioning,** in greater detail. The behavior of the cat in the puzzle box can be diagrammed as shown in Figure 5-14, where R_1, R_2, R_3 . . . R_n are different responses or actions of the animal. R_1 might be meowing, R_2 raising the right paw, R_3 turning to the left, and so on. The response that solves the problem and leads to the food, raising the latch on the door, is labelled R^*.

In instrumental conditioning, one of the animal's many spontaneous, voluntary behaviors is selected for reinforcement. When the chosen behavior occurs, the animal is immediately rewarded. The effect of reinforcement is to increase the likelihood that the animal will emit the chosen response. This is one form of the **Law of Effect,** which generally states that the consequences of a given behavior will alter the likelihood that the behavior will be repeated. This type of learning is called instrumental because the response emitted is instrumental in obtaining the reinforcement. The frequency, or strength, of almost any voluntary behavior can be changed by using the procedures of instrumental conditioning. The principal differences between classical and instrumental conditioning are listed in Table 5-1 (page 218).

One criterion used to measure the strength of learning that takes place in instrumental conditioning is the speed with which an animal makes the instrumental response. Another way to measure learning in such situations is to record the

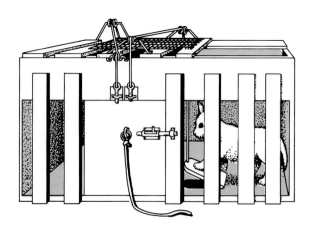
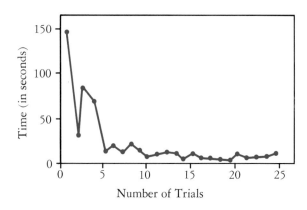

FIGURE 5-12

Thorndike's Puzzle Box for Cats Hungry cats placed inside the box had to learn to press the lever that released the latch in order to reach the food placed outside. The graph shows that the time taken to solve the puzzle decreased rapidly with practice. *Source:* After Thorndike, E. L. (1898). Animal intelligence: An experimental study of the associative processes in animals. *Psychological Review Monograph, 2*(8).

frequency of instrumental responses the animal emits in a given period of time. When instrumental conditioning is assessed in terms of change in the *frequency* or *rate of responding,* we call this type of learning **operant conditioning.** This method of measuring learning is so common that the terms *operant* and *instrumental conditioning* are now used interchangeably by many psychologists. Harvard psychologist B. F. Skinner has made operant conditioning the chief focus of his career.

Operant Conditioning

Experiments in operant conditioning are carried out generally in an operant chamber named after Skinner and known as a **Skinner box** (Figure 5-15). The Skinner box is similar to the puzzle box in that the animal is in control of its own behavior in both cases and voluntary responses are instrumental to attaining the goal. Unlike the puzzle box, however, an animal in a Skinner box is *not* constrained in the number of reinforceable

responses it can emit. For example, in an instrumental situation a cat that has escaped from the puzzle box can make the same response (escape) only if it is put back in the box by the experimenter; in an operant situation a rat can press a lever to obtain food any number of times.

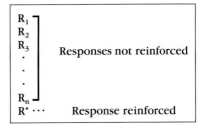

FIGURE 5-14
Instrumental Conditioning The animal spontaneously emits a variety of responses (R_1, R_2, R_3, . . . R_n). Reinforcing one of those responses (R^*) leads to an increase in the frequency with which that response is emitted.

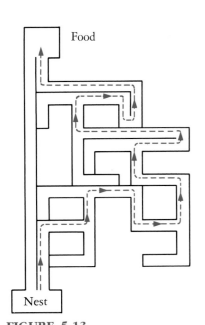

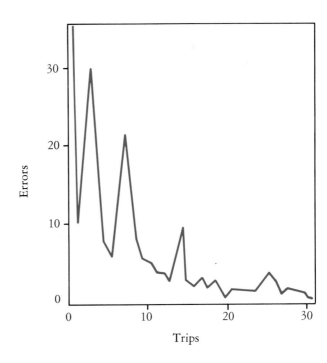

FIGURE 5-13
Maze Learning in Ants The ants must negotiate a maze of alleys in order to travel from their nest to the food. The graph shows the reduction in time taken to travel the maze with practice. *Source:* After Mayer, N. R. F., & Schneirla, T. C. (1965). *Principles of animal psychology* (p. 160). New York: Dover.

TABLE 5-1

Differences between Classical and Instrumental Conditioning

Type of Comparison	Classical Conditioning	Instrumental Conditioning
1. *Response-reward sequence*	1. *US precedes response*	1. *Response precedes reward*
2. *Role of stimuli*	2. *Specific stimulus produces the response*	2. *No specific stimulus produces a response*
3. *Character of response*	3. *Response is elicited*	3. *Response is emitted*
4. *Observed changes*	4. *Change in effectiveness of formerly neutral stimulus on magnitude of response*	4. *Change in speed, force, or frequency of response*
5. *Involvement of nervous system*	5. *Usually involves autonomic nervous system*	5. *Usually involves somatic nervous system*
6. *What is learned*	6. *Emotions such as fears, attitudes, feelings*	6. *Instrumental (goal seeking) behavior*

Source: Adapted from Ellis, H. C. (1978). *Fundamentals of human learning, memory and cognition* (2nd ed., p. 19). Dubuque, IA: Wm. C. Brown.

FIGURE 5-15

Operant Conditioning Apparatus   Skinner boxes for rat and pigeon provide a controlled environment for studying the influence of various schedules of reinforcement on a simple operant response — bar-pressing for the rat and pecking the screen for the pigeon. *Source:* B. F. Skinner.

The operant conditioning of a bar-pressing response in a hungry rat is carried out as follows. The animal is placed in the Skinner box and it typically paws around, sniffs the corners, scratches itself, goes to sleep, then resumes activity. Eventually, by chance, it moves near the food dispenser, at which point the experimenter arranges for a pellet of food to be delivered. That experience keeps the animal near the dispenser and thus close to the nearby bar. When the rat accidentally touches the bar, another pellet of food is delivered. After a few more food reinforcements, each to a response that more closely approximates a bar-press, the rat quickly learns to press the bar, and soon does so at a high and steady rate. As with the puzzle box, we can point to reinforcement — delivery of food after each bar press — as the critical factor responsible for the increase in frequency of responding.

Trainers apply the principles of operant conditioning when they teach elephants, lions, seals, monkeys, and other animals to perform their marvelous "tricks." Specifically, they use a technique called **shaping,** which involves reinforcing successive approximations of the desired behavior. If, following Skinner's (1951) suggestions, you desired to teach your dog to press the doorbell with its nose when it wanted to come in, you would shape your dog's behavior in the following fashion. First, you would make your dog hungry so that food is reinforcing for it. Then you would reinforce the dog with a piece of food for simply staying near the door. After your dog does so reliably, a next step would be to reinforce it only when it faces the door. Later you would reinforce your dog for approaching the bell, and after that for keeping its head at the proper height, until its nose was in front of the button. By now the dog would be spending much of its time with its nose close to the button, and because your dog was active it would eventually push the button.

Source: Animal Behavior Enterprises.

Since that is the desired behavior, you would reward it immediately. Soon your dog would be ringing the doorbell whenever it wanted to come in. Other reinforcers, such as verbal approval, also can be used.

Shaping is a powerful technique that can be used to teach animals a wide variety of behaviors. Pigeons have been trained to play table tennis, dogs to waltz, tigers to jump rope, and dolphins to retrieve devices from the seabed. Shaping also is applicable to human behavior. Swimming instructors use shaping to teach very young children how to swim (although many instructors may not be aware that they are using this technique). Learning to read involves shaping successive approximations to the final target behavior. Procedures based on shaping can be used to toilet train young children with relative ease.

In operant conditioning, as in classical conditioning, timing is a crucial factor in learning and maintaining a desired behavior. When an animal emits the behavior desired by the experimenter, the behavior must be reinforced immediately for learning to take place. However, once the animal is pressing the bar, this may not be the best way to *maintain* the behavior. Would it be better to continue to reinforce every response or would it be better to reinforce only some of the responses? This is the question Skinner studied most intensively in his early work. His findings, refined by extensive subsequent research, reveal marked differences in learning due to variations in the pattern of reinforcement.

Schedules of Reinforcement

The question Skinner addressed is how different schedules of reinforcement affect the rate of responding in an operant situation. In a **continuous reinforcement schedule,** the response is reinforced every time it is emitted. In a **partial reinforcement schedule,** only some of the responses are reinforced. Let us examine the different patterns that can be used when partial reinforcement is applied.

Two basic principles may be used to regulate a partial schedule of reinforcement: the animal can be reinforced for responding after a particular period of time, which is called an **interval schedule,** or it can be reinforced after it has made a particular number of responses, which is called a **ratio schedule.** (Ratio refers to the relationship between the number of responses an animal emits and the number of reinforcements given — for example, 2:1, 10:1, 100:1).

Once a choice is made between the interval and ratio schedules, the experimenter must decide whether to be precise or imprecise. For example, the experimenter might reinforce the animal after every tenth response or for the first response it emits after every ten seconds. These are called **fixed schedules** of reinforcement. Alternatively, the experimenter might reinforce the animal *on the average* after every tenth response or after the first response after an average of ten seconds. Skinner called these **variable schedules** of reinforcement.

These principles can be combined to produce four schedules of reinforcement: *fixed interval, fixed ratio, variable interval,* and *variable ratio.* These four schedules of partial reinforcement are summarized in Table 5-2.

What difference does it make which schedule of reinforcement is used? Typical patterns of responding produced by the four schedules of partial reinforcement are shown in Figure 5-16. These tracings are from a **cumulative recorder** attached to a Skinner box. The recorder has a rotating drum from which a strip of paper is slowly unwound and passed beneath a pen. Each time the rat presses the bar or the pigeon pecks the screen, the pen moves a short distance vertically; each time the bar-press is reinforced, the pen "blips" (producing the short vertical lines shown in the tracing). Because the paper is always moving from left to right, faster responding produces a steeper tracing. By this means a permanent record is created of the cumulative number of bar-presses made by the rat.

Animals reinforced on a fixed interval schedule learn that making a response during an interval does not produce the desired result. They delay responding until toward the end of an interval (just before reinforcement may be obtained) and then respond rapidly. This produces a characteristic scalloping in the cumulative response record. In the variable interval schedule, the animal cannot predict when reinforcement will occur; consequently, it responds at a fairly steady rate in order to receive reinforcement whenever it is available.

When a ratio schedule is used, whether fixed or variable, there is a direct relationship between rate of responding and rate of reinforcement. Because reinforcement is dependent on the number of responses, the subject receives more reinforcement for responding more frequently. Therefore, ratio schedules produce more rapid responding than interval schedules (see Figure 5-16).

TABLE 5-2
Schedules of Partial Reinforcement

	Fixed Schedules	**Variable Schedules**
Interval Schedules	*Fixed Interval* Reinforcement of first response emitted after a fixed interval following last reinforced response (for example, monthly paycheck)	*Variable Interval* Reinforcement of first response emitted after a variable interval following last reinforced response (for example, surprise college quizzes)
Ratio Schedules	*Fixed Ratio* Reinforcement given after a fixed number of responses following last reinforced response (for example, earnings based on piecework)	*Variable Ratio* Reinforcement given after a variable number of responses following last reinforced response (for example, slot-machine payouts)

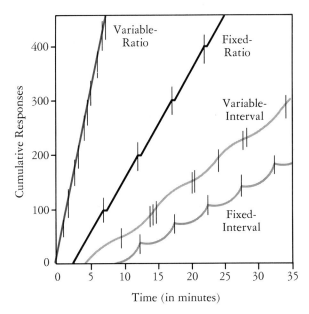

FIGURE 5-16

Patterns of Responding under Different Schedules of Partial Reinforcement Each schedule of reinforcement (explained in Table 5-2) produces a characteristic pattern of bar-press responses in rats. Note that variable schedules produce a consistently higher rate of responses than fixed schedules. *Source:* McGee, M. G., & Wilson, D. W. (1984). *Psychology: Science and application* (p. 146). St. Paul, MN: West.

Operant Conditioning of Human Behavior

Although most of Skinner's research has been conducted on pigeons, the laws of learning that he discovered have significant application to human behavior. For example, there is evidence that productivity is higher for piecework (payment according to the number of pieces produced — a fixed-ratio schedule) than for work that is paid for in equal weekly or monthly installments (a fixed-interval schedule). Consider the effect of signing a long-term contract on the playing time of baseball pitchers shown in Figure 5-17. Skinner's findings also suggest that the rate of studying between exams scheduled at fixed intervals would be initially minimal, but that it would increase dramatically right before the exams are given. On the other hand, the rate of study is likely to be greater and more evenly paced when there is a series of surprise quizzes.

Inasmuch as most of our behavior is not con-stantly approved or disapproved by other people, the reinforcement we receive for our actions is relatively infrequent. Consequently, most of what we know about the effect of reinforcement schedules has been obtained from experiments with animals such as pigeons and rats. It also is difficult, for ethical and practical reasons, to conduct studies with humans in which the rate of reinforcement is manipulated arbitrarily. However, some research in applied settings has been conducted, and what is available confirms, by and large, what has been found with nonhuman animals.

Stephen, Pear, Wray and Jackson (1975) demonstrated that six severely retarded children, aged four through eleven, learned to name pictures twice as quickly when they were reinforced on a fixed ratio schedule of 5 : 1 (one candy given

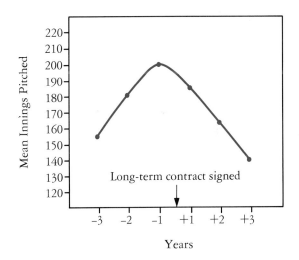

FIGURE 5-17

The Effect of Signing a Long-term Contract on Baseball Pitchers' Performance The number of innings pitched during the three years before signing a long-term contract showed a steady increase. After signing, however, the number of innings steadily declined. For pitchers on one-year contracts during the same period, the number of innings pitched remained roughly constant. The number of wins by pitchers showed a similar pattern. *Source:* O'Brien, R. M., Figlerski, R. W., Howard, S. R., & Caggiano, J. (1981, August). *The effects of multi-year, guaranteed contracts on the performance of pitchers in major-league baseball.* In R. M. O'Brien, A. M. Dickenson, & M. P. Rosow (Eds.). *Industrial behavior modification: A management handbook* (pp. 91–114, p. 101). Elmsford, NY: Pergamon.

for every fifth correct response) than when they were reinforced continuously (one candy given for every correct response).

In another experiment (Mawhinney, Bostow, Laws, Blumenfeld & Hopkins, 1971), twelve college students volunteered to participate in an experiment in which they could consult course material only in a study area that could be monitored through a one-way mirror. The students agreed to organize their studies according to two different schedules. For a few weeks, their achievements were tested at the end of each day. In the subsequent schedule, they were tested only at the end of each three-week period. The daily tests approximated a continuous reinforcement schedule; the testing at three-week intervals followed a fixed interval schedule. The results of this study are shown in Figure 5-18. In accord with predictions from behavior of nonhuman animals, daily study time was roughly constant when tests were given each day, but showed the typical scalloped pattern under the three-week schedule. During the latter phase, there was little work at the start of the three-week period but a lot toward the end.

As a final example of the influence of schedules of reinforcement on human behavior, we offer the study of the work pattern of the United States Congress reported by Weisberg and Waldrop (1972). These investigators simply plotted the cumulative number of bills passed by Congress as a function of the time Congress had been in session. The results are shown in Figure 5-19. Congress passes very few bills at the beginning of each session. As the session draws to a close the legislative pace quickens until, at session's end, bills are passed in rapid succession. A somewhat cynical interpretation of this pattern is that it simply reflects the deliberate stalling that is part of the American political bargaining process. Nevertheless, the pattern is just what would be expected from a fixed interval schedule of reinforcement.

The Partial Reinforcement Effect

We have pointed out that rate of responding is used as an index of learning in operant conditioning. In situations where responding is reinforced by food or other similar stimuli, we tend to assume that the more frequent a response is, the better it has been learned. Another way of determining how well a response has been learned is to assess its **resistance to extinction** — the total

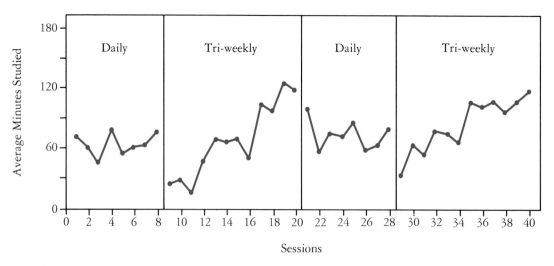

FIGURE 5-18
Students' Studying Behavior under Daily and Triweekly Testing Schedules When students were tested daily, their study time changed little from day to day. However, when tests occurred only every three weeks, study time varied markedly; it was minimal in the early days but substantial just before the test. *Source:* Mawhinney, V. T., Bostow, D. E., Laws, D. R., Blumenfeld, D. J., & Hopkins, B. L. (1971). A comparison of students' studying-behavior produced by daily, weekly, and three-week testing schedules. *Journal of Applied Behavior Analysis, 4,* 257–64.

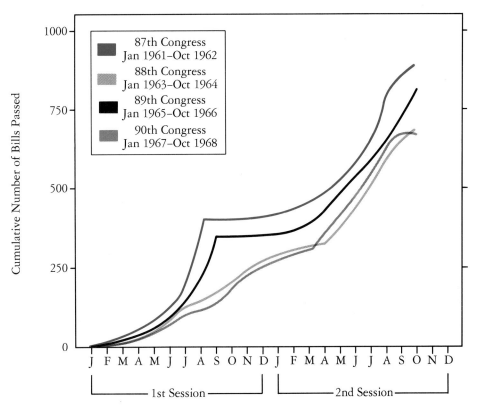

FIGURE 5-19
Changes in the Rate of Passage of Bills in the U.S. Congress During the two-year legislative sessions of Congress between 1951 and 1968, the number of bills passed each month varied dramatically. The pattern is similar to the "scalloping" seen in records of the responses of animals on a fixed interval schedule of partial reinforcement. *Source:* Weisberg, P., & Waldrop, P. B. (1972). Fixed interval work habits of Congress. *Journal of Applied Behavior Analysis, 5,* 93–97.

number of unreinforced responses an animal emits before ceasing to respond altogether. This definition of learning matches our common-sense conception of learning. We generally do not think of learning as measured by rate of responding; we are more likely to assess how well we have learned something by how deeply we feel it is ingrained.

One of the most striking discoveries made by learning researchers is that intermittent or partial reinforcement results in learning that is much more persistent than that produced by continuous reinforcement. This phenomenon has been termed the **partial reinforcement effect.** Suppose that you place two animals in Skinner boxes, then reinforce one continuously for a thousand bar-presses but reinforce the other animal only once every ten bar-presses (100 versus 1000 re-

inforcements). Next, compare the number of times each animal presses the bar *without* reinforcement — how long it takes for the bar-pressing response to be extinguished. You would find that the animal you reinforced only 100 times would continue pressing the bar for much longer than the animal that you reinforced 1000 times. In summary, partial reinforcement leads to more persistent learning than does continuous reinforcement.

The partial reinforcement effect provides an account of certain behaviors that seem to run contrary to the tenets of learning theory, such as the behavior of gamblers who incur heavy losses in the quest for a big win, the behavior of criminals who continue unlawful activity despite punishment, and the extraordinary persistence of undesirable behaviors in "problem" children. Any-

one who has observed the rows of patrons patiently playing slot machines in Las Vegas or Atlantic City should draw an obvious parallel between the behavior of animals in Skinner boxes and the behavior of humans in comparable situations. Partial reinforcement may also account for the persistence of some superstitious behaviors, as outline in Box 5-3.

Generalization and Discrimination

Since there is no apparent eliciting stimulus in operant conditioning, it would seem that the notions of stimulus generalization and discrimination would not apply to this type of learning. Yet consider the following experiment. Guttman and Kalish (1956) conditioned a group of pigeons (reinforcing them with food) to peck at a button that was illuminated with an orange-

Box 5-3
Superstitious Behavior

Baseball players often engage in strange rituals when getting ready to bat. One might invariably tap the tip of the bat on the ground, another might tap his toe with the bat, yet another might regularly tug several times at the peak of his batting helmet. Some people blow on dice before throwing them, carry lucky charms, take part in rain dances, or avoid walking under ladders. Superstitious behaviors such as these tend to be maintained by schedules of partial reinforcement developed by chance. Let us see how this might happen.

Just by chance, a baseball player gets a hit immediately after knocking the dirt off of his shoe. Because this behavior was reinforced by the hit, the player is likely to repeat the behavior next time he is at bat. A subsequent hit that occurred after knocking dirt from the shoe would further reinforce the behavior. As a result, the knocking behavior would be performed more frequently and would therefore be associated more often with hits. Even though batting performance is entirely unaffected by knocking the dirt from a shoe, the power-

ful partial reinforcement schedule is likely to make the ritual a persistent part of the batter's behavior.

The principle is the same for other superstitious behaviors. Even if the initial reason for performing the ritual is to imitate someone else, as it often is, the behavior will be maintained by the accidental intermittent schedule once it is reinforced. In this way, some superstitious behaviors are learned through the chance application of partial reinforcement.

yellow light. After the pigeons learned the task, the experimenters stopped giving the food reinforcement. They left the original orange-yellow color on the light for one group of pigeons, but changed the color by degrees for other groups so that each new color was increasingly dissimilar to the original. They measured the number of responses each group of pigeons made to the new colored button after the reinforcement had been terminated—resistance to extinction. The results, shown in Figure 5-20, revealed that a phenomenon very similar to stimulus generalization took place: the greater similarity the new colors had to the original color to which the pigeons had been conditioned, the longer the pigeons continued to peck. The total number of responses emitted during extinction was used as a measure of **stimulus control**—an indication of the importance of the presence of a particular stimulus in determining the animals' response rate.

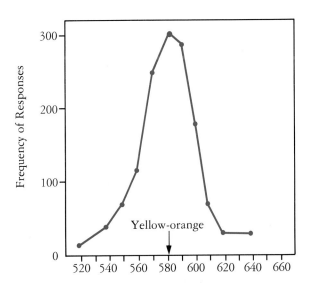

FIGURE 5-20

Operant Generalization Pigeons were reinforced for pecking at a screen illuminated with a yellow-orange light (wavelength: 580 nanometers). Their frequency of responses was determined for illuminations of higher or lower wavelength. The greater the difference in the color of the illuminated light, the lower the pigeons' rate of pecking. *Source:* After Guttman, N., & Kalish, H. J. (1956). Discriminability and stimulus discrimination. *Journal of Experimental Psychology, 51*, 79–88.

Suppose we modify the procedure used by Guttman and Kalish as follows. During the conditioning process, two lights of different colors are projected alternately on a button—an orange-yellow light and a green light. When the orange-yellow light is projected, pecking is followed by food; when the green light is projected, no food is dispensed. In this situation, pigeons soon learn to peck at the orange-yellow light and not at the green light—a phenomenon that is similar to discrimination in classical conditioning. Figure 5-21 illustrates the development of discrimination. In operant conditioning, the stimulus in the presence of which the animal is (or is not) reinforced is called a **discriminative stimulus.** The stimulus is labeled S+ when it signals availability of reinforcement and S− when it signals that reinforcement is unavailable. S+ and S− are analogous to CS+ and CS− in classical conditioning.

Positive and Negative Reinforcers

We have used the terms *reinforcer* (or reinforcing stimulus) and *reinforcement* several times during our discussion of conditioning. Pavlov called the unconditioned stimulus a reinforcer because it served to develop the conditioned response and to maintain its strength. In instrumental and operant conditioning, a reinforcer is a stimulus that increases the likelihood that the immediately preceding response will be emitted again. Reinforcement refers both to the presentation of the stimulus during the conditioning procedure and to the effect of the presentation.

There are two different classes of reinforcer: positive and negative. A **positive reinforcer** is a stimulus whose *presentation* increases the strength of the response that led to the reinforcement. Food is a typical positive reinforcer for a hungry animal. A **negative reinforcer** is a stimulus whose *termination* or *removal* will increase the strength of the response. It is called negative because it is unpleasant, usually evoking pain or other discomfort. Weak electric shock is sometimes used in experimental situations as a negative reinforcer. Imagine a rat in a Skinner box with an electrified floor. An experimenter turns on an electric current that delivers a shock. The animal can turn off the shock by pressing a bar — and quickly learns to do so. Termination of the

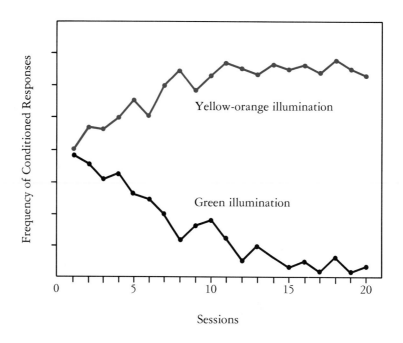

FIGURE 5-21

Operant Discrimination Pigeons were taught to peck at a screen for reinforcement. Then, for one-minute sessions, the screen was illuminated with either orange-yellow light or green light. Reinforcement was provided only under orange-yellow light; responses under green light were not reinforced. At first, stimulus generalization led the pigeons to peck under both types of illumination. But the differential pattern of reinforcement enabled them to discriminate between the two colors within approximately 15 sessions.

shock is reinforcing and increases the strength of bar-pressing.

There are two situations in which the effects of negative reinforcement have been investigated in psychological research. In **escape learning**, an unpleasant stimulus is presented without warning, as in the example just given, and the organism must make a response to terminate it. The unpleasant stimulus cannot be avoided; it can only be escaped. In contrast, in **avoidance learning** a warning signal is given before the unpleasant stimulus occurs, enabling the animal to avoid experiencing it as long as it responds quickly enough. For example, a tone or a light might be turned on two seconds before an electric shock is delivered. If the animal immediately responds to the warning, it avoids the shock.

In both escape and avoidance learning, the removal of an unpleasant stimulus increases the likelihood of the response that terminates it. Negative reinforcement should not be confused with punishment, which is discussed later. Negative reinforcement involves the reinforcement of

a response by *withdrawing* an unpleasant stimulus. Punishment involves *giving* an unpleasant stimulus that causes a decrease in the strength of a response. This distinction is summarized in Table 5-3.

Primary and Secondary Reinforcers

Now that we have defined reinforcement, we can consider what stimulus types are powerful enough to reinforce various responses. The most basic types of reinforcer are stimuli that satisfy a biological need — food, water, sex, escape from pain. We call them **primary reinforcers.** They are innately reinforcing; they require no learning or experience to endow them with the capacity to reinforce behavior. Although primary reinforcers are obviously powerful, a great many behaviors appear to be learned without them. Consider the results of an experiment by Bugelski (1968), in which rats were trained to press a food bar in a Skinner box. When the bar was pressed, the food delivery mechanism made a

TABLE 5-3
Types of Instrumental Conditioning

	Response	Consequence	Change in Behavior
Positive Reinforcer	Rat presses bar	Rewarding stimulus introduced	Bar-press rate increases
Negative Reinforcer	Rat presses bar	Aversive stimulus removed	Bar-press rate increases
Punishment	Rat presses bar	Aversive stimulus introduced	Bar-press rate decreases

clicking noise. After the rats had learned to press the bar at a steady rate, they were divided into two separate groups and extinguished. For the *click* group, bar-pressing during extinction continued to produce clicks, even though food was no longer available. For the *no-click* group, bar-pressing during extinction produced neither food nor clicks. The results showed that the responses of the *click* group took much longer to extinguish than those of the *no-click* group.

A straightforward explanation of such a result is the assumption that during extinction the clicks were reinforcing; in other words, they worked against the extinction effect and motivated the rats to continue pressing the bar. If this is true, the clicks somehow must have acquired reinforcing power during the first part of the experiment. How could this have occurred? The answer lies in the fact that the delivery of food was always accompanied by a clicking noise. While the rats were learning to press the bar, they were also being classically conditioned: the originally neutral CS (clicking noise) always accompanied the US (food delivery).

Stimuli that have acquired reinforcing power through classical conditioning are called **conditioned** or **secondary reinforcers.** Any neutral stimulus that can serve as a conditioned stimulus can become a secondary reinforcer. Because a CS becomes a secondary reinforcer when paired with a primary US, it can maintain its secondary reinforcing power only if it is regularly (though no necessarily always) followed by the US. That is, in the same way that the conditioned response to a CS extinguishes if the CS is no longer followed by the US, so also does the secondary reinforcing power of a CS extinguish.

According to certain learning theorists, such social responses as praise, approval, and scorn are secondary reinforcers. They gain this status be-

cause they are paired with such primary reinforcing (unconditioned) stimuli as food, relief from pain, and cuddling (especially in the early months of a child's life).

Secondary reinforcers are extremely important in human learning. Consider money, for example. Although most money has little intrinsic value (it is just metal or paper), we all learn to perform a variety of behaviors in order to obtain it. Tokens of all kinds can serve a similar function. In a classic experiment, Wolfe (1936) trained chimpanzees to work for tokens that could

FIGURE 5-22
Token Reinforcement of Chimpanzee's Behavior A correct response in a learning experiment earns the chimpanzee a token, which it can then trade for a food reward. *Source:* Yerkes Regional Primate Center, Emory University.

be exchanged for food (see Figure 5-22). Wolfe found that the chimpanzees came to treasure the previously uninteresting tokens for their secondary value and in some cases to hoard them.

A clinical case supplies a good example of the power of secondary reinforcement in humans. A five-year-old girl was brought to a clinic because she could hardly speak a word that made sense (Sulzer-Azaroff & Mayer, 1977). At first the analyst tried to reinforce her by saying "good" or smiling whenever she said or did anything that could be considered appropriate. The analyst assumed that saying "good" or smiling would be reinforcing to this child, as these secondary reinforcers generally are for most children. But the procedure did not work and the child made no progress. The analyst then decided to try primary reinforcers. He gave the child bits of food whenever she said something or responded appropriately at lunch. This procedure worked. The child soon began to say many

appropriate words and to do many appropriate things in the lunch situations and, later, in other situations. However, it would have been impractical to continue to reinforce the child only with food. Thus the analyst arranged to have such words and phrases as "good," "fine," "yes," and "you're doing well" and such actions as nodding, smiling, and hugging, precede the delivery of food. Over time, these words and actions acquired secondary reinforcing value, enabling the analyst to reinforce the child with the single word "yes." After a year of this treatment, the child was able to enter a special education class in a public school. Three years later she was still progressing well. This type of procedure is an example of behavior therapy, a topic discussed in greater detail in Chapter 14.

As this example illustrates, secondary reinforcement is tremendously significant because it extends the range of stimuli that can be used as reinforcers in classical and instrumental conditioning. It permits a flexibility that would be impossible if only primary reinforcers could be used. The example also helps explain the broad variability in human behavior. We all know that some people respond to praise and others do not; some people like to talk, and others to listen; some people pursue wealth, and others pursue knowledge. The range of stimuli that are rewarding to different people is enormous, and would be expected to vary according to their history of learning.

Punishment

To a large extent human society has always been governed by **punishment** or by the threat of it. The "law" generally is interpreted as a set of prohibitions which, when violated, result in punishment (see Figure 5-23). We are not rewarded when we travel within the speed limit, but we are punished when we do not. We are not rewarded for keeping enough funds in the bank to cover our checks, but we are in trouble when they bounce. Of course, we earn money for working, we earn good grades for studying, and we sometimes earn praise and esteem for a job well done. Yet the institutions of society seem to place greater emphasis on what we should *not* do, and the resulting punishments, than on what we should do, and

Edict of Louis XI, King of France
A.D. 1481

"Anyone who sells butter containing stones or other things (to add to the weight) will be put into our pillory, then said butter will be placed on his head until entirely melted by the sun. Dogs may lick him and people offend him with whatever defamatory epithets they please without offense to God or King. If the sun is not warm enough, the accused will be exposed in the great hall of the gaol in front of a roaring fire, where everyone will see him."

FIGURE 5-23

A Medieval Form of Punishment   The methods have varied, but all societies have used punishment to control undesirable behavior.

the resulting rewards. The orientation in our society toward punishment makes it important to understand its effects.

How effective is punishment as a means of regulating behavior? In seeking an answer to this question, we consider a typical problem and some relevant research. Imagine that you are a teacher faced with the challenge of dealing with a student who is disruptive during class. From the point of view of learning theory, you assume that the disruptive behavior is being maintained by one or more reinforcers. Therefore, the first thing you should do is attempt to discover which reinforcers are maintaining the behavior. Once you obtain that information, two courses of action are open to you — withdraw the reinforcer or substitute it with punishment. If the reinforcer is attention, as it often is, you could attempt to extinguish the undesirable behavior by ensuring that all acts of disruption are ignored. Or you could punish the disruptive behavior. Which strategy would work best?

For many years, on the strength of a few early experiments (for example, Estes, 1944), it was believed that punishment had only a temporarily suppressing effect and, therefore, that it was relatively ineffective as a means of controlling undesirable behavior. In the late 1960s, however, this conclusion was challenged by several investiga-

tors (for example, Boe & Church, 1967). There is now a considerable body of evidence suggesting that some types of punishment may be more effective than the extinction that occurs when reinforcers are withdrawn (Axelrod & Apsche, 1983).

The effectiveness of punishment depends primarily on two factors: its intensity and its immediacy. The sooner the punishment follows a behavior and the stronger the punishment is, the more effective it will be (Azrin, 1956). Research also has shown that continuous punishment is more effective than intermittent punishment (Van Houten, 1983). The reason for this is that if a behavior is not punished consistently, it is likely that it will be reinforced on the occasions when it is not punished. The partial-reinforcement schedule is usually powerful enough to outweigh the effects of intermittent punishment.

It is important to recognize that punishment can have undesirable side effects. When punishment is severe, it arouses unpleasant emotions which, through classical conditioning, become associated with aspects of the situation in which punishment occurs, including the people who deliver it. Children who are punished severely often learn to fear the people who punish them, which causes the punishing agents to lose their power to deliver positive reinforcements. A final problem with punishment — one emphasized by social learning theorists — is that when an adult punishes a child physically, the adult presents an aggressive model for the child to imitate. Consider an incident reported by a colleague of ours who saw a neighbor grab his son by the neck for hitting his sister. A short while later, the boy was observed grabbing his sister by the neck in exactly the way that he had just been punished.

Returning to the classroom example, one course of action in this situation would appear to be to ignore the undesirable behavior of the aggressive student and use attention to reinforce desirable behaviors. This method has many advantages. Because you would be associated mainly with positive cues, the student should come to like you, approach you, and respond to you as a source of reinforcement (rather than fearing and avoiding you). In addition, you would create a constructive model for the behavior you desired. We would expect this method to work fairly well with relatively mild cases of undesirable behavior. However, progress using this method might be rather slow, making it unsuitable for more serious cases of troublesome behavior — in which the need for rapid improvement requires more

drastic action. Three examples, which demonstrate the appropriate use of punishment, are described in Box 5-4.

If the same teacher punished the undesirable behavior and reinforced the alternative, de-

Box 5-4
The Appropriate Use of Punishment

Most people disapprove of the use of physical punishment when the only goal is to stop a person from behaving in an undesirable or unacceptable manner. Yet such an approach occasionally is warranted; for example, you probably would not object to the use of punishment if the continued occurrence of the undesirable behavior represented a threat to the person's health. Schwartz (1984) offers three examples to support this contention.

Bucher and Lovaas (1968) describe the treatment of an eight-year-old boy whose self-mutilation behavior was so severe that he had to be restrained continuously. Using what they called an extinction period (equivalent to a time-out), the boy was left unrestrained and in isolation for 90 minutes. During the first session, he was observed to hit himself some 2,700 times. The treatment was continued, however, and by the eighth session of isolation the frequency of self-

mutilations had dropped to zero. The fact that the undesirable behavior had been eliminated by the simple expedient of depriving the boy of an audience confirmed the belief that attention from others had served as a reinforcement of the self-mutilation. Withdrawal of the reinforcer led to extinction of the behavior, albeit slowly.

A similar problem was treated quite differently by Lovaas and Simmons (1969). A single, mild electrical shock applied to the leg caused an immediate cessation of self-destructive behavior in a young boy. The behavior gradually reemerged over the next few days, but was suppressed again by a single shock. After four such treatments, the self-destructive behavior seemed completely eliminated. However, outside the treatment setting — in the presence of people other than the one who administered the shocks — the undesirable behavior still tended to occur. This

problem was solved by having a second person repeat the treatment. This resulted in the full generalization of the punishment, and self-destructive behavior no longer occurred in any setting.

A third study shows how a **conditioned punisher** can be created to facilitate generalization and maintain the suppression of undesirable behavior (Risley, 1968). The case concerns a hyperactive six-year-old girl with an irresistible urge to climb, which had already resulted in several bad falls. The treatment consisted of the application of a mild electric shock whenever she started to climb, with the shock being preceded by a stern "No!" This suppressed climbing, but only in the presence of the therapist. Having the mother continue the treatment at home, using the reprimand "No!" that had become a conditioned punisher, promoted generalization and brought the case to a successful conclusion.

sirable behaviors, the student would be unlikely to develop an aversion to him or her. Another advantage of using both punishment and reinforcement is that they make it easier to discriminate between the behaviors that lead to punishment and those that do not. We are pleased to note that the British government recently voted to ban corporal punishment in schools (July, 1986). A variety of effective noncorporal punishments are available to a teacher, ranging from verbal reprimand (Van Houten & Doleys, 1983) to withdrawal of privileges or "time-outs" (Brantner & Doherty, 1983). In conclusion, punishment can be an effective means of controlling behavior, but must be used judiciously and with caution. Whenever possible, it should be used in conjunction with reinforcement of desirable behavior.

Learned Helplessness

Several decades ago, the learning theorist Hobart Mowrer and his colleague Viek (1948, p. 193) wrote: "A painful stimulus never seems so objectionable if one knows how to terminate it as it does if one has no control over it." The implications of this observation went unexplored for a number of years, until two psychologists, Overmier and Seligman (1967) pursued them. These psychologists experimented with two groups of dogs. They restrained and harnessed the first group, and repeatedly gave them painful shocks. Because the dogs could do nothing to avoid the shocks, they were helpless. The second group of dogs was left at rest while the first group was being punished. Later, both groups of dogs were tested in a shuttle box, which is a chamber with two compartments separated by a barrier. A warning light in the box was illuminated for ten seconds prior to a shock being delivered to the floor of one compartment of the shuttle box. The dogs could avoid the shock simply by jumping into the other compartment before the ten-second interval elapsed.

The results of this experiment, shown in Figure 5-24, revealed that the group of dogs put into the shuttle box without any prior treatment quickly learned to jump to the second compartment. However, most of the dogs that previously had been subjected to unavoidable shocks pas-

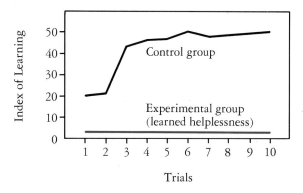

FIGURE 5-24

Learned Helplessness in Dogs Dogs that have experienced inescapable shock — causing them to experience "learned helplessness" — later fail to attempt escape from shock despite an easy means to do so. Control animals that were not given the initial shock treatment quickly learned to escape.

sively accepted the painful shocks without ever learning to move to the other compartment to avoid them. The investigators concluded that these dogs had learned to become helpless. Later experiments showed that the effects of **learned helplessness** can be reversed. Seligman, Maier, and Geer (1968) induced learned helplessness in a group of dogs and then, during the testing phase (while the warning light was illuminated), they dragged the dogs into the safe compartment of the shuttle box. Eventually these dogs learned to avoid the shock.

Abramson, Seligman, and Teasdale (1978) and Peterson and Seligman (1984) have suggested that learned helplessness supplies a good explanation for at least some cases of human depression. From this point of view, depression results less from people's inability to cope with unpleasantness than from their perception that no matter what they do they cannot improve their lot. Interestingly, antidepressant drugs and electroconvulsive shock treatments often administered to depressed human patients have been found effective in ameliorating learned helplessness in rats (Sherman et al, 1982). However, the extent to which learned helplessness is a useful model for human depression is a subject of current debate (Flaherty, 1985, pp. 223–31; Mazur, 1986, pp. 175–77). We discuss this topic further in Chapter 13.

Applications of Operant Conditioning

We have described how operant conditioning procedures can be used to shape the behavior of a pet animal. You can probably imagine dozens of practical uses to which such procedures can be put. Yet, however fertile your imagination, it is unlikely that many of the following applications would have appeared on your list: air-to-ground missile guidance, assembly-line quality control, rescue of people lost at sea, housekeeping for the handicapped. Nevertheless, all of these activities have been accomplished successfully by applying the basic principles of operant conditioning to the shaping of animal behavior.

Skinner (1960) used discrimination training to teach pigeons to peck at a target on a screen in a Skinner box. Three such boxes were then placed in the body of an air-to-ground missile. The view of the target recorded by a camera in the nose of the missile was displayed on the screen in each box. When the pigeons pecked at the target, the location of their pecks on the screens provided information that could be used to correct the flight of the missile as it homed in on its target. Skinner was convinced that his system would be effective, but was unable to persuade military backers to adopt the scheme.

Skinner's work has prompted other efforts. For example, after observing assembly-line workers engaged in the mindless task of watching for defective capsules on a moving conveyor belt, a psychopharmacologist employed by a large drug company taught pigeons to do the job (Verhave, 1966). Using discrimination training, the animals learned to respond to a passing capsule only if it was dented, double-capped, or otherwise defective.

Pigeons were also the animals chosen by the U.S. Coast Guard to assist them in rescuing persons lost at sea (Simmons, 1981). As shown in Figure 5-25, three pigeons were placed in a windowed box attached to the underside of a helicopter. The box was partitioned so that each pigeon faced a different direction. The animals had been trained to peck at a key when presented with a stimulus that was colored orange — the color of lifejackets. When one of the pigeons in the helicopter spotted a lifejacket in the sea, it pecked the key that activated a buzzer, telling the pilot in which direction to fly. Pigeons are particularly

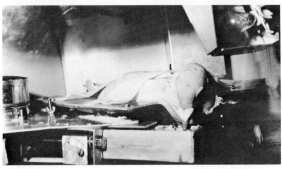

FIGURE 5-25

Pigeons Spot Persons Lost at Sea Pigeons are trained by the Coast Guard to signal when they spot an orange life preserver. *Source:* After Simmons, J. V. (1981). Project Seahunt: A report on prototype development and tests. San Diego: Naval Oceans Systems Center, Technical Report 746.

well-suited to this task because they have good color vision, a broad field of focus, and apparently can stare at stretches of sea for hours without fatigue.

Mack (1981) reported that a capuchin monkey, Hellion, has been trained to serve the needs of Foster, a young man whose quadriplegia prevents almost all physical movement. Using a mouth-operated laser beam, Foster points to objects that he wants Hellion to bring him, and dispenses a food pellet for the animal when this is done. Figure 5-26 shows Crystal, another monkey trained to help the handicapped, brushing a man's hair. Crystal also has been taught to turn the TV on and off, open the door, and even do the grocery shopping!

Operant learning also has been applied to shape human behavior. For example, Wallin and Johnson (1976) reported an operant conditioning scheme to reduce employee absenteeism in a small electronics company. Workers participated in a monthly $10 lottery only if they had maintained a perfect attendance record for the previous month. This variable ratio reinforcement schedule would be expected to maintain steady behavior. Despite the modest size of the reinforcer, absenteeism dropped by 30% the following year — the consequent savings amounting to almost 30 times the total prize money. You might pause to recall our discussion of the placebo effect in Chapter 1 and legitimately complain that Wallin and Johnson's study lacked a control group. You are correct; however, an earlier study by Pedalino and Gamboa (1974) had demonstrated that, in a similar situation, the dilatory behavior of a lottery group improved much more than that of three different control groups.

Most of the human applications of operant learning, including those just described, fall under the heading of *behavior modification,* a subject covered extensively in Chapter 14 (see also Bellack, Hersen, & Kazdin, 1982; Martin and Pear, 1983 for reviews of this area). Behavior modification is a process in which the frequency of the desirable or undesirable behavior is altered by introducing an appropriate schedule of reinforcement.

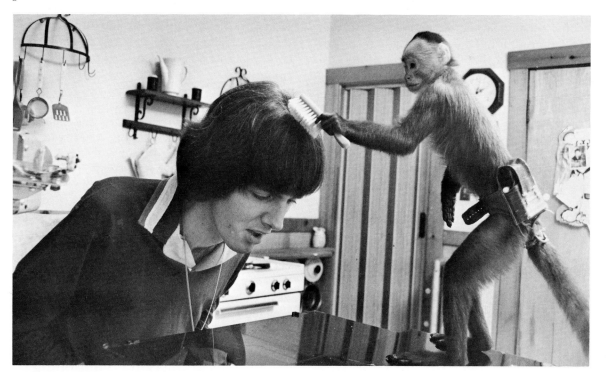

FIGURE 5-26

Monkeys Help the Handicapped Operant conditioning has been used to train monkeys to perform many chores for the severely handicapped.

BIOLOGICAL CONSTRAINTS ON CONDITIONING

Until recently, most learning theorists believed that the basic processes of classical and instrumental conditioning were common across most situations and almost all organisms. Recent evidence, however, requires that we abandon these beliefs. There are limits, set by an animal's biological inheritance, on what it can learn through classical conditioning.

Limitations of Classical Conditioning

One of the ways in which classical conditioning extends the range of learning is to endow previously neutral stimuli with the power to elicit reflexive responses. Buzzers and lights have been used as neutral stimuli in most classical conditioning experiments because they are convenient; for many years most learning theorists assumed that all neutral stimuli were equivalent as potential-conditioned stimuli. However, in a now classic experiment, Garcia and Koelling (1966) showed that this was not the case. The neutral stimulus in their experiment was an unusual one—"bright, noisy water." The investigators produced this stimulus by activating an electrical circuit that produced flashing lights and a distinctive noise whenever a rat drank. The object of the experiment was to see whether bright, noisy water would serve as an equally effective conditioned stimulus for two types of unconditioned stimulus—shock and irradiation by X ray. (The effect of X ray irradiation is similar to that of food poisoning.) Garcia and Koelling presented the bright, noisy water to a number of rats, shocking half when they drank and irradiating the other half. The next day they again offered all rats bright, noisy water. The group of rats that had been shocked drank very little but the group of rats that had been irradiated drank as much as they had the previous day. The experimenters concluded that the bright, noisy water was more effective as a cue for the pain associated with shock than it was for the illness associated with irradiation.

By itself, of course, this experiment does not demonstrate conclusively that the difference in the drinking behavior was caused by the difference in the stimuli. Perhaps it was not possible to condition the illness produced by irradiation to any neutral stimulus. This possibility occurred to the investigators, and they conducted another experiment in which they offered rats water that was sweetened with saccharine. This time the initially neutral cue was a taste cue (sweetness) instead of a visual–auditory cue ("bright, noisy water"). Half these rats were shocked while they drank and the other half were irradiated by X ray. This time the rats given shocks drank as much sweetened water as before but the X ray irradiated rats showed a strong aversion to the water. The investigators concluded that shock is easily associated with some cues (such as auditory and visual stimuli) but not with others (taste stimuli), and that the opposite is true for X ray produced illness. Rats seem to be innately "prepared" to associate externally inflicted pain with audiovisual stimuli and internally inflicted pain with taste stimuli.

Garcia and Koelling's experiment demonstrates that not all stimuli are equally easily associated with all responses *within* a particular species. Another experiment shows that different stimuli may be differentially effective across animal species.

Wilcoxon, Dragoin, and Kral (1971) induced two animal groups—rats and bobwhite quail—to drink blue and salty water, and then injected them with a drug that made them ill. When all animals were given a choice of drinking blue or salty water, the rats avoided the salty water and the quail avoided the blue water. How can this finding be explained? The explanation offered by the experimenters is that rats are more dependent on taste cues and less dependent on visual cues in their natural environment, whereas the opposite is true for bobwhite quail. The study supplies additional evidence that animals are innately prepared to develop conditioned responses to specific stimuli.

Limitations of Operant Conditioning

Some years ago, Keller Breland and Marian Breland, two students of B. F. Skinner, became professional animal trainers. They had amazing success shaping the responses of a variety of animals and teaching them to perform tricks. One of their most famous accomplishments was Priscilla the Fastidious Pig, who starred in her own TV series. Priscilla ate meals at the table, cleaned house, and played quiz competitor by flashing lights marked *Yes* and *No* in response to questions from the audience (Breland & Breland, 1951). Yet during their experiments the Brelands discovered that it was almost impossible to teach some animals certain responses. For example, they attempted to teach raccoons to pick up coins and deposit them in a small box, using food as a reinforcer. When they gave the raccoons one coin, the animals quickly learned to deposit it. But when they tried to teach the raccoons to pick up two coins and deposit them, they found that the raccoons did not learn this response. Rather, they would pick up the coins, rub them against each other, dip them in the container, withdraw them, rub them again, and so on.

The trainers tried making the raccoons hungrier in order to increase the value of food as a reinforcer. But the hungrier the raccoons became, the more they rubbed the coins together. The same sort of problem occurred with roosters, who made scratching movements with their feet that interfered with their training. Similarly, pigs rooted with their noses on the bare floor rather than perform the responses that had been reinforced. What all of these behaviors have in common is that they are associated in each species with eating behavior. Given that raccoons are notorious for the "washing" they perform before eating, Breland and Breland (1961) concluded that in such cases an innately determined behavioral disposition could override conditioned behavior. They termed the phenomenon **instinctive drift.**

The finding that different animals are more or less likely to condition certain responses to certain stimuli makes sense from an evolutionary point of view. After all, "Simple conditioning . . . was already full blown on this planet some 500,000,000 years ago in organisms with no cortex, [and] very little forebrain" (Razran, 1971, p. 9). It is reasonable to suggest that in the same way that natural selection has molded the physical form of animals, it also has molded their capacities to learn. Learning theorists are becoming more fully aware that the subtle interplay between evolutionarily determined biological constraints and environmentally controlled learning must be fully understood before general statements about the "laws" of learning can be made (Mazur, 1986, p. 230). This does not mean that there are no laws of learning; rather it suggests that laws operate within the constraints imposed by the innate capacities of various animals.

COGNITIVE LEARNING

Let us return to the question with which we opened this chapter: What is learning? After discussing habituation and sensitization, we devoted a good deal of attention to classical and instrumental conditioning. But how much learned behavior, especially in humans, is caused by conditioning? Do people learn to drive a car, solve complex equations, put rockets on the moon, write music, and so on, through conditioning? In the heyday of classical and instrumental conditioning, many psychologists believed that this was indeed the case. These psychologists did not deny the existence of thinking but maintained that thoughts were behaviors and, as such, could be conditioned just like any other behavior. Conditioning was assumed to provide *the* model for all learning. Psychologists who held this view attached great emphasis to the role of overt responding, reinforcement, and the automatic strengthening effect of reinforcement. Indeed, some learning theorists even held that learning could not occur unless an organism responded, was reinforced, or both.

Other psychologists, however, disagreed, maintaining that learning may occur in the absence of overt responses, reinforcement, or both. They argued that organisms, especially those with a large cerebral cortex, learn not so much through the reinforcement of specific responses but by the acquisition of information. This kind of learning is characterized as cognitive. In its most elementary form, **cognitive learning** involves forming the expectation (thought, belief) that a particular stimulus situation or behavior will be followed by another stimulus situation or behavior. According to this cognitive view, the only requirement for learning is that the animal pays attention to what occurs in the environment. If it does, it will acquire information—and learning will occur with or without overt responses and/or reinforcement. Support for this view of cognitive learning comes from research on sensory preconditioning, latent learning, learning to learn, and insight.

Sensory Preconditioning

Most early learning theorists believed that an unconditioned stimulus was essential in classical conditioning. For example, they believed that in order to condition a dog to salivate to a buzzer, a researcher must pair the buzzer with a US that elicits salivation in the first place. Yet an experiment by Rokotova (1954) suggests that learning can occur without a US. Rokotova presented a toy that said "cuckoo" to a baboon a number of times. Thus a visual stimulus (toy) was accompanied by an auditory stimulus (the sound, "cuckoo"), with no US or reinforcer. The baboon was not required to make a response. Then Rokotova used a normal classical conditioning procedure to teach the baboon to make a CR to the auditory stimulus "cuckoo." After the baboon was conditioned to respond to the auditory stimulus, Rokotova presented the visual stimulus (the toy) by itself, and found that it too now elicited the CR. These results indicated that the baboon had learned to associate the visual and auditory stimuli when they were originally paired, even though there was no apparent US or "reinforcer" at that time.

In another experiment, Brogden (1939) exposed dogs to paired presentations of lights and tones. The dogs sat quietly as lights flashed and tones sounded. Brogden then employed the light as a conditioned stimulus to signal shock. After the dogs had been conditioned to respond to the light, he presented only the tone. Brogden found

that the dogs responded to the tone as if it were the light. These two experiments demonstrate that when two neutral ("sensory") stimuli closely follow each other in time, animals may form an association between them that affects their behavior. This phenomenon is referred to as **sensory preconditioning.**

The results of the sensory preconditioning studies are easy to interpret if it is assumed that, with repeated pairings, the animal learned to *expect* that the two sensory stimuli would occur together or follow each other closely in time. In contrast, it would be very difficult to account for the results of the sensory preconditioning studies if one were to assume that either an overt response (none was required in the preconditioning phase) or reinforcement (none was provided) were necessary for learning to occur. These experiments demonstrate that organisms can learn what occurs around them by simply observing and, as a result, acquiring information.

Latent Learning

If you put a rat in an unfamiliar maze without any food, it will expend considerable energy exploring the alleys of the maze. Clearly, the rat is responding in the absence of any obvious reinforcement, but is it learning anything? Tolman suggested that learning takes place in situations such as these even though the behavior is not being reinforced. Tolman and Honzik (1930) permitted three groups of rats to run every day for 17 days in a complicated maze. The rats in the first group were always reinforced with food when they reached the goal box—a typical instrumental conditioning procedure. The rats in the second group were never reinforced when they reached the goal box; they were simply removed from the maze. The rats in the third group were not reinforced for reaching the goal box for the first ten days, but received reinforcement for reaching it from the eleventh to the seventeenth day. The experimenters calculated the amount of learning in terms of the number of blind alleys the rats entered before entering the goal box; the fewer the mistakes, the greater the learning.

Figure 5-27 displays the results of the study. As you can see, the rats who were always reinforced for reaching the goal box quickly

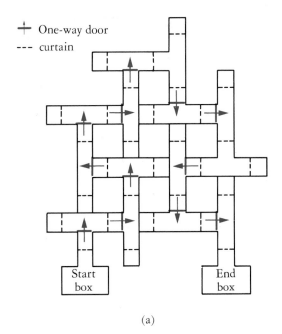

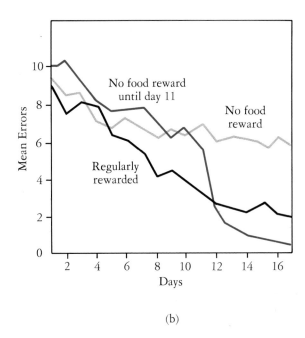

(a)   (b)

FIGURE 5-27

Latent Learning   (a) The maze used by Tolman and Honzik to study latent learning in three groups of rats.   (b) The animals not receiving a food reward on days 1 – 10 nevertheless demonstrated the cumulative effects of learning when rewarded on day 11.   The learning had occurred but remained latent until that time.   *Source:* After Tolman, E. C., & Honzik, C. H. (1930).   Introduction and removal of reward, and maze performance in rats.   *University of California Publications in Psychology, 4,* 257 – 75.

learned to make fewer errors than the other rats. By the twelfth day, they were averaging two errors only.   The rats who were never reinforced improved their performance somewhat, but still entered an average of about six blind alleys by the seventeenth day.   The third group of rats behaved similarly to the rats who were never reinforced during the first eleven days, which is not surprising since they were treated in exactly the same way.   However, after just one reinforcement (received on the eleventh day), the third group performed as well as the rats who had been reinforced on all eleven trials.   Subsequently, the third group performed a little better than the rats who were always reinforced.

According to Tolman and Honzik, this experiment shows that the rats not reinforced during the first ten days were nevertheless "learning."   They were acquiring a "map" of the maze and storing this information in their brains.   As long as they didn't need the information, they didn't use it; as soon as they needed it, they put the

information to good use.   Tolman called this type of learning **latent learning.**

Tolman's experiments have two important implications.   The first is that learning can occur in the absence of reinforcement.   The second is that behavior can sometimes be a misleading criterion of learning.   Tolman insisted on an important distinction — between learning and performance.   *Performance* can be observed — it is overt behavior; but *learning* is an internal process that underlies performance.   We can learn something, but not reveal it in our performance unless motivated to do so.   You may know the material for an examination extremely well, but because you are fatigued or sick or anxious, you may perform poorly.   On the other hand, you may have learned very little, but get lucky in receiving just the right questions.   In neither case does your performance reflect your learning.   According to Tolman, and as we emphasized in the definition given earlier, learning represents the *potential* for change in overt behavior — which may or may not become apparent depending on such factors as food or other reinforcers.

Learning to Learn

Consider the following experiment performed by psychologist Harry Harlow (1949). Harlow trained a group of monkeys to perform numerous discrimination tasks. The format of the tasks was always exactly the same; only the stimuli differed. For example, on the first discrimination task a monkey might have to choose between a box printed with a circle (which contained a peanut) and a box printed with a square (which didn't contain anything) and on the second task, to choose between a box with a triangle and a box with a cross (see Figure 5-28). When it chose correctly, the monkey received a peanut. Harlow presented each discrimination task six times, and recorded the number of errors the monkeys made. Note that although the particular discriminations the monkeys were required to make differed on each set of six trials, the basic structure of the task was always the same — to learn which of two cues signals a reward.

Although the discriminations required of the monkeys are simple for most humans, they are difficult for most nonhuman animals. The animals must learn to disregard irrelevant information — such as the size, color, or position of the stimuli — and focus on shape, the relevant characteristic.

Harlow presented his monkeys with 312 problems, giving them six trials per problem. The results are shown in Fig. 5-29. Look at the average performance of the monkeys on the first set of eight problems. The monkeys did about the same as humans would on the first trial of each problem — they guessed correctly 50% of the time. Now, most people would conclude after the first trial that if the reward was not in one box it must be in the other. Yet Harlow's monkeys improved hardly at all on trial two. However, they did improve steadily from trials three to six.

Now look at the performance of the monkeys on trial two of the second set of eight problems (numbered 9 – 16). They chose correctly

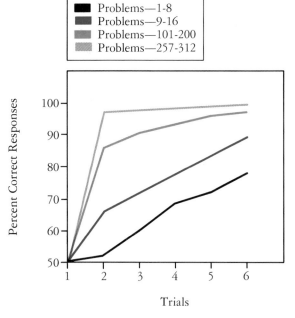

FIGURE 5-29

The Development of a Learning Set Each line shows the rate of success of rhesus monkeys in solving the same problem over six trials. A different version of the problem was given every six trials, for a total of 312 problems. Average performance is shown for problems 1 – 8, 9 – 16, 101 – 200, and 257 – 312. With increasing practice, the monkeys' success rate markedly improved, showing that the monkeys developed an appropriate learning set. *Source:* After Harlow, H. F. (1949). The formation of learning sets. *Psychological Review, 56,* 51 – 65.

FIGURE 5-28

Harlow's Monkey Learning to Learn *Source:* Harlow Primate Laboratory, University of Wisconsin.

approximately 65% of the time, and their performance continued to improve through trial six. Finally, look at the monkeys' average performance over six trials for problems numbered 101–200. By this time they are getting about 86% of the discriminations correct on the second trial of each problem. At the end of the experiment, on the last 56 discrimination problems (numbered 257–312), the monkeys chose the correct box on the second trial almost 100% of the time.

Harlow's experiment shows that when monkeys first approach a particular type of learning task (in this case a two-choice discrimination problem), they perform poorly. After they have had experience with it, their performance improves. In effect, they learn how to learn. The peanut serves as a reinforcer that motivates the monkeys to respond throughout the experiment. However, it accounts for neither the improved ability of the monkeys to make correct discriminations on the second trial nor the fact that such improvement continues after repeated experience with the same type of problem. This suggests that a type of learning not exclusively under the control of reinforcement is taking place — one that is reflected only indirectly in behavior. The learning-to-learn phenomenon was called **learning set** by Harlow.

Extrapolating from Harlow's experience, one would expect that people who enter new occupations or return to school in an attempt to develop new skills must learn not only the specific task or tasks associated with these activities but they also must learn new strategies of learning. When you took your first courses in college, you probably did not know how to prepare effectively for exams, and so wasted considerable time and effort studying irrelevant aspects of the material. With experience, most people learn how to learn more efficiently. You might, for example, learn to prepare in one way for a multiple-choice exam and in a different way for an essay exam. As with Harlow's monkeys, this general type of learning probably takes longer than the learning of a specific skill. Consequently, the next time you begin a new activity, do not become discouraged if it takes you longer to learn new things than it takes people who have had more relevant experience. You are probably not less competent than they are; you simply need more time to learn the general strategies for dealing with the tasks more effectively.

Insight

After Thorndike put his cats into a puzzle box, they scratched around somewhat randomly until, through trial-and-error, they learned to undo the latch. Thorndike believed that his puzzle box was a useful model for all problem-solving situations and that the learning involved was acquired slowly, as shown by the gradual reduction in time it took the cats to escape (see Figure 5-12). However, noted Gestalt psychologist Wolfgang Köhler disagreed with this view. Köhler argued that Thorndike's boxes were not representative of typical problem-solving situations faced by higher animals. According to Köhler, the elements necessary for the solution of problems are clearly and openly available in most cases — which was not true for Thorndike's cats — and all that is needed to produce a solution is to put the elements together in a new way. He and other Gestalt psychologists argued that solutions typically occur rapidly — in a flash of **insight.**

Köhler (1925) studied problem-solving in chimpanzees while confined to the Canary Island of Tenerife during World War I. In one problem, he hung a banana from the ceiling of a cage and placed several boxes on the floor. Typically the chimpanzees engaged in a fair amount of trial-and-error, jumping up to try to reach the banana, throwing boxes at it, and the like. And yet, after a series of futile attempts, a chimp would sometimes suddenly rush to the boxes, deliberately pile them up under the banana, jump on them, and retrieve the fruit (see Figure 5-30). In another problem, Köhler placed a banana a short distance outside the cage and put two short sticks inside the cage that could be fitted together to make a longer stick. After many unsuccessful attempts, a chimp would suddenly seize the sticks, join them together, rush to the bars, and rake in the banana. In both experiments the solution seemed to come to the chimp in a flash, as suggested by the rapidity of its onset and the smoothness of its execution.

Other studies with chimpanzees (Birch 1945) have shown that only chimps with previous experience with sticks show insight on the

FIGURE 5-30

Insightful Learning in Problem-Solving   In contrast to the gradual development of response strength in most instances of animal learning, the solution to some problems seems to come suddenly — in a flash of insight. *Source:* Hess, L.   The Photo Source.

stick problem. Prior experience with the solution itself is not necessary, but it is necessary to have had experience with the components of the solution — in this case, to have used sticks as tools and playthings.

If we observed the behavior of a monkey on problem 300 of Harlow's two-choice discrimination task, we probably would characterize its behavior as insightful because the monkey was capable of extracting all the required information on the first trial of the problem. However, Harlow's experiment showed that this ability develops gradually over a number of problems that are similar in structure. Thus, the evidence suggests that practice with the elements of a problem (previous play with sticks, previous practice with discrimination problems) is necessary for insightful learning to occur.

In conclusion, Thorndike found that practice increased problem-solving ability on particular problems. Köhler found that chimpanzees are mentally capable of reorganizing the elements of a problem to obtain insightful solutions. Harlow and Birch provided the links needed to bridge these two findings; they showed that there is a gradual progression involved in solving many different problems of the same kind. As experience with different problems accumulates, it becomes increasingly likely that the solution to one particular problem will be insightful.

Cognitive Learning in Evolutionary Perspective

You may have noticed that the animals in the experiments we have been discussing are from species with relatively well-developed brains. There is evidence that the more developed is an animal's brain the more kinds of learning it is capable of, and the more cognitive the special types of learning become.

Razran (1971) believes that sensory preconditioning is a higher form of learning than classical conditioning. He suggests that it is possible to condition an earthworm classically but not to precondition it sensorily. Only the higher vertebrates, some birds, and most mammals show sensory preconditioning. Unfortunately, this in-

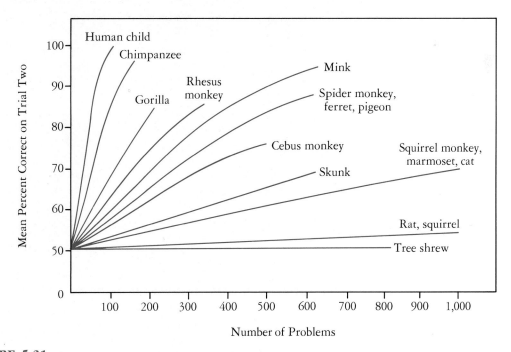

FIGURE 5-31
Differences among Species in Their Ability to Generalize An animal's likelihood of success on the second trial of a problem series improves with practice, but the rate of improvement varies greatly across species.
Source: Hodos, W. (1970). Evolutionary interpretation. *Neurosciences.* Rockefeller University Press.

teresting proposal does not appear to have been investigated systematically. Neither has the capacity of animals from various species to benefit from latent learning been studied extensively. However, there is evidence that only animals with highly developed brains can learn to learn, as defined by Harlow. Figure 5-31 shows the percent of correct responses on trial two made by several different types of animals over a number of discrimination problems. After 1000 problem sets, rats and squirrels learned very little about the structure of the task, cats learned somewhat more, monkeys more yet; then came gorillas and chimpanzees, and then human children. We discuss other aspects of cognitive learning in several of the following chapters.

SOCIAL LEARNING

An important contribution to cognitive learning has been made by Albert Bandura, who has developed a theory that emphasizes the social nature of learning (Bandura, 1977, 1986). His **social learning** theory is wide-ranging and quite complex, but we can sample its flavor by describing his ideas on **modeling.** Most of us are familiar with modeling (we have seen children imitate adult behavior) and surely all of us have tried to copy other things people do. However, modeling may take more subtle forms. Panhandlers may prime their cups with coins in order to increase the likelihood that passersby will contribute. On slack days, shrewd restaurant owners may have the staff park their cars in front of the restaurants.

According to Bandura, four processes must occur in order for a behavior to be learned through modeling: *attention, retention, reproduction,* and *motivation.* An observer must pay attention to the model in order to appreciate the behavior to be imitated. Advertisers show their recognition of this stage when they promote products through such attention-getting personalities as professional athletes and media stars. For the behavior to be imitated when the model is no longer present, the observer must be able to retain the information acquired through paying attention to the model. This requires that the observer somehow code the behavior for storage in memory.

In the third stage, the observer puts the acquired information into practice by attempting to reproduce the model's behavior. If the necessary component skills are already available, the attempt may be reasonably successful. In other instances, practice is required, often guided by feedback from the model. Sometimes attention and retention are insufficient; the observer may lack some necessary skill or may simply not have the motivation to perform.

Bandura's orientation also is reflected in his conception of reinforcement. As we have seen, learning theorists traditionally have viewed reinforcement in terms of its response-strengthening function. Bandura believes that reinforcement has the additional important functions of providing information and incentive. Reinforcement following a particular response provides feedback (information) on the identity of the correct response. This informative function operates whether the reinforcement is experienced directly or indirectly through observation of others. Thus, seeing another person being punished is as informative as being punished directly (although a lot less painful!). Reinforcement also teaches us what to expect as a result of our actions. The experience of reinforcement for a particular action leads to an anticipation of reinforcement that motivates our behavior. As with informative properties of reinforcement, incentives can be experienced directly or indirectly.

SUMMARY

1. Learning is a relatively enduring change in behavior or behavior potential that results from experience or practice.

2. Two primitive forms of learning are habituation (a decreased readiness to respond to biologically irrelevant stimuli) and sensitization (an increased readiness to respond to biologically relevant stimuli).

3. Classical conditioning occurs when a neutral stimulus is paired repeatedly with an unconditioned stimulus that elicits an unconditioned response. After many such pairings, the neutral stimulus becomes a conditioned stimulus that elicits a "new" conditioned response.

4. Classical conditioning is most effective when the conditioned stimulus precedes the unconditioned stimulus. A conditioned response will extinguish if the conditioned stimulus is repeatedly presented alone. However, spontaneous recovery of the conditioned response will occur when the conditioned stimulus is presented again after a rest following extinction.

5. Stimuli that are similar to the conditioned stimulus also elicit conditioned responses, although of reduced strength. This phenomenon is called stimulus generalization. Conversely, an animal may learn to respond to one conditioned stimulus and not to another when the unconditioned stimulus regularly follows the former but not the latter. This process is called stimulus discrimination.

6. In instrumental and operant conditioning, a particular behavior is said to be instrumental or operant if it serves to attain a reward or avoid punishment. We speak of instrumental conditioning when the organism is per-

mitted to make only one response at a time; operant conditioning refers to situations in which the organism is free to respond as frequently as it desires.

7. In operant conditioning, behavior can be reinforced on either a continuous or a partial schedule. There are four basic schedules of partial reinforcement: fixed interval, variable interval, fixed ratio, and variable ratio. Ratio schedules (fixed and variable) produce a greater frequency of responses. Fixed interval schedules characteristically produce a scalloped pattern of responses on a cumulative record. Partial schedules of reinforcement generally lead to a greater resistance to extinction than continuous schedules of reinforcement.

8. An animal rewarded for a behavior performed in the presence of a particular stimulus will perform that behavior in the presence of stimuli similar to the original stimulus. This defines the process of stimulus generalization in instrumental and operant conditioning.

9. An animal will learn to respond in the presence of a stimulus if it is rewarded for doing so and will learn *not* to make that response in the presence of a stimulus when no reward is provided. This defines the process of stimulus discrimination in operant and instrumental conditioning.

10. A reinforcer is a stimulus that, contingent on a response being made, increases the likelihood of the reinforced response being emitted again. A positive reinforcer is a stimulus whose presentation is reinforcing; a negative reinforcer is a stimulus whose removal is reinforcing. Innately reinforcing stimuli are called primary reinforcers. Secondary or conditioned reinforcers are stimuli, not originally reinforcing, that have acquired reinforcing power by having been paired with primary reinforcers.

11. A punisher is a stimulus whose presentation, contingent on a response being made, decreases the likelihood of the punished response being emitted again. Punishment can be an effective method of eliminating undesired behavior when it is strong and administered immediately after the occurrence of the undesired response. However, the incidence of undesirable effects of punishment make its use questionable, especially if it is not used in conjunction with the positive reinforcement of desired behavior. Noncontingent punishment—given regardless of what an animal is doing—engenders learned helplessness. Research on learned helplessness may throw light on at least some forms of human depression.

12. The laws of classical, instrumental, and operant conditioning were long thought to be valid for all stimuli, all responses, and all animals. However, recent evidence indicates that the biological makeup of a species limits the nature and rate of an animal's learning.

13. The traditional view of learning held that reinforcement of overt responses was necessary for learning to occur. According to the more recent cognitive view of learning, however, neither overt responses nor reinforcement are necessary. Learning is viewed as the acquisition of information that occurs whenever the organism pays attention to its surroundings and to the relationship between what it does and the consequences of its actions. Evidence of cognitive learning is found in studies of sensory preconditioning (learning that one neutral stimulus follows another), latent learning (learning in the absence of a reward), learning set (learning how to learn), and insight (learning to solve problems).

14. Social learning occurs when an observer imitates the behavior of a model. The four processes identified by Bandura as necessary for social learning are attention, retention, reproduction, and motivation.

KEY TERMS

Learning
Unconditioned Stimulus (US)
Unconditioned Response (UR)
Habituation
Sensitization
Orienting Response
Classical Conditioning
Neutral Stimulus
Conditioned Stimulus (CS)
Conditioned Response (CR)
Reinforcer
Reinforcement
Delayed Conditioning
Trace Conditioning
Simultaneous Conditioning
Backward Conditioning
Extinction
Spontaneous Recovery
Stimulus Generalization
Semantic Generalization

Discrimination
Stimulus Substitution
Expectancy
Instrumental Conditioning
Law of Effect
Operant Conditioning
Skinner Box
Shaping
Continuous Reinforcement Schedule
Partial Reinforcement Schedule
Interval Schedule
Ratio Schedule
Fixed Schedule
Variable Schedule
Cumulative Recorder
Resistance to Extinction
Partial Reinforcement Effect
Stimulus Control

Discriminative Stimulus
Positive Reinforcer
Negative Reinforcer
Escape Learning
Avoidance Learning
Primary Reinforcer
Conditioned (secondary) Reinforcer
Punishment
Conditioned Punisher
Learned Helplessness
Instinctive Drift
Cognitive Learning
Sensory Preconditioning
Latent Learning
Learning Set
Insight
Social Learning
Modeling

RECOMMENDED READINGS

Flaherty, C. F. (1985). *Animal learning and cognition*. New York: Alfred A. Knopf. A thorough account of theory and evidence related to classical and instrumental conditioning.

Gagne, R. M. (1977). *The conditions of learning* (3rd ed.). New York: Holt. A useful introduction to learning with an emphasis on educational implications.

Mazur, J. E. (1986). *Learning and behavior*. Englewood Cliffs, NJ: Prentice-Hall. An up-to-date and broad-ranging survey of most forms of animal and human learning.

Razran, G. (1971). *Mind in evolution*. Boston, MA: Houghton Mifflin. A comprehensive attempt to integrate the many levels of learning into a coherent evolutionary framework.

Schwartz, B. (1984). *Psychology of learning and behavior* (2nd ed.). New York: W. W. Norton. A solid overview of state-of-the-art learning theory.

Skinner, B. F. (1938). *The behavior of organisms: An experimental analysis*. Englewood Cliffs, NJ: Prentice-Hall. A classic in the field of operant conditioning.

6

MEMORY AND THINKING

When we introduced the topic of *learning* in Chapter 5, we stressed that psychologists typically use the term in a special way. They apply the label *learning* to habituation and sensitization, classical and operant conditioning, behavioral changes following rewards and punishments, and related concepts. Yet, in daily conversation, we often use *learning* to refer to something quite different — the understanding, retention, and application of information that we hear and see. We might talk of learning Spanish verbs, learning the material in Chapter 6, and learning to play chess. The difference in the use of *learning* is the difference between a *habit* system, knowing how . . . , and a *memory* system, knowing that . . . (Mishkin & Petri, 1984). The *knowing-how* type of learning was examined in Chapter 5; we now consider the *knowing-that* type of learning, labeled *cognition* by psychologists. The breadth of topics covered by **cognition** is evident in its definition as "all processes by which the sensory input is transformed, reduced, elaborated, stored, recovered and used" (Neisser, 1967). Our discussion centers on the processes of *memory* and *thinking*. We begin by considering the remarkable abilities of two individuals, both of whom have been studied extensively in the field of memory research.

MEMORY

A patient, whose initials are HM, underwent a new and radical type of brain surgery in 1953. Since the age of 16, HM had suffered increasingly severe epileptic seizures; surgical removal of parts of his hippocampus was undertaken as a last resort. Because the seizures were eliminated, the operation was considered a success; in other respects, however, it was a tragic failure. In removing parts from both sides of HM's brain, the surgeons inadvertently removed his ability to establish new memories. Brain surgeons quickly abandoned this type of bilateral surgery, and HM survived to become a subject for research into memory processes during the next 30 years.

HM can understand and use language, but retaining newly acquired knowledge is impossible. Give him a seven-digit telephone number and he can repeat it correctly — if asked to do so immediately. Wait a few seconds, and all trace of it is gone. Because HM cannot remember directions, he is liable to become lost if alone on a trip. Sometimes he forgets the faces or names of people with whom he is familiar, and sometimes he forgets his age. Conversations with HM are difficult because he forgets information exchanged only moments earlier. This inability to commit information to memory has produced both unexpected costs and benefits for HM. For example, when he inquired about the health of an ailing relative — only to learn that he had died —

HM became quite upset. Because he quickly forgot, however, he was equally grief stricken on each subsequent occasion when he made the same inquiry and heard the same "news." Sometimes, however, there were advantages in being unable to remember. For example, HM maintained fresh interest through endless readings of the same book or magazine.

Despite a severe memory deficit, HM was still capable of learning some new skills. This became evident when he began to play the Tower of Hanoi game (a challenging puzzle in which a tower of six differently sized rings must be moved from one of three posts to another, one ring at a time, while never putting a larger ring upon a smaller one). After many attempts, HM solved the puzzle in the minimum number of moves. Yet, on each occasion he believed he was seeing the puzzle for the first time and professed to having no idea how to solve it!

S is the last initial of a Russian journalist whose memory appeared to be virtually perfect and who was studied for many years by the eminent neuropsychologist Alexander Luria (1968, 1972). S could listen to 70 or more items (numbers, letters, words, or sounds) and repeat them exactly — either forward or backward. And it seems he never forgot such information. On one occasion, S was asked to recall a list of 50 unrelated words that he had seen only once about 15 years earlier. He responded: "Yes, yes. . . .

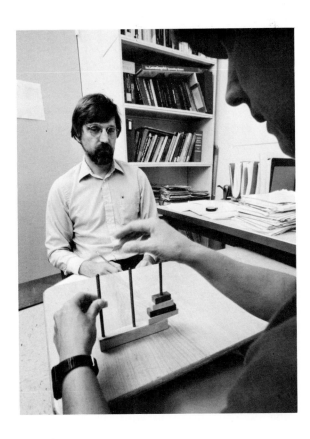

This was a series you gave me once when we were in your apartment . . . You were sitting at the table and I in the rocking chair . . . You were wearing a grey suit and were looking at me like this . . . Now then, I can see you saying . . .'' Then S quickly recalled the entire list of 50 words without a single error.

The amazing feats of memory shown by S seem to be related to his capacity for rich and vivid imagery. When presented with a 2,000 *Hz* tone, he said: ''It looks something like fireworks

tinged with a pink-red hue. The strip of color feels rough and unpleasant, and it has an ugly taste — rather like that of a briny pickle . . . you could hurt your hand on this.'' Although the vivid associations S made to each item no doubt contributed to his phenomenal memory, they also made it very difficult for S to abstract the meaning of even simple sentences. This is how he described his thought processes in one such instance.

> I read that ''the work got underway normally.'' As for *work,* I see that work is going on . . . there's a factory. . . . But there's that word *normally.* What I see is a big ruddy-cheeked woman, a *normal* woman. . . . Then the expression *got under way.* Who? What is all this? You have industry . . . that is, a factory, and this normal woman — but how does all this fit together? How much I have to get rid of just to get the simple idea of the thing!

The cases of HM and S provide a stark contrast. For the one, last-resort brain surgery virtually destroyed the ability to establish new memories; for the other, forming exceptionally rich and detailed associations created an apparently unlimited capacity for remembering experiences. Although the two cases are extreme examples, they raise certain issues that have challenged psychologists attempting to understand how normal human memory works. One such issue is the inability of HM to convert short-term memories into long-term memories — strong evidence that these two stages of memory are fundamentally different. Also, the experiences reported by S strongly suggest that forming elaborate associations to items being memorized greatly increases the likelihood of their being remembered. These and other salient aspects of memory are addressed in the first half of this chapter.

STAGES OF REMEMBERING

Pause for a moment to recall the last telephone call you made. Assuming the call occurred within the last day or so, you probably remember a good deal about the call: the person you talked to, the reason you called, some of the information exchanged, where and approximately when the call was made, what you were wearing, and so on. Doubtless, there are details you cannot recall: perhaps the last four digits of the number you dialed, the precise words spoken and who spoke

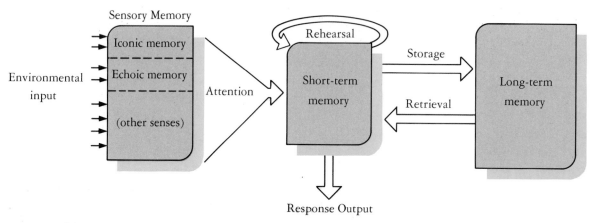

FIGURE 6-1

An Information-processing Model of Memory Input is held briefly in sensory memory before being selectively transferred by the process of attention to short-term memory. Rehearsal maintains items in short-term memory and increases the likelihood of their being stored in long-term memory. *Source:* Adapted from Atkinson, R. C., & Shiffrin, R. M. (1971). The control of short-term memory. *Scientific American, 225,* 82–90.

last. Just how is the knowledge you gain from experiences stored in your memory? What factors determine which information is remembered and which is forgotten? Is the forgotten information truly lost or only mislaid? What can be done to improve memory? These are the central questions addressed by memory researchers, most of whom favor an information-processing approach in their quest for answers.

Figure 6-1 shows a simple example of an information-processing model of memory. An imput, such as a word that is seen or heard, first enters *sensory memory.* There, a reasonably faithful representation of the input is maintained for a very short time. These sensory memories disappear within a second or two and their information is lost unless they are attended to. Paying *attention* transfers information from sensory memory to *short-term memory,* a limited capacity system that provides the contents of conscious awareness. The items in short-term memory are subjected to a variety of coding and organizational processes, such as *rehearsal,* that result in the transfer of some of the information to *long-term memory.* Except for very rare individuals like S, *retrieval* of information from long-term memory is an uncertain process that is prone to error. We now discuss these stages of memory in detail.

SENSORY MEMORY

Neisser (1967) gave the names *iconic memory* and *echoic memory* to the visual and auditory representations briefly held in **sensory memory.** Although such input from the other senses as smells and tactile impressions occasionally does enter into conscious awareness and may even be processed into long-term storage, for most of us memory is dominated by information that enters through our visual and auditory channels.

Iconic Memory

Evidence for the existence and nature of **iconic memory** was provided in a classic series of studies by Sperling (1960, 1967). Subjects in his experiments were shown a display such as that in Figure 6-2. The set of letters was flashed on a screen for about one-twentieth of a second. In the *full report* procedure, the subject was asked to identify as many of the letters as possible, re-

C	F	H	J
L	N	P	R
T	V	X	Z

FIGURE 6-2

Display Based on Sperling's Study of Sensory Memory The digits were displayed to subjects for a fraction of a second. The subjects' task was to identify the set of digits indicated by a signal given as the display was turned off.

gardless of their location. Usually subjects reported four or five letters and sometimes as many as six. Their impression of the remaining letters simply faded from sensory memory before they could be identified.

Sperling (1960) introduced a variation of this task that was to prove highly illuminating. Using a *partial report* procedure, subjects were cued by a tone to report the letters in one particular row (for example, high-frequency tone for top row, mid-frequency tone for middle row, low-frequency tone for bottom row). The tone indicating the row to be reported was not sounded until the moment the letter display was turned off. In the partial-report condition, subjects identified an average of just over three of the four letters in the signaled row, regardless of which row was called for. Subjects had no time to move their eyes in response to the cue so as to fixate the signaled row in the stimulus display. However, they could "look" at the signaled row by attending to the specified part of the iconic image stored in sensory memory. Sperling argued that inasmuch as subjects did not know which row to report until the display was turned off, their iconic storage must have held just over three letters *in each of the three rows*. He concluded, therefore, that at the moment the physical stimulus was removed, the iconic storage held about ten letters —or almost all of the twelve-letter display.

Iconic memories begin fading from sensory storage as soon as they are formed. Sperling measured the rate of fading by delaying the cuing tone for a varying time after the letter display was terminated. Figure 6-3 shows that the number of items available for report dropped from around ten at zero delay to about four at a one-second delay. At some point between one-third of a second and one second after the display is turned off, the iconic image fades and subjects remember only the letters already transferred to short-term memory.

Echoic Memory

It is possible to conduct a study very much like Sperling's in which the input is auditory rather than visual. Darwin, Turvey, and Crowder (1972) used a stereophonic recorder and headphones to provide subjects with three simultaneous messages: one to the left ear, one to the right ear, and one that seemed in the middle. Each message consisted of three letters or three numbers. The subjects' ability to report these messages was compared under full- and partial-report procedures (a visual signal was used to indicate whether the first, second, or third item in each message should be reported). Just as Sperling found for iconic memory, Darwin found that proportionately more letters were recalled under partial-report than under full-report procedures. **Echoic memory** holds auditory input for a short period during which the contents can be reported. Estimates of the length of this period range from less than a second to several seconds, depending on the method of measurement (Crowder, 1978).

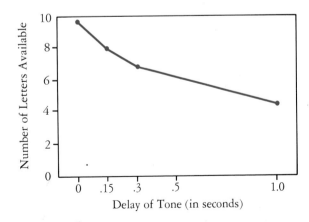

FIGURE 6-3

Fading of Information in Iconic Memory The number of digits a subject can report decreases as the signal indicating the target digits is delayed beyond the offset of the display. *Source:* Adapted from Sperling, G. A. (1960). The information available in brief visual presentations. *Psychological Monographs, 74* (Whole No. 498).

Attention

Iconic and echoic memories are immediate sensory representations of the information picked up from moment to moment by our eyes and ears. At this stage, memory is not particularly selective; all the input detected is registered in sensory storage —but not for long. Unless the observer takes action, the contents of iconic and echoic memory quickly disappear. The action that rescues this sensory information before it is lost is **attention.** You may find it helpful to think of the flashlight as a model for attention. When you shine a flashlight, its beam illuminates a portion of the visual scene. As you move the beam, different portions come into view. Just as the flashlight beam singles out and illuminates the portion at which it is directed, so attention selects a portion of the information in sensory storage for transfer to short-term memory where it then is available to conscious awareness.

What happens if there are competing demands for the spotlight of attention? Can you simultaneously process information from the sights you observe and the sounds you hear? The simple answer is yes, but only under certain conditions and only after considerable practice. Shiffrin and Schneider (1977) divide cognitive processes into *controlled processes,* which require undivided attention, and *automatic processes,* which require little if any attention. Because extracting information from the displays in Sperling's studies required that his subjects engage in controlled processing, it is easy to imagine that if they had had to respond to a simultaneous auditory input, it would have ruined their performance. Yet when they drove home from Sperling's laboratory, the subjects presumably could listen to a passenger or to the radio without impairing their ability to extract information from their iconic images about the road and other vehicles. Once they are sufficiently experienced at the task, drivers engage in a good deal of automatic processing as they monitor their visual input.

Attention is controlled voluntarily: you decide where to look and what to listen to. But attention also is captured by certain environmental events briefly registered in sensory storage. Although movement in peripheral vision remains a potent attention-getter, for humans it is no longer likely to signal the dire threat that made detection of movement so valuable to animals throughout evolution. Loud sounds also are likely to capture attention, as is the mention of your name in a conversation held within earshot. Whether controlled voluntarily or captured, attention usually is regarded as a necessary condition for remembering, at least for verbal material. Some psychologists dispute this view (for example, Dixon, 1983), but most accept that for information or events in sensory memory to receive full cognitive processing, they must be transferred to the next stage of remembering— short-term memory.

SHORT-TERM MEMORY

Short-term memory also has been called *working memory* and *active memory* (Anderson, 1985), labels that emphasize its functional position in the sequence of cognitive processes. The contents of short-term memory are *working* in the sense that they constitute knowledge currently in use; they are *active* in the sense that they are in the forefront of the mental stage: they represent the contents of conscious awareness. Information enters short-term memory from two sources, sensory storage (for example, iconic and echoic memory) and long-term memory. We focus here on the information that is transferred to short-term memory from sensory storage.

The psychologist attempting to study the fate of information in short-term memory faces the problem of how to prevent information in long-term memory from intruding. Suppose I want to know how long an item will remain stored in your short-term memory before the item fades away. I could simply present you with a list of common words, such as the word *elephant,* and vary the length of time that passed after each item before asking that you recall the word. The problem is that you already have the word *elephant* stored in your long-term memory, from where it was automatically and immediately activated by its presentation. We can safely assume that even without thinking about it, your knowledge (long-term memory) of elephants was updated immediately to include the information that the word was used as an item in this test. Consequently, any later recall of the word may well use information from long-term memory rather than from short-term memory.

The way around this obstacle is to ask that you hold some unfamiliar information in short-term memory, items not already stored in your long-term memory. Although it is difficult to suggest completely novel items, we can easily prepare *unfamiliar combinations* of items. The letter sequence *BJDIVAKX* and the nonsense syllables *KAJ, DEX,* and *NIR* are examples. The elements (letters) are familiar and easy to report; presumably, however, these particular sequences of letters are not already stored in your long-term memory. This is why psychologists typically have used verbal input (for example, unrelated letter sequences and nonsense syllables) in studies designed to reveal the characteristics of short-term memory. Before considering what such research has shown about the way items are coded in short-term memory and about the capacity of this storage, you should try to recall — without referring back — the three examples of nonsense syllables. Even though they were at the center of your attention some 15 – 20 seconds ago, they may well have already disappeared from your short-term memory.

Coding

Psychologists are interested in the code employed for storing information in short-term memory. One method used to investigate the **coding** process is to overload people's memory and then analyze the errors they make in attempting recall. Conrad (1964) provides a good illustration of this technique. Conrad had subjects attempt to memorize briefly displayed strings of unrelated letters, such as *RVKSJTLZPMHX,* presented visually. After presentation, the subjects were instructed to write down in correct order as many letters as they could remember. The number of letters presented exceeded the capacity of the subjects'

short-term memory, leading to recall errors being made. Conrad carefully examined the errors and found that subjects tended to confuse some letters but not others. For example, they often recalled the letter B when in fact the letter V had been presented. However, they virtually never recalled the letter X when V had been presented.

What might these errors reveal about the process by which the letters are coded? Note that B and V sound similar, whereas X and V do not. On the other hand, X and V look more alike than B and V. Conrad suggested that when their memories were overloaded, the subjects were forced to make educated guesses about letters they could not easily recall. It seems those guesses were guided by the sounds of the letters, not by their shapes, even though the letters had been presented visually. Subsequent research (Crowder, 1976) has confirmed that verbal information in short-term memory is, for the most part, coded acoustically (by the way it sounds) rather than visually (by the way it looks).

There is some evidence that the physical characteristics of visually presented verbal input (as examples, the shape of letters, whether they are in upper or lower case) initially are represented in a visual code (Posner & Keele, 1967). However, visually coded memories last only a second or two before being recoded in an auditory form (Matlin, 1983). There also is evidence that verbal input to short-term memory is coded semantically (for meaning). The importance of meaning has been demonstrated by Shulman (1972), who used the memory-confusion technique to demonstrate semantic coding in short-term memory. After presenting subjects with a ten-word list they were asked to remember, Shulman gave them a test word and asked whether the test word had been on the list. Shulman was interested in a certain kind of mistake that subjects often made: believing a word *not* on the list *was* on the list. Shulman sought to understand the kind of confusion people experienced: did the confusion lie in words that sounded alike (bored/board) or in words that were similar in meaning (board/plank)? Shulman found that confusion occurred most when the words were synonyms, not when they sounded alike, suggesting the subjects coded the words on the list according to meaning.

Capacity

How much information can we hold in short-term memory? The **capacity** of short-term memory is limited in two critical ways, size and duration. Size of short-term memory usually is measured in terms of **memory span.** Individuals' memory spans may be assessed by presenting them with item lists (commonly strings of unconnected letters or numbers) of various lengths and asking them to recall them immediately. The length of the longest list of items a person can recall without error is that person's memory span. Early experiments showed that the average person's memory span for unconnected letters or numbers is about seven items (Miller, 1956). However, this is not an exact figure; in fact, Miller reported

it as "7 ± 2." You can determine whether your memory span falls within this range by taking the test in Table 6-1.

If meaningfully connected, as letters are in words, many more items can be held in short-term memory. In fact, memory span for simple words is also about seven, even though the words may total 30 or more letters (see Table 6-2). When words are meaningfully connected to form sentences, even more letters can be retained. Clearly, it does not make sense to specify the capacity of short-term memory in terms of the number of individual letters or digits it can hold. Miller suggested the unit we should use is the **chunk**—a meaningful grouping of material (for example, one letter in an unconnected string, one nonsense syllable, one word in a list of uncon-

TABLE 6-1
Test Your Short-term
Memory Span*

6	2	9	7	3					
8	3	5	1	2					
1	5	2	9	7					
4	8	5	2	9	1				
2	6	3	5	1	8				
5	9	8	1	6	3				
7	4	2	1	9	3	5			
8	2	9	3	7	5	1			
6	9	3	7	4	2	8			
3	6	1	4	9	8	2	7		
9	2	8	6	1	7	4	5		
4	8	2	9	1	7	3	6		
3	9	1	4	2	7	5	8	6	
8	5	2	9	3	6	4	1	7	
6	3	7	1	9	8	4	2	5	
8	2	7	5	6	1	4	9	3	6
9	6	4	8	1	5	6	3	7	2
1	8	3	2	7	8	5	9	4	6

* Cover the table of numbers with a sheet of paper. When ready to take the test, slide the sheet down so as to uncover only the first row of numbers. Read the numbers aloud from left to right at the rate of about two digits per second; then immediately cover the row again and write down the digits in their correct order. Keep going until you make an error in recalling all three sequences of the same length. Your memory span, in this case *digit span,* normally is defined as the length of the sequence that you correctly recall about half the time. For this test, compute your digit span as the halfway point between the shortest sequence you got wrong and the longest sequence you got right.

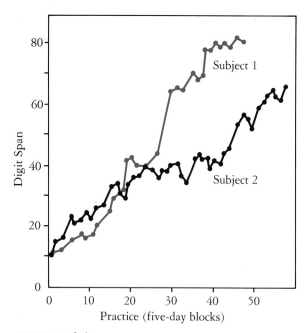

FIGURE 6-4
Practice Increases the Memory Span Two subjects each attempted immediate recall of strings of digits. Over many months of daily practice, the longest string they could recall without error increased dramatically. The improvement was due mostly to the chunking of successive sequences of three or four digits using a personally relevant framework of information. *Source:* Adapted from Chase, W. G., & Ericsson, K. A. (1982). Skill and working memory. In G. H. Bower (Ed.), *The psychology of learning and motivation* (Vol. 16). New York: Academic Press.

TABLE 6-2
Chunking of Information in Short-term Memory*

/	|	\	—	\	|	/
A	R	H	Q	G	I	W
JET	WOE	CRY	DOG	ASH	FIN	POP
Kidnapper	Penultimate	Bitterness	Artificial	Situational	Lip-reader	Redolence
Cost of living	Make my day	Black and white	Ready, set, go	Dean of Arts	Pass the salt	Queen of England
Out of sight, out of mind	Absence makes the heart grow fonder	A stitch in time save nine	He who hesitates is lost	Birds of a feather flock together	Nothing ventured nothing gained	Half a loaf is better than none

* Although the capacity of short-term memory is about seven items, the maximum amount of information that can be carried in short-term memory at one time depends on how informative each chunk is.

nected words, one phrase in a sentence, and so forth). Although the chunk is not a precise measure, it allows us to give an informed estimate of the capacity of short-term memory—one that takes into account the meaningfulness of the material being stored. The typical person's memory span is about seven chunks.

If we can remember many more letters when we chunk them into words (and so on), one way to improve the capacity of short-term memory may be to chunk short-term memory into increasingly larger units. This was the hypothesis tested by Chase and Ericsson (1982). Two subjects listened to digits presented at the rate of one per second and then attempted to recall them in the order presented. They practiced this task daily for about two years, each time measuring their memory span (the longest sequence of digits recalled correctly). Starting at a level of 9 digits, both subjects increased their memory span to an extraordinary sequence of more than 65 digits, with the best performance being an amazing 82 digits (see Figure 6-4). Improvement in the memory span of subjects in the Chase and Ericsson study was due largely to their developing personal chunking techniques: coding particular

groupings of three or four digits in meaningful ways. Thus, for one subject, who had a strong interest in running, the sequence *351* was *3 minutes 51 seconds, the old-world record for the mile.* Ages and dates were also used: *893* became *89.3 years, the age of a very old man* and *1946* became *one year after World War II ended.* Subjects also structured the chunks into groups of chunks, which allowed them to index the information in a way that facilitated retrieval.

Although the performance of Chase and Ericsson's subjects is impressive, their memory span for other items (for example, unrelated letters) remained entirely unaffected by their achievements with numbers. Note also, their performance was heavily dependent on information retrieved from long-term memory, and thus was not a pure test of the capacity of short-term memory.

In addition to being few in number at any one time, short-term memories are also short-lived. Murdoch (1961) showed just how short-lived in a study that used sequences of unrelated letters as stimuli and employed a counting task to prevent subjects from refreshing their memory between presentation and recall. Under such conditions, Murdoch found that a letter sequence

Box 6-1
Flashbulb Memories

Memories often seem to fade with time and eventually to disappear beyond recall. Yet some memories last a lifetime. For example, many people vividly recall such childhood experiences as breaking a limb, being caught misbehaving, or going on the first date. The details of such an event—where it occurred, what was said, who else was present, the emotion—seem as clear as if the event had happened today. What is it about some memories that seems to etch them indelibly in our minds? Although there is no complete answer to this question, some progress has been made in explaining it.

Brown and Kulik (1977) identified the distinguishing characteristics of one type of permanent memory, referred to as **flashbulb memory,** and proposed an explanation for its lasting quality. Flashbulb memories are "memories for the circumstances in which one first learned of a very surprising and consequential (or emotionally arousing) event" (p. 73). The outstanding example of flashbulb memory shared by many of Brown and Kulik's subjects concerns the circumstances in which they first heard of the death of President John F. Kennedy. Chances are you probably do not have a flashbulb memory for this event but probably do have for a more recent dramatic event, such as the explosion of the Challenger spacecraft in January 1986 that killed seven astronauts. Most likely you will find, as did Brown and Kulik, that people vividly recall where they were when they heard the news, what they were doing, who told them, how they and others felt, and what the immediate aftermath was. Ask your grandparents the same question about the Japanese attack on Pearl Harbor and the atomic bombing of Hiroshima and Nagasaki — these events created flashbulb memories for many people.

So far the examples of flashbulb memories concern events known by most adult members of our North American culture. Uniquely personal events also produce flashbulb memories. Hearing of the severe injury or death (by accident or suicide) of a close friend or relative often produces flashbulb memories. Perhaps you can supply your own example.

If you examine the events that produced flashbulb memories, you will notice they share two interesting characteristics. First, the events were unexpected — they created a high level of surprise. Second, the events were personally consequential — people's lives were affected by them; people lived, acted, and felt differently because of them. Extreme unexpectedness and consequentiality seem to be the major distinguishing characteristics of events that give rise to flashbulb memories. The importance of consequentiality was demonstrated nicely by Brown and Kulik, who found that black Americans — but not white

could be recalled correctly only 50% of the time after 5 seconds and only 25% of the time after 10 seconds. After 30 seconds, the chances of recalling the letters were very small (see Figure 6-5).

It might seem a liability to have such a fast-decaying short-term storage system; however, it is highly adaptive. Just as we attend only to a small proportion of the extensive information fleetingly available in sensory storage, so we select only a fraction of the contents of short-term memory for further processing. How many telephone numbers can you remember? Almost certainly

Americans—tended to have flashbulb memories for the death of Martin Luther King, Jr. Presumably this difference occurred because

King's death was more consequential for blacks than for whites.

In addition to describing the characteristics of flash-

bulb memories, Brown and Kulik proposed an explanation for their permanence. Imagine, early in the evolutionary history of *Homo sapiens,* that a cave dweller became involved in a highly unexpected and consequential event—perhaps he or she met a dangerous creature in a location where that creature had not been encountered previously. An event of that type threatens survival. To decrease the chances of harm from reoccurrence of that event, it is important an accurate and detailed record be made for future reference. At that time in history, human memory was the only record-keeping device. Accordingly, a special memory system may have evolved for storing a record of events of physical significance. As human culture evolved, individuals became more and more prone to experience danger second-hand (to hear of it rather than to live it). Brown and Kulik propose that the special memory system that evolved to deal with survival-threatening events in which one was involved directly was extended to cover those events to which one was a witness only.

fewer than a dozen. Yet you probably have had hundreds of them in short-term storage at one time or another. It simply was not worth the effort to commit them to long-term memory. Similarly, much of the detail of the information that passes through the spotlight of conscious aware-

ness is soon forgotten. You may regret this, particularly when studying for exams. However, recall the complaint of S discussed earlier in the chapter: "How much I have to get rid of just to get the simple idea of the thing." For S, the effort lay in forgetting, not remembering! Effective cogni-

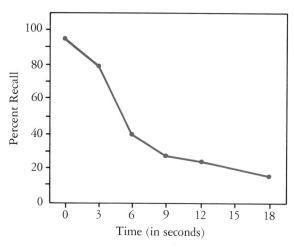

FIGURE 6-5

Decay of Information in Short-term Memory When rehearsal is prevented by requiring subjects to engage in a counting task between the presentation and attempted recall of unrelated letter strings, about half the letters drop from short-term memory after 5 seconds and most of the remainder decay within 30 seconds. *Source:* Adapted from Murdoch, B. B. (1961). The retention of individual items. *Journal of Experimental Psychology, 62,* 618–25.

tive functioning requires selective processing at the stage of short-term memory, and one mechanism for selective processing is rehearsal.

Rehearsal

If you look up a telephone number and want to remember it just long enough to make a call, what do you do? Most people repeat, or rehearse, the number. **Rehearsal** permits us to retain information in short-term memory beyond 15 to 30 seconds, and thus to increase the likelihood of that information being transferred to long-term

memory. An experiment by Rundus (1971) illustrates how this process may work. Rundus presented subjects with a long list of words at the rate of one word every five seconds and instructed the subjects to rehearse aloud any of the words during the five-second gap. By having subjects rehearse aloud, Rundus could record the number of times each word in the list was repeated. After presenting all the words, Rundus asked his subjects to recall as many of the words as possible in any order (termed a **free recall** procedure). Results showed the more often a word was rehearsed, the more likely it was to be recalled. Because the list contained more words than the subjects could hold in short-term memory, Rundus inferred the recalled words must have been transferred to long-term memory.

Subsequent studies (for example, Craik & Watkins, 1973) showed that a distinction must be drawn between two types of rehearsal. **Maintenance rehearsal,** the mere repetition of a to-be-remembered item, is not a particularly effective way of improving memory; **elaborative rehearsal,** the relating of to-be-remembered items to information already existing in long-term memory, is much more effective. As with chunking, elaborative rehearsal involves organizing incoming material in terms of information already in memory. A general finding in memory research is that organizing to-be-remembered material in any coherent way will increase the chances of that material being recalled. We discuss the role of organization in recall in more detail later in the chapter.

Other characteristics increase the likelihood of short-term memory being transferred to long-term memory; one of these, personal importance of event, we discuss in Box 6-1, page 256.

LONG-TERM MEMORY

The third stage of remembering is **long-term memory,** the storehouse of all knowledge and information we extract from a lifetime of experience. Earlier we asked that you recall the last telephone call you made. Assuming you retrieved some information about that call from

your long-term memory, in what form was it stored? Was visual information stored as images and auditory information stored as sounds? Or was the information coded in some other, nonsensory fashion? Cognitive psychologists have developed two different theories to answer these questions. The dual-code theory asserts long-term memory contains both verbal representations and visual images (Paivio, 1971, 1978). A rival theory claims long-term memories are stored as propositions that are neither visual nor verbal in character (Anderson, 1980, 1985; Kintsch, 1974). We now consider the evidence for these alternative views.

Dual-code Memory

According to the **dual-code theory,** we have two storage systems in long-term memory, one verbal and one visual. These systems are basically independent, but there is communication between them. The verbal system contains auditory memories of sounds we have heard and articulatory memories of sounds we have made. In both cases the sounds are generally from speech. When you remember something someone said, for example, you are retrieving the words and sentences stored in long-term memory at that time. Similarly, visual memories are literal representations of visual images experienced at an earlier time. So the dual-code theory seems plausible; after all, at least some of our memories fit these descriptions. Certainly, we remember the words of songs and poems and the vivid images of things we have seen. But remember the discussion of short-term memory: people also remember the *meaning* of experiences.

Eric Wanner (1968) assigned subjects in a memory experiment to a *warned* or an *unwarned* group. The warned group was alerted to listen carefully to the tape-recorded instructions that followed because they would be tested on their ability to recognize sentences taken directly from the instructions. The unwarned group was told nothing of a later recognition test. The instructions that followed consisted of several sentences describing how subjects should score their results, mark those that were wrong, and so on. The final instruction was to "turn the page," where they would find a recognition test. The recognition test contained pairs of sentences: one sentence was exactly as given (heard) in the instructions; the other sentence was the same except for two words. For some sentence pairs, this word difference affected the meaning of the sentence; for other pairs, the difference was stylistic only.

The subjects' task was to identify which sentence of the pair was the one that they had heard in the instructions. Their success rate is shown in Figure 6-6. If Wanner's subjects had remembered the exact wording of the sentences, they should have been equally successful at spotting word differences in meaning-change and style-change pairs. But this was not the case. Memory for meaning was clearly superior, and no warning was necessary to achieve it.

In may seem reasonable to you that we tend to store the general import or gist of verbal input rather than store it word-for-word. Although it may be less apparent that the same should hold for visual input, that does seem to be the case. You may have seen examples of ambiguous drawings called "droodles"; two are shown in Figure 6-7. They provide convenient stimuli for studying visual memory because they can be presented as meaningful or meaningless patterns. Bower and his colleagues (1975) found their subjects correctly drew from memory 70% of a set of droodles that were given meaningful labels [for example, a midget playing a trombone in a telephone booth; see Figure 6-7(a)] but only 50% of droodles that

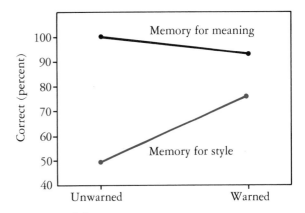

FIGURE 6-6

Memory for Meaning and Style Subjects were either warned or not warned that later they would be asked to recognize sentences they had heard. Key sentences on the recognition test were altered in ways that changed only their style or their style and meaning. Subjects were shown to be better at detecting meaningful changes than stylistic changes, regardless of forewarning. *Source:* Adapted from Wanner, H. E. (1968). *On remembering, forgetting, and understanding sentences. A study of the deep structure hypothesis.* Unpublished doctoral dissertation, Harvard University.

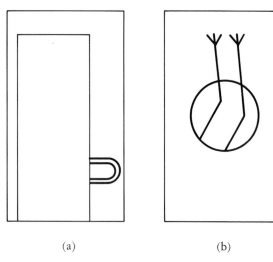

(a)   (b)

FIGURE 6-7

The Effect of Labeling on Memory Subjects are better at reproducing ambiguous figures from memory when the figures have been labeled than when unlabeled. These *droodles* show (a) a midget playing a trombone in a telephone booth and (b) an early bird who caught a very strong worm. *Source:* Adapted from Bower, G. H., Karlin, M. B., & Dueck, A. (1975). Comprehension and memory for pictures. *Memory and Cognition, 3*, 216–20.

were not labeled. Our memory for visual patterns is better if the patterns are meaningful. Mandler and Ritchey (1977) came to a similar conclusion about the influence of meaning on visual memory in a study that used drawings of classroom scenes. Using a paired-item recognition test similar to that employed by Wanner, they showed that subjects were much better at detecting a small change in a drawing when the change affected the picture's meaning (for example, what is drawn on the blackboard) than when it was only a token change (for instance, the pattern of the teacher's dress).

Propositional Memory

Evidence that people remember the meaning of experienced events better than the particular visual and auditory messages that convey the meaning has led some researchers to suggest that long-term memories are coded as propositional representations. This is not an easy suggestion to

understand. The dominance of visual and auditory images in conscious awareness and our practice of describing them in verbal terms make it difficult to think of memories in other terms. However, as we saw with perception, there is substantially more to mental processes than meets the eye (or ear). Anderson (1985) defines the term *proposition* as "the smallest unit of knowledge that can stand as a separate assertion, that is, the smallest unit about which it makes sense to make the judgment true or false" (p. 114). According to propositional-coding theory, knowledge is contained in networks that link associated propositions. A schematic representation of **propositional memory** is shown in Figure 6-8. Because these associations are numerous and link a wide range of propositions at many different levels, the networks are extremely complex. Although beyond the scope of an introductory psychology text, the theory of propositional representation of knowledge is an important contribution. Anderson (1980) has characterized it as "one of the major accomplishments of modern cognitive psychology" and as "a significant breakthrough in our understanding of the nature of human intelligence" (p. 123).

Neither dual coding nor propositional coding alone is likely to supply a complete and sufficient account of long-term memory. Proponents of each continue to accumulate evidence to support their cases (see Box 6-2). Regardless of how memories are coded, however, it has become clear that what is central to the process of remembering is the extraction and storage of the *meaning* of experience.

Memory for Meaning

Have you ever found that someone else remembers an event differently from you, though you both experienced it? The fact that virtually everyone has leads us to suspect that individuals may be more actively involved in the construction of memories than is usually assumed. Several experiments support and exemplify the suspicion that memories often are not a literal, objective record of experience. In one study, Owens and others (1977) had subjects read the account of a water-skiing incident involving two characters

Box 6-2
Visual Images in Long-term Memory — Comparing Clocks

Imagine a clock reading 6:35 (a clock with hands, not a digital device). Now imagine a similar clock reading 11:25. On which clock is the angle between the hour and minute hand longer? This is a simple task, and no doubt you had no trouble performing it. But exactly how did you do it? Many people report they formed a visual image of both clocks, "looked" at these images, and compared the angles between the hands. Since there are no physical representations of the two clocks to compare, the images they report using must be images retrieved from information stored in long-term memory. The ability to perform this task was offered by Paivio (1978) as evidence for the presence of visual encoding in long-term memory.

In an attempt to provide firmer evidence that long-term memory contains visually encoded information and that such information is used in the comparison-of-clocks task, Paivio logged the time it took subjects to say which angle was larger; that is, he used reaction time as a measure of cognitive pro-

cessing. Results indicated the greater the difference between the two angles, the faster subjects responded. For example, subjects responded faster when they compared 6:15 and 11:25 than when they compared 6:15 and 5:15. Another group of subjects was presented with pictures of clock faces, rather than being given the time in words or numbers. As with the earlier subjects, the greater the difference between the two angles, the faster the subjects responded. The similarity of results obtained in the memory condition (when subjects were told the times) and the perceptual condition (when pictures of clocks were presented) suggests that similar processes were occurring. That is, it suggests that subjects were looking at and comparing mental images in the one case, just as they looked at and compared perceptual information in the other.

Paivio offered other evidence in support of his interpretation. On the basis of their performance on a visual imagery test, subjects with high or low visual-imagery ability were identified.

These subjects then took part in the (mental) comparison-of-clocks experiment. What might we expect about the performance of high- versus low-imagery subjects? If visual imagery is employed in this task, subjects with high visual-imagery ability should be better able to create and employ the necessary mental images of clocks than subjects with low visual-imagery ability. In other words, high visual-imagery subjects should be faster (have lower reaction times) than low visual-imagery subjects. Paivio's results confirmed this prediction.

Paivio offers these findings as evidence for a visual code in long-term memory. Critics who believe the long-term memory code is abstract argue the visual images of the clocks were in short-term (working) memory when compared and had been generated from information retrieved from abstract propositions stored in long-term memory. The argument between memory theorists who favor a dual-code system and proponents of propositional representation remains unresolved.

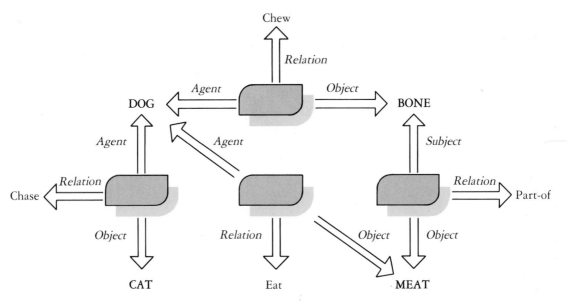

FIGURE 6-8

Propositional Memory A propositional representation of the concept **DOG** in an individual's memory. Note how the concept **DOG** links with other associated concepts. *Source:* From Anderson, J. R. (1985). *Cognitive psychology and its implications* (p. 147). New York: W. H. Freeman.

named Harry and Rick. In the story read by one-half the sujects, Harry was introduced first; for the other one-half, Rick was introduced first. Researchers expected typical subjects to identify with the first character they read about. After reading the otherwise identical stories, subjects were presented with several sentences and asked whether each sentence had occurred in the story they had just read.

At one point in the story, Rick fell while Harry was driving the boat and had difficulty getting hold of the tow rope. The specific sentence relevant to this incident was: "Rick reached for the handle, but it escaped him." The recognition sentences were :(A) "Rick reached for the handle, but he wasn't fast enough to catch it" and (B) "Rick reached for the handle, but the boat hadn't come close enough for him to catch it." Note sentence (A) assigns Rick's failure to grasp the handle to his own inability, whereas sentence (B) assigns the same failure to a situational factor (the boat was out of reach). As predicted, subjects who identified with Rick tended to reject sentence (A) and to accept sentence (B) as having occurred in the story. The reverse was generally true for those subjects who identified with

Harry. Results of this study show how, by varying a person's point of view, it is possible to vary his or her interpretation of events and consequently to shape the memory formed of those events. Although these differing interpretations matter little when they occur in the laboratory, they may be of considerable importance when they occur in the real world (see Box 6-3).

Capacity

Each of the memory stores discussed has had limited capacity in terms of volume and duration. Sensory storage holds the content of a single glance for a second or less (if unattended), whereas short-term memory holds about seven chunks of information for a minute or less (if unrehearsed). What is the capacity of long-term memory? The performance of S, described at the start of the chapter, suggests it may be much greater — perhaps even unlimited. S had what is popularly called a "photographic memory," one capable of retaining virtually all aspects of experience for a seemingly indefinite time.

But most of us do not have photographic memories; we forget things. Yet, forgetting does

Box 6-3
Leading Questions and Eyewitness Testimony

Imagine that you witness an automobile accident. The police arrive and, because you are the only eyewitness not involved in the collision, carefully question you on the details of the accident. Our legal system assumes, until proven otherwise, that your memory of the accident will not be distorted. As we shall see, however, your report of the events is likely to be influenced significantly by the manner in which you are questioned.

One mode of questioning might have you simply say what you saw; another might have you respond to specific inquiries. It is the latter that generates difficulties. It has become increasingly apparent over the past decade that there are numerous ways in which seemingly impartial inquiries can be leading questions—can implicitly suggest a particular version of what happened. For example, you might be asked "How fast was the car going when it ran the red light?" This question assumes the light was red when in fact it may have been amber. Or you might be asked "How fast was the car going when it smashed into the other car?" The verb "smashed" carries the connotation of high speed. Substituting the word "bumped" implies a quite different version of what happened. Although it may seem plausible that leading questions could affect what you say you saw, you probably doubt such questions could actually change your memory of the events. However, studies by Elizabeth Loftus and her colleagues seriously challenge this belief (Loftus, 1979; Loftus & Palmer, 1974).

In one study, subjects witnessed a 30-second video of two cars colliding head-on. Subjects were then asked several questions about the collision. Some subjects were asked "About how fast were the cars going when they smashed into each other?" Others were asked "About how fast were the cars going when they hit each other?" The question containing the word "smashed" is a leading question: the verb "smashed" suggests a rather violent collision and, therefore, a relatively high speed. Estimates of speed were higher when the question used "smashed" rather than "hit." One week later the subjects were asked additional questions about the video they had seen. The critical question was "Did you see any broken glass?" In fact, there was no broken glass visible in the video they had watched. Nevertheless, 32% of subjects in the "smashed" condition reported seeing broken glass compared to 14% of subjects in the "hit" condition.

In another study, Loftus had subjects witness a short video of a car traveling through the countryside. Afterward, some subjects were asked "How fast was the white sports car going when it passed the barn while traveling along the country road?" Others were asked "How fast was the white sports car going while traveling along the country road?" Note the first question presupposes the car passed a barn. In fact, it did not. One week later, subjects were asked a number of questions about the same event, including "Did you see a barn?" Of those who previously answered the question that presupposed the existence of a barn, 17.3% said "Yes." Only 2.7% of the other subjects claimed to have seen a barn. According to Loftus, leading questions may not only produce biased answers, they may also distort memory.

not necessarily mean gone forever. Forgotten items may be mislaid rather than lost. In other words, a forgotten memory may exist yet for some reason cannot be retrieved. A useful analogy is the library. If you go to the library to check out a book (retrieve a memory), you may be unsuccessful for two quite different reasons: the book may be out, or it may be in the library but on the wrong shelf. Although researchers have obtained clear evidence of decay in short-term memory, it has proven extremely difficult to demonstrate a similar fate for items held in long-term storage. Indeed, studies have found that many cases of apparent decay actually are cases of failure in retrieval.

THE RETRIEVAL PROCESS

Have you suffered the embarrassment of forgetting the name of a person you know well just at the moment of introduction or the frustration of being unable to recall important information during an exam (information that comes easily to mind immediately following the exam)? From time to time, we all find ourselves unable to retrieve information once available to us. What factors contribute to these **retrieval** failures? We now discuss several, beginning with some that operate at the time the memory is established.

Depth of Processing

Earlier we noted that the exceptional memory capacity demonstrated by S was probably related to the richness of his mental processes. Presentation to him of a simple stimulus such as a word triggered an entire range of associations to the appearance and meaning of the stimulus. For S, this happened spontaneously. For most of us, however, it requires a conscious effort. When we make the effort — when we engage in what is called a greater **depth of processing** of the input — the investment generally pays handsome dividends.

The beneficial effects on memory of deeper processing have been demonstrated in a study by Craik and Tulving (1975). These experimenters presented subjects with a list of words and asked them to decide whether a word (1) was in capital letters (*visual* decision), (2) rhymed with another word (*auditory* decision), (3) was a member of a semantic category (*category* decision), or (4) would fit into a particular sentence (*sentence* decision). After the subjects heard all the words, they were unexpectedly given a test of their ability to recognize the words. Results indicated that subjects were poorest at recognizing visual-decision words, did progressively better for auditory- and category-decision words, and performed best for sentence-decision words.

Craik and Tulving attribute these performance differences to the varying depth of processing required. For example, consider the word *rain*. To decide whether it is written in capital letters, one must code the word visually. To decide whether it rhymes with *feign,* one must first code the word visually (to identify its component letters) and then code it acoustically (to compare the two words). A semantic-category decision requires visual, acoustic, and semantic coding. Craik and Tulving used such evidence as this to support a theory (originally proposed by Craik & Lockhart, 1972) that the likelihood of retrieving a memory is determined by the depth to which the item has been processed. In general, the deeper the level to which an item is processed, the greater the number of ways in which it is coded and the greater the number of potential retrieval cues that are created.

The performance differences found by Craik and Tulving were impressively large. For example, their subjects were three times more likely to recognize a word if they had questioned its meaning than if they had questioned its physical appearance. Even more potent are questions involving self-reference. Rogers and other (1977) had some subjects answer the question "Does this word describe you?" while other subjects responded to questions that led to words being coded physically, acoustically, or semantically. Their performance on a subsequent recall test is shown in Figure 6-9.

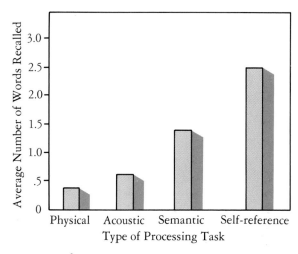

FIGURE 6-9

Level of Processing and Recall As words are processed to deeper levels—first visual, then acoustic, and finally semantic—the probability increases that later the words can be recalled. The best recall is obtained when the semantic processing involves self-reference. *Source:* Based on data reported in Rogers, T. B., Kuiper, N. A., & Kirker, W. S. (1977). Self-reference and the encoding of personal information. *Journal of Personality and Social Psychology, 35,* 677–88.

Organization of Memory

A second factor that influences whether long-term memories are remembered or forgotten is the extent to which the input is organized in some coherent way. Read the following list of words two or three times with the purpose of committing them to memory: *walk, one, around, quite, dog, took, tree, hurt, sunny,* and *tangled.* Now look away, count to 25, and then try to recall the words. If you organized the words into a short story, such as "I *took* my *dog* for his daily *walk one sunny* day but he got his leash *tangled around* a *tree* and *hurt* himself *quite* badly," your memory (recall) would have been much better than if you had treated the list as a series of ten unrelated words. Many studies have shown that when people organize material meaningfully, their ability to remember the information improves. This is true whether the material is organized in terms of semantic relationships, such as in stories (Bower & Clark, 1969), or in terms of visual images (Bower, 1972). Furthermore, this effect has been shown whether people

provide their own organization or whether the organization is provided for them (Mandler & Pearlstone, 1966). The core principle has been stated clearly by Lorayne and Lucas (1974): "You can remember any piece of information if it is associated to something you already know or remember" (p. 7).

What we already know represents a **schema** or framework within which to fit the material to be remembered. The power of a schema to enhance memory is demonstrated by the following passage that Bransford and Johnson (1972) asked their subjects to read.

> The procedure is actually quite simple. First you arrange items into several different groups. Of course one pile might be sufficient depending on how much there is to do. If you have to go somewhere else due to lack of facilities, that is the next step; otherwise, you are pretty well set. It is important not to overdo things. That is, it is better to do too few things at once than too many. In the short run this may not seem important but complications can easily arise. A mistake can be expensive as well. At first the whole procedure will seem complicated. Soon, however, it will become just another facet of life. It is difficult to see any end to the necessity for this task in the immediate future, but then one can never tell. After the procedure is completed one arranges the material into different groups again. They then can be put into their appropriate places. Eventually they will be used once more and the whole cycle will then have to be repeated. However, that is part of life. (p. 722)

If you are like Bransford and Johnson's subjects, you found this paragraph difficult to understand and later would recall no more than 2 or 3 of the 18 distinct ideas it contains. Your difficulty lay in being unable to relate the material to what you already know—you did not have an appropriate schema. When Bransford and Johnson told other subjects in advance that the passage is about washing clothes, the subjects found it much more understandable and could recall twice as many ideas as the uninformed subjects. If you read the passage again, knowing its subject matter, you will appreciate the difference. On the first reading, you probably had no problem understanding the sentence: "First you arrange items into several different groups," but its nonspecific reference made it easy to forget. However, when you know that "items" refers to socks, shirts, and shorts to be washed, the sentence becomes linked to a network of memories that makes the subject matter of the sentence more likely to be remembered.

We now consider some determinants of retrieval that operate at the time of recall.

The Tip-of-the-tongue Feeling

Try the test provided in Table 6-3. If you resemble the subjects in an experiment by Brown and McNeill (1966), there will be times when you cannot recall some of the words referred to, but feel you have them on the *tip of your tongue.* The **tip-of-the-tongue phenomenon** is the feeling that we have the information in memory but cannot retrieve it. Although we cannot recall it at the moment, we feel we certainly would recognize it if we read or heard the information somewhere. To study this phenomenon, Brown and McNeill presented subjects with an extended version of the test in Table 6-3. These researchers found

that when the tip-of-the-tongue phenomenon occurred, subjects often could recall the general sound of the word, the number of syllables, the first letter, and sometimes could give a synonym of the word. For example, when presented with the first description, subjects might say *singsang, simdan, sancan,* when the word they were searching for is *sampan* (the other words described are *sextant, nepotism, cloaca, ambergris,* and *apse,* respectively).

Brown and McNeill found that having subjects recall such information as the word's first letter often helped subjects retrieve a word on the tip-of-the-tongue. You may experience this when you attempt the test suggested by Baddeley

TABLE 6-3
The Tip-of-the-tongue Test*

1. A small boat used in the harbors and rivers of Japan and China, rowed with a scull from the stern, and often having a sail.

2. A navigational instrument used to measure angular distances at sea, especially the altitude of the sun, moon, and stars.

3. Favoritism, especially governmental patronage extended to relatives.

4. The common cavity into which the various ducts of the body open in certain fishes, reptiles, birds, and mammals.

5. An opaque, grayish, waxy secretion from the intestines of the sperm whale, sometimes found floating on the ocean or lying on the shore, and used in making perfumes.

6. An extending portion of a building, usually semicircular with a half dome; especially the part of a church where the altar is located.

* Try to identify the word that fits each definition below. There may be instances when you cannot think of the word being defined, yet you feel that you know it and that it is on the verge of coming to you. When there is a word on the tip of your tongue, see whether you can prompt its retrieval by writing down the following information about the word: (1) number of syllables, (2) initial letter, (3) words of similar sound, and (4) words of similar meaning.
Source: Based on material reported in Brown, R., & McNeill, D. (1966). The "tip of the tongue" phenomenon. *Journal of Verbal Learning and Verbal Behavior, 5,* 325–37.

TABLE 6-4
How Accurate Is the Feeling of Knowing?*

1.	Norway	O
2.	Turkey	A
3.	Kenya	N
4.	Uruguay	M
5.	Tibet	L
6.	Australia	C
7.	Portugal	L
8.	Romania	B
9.	Burma	R
10.	Bulgaria	S
11.	South Korea	S
12.	Iraq	B
13.	Cyprus	N
14.	Philippines	M
15.	Nicaragua	M
16.	Yugoslavia	B
17.	Colombia	B
18.	Canada	O
19.	Thailand	B
20.	Venezuela	C

* Before taking this test, cover the column of letters on the right. Keeping the letters covered, read down the list of countries on the left, attempting to identify each country's capital city. Now go over those you were unable to identify, noting in each case whether you know the answer but cannot retrieve it or do not know the answer. Finally, uncover the right column of first letters of capital city names and see whether this cue prompts the retrieval of the hard-to-remember names. The cue is more effective for cities whose names you feel you know than for those you feel you do not know. The answers are given below.
Source: Baddeley, A. (1982). Memory: A user's guide (p. 96). New York: Macmillan.

Answers   20. Caracas
grade 17. Bogota 18. Ottawa 19. Bangkok
13. Nicosia 14. Manila 15. Managua 16. Bel-
9. Rangoon 10. Sofia 11. Seoul 12. Baghdad
5. Lhasa 6. Canberra 7. Lisbon 8. Bucharest
1. Oslo 2. Ankara 3. Nairobi 4. Montevideo

(1982) and provided in Table 6-4, in which you are asked to name the capital city of various countries. Cover the column of individual letters before trying the test. For some countries you probably knew the answer, but for others the retrieval process was initially unsuccessful. In some of the latter cases, the first letter may have supplied the cue that triggered recall of a name on the tip-of-your-tongue. Baddeley reports that the "feeling of knowing" that accompanies the tip-of-the-tongue phenomenon is quite accurate in this type of circumstance. Using a test similar to that in Table 6-4, Baddeley found the first-letter cue prompted subjects to recall 50% of city names they thought they knew but only 16% of those they felt they did not know.

The parts of the stimulus are not alone in serving as a retrieval cue; the context in which the stimulus is presented also can be an important factor in determining whether later attempts at retrieval are successful.

Context Effects

The role played by context in retrieval was demonstrated in dramatic fashion by Godden and Baddeley (1975) in a study prompted by the difficulty an acquaintance was having in conducting a study of fish behavior. Deep-sea divers observed the actions of fish as they entered or escaped from the nets of trawlers. Yet when the divers surfaced, they were unable to retrieve much information about what they had observed. Although the practical problem was solved by equipping the divers with underwater tape recorders, the experience prompted Godden and Baddeley to look closer at what they saw as evidence of **context-dependent recall.** They examined the evidence under better controlled conditions by having divers memorize lists of unrelated words either on land or under about ten feet of water. Some time later, either on land or under water, the divers were asked to recall the words. As shown in Figure 6-10, retrieval was more successful when the conditions in which recall took place matched those in which the memories were stored. Later research has shown this effect is peculiar to tasks that require recall; it does not occur in tasks that require recognition (Godden & Baddeley, 1980). Research also has shown that impairment of recall due to a changed context can

be avoided if subjects are asked to *imagine* the original context shortly before attempting recall (Smith, 1979).

We have used the term *context* in reference to *external environment,* but *internal environment* also may influence the retrieval process. Such is the basis of the alcoholics' complaint that when sober they cannot remember where they hid their bottle when drunk, and when drunk they cannot remember where they hid their money when sober. When a person's physical state affects recall of information received when in a different state, psychologists refer to the phenomenon as **state-dependent recall.** An example is provided by Eich and his colleagues (1975) who had subjects commit word lists to memory soon after smoking either a regular cigarette or a marijuana cigarette. Four hours later the subjects attempted to recall the words, again after smoking either a regular or a marijuana cigarette. Their performance, shown in Figure 6-11, provides clear evidence of the state dependency of the retrieval process. A similar effect has been demonstrated for changes in mood (Parker, Birnbaum, & Noble, 1976).

We have used the term *recall* to describe successful retrieval of information from long-

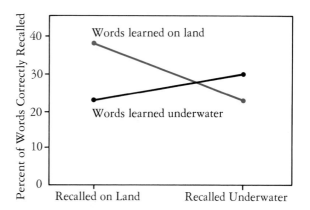

FIGURE 6-10

The Influence of Context on Memory Divers memorized word lists either on land or underwater, and later attempted to recall the words in each environment. The context-dependency of memory is demonstrated by the impairment of recall when the conditions were changed between presentation and retrieval. *Source:* Adapted from Godden, D. R., & Baddeley, A. (1975). Context-dependent memory in two natural environments: on land and under water. *British Journal of Psychology, 66,* 325–31.

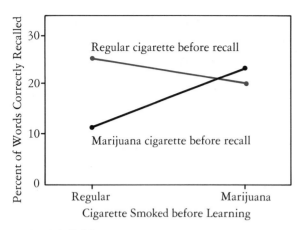

FIGURE 6-11

The Influence of Internal Environment on Memory Subjects memorized word lists after smoking a regular or marijuana cigarette. When later attempting to recall the words—again after smoking a regular or marijuana cigarette—the state-dependency of their memory was demonstrated by the impairment of recall when the conditions were changed between presentation and retrieval. *Source:* Based on data reported in Eich, J., Weingartner, H., Stillman, R. C., & Gillin, J. C. (1975). State-dependent accessibility of retrieval cues in the retention of a categorized list. *Journal of Verbal Learning and Verbal Behavior, 14,* 408–17.

term memory, implying that what is being retrieved is information stored at the time of the experience. However, there is ample evidence that at least some of our memories are *reconstructed* rather than recalled.

Recall or Reconstruction?

What were you doing at 2:00 PM on the second day of January, two years ago? Most likely you cannot respond immediately. Memories of past events —particularly memories not refreshed by recall —tend to fade. However, if you really needed to remember—perhaps because a judge asked you to—you probably could reconstruct a relatively accurate memory of that afternoon. You might start by indentifying the year ("Two years ago— when I was 17. . ."), identifying what you were doing generally ("I was a senior at Central High."), where you were living ("We lived on Laurel Street then."), and what you might have been doing ("I was on Christmas vacation; we usually went to visit our grandparents right after New Year's Eve. Grandmother always served lunch at 1:00, and I usually washed the dishes.

So I probably was washing the dishes at 2:00 that afternoon.") The preceding memory consists of a mixture of events actually remembered and events that must have occurred; we infer the latter from the former. Memory based on fragments of original experiences plus general knowledge about how things typically operate is called **reconstructed memory.**

One source of the discrepancies between actual events and reconstructions of them is people's expectation that the world is more orderly and consistent than it really is. Thus, reconstructed memories often contain more consistent and orderly descriptions than warranted by the actual events on which the memories are based. An experiment by Owens and others (1979) nicely illustrates this point. Two groups of subjects read the following somewhat unexceptional account of a visit to a physician by a person named Nancy.

> Nancy went to see the doctor. She arrived at the office and checked in with the receptionist. She went to see the nurse who went through the usual procedures. Then Nancy stepped on the scale and the nurse recorded her weight. The doctor entered the room and examined the results. He smiled at Nancy and said, "Well, it seems my expectations have been confirmed." When the examination was finished, Nancy left the office.

Some subjects read only the preceding material; for others (those in the theme condition), the story was preceded by a brief additional description.

> Nancy woke up feeling sick again and wondered if she really were pregnant. How would she tell the professor she had been seeing? And the money was another problem.

Twenty-four hours later, all subjects were asked to recall the story as accurately as possible. Results of this study, provided in Table 6-5, show the number of correct and inferred (incorrect) propositions recalled by the subjects in each group. Of most interest is the relatively large number of incorrect propositions reported by the theme group: they apparently used the additional information to interpret the story, and in doing so embellished it. For instance, many theme-group subjects incorrectly recalled reading that Nancy was depressed, although nothing in the story al-

TABLE 6-5
The Embellishment of Memory*

	Control Condition	Theme Condition
Propositions Correctly Recalled	20.2	29.2
Propositions Incorrectly Inferred	3.7	15.2

* Control subjects *misrecalled* (incorrectly inferred) relatively few statements or propositions from a story read a day earlier. However, when the story had been preceded by information that identified its theme, subjects both misrecalled and correctly recalled many more propositions than control subjects.
Source: Adapted from Owens, J., Bower, G. H., & Black, J. B. (1979). The "soap opera" effect in story recall. *Memory and Cognition, 7,* 185–91.

luded to her mood, and many subjects mistakenly recalled the doctor telling Nancy she was pregnant. It seems clear theme-group subjects were recalling a meaningful elaboration of the information presented rather than the information itself. Note this elaboration also aided their *correct* recall of the story elements: theme-group subjects recalled about 50% more correct propositions than control-group subjects.

Given that most of our experiences involve familiar objects and events, remembering is partly a matter of updating previously established memories. If, for example, we learn that one of our single friends has recently married, we update our previously stored knowledge (that he or she is single). However, research has shown that updating memories may cause two types of distortion. First, we tend to remember only those events that support our present interpretation; second, we tend to reinterpret past events in a manner that supports our present interpretation. A study by Snyder and Uranowitz (1978) exemplifies these points.

Snyder and Uranowitz asked subjects to read and remember an extensive case history about a woman called Betty K. Later, the information about Betty that the subjects had memorized was updated. One-half the subjects were informed that Betty was now leading a homosexual lifestyle; the other one-half were informed she was leading a heterosexual lifestyle. One week later, all subjects were given a recognition memory test for factual information about Betty K. The results indicated the update (that she is a homosexual or she is a heterosexual) greatly influenced the subjects' memories for past events in Betty's life. Subjects who were told she was homosexual remembered many more incidents relevant to this characteristic than those told she was heterosexual.

Some insight into the process involved in updating memories was obtained from this study by comparing the memories of people who had read the case study of Betty K. with a set of fabrications constructed by a group of subjects who were told nothing about her except that she was homosexual. Results of this comparison revealed clear differences between updating and fabrication. The researchers concluded that the reconstruction errors of the subjects who had read the case history probably were not due to deliberate fabrication. Instead, they resulted from the normal and necessary process of updating memories, a process that often involves considerable elaboration and embellishment.

In conclusion, our discussion of long-term memory and the retrieval process presents evidence that supports a model of memory in which meaning plays a central role. Just as we actively interpret information that produces perceptions, we actively construct and reconstruct information in memory. Memories are not inscribed on a static microchip in the mind. Rather, they are units in a highly integrated system of knowledge that is constantly undergoing transformation and change.

IMPROVING MEMORY

Most people use devices to help them remember associations that otherwise are easily forgotten. Some devices employ rhyming as a basis of association: "Thirty days hath September. . . ." Others employ spatial association. Make a fist with each hand, then touch your index fingers with palms down. Starting with January, the months are assigned alternately to the knuckles and the spaces between them. Months that fall on a knuckle have 31 days; those in between are shorter. Another spatial aid can help you remember how the axes of a graph are labeled: which of the *ordinate* and the *abscissa* is the vertical axis and which is the horizontal axis. Simply consider the shape made by your lips as you speak the first syllable of each label. Other devices employ sentences or names constructed from the first letters of unrelated words that must be remembered in sequence. The only way many people remember the order of colors in the rainbow (red, orange, yellow, green, blue, indigo, violet) is by storing the sentence *Richard of York Gave Battle in Vain* or the name *ROY G. BIV*. Certain more elaborate memory aids, called **mnemonics** (the first **m** is silent), are described in Box 6-4.

The method of loci and the peg-word technique are designed to help people recall unrelated items in a specific order. Although remarkably effective, both have two limitations. First, they require considerable time and effort to learn. Second, we seldom need to remember unrelated items in a specific order.

The retrieval failures most of us want to avoid typically are quite different from those involved in remembering the specific order of things. The aspect of memory most students would like to improve is the ability to retrieve

BOX 6-4
MNEMONICS

Mnemonics are techniques designed to improve memory. One such device is the *peg-word technique,* which supplies an organized list of retrieval cues. It is particularly useful for memorizing a list of items in exact order: the cranial nerves, the planets (starting at earth), the kings and queens of England, or the presidents of the U.S. Suppose you chose to use the peg-word technique to help remember, in order, the following list of ten words: hat, elephant, lamp, sausage, telephone, bucket, radio, paint, book, cigar. First you would memorize a sequence of cues like that shown in the table. Then you would form a vivid (preferably bizarre) image that asso-

ciated the first word, *hat,* with the first cue word, *bun.* Perhaps you would visualize a hamburger *bun* walking down the street wearing a bowler *hat.* Next you would form an image of the second word, *elephant,* that linked it with the second cue word, *shoe.* And so on for all ten items.

The Peg-word Mnemonic*

1 - bun	6 - stick
2 - shoe	7 - heaven
3 - tree	8 - gate
4 - door	9 - line
5 - hive	10 - hen

* Commonly used pairings between numbers and cue-words rhyming.

To recall the first word on the list, you recall the first cue word, *bun*, and then retrieve the image you associated with it. The image of a bun with a hat walking down the street should spring to mind. The remaining words on the list would be recalled in similar fashion. If you want to remember a list of more than ten items, simply associate more than one item on the list with each peg word. For example, you might connect the word *bun* to an image involving *hat* (the first item) and to an image involving *radiator* (if that is the eleventh item).

One problem with the peg-word technique is the difficulty people have in forming images of such to-be-remembered items as proper names (for example, names of the U.S. presi-

information in textbooks. We turn now to this type of retrieval.

Study Techniques

Memory can be improved by asking questions about the to-be-remembered material, as demonstrated in a study by Frase (1975). This point directly applies to study habits. Frase divided subjects into pairs, and had one member of each pair compose questions relevant to the passages being read in the first one-half of the text. These questions were then given to the other subject in the pair, who tried to answer them as he or she read the same passages. The subjects then reversed roles and worked on the second one-half of the text. Finally, all subjects took a test of their memory for all the material they read. (Frase also had a control group that simply read the text without any special instructions.) Results of Frase's study are shown in Table 6-6. Clearly, material that had been questioned was remembered better than material that had not. The slight superiority of composing questions over answering questions has been confirmed by other researchers (for example, T. H. Anderson, 1978).

Many textbooks contain end-of-chapter questions that prompt readers to review the material they read. Are such questions useful? Would such questions be more or less useful at the beginning of a chapter than at the end? Rothkopf (1966) provided one group of subjects with *pre-*

dents). This problem can be overcome by first forming some readily visualized association to the name (Washington — tons of wash) and then linking this image with the relevant item from the *one-bun* sequence.

Another mnemonic that makes use of organized cues for retrieval is the *method of loci* (*loci* is Latin for *places*). It is similar to the peg-word technique, except that well-known places are used as cues instead of the *one-bun* sequence. To employ this technique, you retrieve from long-term memory visual images of familiar locations and objects and arrange them in a logical sequence. For example, you might imagine entering the front door of your home and walking through the entry and living room on the way to the kitchen. Along the way you would pass several familiar items: an entry closet, a barometer on the wall, a couch, a stereo system, a coffee table, a kitchen door, a refrigerator, a stove, and a kitchen sink. Because you have taken this route many times, it should be easy to image and to remember. Arranged in order, these locations and objects now can be used as cues in the same way as the *one-bun* sequence. The first item on the list you want to remember (for example, the word *hat*) is linked with the first location, the front door. You might visualize a hat hung on the front door. Similarly, the second item is imagined at the second location, and so on. To recall the items, take a mental walk through the rooms. At each location, retrieve the image formed and thus retrieve the item to be remembered.

Although a number of studies have shown the peg-word technique and the method of loci are extremely effective ways of improving memory (Bugelski, Kidd, & Segman, 1968; Crovitz 1970), these and other studies also have shown that to be effective the images formed must be interactive. Simply visualizing a hat and a bun or a hat beside a bun would not have been particularly effective in the preceding example, because such images of the two items are not linked interactively. Also note that even though we have discussed the formation of linked visual images, language also can express a vivid interaction between the items. The critical factor appears to be organizing the peg word and the to-be-remembered item in an integrated structure, be it imaginal or verbal.

TABLE 6-6
The Effect of Questioning on Retention*

	Question-Composing Condition	Question-Receiving Condition	Control Condition
Information Relevant to Questions	70%	67%	
			50%
Information Irrelevant to Questions	52%	49%	

* Subjects read a text while keeping in mind questions that addressed some but not all the information contained in the text. The subjects composed half the questions; the remainder were composed for them. Compared with control subjects who simply read the text, questions — regardless of origin — substantially improved recall of relevant information without impairing retention of irrelevant information.
Source: Adapted from Frase, L. T. (1975). Prose processing. In G. H. Bower (Ed.), *The psychology of learning.* New York: McGraw-Hill.

view questions relating to information in a three-page segment of a textbook chapter and provided a second group with *review* questions on the same material. For both groups, questions covered some of the material in the three-page segment (*relevant*) but not other material (*irrelevant*). A control group simply read the text without benefit of questions. The subjects' performance on a final recall test of relevant and irrelevant material is shown in Table 6-7. As in Frase's study, large gains were made by subjects who used either preview or review questions, compared to subjects in the control group. There was no difference in the effectiveness of preview and review questions for relevant material; however, review questions were significantly better than preview questions at enhancing the recall of irrelevant information.

These and other findings have led to the development of numerous study guides designed to help readers retain information read in textbooks. One example is the popular **PQ4R method** (Thomas & Robinson, 1972), which advises readers to *p*review, *q*uestion, *r*ead, *r*eflect, *r*ecite, and *r*eview the material in each chapter. Although it requires considerable self-discipline to follow this plan, there is clear and convincing evidence that doing so greatly increases the effi-

ciency of study and improves retention of information learned.

1. *Preview*   Familiarize yourself with the range of topics to be covered and identify how each topic is organized into units. Complete the following steps for each unit.

2. *Question*   Prepare questions that focus on the key concepts and issues in each unit (for example: What are the six stages of the PQ4R method?).

3. *Read*   Keeping the questions in mind, read the material in the unit with the goal of learning the answers.

4. *Reflect*   As you read, pause to reflect upon the meaning of the information presented and its relation to what you already know.

5. *Recite*   Try to recall what you have read, using your questions as reminders. Reread sections, as necessary, to refresh your memory of information that proves difficult to retrieve.

6. *Review*   Finally, review in your mind the material covered in the entire chapter, again using the questions to structure this task.

DIRECTED THINKING

We now turn to a consideration of how the knowledge accumulated in long-term memory guides and informs the process of think-ing. Specifically, we are concerned with **directed thinking,** the manipulation of knowledge to achieve some goal. A good example of

TABLE 6-7
Should Questions Preview or Review Material? *

	Questions Previewed Text	Questions Reviewed Text	Control Condition
Information Relevant to Questions	72%	72%	
			30%
Information Irrelevant to Questions	29%	42%	

* Subjects read a text while keeping in mind questions that addressed some but not all the information contained in the text. The questions occurred every three pages; they either previewed the upcoming material or reviewed the preceding material. Compared with control subjects who simply read the text, preview and review questions were equally effective in boosting retention of the information they covered. Review questions also enhanced recall of irrelevant information.
Source: Adapted from Rothkopf, E. Z. (1966). Learning from written instruction materials: An explanation of the control of inspection behavior by test-like events. *American Educational Research Journal,* **3,** 241–49.

directed thinking is detective work. Sherlock Holmes, the fictional private detective created by English author Sir Arthur Conan Doyle, exemplified the qualities of the ideal detective. In addition to possessing broad general knowledge and acute powers of observation, Holmes said, detectives must be able to think logically. Holmes, of course, possessed this ability, and his "cases" are perhaps best known for their demonstration of the power of reasoning (see Box 6-5).

There are two primary types of reasoning, deductive and inductive. **Deductive reasoning** is the process of drawing conclusions from premises according to certain logical rules. **Inductive reasoning** is the process of making general inferences based on particular observations or knowledge. Let us first examine deductive reasoning.

Deductive Reasoning

An example of deductive reasoning follows.

> *Premise 1*   All parrots are birds
> *Premise 2*   All birds can fly
> *Conclusion*   Therefore, all parrots can fly

Two statements called **premises** are combined to produce a third statement, referred to as the *conclusion.* Given that parrots are a member of the class "bird" and that birds have the property "can fly," it may be deduced that "parrots can fly."

You may not be impressed by the intellectual force of this type of reasoning; it seems too simple even to be described as reasoning. After all, we normally do not think of $2 + 2 = 4$ as an example of reasoning. But what does $1,437 + 6,294$ equal? This does require reasoning: you must calculate the answer by using the rules of arithmetic. Similarly, the rules of deductive logic allow you to establish *new* knowledge from *old* knowledge. You may never have seen a parrot fly, but you can deduce the knowledge that it does. The logical rule being applied in this example can be stated in the following general form.

> *Premise 1*   All *A* are *B*
> *Premise 2*   All *B* are *C*
> *Conclusion*   Therefore, all *A* are *C*

Aristotle, the Greek philosopher who wrote the rules of deductive logic, developed several variations on this theme. For example, the second premise can be stated in a negative form: "No *B* are *C*." Can you deduce how this changes the conclusion? It is easier if the problem is stated in concrete form.

> *Premise 1*   All parrots are birds
> *Premise 2*   No birds have teeth
> *Conclusion*   ?

If your answer is ". . . no parrots have teeth" (". . . no A have C"), you are thinking logically.

Now, return to Box 6-5 and look for examples of deductive reasoning in Sherlock Holmes' thinking. One such instance occurs when Holmes combines the observation that the watch is scratched with the premise that scratched watches belong to careless people: deducing that the watch in question was owned by a careless person. Later, Holmes attributes the total accuracy of his reasoning to luck: "I could only say

BOX 6-5
REASONING AS DETECTIVE WORK

Perhaps the most famous of all fictional detectives is Sherlock Holmes. Holmes' talent for reasoning is demonstrated in the following extract from *The Sign of Four,* in which Holmes responds to a challenge from his venerable colleague, Dr. John Watson. Watson speaks first.

"I have heard you say it is difficult for a man to have any object in daily use without leaving the impress of his individuality upon it in such a way that a trained observer might read it. Now, I have here a watch which has recently come into my possession. Would you have the kindness to let me have an opinion upon the character or habits of the late owner?"

I handed him over the watch with some slight feeling of amusement in my heart, for the test was, as I thought, an impossible one, and intended it as a lesson against the somewhat dogmatic tone which he occasionally assumed. He balanced the watch in his hand, gazed hard at the dial, opened the back, and examined the works, first with his naked eyes and then with a powerful convex lens. I could hardly keep from smiling at his crestfallen face when he finally snapped the case to and handed it back.

"There are hardly any data," he remarked. "The watch has been recently cleaned which robs me of my most suggestive facts."

"You are right," I answered. "It was cleaned before being sent to me."

In my heart I accused my companion of putting forward a most lame and impotent excuse to cover his failure. What data could he expect from an uncleaned watch?

"Though unsatisfactory, my research has not been entirely barren," he observed, staring up at the ceiling with dreamy, lack-luster eyes. "Subject to your correction, I should judge that the watch belonged to your elder brother, who inherited it from your father."

"That you gather, no doubt, from the H. W. upon the back?"

"Quite so. The W. suggests your own name. The date of the watch is nearly fifty years back, and the initials are as old as the watch: so it was made for the last generation. Jewelry usually descends to the eldest son, and he is most likely to have the same name as the father. Your father has, if I remember right, been dead many years. It has, therefore, been in the hands of your eldest brother."

"Right, so far," said I. "Anything else?"

"He was a man of untidy habits—very untidy and careless. He was left with good prospects, but he threw away his chances, lived for some time in poverty with occasional short intervals of prosperity, and finally, taking to drink, he died. That is all I can gather."

I sprang from my chair and limped impatiently about

what was the balance of probability," he states. Holmes is referring here to an important characteristic of the second primary type of logical thinking, inductive reasoning.

Inductive Reasoning

From the observation that the watch is expensive, Holmes infers that the owner was "pretty well cared for." Going beyond the evidence in this fashion is called inductive reasoning. It is made possible by the fact that objective properties tend to go together. If a person owns an expensive item, it is likely that he or she is well cared for. But this is only likely, not certain—what Holmes was referring to when he spoke of "the balance of probability." Unlike deductive reasoning, which is sure to produce valid conclusions (pro-

the room with considerable bitterness in my heart.

"This is unworthy of you, Holmes," I said. "I could not have believed that you would have descended to this. You have made inquiries in the history of my unhappy brother, and you now pretend to deduce this knowledge in some fanciful way. You cannot expect me to believe that you have read all this from his old watch! It is unkind and, to speak plainly, has a touch of charlatanism in it."

"My dear doctor," said he kindly, "pray accept my apologies. Viewing the matter as an abstract problem, I had forgotten how personal and painful a thing it might be to you. I assure you, however, that I never even knew that you had a brother until you handed me the watch."

"Then how in the name of all that is wonderful did you get these facts? They are absolutely correct in every particular."

"Ah, that is good luck. I could only say what was the balance of probability. I did not at all expect to be so accurate."

"But it was not mere guesswork?"

"No, no: I never guess. It is a shocking habit— destructive to the logical faculty. What seems strange to you is only so because you do not follow my train of thought or observe the small facts upon which large inferences may depend. For example, I began by stating that your brother was careless. When you observe the lower part of that watch-case you notice that it is not only dented in two places but it is cut and marked all over from the habit of keeping other hard objects, such as coins or keys, in the same pocket. Surely it is no great feat to assume that a man who treats a fifty-guinea watch so cavalierly must be a careless man. Neither is it a very far-fetched inference that a man who inherits one article of such value is pretty well provided for in other respects."

I nodded to show that I followed his reasoning.

"It is very customary for pawnbrokers in England, when they take a watch, to scratch the numbers of the ticket with a pin-point upon the inside of the case. It is more handy than a label as there is no risk of the number being lost or transposed. There are no less than four such numbers visible to my lens on the inside of this case. Inference—that your brother was often at low water. Secondary inference — that he had occasional bursts of prosperity, or he could not have redeemed the pledge. Finally, I ask you to look at the inner plate, which contains the keyhole. Look at the thousands of scratches all round the hole—marks where the key has slipped. What sober man's key could have scored those grooves? But you will never see a drunkard's watch without them. He winds it at night, and he leaves these traces of his unsteady hand. Where is the mystery in all this?"

"It is as clear as daylight," I answered. "I regret the injustice which I did you. I should have had more faith in your marvelous faculty."

Source: Doyle, C. A. (1953). *The Sign of Four.* In *The Complete Sherlock Holmes.* New York: Doubleday.

viding the rules of logic are followed), the products of inductive reasoning are probably but not certainly true.

Inductive reasoning is appropriate for making a general inference based on limited evidence. For example, if you observe that on several occasions good weather follows a red sunset, you might infer that this is a general weather pattern ("Red sky at night, sailor's delight . . ." as the saying goes). Of course, you do not expect this *always* to be so. The same is true for general statements about behavior. Prediction of both weather and behavior patterns is a matter of probability rather than certainty. In fact, there is only one certain law of human behavior: There are exceptions to every rule. Nevertheless, behavior is predictable to some degree, and most predictions are based on generalizations that result from inductive reasoning based on limited evidence. In the following section, we consider how accurate we are in assessing such evidence.

Figuring the Odds   When a researcher employs statistics to measure the probability that an event will occur, values are obtained by objective measurement and computation. But people often draw conclusions quite subjectively about the likelihood that an event will occur by *figuring the odds* mentally. Calculating a statistical probability requires the deductive processes of arithmetic; estimating a **subjective probability** involves inductive reasoning—going beyond the available evidence to reach a general conclusion. Let us consider how accurate we are in making subjective probability judgments. A useful review of the research on this question has been provided by Bourne, Dominowski, and Loftus (1979, p. 290–98). These authors invite the reader to try the following problem.

> You are sitting at a table facing a screen. Behind the screen are two boxes. The box on the left contains 70 red chips and 30 blue chips, while the box on the right contains 30 red chips and 70 blue chips. Behind the screen, the experimenter flips a coin to pick a box, reaches in and grabs some chips, which you are shown. The sample consists of 4 blue chips and 2 red chips. What do you think is the probability that the experimenter took the chips from the box on your left?

Before the coin is flipped, the probability that the left box will be chosen is .50. After the choice is made and you see the evidence, you can adjust your estimate of the probability that the left box was chosen accordingly. Because the sample shown to you by the experimenter contains twice as many blue chips as red chips, you probably favor the right box as the one selected, since you know the right box contains more blue chips than red chips. But the sample is small, and it remains possible that it was drawn from the left box. If you had to estimate the probability that the sample came from the left box, what figure would you give? A probability of .40? Or .30? The correct answer, according to probability statistics, is .14; that is, there is only a one-in-seven chance that the sample was drawn from the left box. If you are like the subjects tested on this type of problem by Slovic and Lichtenstein (1971), you estimated a much higher probability than .14. You undoubt-

edly adjusted the probability in the correct direction, but were probably too conservative in your estimate.

Research on how well our subjective estimates of probability correspond to objectively correct values has suggested that the type of error just described is not simply a matter of sloppy calculation. Rather, we appear to deviate systematically from probability theory. Kahneman and Tversky (1972) believe our estimates of subjective probability are determined by the **psychological representativeness** of the available evidence.

Psychological representativeness, Kahneman and Tversky argue, is different from statistical representativeness. For example, people expect random samples to *look random,* in the sense of reflecting no particular pattern. Probability theory, on the other hand, paints a different picture. Random samples, according to probability theory, quite often reflect apparently systematic patterns. Imagine you have just tossed a coin seven times and each time it came up heads. What is the probability it will come up tails on the next toss? If you believe the chance tails will occur on the next toss is greater than 50/50, you are suffering from what has been called *gambler's fallacy.* You may assume correctly that, if the coin is unbiased, the numbers of heads and tails will tend to balance out in the long run. But eight tosses is a short run, and probability theory tells us that the appearance of systematic patterns is not at all uncommon in short-run series of random events. Furthermore, a gambler typically wants to predict the outcome of just one event—the next one. In games of chance, the next event is not influenced by the preceding events: the coin does not *remember* what happened on previous trials. The likelihood that tails will occur is 50/50 on each and every trial.

Another difference between psychological and statistical representativeness concerns sample size. Although probability theory shows that the smaller the sample the less representative it is likely to be, people seem to expect small samples to be just as representative as large samples. Returning to the example of red and blue chips, assume the experimenter had posed a different problem. The content of the boxes remains the same (mostly red chips in the left box, mostly blue chips in the right box), but this time you are shown two samples. Sample *A* contains 5 red chips and 1 blue chip; sample *B* contains 20 red chips and 10 blue chips. The question now is: Which of these two samples is more likely to have come from the mostly red-chip box? Most people, we suspect, would choose sample *A*. After all, it contains a greater *percent* of red chips than does sample *B* (83% versus 67%) and it is intuitively reasonable that the "redder" of the two samples is more likely to have come from the mostly red-chip box. Probability theory, unlike intuition, takes into account the difference in sample size. The smaller the sample, the more variable its composition is likely to be. In fact,

the difference in size of the two samples is such that, objectively, sample *B* is more likely than sample *A* to have come from the mostly red-chip box. Additional examples of the role of representativeness in reasoning are provided by Matlin (1983).

A different type of mistaken reasoning appears when we fail to take into account all the available evidence on the probability that an event will occur. Box 6-6 describes a situation in which such an error is likely to appear.

It is clear that people's intuitive reasoning in such cases as that described in Box 6-6 does not conform strictly to the principles of probability

BOX 6-6
WHAT ARE THE ODDS?

Although our intuitive estimates of the probability that events will occur are often quite accurate, sometimes they are way off the mark. Test your ability to *figure the odds* on the following problem.

It is known that approximately 5% of the population is afflicted with the disease *rubadubitis*. A diagnostic test has been developed recently that is rather promising. If a person has *rubadubitis,* the test is positive 85% of the time; if a person does *not* have the disease, the test is positive only 10% of the time. All in all, a pretty accurate test. Here's the situation: The test has just been given to John Doe and the result is positive. What is the probability that John has *rubadubitis?* (Bourne,

Dominowski, & Loftus, 1979, p. 295).

Most people estimate the chance of John having the disease at about 85% (odds of 6 to 1). Probability theory, however, shows the correct figure is 31% (odds of 2 to 1 *against* having the disease!). How could such a large discrepancy occur between intuition and probability theory? The answer is that intuition ignores the fact (clearly implied in the first line of the problem) that rubadubitis is a rare disease. This before-the-fact information must be taken into account for a correct after-the-fact estimate to be made.

If you estimated John's chances at 85% and still are not clear how you could have been so far off in your estimate, consider the

following illustration offered by Bourne et al. Assume there are 10,000 people in the population. If rubadubitis afflicts 5% of the population, 500 have the disease and 9,500 do not. Of the 500 sufferers—if all were tested—425 (85%) would test posit9,500 *non*sufferers, 950 (10%) would test positive. So if the entire population was tested, 1,375 (425 plus 950) would test positive. But only 31% (425 of 1,375) of those who tested positive would actually have the disease. It follows that if the only test result you know about is John's, and it is positive, it is more than twice as likely to be one of the 950 false alarms than one of the 425 correct detections.

theory. What, then, does guide intuition? One interesting possibility, raised by Tversky and Kahneman (1973), is that intuitions about the probability that events will occur are guided by *mental effort*. Hence, it takes greater mental effort to imagine how some outcomes might occur than it does for other outcomes, and this difference in mental effort affects judgment of the probability of the outcomes. Although Tversky and Kahneman provide several lines of evidence that converge on this idea, one example is sufficient to show what they mean by mental effort. Imagine you are about to open a book at random and select the first word you see with three or more letters in it. Is it more likely the word will begin with K than that K will be the third letter?

If you answered "yes," Tversky and Kahneman suggest it was because you began by thinking of how many words you knew either beginning with K or with K as the third letter. Finding it easier to think of words beginning with K, you concluded there are more words beginning with K than words with K in the third position. If that were true, your answer would be correct. But it is not true. In fact, words with K in third position outnumber words beginning with K by a factor of three; so "no" is the correct answer.

What we are attempting to do in this discussion of reasoning is to introduce you to the logical and inferential processes that underly thinking. In doing so, we have placed what might seem an unreasonable emphasis on the errors that people make in their thinking. This is not because we think the average person's thinking is riddled with such errors. Rather, it is that errors often illuminate the processes that underlie correct functioning. Nisbett and Ross (1980) draw a parallel with the study of illusions.

> Perception researchers have shown that in spite of, and largely because of, people's exquisite perceptual capacities, they are subject to certain perceptual illusions. No serious scientist is led by such demonstrations to conclude that the perceptual system under study is inherently faulty. Similarly, we conclude from our own research that we are observing not an inherently faulty cognitive apparatus but rather, one that manifests certain explicable flaws. Indeed, in human inference as in perception, we suspect that many of people's failings will prove to be closely related to, or even an unavoidable cost of, their greatest strengths. (p. 14)

In this section we have focused on directed thinking, rather than on daydreaming, autistic, or schizophrenic thinking, because most of our thinking is in fact directed—it has a purpose. The purpose, we have assumed, is to acquire knowledge. But thinking often serves another purpose, and that is to solve problems.

PROBLEM-SOLVING

The history of **problem-solving** can be divided broadly into three approaches. The first major approach to influence problem-solving was behaviorism. For behaviorists, problem-solving was primarily a matter of trial-and-error and accidental success. In their view, problem-solving improved as appropriate habits were learned. A quite different approach was taken by Gestalt psychologists, who believed that problem-solving—particularly in humans—was more likely characterized by insight than by trial-and-error. In the Gestalt view, problems were solved through "meaningful apprehension of relations" rather than "senseless drill and arbitrary associations" (Katona, 1940). More recently cognitive psychology has come of age, with its emphasis on the mind as an information-processing system. A major contribution of cognitive research to problem-solving has been the development of models of thinking that can be tested on computers.

In the following sections, we identify the principal contributions of these three approaches to our understanding of the processes involved in the solution of problems.

The Behaviorist Approach

An experiment that effectively demonstrated the behaviorist approach to problem-solving is the puzzle-box study reported by E. L. Thorndike (1911). Thorndike placed a hungry cat inside a puzzle-box, the door to which was secured by one of several different mechanisms. When food was placed just outside the box, the cat would work to solve the problem of opening the door in order to reach the food. After engaging in a variety of seemingly random behaviors, Thorndike observed, the cat eventually would solve the problem. When later returned to the box, the cat would repeat the same sort of trial-and-error behavior, but would solve the problem more quickly on successive occasions. In Thorndike's view, the cat was gradually learning appropriate habits.

The behaviorist view of problem-solving was developed and extended over the years to encompass the thinking engaged in by humans when they solve problems. Omitting several decades of research and theorizing, we note the comprehensive theory advanced by Berlyne (1965) that treated the thinking engaged in by humans when they solve problems as a chain of stimulus–response associations. An important development in this theory was the notion of symbolic responses. Originally, behavior theorists referred to responses as observable behavior only. But later theorists, including Berlyne, recognized that many responses (particularly those made by humans) are covert, or symbolic, and are not directly observable. According to Berlyne, links in the overall stimulus–response chain are formed as each symbolic response becomes established as the stimulus that elicits the successive response.

The popularity of stimulus–response theories of problem-solving has waned over the years, and such theories have been replaced largely by cognitive, information-processing theories. However, the first attack on the behaviorist approach to problem-solving came from Gestalt psychologists.

The Gestalt Approach

Like behaviorists, Gestalt psychologists have one significant experiment that characterizes their approach to problem-solving: the study on problem-solving in apes conducted by Wolfgang Köhler (1925). Köhler believed that Thorndike's view of problem-solving, as a trial-and-error process, revealed more about the behaviorists' method of research than about the thought processes that underlie problem-solving behav-

ior. Rather than leaving his subjects to figure out the problem entirely by themselves, Köhler found it more useful to allow his subjects to see all the elements of the problem and their interrelationships. Contrary to behaviorist research, Köhler found the solution to problems often came suddenly, in a flash of insight, rather than always by trial-and-error.

Köhler carried out his most famous study on an ape named Sultan, in whose cage he placed a bunch of bananas suspended from the ceiling. The problem was that the fruit was out of Sultan's reach. There were a number of objects in the cage that Sultan could use in attempting to solve this problem. His first attempt involved using a stick to knock down the bananas, but the stick was too short. A second stick proved too heavy to swing effectively. These attempts were interspersed with bouts of cage-rattling and other signs of frustration, but Sultan eventually spied a collection of empty fruit boxes in the back of the cage. He quickly dragged the boxes underneath the bananas, arranged them in a pile, and climbed up to claim his reward.

Although Sultan's problem-solving behavior might not appear much different than that of Thorndike's cat, the following episode convinced Köhler it was different. Köhler placed a box in the corridor leading to the experimental room and made sure that Sultan saw it as he was being taken to his cage. Again, bananas were suspended from the ceiling of the cage, but this time the boxes had been removed from the cage. Sultan's first move was an attempt to extract the long bolt from the open cage door. But then, quite suddenly, he ceased this activity, ran down the corridor, and returned with the box to solve the problem.

Noting that Sultan did not have the box in view at the time he set off to fetch it, Köhler interpreted the ape's behavior to have resulted from a sudden perceptual reorganization of the problem. This, Köhler argued, was an intelligent process of **insight** that was quite different from aimless trial-and-error. Insight occurs when previously unrelated elements come together in an organized whole to form a plan that achieves the desired solution. (You should recognize the correspondence between this view of insight and the Gestalt theory of perceptual organization described in Chapter 4.)

Once insight is achieved, the reorganization appears to be maintained as a plan of action that can be called upon when appropriate. But Köhler also observed use of the plan when it was not appropriate. Thus, on one occasion food was placed on the ground *outside* the cage, and Sultan quickly built a tower of boxes to reach it! Such observations led Gestalt psychologists to investigate the effects of past experience on problem-solving activity. Their studies showed that past experience is a double-edged sword: it can cut both ways. Sometimes experience provides a helpful guide; at other times it misguides attempts to solve a problem.

Positive Effects of Past Experience Few problems are entirely novel; typically, several elements are familiar and some similarity to successfully solved problems is usually evident. Under these circumstances, past experience generally has a positive effect — the more recent the experience the stronger the effect — on the strategy selected to solve the problem.

Maier (1945) studied performance on the hatrack problem (Figure 6-12). Because a problem often seems easier when you are shown the solution than when you are obliged to solve it, you might not think the hatrack problem is particularly difficult. Yet only 24% of Maier's subjects who attempted just the hatrack problem successfully solved it. The beneficial effect of recent past experience was demonstrated by another group of subjects who attempted the hatrack problem immediately after successfully solving the string problem (also Figure 6-12). Having the recent experience of successfully solving a similar problem, this group's success rate doubled (48%) on the hatrack problem. Even more successful (72%) was a third group of subjects who had access to their string problem solution as they attempted to solve the hatrack problem.

In Maier's study, the relevant past experience was closely related to the current problem. Yet even when the similarity is less specific, past experience still can have a beneficial effect on problem-solving performance. Harlow (1949) demonstrated this fact with monkeys by using an oddity problem (a study presented in Chapter 5 as an example of cognitive learning). Oddity problems are difficult for monkeys, typically requiring many trials to solve. But following a lengthy series of such problems, the monkeys' performance had improved to the point that only an occasional mistake was made. Inasmuch as the specific elements of the problems were changed, it seems the monkeys were learning a general strategy for solving this type of problem.

Negative Effects of Past Experience Research by Gestalt psychologists identified two conditions in which past experience hindered rather than helped to solve problems. The first condition occurs when the strategy successfully employed for similar problems in the past is not appropriate to the current problem. In such cases, past experience causes **rigidity** in problem-solving. The second condition occurs when objects required in the solution must serve a different function than in the past. Difficulties of this nature are said to be caused by **function fixedness.**

The classic demonstration of rigidity in problem-solving comes from Luchins (1942). Luchins had subjects attempt the problems shown in Table 6-8. First they were given a simple practice problem involving two jugs and an endless supply of water. They were asked to determine how 20 quarts of water could be obtained by using two jugs, one with a capacity of 29 quarts and the other of 3 quarts. Luchins' subjects quickly solved the problem by filling the 29-quart jug and pouring off enough water to fill the smaller jug three times, leaving exactly 20 quarts in the large jug.

Although problems 2–6 employed three jugs and were more difficult, each problem could be solved by applying the formula: $B - A - 2C$. That is, fill jug B and pour water into jugs A (once) and C (twice). Luchins used these problems to develop in subjects what he called a *set*, a particular solution strategy. Problems 7 and 8 were included to determine whether subjects were indeed set in their ways. Both problems could be solved by the formula just cited, but they also could be solved more simply by a method involving only the two smaller jugs. Even though Luchins' subjects were instructed to find the simplest solution, 81% chose the more difficult solution. Their past experience on problems 2–6 had produced a set that caused rigidity in their problem-solving strategy.

Interested in determining whether this set could be dispelled easily, Luchins constructed the next problem in the sequence (problem 9) so that it could be solved *only* by the easy method

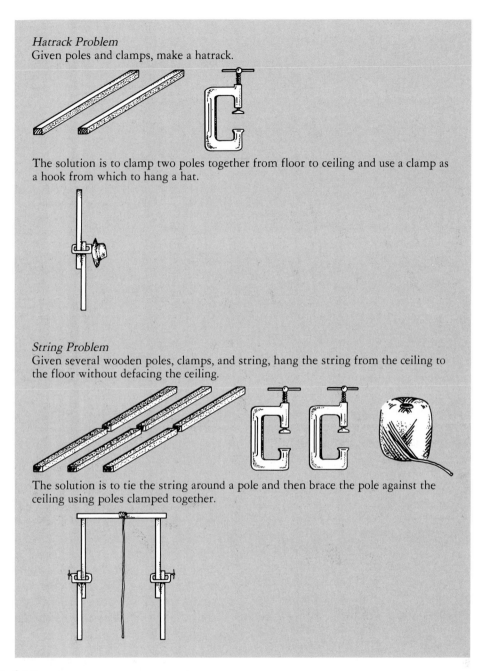

Hatrack Problem
Given poles and clamps, make a hatrack.

The solution is to clamp two poles together from floor to ceiling and use a clamp as a hook from which to hang a hat.

String Problem
Given several wooden poles, clamps, and string, hang the string from the ceiling to the floor without defacing the ceiling.

The solution is to tie the string around a pole and then brace the pole against the ceiling using poles clamped together.

FIGURE 6-12

The Hatrack and String Problems Subjects did much better on the hatrack problem if they had just successfully solved the string problem — demonstrating the benefit of relevant past experience on problem-solving efficiency. *Source:* Adapted from Maier, N. R. F. (1945). Reasoning in humans III: The mechanisms of equivalent stimuli of reasoning. *Journal of Experimental Psychology, 35,* 349–60.

overlooked by most subjects in the two previous problems. However, experience in using the easier method did little to dispell the rigid set the subjects had developed. On the final two problems (10 and 11), which could be solved by either method, 79% of subjects chose the more difficult solution.

Luchins developed the set during trials conducted within the experiment. But we also learn systematic ways of solving certain types of prob-

TABLE 6-8
The Negative Effect of Set on Problem Solving*

Problem #	Purpose of Problem	Capacity of Jars			Desired Volume	Comments on Solution
		A	B	C		
1	Practice	29	3	—	20	Solution is A − 3B
2	Establishing the set	21	127	3	100	Solution is B − A − 2C
3	" " "	14	163	25	99	" " "
4	" " "	18	43	10	5	" " "
5	" " "	9	42	6	21	" " "
6	" " "	20	59	4	31	" " "
7	Testing the set	23	49	3	20	Easy solution is A − C
8	" " "	15	39	3	18	Easy solution is A + C
9	Breaking the set	28	76	3	25	A − C works, but B − A − 2C does not
10	Testing whether set is broken	18	48	4	22	Both A + C and B − A − 2C work
11	" " " " "	14	36	8	6	Both A − C and B − A − 2C work

* In each problem, the challenge is to obtain the desired volume of water by using the available jars in the most efficient manner. The solution that works for earlier problems typically is applied to later problems even when much simpler solutions are available.
Source: Based on material reported in Luchins, A. (1942). Mechanization in problem solving. *Psychological Monographs, 54* (Whole No. 248).

lems over a lifetime of practice. Although this generally translates to efficient problem-solving performance, it sometimes is counterproductive, as shown by Bartlett (1958) in the following study of how people do letter arithmetic.

$$\text{DONALD}$$
$$\underline{+\,\text{GERALD}}$$
$$=\text{ROBERT}$$

The task is to crack a code in which each letter represents a particular number. Thus D could stand for 2 and G for 9 (these are not correct). Then treat the problem as one of simple addition: the number represented by DONALD plus the number represented by GERALD is equal to the number represented by ROBERT. Given that each number from 0 to 9 is represented by a different letter and that D equals 5, can you solve the problem?

You probably began by substituting 5s for the Ds in the last column. Two fives are ten, so T must equal zero. But where do you go from there? Almost certainly your years of experience in going from right to left when adding caused you to decode next the letters in the column second from right. This is what most of Bartlett's subjects did—and it blocked their progress because the solution cannot be reached in this way. In

fact, you must go next to the column second from left and determine the numerical value of E. The steps in the solution to this problem are explained fully by Lindsay and Norman (1977, pp. 544–61); the letter–number code follows.

T = 0, G = 1, O = 2, B = 3, A = 4, D = 5, N = 6, R = 7, L = 8, and E = 9.

The second condition in which past experience hinders problem-solving arises when a key element in the solution must serve an unusual function. The difficulty, function fixedness, was studied in the experiment by Saugstad and Raaheim (1960) described in Figure 6-13. Try to solve the problem before reading further.

The solution to the Saugstad and Raaheim problem follows.

The pliers are used to bend a nail into a hook that is then tied to the string. The hook is thrown out to catch the tray and pull the balls in the glass within reach. The newpaper is rolled into a tube that is held in shape by the rubber bands. The balls can then be poured down the tube into the bucket.

Because you were alerted to look for problem elements serving unusual functions, you may have performed better than Saugstad and Raaheim's subjects, whose success rate was 22%.

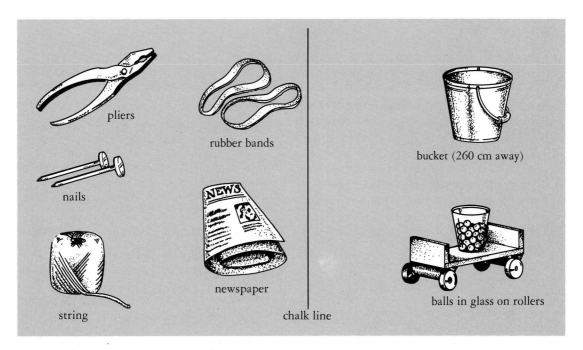

pliers

rubber bands

bucket (260 cm away)

nails

NEWS

newspaper

balls in glass on rollers

string   chalk line

FIGURE 6-13

Function Fixedness The problem involves using the materials shown to the left of the chalk line (pliers, rubber bands, nails, newspaper, and string) in order to transfer the balls from the glass to the bucket without any part of your body crossing the chalk line. (See text for solution.) *Source:* Adapted from Saugstad, P., & Raaheim, K. (1960). Problem solving, past experience and availability of functions. *British Journal of Psychology, 51,* 97–104.

Function fixedness was identified as the principal obstacle to the solution when nearly all the subjects in a second group solved the problem after having been shown how to bend a nail with pliers and how to roll a newpaper into a tube. In a second experiment, the same researchers took a less-direct approach to reducing function fixedness. They first asked subjects to think of all possible uses for a nail and a newspaper. The success rates on the problem were 89% for subjects who thought of both a hook and a tube, 42% for those who thought of one or the other use, and 19% for the least imaginative subjects who thought of neither.

An interesting example of function fixedness occurred partway through Köhler's original study of Sultan. Köhler had, as usual, suspended bananas from the ceiling of the cage, and was standing to one side observing Sultan's attempts to reach it. Sultan suddenly ran over to Köhler, took him by the hand, and pulled him toward the fruit. Köhler thought he was being asked to get the bananas for Sultan (a notably direct solution to the problem). But it was Köhler, not Sultan, whose thinking displayed function fixedness in this case: Sultan proceeded to climb up Köhler and stand on Köhler's shoulders to reach the food!

The contrast between the associationist view of problem-solving taken by behaviorists and the approach of Gestalt psychologists can be summarized as follows. Whereas behaviorists concerned themselves with the reproduction of habits, Gestalt psychologists emphasized the production of new solutions. The latter typically required reorganization of problem elements, as distinct from establishment of stimulus-response links. But where behaviorist theory was stated in considerably detail, Gestalt definitions of such terms as *organized structure* and *insight* remained vague. This vagueness is not characteristic of the problem-solving theories we consider next, those advanced more recently by cognitive psychologists. One explanation is that many cognitive theories have been developed sufficiently to be tested on a computer, and computers demand a precision that disallows the sort of conceptual fuzziness for which Gestalt theorists have been criticized.

The Cognitive Approach

Early behaviorists dealt with mental processes by ignoring them and treating the mind as a closed or "black" box. Behaviorists focused on the relation between observable inputs to the box (stimuli) and observable outputs from the box (responses). Gestaltists, on the other hand, wrote about the contents of the box, both in terms of mind and brain. Unfortunately, as noted, the mental events Gestaltists wrote about were defined imprecisely. And although they attempted to be more definitive about brain processes, their psychological concepts were rather primitive and soon were obsolete. Today, cognitive psychology is dominated by a quite different approach, one that sees the mind as an information-processing system.

We described an information-processing model of memory earlier in this chapter; we now consider how the information-processing approach has been applied to problem-solving. As a first step, we look more closely at the sequence of events that occurs as we attempt to solve problems. Following Bourne, Dominowski, and Loftus (1979), we list the activities engaged in by problem-solvers at three stages: *preparation, production,* and *judgment* (see Table 6-9).

Preparation: Understanding the Problem At this stage, a mental representation of the problem is established and a plan of attack is developed. Obviously, a successful solution depends upon a correct representation of the problem. If vital information is wrong or missing, a solution may simply be unavailable. However, difficulties arising at the problem-representation stage typically are more subtle than those involving incorrect or missing information. It is possible, for example, to mistakenly include in your representation a restriction that is not part of the stated problem. This appears to be the major source of difficulty in solving the problem shown in Figure 6-14. If you cannot solve this problem, it probably is because you are assuming the lines cannot extend beyond the square outlined by the dots; but no such restriction is made in the statement of the problem. Even with this hint, Weisberg and Alba (1981) found that only 25% of subjects solved the problem. Make an attempt to solve the

TABLE 6-9
The Stages of Problem Solving*

Stage 1	Preparation: Understanding the Problem
Activity	- Identifying the initial state of the problem
	- Identifying the goal state
	- Noting restrictions on solution attempts
	- Comparing problem with previously experienced problems
	- Breaking problem into set of subproblems
Outcome	- Representation of the problem
	- Decision regarding plan of attack
Stage 2	Production: Generating Possible Solutions
Activity	- Retrieving facts and procedures from memory
	- Scanning other available information
	- Applying algorithm or heuristic
	- Storing results in memory
Outcome	- A potential solution
Stage 3	Judgement: Evaluating Potential Solutions
Activity	- Comparing potential solution with goal state
	- Judging whether solution is satisfactory
Outcome	- Decision that problem is solved or that potential solution is unsatisfactory

* An analysis of the problem-solving process showing activities and outcomes associated with preparation, production, and judgement stages.
Source: Bourne, L. E., Dominowski, R. L., & Loftus, E. F. (1979). *Cognitive processes.* Englewood Cliffs, NJ: Prentice-Hall.

problem before turning to the solution shown in Figure 6-15, page 286.

The form in which the problem is represented, as distinct from the information provided, also can influence the difficulty of finding a solution. This is demonstrated in the Buddhist monk problem that originated with Duncker (1945). As presented by Glass and Holyoak (1986), the problem reads as follows.

One morning, exactly at sunrise, a Buddhist monk began to climb a tall mountain. A narrow path, no more than a foot or two wide, spiraled around the mountain to a glittering temple at the summit. The monk ascended at varying rates of speed, stopping many times along the way to rest and eat dried fruit he carried with him. He reached the temple shortly before sunset. After several days of fasting and meditation, he began his journey back along

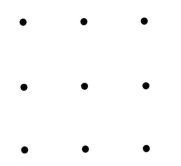

FIGURE 6-14
The Classic Nine-dot Problem The challenge is to draw four straight lines through all nine dots without lifting the pencil from the paper and without retracing. (For solution, see Figure 6-15.)

the same path, starting at sunrise and again walking at various speeds with many pauses along the way. His average speed descending was, of course, greater than his average climbing speed. Show that there is a spot along the path that the monk will occupy on both trips at precisely the same time of day. (p. 373)

You probably attacked this difficult problem at the verbal level, perhaps with a dash of mathematics (average speeds, total times, and the like). But it is unlikely this approach will lead to a quick solution. You will fare better if you visualize the problem—which obviously provided the key to the solution for one successful solver whose thoughts are reported by Koestler (1964).

"I tried this and that, until I got fed up with the whole thing, but the image of the monk in his saffron robe walking up the hill kept persisting in my mind. Then a moment came, when, superimposed on this image, I saw another, more transparent one, of the monk walking down the hill, and I realized in a flash that the two figures must meet at some point in time—regardless of what speed they walk and how often each of them stops. Then I reasoned out what I already knew: whether the monk descends two days or three days later comes to the same; so I was quite justified in letting him descend on the same day, in duplicate so to speak." (p. 184)

Figure 6-16 shows how the Buddhist monk can be visualized in a way that makes the solution appear simple. Although visualizing does not always provide as salient a solution, if you are stymied,

finding an alternative form in which to represent the problem may help. An extensive treatment of the use of *visual thinking* in problem-solving has been provided by McKim (1980).

Another activity of problem-solvers during the preparation stage is formulation of a general plan of attack. One obvious strategy involves recalling similar problems you successfully solved in the past — the beneficial effects of past experience on analogous problems covered earlier. Another preparation activity involves dividing the total problem into subproblems. This lightens the volume of information that must be kept in mind and may reduce a large, unmanageable problem to a number of smaller, more manageable problems. Once a strategy has been decided, it must be implemented in an attempt to generate a solution.

Production: Generating Possible Solutions
One way to ensure production of the correct solution to a problem is to generate *all* possible solutions. Such a procedure is called an **algorithm.** If a friend loans you her car, you may have difficulty deciding which of several similar keys fits the ignition. The number of possible solutions probably is small enough to make the algorithm of trying each key an efficient strategy. It would be laborious, however, to use the same approach to solve the problem of opening a combination lock whose combination you had forgotten. And algorithms clearly are not going to be effective with problems like winning a game of chess, where the number of alternative moves is astronomical.

Although the term *algorithm* often is used to refer only to problem-solving procedures guaranteed to produce a correct solution, it is better understood as meaning any well-defined procedure for attacking a problem. The important characteristic of an algorithm is that it requires very little thinking. When there is no efficient, well-defined procedure for solving a problem, we are likely to use a **heuristic** strategy: a rule-of-thumb. A heuristic is likely to involve intuition, judgment based on past experience, and any other relevant information. Unlike the well-defined algorithm, a heuristic is a *fuzzy* procedure. Although heuristics typically provide no guarantees of success, by playing the percentages they often help problem-solvers avoid wasting time in blind

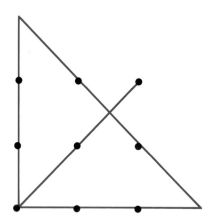

FIGURE 6-15

Solution to Nine-dot Problem Shown in Figure 6-14 Many people fail to solve this problem because they assume erroneously that the lines must stay within the square outlined by the dots.

alleys. In a study that examined the effectiveness of different approaches to problem-solving (de Leeuw, 1978), schoolchildren were given either a series of decisions to make to reach the solution (provided an algorithm) or obliged to make their own decisions (find a heuristic). The algorithm performed better initially, but after a few days the heuristic proved more effective.

One heuristic mentioned earlier is to use a solution that worked successfully in the past for a similar problem. Another sometimes helpful heuristic is to work backward from the result you are trying to achieve to the start of the problem. A third heuristic device is **means–end analysis.** The *end* is the correct solution, sometimes called the goal. The *means* are the steps you must take to get from where you are—a problem on your hands—to the goal. Thinking of a problem in this way often makes it easier to identify the moves required to reach a solution.

Let us apply means–end analysis to a type of problem you may well have encountered in the past. Assume you normally travel to work by bus, but a problem has arisen: the bus drivers have just gone on strike. First you establish your goal—to get to work on time tomorrow. Then you consider alternative means available that might achieve this goal. Hitchhiking, riding in a coworker's car, taking a taxi, and cycling are examples. Next you investigate these alternatives.

Perhaps you rule out the taxi (too expensive), consider help from a coworker unlikely (he lives across town), and judge hitchhiking a risky business. So your solution is to cycle to work. As noted, however, heuristics do not guarantee successful solutions. You might find, for example, that your bicycle has a flat tire and that you have no pump to inflate it.

Few textbook discussions of problem-solving talk about what to do when you run out of possible solutions. A last-ditch heuristic that sometimes helps in such a situation can be summarized as follows: If all else fails, change the problem. In the preceding example, you could change your goal of getting to work on time to being absent with pay. This new problem may have a quick solution: take a day's vacation (use the time to purchase a bicycle pump).

Judgment: Evaluating Potential Solutions
The final stage of problem-solving involves determining whether any of the possible solutions generated in fact solves the problem. This is what Koestler's subject was doing when she said, "Then I reasoned out what I already knew." In many cases this determination is a relatively simple process, particularly where the problem and the goal are stated precisely; most examples in

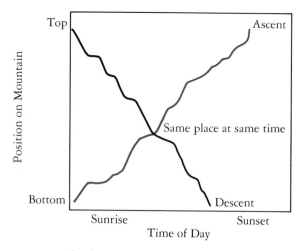

FIGURE 6-16

The Buddhist Monk Problem Visualizing the Buddhist monk problem from this perspective usually leads to its solution. (See text for statement of the problem.) *Source:* Glass, A. L., & Holyoak, K. J. (1986). *Cognition* (2nd ed., p. 375). New York: Random House.

this chapter fall into this category. But there is another class of problems in which evaluating the solutions generated may be a major task. These are called "ill-defined problems" (Reitman, 1964; Simon, 1973). The challenge of winning a game of chess is an example of such a problem.

At any stage of a chess game, the player's problem is to move nearer the desired goal — checkmate. Although this goal can be defined generally, there are tens of thousands of arrangements — patterns of chess pieces — that each constitute a correct solution. Given such an ill-defined goal, how does a player decide which move to make next?

You might think an expert chess player has an advantage over an averge player at this stage because the expert generates more alternative solutions and can evaluate their consequences better. Surprisingly, de Groot (1965) has shown this is not the case. Chess masters actually evaluate fewer alternative moves than weaker players and typically do not look farther ahead than two to three moves. It appears the expert's advantage in chess lies in having better developed and more appropriate heuristics and a better memory for meaningful arrangements. De Groot showed this second advantage was not the result of a superior ability for remembering patterns in general. In

fact, chess masters are no better than average players at remembering patterns of chess pieces *randomly* arranged on the board. Their superiority lies in a better memory for *meaningful* arrangements that are likely to occur in the course of a game. From their work on computer simulation of chess playing, Simon and Gilmartin (1973) estimate that chess masters may have from 10,000 to 100,000 such arrangements stored in memory.

It should be apparent now why information-processing models are generally more highly regarded than behaviorist or Gestalt theories of problem-solving. By dividing the overall process into the stages of preparation, production, and judgment and by defining the various activities that occur at these stages, cognitive theorists have provided detailed accounts of the mental events that take place during problem-solving. In the following section, we consider another reason why information-processing models are regarded highly: many have survived the test of a theory suggested by the adage — you don't really understand something until you build a machine that will do it. In this case, the machine is a computer.

Computers and Cognitive Psychology

The evolution of computer technology over the last 30 years has had a powerful influence on psychology. Nowhere has this influence been felt more strongly than in cognitive psychology. There are two related reasons for this: the mind is, *in a sense,* a computer, and computer models have proved an excellent means of developing and testing theories of how the mind works. The similarity between minds and computers is exemplified by reference to computers as *brains*. But several myths have developed concerning this similarity. To give you an appreciation of what computers are, and what they can and cannot do, Box 6-7 raises and then dispels certain of these myths.

Computer simulation, sometimes referred to as artificial intelligence (or AI), is the study of human functions by means of computer models. In the context of cognitive psychology, a computer model essentially is a program that instructs the computer to generate output that

Box 6-7
Selected Myths about Computer *Brains* and Human *Minds*

If you have suffered the frustration of corresponding with a computer to correct an error in your credit card account, you probably have a negative image of computers and of the ever-increasing role they play in human affairs. Perhaps you feel computers are mindless number-crunchers too dumb to answer a simple question. Or perhaps your image of computers has been shaped by reports that today's computers are so intelligent they can beat all but the world's finest chess players. The following discussion is intended to dispel certain of the more common myths about computers and their similarity to the human mind.

Myth I *Computers Are Just Number-crunchers*

 File   Edit   Level   Options   Features   Screen   Special

Sargon III

PLAYER	SARGON
1. e2-e4	e7-e5
2. g1-f3	b8-c6
3. f1-c4	f8-c5
4. b2-b4	c5xb4
5.	

Window on the Search

Current	Previous
Depth: 4/9	Depth: 3/0
Score: 73	Score: 73

g8-f6	c5-b4
c2-c3	e1-g1
b4-e7	
d2-d3	

Fact This is rather like saying mothers are just diaper-washers or that Freud was just a psychoanalyst. The error lies in the word *just*. Certainly computers *can* be used for computation, but that is only a minor capability. Computers are general-purpose symbol manipulators, and symbols can represent any manner of things—not just numbers. Thus, computers exist that can follow spoken instructions, prove theorems in

matches the output of human subjects given the same task. Two examples should clarify the notion of computer simulation.

Newell and Simon (1972) modeled the mental processes of subjects attempting to solve the letter arithmetic problem presented earlier. To reveal how they went about figuring the solution, subjects were asked to think aloud as they attacked the problem. The result was a protocol, or statement of thoughts, a fragment of which is shown in Figure 6-17, page 290. Newell and Simon then analyzed the protocol to identify the sequence of steps that led to eventual solution.

For example, in steps 5 and 6 the subject is plugging known information into the equation, whereas step 7 involves drawing an inference based on having two numbers in a column. In steps 10 and 12, the subject is employing the strategy of searching for letters already decoded. Although painstaking work, Newell and Simon eventually learned enough about the strategies and tactics of human problem-solvers to devise a computer model that simulated the processes with remarkable accuracy.

Slightly earlier, Ernst and Newell (1969) had boldly attempted to design an all-purpose

logic, and counsel patients—none of which involves numbers.

Myth II *Computers May Be Quick, but They Are Not Intelligent*
Fact Modern computers can execute millions of operations in a second, so it certainly is correct to say they are quick. Although many people are unwilling to describe computers as intelligent, consider this: What makes other people think *you* are intelligent? The answer lies in the things that you do—your output. They infer intelligence from your behavior. Computers can be programmed to provide output remarkably similar to intelligent human behavior. So it seems reasonable to describe computers as intelligent when they do things we would regard as intelligent if done by a human.

Myth III *Computers Cannot Think for Themselves; They Do Only What They Are Told to Do*
Fact Computers are obedient in the sense that they follow instructions given them by human programmers. Nevertheless, a computer can demonstrate skills and knowledge that exceed those of its human operator. This fact was discovered by an early researcher in this field (Samuel, 1963) when he programmed a computer to play checkers. After a few practice games with itself, the computer soon began to beat Samuel consistently. Computers also can be programmed to solve problems using procedures analogous to deductive and inductive reasoning (Boden, 1977). Such procedures enable computers to acquire knowledge beyond that explicitly given them by their human designers.

Myth IV *Building Computers that Act Like People Means Building Robots*
Fact Most computers look nothing like humans. Very few cognitive psychologists who use computers intend to build robots; their goal generally is to simulate the processes of the mind, not the anatomical structure of the human brain or body. Cognitive psychologists do this by attempting to program computers to function in a way that is similar to the way the mind works. To the degree they are successful, the rules employed in the computer program provide insight into the rules that govern the way we think.

computer model they called the General Problem Solver (GPS). The following description (based on Mayer, 1977) sets forth the problem-solving principles employed by GPS.

1. GPS translates the problem into an initial state, a goal state, and into a set of steps available for moving from one state to the other.

2. GPS first breaks down the problem into a series of subgoals, each of which brings the problem nearer to a solution.

3. GPS then applies the heuristic of means–end analysis, reducing the difference between the present state and the desired subgoal state.

4. When one subgoal is reached, GPS moves to the next, and so on until the problem is solved.

5. The entire process is presided over by a *problem-solving executive* that controls the order of steps, monitors the success of these operations, and decides how to proceed when an operation fails to bring the problem closer to a solution.

GPS was successful in solving a variety of problems—including the water-jar puzzle (see

1. Each letter has one and only one numerical value. . . .
2. (E: One numerical value.)
3. There are ten different letters.
4. And each of them has one numerical value.
5. Therefore, I can, looking at the two D's . . .
6. each D is 5;
7. therefore, T is zero.
8. So I think I'll start by writing that problem here.
9. I'll write T, T is zero.
10. Now, do I have any other T's?
11. No.
12. But I have another D.
13. That means I have a 5 over on the other side.
14. Now I have 2 A's
15. and 2 L's
16. that are each
17. somewhere
18. and this R
19. 3 R's

     ⋮

321.

FIGURE 6-17

Fragments of a Protocol A partial transcript (steps 1 through 19 of 321) of steps taken by a subject attempting to solve the letter arithmetic problem: DONALD + GERALD = ROBERT. *Source:* Newell, A., & Simon, H. (1972). *Human problem solving.* Englewood Cliffs, NJ: Prentice-Hall.

Table 6-8), letter arithmetic, and problems in calculus. Although the match between GPS and human protocols was by no means perfect, the value of computer simulation is that it clearly specified areas of mismatch between theory and practice. As noted earlier, computer models require that theories of mental functioning be stated quite precisely. Even though we are still far from being able to provide a comprehensive account of the thought processes involved in problem-solving, the information-processing approach of cognitive psychologists represents a considerable advance over the behaviorist and Gestalt treatments of this topic.

CREATIVITY

Of all the faculties of mind, the one perhaps most admired yet least understood is **creativity.** In his book *The Act of Creation* (1964), Arthur Koestler examines numerous examples of creative work drawn from the sciences, literature, and even humor. The property Koestler identifies as the defining characteristic of these diverse examples of creativity is *the synthesizing of a novel combination of ideas.* Each idea in the mix may be entirely familiar; the creative act is to combine these familiar elements in an unfamiliar way. Artists who paint familiar scenes and poets whose work arouses memories of past events and feeling may be admired for their evocative techniques, yet we do not think of them as particularly creative. A creative work makes us see things in a different light; it makes, in artistic or scientific terms, a novel statement about the world.

Attempts to analyze creativity typically have involved identifying stages of the creative process. We examine two such efforts, and then consider their implications that we might be able to improve our ability to think creatively.

Stages of the Creative Process

One popular analysis of creativity holds that the process can be separated into four successive stages: preparation, incubation, illumination, and verification. Graham Wallas (1926) originated this theory and developed it after reading an account of how French mathematician Jules-Henri Poincaré discovered the solution to a puzzling problem. Poincaré had struggled for more than two weeks on the problem, but to no avail. Then, as Poincaré (1913) tells it, he literally stumbled upon the solution.

> Just at this time I left Caen, where I was then living, to go on a geological excursion under the auspices of the school of mines. The changes of travel made me forget my mathematical work. Having reached Coutances, we entered an omnibus to go some place or other. At the moment when I put my foot on the step the idea came to me, without anything in my former thoughts seeming to have paved the way for it, that the transformations I had used to define the Fuchsian functions were identical with those of non-Euclidean geometry. I did not verify the idea; I should not have had the time, as, upon taking my seat in the omnibus. I went on with a conversation already commenced, but I felt a perfect certainty. On my return to Caen, for conscience sake I verified the result at my leisure. (p. 383)

In this case the **preparation** stage continued for more than two weeks, after which the problem was not pursued consciously for some time. This **incubation** period was broken quite unexpectedly when the answer Poincaré had been seeking came to him in a flash of **illumination.** The **verification** stage came when he confirmed that the idea that had come so suddenly really did provide a solution to the problem.

The first and last stages, preparation and verification, appear to be little different in Poincaré's case than in the solutions to the more routine problems discussed in the previous section. Furthermore, as Gestalt psychologists demonstrated in certain studies on insight, quite ordinary and noncreative solutions also may be illuminated

suddenly. What led Poincaré's experience to be regarded as a classic example of the creative process was the occurrence of the second stage, incubation.

Two questions must be asked of Wallas' incubation stage: Why is the problem more likely to be solved after it has been set aside? Is this stage critical to the creative process? An intriguing answer to the first question is the possibility that attempts to solve the problem continue during an incubation period, but at an unconscious level. In Chapter 4 we argue that unconscious processes seem to occur during perceptual activity. Perhaps it also is the case, as Neisser (1963) has suggested, that multiple trains of thought occur beyond the spotlight of awareness at the cognitive level of mental activity. Note, however, that unconscious processes must be inferred — they cannot be observed directly. As Weisberg (1986) has argued, it is unreasonable to infer the existence of unconscious processes when simpler explanations are available.

There are simpler explanations of the incubation effect than unconscious problem-solving. Posner (1973) suggests two candidates; the first is recovery from fatigue. When a problem is particularly difficult and attempts at its solution continue for some time, the incubation period may serve simply to refresh a tired problem-solver. The second candidate suggested is that taking an extended break from a problem allows a problem-solver to forget inappropriate approaches. When we benefit from looking at a problem with a fresh mind after sleeping on it, either of these two possibilities provides a simpler explanation of the benefit than that of unconscious problem-solving. The possibility of unconscious problem-solving cannot be ruled out, but as Wickelgren (1979) succinctly observes: "There isn't a shred of evidence to support it" (p. 381).

The second question raised about the incubation period concerns its relevance to the creative process. Although little systematic evidence has been collected on the point, we suspect an incubation period is not a *necessary* condition for creativity. That is, creative outcomes are no more likely to follow incubation periods than to result directly from continued hard thinking.

A quite different view of the creative process from that proposed by Wallas has been developed by Wickelgren (1974, 1979), who argues there are two important processes that underlie creative thinking. The first concerns **generation** of novel ideas (or novel combinations of ideas); the second involves **evaluation** of these products. Wickelgren endorses the theory proposed by Campbell (1960), that all creative accomplishment is "blind variation and selective retention." Although the notion that creative achievements result from blind or chance variation in the combination of ideas may seem unlikely, Campbell emphasizes "the tremendous number of unproductive thought trials" that precede genuine accomplishment. Thus, when Thomas Edison was questioned about his progress on a particular invention, he is credited with replying that he now knew 100 ways that would *not* work. One suspects that Poincaré might have offered a similar response prior to his illumination experience.

Generating new combinations of ideas is only half the battle. An equally or perhaps more important aspect of creativity, in Wickelgren's view, is the evaluation of these new ideas. This is the "selective retention" part of Campbell's thesis, wherein only those products with the potential for making a creative contribution are pursued. The critical idea responsible for a creative accomplishment may well have been generated by others before, but it would have gone unrecognized if those previous thinkers lacked the ability to evaluate the creative potential of the idea.

Can We Learn to Be More Creative ?

The four-stage model proposed by Wallas remains a popular view of the creative process. Although it usually is cited in discussions of creativity, scant mention is typically made of the dearth of empirical support for its critical second stage, incubation (particularly if incubation is interpreted as an opportunity for unconscious problem-solving). Another weakness of Wallas' formulation is that it provides little useful guidance to people who want to improve their creative thinking.

The first stage of Wallas' model, preparation, includes not only thinking about the problem at hand but also includes prior acquisition of knowledge gained through reading and listening. But does acquisition of knowledge necessar-

ily enhance creativity? One cynical answer was given by author George Bernard Shaw, who wrote that "Reading rots the mind." A directly opposite view was taken by Louis Pasteur, the famous French microbiologist, who said "Chance favors only the prepared mind." In fact, the most reasonable answer is twofold: knowledge is a necessary but not a sufficient condition for creativity; however, knowledge sometimes is an impediment to creativity when it perpetuates a familiar view of the world. Einstein felt his lack of formal training in physics facilitated his creativity, presumably by allowing him to think in unconventional ways. Similarly, a conventional education in music or an apprenticeship in dance may cultivate craftmanship but impede creativity.

One approach to creativity with practical implications is based on **reasoning-by-analogy** (Gordon, 1961). In his book *Synectics,* Gordon suggests creativity depends on making the strange familiar and making the familiar strange. In making the strange familiar, one comes to understand the problem. Although traditionally the first step in problem-solving, it is one Gordon thinks is much less important to creativity than his second process—making the familiar strange. Gordon identifies four types of reasoning-by-analogy that are designed to improve one's ability to think creatively by making the familiar strange.

Personal Analogy This technique requires that you involve yourself personally in imagining a variety of ways in which the elements of the situation may be restructured. For example, if the problem is to determine what happens to a gas when heated, imagine yourself a gas molecule inside an enclosed metal box suspended over a fire. As the temperature rises, you hop around more and more — as do your friends (other gas molecules). This activity causes you to hit the sides of the box more often, which . . . and so on. Perhaps this is how Robert Boyle discovered the law relating the volume, pressure, and temperature of gases!

Direct Analogy This method compares the elements of the problem to a parallel set of facts. Gordon gives the example of Sir March Isumbard-Brunel, who invented the caisson that revolutionized underwater construction of bridge supports. Brunel hit upon the idea while watching a shipworm tunneling into lumber, making a tube for itself as it moved forward.

Symbolic Analogy This approach uses impersonal or objective images to describe the problem. When an appropriate symbolic analogy is found, the elements of the original problem typically condense into a restructured form more likely to suggest a creative solution.

Fantasy Analogy This type of analogy requires that you set aside the constraints of reality and imagine how a problem could be solved if anything goes. This permits one "to sneak in a new way of thinking," argues Gordon.

> The immutable laws usually do hold, but by pushing them out of phase for a moment one can peek in between. By the time the laws are permitted by the mind to snap back into control, the mind has derived a new viewpoint and can discover useful aberrations of the laws underlying the new viewpoint so essential for basic solution. (p. 53)

For final tips on how to improve creativity, we again turn to the work of Wickelgren (1974, 1979). Recall his view that the two processes involved in creative thinking are the generation of novel combinations of ideas and their evaluation. Wickelgren's advice on improving one's chances of generating a novel idea is summed up in a line he quotes from the writings of double Nobel prize winner, Linus Pauling: "The best way to have a good idea is to have lots of ideas." The chances of generating a creative combination of ideas are in proportion to the number of ideas generated. Wickelgren attacks the belief that creativity cannot be forced: he argues that it can be forced, sometimes, and identifies four conditions that favor creativity.

> You must have prepared your mind with a critical mass of long-term knowledge, ideas, and questions on a particular topic. You must deliberately warm up (prime or set) your mind at the beginning of the thinking time by going over some of your previous thoughts and other people's thoughts on the matter. You must be in a suitable mood — task oriented and not distracted by other problems or worries. And you must employ creative plans for the combination of ideas. This is called *playing with ideas* or *mental gymnastics*. (1979, p. 385).

Our understanding of mental processes in general, and creative thinking in particular, is too limited to offer these suggestions as anything more than tips that may be helpful. Although there is no guarantee they will improve your thinking dramatically, they are worth trying — whether the challenge you face is writing an essay or solving a financial problem.

SUMMARY

1. Cognition is the set of mental processes through which information is transformed, reduced, elaborated, stored, recovered, and used. Research on the cognitive function of memory typically employs an information-processing approach in which sensory memory, short-term memory, and long-term memory are the principal stages of remembering.

2. Iconic memory and echoic memory are the sensory memory stores for visual and auditory input, respectively. Sensory memory is unselective and brief; unless attended to, its contents typically decay in a second or two. Attention is a highly selective process that transfers information from sensory memory to short-term memory.

3. Short-term memory stores information that supplies the contents of conscious awareness. Verbal input from iconic memory is coded both auditorily and semantically (for meaning). The capacity or span of short-term memory is limited to about seven items, but chunking can increase the amount of information carried by an item. Unless rehearsed and thereby transferred to long-term memory, unfamiliar items will disappear from short-term memory within a few seconds.

4. The dual-code theory suggests that knowledge in long-term memory is stored in either a visual or verbal code. An alternative theory is that knowledge is coded in the more abstract form of a network of associated propositions.

5. The deeper the level to which an item of input is processed, the easier it is to retrieve from long-term memory. Shallow processing considers only the form of the item; deeper processing considers its meaning. Another important determinant of retrieval is knowledge, in the form of a schema, that associates incoming information with existing information.

6. Both external and internal environments can influence whether information committed to memory can be retrieved. Context-dependent recall occurs when a change in external environment between memorizing and recall impairs retrieval. State-dependent recall occurs when a change in a person's mood or physiological state has a similar negative effect.

7. Retrieved memories do not always faithfully recapture original experiences. The intervening receipt of information typically results in relevant memories being updated, which causes their later retrieval to be more a process of reconstruction than one of simple recall.

8. Memory can be improved by employing techniques called mnemonics, which range from simple rhymes and first letters to more elaborate sets of retrieval cues. More relevant to everyday needs is the PQ4R method for efficient studying: preview, question, read, reflect, recite, and review.

9. Deductive and inductive reasoning are instances of directed thinking. Deduction follows logical rules to combine the information in premises to yield a particular conclusion. Induction is the process of drawing general inferences from limited evidence. A common error of inductive reasoning arises from the tendency to regard a small sample of evidence as just as representative as a large sample.

10. The behaviorist approach to problem-solving was based on trial-and-error and accidental success. The Gestalt approach emphasized the reorganization of elements of the problem, sometimes resulting in a sudden solution termed insight. Although past experience often is a benefit in problem-solving, it may be a disadvantage if it leads to a rigid solution set or to function fixedness.

11. The cognitive approach to problem-solving distinguishes three stages. Preparation is important for understanding the problem. Production is the stage at which potential solutions are generated, either by an all-encompassing algorithm or by a rule-of-thumb heuristic, such as working backward from the solution or means–end analysis. Finally, potential solutions are evaluated at the judgment stage. Today, computers are widely used to test cognitive theories and to simulate intelligent human behavior.

12. Creativity is the synthesizing of a novel combination of ideas. The long-held belief that creative insights occur as flashes of illumination following periods of incubation has only anecdotal evidence to support it. An approach to the creative process with more practical implications focuses on the multiple generation and selective retention of ideas. Reasoning-by-analogy to make the familiar strange is one method suggested for improving one's creative thinking.

KEY TERMS

Cognition
Sensory Memory
Iconic Memory
Echoic Memory
Attention
Short-term Memory
Coding
Capacity
Memory Span
Chunk
Flashbulb Memory
Rehearsal
Free Recall
Maintenance Rehearsal
Elaborative Rehearsal
Long-term Memory
Dual-code Theory
Propositional Memory

Retrieval
Depth of Processing
Schema
Tip-of-the-tongue
　　Phenomenon
Context-dependent Recall
State-dependent Recall
Reconstructed Memory
Mnemonic
PQ4R Method
Directed Thinking
Deductive Reasoning
Inductive Reasoning
Premise
Subjective Probability
Psychological
　　Representativeness
Problem-solving

Insight
Rigidity
Function Fixedness
Algorithm
Heuristic
Means – End Analysis
Computer Simulation
Creativity
Preparation
Incubation
Illumination
Verification
Generation
Evaluation
Reasoning-by-Analogy

RECOMMENDED READINGS

Anderson, J. R. (1985). *Cognitive psychology and its implications* (2nd ed.). New York: W. H. Freeman. An excellent treatment—rigorous yet accessible—by one of the most-respected cognitive theorists.

Baddeley, A. (1982). *Your memory: A user's guide.* New York: Macmillan. A lively account of the way memory functions—and misfunctions—at a researcher equally at home in the laboratory and in the field.

Glass, A. L. & Holyoak, K. J. (1986). *Cognition* (2nd ed.). New York: Random House. Provides an integrated, up-to-date coverage of most aspects of cognition, with an extensive set of references.

Koestler, A. (1964). *The act of creation.* New York: Macmillan. A lengthy classic in which the author attempts to distill the essence of creativity through examples drawn from a wide range of arts and sciences.

Stern, L. (1985). *The structures and strategies of human memory.* Homewood, Illinois: Dorsey. Uses retrieval as a unifying theme in a straightforward account of memory processes.

Weisberg, R. W. (1986). *Creativity.* New York: W. H. Freeman. A critical account of such myths as genius and the role of the subconscious in creativity that provides a counterpoint to Koestler's text.

7

MOTIVATION AND EMOTION

Imagine that you have been banished for a month to a barren desert island and that you are permitted to take only ten items with you. What would they be? The itemized lists people supply in answer to this question are generally quite similar. Consider the three examples shown in Table 7-1. Note that all three lists contain similar basic *necessities*—items we need to survive. Also selected are a variety of *luxuries*—items that make survival worthwhile. Everyone would take food and water; yet whereas one person might refuse to leave home without a guitar, another person's life would lack meaning without a copy of the Bible.

Much of your time on the desert island would be devoted to fulfilling your needs, while most of the remaining time would be used to satisfy your desires. But if you think about it, that's how you spend your time now! Eating, drinking, keeping warm, earning money, procreating, recreating—all these varied activities have the common goal of satisfying needs or wants. Such behaviors are grouped by psychologists under the heading of *motivation*, which is the topic we consider in the first half of this chapter.

THE MEANING OF MOTIVATION

We use the term *motivation* in several ways. Sometimes we use it to mean striving for goals, such as when we are motivated to earn good grades, excel at a job, or win at sports, or when we say on some days that we lack the motivation to do anything. Sometimes we speak of *hidden motives,* implying either that a person is being deceitful or is not conscious of the forces guiding his or her actions. In psychology the term **motivation** is used more generally to refer to "the dynamics of behavior, the process of initiating, sustaining and directing activities of the organism" (Goldenson, 1970).

Conscious and Unconscious Motives

Psychology inherited from philosophy an age-old debate concerning the role of consciousness in motivation. Some philosophers have maintained a strict dichotomy between human motives and those of other animals. Lower beasts were seen to be directed primarily by inborn, automatic reactions called **instincts;** humans, endowed with rational thought, were considered to be motivated exclusively by conscious choices. As a discipline that has been guided by evolutionary theory (see Chapters 1 and 2), psychology recognizes the role in human motivation of both naturally selected biological mechanisms without a conscious component and purely conscious deliberations made possible by more recently evolved brain structures. Although we do not have to think about perspiring or shivering to maintain normal body temperature, we might consciously decide to open a window or put on a sweater to help achieve that goal. Depending on the type of motive being studied, the relative mix of innate unconscious determinants and acquired conscious determinants will vary.

Primary and Secondary Motives

Psychologists have found it helpful to distinguish two types of motives—**primary motives** and

TABLE 7-1
Lists of Items for Desert Island*

water	food	water
food	water	food
warm clothing	machete	sleeping bag
tent	gun and ammunition	plastic sheet
knife	medical supplies	ax
medical kit	radio	a friend
fishhook	matches	generator
female companion	needle and thread	radio
television	soap	art supplies
guitar	wine	Bible

* When people choose a limited number of items for an extended stay on a barren desert island, they typically select the same basic needs followed by a variety of desirable items.

secondary motives. All living creatures share such physical requirements as breathing, eating, drinking, maintaining body temperature within certain limits, eliminating wastes, and avoiding pain. From these physical requirements arise such primary motives as hunger, thirst, and safety needs — primary in the sense that ignoring them eventually will lead to death. In addition to primary motives that sustain individual life, there are others that help individual species propagate their genes. For this reason, sexual motivation usually is considered primary. As part of our biological makeup, primary motives are unlearned, although the behaviors that satisfy them may be learned. Thus, while the drive for sexual activity is natural, its expression — at least in humans — is clearly a matter of learning (see Chapter 8). Secondary motives relate to the acquisition of what we have referred to as luxury items. People are motivated not only to obtain food, shelter, and clothing but also to acquire money, status, friendship, understanding, approval, and various personal achievements.

Several terms are closely associated with the concept of motive. A **primary need** is a state of physical deprivation within the body that serves to direct the organism toward a goal object that will relieve the need. Some psychologists speak of **secondary needs,** by which they mean secondary motives. A **drive** is an aroused state produced by deprivation of a needed substance or by noxious stimuli in the environment. For example, the need for nutrition, warmth, or to escape from a painful stimulus produces a state of arousal or tension (the drive) that the organism attempts to reduce by seeking food and shelter or by making avoidance responses, respectively. A drive is an internal state that is not directly observable; it is inferred from observing an organism's behavior.

Closely linked to the notion of drive is the concept of **homeostasis.** Homeostasis refers to the optimal balance of internal functions. When factors that affect this optimal balance are either in short supply or are overabundant, homeostatic mechanisms become active and restore them to normal levels. For instance, if the body becomes too cold, constriction of peripheral blood vessels and shivering help restore body temperature. The thermostat that controls home heating is a mechanical homeostatic device that works in a similar way to maintain the optimal temperature range selected for the house.

Thus far we have characterized motivation largely in terms of needs that "push" behavior toward certain goals. However, the stimuli in the environment that signal these goals also seem to attract or exert a "pull" on us. Having fully satisfied your need for food by the main course of a meal, you probably have been tempted to try a tasty-looking dessert. Food not only reduces the hunger drive but also serves as an **incentive** that prompts you to eat regardless of need. In this instance your behavior (eating) was initially motivated by a drive (hunger) that had developed over time as your body became deprived of its principal energy source. Subsequently, even though the need for food was satisfied, an incentive (the dessert) maintained your goal-directed behavior. Goal-directed behavior is usually motivated by a blend of "pushes" and "pulls."

Psychologists refer to objects or conditions in the environment that satisfy primary or secondary motives as *incentives.* As we have seen, food has incentive value. Schools and businesses frequently adopt various incentive schemes to motivate students and employees to increase production. The achievement of goals that satisfy primary or secondary motives is rewarding, or as psychologists put it, *reinforcing.* In Chapter 5 we discussed how reinforcers such as food affect learning and performance. The study of motivation and the study of learning are linked closely by their mutual interest in the concepts of incentive and reinforcement. Learning theorists are concerned primarily with the effect of reinforcement on behavior; motivational theorists are concerned with understanding the nature of reinforcement itself. We now turn to this important issue.

The Nature of Reinforcement

At first glance it seems that at least part of what is meant by *reward, positive reinforcer,* or *incentive* is something that produces a sense of pleasure. The idea that the essential quality of things that motivate us lies in their capacity to produce pleasure is as old as Aristotle and the doctrine of *hedonism.* But what is pleasure? To one of the most influential psychologists in the first half of this century, the answer, in essence, was "the absence of tension." In the spirit of the person who banged his head against the wall because it felt so good when he stopped, Clark L. Hull (1943) maintained that positive reinforcement is nothing more than relief from the unpleasant tension associated with an unsatisfied drive. Such drives as hunger and thirst arouse an organism to seek whatever will relieve the biological need that created the arousal (food or water) and return the body to a state of homeostatic balance. According to Hull, it is the satisfaction inherent in **drive reduction** that supplies reinforcement. Hull held that drive reduction leads to learning by strengthening the association between stimuli in the situation and responses leading to drive reduction. For Hull, learning involved biologically useful behaviors becoming habits through the reinforcing effects of drive reduction. Hull's drive reduction theory is relevant to many primary motives, but it proved vulnerable to three main criticisms. We consider each in turn.

Secondary Drives and Secondary Reinforcers

As long as we focus on behaviors that serve to reduce hunger or thirst or to terminate painful stimuli, drive reduction theory makes sense; such behaviors seem clearly aimed at reducing tension from drives. However, a large proportion of human behavior is not directed in any obvious fashion at satisfying primary needs. What drives are reduced, for instance, when we play a guitar, watch television, or enjoy a spectacular sunset? Critics of drive reduction theory argue that activities such as these are rewarding in and of themselves, not because they reduce any drives.

In response to these criticisms, drive reduction theorists frequently fell back on the concepts of **secondary drives** and **secondary reinforcers.** As shown in Chapter 5, neutral stimuli that initially are not reinforcing in any way can themselves, through repeated association with primary reinforcers, acquire reinforcing properties. As reinforcers, animals will work to obtain them. An early experiment by Wolfe (1936) demonstrates how a secondary drive — the learned need for a secondary reinforcer — might originate.

As mentioned in Chapter 5, Wolfe trained chimpanzees to insert poker chips into a machine

that dispensed food. The food is a primary reinforcer and capable of reducing the hunger drive. Over the course of many trials, however, Wolfe found that the poker chips began to take on a value in and of themselves — the chimpanzees working to obtain them even after they could no longer be exchanged for food. Through their association with a primary reinforcer, the poker chips had acquired (secondary) reinforcing qualities. Obtaining them appeared to reduce a learned, secondary drive. A parallel between the chimpanzee's poker chips and money in human society suggests itself. Secondary reinforcement may help to explain why some miserly people hoard money that they refuse to exchange for food, shelter, or other primary reinforcers.

Sensory Deprivation and the Need for Stimulation

Hull's drive reduction theory implied that the most desirable state an organism can attain is the tranquility resulting from the complete satisfaction of all needs. While Hull's critics conceded that organisms strive to reduce excessive stimulation, they created problems for the theory by demonstrating that complete tranquility can also be unpleasant. Heron (1957) describes work he and others carried out under the supervision of Donald Hebb at McGill University, in which they assessed the effects of a drastic reduction in physical stimulation. Subjects were placed in a chamber like the one shown in Figure 7-1. They wore translucent goggles that admitted light but allowed no patterned vision and wore padded cuffs over their hands. They lay on soft foam pads to reduce tactile stimulation to a minimum. A monotonous drone from the air conditioner masked most auditory stimuli. It was not difficult to find healthy students who were happy to be paid an hourly sum simply to lie in the chamber and do nothing for as long as they wished. They were permitted to leave the chamber for brief intervals to be tested, and to eat and to relieve themselves. Most of the volunteers anticipated a long, relaxing vacation in this completely undemanding setting. However, they soon found that the effects of such seemingly innocuous experience can become rather unpleasant.

As time wore on, the subjects found it increasingly difficult to maintain any coherent train

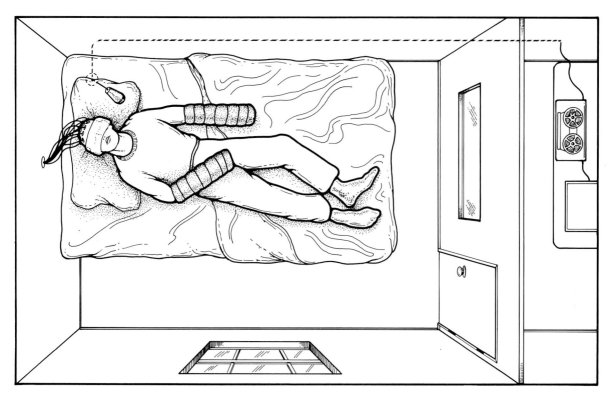

FIGURE 7-1

Sensory Deprivation Chamber Volunteers have spent hours and sometimes days in total isolation, cut off from almost all patterned sensory stimulation. The effects of long-term sensory deprivation typically are unpleasant and may be quite disturbing. *Source:* Heron, W. (1957, January). The pathology of boredom. *Scientific American, 196,* pp. 52–56.

of thought. Their performance on standard tests of mental ability deteriorated and they began to behave as if they had a need for stimulation. Some subjects began to sing aloud and bang on the chamber walls to relieve the monotony. Many even requested repeated replays of outdated weather reports when they were made available. Subjects found that their mood fluctuated erratically between hilarity and irritability. Some exhibited abnormal brain activity on the electroencephalograph, but this varied considerably from individual to individual. A few subjects even experienced hallucinations similar to those produced by psychedelic drugs. Although most subjects did not experience such spectacular effects, lesser sensory distortions were not uncommon. The surprising unpleasantness of sensory deprivation led most subjects to ask for release from the experiment after only a few days in the chamber.

The results of laboratory studies of sensory deprivation are consistent with real-life reports, some dating back to antiquity, of the experience of people during religious and political conversion rites (see Zubek, 1969). Literature contains accounts of similar effects from cloistered monks, arctic explorers, long-distance solo drivers and pilots, and those imprisoned in solitary confinement. Monotony can be a strong motivator.

The **sensory deprivation** experiment supplied strong evidence against the view that we are motivated only to reduce drives. We seem also to be motivated to maintain at least some sensory input. We tend to think of such input as informing us about our environment, but it also serves another function—to keep us aroused. It has been suggested that we need stimulation from the environment to keep arousal at an optimal level for mental and physical performance and that we act so as to increase or reduce our internal arousal, depending on the circumstances. This idea was proposed in 1908, by two psychology pioneers, as the **Yerkes–Dodson Law.** It was cast in terms of an optimal level of motivation, but Hebb reformulated it in the 1950s as an **optimal arousal theory** (Hebb, 1955). As evident from the inverted-U curve shown in Figure 7-2, behavioral efficiency suffers if arousal is either too high or too low.

The optimal level of arousal depends on the difficulty of the task to be performed. The harder the task, the sooner performance drops off as the level of arousal increases. Athletic performance that involves simple motor skills such as running is likely to continue improving with increasing arousal, even at very high levels. By contrast, many athletes who attempt more complex skills try to avoid very high levels of arousal. They are not always successful, of course, and overarousal may be responsible for the poor performance called "choking" that is sometimes seen at crucial times. Some support for this was found by Sokoll and Mynatt (1984), who determined that basketball players' free-throw accuracy was reduced when they were highly aroused by the crowd. This suggests that while the home team is generally considered to have an advantage in most sports, fan support may become a liability when the stakes (and thus arousal) are very high. Baumeister (1985) observed that home teams win over 60% of the first two games of championship baseball series but win less than 40% of the crucial remaining games (in which the winner is decided).

A Reinforcement System in the Brain The third criticism of drive reduction theory concerns the premise that reinforcement consists only of relief from unpleasant drive states, not the experience of pleasure in and of itself. From studies of electrical self-stimulation of the brain in rats, it is clear that direct stimulation of certain brain structures provides a powerful positive reinforcement for these animals. Even when extremely hungry and tired, they will ignore food and rest in order to press repeatedly on a bar to produce pulses of electrical stimulation. The few studies that have investigated electrical stimulation of comparable brain structures in humans have found that it does produce pleasant sensations (Deutsch, 1973).

The issue to which research on secondary reinforcement, sensory deprivation, and electrical stimulation of the brain is relevant relates to the essential qualities that all motives have in common — their capacity to energize people and to direct their behavior. However, most psychologists interested in the study of motivation specialize in the investigation of particular motives such as hunger, sex, or need for approval. Significantly, psychologists who study motivation may come from almost any area in psychology. Physiological psychologists tend to study the brain and nervous system mechanisms that mediate primary motives. Social and personality psychologists tend to study such motives as the needs for affiliation, achievement, and approval. Typically, researchers from different areas tend to employ different methods, different subjects, and different equipment, and they tend to communicate mainly among themselves. Thus, the study of motivation tends to be almost as variable as the type of motive that is being investigated. We devote an entire chapter to the sexual drive, one of the most important of all motives (Chapter 8); we consider the biological basis for the motive to behave altruistically (Chapter 2); and near the end of the book we discuss aggression (Chapter 14). Here we focus on a representative group of motivations: hunger, the avoidance of pain, interpersonal needs, and two "higher" motives, curiosity and self-actualization.

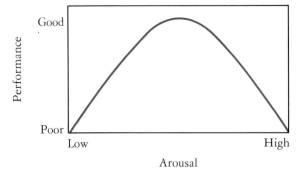

FIGURE 7-2

Hebb's Version of the Yerkes–Dodson Law
Performance on most tasks is generally best at intermediate levels of arousal. Behavioral efficiency drops off as arousal becomes too low or too high.

THE CLASSIFICATION OF MOTIVES

In many fields the early stages of development are largely concerned with taxonomy — the exhaustive listing and classification of the things that are to be studied. This was the case in the study of motivation; but how can we classify motives that involve things as diverse as hunger and money, thirst and music, or conducting scientific research and watching TV? As we have seen, investigators made a start by distinguishing between unlearned primary needs and learned secondary needs. However, this distinction does not take us far enough. A more elaborate scheme, developed by Abraham Maslow, introduces several subclassifications and arranges the major motives in a hierarchical order.

Maslow's Hierarchy of Needs

Maslow (1970) proposed that motives (to which he referred as *needs*) could be arranged in a hierarchy or pyramid (see Figure 7-3). At the base of the pyramid are the most basic biological needs, called **deficiency needs** or primary needs. Toward the peak of the pyramid are intellectual and spiritual needs, called **growth needs** (secondary needs). Maslow's hierarchy is anchored by the physiological needs. If these needs are denied, we perish. Thus we are strongly motivated to satisfy them. Only when our physiological needs are satisfied do organisms focus on the safety needs, those related to the avoidance of discomfort and pain — signals of potentially life-threatening situations — and only when these lower level needs have been dealt with, Maslow argued, do we attend to higher needs. As a humanistic personality theorist devoted to promoting the maximization of human potential, Maslow was concerned primarily with the needs at the upper end of his hierarchy: **interpersonal needs, esteem needs, cognitive-aesthetic needs,** and the pinnacle of development in his

scheme, need for **self-actualization.** (We discuss each of these motivational types in subsequent parts of this chapter.) Although Maslow's scheme is not without its shortcomings and its critics (for example, Wertheimer, 1978), it nonetheless provides a useful framework for organizing the many diverse topics that come under the general heading of motivation. The usefulness of Maslow's classification can be demonstrated by looking again at the answers to the desert-island question. Such lists often parallel the hierarchy proposed by Maslow.

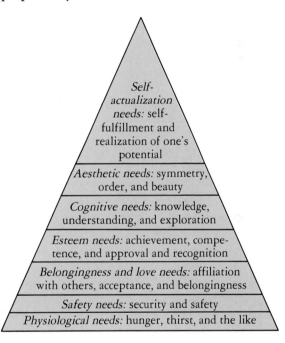

FIGURE 7-3
Maslow's Hierarchy of Needs At the bottom of the pyramid are basic survival needs; these dominate behavior until they are satisfied. Higher level needs then take over as sources of motivation. Highest level needs stem from motives that are unique determinants of human behavior. *Source:* Maslow, A. H. (1970). *Motivation and personality* (2nd ed.). New York: Harper & Row.

PHYSIOLOGICAL NEEDS

Hunger

The need for food is surely one of our most basic needs. Initially it might seem there would be little to say about it, psychologically at least. We feel hungry, so we eat. That's it. However, as with so many aspects of our nature, the motivation to eat is more complex than it may seem.

When you are hungry, you almost certainly would be willing to eat fruits and nuts, would probably eat beef, and might eat pork. However, you would be less likely to eat horse meat and you would probably feel unable to eat dog meat or grasshoppers. Yet these food preferences are quite different in other parts of the world. Although it might seem that something as basic and essential as eating would be part of our inherited makeup, this is so only after food is in the mouth. The social conventions that govern what, when, how, and with whom one eats are at least as important in regulating food intake as are physiological systems (Bates, 1958). We share food as a sign of friendship; we go on hunger strikes as a symbol of protest. The devout eat prescribed foods on ceremonial occasions and fast during certain holidays. To make any sense out of this web of things that affect eating, we must examine the interplay of physiological and psychological determinants of hunger. In this respect, eating is a good model for understanding other human motivational systems.

Physiological Factors in Hunger and Satiation

If you were to ask most people how they know when nutritional stores in their bodies are becoming depleted and how they know when they have eaten enough to make up the deficit, they are likely to tell you that first they feel hungry and then they eat until they feel full. If you pressed them further about what makes them feel hungry and full, they would probably tell you that the start-and-stop signals are an empty and a full stomach, respectively. This makes sense because hunger pangs do seem to arise from an empty stomach and bloated feelings after a large meal discourage most of us from overindulging. However, feelings that arise from neural messages sent by the stomach to the brain prove to be a useful but not an essential part of the physiological system that controls eating. That we can get along without these signals, if need be, is shown by the fact that cancer patients who have had their stomachs removed still experience feelings of hunger and, with practice, learn to regulate their food intake adequately. Thus, factors other than an appreciation of stomach fullness must also be in-

volved in hunger and satiety. Examining these in greater detail, it is useful to distinguish between *central* controls — originating in the brain, and *peripheral* controls — existing in various parts of the body that send messages back to the brain.

Peripheral Controls for Eating   There are three main peripheral hunger mechanisms.

1. Receptors in the mouth and throat monitor taste and the amount of chewing and swallowing that has taken place.
2. Sensors gauge the fullness or emptiness of the stomach.
3. Receptors in the liver inform the brain of the absorption of nutrients from the intestine into the bloodstream.

To assess the relative contributions of these three parallel systems to the control of eating, researchers have performed animal operations that allow them to study the workings of each system in isolation.

The role of mouth and throat mechanisms in hunger and satiation can be studied by preventing food that has been tasted, chewed, and swallowed from reaching the stomach and intestine. When animals that have undergone this bypass operation are made hungry, they initially eat their customary amount and then stop. Soon, however, they show renewed signs of hunger and resume eating. This shows that the mouth and throat sensors are able to produce feelings of satiation by themselves, probably to inhibit excessive eating while the much slower processes of digestion take place (Mook, 1963).

The independent contributions of stomach expansion and contraction to feelings of hunger and satiation can be assessed by injecting food directly into the stomach, bypassing the mouth and throat sensors (Epstein & Teitelbaum, 1962a). If a nonnutritive substance is injected into the animal's stomach when it is hungry, it initially shows signs of satiation. These results confirm that sensors attuned to the fullness of the stomach can, by themselves, contribute to the inhibition of hunger (Deutsch & Wang, 1977). This fact has been seized on recently by manufacturers of a nonnutritive bread made from sawdust that is intended to give dieters a satisfying feeling of fullness without unwanted calories. Direct stomach-loading experiments such as these lead to two main conclusions about the short-term determinants of eating. First, animals normally use information from sensors in the mouth and throat to stop eating before digestion has taken place; if necessary, however, they can manage without this information. Second, information about stomach fullness is normally used to regulate food intake. In the long term, however, eating is controlled by the nutritional quality of food—detected by the liver—rather than by its taste or volume.

It has long been known that, among its many other functions, the liver acts as a storage site for sugar and fat. It stores them when intake temporarily exceeds the metabolic needs of the body and releases them when energy is needed quickly. More recently, it has become known that the liver also contains a number of sensory receptors important for feelings of hunger and satiation (Friedman & Stricker, 1976; Russek, 1971). After being digested, food is emptied from the stomach into the small intestine where its useful constituents are absorbed through the intestinal wall into the bloodstream. Among the first organs to receive the blood bearing these newly absorbed nutrients is the liver. A rise in various nutrients after a meal, or a drop after fasting, is detected in the liver and signalled to the hypothalamus (in the brain) where it is coordinated with messages from sensors in the mouth, throat, and stomach (Novin et al., 1976).

Central Controls for Eating The task of maintaining a stable body weight over extended periods is one we rarely devote much thought to until something goes awry and we can no longer manage to do it. If you consider that a weight gain of merely an ounce a day would result in nearly 23 pounds in a year, you begin to appreciate the precision of the regulatory mechanisms involved and the extremely fine adjustments they must make in order to balance daily intake with often highly variable rates of energy expenditure. You should not feel particularly hungry after lounging about all day; you should have a voracious appetite after a day of hard physical labor.

The first theories that progressed beyond the notion that stomach fullness alone determines how hungry we feel assumed that the primary control for hunger is a brain mechanism that operates like a thermostat. That is, it keeps track of the levels of nutrients dissolved in the blood and triggers hunger and food-seeking behaviors when they drop below prescribed levels. Some early research suggested that sugar concentration in the blood was the crucial indicator, but other research focused on fat content, amino acid levels, and even blood temperature. Over the years, evidence has accumulated to suggest that each of these factors affects hunger in some way. We know from studies of damage to animal brains that the mechanisms that monitor glucose in the blood are distinct from those that are sensitive to the amount of fat stored in the body. Some of these sensors are in the brain; others are in the periphery and feed their measurements back to centers in the brain.

The experimental search for brain centers that receive and act upon nutritional information was guided initially, as is often the case, by clinical data derived from brain-damaged patients—in this instance patients with tumors in the hypothalamus. When the tumors encroached on a region of the hypothalamus concerned with control of eating and drinking (called the *ventromedial nuclei*), patients exhibited marked increases in appetite and body weight. Research on animals (Powley et al., 1980) confirmed that if the ventromedial nuclei are destroyed, animals overeat until, several weeks after the lesion, they reach a new stable level several times their original weight (see Figure 7-4). When the experimental lesions were placed a few millimeters away (in the region called the *lateral hypothalamus*), the animals ceased eating and drinking altogether, and would have perished had they not been force-fed. After a period of forced-feeding, these animals gradually began eating on their own—but only enough to maintain a drastically lowered body weight. This prompted Epstein and Teitelbaum (1962b) to suggest that secondary eating control mechanisms gradually substituted for the destroyed ones. Hypothalamic mechanisms seem to set the *natural* body weight that a person establishes. However, major nerve tracts from the limbic system that pass close to the hypothalamus also seem to play a role in controlling eating. Antelman and Szechtman (1975) suggest that these pathways could be involved in

FIGURE 7-4
Hypothalamus and Control of Body Weight
Damage to the *ventromedial nuclei* in the hypothalamus can cause an animal to eat so much that it becomes grossly overweight. A hypothalamic lesion caused this rat to triple its normal body weight.

"nervous eating" and the loss of appetite that often accompanies depression.

The Psychology of Eating

The physiological mechanisms that underlie hunger are similar in all normal people and in many nonhuman animals. However, there are tremendous differences among people in the ways in which they satisfy the hunger need. Some eat only one meal a day; others are constant "nibblers," always snacking on something. Some people seem powerless to control their appetites; others seem to waste away, with practically no desire to eat. As Marston Bates (1958) once commented, it is extremely rare to find a society that is rational in its choice of diet, if we define *rational* as eating the greatest amount of

the most plentiful and nutritious food available when it is most needed. There is much more to eating than simply satisfying nutritional needs. We have alluded to the important role played by learning, custom, and taboo in selecting diets. Social psychologists have examined how individuals differ in the relative importance of internal and external factors that affect their eating habits. To appreciate their findings, we must begin by reviewing certain research on nonhuman animals.

Research on animals with lesions in the region of the ventromedial hypothalamus produced a somewhat puzzling finding. Although animals with these lesions typically gorge themselves when good food is freely available (suggesting that the lesions make them very hungry), they actually eat *less* than normal animals when they are compelled to work for their food or when the taste of the food is even slightly unpleasant (Ferguson & Keesey, 1975). These findings led several researchers to question whether the lesions in fact made the animals hungry. Some suggested instead that the lesions produced a state in which eating came under the control of such external factors as the availability and taste of food rather than internal cues about stomach fullness and nutritional needs of the body. The lesioned animals become much more finicky about their food and less able to tolerate even minor frustrations placed in their way. Columbia University social psychologist Stanley Schachter had the insight to investigate whether obese humans share some of the unusual feeding habits observed by physiological psychologists when rats are made obese by hypothalamic lesions.

Schachter devised a series of experiments that compared the eating behavior of normal and obese subjects (Schachter & Rodin, 1974). In these studies, food was introduced casually into experimental settings while subjects were engaged in irrelevant tasks, tasks they were led to believe were the actual purpose of the experiment. Schachter found some interesting parallels between behaviors of nonhuman animals with ventromedial hypothalamic lesions and obese humans. For example, he found that obese people would eat *less* than people of normal weight if they had to work for their food (if, for example, they were required to crack nuts before

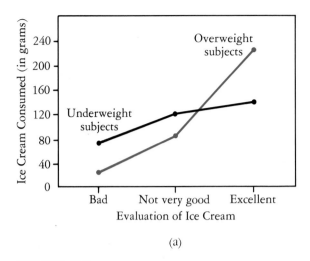

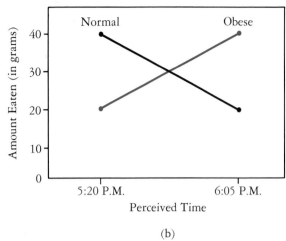

(a)

(b)

FIGURE 7-5

Obesity and the Perception of Food   (a) Varying the taste of ice cream changes the amount eaten much more for overweight than for underweight people.   (b) The erroneous belief that it is time to eat affects obese people more than people of normal weight (see text for explanation).   *Sources:* (a) Nisbett, R. E. (1968).   Taste, deprivation, and weight determinants of eating behavior.   *Journal of Personality and Social Psychology, 10,* 107–16.   (b) Schachter, S., & Gross, L. P. (1968).   Manipulated time and eating behavior.   *Journal of Personality and Social Psychology, 10,* 98–106.

eating them rather than receiving nuts already shelled).   Similarly, it was found that obese people rejected food at a lower concentration of a bad-tasting additive than did people of normal weight.   On the other hand, obese people seemed compelled to eat more than "normals" if the food was made attractive to eye and palate [see Figure 7-5(a)].

Another experiment examined the role of time cues in prompting eating (Schachter & Gross, 1968).   Normal and overweight students were observed in a setting where the wall clock was rigged to run about half as fast or twice as fast as it usually did.   A sham activity served to get the subjects to remove their own watches and to divert their attention from the real measure — the number of crackers they consumed when the crackers were casually offered.   Subjects entered at 5:00 p.m. and were exposed to the irrelevant activity until 5:30 p.m.   By that time the rigged clock for the "fast" group read 6:05 p.m. but for the "slow" group read only 5:20 p.m.   Figure 7-5(b) shows that normal weight and obese people reacted quite differently if they were led to

believe it was earlier or later than it really was. Obese people who thought it was 6:05, and therefore "time to eat," consumed more crackers than similarly overweight people who thought it was only 5:20, and therefore not yet "time to eat."   By contrast, people of normal weight either ate no more or decreased their intake when they were led to believe it was approaching dinnertime — presumably not wanting to spoil their appetites.

The work of Schachter and his colleagues suggests that obese people rely more heavily on external cues than internal (need-related) cues to know when to start and to stop eating.   They seem more affected by habit, the proximity, appearance, and taste of what they eat, and by the effort they must expend to obtain food, than by signals from within that should inform them of their nutritional needs.   Although normal-weight people might skip a meal if they didn't feel hungry or decline the offer of a tempting treat if they had just recently finished lunch, obese persons would be much less likely to abstain.   If the obese are likely to eat whether they need it or not — "just because it's there" or "because it's time" — knowing this

Obese individual

could be very valuable in restructuring their environments to help them "stick to their diets." Franken (1982, pp. 136–41) has done service to would-be dieters by distilling the implications of the research we have been discussing into a number of practical strategies for everyday use. Franken's Six Rules for Dieting are given in Table 7-2. Current work on obesity points to the important role played by genetic factors (Bray, 1981) and suggests that the internal–external hypothesis is too limited a notion to account for all the data on obesity (Rodin, 1981).

Eating and Energy Expenditure The effort we must expend to get food in modern societies is insignificant compared to that of our ancestors in hunting and gathering societies. Is it possible that our technological cleverness has outstripped our naturally selected mechanisms for dealing with hunger? The abundance and ease of access to food most of us enjoy and the constant bombardment of our senses with food-related stimuli are very recent developments, considered in an evolutionary time frame. During most of our evolutionary history, food was comparatively scarce and difficult to obtain (which is still the case for most inhabitants of our planet). Thus, pressures to evolve powerful mechanisms to turn off eating would have been relatively slight.

Overabundance was not a problem for early humans; in fact, the best survival strategy for a people faced with precarious food supply would have been to eat as much as possible because of the uncertainty of the next opportunity. Ideally, the amount you eat should be related to how

TABLE 7-2
A Psychologist's Rules for Dieting*

Rule 1 *Eat only in one place and only at regular times.* Overweight people generally overeat, particularly by snacking between meals. They eat in a variety of places, often while engaged in such other activities as watching television. Eliminating snacks narrows the problem of controlling intake to mealtimes. People usually can pay full attention to the amount they eat at mealtimes when in the company of others who can act as their "social conscience."

Rule 2 *Eat slowly.* Obese people tend to devour food rather than savor it; eating slowly aids dieting both directly and indirectly. The quantity of food eaten depends in part on signals triggered by food in the mouth. Slower eating allows "full" signals to be triggered after eating less food. Similarly, "full" signals from the relatively slow digestive process have a greater opportunity to limit consumption. Finally, because eating is a pleasurable process, savoring food as it is eaten extends the period of pleasure at mealtimes.

Rule 3 *Do not eat or buy problem foods.* Most overweight people have a favorite food they find impossible to eat in small quantities. Often the food is high in caloric content, such as chocolate or peanuts. A simple but effective aid to dieting is to cut out this problem food entirely. If that is unacceptable, its consumption should be limited to a predetermined amount at only one meal each day.

Rule 4 *Vary your diet.* Substantially reducing the range of sensory cues encountered during eating is a form of sensory deprivation—an experience that may be even more aversive for obese than for nonobese people. Overweight people should reduce the amount of food consumed without reducing the range of sensory stimulation they experience.

Rule 5 *Make food hard to get.* Although psychologists still debate the underlying reasons, it seems clear that one of the primary determinants of overeating is easy availability of food. For example, obese people eat far fewer nuts if they must shell them first than when already shelled and eat fewer sandwiches if they must get them from the refrigerator than when they are on the table (Schachter, 1971). For effective dieting, choose foods that take time and effort to prepare, and keep other foods out of sight and out of reach.

Rule 6 *Exercise.* There is some evidence that exercising before meals reduces appetite (Stuart & Davis, 1972). Also, exercising tends to improve mood, aiding the dietary motivation of individuals whose overeating stems from anxiety or depression. However, the primary virtue of exercise for dieters is that it helps burn off fuel that would otherwise be converted to fat. The following durations of specific activities are required to expend the calories acquired through consumption of specific foods (Konishi, 1965).

Food	Calories	Minutes of Activity				
		Reclining	Walking	Cycling	Running	Swimming
TV dinner (chicken)	542	417	104	66	48	28
Milk shake	421	324	81	51	38	22
Strawberry shortcake	400	308	77	49	36	21
Apple pie (1/6th)	377	290	73	46	34	19
Hamburger	350	324	81	51	38	22
T-bone steak	235	181	45	29	21	12
Ice cream (1/6 qt)	193	148	37	24	17	10
Milk (1 glass)	166	128	32	20	15	9
Doughnut	151	116	29	18	13	8
Beer (1 glass)	114	88	22	14	10	6
Cheddar cheese (1 oz)	111	85	21	14	10	6
Fried egg	110	85	21	13	10	6
Potato chips (1 bag)	108	83	21	13	10	6
Apple (large)	101	78	19	12	9	5
Skim milk (1 glass)	81	62	16	10	7	4
Cookie (chocolate chip)	51	39	10	6	5	3
Carrot (raw)	42	32	8	5	4	2
Cottage cheese (1 tbs)	27	21	5	3	2	1
Cookie (plain)	15	12	3	2	1	1

* Robert Franken has distilled psychological knowledge about eating behavior into six rules for persons who want to diet effectively.
Source: Adapted from Franken, R. E. (1982). *Human motivation* (pp. 136–41). Belmont, CA: Brooks/Cole.

much energy you expend, a factor that may vary greatly from day to day (see Figure 7-6). For instance, an office worker who enjoys cross-country running probably uses much less energy on normal workdays than on days off. What records this difference and translates it into the appropriate increases or decreases in appetite? We do not yet know the answer to this question; however, whatever the mechanism, it is apparent that a certain amount of physical exertion is required for it to operate effectively. Paradoxically, humans and animals who fall below a minimum level of exer-

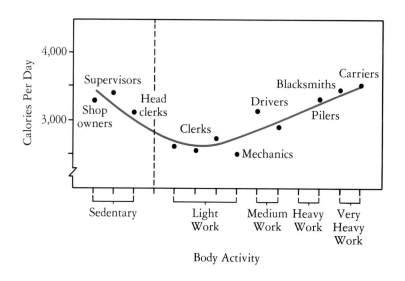

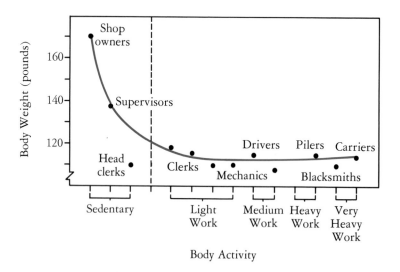

FIGURE 7-6

Caloric Intake and Body Weight for Various Jobs Workers in West Bengal, India had their daily caloric intake (a) and body weight (b) recorded. For those whose jobs required at least some heavy work (shown to right of vertical broken line), the amount eaten increased with increased physical effort; however, their body weight remained roughly constant, indicating the additional calories supplied only the additional energy required. In contrast, because sedentary work required little effort, eating more led to substantial increases in body weight (shown by curve to left of vertical broken line), indicating the extra calories were not burned off. *Source:* Mayer, J., Roy, P., & Mitra, K. P. (1956). Relation between caloric intake, body weight, and physical work: Studies in an industrial male population in West Bengal. *American Journal of Clinical Nutrition, 4,* 169–75.

tion often suffer an increase in appetite, with a subsequent tendency to become considerably overweight. This often occurs among caged animals with limited opportunity to exercise and is all too apparent in the populations of modern industrialized societies.

Eating and Learning As indicated by the number of cultural conventions that affect eating behavior, much of our control over eating is learned. Certain kinds of learning concerned with food (particularly with its taste) are different from other kinds of learning. Most learning is acquired in small steps and with repeated practice (see Chapter 5); learning about taste seems to occur in a single exposure and to last almost indefinitely. Trappers have long known that animals who survive poisoned bait will avoid similar bait for an extremely long time. Studies by John Garcia and co-workers indicate that novel foods that cause an animal to become ill, even several hours after consumption will be avoided in the future. Box 7-1 (page 312) describes this phenomenon and its implications for normal dietary selection.

SAFETY NEEDS

The Avoidance of Pain

Think of the last time you had a severe toothache, earache, migraine headache, burn, or other serious injury. Sometimes people will do almost anything to obtain relief from these painful stimuli. Avoidance of pain appears to be a powerful motivator—people spend billions of dollars every year on medicines and surgical procedures to prove it. In general terms, avoiding pain can be considered one of the primary motives of life.

Pain is both a sensation (like seeing and hearing) and an emotional experience (like fear and anger), and the experience of pain is determined by both physical and psychological factors. We discussed the sensation of pain in Chapter 4, noting how noxious stimuli from the environment are received by sensory receptors, coded, and transmitted to the brain. Here we are concerned with the psychological experience of pain (the "agony" component) and the effects of this experience on behavior.

Social and Cultural Factors

Research has shown that pain sensation thresholds (the ability to detect noxious stimuli) are much the same among people of all cultures (Sternbach & Tursky, 1965, p. 241). However, the painfulness of an experience with a given level of sensation (or amount of tissue damage) has been shown to vary with prior learning, personality, attention, arousal level, and with the social and cultural backgrounds of the perceiver (Melzack, 1973; Weisenberg, 1977). For instance, Clark and Clark (1980) studied a group of Nepalese porters, who are famous for their endurance in carrying heavy loads up steep Himalayan slopes. While it had seemed to some Western observers that these remarkable people might be relatively insensitive to pain, tests showed no difference in their sensory responses. Instead, they were found to differ from people in our culture with respect to their criteria for defining these sensations as painful.

Studies on animals reared in social isolation suggest that early experience plays a role in the development of an individual's characteristic level of tolerance for pain. Melzack and Scott (1957) found that puppies that matured in isolation reacted differently to noxious stimuli than other puppies. Their reflexive reactions to the stimuli were normal—suggesting their sensations were unaffected—but their ability to learn avoidance responses and their emotional reactions to the stimuli were grossly abnormal.

Safety Needs versus the Need for Stimulation

If **safety needs** are basic to motivation, it may seem paradoxical that some people are attracted to skydiving, mountain climbing, and contact sports. Why do such people appear to take their

BOX 7-1
AN ANALYSIS OF BAIT SHYNESS

People who have the responsibility for poisoning rats know that it is often a difficult job. Rats and other mammals have evolved highly adaptive responses to novel foods. Even if very hungry, they sample only a small amount of a new substance and then wait, often for several hours. Only if no signs of illness arise will they consume the remainder of the food. Any adverse symptoms during the waiting period will produce a strong aversion to the new taste that lasts virtually indefinitely.

A group working with learning psychologist John Garcia became interested in this "bait shyness" phenomenon because of its evolutionary significance as a poison-avoidance mechanism and its implications for learning theory. They soon realized that it can also teach us important things about how we normally learn to regulate our internal bodily processes. The investigators discovered that the ways in which animals learn about what improves or impairs their *internal* equilibrium are different from the process of learning to avoid noxious stimuli in the world around them (Garcia et al., 1974).

Because things that affect internal processes generally enter the body by mouth, their effects become associated with their tastes. Objects and events in the external environment that have consequences of importance for an animal usually become associated with their sounds or visual appearance. Learned associations that involve visual or auditory cues most often are acquired gradually and with repeated practice. However, animals that required several trials to learn to avoid poisons clearly were not adapted to an environment that contained edible but poisonous substances. A learning process therefore evolved in which a single exposure became sufficient to produce aversion to a taste. A visual or auditory stimulus that preceded its consequences by more than a few seconds produced a weak association, if any. However, a novel taste followed by illness several hours later (whether or not it was the real cause of the symptoms) could still produce the very strong avoidance response called **bait shyness.**

safety needs so lightly? One hypothesis that may account for their willingness to risk life and limb in these pursuits is that some individuals require more than the average amount of stimulation from their environments in order to maintain their preferred level of arousal. The sensory deprivation studies we discussed earlier and the novelty experiments that we will discuss shortly suggest that underarousal can be as detrimental to performance as overarousal. If some people naturally tend to be underaroused, perhaps because of some difference in their nervous systems, they would be more dependent on their environment to supply external boosters. Conversely, there may be others chronically high in arousal who are generally motivated to limit the amount of external stimulation in their surroundings.

To test the usefulness of the foregoing assumptions, Marvin Zuckerman (1978) compared people who were attracted to thrills of various sorts to people who tended to avoid them. He developed a *sensation-seeking scale* that ranks people according to their preference for such diverse interests as scary movies, risky sports, mind-

Taste aversions involve making the offending substance less pleasurable; however, raising the pleasurableness of things the body needs is equally important for maintaining a healthy internal environment. It was once thought that the body somehow "knew" exactly which nutrients it lacked and that animals were motivated by *specific hungers* to seek foods that contained them. While this is true for a few essential nutrients, we now know that most of these behaviors are really learned responses that are the converse of the bait-shyness phenomenon. When animals experience symptoms of illness due to a shortage of an essential nutrient, this may lower the pleasurableness of the deficient diet and prompt a tentative broadening of the range of acceptable foods. If the animal happens to sample a new food and feels better following the experience, the food's pleasurableness (and hence its incentive value) is raised and the animal becomes motivated to seek more of it (Rozin & Kalat, 1971). Attempts to condition similar food preferences or aversions by using visual or auditory cues rather than tastes have proved extremely difficult.

That separate systems may control learning about the internal and external environments is suggested by the fact that an animal need not even be consciously aware of symptoms caused by a tainted food for a taste aversion to be established. The animal can be rendered unconscious while the nausea and vomiting run their course, but the aversion to the novel taste is established anyway (Garcia & Rusiniak, 1980).

A practical outcome of the bait-shyness research may provide a way of controlling wild animals that prey upon domestic livestock. Environmentalists have stressed the value of wolves, coyotes, and other carnivores for maintenance of ecological balances (for example, in controlling rodent populations), but their attacks on sheep and cattle represent a considerable economic loss for ranchers. Gustavson et al. (1974) suggested an alternative to killing predators: feeding coyotes minced lamb flesh, skin, and wool laced with apomorphine—a drug that induces severe nausea. Following Gustavson's suggestion, when the coyotes recovered from the nausea and vomiting they were reluctant to attack lambs but were still quite willing to attack rabbits. The results offer hope for reconciling the concerns of environmentalists and ranchers.

altering drugs and exotic forms of food, art, travel, and sexual practices. When high and low responders were compared, high-sensation seekers were found to prefer excitement and diversity in many areas of their lives—for example, their adventuresome tastes were evident in their choice of sports, jobs, diets, and sexual partners. They felt trapped by routine and unchallenging tasks, and did poorly in jobs or schools that permitted little room for variety or creativity. As a group, they were somewhat prone to seek escape from boredom in alcohol or other drugs. People low on the sensation-seeking scale lacked this strong drive for stimulation. They tended to disapprove of the high-sensation seekers, and even thought them bizarre. The free-wheeling "highs," on the other hand, tended to see the "lows" as stuffy and inhibited.

There is some evidence to suggest that individual differences in motivation for sensation-seeking are related to inherited differences in personality. Eysenck (1973) found that people he classified as extraverts were inclined to be sensation-seekers and those he classified as introverts

were more likely to be sensation-avoiders. Eysenck attempted to relate these personality and behavioral differences to levels of brain arousal measured by EEG (electroencephalography). He found some support for the notion that extravert sensation-seekers live in a chronic state of mild underarousal, and thus constantly comb their environments for stimulation. We return to this issue later in this chapter when we discuss curiosity.

INTERPERSONAL NEEDS

The Need for Affiliation

In earlier times, people in our society who committed crimes were punished physically—their safety needs were violated. This remains the case in many parts of the world. Today, however, we punish convicted criminals by imprisoning them, and within the prison punish them further by putting them in solitary confinement. Why is solitary confinement considered so aversive? From what we have learned already in this chapter, one answer is that it is a form of sensory deprivation, and that experience can be quite unpleasant. More than that, however, it prevents interaction with other people. Psychologists call the motive to be with other people the **need for affiliation.**

It is quite obvious that most people feel the need to affiliate with others — but why? In Chapters 2 and 10 we discuss how the benefits of affiliating with others for purposes of mating and rearing offspring, for hunting and food gathering, and for mutual grooming and protection are believed to have played an important role in the evolution of the human species (Barash, 1977, p. 126–27). Members of many (though not all) species raised in isolation nonetheless exhibit affiliative behavior as adults. This suggests that the affiliation motive is inborn. However, like other dispositions with an unlearned basis, experience inevitably exerts a profound influence on how individuals go about satisfying the need. Some people constantly seek the company of others by joining clubs, visiting friends, talking on the telephone; others covet their privacy.

While most research on deficiency needs has been conducted by physiological psychologists, research on interpersonal needs generally has been conducted by social and personality psychologists. The focus of this research has been on the circumstances under which the need to affiliate is aroused and the differences among people regarding its intensity. The question that has guided this research centers on what causes people to feel a strong need to affiliate with others. The most obvious answer is "social isolation"; however, social isolation is not the only condition that affects the need for affiliation. The condition that has received the most attention from social psychologists is somewhat less obvious — anxiety.

Anxiety and Affiliation Noting that people frequently report feeling anxious when they are isolated from others for long periods, Stanley Schachter (1959) arranged to make a group of women anxious in an experimental setting to see whether it would increase their need to be with others. To induce anxiety he used the threat of electric shock. Although no one actually received any shocks, Schachter assumed that the anticipation of receiving them would be anxiety-provoking. On entering the experiment, the student volunteers were assigned randomly to one of two groups. Subjects in the *high-anxiety* group were met by an austere individual purporting to be a medical researcher studying the physiological effects of electric shock. He empha-

sized that the shocks would be exceedingly painful, though not permanently damaging. With the *low-anxiety* group, the same "experimenter" adopted a more humane manner and told them the shocks would produce only a mild tingling sensation. Following these introductory remarks, the subjects in both groups were told they must wait about ten minutes for the equipment to be set up and were asked if they preferred to wait alone or in the company of others. Schachter found that approximately twice as many women in the high-anxiety group preferred to wait with other subjects than to wait alone. The reverse pattern was found in the low-anxiety group.

An interesting sidelight on these experiments revealed that subjects who were firstborn children exhibited a significantly greater need to affiliate than subjects who were later-born members of their families. Schachter's explanation for this finding was that the typically greater indulgence of firstborn children by their parents makes them more likely than later-born children to turn to others when they wish to reduce anxiety in stressful situations.

Fear and Affiliation After the publication of Schachter's work on anxiety and affiliation, several other researchers conducted similar experiments. Although most of them obtained similar findings, some disagreed with Schachter's assumption that it was anxiety that increased affiliation under these conditions. For example, Sarnoff and Zimbardo (1961) argued that subjects who expected severe electric shocks became fearful, not anxious. *Fear* is the emotion we experience when confronted by a real danger in the environment, one that might produce pain; *anxiety* is the feeling of unease aroused by some ill-defined risk or by innocuous stimuli that are subjectively upsetting to us but not likely to be dangerous in an objective sense. Sarnoff and Zimbardo (1961) attempted to produce anxiety rather than fear by telling male college students in an experiment that they might have to do some embarrassing things in public, such as suck on pacifiers. Under these conditions, most subjects preferred to wait alone instead of together. Thus, they concluded, while anxiety decreases the desire to affiliate, fear is actually more likely to have the opposite effect.

Why might those in fear-provoking situations prefer to be with others? A number of possibilities exist. People in these circumstances may have learned to associate the presence of others with protection, comfort, or reassurance (safety in numbers). Or being with people may divert attention from unpleasant feelings of fear. These possibilities have been tested experimentally, but another possibility has received the strongest support — namely that affiliating allows people to compare their perceptions, feelings, and expectations with those of others facing similar circumstances. Situations in which we feel fearful often involve great uncertainty about what is going to happen and how we should react. The idea that the major function of affiliating is to reduce uncertainty by arriving at a consensus about what the situation means and what should be done about it derives from the *social comparison theory* of Leon Festinger (1954). The theory states that people try to verify their beliefs about the world and about themselves by examining them in relation to the opinions and behaviors of others. In one experiment, for example, Schachter (1959) gave subjects a choice between waiting alone or waiting either with other subjects or with students waiting to see their academic advisors. Schachter found that subjects were much more likely to choose to affiliate when they could wait with people who were about to undergo a similar experience. From these results, Schachter (1959) concluded that "misery doesn't love just any kind of company; it loves only miserable company."

As more and more studies on affiliation have been conducted, it has become clear that small variations in the circumstances that surround the arousal of the need can affect the behavior of subjects. For example, whereas Schachter found that subjects threatened with electric shock preferred to wait with other subjects who faced a similar fate, Firestone et al. (1973) found that subjects threatened with embarrassment preferred to wait with strangers rather than with subjects in the same situation, apparently because the strangers would supply more of a diversion.

There is also evidence that people's characteristic level of need for affiliation can affect their performance in different social settings (McKea-

chie et al., 1966). McKeachie and his colleagues set up two college psychology classes that differed in the level of affiliative cues present. In one class, student contact with the instructor and contact among students were frequent, and the atmosphere was personal and friendly. In the second class, the instructor was much less accessible to students, and the atmosphere was decidedly less social and more reserved. You might expect that student performance was better in the friendly setting than in the reserved atmosphere. That was the case for students with a high need for affiliation, McKeachie found, but just the opposite pattern was true for students with a low need for affiliation (see Figure 7-7).

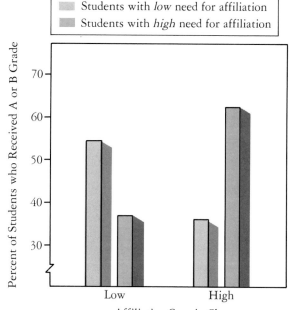

FIGURE 7-7

Individual Differences in Need for Affiliation Students in a college psychology course were assigned to classes either high or low in affiliative cues (for example, personal attention by instructor, number of contacts with instructor, friendly atmosphere). Students concerning whom tests had shown were high in need for affiliation earned better grades in the class with more affiliative cues; students who had shown a lower need for affiliation fared better in the less friendly and less personal environment. *Source:* McKeachie, W., Lin, Y. G., Mulholland, J., & Isaacson, R. (1966). Student affiliation, motives, teacher warmth and academic achievement. *Journal of Personality and Social Psychology, 4,* 457–61.

ESTEEM NEEDS

The Need for Approval

One of the best-selling "How to . . ." books of all time is Dale Carnegie's, *How to Win Friends and Influence People.* The subtitle of the book is "How to make people like you instantly." However we may feel about the advice given by Dale Carnegie, most people know, deep down, that they need to be liked. In psychology, the motivation to be liked has been studied primarily as it is revealed in the **need for approval,** and the need for approval has been studied primarily by personality psychologists. The focus of their research has been on individual differences — how people differ in the need for approval, and why.

The major early work on need for approval was done by Douglas Crowne and David Marlowe (1964). In the process of considering biases in answering questions on personality tests, these psychologists noted that some people consistently give socially desirable answers. They collected a number of socially desirable statements and included them in a true/false test. Some of the statements were those that people often wish were true of themselves but which, in reality, are untrue of most of us (for example, "I have never intensely disliked anyone.") Other statements described characteristics that are socially objectionable but are nonetheless true of most people (for example, "I like to gossip at times.") Crowne and Marlowe hypothesized that a tendency to make socially desirable responses and to avoid undesirable ones would be a good measure of the person's need for approval.

The *Marlowe-Crowne Social Desirability Scale* has been given to large numbers of people. People who score high on this scale have been found to have an interesting group of traits. As you might expect, they tend to be very susceptible to social pressures. They tend to be cautious, conforming, and easily swayed by group opinions. They are unlikely to express their hostility, even when provoked, and are likely to change their attitudes when presented with a persuasive argument. In short, they try to present an idealized picture of themselves to the world. To some

degree, this orientation is probably necessary for successful social interactions, but those who carry it to extremes may produce the opposite effect from the one they intend. Crowne and Marlowe (1964) report that people who score highest on the scale tend to be viewed by others as sanctimonious, subservient, and *less* likeable than others. Our language contains several unflattering terms (such as "brownnose") used to describe this type of individual.

The Need for Self-esteem

Advice columns such as that of Ann Landers frequently print letters from distressed individuals who admit having violated some personal standard of behavior and whose opinion of themselves has been lowered as a result. Liking oneself usually depends on living up to a set of ideals that define one's sense of self-worth. The feeling that one has failed to meet one's own standards is among the most common symptoms of psychological depression. Personality researchers and developmental psychologists have long been interested in how we acquire these ideals and why people differ in their apparent need to be faithful to them.

Research has shown that preschool and early-school years are important in forming children's estimates of their own competence and self-worth. As you might predict, family relationships play a large part in shaping these feelings and needs. Coopersmith (1967) found that children with high self-esteem tended to come from families where they were treated early on as responsible individuals. Parents were highly involved with their children; accomplishments were both expected and rewarded. Within an atmosphere of loving acceptance, discipline was nonetheless strict and consistent. Within well-defined boundaries, children were encouraged to explore, question, and experiment.

In contrast, Coopersmith found that low self-esteem children did not come from environments where achievements and self-confidence became second nature. Thus, in later years they were less likely to utilize their talents to the fullest in school, sports and group activities. They were more anxious and they were less willing to assume leadership roles. Such behavior often produces a vicious circle where initial low self-esteem inhibits the use of talents one may actually have, which, in turn, precludes the achievements that could bolster self-esteem.

Cognizant that feelings of self-worth typically are well established early in the lives of children, Baumrind (1972) set out to study the ways in which this need is met in preschool children. When she compared measurements of pre-schooler self-esteem, Baumrind found that those with positive self-regard tended to be more self-reliant and more inclined to question and explore. Their home lives conformed to the pattern described earlier by Coopersmith (1967). Interestingly, Baumrind found that children of permissive parents, who were warm and affectionate but undemanding, were less self-reliant and lower in self-esteem than those of parents who had firm expectations and set clear limits. Apparently the best way to fulfill the need for self-esteem is to acquire the ability to live up to expectations of achievement—first those imposed by parents and later those internalized by oneself.

COGNITIVE-ESTHETIC NEEDS

We have suggested that most motives result from an interaction between innate dispositions and learned experiences. We demonstrated the effect of learning and experience on the basic physiological need for food and we speculated about the biological origins of social needs, such as the need for affiliation. However, because psychological research on esteem needs has almost exclusively treated them as personality traits, we said little about how biologically based dispositions affect the need for approval. Ascending to the next category of need in Maslow's hierarchy, however, we are able, once again, to demonstrate the joint contributions of biology and experience as we examine the needs to explore and manipulate the environment.

The Curiosity Need

At the University of Wisconsin in the 1950s, Harlow and his associates were studying problem-solving with monkeys (Harlow, 1976). Like many other psychologists of that era, they were influenced by the dominant theory of motivation discussed earlier—that all reinforcers reduce drives (physical needs) and that in the absence of drives to reduce, an animal would not be motivated to engage in any behavior. Consistent with these assumptions, Harlow conducted a study with monkeys in which he used a primary reinforcer (food) to reward the unlocking of puzzle-box compartments. During one night an interesting incident occurred. A naive monkey was left inadvertently with a box whose compartments had not been filled with food. The following morning, the staff returned to find that even without food reinforcement the monkey solved all the lock problems. Instead of ignoring this serendipitous finding, Harlow was struck by its implications. What reinforced the monkey's problem-solving behavior? No drive seemed to be reduced. Ultimately, Harlow concluded that the monkey was motivated to satisfy a curiosity need, to explore its environment, and to gain information. Later experiments by Harlow and his students directly investigated how exploration, manipulation of objects, satisfaction of curiosity, and, in general, acquisition of information could serve as reinforcers for monkey behavior. Harlow and his students found that these reinforcers often sustained interest in tasks much longer than such primary reinforcers as food. They found, for instance, that monkeys would work extraordinarily hard for the opportunity to peer out of a boring compartment into another that contained toys, people, or other monkeys.

Examining curiosity from an evolutionary perspective, a number of scientists have wondered why it would evolve and whether it should evolve more in some species than in others.

FIGURE 7-8
Primates Showing Curiosity Animals of most species exhibit curiosity that leads them to observe, explore, and manipulate their environment. This drive seems strongest in primates.

Comparative psychologist Stephen Glickman embarked on a program of research at Chicago's Lincoln Park Zoo to investigate these questions. Glickman and Sroges (1966) devised a series of standardized tests of curiosity and manipulatory behavior that could be used with the diverse species in the zoo. These tests involved introducing simple but novel objects into the animals' home cages and observing their responses to them. Among the species compared, mammals showed the most curiosity. In general, the most curious species were found to be those that possessed the following characteristics.

1. A large, well-developed brain
2. The bodily apparatus and abilities necessary for manipulating objects
3. A varied diet in the natural habitat
4. The relative freedom from danger of predation in the natural habitat

There are several selection pressures at work that could foster the evolution of curiosity in some species and not in others. One advantage of exploratory behavior is that it promotes incidental discovery of things in the environment that could prove useful in the future. New sources of food, potential hazards, or possible escape routes could all be discovered in this way. However, exploring also has potential costs. It could increase the danger of being caught by predators and consume time and energy that could be devoted to the satisfaction of basic physical needs. The ways in which these factors interact in the habitats of particular species serve to promote or hinder the evolution of curiosity. Laboratory studies have determined that the objects and events likely to evoke the most exploration are ones that are newer than those already explored but not so novel as to evoke fear (Valle, 1975, Chapter 11). The adaptive advantages of thoroughly exploring one's environment is at some point outweighed by the advantages of developing a healthy wariness of the unknown.

Research on curiosity also has looked at the time of life in which exploratory behavior is most prevalent. As indicated by Glickman (1973), in most species exploratory behavior peaks between childhood and early adulthood. This makes sense because this is the age range in which individuals usually are mature enough to avoid dangerous situations but are still within the optimal age range for learning. The parallels between animal studies of curiosity and human studies of children's play are many. Play in humans offers considerable opportunity for incidental learning that will be of use later in life (see Figure 7-8).

In addition to serving several biological functions, the need to explore the environment also is believed to serve psychological functions. Theorists such as Berlyne (1960) point out that novelty in the environment can contribute to maintaining an optimal level of arousal in an organism. Berlyne (1960) assumed that between the boring extreme of sensory deprivation and the fear-arousing extreme of too much novelty there is an optimal range that animals seek to achieve. Exploration is seen as one means of maintaining the optimal complexity of the environment (Valle, 1975, p. 202).

The needs we have been discussing — need for self-esteem, need for approval, and need to explore, understand, and manipulate the environment — all share a common characteristic. They represent a disposition to grow, improve, and become more competent — needs that become increasingly important in conjunction with enhanced language and cognitive abilities in mammals with complex brains. The ultimate need in Maslow's hierarchy represents the culmination of these tendencies, recognizing, as we are so often told, that "man does not live by bread alone." According to humanistic psychologists such as Maslow, human self-awareness and our capacity for contemplating meaning and choices in our lives make us in some important sense more than just highly developed animals. Let us, then, proceed to the top of Maslow's pyramid and examine his belief that we humans possess a tendency that sometimes overrides our lower needs — the need for *self-actualization,* or the drive to reach our full inherent potential.

SELF-ACTUALIZATION

How could you study a need as broad and intangible as the need for *self-actualization?* Maslow studied it in a rather circular fashion by starting with some rough assumptions about the attributes he believed should characterize the few people who were able to beat the odds and reach the pinnacle of his hierarchy. Then Maslow sought to identify people, both from the present and the past, who possessed most of these attributes. Included in his list were such people as Eleanor Roosevelt, Martin Luther King, Jr., Barbara McClintock, Albert Einstein, Mother Teresa, and Mahatma Ghandi. Finally, Maslow examined these people to see what attributes they did in fact possess and, on that basis, refined his list.

Over many repetitions of this procedure, Maslow sharpened both his criteria for self-actualization and the list of people he believed had fulfilled them. Maslow's self-actualizers were judged to possess an overriding motivation to pursue abstract qualities such as justice, beauty, order, understanding, and unity. They seemed oblivious to the lesser concerns that occupy so much of the lives of those motivated primarily by deprivation needs. Despite these other-worldly devotions, however, self-actualizers proved to be firmly planted in reality and quite accurate in their perceptions of it. They exhibited a philosophic acceptance of themselves, of others, and of the world at large. Nevertheless, this accepting attitude did not prevent them from leaving their mark.

Maslow characterized self-actualizers as spontaneous, open, and creative; as able to care about others while remaining detached and self-sufficient; as democratic and somewhat nonconforming. Although many self-actualizers achieve renown in the arts, sciences, professions, or in politics, not all seek or achieve fame. Many are content to seek the maximization of their potential in more private ways. Such individuals stand out because of their full lives and satisfied minds. According to humanistic psychologists, the thwarting of the natural motive to pursue self-actualization leads to the alienation, cynicism, and apathy characteristic of so many people in our society today.

Although many psychologists and lay people agree that we should strive to fulfill our potential, the theoretical positions of humanistic psychologists such as Maslow have met with harsh criticisms from more scientifically minded psychologists. For example, Weiner (1980) has argued that the central concepts of Maslow's theory are formulated so vaguely that firm predictions and experimentally testable hypotheses are impossible to derive. Given the fairly widespread resistance among humanistic psychologists to quanti-

Some of Maslow's self-actualizers

fication and empirical investigation (on the ground that it is dehumanizing — see Chapter 1), it is not surprising that they have not conducted much research on their theories. In issuing his indictment, Weiner (1980) nonetheless credits humanistic psychology with drawing attention to important areas of human motivation that could benefit from thorough empirical study. For example, Maslow assumed that the need for self-actualization is innate, but no systematic effort has been made to document this assumption or to rule out other possible origins of the need. Is it not at least possible that self-actualization needs are acquired in much the same way as, say, the need for achievement?

Such other critics as Michael Wertheimer (1978) have pointed out that it is quite possible to be in sympathy with the personal and social aims of humanistic psychology yet still feel that objective psychological research is more likely, in the long run, to arrive at the understanding that will allow us to achieve our potential more effectively. In defending the position that the traditional methods of psychological analysis and experimentation will provide a more useful understanding of these complex issues, Wertheimer concludes:

> Paradoxical as it may seem at first glance, a dispassionate scientific approach is, in the last analysis, also the most humanitarian one. We will be in the best position to help people if we know what works, what effects something has when we are trying to help troubled souls get along in this world. Tough-minded, humane science is apt to be more helpful in this endeavor than are magic, wishful thinking, nonempirical speculation, blind faith, or dogma. (1978, p. 475)

THE ORIGINS OF EMOTION

We have explored the topic of motivation — examining the range of forces that energize and direct our behavior. We now consider **emotion,** the range of feelings that accompany motivated behavior. Emotion has always been a controversial topic in psychology, and remains so today. How many emotions are there? Is each emotional experience different, or can all emotions be described in terms of a small number of underlying dimensions? Do emotional responses occur before or after we think about the experience that prompts them? Are the expressions of emotion universal or are they culturally determined? Let us consider the answers that psychologists have given to these questions and to others.

To appreciate what it means to have something, imagine being without it. Can you imagine what it would be like to have no emotions? William James tried this exercise almost 100 years ago.

> Conceive yourself, if possible, suddenly stripped of all the emotions with which your world now inspires you. . . . It will be almost impossible for you to realize such a condition of negativity and deadness. No one portion of the universe would then have importance beyond another; the whole collection of its things and series of its events would be without significance, character, expression, or perspective. Whatever of value, interest, or meaning our respective worlds may appear endowed with are thus pure gifts of the spectator's mind. The passion of love is the most familiar and extreme example of this fact. If it comes, it comes; if it does not come, no process of reasoning can force it. Yet it transforms the value of the creature loved as utterly as the sunrise transforms Mont Blanc from a corpse-like gray to a rosy enchantment; and it sets the whole world to a new tune for the lover and gives a new issue to his life. So with fear, with indignation, jealousy, ambition, worship. If they are there, life changes. (1890)

According to James, emotions endow events with richness, color, and meaning. But what is an emotion? One way of answering this question is to identify the markers of emotion, the aspects of experience that lead you to say "I'm afraid," "I'm in love," or "I'm angry." If you have ever walked alone at night in a strange neighborhood, you have probably experienced fear. One way of knowing that you were afraid in that situation is from feeling your heart beating faster, the hairs on the back of your neck rising, and your hands sweating. These are *physiological responses,* and they constitute one important aspect of emotion. A second basis for knowing that you are afraid is your thoughts. As you were walking along, such ordinary events as a car backfiring and a person crossing the street may have triggered thoughts that made you feel frightened. Thus an emotion also involves a *subjective response.* Finally, let us suppose that just as you were nearing your destination, a tall figure unexpectedly appeared from a dark doorway and moved quickly toward you. In a state of near panic, your eyes widened, your mouth opened, your muscles tensed, and you turned and ran. *Behavioral responses* such as these represent the third component of emotional experience. Let us examine how psychologists have attempted to measure emotions by tapping into the physiological, subjective, and behavioral dimensions of emotional experience.

THE MEASUREMENT OF EMOTION

It is difficult for psychologists to measure emotions of such compelling and intense character as fear, jealousy, rage, and the like. Methodological concerns lead them to conduct their research in the laboratory with volunteer subjects and ethical concerns prevent them from arousing extreme emotional states. Nevertheless, it is possible to measure subjects' responses to provocative stimuli that are assumed to be similar to, but generally paler than, the emotions that we experience in our daily interactions (see the following passage and Figure 7-9).

"No! Don't kill him yet!" screamed the delirious mob. "Killing's too good for the likes of him."

> The mobsters decided on a protracted torture for Stevens—a torture that lasted for some ten hours during Friday, June 20. Stevens was tied, suspended from his thumbs from the overhanging lamp post, his feet only inches from the ground, struggling to reach the earth. In a calculating manner Brady approached the trembling Stevens and, without undue ceremony, ripped off the boy's pants . . . an anxious titter arose from the crowd. From his boot Brady withdrew a long knife . . . Stevens gasped for breath . . . he whispered, "Let me die! Please, let me die!" "You wish!" retorted Brady. "The fun has just begun . . . " (Cantor, Bryant, & Zillman, 1974)

Although we have deleted some of the horrible details, nonetheless this passage demonstrates the

"Dinner was wonderful and I really enjoyed the movie, Arthur. You may touch one of my breasts."

FIGURE 7-9

Stimulus for Provoking Amusement Reprinted courtesy of *Penthouse* Magazine © 1980.

power of particular events to make us experience certain feelings. In the following sections, we describe emotional responses in their various forms and how they can be measured.

Physiological Responses

In the physiological measurement of emotion, attention is paid to activity in different parts of the nervous system. As noted in Chapter 3, we possess more than one nervous system. The central nervous system (CNS) includes the brain and spinal cord; the peripheral nervous system (PNS) connects the CNS to the rest of the body. The PNS is divided into two major components: the somatic nervous system (SNS), which controls skeletal muscles, and the autonomic nervous system (ANS), which controls internal bodily functions. Each plays a role in emotional experience.

Central Nervous System (CNS) Attempts to identify CNS structures that are associated with particular behaviors and to describe the way in which they function have produced some interesting results, but they also have left many questions unanswered. Most of the research on central nervous system processes has used nonhuman

animals as subjects for study. Researchers have stimulated sites in the brain electrically or injected minute amounts of chemical substances into them, then observed their effects on behavior. A dramatic demonstration of the power of electrical stimulation to initiate and terminate emotional responses was provided by Spanish neuroscientist Jose Delgado (1969). Using a bull as his subject, he implanted an electrode in what he believed to be the area of the hypothalamus responsible for terminating aggression. Delgado then joined the bull in a bullring, armed only with a button that would trigger an electrical pulse through the implanted electrode. The bull charged. Delgado stood his ground and pressed the button. The bull immediately pulled up and turned away. From this type of research, we know that the hypothalamus plays a significant role in aggression but we do not yet know precisely what that role is. For example, it is not known whether the bull that attacked Delgado experienced a change in its emotional state as a result of the electrical stimulation. It has even been suggested that Delgado implanted the electrode in an area of the bull's brain that controls motor function (Valenstein, 1973), in which case the bull stopped because of signals to its muscles rather than a reduction in aggression.

Other information about CNS processes in human emotion has come from observation of individuals with brain damage in particular areas and from research with severe epileptics. These studies indicate that the structures that seem central to motivational processes, the hypothalamus and the limbic system, also play a major role in emotion. It has been hypothesized that the hypothalamus is associated primarily with the expression of emotion (for example, laughing) and that the limbic system is associated with emotional experience (for example, feeling amused) (Buck, 1976).

Somatic Nervous System (SNS) Activity in the SNS determines facial and postural expressions. Of the two modes of expression, facial activity has received the most attention from emotion researchers (see Figure 7-10). One group of investigators (Schwartz et al, 1976) attached electrodes to several places on subjects' faces to record the electrical activity of four distinct facial muscles. The subjects were asked to imagine situations in which they were happy, sad, or angry,

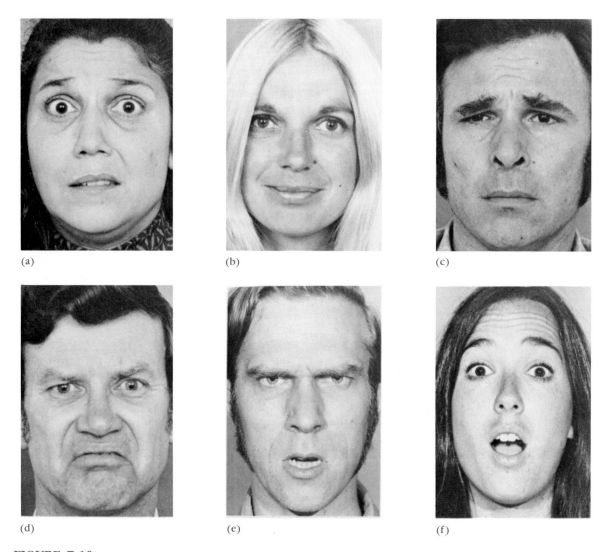

(a)   (b)   (c)

(d)   (e)   (f)

FIGURE 7-10

Facial Expression Accompanying Different Emotions When asked to effect (pose) common emotions, actors' facial expressions are recognized immediately as showing (a) fear, (b) happiness, (c) sadness, (d) disgust, (e) anger, and (f) surprise. *Source:* Ekman, P., & Friesen, W. V. (1976). *Pictures of facial affect.* Palo Alto, CA: Consulting Psychologists Press.

and to try to generate the appropriate emotion. They also were asked to imagine a typical day in their lives. The investigators found distinctive patterns of minute facial muscle movement for each of the three emotions. Furthermore, their research indicated that when subjects who had been diagnosed as depressed imagined a typical day, their profiles looked more like their sad or angry patterns than their happy patterns. The profiles of nondepressed subjects looked like their happy profiles. This study illustrates that different emotions are associated with distinctive patterns of facial muscle movement and that this movement can be identified by using psychophysiological techniques.

Autonomic Nervous System (ANS) The term *autonomic* means *self-governed.* The bodily functions controlled by the ANS are those that run largely on automatic pilot, such as the salivary glands, heart, lungs, and stomach. Each of these organs is supplied with nerves from both the *sym-*

PARASYMPATHETIC   SYMPATHETIC

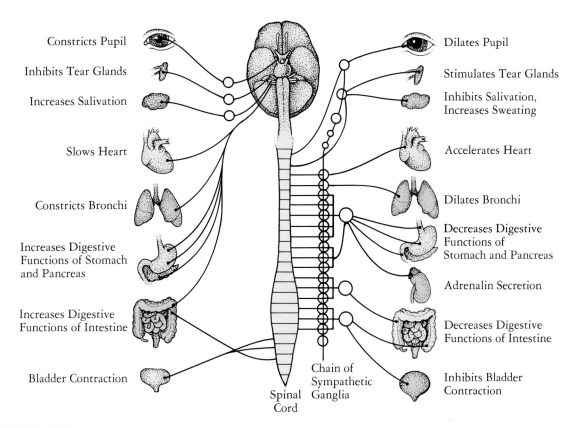

Constricts Pupil   Dilates Pupil

Inhibits Tear Glands   Stimulates Tear Glands

Increases Salivation   Inhibits Salivation,
                                                                  Increases Sweating

Slows Heart   Accelerates Heart

Constricts Bronchi   Dilates Bronchi

Increases Digestive   Decreases Digestive
Functions of Stomach   Functions of
and Pancreas   Stomach and Pancreas

                                                                  Adrenalin Secretion

Increases Digestive   Decreases Digestive
Functions of Intestine   Functions of Intestine

Bladder Contraction   Inhibits Bladder
                                                                  Contraction

Chain of
Sympathetic
Ganglia

Spinal
Cord

FIGURE 7-11

The Autonomic Nervous System (ANS) The ANS has two branches, *sympathetic* and *parasympathetic,* that exert opposing influences on the pupil of the eye, tear and salivary glands, heart, lungs, stomach, and other mechanisms of involuntary behavior associated with emotional experience. The emotional response of fear causes sympathetic activity leading, for example, to dilation of the pupil, sweating, accelerated heart rate, and decreased stomach activity. As the fear response diminishes, parasympathetic activity restores the normal balance between the two branches.

pathetic and *parasympathetic* branches of the ANS. The balance between the opposing influences of the two branches determines the state of the organ (see Figure 7-11). The ANS serves two functions that are particularly relevant to emotion: it helps to "maintain homeostasis, a constant internal environment within the body that supports life . . ." and it ". . . prepares the body for emergencies and stress by activating bodily defense mechanisms" (Buck, 1976, p. 23). Because potential emergencies often trigger emotions, the ANS is particularly active when emotions are elicited.

The "feelings" we associate with emotion tend to be associated with changes in the auto-

nomic nervous system. A pounding heart, butterflies in the stomach, sweaty hands, and flushing are all symptoms of ANS activity. Psychologists interested in the autonomic component of emotion generally measure two ANS functions. First, they assess circulatory or vasomotor responses by measuring heart rate, blood pressure, and dilation and constriction of blood vessels in specific parts of the body. Blushing reflects a vasomotor response in which the blood vessels of the face dilate. Second, they assess electrodermal responses by measuring the resistance of the skin to a weak electrical current. Sweat-gland activity results in a temporary increase in skin conductance of electrical current. By recording these indicators of ANS activity, psychologists can monitor the changing physiological state of a person experiencing an emotion.

Subjective Reports

The easiest way to determine if people have experienced an emotion is to ask them. You could, for example, simply ask people to describe their experience and then score their responses concerning particular feelings or emotions. Or you could employ a rating scale (like the one that follows) on which people are asked to indicate the degree to which they are experiencing a specified emotion.

1 —— 2 —— 3 —— 4 —— 5 —— 6 —— 7
not at all   extremely
disgusted   disgusted

Alternatively, subjects can be asked to indicate whether or not each of several emotionally relevant statements applies to them; this is the basis of commonly used tests of anxiety. Mood tests that use adjective checklists also have been developed (Howarth & Schokman-Gates, 1981) and techniques are available for analyzing the emotional content of verbal reports (Lyman, 1984).

There are two primary problems with measures of subjective experience that use self-report. This first is probably obvious; people may not say how they feel. Indeed, they may even intentionally mislead an interviewer, particularly if expression of the emotions in question is not culturally acceptable. For example, some men do not want anyone to know that they are afraid. Or, in view of social pressure on women to believe that they do not experience sexual desire, women may believe they experience less sexual desire than men even though their involuntary physiological reactions to sexual stimuli are every bit as strong (see Chapter 8).

Other problems with subjective reports are that people may not know whether they are experiencing an emotion and they may misidentify an emotion. Women exposed to sexual stimuli may in fact believe they are not aroused — and we have all encountered people apparently seething with anger who have insisted, perhaps violently, that they are not upset.

Behavioral Measures

Some psychologists are more interested in what people do than in what they say about their feelings and thoughts. These psychologists focus on the behavioral results of emotional experiences rather than on the subjective reports of emotions. For example, they might show people a film that contains scenes of violence in an effort to determine whether the viewers subsequently behave more aggressively. Or they might lead people to believe that they succeeded or failed at some task in an effort to determine whether the outcome affects their willingness to help someone in an emergency. In such cases as these, the investigators may infer that emotions of anger and elation mediated the effect of the stimulus on the response (see Krebs & Miller, 1985).

Other behavioral scientists focus exclusively on the relationship between observable events. For example, they might conclude that witnessing violent episodes increases the probability of exhibiting aggressive behavior or that experiencing success induces people to behave cooperatively. Psychologists such as these believe that invoking the rather fuzzy concept of emotional state adds little to our understanding of the behaviors being studied. This view was prevalent until the 1950s, when several individuals began the difficult process of developing precise and objective methods of quantifying the behavioral expression of emotion. We now turn to the work of one such individual, Paul Ekman, and that of his colleagues.

Ekman's Studies of Facial Expression The aspect of emotion focused on by Ekman is facial expression. He devoted his early work to the creation of a method for measuring facial expressions of emotion. In one of their earliest studies, Ekman and his colleagues divided the face into three sections: eyebrow–forehead, eyes–lids, and lower face. Then they wrote descriptions and compiled a set of criterion photographs of all the variations in each section of the face for each of the six emotions.

More recently, Ekman and his colleagues have developed increasingly sophisticated methods for measuring the changes that occur during the facial expression of emotions. One such method is called the **Facial Action Coding System (FACS)** (Ekman & Friesen, 1978). With impressive dedication, the authors first spent many months observing their own faces in a mirror as they posed various emotions. This enabled them to identify 44 facial muscles, called **action units (AUs),** that seemed capable of independent action. Added to these were 22 AUs corresponding to various eye and head positions. The resultant 66 distinct facial actions or postures constituted the elements of facial expression. With the bene-

fit of frame-by-frame analysis of videotaped faces, observers were trained to identify the particular AUs, singly and in combination, that occurred in the formation of different facial expressions. In this manner, Ekman and Friesen provided an objective means of coding a familiar manifestation of emotion that had previously seemed resistant to measurement.

THEORIES OF EMOTION

Given these means of measuring emotional experience, what sort of theories have been developed to explain emotion? Perhaps not surprisingly, there have been three important theoretical thrusts that correspond roughly to the three categories of measurement. We consider, in turn, theories that have emphasized the physiological, evolutionary, and cognitive components of emotion, and complete our coverage with a discussion of a theory that attempts to integrate these different views.

The Physiological Emphasis

The James–Lange Theory of Emotion One of the earliest theories of emotion was advanced by Harvard psychologist William James (1884). His theory contained two central assumptions. First, the essence of emotion lies in our recognition of a unique pattern of responses within ourselves. Second, the type of responses that are most important are visceral or "gut" responses. If you are faced with a dangerous situation, your heart may pound, your stomach may feel knotted, your muscles may feel tense, and you may take action to confront or evade the problem. According to James, it is the individual's perception of these events that constitutes the emotion. While most of us assume that we run away because we are afraid, James took the opposite position. He suggested that we are afraid because we run away. Put another way, our appreciation of the visceral and behavioral responses to a provocative stimulus instills in us the emotion of fear. At about the same time that Williams James published his ideas, another investigator, Danish physiologist

Carl Lange, proposed a similar theory. Thus, the view proposed by James is often called the James–Lange theory of emotion.

The Cannon–Bard Theory of Emotion Walter Cannon, a Harvard physiologist, was not convinced by the James–Lange theory. He doubted that a set of similar bodily reactions could be responsible for such a variety of distinct emotional experiences. Further, he argued, the bodily changes that occur in emotion develop too slowly to play a causal role. Finally, Cannon noted that these same bodily changes occur in other situations — such as strenuous exercise or through injection of certain drugs — where they typically do not result in the experience of emotion. Contrariwise, individuals who are not in touch with their bodies because of paralysis can still experience emotions.

Cannon's theory (1927), further developed by Bard (1934), was that emotions are a direct reflection of activity in certain brain centers. Specifically, Cannon and Bard proposed that an emotional stimulus results in activity in the thalamus (although more recent research has indicated that the hypothalamus and limbic system are the brain centers principally responsible for emotion). This activity in key brain structures causes two simultaneous messages to be sent, one to the autonomic nervous system and one to the cerebral cortex. The message to the autonomic nervous system triggers the visceral actions and bodily sensations that we experience during an emotionally toned interaction. That same autonomic activity is the basis for the controversial lie detector test (see Box 7-2). The second message, relayed to the cortex, elicits the subjective

BOX 7-2
THE LIE DETECTOR TEST

The *lie detector test* is based on the premise that telling a lie is an emotional action. The test involves the measurement of several indices of activity in the autonomic nervous system, the system that is activated by emotionally arousing stimuli. Heart rate, respiration rate, and the electrical activity that underlies sweating (electrodermal response or EDR) are the measures normally recorded. Electrodes attached to the subject pick up the autonomic activity and translate it into pen tracings on a *polygraph* (see figure). In its simplest application, the test is given to a subject who is suspected of having committed an offense. After being "hooked up" to the polygraph, the subject is asked a series of questions. Control questions are used to establish the strength of the subject's response to a little lie. "Up to age 18, did you ever deceive anyone?" is such a question. When subjects respond "No" to this, as they typically do, they must surely be telling a little lie. The strength of response to

questions relevant to the offense ("Did you do it?") is measured against the baseline of responses to control

questions. If the answer is truthful, the subject's response on the polygraph is expected to resemble closely the baseline responses. If the subject lies, however, the emotional arousal that accompanies the lie should be evident in increased autonomic activity that shows up as a larger response on the polygraph. (See polygraph tracings in figure.)

That is how the lie detector test is supposed to

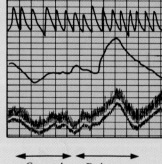

| Control Question | Relevant Question | Control Question | Relevant Question |

Polygraph Tracing in Lie Detector Test The chart on the left shows the responses of an innocent witness who provided an accused murderer with an alibi. A moderately sized response was given to the control question that elicited a white lie. The response to a question relevant to the alibi was much smaller, leading the examiner to judge the witness' response as truthful. The chart on the right shows the responses of an accused murderer who pleaded self-defense. He was judged to be lying to the relevant question because his response to it was larger than that to the control question. *Source: Science* (1982, June). pp. 24–27.

feelings associated with the emotion. The contrast between the role of bodily feelings in the James – Lange and Cannon – Bard theories of emotion is shown in Figure 7-12, page 330.

While the Cannon – Bard theory of emotion has some strong supporting arguments, there is evidence that feedback from autonomic activity does play a role in determining emotional experi-

work; but how well does it work in practice? The answer is that it does not work very well at all. You can probably think of a number of reasons to be suspicious of the polygraph test. Perhaps some individuals, such as "cold-blooded" criminals, are not upset by the act of lying. If it does not disturb them emotionally, then they may escape detection by the polygraph. Conversely, most innocent people would be quite upset if they were suspected of a crime and their concerns would probably be magnified by the experience of undergoing the test. Many innocent persons would surely find the answering of the critical question to be a disturbing experience, even though they were telling the truth ("Did I sound convincing?" "I wonder what the polygraph showed").

Proponents of the lie detector test argue that there are very few individuals who can beat the test by disguising their true emotions. Furthermore, they point out that several safeguards are built into the test that make it unlikely an innocent person would appear guilty. Indeed, the accuracy claimed by such organizations as the American Polygraph Association is generally about 90%. Skeptics such as Lykken (1981) believe that the success rate is actually much lower. The relevant evidence must come from a study to determine whether the lie detector test can correctly categorize persons *known* to be innocent or guilty. Precisely that experiment was performed by Kleinmuntz and Szucko (1984). They obtained the judgments of expert polygraph operators who had tested hundreds of suspects. The authors then separated the cases of 50 individuals who later confessed to their guilt from 50 individuals who were subsequently proven innocent by the confessions of others. Almost one-quarter of the guilty individuals were judged to be innocent on the basis of the lie detector test. More disturbingly, over one-third of the innocent persons were judged guilty by the polygraph operators.

It is obviously a serious problem when such an an unreliable test is used to establish the guilt or innocence of individuals suspected of crimes. Fortunately this flaw is recognized, and most judicial systems refuse to accept polygraph evidence in criminal cases (Meyer, 1982). In nonlegal settings, however, the magnitude of the problem is even more serious and growing. One estimate puts the annual number of lie detector tests administered in the U.S. at "a million or more" (Myers, 1986, p. 372). A large proportion of these tests are given to the employees of businesses and corporations as a routine screening measure. The use of these tests was promoted by President Ronald Reagan who, in 1983, established a requirement that government employees take a polygraph examination during investigations of leaks of classified information (Associated Press, 1983). Notwithstanding the concerns of psychologists (Katkin, 1985) and legislators (Brooks, 1985), polygraph use may become even more widespread if a later presidential suggestion to give routine tests to *all* government employees is heeded.

ence. Hohmann (1966) tested the emotional responsiveness of war veterans paralyzed from the waist down due to spinal injury. The veterans were asked to compare their pre-injury and post-injury memories of events that aroused fear, anger, grief, or sexual excitement. As Figure 7-13 shows, the higher up the spinal cord the location of injury—and thus the less bodily

James-Lange theory   Cannon-Bard theory

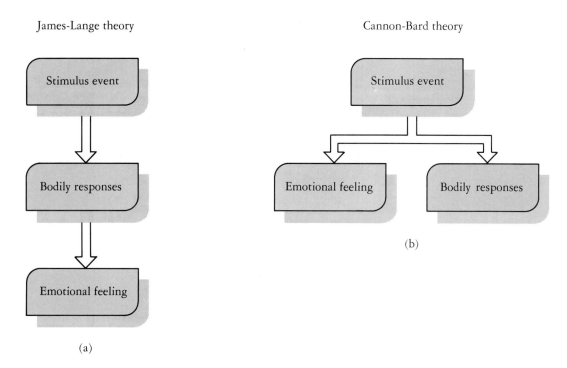

(a)

FIGURE 7-12

James – Lange and Cannon – Bard Theories of Emotion   A contrast of the sequence of events hypothesized in the James – Lange and Cannon – Bard theories of emotion.   *Source:* Adapted from Myers, D. G. (1986). *Psychology.* New York: Worth.

feeling experienced — the greater the loss in emotionality. Although similar results for sexual arousal were obtained by Jasnos and Hakmiller (1975), Reisenzein (1983) notes how vulnerable this type of study is to experimenter bias and social desirability effects. It is also possible that victims of spinal cord injury tend to suppress their feelings as a way of coping with their depressing circumstance (Trieschmann, 1980).

The enormous advances in brain research since the Cannon – Bard era have shed considerable light on the brain mechanisms that underlie emotional experience (Gray, 1982; Panksepp, 1981, 1982). For example, we know that parts of the limbic system, particularly the hypothalamus, play an important role in anger and aggression. Electrical stimulation of a cat's hypothalamus turns it into a raging beast; destruction of the same area renders the animal abnormally placid (Valenstein, 1973). Other components of the limbic system also have been implicated in aggressive behavior, sometimes by tragic demonstration. In 1966, after killing his wife and

mother, Charles Whitman killed 15 people and wounded 24 others on the campus of the University of Texas before dying in a hail of police bullets. Whitman was well aware of his aggressive tendencies. In a letter written just before the killings, he revealed some of the personal agony that he was experiencing.

> I don't quite understand what it is that compels me to type this letter . . . . I am supposed to be an average, reasonable and intelligent young man . . . . However, lately I have been a victim of many unusual and irrational thoughts . . . . I talked with a doctor once for about two hours and tried to convey to him my fears that I felt overcome (sick) by overwhelming violent impulses. After one session I never saw the doctor again and since then I have been fighting my mental turmoil alone, and seemingly to no avail. After my death I wish that an autopsy would be performed on me to see if there is any visible physical disorder. (Quoted in Johnson, 1972, p. 79.)

An autopsy was performed, and it revealed a walnut-sized tumor in Whitman's brain (Franken,

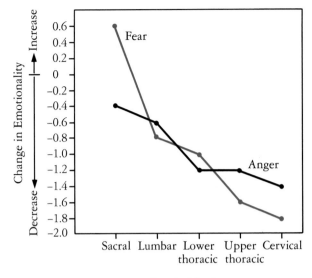

FIGURE 7-13
Emotionality after Lower-body Paralysis
People with spinal-cord lesions were asked to report whether the intensity of emotion they experienced had increased, decreased, or remained unchanged since their injury. Most reported a decreased intensity of emotion for both fear and anger, the extent of decrease being greater the higher the locus of the lesion.
Source: Adapted from Hohmann, G. W. (1962). Some effects of spinal-cord lesions on experienced emotional feelings. *Psychophysiology, 3,* 143–56.

1982). Although bullet wounds made it difficult to establish the precise location of the tumor, it was apparently in or close to the amygdala (Sweet et al., 1969).

The Evolutionary Emphasis

Darwin's Study of Emotion The first comprehensive theory of emotion — presented by Charles Darwin (1872) in a book titled *The Expression of the Emotions in Man and Animals* — focused on behavioral expressions of emotion, especially in the face. Darwin held that emotional expressions originally were associated with adaptive responses and that they evolved because of the survival value of those adaptations. Consider, for example, the startle reflex that occurs in response to an unexpected event. Because it prepares the body for action, it serves an important adaptive function. If the unexpected event represents a threat, the startled animal is

better prepared for fight or flight than the animal that is not aroused. Thus, the members of a species that have the best developed startle reflexes would be most likely to survive, to reproduce, and to transmit the response to subsequent generations.

Darwin felt that adaptive behaviors such as the startle reflex came to be associated with particular states of mind. When these states of mind were experienced, they would elicit both a corresponding expressive behavior and what he called a *neural discharge.* Together, these experiences comprised the emotion — *fear,* in the case of the startle reflex. Regarding two other examples, Darwin believed that the origin of the emotion *disgust* was found in the adaptive behaviors associated with rejecting food from the mouth. (If you imagine someone "spitting in disgust," the analogy becomes clear.) And, according to Darwin, *sneering* originated in the baring of fangs.

You might argue that such emotions as disgust, as we know them, seem far removed from their original purpose as Darwin described it. Darwin hypothesized that the expression of such emotions as disgust are adaptive for a purpose other than the one they originally evolved to serve, namely as a means of communication. The ability to communicate feelings and to interpret the expressive behaviors of others increased the probability of survival. In support of Darwin's theory of emotion, some contemporary ethologists and psychologists have noted that nonhuman animals display facial expressions and gestures that are similar to those of humans (Eibl–Eibesfeldt, 1975). In the words of Hebb: "The dog is definitely capable of jealousy and occasionally, in some dogs, there are signs of sulking. In the chimpanzee, however, we have the full picture of human anger in its three main forms: anger, sulking, and the temper tantrum" (cited in Plutchik, 1980, p. 71). However, human emotional expression is considerably more varied than emotional expression in other primates.

An interesting inducement to emotion that is shared by humans and other primates is eye contact. We have all experienced emotional feelings when someone "looks us in the eye." Box 7-3 discusses some similarities between the role of eye contact in the emotional behavior of humans and in a variety of other animals.

BOX 7-3
THE POWER OF A STARE

In the animal kingdom, a face-to-face, "look-them-in-the-eye" approach to another animal is often a threatening gesture. In fact, some moths and fish have large, eye-like designs on wings and bodies that have been found to help intimidate predators (see figure) Are stares also threatening to humans? There is evidence that they are.

The next time you meet a small child who is going through a stage of being afraid of strangers, look directly at the child in your friendliest manner and see what happens. Then try not to look right at the child. You will probably find that the child will back off and seem timid when you stare at him or her, but will approach you and want to play with you when you do not. Ellsworth, Carlsmith, and Henson (1972) demonstrated that staring at drivers stopped at intersections caused them to drive off more rapidly when the light changed. Fisher and Byrne (1975) found that male college students were more uncomfortable and felt greater dislike for a stranger who sat down directly across from them at a library table (where they could look her or him in the eye) than for one who sat down beside them. The "evil eye" is an object of fear in many societies.

We could conclude that stares are only threatening were it not for another interesting fact. Among primates, including humans —but no other species— looking directly in the eye can also signal and elicit affectionate and sexual responses. Rubin (1970) reported that couples who said they were strongly in love gazed longer and more frequently into one another's eyes than couples who were weakly in love or were strangers.

No one knows why the eyes are such powerful agents of emotion, but studies of primates have established clearly that eye contact elicits powerful reactions.

Animal "Stares"   This animal has "eyespot" markings that intimidate predators.

Cross-cultural Similarities in Facial Expression of Emotion   Ekman and his co-workers have attempted to evaluate the idea that emotional expressions are innate by assessing facial expressions of emotion in people from other cultures. They selected 30 photographs that their research had shown were particularly representative of the six emotions (happiness, sadness, disgust, anger, fear, and surprise) and showed them to people in the U.S., Brazil, Argentina, Chile, and Japan (Ekman, 1973). These investigators found that participants from all five nations were able reliably to identify each emotion, as indicated in Figure 7-14. Finding that people from different

	United States	Brazil	Chile	Argentina	Japan
Percentage Agreement in How Photograph Was Judged Across Cultures					

	United States	Brazil	Chile	Argentina	Japan
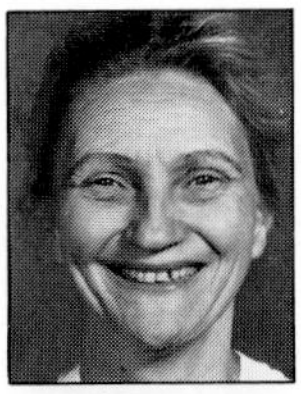	97% Happiness	95% Happiness	95% Happiness	98% Happiness	100% Happiness
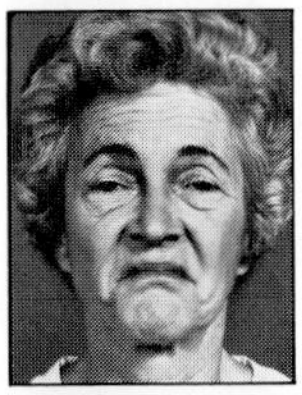	92% Disgust	97% Disgust	92% Disgust	92% Disgust	90% Disgust
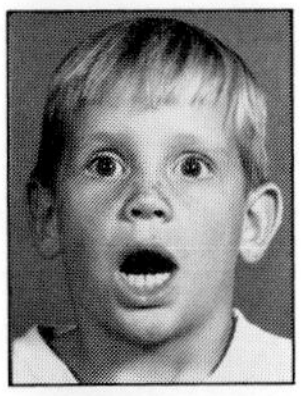	95% Surprise	87% Surprise	93% Surprise	95% Surprise	100% Surprise
	84% Sadness	59% Sadness	88% Sadness	78% Sadness	62% Sadness
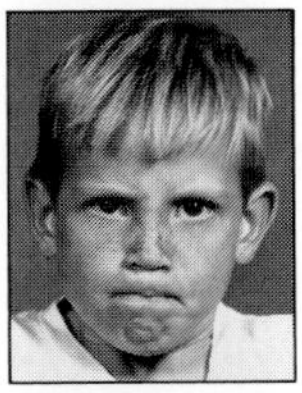	67% Anger	90% Anger	94% Anger	90% Anger	90% Anger
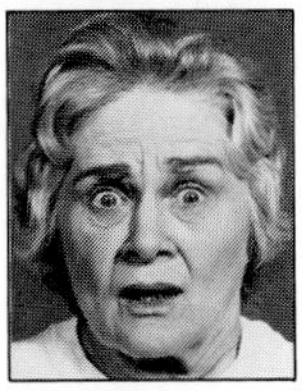	85% Fear	67% Fear	68% Fear	54% Fear	66% Fear

FIGURE 7-14

Cross-cultural Identification of Facial Expression Six photographs of faces of individuals experiencing different emotions were shown to subjects in five different countries. The values listed indicate the percent of agreement among subjects in each country as to the identity of the emotion. *Source:* From Ekman, P. (1973). *Darwin and facial expression.* New York: Academic Press.

cultures identified the same emotions is consistent with the idea that these emotions are innate. However, the possibility that facial expressions are learned is not ruled out by this study.

With so much international communication, it is possible that expressions are transmitted across cultures. To examine this possibility, the investigators looked for cultural groups that had little contact with the modern world, and selected two isolated tribes in New Guinea (Ekman & Friesen, 1971). When members of these tribes were shown two or three faces and asked to select the one that best depicted the emotion described in a brief story (for example, "His friends have come and he is happy."), they were able to identify happiness, sadness, disgust, and surprise easily, although sometimes anger was mistaken for disgust and fear for surprise.

Ekman and Friesen also asked members of the two New Guinea tribes to portray the emotions described in the stories. They videotaped their portrayals and showed them to American students. The students were able to identify happiness, sadness, anger, and disgust but, like the New Guineans, were unable to reliably distinguish between fear and surprise.

Ekman's findings suggest that there are several emotions, with associated facial expressions, that can be regarded as universal. His findings also suggest that these emotional expressions are innate. Evidence from other studies supports this conclusion. If facial expressions of emotion are innate, they should be displayed very early in life, before infants have much opportunity to learn them. Certainly, newborns smile, cry, show a startle response, and appear to show disgust (Steiner, 1977), and infants receiving inoculations show facial expressions that are recognized easily as pained (Izard et al, 1983). It has been reported also that infants only a few minutes old can imitate an adult's emotionally expressive gestures (Meltzoff & Moore, 1983). These results support the idea that young children express basic emotions naturally, without learning them.

Research demonstrating that facial expressions of emotion in blind and deaf children are similar to those of normal children has provided additional evidence that basic emotional expressions are unlearned (Eibl-Eibesfeldt, 1973). In an older study (Thompson, 1941), judges were able to identify spontaneous expressions of joy, sadness, and anger in photographs of blind children even though the children could not have copied them (the expressions did, however, occur less uniformly than among sighted children). In another study, blind and sighted children were asked to pose the expressions of anger, fear, sadness, and happiness (Fulcher, 1942). Although the expressions of blind children were less distinct than those of sighted children, their facial movements followed the same patterns. The expressive patterns of blind and sighted children also did not vary with age (4 to 16 years), supplying additional evidence that they were there from the start, and were thus inborn.

The results of the studies with blind children support the idea that the patterns of expression of basic emotions are innate; however, they also suggest that the expression of these emotions can be affected by learning. Experiments on animals add additional support. One group of researchers trained a group of normal rhesus monkeys and a group of rhesus monkeys that had been raised in isolation to press a bar after a light came on in order to avoid electric shock (Miller, Caul, & Mirsky, 1967). Then pairs of monkeys were placed in separate rooms. One member of the pair, the sender, could see the light that signalled shock, while the other, the observer, could see only the (televised) face of the sender. The observer (and not the sender) had access to the bar. The observer had to be able to "read" the sender's facial expression correctly in order to know when to press the bar to avoid shock to both of them. When normal monkeys were paired, the observer learned to read the face of the sender, and thus to avoid shock very efficiently, suggesting that the sender expressed fear accurately and that the observer was able to perceive it. However, when isolated monkeys were observers, they were unable to read the expressions of normal monkey senders and avoid the shock. When the isolates were senders, they communicated fear at both appropriate and inappropriate times, causing their normal observer partners to press the bar many more times than necessary.

These findings suggest that normal, early social experience is a prerequisite for both the ability to send and the ability to read the emotional expressions of others. It is possible that deficiencies in the ability to send emotions may reflect deficiencies in the ability to experience them and that deficiencies in the ability to read them may relate to deficiencies in the ability to empathize. It is interesting to note in this respect that shallow emotional experiences (especially as related to fear) and lack of empathy are two of the defining characteristics of psychopaths (see Chapter 13).

Cross-cultural Differences in Facial Expression of Emotion Although there clearly are fundamental cross-cultural similarities in the facial expression of emotion, it is also well known that the same gesture or action can signify quite different emotions in different cultures. For example, in our culture sticking out the tongue is an insulting gesture of defiance or contempt, used mainly by children. But LaBarre notes that in other cultures it may signify anger, shock, or embarrassment. In our culture, hissing expresses contempt, but according to LaBarre, "Hissing in Japan is a polite deference to social superiors, and the Basuto [Lesotho natives] applaud by hissing" (1947, p. 56).

Societies differ in the extent to which they encourage and discourage the expression of various emotions. This became evident in a study by Ekman (1972) of the facial expressions of American and Japanese adults as they watched an extremely bloody film on eye surgery. For the first part of the film, the subject was alone; for the remainder, an interviewer joined the subject. A hidden camera revealed that the facial expressions of disgust shown by American and Japanese subjects were no different when they were alone. When they had company, however, the Japanese (but not the Americans) tended to mask their negative emotions, often adopting a polite smile.

Societies also differ in the way they interpret the absence of emotional display. For example, anthropologist E. T. Hall (1966) points to misunderstandings caused by the American custom of controlling anger and employing the "silent

Box 7-4
Interpreting Smiles

One way in which culture influences behavior is through its differential influence on the two sexes. A consequence of sex-role stereotyping for emotional expression is illustrated in a study by Bugental, Love, and Gianetto (1971). In an earlier study, they had found that five- to eight-year-old children regarded women's smiles as relatively neutral in emotional content when compared with men's smiles. They commented that: "The traditional female role demands warm, compli-ant behavior in public situations; the smiling facial expression may provide the mask to convey this impression" (p. 318). If this were so, they continued, "there may be little or no relationship between smiling and the evaluative content of verbal messages in females, but not in males." To test this idea, the authors in the later study had judges view fathers' and mothers' smiles on silent videotapes of families interacting in a clinic waiting room. They transcribed the conversations that were recorded when the videotapes were made and had different judges rate the statements made by the parents as positive, negative, or neutral. They found that fathers' smiles were associated with positive verbal communications, but that mothers' smiles occurred in conjunction with neutral or slightly negative verbal content. Apparently the young children in their previous research had been correct in their interpretation of women's smiles.

treatment.'' He notes that in some cultures (for example, English and Arab), individuals typically do not have private rooms where they can go to be alone, even at home. Therefore, when they need to be alone, they simple tune out their surroundings and people who are present. Hall describes an incident involving an English student's difficulty with an American roommate. Whenever the English student wanted to be alone with his thoughts, his roommate would get worried, try to engage him in conversation, and eventually ask whether he was angry. Hall noted that ''for an American to refuse to talk to someone else present in the same room, to give them the 'silent treatment,' is the ultimate form of rejection and a sure sign of great displeasure'' (p. 140). In other words, the expression of a need to be alone was interpreted as suppressed anger. Quite the opposite was the case in another situation: '' . . . an Arab exchange student visiting a Kansas farm failed to pick up the cue that his American hosts were mad at him when they gave him the 'silent treatment.' He discovered something was wrong only when they took him to town and tried forcibly to put him on a bus to Washington, D.C.'' (Hall, 1966, p. 159). A surprising example of cultural influence on emotional expression is provided in Box 7-4, page 335.

Universal Consistencies versus Cultural Differences There is really no contradiction between the culture-specific and universal points of view if we conclude that a set of universal, innate, basic patterns of emotional expression exist upon which different cultures superimpose idiosyncratic patterns and rules (Scheff, 1983). In summary, you don't wiggle your nose to express happiness, but you could learn to if it were normal in the culture in which you were raised. However, it is doubtful that you could learn to express joy by adopting the facial expression universally associated with anger.

There do seem to be certain basic emotions that are expressed spontaneously and naturally — without any learning — but which emotions belong in that category has been the subject of much debate. There are plenty to choose from, since over 400 English words exist that describe emotions (Davitz, 1969). Descartes, the early 17th century philosopher, believed there to be six primary ''passions'': love, hatred, desire, joy, sadness, and admiration. All other emotions were mixtures of these. Spinoza assumed only three emotions were primary: joy, sorrow, and desire. Hobbes later increased the number to seven, a number with which Darwin seemed to agree. Common to these theorists was the absence of a rational basis for defining primacy of emotions. That lack was addressed by the next theorist we consider.

Plutchik's Theory of Emotion Plutchik (1980, 1983) has proposed a *psychoevolutionary* theory of emotion in which he suggests that there are eight essential adaptive functions, each associated with a basic emotion. Table 7-3 shows

TABLE 7-3
Plutchik's Taxonomy of Emotions

Adaptive Process	Associated Behavior	Emotion
Protection	avoiding danger or harm	fear
Destruction	eliminating a barrier to satisfying an important need	anger
Incorporation	accepting a beneficial stimulus from the outside world	acceptance
Rejection	expelling something harmful that has been ingested	disgust
Reproduction	providing contact with sex in order to perpetuate one's gene pool	joy
Reintegration	facing the loss of someone who has provided important nurturance	sadness
Orientation	reacting to contact with a new, unfamiliar stimulus	surprise
Exploration	providing the organism with contact with many aspects of its environment	anticipation

Source: Adapted from Plutchik, R. (1980). *Emotion: A psycho-evolutionary synthesis.* New York: Harper & Row.

the adaptive functions, the behaviors that serve those functions, and the labels commonly given to the subjective experiences that accompany the behaviors. Thus the adaptive process of *protection* involves *avoiding danger or harm* and is accompanied by the feeling of *fear; orientation* is a *reaction to an unfamiliar stimulus* and is accompanied by *surprise.*

What about all of the other emotions? Plutchik suggests that the eight primary emotions, like primary colors, can be combined in any number of ways to produce a wide variety of "blends." They may also vary in *intensity* (anxiety versus panic), *similarity* (shame and guilt versus sadness and joy), and *polarity* (love versus hate). It is difficult to capture all these features in a model, but Plutchik has attempted this with his *emotion solid* (see Figure 7-15). The top face of the solid contains the eight primary emotions; the outside face contains facets of corre-

sponding but less intense emotions. Again borrowing from color models, Plutchik also offers an *emotion wheel* that emphasizes the polarity of emotions (see Figure 7-16). It, too, shows how emotional blends (the labeled spokes) are derived from adjacent primaries.

What evidence is there that humans experience the primary emotions that Plutchik believes stem from the eight essential adaptive functions; what evidence is there for the existence of emotional blends as he describes them? We have seen already that Ekman and his colleagues found evidence of facial expression for six of the emotions in Plutchik's list, and that such expressions appear to be universal. In addition, Plutchik and his colleagues asked subjects to rate the similarities among more than 140 words that describe emotions and found that the ratings corresponded with the *emotion wheel* in Figure 7-16. Finally, Plutchik asked people to indicate what emotion

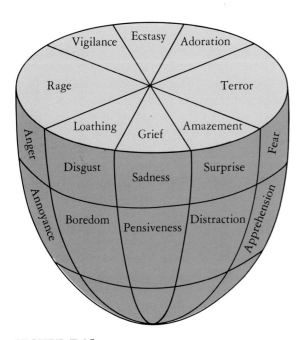

FIGURE 7-15
Plutchik's Emotion Solid The solid figure shows eight emotions that Plutchik believes are primary. The most intense forms of these emotions (for example, rage, grief, terror) are shown on the top surface. Milder forms (for example, anger, sadness, fear) are revealed in successive cross-sectional slices of the solid. *Source:* Plutchik, R. (1980). *Emotion: A psychoevolutionary synthesis.* New York: Harper & Row.

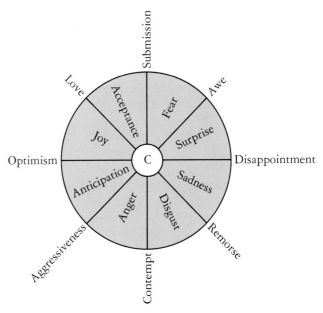

FIGURE 7-16
Plutchik's Emotion Wheel Plutchik asked people to rate the similarity of emotions. Those rated as similar were placed in the same quadrant of the emotion wheel; those rated as dissimilar were located in opposite quadrants. Emotions rated as neither similar nor dissimilar were placed in adjacent quadrants. Plutchik found that the emotion terms were distributed around the entire circle with no appreciable gaps. *Source:* Plutchik, R. (1980). *Emotion: A psychoevolutionary synthesis.* New York: Harper & Row.

would result by combining specific primary emotions. He found that the people chose the same emotions that had been derived through different means. For example, if you asked people to imagine what emotion they would experience if they felt both joy and acceptance, Plutchik's theory says they would answer "love"; if you asked them how they would feel if they experienced both anticipation and anger, they should say "aggressive." Similarly, people should be able to break down emotional blends into the primary emotions if asked to say what basic emotions contribute to such feelings as love and aggressiveness.

There are four components, in Plutchik's theory, to an emotional reaction: stimulus, thought process or cognition, feeling, and behavior. The way this "chain reaction" works for *fear* is outlined in Figure 7-17. The top row shows the order of events for a particular function, leading from stimulus to behavior. The second row gives an example of this sequence for the function of *protection*.

Plutchik places greater emphasis than Darwin does on the significance of thought in emotional reactions. He takes the position that " . . . cognitive capacities have evolved with the development of the brain — and largely in the service of the emotions" (Plutchik, 1980, p. 74). As noted in our discussion on communication (Chapter 2), nonhuman animals tend to react impulsively and stereotypically to stimuli; humans interpret, process, and analyze information. Thus, to a great extent the emotional reactions of humans are based on their interpretations of situations rather than on the physical stimuli themselves. This emphasis on cognitive appraisal is characteristic of the theories of emotion to which we now turn.

The Cognitive Emphasis

Schachter's Theory of Emotion One of the most influential cognitive theories of emotion proposed since that of William James is that of Stanley Schachter (Schachter & Singer, 1962; Schachter, 1971). In Schachter's theory, emotions consist of two components — *physiological arousal* in the autonomic nervous system and *cognitive appraisal* of the arousing situation. The degree of arousal determines the intensity of the emotion; which particular emotion is experienced is determined by cognitive appraisal. Both components are required for emotion to be experienced. If either is absent, so is emotion. If you experience autonomic arousal without the cognitive appraisal that usually accompanies such an experience (after taking some medication, for example), you might say "This stuff sure speeds up my system" or "I feel as if I were excited," but you probably would not say "I am excited." On the other hand, if your cognitive appraisal reveals a situation that normally provokes an emotion but you do not experience arousal (when you are "too tired to care," for example), you should not experience an emotion.

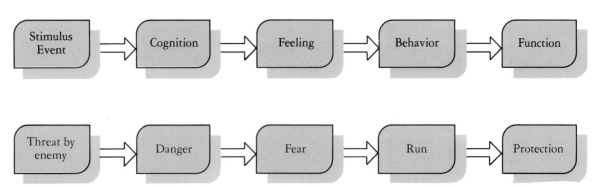

FIGURE 7-17
Plutchik's Chain Reaction of Emotion Plutchik suggests the sequence of events that define an emotional experience is a chain reaction. As shown in the upper sequence, the precipitating stimulus event is recognized, leading to feelings that trigger behavior that has evolved to serve some basic adaptive function. *Source:* Adapted from Plutchik, R. (1980, February). A language for the emotions. *Psychology Today,* pp. 68–78.

In postulating a large number of possible emotions and in viewing emotions as resulting from subjective reactions to physiological and behavioral signs of arousal, Schachter agrees with William James. However, he disagrees with James about the basis on which different emotions are distinguished. Whereas James believed that people base their perceptions of different emotions on the recognition of different patterns of visceral responses, Schachter assumes that the physiological changes that underlie all emotions are essentially the same and that it is the meaning that people attribute to their arousal that generates different emotional experiences. A number of experiments have supported the basic assumptions of Schachter's theory, but some also have called it into question.

In their defining experiment, Schachter and Singer (1962) recruited subjects for a study "to test the effects of a vitamin compound on visual acuity." In reality the subjects were injected with **epinephrine,** a drug that induces the type of autonomic arousal characteristic of emotional experience. One group of subjects was informed accurately about the symptoms they would experience as a result of the injection ("Your hands will start to shake, your heart will start to pound, and your face may get warm and flushed."); a second group of subjects was not informed about any possible symptoms. A third group of subjects, in the placebo-control condition, was injected with a saline solution that would not produce symptoms of arousal; they too were told nothing about any symptoms. After the subjects received their respective injections, they were taken to another room to wait for the substance to take effect. There they were introduced to another subject — really a confederate of the experimenter — who behaved playfully in the presence of half the subjects of each group and behaved angrily in the presence of the other half of the subjects of each group.

Schachter and Singer predicted that subjects in the *accurately informed group* (who had received an injection of epinephrine and were informed accurately about its symptoms) would attribute the arousal they experienced to the drug rather than to the emotion-provoking situation, neither feeling emotional nor behaving emotionally. In contrast, they expected subjects in the *not-informed group* to feel aroused and to interpret their arousal in terms of the situations they were placed in: they expected the subjects who observed the playful confederate to feel happy and to act playfully and they expected the subjects who observed the angry confederate to feel angry and to behave accordingly. Subjects in the control condition who received injections of a placebo were expected to be relatively unaroused and therefore unemotional.

The results of the study generally confirmed these predictions. Figure 7-18 shows Schachter and Singer's experimental groups and summarizes the effect of their manipulations on the subjects' emotional state. When subjects rated their moods following their experience in the waiting room, those who had not been informed of the effects of epinephrine and who observed the playful confederate reported that they felt happier than the informed subjects who observed the playful confederate. Similarly, the uninformed subjects who observed the angry confederate felt angrier than the informed subjects. The subjects in the control condition consistently reported emotional experiences that fell between those reported by the other two groups. These results lent support to Schachter's theory that emotion occurs when a state of general arousal is associated with an "emotional" cognitive appraisal of the source of the arousal.

Although it was not made explicit in the original formulation of Schachter's theory of emotion, he is arguing that there are really *two* cognitive components that must be present for emotion to occur (Reisenzein, 1983). First, there must be a cognitive appraisal that interprets the situation in an emotional way. Second, the cognitive appraisal must "connect up" (Gordon, 1978) with the arousal. That is, the person must attribute arousal to the emotional source. This dependence of emotion on correct attribution has been the focus of several applications of Schachter's theory.

Applications of Schachter's Theory Schachter's theory has generated considerable research. One writer has suggested that it helps explain passionate love that, she suggests, occurs when we experience intense arousal (from any source) in the presence of a specific other person and

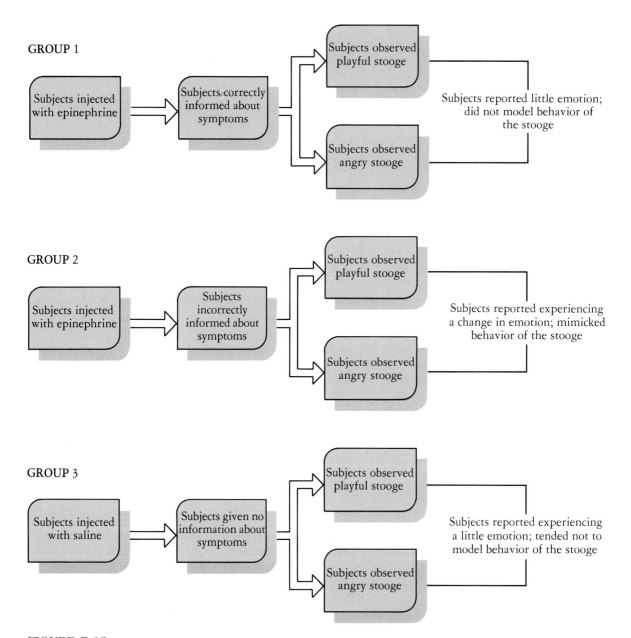

FIGURE 7-18

Design and Results of Schachter and Singer's Study See text for a description of the conditions and findings of this test of Schachter's theory of emotion.

label our feelings love (Walster, 1971). Other investigators have employed Schachter's theory as the basis of a new form of therapy, called **misattribution therapy,** for people with strong, irrational fears (Ross, Rodin, & Zimbardo, 1969). Consider a person with an intense fear of spiders, for example. A misattribution therapist might give the person a placebo, tell him the pill would cause symptoms of intense arousal, and then expose him to a spider. The person would, of course, become aroused, but he would attribute his arousal to the drug rather than to the insect. In other words, he would misattribute his arousal and therefore not label it as fear. After a program of exposure to spiders under these conditions, he would find spiders less frightening.

One test of misattribution therapy was carried out by two researchers (Storms & Nisbett, 1970) who noted that people suffering from insomnia often report experiencing symptoms such as mind racing, fast heart rate, and elevated body temperature. They hypothesized that if insomniacs thought that the symptoms were caused by something neutral such as a pill, they would be less anxious about their insomnia and thus fall asleep quicker. To test this hypothesis, they recruited insomniacs ostensibly for a study on dreams. They gave one group a pill that, they said, should cause the symptoms of insomnia just described and asked them to take it on certain nights. The subjects in this group reported that they got to sleep faster on the nights when they took the pill. No such difference was reported by subjects in a control group.

Objections to Schachter's Theory Although Schachter's theory has received a considerable amount of attention and some support, a number of investigators have raised serious questions about it (see Reisenzein, 1983, for a review). One attempt to replicate Schachter's and Singer's original experiment failed (Marshall & Zimbardo, 1979). Other investigators have been unable to replicate Storms and Nisbett's results with insomniacs (Kellogg & Baron, 1975). Furthermore, Calvert-Boyanowsky and Leventhal (1975) noted that in all of the experimental demonstrations of Schachter's theory, the subjects given a neutral explanation for their arousal (for example, the effects of the pill) were the only ones given a list of arousal symptoms. These researchers showed that thinking about the symptoms of arousal results in a reduction in emotional behavior, regardless of whether the symptoms are attributed to a neutral but plausible source or to a true emotional source. In other words, the critical difference between subjects who expressed less fear of spiders or fell asleep quicker may have been that they were encouraged unintentionally to think about the symptoms of arousal, not that they misattributed the causes.

The Primacy of Cognition On balance, the results of research directed at testing Schachter's

theory suggest that some of its propositions are not well supported (Reisenzein, 1983). Nevertheless, the notion of **cognitive appraisal** as a necessary determinant of emotion continues to play a central role in cognitively oriented theories of emotion (Averill, 1980; Lazarus, 1982, 1984; Mandler, 1975; Weiner, 1980). Lazarus has articulated this view clearly.

> In my view, emotion reflects a constantly changing person-environment relationship. When central life agendas (e.g. biological survival, personal and social values and goals) are engaged, this relationship becomes a source of emotion. . . . Cognitive activity is a necessary precondition of emotion because to experience an emotion, people must comprehend — whether in the form of a primitive evaluative perception or a highly differentiated symbolic process — that their well-being is implicated in a transaction, for better or worse.

In some situations and with some emotions, the process of cognitive appraisal is conscious, rational, and deliberative. We are, at least to a degree, able to exercise conscious control over our emotions. Without that possibility, there would be little prospect of success in many therapeutic programs designed to help individuals gain some control over disabling emotional states (see Chapter 14). Other emotional responses, particularly more primitive ones such as fear, may require only the rapid and unconscious appraisal that Lazarus refers to as a *primitive evaluative perception*. In both cases, however, cognition appears to have primacy over emotion.

The Primacy of Emotion One theorist who disagrees with the proposition that cognition has primacy over emotion is Robert Zajonc (1980, 1984). Zajonc has marshalled a considerable body of evidence in support of the primacy of emotion, or *affect* as he prefers to label it. Briefly, he argues that the affective and cognitive systems are not so closely intertwined as Lazarus and others believe. In particular, affective responses to external stimuli can precede the onset of cognition and, under certain circumstances, can occur in the absence of any type of cognitive appraisal.

In Chapter 4 we considered a theory of direct perception proposed by Gibson (1979). In this view, our perceptual systems have evolved the capacity to detect or pick up perceptual attributes of the external world in a direct fashion, without the need for intervening inferential or cognitive processes. The same argument can be applied to the affective attributes of objects and events (Buck, 1984); that is, we have evolved the capacity to detect affective qualities without cognitive mediation. Although this is an extremely difficult theory to confirm, there is a good deal of evidence that is consistent with it. Zajonc (1984) believes the evidence favors five significant assertions regarding the relation between affect and cognition.

1. Affective reactions show phylogenetic and ontogenetic primacy.
2. Separate neuroanatomical structures can be identified for affect and cognition.
3. Appraisal and affect are often uncorrelated.
4. New affective reactions can be established without apparent appraisal.
5. Affective states can be induced by noncognitive and nonperceptual procedures.

As the debate over the primacy of cognition and emotion demonstrates, there remains considerable disagreement about the nature of emotional experience. One significant contribution would be a theory of emotion that encompassed the three emphases we have discussed: physiological, subjective, and behavioral. Recently a theory was proposed that claims to do just that (Buck, 1985). Even better, it offers a role for motivation in the same model.

An Integrated Theory of Motivation and Emotion

The central elements in Buck's theory are **primes,** which he defines as "biologically based primary motivational/emotional systems [that] have evolved within each species with the basic role of bodily adaptation and maintenance of homeostasis" (1985, p. 390). Primes are innate, special-purpose systems located primarily in old brain structures, such as the limbic system, that have developed to help animals adapt to their environments and to help maintain their health and welfare.

Primes exist at various levels of organization, Buck argues. At the most primitive level are *reflexes,* which are stereotyped behaviors triggered by specific stimuli. At the next level are **primary drives,** which are activated when such basic needs as food, water, sleep, sex, air, temperature regulation, and pain avoidance develop. The goals of these drives are fixed but the specific behaviors that satisfy the needs may be shaped by learning. Buck notes in the case of *secondary drives* that "the organism learns not only the sequence of behavior needed to satisfy the goal, but also the value of the goal itself: initially neutral stimuli in the environment that are associated with the reinforcement of a biological drive come to be reinforcing (incentives) in themselves" (p. 391). Next are **primary affects** that Buck, like Ekman and Friesen (1975), identifies as happiness, sadness, fear, anger, surprise, and disgust. Buck believes that the capacity to experience and express primary affects is "hard-wired" in the brain but involves general response tendencies rather than specific behaviors. At higher levels are *prime systems* that, although similar to drives, are difficult to relate directly to bodily needs. The drives of curiosity, exploration, and sensation-seeking are examples offered by Buck.

In Buck's model, motivation is the *potential inherent in the primes for activating and directing behavior.* Just as a coiled spring or a lifted weight has potential kinetic energy, so primes have potential motivational energy that is released when animals experience certain internal and external stimuli. In Buck's model, emotion is a "readout mechanism" associated with motivation. The idea that "emotion has evolved as a readout mechanism carrying information about motivation—that is, about the state of the primes—in a kind of running progress report" (p. 396) is a major contribution of Buck's theory. Thus motivation and emotion are seen by Buck to be two aspects of the same process—the activation of primes.

Buck believes that three emotional readout systems have evolved successively during the course of evolution; he labels them Emotion I, II, and III. The readout process for these three systems is shown in Figure 7-19. *Emotion I* in-

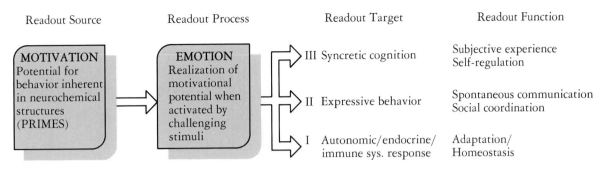

FIGURE 7-19
Buck's Readout System for Emotion The emotional expression of basic motives (primes) is channeled to three separate targets (cognition, external behavior, internal organs), each serving a different adaptive function. *Source:* Buck R. (1985). Prime theory: An integrated view of motivation and emotion. *Psychological Review, 92(3),* 389–413.

volves readout of the state of the primary drive systems to the autonomic nervous system and to the body's endocrine and immune systems. *Emotion II* is an external readout wherein the state of the primes is reflected in overt expressive behavior (particularly facial expression). This latter readout system evolved in response to the need for communication between members of a species (for example, concerning reproduction and caring for the young).

Emotion III is an internal readout system in which the animal itself is made aware of the state of its primes. The readout takes the form of what Buck calls **syncretic cognition,** as distinct from **analytic cognition.** This is a highly speculative but provocative notion that captures several distinctions we have touched on in this and in prior chapters. Although it should not be taken too literally, we can characterize analytic cognition as linear, sequential, verbal, conscious, intentional, indirect, and based in the left hemisphere. By contrast, syncretic cognition is nonlinear, holistic, nonverbal, unconscious, spontaneous, indirect, and based in the right hemisphere. There is much evidence to link the right hemisphere with the recognition and expression of emotion (for example, Buck & Duffy, 1980; Tucker, 1981). Buck speculates that Emotion III messages are received as syncretic cognitions in the right hemisphere, where they are available to the processes of analytic cognition based in the left hemisphere. They thus serve as the basis of subjective experience and provide a means for in-

tentional control over the outward expression of emotion.

The various elements of Buck's theory are sketched in Figure 7-20. The easiest way to appreciate how this model works is to demonstrate its application by means of a familiar experience. Imagine that you have spent a considerable amount of time and effort on your appearance in order to impress someone you are about to meet. No doubt your efforts resulted in part from a need for approval (a high level *prime*). This need *motivated* you—stirred you into action and directed your behavior toward the goal of making yourself presentable. When at last you meet, the person compliments your appearance. This *external affective stimulus* satisfies your need for approval and triggers messages in the emotional readout systems. The *Emotion I* system prompts autonomic activity in your *adaptive and homeostatic mechanisms*—your heart beats a little faster, your breathing rate increases, your pupils dilate, and you blush. The *Emotion II* message elicits a *spontaneous expressive tendency*—you smile—which is considered acceptable under the circumstances. However, since this person is an acquaintance only, the **display rules** that you have learned inhibit other expressions—ones you might have shown your best friend, for example. Finally, the *Emotion III* system provides *subjective experiences* that your *cognitive appraisal* labels as pride and satisfaction, although the social conventions may prevent you from displaying such feelings.

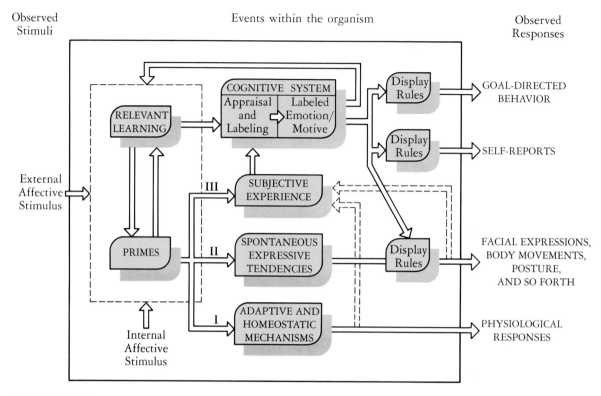

FIGURE 7-20

Buck's Theory of Motivation and Emotion   Emotional expressions at various levels result from complex interactions among motivation, cognition, and social constraints.   *Source:* Buck, R. (1985). Prime theory: An integrated view of motivation and emotion. *Psychological Review, 92(3),* 389–413.

Although speculative on several counts, Buck's theory is valuable in at least three ways. First, it helps organize a wide array of facts and observations about motivation and emotion. Second, it provides a basis for resolving debates and disputes. (For example, Buck believes that his distinction between syncretic and analytic cogni-

tion is highly relevant to the argument between Lazarus and Zajonc as to the primacy of cognition.) Third, a good theory should offer the opportunity to advance knowledge. There is ample room for such a theory in the complex area of motivation and emotion.

SUMMARY

1. Motivation concerns the processes of initiating, sustaining, and directing behavior. Psychologists who study motivation seek to understand why organisms expend energy to achieve goals and how their behavior is

pushed by internal needs and pulled by external incentives.

2. Primary motives, which serve to ensure survival of the individual or species, lead to such

behaviors as eating, drinking, pain avoidance, and sexual activity. Secondary motives, responsible for behaviors that enrich life, are learned.

3. Motives can be organized hierarchically. Those at the base — such as hunger and thirst — dominate behavior until the corresponding needs are satisfied, thus freeing the individual to respond to such higher-level motives as curiosity, affiliation, and self-actualization.

4. Eating is motivated by hunger, a drive state induced by a need for food; ingestion of food reduces the drive and satisfies the need. In humans, however, food typically retains some incentive value even when the need for it has been satisfied. Sensors in the mouth, throat, stomach, and liver report to specific brain centers on the ingestion and digestion of food. These centers exercise short-term control over eating; taste exercises longer-term control.

5. Hull's drive-reduction theory is a historically important explanation of motivated behavior. However, his theory was inadequate to account for secondary motives and reinforcers, the need for an optimal level of sensory stimulation, and the reinforcing effect of direct electrical stimulation of the brain.

6. Animals are motivated to keep their level of arousal from rising too high or from dropping too low. This typically is achieved by varying the level of sensory stimulation experienced. Individuals vary in their optimal level; those with a higher level are more likely to engage in risky pursuits.

7. Individuals exhibit such interpersonal and personal needs as those for affiliation, approval, self-esteem, achievement, and self-actualization, needs which energize and direct much of human behavior. Also evident is a curiosity need, which prompts exploration and manipulation of the environment.

8. Emotions are states that are inferred from both subjective and objective indices. Measures of emotion fall into three categories:

physiological responses, subjective responses, and behavioral responses.

9. Physiological measures of emotion include activities in the central, somatic, and autonomic nervous systems (CNS, SNS, and ANS). CNS structures involved in emotions lie principally in the hypothalamus and in components of the limbic system. An SNS activity that has proved particularly revealing of emotional state is facial expression. Similarly revealing are ANS responses that involve coronary activity and electrical properties of sweat glands.

10. Subjective reports are obtained from individuals asked to describe their feelings as they experience an emotion. However, problems arise from this form of measurement relating to cultural variation in willingness to disclose such information and to the difficulty we often experience in accurately identifying our emotions. These problems are less evident when measurement of emotion is focused on behavioral responses.

11. Theories of emotion tend to have a physiological, evolutionary, or cognitive emphasis. An early example of the physiological emphasis is the James–Lange theory, which asserts that the essence of emotion is the recognition of a distinctive pattern of visceral or "gut" responses to an emotionally arousing stimulus. A different theory was advanced by Cannon and Bard, who proposed that an emotional stimulus causes activity in the thalamic area of the brain, which in turn triggers both subjective feelings and visceral responses.

12. Darwin, Ekman, and Plutchik each provided theories of emotion with an evolutionary perspective. Darwin held that emotional expressions originally were associated with adaptive responses, and evolved because of the survival value of those adaptations. Ekman has demonstrated the universal nature of the facial expressions of primary emotions. Similar evidence on emotions in newborn infants and in blind children suggests that primary emotions are innate; however,

in different settings cultural factors may constrain the expression of emotions. Plutchik's psychoevolutionary theory postulates eight essential adaptive functions, each associated with a basic emotion.

13. Schachter, Lazarus, and Zajonc each offer a theory of emotion with a cognitive focus. For Schachter, the degree of autonomic arousal determines the intensity of experienced emotion and a cognitive appraisal of the situation determines which emotion is experienced. While recent evidence casts some doubt on this theory, the notion of cognitive appraisal plays a central role in several other cognitively oriented theories, such as that of Lazarus. An opposite view is taken by Zajonc, who believes in the primacy of emotion — affect over cognition.

14. Buck has developed an integrated theory of motivation and emotion, the core concept of which is the prime. Primes are biologically based systems that have evolved within each species to serve bodily adaptation and to maintain homeostasis. Motivation is the potential inherent in primes that activate and direct behavior. Emotions are readouts of the state of the primes to the autonomic nervous system, to expressive behavior, and to conscious awareness.

KEY TERMS

Motivation
Instinct
Primary Motive
Secondary Motive
Primary Need
Secondary Need
Drive
Homeostasis
Incentive
Drive Reduction
Secondary Drive
Secondary Reinforcer
Sensory Deprivation

Yerkes-Dodson Law
Optimal Arousal Theory
Deficiency Need
Growth Need
Interpersonal Need
Esteem Need
Cognitive-aesthetic Need
Self-actualization Need
Safety Need
Bait Shyness
Need for Affiliation
Need for Approval
Emotion

Facial Action Coding System
  (FACS)
Action Unit (AU)
Epinephrine
Misattribution Therapy
Cognitive Appraisal
Prime
Primary Drive
Primary Affect
Syncretic Cognition
Analytic Cognition
Display Rule

RECOMMENDED READINGS

Arkes, H. R., & Garske, J. P. (1982). *Psychological theories of motivation* (2nd ed.). Belmont, CA: Wadsworth. A well-organized survey of the full range of motivation theories.

Buck, R. (1983). *Human motivation and emotion* (2nd ed.). New York: Wiley. A broadly based integration of ideas and findings from most areas central to motivation and emotion.

Eckman, P. (Ed.). (1982). *Emotion in the human face* (2nd ed.). New York: Cambridge University Press. A detailed account of research on the facial expression of emotion, including cross-cultural studies of similarities and differences of expression.

Franken, R. E. (1982). *Human motivation.* Monterey, CA: Brooks/Cole. A highly readable review of the phenomena of motivation from the standpoints of biology, learning, and cognition.

Izard, C. E. (1977). *Human emotions*. New York: Plenum Publishing. A challenging examination of human emotion that focuses on expressive aspects, with particular emphasis on nonverbal factors.

Lykken, D. T. (1981). *A tremor in the blood: Uses and abuses of the lie detector*. New York: McGraw-Hill. A leading authority on the subject argues that the lie-detector test is less valid and more limited in its applications than proposed by most of its advocates.

Plutchik, R. (1980). *Emotion: A psychoevolutionary synthesis*. New York: Harper & Row. Appeals to both animal and human data in presenting a theory of emotion rooted in Darwin's conception of emotions as adaptive responses that possess survival value.

8

HUMAN SEXUALITY

O
h Lord, give me the strength to give up my lust; but not just yet.'' So, apparently, prayed St. Augustine. To the delight of some and to the consternation of others, sexual desire is an essential part of human nature. Human sexuality involves psychological processes that are discussed in every chapter of this text. Sexual urges are among our most basic biological dispositions—without them the human species would not have evolved—yet they are shaped by learning and culture in a variety of fascinating ways. Human sexuality is determined by the interaction between nature and nurture. It involves neurological and psychophysiological responses mediated by centers in the brain. Human sexuality involves certain powerful sensations, and it is activated by particular perceptions. Sexual behaviors may be shaped through classical and operant conditioning (in much the same way as other behaviors), but sex is also strongly affected by the ways in which people think. Sexual desire is both a motive and an emotional state. Human sexuality is affected by the physical, cognitive, and social changes that people experience as they develop. Sex is a social

TABLE 8-1

Twenty Commonly Held Misconceptions about Sexuality

Myth	More Accurate
In virtually all cultures, monogamy is the primary form of marriage.	The primary form of marriage in most cultures is polygamy.
Compared to other cultures, ours is very sexually permissive.	Although there is a great deal of variation among subcultures, our culture is among the most sexually restrictive.
Masturbation is an act that may lead to mental illness, hairy palms, blindness, and so forth.	Masturbation is a natural act practiced universally by most males and females. Rather than cause physical damage, there is evidence that it may help to improve sexual functioning in some persons. Moreover, it is often more physiologically pleasurable than intercourse.
Young people today are more promiscuous than young people in the past.	Although there has been an increase in premarital sex, most young people today confine their sexual relations to people with whom they have a close relationship and whom they intend to marry.
Most children learn about sex from their parents.	Most children learn about sex from their peers.
Elderly persons should beware of a ''coital cardiac.''	A heart attack during sex is very rare at any age and is usually associated with a preexisting heart condition, a recent heavy meal, and an extramarital sex partner.
A small penis is less efficient than a longer penis in producing female orgasms.	The size of the *erect* penis is somewhat uniform (about 5.5–6.5 inches); even when there are size differences, they do not appear to correlate with orgasmic frequency or with the satisfaction reported by females. The vaginal barrel adapts to the size of the penis; however, if the female believes she needs an uncommon penis, she may fulfill her own prophecy.
The length of the penis can be predicted by race and by finger length.	At the present time there are no reliable predictors of the size of the erect penis—including race, height, weight, and finger length. Black males do tend to have a longer limp penis (which may account for some racial myths), but this difference disappears with erection.
Simultaneous orgasm is a sexual ideal.	The pursuit of simultaneous orgasm may interfere with sexual satisfaction because the male usually desires sustained deep penetration at the point of orgasm while the female often desires continued pelvic thrusting. Pursuit of this goal also may create performance anxieties and detract from spontaneity.
There are significant differences between the experience of orgasm in males and in females.	The similarities outweigh the differences.
Orgasm and ejaculation always go together in males.	Men may have an orgasm without ejaculation, although they usually occur together.

behavior; indeed few social relationships are more significant than those determined by love and sanctioned in marriage. According to Freud and other personality theorists, the ways in which people deal with their sexual urges guide the development of their personalities. Finally, no other type of behavior is more closely related to psychopathology.

Considering the significance of sex, you might assume that we would know a lot about it. However, for many centuries the topic of sex was taboo in our society. Indeed, as we shall see, even today attempts to include sex-education programs in high school curricula are often opposed by various groups of concerned citizens. One unfortunate consequence of the taboo against sex is the relative lack of scientific research on the topic. As late as 1967, Reiss wrote that "Probably no other area in social sciences has such a poor pedigree as the study of human sexual relationships," adding that the number of objective studies on the issue could be counted "on one's fingers and toes" (p. 1). Another unfortunate consequence is that sex is shrouded in myth (see Table 8-1).

Myth	More Accurate
The penis must be erect (tumescent) for orgasm to occur.	Orgasm and ejaculation can occur without erection. Recent research on handicapped persons incapable of erection suggests that orgasm is as much a cognitive achievement as a genital one.
Penis captivus is common during sexual intercourse with virgins.	The "captivation" of a penis by a vagina has never been documented in humans. This myth probably stems from the fact that the dog's penis—which contains a bone—is captivated by the bitch when her vaginal opening constricts over it, and releases only following ejaculation.
It is natural for women to require a longer time to reach orgasm than men.	With appropriate setting and stimulation, most women can reach orgasm within four minutes.
When males complain of "stone ache" (testicular pain from prolonged arousal without sexual relief), this is simply a ploy to persuade females to have sex.	While their motives at times may be seductive, males may in fact suffer pain from prolonged vasocongestion in the genitals.
Castrating males, and therefore halting the supply of male sex hormones, causes a reduction in their sexual activity.	Castration of adults does not necessarily affect sexual appetite.
Spanish Fly is a potent aphrodisiac.	The drug (cantharis) may cause irritation of the mucous membranes and the genitourinary tract. The erection and inflammation that follow may mimic arousal, but there is no real sexual stimulation. Other alleged aphrodisiacs (for example, yohimbine) are equally ineffective at increasing genital responsiveness, as are drugs intended to reduce it (for example, saltpeter).
Alcohol increases sexual desire and activity.	The expectation that alcohol will enhance sexual desire and activity is more important than the effect of alcohol itself, which is a depressant.
People are either heterosexual or homosexual.	"The world is not divided into sheep and goats" (Kinsey et al., 1953).
Some women are nymphomaniacs and have virtually insatiable sexual appetites.	Nymphomania is an archaic term remaining from a time when any woman who asserted her sexual needs was considered "sex-crazed." The male counterpart (satyriasis) is also mainly mythical. Differences in sexual appetite are common and do not necessarily reflect disturbance. Extreme promiscuity usually reflects a psychological problem.

Source: Adapted from Mahoney, E. R. (1983). *Human sexuality.* New York: McGraw-Hill.

TABLE 8-2
Landmark Publications on Human Sexuality

Date	Author(s)	Publication	Topic
1886	Richard von Krafft-Ebing	*Psychopathia Sexualis*	Sexual deviance and psychopathology
1895	Sigmund Freud and Joseph Breuer	*Studies in Hysteria*	The relationship between the sexual instinct and psychopathology
1896–1928	Havelock Ellis	*Studies in the Psychology of Sex*	Seven volumes on human sexuality
1907	Sigmund Freud	*Three Essays on the Theory of Sexuality*	The nature of human sexuality
1929	Katherine B. Davis	*Factors in the Sex Life of Twenty-Two Hundred Women*	Female sexuality
1933	Robert Dickinson	*Human Sex Anatomy*	Sexual anatomy
1948	Alfred Kinsey et al.	*Sexual Behavior in the Human Male*	A survey of the sexual practices of American males
1953	Alfred Kinsey et al.	*Sexual Behavior in the Human Female*	A survey of the sexual practices of American females
1966	William Masters and Virginia Johnson	*Human Sexual Response*	The physiology of sexual arousal
1970	William Masters and Virginia Johnson	*Human Sexual Inadequacy*	Clinical studies on the treatment of such sexual problems as frigidity, impotence, and premature ejaculation

Source: Adapted from Elwood, A., et al. (1975).   Uncensored highlights in the history of sex in the last 500 years.   In D. Wallechinsky & I. Wallace (Eds.), *The people's almanac* pp. 964–970.   Garden City, NY: Doubleday.

Until the second half of the twentieth century, scholarly works on sexual behavior consisted primarily of research on animals, clinical reports of sexual dysfunctions, and basic facts about anatomy and physiology (see Table 8-2).   In the early 1950s, entomologist Alfred Kinsey and his colleagues altered this long-standing trend by publishing the famous *Kinsey Reports,* which described the incidence of various forms of sexual behavior in normal American people.   For the most part, the *Kinsey Reports* are descriptive; they make no attempt to explain human sexuality.   Only recently have researchers begun to study the psychological determinants of sexual behavior.   In the words of Peplau and Hammen (1977):

> In the past 10 years, the study of human sexuality has altered greatly.   The quality of sex research has expanded dramatically, and . . .   the respectability of sex as a subject for scholarly investigation has increased, encouraging university researchers to venture into the area.

In this chapter we cover four fundamental aspects of human sexuality.   First, we consider the evolution of sex and the relationship between biological and cultural determinants of sexual behavior.   Second, we examine the sexual practices of people in our society and discuss how socialization affects the development of sexual behavior in children.   Third, we study the nature and causes of sexual arousal.   And, finally, we examine sexual deviations, focusing on homosexuality and rape.

THE EVOLUTION OF SEX

It is appropriate to open a discussion of human sexuality by posing the most basic of all questions: "Why sex?"   Why do members of so many species engage in sexual relations?   The answer to this question may seem obvious — to reproduce — for without sex the species would become extinct. But not all species must engage in sex to reproduce; many species reproduce asexually. Their cells divide, producing replicas of themselves (see Figure 8-1). So the question focuses then on why individuals engage in sexual rather than **asexual reproduction**?

Viewed from an evolutionary perspective, the general answer to the question "Why sex?" is that **sexual reproduction** evolved through natural selection because, at some point in the evolutionary history of the species that acquired it, it was more adaptive than its alternatives. Sexual reproduction fostered the propagation of genes more effectively than asexual reproduction. Yet, on the face of it at least, the disadvantages of sexual reproduction are more apparent than its advantages. Locating, attracting, and winning a mate all involve investments of time and energy —as does the act of mating itself—and sexual reproduction generally increases vulnerability to predators. Moreover, individuals who reproduce asexually are virtually guaranteed viable replicas of themselves; individuals who reproduce sexually may produce a lethal or nonadaptive combination of genes. More significantly, individuals who engage in sexual reproduction transmit only 50% of their genetic materials to their offspring; whereas those who reproduce asexually transmit 100% of theirs. In view of

these disadvantages, then, why has sexual reproduction evolved in so many animals? What advantages outweigh these disadvantages?

The fundamental difference between sexual and asexual reproduction lies in the genetic variability produced by sexual reproduction. When male and female sex cells unite, genetically unique individuals are produced. Inevitably some of these unique individuals are less well-adapted than are their parents, and some do not survive. However, some are better adapted, and therein lies the gain. In uncertain and changeable environments, individuals hedge their bets through sexual reproduction. Although it costs them a 50% loss in genetic materials to reproduce sexually, sexual reproduction enables them to distribute their genetic investments among several different options rather than to one option and its replicas.

As an analogy, consider the game of roulette. In asexual reproduction, you put all your chips on one number. You have a relatively small chance of winning—but if you win, you win big. In sexual reproduction, you put one chip on as many numbers as possible. You will not win as big—but you will minimize the chances of going broke. In cases where a spin of the wheel (the environment, or the natural selector) is predictable, you are better off betting all your chips (genes) on the number (type of offspring) that has paid off in the past. However, in cases where it is unpredictable—like a game of chance—the best way to ensure solvency (to ensure that some of your genes are propagated) is to cover as many options as possible.

If the reason for sex stems from the value of variation in offspring created by environmental uncertainty, then there should be a positive correlation between sexual reproduction and environmental uncertainty in existing species, and indeed this seems to be the case (Glesener & Tilman, 1978). Interestingly, this also seems to be the case in certain species that reproduce both sexually and asexually. Many parasites reproduce asexually when they first invade the body of a host animal (a common environment). Asexual reproduction leads to an exponential increase in offspring ($2 \times 2 = 4$, $4 \times 4 = 16$, $16 \times 16 = 256$, etc.) that causes a population explosion that makes it adaptive for individuals to leave the host. At this point the parasites reproduce

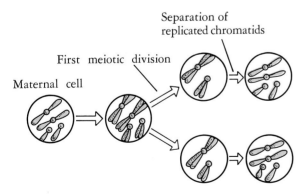

FIGURE 8-1

Asexual Reproduction through Parthenogenesis Organisms may produce in several ways. In the type of asexual reproduction demonstrated here, the chromosomes within a cell replicate, the cell divides through meiosis, and then the chromatids separate to form replicas of the chromosomes in the original cell. *Source:* Bernstein, R. A., & Bernstein, S. (1982). *Biology: The study of life.* New York: Harcourt Brace Jovanovich.

Separation of replicated chromatids

First meiotic division

Maternal cell

sexually, creating the variation that is adaptive to the uncertain environments into which they disperse. Some biologists have speculated that sexual reproduction in humans is a sort of evolutionary vestige that evolved when their environment was uncertain—that if anyone ever developed the capacity for asexual reproduction, it would preempt sexual reproduction. "Should some women develop the ability to reproduce without sex, the trait might indeed enjoy a selective advantage, and sex (and men!) could be consigned to oblivion" (Daly & Wilson, 1978).

Why Two Sexes?

The question "Why sex?" raises another related question: "Why two sexes?" Why are most species divided into males and females? Again, the answer to this question might seem obvious: you need two sexes in order to effect sexual reproduction. But this is not, strictly speaking, the case—because unisex individuals can unite with one another. To explain why there are two sexes in most sexually reproducing species, we must define *sex* (meaning gender). Most people assume that the fundamental difference between the sexes lies in the anatomical differences between their bodies, but this assumption is inexact.

In some species—sparrows and oysters, for example—the bodies of males are virtually identical to the bodies of females. Indeed, among humans, people sometimes are born with the sexual characteristics of both males and females (see Chapter 2). The fundamental difference between the sexes lies in the sex cells, or **gametes,** they produce. Females produce ova; males produce sperm. Sperm are smaller and more mobile than ova. In humans, a sperm is only a fraction of the size of an ovum (see Figure 8-2) and it leaves the male body to enter the female body. Human females are born with a fixed number of immature eggs, which normally are released at a rate of only one per month. In contrast, human males produce several billion sperm each year, which may be released at the rate of thousands per day.

No one knows for sure how two sexes evolved, but Parker, Baker, and Smith (1972) have offered an interesting theory. They imagine that at the dawn of life there was only one type of sex cell that combined with other sex cells of its type. Inevitably the offspring of such combina-

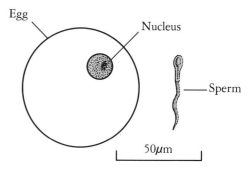

FIGURE 8-2

Ovum and Sperm (drawn to same scale) Although the human ovum is significantly larger than the human sperm, males tend to be physically larger than females. *Source:* Daly, M., & Wilson, M. (1978). *Sex, evolution and behavior.* North Scituate, MA: Duxbury Press.

tions varied, rendering some more fit than others. Parker et al. suggest that two important dimensions of this variation were size and number. Large sex cells would have an adaptive advantage over smaller ones because they could store more food (yolk) for subsequent cell division; small sex cells would have the advantage of mobility. These theorists show how, over generations, **disruptive selection** could have led to the evolution of two types of sex cell—large sex cells produced in small numbers and small sex cells produced in large numbers (see Figure 8-3). According to the Parker team, the two sexes originated through this process. At first, they speculate, large (female) sex cells may have combined with other large sex cells, but the odds favoring such combinations would have been low in view of their small number and immobility. Small sex-cell combinations would have been lethal because there would have been insufficient nourishment to support the union. The ideal combination would have involved unions between large and small sex cells, which—according to Parker, Baker, and Smith—is why sex as gender became necessary for sex as mating.

Note that we speak here of sex cells, not individuals. Although the ova of mammals are significantly larger than sperm, the females of a species are not necessarily larger than the males. Indeed, males are larger than females in most, but not all, mammals. It is the size of sex cells that determines whether they are male or female, not the size of the individuals who produce them.

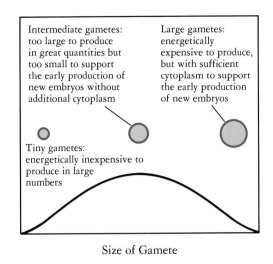
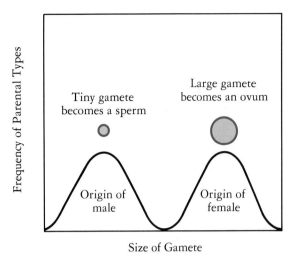

FIGURE 8-3

Disruptive Selection Through the process of natural selection, intermediate size gametes become extinct. Tiny and large gametes prevail and produce, over time, sperm and ova. *Source:* Adapted from Daly, M., & Wilson, M. (1978). *Sex, evolution and behavior.* North Scituate, MA: Duxbury Press.

Sex Differences in Mating Strategies in the Animal Kingdom

The basic biological differences between the sexes have important implications for sexual behavior. Consider our own species, for example. Physically, males are capable of siring many more offspring then females. As stated in the *Guinness Book of World Records,* the most children ever produced by a female is 69 — a record held by a Muscovite woman who became pregnant 27 times and bore twins, triplets, and quadruplets. The record for males was established by Moulay Ismail the Bloodthirsty, an emperor of Morocco, who sired 888 children. Because females nurture fetuses inside their bodies, give birth, and lactate, initially they make a considerably greater investment in their offspring than do males. Females know that the offspring they bear are theirs; males are much less certain of their paternity. According to some evolutionary theorists, such sex differences give rise to significant differences between the mating strategies and sexual orientations of males and females and pave the way for a fundamental conflict between the sexes. Although it is always in an animal's best evolutionary interest to mate with a high-quality partner (quality defined here in terms of potential for fostering the propagation of genes, or **reproductive fitness**), it is usually more in the interest of

females than of males. In general, therefore, females should be more selective than males in their choice of mating partners. Because females (or more exactly their ova) are relatively finite resources, males should tend to compete for them.

Males compete for females in two primary ways: by wooing them and by defeating other males. A survey of mammalian species reveals that males are almost always more ostentatiously ornamented than females and that males virtually always take the initiative during courtship, putting on behavioral displays of aggression, aerial acrobatics, parading, croaking, cooing, singing, and, as a rule, showing off. When there is competition for a mate, it is the males who usually compete. The trumpeting of bull elk, the roaring of elephant seals, the territorial songs of birds, the head butting of rams, and the ferocious battles of tigers and lions are familiar examples. Given the advantages of size in such exchanges, it is not surprising that males are larger than females in most species — and that the largest males mate with the most females.

These generalizations do not, of course, mean that females are always more selective than males or that females never compete for males. We would expect females to compete for males when, for whatever reason, males — or more ex-

The sexual behavior of gorillas: (a) female "presents" to male, soliciting copulation; (b) rear-mount position copulation; (c) face-to-face copulation position — rare among nonhumans *Source:* R. D. Nadler. Atlanta, GA: Yerkes Regional Primate Research Center.

actly fit males — are a finite resource. "As a general rule, when environmental resources are sometimes limiting, such that reproduction of one female decreases the likely reproductive success of another, we can expect to find female–female competition" (Barash, 1982, p. 242). And, for species in which offspring require assistance from their fathers to ensure their survival, males would be expected to produce fewer offspring and invest more in those they produce. "With increasing male **parental investment,** males should be more selective and females less so. When males provide most of the parental investment, they should be very selective, with the females being hardly selective at all" (Barash, 1982, p. 271). Among stickleback fish, for example, males build nests and care for the eggs the females lay; in this species there appears to be as much female–female competition as male–male competition, with dominant females mating more than subordinate females (Li & Owings, 1978).

Pair-bonding

The basic biological reason why animals form social bonds that extend beyond the reproductive act is because such bonds are necessary to foster their reproductive fitness. Males and females may form ongoing unions in order to protect a territory or in order to engage in mutual defense or hunting, but the primary value of **pair-bonding** relates to care of offspring. Species whose offspring are born mature rarely pair-bond. Even among species whose offspring are born immature, pair-bonding usually occurs only when the female is unable to nurture the offspring successfully by herself.

Among species that pair-bond, some are **monogamous** — they pair up with one mate, either for life **(perennial monogamy)** or for a mating season **(annual monogamy).** Other pair-bonding species are **polygamous** — a member of one sex forms a bond with more than one member of the opposite sex. There are two types of **polygamy** — **polygyny,** where a male forms a bond with several females, and **polyandry,** where a female forms a bond with several males. Table 8-3 outlines the most prevalent mating systems observed in the animal kingdom. In species that pair-bond, males tend to favor polygyny (as long as they have the resources to support several mates) and females tend to favor mo-

TABLE 8-3
Classification of Animal Mating Systems

System	Definition	Example
Monogamy	Reproductive unit of one male and one female; pair-bond formed	
Annual monogamy	Bonds formed anew each year	Small passerine birds: sparrows, warblers, chickadees
Perennial monogamy	Bond retained for life	Swans, geese, eagles, gibbons
Polygamy	Reproductive unit of one individual of one sex and several of another; pair-bond formed	
Polygyny:	One male bonded with several females	
serial	One male bonded with several females during a breeding season, but only one at a time	Pied flycatchers
simultaneous	One male simultaneously bonded with several females during the breeding season	Red-winged blackbirds, fur seals, elk
Polyandry:	One female bonded with several males	
serial	One female bonded with several males during a breeding season, but only one at a time	Rheas
simultaneous	One female bonded with several males simultaneously during the breeding season	Jacanas, Tasmanian native hen
Promiscuity	No bonds formed	Grouse, bears, wildebeests

Source: Adapted from Barash, D. P. (1982). *Sociobiology and behavior* (2nd ed.). New York: Elsevier.

nogamy. In the words of William James (supposedly inspired by a dose of opium), "Higamous hogamous, woman monogamous; hogamous, higamous, man is polygamous!"

Except among birds, monogamy is relatively rare in the animal kingdom. More than 90% of known bird species are monogamous. Considering that newly hatched birds are helpless and have voracious appetites, it is unlikely they would survive without the assistance of both parents — and this appears to be the reason why they form monogamous unions. As indicated, however, most mammals are polygynous. Although the offspring of most mammals require a great deal of care at birth, females, who supply milk, usually care for them by themselves. Among mammals, monogamy is most prevalent in such carnivores as wolves, foxes, and coyotes. In these species males assist their mates by bringing them meat.

Although polygyny (one male, several females) and polyandry (one female, several males) may appear to be equally functional alternatives, biologically they are not. Even though a female's mate may have several "wives," she still knows which offspring are hers and, in virtually all species, assumes responsibility for rearing them. However, this is not the case when several males mate with the same female. Because paternity is uncertain in polyandry, males should avoid it. And in virtually all species they do. There are only two documented cases of simultaneous polyandry in the animal kingdom (see Table 8-3) — among jacanas and Tasmanian native hens. It is significant that, in both cases, the males involved in the polyandrous unions are brothers. Because brothers share 50% of their genes, each "husband" is assured that at least 25% of his genes will be propagated in the offspring of any union.

BIOLOGY AND CULTURE IN HUMAN SEXUALITY

Our primary concern here is human sexuality. Of what relevance are the theory of evolution and the behavior of nonhuman animals to the sexual behavior of humans? The strongest answer to this question would seem to be "some relevance, but only very general." Humans are the products of millions of years of evolution, and they bear the imprint of the process. In view of the essential significance of sex in genetic propagation, we should expect human sexual behavior to be rooted deeply in evolved dispositions. Like other animals, humans engage in sex and form sexual relationships. They court, compete, select, pair-bond, and invest time and effort in rearing their offspring. Looking at humans through the broad lens of evolutionary biology supplies a useful perspective: the human species is one of many. But the human species also is unique. The ability of humans to learn, to adapt, to control the environment, and to create culture is not even faintly approached by any other species. Indeed, some biologists have suggested that in the human species **cultural evolution** has preempted **biological evolution** (see Barash, 1982, Chapter 7; Dawkins, 1976, Chapter 11).

As demonstrated in Chapter 3, the primary way in which humans differ from nonhumans is that they possess additional and overriding mental structures. We humans possess the same basic *primitive* brain structures and capacities to learn as other animals, but we possess considerably more cortex. Thus, to quote Beach (1977), "Man is no more a naked ape than chimpanzees are hairy people, but he is a mammal and a primate, and as such shares certain physical and behavioral characteristics with other members of his class and order" (p. 297). We would expect all humans to possess basic, general, deep-seated sexual dispositions that give rise to broad consistencies in their sexual behavior. However, we also would expect the demands of different environments, the evolution of different cultures, and the inevitable differences in individual experiences to produce more variation within the human species than within any other species in the animal kingdom. Davenport (1977) draws an instructive analogy between human sexual behavior and language:

> both have psychobiological foundations that require lengthy social learning and reveal maturational changes; both are made up of many behavioral components which by implicit rules are combined into acceptable (or unacceptable) patterns of action; in both, the salience and meaning of any and all acts can be fully grasped only with complete knowledge of the cultural context in which they occur. (pp. 120–21)

Biological evolution has shaped the deep structure of sexual behavior in much the same way as it has, according to some linguists, shaped the deep structure of language (see Chapter 9). However, the vocabulary of sex (the specific customs of a people) may differ as widely from culture to culture as the vocabulary of language.

Pair-bonding in Humans — Marriage

Few, if any, other species invest more in their offspring than do humans. Females carry and nourish human fetuses for nine months before they are born, and the average human child requires more than a decade of care before reaching sexual maturity. Many children remain dependent on their parents for 20 or more years. We can safely say that raising children, until very recently in our evolutionary history, has required two parents. It is not therefore surprising that human males and females are unusual among mammals in their tendency to form long-term alliances (Lovejoy, 1981). There is no known human culture in which males and females do not establish formal partnerships based on maternity and paternity. And although biological dispositions lay the substructure for the basic unions established by all humans, culture determines the particular form the unions take.

If you examine the various cultures of the world, you find significant differences in the nature of the bonds we call marriage. In terms of number, most of the marriages formed among humans are monogamous; however, polygyny is the primary form marriage takes in most cultures (see Figure 8-4). In most polygynous societies, monogamy is a fallback option for men who cannot afford more than one wife. Consistent with the practices of other species, polyandry is rare among humans.

Why do some people practice monogamy and others practice polygyny? And why is polyandry practiced at all? From an evolutionary perspective, there is little difficulty explaining monogamy and polygyny. Monogamy should occur in egalitarian societies where resources are distributed relatively equally, the number of males

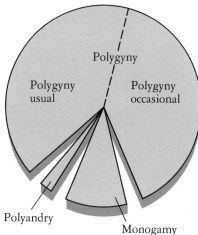

FIGURE 8-4

Human Mating Systems Of a sample of 849 societies studied by Murdock (1967), the majority were primarily polygymous. *Source:* Murdock, G. P. (1967). *Ethnographic atlas.* Pittsburg, PA: University of Pittsburg Press. Modified slightly from Daly, M., & Wilson, M. (1978). *Sex, evolution and behavior.* North Scituate, MA: Duxbury.

and females is approximately equal, and women have control over their marital choices. The biological decision faced by many women of other cultures is whether their offspring will be better off with an unmarried man with relatively few resources or with a married man with many resources. There is a high positive correlation between the number of wives of men in polygynous societies and their wealth and social status.

As it turns out, polyandry does not present as much of an exception as it seems. Most of the societies classified as polyandrous are legally but not biologically polyandrous. The purpose of these unions is to keep land in the family and to avoid inheritance taxes. Although several males may be legally married to the same woman, the woman does not have sex with them simultaneously, so there is little question of paternity. Further, virtually all males in polyandrous marriages are brothers. Finally, all societies that sanction polyandry also sanction polygyny and, indeed, may practice it simultaneously (producing group marriage, or *polygnandry*) (see Daly & Wilson, 1978, pp. 266–69).

Mate Selection

We have seen that, in general, females are more selective than males in the animal kingdom. What about humans? In general, males tend to take more initiative in courting than females, but not always. There is evidence that when females are able to choose their sexual partners, they are more discriminating than males; however, most of the females in the world do not have much choice about whom they marry. In most societies, fathers control the marriages of their daughters (Murdock, 1965); indeed, in effect, they sell their daughters to the highest bidder (see Figure 8-5). In the somewhat rare cases where a dowry is paid, the dowry remains with the newlyweds.

Studies investigating the criteria employed by males and females in the Western world for evaluating potential mates have revealed that females are more likely than males to base their preferences on such characteristics as earning power, career orientation, possession of a college degree, social status, and wealth; whereas males are more likely to base their preferences on only one characteristic — physical attractiveness (Buss, 1985). Studies investigating who marries whom have found significant positive correlations between physical attractiveness in females and occupational status in males, especially among females from working-class backgrounds (Elder, 1969). According to Buss (1987), these findings are consistent with evolutionary theory.

> Females, showing large parental investment and biological constraints on number of offspring, should select mates most capable of investing resources in their children. Males, investing less in offspring but being limited by access to reproductively valuable females, should seek females whose qualities closely correlate with reproductive value. In humans, this can be reduced largely to valuation of the strongly correlated features of earning power, status, and ambition in males and physical attractiveness in females. The data show strongly that males and females differentially value these attributes in potential mates. Furthermore, attractive females and high status males appear to

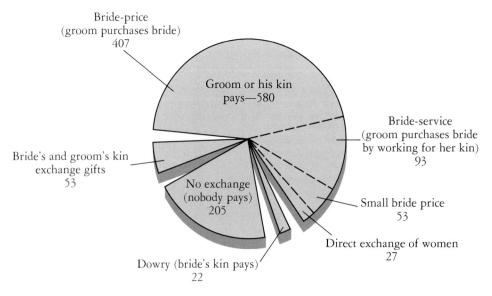

FIGURE 8-5

Bride-price A study of 860 societies reveals that bride-price ranges from no exchange in some societies to the payment of goods, money, or services in other societies. *Source:* Murdock, G. P. (1967). *Ethnographic atlas.* Pittsburg, PA: University of Pittsburg Press.

be able to command one another on the marriage market.

Reproduction

Humans have one of the lowest **reproductive rates** of all species, one of the longest **gestation periods** (surpassed only by such species as camels, giraffes, whales, and elephants), one of the longest **lactation periods,** and, as mentioned earlier, one of the longest durations of infant dependency.

During the past century, the industrialized countries of the West have been undergoing two highly significant changes: more women have been bearing children, but the number of children borne by the average woman has declined. In 1909, 23% of 35-year-old women in the United States were childless; in 1975, the figure had fallen to about 6% – 7%. As a result of these two trends, and for such other reasons as increasingly low mortality rates, there is extremely little variation in the number of offspring produced by American women. Since natural selection cannot operate without variation, it can be said that there is extremely little natural selection in the American population.

Premarital and Extramarital Sex

Although most sexual reproduction occurs within the bonds of marriage, in all cultures some people engage in **premarital** and **extramarital sexual relationships.** Cross-cultural studies have revealed that although there is a great deal of variation, premarital and extramarital relations are quite common in most cultures (see Table 8-4). In cultures that impose sanctions, punishment for transgressions tend to be more severe for females than for males — as is the case in our own society. For example, in many cultures brides-to-be must prove virginity. Unfortunately for many virgins, the typical virginity test in most preliterate societies — the presence of blood during first intercourse — is invalid. Among the Kurd, for example, women who did not bleed on their wedding night were subjected to public humiliation; whereas the husbands of those who passed the test paraded through the streets proudly displaying the bloodstained sheets. There are, however, some societies — such as East Bay — where men are held responsible and punished for premarital liaisons.

The double standard is also prevalent when it comes to extramarital sex: most cultures impose more severe sanctions on the wife than on the husband (see Table 8-5). According to evolutionary theorists, this double standard occurs because "maternity defines parenthood. A man can be cuckolded, whereas a woman cannot" (Daly & Wilson, 1978, p. 281). Cross-cultural surveys supply other evidence that males are less discriminating than females in their sexual behavior: the

TABLE 8-4

Percent of Cultures Surveyed in which Premarital and Extramarital Sex Occur in Varying Degrees

	Premarital*		Extramarital**	
	Males	**Females**	**Males**	**Females**
Very Common	60	49	13	13
Not Uncommon	18	17	56	45
Occasional	10	14	11	16
Uncommon	12	20	20	27

* Based on 186 cultures.

** Based on 56 cultures.

Source: Adapted from Mahoney, E. R. (1983). *Human sexuality.* New York: McGraw-Hill.
Data: Broude, G. J., & Green, S. J. (1976). Cross cultural codes on twenty sexual attitudes and practices, *Ethology, 15,* 409 – 29.

TABLE 8-5
Percent of Cultures that Demonstrate One of Four Patterns of Approval and Disapproval of Extramarital Sex

Pattern	Percent
Extramarital sex is allowed for both husband and wife.	11
Extramarital sex is allowed for the husband and condemned for the wife.	43
Extramarital sex is condemned for both sexes but the wife's activities are more severely punished.	22
Extramarital sex is condemned for both sexes and punishment is equally severe for both.	23

Source: Adapted from Mahoney, E. R. (1983). *Human sexuality.* New York: McGraw-Hill.
Data: Broude, G. J., & Green, S. J. (1976). Cross cultural codes on twenty sexual attitudes and practices, *Ethology, 15,* 409–29.

incidence of male homosexuality tends to be higher than the incidence of female homosexuality, males masturbate more than females, and males engage in more "perversions" (such as those that involve contact with animals) than do females.

Although most preliterate societies seem permissive by Western standards, it is important to note that permissiveness and preliteracy do not necessarily go together. Some preliterate societies impose extraordinarily severe prohibitions on sexual activity. For example, the early Manus considered sexual intercourse an abomination, even between husband and wife. They avoided the topic of sex in all of their discussions and engaged in sexual relations only in the highest secrecy. Manus believed that the spirits were aware of extramarital liaisons, that the spirits considered them criminal acts, and punished the guilty parties severely. It is not surprising that in such an atmosphere ignorance about sex would prevail—and indeed this was the case. For example, the men of the society were unaware that women menstruated and denied it vehemently when told.

It is, of course, difficult to obtain accurate information about the sexual practices of people of other cultures, but the data that anthropologists have been able to collect are consistent with two principles: males and females inherit somewhat different sexual dispositions and these dispositions are shaped into sexual practices by the customs, norms, and values of different cultures. Inherited tendencies steer females and males in the general directions that have been adaptive for their sex in their evolutionary past, but the precise form of their sexual behavior is determined by the socialization practices in the culture and by individual experiences.

SEX IN THE WESTERN WORLD

We opened this chapter with an examination of the sexual practices of animals from a variety of species and then narrowed our focus to the human species, examining the sexual practices of people from a variety of cultures. It is time to adjust our lens again, narrowing our focus to one of the many societies of humans—our own. We now examine the general trends in our culture, keeping in mind that the dominant attitudes, values, and practices are not internalized to the same extent by everyone. "In large, complex societies such as the United States, there is not a single culture of sex. Rather, there are many obvious subcultural differences that exert demonstrable effects on different segments of the society" (Davenport, 1977, pp. 118–19).

When the anthropologist Murdock (1949) compared the attitudes and practices of 60 cultures, he classified ours as one of the three most restrictive. Religion was an important force in shaping the sexual attitudes and practices of our forefathers. For example, in the early years of Roman Catholicism, celibacy was viewed as a chief virtue; sex was condoned only for the purpose of procreation, and sexual enjoyment was considered a sin. Remnants of this ambivalence are evident in contemporary society—but things have changed. Indeed, many writers have suggested that during the past three decades we have undergone a *sexual revolution,* citing as support an increasingly direct and casual approach to sex, the use of sex in advertising, the greater availability and popularity of pornography, the "pill," "free love," and the growing number of common-law relationships. Other writers have disagreed, arguing that people are behaving in much the same way they always did, only more openly.

THE *Kinsey Reports* AND THE *Hunt Survey*

Alfred C. Kinsey

The first large-scale investigation of the sexual attitudes and practices of people in America was conducted three decades ago by Alfred Kinsey, Ward Pomeroy, Clyde Martin, and Paul Gebhard. Kinsey and his colleagues interviewed more than 16,000 people, with Kinsey himself interviewing more than 7,000 subjects. The general goal of Kinsey's research was to determine how often people in America have sex and what forms of sexual behavior they practice. More precisely, Kinsey attempted to determine how often the people in his sample reached orgasm through heterosexual intercourse (which he divided into such categories as marital, extramarital, premarital, intercourse with prostitutes), masturbation, oral-genital sex, anal sex, homosexuality, petting to climax, nocturnal emissions ("wet dreams"), and animal contacts. Kinsey determined the incidence of these practices for people of different age, sex, marital status, and educational background, thereby attending, in part, to subcultural differences. Kinsey and his colleagues published their findings in two books: *Sexual Behavior in the Human Male* (1948) and *Sexual Behavior in the Human Female* (1953).

In 1972, the Playboy Foundation commissioned a nationwide survey of the sexual attitudes and practices of 2,026 randomly selected adults in 24 cities across the United States. The survey was conducted by the Research Guild Inc., an independent research organization. Professional journalist Morton Hunt and his wife, Bernice Kohn, interviewed an additional 200 subjects in greater depth. The *Hunt Survey* represents the most comprehensive investigation of the sexual attitudes and behaviors of a large sample of subjects since Kinsey's reports, although some more recent surveys have investigated particular sexual practices in selected groups in even greater depth.

We compare the results in the Kinsey and Hunt surveys to obtain an idea of the sexual behavior of typical Americans and to see whether sexual practices in America have changed in any significant ways since Kinsey's survey. However, bear in mind that both surveys are limited in certain respects. First, neither survey obtained a representative sample of people. In the Hunt Survey, four of every five people contacted initially by telephone refused to participate. Critics have argued that people who volunteer to participate in sex surveys are different from people who do not. Second, critics have argued that people are not inclined to tell strangers the truth about their sex lives. Third, however valid the results of the *Kinsey Reports* and the *Hunt Survey* are in themselves, the two surveys are not directly comparable. They tested different samples of people, asked different questions, and used different procedures for gathering data. In particular, the primary data from the Kinsey study came from indepth interviews, whereas the primary data from the Hunt study came from a written questionnaire. Yet, in spite of these limitations, it is generally agreed that the *Kinsey Reports* and the *Hunt Survey* supply the best available evidence on the sexual attitudes and practices of people in America.

Frequency of Total Outlet

The average number of **orgasms** per week reported by white males aged 18–85 interviewed by Kinsey was about three (see Figure 8-6). Kinsey did not report a comparable figure for females; however, he estimated that most females between the ages of 26 and 45 experience an average of about one and one-half orgasms every week (see Figure 8-7). It is important to recognize that such figures as three orgasms per week represent average group scores and not the typical behavior of the average person. As shown in Figures 8-6 and 8-7, there is considerable variation in

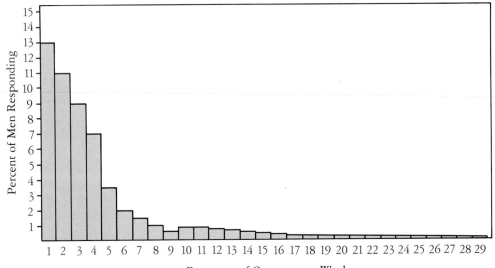

FIGURE 8-6

Percent of Men Reporting Various Numbers of Orgasms per Week The number of orgasms most frequently experienced by males is one per week; however, only 13% of males reported this number. The larger the number of orgasms reported, the lower the percent of men reporting it. *Source:* Kinsey, A. C., Pomeroy, W. B., & Martin, C. E. (1948). *Sexual behavior in the human male* (p. 198). Philadelphia, PA: Saunders.

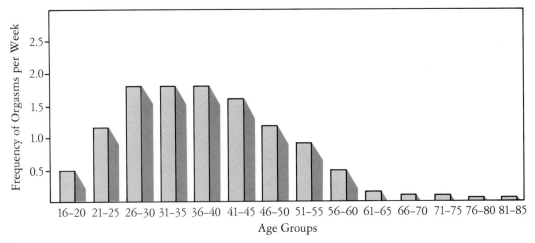

FIGURE 8-7

Average Frequency of Orgasms for Women of Various Age Groups The highest average number of orgasms is less than two per week for women between the ages of 26 and 45. Younger and older women tend to experience fewer than one orgasm per week. *Source:* Kinsey, A. C., Pomeroy, W. B., Martin, C. E., & Gebhard, P. H. (1953). *Sexual behavior in the human female* (p. 548). Philadelphia, PA: Saunders.

the number of orgasms experienced by the men and women interviewed by Kinsey.

The Sexual Behavior of Single Women and Men

Kinsey found significant differences in patterns of sexual behavior between married and single women, and so analyzed each group separately. As shown in Figure 8-8, young single women reported achieving orgasm most often through masturbation. With age, coitus replaced masturbation as the primary source of orgasm. Petting to climax and homosexuality peaked between ages 31–40. The educational level of women was not a particularly important source of difference in their sexual behavior. In contrast, as revealed in Figures 8-9 and 8-10, Kinsey found significant differences in the sexual behavior of men of different educational levels. For example, college-educated men reported that they engaged in sexual intercourse with companions and prostitutes

less frequently than did men with elementary school educations, relying more on masturbation.

Marital Sex

Kinsey found that young married couples engage in sexual relations more frequently than older married couples. Married couples aged 16–25 reported that they had sexual intercourse about two and one-half times per week compared to less than once a week (0.85) for couples aged 45–55. In a more recent survey, Hunt found that the rate reported by 18 to 24-year-olds had increased to about three and one-half times per week and the rate for 44 to 54-year-olds was about once per week. Aside from frequency, the most notable change in marital sex over the past several decades appears to be the use of a greater variety of techniques. For example, the husbands and wives interviewed by Hunt reported spending more time at foreplay and intercourse, utilizing a greater variety of positions, and engaging in more

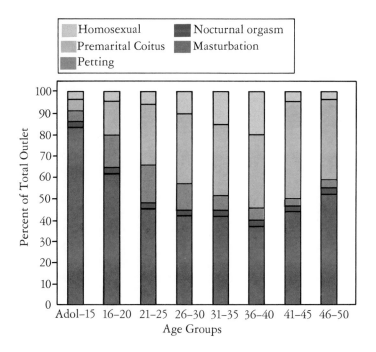

FIGURE 8-8

Sources of Orgasm among Single Females   The most frequent source of orgasm for the single women interviewed by Kinsey was masturbation, with premarital coitus second in frequency. Petting to climax occurred most frequently in women from 16–30 years of age. Achieving orgasm with another woman increased in frequency from adolescence until age 36–40, then diminished significantly. *Source:* Kinsey, et al. (1953). *Sexual behavior in the human female* (p. 562). Philadelphia, PA: Saunders.

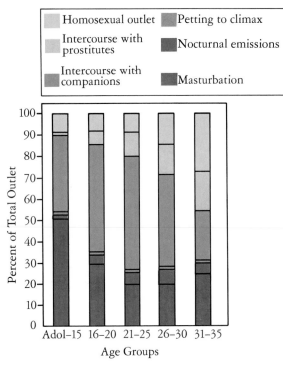

FIGURE 8-9
Sources of Orgasm among Elementary-school-Educated Single Men The most frequent source of orgasm reported by single males with an elementary-school education interviewed by Kinsey was intercourse with a female companion, followed by masturbation (especially among adolescents), and intercourse with prostitutes (especially among older men). Homosexuality tended to increase with age. *Source:* Kinsey, A. C., Pomeroy, W. B. & Martin, C. E. (1948). *Sexual behavior in the human male* (p. 490). Philadelphia, PA: Saunders.

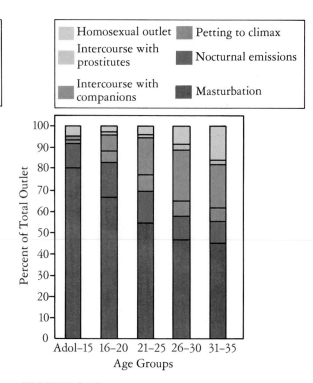

FIGURE 8-10
Sources of Orgasm among College-educated Single Men The most frequent source of orgasm reported by single males with a college education interviewed by Kinsey was masturbation. Nocturnal emissions accounted for approximately ten percent of the orgasms of males in this sample. Adolescents rarely reported achieving orgasms with female companions, but this source became the second-most frequent by age 21. Homosexuality increased with age. *Source:* Kinsey, A. C., et al. (1948). *Sexual behavior in the human male* (p. 491). Philadelphia, PA: Saunders.

oral-genital and anal intercourse than those interviewed by Kinsey.

Premarital Sex

Kinsey reported that by age 25, one-third of the women he interviewed had engaged in premarital sexual intercourse—a statistic that shocked many of his contemporaries. Among men, the range extended from 68% for college-educated men to 98% for elementary-school-educated men. Hunt reported a much higher incidence of premarital intercourse for young people of both sexes—about 75% for 18 to 24-year-old single females and 90–95% for 18 to 24-year-old

males. However, this apparent increase in premarital sex did not apply to older women; only 36% of the women aged 35–54 reported having premarital sexual experience.

Several recent studies have investigated the incidence of premarital sex among adolescents and college students. On the basis of a careful review of the surveys conducted between the 1930s and the 1970s, Hopkins (1977) maintains that three conclusions are warranted. First, college students are more sexually active and sexually experienced than those of previous generations. Second, there has been a greater increase in the incidence of premarital intercourse for women than for men, although the absolute incidence for men remains higher. Third, there is a general trend toward earlier sexual experience.

The diminishing gap between the frequency of premarital sex in males and females appears to reflect a loosening of the double standard that is so prevalent in other cultures and that has long held sway in our own. The **double standard** prescribes that premarital sex is acceptable — even necessary — for men, but that women are expected to preserve their virginity until marriage. One reason why the double standard is declining is because reliable methods of birth control have reduced greatly the fear of unwanted pregnancy and, thus, provided a degree of female sexual freedom not possible in the past.

Permissiveness with Affection   The increased incidence of premarital sex among young women does not necessarily signal an increase in **promiscuity.** Kinsey found that the majority of women who engaged in premarital sex reported engaging in it either with the one man they loved and intended to marry (40%) or with a man they loved and just one other man (40–45%). The *Hunt Survey* suggests that this norm is equally true of young women today. Only 8% of the women in Hunt's sample reported engaging in premarital sex exclusively with men they did not intend to marry. Reiss (1960) has described the trend as "permissiveness with affection." Research suggests that the changes in values associated with the increase in premarital sex do not reflect a greater tolerance for promiscuity. For example, Janda et al. (1981) found that female college students who do not limit intercourse to relationships involving a strong degree of affection were viewed negatively by both male and female peers (see Table 8-6).

Extramarital Sex

One standard that appears to have undergone virtually no change since Kinsey's time relates to marital fidelity. Contrary to popular belief, the overall rate of extramarital sex does not seem to have increased. The overall figures presented by both Kinsey and Hunt are very similar. From 30–40% of the men and from 18–20% of the women in both samples, aged 35–44, reported engaging in extramarital sex. The sex difference is consistent with the trend in most other cul-

TABLE 8-6

Percent of College Students who Approve of Sex in Various Kinds of Relationship*

Type of Relationship between the Two Partners	Males	Females
Married to each other	100	99
Engaged to each other	90	83
In love with each other	85	74
Not in love, but really like each other	67	42
Friends	42	13
Casual aquaintances	34	9
Do not know each other	37	7

* Although males report a somewhat greater tolerance for premarital sex than do females, the best predictor of approval is the nature of the relationship between the two partners.
Source: Adapted from Mahoney, E. R. (1979). *Patterns of sexual behavior among college students.* Unpublished research report. Bellingham, WA: Western Washington University, Department of Sociology.

tures. There does, however, appear to have been one change in America since Kinsey's time: for women under 25 the rate of extramarital affairs has increased threefold (from 8% to 24%). Although this increase appears to reflect a culturally sanctioned break with the double standard, it does not appear to reflect a change in attitudes toward marital fidelity. From 80–90% of the couples surveyed by Hunt expressed disapproval of extramarital relations. In a more recent survey, Davis (1980) found that 70% of individuals surveyed felt that extramarital sex is always wrong — a figure comparable to earlier figures. Interestingly, younger respondents expressed as much disapproval of extramarital sex as did older respondents, even though they were more likely to engage in it (Edwards & Booth, 1976). Other surveys have found that both men and women are significantly more tolerant of extramarital relations in males than in females (Schoof-Tams, Schlaegel, & Walczak, 1976).

Most people who have extramarital affairs do not appear to enjoy them. Hunt found that they described them as less free, less varied, and less satisfying than sex within marriage. Only 39% of the women surveyed said they were able to experience orgasm outside marriage, compared to 53% who reported experiencing orgasm within marriage. Hunt concluded that the vast majority of adults continue to maintain the traditional conviction that sex and marriage go together.

One of the most pronounced changes that has occurred in America during the past three decades is the frequency of divorce and the increase in sexual activity among those who are divorced or widowed. Only a small percentage of the widowed or divorced men and women who took part in the Hunt study said they had been sexually inactive within the last year. Divorced men averaged about eight sexual partners a year and divorced women about three and one-half. Both men and women averaged about two sexual interactions a week — a fourfold increase over the frequency reported by Kinsey. More recent studies (for example, Zeiss & Zeiss, 1979; Cargan, 1981)

report similar frequencies. However, it is important to note that the sexual relations of divorced people tend to be sequential — divorced people tend to date only one partner at a time (Zeiss & Zeiss, 1979).

Masturbation

Most of us are familiar with the justifications that have been used traditionally in our society as prohibitions against **masturbation.** They range from religious injunctions (masturbation is a sin against God) to warnings of physical or mental debilitation (blindness or even insanity; see Box 8-1). Although we know now that masturbation is not related to physical or mental deterioration in any direct way, the taboo against it still evokes

---

Box 8-1
NAIVE JUSTIFICATIONS OF SEXUAL PROHIBITIONS

People from a wide range of preliterate and modern cultures justify their belief that humans should show sexual restraint by claiming that sex, especially in excess, causes physical weakness and ill health. In the early part of the present century in our society, it was commonly assumed that masturbation caused warts or blindness. In the nineteenth century, the belief that sexual excesses caused physical maladies was even more prevalent.

Consider, for example, this quote from a certain Graham, the inventor of Graham crackers.

Husbands and wives who over indulged in sex would

soon be afflicted with languor, lassitude, muscular relaxation, general debility and heaviness, depression of spirits, loss of appetite, indigestion, faintness and sinking at the pit of the stomach, increased susceptibilities of the skin and lungs to all the atmospheric changes, feebleness of circulation, chilliness, headache, melancholy, hypochondria, hysterics, feebleness of all the senses, impaired vision, loss of sight, weakness of the lungs, nervous cough, pulmonary consumption, disorders of the liver and kidneys, urinary difficulties, disorders of the genital organs, spinal diseases, weakness of the brain, loss of memory, epilepsy, insanity, apoplexy:—abortions,

premature births, and extreme feebleness, morbid predispositions, and early death of offspring. (Graham, 1948, pp. 82–84)

Although we may smirk at Graham's ignorance, the remnants of his assumptions influence the behavior of many people in our society today. Witness, for example, the popular practice of restricting the sexual activity of athletes before important contests. It seems reasonable to suspect that the belief that sexual excesses cause illness is more an attempt to supply an acceptable justification for a deeply entrenched attitude than a real reason in itself.

strong feelings of guilt and anxiety in many people. Nevertheless, most people masturbate.

Kinsey reported that 92% of the men and 58% of the women he interviewed had masturbated at some time in their lives. Most males reported masturbating by age 15 and there was a steady increase in the number of females who reported masturbating from age 5 to 35. The figures reported by Hunt (94% and 62%, respectively) are remarkably similar to those reported by Kinsey; however, there appear to have been some changes since Kinsey's time. Masturbation appears to be initiated at an earlier age (see Figure 8-11) and to be practiced more regularly by adult women. The *Hite Report* (1977), which surveyed the sexual practices and attitudes of 1,844 women, found that 82% of the women who responded to the survey reported masturbating with some regularity. Of particular interest is Hite's finding that almost all (95%) of the women said that they were able to achieve orgasm easily and

regularly through masturbation (compared to only 31% who regularly reached orgasm during heterosexual foreplay and intercourse). Because the report has been criticized severely on methodological grounds, the Hite figures should be accepted only tentatively. Nevertheless, these numbers suggest that the practice of masturbation has gained much greater acceptance as a legitimate form of sexual behavior among American women and that it may lead to orgasm more consistently than sexual intercourse.

A Sexual Revolution?

The findings of Kinsey, Hunt, and others suggest that various sexual practices have become increasingly acceptable in our society and, in particular, that many of the restrictions on women's sexual behavior have been eased. At the same time, they indicate that the traditional values that discourage the separation of sex from love and marriage seem firmly entrenched. For those with traditional sexual attitudes, the apparent trend toward greater permissiveness is a matter of concern; indeed, some have interpreted it as a sign of moral and social decay. On the other hand, less traditionally oriented people have welcomed increased sexual permissiveness as a necessary and long-awaited move toward a more enlightened and more rational approach to one of humanity's most basic and important means of expression and fulfillment. Still others — perhaps the majority — have reacted to the changes with ambivalence and with a certain amount of confusion.

Although sex is discussed more openly and although information about sex is more readily available today than it has been in past years, many individuals still experience conflict, confusion, and guilt about sex (see Figure 8-12). Major differences in expectations about appropriate male and female sexual behavior still exist. Premarital female chastity is still expected by many men and women. Religious beliefs and family values also continue to be powerful determinants of sexual behavior in both sexes. At the same time, there are increasing social pressures on many young people to accept more liberal standards and to avoid appearing old-fashioned or narrow-minded. In this sense, North America has been described as a sexually polarized society (see Kirkendall & Whitehurst, 1971, p. 2).

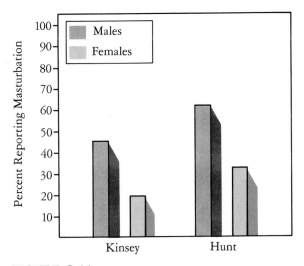

FIGURE 8-11
Percent of Males and Females who Reported Masturbating before Age 13 — Kinsey versus Hunt More males than females reported masturbating before age 13 in both the Kinsey and Hunt surveys. However, the frequency increased only by about one-third for males and almost one-half for females in the Hunt survey. *Sources:* Adapted from Hunt, M. (1974). *Sexual behavior in the 1970s.* Chicago: Playboy Press. Kinsey, A. C., Pomeroy, W. B., & Martin C. E. (1948). *Sexual behavior in the human male* (p. 502). Philadelphia, PA: Saunders. Kinsey, A. C., Pomeroy, W. B., & Martin, C. E. (1953). *Sexual behavior in the human female* (p. 141). Philadelphia, PA: Saunders.

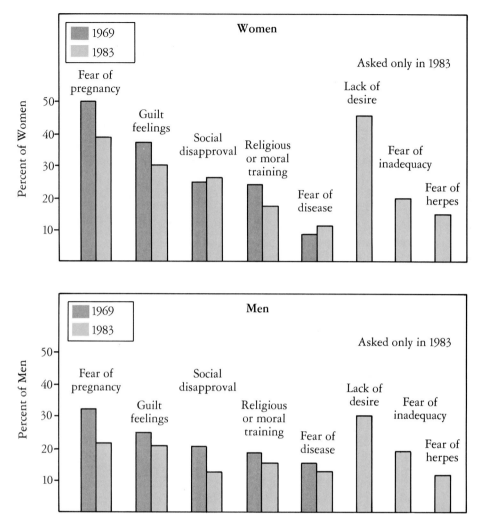

FIGURE 8-12

Reasons Given for Sexual Problems These data were obtained from surveys conducted in 1969 and 1983 that asked women and men to state why they did not freely express their sexuality. Fear of pregnancy was the most popular reason in 1969, especially for women. Lack of desire and guilt feelings were stated as often as or more often than fear of pregnancy in 1983. *Source: Psychology Today,* July 1983, p. 47.

THE SOCIALIZATION OF SEXUAL BEHAVIOR

Biologically based sexual dispositions are shaped by three main factors: the norms and values of a culture and its subcultures, social roles, and individual learning experiences. Children are exposed to the norms and values of their culture and, in most cases, internalize them as their own. Young children learn the meaning of sex from older children and from adults — directly, through the things they preach, and indirectly, by the models implicit in their behavior. As detailed in Chapter 10, from the time they are born, children are taught to behave like members of their sex, but pressure to adopt an appropriate sex role becomes particularly acute during adolescence. Typically, the learning environments of males and females differ in significant ways.

One way to view the socialization of sexual behavior is in terms of **sexual scripts** — sequences of acceptable behavior in familiar settings. Sexual scripts are analogous to the scripts of plays and movies, except they are more abstract and flexible. A script is like the basic structure of a musical score, which musicians may adapt to different instruments and improvise upon in varying ways. People generally learn scripts without being consciously aware that they are learning them; scripts are simply the way it is done. Sexual scripts supply general guidelines for what sex involves, where it takes place, when it is appropriate, who is an eligible sex partner, and why it happens. In the Western world, the dominant sexual script involves foreplay and intercourse between consenting adults in a bedroom with a partner of the opposite sex with whom one has an ongoing relationship. The purpose of sex is to produce children, to express love, and/or to relieve sexual tension. But there are many subgroups in the Western world that learn different scripts. Sex may involve practices other than coitus, people other than adults, and places other than the bedroom. Individuals may form homosexual relationships; adults may go to prostitutes; couples may swap partners; people may practice *S and M* (sadism and masochism). All these practices and many more are guided by the sexual scripts of the subcultures or groups involved.

Sexual Socialization in Childhood

In our culture, most adults assume that children are either not interested in sex or that they shouldn't be. The socialization of sexual behavior seems to entail as much suppressing and distorting information as it does teaching the "facts of life." A strikingly small proportion of children learn about sex from their parents and from other socializing agents (see Figure 8-13). Adults tend not to use sexual words when talking to children, often avoiding even the words that label their genital organs. As far as children can perceive, their genitals are for "peeing," or "number 1" — unnamed or "dirty" functions. When children touch their genitals, many parents indicate undefined disapproval by saying such things as "Don't do *that*"; when children ask such questions as "Where do babies come from?" many parents

avoid answering ("Ask your father/mother") or give incorrect information ("The stork"). Words that refer to or describe sexual acts are often spoken as swear words, included in "dirty" jokes, or employed in a negative context.

The manner in which children are socialized about sex in our culture has four primary consequences. First, it makes sex a "forbidden fruit," whetting children's curiosity and, perhaps, their appetites for it. Second, it encourages children to fantasize about this fascinating but mysterious matter, letting their imaginations fill in the many gaps in their knowledge. Third, it leads to the development of misconceptions that are fostered and exacerbated in conversations with other equally misinformed and imaginative children. For example, Petras (1973) describes a women who feared she had become pregnant because she had fallen asleep next to a man on a bus — and therefore "slept with him." Mosher (1979) found that 55% of a sample of males and 43% of a sample of females thought people could become stuck together during intercourse and that 40% of the males and 23% of the females thought the probability of pregnancy greater if partners experience mutual orgasm. Finally, some children grow up thinking that sex is dirty and shameful. Most children are appalled to discover that their parents actually "did it" and refuse even to entertain the idea that they still might be "doing it" (see Table 8-7).

In spite of their cultural constraints, most children eventually acquire reasonably accurate information about sex. Natural curiosity appears to prevail over cultural inhibitions. And, of course, many children experiment with sex. In a study conducted in 1969, Elias and Gebhard found that among the white American males aged 4–14 they surveyed, 52% had experimented sexually with a same sex peer, 34% had engaged in some form of sex play with a member of the opposite sex, and 56% had masturbated. Comparable figures for females were 35% for homosexual activity, 37% for heterosexual activity, and 30% for masturbation.

Sexual Guilt

Although, in general, our culture tends to be restrictive, some parents are more restrictive than

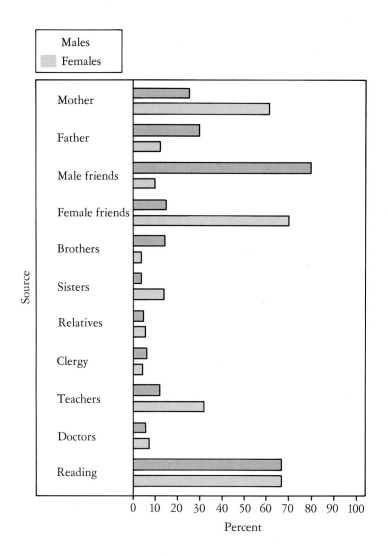

FIGURE 8-13

Where Children Learn about Sex   Children's primary sources of information about sex are friends and books.   Girls learn more about sex from their mothers than boys do and boys learn more about sex from their fathers than girls do.   *Source:* Spanier, G. B. (1977).   Sources of sex information and premarital sexual behavior. *Journal of Sex Research,* 13, 73–88.

others.   One recognized consequence of exposure to prohibitive and/or punitive attitudes and practices is **sexual guilt** (Abramson et al., 1977), defined as "a general expectation that an individual has to experience self-induced punishment for approaching or thinking about sex" (Mosher, 1968).   Sexual guilt is a personality characteristic measurable by a personality test (Mosher, 1961, 1968).

Investigators have found that people who are high in sexual guilt experience strong nega-tive feelings when they think about, are exposed to, or become involved in sex.   As we would expect, people high in sexual guilt are aroused less by sexual stimuli, are more likely to avoid sexually arousing situations, and are more likely to deny the existence of sexual desire than people low in sexual guilt (see Figure 8-14) (Gibbons, 1978; Mosher & White, 1980).   People high in sexual guilt tend to have traditional moral standards, tend to avoid erotic stimuli, and are disinclined to perceive sexual meanings in things.

TABLE 8-7
Students' Conceptions of their Parents' Sexual Behaviors*

Sexual Behavior	Daughters Thinking Mothers Had Engaged in Behavior (%)	Kinsey Findings Mother's Generation Had Engaged in Behavior (%)	Sons Thinking Fathers Had Engaged in Behavior (%)	Kinsey Findings Father's Generation Had Engaged in Behavior (%)
Premarital petting	63	99	81	89
Premarital intercourse	10	50	45	92
Extramarital intercourse	2	26	12	50
Oral-genital sex	25	49	34	59
Masturbation	31	62	73	93

* The results of a survey of 646 college students' conceptions of their parents' sexual behaviors were compared with findings of a Kinsey report concerning people of the parental age group. The comparison revealed that sons and daughters underestimated the frequency with which their parents had engaged in all types of sexual behaviors, especially premarital and extramarital sex.
Source: Adapted from Pocs, O., & Godow, A. G. (1977). Can students view parents as sexual beings? *The Family Coordinator,* 26, 31–36.

They tend to avoid premarital sex and are restrictive in terms of the behaviors in which they engage when they do have sex (Mosher & Cross, 1971). It might be expected that feelings of guilt resulting from early negative learning diminish as individuals undergo positive sexual experiences. However, one study found that when "high sex guilt subjects are exposed to situations which are systematically stimulating, their levels of guilt and anxiety are increased creating a cycle of guilt, punishment, and further inhibition of behavior to avoid guilt" (Lenes & Hart, 1975, p. 447). Interestingly, during the past decade the level of sexual guilt in America appears to be declining steadily among college students (Abramson & Handschumacher, 1978).

Sexual Socialization in Adolescence

At the onset of adolescence, boys and girls develop the bodies of men and women and they acquire the capacity for reproductive sex. The physical and hormonal changes that occur during adolescence are problematic for adolescents in our society because our norms do not permit unmarried adolescents to engage in the sexual be-havior for which they have become biologically prepared. If the central focus of the sexual socialization of children is on the avoidance of sexual issues, the central focus of the sexual socialization of adolescents is on **sex roles** (see

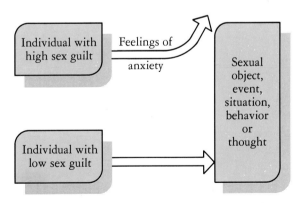

FIGURE 8-14
Sexual Guilt Individuals with high sexual guilt feel anxious when presented with sexual stimuli. Consequently, they avoid sexually arousing objects, events, and so forth, and deny the existence of their sexual desires. *Source:* Mahoney, E. R. (1983). *Human sexuality.* New York: McGraw-Hill.

Box 8-2
Sexually Transmitted Diseases

Over the past two decades, during which birth control pills and intrauterine devices (IUDs) have replaced condoms as the most popular methods of contraception, there has been a drastic increase in venereal — sexually transmitted — diseases. It is sobering to realize that in the United States **nongonococcal urethritis (NGU)** and **gonorrhea** are the two most-common infectious diseases, and that **syphilis** is fourth. The third most-common infectious disease is the common cold! In addition, it is estimated that no less than 20 million Americans have some form of **herpes,** and acquired immune deficiency syndrome **(AIDS)** is becoming an epidemic, at least among high-risk groups.

Gonorrhea

Gonorrhea is the oldest recorded sexually transmitted disease. It was named by the Greek physician Galen in 140 B.C. after the Greek words *gonos,* meaning *seed* and *rhoia,* meaning *flow.* Galen mistakenly thought that the fluid discharged from the urethra (the canal that carries off urine from the bladder) of most men

who contract gonorrhea was semen.

Like NGU and syphilis, gonorrhea is caused by a contagious bacterium; in the case of gonorrhea the bacterium is called the **gonococcus.** The bacteria usually are passed from an infected individual to another individual through genital–genital contact, but they also may be passed through oral–genital and anal–genital contact. Indeed, gonorrhea may be contracted from a toilet seat or towel (especially a wet one), although nonsexual sources are rare. The chance of contracting gonorrhea

through sex with an infected individual is about 33%.

It is very difficult to obtain precise estimates of the incidence of sexually transmitted diseases. Public health officials believe that only about 25% of the cases are ever reported. The figure displays the number of reported cases of gonorrhea and syphilis in the United States from 1950 to 1976. The figure shows that the incidence of gonorrhea increased far faster than the incidence of syphilis (although there is evidence that the incidence of gonorrhea is beginning to level off). The reason for the difference in

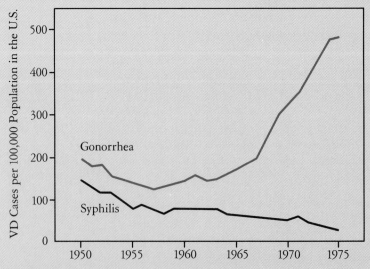

Rates of Syphilis and Gonorrhea (1950–1975) *Source:* Adapted from Mahoney, E. R. (1983). *Human sexuality.* New York: McGraw-Hill.

rates probably stems from the fact that gonorrhea is more difficult to diagnose and to treat than syphilis.

Gonorrhea is most prevalent among people between the ages of 15 and 30. About 85% of the males who contract gonorrhea display symptoms within the first two weeks, compared to only about 15–20% of the females. Because women may unknowingly pass the disease on to others and because they may fail to obtain treatment, gonorrhea is much more dangerous in women. It follows that men who discover they have the disease have a special moral obligation to inform the female(s) with whom they have had sex.

The first symptom of gonorrhea in males is a thin clear or yellow discharge from the urethral opening in the penis that becomes thicker, creamier, and usually yellower within a day or two. Males may experience a burning sensation during urination and the urine may contain pus or blood. When women display symptoms, the most common is a thick yellow-green vaginal discharge that originates from the cervix. In some cases the infection may spread to the urethra, causing a burning sensation during urination. If the infection is not treated — in males and females — it spreads internally to such other organs as the prostate, bladder, lymph glands, and uterus, and then to the joints, heart, and spine. Approximately 50% of untreated women become sterile and the disease may affect the newborn children of infected mothers. In the "old days," many children of infected women were born blind; however, the common practice of putting silver nitrate or an antibiotic in the eyes of newborn infants has largely controlled this tragic consequence.

There are two primary methods of detecting gonorrhea, through a blood test and through an analysis of the discharge from the penis or vagina. In the 1960s, gonorrhea was treated with relatively mild injections of the antibiotic penicillin, but the gonococcal bacterium developed a resistance to it. Today large doses of penicillin or other more powerful antibiotics supply effective early-stage treatments.

Nongonococcal Urethritis (NGU)

NGU is a generic term for inflammations of the urethra not caused by gonococcal bacteria. The primary symptom of NGU is a thin white discharge from the urethra. Most sexually transmitted diseases treated in college health services are of this nature. It is estimated the incidence of NGU is at least twice as great nationwide as that of gonorrhea and syphilis. Indeed, the most prevalent type of NGU, **Chlamydia,** appears to be increasing to epidemic proportions. Although this type of bacterium is generally transmitted sexually, it also may be transmitted through nonsexual contact. The bacteria that cause NGU may be resistant to penicillin, but they succumb to other antibiotics.

Syphilis

Although syphilis is more familiar to most people than is gonorrhea, syphilis is less prevalent (see figure). It is most prevalent among 20- to 30-year-old males, and males are approximately three times as likely to contract it than are females.

Although syphilis is less prevalent than gonorrhea, it is highly contagious; there is about a 50% chance of contracting it through intercourse with an infected partner. Four stages have been identified in the development of syphilis. Within ten days to three months following contact with an infected partner, males usually develop a **chancre** (pronounced *shank-er*) on the glans of the penis. The chancre may

(continued on next page)

(continued from pp. 374–375) resemble a pimple or a small crater, and is not painful. In females the chancre is usually not visible because it develops on the walls of the vagina or cervix. Oral or anal intercourse with an infected person may give rise to chancres on the mouth or anus. If untreated, the chancre will go away within from one to five weeks after it appears.

The second stage begins within a month or two after the disappearance of the chancre, when the infection moves into the bloodstream. The primary symptom of the second stage is a nonitchy rash. Approximately 25% of people infected with syphilis also develop a fever, head-aches, and/or sore throat, ex-perience fatigue and nausea, constipation, sore joints, and hair loss. Because many of these symptoms are symp-toms of other diseases, syphilis has been called the *great imitator*. The second stage usually lasts from two to six weeks only.

Although the third stage seems innocuous — there are no symptoms — the infection continues to spread. After the first year or so, the disease is no longer conta-gious but a pregnant woman may still pass it on to a fetus. From 50–66% of the people who enter the third stage remain in it for the rest of their lives, experiencing

no further complications. The remaining 33–50%, however, may reenter earlier stages and, eventually, enter the fourth stage. In the fourth stage, the bacteria destroy internal organs and structures — causing heart, liver, and lung ailments, blindness, bone damage, brain damage, and death.

As with all sexually transmitted diseases, the ear-lier syphilis is treated, the better. Syphilis may be detected through a blood test and is usually responsive to treatment by antibiotics, such as penicillin.

Herpes

Unlike the bacterial diseases we have been discussing, herpes is a virus, and as such, at the time of writing, is unresponsive to treatment. The word herpes is derived from *herpein,* which means "to creep," and this is an apt description of the virus. There are five kinds of herpes. Type I is well-known as the common cold sore or fever blister. Type II is sexually transmitted through oral, anal, or genital contact. The symptoms of herpes include fluid-filled blisters that resemble cold sores and that erupt and spread within 10 to 20 days of formation. These painful sores usually form on the penis or the labia, clitoris, thighs, buttocks, and cervix,

and appear from two days to three weeks after contact with an infected person. The herpes virus invade ganglia in the spinal cord, where they may lie dormant for indeterminant periods of time. In approximately 80% of herpes carriers, the virus reactivates, traveling back along the nerves to the skin, where they produce painful sores. Herpes seems to erupt in carriers during times of stress, menstruation, sexual activity, and exposure to the sun, and there is some indication that herpes may be linked to cancer. Ap-proximately 20 million Americans suffer from herpes, which constitutes approximately 13% of all veneral diseases. Although as a general rule people with herpes should not have sex with people who do not have herpes, Type II herpes can be transmitted sexually by the carrier only when he or she is inflicted with the sores. In other words, when no sign of the virus exists, it is dormant and cannot be transmitted. But if you contract it, you have it for life.

AIDS

Although AIDS appears to be sexually transmitted, no one knows for sure how it is acquired. And although the incidence of AIDS is low compared to other sexually transmitted diseases (in

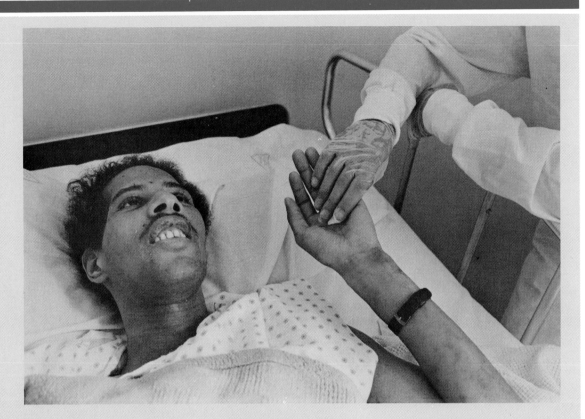

1986, approximately 15,000 Americans had the disease and another 11,500 showed symptoms; now between 1 and 2 million are susceptible), it is significantly more deadly. About 86% of AIDS sufferers die within three years of diagnosis (Time, 1986).

Most people with AIDS are male, and approximately three-fourths of them are homosexual. AIDS also infects drug addicts, recipients of blood transfusions, and hemophiliacs, and — more recently — women. Moreover, it appears to be disproportionately high in Haitian immigrants.

As its name indicates, AIDS breaks down the processes that render people immune to disease, especially the T-lymphocytes — a type of white blood cell that fights parasites, viruses, fungi, and other infectious organisms. Because of lowered immunity, AIDS sufferers initially display such symptoms of other disorders as fatigue, fever, diarrhea, swollen lymph glands, and a recurrence of such virus infections as herpes, colds, and the flu. Eventually, AIDS victims develop more serious disorders that cause their death.

It is thought that AIDS is transmitted through such body fluids as semen, saliva, mucus, blood, and perhaps sweat and tears. There is no evidence that anyone has contracted AIDS except through intimate contact or through an infusion of someone else's blood. Among homosexuals it is almost certainly transmitted sexually, and the most sexually active homosexuals seem to be at greatest risk. The incubation period for AIDS is estimated to extend from two months to approximately two years.

Chapter 10). Following the development at puberty of **secondary sexual characteristics** (see Chapter 9), boys are encouraged to begin acting like men and girls are encouraged to act like women.

In our culture, there are significant differences in the sexual socialization of males and females. In general, males are encouraged to adopt a quantitatively oriented, genital, and even somewhat predatory approach to sex; females are encouraged to be more quality oriented, interpersonal, and selective (see Gross, 1978). There are, of course, significant differences in the orientations of different people. Salient in the sexual orientation of adolescent males is the desire to "score" (Mahoney, 1983). When they do, they are more likely than females to brag about it to their friends (Carns, 1973). Males tend to praise peers who have their first sexual experiences with physically attractive females; females are more likely to praise peers who have their first sexual experiences with a loved fiancé (Mendelsohn & Mosher, 1979). Adolescent males tend to think about sex in physical terms, orienting to aspects of the female body and characterizing sexual acts in aggressive-dominant four-letter terms. In contrast, females orient to interpersonal characteristics and relationships, characterizing sex in such terms as "making love" (Walsh & Leonard, 1974). To the typical adolescent male, sex focuses on the physical act of intercourse and the genitals; sex is goal-oriented and is viewed in terms of a sequence that leads to orgasm. For the typical adolescent female, sex is more diffuse, involving the whole body and the whole person. For example, Houston (1981) found that males tend to view kissing as a preliminary activity, whereas females tend to enjoy it in and of itself. Adolescent females are less likely to achieve orgasm than adolescent males. Indeed, one investigator found that 33% of the adolescent females he interviewed didn't even know whether or not they had ever experienced an orgasm (Hass, 1979).

One of the defining aspects of the male sex role in America is dominance and control; males are expected to initiate sexual encounters and to guide the flow of events (Allgeier, 1981). As a consequence, many males react negatively when

"Women kiss women good night. Men kiss women good night. But men do not kiss men good night—especially in Armonk."

Drawing by Handelsman; ©1979 The New Yorker Magazine, Inc.

females initiate sex (Komarovsky, 1976). The responsibilities intrinsic to the adolescent male sex role place considerable pressure on adolescent males who feel compelled to initiate sexual exchanges they do not really desire (Hass, 1979). Because many adolescent males do not have the knowledge or experience demanded by the roles they are expected to play, they find themselves forced to "fake it." This leads to a vicious circle that perpetuates their ignorance — sometimes at the expense of females on whom their myths and misconceptions are imposed.

Sex Education

Most of the knowledge that individuals in our culture acquire about sex is learned informally from friends, parents, and books (see Figure 8-13), but some is acquired formally as part of sex-education programs. Approximately three-fourths of U.S.

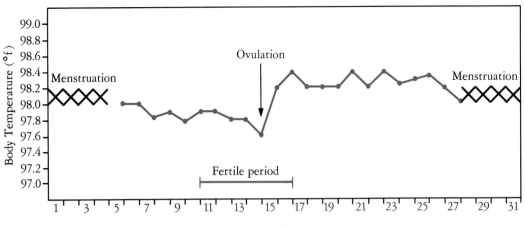

FIGURE 8-15

The Relationship between Body Temperature and Fertile Period For some women, an increase in body temperature follows **ovulation.** Intercourse prior to and during this change in body temperature may result in pregnancy. This fertile period usually occurs between the eleventh and sixteenth days of the menstrual cycle. However, some women ovulate irregularly or at an earlier or a later stage of their cycle. *Source:* Bernstein, R., & Bernstein, S. (1982). *Biology: The study of life* (p. 595). San Diego: Harcourt Brace Jovanovich.

schools offer some instruction on sexual matters; however, only about one-third offer a separate course in sex education and only about 10% offer a formal program. The history of **sex education** in schools is a stormy and bitter one (Haims, 1973). Although most parents support the concept of sex education (Davis, 1980), many worry that discussions of sex may disinhibit their children, give them "ideas," and stimulate them to experiment. Individuals opposed to sex education tend to have a traditional orientation toward the family, to oppose premarital sex, and to agree with such statements as "A woman's place is in the home" (Richardson & Cranston, 1981). Although a minority, they are often very vociferous and successful in resisting proposed or planned programs.

The results of studies on the effects of sex education suggest that opponents of sex education may be worrying themselves needlessly. Many, if not most, sex education programs are innocuous, supplying instruction on matters largely irrelevant to the interests of the students who study them. In the words of Mahoney (1983), "Many sex education courses are history lessons in which the teacher tells students about

things they have already done as if they had not" (p. 113). Sex education courses tend to teach family living and traditional values, whereas students want to learn about such topics as abortion, sexual molestation, contraception, and dating (McCormick, 1979). Only about one-third of the 13- to 18-year-old adolescents, sampled by Gallup (1978), who had taken a sex-education course received instruction in methods of birth control (see Table 8-8 for an evaluation of commonly used methods of birth control). Only 63% of a sample of females who had taken a sex-education course knew what time of the month they were at greatest risk for pregnancy (Zelnik, 1979) (see Figure 8-15). Further, the evidence suggests that formal sex-education programs have little effect on the sexual behavior of the students who take them (see Spanier, 1977), although sex-education courses in college appear to make students more accepting of their own and others' sexual behavior (Story, 1979).

One of the commonly discussed issues in sex education classes, and one of growing importance to many students, concerns **sexually transmitted diseases.** We supply a brief overview of this issue in Box 8-2, page 374.

TABLE 8-8
Comparing a Selection of the Most Commonly Used Methods of Birth Control

Method	Where/How Obtained	Reliability	Advantages	Drawbacks
Rhythm	Available to anyone	Depends on regularity of menstrual cycle	Only method sanctioned by the Roman Catholic Church	Frequent failures; requires abstinence during the female's fertile periods
The Pill	Prescription	99.5% effective	Affords sexual freedom; highly reliable	May cause cancer, blood clots, and liver and/or heart disease; must be taken regularly
Mini-pill	Prescription	97% effective	Does not contain estrogen, eliminating many side effects of the pill	Long-term effects unknown
Vasectomy	Physician's office or hospital	Fail proof once absence of sperm in ejacula is established	Minor operation; sexual freedom; full reliability	Difficult to reverse; may contribute to arteriosclerosis
Condom	Over the counter	98% effective	No health hazards	Can slip or break; interrupts foreplay and may lessen male pleasure
Tubal Ligation	Physician's office or hospital	Almost 100% effective	Sexual freedom; full reliability	Operation usually requires hospitalization; difficult to reverse
Diaphragm	Prescription	98% effective when used consistently with spermicide	No health hazards; does not diminish sexual pleasure	Must be inserted properly; may inhibit spontaneity
Aerosol Foams	Over the counter	80% effective	No prescription required; no health hazards	Must be applied shortly before intercourse
Jellies, Creams, and Suppositories	Over the counter	Varies (but less effective than foams)	No health hazards	Not fully reliable

Source: Adapted from Bernstein, R., & Bernstein, S. (1982). *Biology: The study of life* (p. 594). San Diego: Harcourt Brace Jovanovich.

SEXUAL AROUSAL

Two overriding questions have guided research on sexual arousal. The first question is somewhat academic: what is sexual arousal? The second question is one that virtually everyone has pondered during his or her life: what causes people to become sexually aroused? We consider each question in turn.

Method	Where/How Obtained	Reliability	Advantages	Drawbacks
Intrauterine Device (IUD)	Prescription	98% effective	Sexual freedom; no side effects from drugs	May puncture uterus; may cause bleeding, cramps, and other discomforts; may be unknowingly expelled
Morning-after Pill	Prescription	98% effective	Eliminates pregnancy following intercourse	Not recommended for regular use; may cause serious nausea and vomiting; if ineffective, may cause vaginal cancer in female children of women who use it
Abortion by Early Uterine Evacuation	Physician's office or clinic	*Not a preventative*	Ends unwanted pregnancies; painless, relatively inexpensive procedure	Should be performed within *two months* of pregnancy; possible complications include uterine perforation, infection, cervical lacerations, hemorrhaging
Abortion by Dilation and Evacuation	Physician's office or clinic	*Not a preventative*	Ends unwanted pregnancies after first trimester; relatively inexpensive procedure	Should be performed within *five months* of pregnancy; possible complications include uterine perforation, infection, cervical lacerations, hemorrhaging

THE NATURE OF SEXUAL AROUSAL

When most people think about being sexually aroused, they think about it in emotional and physical terms: they *feel* sexually aroused; they are aware of such changes in their body as increased heart rate, penile erection, or vaginal lubrication. Sexual arousal does indeed involve physical and emotional changes but there is more to it than that. The awareness of physical and emotional changes and the way in which people think about them play a significant role in how aroused they feel.

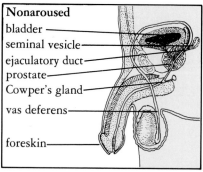

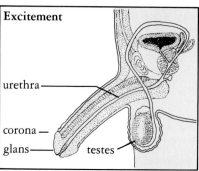

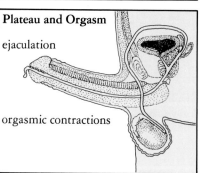

The Physiology of Sexual Arousal: Phases of Sexual Responsiveness

Until the 1960s, little was known about the physical changes that occur in humans during sexual arousal and sexual intercourse — undoubtedly because of the social and ethical difficulties of conducting such research. A major breakthrough occurred in 1966, when William Masters and Virginia Johnson published the book *Human Sexual Response*. Employing prostitutes and other research volunteers, Masters and Johnson observed the sexual organs of males and females as they prepared for, engaged in, and recovered from **coitus** (sexual intercourse) and masturbation. Although many objected to this scientific intrusion into the most intimate of human experiences, the bold research of Masters and Johnson remains the major factual source of information about the physiological changes that take place before, during, and after sex.

Before discussing the findings of Masters and Johnson, it is important to recognize that their research is limited in two significant ways. First, they focused almost exclusively on physiological aspects of sexual behavior and ignored the crucial roles played by social, emotional, and psychological factors. Second, they described the average sexual behavior of the men and women they studied. Because there is considerable variation in people's physiological responses during sex, the "average" may be misleading. This is especially the case with females. As Masters and Johnson themselves warn, the patterns they describe in females "are simplifications of the most frequently observed and are only representative of the infinite variety in female sexual response" (pp. 4–5).

Masters and Johnson divide the sexual response cycle into four phases — *excitement, plateau, orgasm,* and *resolution.* The first phase parallels the foreplay phase described by Ford and Beach (1951) in nonhuman animals; the second two phases parallel Beach's copulation phase; the final phase corresponds to Beach's recovery phase. Masters and Johnson recognize that any division of the sexual cycle into phases is necessarily rough and arbitrary; in actual practice the phases overlap and merge in different ways for different people.

FIGURE 8-16

Changes in Male Genitals from Nonaroused State through Excitement, Plateau, and Orgasm *Source:* Adapted from Mahoney, E. R. (1983). *Human sexuality.* New York: McGraw-Hill.

The Excitement Phase Although sexual excitement can be initiated in a wide variety of ways, the pattern of physical changes that accompany it is quite constant. In both males and females, the excitement phase is marked by two major physical reactions — engorgement of blood vessels and muscle tension. In the male, excitement is first indicated by the erection of the penis (see Figure 8-16) as it becomes engorged with blood (called

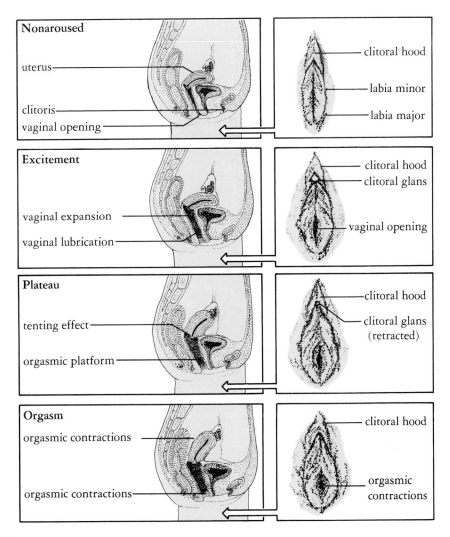

FIGURE 8-17
Changes in Female Genitals from Nonaroused State through Excitement, Plateau, and Orgasm   *Source:* Adapted from Mahoney, E. R. (1983).   *Human sexuality.*   New York: McGraw-Hill.

vasocongestion).   In the female, the *vagina* (see Figure 8-17) becomes lubricated.   As the excitement phase progresses, a variety of other physical changes occur in the sexual organs.   The *clitoris*, like the penis, contains erectile tissue and is similar to the *glans* of the penis.   The clitoris is richly endowed with nerves and is a central focus of sexual sensations.   During sexual excitement it becomes engorged with blood and increases slightly in size.   Curiously, at the height of sexual tension, just prior to orgasm, the clitoris retracts beneath its hood.   In addition, physiolog-

ical changes take place in other areas of the body. For example, when the female breast is stimulated, the nipples may become erect and, during later stages of excitement, the breasts may swell. Late in the excitement phase (or early in the plateau phase), both males and females may experience a superficial skin flush.

The Plateau Phase   The **plateau phase** is an extension of the excitement phase.   In the male, increased excitement is manifested by an increase in the circumference of the penis at the *corona.*

In the female, the vagina expands fully and the *cervix* and *uterus* are elevated (see Figure 8-16). In both males and females, the muscles of the entire body become taut in response to increasing sexual tension. The musculature of the legs, arms, abdomen, neck, and face may twitch and contort involuntarily in the late plateau phase and early orgasm phase. The superficial skin flush that often appears in the excitement phase typically deepens. Other physiological changes include a marked inrease in blood pressure and heart rate (from approximately 100 to 160 beats per minute), heavier breathing, and increased perspiration.

The Orgasmic Phase As sexual tension mounts to climax, voluntary control of sexual response decreases and, at the moment of orgasm, is lost altogether. An orgasm involves one of the most profoundly intense and pleasurable human sensations. In physiological terms, it consists of the explosive discharge of accumulated nerve and muscle tension. The intensity and pattern of responses during orgasm vary among individuals and are affected by such factors as age, fatigue, and length of sexual abstinence.

Until recently it was believed that there were major physiological differences between the orgasms of males and females; however, research has cast doubt on this belief (see Box 8-3). Many people appear to confuse orgasm and ejaculation. "Orgasm is a neuromuscular release of built-up sexual tension which peaks in the late plateau stage. **Ejaculation** is the muscular contraction of certain tissues in the body which transports ejaculate" (Mahoney, 1983, p. 128). Masters and Johnson failed to make this distinction and, accordingly, equated the male orgasm and ejaculation. More recent research reveals that males may experience orgasm without ejaculating (Robbins & Jensen, 1978).

The confusion between ejaculation and orgasm also led Masters and Johnson to conclude that only males have a **refractory period** following orgasm—a period in which they are not capable of further orgasm. Current evidence suggests that the refractory period follows ejaculation, not orgasm, in males, and perhaps females as well (see Box 8-3). Therefore, the refractory period is best defined as the time required to ejaculate a

second or third time, not the time in which a second or third orgasm can be experienced.

One Type of Orgasm — or Many? Some years ago, Freud advanced the theory that women experience two kinds of orgasm. He maintained that during an immature phase of psychosexual development, women focus on the clitoris as the center of sexual pleasure. Some women become fixated at this phase; others move to a more mature phase marked by vaginal orgasm. Masters and Johnson concluded that Freud was wrong—"clitoral and vaginal orgasm are not separate biological entities" (1966, p. 67). However, recent research by Ellison (1980) indicates that women may well experience two kinds of orgasm—an orgasm induced by stimulation of the clitoris alone and an orgasm induced by deep penetration of the vagina. Neurological research reveals that there is a physiological basis for the experiences of two kinds of orgasm—the body contains two separate sets of nerve pathways to the genitals. There is, however, no support for Freud's contention that the vaginal orgasm is more mature than the clitoral orgasm.

It is commonly assumed that men respond more quickly to sexual stimulation and are able to reach orgasm more rapidly and more easily than women. In fact, the majority of women do not achieve orgasm as consistently or as rapidly as men during intercourse; however, the reason may not be physiological. According to Masters and Johnson, women are equipped to respond just as quickly as men to sexual stimulation and are potentially as capable (if not more so) of achieving orgasm. They base this conclusion primarily on their finding that through masturbation women in their study were able to reach orgasm as quickly and as easily as men. Masters and Johnson suggest that the disparity in achieving orgasm between men and women stems mainly from techniques of intercourse and psychological factors—not from the physiological differences between the sexes. While it is relatively simple to stimulate males sexually, it is more difficult to ensure that females receive effective stimulation. This is due, for the most part, to the differences in male and female anatomy; in addition, however, it may be caused by the tendency of men to regulate sexual movements to their personal satisfaction during intercourse, failing to provide women with sufficient clitoral stimulation to achieve orgasm.

The Resolution Phase The resolution phase begins at the termination of orgasm or ejaculation, but its duration varies. During this phase the body returns to a relaxed state. In both males and females the muscles of the body relax, the sexual flush dissipates, and blood pressure, heart rate, and breathing return to normal. The release of accumulated muscular tension during orgasm and the body's return to a quiescent state typically are accompanied by feelings of relaxation and satiation.

Cognitive and Affective Components of Sexual Arousal

There is more to sexual arousal than the changes in the body studied by Masters and Johnson. Sexual arousal involves changes in the way people think as well as changes in how they feel, and each factor influences the other. Sexual ideas may cause an increase in physical arousal and physical arousal may cause an increase in sexual ideas. In this respect it is important to note a fundamental difference between males and females. The signs of physical arousal (penile erection) are more obvious in males than in females. For this reason, physiological arousal is more apparent to most males than to most females, especially when they are first becoming conscious of their sexuality.

The Perception of Arousal Evidence from social psychological studies indicates that when people are aroused physiologically, they will not feel sexually aroused unless they label the arousal as sexual. Schachter's theory of emotion, which we considered in the previous chapter, suggests that people experience emotions only when they are physiologically aroused and label the arousal as an emotion. The labeling process is influenced by people's past experiences with similar situations and their appraisal of the context in which the arousal occurs. Thus, depending on the circumstances, the "same" physiological arousal may be labeled as anger, anxiety, or joy, depending on which experience is most consistent with the individual's past history and present social context.

Physiological arousal must occur, it must be detected, and it must be ascribed erotic meaning for an event to be experienced as sexual. These would seem to be the minimum requirements, although the precise sequence of events may be quite variable within and between persons. That is, sexual arousal has both physiological and subjective components which are reciprocally related. (Rook & Hammen, 1977, p. 11)

Consider certain evidence in support of this position. Adamson et al. (1972) failed to find any difference in the autonomic reactions of women who watched explicit sex films and women who watched films of atrocities in Nazi concentration camps, suggesting that there is no physiological difference between arousal evoked by sexual and disgusting events. Cantor et al. (1975) found that male subjects who viewed erotic photographs five minutes after exercising vigorously became more sexually aroused than subjects who had not exercised. These investigators suggest that the residual arousal of the exercise became associated with the sexual cues. Interestingly, males who were shown erotic pictures immediately after exercising did not feel they had become more sexually aroused than control subjects, apparently because they attributed their arousal to the exercise.

Other studies have found an association between sexual arousal and aggression. For example, in a study by Zillman (1971), subjects received an electric shock and were then divided into three groups, each of which watched a different movie. Zillman found that the subjects who watched an erotic movie subsequently delivered stronger retaliatory shocks (behaved more aggressively) than the subjects who watched a prizefight and that the latter subjects delivered stronger retaliatory shocks than the subjects who watched a nonarousing travel film. Still other studies have found an association between sexual arousal and fear. For example, Dutton and Aron (1974) arranged for an attractive woman to approach men as they were crossing either a rocking suspension bridge over a deep canyon or a low, solid bridge, and ask them to fill out a questionnaire and write a story about a picture. The woman gave the subjects her name and telephone number so they could call her if they wanted more information about the research. Dutton and Aron found that

BOX 8-3
ORGASM — MALE AND FEMALE

Most males achieve orgasm during coitus virtually all the time; fewer females obtain this result (see figure). Male orgasm is usually accompanied by ejaculation and therefore is easy to perceive; female orgasm is more subtle. Mould (1980) suggests that a certain degree of vasocongestion must occur in females before they can obtain orgasm. According to Mould (1980), vasocongestion causes the pelvic muscles to stretch, and when they become sufficiently congested, they undergo *clonic contraction*—repetitive involuntary contractions. Vasocongestion is caused both by physical stimulation and cognitive factors. Women with strong pelvic muscles are more likely to achieve orgasm than women with weak pelvic muscles.

Most authorities do not believe that women are capable of ejaculation, but at least one authority disagrees. Consider the following letter from Martin Weisberg, published in the *Journal of Sex Research* in 1981:

I first learned about female ejaculation at an American Association for Sex Educators, Counselors, and Therapists meeting. The

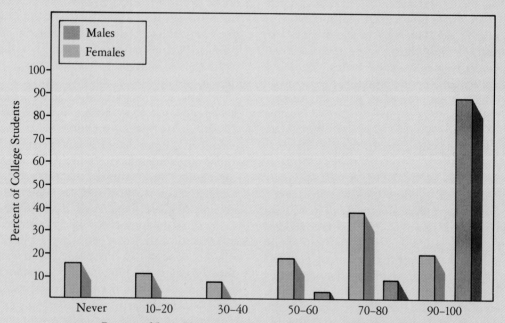

Frequency of Orgasm during Intercourse   A study of male and female college students reveals that 88% of males and 20% of females experience orgasm 90 – 100% of the time they engage in sexual intercourse. *Source:* Mahoney, E. R. (1979). Patterns of sexual behavior among college students. Unpublished research report, Western Washington University, Department of Sociology.

presentation was full of foreign-sounding phrases like Grafenberg spots and female ejaculation.

"Bull," I said. "I spend half of my waking hours examining, cutting apart, putting together, removing or rearranging female reproductive organs. There is no prostate and women don't ejaculate."

After the presentation, I, along with two other physicians and a registered nurse (all sex therapists), challenged the presenters. "Show us," we said. And they did.

Strange as it sounds, the whole group went up to a room in the hotel and had the opportunity of examining one of the subjects about whom the paper was written. [Weisberg describes observing a female ejaculate, but we spare you the details.] . . .

I was really confused. I checked with several anatomists, all of whom thought I was crazy. But my patients didn't think I was crazy. A few told me that they ejaculate. Some knew about the erotic area around the urethra. . . .

Years from now I am sure that a medical school lecturer will joke about how it wasn't until 1980 that the medical community finally accepted the fact that women really do ejaculate (1981, pp. 90–91).

These are the physiological facts (or, perhaps,

theories). Sex differences in the psychological experience of orgasm, or at least reports of the experience, are much clearer—orgasm feels the same to males and females.

In a study published in 1974, Proctor, Wagner, and Butler obtained descriptions of "what an orgasm feels like" from male and female college students. They selected a sample of 24 male and 24 female descriptions and asked groups of medical students, obstetrician-gynecologists, and clinical psychologists to attempt to determine whether they were written by males or females. The results indicated that "these professionals were unable to determine the sex of the writer, and thus, to distinguish between the descriptions of male versus female orgasm." The following are some of the statements they used:

1. _____ I really think it defies description by words. Combination of waves of very pleasurable sensations and mounting of tensions culminating in a fantastic sensation and release of tension.

2. _____ Physical tension and excitement climaxing and then a feeling of sighing, a release of tension-like feeling.

3. _____ It is a pleasant,

tension-relieving muscular contraction. It relieves physical tension and mental anticipation.

4. _____ It is a very pleasurable sensation. All my tensions have really built to a peak and are suddenly released. It feels like a great upheaval, like all of the organs in the stomach area have turned over. It is extremely pleasurable.

5. _____ Orgasm gives me a feeling of unobstructed intensity of satisfaction. Accompanied with the emotional feeling and love one has for another, the reality of the sex drive, and our culturally conditioned status on sex, an orgasm is the only experience that sends my whole body and mind into a state of beautiful oblivion.

6. _____ Tension builds to an extremely high level—muscles are tense, etc. There is a sudden expanding feeling in the pelvis and muscle spasms throughout the body followed by release of tension. Muscles relax and consciousness returns.

the men who were approached as they crossed the frightening suspension bridge wrote stories containing more sexual imagery and were more likely to call the attractive woman and ask her for a date than the men who were approached on the safe bridge. These results were not obtained when the subjects were approached by a male. The results of this study suggest that arousal evoked by fear may heighten sexual arousal in situations containing sexual cues.

Predictably, anxiety is an emotion commonly believed to interfere with sexual arousal, which it does when the cues that evoke anxiety are sexual in nature — when people are afraid of sex. However, if people are made fearful or anxious and then exposed to sexual cues, they may become more sexually aroused than otherwise. For example, Hoon et al. (1977) found that women who watched graphic films of automobile accidents became more sexually aroused by erotic films they watched immediately afterward than women who did not watch the graphic films. Wolchik et al. (1980) found a similar effect in men. However, it is important to note that not all emotional states have been found to enhance sexual arousal. Wolchik et al. also found that those men who felt depressed after watching the graphic films of the accidents became less sexually aroused than men who did not watch the films.

Sex Differences in Perception of Sexual Arousal   Early research comparing sexual arousal in males and females found that women reported feeling less aroused than males when exposed to the same sexual stimuli. Accordingly, the researchers who conducted these studies concluded that females were less sexual than males. Recent research, however, points to a different conclusion — that women experience as much physiological arousal as men but are less likely to notice it, more likely to deny it, and more likely to attribute it to nonsexual sources. In one experiment Heiman (1975) measured the physiological and subjective responses of university males and females as they listened to tape recordings of erotic stories. She found that both males and females became physiologically aroused while listening to erotic material but that females were less likely than males to detect, to acknowledge,

and to report it. The tendency of females not to notice signs of physical arousal or not to interpret them as sexual has been linked to their relative difficulty in achieving orgasm. Hoon and Hoon (1978) found that nonorgasmic women were relatively unaware of the changes that occurred in their bodies in response to sexual stimulation; Kaplan (1974) found that teaching women to be sensitive to the physical changes that take place during sexual stimulation increases their ability to experience orgasm. It should be noted, however, that self-consciousness tends to reduce sexual arousal in both women (Wilson & Lawson, 1978) and men (Farkes et al., 1979), especially when it relates to the evaluation of sexual performance.

Expectations   In addition to the perception and interpretation of sexual arousal, expectations about what will happen during sex affect the arousal experience. According to Rook and Hammen (1977), an

> individual who engages in sexual activity may have expectations about the specific pattern of physiological responses that will occur, the probable intensity of such responses, the cause of arousal, the duration and sequencing of specific arousal responses, and the symbolic meaning of sexual activity. (pp. 21–22)

The confirmation or disconfirmation of these expectations is likely to affect the perception of how intensely aroused an individual is, as well as how much enjoyment he or she derives from subsequent sexual activity. For example, many drug users report an intensification of sexual excitement after taking drugs; however, as we will see, there is little evidence that drugs actually increase sexual arousal. The important factor appears to be the *expectation* that the drug will enhance sexual pleasure.

Of course, expectations can be disconfirmed. The individual who expects drugs or alcohol to enhance sexual arousal may find that it does not. If the person attributes the failure to the ineffectiveness of the drug, it probably will not have serious consequences to his or her future sexual experiences. However, if the person attributes the failure to himself or herself, ensuing feelings of inadequacy may become problematic. We consider the important influence of expectations on the sexual arousal experience further when we review the effects of alcohol.

Having discussed the nature and experience of sexual arousal, we turn to a related question: What causes people to become sexually aroused? We open with a brief look at sexual arousal in nonhuman animals. With that as a context, we then examine the internal and external stimuli found to induce sexual arousal in humans.

The Role of Hormones

In approximately 90% of mammalian species, the females copulate only when they are in "heat" or **estrus** (*mad desire* or *frenzy* in Greek); thus, they engage in sexual activity only during certain periods of the month or year. Estrus is induced by hormonal changes associated with ovulation, and the usual outcome of **copulation** during estrus is pregnancy. Different species differ in the frequency and duration of estrus, and therefore in the frequency with which they copulate. For example, dogs and cats usually come into heat twice a year, estrus lasting a few days. Chimpanzees come into estrus approximately once a month (chimpanzees have menstrual cycles similar to those of humans). Rats and mice come into estrus approximately once every four days.

Although some nonhuman primates have been observed copulating with female primates not in estrus, human sexual behavior is unique among mammals in its independence from this biological imperative. Humans engage in sexual intercourse at any time during a woman's menstrual cycle, whether or not it leads to pregnancy. Indeed, it has been estimated that the human copulation-to-pregnancy ratio is about 351 : 1 (Katchadourian & Lunde, 1975, p. 209). An interesting question arises from these observations: Why do human females not experience estrus? No one knows the answer for sure. However, evolutionary theorists have speculated that hidden ovulation and absence of estrus in humans might have evolved because they encourage pair-

bonding, which appears to have been an important adaptation in the evolution of the species (see Daly & Wilson, 1978).

Is there any evidence that human females retain a vestige of estrus? Do females become more aroused during ovulation than during other times in their reproductive cycle? Studies have found peaks of sexual arousal during particular times in the **menstrual cycle;** these peaks do not, however, always correspond to ovulation (McCauley & Ehrardt, 1976). Some women appear to experience increased sexual arousal and sexual enjoyment midway through their cycle, during ovulation, but other women appear to experience peaks of arousal just before and just after **menstruation.** And, to complicate matters even more, some studies have not found any consistent trend at all (Hoon, Bruce & Kinchloe, 1982).

Researchers have investigated the effects of hormones on sexual arousal in three primary ways — by determining the correlation between naturally occurring hormonal levels and sexual activity, by observing what occurs when hormonal levels are decreased, and by observing what happens when hormonal levels are increased. Many studies have found that in both males and females high levels of **testosterone** are correlated with high levels of sexual activity (see Offir, 1982, pp. 102–106 for a review); nevertheless, it is unclear whether high levels of testosterone cause high levels of sexual activity or the reverse. There is no evidence that females experience any reduction in sexual interest after their ovaries are removed. Indeed, sexual interest and activity may actually increase, presumably because fear of pregnancy is eliminated. There is evidence, however, that **castration** produces a decrease in the sexual behavior of human males, partly because a certain amount of testosterone is necessary to maintain sufficient tone in the penile muscles to achieve erection. Yet, some studies have found that castration has little effect on men's sexual appetites. For example, Heim (1981) found that 73% of a sample of rapists who were castrated continued to masturbate and to engage in sexual intercourse.

The emerging mammalian independence from rigid hormonal control of sexual activity that accompanies increasingly elaborate brains is illustrated in Figure 8-18, which shows the length

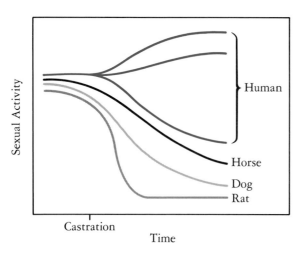

FIGURE 8-18

The Effects of Castration Animals that require more learning for adequate performance continue to be active for longer periods after gonadal hormones are removed by castration. In humans, for whom learning plays the greatest role, the amount of sexual activity after castration is highly variable (as shown by three patterns). *Data:* From Beach, F. A. (1976). Hormonal control of sex-related behavior. In F. A. Beach (Ed.), *Human sexuality in four perspectives.* Baltimore, MD: Johns Hopkins University Press.

of time sexually experienced males of different species continue to engage in sexual activity after they have been castrated. Although castration is devastating to the sexual behavior of simple species, it has relatively little effect on species whose sexual behavior is shaped by learning.

Aphrodisiacs, Drugs, and Alcohol

Rare is the adolescent male in our society who, at one time or another, has not fantasized about acquiring a drug that will turn all women into **nymphomaniacs.** Many people eat special foods — oysters and bull testicles ("prairie oysters"), for example — that they believe will increase their sexual appetite, performance, and pleasure. Other people ingest drugs and consume alcohol for the same reason.

An **aphrodisiac** is a substance that creates or increases sexual arousal. No true aphrodisiac has as yet been discovered (Kaplan, 1974). Some drugs, such as *cantharis* or "Spanish Fly" (so named because it is derived from a beetle found in Spain and other Southern European

countries), irritate the **genitourinary tract,** causing dilation of nearby blood vessels; other drugs, such as *yohimbine,* stimulate the erection center in the spine of men. Although such drugs as these induce certain signs of sexual arousal, they do not increase sexual desire. In fact, they are potentially dangerous irritants to the nervous system.

It is popularly believed that marijuana enhances sexual experience. Marijuana does not induce sexual arousal directly; however, it may affect sensory and perceptual experiences in ways that enhance sexual pleasure. Because marijuana induces a state of relaxation in many people, it may lower their inhibitions and make sex more enjoyable. Research indicates that the effects on sexual behavior of such drugs as marijuana are more psychological than physical in nature. People who expect marijuana to enhance their sexual experience are disposed to interpret its effects as support for their expectation. For example, Koff (1974) found that after smoking marijuana males reported an increase in sexual desire and that females reported an increase in sexual enjoyment. According to Koff, the physical relaxation induced in females by marijuana helped reduce inhibitions and in males helped reduce performance anxiety. In line with these findings, other studies have found that the disinhibiting effect of sedatives is greatest for females and people high in sex-guilt (Ugerer et al., 1976).

Such other drugs as **amyl nitrate** ("poppers"), **cocaine,** and **amphetamines** have been said to affect sexual arousal and performance. There is some self-report evidence that amyl nitrate prolongs orgasm (Everett, 1975) — probably due to the sudden drop in blood pressure caused by the drug — and that amphetamines prolong erection, delay ejaculation, and facilitate repeated orgasms in males (Mims & Swenson, 1980); however the side effects of both drugs, especially with repeated use, may be very harmful.

According to Shakespeare, alcohol "provokes the desires but takes away the performance" (Macbeth, Act II, scene iii, line 34). Recent research indicates that Shakespeare's maxim is close, but not exact. Small quantities of alcohol increase sexual arousal (as revealed by penile erection in males), but large quantities decrease

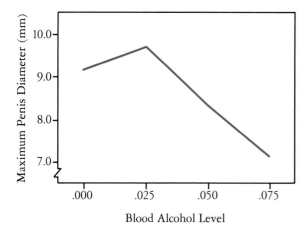

FIGURE 8-19

The Effects of Alcohol on Sexual Arousal A small amount of alcohol in the bloodstream produces an increase in penis diameter (size of erection) but increasing amounts of alcohol in the bloodstream produce a rapid decrease in penis diameter. *Source:* Farkas, G. M., & Rosen, R. C. (1976). Effect of alcohol on elicited males' sexual response. *Journal of Studies on Alcohol, 37,* 265 – 72.

the response (see Figure 8-19). In contrast, alcohol causes a steady decrease in physiologically measured sexual arousal in women (Wilson & Lawson, 1978).

To understand the effect of alcohol and other drugs on sexual arousal, we must consider cognitive as well as physiological factors. Although in females alcohol induces a decrease in vasocongestion, it also may induce an increase in their perception of sexual arousal; females report feeling more aroused while drinking than while not, and they are more likely than men to report feeling sexy and romantic after a couple of drinks (Wilsnack, 1974). As we mentioned earlier, because the physiological changes that accompany sexual arousal in females (vasocongestion) are much less noticeable than the physiological changes that accompany sexual arousal in males (erection), females tend not to notice the decrease in physiological responsiveness caused by alcohol. The reason why they report feeling more aroused probably relates to the disinhibiting effect of alcohol and the expectation that alcohol will make them feel sexier.

Several studies have found that people need not actually consume any alcohol to experience the effect they expect it to have on their sexual experience — they need only think they have. Interestingly, this effect is especially pronounced in males. For example, Wilson and Lawson (1976) gave males tonic water, told them that they were drinking vodka and tonic, and found that they became more physiologically aroused (measured by penile erection) when watching erotic slides than males who actually consumed alcohol but believed it was only tonic water. We saw earlier that people who score high in sexual guilt tend to avoid sexual stimuli. However, Lang et al. (1980) found that after they were led to believe they had consumed alcohol, males who were high in sex-guilt spent more time watching erotic slides than men low in sex-guilt.

Sensory Stimuli

From an evolutionary perspective, we would expect humans to be prepared biologically to respond sexually to certain types of sensory stimulation. We know that female primates secrete chemical substances called **pheromones** whose odors evoke sexual responses in males. Researchers have found similar chemicals in the vaginal secretions of human females (Michael, et al., 1974); however, existing evidence fails to support the popular idea that they evoke sexual arousal in males (see Morris & Udry, 1978).

In addition to **olfactory stimuli,** nonhuman animals become sexually aroused through tactile, auditory, and visual stimuli. **Tactile stimulation** appears to be the most basic; people with higher brain-center damage may nevertheless show signs of sexual arousal when tactilely stimulated. Sexually sensitive areas of the body are called **erogenous zones.** The genitals are the primary erogenous zone, but many other parts of the body can be sexually sensitive. In general, areas rich in nerves are more sensitive to stimulation than areas not rich in nerves. There are no special sexual receptors in the skin — *erogenous zones* are areas sensitive to any kind of touch — what makes a physically sensitive area sexually sensitive is the meaning attached to the touch. For example, although lips are very rich in nerve endings, the stimulation they receive from eating does not induce sexual arousal. Moreover, there are pronounced individual differences in the areas of the body people find stimulating.

Most people become sexually aroused by the sounds of sexual activity and the sight of sex organs. As discussed, sex researchers use erotic pictures and films to evoke sexual arousal in the subjects of their experiments. Although there is considerable variability in the auditory and visual stimuli that evoke sexual arousal in people from different cultures and in different people from the same culture, among undergraduate students explicit and intense sexual scenes appear to evoke more arousal than more moderate scenes (see Figure 8-20).

The magazine counters of our society are laden with books intended to titillate readers, and sections in most of our large cities are replete with "topless" and "bottomless" shows. Certain aspects of the human body are considered erotic in all cultures, but there is considerable variation in exactly which aspects. In other societies, most males would be quite turned-off by our top fashion models, considering them anemic and malnourished. In some cultures, such as the old aristocracy of Hawaii, extreme female obesity was considered the height of eroticism.

The sight of genitals appears to evoke erotic responses in most cultures. People from almost every society cover their genitals; even in societies where people go naked, there are prohibitions against looking directly at the genitals (Ford & Beach, 1951). And people from all cultures manipulate aspects of dress, appearance, and posture to enhance their sexual attractiveness; however, the precise form of these manipulations differs from place to place. For instance, in East Bay the inside of a woman's thigh is considered highly erotic, and women make their thighs even more erotic by tattooing them.

Physical Attractiveness Physically attractive people tend to be sexually arousing; Mathes and Edwards (1978) found that just seeing a physically attractive person may stimulate erection in males and vaginal secretions in females. Within particular cultures there is a fair amount of con-

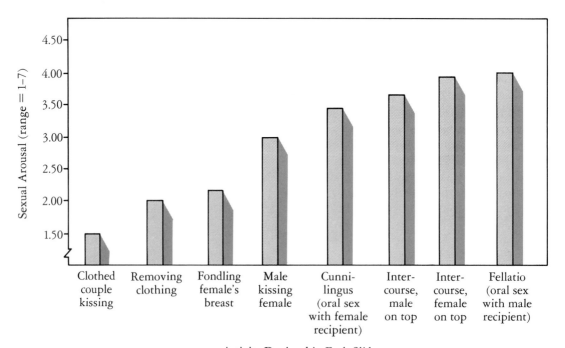

Activity Depicted in Each Slide

FIGURE 8-20

Sexual Arousal in Response to Stimuli that Vary in Degree of Explicitness The more explicit the scene depicted, the greater the degree of sexual arousal in males and females. *Source:* Adapted from Miller, C. T., Byrne, D., & Fisher, J. D. (1980). Order effects on sexual and affective responses to erotic stimuli by males and females. *Journal of Sex Research, 16,* 131–47.

sistency in the norms for beauty, yet there are notable individual differences. In general, American males prefer moderately sized breasts, buttocks, and legs in females (Wiggins et al., 1968) and females prefer relatively small buttocks and moderately large (but not muscle-bound) chests in males (Beck et al., 1976). Asked to indicate which aspect of the male anatomy is most sexually arousing (candidates being penis, legs, buttocks, chest), female college students chose the chest (51%), followed by penis (23%), buttocks (9%), and legs (1%) (Wildman et al., 1976). Among males there was more variation in preference, with 38% selecting breasts, 24% buttocks, 21% genitals, and 18% legs. It is interesting to note a certain male ambivalence toward large breasts. Although many males find large-breasted women sexually attractive, they tend to perceive such women as less intelligent, less competent, less moral, and less modest than small-breasted women (Kleine & Staneski, 1980).

The Role of Learning

Although humans appear to be prepared biologically to respond sexually to certain types of stimuli, their basic biological dispositions must be activated by experience. As adults, male rats isolated from other rats since a very young age are able to copulate successfully on their first exposure to females in heat; yet, as adults, members of such species as monkeys — with advanced capacities to learn — when reared in isolation, may never acquire the capacity to engage in normal sexual behaviors (Harlow et al., 1972). Classical conditioning undoubtedly plays a major role in expanding and refining the range of stimuli that elicit sexual arousal in different people (see Chapter 5). Any neutral stimulus consistently paired with an unconditioned stimulus may, through conditioning, come to evoke sexual arousal. For example, a teenage girl who experiences intense arousal while necking with a tall, blond boyfriend subsequently may prefer men with these characteristics. Or a man may be aroused by large breasts because the first teenage girl to excite him was large-breasted. If Freud is correct, children may become sexually attracted to people who resemble their opposite-sex parent. As we will see, classical conditioning also may account for sexual deviations.

Learning theorists also have suggested that the reinforcement involved in orgasm plays an important role in shaping sexual arousal. Research on sex offenders demonstrates that they frequently masturbate while fantasizing about deviant sexual activities (Gebhard, Gagnon, Pomeroy & Christensen, 1965). According to behaviorally oriented sex therapists, the pleasure that accompanies and follows these events may cause the fantasies to become deeply entrenched. Behavioral treatments for sexual deviations are based on procedures that attempt, through conditioning, to extinguish inappropriate responses and instill appropriate ones (see Chapter 14). Modeling also may play an important role in the learning and relearning of sexual behavior (see Bandura, 1977).

The Role of Cognition — Especially Fantasy

We suggested earlier that the labels people give to physiological arousal play an important role in determining whether the people feel sexually aroused or not. Certain kinds of cognition — imagining sexual experiences and remembering past encounters, for example — also may play an important role in evoking and sustaining sexual arousal. To many, thinking about sex is as sexually arousing as experiencing sexual stimulation directly. Indeed, some researchers have found that sexual fantasies produce more sexual arousal than erotic material (Byrne & Lambreth, 1971); other researchers have suggested that **sexual imagery** may be a necessary component of sexual arousal. For example, Geer and Fuhr (1976) suggest that exposure to erotic stimuli does not evoke physiological arousal directly; rather, they suggest that erotic stimuli initiate thought processes that, in turn, evoke arousal.

Sexual fantasies may range from fleeting daydreams (Mednick, 1977) to elaborate and vivid constructions (Coleman, 1978). Studies have found that approximately 60% of the people surveyed reported entertaining sexual fantasies while having sex with their partners (Hariton & Singer, 1974; Sue, 1979); however, only half that figure reported fantasizing most of the time and only between five and six percent reported fantasizing during every sexual experience. Several studies (for example, Coleman, 1978; McCauley

& Swann, 1980) have found that females are more likely than males to fantasize in order to enhance their sexual experiences and to reduce their anxiety, that females have more vivid and complex fantasies than males, and that females tend to become more physiologically aroused by sexual fantasies than males. Brown and Hart (1977) have found that women with liberal attitudes toward the female role tend to fantasize more than those with more traditional attitudes.

What do people fantasize about? Do males fantasize about the same things as females? Several researchers have compared the content of female and male sexual fantasies; the results of a study by Sue (1979) are given in Table 8-9. Like Sue, other investigators have found that females tend to fantasize about receiving a male's advances, whereas males tend to fantasize about making the advances (Mednick, 1977). However, although Sue (1979) found that males were more likely than females to fantasize about an imaginary lover (see Table 8-9), other investigators have found the opposite (McCauley & Swann, 1976).

In summary, such basic biological factors as hormones play a less significant role in determining sexual arousal in humans than they do in regulating the sexual behavior of nonhuman animals. Some drugs, including alcohol, affect human sexual behavior, but the effect of these drugs appears to stem more from the expectations people have about them than from their physiological effects. The learning history of individuals and the way they think about sex appear to exert the primary influence on their sexual experiences.

TABLE 8-9
Sexual Fantasies — Male and Female

Theme of Fantasy	Percent of People Having that Type of Fantasy	
	Males	Females
1. *Having intercourse with a stranger*	47	21
2. *Having sex with more than one person at the same time*	33	18
3. *Doing sexual things one would never do in reality*	19	28
4. *Being forced to have sex*	10	19
5. *Forcing someone to have sex*	13	3
6. *Having sex with someone of the same gender*	7	11

Source: Adapted from Hunt, M. (1974). *Sexual behavior in the 1970s* (pp. 92–93). Chicago: Playboy Press.

SEXUAL DEVIATIONS

For some people, anything other than sexual intercourse for the purpose of procreation is wrong; for others, almost everything goes. **Sexual deviations** are sexual practices that deviate from cultural norms. Some people think that sexual deviations are perverse and "sick"; others view them as creative variations of a normal biological urge. Sexual deviations may involve variations in the *object* of sexual desire or variations in the sexual *act*. Most sexual deviations involve variations in sexual object. The most prevalent deviation of this type is **homosexuality,** where the variant object is a member of the same sex. Other rarer deviations include **pedophilia,** where the variant object is a child; **incest,** where the variant object is a close relative; and **fetishism,** where the variant object is a particular part of the body or a particular physical article. The primary deviations of sexual act include **voyeurism,** achieving sexual excitement from observing people who would be offended if they knew they were being watched; **exhibitionism,** exposing one's genitals; **sadism,** inflicting pain; **masochism,** receiving pain; and **rape,** forcing sex on an unwilling partner. These practices are considered deviant only when they are the primary or exclusive means of sexual arousal and sexual satisfaction and when mutual consent is absent. There is relatively little research on pedophilia, incest, fetishism, voyeurism, exhibitionism, sadism, and masochism (Box 8-4); there is considerably more research on homosexuality and rape.

HOMOSEXUALITY

Homosexuality has been called, among other things, a sin, an illness, a way of life, a normal variant of sexual behavior, a behavior disturbance, and a crime. Homosexuals are said to have been "born that way," been enticed into homosexuality by an adult, been turned to homosexuality by a lack of a strong parent, been made homosexuals by a dominating parent, been trapped in the gang stage of development, been unable to attract a person of the opposite sex, been oversexed or sexually deficient, been at a lower level of human evolution, been rebels against a bourgeois materi-

alistic society, or been victims of various kinds of traumatic experiences. (Bullough, 1979, p. 1).

Homosexuality involves a sexual orientation based on a preference for same-sex partners. A homosexual (from the Greek *homo,* meaning *same*) may be either male or female, but the term *homosexual* usually is applied to males and the term *lesbian* to females (from Lesbos, the island home of Greek poetess Sappho). There is no absolute division between homosexuals and heterosexuals; in Kinsey's words, "The world is not divided into sheep and goats" (p. 639). To illustrate this fact, Kinsey (1953) developed a six-point rating scale that ranges from exclusive **heterosexuality** to **bisexuality** (a preference for both male and female partners) to exclusive homosexuality (see Figure 8-21). More recently, Storms (1980) has presented a two-dimensional model of sexual orientation, where *homoeroti-*

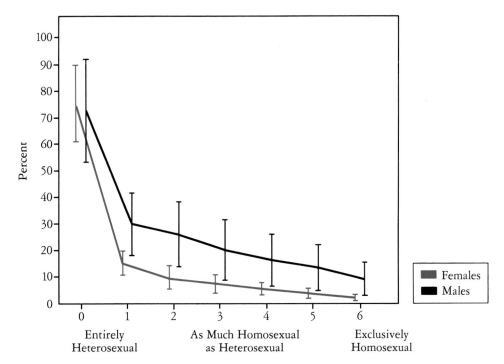

FIGURE 8-21

Kinsey's Heterosexual–Homosexual Rating Scale (percent of females and males scoring in each category) Vertical lines indicate the range of responses—caused in part by analyzing the responses for married people separately from single people. Most respondents reported being entirely heterosexual. From 11–20% of the females and from 18–42% of the males reported at least one homosexual experience (1 on the scale). From 1–3% of the females and from 3–16% of the males reported being exclusively homosexual. *Source:* Kinsey, A. C., et al. (1953). *Sexual behavior in the human female* (pp. 470 and 488). Philadelphia, PA: Saunders.

Box 8-4
Sexual Deviations

*P*edophilia (from the Greek *love of children*) refers to the use of children for sexual gratification. Pedophilia is almost exclusively practiced by men and may involve homosexual or heterosexual contacts. Homosexual contacts tend to be more aggressive than heterosexual ones, and the prognosis for homosexual pedophiles tends to be poorest. Although the age of the child may vary, pedophilia usually refers to sexual relations with children under the age of twelve (before physical maturation). There are no reliable estimates of the incidence of pedophilia; however, Kinsey found that 24% of the women he interviewed had been approached sexually by an older male and Landis (cf. McCaghy, 1968) found that 30% of the male and 35% of the female university students he surveyed had been approached sexually by an adult during their childhood.

The idea of a pedophile typically evokes the image of a child molester lurking in park bushes, awaiting an opportunity to rape and torture. This is not entirely valid. In a study of various types of sex offenders, Gebhard et al. (1965) found that in 85% of the incidents

they reviewed, the pedophile was known to the child and was most often a relative, neighbor, or family friend. Most episodes were brief and took place in the home of either the child or the initiator. Typically, the male pedophile fondled the child's external genitals and induced the child to fondle his. Intercourse was rarely attempted, in part because many pedophiles are impotent. About half the pedophiles have a criminal and psychiatric record and come from a home where immediate relatives also have criminal records; many are raised in a milieu of physical violence and alcoholism; but the majority do not appear to be seriously psychologically disturbed. Many are married or have been married, and many have children of their own. Male pedophiles, whose average age is between 30 and 40, tend to be conservative and moralistic in their general outlook. Most have had infrequent and inadequate heterosexual experiences. As a result, they suffer from a fear or distaste of adult women and from feelings of sexual inadequacy. Thus, a representative image of a typical pedophile who has come to the attention of authorities is

a pathetic, immature person who lacks the confidence and competence to pursue sexual relations with adults.

The most powerful and universal basis of restriction on sexual partners is called the *incest taboo*—a prohibition against engaging in sexual relations with close relatives. However, incest taboos take different forms in different cultures. In most societies they apply only to direct relatives (parents and children, siblings, uncles and nieces, and aunts and nephews); in others, such as our own, they extend to first cousins. In many cultures they apply only to parallel cousins and not cross-cousins; in others they apply to all relatives or members of totemic clans. In most other cultures, incest prohibitions are more severe than in our own. Ford and Beach (1951) estimate that 72% of the societies they studied have more severe restrictions, in some cases extending to "half the available population" (p. 113). Moreover, in other societies, the form that the incest taboo takes is often more severe than in ours. In many cultures the incest taboo is applied most strongly to parents and children; in some it is applied more strongly to maternal uncles and their nieces. In some societies brothers and sisters are not permitted to eat at the same table, inasmuch as eating together is considered a symbol of a marital relationship. And in still others, some relatives are not even permitted to look at one another.

Interestingly, the only documented exceptions to cultural prohibitions on sexual relations among close relatives have occurred among royalty—to preserve the genetic purity of lineages. The matings of brothers and sisters in Ancient Inca and Ancient Egypt are well known. Early aristocratic Hawaiians (those who governed the islands prior to 1820, when the American Congregational missionaries arrived) arranged special matings between half siblings, uncles and aunts, and nieces and nephews, and sometimes even full siblings, for the purpose of producing "purebred" offspring (Davenport, 1977, p. 119).

In his studies on American sexual practices, Kinsey was able to gather almost no information on incest when it was defined as sexual intercourse between parents and children. However, when he extended his definition to include any form of intimate sexual contact between relatives, he found that 13.5% of the males and 8.1% of the females had had heterosexual incestuous relationships. Hunt (1974) found that approximately 7% of his American sample had engaged in incestuous practices, which he describes as consisting primarily of "early, exploratory, noncoital behavior, the greatest part of which takes place between cousins, and much of the rest between siblings" (pp. 346–47). Gebhard et al. (1965) found that brother–sister incest outnumbered father–daughter contacts by about five to one in the U.S.

Gebhard et al. (1965) found that fathers who become sexually involved with their daughters are usually passive, ineffectual, preoccupied with sex, and heavy drinkers. Their sexual contacts with younger daughters consist mainly of fondling the girl's genitals and, sometimes, oral–genital contacts; with physically mature daughters, sexual activity typically includes sexual intercourse. To the surprise of many authorities, relationships between parents and children often exist for a long time before discovery.

Fetishism is a deviation in which sexual excitement is aroused by an inanimate object or by a body part that is not a primary or secondary sex characteristic. It occurs almost entirely in males. The distinction between normally erotic objects or body parts and true fetishes is often confused. Most people find certain articles of clothing and certain nongenital parts of the body arousing—but these objects are arousing because they are associated with a sexual partner. In contrast, fetishes are arousing in themselves. According to most authorities, fetishists are aroused exclusively by inanimate objects or body parts. The objects of fetishes vary, but some, such as female underwear, are more commonly employed than others. Katchadourian and Lunde (1975) distinguish between two classes of fetishes— feminine objects that are soft, furry, or lacy and masculine objects that are hard, smooth, or black (such as leather, chains, and the like). While the sexual significance of some fetishes is fairly obvious, the significance of many others is obscure to the casual observer.

Rachman (1966) demonstrated how a fetish could be learned through conditioning. He showed a subject a photograph of a women's boots at the same time he showed slides of female nudes. After repeated pairings, the subject evidenced sexual arousal (a

(continued on next page)

(continued from pp. 396–397) mild erection) when the photograph of the boots was shown separately. The subject also displayed sexual arousal to pictures of other types of boots (stimulus generalization).

Concerning variations in sexual aim, it is difficult to draw the line between deviant and nondeviant practices because so many people engage in sexual acts other than coitus — such acts as mutual masturbation, oral-genital sex, and anal intercourse — in order to obtain sexual relief and pleasure, and because so many people experience some degree of sexual arousal when they engage in mild versions of what in more extreme forms are considered deviations. Feigelman

(1977) found that high-rise construction workers routinely watch women undress when given the opportunity; however, true *voyeurism* involves compulsive peeping that is the primary source of sexual excitement. Most voyeurs are men, and most of those who have been studied have a history of grossly deficient experiences in heterosexual relationships. As a result of this socialization, the voyeur typically feels uneasy with women and uncertain of his competence. Many voyeurs are also *exhibitionists* ("flashers") (Langevin et al., 1979). Although some women dress provocatively, exhibitionism as a compulsive means of sexual expression is confined almost exclusively to men. Approximately one-third of

all arrests for sex offenses involve exhibitionism (Allen, 1969).

Why do exhibitionists expose themselves? Research indicates that they give two reasons — to shock the women they encounter and to attempt to impress them with the size of their penis (Langevin et al., 1979). Like voyeurs, exhibitionists tend to be uneasy with women and insecure about their masculinity. Most exhibitionists do not engage in serious antisocial behavior; however, it is estimated that one in ten has attempted or contemplated rape. An intensive study of exhibitionists failed to reveal any characteristic other than exhibitionism that distinguished them from other males (Langevin et al., 1979).

---

cism is one dimension and *heteroeroticism* the other (see Figure 8-22). Homosexuals are defined as individuals who score high on homoeroticism and low on heteroeroticism.

Homosexuality is sometimes confused with **transsexuality** and **transvestism**. A **transsexual** is a person (usually a male) who wishes to be and sincerely believes that he or she is a member of the opposite sex. Male transsexuals feel that they are females trapped in a male body, and some have undergone hormone treatments and surgical operations to alter their sexual anatomy (see photographs). Although male transsexuals engage in sex with male partners, they think of themselves as female and are attracted to males as members of the opposite sex. Thus, in their view, their sexual orientation is heterosexual. *Transvestism* ("cross-dressing") is a form of deviance in which a man is aroused by wearing women's clothing (see the case of Scobie, Chapter 13). Pomeroy

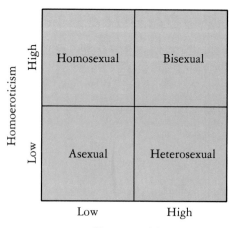

FIGURE 8-22
Storms' Two-dimensional Model of Sexual Orientation Individuals high on homoeroticism and low on heteroeroticism are homosexual. *Source:* Storms, M. D. (1980). Theories of sexual orientation. *Journal of Personality and Social Psychology, 38,* 783–92.

Kinsey found that 25% of the males and females he studied experienced sexual arousal from mild biting and pinching and that 4% enjoyed other types of pain. Hunt (1974) found that 6% of males and 3% of females under 35 years of age obtained sexual pleasure from inflicting pain on another person and that 4% of the males and 6% of the females experienced sexual pleasure from having pain inflicted on them. Although there appears to be an increase in the acceptability of fictional and dramatic portrayals of *sadism* and *masochism (S and M)* in Western society, especially as it involves bondage, the type of activity depicted is usually mild and not physically damaging.

There is a minority of people whose sexual lives revolve around *S and M* or *B and D* (bondage and discipline). Couples contact one another through ads in newspapers and covert means. The behaviors in which these people engage are quite ritualized and governed by sexual scripts. They usually involve only mild forms of pain; sexual pleasure derives more from the fantasy of giving and/or receiving pain than from the actual pain itself (Gosseling & Wilson, 1980). In some cases, one individual (usually the man) assumes the dominant role while the other individual (usually the woman) assumes the submissive role; however, the roles are often reversed (Gosseling & Wilson, 1980).

Mild forms of sadism and masochism are extremely different from severe forms. Truly sadistic people do not seek receptive masochistic partners to act out fantasies — they seek someone whom they can hurt and degrade. Similarly, true masochists need an assailant who acts out of brutality — not out of sexual need (Stoller, 1975). Interestingly, the same person often derives pleasure from both sadism and masochism. Psychoanalytically oriented theorists believe that masochism arises as an expression of sadism — impulses that are unacceptable are turned against the self (Randall, 1969).

James Morris (left photo) was a foreign correspondent and the father of four children before undergoing a sex-change operation and becoming Jan Morris (right photo)

(1975) considers transvestism a type of fetish — transvestites are sexually aroused by women's clothing. In contrast to transsexuals, transvestites regard themselves as men and, although they wear female attire, do not think of themselves as female. Most transvestites are married men and most do *not* engage in homosexual activities (Prince & Bentler, 1972). Typically, transvestites obtain sexual release by dressing in women's attire and masturbating while watching themselves in a mirror or engaging in sexual intercourse with their wives.

Incidence of Homosexuality

Kinsey reported that from 18–42% of the males and from 11–20% of the females he interviewed had at least one homosexual experience. Kinsey also reported that from 3–16% of the males and 1–3% of the females in his study were exclusively homosexual. These findings shocked his contemporaries, perhaps inappropriately. More recent estimates fix the percent of males who have had at least one adult homosexual experience at about 20% (Hunt, 1974) and the percent of the male population who are primarily homosexual at from 1–3% (Hunt, 1974; Katchadourian & Lunde, 1977). Comparable estimates for females are 10–20% and slightly less than 1%. The common perception that homosexuality is on the increase appears to be more a reflection of the willingness of homosexuals to "come out of the closet," and of the resulting publicity, than a genuine increase in the proportion of homosexuals in the population.

Attitudes Toward Homosexuality

Broude and Green (1976) surveyed attitudes toward homosexuality of people in 52 cultures and found a wide range of variation. Homosexuality was accepted or ignored in approximately 20% of the cultures, strongly disapproved and punished in about 40%, with the rest following somewhere between these two extremes. Our culture is one in which homosexuality has re-

ceived and continues to receive strong disapproval, with almost three-fourths of adult Americans viewing sexual relations between two adults of the same sex as "always wrong" (see Table 8-10). Bullough (1979) has reviewed the history of homosexuality, and identifies religion as the most powerful determinant of negative attitudes toward it in Western culture.

Homosexuals tend to be stereotyped in our culture (see Table 8-11). As noted by Katchadourian and Lunde (1977):

Probably the most common misunderstanding of male homosexuals is reflected in the stereotypes that portray them as "effeminate," "swishy," "faggots," or "fairies." There are individuals who fit these stereotypes, to be sure, and within the gay crowd they are known as "queens." But these men represent only a very small proportion of the homosexual population and are by no means appreciated by the rest. (p. 325)

Similarly, research has shown that most lesbians are not masculine, or "butch," in appearance and behavior.

In many states homosexual practices are illegal and for many years homosexuality was con-

TABLE 8-10
Adult American Attitudes toward Homosexuality — 1973–1980

Attitude	Percent of National Sample				
Are sexual relations between two adults of the same sex:	1973	1974	1976	1977	1980
always wrong?	74	73	70	72	73
almost always wrong?	9	5	6	6	6
wrong only sometimes?	10	8	8	8	6
not wrong at all?	15	13	16	15	15
Should an admitted male homosexual be allowed to make a speech in your community?					
Yes	63	65	64	64	68
No	37	35	36	36	32
Should an admitted male homosexual be allowed to teach in a college or university?					
Yes	49	55	54	51	59
No	51	45	46	49	41

Source: Adapted from Davis, J. A., & Smith, T. W. (1980). *General social surveys, 1972–1980: Cumulative Codebook.* Chicago, IL: National Opinion Research Center; New Haven, CT: Yale University, Roper Public Opinion Research Center.

sidered a mental disorder by the psychiatric community. However, on December 15, 1973 the American Psychiatric Association voted to declassify homosexuality as a mental disorder and classify it as an alternative sexual behavior. Because of this vote, many people obtained an instantaneous "cure." Although the evidence is somewhat mixed, most studies have failed to support the hypothesis that homosexuals are more disturbed than heterosexuals (see Rosen, 1974, for a review of the literature). In one well-known study, Hooker (1957) gave 30 homosexual and 30 heterosexual men matched for age, education, and IQ a battery of psychological tests [including the Rorschach (ink blot) and TAT, discussed in

Chapter 12], and then asked several clinicians to rate the protocols for evidence of psychopathology. The clinicians, who were not told that half the group were homosexual, failed to find any systematic difference between the two groups. Although serious questions have been raised about the validity of such **projective tests** as the Rorschach and TAT (see Chapter 12) and although many authors disagree with Hooker's conclusion (see, for example, Bieber et al., 1962), Hooker's study supplies a useful example of one way in which such issues can be investigated scientifically.

Homosexual Behavior

Homosexual behavior includes everything involved in heterosexual behavior—except vaginal intercourse. What characterizes an act as homosexual is not the act itself, but the fact that the people performing the act are of the same sex. Some investigators have attempted to classify homosexuals according to whether they primarily adopt a dominant or passive role during sexual activity; however, only a small minority of homosexuals prefer one role or the other, with most assuming the dominant role on some occasions and the passive role on others.

There are, however, well-documented differences between the sexual life-styles of homosexuals and lesbians. Males are more likely than females to frequent bars and other known homosexual hangouts for the primary purpose of a quick sexual encounter. In a ten-year study of 1,500 homosexuals in the San Francisco area, Bell and Weinberg (1978) found that 43% of the male homosexuals they studied had had 500 or more different partners and that 28% had had 1,000 or more, compared to between five and nine partners for male heterosexuals. In contrast, lesbians are less motivated to pursue short-lived affairs and are more likely to enter into permanent living arrangements with another female.

Bell and Weinberg (1978) identified five homosexual life-styles; the percent of males and females adopting each are displayed in Table 8-12.

What makes people become homosexual, especially in view of the social censure it evokes in our society? Before attempting to answer the

TABLE 8-11
Stereotypes of and Attitudes toward Homosexuals

Stereotype	People Agreeing (%)
Homosexuals act like the opposite sex.	69
Homosexuals have unusually strong sex drives.	59
Homosexuals are afraid of the opposite sex.	56
It is easy to tell homosexuals by how they look.	39
Homosexuals are dangerous as teachers or youth leaders because they try to get sexually involved with children.	73
Homosexuals tend to corrupt their fellow workers sexually.	38
Homosexuality is a social corruption that can cause the downfall of a civilization.	49
A homosexual *should not* be allowed to work as a	
government official	67
medical doctor	68
minister	77
schoolteacher	77
jurist	77
A homosexual *should* be allowed to work as a	
beautician	72
artist	85
musician	85
florist	87

Source: Levitt, E. E., & Klassen, A. D., Jr. (1974). Public attitudes toward homosexuality. *Journal of Homosexuality, 1,* 29–43.

TABLE 8-12

Percent of San Francisco Homosexuals Reporting Various Life-styles*

Life-style	Males (percent)	Females (percent)
Closed couples	10	28
Open couples	18	17
Functionals	15	10
Dysfunctionals	12	5
Asexuals	16	11
Other**	29	29

* *Closed couples* maintain an exclusive relationship. *Open couples* live with a partner but maintain other relationships. *Functionals* are "swingers" who adopt a carefree attitude toward sex. *Dysfunctionals* are tormented by and regretful of being homosexual. *Asexuals* maintain a low level of sexual activity and have no close relationships.
** This group was too diverse to be categorized.
Source: Bell, A. P., & Weinberg, M. S. (1978). *Homosexualities: A study of diversity among men and women.* New York: Simon & Schuster.

question, we must recognize that homosexuality is not *one* thing caused by *one* factor; people engage in homosexual behavior for many different reasons. Most homosexual behavior is determined by a complex array of interacting factors, some of which are biologically based and some of which are derived from the environment.

Genetic Determinants

In a study of twins, Kallmann (1952) reported dramatic evidence that genetic factors may give rise to homosexual behavior. Kallmann found that all identical twin brothers of the homosexual males he studied also were homosexual, but that the concordance rate for fraternal twins was only 15%. If these findings were valid, they would supply compelling support for the genetic determination of at least one type of homosexuality. However, Kallmann's methods have been criticized severely by a number of investigators, and at least one study has failed to replicate his findings (Heston & Shields, 1968).

Hormones and Brain Circuits

It is probably not surprising to learn that most sexually aroused male mammals will try to mount a female who presents a sexually receptive posture; however, it may be surprising to learn that aroused animals of *both* sexes will mount animals of *either* sex who present a sexually receptive posture (Beach, 1977). There is considerable evidence to suggest that in most species males and females possess dispositions to display the sexual behavior of both sexes, depending on the eliciting stimulus. Frank Beach, an authority on sex in nonhuman animals, speculates that both male and female animals possess brain circuits capable of producing male and female sexual behavior, but that heterosexual responses are dominant. Clearly, human sexual behavior is a good deal more complex than that of nonhuman animals. Yet, inasmuch as the brain circuitry that affects human sexual behavior is housed in primitive parts of the brain (see Chapter 3), humans may possess a primitive tendency toward bisexuality, which, in most cases, is overridden by learning.

One plausible explanation for homosexuality is an imbalance in sex hormones—a deficiency in testosterone or a surplus of **estrogen** in males and a surplus of testosterone or a deficiency of estrogen in females. However, research has failed thus far to support this idea (see Rose, 1975). Some scientists have hypothesized that if testosterone were injected into homosexual males (and estrogen into lesbians), it would produce normal sexual preferences. Although studies have found that injections of sex-specific hormones sometimes cause an increase in the sex drive of homosexuals this increase causes them to engage in more *homosexual* activity.

Experience-based Determinants of Homosexuality

Although psychologists recognize the possibility of a biologically based disposition toward homosexuality, most psychological research has focused on aspects of experience—in particular, family interactions, learning histories, and social influences. The psychological theories that have provided the most popular explanations for homosexuality are psychoanalysis and learning theory.

Psychoanalytic Explanations of Homosexuality Psychoanalysts tend to attribute homosexuality to abnormal family relations. Thus, Bieber

et al. (1962) describe the typical family of a male homosexual as one with a dominant mother who is overly protective and intimate with her son and a passive father who is ineffectual or openly hostile. Some studies support these ideas; others do not. A study of 100 lesbians (Wolff, 1971) found that they typically come from families with rejecting or indifferent mothers and distant or absent fathers. Considered as a whole, the evidence suggests that certain family patterns are conducive to homosexuality in some people; however, homosexuals come from a wide variety of families and most members of families conducive to homosexuality do not become homosexual.

Learning Explanations of Homosexuality
Learning theorists attribute homosexuality to early conditioning. Most children experiment with sex. In cases where the experimentation involves either highly pleasureful contacts with a member of the same sex or highly unpleasant contacts with members of the opposite sex, a homosexual preference may develop. Research has shown that sexual arousal to homosexual objects

can be modified through aversive conditioning (Masters & Johnson, 1979). In a typical study, a homosexual patient is shown a picture of a same-sexed person in a provocative sexual posture and given an electric shock or an emetic (a substance that induces vomiting) when he displays signs of sexual arousal. With repeated association, the homosexual pictures become conditioned stimuli for aversive reactions. Alternatively, the patients may be shown heterosexual pictures and reinforced for responding sexually to them. However, changing a homosexual orientation through conditioning does not establish that it originally developed through conditioning. In addition, recent evaluations indicate that the long-term success rate of behavior therapy on homosexuals (as opposed to bisexuals) is very low (Coleman, 1982).

An Interactive Approach

Recently, Green (1980) has published an interactive theory of homosexuality. Green suggests that inborn temperamental factors and behavioral tendencies predispose certain people to homosexuality and that these factors may be linked to prenatal hormones. Whether an individual eventually practices homosexuality or not, however, depends on the way he is treated by his parents and peers and on his early sexual experiences. Interestingly, Green (1982) found that three-fourths of a group of boys who were notably effeminate in childhood became effeminate homosexuals.

In summary, we do not know as yet what causes homosexuality, although the evidence seems most consistent with an interactive model. In a recent review of the literature, Bell, Weinberg and Hammersmith (1981) concluded that there was not enough evidence to support any one theory of homosexuality, but that there was sufficient evidence to conclude that homosexual preferences usually become apparent by early adolescence.

RAPE

Rape can be the most terrifying event in a women's life. The sexual act or acts performed are often intended to humiliate or degrade her: bottles, gun barrels, and sticks may be thrust into her vagina or anus. She may be compelled to swallow urine or perform fellatio with such force that she thinks she might strangle or suffocate; her breasts may be bitten or burned with cigarettes. In many instances, her hope is to save her life — not her chastity. Her terror may be so overwhelming that she urinates, defecates, or vomits. If she escapes without serious outward signs of injury, she may suffer vaginal tears or infections, contract veneral disease, or become impregnated. For months or years afterward, she may distrust others, change residences frequently, and sleep poorly. Her friends and family may blame or reject her. (National Institute of Law Enforcement and Criminal Justice, 1978, p. 15)

Rape involves forcing someone to submit to sex against his or her will. It may involve a deviation in object — males may rape males; it may involve a deviation in aim — it may supply a means to express hatred, anger, and aggression rather than sexual desire. Whatever form it takes, the essence of rape lies in the unwillingness of the victim to take part in a sex act and in the fusion of sex and aggression on the part of the rapist. The unwillingness of the victim may extend from a wife's "I'm not in the mood tonight" to a terror-filled attempt to escape from a sadistic killer.

The stereotype of rape includes an unprovoked attack by a male on a female whom he does not know. Such incidents, however, constitute

TABLE 8-13
Percent of Students Endorsing Forced Sexual Intercourse with a Female for Various Reasons

Condition	High School Students		College Students	
	Males	**Females**	**Males**	**Females**
He spends a lot of money on her.	39	12	13	8
He is so turned on he cannot stop.	36	21	15	9
She has had sexual intercourse with other males.	39	18	25	7
She is stoned or drunk.	39	18	21	6
She lets him touch her above the waist.	39	28	36	12
She is going to have sex with him and changes her mind.	54	31	40	22
They have dated for a long time.	43	32	42	17
She has led him on.	54	26	42	28
She gets him sexually excited.	51	42	45	25

Sources: (high-school data) Giarrusso, R., Johnson, P., Goodchilds, J., & Zellman, G. (1979, April). *Adolescents' cues and signals: Sex and assault.* Paper presented at the Western Psychological Association meeting, San Diego, CA. *(college-student data)* Mahoney, E. R. (1983). *Human sexuality.* New York: McGraw-Hill.

only a small portion of all rapes; most rapes involve men and women who know one another, at least minimally. Consider the following findings, for example. Kanin (1957) found that 62% of the females he surveyed had been victims of sexually aggressive and offensive behavior from a male in their last year of high school. Of these incidents, 44% of the males involved were boyfriends or fiancés and 21% of the acts involved attempted or completed forced intercourse. Kanin (1967) found that 25% of a sample of college males admitted at least one attempt to force a female to have sex against her will. Burt (1980) found that 27% of a sample of female adults in Minnesota reported that at least one male had attempted to force them to have sex, 4–8% reported that they were forced to have sex against their will, and 10% reported that they had submitted to sexual advances out of fear. And Russell (1982) found that 14% of 930 women she studied reported being raped by their husbands.

These figures are appalling. The frequency with which forced sex occurs could not prevail unless the practices were in some ways condoned in our society—and there is evidence that this is the case. Giarusso et al. (1979) found that a high percentage of 14- to 18-year-old males and females condoned, under certain conditions, the use of physical force for the purpose of sex (see Table 8-13).

Social psychology research indicates that a surprisingly high proportion of males are disposed to force women to have sex under certain circumstances. Malamuth et al. (1980) found that 17% of a sample of males who listened to taped descriptions of a rape said that they would be at least "somewhat likely" to engage in the behavior; the percentage rose to 69% when they assumed they would not be punished! Crepault and Couture (1980) found that 33% of the males they studied reported that they fantasized about raping a women during sex with their regular partner. There is evidence that male college students with a proclivity to rape have a callous attitude toward women and that alcohol, or even the belief that one has consumed alcohol, increases sexual arousal associated with rape and other deviant behaviors (Briddell et al., 1976). These findings do not, however, mean that the males in question prefer violent sex to nonviolent sex.

Malamuth consistently has found that males experience more sexual arousal while watching scenes of mutually consenting sex than while watching scenes of forced sex.

Because the vast majority of rapes go unreported (see Table 8-14), it is difficult to estimate the incidence of rape. What we do know, however, is that from 1973 to 1979 the number of reported rapes increased faster than any other major crime and that the number continues to increase. In 1979 the FBI estimated that a women is raped in the United States every seven minutes. It is sobering to note that of reported rapes, only half the rapists are apprehended and only a minority of those apprehended are convicted of rape (Horos, 1974). The major patterns of reported rape, their locations, and attendant behaviors are outlined in Tables 8-15 and 8-16.

TABLE 8-14

Reasons Given by Women for Not Reporting Rape to the Police

Reason for Not Reporting	Persons Giving this Reason	
	Attempted Rape (%)	Completed Rape (%)
Nothing could be done	49	23
Not important enough	15	4
Police would not want to be bothered	7	14
Didn't want to take time; inconvenient	4	1
It was a private or personal matter	19	53
Didn't want to get involved	6	14
Fear of offender retaliation	10	19
Reported it to someone else	12	7
Other reasons	14	11

Source: McDermott, J. (1979). *Rape victimization in 26 American cities.* Washington, DC: U.S. Department of Justice, Law Enforcement and Assistance Administration, Table 35.

TABLE 8-15
Major Patterns of Rape

	Anger Rape	Power Rape	Sadistic Rape
Assault plans and length	Impulsive and of relatively short duration	Premeditated and preceded by persistent rape fantasies; assault may continue for extended time period during which victim held captive	Calculated, preplanned, and of extended duration; victim kidnapped, assaulted, and disposed of
Offense pattern	Episodic	Repetitive and may show increased aggression over time	Ritualistic, usually involving torture, bondage, and bizarre acts interspersed with nonsadistic assault
Offender's mood	Anger and depression	Anxiety	One of intense excitement
Offender's language	Abusive	Unstructured and manipulative — offender gives orders, asks personal questions, tells victim to say things, asks about victim's responses	Commanding and degrading
Dynamics, motivating factors	Retribution for perceived wrongs or injustices against offender; feels "put down"	Compensation for offender's depreciated feelings of inadequacy and insecurity	Symbolic destruction and elimination
Aggression	More physical force than necessary used to overpower victim; victim battered	Offender uses whatever force or threat is necessary to control victim	Physical force (anger and power) is eroticized
Victim's injury	Physical trauma to all areas of body	May be physically unharmed; bodily injury usually not intentional	Physical trauma to sexual areas of victim's body; in extreme cases victim mutilated and murdered

Source: Adapted from Groth, A. N. (1979). *Men who rape: The psychology of the offender.* New York: Plenum Press.

Groth et al. (1977) outline a continuum along which rapists may be classified, ranging from those who rape primarily for sexual gratification through those who rape primarily to exert power and/or to express anger. Males who rape to obtain sexual release are the least likely to be reported or convicted, and they usually rape women whom they know. The primary goal of the power rapist is to induce women to submit to him and to perform the sexual acts he demands as proof of his dominance. Groth and Burgess estimate that 65% of convicted rapists engage in **power rape,** although power rape constitutes only a small portion of all rapes. Men who engage in power rape tend to possess a stereotyped, macho view of the masculine role. Men who engage in **anger rape** are not motivated to obtain sexual gratification — they use sex to humiliate, degrade, and hurt women. Groth and Burgess (1977) estimate that 30% of convicted rapists engage in anger rape. Many of these men have a history of being rejected by females, and they rape strangers to get even.

The most dangerous rapist is the sadist, for this person must hurt his victim in order to experience sexual excitement. Typically he is psychopathic, maintains few ongoing relationships, uses other people for his own ends, experiences little guilt, and has a history of violence toward those weaker than he. **Sadistic rapists** are the most likely to injure, mutilate, desecrate, and kill the women they rape. It is fortunate indeed that this type of rapist is rare (representing only 5% of all convicted rapists).

TABLE 8-16
Where Stranger–Stranger Rapes Occur*

Location	Percent of Stranger–Stranger Rapes
On street, in park, playground, and the like	47
At or in the victim's home	18
Near the victim's home	14
Inside a commercial building	9
Inside an office or factory	1
In a vacation home, hotel, or motel	1
In a school	1
Other places	9

*Stranger–stranger rapes occur most frequently out-of-doors, but a significant percent occur in or near the victim's home (reflecting some planning by the rapist).
Source: McDermott, J. (1979). *Rape victimization in 26 American cities*. Washington, DC: U.S. Department of Justice, Law Enforcement and Assistance Administration, Table 10.

TABLE 8-17
Percent of Rape Victims Reporting Various Behaviors Before and After Rape

Impact	Before Rape (%)	After Rape (%)
Symptom		
difficulty sleeping	13.5	83.7
appetite/eating problems	19.2	63.8
cystitis	07.4	18.0
menstrual irregularity	20.2	28.6
headaches	23.2	40.0
rapid mood changes	29.4	63.6
depression	30.4	79.6
excitability	24.1	42.9
frequent crying	13.2	59.1
loss of temper	18.6	42.7
Reclusiveness (never going out alone)		
movies, concerts	65.7	91.9
restaurants	41.1	75.4
bars	71.3	89.5
public places (such as parks)	28.6	64.7
Sexual Behavior	No decrease after rape	Decrease after rape
frequency of oral sex	74.5	25.5
frequency of intercourse	71.1	29.9
frequency of orgasms	79.3	21.7
overall sexual satisfaction	67.3	32.7

Source: Norris, J., & Feldman-Summers, S. (1981). Factors related to the psychological impacts of rape on the victim. *Journal of Abnormal Psychology, 90,* 562–67.

It is difficult to discuss rape dispassionately. Few people, especially men, understand the immense trauma it inflicts on its victims. Power, anger, and sadistic rape typically leave deep psychological and emotional scars on their victims. Burgess and Holmstrom (1974), who interviewed 92 victims of rape within 30 minutes of their arrival at Boston City Hospital and followed up most of them afterward, found that most women experienced what they term **rape trauma syndrome.** This syndrome has two phases, acute and reorganization. In the *acute phase,* which lasted from several weeks to several months, the women experienced such emotional reactions as fear of additional violence, shock, anger, anxiety, revenge, shame, humiliation, and sometimes guilt. The women also experienced such physical problems as muscle tension, soreness, headaches, difficulty sleeping, nausea, and a variety of genital and urinary problems. Burgess and Holmstrom found that women in the acute phase dealt with the experience in one of two ways — by expressing their emotions or by controlling them. During the *reorganization phase,* many women changed residence, experi-enced nightmares, developed phobias toward situations similar to the rape, and suffered severe depression. Table 8-17 outlines the major reactions of 179 women, studied by Norris and Feldman-Summers (1981), who were raped but did not report it.

As expected, being raped has a profound ef-

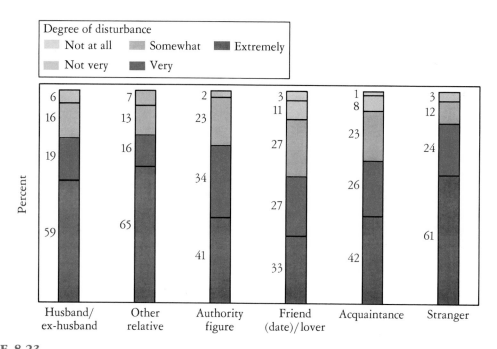

FIGURE 8-23

Degree of Disturbance a Rape Victim Experiences According to Relationship with Assailant
Women raped by relatives, strangers, or husbands (or ex-husbands) reported feeling the most disturbed. Women raped by authority figures, friends, or acquaintances also reported feeling extremely or very disturbed, but some reported low degrees of disturbance. *Source:* Russell, D. E. H. (1982). *Rape in marriage.* New York: Macmillan.

fect on the victim's sexual behavior. Burgess and Holmstrom (1979) reported that 71% of the women they studied engaged in sex less frequently after being raped, and that 38% refrained from sex entirely for at least three months following the rape. (Interestingly, 9% of the women in this study reported an increase in sexual activity. Burgess and Holmstrom attribute the increase to two factors — an attempt to reestablish a normal sexual orientation and a change in sexual identity). In addition to the decrease in sexual activity among women following rape, there is a decrease in enjoyment derived from the sexual activities in which they do engage (Feldman-Summers et al., 1979).

The fear and sexual inhibition that follow rape are determined in large part by classical conditioning. Cues that accompany the rape — especially the sexual behavior of the rapist — become conditioned stimuli, evoking the horror and disgust experienced during the rape. It follows that one antedote to the trauma of the experience is to extinguish and countercondition the

aversive responses by engaging in enjoyable sexual activities, starting with those that are least similar to the behaviors that occurred during the rape. For many women, this is a slow process that works only when initiated by them, and one that requires a great deal of patience from their partner.

The sexual fantasies of some people notwithstanding, there is little evidence that rape is anything other than an aversive experience for females. However, not all women experience the rape trauma syndrome associated with violent rape by a stranger. As indicated in Figure 8-23, the degree of disturbance experienced by a rape victim is closely associated with her relationship to the rapist. Rapes by friends and acquaintances tend to be less aggressive and more situational than rapes by strangers, husband, and ex-husband(s). Rapes by other relatives are disturbing because they are incestuous. Women raped by strangers tend to develop a more generalized fear of men (most of whom are strangers) than women raped by acquaintances.

SUMMARY

1. Traditionally, the scholarly study of human sexuality has been shunned; consequently, there are many myths about sex. Recently, however, psychologists have begun to investigate this aspect of human nature in greater detail.

2. Asexual reproduction has certain advantages. The fundamental reason why some species reproduce sexually is because sexual reproduction produces greater variation in offspring, which is adaptive in uncertain environments.

3. The basic biological differences between the sexes have important implications for their sexual behavior. Females are more certain of their maternity than males are of their paternity, and the females of most mammalian species invest more in their offspring than do the males. Therefore, in most species females tend to be more selective than males.

4. Although most marriages among humans are monogamous, polygyny is the primary system in most cultures; every male may have numerous wives, but not many can afford to pay for them. Few cultures practice polyandry. In most cultures of the world, women are not permitted to choose their husbands. Notwithstanding substantial variation among cultures, premarital and extramarital sexual relations occur in most societies.

5. A comparison of the *Kinsey Reports* and *Hunt Survey* suggests that the frequency of premarital sex, sex in marriage, and sex among the divorced and widowed has increased over the past three decades, particularly for women. However, the frequency of premarital sex for females appears to be associated with affection toward the partner rather than with promiscuity.

6. Biologically based sexual dispositions are shaped by three primary factors: the norms and values of a culture and its subcultures, social roles, and individual learning experiences. The socialization of sexual behavior in children involves the suppression and distortion of information. The central focus of sexual socialization in adolescence involves the learning of sex roles. Sex education courses often fail to address the concerns of the students who take them.

7. William Masters and Virginia Johnson have conducted the most extensive investigation of human physiological changes during the sex act. They divide human sexual behavior into four phases—excitement, plateau, orgasm, and resolution. Although these investigators emphasize the similarities between males and females, they report greater variation among females during the orgasmic phase and longer recovery periods for males.

8. Sexual arousal involves changes in the way people think as well as changes in how they feel. Studies have found that people must label their physiological arousal as sexual before they can feel sexually aroused. Recent research indicates that females experience as much physiological arousal to sexual stimuli as men but are more likely to deny it or to attribute it to nonsexual sources.

9. The more complex the brain of an animal, the more independent from hormonal control its sexual behavior. There are no drugs that induce sexual arousal, although some drugs stimulate erection, irritate the genitourinary tract, prolong orgasms, and reduce inhibitions. The expectation that drugs will enhance sexual arousal and performance appears to be more important than any physiological effect. The learning history of individuals and the ways in which they think about sex exert significant influences on their sexual behavior.

10. Like normal sexual behavior, sexual deviations probably result from an interaction between biological and learned factors. However, the evidence suggests that although biological forces may affect the intensity of sexual drive, experience determines

whether or not it will result in a sexual deviation — and if so, which type.

11. Surveys indicate that about 20% of American males and 10 – 20% of American females have had at least one homosexual experience; however, only from 1 – 3% are primarily homosexual. The majority of people in America strongly disapprove of homosexuality and harbor stereotypes of homosexuals. At present we do not know what causes people to adopt a homosexual orientation, although the evidence suggests that both inborn temperamental factors and early learning experiences are involved.

12. The incidence of rape is much higher than most people suspect; the vast majority, however, go unreported. Most rapes involve men and women who are acquainted with one another. Social psychological research indicates that a surprisingly high proportion of males are disposed to force women to have sex under certain circumstances. The motivation underlying the most brutal kinds of rape is not sexual gratification; it is to express power and anger. Victims of violent rape usually experience the rape trauma syndrome. The degree of disturbance experienced by a rape victim is associated with her relationship to the rapist.

Key Terms

Asexual Reproduction
Sexual Reproduction
Gamete
Disruptive Selection
Reproductive Fitness
Parental Investment
Pair-bonding
Monogamous
Perennial Monogamy
Annual Monogamy
Polygamous
Polygamy
Polygyny
Polyandry
Cultural Evolution
Biological Evolution
Reproductive Rate
Gestation Period
Lactation Period
Premarital Sex
Extramarital Sex
Kinsey Reports
Hunt Survey
Orgasm
Double Standard
Promiscuity
Masturbation
Biologically Based Sexual
  Disposition
Sexual Script
Sexual Guilt

Sex Role
Nongonococcal Urethritis
  (NGU)
Gonorrhea
Syphilis
Herpes
Acquired Immune Deficiency
  Syndrome (AIDS)
Gonococcus
Chlamydia
Chancre
Secondary Sexual Characteristic
Sex Education
Ovulation
Sexually Transmitted Disease
Coitus
Excitement Phase
Vasocongestion
Plateau Phase
Orgasmic Phase
Ejaculation
Refractory Period
Resolution Phase
Estrus
Copulation
Menstrual Cycle
Menstruation
Testosterone
Castration
Nymphomaniac
Aphrodisiac

Genitourinary Tract
Amyl Nitrate
Cocaine
Amphetamine
Pheromone
Olfactory Stimula
Tactile Stimulation
Erogenous Zone
Sexual Imagery
Sexual Deviation
Homosexuality
Pedophilia
Incest
Fetishism
Voyeurism
Exhibitionism
Sadism
Masochism
Rape
Heterosexuality
Bisexuality
Transsexuality
Transvestism
Transsexual
Projective Test
Estrogen
Power Rape
Anger Rape
Sadistic Rape
Rape Trauma Syndrome

RECOMMENDED READINGS

Beach, F. A. (Ed.) (1977). *Human sexuality in four perspectives*. Baltimore, MD: Johns Hopkins Press. A selection of ten articles by leading authorities on sexuality. In particular, Beach's chapter on sex in nonhuman animals and Davenport's article on cross-cultural patterns are excellent.

Daly, M., & Wilson, M. (1978). *Sex, evolution, and behavior*. Belmont, CA: Wadsworth Publishing Company, Inc. A sociobiological analysis of the evolution of sex and related behaviors.

Ford, C. S., & Beach, F. A. (1951). *Patterns of sexual behavior*. New York: Harper & Row. A classic in the field (although somewhat dated), this book supplies the most complete survey of sexual practices in other cultures and among nonhuman animals.

Mahoney, E. R. (1983). *Human sexuality*. New York: McGraw-Hill. An excellent textbook that served as a primary reference for this chapter.

Masters, W. H., & Johnson, V. E. (1966). *Human sexual response*. Boston, MA: Little, Brown. This book describes quite technically the phases of sexual responsiveness in males and females. Physiological in orientation.

Peplau, L. A., & Hammen, C. L. (1977). Sexual behavior: Social psychological issues. *Journal of Social Issues, 33*. Selections from the sexual research of social psychologists, including topics on cognitive factors, bisexuality, moral reasoning, intimacy in dating, sex and aggression, sex and culture, and the ethics of sex research.

Pocs, O. (Ed.) (1985). *Human sexuality*. Guilford, CT: The Dushkin Publishing Group, Inc. A collection of recent articles drawn from the public press covering a wide array of interesting and often controversial topics on sexuality.

9

PHYSICAL AND COGNITIVE DEVELOPMENT

Examine the following photographs. Which are photographs of the same person? These photographs illustrate an obvious point: as people go through life, they change. But how far can this point be taken? How different are you now from the way you were when you were a child or an adolescent? Do people ever change so drastically that, in effect, they become a different person? What, if anything, remains the same?

Such physical changes as those displayed in the photographs are obvious and easy to recognize; however, people also change in other, less obvious ways. Consider, for example, the following changes in the way children think. Anne Bernstein (1976) asked three- to twelve-year-old children a simple question: "How do people get babies?" You might expect the answers of the children to reflect what they had been told about reproduction, but this was not the case. "To get a baby, go to a store and buy a duck," said Susan, a four-year-old. Apparently Susan had been told something about the birds and the bees (and perhaps the stork, which she classified as a duck), yet clearly interpreted the information in a way unintended by her informants.

Bernstein found that from age three to twelve children's ideas about reproduction change in a fairly predictable way. Typically, three- and four-year-olds regard reproduction as a geographical matter: babies come from certain places — *stores, tummies, "God's place."* The average five-year-old believes that babies, like cars and TVs, are products of modern technology.

By the age of seven or so, most children have begun to think of reproduction in physiological terms — but their ideas are muddled. "The sperm comes from the daddy. It swims into the penis — and I think it makes a little hole — and then it swims into the vagina" said one seven-year-old. It is

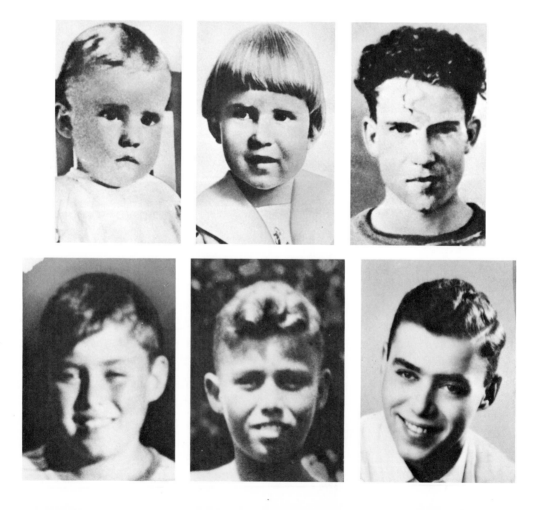

usually not until around twelve years of age that children give essentially accurate explanations of reproduction.

The differences in the way in which children think about reproduction suggest that young children may, in effect, have qualitatively different minds from older children and adults. Yet, some of the ways in which we think and many of the things we learn and remember stay with us throughout our lives. In this chapter we examine the major changes that occur in physical, sensory, and perceptual development from infancy through old age; then we examine the development of language and the growth of knowledge in children and adults.

PHYSICAL DEVELOPMENT

FROM CONCEPTION TO BIRTH — THE PRENATAL PROCESS

Human beings undergo the most rapid physical changes of their lives during the period between conception and birth (see Figures 9-1 and 9-2). The weight of an **embryo** increases by almost 5,000% between the first and second months. By the end of the second month a one-inch-long embryo has eyes, ears, a nose, a mouth, arms, legs, fingers, toes, a liver, a heart, a circulatory system, a spinal cord, bones, and a *tail*. The first six months are devoted primarily to the growth of the basic bodily systems and to the replacement of cartilage by bone cells. The major development of the brain and nervous system takes place during the final three months of the prenatal process. During this time all the basic structures are established (see Figure 9-2). However, additional important changes, such as increased complexity in the pattern of neural connections, occur after birth and during childhood.

PHYSICAL DEVELOPMENT DURING INFANCY

The Development of the Body

At birth, the average full-term infant weighs approximately 7 – 7.5 pounds and is between 19

←

The photographs in the top row are of Richard Nixon; the photographs in the botton row are of another person.

and 22 inches long (see Table 9-1). On the average, boys are slightly larger than girls at birth and throughout the life span, but girls typically develop faster than boys. In our culture, most infants gain approximately two pounds per month during the first six months. Genetic factors primarily are responsible for physical development, although such environmental factors as nutrition, prenatal and postnatal care, and social-emotional stimulation can exert an important influence on growth.

The Development of Motor Skills

Although there are many things newborns cannot do, they are capable of certain reflexive behaviors and some voluntary behaviors. **Reflexive behaviors** are automatic and triggered involuntarily by specific stimuli. For example, if you were to touch an infant on the cheek, close to the mouth, she would turn her head and root around in order to bring her mouth into contact with the object that touched her cheek. This is called the **rooting reflex.** Babies also have **sucking reflexes,** and automatically suck on anything that touches or is inserted into the mouth. Because they are related to feeding, such reflexes clearly have survival value.

In addition to reflexes, newborn infants display many voluntary behaviors — looking around, turning their bodies, and opening and closing their hands and mouths. Such **motor skills** develop rapidly and in an orderly sequence during the early years of life (Figure 9-3). The newborn who initially could not lift his or her head has come a long way when at four years he or

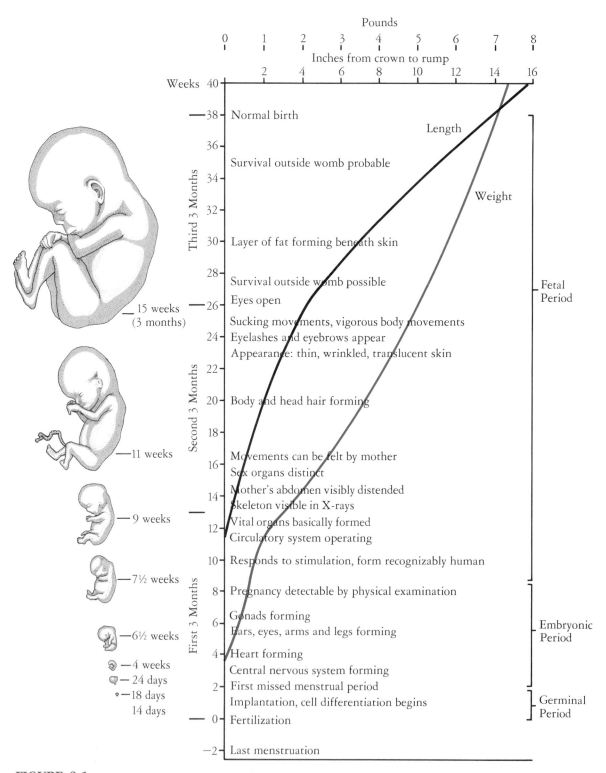

FIGURE 9-1

Growth of Embryo and Fetus *Source:* Adapted from Fisher, K. W., & Lazerson, A. (1984). *Human development: From conception through adolescence.* New York: W. H. Freeman.

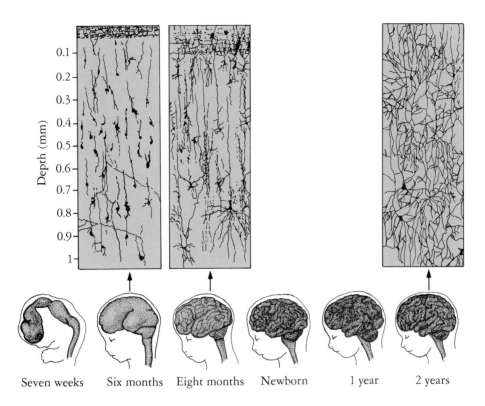

FIGURE 9-2

The Development of the Brain   As the brain enlarges, the cerebral hemispheres overgrow the cerebellum and other regions.   The brain continues to grow after birth.   An infant brain weighs from 300–350 grams at birth, 900 by one year, 1,000 by two years, and from 1,300–1,400 grams by adulthood.   As the brain grows, the dendrites — which mediate the transmission of nerve impulses between neurons — increase in number and length.   *Source:* Adapted from Grobstein, C. (1979).   External human fertilization.   *Scientific American, 240,* pp. 57–68.

TABLE 9-1
Physical Growth of the Average Child during the First Two Years

	At birth	6 months	12 months	18 months	24 months
Height (inches)	20	26	29.50	32	34.25
Weight (pounds)	7.25	16.25	21.50	24.75	27.50
Relative head size (percent of body length)	25			20	
Number of teeth	0	1*	8	16	20*
Brain weight (pounds)	0.75	1.5	2.0		2.5
Brain weight as percent of average adult brain	25	50	67		75

* The teeth mature below the gums.   The first baby tooth erupts from between 6–9 months; the full set of 20 is in place from between 24–28 months.   *Source:* Adapted from Sarafino, E. P., & Armstrong, J. W. (1980).   *Child and adolescent development.*   Glenview, IL: Scott, Foresman.   *Data:* Kessen, W., Haith, M., & Salapatek, P. H. (1970).   Human infancy: A bibliography and guide.   In P. H. Mussen (Ed.), *Carmichael's manual of child psychology* (3rd ed., Vol. 1).   New York: Wiley & Sons.   Tanner, J. M. (1970).   Physical growth.   In P. H. Mussen (Ed.), *Carmichael's manual of child psychology* (3rd ed., Vol. 1).   New York: Wiley & Sons.   Watson, E. H., & Lowrey, G. H.   (1967).   *Growth and development of children* (5th ed.).   Chicago, IL: Year Book Medical Publishers.

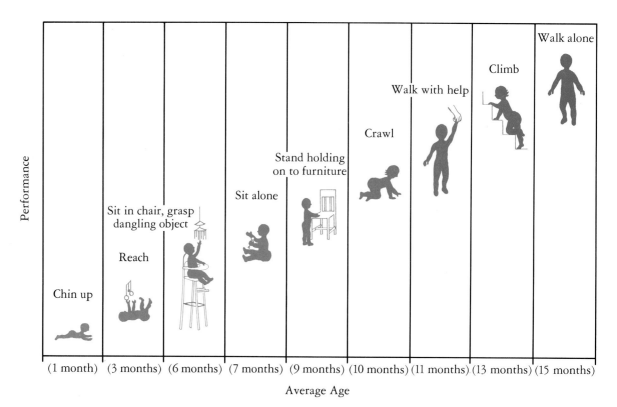

FIGURE 9-3

Milestones in Motor Development Although some infants acquire these motor skills sooner than others, most infants acquire them in the order displayed. *Source:* Adapted from Rubin, Z., & McNeil, E. B. (1981). *The psychology of being human* (3rd ed.) New York: Harper & Row.

she can walk forward, sideways, backward, stand on one foot, walk on tiptoes, jump two feet in the air, hop on one foot, throw a ball, and ride a tricycle. **Fine motor skills** — those that involve manipulation of the thumb and fingers — and hand–eye coordination also develop rapidly during the early years.

Two general principles — **differentiation** and **integration** — describe the orderliness of development (physical development and development of cognitive and social abilities). At first, infants reach for objects with both hands, their arms moving together. With development, infants differentiate these responses by reaching for an object with one hand and integrate these responses with such other responses as looking and grasping. It is interesting to note that infants progressively acquire motor control of responses beginning at the center of their bodies and moving to the periphery and beginning at the head and moving to the toes. For example, infants acquire con-

trol of their arms before their fingers and they acquire control of their arms before their legs.

The Acceleration and Retardation of Motor Development Clearly, the role of heredity is strong in reflexive behaviors; but what about the development of such voluntary motor behaviors as walking? Do motor skills develop in the absence of any opportunity to practice them? Do children learn motor skills faster if they are encouraged to practice?

Although psychologists began investigating the effects of *restriction* and *special practice* on the development of motor skills almost a half century ago, the answers to these questions have not been as decisive as you might expect. In one early study, Wayne and Margaret Dennis (1940) examined walking skills in Hopi Indians. In traditional Hopi society, babies were carried on their mothers' backs during the early months of life and tightly strapped to a flat board so they could move only their heads. They were taken out of the backpacks only for a short period at night, when their parents played with them. When the Dennises compared Hopi children raised in the traditional way to Hopi children raised without cradle boards, they failed to find any difference in the age at which the children started walking. Note, however, that some practice was available to the infants raised on cradle boards, which may have been enough for them to develop the coordination necessary for walking. In a later study, the Dennises (1960) found that children raised in Iranian orphanages had almost no opportunity to practice motor skills and did not learn to walk until up to a year later than other Iranian children. The results of these studies and others suggest that severe restriction in motor activity early in life may retard motor development but moderate restriction does not.

What about extra practice? In two early studies on pairs of identical twins, Gesell and Thompson (1929) and McGraw (1935) attempted to determine whether special training enhances motor development. In both studies, one twin was given special training in particular motor skills (for example, walking and stair climbing) but the other twin was permitted to develop these skills at a natural pace. The results of these studies failed to support the idea that special training accelerates motor development. Although twins who had received special training sometimes acquired a motor skill before twins who had not received special training, the untrained twins developed the skill spontaneously and caught up very rapidly after a small amount of practice. More recent evidence, however, casts some doubt on these conclusions, at least as they apply to walking.

Until infants are about eight weeks old, they perform well-coordinated walking movements —known as the **walking reflex**—when held under the arms with their feet touching a flat surface. Infants also lift and place their feet in a way similar to the movements displayed by kittens— the **placing reflex.** Zelazo and his associates (1972) conducted a study on the walking and placing reflexes of infants to see whether active exercise of these reflexes during the first eight weeks would accelerate the acquisition of walking. Twenty-four one-week-old babies were di-

vided into four groups. Infants in the first group (the active exercise group) were given practice in walking and placing every day for seven weeks. Infants in the second group were given passive exercise (their limbs were pumped gently back and forth while they lay on their backs). Infants in the third group did not receive any special training but, like the infants in the other groups, were tested at weekly intervals. Finally, infants in the fourth group (the control group) were tested at eight weeks of age to determine whether the testing to which the third group was exposed had any effect on their walking and placing reflexes. The results of the study showed that the infants in the active-exercise group learned to step before the infants in the other groups (see Figure 9-4). Zelazo and his associates concluded that active exercising of the primitive walking and placing reflexes accelerates the age at which walking begins.

It seems reasonable to assume that accelerating such skills as walking is beneficial to children. However before giving your own children such special attention, you should consider the possibility that it may have some undesirable consequences. For example, Fitzgerald, Strommen, and McKinney (1977) have suggested that early

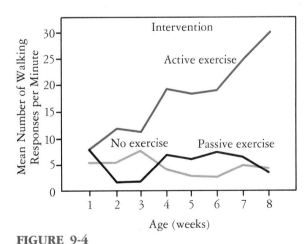

FIGURE 9-4

The Effect of Practice on the Reflexive Stepping Pattern A few minutes of practice each day increases the number of steps transforming the reflexive stepping pattern to an instrumental response and accelerating the age at which unaided walking begins. *Source:* Adapted from Zelazo, P. R., Zelazo, N. A., & Kolb, S. (1972). ''Walking'' in the newborn. *Science, 176,* 314–15.

acceleration of motor skills may block or delay intellectual development, especially in hyperactive children.

PHYSICAL DEVELOPMENT IN ADOLESCENCE

Like many aspects of development, growth in height and weight is not uniform throughout the life span. The first two or three years of life are characterized by rapid growth; this is followed by a period of steady and regular growth. At about eleven years of age, the **adolescent growth spurt** begins and the child grows about two to four inches a year for several years (see Figure 9-5). Females generally begin their adolescent growth spurt before males, and they generally stop sooner.

During the last century, the adolescent growth spurt has begun at progressively earlier ages. Today's adolescents grow faster and bigger than they used to, and they also attain full adult stature earlier. The trend toward larger size and

earlier maturation is known as the **secular trend** because it has occurred among children in the whole population over many centuries. The most obvious contributing factor to the secular trend appears to be diet and health care. Another contributing factor may be related to the increased mobility of our society. Because people travel much more easily than they used to, they tend to marry people from more distant communities. Thus, on the average, people are choosing mates with more genetic differences than they were in the past. The offspring of parents who differ in genetic characteristics are likely to be healthier because genes for recessive, often harmful, traits from one parent are counteracted by correspondingly dominant genes from the other parent. The resulting increase in general fitness may be responsible for the increase in average height of the population at large.

Puberty

Except for the prenatal process, development during puberty is accompanied by greater bodily changes than at any other period. At puberty, there is a sharp increase in the level of certain hormones that triggers final maturation of the reproductive system and of **secondary sex characteristics** (Figure 9-6). Although, on the average, females start and complete puberty earlier than males, there is considerable individual variation within each sex in both age of onset and duration of puberty.

As the average height of people has been increasing over the years, the average age of **menarche** (the onset of menstruation) has been decreasing — on the average, by four months each decade during the past century. One explanation for the progressively earlier onset of menstruation suggests that the sharp increase in hormonal production associated with puberty is triggered by the acquisition of a certain height. Because the average height of girls is increasing, they reach the height programmed for the release of hormones earlier and thus enter puberty at an earlier age. This explanation, although attractive, is probably too simple. The positive correlation between height and age for the onset of puberty does not necessarily reflect a cause-and-effect relationship. It is quite possible that some third

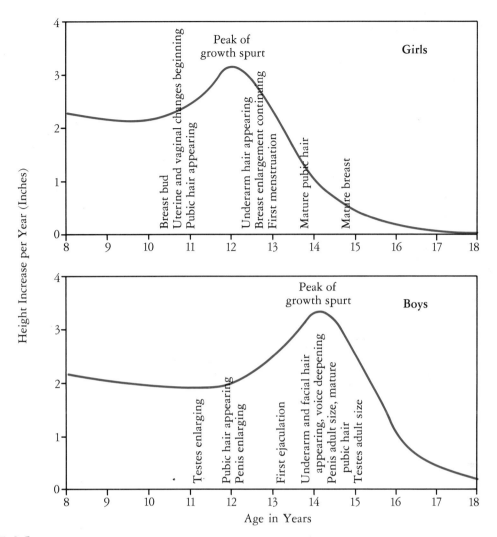

FIGURE 9-5

Secondary Sex Characteristics   The curved lines represent the average increase in height from age 8–18. The secondary sex characteristics listed may occur earlier or later in an individual's development but usually follow this order.   Note the relationship between secondary sex characteristics and adolescent growth spurt.   In girls the growth spurt signals the onset of menstruation; in boys the growth spurt is preceded by enlargement of the testes and the penis.   *Sources:* Tanner, J. M. (1978).   *Fetus into man: Physical growth from conception to maturity.*   Cambridge, MA: Harvard University Press.   Tanner, J. M., & Whitehouse, R. H. (1976).   Clinical longitudinal standards for height, weight, height velocity, weight velocity, and the stages of puberty, *Archives of Disease in Childhood, 51,* 170–79.

factor (for example, improved nutrition) is responsible for both the early adolescent growth spurt and for the early onset of puberty.   Alternatively, it is possible that separate factors are responsible for each.   For instance, increase in height may be caused by improved nutrition and early menstruation may be caused by early exposure to adult social experiences.

Psychological Effects of Physical Development in Adolescence   The process of sexual maturation that occurs during puberty is closely associated with the adolescent sense of identity.   Studies suggest that reaching sexual maturity earlier or later than other members of the same sex may have significant psychological effects.   In one study on adolescent males aged 12–17, Jones

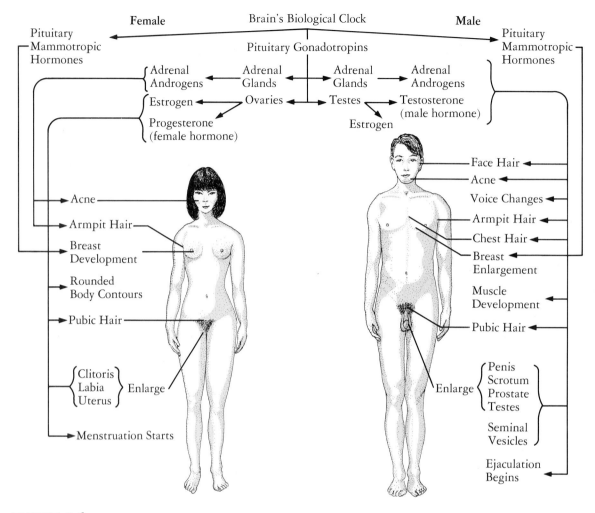

FIGURE 9-6
Physical Development in Adolescence   *Source:* Adapted from Sarafino, E. P., & Armstrong, J. W. (1980). *Child and adolescent development.* Glenview, IL: Scott, Foresman.

and Bayley (1950) found that early-maturing males were rated by their peers and by adults as more self-possessed and reserved, more likely to behave in socially appropriate ways, and better able to laugh at themselves than late-maturing males. This study also found that late-maturing males were rated as less attractive, less popular, more tense and eager, and more restless, talkative, and bossy. Jones (1957) followed up certain of the subjects from the study at age 33, and found that many of the differences between early and late maturers persisted over the years. More recent studies have supported these findings (for example, Apter et al., 1981).

For females, the case is not as clear-cut. Faust (1960) found that early-maturing girls were rated lower on desirable personality characteristics than girls who had not yet reached puberty. However, Jones and Mussen (1958) found that late-maturing girls had lower self-esteem and a greater need for recognition than girls who had matured at the "normal" time. These findings suggest that it is more important to their peers for females than for males to be "in phase" developmentally. Another study suggests that it also is more important to adolescent females themselves. Frazier and Lisonbee (1950) questioned 580 tenth-grade boys and girls regarding their concerns about physical development. While the boys said that they preferred to develop early, to be tall, and to be moderately heavy, the girls did not want to be too tall or too short, too fat or too thin, or to develop too slowly or too early.

PHYSICAL CHANGES IN ADULTHOOD AND OLD AGE

The body grows from birth until about age 30; then, typically, it begins to lose efficiency. Nathan Shock (1977) and his associates have found that most bodily functions lose about one percent of their original capacity each year after age 30. It is not surprising that about 120 years is the greatest age attained by anyone for whom we have adequate birth and death records, since, according to Shock's estimates, the reserve ability of the body would run out at about 120 years.

The Climacteric

Perhaps the most significant biological change that occurs during adulthood relates to people's reproductive capacities. *Climacteric* and *menopause* are terms often used interchangeably, but there is a useful technical distinction between them. The **climacteric** is the period during which reproductive capacity in men and women decreases, culminating, for women, in the menopause. The **menopause,** usually occurring between the ages of 45 and 55, is the time in which menstruation becomes sporadic and finally ceases. The average age of the onset of menopause has been rising slowly and is currently in the early fifties (Cherry, 1976). For most men, the climacteric occurs later in life, when there is a marked decline in the production of fertile sperm. Levels of female hormones (called **estrogens**) drop sharply at menopause; however, levels of testosterone and other male hormones (called **androgens**) decline more gradually.

It is commonly believed that menopause is accompanied by such experiences as depression, emotional volatility, hot flashes, and urinary dysfunction. However, Neugarten (1967) interviewed several hundred middle-aged women and found that they did not experience most of these symptoms. Fifty-eight percent of the women asserted that menopause had no effect on their physical and emotional health; ten percent felt that it was accompanied by improvements in these areas. According to Neugarten's respondents, the worst thing about menopause was not knowing what to expect. These findings were supported by a later study on Caucasian and Japanese women (Goodman, Stewart, & Gilbert, 1977). Interestingly, although most women in the Neugarten study felt they had not experienced great difficulty with menopause, they still believed other women did. It appears that commonly held beliefs about the nature of menopause are not easily altered by personal experiences. Beliefs about the constellation of symptoms that allegedly accompany menopause probably have arisen from the fact that menopausal women who experience these symptoms are the ones most likely to contact a doctor.

In conclusion, we emphasize that although the evidence suggests that menopause need not be especially stressful, it is clearly an important developmental milestone. For some women it brings an end to concern about pregnancy; for others it brings a perceived onset of old age; for all it brings the recognition that a unique phase of development is ended. Notman (1979) points out that the total context of midlife changes must be considered when assessing the impact of menopause.

Aging

Aging involves the gradual lessening in efficiency of numerous physical functions (see Figure 9-7) and such changes in physical appearance as wrinkling skin, thinning hair, and graying color of hair; there are, however, significant individual differences. Many changes associated with age are now clearly recognized as resulting from degenerative diseases that are neither universal nor inevitable and, in many cases, can be treated or prevented.

Many people believe that aging is accompanied by a loss of brain cells; some even provide a number. "After you reach 30, you lose 1,000 (or 10,000, or 100,000) brain cells a day." This belief is false (Diamond, 1978). There is no evidence that brain cells die in old age, although

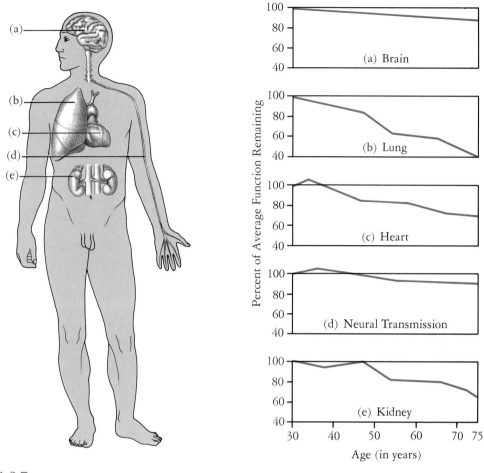

FIGURE 9-7

Physical Changes with Age   Between the ages of 30 and 70, adults experience a gradual decrease in many physical responses   *Source:* After Leaf, A. (1973, September).   Getting old.   *Scientific American, 299,* 52.

there may be a slight decrease in the number of branches on dendrites (Buell & Coleman, 1979). Senility is not caused by the systematic loss or deterioration of brain cells; it is caused by such degenerative processes as Alzheimer's disease (Henig, 1981), inhibited circulation of blood in the brain, poor diet, and the large quantities of drugs sometimes prescribed for the aged (Smith, 1979).

No one knows for sure what causes aging. All species have a typical life span, but individuals in most species do not die of old age. Although most humans live longer today than they lived in past decades, the maximum life span has not changed. Some scientists believe that in humans,

aging and death are programmed genetically. Others believe that they are just a matter of wear and tear — that is, due to such factors as cell loss, waste accumulation from cell activity, cessation of cell reproduction, damage to genetic information stored in cells, lowering of immunity to disease, and changes in the endocrine system (see Timiras, 1972, for a review).

Figure 9-8 outlines the tremendous increase in the number of elderly people in the population. A 65-year-old man may now expect to live to 79 and a 65-year-old woman to 83. The increase in the number of elderly people has stimulated an interest in **gerontology,** or the study of aging. Gerontologists point out that many peo-

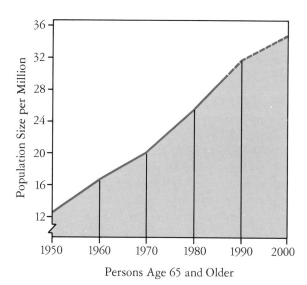

FIGURE 9-8

Increase in the Number of Elderly The number of persons in the United States over the age of 65 is increasing at a rapid rate. *Source: U.S. News & World Report,* (1984, July 2). p. 53.

ple harbor stereotypes and prejudices about old people, and identify numerous ways in which our society neglects the elderly.

It is obvious that the aging process does not affect all persons at the same rate or to the same extent. Aging is modified by such factors as genetic inheritance, physical environment, quality of nutrition (throughout earlier years and in old age), medical care, physical activity, and levels of short-term and long-term stress. Because people vary widely concerning these kinds of factors, among older people individual differences are often more marked than at any other time during development. Some older people reflect many of the symptoms popularly thought to be associated with old age; others continue to be healthy and active, demonstrating that certain of the unavoidable physiological changes associated with aging need not necessarily prevent one from leading a fulfilling life. Artist Georgia O'Keeffe took vigorous daily walks in the New Mexico desert and took up pottery in her nineties, while others, years younger than O'Keeffe, lose all interest in life, isolate themselves from human relationships, and simply await death. Although it is not true that aging is a state of mind, it is probably true that aging is affected by one's state of mind (Kalish,

1975). Neugarten (1967) found that 75% of a group of 75- to 79-year-olds were active, social, intellectually acute, and satisfied with their lives.

As the results of research on aging accumulate, it is increasingly apparent that although aging involves certain inevitable losses in physical ability, it need not impair intellectual and social functioning. Many older people suffer more from decreases in environmental, intellectual, and social stimulation — especially decreases in stimulation associated with the death of a spouse, retirement, or confinement to an "old-age home" — than from the actual physical impairments of aging. In some cases, however, it is difficult to separate cause from effect. For example, loss of hearing and visual acuity may be related to older people's preference for familiar environments; yet it may also be the case that withdrawal from the challenge of dealing with new and demanding physical and social situations contributes to such decrements. Research indicates that elderly people can improve their memories and problem-solving abilities when they are given incentives (Langer et al., 1979) and when they are taught to use different strategies (Poon et al., 1980; Giambia & Arenberg, 1980). Recently, some scientists (for example, Fozard & Popkin, 1978) have advocated designing environments for the elderly that are attentive to the developmental changes that

accompany old age. Consequently, with proper diet, medical attention, exercise, and intellectual and social stimulation, the losses associated with aging can be held to a minimum.

DEATH

Deciding when someone is dead is occasionally a complex matter (see Chapter 3). However, death normally occurs when one or more of the body's vital systems ceases to function. Although death is essentially a physical matter, social and emotional factors may contribute to the processes that lead to death. For example, depressed people may fail to eat properly and thereby predispose their bodies to disease. Or, as we describe in Chapters 7 and 13, stress may exact a physical

toll. The marked tendency of people to die within the first three months following their birthday and shortly after the death of a spouse may reflect psychological factors.

People are most vulnerable to death during infancy and old age (Kalish, 1982). As people grow old, they typically suffer a series of illnesses, become infirm, and finally enter a terminal phase of life from which no recovery is possible (Kimmel, 1980). An automobile accident is the leading cause of death for young people (ages 25 – 34); cancer and heart disease are the leading causes of death for older people. Among those who die of old age, the last four or five years are often a period of declining physical and intellectual ability, with a marked reduction of energy and a tendency to withdraw in the months immediately preceding death (Riegel & Riegel, 1972; Lieberman, 1966). We discuss research on the process of facing death in Box 9-1.

BOX 9-1
CONFRONTING DEATH

How do people feel as they approach death? Although it is among the most ancient of topics, only recently have psychologists and others in related fields begun to study the process of death. Therapist Elizabeth Kubler-Ross has studied people who are dying, and her work has been influential in evoking concern for their psychological needs. According to Kubler-Ross (1969), dying people go through a number of psychological stages. During the first stage, they deny the seriousness of their condition. During the second

stage, dying individuals experience anger ("Why me?"), which is directed toward other people in general. Following this, they go through a bargaining stage, attempting to make a deal with fate ("If you let me recover, I will do such and such"). When this fails, dying people experience a profound sense of loss and become severely depressed. Finally, if they successfully pass through all of the previous stages, dying individuals may reach a stage that involves acceptance of their fate, readiness to die, and preparation for the event.

Kubler-Ross' stage theory of dying has been questioned by other scholars. For example, Richard Kastenbaum (1979) points out that there is no strong evidence that a person actually passes through such a sequence of stages during the process of dying. People who are dying may react in any or all the ways suggested by Kubler-Ross, but, Kastenbaum cautions, these stages should not be viewed in isolation from the total context of the person's life. There is a danger that family and medical staff may feel that "He's just going through

SENSORY AND PERCEPTUAL DEVELOPMENT

When newborn infants enter the world, can they see and hear things the same way they do when they are older, or must they learn these abilities? This question has a long history in psychology. Although it is obvious that infants are born with sensory organs that prepare them to perceive things in the environment, such early psychologists as William James (1890) believed that the perceptual world of infants is "one great blooming, buzzing confusion" (p. 488) and such early behaviorists as J. B. Watson believed that the mind of the newborn infant is a *tabula rasa,* "blank slate," on which experience inscribes its lessons. In opposition to these environmentalist views, other psychologists and philosophers have insisted that infants inherit at least a rudimentary ability to perceive the basic properties of the physical world. We now review the evidence on the sensory and perceptual worlds of the infant, and then consider the age-old question of what infants inherit and what they learn.

THE INFANT'S SENSORY WORLD

Research has established that newborn infants can see and hear things (although their visual and auditory systems do not function at a mature level), can locate and follow moving objects with their eyes, and spend from 5–10% of their waking hours scanning the environment. Scanning

the anger stage," and fail to show an understanding of real grievances and concerns. Kastenbaum also questions whether Kubler-Ross' theory should be taken as a model for the way people should die. He points out that just as people react differently to physical and psychological events throughout their lives, they react in different ways to this ultimate event.

According to Kalish and Reynolds (1976), people change their attitude toward death as they grow older. These researchers compared the responses of people in three age groups: 20–39, 40–59, and over 60, to such questions as where they would prefer to die, how often they thought about death, and how frightening death was to them. The results of this study showed that people over 60 years of age think about death more often and are less frightened by it than those younger than them. However, although thinking about death may help a person accept death (Kalish, 1976) and even though elderly people as a group think about death more than younger people, it is not the case that all elderly people respond to death with acceptance (Kastenbaum & Weisman, 1972).

Often people simply do not know how to react to the terminally ill. In response to this quandary, usually it is best to consider the patient's needs. Schulz (1978) identifies three major needs of the dying person: the control of physical pain, the maintenance of a sense of dignity and self-worth, and the need to receive love and affection. It is often difficult, however, to satisfy these needs — especially in hospitals and nursing homes. In recognition of the problems attendant to caring for the needs of a dying person in an institutional setting, hospices have been designed to provide the unique care required by the dying. Hospices are structured to ensure that the terminally ill die without pain, with dignity, and surrounded by loved ones.

movements are more likely to be horizontal than vertical, and scanning is often adjusted to the size of the object under consideration. However, the muscular control necessary for efficient accommodation is poorly developed in newborns and their scanning movements are not well controlled. Of all the objects that psychologists have given newborn infants to look at, vertical lines have been most successful in capturing their attention.

One of the methods employed by psychologists to explore the perceptual abilities of newborns is to examine their ability to discriminate between different kinds of objects. Early research established that infants could distinguish between human faces and other objects, and that they preferred to look at faces (Fantz, 1966; see Figure 9-9). However, later research indicated that infants' preference for human faces is only one instance of their more general preference for patterned stimuli over nonpatterned stimuli (see Figure 9-10).

The visual system matures rapidly. By two months infants can discern hue and brightness (Teller & Bornstein, 1984). By four months scanning occupies about 35% of infants' waking hours, and their ability to focus at varying distances is almost as good as that of an adult. Four-month-old infants show a preference for natural over distorted faces and gaze longer at certain features, such as eyes. This and other preferences displayed by infants reflect an ongoing preference for stimuli that are slightly more complex and novel than those with which the infant is familiar. By six months the visual acuity of most infants is 20/20 (Banks & Salapatek, 1983).

Although the visual system takes some time to mature, the auditory system is essentially complete at birth; indeed, it is known to be functional well before birth. A seven-month-old fetal heart

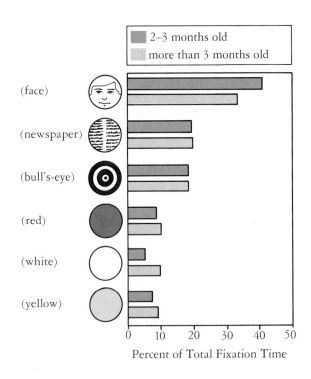

FIGURE 9-9

Fantz's Apparatus: A Measure of Pattern Perception Robert Fantz designed this apparatus to study what babies like to look at. The babies were situated beneath a stand that held pattern cards. From above the stand a researcher could observe the amount of time the babies' eyes were directed at each pattern. This procedure demonstrated that babies prefer patterns over solid colors and faces over patterns. *Sources:* Adapted from Fantz, R. L. (1961). The origin of form perception. *Scientific American, 204,* 66–72. Fantz, R. L. (1963). Pattern vision in newborn infants. *Science, 140,* 296–97.

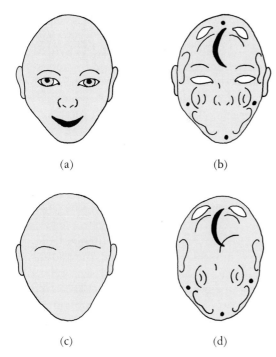

(a)   (b)

(c)   (d)

FIGURE 9-10

Scrambled Faces Although infants younger than four months of age prefer looking at the drawing that resembles a face (a), Haaf (1974, 1977) maintains that they prefer it because it is moderately complex and not because it resembles a face. Facial resemblance, according to Haaf, does not become an important feature of pattern perception until after four months of age. *Sources:* Haaf, R. A. (1974). Complexity and facial resemblance as determinants of response to face-like stimuli by 5- and 10-week-old infants. *Journal of Experimental Child Psychology, 18,* 480–87. Haaf, R. A. (1977). Visual response to complex facelike patterns by 15- and 20-week-old infants. *Developmental Psychology, 73,* 77–78.

rate will accelerate to certain sounds. Newborn infants show a startle response to loud sounds, turn in the direction of a sound (Field, Muir, Pilon, Sinclair, & Dodwell, 1980), and can distinguish between sounds of varying duration and intensity. By three weeks of age, infants can distinguish between their mothers' voices and the voices of other women (Carpenter, 1973). Very young infants appear to be soothed by rhythmic sounds, particularly those in the low-frequency range. However, they do not appear to show a special preference for their mothers' heartbeats, as once believed (Salk, 1962).

In summary, while there is no doubt that the major human sensory systems are functional at birth and that babies therefore have the capacity to register a great deal of the information necessary for perception, infant control over the use of sensory systems is limited by an initial weakness of muscular coordination. The course perceptual development follows moves from an interest in the simple to an interest in the familiar and on to an interest in slightly more complex and novel stimuli than those the infant has come to "understand."

THE INFANT'S PERCEPTUAL WORLD

Assume that infants are born with some perceptual abilities — but not others. On what basis might you predict which capacities the infant inherits? One promising candidate is natural selection; infants should inherit those perceptual abilities most important to ensuring their survival. We can identify three such abilities:

1. It is important to perceive movement in the environment in order to locate both dangerous and desirable animate objects.

2. It is important to perceive depth in order to avoid dangerous irregularities, such as cliffs.

3. It is important to perceive the world as containing objects that retain their identity even though the retinal images they cast from different distances and positions may vary.

Let us examine the evidence that infants inherit these three perceptual abilities.

Movement Perception

Evidence from nonhuman animals suggests that the perception of movement, *where* an object is, is a more primitive process than the perception of detailed information about stationary objects, *what* an object is. Animals, such as frogs, that catch their prey in midflight have visual systems highly sensitive to movement but relatively insensitive to form and pattern. More complex animals, such as hamsters, usually perceive both movement and form. However, if the visual

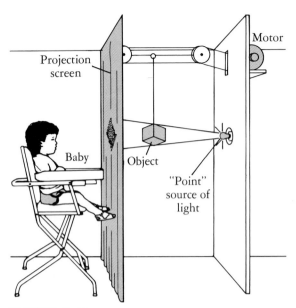

FIGURE 9-11

Shadow-casting Apparatus This apparatus presents a baby with either an expanding or contracting shadow pattern. The baby sees a pattern that becomes larger as the square is pulled closer to the source of light and becomes smaller as the square is moved away from the light. *Source:* Haber, R. M., & Hershenson, M. (1980). *The psychology of visual perception* (2nd ed.). New York: Holt, Rinehart & Winston.

cortex—a late evolutionary acquisition in hamsters—is removed, the hamster becomes essentially blind to the identity of objects yet retains its ability to detect movement (Schneider, 1967).

Research on human infants has shown that when an object is moved rapidly toward their faces, they raise their hands and turn their heads, apparently to protect themselves (Bower et al., 1970). Other research that employs an expanding shadow on a screen (see Figure 9-11) has obtained similar results (Ball & Tronick, 1971). Interestingly, this protective response disappears shortly after birth and returns at about five months of age (Yonas et al., 1978). These findings suggest that infants inherit a reflexive ability to perceive movement and that this ability is located in early developing centers of the brain. However, the ability is later overridden by a less-reflexive ability mediated by later-developing centers in the cortex of the brain.

Depth Perception

In a classical study of the infant's ability to perceive depth, Gibson and Walk (1960) employed a device called the **visual cliff.** As shown in Figure 9-12, a visual cliff consists of two solid surfaces, one lower than the other, divided by a wooden center strip and covered by a nonreflecting glass surface. Gibson and Walk placed babies who were just able to crawl on the center strip and encouraged them to "Come to Mom." Their mothers stood alternately beyond the "deep" or the "shallow" side of the apparatus. Gibson and Walk found that 24 of 27 babies crawled over the shallow surface to their mothers but that only 3 crawled over what appeared to be a cliff. The results of this study are consistent with the assumption that the capacity to perceive depth is innate; however, because the infants were more than six months old when tested, the finding is not conclusive. Unfortunately for this type of research, newborn infants cannot crawl.

In order to counteract the problem of young infants' immobility, some investigators have tested animals that can crawl at birth or shortly thereafter (see Walk, 1966, for a review), and others have recorded changes in the heart rates of infants placed on the deep and shallow sides of

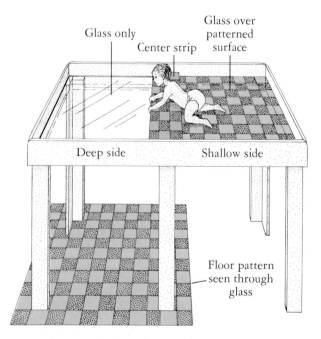

FIGURE 9-12

Visual Cliff Infants as young as six months of age demonstrate they can perceive depth by their reluctance to crawl over the visual cliff. *Source:* Vandivert, W. (1961). *Scientific American, 202,* 80–92.

visual cliffs (Campos et al., 1978). The results of studies on nonhuman animals have revealed that such land-based species as rats, kittens, chicks, and goats tend to avoid the deep side of the visual cliff at birth or shortly thereafter but that such water-based species as the sea turtle (for which cliffs are no danger) do not. Studies on human infants placed on the deep side of the visual cliff before they can crawl have revealed that they do not display signs of distress. Campos (1976) found that the heart rates of two-month-old children decreased when put on the deep side of a visual cliff — a sign of attention — suggesting that they were aware of the "cliff" but were not afraid of it (fear evokes an increase in heart rate). In a recent study, Richards and Rader (1981) found that infants who learn to crawl before they are normally ready to crawl do not avoid the deep side of the visual cliff. Taken together, these findings suggest that animals acquire the ability to perceive depth if and when they need it to enhance their chances of surviving. For most species, this coincides with the time they acquire the ability to move: for chickens and goats, at birth; for rats and kittens, during the first weeks of life. Human infants appear to acquire the ability to detect differences in depth by two months but do not avoid cliffs until some time after six months of age.

Size and Shape Constancy As explained in Chapter 4, our perceptual apparatus is geared to produce the impression that objects viewed from different distances and angles (thus producing different images on our retinas) remain the same objects. These phenomena are referred to as **size constancy** and **shape constancy**. Do infants possess size and shape constancy? Or do they think objects that look different because they are farther away or in different positions are different objects? Although the obvious problems involved in studying an infant's perceptual world have made it difficult to answer this question, an ingenious attempt was made by Bower (1964, 1965). Bower trained babies approximately two months old to turn their heads in the presence of a 30-cm cube placed one meter away from them. Bower then divided the babies into three groups and retested them. He presented a 30-cm cube to the first group — the same object they had seen originally — but held it nine meters away. At this distance, the cube created a retinal image nine

times smaller than it created at one meter. To the second group Bower presented a 90-cm cube from three meters away, thus producing the same size of retinal image as did the original cube even though the object was three times as large. To the third group he presented a 90-cm cube held one meter away, thus creating a retinal image three times as large as the retinal image produced by the original cube (see Figure 9-13).

Bower found that the babies in the first group turned their heads most often, followed by the babies in the third group, then the babies in the second group. These findings revealed that the babies generalized most to the *same object,* next to an object at the *same distance,* and least to an object that produced the same *retinal image.* Although Bower's results appear to provide compelling support for the existence of size constancy in young infants, later research has raised doubts. For example, in three separate attempts Day and McKenzie (1973) were unable to demonstrate that very young infants show size constancy. After thoroughly reviewing research findings on this topic, Day and McKenzie submit that the situation regarding the possibility of size constancy in infants is "confused and unsettled" (p. 313).

The evidence on the question of whether or not infants show shape constancy is clearer. Bower (1966) trained babies to turn their heads in the presence of a wooden block viewed at a particular angle. They were then tested in the presence of blocks that were either the same as or different from the training block in terms of physical shape and shape projected on the retina. The babies responded more to blocks of the same physical shape, even though the blocks differed in orientation and thus in retinal shape from the training block. The conclusion that babies can maintain shape constancy also has been confirmed by a more recent study employing a different method (Caron, Caron, & Carlson, 1979).

There is evidence also that babies display what is called **object-identity constancy.** For example, when a feeding bottle is tilted laterally, it still retains its identity for the baby (Day & McKenzie, 1973). The possibility that babies also show such other visual constancies as those for position, lightness, and color has received little attention from researchers — no doubt because research of this type is so difficult to con-

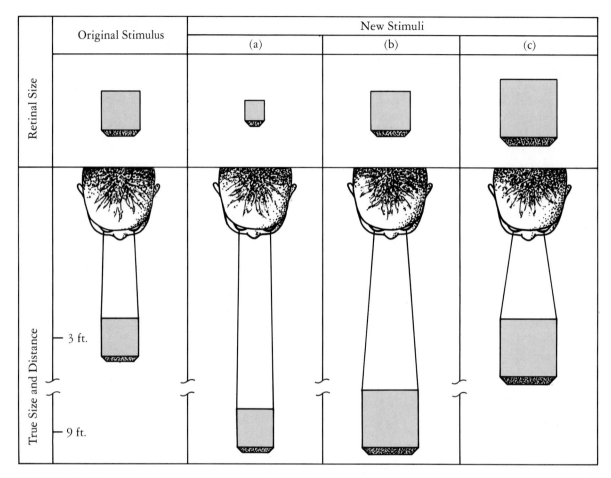

FIGURE 9-13
Bower's Cubes Bower trained babies to turn their head when shown a 30-cm cube from a distance of one meter. He then divided the babies into three groups to determine if they possessed size and shape constancy. Bower's study revealed that babies do in fact possess size and shape constancy. The babies responded most to the same object (a) even though it produced a smaller retinal image, next to an object at the same distance (c) even though it produced a larger retinal image. The infants responded least to an object producing the same retinal image (b).

duct. The milestones achieved by infants in sensory and perceptual development are outlined in Table 9-2.

The results of research on the infant's perceptual world favor a compromise between the extreme heredity and environmental positions. Although evidence for the existence at birth of many constancies is mixed, it is quite clear that the baby's world is not a "blooming, buzzing confusion." Infants can engage in perceptual processing at or soon after birth; however, their abilities are unrefined. With experience these abilities become more differentiated and integrated.

ACQUIRING LANGUAGE

The definitive sign of life in a newborn infant is a sound—a loud and compelling cry. As every parent knows, the sounds that infants make communicate important information. As important as these sounds may be, however, they are not language. In one sense, we all know what lan-

TABLE 9-2
Milestones in Sensory and Perceptual Development

First Week

See patterns, light, dark
Sensitive to location of sounds
Distinguish volume and pitch
Prefer high voices
Grasp object if touched accidentally

First Month

Look at objects only if in line of vision and for short periods
Prefer patterns to color, brightness, or size
Coordinate eyes sideways, up and down
Follow slowly moving object

Second Month

Prefer people to objects
Stare at human face, become quiet to human voice
Startle at sounds and make facial response
Reach out voluntarily instead of grasping reflexively
Focus on large or moving objects at several feet
Perceive depth
Coordinate eye movement in a circle when looking at light or object
Discriminate among voices, people, tastes, and objects

Third Month

Follow moving object with eyes for at least ten seconds
Glance from one object to another
Stop sucking to listen
Distinguish near objects from distant ones
Search for sound with eyes
Show signs of memory by waiting for expected rewards (like feeding) and by recognizing and differentiating family members

Four to Seven Months

See world in color and with near-adult vision, lens of eye adjusting to objects at varying distances
Pull dangling objects toward body, bring object to mouth
Follow dangling or moving objects
Alert one to two hours at a time
Turn to follow sound, vanishing object
Visually search for fast-moving or fallen objects, familiar objects
Become aware of and compare size differences of similar objects
Begin to anticipate a whole object by seeing only part
Deliberately imitate sounds and movements

Eight to Twelve Months

Put small objects into and remove from containers
Hold and manipulate one object while looking at a second
Recognize dimensions of objects
Recognize regions of differing depth

At One Year

Group objects by shape and color
Clearly perceive objects as detached and separate

Source: Adapted from Clarke-Stewart, A., Friedman, S., & Koch, J. (1985). *Child development: A topical approach.* New York: Wiley & Sons.

guage is; after all, we use it every day. But what exactly is language? How does the babbling of infants become the language of adults? We turn now to these difficult questions.

WHAT IS LANGUAGE?

Language can be defined as a mode of communication that employs symbols to convey meaning. As such—it is social, it is a tool, it is symbolic, and it consists of ideas. The ability to communicate is a valuable adaptation, especially in a species as social as ours (see Chapter 2). Language enables individuals to engage in cooperative activities, to transmit information, and, in general, to share their thoughts, feelings, plans, and intentions with others. In the same way that a shovel can be used to extract a potato from the soil, a word ("please") can be used to obtain things from other people. It probably is no coincidence that the emergence of the ability to name things is linked closely to the ability to use tools in problem-solving (Bates, Benigni, Bretherton, Camaloni, & Volterra, 1979).

Words are symbols that stand for objects, events, properties, and relationships; the capacity to employ symbols is integral to the capacity to think. Thus, in addition to the social function of language (to communicate), language plays a more private role in the ability to think.

Different languages convey meaning in different ways. For example, consider the following two sentences:

Where did you go with grandpa?

Dedenle nereye gittin sen

The second sentence is Turkish and expresses exactly the same meaning as the first. The first word in the Turkish sentence is complex, consisting of three meaningful units: *dede* (grandpa), *n* (your), and *le* (with). The *ne* in the second Turkish word is a question mark, the *re* means place, and the *ye* means *to* (as in *to* go). The *git* in the third Turkish word means *to*, the next *t* means past tense, and the *in* means second person (in English, past tense is not marked for person). The fourth Turkish word, *sen,* means you. Thus, the four-word Turkish sentence—in

which the following sequence of meaningful units occurs: "grandpa, your, with, question, place to, go, past, second-person, you"—is equivalent to the seven-word English sentence.

In spite of their differences, all languages have at least four features in common. If you wanted to say "Where did you go with grandpa?" in Turkish, first you would have to know how to translate into words your meaning—the idea(s) you wanted to express. This is a question of **semantics**—how meaning is represented in language. Second, you would have to know the rules followed in the Turkish language to construct sentences. This is a question of grammar, or **syntax**—the set of rules for combining words into appropriate and acceptable sentences. Third, you would have to be able to translate the words into a string of sounds; this is a question of **phonology.** Finally, you would have to anticipate the effect of the utterance on your listener; this is a question of **pragmatics,** or the social purposes of language. The task you face as a speaker or producer of language, then, can be characterized as one in which you attempt to translate meaning into sound (Chomsky, 1968). Conversely, the task you face as a listener or comprehender of language involves translating sounds into meaning (see Figure 9-14).

When you think about it, this is really quite a formidable task—especially for a child who has barely begun to walk, is still probably not toilet trained, and must be fed by others.

HOW DOES LANGUAGE DEVELOP?

First Sounds

To speak a language, children must be able to distinguish between the sounds they hear, and they must be able to make particular kinds of sound themselves. How well do newborns distinguish between sounds? Can they distinguish between the sound of the human voice and other sounds; if so, can they distinguish between different words or syllables? It might seem impossible to answer these questions because infants cannot tell you what they hear. Yet, as developmental

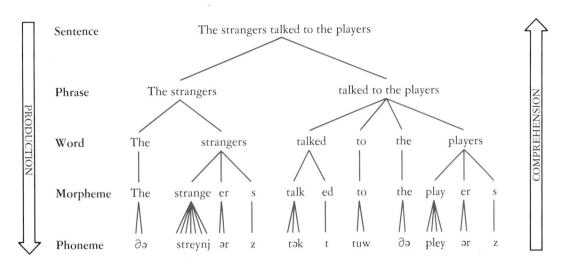

FIGURE 9-14
The Structure of Language: Production and Comprehension When people produce language, they go from ideas to sounds; when people comprehend language, they go from sounds to ideas. *Source:* Adapted from Clarke-Stewart, A., Friedman, S., & Koch, J. (1985). *Child development.* New York: Wiley & Sons.

psychologists have discovered, infants can indeed "tell" you what they hear if you "ask" them in the right way. Although infants cannot talk, they can suck, look, grasp, and perform other behaviors. By examining changes in these behaviors, psychologists are able to draw inferences about their mental processes.

For example, research has established that the rate at which infants suck increases when they experience a change in stimulation or when more rapid sucking produces a stimulus that interests them. Employing a pacifier with electronic sensors, investigators have found that babies prefer the sound of the human voice to other sounds (Butterfield & Siperstein, 1974) and that by one month of age babies are able to distinguish between such sounds as *ba* and *pa* (Eimas & Tarter, 1979). Interestingly, until about nine months of age infants can distinguish between sounds used in languages other than the one they will acquire, but lose the ability as they begin to learn a particular language (Jusczyk et al., 1980). Research on the abilities of infants suggests they are prepared biologically to attend to and distinguish the sounds that make words in all languages.

The ability to distinguish between the sounds of language, however, is much more highly developed in infants than is their ability to produce such sounds. The first sound that the infant makes is a cry; in fact, infants typically produce three different kinds of cry—a hunger cry, an anger cry, and a pain cry. By their second or third month, babies produce a wide variety of such other sounds as squeaks and coos; by five or six months, babies begin to babble. The primary function of babbling appears to be to provide motor practice for the muscles that must develop to produce speech. There is no difference between the babbling of children from different countries, or between the babbling of deaf children and children who can hear (Lenneberg, 1967).

It is not until infants near their first year that their babbling begins to resemble the language they will acquire. During this time, the patterns of **intonation** of American babies begin to sound like English, the babbling of Chinese babies like Chinese, and so on. Intonation is important to language because it is one of the devices that people employ to communicate meaning. Consider, for example, the difference between "How do *you* feel?" and "How do you *feel*?"

First Words

Children understand what many words mean before they utter their first word. The first words spoken by infants tend to be short and to consist of one or two consonants followed by a vowel. *Ma* or *ma-ma* and *ba* or *ba-ba* are favorites. Up to one-third of the words children acquire are used to convey several different meanings (Nelson et al., 1978). Thus, *da* may mean "dog," "cat," "Dad," "There's a dog," "I see Dad," or "I want the cat." This phenomenon is called **overextension.** In addition, one-year-olds may pronounce words like *ba* in a variety of different ways. The context in which babies say words, the intonation of their voices, and their gestures — especially reaching, pushing away, and pointing — enable adults to understand what they mean.

Children also understand distinctions before they are able to make them in speech. For example, Gruendel (1977) found that children who use *bow-wow* to refer to all animals nonetheless pick a dog rather than a cat or a cow when asked to point to a *bow-wow*. This exemplifies the difference between children's comprehension of language and their ability to produce it.

With development, children learn new words and employ them to make increasingly fine distinctions. At first, *bow-wow* may refer to most animals; later the child might use *moo* to apply to large animals and *bow-wow* to small animals, and so on. By the first birthday, the vocabulary of most children is only about three words. However, before reaching their second birthday, they begin acquiring words at the rate of about 20 a day (G. Miller, 1978).

Nelson (1973) studied the first 50 words spoken by 18 different children and found that 65% of them consisted of nouns such as *duck, doggie, milk,* the names of pets, and the like (see Table 9-3). Thirteen percent of the words described or demanded actions: *byebye, give, up,* and so forth. Nine percent of the words were modifiers: *red, dirty, outside,* and so on. The remainder consisted of what Nelson called personal-social words (for example, *yes, no, please*) and function words (for example, *what, for*).

When you consider the first words used by most children (*ball, doggie,* and the like), you might assume they are a straightforward reflection of the words used by adults to name the objects most familiar to them. However, young children do not say such words as *pants, sweater, mittens, diapers, blanket,* or *soap,* even though these words are used just as frequently by the adults

TABLE 9-3
First 50 Words*

Number of times Noun used	Noun(s)
10 – 16	Dog, Cat, Car, Juice, Milk, Cookie
7 – 9	Duck, Water, Toast, Blocks, Clock, Bottle
5 – 6	Boat, Truck, Light, Key, Book, Apple, Cake, Horse, Hat
4	Bear, Bird, Cow, Doll, Blanket, Socks, Cup, Snow
3	Banana, Drink, Chair, Door, Watch, Pool
2	Bread, Butter, Cheese, Egg, Peas, Lollipop, Boots, Belt, Coat, Teddy Bear, Bike, Bus, Spoon, Flower, House, Moon, Rock

* Nelson kept a record of the first 50 words spoken by 18 children. The table shows how many times a particular noun was used.
Source: Adapted from Nelson, K. (1973). Structure and strategy in learning to talk. *Monographs of the Society for Research in Child Development, 38,* 1 – 2, Table 8.

around them as are the words the children say. Why the difference? Nelson noted that the words children use symbolize the things with which children interact, especially things that move or can be moved *(dog, cat, ball)* and things they can demand *(juice, milk, cookie).* Young children typically do not say the names of objects over which they have no control.

The things young children talk about tend to be immediate and concrete, and they talk about them in the most direct and simple way possible. Thus, a child who wants to convey delight at the movement of a car says something like "Go!"; a child who wants to convey a desire to hold the car says "Car?" (perhaps with outstretched hands). Table 9-4 outlines some of the highlights of language development during the first two years.

First Sentences — The Acquisition of Grammar

Most children acquire a vocabulary of about 50 words before they begin to say two words in a row. When children first begin combining words, they do not use such connecting words as articles *(the, a)* or prepositions *(to, for)*

TABLE 9-4
Highlights of Language Development During the First Two Years*

Average Age in Months

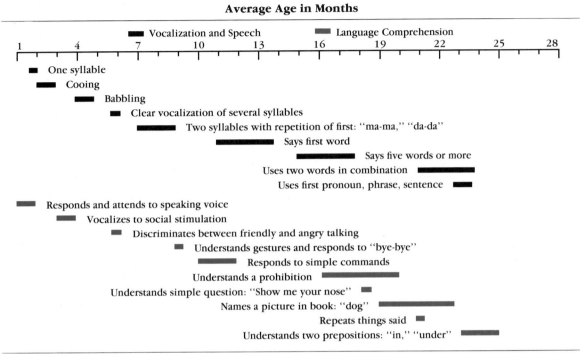

■ Vocalization and Speech   ▬ Language Comprehension

|1 | 4 | 7 | 10 | 13 | 16 | 19 | 22 | 25 | 28|

One syllable
Cooing
Babbling
Clear vocalization of several syllables
Two syllables with repetition of first: "ma-ma," "da-da"
Says first word
Says five words or more
Uses two words in combination
Uses first pronoun, phrase, sentence

Responds and attends to speaking voice
Vocalizes to social stimulation
Discriminates between friendly and angry talking
Understands gestures and responds to "bye-bye"
Responds to simple commands
Understands a prohibition
Understands simple question: "Show me your nose"
Names a picture in book: "dog"
Repeats things said
Understands two prepositions: "in," "under"

* Some infants may not display all the linguistic developments indicated. The average ages given are approximations and the length of the bars reflects the range (in average ages) that different researchers have reported for a particular linguistic development.
Sources: McCarthy, D. (1954). Language development in children. In L. Carmichael (Ed.), *Manual of child psychology* (2nd ed.). New York: Wiley & Sons. Lenneberg, E. H. (1967). *Biological foundations of language.* New York: Wiley & Sons. Bayley, N. (1969). *Bayley scales of infant development.* New York: Psychological Corporation.

—saying things like "Mommy ball" and "car go." This means of communicating has been called **telegraphic speech.** Slobin (1979) and others examined the two-word sentences of children from many different countries, and concluded that they serve seven basic functions (see Table 9-5).

To acquire language, a child must learn more than the meaning of words. He or she also must learn how to combine the words in meaningful ways, how to change their tense, how to make them plural, and so forth. In short, the child must learn **grammar.** When language scholars speak of children learning grammar, they do not mean that children sit down and learn the rules of grammar in the way you were taught in school. That is not how children learn grammar. By the age of four, most children possess sufficient implicit knowledge of how to convey

meaning through word order and inflection to construct sentences as grammatically correct as those of most adults; yet they cannot tell you even one grammatical rule.

The first grammatical device children use is intonation: they vary the tone of their utterances to convey the meaning behind words. When they begin to say two words in a row, they begin to vary the order of those words to convey their intentions—saying things like "Daddy kiss" to signal that it is Dad doing the kissing and "Kiss Daddy" to signal that Dad is the lucky recipient. Another way young children display a knowledge of grammar is through the use of such inflections as -*ed* to form the past tense and -*s* to form a plural.

Psychologist Roger Brown and colleagues studied the development of grammar in three children by visiting them regularly over a period of several years and recording what they said.

TABLE 9-5

Functions of Two-word Sentences in Child Speech (examples from several languages)

Function of Utterance	Language					
	English	**German**	**Russian**	**Finnish**	**Luo (spoken in Kenya)**	**Samoan**
Locate, Name	*there book* *that car* *see doggie*	*buch da* [book there] *gukuk wauwau* [see doggie]	*Tosya tam* [Tosya there]	*tuossa Rina* [there Rina] *vettä siinä* [water there]	*en saa* [it clock] *ma wendo* [this visitor]	*Keith lea* [Keith there]
Demand, Desire	*more milk* *give candy* *want gum*	*mehr milch* [more milk] *bitte apfel* [please apple]	*yeshchë moloko* [more milk] *day chasy* [give watch]	*anna Rina* [give Rina]	*miya tamtam* [give-me candy] *adway cham* [I-want food]	*mai pepe* [give doll] *fia moe* [want sleep]
Negate	*no wet* *no wash* *not hungry* *allgone milk*	*nicht blasen* [not blow] *kaffee nein* [coffee no]	*vody net* [water no] *gus' tyu-tyu* [goose gone]	*ei susi* [not wolf]	*beda onge* [my-slasher absent]	*le 'ai* [not eat] *una mea* [allgone thing]
Describe Event or Situation	*Bambi go* *mail come* *hit ball* *block fall* *baby high-chair*	*puppe kommt* [doll comes] *tiktak hängt* [clock hangs] *sofa sitzen* [sofa sit]	*mama prua* [mama walk] *papa bay-bay* [papa sleep] *korka upala* [crust fell]	*Seppo putoo* [Seppo fall] *talli 'bm-bm'* [garage 'car']	*chungu biro* [European comes] *odhi skul* [he-went school]	*pa'u pepe* [fall doll] *tapale 'oe* [hit you] *tu'u lalo* [put down]
Indicate Possession	*my shoe* *mama dress*	*mein ball* [my ball] *mamas hut* [mama's hat]	*mami chashka* [mama's cup]	*täti auto* [aunt car]	*kom baba* [chair father]	*lole a'u* [candy my] *polo 'oe* [ball your]
Modify, Qualify	*pretty dress* *big boat*	*milch heiss* [milk hot]	*mama khoro-shaya* [mama good]	*rikki auto* [broken car] *torni iso* [tower big]	*piypiy kech* [pepper hot]	*fa'ali'i pepe* [headstrong baby]
Question	*where ball*	*wo ball* [where ball]	*gde papa* [where papa]	*missä pallo* [where ball]		*fea Punafu* [where Punafu]

Source: Adapted from Slobin, D. I. (1966). The acquisition of Russian as a native language. In F. Smith & G. Miller (Eds.), *The genesis of language* (pp. 129–48). Cambridge, MA: MIT Press.

Brown (1973) found that all three children's use of particular grammatical rules developed in an orderly fashion. First they mastered the use of the present progressive (adding *-ing* to words), then they began to employ the preposition *in,* and so on. In all, Brown (1973) found that children acquire the ability to use 14 suffixes and function words in a consistent order (see Table 9-6).

Why should children acquire the ability to use *-ing* before they acquire the ability to use *in?* Perhaps the first modifiers children master are those used most frequently by adults and the next mastered are those used almost as frequently, and

so forth. Brown found no support for this possibility—the frequency of modifier use by adults was unrelated to the order of their emergence in children. A second possibility relates to the complexity of the meaning of the modifiers. That is, a modifier such as *-ing* may represent or map a single aspect of meaning and later-developing modifiers may represent or map more aspects of meaning. The aspects of meaning represented or mapped by each modifier are listed in column two of Table 9-6. As you move down the column, the number of aspects of meaning represented or mapped by each modifier tends to increase. Ac-

TABLE 9-6
Fourteen English Suffixes and Function Words

Form	Meaning	Example
Present progressive: -**ing**	Ongoing process	He is sit*ting* down.
Preposition: **in**	Containment	The mouse is *in* the box.
Preposition: **on**	Support	The book is *on* the table.
Plural: -**s**	Number	The dog*s* ran away.
Past irregular: e.g., **went**	Earlier in time relative to time of speaking	The boy *went* home.
Possessive: -**'s**	Possession	The girl*'s* dog is big.
Uncontractible copula **be**: e.g., **are, was**	Number; earlier in time	*Are* they boys or girls? *Was* that a dog?
Articles: **the, a**	Definite/indefinite	He has *a* book.
Past regular: -**ed**	Earlier in time	He jump*ed* the stream.
Third person regular: -**s**	Number; earlier in time	She run*s* fast.
Third person irregular: e.g., **has, does**	Number; earlier in time	*Does* the dog bark?
Uncontractible auxiliary **be**: e.g., **is, were**	Number; earlier in time; ongoing process	*Is* he running? *Were* they at home?
Contractible copula **be**: e.g., -**'s, -'re**	Number; earlier in time	That*'s* a spaniel.
Contractible auxiliary **be**: e.g., -**'s, -'re**	Number; earlier in time; ongoing process	They*'re* running very slowly.

Sources: Brown R. A. (1973). *A first language: The early stages.* Cambridge, MA: Harvard University Press. Clark, H. H., & Clark, E. V. (1977). *Psychology and language: An introduction to psycholinguistics.* New York: Harcourt Brace Jovanovich.

cording to Clark and Clark (1977) "The more ideas that had to be mapped onto a morpheme [a meaningful unit of speech], the later it was acquired" (p. 346).

Although children learn to make grammatically correct statements amazingly fast, they do not accomplish this task without making mistakes. In some ways, the mistakes that children make are more telling than the things they say correctly. Indeed, acquiring the ability to make certain mistakes is an accomplishment. Perhaps this is a principle of life. Consider the development of children's ability to use the past tense, for example.

In learning to use verbs in the appropriate tense, children go through five stages. First, they make slight use of past-tense forms. Second, they make sporadic use of correct irregular forms they hear often (for instance, "I broke the toy", "He ran away"). At the third stage — usually reached during the third and forth years — children learn to use the regular suffix *ed* for all past-tense forms. Although this is clearly an accomplishment, it leads children to a consistent set of errors: they add -*ed* to irregular verbs, uttering such sen-

tences as "I breaked the toy" and "He runned away." This phenomenon is called **overregularization.** In the fourth stage, as children continue to develop during their fifth and six years, they may be heard saying such things as "I broked the toy" and "He ranned away" — utterances that include both regular and irregular constructions, with the past tense doing double duty (Kuczaj, 1978). Finally, in the fifth stage children use regular and irregular forms correctly.

Beyond the Initial Stages

As language development continues, children master more and more syntactical fine points of the language they are learning. For example, in English the child learns to produce well-formed negative sentences, to ask questions, to use various kinds of relative clauses, and to combine sentences in meaningful ways. Nevertheless, children have more difficulty with, and take longer to master, some constructions than others. Mastering the passive voice is particularly difficult. Most English sentences are organized in an actor-action-object sequence ("Jane hugs Dick"); the meaning of the sentence is conveyed through word order. In passive constructions, such as "Dick was hugged by Jane," word order is reversed. If you give a four-year-old child the sentence "The horse is kissed by the cow," he or she will think it is the horse doing the kissing (Bever, 1970). It is not until age five or six that children understand passive constructions containing a verb that does not denote action, such as "The horse was liked by the cow" (Maratsos et al., 1984).

LANGUAGE AND THOUGHT

Words represent ideas, and combinations of words represent relationships among ideas. Obviously there is a close association between language and thought, but what is the nature of the association?

The languages of people from different lands differ in ways other than the sounds they employ; many languages have words for things for which we have none. For example, Eskimos employ some 20 different words for the substance we call "snow." Similarly, although we distinguish between eleven basic color categories (black, white, red, green, yellow, blue, brown, purple, pink, orange, and grey), the Ibo of Nigera have only four words for colors and the Jale of New Guinea have only two.

There also are significant differences in the rules of grammar of different languages. For example, the Hopi Indian language does not distinguish between past, present, and future. In Hopi, inflections are employed to indicate whether a speaker is reporting an event that actually occurred, an event that is expected to occur, or a generalization about events.

These observations raise an interesting question: do the words and grammar of the languages people use determine how they think about the objects and events in their worlds? If we do not have different words for different kinds of snow, does that mean that we cannot distinguish them or think about them in the same way an Eskimo can? Are Hopi people unable to think about time in the way we do? If you could delete words from a language, as suggested by George Orwell in *1984*,

could you control people's thoughts? Linguist Benjamin Lee Whorf (1956) argued eloquently that the language we use determines what we see and think. According to Whorf (1956, p. 213) "We dissect nature along lines laid down by our native languages."

A somewhat less radical view of the relationship between language and thought was advanced by Russian linguist Vygotsky. Vygotsky (1962) suggested that until about two years of age speech and thought develop independently. During this time children can think only in sensory-motor terms, primarily with images, and their speech consists mainly of labeling objects — which Vygotsky did not consider language. It is only when speech and thought join, suggested Vygotsky, that children acquire language in the true sense. Language frees children from the immediate situation, permits them to represent relationships in their heads, and therefore to plan, anticipate, and reconstruct events. When speech and thought join, suggested Vygotsky, children are able to understand grammar. And, in his words, "Grammar precedes logic" (see Figure 9-15).

Although few psycholinguists (scholars who study the psychology of language) accept the **Whorfian hypothesis** or the prominence that Vygotsky gives to language, most psycholinguists agree that language facilitates thinking. Of course, language is not the only system of symbols people employ when they think, but it is probably the most important one. Language helps free people from their immediate perceptual experiences, and may be as much an effect of thought as a cause. Research indicates that the capacity of children to represent experience mentally reveals itself in several forms and at about the same time — language is one; **delayed imitation** (for example, imitating a behavior observed the day before) and **make-believe play** are others (Bates, 1979).

THEORIES OF LANGUAGE ACQUISITION

As is the case with so many aspects of human development, psychologists have tended to favor one of two opposing types of theory of how chil-

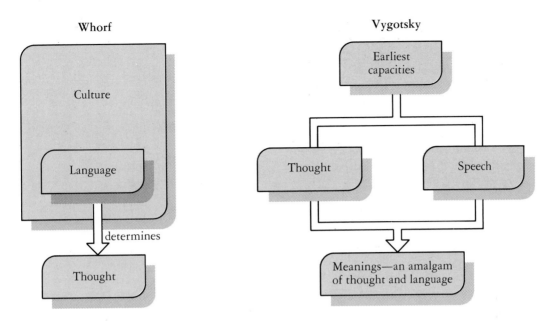

FIGURE 9-15
Theories of Language and Thought Benjamin Whorf and Lev Semenovich Vygotsky each had a different view of the relation between language and thought. *Source:* Gardner, H. (1978). *Developmental psychology: An introduction.* Boston, MA: Little, Brown.

dren acquire language: theories that attribute language development primarily to environmental input and learning, and theories that attribute it primarily to genetic factors and the maturation of the brain. Such learning theorists as Skinner (1957) and social learning theorists as Bandura (1977) maintain that children learn language when the sounds they babble are reinforced selectively by adults and when they imitate what adults say. Other theorists maintain that although the environment may supply the content of language — for example, the specific words that children learn, the structure of language — its grammar is innate. According to such theorists as Chomsky (1975) and Lenneberg (1967), children learn to talk in much the same way they learn to walk. We now outline and evaluate these two approaches, and then consider integrative positions that draw from both.

The Environmental Approach

Some years ago, a friend of mine asked his son (then five years old) how people learn to speak. The process was perfectly obvious to the boy: kids listen to their parents and copy what they say. When my friend asked his son why kids cannot

speak like their parents right away, his son said that kids have to practice to get better, in the same way as when they learn other skills. Behaviorist B. F. Skinner (1957) would add another crucial component to the theory: children are reinforced (receive praise, attention, and sometimes candy) for saying correct sentences and are not reinforced, or even mildly punished, for saying incorrect ones. This environmental view of how children acquire language assigns to children a rather passive role: they repeat what they hear, retain the sentences that are reinforced, and forget those that are not. Although this theory of language development is plausible, its limitations have become apparent.

First, even though children undoubtedly learn new words through imitation, it is difficult to imagine how this process explains all the things they say. For example, children say things like "all gone sticky" or "no wet"; clearly such utterances are inventions by the children. If language is learned through imitation, why would a child first use the past tense correctly ("I saw") but later use it incorrectly ("I see'd")? No parent would change the form of his or her speech in this manner.

To know a language you must know its syntax — the rules for combining words to form sentences. Children's overregularizations demonstrate that they are not passive recipients of linguistic information; rather, they are active processors who attempt to discover the regularities (the rules) underlying language. Children rarely are told how to form past tenses. The fact that they learn how to do so appears to be a genuine discovery, made possible by their active search for regularities in speech.

Second, when children imitate language, they do so selectively. Children do not imitate sentences that go beyond the level of their linguistic ability; in fact, the sentences children imitate are less advanced than the ones they produce themselves (cf. Ervin-Tripp, 1964; Bloom, Hood, & Lightbown, 1974). If children can and do imitate only language they already use spontaneously, imitation cannot account for the acquisition of new linguistic structures.

Third, research has shown that parents do not usually reinforce their children for *saying* grammatically correct sentences; rather, they reinforce them for *meaning* the right thing (Brown, Cazden, & Bellugi, 1969). For example, when a child expressed the opinion that her mother was a girl by saying "He a girl," the mother reinforced her by saying "That's right" (Brown, 1973). However, the perfectly good sentence "Walt Disney comes on on Tuesday" was disapproved because in fact Walt Disney aired on another day. Attempts to teach children correct forms usually fail (McNeill, 1966, see Table 9-7).

A similar case is reported by Braine (1976, see Table 9-8).

TABLE 9-7
Attempts to Correct Grammar

Child	Nobody don't like me.
Mother	No, say "Nobody likes me."
Child	Nobody don't like me.
	(eight repetitions of this dialogue)
Mother	No. Now listen carefully, say "Nobody likes me."
Child	Oh! Nobody don't LIKES me.

Source: Adapted from McNeill, D. (1966). Developmental psycholinguistics. In F. Smith, & G. A. Miller (Eds.), *The genesis of language: A psycholinguistic approach.* Cambridge, MA: MIT Press.

TABLE 9-8
Attempts to Correct Grammar

Child	Want other one spoon, Daddy.
Father	Can you say "the other spoon?"
Child	other . . . one . . . spoon
Father	Say . . . "other."
Child	Other.
Father	Spoon.
Child	Spoon.
Father	Other . . . spoon.
Child	Other spoon. Now give me other one spoon.

Source: Adapted from Braine, M. D. S. (1976). Children's first word combinations. *Monographs of the Society for Research in Child Development, 41,* 266.

In summary, to learn a language children must, among other things, acquire an implicit knowledge of its rules. To infer these rules, they must go beyond what they hear and beyond what is reinforced. Once a rule has been learned, it can be used to construct (or to understand) sentences never before spoken or heard. This creativity makes it possible to produce and to understand a potentially infinite number of good sentences because the rules of language can be used to combine all the words of the language in a potentially infinite number of ways.

In response to criticisms of the role of imitation in language acquisition, some researchers have broadened the concept of imitation. Although these researchers agree that the immediate, mechanical, and exact imitation of particular sentences plays a relatively minor role in the acquisition of language, they argue that children may imitate the general form of sentences, filling these forms with a variety of words (Bandura, 1977). Snow (1983), for example, presents evidence that a relatively high proportion of children's utterances consist of deferred and expanded imitations. **Deferred imitations** are sequences of words and language structures that are stored in children's memory for several hours or days before they are used, often being used when children are in the same situation as when they first head them. **Expanded imitations** are repetitions of sentences and phrases that contain words that were not present in the original form. Snow observes that children imitate forms of language they do not really understand — their performance exceeds their competence. She suggests that the ability to store examples of adult language in memory and to produce it at a later time supplies an "instant or delayed replay" that helps the child acquire language.

The Genetic Approach

No one believes that children can acquire language without some environmental input; however, according to some theorists, the environment plays only a minor role in the development of language. These theorists view language development as a species-specific process controlled mainly by genetic factors. Several argu-

ments have been used to support this view; consider three. First, no nonhuman animal possesses language. It is true that captive chimpanzees and gorillas have been taught a signing system that is similar to language (see Chapter 2); however, no nonhuman species has been observed using language in its natural environment. Thus humans clearly inherit structures that prepare them to learn a language. We know that areas in the left hemisphere of the human brain are specialized for language (see Chapter 3; Figure 9-16).

Second, unless brain damaged or reared in complete social isolation, all human beings learn to talk despite enormous variations in their ability

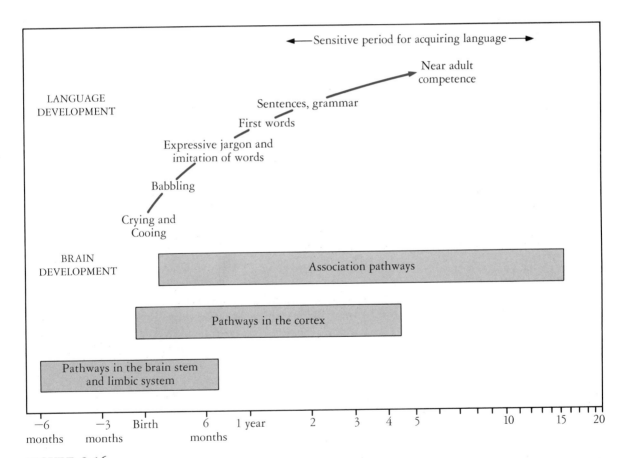

FIGURE 9-16

Language Development and Brain Development This figure shows how the development of brain pathways parallels the development of language. The pathways in the brain stem and the limbic system seem to be involved with the development of babbling. Early speech corresponds with the development of pathways in the cortex. More advanced speech is not possible until the association pathways have matured. *Source:* Adapted from Fischer, K. W., & Lazerson, A. (1984). *Human development: From conception through adolescence.* New York: W. H. Freeman.

to learn other skills (Lenneberg, 1967). Lenneberg has pointed out that although people may vary widely in IQ, virtually everyone masters language. People with an IQ of 50 may have difficulty learning elementary tasks but they still learn to talk. This indicates that the task of learning to speak develops independently from factors that affect the learning of other tasks. Lenneberg concludes that language acquisition must be controlled by genetic factors that are relatively independent of those that control general intelligence.

Lenneberg suggests also that there is a sensitive period in learning language that extends from about the age of two until sexual maturity. To evaluate this idea, we would have to observe children who were not exposed to language until after puberty. Curtiss (1977) reports just such a case. In California, a girl named Genie was discovered who had been reared in almost total isolation until she was 14 years old. During the day she was strapped to a potty chair; during the night she was bound in a sleeping bag. She was spoon-fed by a silent, almost blind mother and growled at by a brutal father. Apparently no one had ever spoken to her. After she was rescued, instructors attempted to teach her to speak. By age 18 Genie could understand language and produce some of its basic forms, but she did not learn to speak in a normal way. Although this case is consistent with the idea that there is a sensitive period for learning language, many special features of Genie's experience make hers an unsatisfactory test of the general proposition.

Genie's experience is significant because it supplies a rare example of someone who was not exposed to language until after sexual maturity. Other studies have found that children develop a language even if they are not taught one by adults, as long as they have someone with whom they can communicate. For example, Goldin-Meadow and Feldman (1977) discovered six deaf children whose parents refused to teach them sign language in the hope this would motivate them to speak. Although these children did not learn any existing language, they invented one of their own.

A third argument advanced by theorists who believe language development is primarily innate concerns an important commonality among all languages of the world — the **deep structure** of grammar. In their view, although different languages may employ different sounds and surface rules, the deep structure of grammar is universal. Noam Chomsky (1975) insists that deep structures are innate, that they are inborn aspects of the organization of the human brain. In support of this view, Chomsky points out that all languages are governed by certain grammatical rules and not by others. For example, no language employs the rule "To form a question, invert the sentence" (which would produce an utterance such as "Home at are you?").

Critics of the genetic approach to language development generally do not deny that humans inherit a special capacity to learn language, but they take exception to the idea that the capacity to acquire language is as separate from other cognitive abilities as Chomsky and others have suggested. They suggest that the reason why certain aspects of language are universal is because all human beings inherit similar nervous systems and because all humans experience environments that are basically the same. For example, all people must form concepts for things that perform actions (actors), for the objects of actions, and for the relationships between actors and objects of actions. In addition, all children in the world develop concepts that enable them to locate objects, demand things, describe events, and so on.

Critics of the genetic approach have pointed out ways in which environmental factors facilitate the acquisition of language. For example, some researchers have shown that adults speak to children in a way that is different from the way they speak to one another. Speech directed to children — sometimes called *motherese* — is not baby talk, but it is not adult speech either. It is generally spoken at a lower rate and higher pitch, is more repetitive, and is grammatically and semantically simpler than speech addressed to adults (Phillips, 1973; Snow, 1972). When talking to children, the level of complexity adults use seems always to be just one step ahead of the children's level. This would seem ideal for providing children with input they can use to improve on what they already know. Thus adults appear to simplify the children's task by making it easier for them to detect the rules of language.

An interesting study that bears on this hypothesis was reported by Sach and Johnson (1976). These investigators studied the language development of a three-year-old hearing child of deaf parents. The child had been exposed to speech on TV and to people talking to one another, but the speech had not been directed at him. When people began talking to him, his language showed a rapid spurt of development. One of the characteristics of the speech directed to him may have been that it was geared more to his level than was the adult speech to which he had been exposed. And there probably were other differences as well.

Integrative Positions

If there is a "new look" in theories of language development, it is characterized by attempts to specify the ways in which innate and environmental factors interact to produce language. Integrative theorists tend to agree that children cannot acquire language until they reach an appropriate maturational level, yet depart from strong maturational positions by viewing language development as more strongly tied to cognitive development and more strongly affected by environmental input. According to integrative theorists, learning theorists err by focusing so exclusively on reinforcement and imitation; they insist that language is affected by a much broader array of social experiences—such experiences as turn-taking, joint attention, and shared assumptions about the context in which ideas are exchanged.

Although there are many new theories of language development, each with its own set of as-

sumptions, a consensus among scholars in the field of language acquisition appears to be emerging about the acquisition of grammar. Maratsos (1983) identifies the following five points of agreement:

1. Children are highly motivated to communicate and are, therefore, active rather than passive learners of language.

2. Children are able to learn the major aspects of grammar because they have already acquired such important concepts on which grammar is based as that events involve agents, actions, objects of action, take place in a particular location, and so forth.

3. For this reason learning a grammar requires very little information processing, which is a good thing because the child has very little.

4. Other aspects of language can be explained by the language parents use to talk to children.

5. The few rules of grammar that do not fit with the child's natural cognitive processes and that are not conveyed adequately through parental input are unnatural, difficult for the child, and acquired very late (for example, passive voice in English).

As mentioned earlier, language and thought are closely related. We now examine the development of children's ability to think and the resulting growth of knowledge in the child.

COGNITIVE DEVELOPMENT

A COMMON-SENSE ACCOUNT OF COGNITIVE DEVELOPMENT

Like most people, you probably assume that adults possess more knowledge than children. Yet if someone challenged that assumption, how could you establish you were correct? One way might be to gather a group of children and a group of adults and ask them some factual questions—Who discovered America? What is 16×9?

Where does rubber come from? Who is the Prime Minister of Canada?—the kind of questions that appear on intelligence tests. Most adults answer such questions correctly; most young children do not. You might conclude from this that cognitive development consists of the acquisition of knowledge demonstrated by the learning of facts. In its extreme form, this approach assumes that cognitive development consists of the gradual accumulation of knowledge that is "stamped in" by specific environmental experiences. In other words, as children experience more and more of the world, they acquire a larger and larger store of knowledge. So the difference between the knowledge possessed by children and by adults is primarily a matter of degree.

Obviously this common-sense approach is sensible and correct in many ways: we learn from experience, and the more we know the smarter we seem. Yet recall the ideas expressed by young children about where babies come from. The common-sense approach does not account for the fact that children possess many ideas they have not learned from observing others or from experience. And it does not account for the fact these ideas may differ from those of adults. For example, a young girl may say—as many do—that when she grows up she is going to be a boy; a three-year-old may line up ten toy people next to ten toy cars, place the people and the cars in separate piles, and insist there are more cars than people because the pile of cars is bigger. Such occurrences suggest the difference between the knowledge possessed by children and the knowledge possessed by adults is a matter of kind as well as degree. So cognitive development appears to consist of more than accumulation of information; it also appears to involve growth in the ability to think and changes in how information is processed. This latter position is central to the theory of cognitive development proposed by Jean Piaget.

PIAGET'S COGNITIVE-STRUCTURAL THEORY OF DEVELOPMENT

No theorist has had greater impact on developmental psychology than Jean Piaget (1896–1980). Piaget's background supplies a basis for understanding his theory. As a child, Piaget developed an interest in biology and observed animals in their natural habitats. He established his intellectual prowess at an early age, publishing a letter reporting observations of an albino sparrow when he was only eleven years old. At the age of 15, Piaget's reputation led to his being offered the position of curator of the mollusk collection at the Geneva natural history museum (he declined in order to finish high school). In early adolescence, inspired by his godfather, Piaget de-

veloped an interest in philosophy, particularly in epistemology, the study of the nature of knowledge. Eventually Piaget integrated his two interests, developing **genetic epistemology,** the study of the growth of knowledge.

Although Piaget received his doctorate in biology, he soon became interested in psychological issues. He collaborated with Theodore Simon to produce a standardized French version of some English intelligence tests. While working on this project, Piaget become convinced that older children were not only more intelligent than younger children, they also thought in qualitatively different ways (different in kind, not in degree). Thus Piaget rejected the idea that intelligence is a quantitative ability that can be assessed by the number of correct answers on a given test, and resolved to discover the different ways in which children at different ages think—a problem that engrossed him for the next 50 years.

In general terms, Piaget views people as active and creative organisms, seeking interactions with the environment and learning from these interactions to adapt to increasingly complex environmental events. To Piaget, intelligence is

Jean Piaget

knowing how to act on objects and ideas so as to modify them, transform them, and understand their transformations. At birth, infants physically interact with the environment by sucking, looking, grasping, and so on. In Piaget's theory, these are intelligent behaviors. Later, children act on the environment in more complex ways. Classifying animals on the basis of food habits (for example, herbivores versus carnivores) is a complex way of acting intelligently; counting, putting things in a series, and measuring are other ways of acting intelligently.

Because Piaget's explanation of cognitive development differs from the explanation advanced by learning theorists, some scholars have inferred that Piaget believed that cognitive development unfolds in a predetermined, genetically controlled way. For instance, some reviewers attribute to Piaget the position that new forms of reasoning develop at particular ages in the same way that new physical structures and skills appear. This most certainly was not Piaget's position. Piaget was insistent on the point that cognitive development occurs through the interaction between innate capacities and environmental events.

According to Piaget, all species inherit two basic tendencies — to adapt to their environment and to organize their thoughts and actions. Because these processes form the foundation of his theory, it is essential to understand what Piaget meant by **adaptation** and **organization.**

Adaptation

According to Piaget, species adapt to their environment in two interdependent ways — by **assimilating** information into existing systems of understanding and by **accommodating** to information by changing the systems of understanding. To appreciate these processes, consider the simple analogy of what happens to the body during digestion. As a person eats, two primary reactions occur — the stomach muscles contract in order to take in (accommodate to) food and the acids in the stomach cause food to change into a form that can be absorbed (assimilated) by the body. In the analogy, the stomach is like the mind and food is like information.

Accommodation refers to the tendency to change a behavior or a thought in response to

features of the event being understood. *Assimilation* refers to the tendency to use existing behaviors or ways of thinking to understand events. Accommodation and assimilation are complementary and are present simultaneously in every act. Consider now one of the most adaptive behaviors that newborn infants come equipped to perform and how the processes of assimilation and accommodation affect it.

The Development of Sucking

Many of us have observed infants sucking and, like so many other things we look at, have seen only what is obvious. Piaget observed his own children in much the same way that he observed sparrows and other creatures in their natural habitat, and saw a great deal more than meets the eye. The following notes were made by Piaget while observing his son Laurent.

First Day "A few hours after birth . . . contact of the lips and probably the tongue with the nipple suffices to produce sucking and swallowing" (Piaget, 1952, p. 25).

Second Day " . . . Laurent seizes the nipple with his lips without having to have it held in his mouth. He immediately seeks the breast when it escapes him as a result of movement" (Piaget, 1952, p. 25).

Ninth Day "Laurent is lying in bed and seeks to suck, moving his head to the left and to the right. Several times he rubs his lips with his hand which he immediately sucks. He knocks against a quilt and a wool coverlet; each time he sucks the object only to relinquish it after a moment and begins to cry again" (Piaget, 1952, p. 26).

Twentieth Day " . . . He bites the breast which is given him, 5 cm from the nipple. For a moment he sucks the skin which he then lets go in order to move his mouth about 2 cm. As soon as he begins sucking again he stops. In one of his attempts he touches the nipple with the outside of his lips and he does not recognize it. But, when his search subsequently leads him accidentally to touch the nipple with the mucosa of the upper lip (his mouth being wide open) he at once adjusts his lips and begins to suck" (Piaget, 1952, p. 26).

It should be evident from these observations that by three weeks sucking is far more than a reflex reaction. As soon as Laurent employed the sucking reflex in order to interact with his environment, the reflex became modified. Laurent sucked objects other than those presented to his lips (assimilation). The sucking changed, and searching behavior was added (accommodation). These observations reveal the infant as an organism actively learning to adapt to the environment.

It may have occurred to you that the modification of sucking behavior described by Piaget bears a remarkable resemblance to discrimination learning: successful sucking responses are reinforced and tend to be repeated; unsuccessful sucking responses tend to disappear (Chapter 5). But, in Piaget's words, "This manner of speaking seems to us more convenient than precise" (1952, pp. 130–31). The difference between Piaget's explanation of sucking behavior and the explanation provided by learning theorists is apparent in the language Piaget used to describe Laurent's behavior on the twentieth day: the infant *searches, recognizes, adjusts.* The source of the behavior is construed as being in the infant, not in the environment.

Consider what happened to the sucking reflex by the end of Laurent's third week of life.

> "Laurent . . . is lying on his right side, his arms tight against his body, his hands clasped, and he sucks his right thumb at length while remaining completely immobile . . ." (Piaget, 1952, p. 27)

Learning theorists would explain thumb sucking in terms of the association between the sucking response and the powerful primary reinforcer, mother's milk. In contrast, Piaget argues that sucking has a more general function, namely as a means through which infants learn to understand their world. According to Piaget, Laurent was acquiring knowledge about an object (his thumb) by sucking it. And, as anyone who has attended infants knows, it does not take long before everything goes in their mouth.

Schemes   According to Piaget, sucking is one example of a scheme or schema. (Piaget used both terms but defined them in somewhat different ways; for our purposes the term *scheme* suffices.) The concept of **scheme** refers to an organized pattern of behavior or potential to behave in a way that tends to be repeated and applied to new objects and situations. The sucking reflex is a primitive scheme. When infants suck on, grasp, or look at objects, they are acquiring knowledge about their world. Through assimilation and accommodation, schemes develop into increasingly complex systems. At first, children's schemes involve overt behaviors; however, as children grow older and become capable of symbolic thinking, the schemes involve cognitive processes. Piaget believed there is a parallel between the infant who acquires knowledge about an object by, say, grasping it, and an older child who acquires knowledge about the object by thinking about how it could be grasped. Indeed, Piaget believed that cognitive processes are best conceptualized as behaviors. Thus Piaget employed the concept of scheme to refer to phenomena as different as the sucking reflex of the newborn infant and the cognitive processes through which an adult classifies animals.

Organization

Piaget's observations of sucking behavior suggested to him that in the process of adapting to the environment, children organize their actions. The sucking behavior of a one-month-old infant is more organized than the sucking behavior of a newborn. In addition to the organization within a system such as sucking, organization involves the coordination of different systems of behavior. Consider an infant who can look at things at one time and can grasp them at another. As these two systems become efficient, the infant will begin to combine them. He or she will look at something, then reach out and grasp it.

The principle of organization also applies to internal acts, the behaviors we call thoughts. One example of mental organization is classification. Very young children can identify apples, oranges, and bananas, but they do not realize that *fruit* is a superordinate category that includes apples, oranges, bananas, and other fruits. A young child would be quite comfortable saying, "We have oranges and fruit at our house."

Some of the many ways in which things can be organized are in terms of their similarities, differences, hierarchies, causes, and correlations. We encounter examples of these kinds of organization later; however, for now keep in mind that Piaget views the tendency to organize our thoughts and actions as one of the fundamental principles of cognitive development.

Equilibration According to Piaget, development consists of a continuous process of organizing and reorganizing actions. He hypothesized that the goal of development is to obtain increasingly elaborate states of balance between people's mental actions and the environment. Piaget called the hypothesized process through which actions change from one state of organization to another **equilibration,** the process of seeking mental balance. The result of the process is called **equilibrium.**

To illustrate what Piaget meant by equilibration, consider how a child learns that the quantity or amount of a thing remains the same regardless of changes in its shape or arrangement. Piaget called this process **conservation.** Suppose we shape some clay into a ball that we then roll into a hotdog while the child is watching. When asked if the amount of clay has remained the same or has changed, young children almost always say the quantity has changed (see Figure 9-17). Jessie, age five, gives a typical answer.

Adult Now, is there as much clay in this one as in that one, or does one have more?

Jessie The hotdog has more.

Adult Why?

Jessie Because it's so long, it has more.

Jessie focuses on only one dimension, length. Because this is not a problem for him, his thinking can be described as being in a state of equilibrium. However, if we were to continue to roll the hotdog so it became increasingly thin, Jessie might reach a point where he noticed the diminishing width and changed his mind, claiming that there was now less clay in the hotdog than in the ball. If we continued to elongate the hotdog, he might experience disequilibrium and vacillate between attending to the dimensions of width and length. One moment he might attend to the narrowness of the hotdog and decide that the hotdog must have less clay than the ball; the next moment he might attend to the length of the hotdog and conclude that the hotdog must have more. There is, of course, a way for Jessie to resolve his confusion; he can realize that as the hotdog gets longer it also gets thinner—but that

I	Make two equal balls of Play-Doh (each three ounces), saying: (If the subject says they are both the same, go on to II) If the subject says one ball is larger, say: (Continue to adjust the balls until the subject says they are the same.)	"Here are two balls of Play-Doh. There is the same amount of Play-Doh in each ball. They are both alike. Is there as much Play-Doh in *this* ball as in that one, or does one have more?" "Let's make them the same. I am taking a little bit away from this one and adding it to that one. Now, is there as much Play-Doh in *this* one as in *that* one?"	2 equal balls a b
II	Roll one ball into a hotdog (six inches long—use ruler), saying: When finished, ask: Record and ask: Record.	"Now watch what I do. See, I am making this ball into a hotdog." "Now, is there as much Play-Doh in *this* one as in *that* one, or does one have more?" "Why?"	ball vs. hotdog a b

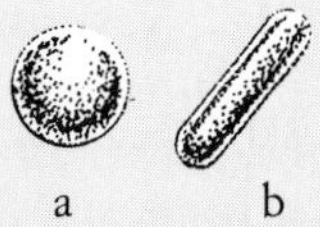

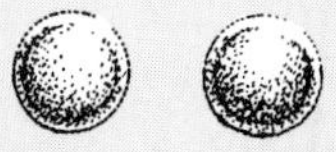

FIGURE 9-17

A Procedure for Testing Conservation of Quantity *Source:* Adapted from Goldschmid, M. L., & Bentler, P. M. (1968). *Concept Assessment Kit—Conversation.* San Diego, CA: Educational and Industrial Testing Service.

the total amount of clay in the hotdog remains the same. Changes in length compensate for changes in width. If he achieves this resolution, he will reach a new state of equilibrium in which he grasps the principle of conservation.

The example of conservation illustrates how disequilibrium fosters cognitive development. At first the child understands something in a well organized but incomplete way; later comes the discovery that the system of ideas or assumptions fails to explain a related phenomenon or leads to inconsistencies. Accordingly, the child is cast into a state of disequilibrium, which prompts a search for a new and better system of understanding. In striving to achieve mental balance, to reconcile two or more opposing perceptions, the child is forced to a higher level of organization and to a greater intellectual understanding.

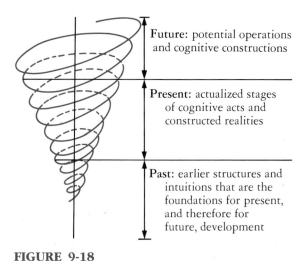

FIGURE 9-18

The Growth of Knowledge Cognitive-developmental theorists believe that knowledge builds on itself. Early rudimentary understandings provide the foundation for more complex cognitions. *Source:* Adapted from Langer, J. (1969). *Theories of development* (p. 96). New York: Holt, Rinehart & Winston.

STAGES OF COGNITIVE DEVELOPMENT

The most controversial aspect of Piaget's theory is the assumption that cognitive development progresses in a series of hierarchical stages. Among the several stage-theories of development described in this book are those of Freud and Erikson (see Chapter 12); however, Piaget's conception of stages is different from these. Piaget's stages are defined by growth in the form or structure of thought and its logic and organization. For this reason, stages are both independent of specific content and universal. In other words, stages are defined by how people think, not by what they think about. According to Piaget, even though their environments may be quite different, all people develop the ability to interpret their worlds in essentially the same way. An Eskimo may learn to classify types of snow but not camels; an Arab may learn to classify types of camel but not snow. Nevertheless, both learn to classify.

In Piaget's theory, stages build upon each other; they form a hierarchy (see Figure 9-18). The logic and organization of Stage 2 is not only different from the logic and organization of Stage 1, but better because it includes and improves on the previous way of thinking. For example, a young child who has learned what apples, or-

anges, and bananas are will retain this knowledge; however, when he or she comprehends that all these foods can be classified as fruit, the child will have improved his or her knowledge in a significant and permanent way. Moreover, once the ability to form classifications is acquired, it is not confined to particular content categories (here, fruit), rather, it is generalized to other objects (such as cars and animals) as well.

The hierarchical nature of Piaget's stages contains two implications: children must go through the stages in order, without skipping any stage; children do not regress (return to an earlier stage), except in such pathological cases as brain damage. Once we acquire the ability to understand such ideas as "apples and oranges are fruit" and "all birds have feathers," they are never forgotten; rather than being isolated beliefs, such concepts become part of the way we think. Although they may differ in the speed with which they progress through the stages, all children must pass through each stage in order to achieve cognitive maturity. Thus age is only a rough indicator of the development of children's thought processes.

Obviously, children do not move from one stage to another overnight; they go through **transitional periods** during which their thinking is a mixture of two stages. Piaget's stages describe the point at which children reach an equilibrium characteristic of the stage to which their thinking is headed. In a sense, then, stages are ideal types. During the transitional periods, children's thinking may be characterized by one stage in one area of functioning and by another stage in another area. In other words, even though a child may have mastered a particular principle in one content area (for instance, the classification system for animals), he or she may not understand how the principle can be applied in another area (for instance, to plants).

Piaget outlined four stages of cognitive development: sensory-motor, preoperations, concrete operations, and formal operations. Each stage begins with a period of formation and is followed by a period of attainment. During the attainment period, a child makes greater and greater use of the knowledge and understanding that defines the stage.

Sensory-motor Stage

The **sensory-motor stage** extends from birth until approximately 18 months, and is called *sensory-motor* because the infant understands the external world in terms of sensations and motor actions. At birth, infants react to the world with inborn reflexes; however, as we saw with the sucking reflex, infants immediately begin to acquire knowledge about their environments that modifies their sensory and motor behavior. Ultimately children progress to the point where they are reacting to the world on the basis of an internal, or mental, representation of its components. Milestones of the sensory-motor stage are outlined in Table 9-9.

A significant milestone during the sensory-motor stage of development is the understanding of **object permanence.** The idea that objects continue to exist regardless of whether anyone is looking at them seems quite obvious to adults.

TABLE 9-9
Milestones of the Sensory-motor Stage

Primary Circular Reactions		Secondary Circular Reactions		Tertiary Circular Reactions	
Exercising Reflexes (birth–1 month)	*Extending Reflexes* (1–4 months)	*Integrating Senses* (4–10 months)	*Coordinating Reactions* (10–12 months)	*Searching for Novelty* (12–18 months)	*Beginning of Thought* (18–24 months)
child practices reflexes until they function smoothly	child extends reflexes to new objects	child achieves fluid coordination of all senses	child represents objects in the mind	child searches for novelty in the environment	child thinks about the problem before acting
child practices built-in patterns of behavior	child coordinates simple schemes (like grasping and looking)	child attains *object concept* in last months of this stage	child demonstrates the beginning of symbolic behavior and memory	child uses several interchangeable schemes to achieve goals	child's thought begins to dominate action
child has no intentionality	child repeats behaviors that cause specific events	child anticipates events and results of actions	child decides on goal, then acts to achieve goal	child conducts experiments to see what will happen	child mentally manipulates objects to reach goals
child has no understanding of an object	child looks where object disappears (for a few moments)	child finds partially hidden object	child finds completely hidden object	child finds objects hidden under one of several covers	child finds objects placed in a container and then hidden

Source: Adapted from Tomlinson-Keasey, C. (1985). *Child development: Psychological, sociocultural, and biological factors.* Chicago: Dorsey Press.

Consider, however, the following observations by Piaget of his son, Laurent.

> At six months and nineteen days Laurent immediately began to cry from hunger and impatience on seeing his bottle (he was already whimpering, as he does quite regularly at mealtime). But at the very moment when I make the bottle disappear behind my hand or under the table—he follows me with his eyes—he stops crying. As soon as the object reappears, a new outburst of desire; then flat calm after it disappears. I repeat the experiment four or more times; the result is constant until poor Laurent, beginning to think the joke bad, becomes violently angry. (Piaget, 1954, p. 30)

When the bottle is no longer visible to Laurent, he behaves as though it has ceased to exist. "Out of sight" is not only "out of mind" but also "out of existence." According to Piaget, objects and infants' actions upon them are inseparable. In other words, when children are looking at or touching objects, the objects exist; otherwise, the objects do not. Only later can infants think of objects apart from their actions and, therefore, imagine the objects when they are out of their presence.

The beginning of the comprehension that objects have permanence can be visualized in somewhat older infants when they watch a toy train going around a track and through a tunnel. If infants anticipate the emergence of the train from the tunnel, they are showing signs that they know the train exists even when it is not wholly visible to them. Infants usually attain the concept of object permanence at nine or ten months of age. Thus if we hid a ball under an opaque cloth while a ten month old was watching, the infant would likely pull aside the cloth to retrieve the ball; yet even at this age, the infant's idea of the permanence of objects is limited. For example, if we placed a toy under a familiar blanket several times, the infant would remove the blanket each time to retrieve the toy. But if we placed the toy under one blanket, then removed it and placed it under a different blanket—even while the infant was watching—he or she would still look under the first blanket rather than under the one concealing the toy (see Figure 9-19).

Attaining the understanding that objects continue to exist when out of sight is extremely significant and indicates the child has developed the capacity to form an inner representation of objects. Development of this ability signals the beginning of symbolic thinking and marks the end of the sensory-motor stage. At this point most children have learned that certain actions have certain consequences and they have become active experimenters, dropping objects to watch them fall, pulling toys toward them by strings attached, using sticks to push things, and so on. By such experimentation, children demonstrate they have laid the necessary groundwork for moving into Piaget's next stage.

Preoperational Stage

During the **preoperational stage,** which begins around the middle of the second year and generally lasts until about age six, the child begins to use language to develop what Piaget calls the **symbolic function**—the ability to use words and images to represent objects and events. If you saw the movie *The Miracle Worker,* you may remember the dramatic scene in which Helen Keller—severely impaired in sight, speech, and hearing as a child—suddenly makes the connection between a sign for water and the actual water spurting from a pump. Although for most children this connection does not occur in such a dramatic form, the realization that things entirely different from an object can represent it is an extremely significant discovery that enables the child to think about things without actually doing them (that is, without performing sensory-motor behaviors on them).

Piaget used the term *preoperational* to emphasize that children at this stage cannot perform logical operations. Piaget defined the term **operation** in a very specific way: an action that is reversible, one that can be returned to its starting point. Addition and subtraction are examples of operations. We can add three and five to make eight, and we can reverse the operation by subtracting five from eight to make three. Another example of an operation is the principle of conservation. As adults we know that if we pour a liquid from one container into another container of a different shape, we still have the same amount of liquid because we can reverse the operation by pouring the liquid back into the original con-

PRIMARY CIRCULAR REACTIONS If something disappears from sight, the infant does not even look for it. It is as if the object ceased to exist.

SECONDARY CIRCULAR REACTIONS If an object is partly hidden, the infant will search for it. However, the infant will not search for the object if it is completely hidden — even if the infant sees it being hidden.

COORDINATION OF SECONDARY CIRCULAR REACTIONS If an infant sees an object being hidden, the infant will search the area in which it was hidden. However, if the object is moved to a second hiding place, the infant will still search in the first hiding place, even if the infant watched while the object was moved to the second hiding place.

BEGINNINGS OF REPRESENTATIONAL THOUGHT The infant will continue to search for objects even if they have been secretly hidden, showing that he or she knows the object must exist somewhere.

FIGURE 9-19
Milestones in Understanding Object Permanence *Source:* Adapted from Fischer, K. W., & Lazerson, A. (1984). *Human development: From conception through adolescence.* New York: W. H. Freeman.

tainer. Preoperational children do not understand the principle of conservation; their thinking is still dominated by immediate perceptual events.

According to Piaget, the thinking of preoperational children is **egocentric.** In the sensory-motor stage, children learn to distinguish themselves from the objects in the world. In the preoperational period, children cannot distinguish their own view of the world from that of another person; that is, they believe that other people's viewpoints are the same as theirs. Thus, you might find a preoperational child sitting by herself in a room with the door closed yelling "What is this?" to her father. By the end of the preoperational stage, children acquire the ability to distinguish their perspective on concrete things from those of others (see Box 9-2).

Concrete-operations Stage

In the third stage, which lasts from roughly seven to twelve years of age, children master several operations. Piaget calls them **concrete operations** because children at this stage operate effectively only on concrete objects, not on abstractions.

During the **concrete-operations stage**, children learn principles of **classification;** for example, they learn that dogs and cats are both

---

Box 9-2
PREOPERATIONAL THINKING AND WINNIE-THE-POOH

In an article entitled "Piglet, Pooh, and Piaget," Dorothy Singer (1972) points to many examples of preoperational thinking in A. A. Milne's classic children's book *Winnie-the-Pooh.* *Winnie-the-Pooh* concerns the adventures of Milne's son, Christopher Robin, and his son's friends, Winnie-the-Pooh, Kanga, Roo, and others (actually Christopher Robin's stuffed toys).

Egocentrism   In one chapter a great flood comes. Pooh discovers a note in a bottle floating past his house with a message from Piglet: "Help Piglet (me)." On the other side it says: "It's me, Piglet. Help, help." Since Piglet is egocentric, he believes that everyone must know where he is. Since Pooh is also egocentric and "a bear of little brain," he only recognizes the letter 'p' which must, of course, mean " 'Pooh,' so it's a very important message to me."

Inability to Conserve   Piglet plans to give Eeyore, the donkey, a large red balloon for his birthday. On the way to Eeyore's place Piglet trips

and the balloon bursts. When Piglet gives Eeyore the "small piece of damp rag," the following conversation ensues.

"Eeyore, I brought you a balloon." "Balloon?" said Eeyore . . . "one of those big coloured things you blow up? Gaiety, song-and-dance, here we are and there we are?"

"Yes . . . but I fell down . . . and I burst the balloon."

"My birthday balloon?"

"Yes, Eeyore," said Piglet, sniffing a little. "Here it is. With—with many happy returns of the day."

"My present?"

Piglet nodded again.

"The balloon?"

"Yes."

"Thank you, Piglet," said Eeyore, "you don't mind my asking," he went on, "but what color was this balloon when it—when it was a balloon?"

Eeyore does not realize that the color of the balloon will remain the same regardless of the size and shape of the balloon.

Animism   Preoperational children believe that some inanimate objects are alive. In chapter one, Pooh plans to steal honey from a bee's nest by disguising himself as a cloud in the sky. In order to resemble a thunder cloud, he coats himself with mud, attaches himself to a sky-blue balloon and floats upwards. He approaches the bee's nest in the tree, singing:

"How sweet to be a Cloud
Floating in the Blue!
Every little cloud
Always sings aloud."

Pooh believes that clouds are alive and that the bees must be completely deceived. When Christopher Robin informs him that he just looks "like a bear holding on to a balloon," a disappointed Pooh suggests that Christopher Robin should walk below with an umbrella muttering, "Tut, tut, it looks like rain." This, he believes, will surely serve to convince the bees that he is a "little dark cloud."

Source: Singer, D. (1972). Piglet, Pooh, and Piaget. *Psychology Today. 1,* pp. 70–74 and 96.

animals, and that in this respect both are the same. The children learn how to order, or **seriate,** things; for instance, they can line up a series of sticks according to the differing lengths. They acquire an understanding of the **reciprocity** of relationships; for example, if you add one to three you get the same amount as if you take one from four. They also acquire the ability to understand that objects can belong to more than one class—that Jim can be Sam's brother, Helen's best friend, a skinny boy, and the smartest student in his class, all at the same time.

Most important, and central to the development of concrete thinking, is the child's grasp of the **principle of conservation.** We already have explored examples of conservation of quantity and conservation of number, and know that conservation implies the ability to recognize that a particular dimension of an object does not change in the face of irrelevant changes in other dimensions of the object. The number of poker chips remains the same whether they are spread out on a large table, stacked in one spot, or have

dots painted on them; similarly, the amount of clay remains the same regardless of the way it is shaped. During the concrete-operations stage, the child learns several different conservations in specific order: number (acquired at approximately five to seven years), liquid and nonliquid quantity (six to eight), and weight (eight to nine). Conservation of volume, the most complex conservation, usually is acquired at eleven years or later. Conservation of volume refers to understanding that an object, no matter how its shape is changed, will continue to displace the same amount of liquid. Figure 9-20 summarizes four of the differences between the way children think in the preoperations and the concrete-operations stages.

Can Children Be Taught to Conserve? According to Piaget, deliberate instruction on how to perform specific tasks is not a particularly effective way to foster cognitive development. Attainment of a new stage of development is not, in Piaget's view, dependent on the acquisition of

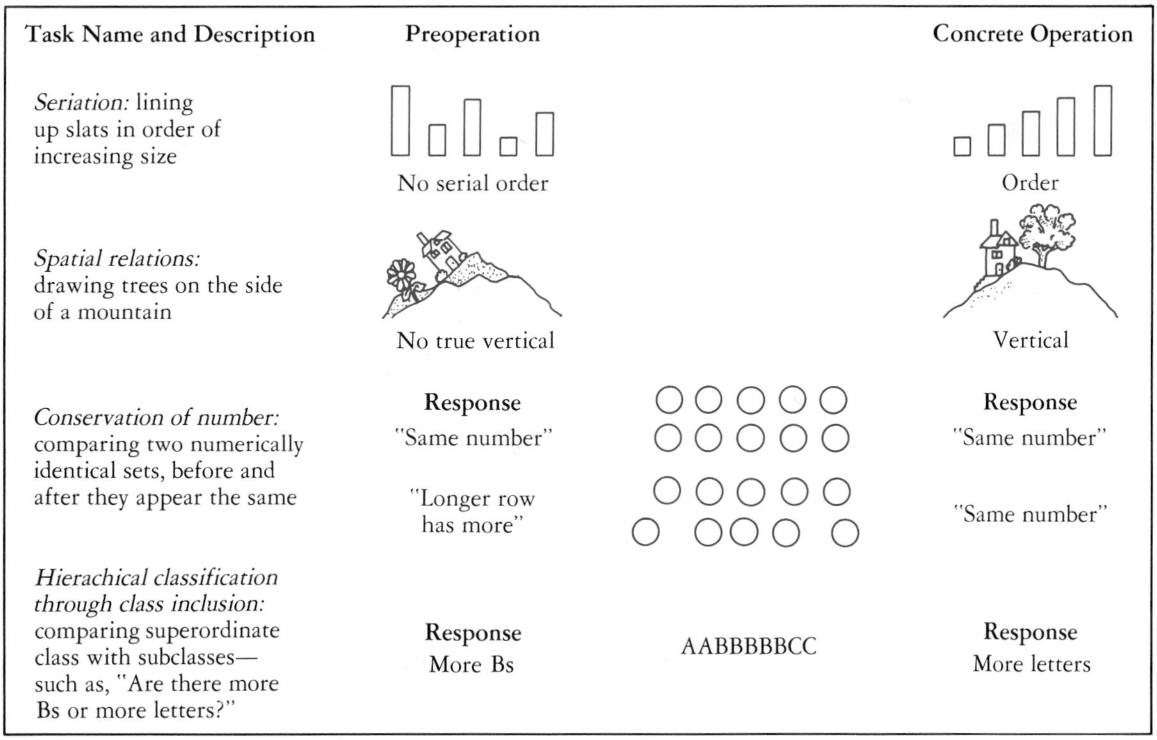

Task Name and Description	Preoperation		Concrete Operation
Seriation: lining up slats in order of increasing size	No serial order		Order
Spatial relations: drawing trees on the side of a mountain	No true vertical		Vertical
Conservation of number: comparing two numerically identical sets, before and after they appear the same	**Response** "Same number" "Longer row has more"		**Response** "Same number" "Same number"
Hierachical classification through class inclusion: comparing superordinate class with subclasses— such as, "Are there more Bs or more letters?"	**Response** More Bs	AABBBBBCC	**Response** More letters

FIGURE 9-20

Acquisitions in Concrete Operations *Source:* Adapted from Hothersall, D. (1985). *Psychology.* Glenview, IL: Scott, Foresman.

new skills; rather, it arises from a major reorganization of mental operations. Piaget did not believe that such a thorough reorganization of thinking could be speeded up by applying specific teaching methods or by otherwise altering the child's environment in specific ways. Other investigators have disagreed, attempting to show that nonconserving children can be taught to conserve.

One approach (for example, Gelman, 1969) involves training the child to attend only to aspects of tasks that are relevant to understanding them, and to ignore others. For instance, you might teach a child to ignore color and shape when the relevant dimension is weight. Although this approach has been found to improve children's performance on conservation tasks, it does not appear to be particularly effective in advancing children's general understanding of the principle of conservation.

Another approach involves an attempt to induce in the child an understanding of the kinds of operation underlying conservation. Some studies (for example, Wohlwill & Lowe, 1962; Brainerd & Allen, 1971) have focused on teaching the child a single operation, such as addition-subtraction, which involves the idea that if nothing has been added or subtracted, weight must remain the same even if shape has been changed. The results of these studies seem to suggest that training a child to understand one operation does help in the acquisition of conservation. One might expect, then, that training in multiple operations would be even more helpful. However, studies that have tried to train more than one operation (for example, reversibility and addition-subtraction) have not met with success (for example, Siegler & Liebert, 1972). Perhaps providing a nonconserver with more than one operation to apply leads to confusion because the child has too much information with which to deal.

A third approach termed *cognitive conflict* deliberately attempts to throw the child into a specific kind of confusion (Smedslund, 1961). This approach builds on Piaget's contention that development occurs when the child notices but cannot resolve inconsistent evidence, a conflict that forces the child to a higher level of cognitive development. Studies along these lines (for instance, Beilin, 1971) typically involve asking children to make predictions on conservation

tasks and then showing them their predictions are wrong. Brainerd (1973) evaluated these attempts to teach conservation and concluded they were not successful.

The results of studies on teaching the principle of conservation parallel the results of studies on the acceleration of motor development: special training techniques may speed children's understanding of conservation but only if the children have reached the necessary stage of development. At most, such teaching appears to move children through the period of formation and into the period of attainment more quickly than they would otherwise progress.

Formal-operations Stage

According to Piaget, children begin to enter the final stage of cognitive development, the **formal-operations stage,** around eleven or twelve years of age. Piaget believes this stage involves a long period of preparation and typically is not reached for many years. During the formal-operations stage, children acquire the ability to reason in symbolic terms in the absence of concrete objects. This makes it possible for them to think about abstract things that may have no basis in the real world, to think about things that are hypothetically possible as well as things that actually occur. When children reach this stage, they acquire the ability to reject hypotheses without physically trying them out. They can analyze their own thoughts and formulate theories about themselves, society, and the world. They can reason deductively, from general statements to specific conclusions (for example, all birds have wings; a penguin is bird, therefore a penguin has wings), and they can reason inductively, from specific events (apples fall toward the ground) to general laws (the law of gravity).

An example of formal operational thinking is seen in Archimedes' law of floating bodies: An object will float if its density is less than that of water. Density is defined as weight divided by volume. To decide if an object will float, a person must understand the concept of weight and the concept of volume — both of which require operations — and then must place these operations in a logical relationship to each other so that he or she can determine whether the density of the object is less than the density of the water. By

Box 9-3
Operations on Operations

What would happen if two young children, one large and one small, attempted to play together on a seesaw? The larger child would remain on the ground and the smaller child would be held in the air. In an attempt to seesaw, the larger child may try jumping up or lifting his or her feet off the ground. Eventually, the two children may find that if they reposition themselves slightly they can enjoy the up-and-down movements of the seesaw. However, even if these children successfully compensate for the weight imbalance, they cannot explain why the larger child must sit closer to the center of the seesaw than the smaller child because they do not possess the ability to understand the proportionality between weight and distance.

The **principle of proportionality** is not acquired until the formal-operations stage. Weight and distance from the pivot determine whether or not a balance is struck; equal weights must be placed at equal distances from the pivot to create a balance. However, if one weight is greater than the other, the lesser must be moved farther away from the pivot point. But how much farther?

What is the relationship between weight and distance? Examine the scales in the figure. On which hook must the weight be hung to reach an equilibrium?

When one weight is greater than the other, the distance of the lighter weight from the pivot point must be equivalent to the difference between the two weights. Therefore, if one weight is double the other (as represented in the figure), the distance between the pivot point and the lighter weight must be double the distance between the pivot point and the heavier weight. Thus weight may be exchanged for distance — the principle of proportionality.

Because the young children on the seesaw can experience the effects of, but cannot understand, proportionality, it is reasonable to

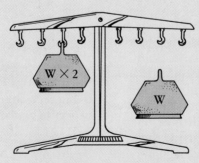

The Principle of Proportionality On which hook must weight **W** be hung to maintain a balance with weight **W×2** (which weighs twice as much)?

expect, for example, that the heavier child may select the same forward position at a later date when playing with a child heavier than himself — demonstrating the effects of learning rather than a knowledge of proportionality.

Children of virtually any age could solve the problem presented in the figure, provided the scales were actually available to them. However, at the formal-operations stage it is not necessary to have the scales actually present to solve the problem correctly and to have confidence in the solution, since the ability to solve problems, or perform operations, by thinking them through is developed at this stage. This ability, *operations on operations,* in this example involves envisioning what would happen if weight is manipulated, what would happen if distance is manipulated, and the ability to put the two together — to envision what would happen if both weight and distance were manipulated. Some of the operations on operations identified by Piaget include *implication* (if-then), *disjunction* (either-or, *or* both), *exclusion* (either-or), and *incompatibility* (either-or, *or* neither-neither) (Piaget & Inhelder, 1969, pp. 135–36).

relating these operations in a logical way, the person is doing what Piaget calls *operating on operations.* Another illustration of formal operational thinking is provided in Box 9-3.

PIAGET'S METHODS OF RESEARCH

Piaget's method of investigation has been labeled the **clinical method,** but seems more accurately described as the *method of critical exploration.* In adopting an approach that was flexible and unstructured, Piaget drew on his experiences in abnormal psychology. He attempted to follow children's thinking as they revealed it; instead of directing the course of interaction with children, Piaget allowed their answers to guide the interaction. If a child said something interesting, Piaget pursued that line of thought.

When Piaget was working on the standardization of intelligence tests, he created performance tests as a way of overcoming deficient verbal abilities in abnormal children. Later, he used similar tests to supplement his verbal exchanges with children. The conservation tests described earlier are examples of performance tests.

PIAGET'S THEORY — AN EVALUATION

Piaget has offered us a rich store of observations and insights about the way in which children think. Moreover, he has provided us with an elaborate theoretical framework for understanding the development of thought and has inspired an enormous amount of research on cognitive development in children. Nevertheless, Piaget could not and certainly did not provide the final word on the development of knowledge; nor has everyone agreed with his conclusions. Indeed, Piaget's theory probably has evoked more criticism than any other theory in developmental psychology. The criticisms tend to focus on five aspects of Piaget's work:

1. his methods of research
2. the ambiguity of certain of Piaget's concepts
3. the assumption that cognitive development progresses in stages
4. the assumption that young children have not acquired certain mental abilities
5. the assumption that older children and adults are able to use formal operations with facility

We consider each criticism in turn.

Problems with Methodology Compared to the more controlled experimental methodology that characterizes most psychological research, many North American scholars find Piaget's methodology loose and incompletely reported (Brainerd, 1978). Piaget made no attempt to test representative samples of children; instead, he observed individual children, often his own, and selected particular observations to demonstrate general points. We discuss the shortcomings of the case-study approach in Chapter 1.

Ambiguity of Concepts You may have found certain of Piaget's concepts difficult to understand; many psychologists have shared that experience, some even suggesting that key Piagetian concepts are too loosely defined to be of any practical use.

> The most interesting concepts in the theory—assimilation, accommodation, and equilibration—which are used to explain how progress is made in development, are tricky to pin down operationally, despite their theoretical glitter. Despite work over the years to flesh out these concepts and anchor them in concrete procedures, not much progress has been made. (Yussen & Santrock, 1982, p. 189)

Virtually all evaluators agree that Piaget has supplied brilliant descriptions of the way children think, yet many question whether the concepts he evokes to explain development are useful (Brainerd, 1978).

Problems with Stages The idea of stages of development implies a certain homogeneity or commonality of abilities. In the ideal case, for example, a child who has reached the concrete-operations stage should be able to conserve number, quantity, weight, and volume. Moreover, children who are able to conserve should be able to perform the other tasks that demonstrate concrete operations, but this often is not the case. According to some psychologists (Fischer, 1980; Kuhn, 1980), unevenness and lack of commonality is the rule in development, not the exception; children acquire specific abilities at different times, not as a unified group as implied by the idea of stages of cognitive development.

In addition to a commonality of abilities, the idea of stages also implies a sequence of development. The assumption that there is an orderly progression in the development of thought that roughly parallels the one outlined by Piaget generally has been supported by research (see Flavell, 1977; Shaffer, 1985).

Cognitive Abilities of the Preschooler Research indicates that Piaget underestimated the abilities of preschool children. If the test conditions for young children are made more optimal than those under which children were tested by Piaget, the children make fewer mistakes and demonstrate abilities that they shouldn't, according to Piaget, possess (Gelman, 1978). Consider what occurred when Piaget asked three- to five-year-olds whether there were "more Smarties or more candies" in the following array:

Top Row = Smarties
Bottom Row = Other kinds of candy

The children answered "more Smarties." Based on this answer, Piaget concluded that the children did not understand the concept of **class inclusion.** However, when Hodkin (1981) altered the question slightly and asked children of the same age whether there were "more Smarties or more of all of the candies," they answered "more of all of the candies," indicating that they could in fact understand class inclusion.

Cognitive Abilities of the Adolescent and of the Adult Although the evidence suggests that Piaget underestimated the abilities of preschoolers, it indicates that he overestimated the abilities of adolescents and adults. Piaget revised the age at which children typically reach the formal-operations stage upward, from 11 to about 15, as he tested more children. However, an extensive study of formal operational thinking conducted by Kuhn et al. (1977) on people from 10 to 50 years of age found that none of the subjects fully achieved the formal-operations stage. Interestingly, those in the 21–30 age range performed better than both younger and older subjects.

Although the thrust of most criticisms of Piaget's final stage of development is that most people never attain it, some psychologists have suggested that there are stages beyond formal operations. Such theorists as Riegel (1976) and Labouvie-Vief (1980) speculate that some adults may reach a stage of development (following the formal-operations stage) that is characterized by the ability to understand the nature of formal operational thinking itself — at least in such specific areas of their expertise as physics, law, or medicine. Indeed, some scholars suggest that Piaget himself must have reached such a stage in order to outline the logic of thinking at the formal-operations stage.

During the 1960s and 1970s, Piaget's theory was the central focus of attention in the field of cognitive development. During the past few years, however, contemporary developmental psychologists are voicing the need to move on. As John Flavell (1980) said in his eulogy to Piaget, upon Piaget's death in 1980 at the age of 84, "Our task is now to extend and go beyond what he began so well." Recently, a number of researchers have done just this. We briefly review certain of these extensions of Piaget's theory.

A NEO-PIAGETIAN APPROACH TO COGNITIVE DEVELOPMENT

Pascual-Leone (1970, 1973, 1980) and Case (1974) have outlined a theory that, although parallel and complementary to Piaget's in orientation, attends to some of the criticisms of Piaget's theory. The approach advanced by Pascual-Leone and Case departs from that of Piaget in three main ways. First, Pascual-Leone and Case assume that children employ several cognitive strategies to solve Piagetian problems, not just one type of overriding strategy as believed by Piaget. Pascual-Leone and Case assume that the difficulty of a problem is determined, in part, by the number of strategies required to solve it. Second, Pascual-Leone and Case assume that a certain amount of space is required in short-term memory to store the information necessary to solve problems, and that complex problems require more storage space than simple problems. Further, they assume that the amount of space available in short-term memory increases during childhood. Third, Pascual-Leone and Case assume that with practice many strategies become automatic or habitual, thus requiring less space in short-term memory. For example, you may automatically see that $(5 + 2) - (5 + 2)$ is equal to 0, whereas a child must store each component in memory before he or she can figure it out.

Central to the theory of Pascual-Leone and Case is the concept of intellectual power. These theorists assume that intellectual power increases with age, and that older children have more stored information, rules, and plans than do younger children. However, people of the same age may differ in their approach to problem-solving in two basic ways: responding in the simplest way possible versus using their full intellectual power and attending to immediate perceptual cues versus viewing events in a broader context.

Pascual-Leone and Case believe that the tendency to respond to problems in the simplest way is correlated positively with attending to perceptual cues; such problem-solvers are called **field-dependent.** Similarly, the use of full intellectual capacity in problem-solving is correlated positively with attending to nonperceptual cues; such problem-solvers are called **field-independent** (Witkin et al., 1962). Figure 9-21 shows a typical test that measures field-dependence and field-independence.

Pascual-Leone and Case have been quite successful in predicting the age at which a child will perform correctly on Piagetian tasks. Their success is due to an assessment of the child's cogni-

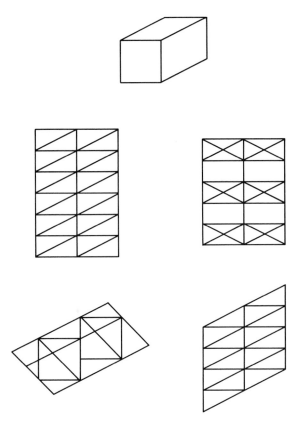

FIGURE 9-21

Witkin's Embedded-figures Test of Field-dependence A subject is shown one of the four complex figures in the lower two rows. He or she is then shown the simple figure in the top row. The simple figure is then removed from view and the subject is asked to find it embedded in the complex pattern. The longer the subject takes to find it, the more field-dependent the subject is. *Source:* Adapted from Rogers, L. (1976). Male hormones and behavior. In B. Lloyd & J. Archer (Eds.), *Exploring sex differences* (pp. 169–70). New York: Academic Press.

tive style (field-dependence or field-independence) and the intellectual capacity needed to perform correctly on a particular task. Consider the following imaginary situation.

Gerry and Judy are both in the same fifth grade class. The boys in the class decide to have a relay race against the girls in the class. They win the race, but not by too much. Turning to Judy, Gerry says, "See, I told you the boys were better runners than the girls; now we've proved it." Judy replies, "Oh, come off it. You boys are not better runners. The only reason you won was because your team was wearing running shoes. You didn't prove a thing!" "Didn't prove a thing?" Gerry replies. "We won, didn't we?" "Yeah, but you can't be sure it was because you were better runners." (Case, 1974, p. 556)

A young child who overheard the argument could conclude either that boys are faster runners than girls or that you cannot be sure. What must a child do in order to reach the second (correct) conclusion? According to Pascual-Leone and Case, the child must first have a plan for evaluating each person's argument. Second, he or she must consider the information contained in each person's argument and apply a rule to generate a conclusion. A possible rule in this case is: given two reasonable opposing possibilities, you cannot be sure. It may be that boys are faster runners or that boys are slower runners but that running shoes help. Third, the child must have sufficient intellectual capacity to process all the information. Finally, the child must be sufficiently field-independent so that he or she will not be misled by such perceptual cues as the possibility that the boys looked faster.

Other neo-Piagetian approaches (for example, Flavell, 1981; Fischer, 1980, 1982) have focused on the problem of describing and explaining developmental changes in the intellectual capabilities of children. These approaches have been less encompassing than Piaget's, tending to center on the development of individual skills. For example, Fischer suggests that children, depending on context, employ several different skills in the development of object permanence. The skill the child demonstrates in following the path of an object that is hidden is different from the skill demonstrated in searching for that object once it is hidden. The skills identified by Fischer undergo a series of transformations in the course of development, but each skill develops at a different rate and is not part of an overriding system of stages.

INFORMATION-PROCESSING APPROACHES TO COGNITIVE DEVELOPMENT

Piaget's theory pertains to how the child thinks and represents the world; another way to view cognitive development is from the perspective of information processing (Sternberg & Powell, 1983; Hunt, 1983). This approach focuses on the kinds of information children are capable of acquiring from the surrounding environment and what they are capable of doing with it.

In information processing, the computer is used as a metaphor for understanding how humans process information (Klahr & Wallace, 1976; Newell & Simon, 1972); however, both computers and humans have limitations on how much and what kinds of information they can handle. Thus the computer can be used to model the steps involved in solving the kinds of problems that confront children and adults, including the kinds of problems with which Piaget dealt, such as conservation (Siegler, 1978) and arithmetic problems (Gelman & Baillargeon, 1983).

The information-processing approach involves careful task analysis. Advocates of this approach believe that it is necessary to understand the component steps involved in a task in order to describe the nature of the problems that children face and to understand why they fail tasks that adults pass. In addition, information-processing theorists believe that it takes some time to complete each step necessary to solve a problem. Some theorists have produced fairly detailed claims about which processes unfold over time and how long each one takes.

As a means of contrasting Piaget's approach and the information-processing approach, consider again the problem of class inclusion, one often used by Piaget. In this type of problem the child must compare the relative number of objects in a subset (for instance, roses) with the number of objects in a larger set (for instance, roses and daffodils) and answer such questions as "Are there more roses than flowers?" According to Piagetian theory, a wrong answer indicates the child does not yet possess the cognitive skills and understanding to respond otherwise — that he or she does not yet understand hierarchical relationships. According to information-processing theory, we must understand the steps required to solve this task. First, the child must **encode** the important elements of the question; in other words, the child must **attend** to the question and store the critical aspects in memory. Next, the child must formulate a **plan** for answering the question. A possible plan might involve counting the number of objects in the two sets and then comparing the two numbers to reach an answer.

According to information-processing theorists, there are many reasons why children fail at such tasks as these. They may encode the problem incorrectly (Trabasso, 1977). The children may have difficulty counting (Wilkinson, 1976). They may be unable to remember the problem long enough to solve it. In other words, if it takes a certain amount of time to plan, count, and compare, a child may not be able to hold information in memory long enough to process it, or the attempt to hold it in memory may interfere with the execution of the other tasks.

Thus far information-processing approaches have supplied sensible analyses of various cognitive tasks, have produced suggestions for teaching children important skills, and have led to the discovery of some surprising competencies in young children. The influence of the information-processing approach is apparent in the attention paid by neo-Piagetian theorists to such aspects of thinking as task analysis and short-term memory.

COGNITIVE DEVELOPMENT IN ADULTHOOD

Although Piaget considered the attainment of formal operations to be the final developmental stage — lasting from adolescence throughout the rest of life — his research on this stage was confined to the adolescent years. Studies that have used Piagetian tasks to assess adult intellectual functioning shed little light on the question of whether there is intellectual growth or decline in the adult years. Past studies (for example, Doppelt & Wallace, 1955; Miles & Miles, 1932), primarily using standard tests of intelligence, found that intelligence increased through childhood, peaked somewhere between adolescence and the middle twenties, and declined thereafter. Should we conclude that as people grow older they become less intelligent? Recent reevaluations of earlier studies and certain new studies have suggested that this conclusion may be inaccurate.

Two factors have contributed to the reevaluation of whether intellectual performance declines with advancing age. The first pertains to *how* information on intelligence is collected

(there are several different ways). Using the **cross-sectional method,** the researcher measures intellectual performance in groups of people who differ in terms of their birth date. For example, the subjects in group one may be born in 1920; the subjects in group two, 1930; those in group three, 1940; and so on. These groups are compared on the basis of their average performance on some test of intellectual ability. Studies using the cross-sectional method usually have found a general decline in intelligence with increasing age.

However, this conclusion is problematic inasmuch as it is based on two questionable assumptions: that the older subjects in these studies would have performed like the younger subjects if they had been tested when they were younger and that the younger subjects will perform like the older subjects when they reach that age. Both these assumptions may be false. The older subjects do not differ from the younger subjects in age alone, but also in such other ways as amount of education, quality of health care and nutrition, socialization experiences, life-styles, and motivation to do well on the tests. Furthermore, historical events — such as experiencing a world war — have a complex differential impact on people, depending on their age at the time. It is impossible to separate the effects of aging from all the other factors that may be related to age changes.

A better method for collecting information on intellectual development in adulthood is the **longitudinal approach,** by which the same group of people is tested over regular intervals. For example, a group may be tested in 1940, again in 1950, and again in 1960. This is more effective than the cross-sectional method because age changes, and not just age differences, can be examined. Studies using this approach have *not* found a general decline in intelligence with age, but rather a slight increase up to almost age 50, and stable scores thereafter, at least up to age 61 (for example, Owens, 1966).

The second factor that has changed our thinking about adult intellectual development concerns the kinds of intelligence test used. For a long time, intelligence was assessed through tests (called omnibus tests) that derived a single intelligence score for each subject by combining scores from a variety of tests. In recent years, a new model of intellectual abilities has been proposed (Cattell, 1971; Horn & Donaldson, 1976). According to this model, there are two major types of intelligence. The first, called **crystallized intelligence,** consists of abilities that arise from learning facts, having experiences, and practicing the application of problem-solving techniques. The second, called **fluid intelligence,** is assumed to reflect physiological capacity (which varies considerably even among healthy young adults) and early experiences of a universal kind. Fluid intelligence involves the ability to organize and reorganize information in the process of solving problems—that is, to be flexible. Examples of items used to assess fluid intelligence are shown in Figure 9-22.

Horn and Donaldson (1976) believe that starting in adolescence fluid intelligence shows a steady decline as a result of the normal aging process but that crystallized intelligence, which depends on stored information, actually increases as a person ages. The results of a study by Horn (1975), which attempted to assess the two types of intelligence separately, support these ideas (see Figure 9-23). Because general intelligence tests reflect both types of intelligence, the scores remain relatively stable following adolescence.

It appears that answers to questions concerning the course of intellectual development in adulthood depend on the manner in which information on intelligence is collected and the way in which intelligence is defined. According to Horn and Donaldson, if intelligence is defined as fluid intelligence, it appears to decline with age; if intelligence is defined as crystallized intelligence, it increases.

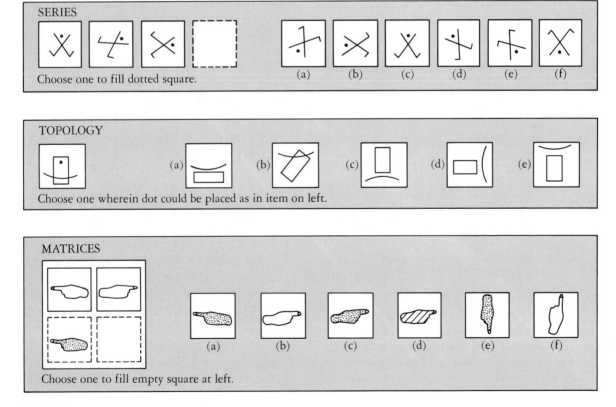

FIGURE 9-22

Sample of Items Used to Test for Fluid Intelligence The items require inference and induction to solve, and contain relatively little culture-specific information. Answers: e, b, c. *Source:* Selections from Tests 1 – 4, Scale III, (1961). *Culture fair intelligence test.* Champaign, IL: Institute for Personality and Ability Testing. Copyright © 1950, 1961 by the Institute for Personality and Ability Testing, Inc. All rights reserved. Reproduced by permission.

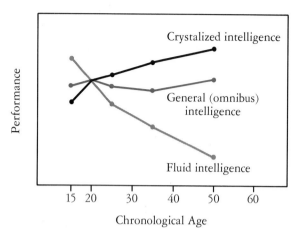

FIGURE 9-23

Differences between Crystallized, General, and Fluid Intelligence As people age, their scores on tests of crystallized and fluid intelligence change. *Source:* Adapted from Horn, J. L. (1978). The nature and development of intellectual abilities. In R. T. Osborne, C. E. Nobel, & N. Weyl (Eds.). *Human variation.* New York: Academic Press.

Riegel and Riegel (1972) have suggested that until approximately the last five years before a person dies intelligence does not decline at all. The Riegels tested a group of older people and retested them some time later. By comparing the initial scores of those who had been retested with the scores of subjects who had died before the second testing, the researchers discovered the phenomenon of **terminal drop.** The people who were retested showed no decline in intelligence; those who had died showed lower scores on the initial test than did the survivors. Terminal drop, however, is not necessarily a function of age because it is also seen in terminally ill younger subjects. Nevertheless, since more old people than young people are likely to be in a period of decline at the time of intelligence testing, their poor performance in cross-sectional studies may explain the larger proportion of the older group showing terminal drop.

In conclusion, some people think there is a decline in intelligence during adulthood; some people think there is no decline; some people think there is a decline in one form of intelligence but not in another. Clearly a great deal remains to be learned about intellectual changes in middle and late adulthood.

SUMMARY

1. Developmental psychologists attempt to describe important changes that occur throughout the life span, from conception to death, and to learn what causes them. Principal questions address whether such changes occur in a fixed sequence and how they are related to one another.

2. The most rapid developmental changes occur between conception and birth. The newborn displays such reflexes as sucking and rooting, as well as nonreflexive activities of many kinds. Although motor development may be retarded by lack of opportunity for exercise, unless the deprivation is severe, children soon catch up to their age-mates. There is rapid growth during the first two to three years, then steady growth until about eleven, when the adolescent growth spurt begins. Adolescents grow larger and achieve full adult stature earlier than in the past.

Increases in hormonal levels trigger sexual maturation; females start and complete puberty earlier than males. The average age of menarche has been decreasing and is now under 14. Reaching sexual maturity early is advantageous for males; being "in phase" is most beneficial for females.

3. Both sexes experience a climacteric—a marked decline in reproductive capacity. For women this culminates in menopause. Aging involves a gradual decrease in the effectiveness of many bodily functions. Outward physical changes are likely to have less effect than changes at the physiological level that decrease adaptive responsiveness to the environment. In late old age there is typi-

cally a terminal decline phase, ending in death. The dying person may welcome the opportunity to discuss his or her condition. There may be a five-step pattern of reaction to one's own death: denial, anger, bargaining, depression, acceptance.

4. Although newborn infants can see, their visual systems do not function at a mature level. However, their auditory systems are essentially complete at birth. The direction taken by sensory and perceptual development is from an interest in simple to an interest in slightly more complex and novel stimuli.

5. Infants appear to inherit a reflexive ability to perceive movement; this ability is later overridden by abilities mediated by later-developing centers in the brain. Infants show evidence they can perceive depth by two months of age, but do not avoid heights until six months. Although the evidence as to size constancy is unclear, infants can maintain shape constancy and object identity constancy. In general, infants can perceive things at or soon after birth, but such abilities are refined with experience.

6. Language is a mode of communication that employs symbols to convey meaning. Infants appear to be prepared biologically to distinguish the sounds that make words in all languages. Children's first words symbolize things with which children interact, especially things that can be moved and that they can demand. Children acquire the ability to employ grammatically correct constructions in an orderly sequence and in accordance with the complexity of the meanings conveyed.

7. Although theories of language development may emphasize the effect of heredity or environment, the evidence suggests that both factors are involved. Children cannot acquire language until they reach an appropriate maturational level and a broad range of environmental inputs are necessary for adequate language development.

8. Cognitive development involves growth of the ability to think. The learning approach views development as acquisition of responses: development is quantitative. In Piaget's cognitive-structural theory, development is qualitative: marked by distinctively different ways of thinking. The first intelligent behaviors are sucking, looking, and grasping. An organism adapts by assimilating information into its existing systems of understanding and accommodating to new information by changing those systems. The organism seeks consistency or equilibrium between its mental acts and the environment; seeking balance leads to cognitive development.

9. In Piaget's view, thinking is restructured at each stage. Stages may be reached at slightly different ages, depending on individual and cultural variation, but their order is fixed and identical in all cultures. Movement from stage to stage is gradual and once the transition to a new stage is completed, the child does not regress to earlier forms of understanding.

10. In the sensory-motor stage, which lasts from birth to about 18 months, infants progress from reflexive reactions to the beginnings of internal representations of their environment. By the end of this stage, object permanence is achieved. In the preoperational stage, which lasts from 18 months until approximately six years, children start to use language; however, thinking is still dominated by immediate perceptual cues and is egocentric — children do no distinguish clearly between their viewpoints and the viewpoints of others until the end of this period.

11. In the concrete-operational stage, lasting roughly from six to eleven years, children learn the operations of classification, ordering, reciprocity, and most importantly, conservation. However, they can make these logical, reversible operations with materials only, not with symbols or abstractions.

Can a child be taught to conserve? Piaget doubted that the pervasive mental reorganization required for conserving can be brought about by teaching. Although one method, teaching the child to apply a rule, has had some success, conservation can be induced only in children who are ready.

The final stage, formal operations, is attained between 11 and 15 years. The formal-operations stage involves reasoning in symbolic terms in the absence of concrete objects and is exemplified by the formulation of scientific propositions.

12. Criticisms of Piaget's theory have tended to focus on his case study and interview methods of research, the ambiguity of some of the central concepts in his theory, the degree of homogeneity in abilities characteristic of stages, his contention that young children are not able to understand certain concepts, and Piaget's belief that most people reach the formal-operations stage.

13. The theory of cognitive development advanced by Pascual-Leone and Case departs from that of Piaget in three main ways. Pascual-Leone and Case assume that children employ several cognitive strategies to solve problems; that the amount of space in short-term memory increases with age and that complex problems require more space in short-term memory than simple problems;

and that certain strategies become habitual, requiring less space in short term memory.

14. Information-processing methods focus on the kinds of information children are capable of acquiring from the surrounding environment and what they are able to do with it. The computer is used as a metaphor for understanding how people process information.

15. Early studies indicated that intelligence declined in adulthood; however, the studies were cross-sectional — they compared groups born at different times. But group differences other than those caused by age differences could have accounted for the decline in intelligence-test scores. Consequently, a longitudinal approach is preferable. And longitudinal studies have not found a decline with age until at least late adulthood.

Intelligence can be conceived as being of two kinds — crystallized and fluid. The former consists of stored information and is believed to accumulate with age; the latter is based on physiological capacity and shows a steady decline after early adulthood.

KEY TERMS

Embryo	Androgen	Delayed Imitation
Reflexive Behavior	Gerontology	Make-believe Play
Rooting Reflex	Visual Cliff	Deferred Imitation
Sucking Reflex	Size Constancy	Expanded Imitation
Motor Skill	Shape Constancy	Deep Structure
Fine Motor Skill	Object-identity Constancy	Genetic Epistemology
Differentiation	Language	Adaptation
Integration	Semantics	Organization
Walking Reflex	Syntax	Assimilation
Placing Reflex	Phonology	Accommodation
Adolescent Growth Spurt	Pragmatics	Scheme
Secular Trend	Intonation	Equilibration
Secondary Sex Characteristic	Overextension	Equilibrium
Menarche	Telegraphic Speech	Conservation
Climacteric	Grammar	Transitional Period
Menopause	Overregularization	Sensory-motor Stage
Estrogen	Whorfian Hypothesis	Object Permanence

Preoperational Stage	Reciprocity	Encode
Symbolic Function	Principle of Conservation	Attend
Operation	Formal-operations Stage	Plan
Egocentric	Principle of Proportionality	Cross-sectional Method
Concrete Operations	Clinical Method	Longitudinal Approach
Concrete-operations Stage	Class Inclusion	Crystallized Intelligence
Classification	Field-dependent	Fluid Intelligence
Seriate	Field-independent	Terminal Drop

RECOMMENDED READINGS

Eliot, A. J. (1981). *Child language.* Cambridge, Eng.: Cambridge University Press. A readable text outlining the acquisition of language in first years.

Flavell, J. H. (1985). *Cognitive development.* (2nd ed.). Englewood Cliffs, NJ: Prentice-Hall. A leading developmental psychologist's general introduction to cognitive development.

Ginsberg, H. & Opper, S. (1979). *Piaget's theory of intellectual development* (2nd ed.). Englewood Cliffs, NJ: Prentice-Hall. A well-written introduction to Piaget's theory, with many examples of how children think at each stage of development.

Leach, P. (1980). *Your baby and child from birth to age five.* New York: Alfred A. Knopf. Written by a developmental psychologist, the book supplies a scholarly but readable overview of the skills and limitations of children in the early years of their lives.

McCall, R. C. (1979). *Infants.* Cambridge, MA: Harvard University Press. Cast at a level appropriate for parents, this volume presents a clear overview of milestones in development.

Poon, L. W. (Ed.) (1980). *Aging in the 1980's.* Washington, D. C.: American Psychological Association. A collection of readings on all facets of the aging process.

10

SOCIAL DEVELOPMENT

"**I**f everybody minded their own business," said the Duchess in *Alice in Wonderland,* "the world would go round a deal faster than it does." This is a rather edgy comment on the value of social relations. It also is quite incorrect. If everybody minded "their" own business, the world as we know it wouldn't go around at all.

It often has been said that humans are the most social of all animals. Because our social relations seem so natural to us, it is difficult to appreciate just how social we are. However, if you were to observe humans in the detached manner that ethologists observe such animals as geese and gorillas, you undoubtedly would be struck by the extent and complexity of the social bonds formed by members of the human species. Mammals are biologically disposed to remain with their parents longer than the children of almost every other species. All people form elaborate networks of family relations and virtually everyone belongs to at least one formal group. The children of all cultures create clubs, form gangs, and band together in an endless variety of ways. In industrialized countries, the social context of

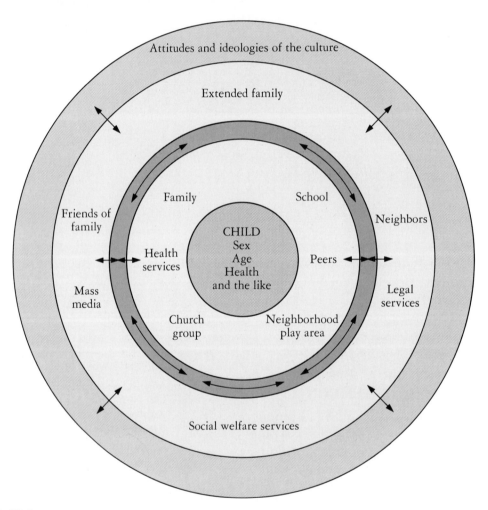

FIGURE 10-1

The Social Context of the Child Within the social world of the child, there is an expanding series of social systems. The innermost system consists of relations between the child and his or her immediate environment. The next system consists of the interrelationships between the items in the first system (family, school, peers, and so forth). The next system consists of agencies, social groups, and services that affect the child. The outermost system consists of the cultural values and beliefs in which other systems are embedded. *Source:* Adapted from Garbarino, J. (1982). Sociocultural risk: Dangers to competence. In C. Kapp & J. Krakow (Eds.), *The child* (p. 648). Reading, MA: Addison-Wesley.

the child includes interactions with such institutions as the mass media and health and legal services (see Figure 10-1). If you doubt the significance of social relations in your own life, try spending a few days completely alone.

Why are humans so social? Some theorists have suggested that social dispositions evolved because early humans were poorly equipped to survive on their own. Compared to the species with which early humans competed, humans were not particularly strong or fierce; they banded together to enhance their chances of survival. Because dispositions that fostered cooperation were adaptive, individuals who possessed them prevailed and passed them on to their offspring, while less social individuals (and their less social dispositions) perished. Through this process of natural selection, humans came to be social by nature.

It is possible that in early humans the adaptive value of social relations stimulated the evolution of their most distinguishing physical structure, the brain. Some theorists have suggested that the primary reason why the brain developed into its present elaborate structure is because it facilitated communication among our early ancestors (Lovejoy, 1981). For this reason, argue some theorists, the development of language — the ability to engage in the social act of communication — related closely to the development of thought (see Chapter 9). Of course, the fact that human infants inherit social needs and dispositions does not mean they specifically inherit the urge to chat on the phone, go to a party, or engage in a heart-to-heart talk. The social dispositions that people inherit are general — the need for social contact, the need to have friends, the need for physical intimacy — and are shaped into specific behaviors through learning.

In this chapter we describe the types of social dispositions that human infants inherit, examine how these dispositions are shaped by early experiences, and outline the ways in which they guide behavior from infancy to adulthood. More specifically, we discuss four aspects of social development: how infants form attachments, how parents and other caretakers socialize their children, how children

TABLE 10-1

Four Theoretical Perspectives on Social Development — An Overview

Evolutionary Theories	Evolutionary theories derive from Darwin's theory of evolution. They focus on evolved dispositions that affect social behavior and on environmental factors that caused them to evolve in the past (*selected* them) and evoke them in the present. Evolutionary perspectives postulate genetically programmed behaviors but recognize the importance of environmental factors that elicit them; the perspective is phylogenetic (the evolution of species) rather than ontogenetic (the development of individuals). Ethology focuses on innately programmed social responses (fixed-action patterns) elicited by particular environmental stimuli. Sociobiological theory focuses on relations among genetically related individuals and on biologically rooted systems of interaction, such as attachment, that protect and benefit the social organism.
Psychoanalytic Theory	Psychoanalytic theory focuses on the conflicts experienced by children in dealing with their sexual and aggressive instincts, especially in relation to their parents. It postulates four stages of development based on the zones of the body through which sexual tension is released.
Social Learning Theory	Social Learning theory focuses on the learning environment of children —the rewards and punishments they experience and the models to whom they are exposed. Social learning theorists view social development as continuous and without stages. They focus on the methods used by such agents as parents to socialize children.
Cognitive-developmental Theory	Cognitive-developmental theorists focus on the development of knowledge in children and the effect of children's increasing cognitive sophistication on their social behavior. Cognitive-developmental theorists postulate stages of cognitive development that involve transformations in the structure of thinking.

come to adopt identities and roles that are appropriate to their gender, and how children develop a sense of morality. In addition, we examine stages in the social development of adults.

When psychologists study the various facets of social development, they tend to view them from one or more broad theoretical perspectives. Four theories are especially useful in this regard: evolutionary theory (see Chapter 2), psychoanalysis (see Chapter 12), social learning theory (see Chapters 5 and 12), and cognitive-developmental theory (see Chapter 9). As we examine the various facets of social development, we view them, when appropriate, from each of these perspectives (see Table 10-1).

ATTACHMENT

Infants form their first social and emotional bond with their primary caretaker, usually their mother. Although this bond has been called many things, most notably love, in psychology it is commonly referred to as **attachment.** According to one theorist, ''No form of behavior is accompanied by stronger feelings than is attachment behavior. Infants greet those to whom they are attached with joy, and become anxious, angry and sorrowful when they leave, or even threaten to leave'' (Bowlby, 1971, p. 257).

Psychologists have attempted to determine what is involved in the formation of attachments, how they develop, and the different forms they take. Most research has involved the observation of children in normal environments; however, some researchers have examined orphaned, institutionalized, and neglected infants in order to evaluate the effect of early deprivation on the development of later social relations. What happens to children who receive inadequate social contact early in their lives? Do they lose the capacity to love? To what extent do the early attachments of infants determine the kinds of bonds they form in later life? What role do fathers play in the process of attachment?

An Ethological Account of Attachment

The concept of attachment — indeed the label itself — was introduced to psychology by **ethologists.** Ethologists are researchers (usually zoologists) who observe animals in their natural environments; they are guided by evolutionary theory. In ethology the concept of attachment was derived from the concept of **imprinting** (see Chapter 2). Newly hatched birds and many newborn mammals start to follow their mothers shortly after birth; however, if the mother is absent, the animal will follow another moving object, including a human. The following response signals the formation of an emotional bond between the infant and the individual or object on whom it has imprinted; this *attachment* appears to pave the way for subsequent attachments. When animals that have imprinted on members of other species reach sexual maturity and are faced with the choice of a sexual partner, they may show a preference for members of the species on which they imprinted. Indeed, ethologists have observed ducks that have become imprinted to a box dangling from a string make amorous advances to it when they reached sexual maturity — even while receptive and available mates stood nearby.

The most influential ethological theory of attachment, however, was published by psychoanalyst John Bowlby. Bowlby's early book *Maternal Care and Mental Health,* published by the World Health Organization in 1952, and his subsequent volumes *Attachment and Loss* stimulated a spate of research on the issue. At first blush it may seem that ethology and psychoanalysis have little in common, yet they do. Both theories are based on the assumption that human motivation is instinctual and that instincts operate in a closed energy system. Both assume that there is a direct relationship between the performance of certain behaviors and the satisfaction of instinctual needs. Both theories assume that needs may be partially satisfied by related activities. And both theories attach considerable importance to early experiences.

The central assumption of Bowlby's theory is that infants inherit a *genetic blueprint* that causes them to behave toward their mothers in a manner that ensures their survival. Infants employ such built-in signaling systems as crying, clinging, sucking, smiling, and following. In turn, mothers inherit a genetic blueprint with which to respond appropriately to the signals of infants. According to Bowlby, there is a **sensitive period** during which the *synchrony* of action between mother and child produces an attachment. Once formed, this bond activates an internal system that regulates such behaviors as how far away from the mother a child will move and the amount of fear the child will show toward strangers.

Although Bowlby's theory has been influential, critics have questioned whether the formation of attachments is as genetically preprogrammed as Bowlby implies, whether it occurs only during a sensitive period in infancy, and whether mothers are as important in the process as Bowlby suggests.

A Psychoanalytic Account of Attachment

According to psychoanalytic theory, young infants develop an attachment to their caretakers (usually their mother) because the caretakers satisfy their instinctual needs. Psychoanalytically oriented theorists emphasize the significance of feeding practices, especially breast-feeding, in the formation of attachments during the oral stage of development. Correspondingly, they also stress the importance of the *maternal* figure as essential to attachment. According to psychoanalytic theorists, healthy attachments are formed when feeding practices satisfy infants' needs for food, security, and oral sexual gratification; unhealthy attachments occur when infants are deprived of food and oral pleasure or when they are overindulged. In the latter cases, children may fixate at the oral stage of development, developing either a dependent personality (becoming overattached) or withdrawing from social relations (becoming underattached).

Psychoanalytic theory stimulated a great deal of research on the effects of various feeding practices — especially breast-feeding versus bottle-feeding and schedule-feeding versus demand-feeding — and on the consequences of weaning children at different ages. In general, the research did not confirm predictions derived from psychoanalytic theory. The evidence suggests that it makes little difference to the social development of children whether they are breast-fed or bottle-fed, fed on demand or by schedule, weaned early or late. Rather, research indicates that infants are most likely to form secure attachments to those who supply them with the highest quality and the most consistent nurturance and social stimulation (Schaffer & Emerson, 1964).

A Social Learning Account of Attachment

In contrast to ethological and psychoanalytic theorists, social learning theorists do not assume that attachment is a special phenomenon governed by special laws; they believe young infants approach their caretakers because the caretakers reinforce their approach behaviors. Caretakers give food, relieve pain, and supply comfort. Through the repeated association of caretakers with pleasure, caretakers become rewarding in themselves — they become secondary reinforcers (see Chapter 5).

A classic series of studies by Harlow and his colleagues (Harlow, 1958; Harlow & Zimmerman, 1959) revealed the limitations of the social learning explanation of attachment. Harlow isolated infant rhesus monkeys at birth and reared them with either terry cloth or wire surrogate mothers (see Figure 10-2). Regardless of which "mother" supplied the primary reinforcement (a bottle of milk) in infancy, the monkeys showed a clear preference for the terry cloth mother at a time later in their lives when they were given a choice. They used the terry cloth mother as a base for exploration and ran to "her" when frightened. The monkeys appeared to need the security associated with the **contact comfort** supplied by the terry cloth, independently from its association with the primary reinforcement supplied by the milk.

A Cognitive–Developmental Account of Attachment

In contrast to theories that emphasize the emotional bond involved in attachment, cognitive-developmental theory emphasizes the cognitive relationship between infants and caretakers. It

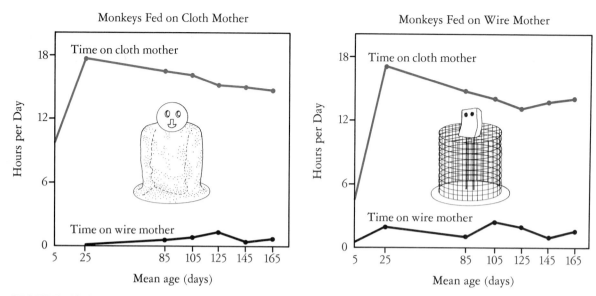

FIGURE 10-2

Contact Comfort Both the monkeys fed by a cloth mother and the monkeys fed by a wire mother preferred to spend time with the cloth mother. *Source:* Adapted from Harlow, H. F., & Zimmerman, R. R. (1959). Affectional responses in the infant monkey. *Science, 130,* 421–22.

focuses on the growth of the infant's ability to distinguish between self and other and, once that ability is acquired, to distinguish between caretakers and strangers. In addition, the theory attends to the ways in which caretakers stimulate the growth of knowledge. According to this theory, infants become attached to their parents because their parents provide the most interesting, informative, and cognitively challenging events in their lives.

The research of Schaffer (1971) exemplifies a cognitive-developmental account. Schaffer believes that the growth of attachment depends upon infants' expanding perceptual and cognitive abilities. Schaffer points out that infants do not become attached to a specific person until they are able to distinguish between that person and other people. He attributes the satisfaction derived from attachment to the rewards associated with effective mutual stimulation of caretaker and child and the child's growing sense of social competence and mastery. According to this perspective, the pleasure a child experiences when forming an attachment derives from the development of increasingly organized and integrated conceptions of the social world, not from physical pleasure or satisfaction of instinctual needs.

Four Theories of Attachment — Which One?

Each theory we have considered focuses on a particular aspect of the attachment process — genetic blueprint, relief from instinctual tension, primary reinforcement, secondary gains, cognitive growth. Some theories emphasize innate capacities and some emphasize learning (see Table 10-2). As research on attachment has progressed, however, it has become increasingly clear that all factors are implicated in the process. But this does not mean that the particulars of all theories are correct. Indeed, considering that the assumptions of certain theories are inconsistent with the assumptions of others, they cannot all be correct. The best evidence suggests that attachment involves both innate dispositions and learned associations as well as both emotional and cognitive bonds.

The general theoretical orientations we have outlined are useful mainly as contexts from which to view attachment and as means of directing researchers' attention to different aspects of the process.

Mutual Coordination

For years it was assumed that infants are helpless at birth and do little or nothing to promote their

TABLE 10-2
Four Theories of Attachment

Point of Comparison	Ethological Theory	Psychoanalytic Theory	Social Learning Theory	Cognitive-developmental Theory
Attachment behaviors	behaviors that promote proximity between infant and caretaker	oral behaviors and dependence on person providing oral gratification	learned behaviors	exploratory, cognitively stimulating behaviors
Motivation	instinctual	relief of tension from physical sexual drives	reinforcement	enhance understanding and acquire a sense of competence
Time frame	sensitive period	oral stage	continuous throughout life	associated with stage of cognitive development
Object of attachment	emphasis on mother as typical caretaker	person who breast-feeds (usually the mother)	anyone who reinforces approach behaviors	anyone who provides consistent and engaging cognitive stimulation
Degree of reversibility	relatively irreversible	relatively irreversible: inadequate attachment causes fixation that affects later development	reversible	reversible
Effect on later development	affects ability to love and sexual preferences	affects formation of adult personality and all other intimate relationships	minimal if environment changes	paves the way for subsequent stages of social development

survival; we now know this is not at all the case. With the use of increasingly precise methods of observation, especially videotapes, it has become clear that infants interact with and guide their caretakers in a variety of adaptive ways. As demonstrated in Chapter 9, infants are born with abilities that enable them to distinguish between social and nonsocial objects, and considerable research reveals that infants show preferences for certain social stimuli from the time of birth. As evidence of the infant's role in early social interactions accumulated, some researchers suggested it is the infant, not the caretaker, who initiates the process of attachment (see Rheingold, 1968). Cited as evidence were reports of mothers who said they did not experience intense feelings toward their babies until the end of the second or third month, when the infants made and maintained eye contact (Robson & Moss, 1970). Researchers also described mothers of blind children who felt less attached to their children than

mothers of sighted children until corrective measures were taken (Fraiberg, 1977). However, it must be remembered that the capacity of the infant to evoke reactions from his or her caretaker depends on the disposition of the caretaker to respond.

Today most researchers recognize that infants and caretakers each contribute to the pattern of interaction between them, and that the contribution of one cannot be separated from the contribution of the other (see Figure 10-3). Relations between infants and caretakers involve mutually coordinated systems of behavior: alert, responsive mothers evoke responsiveness in their infants; alert, responsive infants evoke stimulation from their mothers (Osofsky & Danzger, 1974). Who begins the sequence is not as important as the rhythm and mutual coordination of the behaviors. This coordination is seen perhaps most clearly in such an early game between infants and caretakers as peekaboo, which is based

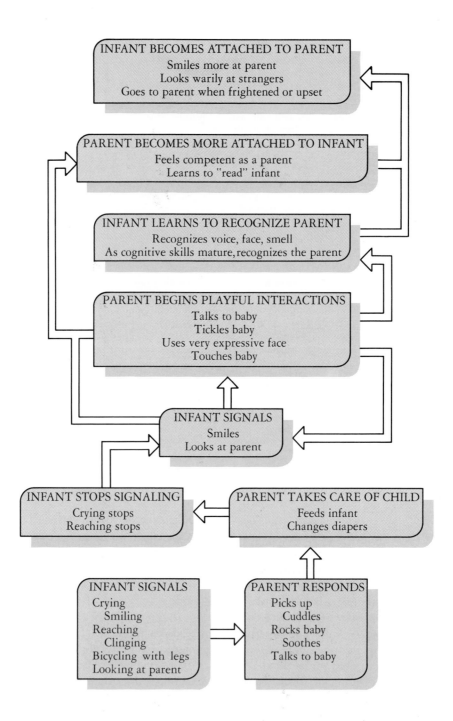

FIGURE 10-3

The System of Mutual Interaction that Fosters Attachment The attachment behavioral system encompasses all of the behaviors the infant uses to keep the parent close. Starting at the bottom of the figure, during the early days, crying is the most effective behavior. Later, the infant is able to keep the parent close by smiling, reaching, clinging, looking, and bicycling with the legs. Once infants can walk or crawl, they can play a more active role in staying near the parent. The infant's attachment behavioral system meshes with parental behaviors to promote attachment. *Source:* Adapted from Tomlinson-Keasey, C. (1985). *Child development* (p. 285). Homewood, IL: Dorsey Press.

on simple principles of reciprocity. Games like this pave the way for the infant to learn social conventions and rules of social exchange (Bruner, 1974).

Research on Attachment

In the early years of research on attachment, investigators separated babies from their mothers for brief periods of time and recorded how much the babies protested. They found that babies from a variety of cultures protested most vigorously when separated from their mothers at the approximate age of one year (see Figure 10-4). Early researchers assumed the more a baby cried when separated from his or her mother, the stronger the attachment between them, but there is a problem with this assumption. Infants who have formed the strongest attachments might feel the most secure and, therefore, protest the least when their mother is not present.

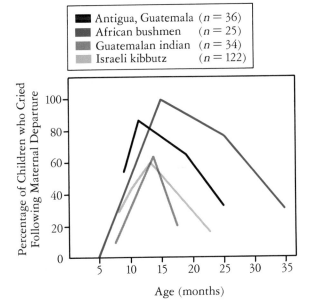

FIGURE 10-4

Separation Protest in Different Cultures In a variety of cultures, infants are most sensitive to being separated from their parents between 12 and 15 months of age; however, the intensity and duration of their crying may vary. *Source:* Adapted from Mussen, P. H., Conger, J. J., & Kagan, J. (1980). *Essentials of child development and personality* (p. 104). New York: Harper & Row.

In the 1960s, Mary Ainsworth, a colleague of John Bowlby, developed a new technique for studying attachment called the **strange situation,** where the baby is exposed to a series of eight increasingly stressful experiences. First, the baby and mother are brought into an unfamiliar setting that contains three chairs and several toys. Then a series of events take place: a stranger enters the room, the mother leaves, and so on (see Figure 10-5). On the basis of observations of infants placed in the strange situation, Ainsworth developed a detailed description of behaviors that reflect attachment (see Table 10-3).

Phases in the Process of Attachment Ainsworth (1973) and Schaffer and Emerson (1964) divide the process of attachment into four phases:

Phase 1: *Preattachment* (birth to three months) The infant responds to social stimuli, but does not discriminate between people and such people-like objects as mobiles and teddy bears.

Phase 2: *Indiscriminate Attachment* (three to six months) The infant is especially responsive to people, and will smile and coo when picked up and protest when put down. Although the infant can tell the difference between familiar and nonfamiliar people (Maurer & Salapatek, 1976), he or she is as content with a stranger as with a caretaker.

Phase 3: *Discriminate Attachment* (six months to two years) The infant reacts differently to familiar and unfamiliar adults and will laugh, smile, cuddle, invite play, and approach familiar adults. He or she may protest when handed to an unfamiliar adult and may show signs of fear when a stranger appears.

Phase 4: *Multiple Attachments* (two years on) The child becomes increasingly independent from his or her caretaker and forms attachments to other individuals. For example, Rheingold and Eckerman (1973) found that one-year-old children traveled only about 7 meters from their mothers when they were in a strange yard, but by age four they traveled an average of about 20 meters. During this phase, children typically spend more and more time with their peers.

Quality of Attachment According to Mary Ainsworth and her colleagues (Ainsworth, Blehar,

Stranger   Mother

Episode	Persons Present	Duration	Brief Description
1	Mother, baby and observer	30 seconds	Observer introduces mother and baby to experimental room, then leaves.
2	Mother and baby	3 minutes	Mother is nonparticipant while baby explores; if necessary, play is stimulated after 2 minutes.
3	Stranger, mother, and baby	3 minutes	Stranger enters. First minute: stranger silent. Second minute: stranger converses with mother (see illustration). Third minute: stranger approaches baby. After 3 minutes, mother leaves unobtrusively.
4	Stranger and baby	3 minutes or less*	First separation episode. Stranger's behavior is geared to that of baby.
5	Mother and baby	3 minutes or more†	First reunion episode. Mother greets and/or comforts baby, then tries to settle the baby again in play. Mother then leaves, saying "bye-bye."
6	Baby alone	3 minutes or less	Second separation episode.
7	Stranger and baby	3 minutes or less	Continuation of second separation. Stranger enters and gears her behavior to that of baby.
8	Mother and baby	3 minutes	Second reunion episode. Mother enters, greets baby, then pickes up baby. Meanwhile, stranger leaves unobtrusively.

* Episode is curtailed if the baby is unduly distressed.
†Episode is prolonged if more time is required for the baby to become reinvolved in play.

FIGURE 10-5

Ainsworth's *Strange Situation* The procedure involved in Ainsworth's *strange situation* involves eight episodes. *Source:* Ainsworth, M. D. S., Blehar, M. C., Waters, E., & Wall, S. (1978). *Patterns of attachment* (p. 37). Hillsdale, NJ: Lawrence Erlbaum Associates.

Waters, & Wall, 1978), infants form one of three basic types of attachment (see Table 10-4). Although the **secure attachment** pattern seems like the optimal type of attachment (almost 70% of the infants studied by Ainsworth displayed this pattern), Ainsworth insists that it does not entail more or less attachment than the other types. It is qualitatively, not quantitatively, different.

What events maximize the probability that an infant will form an adequate attachment? A few years ago an idea derived from ethological research on animals gained currency — there was a critical period after the animal's birth when the mother formed a bond with it and that if the infant were taken away from the mother during this period, the mother would not "bond" (Klaus & Kennell, 1976). Although such **bonding** appears to occur in most animals, the evidence suggests that it does not occur in humans. As discussed, the process of attachment involves a complex coordination between caretaker and child; however, the strength of the attachment

TABLE 10-3
Attachment Behaviors

Behaviors	Description
Differential crying	The infant cries when held by someone other than the parent but usually stops crying when taken by parent.
Differential smiling	The infant smiles more readily and more frequently in interaction with parent than with others.
Differential vocalization	The infant vocalizes more readily and more frequently in interaction with parent than with others.
Visual-motor orientation	When apart from parent but within sight of parent, the infant maintains an orientation toward parent.
Crying when parent not seen	The infant often cries when parent leaves infant's range or sight.
Following	Once able to crawl, the infant attempts to pursue parent after separation from parent.
Scrambling	The infant climbs over parent, explores and plays with parent's face, hair, or clothes.
Burying the face	The infant buries his or her face in parent's lap.
Parent-based exploration	The infant takes little excursions away from parent, briefly returning and glancing back from time to time.
Clinging	The infant may display excessive holding and grasping, particularly in the presence of strangers.
Greeting (lifting arms)	The infant raises arms, smiling and vocalizing toward parent after brief absence.
Greeting (clapping hands)	The infant claps hands in response to parental reappearance.
Approach	Once able to crawl, the infant terminates greeting responses by quickly crawling to parent.

Source: Adapted from Ainsworth, M. D. S. (1964). Patterns of attachment behavior shown by the infant interacting with his mother. *Merrill-Palmer Quarterly, 10,* 51–58.

depends on a system of interaction that grows throughout the child's early life.

The mother's attitude toward her role as a mother has been found to have an important effect on the quality of attachment (Kennedy, 1973). If a woman feels negative about being a mother, she is likely to ignore or punish her infant; this, in turn evokes negative behavior. The pattern also may originate with an infant. An irritable or demanding infant may evoke harsh responses in his or her caretaker; these, in turn, may lead to increased negative behaviors.

Research on attachment suggests that although it is necessary for caretakers to spend some time with infants (the exact amount differs with different infants), the quality of parent-child interactions is more important than the quantity. The warmer and more responsive caregivers are to infants' overtures, the stronger the attachment

(Schaffer & Emerson, 1964). In the pioneer collective settlements of Israel (*kibbutzim*), parents normally saw their children only in the evenings and on weekends; yet children from *kibbutzim,* like children in day-care centers, formed perfectly normal attachments to their parents (Caldwell et al., 1970). Although some learning theorists would predict that parents who respond sympathetically to infant crying would reinforce crying in their children, research has not supported this prediction (Bell & Ainsworth, 1972). Apparently, parents who are responsive to infant crying are responsive to other social signals from their children as well and, therefore, induce stronger attachments in them than parents who are not.

Social Deprivation   In Chapter 2 we reviewed studies that investigated the effects of early expe-

TABLE 10-4
Three Types of Attachment

	Anxious/Avoidant Attachment	Secure Attachment	Anxious/Resistant Attachment
Infant exploration	*Independent exploration*	*Exploration from secure base of caregiver*	*Poverty of exploration*
	1. readily separates to explore during preseparation	1. readily separates to explore toys	1. has difficulty separating to explore; may need contact even prior to separation
	2. readily explores	2. readily explores	2. wary of novel situations
	3. little affective sharing	3. affecting sharing of play	3. little affective sharing
	4. affiliative to stranger, even when caregiver is absent (little preference); no avoidance of strangers	4. affiliative to stranger in mother's presence	4. wary of strangers
	5. distress as easily comforted by stranger as by caregiver	5. readily comforted by caregiver when distressed (promoting a return to play)	5. not easily comforted by caregiver or by stranger
Reunion with mother	*Active avoidance upon reunion*	*Active seeking of contact or interaction upon reunion*	*Difficulty settling upon reunion*
	1. turns away, looks away, moves away, ignores	1. seeks caregiver; knows caregiver will be there if needed	1. may show striking passivity
	2. may mix avoidance with proximity	2. if distressed, immediately seeks and maintains contact, which is effective in terminating stress	2. may simply continue to cry and fuss
	3. avoidance is more extreme on second reunion	3. if not distressed, shows active greeting behavior (happy to see caregiver and strong initiation of interaction)	3. may mix contact seeking with contact resistance (hitting, kicking, squirming, rejecting toys)

Source: From Sroufe, Alan L. (1981, October). Infant-caregiver and patterns of adaptation in preschool: The roots of maladaptation and competence. Presented at the Minnesota Symposium in Child Psychology.

rience on later development; this issue has been of particular interest to investigators concerned with attachment. Researchers have wondered whether infants deprived of social contact—for example, orphaned, institutionalized, or neglected children—suffer permanent deficiencies in their ability to form fulfilling relationships in later life. In Bowlby's 1952 report to the World Health Organization, he reached the strong conclusion that a normal relationship between mother and infant was necessary for adequate social, emotional, and intellectual development.

In the years following Bowlby's report, researchers studied the effects of social deprivation in human and other animals; the results of the studies suggested several qualifications to

Bowlby's conclusions. Some studies found that it was more the lack of physical stimulation than social isolation that produced adverse effects in deprived children (Dennis, 1960; Yarrow, 1964). Other studies found that the adverse effects of early deprivation could be overcome if appropriate sensory and social experiences were provided in later years (Skeels, 1966). In a recent review of studies on maternal deprivation, British psychiatrist Michael Rutter (1979) distinguishes four kinds of early adversity and links them to four kinds of behavior disorder in later life (see Table 10-5).

The weight of the accumulated evidence suggests that there are several processes involved in the formation of attachments and that adequate

TABLE 10-5
Consequences of Adversities in Caregiver – Child Relations During Infancy

Nature of Caregiver – Child Adversity	Antecedent Conditions to Adversity	Behavioral Disorder in Child's Later Development
Interference with Attachment Behavior	Separation, coupled with poor quality social interactions during the separation and vulnerability on the part of the child	Acute distress syndrome (for example, severe psychological reactions during extended hospitalization)
Conflictual Interpersonal Relations	Family conflict, caregiver-child disharmony	Conduct disorders in interactions with adults and peers
Lack of Meaningful Social Experiences	Impoverished social environment, little or no social stimulation	Intellectual retardation
Insecure Early Attachment	Characteristics of caregiver (coldness, noninteractiveness) combined with characteristics of the child ("noncuddliness," passivity, behavioral difficulties associated with particular temperaments, premature birth, illness, and so forth)	Affectionless psychopathology

Source: From Rutter, M. (1979). Maternal deprivation 1972 – 1978: New findings, new concepts, new approaches. *Child Develoment, 50,* 283 – 305.

physical, intellectual, and social stimulation are necessary for optimal development during infancy. There is little doubt that severe deprivation in the early years makes children susceptible to a variety of social, emotional, and/or intellectual problems in later life; however, we do not know yet the precise role the social aspect of deprivation plays in the process.

Infants and Their Fathers

Early researchers focused almost exclusively on attachments between mothers and infants; they seemed to agree with Margaret Mead that "Fathers are a biological necessity, but a social accident" (see Hetherington & Parke, 1979, p. 227). In one sense, the focus on mothers was warranted; after all, in most societies mothers are the primary caretakers. Indeed, in a study conducted in 1972, Rebelsky and Hanks found that American fathers averaged only about 38 seconds of verbal interaction with their infants a day! Yet it is becoming increasingly apparent that fathers can and often do play an important role in the early development of their children, and that infants may

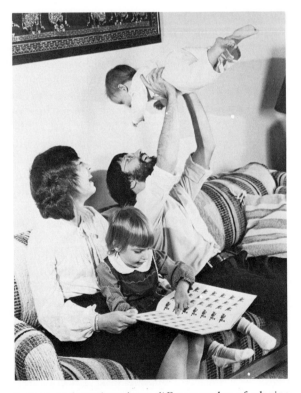

Fathers and mothers have different styles of playing with infants

become as strongly attached to their fathers as to their mothers.

In recent years, researchers have found that fathers and mothers interact with their children in somewhat different ways. For example, Lamb (1977, 1981) found that fathers spend at least four times as much time playing with their infants as they do taking care of them. According to Lamb, "Fathers were more likely to initiate physically stimulating and idiosyncratic types of play" than mothers. Lamb also found that infant boys showed a slight preference for interacting with their fathers over their mothers during their second year, but that girls showed no preference for either parent.

For the first few months of an infant's life, the parental role primarily involves providing love and care. However, as infants become toddlers, they begin to make significantly different demands on their caretakers. The infant's increasing sense of autonomy is accompanied by an increasing capacity for mischief and mayhem. As young children become more and more independent, the emphases in childrearing change. In addition to ensuring the physical, intellectual, and social needs of children are met, parents must also teach them to behave in socially acceptable ways. We turn now to an examination of the methods used by parents and other people to socialize children.

SOCIALIZATION

According to developmental psychologists Hetherington and Parke (1979), "Socialization is the process whereby an individual's standards, skills, motives, attitudes, and behaviors are shaped to conform to those regarded as desirable and appropriate for his or her present or future role in society." This characterization appears to imply that **socialization** is something that is imposed on children by adults. However, in recent years the role of the child and the significance of mutual exchanges between children and adults (and, indeed, between children and other children) have been recognized. Many psychologists (for example, Rheingold, 1968) believe that infants socialize adults at least as much as adults socialize infants.

Socializing a child involves a paradox. Although the ultimate goal of socialization is to foster an independent adult who respects and practices the values and principles of his or her society, parents inevitably feel compelled to control, suppress, constrain, and indoctrinate their children. Negotiating the delicate balance between police officers and emancipator — simultaneously instilling in a child a sense of social responsibility and a sense of independence — is clearly a difficult task. In considering the ways in which parents attempt to resolve this paradox, we first examine the methods they

employ to discipline their children. We next explore the tendency of children to do what their parents *do* rather than what they *say*. Finally, we examine research on the role that peers play in the socialization process.

Relations between Parents and Children

The most obvious way in which parents control and shape the behavior of their children is through reward and punishment. Rewarding desirable behavior is generally more effective than punishing undesirable behavior (see Chapter 5). There are four main problems with punishment:

1. The punishing agent (parent) presents an aggressive model.
2. The bad feelings elicited by punishment become associated with the surrounding cues (making it less likely the child will turn to the parent in times of conflict or doubt).
3. Punishing a child may teach the child what not to do, but it does not teach positive alternatives.
4. Frequent punishment may make the child insecure about himself or herself and erode his or her sense of autonomy and self-esteem.

Research has shown that punishment is most effective in suppressing behavior when it is emphatic and when it is administered immediately following an undesirable behavior (Aronfreed, 1976). Punishment is particularly effective when the child feels it is judiciously applied and when the punishing agent is seen as warm and loving (Martin, 1975).

Traditionally, psychologists have classified the methods of discipline employed by parents into three types: **power assertion, love-withdrawal,** and **induction.** Power assertion involves coercing children to comply by overpowering them and intimidating them, typically through the threat or use of physical punishment. Love-withdrawal involves the explicit or implicit message: "If you do (or don't do) this, I won't love you anymore." Induction involves explaining to children the reasons why their behavior is wrong, usually by pointing out how it violates a principle or rule. The first two methods of discipline emphasize external control; the third aims at inducing the child to exert internal control over his or her own behavior and to develop his or her own standards. Induction has been found most effective for resolving the paradox involved in cultivating both autonomy from and respect for others (Staub, 1979).

To be effective, discipline must be consistent (the parent should follow through) and predictable; the parent's pattern of discipline should enable the child to anticipate which behaviors will be rewarded and punished. Again, inductive techniques are effective both because they supply the child with reasons and explanations that he or she can employ when parents or other authorities are absent and because they supply a model of self-control.

Styles of Parenting Although type of discipline is an important aspect of parental style, rearing children involves more than disciplining them. Diana Baumrind and her colleagues observed families in their homes and found that parents tended to employ one of three styles of child rearing — **authoritarian, authoritative,** and **permissive** (see Table 10-6; Baumrind, 1973, 1977).

Which style of child rearing is most effective? Baumrind selected as the optimal outcome of child rearing a cluster of traits she called **instrumental competence,** which consists of four dimensions: social responsibility, independence, achievement orientation, and vitality. Research has revealed that *authoritative* parents have children who score highest on all dimensions of instrumental competence (see Baumrind, 1971, 1977; Maccoby, 1980). The children of authoritative parents tend to be self-assertive, independent, friendly, cooperative, successful, and achievement-oriented. In contrast, the children of *authoritarian* parents tend to be withdrawn, low in vitality, shy, and tense around peers. The girls of authoritarian parents tend to be dependent and unambitious; the boys tend to be hostile. Children of *permissive* (indulgent) parents are more positive in their moods and show more vitality than the children of authoritarian parents, but they score low on most dimensions of instrumental competence (see Table 10-6).

It is interesting that although the authoritarian and permissive patterns of parenting seem op-

TABLE 10-6
Parental Control and Children's Competencies

	Competencies	
Patterns of Parenting	**Girls**	**Boys**
Authoritative	Very high cognitive and social competencies	High cognitive and social competencies
Authoritarian	Average cognitive and social competencies	Average social competencies; low cognitive competencies
Permissive	Low cognitive and social competencies	Low social competencies; very low cognitive competencies

Source: Adapted from Shaffer, D. R. (1985). *Developmental psychology: Theory, research, and applications* (p. 615). Monterey, CA: Brooks/Cole.

posite one another, the children of parents who employ either style have low instrumental competence. One explanation is that both patterns of parenting fail to give children the opportunity to develop internal standards — authoritarian parents by controlling their children from the outside and permissive parents by failing to hold children responsible for the consequences of their actions.

Before leaving the discussion on methods of child rearing, it is important to note that the associations found by virtually all researchers are correlational in nature. Although there is a tendency to conclude that different child-rearing methods produce different types of children, it is undoubtedly also the case that different types of children evoke different types of child rearing. Like so many aspects of child development, each factor interacts with the other. This is as true for children raised in respectable ways as for abused children (see Box 10-1, page 486).

Parents as Models To some people, raising children means telling them what to do. Yet parents influence the socialization of their children in other, indirect ways, often without intending to do so. Children watch their parents; they learn from observing them; they model parental behavior. What parents do may influence their children's behavior as much as or more than what they say.

Parents often verbalize one set of values but act out another. How does the child resolve the conflict implicit in this kind of mixed message? In the words of Hetherington and Morris (1978):

A "do as I say, not as I do" approach to socialization is ineffective. If the child sees a church-going platitude-spouting, moralizing parent lie about his golf score, cheat on his income tax, bully his children, and pay substandard wages to his help, the child may emulate his parent's behaviors rather than his hypocritical words. (p. 9)

Worse yet, the child may learn to say what the parent says and do what the parent does.

In a series of laboratory studies, James Bryan and his colleagues found that when children are faced with a choice between doing what an adult says and what the adult does, they are more likely to do what the adult does (Bryan & Walbek, 1970; Bryan & Schwartz, 1970). These researchers showed children films of adults who behaved either selfishly or altruistically and who verbalized one of three messages: a message consistent with the selfish or altruistic behavior, a message inconsistent or hypocritical (for example, a selfish model saying, "It is good to donate."), or a neutral message. After watching the films, the children were given an opportunity to donate money to needy children and were asked how much they liked the model they had observed. The results of the study showed that the behavior of the children — how much they donated — was influenced much more by what the model did than by what the model said: practice won out over preaching. However, the children tended to like the model who verbalized generosity more than they liked the model who verbalized selfishness.

Research on modeling has shown that nurturant and/or powerful adults are the most influential models for children. Typically, parents are the most nurturant and powerful adults in young children's lives; as children grow older, however, peers begin to assume more and more influence.

Relations between Children

As children grow, they typically spend more and more time with their peers. This tendency for children to move away from the family nest and to spend increasing amounts of time with individuals of their own age is typical of most primate species. Observations in day-care centers reveal that the amount of time children spend interacting with adults stays constant or declines from the first to the third or fourth year, but that the amount of time they spend interacting with peers increases. One study found that when pairs of ten- to twelve-month-old infants were given a choice between playing with each other or with their mothers, they usually chose to play with one another; moreover, this preference grew stronger during the second year of life (Eckerman, Whatley, & Kutz, 1975; see Figure 10-6). Other studies have found that by age three to four, children spend approximately the same amount of time with peers as they do with adults (see Holmberg, 1980).

How significant are peer interactions during the early years? Research indicates that although infants begin responding to other infants in a social manner around nine months of age, these early interactions center around objects. It is not until the second year that toddlers begin to engage in reciprocal social exchanges, most of which involve disputes over toys (Bronson, 1981). Although object-centered social interactions predominate through the period of infancy, peer-centered exchanges assume increasing significance (Mueller & Vandell, 1978). Yet even at their most sophisticated, the early interactions between infants do not approach the sophistication of interactions between infants and adults. This should not be surprising: it is more difficult for two novices to coordinate their actions than for a novice to coordinate his or her actions with those of an expert in social exchanges.

When young children get together, they usually play. Although play may seem frivolous by its very definition, it may be instrumental to the social development of children. Let us examine

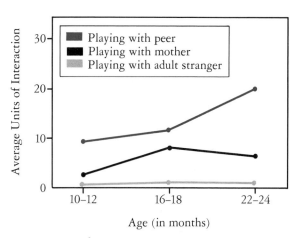

FIGURE 10-6

Interaction Comparisons Although there is a steady increase in the number of interactions in which 10- to 12-month-old children engage with peers, interactions with mother tend to peak at 16 to 18 months. *Source:* Adapted from Eckerman, C. O., Whatley, J. C., & Kutz, S. L. (1975). Growth of social play with peers during the second year of life. *Developmental Psychology, 11,* 42–49.

the functions of play from an ethological, psychoanalytic, social learning, and cognitive-developmental perspective.

An Ethological Account of Play

As discussed, observations of primates and other mammals reveal that it is common for infants to spend most of their early days in close contact with their parents but, as they mature, to spend more and more time with their peers. Observers of children in their natural environments have found that the groups formed by children tend to be organized in **dominance hierarchies** similar to those of other primates (Edelman & Omark, 1973; Savin-Williams, 1979; Strayer & Strayer, 1976). These hierarchies organize the power relations so that those at the top have first access to the resources (food, play materials, choice of territory, and so forth) and thus help reduce conflict in the group.

In addition to dominance hierarchies, some aspects of human group formation may parallel that of primates. Observations of primates and humans in hunter-gatherer societies suggest that males, but not females, go through a subadult stage in which they are apart from the main group

Box 10-1
Perspectives on Child Abuse

Child abuse is a special and socially critical example of the power of mutual interactions in parent-child relations. The definition of child abuse varies across social classes and cultures, but it generally includes psychological as well as physical or sexual abuse. Parke and Collmer (1975) offer a thorough review of studies in the area and discuss some of the complex issues involved.

One explanation for child abuse focuses on the personality traits of parents. What kinds of parents abuse their children? Do abusive parents have psychiatric or personality disturbances? Although it seems plausible that anyone who would abuse a child would be seriously disturbed, less than ten percent of the parents reported for child-abuse can be classified psychotic (Blumberg, 1974; Kempe, 1973).

Do parents who abuse their children have any personality characteristics that set them apart from other parents? This is not a simple question to answer. It requires several well-controlled studies of the personality characteristics of abusive and normal parents, and such studies have not been conducted. One small but systematically controlled study (Melnick & Hurley, 1969) compared ten abusive and ten control mothers matched for age, education, and social class on 18 personality measures. The abusive mothers were found *not* to differ from the nonabusive mothers on 12 of the 18 personality measures; however, mothers who abused their children did show lower self-esteem, higher frustration of their dependence needs, less family satisfaction, less need to give nurturance, and less ability to recognize or admit feelings of rejection toward their children. Whether or

not even these findings can be generalized to a broader sample of parents remains questionable. There is some agreement in case-history descriptions that abusing parents show less impulse control and less willingness to take responsibility for their decisions, particularly with regard to aggression (Spinetta & Rigler, 1972; Young, 1964). But these findings fail to explain abuse inasmuch as poor impulse control and aggression describe the abusive event. We are left with the question of how this problem originates: do personality characteristics cause abuse or do they develop in response to particular environmental circumstances or particular types of children?

In contrast to placing the blame for child abuse directly on parents, a more prevalent and sympathetic view suggests that abuse results from stresses that originate from the socioeco-

and associate in subgroups or *gangs* of same-sex peers (Hrdy, 1977; Konner, 1977). Lockard and Adams (1980) observed people as they walked along paths to shopping malls and found there were many more groups of juvenile males (18 to 20 years of age) than juvenile females. According to Lockard and Adams, males of this age are at a competitive disadvantage for females

and other resources vis-à-vis older males, they are less likely to have formed heterosexual relationships, and they bunch together for mutual support. Although such juvenile males are too old to stay in the parental "nest" and too young to start families of their own, they may form security groups until ready and able to assume the responsibilities of adulthood.

nomic environment and particular patterns of family interactions. The most consistent picture that emerges from the cases of repeated child abuse is that abusive parents, themselves, were subject to abuse as children. Experiments with monkeys (Mitchell & Schroers, 1973) have shown that infants experimentally isolated from their mothers at birth tend, as adults, to ignore or mistreat their first offspring.

Some children appear to participate actively in the pattern that produces and sustains their own abuse. Certain infants, in particular, place heavy demands on their caregivers. Such demands, accompanied by any number of additional strains, may lead to abuse. For example, there is a greater incidence of child abuse for premature infants, who demand more care and mature more slowly; for colicky infants or infants considered unattractive; and for infants whose temperaments are not interpreted as "loving" (Parke & Collmer, 1975).

The cultural values and institutions that operate in a community or a society as a whole may also encourage child abuse. Cultural attitudes toward violence, the level of social stress and isolation in a particular society or social class, and the presence or absence of community support systems for individuals and families are all important. For example, if violence is considered an appropriate means of asserting authority and resolving conflict, then violence tends to be reported by the media, to be prevalent in the disciplinary and correctional institutions of that society, and to be adopted by families as well. The use of physical punishment as a child-rearing method is more prevalent in some cultures, including the U.S., then in others (Parke & Collmer, 1975).

The incidence of reported child abuse tends to be highest in the lower socioeconomic groups, where educational opportunities are limited and stress from economic and living conditions is greatest.

Unemployment, marital stress, social isolation, large families, limited education, and poor living conditions are all associated with child abuse.

Rather than focus on any one cause, researchers investigating child abuse now rely heavily on a multiple approach that emphasizes not only the parent, but the entire social context. Many investigators feel that if the incidence of child abuse is to be lowered significantly, public attitudes toward violence must be modified, responsibilities and stresses of parenthood must be changed, and community-care settings must be provided for children at risk. From a community standpoint, preventive programs may involve identication of high-stress families and high-risk infants. Crisis services, home support assistance (for example, parent-aids), and public education services are increasing in communities concerned with child neglect and abuse.

A Psychoanalytic Account of Play

Psychoanalysts focus on the emotional release that children experience during play. Freud (1920) held that one of the primary functions of play is to enable children to work out emotional conflicts in a safe context. Lili Peller (1954) has elaborated on Freud's view of play, suggesting that it serves four main functions:

1. It enables children to deal with distressful feelings from present or past events in a symbolic or disguised way, thus releasing instinctual tension in a socially acceptable manner.

2. It enables children to fulfill socially inappropriate wishes in an imaginary way.

3. It helps drain sexual and aggressive urges through catharsis (see Chapter 14).

4. It enables children to develop positive self-concepts by adjusting activities to their level of competence.

A Cognitive–Developmental Account of Play

Piaget (1932) suggested that interactions among peers are essential in freeing children from their egocentric views of the world and in compelling them to adopt the perspectives of others. According to Piaget, adults unintentionally reinforce young children's **egocentricity** in two ways: by anticipating their desires and by exerting power over them. There is little incentive for young children to understand the point of view of adults because it is so discrepant from their own and because it typically is imposed upon them without explanation. In contrast, when interacting with peers, children must take some responsibility for coordinating the interaction, express their views in a way that can be understood by others, and assume the role of others in order to understand what they are trying to say. When interacting with peers, children must consider the fact that their listeners are not all-knowing or all-powerful. And because children are less inclined than adults to accommodate to one another's desires, the conflicts of interest that inevitably occur among peers induce children to understand that others possess points of view that may differ from their own. As a result, children develop principles of fairness with which to resolve the conflicts in mutually acceptable ways. Thus, according to Piaget, peer interaction is integral to the development of **perspective-taking** skills and to the development of moral reasoning.

In addition to freeing children from their egocentricity, play serves another more general cognitive function—it enhances their ability to

Learning aggressive behavior

engage in symbolic thinking. Russian psychologist Lev Vygotsky (1976) placed great significance on the symbolic aspect of play, arguing that it makes a unique contribution to the development of children's ability to imagine how things could be, as opposed to how they actually are, and to understand the meaning of social relations. According to Vygotsky, play is the "leading source of development in the childhood years."

Peers also play an important role in determining how children think about themselves. During the school years, children's self-concepts become increasingly dependent on how they are perceived by their peers (Ruble, Feldman, & Boggiano, 1976). Several studies have investigated the factors that affect peer acceptance and popularity. Among those that have been found to be important are physical attractiveness (Lerner & Lerner, 1977) and such social skills as the ability to initiate interactions, the ability to communicate effectively, and the tendency to reinforce others (Gottman, Gonso, & Rasmussen, 1975; Hartup, 1978).

A Social Learning Account of Play

Anyone who has watched young children knows how important imitation is to the development of their social behavior. As is the case when they imitate adults, children are most likely to model the behavior of peers who are nurturant, warm, powerful, and rewarded by others. In addition, children tend to imitate peers who are similar to them (Hartup & Coates, 1967). Although children learn such socially desirable behaviors as helping, sharing, and a variety of social skills through modeling, they also learn socially undesirable and aggressive behaviors in the same way (see O'Conner, 1969; Krebs & Miller, 1985).

Hartup (1978) suggests that children live in two social worlds, the world of parents and family and the world of peers, each with its own rules, roles, and conventions. For certain purposes peers have been found to serve as more effective models than adults. For example, researchers have found that exposing children to a *fearless-peer* model who is interacting with a friendly dentist is especially effective in reducing fear of dentists (Melamed, Hawes, Heiby, & Glick, 1975). Other researchers have found that peer models are especially effective in the treatment of dog phobias (Bandura, Grusec, & Menlove, 1967).

Friendship

Friendships are the fruit of peer relations, but take many years to ripen. During infancy, peers seem to be of interest more because they are complex and interesting objects than for any other reason, and there is little give and take in their interactions (Hartup, 1983). Sometime after the first year, when children become toddlers, they may begin to interact with one another in a more coordinated manner; however, friendships do not usually begin to develop until the preschool years (see Table 10-7). Corsaro (1981) observed three- to four-years-olds at a nursery school and reported that although they spent a great deal of time interacting with one another, the interactions tended to be brief and unstable. "Friends" were those with whom the children were playing at the moment. In nursery school, children typically interact in pairs, with other children in the periphery, and show a preference for same-sex partners and children who are like them in other ways (Rubin, 1980)—a pattern of preference that grows even stronger in adolescence. Selman (1981) labels friendship among preschoolers **playmateship** (see Table 10-7).

During the early school years, children form more enduring friendships, but friends are valued primarily for what they can do—the **one-way assistance** they can offer and the support they can give. When asked what a friend is, children of this age are likely to say "someone you have fun with." Following this period, children form more reciprocal friendships (more give and take), but there is little long-term stability. Selman (1981) terms this stage of friendship formation **fairweather cooperation.**

In late childhood and early adolescence, the meaning of friendship deepens; for example, sixth graders define friendship primarily in terms of trust, loyalty, and the sharing of inner thoughts and feelings (Berndt, 1981). At this age, children tend to form more **intimate and mutually shared friendships** (Table 10-7). Friendships entail obligations as well as expectations; they become more exclusive—especially among girls (Rubin, 1980)—and friends tend to become

TABLE 10-7
Friendship Formation Stages

Stage	Approximate Time Period	Description
Playmateship	Preschool period	A friend is someone who lives nearby and with whom one is playing at the moment.
One-way assistance	Early school years	A friend is important because he or she does specific things that the child wants done. A close friend is someone who is known better than other people, where "known" means being aware of the other person's likes and dislikes.
Fair-weather cooperation	Later school years	There is a new awareness of the reciprocal nature of friendship and a new willingness to adjust to the likes and dislikes of the other person. But there is no long-term continuity—arguments are seen as a cause for breaking off the relationship.
Intimate and mutually shared relationships	Late childhood or early adolescence	There is a closer bond between friends and a new awareness of the continuity of the relationship. Friendship is not seen merely as a way to avoid being bored or lonely, but as a basic means of developing intimacy and mutual support. Friends share intimate problems. Conflicts do not necessarily bring an end to the relationship.

Source: From Selman, R. (1981). The child as friendship philosopher. In S. R. Asher & J. M. Gottman (Eds.), *The development of children's friendships.* Cambridge, England: Cambridge University Press.

possessive of one another. In a study comparing fourth- and eighth-grade children, Diaz and Berndt (1981) found that although friends from each grade were equally likely to know such external things about one another as their friend's birthday, older children were significantly more likely to know more personal things about their friends, such as the kinds of things they worry about. In a large-scale study of girls from 11 to 18 years of age, Douvan and Adelson (1966) found a consistent tendency for friendship to become deeper and more mutual with age. In the younger girls, friendships centered around such shared activities as shopping; in the older girls, security and loyalty were prime concerns.

DEVELOPMENT OF A SENSE OF MASCULINITY AND FEMININITY

There was a little girl who insisted that she was a turtle; she demanded that she be called "Turtle" instead of Danielle, her given name. Whether Danielle really thought that she was a turtle is unclear, but the apparent identification she professed raises an interesting possibility—young children may not distinguish clearly between human and nonhuman animals nor understand they are immutably a member of the former class. Indeed, young children may not even distinguish clearly between animate and inanimate objects; they often seem more concerned about the welfare of their stuffed animals and pets than they do about the welfare of their friends.

The process of learning about one's self involves making several increasingly fine distinctions (see Box 10-2). Children must learn to distinguish between animate and inanimate objects, between ''big people'' and ''little people,'' and between boys and girls. Although children are born physiologically male or female, they are not born with the knowledge that they are *male* or *female;* they must learn which sex they are. And even after they learn to classify themselves correctly, they must learn what it means to be male or female. At a very young age, boys may assume that if they let their hair grow and wear a dress they will become a girl.

We now examine the processes involved in **sex-typing,** which includes both discovering that one is male or female (acquiring a **sex** or **gender identity**) and learning how to behave in the ways appropriate to one's gender (adopting an appropriate **sex role**). We first outline the explanations of these processes given by evolutionary theorists, psychoanalysts, social learning theorists, and cognitive-developmental theorists. We then explore the answers they offer to such questions as:

1. What are the most significant ways in which boys and girls differ?
2. Are sex differences determined mainly by heredity or mainly by environment?
3. How do children learn they are male or female?
4. In what ways do children's conceptions of masculinity and femininity change as they develop?
5. What role do parents and other socializing agents play in the process through which children come to adopt a sex identity and acquire a sex role?

An Evolutionary Account of Sex-typing

Evolutionary theorists focus on the evolution of genetically based differences between the sexes and the adaptive functions they serve, or once served, in various species. (In Chapter 8 we considered the answers given by evolutionary theorists to such fundamental questions as ''Why are there two sexes in most species?'') According to evolutionary theorists, natural selection has determined the basic physical and behavioral differences between the sexes. For example, males are larger than females in most, but not all mammals, and we know that physical size is largely determined by heredity (see Chapter 2). Evolutionary theorists believe that males tend to be larger than females because size and strength were more adaptive for males than for females in the early history of the species. Therefore large males tended to prevail in the struggle for survival, producing other males like themselves (Lumsden & Wilson, 1983). These theorists also argue that sex differences in social behavior were selected in the same manner.

Because really, no one knows for sure what characteristics were and were not adaptive for males and females in the early years of the species, no one knows for sure why sex differences were selected. However, most authorities agree that the basic differences between the sexes originated because females bear and nurse children and males do not. According to some authorities,

Box 10-2
The Origins of Self-awareness

Jean Piaget and Sigmund Freud have very different views on infant development, but they agree on one point: both theorists believe that the newborn baby has no concept of self, no concept of the distinction between "me" and "not me." The baby at first doesn't realize that the sounds he hears are his own cries, that the moving thing passing in front of his eyes is his own hand. Piaget puts it very well.

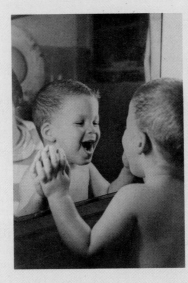

> When a baby discovers his own body—his fingers, feet, arms—he looks at them no differently than he regards other objects, without any idea that he himself is the one responsible for moving the particular objects that he is admiring. . . . To begin with a baby has no sense of self at all. (1927/1977, p. 200)

The concept of self develops gradually during infancy. Many aspects of the baby's experience are responsible for this development. He discovers that he can control the movements of his hands and feet, but that he can't make the wall move, nor the table, nor the family dog. He discovers that his hands and feet and mouth and chest are always there, while other things—such as Mommy and Daddy—come and go. (This, according to Freud, is how the baby learns to distinguish himself from his mother.) He learns that certain sensations derive from the "me" parts of the world and not from the other parts—biting down hard on his toe feels dramatically different from biting down hard on a teething ring!

By the second year of life, most babies in our society have access to another way of finding out about themselves: mirrors. Babies' reactions to their own mirror images change as they get older (Rheingold, cited in Lewis and Brooks, 1975). A 4-month-old baby seems to regard his mirror image as an entertaining playmate—as another baby who is playing an exciting contingency game called "I do everything that you do." Naturally, he smiles enthusiastically at this appealing companion. (He'll smile less vigorously at a motion picture of a baby, since the movie doesn't act contingently.)

In the second half of the first year, babies begin to make deliberate, repetitive movements in front of a mirror, apparently in an effort to explore the mirror's possibilities. They also look behind the mirror. Later in the second year there may be a time when the child avoids looking at himself in the mirror (Amsterdam, cited in Lewis and Brooks, 1975). This seems to be the beginning of that kind of embarrassment commonly called "self-consciousness."

Can we tell when the baby first recognizes that the image in the mirror is "me"? There is a clever technique that psychologists have used to answer this question: a red mark is put on the baby's nose without his knowing it — his mother puts it on while pretending to wipe his face. Then the baby is shown his face in a mirror. What will he do when he notices the red mark? If he just stares, or if he touches the mirror, we haven't found out anything. But if he touches his *own* nose when he sees his mirror image, he must realize that the red-nosed baby in the mirror is himself.

This experiment was tried on 96 babies (Lewis and Brooks, 1975). The results are given in the table. You can see that self-recognition increases as the baby grows older: no babies under a year touched their reddened noses, but 75 percent of the babies over 1½ did so.

An experiment of this sort (Gallup, 1970) has also been tried on rhesus monkeys and chimpanzees. (Chimpanzees are apes. Apes are considered to be higher on the evolutionary scale than monkeys.) The monkeys and chimpanzees were given a general anesthetic, and red dye was painted on one ear while they were unconscious. Then each animal was put in front of the mirror. The chimpanzees immediately reached for the offending ear;

Self-recognition of Mirror Image in Babies of Different Ages

Age	Number Tested	Percent of Babies Who Touched their Noses
9 and 12 months	32	0
15 and 18 months	32	25
21 and 24 months	32	75

Source: Adapted from Lewis, M., & Brooks, J. (1975). Infants' social perception: A constructivist view. In L. B. Cohen & P. Salapatek (Eds.), *Infant perception: From sensation to cognition* (Vol. 2). New York: Academic Press.

the monkeys didn't. So we can say that, in this respect, a year-old baby is still at the level of a monkey, whereas a 21-month-old has reached the more advanced level of the chimpanzee!

By 21 months, many toddlers can also recognize photographs of themselves, and can even discriminate such photos from photos of other babies of the same sex and age. A 21-month-old named Erika was shown a photo of herself, and her mother asked, "Who is that?" "Erika," she replied. When she was shown a photo of a different 21-month-old girl, her response was "No, not Erika." Erika also recognized a photo of her mother ("Mommy," she said) and labeled a photo of another woman "lady." Not all the children in this study (Lewis and Brooks, 1975) did as well as Erika. Only 7 out of 25 toddlers correctly identified photos of themselves —

six gave their own names and one said, "Me." But these toddlers did just about as well in identifying themselves as they did in identifying their mothers. That's rather remarkable, since babies presumably spend much more time looking at their mothers than they do looking at themselves.

Piaget believes that the development of the child's self-image progresses hand-in-hand with his development of the concepts of object and person permanence. Once representation is possible, Piaget says, the child can visualize his own body as "an object among other objects," localized in space and existing through time (1954, p. 86).

Source: From Harris, J. R., & Liebert, R. M. (1984). *The child: Development from birth through adolescence* (pp. 226–28). Englewood Cliffs, NJ: Prentice-Hall.

a division of labor in early humans — males hunted and defended territory while females gathered food and cared for children — was maximally adaptive (Hoyenga & Hoyenga, 1979). For this reason, more aggressive dispositions evolved in males than in females, and more nurturant and domestic dispositions evolved in females than in males (Lovejoy, 1981).

Some theorists have suggested that natural selection has caused the brains of females to evolve in significantly different ways from the brains of males. For example, it has been argued that parts of the left hemisphere of the brain are more dominant in females than in males (therefore females tend to perform better on verbal tasks) and, conversely, parts of the right hemisphere of the brain are more dominant in males than in females (therefore males do better on visual-spatial tasks; see Figure 10-7; McGee, 1979).

It is important to note that although evolutionary theorists insist there are significant biologically based differences between the social behaviors of males and females, humans are much

Examine this block.

Now look below and pick the block that is the same as the block above, except that it has been rotated and presented from a different point of view.

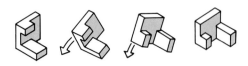

The following illustration sketches out the transformation.

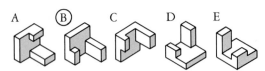

FIGURE 10-7

Spatial Abilities Problem   A modified version of the type of problem used to test spatial abilities features the transformation that leads to a solution. *Source:* Adapted from Stafford, R. E. (1962). Form AA, *Identical Blocks.*

less differentiated by sex than members of most other primate species. In the same way as there is considerably greater overlap between the size of males and females in the human species than in most other primate species — many males are smaller than many females — there is considerably greater overlap in their social behaviors. **Plasticity** — the ability to behave in a variety of different ways (for example, to behave in both masculine and feminine ways) — is adaptive. Husbands disposed to assume a maternal role and wives disposed to assume a paternal role when the situation necessitates it are more likely to foster the fitness of their offspring than parents not so disposed.

Although evolutionary approaches to sex differences supply ultimate explanations of fundamental differences between the sexes, they are difficult if not impossible to test. Because we know so little about the ways in which our early ancestors adapted to their environments, we can only make educated guesses about which characteristics were adaptive and why particular differences between the sexes evolved. Even though evolutionary theorists assume there are genetically based differences between males and females that affect their social behavior, they generally do not attempt to assess these differences. Other researchers, however, do. We supply an overview of the controversy concerning the heritability of sex differences in social behavior in Box 10-3, page 496.

A Psychoanalytic Account of Sex-typing

The psychoanalytic account of how males and females acquire a sex identity is related closely to Freud's explanation of how they acquire a conscience. According to Freud, at some point between the age of three and five, when young boys are in the phallic stage of psychosexual development (see Chapter 12), they begin to direct their sexual desires to the primary love object in their lives — their mother. Boys watch their father interacting with their mother and desire to replace him. They may, for example, insist on climbing in bed between their parents, show glee when their father goes away, and tell their mother they want to marry her when they grow up. In addition to the mother's reluctance, there is an ominous obstacle to the fulfillment of their impossible dream—their father, whom they fear. Thus, suggested Freud, young boys in this stage develop a conflict that he called the **Oedipus Complex** (after the Greek hero Oedipus who blinds himself after learning that he has inadvertently killed his father and married his mother). Young boys resolve this conflict by, in Freud's words, "identifying with the aggressor." In other words, boys identify with their father, view themselves as like him, and thus vicariously satisfy their urge to possess their mother while at the same time assuaging their father. In resolving the Oedipus conflict, young boys make two important developmental gains—they introject their version of their father's conscience into their ego, thereby acquiring a **superego** (conscience), and they acquire a **sex-typed identity.**

But what about females? Freud suggested that, like young boys, young girls also direct their sexual energy toward their mother. However, at some point between the age of three and five they make a horrifying discovery—they do not have a penis. They blame their mother for this "loss," turn against her, direct their sexual desires toward their father, and, as part of a subconscious process, become embroiled in an **Electra Complex** (after the tragic Greek heroine who led a plot to kill her mother). This conflict is resolved when girls identify with their mother, thereby acquiring some of her attributes. However, according to Freud, young girls typically do not resolve the Electra conflict as effectively as boys resolve the Oedipus conflict; accordingly, females acquire neither as strong a superego nor as strong a sex-typed identify as do males.

Freud's theory has had only minimal impact on psychological research on sex-typing; the theory has been criticized as logically inconsistent and empirically invalid. In particular, researchers have failed to support the assumption of psychoanalytic theory that young children of a certain age acquire a sex identity in one fell swoop (Hoffman, 1970).

A Social Learning Account of Sex-typing

Social learning accounts of sex-typing suggest that boys and girls learn to behave differently because people treat them differently and because they are exposed to different models. Boys are reinforced for modeling the behavior of males, and girls are reinforced for modeling the behavior of females (see Bandura, 1977; Mischel, 1968). Although parents are the most influential models in the early years of a child's life, children also learn sex-typed behaviors from other adults and from peers, television, books, and the like. Of course, what children learn depends on the assumptions that exist in their society about what is masculine and what is feminine. Many of these assumptions are implicit: although they affect the behavior of people, people do not realize they are making them. We examine some of the implicit assumptions that people in our society make about masculinity and femininity in Box 10-4, page 500.

Parents and other people begin treating young boys differently from young girls at birth by distinguishing them with blue and pink blankets. Observations of infants suggest that parents are more physical with boys than with girls. As infants reach the toddler stage, parents tend to give boys more positive reinforcement than girls for behaviors that reflect independence, self-reliance, and emotional control. In contrast, they give girls more positive reinforcement than boys for compliance, dependency, nurturance, empathy, and expressions of feeling (Block, 1973; Minuchin, 1965; Mischel, 1968). In one study of two-year-old infants, Fagot (1978) found that parents responded negatively when girls played with blocks but positively when they played with dolls and soft toys. The opposite was true for boys.

Even though research has shown that most parents treat their sons differently from their daughters, it is interesting to note that parents may not realize they make a major distinction. For example, although most parents believe they react to acts of aggression in the same way whether the aggressive acts are emitted by boys or girls, observations of parents have shown they intervene much more frequently and quickly when girls behave aggressively than when boys behave aggressively. Indeed, studies have found that parents react more negatively when their daughters engage in vigorous physical activity than when their sons do; however, they react more negatively when their sons ask for help (Fagot, 1978; Huston, 1983).

Box 10-3
Genetically Based Differences between the Sexes

Evolutionary theory predicts genetically based differences between the sexes. To evaluate this expectation, investigators must first establish that there are systematic differences between the sexes and then establish that the differences have a genetic basis. A large number of studies have assessed sex differences; although the results of these studies have not been notably consistent, the strongest evidence supports the ten differences listed in the box table.

Assume these differences do in fact exist. How can we determine whether they are learned or inherited?

One line of evidence derives from cross-cultural research. If the differences observed in Western cultures also occur in cultures with different customs, habits, norms, and values, the assumption that the differences are not taught to children — and therefore have a biological basis — would be supported. Unfortunately, there has been only modest cross cultural research on sex differences. What evidence there is suggests that boys are more

aggressive and more dominant than girls in virtually all cultures (see Maccoby & Jacklin, 1974) and that girls are more nurturant than boys (Whiting, 1983). In evaluating the results of a comparison between the social behavior of two- to twelve-year old boys and girls in seven different cultures, Whiting (1983) concluded that "The motivation to be responsive to the needs and desires of an infant, in our opinion, is the best candidate for preprogramming — an innate response to the physical characteristics of infants" (p. 239). However, Whiting goes on to emphasize that in all cultures the social experience and self-concepts of girls reinforce girls' natural tendency to behave nurturantly. Whiting concludes that "Since there are cognitive-developmental and direct experiential variables that are involved in the genesis of nurturance, we cannot as yet separate the unique contribution of biology" (p. 239).

A second type of evidence adduced in support of the notion that observed differences between the sexes, especially aggression,

have a biological basis derives from research on primates. Observations of species closest to humans on the evolutionary tree indicate that males are quite consistently more aggressive and more dominant than females are.

A third type of evidence comes from research on the effects of hormonal injections in nonhuman animals. In one study, for example, Phoenix (1974) found that the female offspring of monkeys who were given injections of male hormones while they were pregnant were more aggressive in later life than the female offspring of monkeys not given such injections.

In Chapter 2 we described the research of Money and Ehrhardt (1972) on genetic males raised as females and genetic females raised as males. In some of the cases they investigated, females exposed prenatally to excessive doses of testosterone, but reared as females nonetheless, displayed a greater fondness than average for vigorous athletic activities, preferred boys for playmates, shunned nurturant types of play, and in general displayed the identity of a tomboy. As elaborated in Chapter 2, however, these conclusions have not gone unchallenged.

What, then, should we conclude from the available evidence? In general, the evidence tends to support the evolutionary position that males and females have evolved in somewhat different ways — in particular, that females tend to inherit dispositions that dispose them more than men to the nurturant activities associated with child rearing and that men naturally tend to be more aggressive. However, it is important to note that all conclusions about sex differences relate to average differences; no one disputes the existence of overlap between every characteristic that has been studied of male and female — some males are more nurturant than some females and some females are more aggressive than some males. In conclusion, all researchers agree that whatever role heredity plays in determining differences between the sexes, observed differences always result from interaction between biological and environmental influences.

Assessment of Ten Sex Differences

Behavior	Kind of Difference
Aggression	Boys are more often the aggressors and the victims of peer aggression than girls, particularly of physical aggression, beginning as early as age two.
Spatial Relationships	Boys and men, from about age ten, are better at visualizing spatial relationships than girls.
Mathematical Reasoning	Boys generally perform better than girls in mathematics beginning at about age twelve.
Verbal Skills	Even in infancy girls are superior in verbal abilities, and this superiority increases markedly in the high-school years. Verbal abilities include vocabulary, reading comprehension, and verbal creativity.
Dominance	From preschool age on, boys show more dominance than girls.
Confidence	Boys are more confident about new tasks than girls.
Rate of Maturation	Girls are physically and neurologically more advanced at birth, and they walk and attain puberty earlier than boys; the difference in time is about six weeks for infancy and two years for adolescence. Boys have a more mature muscular development than girls.
School Grades	Girls get better average grades throughout the school years than boys.
Atypical Development	Boys are more likely to have school problems, reading disabilities, speech defects, and emotional problems than girls.
Emotional Development and Nurturance	As early as two years of age, girls are more compliant than boys to the demands of parents and other adults. Boys are more variable than girls in their responses to adult direction. Girls are more nurturant toward younger children than boys are.

Source: Adapted from Hetherington, E. M., & Parke, R. D. (1986). *Child psychology: A contemporary viewpoint* (3rd ed., p. 626–27). New York: McGraw-Hill.

Social reinforcement of sex-typed behaviors is not confined to childhood; it continues throughout life. In a study of adolescents, Block (1978) found that parents endorse different statements that describe the ways they treat their sons and daughters. For boys they endorsed such statements as

> I encourage my child always to do her/his best.
> I believe physical punishment to be the best way of disciplining.
> I teach my child to keep control of her/his feelings at all times.

In contrast, parents endorsed the following statements for girls:

> I feel a child should be given comfort and understanding when she/he is scared or upset.
> I believe in praising a child when she/he is good, and think it gets better results than punishing her/him when she/he is bad.
> I encourage my child to talk about her/his troubles.

Fathers tend to react more negatively than mothers when their sons engage in such feminine behaviors as playing with dolls (Lansky, Crandall, Kagan, & Baker, 1961).

We can safely conclude that social reinforcement plays an important role in the sex-typing of young children; the evidence is not, however, as supportive of the social learning view of modeling. Although there is no question that modeling plays an important role in the socialization of children, children do not appear to show a consistent preference for the behavior of their same-sex parent (Hetherington, 1967); rather, they prefer to model the behavior of adults with whom they have the most contact, usually their mother. In addition, studies have failed to find a significant correlation between the degree to which parents engage in sex-typed behaviors and the strength of sex-typing in their children (Smith & Daglish, 1977).

A Cognitive–Developmental Account of Sex-typing

Cognitive-developmental theorists suggest that the process of discovering there are two sexes and

that they differ in immutable ways is a gradual one that occurs in stages. According to this account, the discovery that one is male or female causes young children to identify with members of their own sex, not vice versa as suggested by psychoanalytic and social learning theories (see Figure 10-8). Once children acquire a sense of **gender permanence** — the idea that they are and always will be male or female (typically around the age of five or six) — they come to value the behaviors and attitudes associated with their sex. It is only at this point, according to cognitive-developmental theorists, that children identify with the adult figures who possess the qualities they view as most central to their concepts of themselves (as male or female) (see Perry & Busey, 1979). In effect, young girls say, "I am a female; therefore, I want to be like other females and want to do female things." The same sequence — from knowledge that one is male, to identification with males, to masculine behavior — occurs in boys.

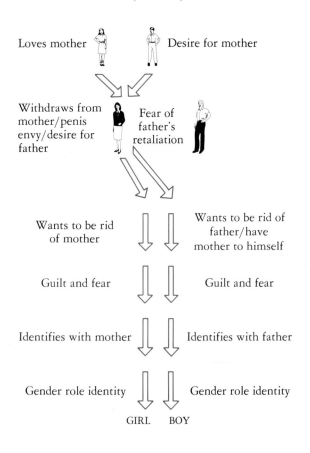

PSYCHOANALYTIC
(Freudian)

Loves mother / Desire for mother

Withdraws from mother/penis envy/desire for father / Fear of father's retaliation

Wants to be rid of mother / Wants to be rid of father/have mother to himself

Guilt and fear / Guilt and fear

Identifies with mother / Identifies with father

Gender role identity / Gender role identity

GIRL BOY

Studies have found that children can distinguish between males and females by age two; however, they cannot apply these distinctions to themselves until about 30 months of age (Thompson, 1975). And by age three, most children have learned cultural stereotypes about sex-appropriate behavior (Kuhn, Nach, & Brucken, 1978). For example, they can sort clothing, tools, and appliances into masculine and feminine boxes (Thompson, 1975). However, children do not usually acquire the idea of gender permanence until they are five or six years of age (Emmerich, 1977). Interestingly, children are much more rigid in their sex-role stereotypes and in their insistence on behaving in accordance with them prior to understanding their gender is permanent (Van Parys, 1983) — presumably because when they are young they assume that if they do not behave like members of their sex, their sex will change. For example, at this stage a young girl may resist having her hair cut short because she is afraid that if she does, she will become a boy.

Masculine and Feminine — Two Sides of the Same Coin?

Research has shown that preschool children conform to traditional sex-role stereotypes even when the stereotypes are arbitrary or inappropriate. For example, one investigator found that young girls showed a preference for games labeled appropriate for girls and that young boys showed a preference for games labeled for boys, even though the labels were attached to the games arbitrarily (Montemayor & Eisen, 1977). Other investigators have found that children's performance is affected by whether they think the tasks they are performing are masculine or feminine: boys do better at tasks labeled *for boys* and girls do better at tasks labeled either *for girls* or *for boys and girls* (Stein et al., 1972), even though the tasks are not, in fact, sex-typed.

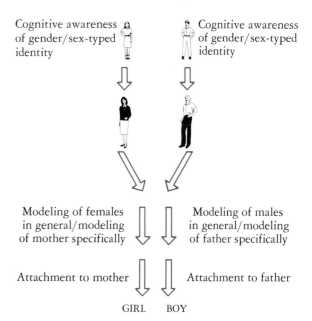

FIGURE 10-8

Theories on the Acquisition of Sex Role Identity The process through which children acquire a sex-role identity starts with sexual desire according to psychoanalysts, with rewards according to social learning theorists, and with awareness of one's own sex according to cognitive-developmental theorists. *Source:* Adapted from Kohlberg, L. (1966). A cognitive-developmental analysis of children's sex. In E. E. Maccoby (Ed.), *The development of sex differences.* Stanford, CA: Stanford University Press.

Box 10-4
Sex-role Stereotypes — Fiction and Fact

Consider the following riddle:

A boy was injured seriously in an automobile accident and rushed to surgery. Before the surgeon began to operate, a nurse recited a brief history of the patient that included information that the boy's father was dead. Upon entering the operating room to perform the procedure, the surgeon saw the boy's face for the first time, gasped, and said, "Oh no, it's my son!"

Although many people have difficulty solving this riddle, the solution is embarrassingly simple — the surgeon is the boy's mother. The elusiveness of this solution dramatically demonstrates the pervasiveness of **sex-role stereotypes.** Interestingly, if the surgeon is described as breaking into sobs when seeing the boy's face, more people solve the riddle. We tend to view certain jobs — surgeon, engineer, truck driver, astronaut — as masculine; others — nurse, flight attendant, secretary, babysitter — as feminine. Similarly, we develop extensive covert assumptions about what characteristics are "feminine" or "masculine."

All stereotypes are oversimplifications; although they usually have some rough validity, they fail to account for characteristics that make individuals unique. We all employ stereotypes — at least to some extent; think of your personal perception of what characterizes a "typical" male and a "typical" female. Stereotypes of American men and women are outlined in the table. The problem with these stereotypes is not that women are viewed as different from men, but that they are viewed less favorably. Greater esteem, status, and privileges are assigned to "masculine" characteristics and to the "masculine role" (D'Andrade, 1966) by both men and women in our society.

The traits associated with each sex reflect value judgments. Broverman et al. (1972) found that only 11 of 41 items that differentiate males and females were considered feminine *and* valued positively. These items clustered around the traits of warmth and expressiveness, and included such characteristics as *gentle, tactful, aware of others' feelings, neat, quiet, strong need for security,* and *enjoys art and literature.*

Broverman et al. asked three similar groups of practicing mental-health clinicians (both men and women) to complete a questionnaire. The first group was asked to choose the characteristics that best described a "mature, healthy, socially competent adult man"; the second group was asked to describe a woman having those characteristics; the third group was asked to describe an adult person having those characteristics. When the investigators compared the results, the

It is interesting to note in the Stein et al. study that boys were more rigid in the distinctions they made than girls were (boys shunned both the tasks labeled *for girls* and *for boys and girls*). A number of studies have found that girls are more flexible than boys in their preference for sex-typed characteristics and activities (see Maccoby & Jacklin, 1974). One price males pay for the greater value placed on their role in our society is the greater pressure on boys to behave in a masculine way than on girls to behave in a feminine way. Young girls may be permitted to wear jeans,

Sex-role Stereotypes

The Male Stereotype— Competence		The Female Stereotype— Warmth and Expressivness
Males are Thought to Be:		**Females are Thought to Be:**
Aggressive	Able to make decisions easily	Talkative
Independent	Self-confident	Tactful
Unemotional	Leaders	Gentle
Objective	Ambitious	Aware of others' feelings
Dominant	Skilled in business	Religious
Not easily influenced	Interested in math and science	Interested in their appearance
Competitive	Unexcitable in minor crises	Neat
Logical	Active	Quiet
Direct	Worldly	In need of security
Not easily hurt	Able to separate feelings and ideas	Interested in art and literature
Adventurous	Not conceited about their appearance	Able to express tender feelings easily

Source: Adapted from Broverman, I. K., Vogel, S. R., Broverman, D. M., Clark-Stewart, F. E., & Rosenkranz, P. S. (1972). Sex-role stereotypes: A current appraisal. *Journal of Social Issues, 28,* 59–78.

descriptions of a healthy man matched the descriptions of a healthy adult person—the descriptions of a healthy woman did not. The difference in the way men and women are perceived and evaluated has far-reaching implications for the development of self-concept, the choice of career, the way performance is evaluated, and even public policy decisions (Deaux, 1985).

Why do sexual stereotypes persist? Certainly we can all think of women who are aggressive, ambitious, or logical and not at all tactful, neat, or quiet, and men who are concerned about their appearance, talkative, or aware of others' feelings and not at all adventurous, competitive, or skilled in business. So why don't sexual stereotypes wither away? One explanation argues that stereotypes are the products of biases in exposure (Berry & Mitchell-Kernen, 1982): stereotypes persist because of greater exposure to stereotypical portrayals of males and females than to individuals who are "exceptions to the rule." Television, in particular, is charged with having fostered sexual stereotypes by its depiction of women as passive, immature, and powerless (Downs, 1981) and by its underrepresentation of women and overrepresentation of men on the screen, thus giving the impression that women comprise a minority of the population (Davis & Kubey, 1982; Gerbner et al., 1980; Greenberg et al., 1983). Viewing television often provides increased exposure to "competent" males and "warm and expressive" females, all of which serves to maintain the stereotypes.

to be tomboys, and to want careers as forest rangers; boys who stray from the prevailing male stereotype—for example, by wearing dresses, playing with dolls, and wanting to be ballet dancers—are labeled *sissies* (Fling & Manosevitz, 1972; Lansky, 1967).

The differential pressure on males and females to behave in sex-typed ways continues into adulthood as well. Members of both sexes who behave in ways that run counter to prevailing sex-role stereotypes tend to be liked less than those who conform to them. However, women who perform "male" tasks well and who receive recognition for their performance from a reputable source are considered more deserving than men who excell in activities that are considered feminine (Costrich et al., 1975; Taylor & Deaux, 1975).

One flaw in the sex-typing of activities is that it may constrain people unnecessarily; another is that it may feed false stereotypes. It has become increasingly apparent that males and females can perform equally well on many if not most of the tasks and occupations traditionally considered "for men (or women) only"; however, the psychological costs of women competing in the "man's world" may be high. There is evidence that competent women who pursue careers traditionally restricted to men experience significant stress; indeed, it even has been suggested that many competent women harbor a "fear of success" that inhibits their tendency to excell (Horner, 1972).

No question about it, there are two sexes. And there are fundamental differences between the sexes. Yet according to some psychologists, the tendencies to view masculinity and femininity as polar opposites and to socialize boys to behave in masculine ways and girls to behave in feminine ways are misguided (see Spence, Deaux, &

Helmreich, 1985). These psychologists argue that everyone has both masculine and feminine sides to his or her personality, and that we should encourage the development of each in everyone. This idea is consistent with the emphasis on the plasticity of human behavior acknowledged by evolutionary theorists and the flexibility inherent in social learning.

MORAL DEVELOPMENT

Over the years, philosophers have made two basic assumptions about human nature. French philosopher Jean Rousseau (1712–1778) popularized one idea—that people are born naturally benevolent. According to this assumption, if you let children be, they will be good. The other assumption, commonly called "original sin" (see Krebs & Miller, 1985), was stated forcefully by the prominent colonial preacher Jonathan Edwards (1703–1758), who argued that children are "young vipers and infinitely more hateful than vipers" (Elkind & Weiner, 1978, p. 12). Edwards insisted that in order to socialize children, parents must break their wills.

Although the theories of moral development we now consider tend to be more or less consistent with *natural-goodness* or *original-sin* conceptions of human nature, they take a middle course. Evolutionary theorists assume that individuals are inherently selfish, at least at a genetic level, but that altruistic and moral dispositions may evolve in species when they foster the inclusive fitness of those who inherit them. Psychoanalytic theorists view children as inherently amoral, driven by sexual and aggressive instincts. According to Freud, children acquire a conscience when they identify with their parents during the early school years. And according to social learning theorists, children are not born moral or immoral; they learn to behave morally or immorally in the same manner they learn to behave in other ways, through reinforcement and modeling. Finally, cognitive-developmental theorists, who have stimulated the most research on moral development, focus on the growth of moral reasoning in the child. We now consider each of these perspectives in greater detail.

An Evolutionary Account of Moral Development

Whereas the psychoanalytic, social learning, and cognitive-developmental accounts focus on the development of morality in children, the evolutionary account focuses on the evolution of morality in the human species. Most scholars agree that morality involves a system of rules that compels people to forgo opportunities to maximize their gains in order to behave fairly toward others. A central assumption of evolutionary theory is that dispositions evolve because they maximize the **inclusive fitness** of the individuals who possess them — that is to say, they maximize their genetic representation in future generations (see Chapter 2). At first glance, it would seem the acquisition of a sense of morality is inconsistent with the principle of natural selection —individuals who resist the temptation to maximize their gains should fare less well than individuals who maximize their gains without constraint. According to some prominent evolutionary theorists, however, this is not necessarily the case. For example, Trivers (1983) and Alexander (1985) believe that moral dispositions enhanced the inclusive fitness of our ancestors and, therefore, have evolved in the human species.

Evolutionary analyses of morality center around the costs and gains of social reciprocity. In an early article, sociobiologist Robert Trivers (1971) suggested that in certain circumstances it makes sense for people to help others if, through helping, they are more likely to receive aid at some later time from those they helped. Trivers suggested that the disposition to engage in **reciprocal altruism** was particularly adaptive in the early years of the human species, and so has become part of human nature. Computer simulations have established that in two-person games, the net benefits obtained by individuals in groups that engage in **tit-for-tat reciprocity** are greater than those obtained by individuals in groups of selfish individualists (Axelrod & Hamilton, 1981). This makes sense because often it is possible to render considerable assistance at little personal cost — for example, by throwing a life preserver to someone who is drowning — and, by the same principle, to receive considerable benefit at little cost in return.

But tit-for-tat reciprocity is limited: it requires that at some later time individuals encounter the people they helped. Trivers (1983) and Alexander (1985) suggest a more general disposition may have evolved in the human species: help those one sees helping others. Alexander (1985) calls the system of reciprocity to which this disposition gives rise **indirect reciprocity,** and argues that it constitutes "the essence of moral systems" (p. 10). Alexander outlines the process through which indirect reciprocity may promote the spread of altruism as follows:

1. A helps B
2. B helps (or overhelps) A
3. C, observing, helps B, expecting that
4. B will also help (or overhelp) C
5. (and so on)

or

1. A helps B
2. B does not help A
3. C, observing, does not help B, expecting that if C does
4. B will not return the help
5. (and so on)

According to Alexander (1985), indirect reciprocity of punishment may also promote the spread of rules:

1. A hurts B
2. C, observing, punishes A, expecting that if C does not,
3. A will also hurt C

or that

4. someone else, also observing, will hurt C, expecting no cost

Ultimately, suggests Alexander, the tendency to make **indiscriminate social investments** — to risk relatively small expenses to help people who need help — might evolve in such large complex societies as our own. Although many of the indiscriminate social investments people make may not "pay off," individuals who behave altruistically and fairly toward others would acquire good reputations that would, in the long run, contribute more to their inclusive fitness than would the bad reputations of those who behave selfishly and unfairly. Thus according to Alexander (1985), even though most people assume that behaving morally entails a net cost to individuals, in the end moral behavior actually pays off — at least at a genetic level. Those perceived as altruistic and moral ultimately leave more replicas of their genes in future generations than those seen as immoral.

Note it is the perception of morality that counts in evolutionary theory, not moral behavior in and of itself. Therefore, dispositions that cause people to be perceived as helpful and fair, even though they are not, should have the greatest adaptive potential of all; people with such dispositions would reap the benefits of both selfishness and a good reputation. In view of the costs of being taken in by such fakers and cheaters, we would expect counteracting sensitivities to evolve that enable individuals to detect them. Indeed, Trivers (1983) suggests that "a sense of fairness [may have] evolved in human beings as the standard against which to measure the behavior of other people, so as to guard against cheating in reciprocal relationships" (p. 46).

In summary, evolutionary theorists suggest a sense of morality has evolved in the human species because it is adaptive — it enhances the inclusive fitness of the individuals who possess it. However, for fairness to make sense (pay off), individuals must also inherit dispositions that enable them to detect and punish cheaters. Therefore, humans inherit both a sense of fairness and such emotions as moralistic aggression — emotions necessary to protect their sense of fairness from exploitation. Sociobiological ideas about morality and moral development are relatively new and, as with much evolutionary thinking, raise provocative possibilities — but they must remain only provocative ideas until tested more systematically.

A Psychoanalytic Account of Moral Development

According to Freud, morality is among the weakest components of human nature. In his words, "As regards conscience God has done an uneven

and careless piece of work, for a large majority of men have brought along with them only a modest amount of it or scarcely enough to be worth mentioning" (1963, p. 61). The basic tenet of psychoanalysis is that life involves an ongoing conflict between the sexual and aggressive instincts on the one hand and the constraints of society on the other. Again according to Freud, the part of the psyche he called the **ego** developed in order to negotiate necessary compromises between the need to relieve instinctual tension and the need to conform to social rules and conventions (see Chapter 12). But these compromises are practical, not moral: individuals with a strong ego might behave immorally if convinced they would not be caught and punished. Freud believed the moral aspect of human nature is rooted in an "outgrowth" of the ego called the *superego,* the aspect of personality that makes moral judgments about our behavior and makes us feel guilty when we violate social standards. In addition, it compels us to do our best. Freud's superego is similar to what most of us call conscience.

But where does this component of personality come from? And why does it develop? Freud invites us to think back to our past and ask ourselves who in our childhood made judgments about our behavior, punished us when we were bad, and rewarded us when we were good. "Our parents," he concludes. Accordingly, our superegos consist of internalized, or in Freud's words **introjected,** embodiments of our parents; our "voice of conscience" is, in effect, the voice of our parents rebuking, praising, criticizing, commending, punishing, and rewarding us. In recognition of the fact that children's moral orientation usually changes with development, Freud suggested that children come to identify with other figures.

> The course of childhood development leads to an ever-increasing detachment from parents, and their personal significance for the superego recedes into the background [to be linked to] the influences of teachers and authorities, self-chosen models, and publicly recognized heroes. (Freud, 1976, p. 168)

Freud developed a rather elaborate explanation of how children come to introject an embodiment of their parents into their egos. (We outlined the central assumptions of this theory in the

Miss Peach by Mell Lazarus.   Courtesy of Mell Lazarus and News America Syndicate.

earlier discussion of sex-typing.)   When young children identify with the parent of the opposite sex in order to resolve their Oedipus or Electra conflicts, they introject their image of that parent into their ego, and this becomes their superego (or conscience).   Critics have questioned the logic of Freud's theory of moral development (Kohlberg, 1969), and the relatively sparse research it has stimulated has not been consistently supportive (see Hoffman, 1970; Chapter 12).

A Social Learning Account of Moral Development

According to learning theorists, moral behaviors, like other kinds of behavior, are acquired through conditioning.   The reason why people resist temptation is because they have been rewarded for resisting temptation and punished for transgressing.   In other words, morals are habits ingrained in people through experience.   According to learning theorists, techniques of parental discipline are particularly important in establishing moral habits.

Social learning theorists accept the proposition that much moral behavior is learned through conditioning, but they emphasize the internal control of behavior and the effect of modeling. They suggest that such emotional reactions as anxiety, shame, and guilt may be evoked by thoughts of doing wrong or by the intention to transgress (Aronfreed, 1976) and that individuals learn to behave morally by modeling the moral behavior of others (Bandura, 1977).   Social learning theorists suggest that when a child models the behavior of an adult, the child constructs an internal image of the behavior that serves as a guide for that type of behavior in the future.   They tend to endorse child-rearing techniques based on induction because they believe explaining why particular behaviors are wrong induces children to understand the principles underlying moral behavior rather than simply how to avoid punishment or how to maximize reward (Hoffman, 1970).

Social learning theory has stimulated considerable research on morality (Aronfreed, 1976).   Critics of the social learning account argue that it equates morality with conformity — for example, as revealed in the tendency of children to model the behavior of adults — and that it does not offer an adequate explanation of how children develop internal moral standards.   How, critics argue, can social learning (and psychoanalytic) theory explain where the standards that parents attempt to instill in children originate?   And why, they ask, do many adolescents (not to mention such moral leaders as Socrates, Christ, Gandhi, and Martin Luther King Jr.) defy the traditional moral and legal standards of their countries?   The following theory attempts to answer such questions as these.

A Cognitive – Developmental Account of Moral Development

Shakespeare's Hamlet observed: "There is nothing either good or bad but thinking makes it so." These words underscore the distinction between what people do, which according to Hamlet is neither good nor bad, and what people think about what they do — the reasons, motives, intentions, and purposes they attribute to behavior. Although somewhat before his time, Hamlet captures the cognitive-developmental approach to moral development. Cognitive-developmental theorists insist the reasons that underlie behavior, not the behavior itself, make it right or wrong.

The Early Work of Jean Piaget More than a half century ago, the founder of cognitive-developmental theory, Jean Piaget (see Chapter 1), published a book entitled *The Moral Judgment of the Child* (Piaget, 1932). In his book, Piaget presented an elaborate account of the development of standards of morality in children. He based his original theory of moral development on an unusual series of observations — children playing marbles. Piaget observed children in this context because of his belief that the essence of morality lies in rules and that marbles is a game in which children create and enforce their own rules. In addition to watching children play marbles, Piaget explored their conceptions of morality by telling them little stories and examining their reactions to them (see Box 10-5).

On the basis of the behavior displayed by children playing marbles and the ideas they disclosed in response to his stories, Piaget concluded that young children typically develop a view of morality oriented to authority and based on what he called **unilateral respect** for adults. According to Piaget, young children's conceptions of morality are based on such assumptions as "People should obey authority," "People should preserve the letter, not the spirit, of the law," and "Wrongdoers should be punished severely." However, suggested Piaget, as children get older, their moral orientation changes to one based on cooperation and **mutual respect** for peers. Older children believe that rules are invented by people for the purpose of preserving order and fairness, that it is proper to change them if everyone agrees, and that exceptions should be made in appropriate circumstances.

What causes children to change their moral orientation? Piaget emphasized three factors:

1. increasing sophistication of children's understanding of the world, as reflected, for example, in their ability to understand such concepts as reciprocity

Box 10-5
INTENTIONS AND CONSEQUENCES

John was in his room when his mother called him to dinner. John goes down and opens the door to the dining room. But behind the door was a chair and on the chair was a tray with 15 cups on it. Johnny did not know the cups were behind the door. He opens the door, the door hits the tray, bang go the 15 cups, and they all get broken.

One day when Henry's mother was out, Henry tried to get some cookies out of the cupboard. He climbed up on the chair, but the cookie jar was still too high, and he couldn't reach it! But while he was trying to get the cookie jar, he knocked over a cup. The cup fell down and broke! (Piaget, 1932, p. 100)

Piaget asked the children which boy they thought had been naughtier, and why. He suspected that young children would orient to the amount of external damage or to the severity of the external consequences of an act, but older children — who understand more about the internal subjective states of others — would orient to the intentions of the actors. As predicted, he found that young children tended to say the child who broke 15 cups was the naughtier and older children tended to choose the child who broke one cup.

Source: From Piaget, J. (1932). *The moral judgment of the child* (p. 100). Glencoe, IL: Free Press.

2. development of the ability to take the role of others, which Piaget believed was fostered in interactions with peers

3. freedom from the feelings of unilateral respect and adult constraint

Lawrence Kohlberg's Theory of Moral Development Piaget's early work laid the foundation for development of the theory that has had the greatest impact on the study of moral development—the theory of Lawrence Kohlberg. Kohlberg began where Piaget left off, but employed a significantly different method. In 1958, Kohlberg created a number of moral dilemmas like the one displayed in Table 10-8. He presented these dilemmas to a group of 72 males from 10 to 16 years of age and recorded their responses. In scoring them, Kohlberg was less interested in what the boys thought was right and wrong than in why they thought particular courses of action were morally superior to others. For example, he was less interested in whether his subjects thought the character Heinz in the dilemma presented in Table 10-8 should or should not steal a drug to save his dying wife than he was in the reasons they gave to support their opinions.

In interpreting the samples of moral reasoning he obtained from his subjects, Kohlberg reached the provisional conclusion that there were six qualitatively different ways of viewing moral issues. Put another way, a given individual may espouse one of six implicit theories of morality. Kohlberg outlined these six types of moral reasoning in a scoring manual. Using the manual as a guide, other scorers were able to identify, with reasonable reliability, the six types of moral reasoning.

There were two noteworthy features of the six moral orientations observed by Kohlberg. First, they differed in complexity; second, older children tended to employ more complex types of moral reasoning than younger children. These features led Kohlberg to suspect that the six types of moral reasoning he observed constituted stages in the development of children's understanding of morality roughly equivalent to Piaget's stages of cognitive development (see Chapter 9; Table 10-9). To test this hypothesis, Kohlberg followed up his original sample, retesting them to determine whether subjects who, for example,

TABLE 10-8
A Moral Dilemma from Kohlberg's Test

In Europe, a woman was near death from a special kind of cancer. There was one drug that the doctors thought might save her. It was a form of radium that a druggist in the same town had recently discovered. The drug was expensive to make, but the druggist was charging 10 times what the drug cost him to make. He paid $400 for the radium and charged $4000 for a small dose of the drug. The sick woman's husband, Heinz, went to everyone he knew to borrow the money, but he could only get together about $2000, which is half of what it cost. He told the druggist that his wife was dying and asked him to sell it cheaper or let him pay later. But the druggist said, "No, I discovered the drug and I'm going to make money from it." So Heinz gets desperate and considers breaking into the man's store to steal the drug for his wife.

1. Should Heinz steal the drug?

1a. Why or why not?

2. If Heinz doesn't love his wife, should he steal the drug for her?

2a. Why or why not?

3. Suppose the person dying is not his wife but a stranger. Should Heinz steal the drug for the stranger?

3a. Why or why not?

4. (If you favor stealing the drug for a stranger.) Suppose it's a pet animal he loves. Should Heinz steal to save the pet animal?

4a. Why or why not?

5. Is it important for people to do everything they can to save another's life?

5a. Why or why not?

6. It is against the law for Heinz to steal. Does that make it morally wrong?

6a. Why or why not?

7. Should people try to do everything they can to obey the law?

7a. Why or why not?

7b. How does this apply to what Heinz should do?

Source: From Kohlberg, L. (1984). *Essays on moral development: The psychology of moral development* (Vol. 2, p. 641). New York: Harper & Row.

were at Stage 1 when originally tested had advanced to Stage 2, and so on. Over the past three decades, Kohlberg has retested the subjects in his original sample every two to five years.

For the primary results of Kohlberg's longitudinal study on moral development, see Figure 10-9, page 510 (Colby, Kohlberg, Gibbs, & Lieberman, 1983). According to Kohlberg, the results support the claim that the first five types of moral reasoning he identified constitute universal stages of moral development and that all people

TABLE 10-9
Six Stages of Moral Judgment

Level and Stage	Content of Stage		
	What Is Right	**Reasons for Doing Right**	**Sociomoral Perspective of Stage**
Level 1: *Preconventional* Stage 1: *Heteronomous Morality*	To avoid breaking rules backed by punishment, obedience for its own sake, and avoiding physical damage to persons and property.	Avoidance of punishment and the superior power of authorities.	Egocentric point of view. Doesn't consider the interests of others or recognize that they differ from the actor's, doesn't relate two points of view. Actions are considered physically rather than in terms of psychological interests of others. Confusion of authority's perspective with one's own.
Stage 2: *Individualism, Instrumental Purpose, and Exchange*	Following rules only when it is to someone's immediate interest; acting to meet one's own interests and needs and letting others do the same. Right is also what's fair, what's an equal exchange, a deal, an agreement.	To serve one's own needs or interests in a world where you have to recognize that other people have their interests, too.	Concrete individualistic perspective. Aware that everybody has his own interests to pursue and these conflict, so that right is relative (in the concrete individualistic sense).
Level 2: *Conventional* Stage 3: *Mutual Interpersonal Expectations, Relationships, and Interpersonal Conformity*	Living up to what is expected by people close to you or what people generally expect of people in your role as son, brother, friend, etc. "Being good" is important and means having good motives, showing concern about others. It also means keeping mutual relationships, such as trust, loyalty, respect, and gratitude.	The need to be a good person in your own eyes and those of others. Your caring for others. Belief in the Golden Rule. Desire to maintain rules and authority which support stereotypical good behavior.	Perspective of the individual in relationships with other individuals. Aware of shared feelings, agreements, and expectations which take primacy over individual interests. Relates points of view through the concrete Golden Rule, putting yourself in the other guy's shoes. Does not yet consider generalized system perspective.

Source: Kohlberg, L. (1976). Moral stages and moralization: The cognitive-developmental approach. In T. Lickona (Ed.), *Moral development and behavior: Theory, research, and social issues* (pp. 34–35). New York: Holt, Rinehart & Winston.

pass through them in an **invariant sequence.** This means that all people start with a Stage 1 orientation to morality and, if they progress, move next to Stage 2; then, if they progress further, they move to Stage 3, and so on. Although people may fixate at any stage — for example, an adult may employ Stage 1 reasoning — people never skip stages and, except for such abnormal occurrences as brain damage, they never regress. Of course, people do not advance from one stage in the sequence to the next overnight. And although most ideas people espouse stem from their major stage

	Content of Stage		
Level and Stage	**What Is Right**	**Reasons for Doing Right**	**Sociomoral Perspective of Stage**
Stage 4: *Social System and Con- science*	Fulfilling the actual duties to which you have agreed. Laws are to be upheld except in extreme cases where they conflict with other fixed social duties. Right is also contributing to society, the group, or institution.	To keep the institution going as a whole, to avoid the breakdown in the system "if everyone did it," or the imperative of conscience to meet one's defined obligations.	Differentiates societal point of view from interper- sonal agreement or motives. Takes the point of view of the system that defines roles and rules. Considers individual relations in terms of place in the system.
Level 3: *Postconven- tional, or Principled* Stage 5: *Social Con- tract or Utility and Individual Rights*	Being aware that people hold a variety of values and opinions, that most values and rules are relative to your group. These relative rules should usually be upheld, however, in the interest of impartiality and because they are the social contact. Some nonrelative values and rights like life and liberty, however, must be upheld in any society and regardless of majority opinion.	A sense of obligation to law because of one's social contract to make and abide by laws for the welfare of all and for the protection of all people's rights. A feeling of contractual commitment, freely entered upon, to family, friendship, trust and work obligations. Concern that laws and duties be based on rational calculation of overall utility, "the greatest good for the greatest number."	Prior-to-society perspec- tive. Perspective of a rational individual aware of values and rights prior to social attachments and contracts. Integrates perspectives by formal mechanisms of agree- ment, contract, objective impartiality, and due process. Considers moral and legal points of view; recognizes that they sometimes conflict and finds it difficult to integrate them.
Stage 6: *Universal Ethical Principles*	Following self-chosen ethical principles. Par- ticular laws or social agreements are usually valid because they rest on such principles. When laws violate these principles, one acts in accordance with the principle. Principles are universal principles of justice: the equality of human rights and respect for the dignity of human beings as individual persons.	The belief as a rational person in the validity of universal moral principles, and a sense of personal commitment to them.	Perspective of a moral point of view from which social arrangements derive. Perspective is that of any rational individual recognizing the nature of morality or the fact that persons are ends in themselves and must be treated as such.

of moral development, they also may espouse ideas from the stages above and/or below their major stage.

The six stages of moral development de- scribed by Kohlberg are outlined in Table 10-9 and compared to the stages outlined by Piaget in Figure 10-10. Note that although Kohlberg has retained the highest stage, Stage 6, in his theoreti- cal scheme, he has not obtained enough support for it from his longitudinal study to state with authority that it marks the pinnacle of moral de- velopment. The highest stage reached by any of

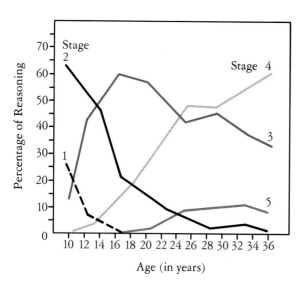

FIGURE 10-9

The Relationship between Age and Kohlberg's Five Stages of Moral Development   In Kohlberg's longitudinal study, there was a systematic decrease in Stage 1 and Stage 2 moral reasoning from age 10 on.   Stage 3 reasoning peaked at age 16, and declined thereafter.   There was a steady increase in Stage 4 reasoning starting at age 10 and a steady increase in Stage 5 reasoning starting at age 18.   *Source:* Colby, A., Kohlberg, L., Gibbs, J., & Lieberman, M. (1983).   A longitudinal study of moral judgment.   *Monographs of the Society for Research in Child Development, 48,* p. 53.

his subjects is Stage 5.   Time will tell whether any of them progresses to Stage 6.

The **preconventional level** (stages 1 and 2) outlined by Kohlberg is somewhat similar to the *morality of constraint* described by Piaget. At these stages, children (and morally immature adults) view rules and social expectations as external to themselves: they believe rules should be obeyed because they are imposed by people in authority.   At Stage 1, people define right and wrong in terms of rewards and punishments.   At Stage 2, people define morality in terms of a you-scratch-my-back-and-I'll-scratch-yours principle.   Most children and some adults are at the *preconventional* stages of morality.

People who view morality from a Stage 3 perspective assume that morality consists of living up to the expectations of others, especially as those expectations are embedded in social roles. Individuals at Stage 3 assume that morality involves being a good daughter, good husband, good employee, and so on.   Such concepts as love, empathy, and altruism are prominent in the

moral reasoning of people at Stage 3.   The perspective of individuals at Stage 4 is somewhat broader than that of individuals at Stage 3.   At Stage 4, people define right and wrong in terms of behaviors that maintain the social system of their society.   People at Kohlberg's fourth stage typically endorse principles of law and order.   Most adolescents and adults are at the **conventional level** (Stages 3 and 4) of moral development.

At the **postconventional level** of moral development (Stages 5 and 6) people orient to the principles of justice on which laws are based and to the rights and duties of individuals.   People at Stage 5 base their moral decisions on such principles as "Do that which produces the greatest good for the greatest number."   The principles of Stage 6 moral reasoning are more absolute — such principles as philosopher Immanual Kant's categorical imperative: "I ought never to act except in such a way that I can also will that my maxim should become a universal law, and I should treat all people as ends in themselves, not means." Sometimes these moral imperatives demand action that runs counter to the rules of society. Virtually all great moral leaders — Christ, Gan-

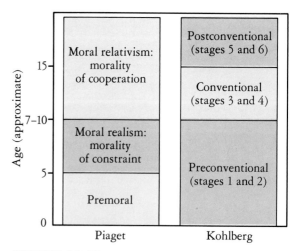

FIGURE 10-10

Piaget's and Kohlberg's Stages of Moral Development   Kohlberg's Stages 1 and 2 overlap Piaget's premoral and moral realism stages.   Kohlberg divided Piaget's second stage into two sets of two stages (conventional and postconventional).   Piaget's and Kohlberg's stages are only roughly comparable. *Source:* Adapted from Helms, D. B., & Turner, J. S. (1981). *Exploring child behavior* (2nd ed., p. 285).   New York: Holt, Rinehart & Winston.

dhi, and Martin Luther King Jr., for example — defied the laws and conventions of their times. According to Kohlberg, only a few people ever reach the postconventional stages, almost all of whom are adults.

In answer to the question "What causes moral development?" Kohlberg places more emphasis on the growth of moral reasoning than Piaget does, and less on peer relations. Kohlberg believes events that place people in moral conflicts, that evoke moral reasoning, and that induce them to take the role of others stimulate moral development.

Criticisms of Kohlberg's Theory Although Kohlberg's theory has stimulated more research than any other theory of moral development, it has not gone without criticism. In a review published in 1974, Kurtines and Grief raised several questions about Kohlberg's test and concluded that it did not meet acceptable criteria for reliability and validity. Since the 1974 review, Kohlberg has revised his test and scoring manual, producing evidence that supports the contention his test is both reliable and valid and that his first five stages of moral development form an invariant sequence (Colby, Kohlberg, Gibbs, & Lieberman, 1983).

Kohlberg's claims that the stages form a hierarchy in which the higher stages are morally superior to the lower ones and that this hierarchy is the same for all people in all cultures have proven the most controversial aspects of his theory. Some critics have argued that the stages described by Kohlberg are more a reflection of his Western cultural upbringing and ethical standards than a description of a universal sequence (Simpson, 1974). Others have challenged the assumption that the essence of morality lies in principles of justice, arguing that such virtues as love and altruism may be equally or more important (Puka, 1983). Related to these criticisms are allegations that Kohlberg's test is biased toward males, and that the types of moral reasoning revealed by the males in the longitudinal study on which his theory is based differ in important ways from the types of moral reasoning employed by females (see Box 10-6, page 512).

Other criticisms of Kohlberg's theory focus on his almost exclusive concern with moral thinking. It has been suggested that Kohlberg's test assesses only storybook morality — the way people reason about relatively unusual hypothetical dilemmas. One critic has developed a test to assess the type of practical moral reasoning that people employ in real-life situations, claiming this type of reasoning is different in important ways from the hypothetical reasoning assessed by Kohlberg's test (Haan, 1978). In addition, social learning theorists have argued that the primary criterion of moral development is what people do, not what they say (Mischel & Mischel, 1976), and that such moral feelings as empathy and guilt exert a much stronger influence than moral reasoning on moral behavior (Aronfreed, 1976).

This issue of the relationship between moral reasoning and moral behavior is a complex and significant one, and one to which Kohlberg recently has turned his attention. For that reason, we consider it in greater detail.

The Relationship between Moral Reasoning and Moral Behavior At least two dozen researchers have administered Kohlberg's test of moral development to groups of children or adults, placed them in a situation that required they make a moral decision, and assessed the relationship between their stage of moral reasoning and their tendency to behave morally. For example, in one study (Mendinnus, 1966) children were promised candy for obtaining a certain number of points on a ray-gun game rigged to fall just short and then observed to see whether they cheated to obtain the necessary scores. In other studies, investigators have assessed the relationship between stage of moral development and people's willingness to: deliver electric shocks to an innocent victim on the command of a person in authority (see Chapter 11; Kohlberg, 1969), intervene in emergencies (McNamee, 1977; Staub, 1975), engage in political protest (Haan, Smith, & Block, 1968), and honor a contract (Krebs & Rosenwald, 1977). Such studies have found quite consistently that the higher the stage of moral reasoning displayed by subjects, the more likely they are to behave morally. Other studies have found that juvenile delinquents and mentally retarded children score at lower stages of moral development than their peers (see Blasi, 1980, for a review).

The results of these studies would seem to support Kohlberg's theory and affirm the validity

BOX 10-6
MORAL DEVELOPMENT FROM A FEMININE POINT OF VIEW

The original interviews on which Kohlberg's theory is based were conducted with 10- to 16-year-old boys. What if the original interviews had been conducted with females instead? Would the stages of moral development outlined by Kohlberg be different? A number of investigators think they would have been.

Constance Holstein (1976) and Carol Gilligan (1977) have raised the possibility of a masculine bias in Kohlberg's scoring system that places the societal, or law-and-order, moral orientation (Stage 4) above reasoning based on interpersonal concordance (Stage 3). These psychologists suggest research has revealed that most adult women tend to reach Kohlberg's Stage 3 moral development but that most adult

men reach Stage 4. They argue that Kohlberg's placement of the "feminine" concerns characteristic of Stage 3 (interpersonal relations, family ties, love, empathy, altruism) below the "masculine" concerns characteristic of Stage 4 (maintaining the social system, upholding the law) is mistaken.

Carol Gilligan (1977) argues that inasmuch as both socialization experiences and domains of decision-making differ for females and males, Kohlberg's male-derived hypothetical dilemmas are inadequate to identify and define the developmental structure of moral reasoning in females. She recommends that investigators find content areas in which females have moral decision-making power, and assess their reasoning in these

moral domains. Gilligan's own research has focused on women's reasoning concerning the dilemma of birth control and abortion because, in Gilligan's words, this dilemma reflects the central moral problem for women: "the conflict between compassion and antonomy, between virtue and power" (Gilligan, 1977, p. 491).

Gilligan studied the moral reasoning of 29 women faced with the decision to have an abortion. She researched both the moral reasoning underlying their decision and their reasoning on three of Kohlberg's hypothetical dilemmas. Gilligan described women's moral judgments concerning abortion as falling within one of four levels. The first level involves an "orientation to

of his test of moral develoment; however, there are certain logical problems with this conclusion. First, Kohlberg does not accept such behaviors as keeping promises, honoring contracts, and refraining from lying, cheating, and stealing as inherently moral. Consider the dilemma in the story about Heinz in Table 10-8. People at both high and low stages of moral development tend to say it is right for Heinz to steal (the drug). In other words, both morally mature and morally immature people tend to advocate stealing—a behavior that is conventionally considered immoral. According to Kohlberg (and Hamlet), it is

not people's choices of behaviors that are right or wrong, it is the reasons that underlie them. For example, one person might say it is right for someone to steal a drug to save his dying wife because he needs her to cook for him; another person might reach the same conclusion because he or she places the value of life above the value of property. According to Kohlberg, the latter answer is more moral than the former even though they share the same conclusion.

A second problem concerning Kohlberg's theory relates to the association between knowing what is right and doing what is right—the associ-

individual survival," and decisions center on pragmatic self-interest. At the second level, a transition "from selfishness to responsibility," women try to balance selfish concerns with concern for interpersonal issues of attachment, including responsibility for future generations. At the third level, a transition "from goodness to truth," women further clarify the dilemma of responsibility by recognizing that caring for others ("goodness") must be balanced by caring for oneself. The last level, described as "the morality of nonviolence," is marked by equal application of the principle of nonviolence to oneself and to others. At this fourth level, women assume personal responsibility for moral deliberations that may go against conventions of both morality and femininity, but which minimize violence and hurt to oneself and to others.

On the basis of Gilligan's comparison of women's moral reasoning on the abortion dilemma to their moral reasoning on Kohlberg's hypothetical dilemmas, she concluded: "The morality of responsibility which women describe stands apart from the morality of rights which underlies Kohlberg's conception of the highest stages of moral judgment" (p. 509). Gilligan argues that women, indeed, reach high stages of moral development (as typified by responses given to the abortion dilemma), but that this is not acknowledged in Kohlberg's scheme. Rather than pit the systems against each other, Gilligan proposes the viewpoints be integrated so that criteria of moral development contain simultaneous consideration of both the impersonal principles derived from the masculine viewpoint and the interpersonal principles derived from the feminine viewpoint.

Kohlberg is sympathetic to certain of Gilligan's points but not to others (for example, see Levine, Kohlberg, & Hewer, 1985). He accepts her argument that he has not attended sufficiently to people's ideas about care, responsibility, and the special relationships that exist among loved ones and families. However, Kohlberg insists that, in fact, women are not any more likely to score at his Stage 3 than are men, especially when evaluated by his revised scoring system. A recent meta-analysis of sex differences in moral reasoning (Walker, 1986) supports Kohlberg's claim. Kohlberg views the care and responsibility orientation described by Gilligan as a "soft stage": it does not develop as part of an invariant sequence.

ation between thinking and behaving. Why should people who give sophisticated solutions to Kohlberg's hypothetical moral dilemmas be disposed to live in accordance with their principles? Should we expect ethical philosophers to be (to behave) any more moral than anyone else? In a recent paper, Kohlberg and Candee (1984) attempt to answer these questions. They present a flowchart that outlines a series of steps they suggest occur from the time an individual makes a moral judgment to the time he or she engages in moral action (see Figure 10-11). The first step involves making what Kohlberg and Candee call a **deontic choice** — reaching a conclusion about what is right (for example, to steal the drug or not to steal the drug). After people reach a conclusion about what is right, they make a **judgment of responsibility** or personal moral obligation in the situation at hand. Even though two people may reach the same decision (it is right to steal the drug), they may differ in their sense of personal responsibility. Kohlberg and Candee adduce evidence indicating that as people ascend the hierarchy of moral development, they feel more and more personally responsible for behaving in a manner that is consistent with their moral

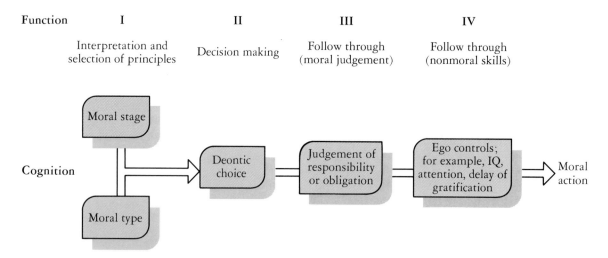

FIGURE 10-11

The Relationship between Moral Judgment and Moral Behavior In this model, people's stage of moral reasoning and their type of moral orientation (autonomous or other-oriented) combine to give rise to a decision about what is right. People who feel they are responsible for doing what is right and who possess high ego strength behave in ways consistent with their judgments. *Source:* Kohlberg, L., & Candee, D. (1984). The relationship of moral judgement to moral action. In W. M. Kurtines & J. C. Gewirtz (Eds.), *Morality, moral behavior, and moral development* (p. 71). New York: Wiley & Sons.

decisions. Yet, acknowledge Kohlberg and Candee, even a sense of personal responsibility may not be enough to induce people to do what they know is right. People may lack such nonmoral qualities as ego-strength, intelligence, or courage required to translate thought into action (see Figure 10-11).

Comparison of the Four Theories

By now it should be apparent that morality is a complex phenomenon interpreted in different ways by different theorists. In Table 10-10, we summarize and compare the similarities and the differences of the four theories of moral development we have just examined.

ADULT DEVELOMENT—A LOOK AHEAD

Who am I?
I go to the mirror . . . The mirror holds a face. I do not recognize it as mine. It no more fits my inner light than the shade of a bridge lamp fits its bulb . . . Not mine. But it winks when I will wink; it occupies, I see by the mirror, the same volume of space wherein the perspectives at which I perceive various projecting edges of the room would intersect . . . These teeth are mine. Every filling and inlay is a mournful story I could sing. These eyes—holes of a mask.

—John Updike (*A Month of Sundays,* 1974)

Most theories of development focus on the changes that occur in children from infancy to adolescence. Psychoanalysis assumes that the fabric of our adult personality is well-woven by early childhood. Cognitive-developmental theory assumes that most people reach the pinnacle of cognitive development with the advent of formal operations during adolescence. Social learning theory assumes that the habits people form early in life become deeply ingrained and resistant to change. Yet the man in Updike's novel is 47 years old, and he appears to be undergoing some significant changes. Recently, psy-

TABLE 10-10
Four Theories of Moral Development—A Comparison

Theory	Sociobiological	Psychoanalytic	Social Learning	Cognitive-developmental
Moral Development is . . .	the phylogenetic evolution of dispositions that induce others to behave some-what altruisti-cally and fairly in order to enhance their inclusive fitness.	abiding by the dictates of the internalized representations of one's parents in one's superego.	behavioral conformity to society's rules (doing the right thing).	the cognitive ability to understand why certain acts are right or wrong.
Morality's Basic Motivation is . . .	to foster one's inclusive fitness.	avoiding guilt and retaining internalized parental approval.	to avoid punish-ment and reap rewards (especially social approval); to model the behavior of others.	to behave in a way that is consistent with one's principles; self-realization; to understand one's world; cognitive consistency.
Morality is . . .	universal—an evolved disposition.	culturally and personally relative—a re-flection of the morality of one's parents.	culturally relative—a reflection of the values of one's social envi-ronment.	universal, inasmuch as it consists of basic principles that dictate rights and duties.
Moral Development In-volves . . .	the maturation of dispositions that promote moral behavior.	introjecting the parents' superego during the phallic stage of development.	internalizing moral norms (for example, thou shalt not steal) that existed originally outside the child.	constructing principles of morality from one's own experience.
The Major Environmen-tal Influences on Moral Development are . . .	stimuli that evoke inherited dispositions.	parents, especially of the opposite sex.	rewards, punish-ments, prohibi-tions, and models.	experiences with moral issues and dilemmas that cause children to think—cogni-tive conflict, difficult decisions, and role-taking opportunities.

chologists have begun to recognize that social de-velopment does not cease after adolescence.

The theory that has influenced most of the research on adult social development is Erik Erikson's **psychosocial theory** (see Chap-ter 12). Erikson (1968) revised Freud's stages of development in two significant ways. First, he elaborated on Freud's oral, anal, phallic, and gen-ital stages. Second, he added several stages, ex-tending the description of development into adulthood. The result of Erikson's extension of Freud's early work is a theory that outlines eight (as opposed to Freud's four) major stages of devel-opment. One might say that Erikson was to Freud what Kohlberg was to Piaget.

According to Erikson, each of the eight stages of social development is marked by a major crisis or critical issue. Whether people resolve the crisis, and how, determines whether they grow socially and psychologically, and in which direction. The first four stages in Erikson's theory are described in Chapter 12. In addition, people typically experience one major crisis in adolescence and three in adulthood. We briefly consider Erikson's description of the final four stages here.

Identity versus Role Diffusion   The crisis experienced by most people during late adolescence involves the formation of an identity; at no other stage of development is there more self-consciousness and brooding about oneself (see Box 10-7). The central questions of this phase of life are "Who am I?" and "Where am I going?" Adolescents who resolve this crisis develop a secure sense of personal wholeness and integration;

those who do not resolve it experience an unintegrated, scattered sense of who they are and their role in life.

Marcia (1966; 1976) has identified four ways in which adolescents resolve the identity crisis — **identity achievement, moratorium, foreclosure,** and **identity diffusion** (see Table 10-11). To *achieve an identity* (resolve the crisis of adolescence through identity achievement), an individual must make a commitment to self-chosen values and goals, especially as reflected in choice of career, philosophy of life, and interpersonal relations. A person in *moratorium* is in the midst of a decision-making crisis,

Box 10-7
ADOLESCENT EGOCENTRISM

Adolescents go through a period when they think everybody's thoughts are focused on them — because their thoughts are focused on themselves. For example, an adolescent who spills a small amount of cola at a restaurant may express inordinate embarrassment over this rather ordinary accident and believe everybody in the restaurant was watching. This is the nature of adolescent egocentrism. Unlike younger children who have difficulty thinking abstractly and taking the perspective of others — and are therefore often aware only of their own thoughts and experiences — adolescents are both aware of their own thoughts and experiences and capable of taking the perspective of others. But adolescents attribute their

own thoughts — because their thoughts are the most salient to them — to others. Consequently, adolescents are painfully conscious of such things as whether they have acne, are too fat, too thin, their hair is messed, or their teeth crooked.

Because adolescents believe they are the focus of others' interest, they act as though they have an imaginary audience. So it is common to see young people strutting about, acting "super cool." Parents of egocentric adolescents may recognize this period as the stage when their children dart behind shopping aisles when somebody they think they know might see them out with Mom or Dad or when they slouch down in the car on the way to a movie to avoid the possibility of

being seen by friends. In addition to these behavioral cues, parents of egocentric adolescents may be recipients of such statements as "You can't possibly know how I feel" (Elkind, 1967).

Although most people can probably remember this stage, it is difficult to say just when, or why, it ends. According to Elkind (1967), adolescent egocentrism begins to diminish when the final stage of cognitive development, formal operations, is achieved. Developing a genuine, intimate relationship with another — where it is essential to understand accurately the other person's perspective (Piaget, 1967) — may also bring adolescents out of this stage.

struggling to formulate a consistent and fulfilling identity. *Foreclosure* involves short-circuiting the process of identity formation by adopting an identity and ideology given by parents or other authorities. People in a state of *identity diffusion* have yet to face up to the challenge of the stage; they have made no commitment to anything and seem to be "just drifting."

Researchers have found that adolescents who experience each of the four identity states typically come from different types of family (Donovan, 1975; Matteson, 1975). Those who foreclose describe their families as "just perfect"; adolescents from such homes find it difficult to leave the family nest and establish identities of their own. In contrast, families of adolescents who achieve an identity are marked by conflict; these families recognize and accept differences among members, and expect differences of opinion. Families of individuals in moratorium are characterized by ambivalence—both positive and negative. The family portrait of adolescents experiencing identity diffusion is the bleakest; the families of these adolescents seem not to exist. Often such families consist of a powerful but emotionally unavailable parent of the same sex and a weak, nonsupportive parent of the opposite sex.

It is important to note that however an adolescent resolves (or fails to resolve) an identity crisis, social development continues nevertheless. Even after people have passed through a major identity crisis, they are likely to experience changes in their lives and outlooks that cause them to reevaluate and change their definitions of themselves, their life-styles, their values, and their commitments. For example, an adolescent who adopts the ready-made personal styles, values, and occupational and/or marital choice of his or her parents may in later years face dissatisfaction with these established patterns and experience another identity crisis.

Intimacy versus Isolation As adolescents resolve the issue of identity, they pass into adulthood. According to Erikson, the first crisis of adulthood involves decisions about **intimacy.** Between the ages of 20 and 30, young adults typically feel the need to make an emotional commitment to another person in a sharing and loving relationship. Those who fail to satisfy this need experience a sense of **isolation.** As with all of Erikson's stages, it is rare that people completely succeed or completely fail to resolve the crisis; rather, different individuals may feel more or less connected to others and more or less isolated.

Generativity versus Stagnation As people approach middle adulthood, in their forties and fifties, they typically seek to extend their personal commitment to a broader range of people than they did at earlier stages. Dominant concerns at this stage often involve activities in which people can make a lasting contribution to future generations—**generativity**—especially through

TABLE 10-11
Marcia's Categories of Identity Status

Status and Definition	Answer (showing occupational commitment)*
Identity Achievement—a successfully developed identity has emerged after a moratorium of self-evaluation and trying on roles.	"Probably not very willing. I've given it a lot of thought. If I could see that there might be 'something better,' I'd consider it."
Identity Foreclosure—career and value commitments have been made *without* undergoing the moratorium processes. These commitments are premature and often unstable.	"I doubt that I'd be willing. I've always known what I wanted to do. My parents and I have agreed, and we're happy with it."
Identity Moratorium—the moratorium process is still in effect; commitments are not yet established.	"It's possible. I kind of like a couple of fields—and if something else was related, I'd want to think about it and get some information."
Identity Diffusion—commitments have not been made, but there is no active search either.	"Sounds like a good idea. I haven't thought much about it, but I'll try anything once. I could switch just like that" (snapping his fingers).

* Included are examples of how adolescents from each status might answer the question: "How willing do you think you'd be to give up going into [occupation] if something better came along?"
Source: Sarafino, E. P., & Armstrong, J. W. (1980). *Child and adolescent development* (p. 512). Glenview, IL: Scott, Foresman.

their children and their work. This period marks the turning point from a forward-looking, youthful perspective to a time frame that includes half a lifetime already lived and half a lifetime still to come. It is at this time that parents must face the changes associated with their children leaving home. Failure to resolve this crisis in a positive manner may result in excessive self-indulgence, depression, a sense that little matters anymore, and **stagnation.**

Ego-integrity versus Despair   During the senior years, in the sixties and seventies, people face the challenge of integrating their life experiences, accepting what they are, and facing the inevitability of death. Those who successfully resolve the crisis of this stage come to feel they have done their best (they acquire **ego-integrity**)—whether or not they have achieved all their goals—and to believe their lives have

made sense. Those who fail to resolve the crisis reach the painful conclusion that their lives have mattered little, and lapse into **despair.** Compared to people of other societies, we present the elderly with few opportunities and statuses to help them acquire a sense of integrity (Comfort, 1976; Stewart & Smith, 1983).

In comparison to research on early stages of development, there has been relatively little research on the stages that occur during adulthood. Perhaps the best known study of the crises experienced by adults was conducted by Daniel Levinson et al. (1978), which formed the basis for the best-selling book *Passages,* written by Gail Sheehy. Levinson and his colleagues interviewed some 40 men from 35 to 45 years of age, following up the subjects after two years. The stages of adult development that emerged from Levinson's study are compared to Erikson's stages in Figure 10-12. The developmental aspects that have re-

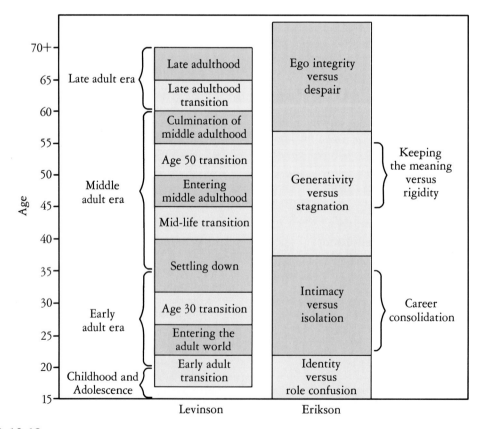

FIGURE 10-12

A Comparison of the Adult Stages Proposed by Levinson and Erikson   Levinson's stages are defined primarily by age; Erikson's stages are defined by crisis. *Source:* Adapted from Santrock, J. W. (1986). *Psychology: The science of mind and behavior* (p. 391). Dubuque, IA: William C. Brown.

ceived the most attention are the transition periods within and between stages, in particular the mid-life transition. Levinson reports that about 80% of the men in his sample experienced a mid-life crisis in which they questioned virtually every aspect of their lives. In Levinson's model, adult development involves a continuing series of readjustments and reappraisals.

At present there is a controversy in psychology about the stability of personality throughout the life span. On the one side are those who emphasize change, either continuously as it occurs through learning (Mischel, 1968) or discontinuously as it occurs when people enter new stages of development; on the other side are those who emphasize the consistency of personality throughout life. Recent studies on the personality profiles of people at various points in their lives have concluded that at least some things do not change much. For example, Block (1981) found that moody teenagers became moody adults; Costa and McCrae (1980) concluded that even at the age of 82, people are "still stable after all these years."

In summary, adult development typically is marked by a series of crises; although each crisis involves risks, it also supplies the opportunity for personal and interpersonal growth. As individuals prevail over each crisis, they develop more mature and more complete senses of themselves, both in terms of their **differentiation** from others (their sense of autonomy) and their **integration** with others (their sense of togetherness and mutuality). They become increasingly able to give to and accept from others, and they show more respect for those who choose ways that differ from their own. According to some theorists, the end point of the process is self-actualization (see Chapter 7). According to Maslow (1970), a self-actualized person is one who has the courage to determine and resolve with honesty, integrity, generosity, and kindness "who he is, what he is, what he likes, what he doesn't like, what is good for him and what bad, where he is going and what his mission is" (pp. 48–49). When faced with a difficult choice, such a person chooses the path that presents the greatest potential for growth.

SUMMARY

1. The first social and emotional bond that infants form with their primary caregivers, usually the mother, is called attachment. When infants are separated from their parent, they may display separation protest. Separation protest, measured by the amount of infant crying, is most prominent between the ages of 12 and 15 months and has been observed cross-culturally.

2. The ethological account of attachment popularized by John Bowlby assumes that infants inherit a "genetic blueprint" that causes them to behave toward their mothers in a manner that ensures their survival. Attachment behaviors include crying, clinging, sucking, smiling, and following caregivers. According to Bowlby, mothers inherit a genetic blueprint to respond to these behaviors. Critics of Bowlby's theory question the assumption that attachment behaviors are preprogrammed biologically.

3. According to the psychoanalytic account, infants become attached to their primary caregivers because the caregivers satisfy their instinctual needs, especially their needs for food and for oral gratification. Psychoanalytically oriented theorists focus on the effect of feeding practices on the formation of attachments during the oral stage of development. Research has not supported predictions based on psychoanalytic theory; the evidence suggests that feeding practices make little difference to the social development of children.

4. The social learning account maintains that attachments are formed when such behaviors as smiling, vocalizing, and crying are reinforced by caregivers when they feed, soothe, or relieve the pain experienced by infants. With repeated associations between these behaviors and responses, caregivers become rewarding in themselves. Studies testing this theory have produced inconsistent results.

5. The cognitive-developmental account of attachment emphasizes the cognitive relation-

ship between infants and caregivers. This approach suggests that the age at which infants become attached corresponds with the age at which their perceptual abilities enable them to distinguish between their parents and others. Attachments are formed because of the cognitive challenge and interest they provide.

6. Socialization is the process of shaping the values, skills, motives, attitudes, and behaviors of individuals to correspond with those regarded as appropriate for their roles in society. Methods of discipline are important in the socialization of children. Parents tend to discipline their children in one of three ways: through power assertion, love withdrawal, or induction. The type of discipline used by parents constitutes an important aspect of their parenting style. Other aspects of parenting style include parental control, clarity of parent-child communication, maturity demands, and nurturance. These characteristics are combined in ways that give rise to three styles of child rearing: authoritarian, authoritative, and permissive. These styles of child rearing are correlated with particular characteristics of children.

7. The time that children spend playing together is believed to be instrumental to their social development. From an ethological view, play serves to organize group dominance hierarchies so that the most dominant children have first access to toys, choice of games, and the like, which serves to minimize aggression. According to psychoanalysts, the main function of play is to provide a safe emotional release for conflicts children may be experiencing. From a cognitive-develomental perspective, play forces children to express their views in a way that can be understood by others, compels them to take the role of others in order to understand what the others are trying to say (thus freeing them from their egocentricity), influences their self-concept, and enhances their ability to engage in symbolic thinking. Social learning theorists emphasize the role of imitation in play and its effect on socially desirable (and undesirable) behaviors.

8. As children develop, the meaning of friendship changes. Among preschoolers, a friend is someone with whom a child is playing at the moment. In the early school years, friends tend to be valued for the things they can do. Later in the school years, children form more enduring friendships, but ones that tend to be fickle and easily broken. In late childhood and early adolescence, friendships are marked with much more mutuality, intimacy, and self-disclosure.

9. There are several theories of how children develop a sense of masculinity and femininity. Evolutionary theorists account for sex-differences in social behavior by the process of natural selection. Psychoanalysts view sex-typing as the product of the resolution of the Oedipus or Electra conflict. Social learning theorists suggest that boys and girls behave differently because they are treated differently — boys are reinforced for modeling masculine behaviors and girls are reinforced for modeling feminine behaviors. Cognitive-developmentalists suggest that sex-typing occurs when children learn which sex they are and come to value the behaviors and attitudes associated with their sex.

10. Evolutionary theorists believe that moral dispositions evolved because they enhanced the inclusive fitness of individuals who possessed them. The psychoanalytic and social learning accounts, however, view morality as imposed on people by parents and other socializing agents. The cognitive-developmental account of moral development, founded by Piaget and developed further by Kohlberg, focuses on the structures of reasoning that underlie behavior, not the behavior itself. Cognitive-developmental theorists assume that moral reasoning develops in qualitatively different stages.

11. Social development after adolescence has received relatively little attention in the past. However, recently psychologists have begun to emphasize that social development does not cease in adulthood. Erikson has outlined eight stages of development, four of which are marked by crises in adulthood. One crisis occurs in adolescence (identity versus role diffusion) and three occur in adulthood (intimacy versus isolation, generativity versus stagnation, and ego-integrity versus despair).

Attachment	Fairweather Cooperation	Unilateral Respect
Ethologist	Intimate and Mutually Shared	Mutual Respect
Imprinting	Friendship	Invariant Sequence
Sensitive Period	Sex Typing	Preconventional Level
Contact Comfort	Sex (or Gender) Identity	Conventional Level
Strange Situation	Sex Role	Postconventional Level
Secure Attachment	Plasticity	Deontic Choice
Bonding	Oedipus Complex	Judgment of Responsibility
Socialization	Superego	Psychosocial Theory
Power Assertion	Sex-typed Identity	Identity Achievement
Love-withdrawal	Electra Complex	Moratorium
Induction	Gender Permanence	Foreclosure
Authoritarian Parenting	Sex-role Stereotype	Identity Diffusion
Authoritative Parenting	Inclusive Fitness	Intimacy
Permissive Parenting	Reciprocal Altruism	Isolation
Instrumental Competence	Tit-for-tat Reciprocity	Generativity
Dominance Hierarchy	Indirect Reciprocity	Stagnation
Egocentricity	Indiscriminate Social	Ego-integrity
Perspective-taking	Investment	Despair
Playmateship	Ego	Differentiation
One-way Assistance	Introject	Integration

RECOMMENDED READINGS

Ainsworth, M. D. S., Blehar, M. G., Waters, E., & Wall, S. (1978). *Patterns of attachment: A psychological study of the strange situation.* Hillsdale, NJ: Lawrence Erlbaum Associates. This volume outlines in detail Ainsworth's procedure for assessing attachment and reviews the results of research using the strange situation.

Bowlby, J. (1969). *Attachment and loss,* Vol. 1. New York: Basic Books. A classic statement of the ethological view of attachment.

Damon, W. (1983). *Social and personality development: Infancy through adolescence.* New York: W. W. Norton. A well-written overview of all aspects of social development, with a particularly good account of the cognitive-developmental approach.

Erikson, E. H. (1950). *Childhood and society.* New York: W. W. Norton. A classic work that describes life-span sociopersonal development from the perspective of a major conributor to ego-psychoanalytic theory.

Hartup, W. (1983). Peer relations. In P. H. Mussen (Ed.), *Carmichael's manual of child psychol-ogy.* New York: Wiley & Sons. A comprehensive review of theory and research on peer relations in childhood.

Levinson, D. J., et al. (1978). *The seasons of a man's life.* New York: Knopf. This book represents a first-hand account of a psychological investigation of adult life crises faced by men in our society. *Passages* (New York: Dutton, 1976) is a popular and personalized account of adult crises faced by a select sample of men and women interviewed by journalist Gail Sheehy.

Rest, J. (1983). Morality. In P. H. Mussen (Ed.), *Handbook of child psychology* (4th ed., vol. 3). New York: Wiley & Sons. A balanced review of cognitive-developmental accounts of moral judgment.

Spence, J. T., Deaux, K., & Helmreich, R. L. (1985). Sex roles in contemporary American society. In G. Lindzey & E. Aronson (Eds.), *Handbook of social psychology* (3rd ed.), Vol. II. New York: Random House. A relatively brief, clear, and comprehensive overview of research on sex roles by leading researchers in the field.

11

SOCIAL PSYCHOLOGY

S ocial psychology is one of the most diverse areas in psychology and, perhaps, one of the least cultivated. The study of social psychology began at the end of the nineteenth century with attempts to explain why individuals sometimes behave so differently in mobs than when alone. In 1898, Norman Triplett published the first experiment in social psychology. Triplett compared the athletic performance of subjects in the presence of others to their performance when alone. In the mid-1900s, the phenomenon of conformity captured the interest of social psychologists. In general, then, early social psychologists attempted to demonstrate that the presence of others influences individual behavior—and why (see Table 11-1). Social psychologists continue to study the influence of groups on individuals, as well as such other forms of **social influence** as bystander intervention in emergencies and obedience to authority. In addition, social psychologists study a quite different (yet ultimately related) phenomenon: how people think about social issues, or **social cognition.**

While some early social psychologists were studying conformity, other social psychologists were developing ways to measure attitudes and to assess their relationship to behavior (see Table 11-1). With the advent of World War II, this academic endeavor evolved into the more practical concern of understanding the dynamics of propaganda, persuasion, and brainwashing. After the war, social psy-

TABLE 11-1
Milestones in Social Psychology

1895	Gustave LeBon studies the behavior of *The Crowd.*
1897	Norman Triplett conducts the first social psychological experiment on social facilitation.
1926	Muzafer Sherif studies norm formation using the autokinetic effect (the illusion of movement given by a stationary pinpoint of light in a totally black room). Subjects' judgment of how far the light moves is influenced by the judgments of other observers.
1927	L. L. Thurstone demonstrates that attitudes can be measured using scaling techniques.
1934	R. T. LaPiere demonstrates that attitudes and behavior are not always consistent.
1936	Sherif explains the process of conformity in *The Psychology of Social Norms.*
1939	Kurt Lewin et al. investigate the effect of leadership styles on group performance.
1945	Lewin founds the Research Center for Group Dynamics, located first at MIT and later at the University of Michigan.
1946	Solomon Asch demonstrates the influence of cognitive set in impression formation (see Chapter 12).
1949	Hovland and his Yale collaborators publish *Experiments on Mass Communication,* the first of five influential volumes on attitude change and persuasion.
1951	Solomon Asch demonstrates conformity to erroneous peer judgments in a line-judging task.
1953	The Yale group under Carl Hovland publishes its findings on persuasion and attitude change.
1957	Leon Festinger proposes a theory of cognitive dissonance, a model of attitude change based on the principle that individuals strive for consistency.
1958	Fritz Heider offers another consistency model in his book *The Psychology of Interpersonal Relations,* which lays the foundation for attribution theory.
1962	Stanley Schachter and Jerome Singer offer a theory that emotions are a function of both physiological arousal and social cues (see Chapter 7).
1963	Stanley Milgram reports the first in a series of studies on obedience to authority, showing that subjects will obey an experimenter's command to administer intense electric shock to another human being.
1967	Harold H. Kelley publishes "Attribution Theory in Social Psychology," one of the earliest works on attribution theory. Attribution research is a dominant theme of the 1970s.
1968	Bibb Latané and John Darley report their research on bystander intervention, explaining why bystanders often fail to help people in emergencies.
1970	Philip Zimbardo and his associates conduct the famous prison simulation study in the basement of Stanford University's psychology department.
1980s	Attribution theory gives way to other aspects of social cognition; applied social psychology grows in importance.

Sources: Adapted from Penrod, S. (1985). *Social psychology.* Englewood Cliffs, NJ: Prentice-Hall. Perlman, D., & Cozby, P. (1983). *Social psychology.* New York: CBS. Deaux, K., & Wrightsman, L. S. (1984). *Social psychology in the 80s* (4th ed.). Monterey, CA: Brooks/Cole.

chologists returned to more theoretical issues — especially the study of how attitudes are organized and how they affect and are affected by social behavior, an area of research still very much alive today.

During the 1970s, another aspect of social cognition captured the interest of social psychologists — the study of **attribution.** First introduced to social psychology in 1958 by Fritz Heider, attribution is the cognitive process through which individuals reach conclusions about the causes of behavior. Today, many social psychologists study the process of attribution as well as other types of social inference.

Although Table 11-1 outlines the major milestones in the history of social psychology and supplies a brief overview to this chapter, it is necessarily incomplete. In addition to investigating the processes involved in conformity, attitude change, and attribution, social psychologists study the products of these and other processes, especially as they relate to helping and harming others. Here we examine the various areas of research within social psychology in the approximate order of their evolution, focusing, when appropriate, on their implications for both prosocial and aggressive behaviors.

SOCIAL FACILITATION

In 1954, Roger Bannister accomplished a feat many people thought was impossible — he ran a mile in under four minutes. When Bannister first ran the "miracle mile," he did so under specifically orchestrated circumstances: he had a different runner pace him at just under 60 seconds for each quarter-mile lap. Would he have broken the record if he had run the race alone?

During the late nineteenth century, bicycle racing was a popular sport; Norman Triplett was an avid fan. Noting that cyclists consistently achieved faster times when paced by a cyclist than when racing against the clock, Triplett set up an experiment to find out whether there was a general tendency for people to perform better in the presence of others than when performing alone. He assessed the peak performance of ten- to twelve-year-old children winding fishing reels alone and compared the results to their peak performance when working with another child. Triplett found that 50% of the children performed better when working with another child than when working alone, 25% performed the same, and 25% performed worse.

Although Triplett's findings may seem obvious in view of the common wisdom that people perform better when competing with others, this belief is misguided in two respects. First, people sometimes perform better in the presence of others even when not competing. Second, they sometimes perform worse. In 1924, Floyd Allport asked subjects to perform a variety of tasks while alone and while in the presence of others. Allport found the subjects performed better in the presence of others on most of the tasks — such tasks as canceling vowels and multiplying simple numbers — even when there was no competition involved. Unexpectedly, however, Allport's subjects performed worse in the presence of others on such other tasks as refuting Greek epigrams (short witty sayings).

Following the research of Triplett and Allport, many psychologists conducted studies on the effects of the mere presence of others; indeed, this virtually was the only problem studied in experimental social psychology for several decades. Some studies found the presence of others produced **social facilitation:** it facilitated or improved performance in humans as well as in such nonhuman species as dogs, rats, ants, and cockroaches (see Box 11-1). Other studies, however, found the presence of others produced **social inhibition.**

In 1965, Robert Zajonc published an article that supplied a resolution of the conflicting results from research on social facilitation and social inhibition. Zajonc suggested that the presence of others (from the same species) produces

Box 11-1
Social Facilitation in the Lowly Cockroach

Zajonc's theory requires that for social facilitation to occur, the others present must be of the same species as the organism being studied. In an experiment by Zajonc, Heigartner, and Herman (1969), the organisms were cochroaches. The experimenters put the cochroaches into the front end of a plexiglass tube that was dark and then lit the front end only. Because cockroaches are photophobic — they avoid light — when the front end was lit, they raced to the dark end of the tube. Zajonc and his colleagues recorded both the time it took the cockroaches to run the length of the tube and their maximum speed. Then the experimenters placed an egg carton of cockroaches beneath the plexiglass tube — an audience, if you wish — and repeated the procedure. They found the cockroaches ran faster with an audience than without one.

The dominant response of this task is to run to the dark — a correct and well-learned response for cockroaches. As expected, the presence of others produced social facilitation. If Zajonc's theory is right, the cockroaches should perform worse in the presence of others on a task for which their dominant response is incorrect. To test this, he placed the cockroaches in a plexiglass T-maze that contained a darkened compartment at the end of one of the T junctions. Learning where to turn to reach the dark is difficult for a cockroach: the dominant response is not necessarily the correct response. As with the first task, the cockroaches practiced alone in the T-maze until their performance reached a peak; then the experimenters introduced an audience of cockroaches. As predicted, the cockroaches ran slower and made more errors in the presence of an audience than when alone. The presence of others produced social inhibition for this less deeply ingrained response, demonstrating a perhaps uncomfortable parallel between the behavior of humans and the behavior of cockroaches.

---

an elevation in the level of arousal of individuals performing tasks and that elevated arousal increases the probability individuals will make a dominant response. A **dominant response** is one that is habitual, well-learned, or innate. In situations where the dominant response is correct (for example, on such simple tasks as winding fishing reels and canceling vowels), increased arousal (evoked by the presence of others) facilitates performance. In situations where the dominant response is incorrect, as is likely for such difficult tasks as refuting Greek epigrams, increased arousal produces social inhibition. But why does the mere presence of others evoke arousal? According to Zajonc (1980), the reason is that it creates uncertainty: the presence of others makes people alert and prepared to respond.

Zajonc's suggestion that the presence of others increases arousal and that heightened arousal facilitates some tasks and inhibits others is generally accepted. Some psychologists, however, question Zajonc's explanation of why the presence of others evokes arousal. Three other explanations have been advanced. First, Cottrell (1972) suggested that people become aroused in the presence of others because they become apprehensive of being evaluated by them. In support of this idea, Cottrell and his colleagues showed that social facilitation does not occur

Box 11-2
Social Loafing

Social-facilitation research focuses on the performance of tasks reached by individuals working alone. When several individuals are required to work together on a common task, the presence of others tends to produce *social loafing* — individuals tend to expend less effort to complete a common task than an individual task. For example, studies have found that individuals put forth less effort when they are part of a group pulling on a rope and part of a group charged with making noise by applauding or shouting than when they perform the activities alone (Latané, Williams, & Harkins, 1979). The key to social loafing appears to lie in the anonymity provided by group membership. People expend less effort to complete a task when their individual performance cannot be identified; when each contribution can be identified, they put forth more effort.

when subjects perform tasks in the presence of others who are blindfolded (and therefore cannot evaluate their performance). Second, Sanders, Baron, and Moore (1978) proposed that the presence of others competes with the demands of tasks for a performer's attention, and that the ensuing conflict produces arousal. According to Sanders and his colleagues, the performance of well-learned tasks is enhanced through the arousal produced by distraction but the performance of poorly learned tasks is inhibited by the interference with attention. Studies showing that noise and other types of nonsocial distraction enhance and inhibit performance in much the same manner as the presence of others support this explanation (Sanders, 1981). Third, Bond (1982) suggested that when people perform before an audience, they are motivated to project an image of competence. When this image is supported (on easy tasks), people gain confidence and their performance improves; when people make mistakes (on difficult tasks), they become embarrassed and their performance deteriorates. Zajonc's theory and the three competing theories are outlined in Figure 11-1.

All four explanations of social facilitation are plausible — at least for human subjects — but which is correct? Recently, Bond and Titus (1983) performed a **meta-analysis** of some 241 studies on social facilitation in human subjects. A meta-analysis involves determining the statistical significance of the combined results of all available studies on an issue. The results of Bond and Titus' meta-analysis provide the strongest support for Zajonc's *mere presence theory,* with Cottrell's *evaluation apprehension theory* receiving the weakest support. There was insufficient evidence to evaluate the distraction-conflict or self-presentation theories. No doubt the last word has yet to be written; nevertheless, it appears that people may facilitate and inhibit the performance of others by their mere presence — even when they are unable to evaluate it.

Although research on social facilitation has focused primarily on such nonsocial tasks as winding fishing reels and solving verbal problems, we also would expect the mere presence of others to affect people's tendency to engage in antisocial and prosocial behaviors. Let us therefore examine this possibility by considering the effect of crowds and mobs on people's tendency to engage in antisocial behaviors and then consider the effect of bystanders on people's tendency to help others in emergencies.

Zajonc's Drive Theory

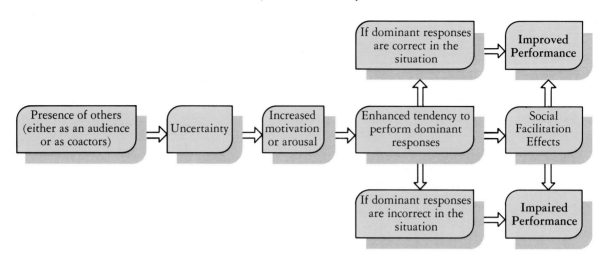

Cottrell's Evaluation Apprehension Theory

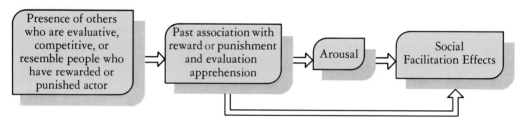

FIGURE 11-1

Theories of Social Facilitation *Source:* Adapted from Baron, R. A., & Byrne, D. (1981). *Social psychology* (3rd ed., pp. 413 and 420). Boston: Allyn and Bacon.

MOB PSYCHOLOGY — ANONYMITY, DEINDIVIDUATION, AND SELF-AWARENESS

In 1930, a black man named James Irwin was chained to a tree; and while approximately one thousand people watched, "members of the mob cut off his fingers and toes joint by joint," pulled his teeth out with wire pliers, castrated him, hung "his mangled but living body . . . on a tree by the arms," lit him on fire, and shot him. (Raper, 1933, pp. 143–44) James Irwin was one of 3,000 black people lynched by mobs in the southern United States.

In 1967, a major black neighborhood in Detroit exploded in a riot that lasted for several days. In the end, 43 people were killed, and 683 buildings were damaged or destroyed by fire.

In the spring of 1985, a mob of British soccer fans broke through a barrier at a soccer stadium; in the resulting melee, several fans were killed and injured.

Sanders, Baron, and Moore's Distraction-Conflict Theory

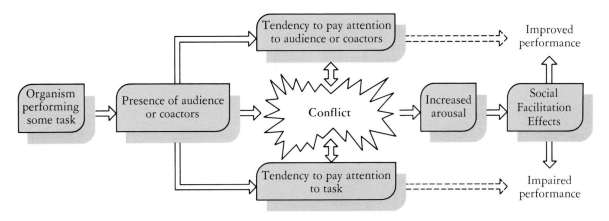

Bond's Self-image Theory

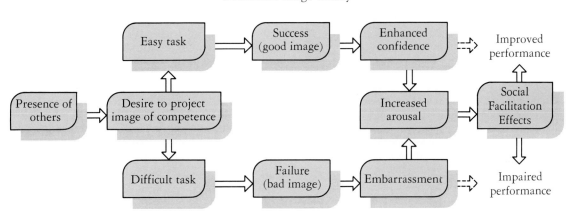

People sometimes behave in utterly cruel and malicious ways when they are in crowds or mobs. In 1895, French physician Gustav LeBon suggested that when individuals form a crowd, they become possessed by "a sort of collective mind which makes them feel, think, and act in a manner quite different from that in which each individual of them would feel, think, and act were he in a state of isolation" (1968, pp. 22–23). LeBon's analysis influenced Freud, who suggested that people possess a need—derived from their relationship to their fathers, to submit to more powerful forces, whether embodied in author-

ities or groups. Both LeBon and Freud emphasized the suggestibility of human nature (consider again the role of hypnosis in Freud's early work; see Chapters 1 and 14) and the tendency for people in groups to regress to primitive states.

Two decades after the publication of LeBon's book on crowds, Floyd Allport (1924) opened his early text on social psychology with an attack on what he called the "group fallacy," with LeBon's idea of group mind his primary target. Allport suggested that several factors contribute to collective behavior, including social facilitation, emotional contagion, feelings of anonymity,

When a dominant ethnic group cannot maintain social control through ordinary, legal means, it sometimes employs extraordinary, illegal means.

diffusion of responsibility, imitation, and **deindividuation** — the loss of a sense of personal identity.

Recent analyses of collective behavior have expanded on Allport's early suggestions. Imagine yourself a member of a crowd or mob; three aspects of this position could affect your social behavior. First, as one of many, you would be difficult to identify individually. This might make you feel anonymous and reduce your sense of accountability. Second, if other group members were engaging in antisocial behavior, there also would be a diffusion of responsibility. You alone could not be blamed for the consequences of the group's actions. Third, the behavior of other group members would set a sort of standard or norm for your behavior (see section on conformity) and supply models to imitate.

Together, these factors create a reduced sense of **public self-awareness:** the sense that other people are watching you and will hold you accountable for your behavior.

Now imagine your group is a dynamic, intense, cohesive unit involved in some arousing activity — such as a rock concert. This situation would be expected to evoke a somewhat different experience from the one we just considered. Your attention would be directed outward and toward the activity; you would tend to lose consciousness of your self. You might become so engrossed in the group's activities that you would forget who you are — losing your sense of identity, self-consciousness, and **private self-awareness.** The subjective state associated with a loss of private self-awareness is called *deindividuation.* Singing, dancing, chanting, and alcohol (and other drugs) would be expected to help induce this state.

According to Prentice-Dunn and Rogers (1983), both a loss of public self-awareness and a loss of private self-awareness may lead to deviant behavior, but through different routes (see Figure 11-2). Public self-awareness leads to rational calculations of the probability of being punished; deindividuation involves an irrational state of altered consciousness. Note that in their model neither factor (lowered public and lowered private self-awareness) is expected to produce deviant behavior by itself; both factors make people susceptible to the influence of what Prentice-Dunn and Rogers call **behavioral cues** — such as the behavior of other people in a group, especially leaders (models). For example, most people at rock concerts dance, but if someone were to start a fight, fighting might replace dancing as a dominant behavioral cue.

What evidence is there for the model presented in Figure 11-2? Several studies have found that conditions that increase anonymity lead to increased antisocial behavior. For example, Zimbardo (1970) found that female undergraduate students who wore hoods over their heads, were not allowed to refer to one another by name, and interacted in a darkened room administered electric shocks to a peer that were twice as long as those administered by subjects who wore large name tags, were encouraged to refer to each other by name, and interacted in a well-lit room. In a

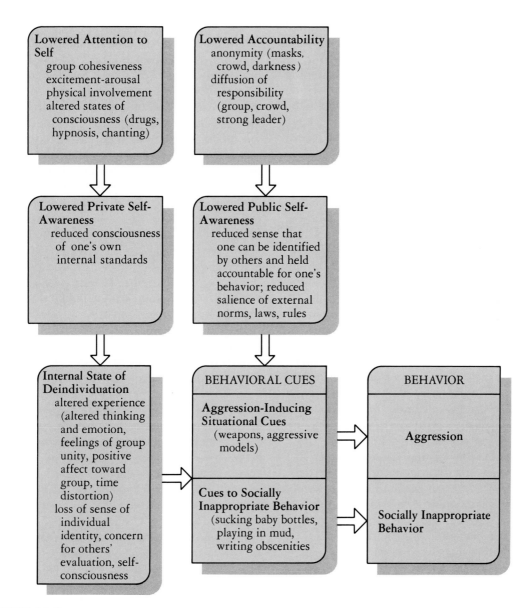

FIGURE 11-2

A Model of Deindividuation and Antisocial Behavior   According to this model, there are two often-confused paths to deviant behavior.   Individuals may engage in deviant behavior because they feel anonymous and unaccountable or because they lose their sense of private self-awareness and become deindividuated.   Low accountability and low self-awareness lead to antisocial behavior only in the presence of appropriate behavioral cues.   *Source:* Adapted from Prentice-Dunn, S., & Rogers, R. W. (1983).   Deindividuation in aggression.   In R. G. Geen & E. I. Donnerstein (Eds.), *Aggression: Theoretical and empirical reviews* (Vol. 2).   New York: Academic Press.

naturalistic study of some 1,300 children who were tricking and treating on Halloween, Diener et al. (1976) found that children who were the most difficult to recognize were the most likely to steal money and candy.   These investigators also found that children were more likely to steal when they were in groups than when they were alone.   In a study involving some 23 cultures, Watson (1973) found a strong positive correlation between the extent to which warriors masked their identities through disguise, face paint, and other means and their tendency to torture and execute their captives. And in an analysis of 21 incidents of a potential suicide victim threatening to jump from a building, Mann (1981) discovered individuals were most likely to bait the victim by yelling "Jump!" when they were part of a large crowd and when it was dark. Size of the crowd and darkness helped obscure the identities of individuals in the group.

In all these studies, the individuals involved were relatively anonymous and engaged in harmful or deceptive behavior. A study by Gergen, Gergen, and Barton (1973) demonstrates that other, more affiliative types of urges may be released in circumstances where people cannot be identified. Gergen, Gergen, and Barton (1973) placed groups of six men and six women in a completely dark room, told them there was nothing special they wanted them to do, and ensured they understood they would never meet the other individuals in the experiment. The experimenters left the subjects in total darkness for one hour, tape recorded what they said, and asked them what happened after the experience ended. The results revealed that during the first 15 minutes, subjects primarily explored the room and engaged in idle chatter. During the next 30 minutes, the conversation concerned more serious matters. During the final 15 minutes something interesting occurred: most of the subjects got physical. Half of the subjects hugged another person, some becoming quite intimate, and 80% reported feeling sexually aroused.

It is important to note that in all the studies under consideration, there are factors other than anonymity that may have evoked deviant behavior. For example, the hoods and white coats worn by subjects in Zimbardo's 1970 study resembled Ku Klux Klan costumes, which perhaps caused subjects to assume the experimenter expected them to behave aggressively. In support of this criticism, Johnson and Downing (1979) found that subjects dressed in surgical masks and surgical gowns were *less* likely to administer shock than subjects whose names and identities were emphasized. The Ku Klux Klan hoods apparently supplied different behavioral cues than the surgical garb provided.

Researchers also have found that conditions that lower private self-awareness induce individ-

uals to engage in aggressive and socially inappropriate behaviors. In an early study, Festinger, Pepitone, and Newcomb (1952) found that small undergraduate groups, meeting to discuss the implications of a survey that ostensibly demonstrated that 87% of college students harbor deep-seated negative feelings toward their parents, were most critical of their parents in those groups that were the most engaging and lively. These investigators also found that individuals in uninhibited, critical groups were less likely to remember who made the criticisms and more likely to enjoy the groups than those in more restrained groups. Other studies have found that members of groups who engage in heated discussions of sex or who engage in such lively activities as singing and chanting lose their self-consciousness and, in addition, become increasingly inclined to engage in such uninhibited activities as painting their face, playing in mud, and writing obscenities (Diener, 1977).

If reduced private self-awareness and deindividuation lead to impulsive, uninhibited, and immoral behaviors, then factors that increase self-awareness should produce the opposite effect. Duval and Wicklund (1972) have suggested that a state they call **objective self-awareness** — being aware of one's self as an object — encourages people to evaluate their behavior in terms of their internal standards. These investigators and others have induced objective self-awareness in subjects by playing tape recordings of their voices, positioning them in front of cameras, and exposing them to their images in mirrors (see Ickes, Layden, & Barnes, 1978). Studies have found that when objective self-awareness is increased, subjects are less likely to cheat on tests (Diener & Wallbom, 1976) and more likely to do what they say they will do (Froming, Walker, & Lopyan, 1982), to accept blame for a hypothetical car accident (Duval & Wicklund, 1972), and to be self-critical (Ickes, Wicklund, & Ferris, 1973). It is interesting that the state of objective self-awareness typically is not a pleasant one. Feeling self-conscious can be awkward and inhibiting; when self-reflection makes people aware of their shortcomings, they may shun it (Duval & Wicklund, 1972).

In many situations the conditions that give rise to reduced public self-awareness also give rise to reduced private self-awareness. Engaging in intense group discussions, such as those studied by Festinger et al., is a case in point. However, there also are circumstances in which one type of self-awareness is reduced while the other type is increased. For example, Mathes and Guest (1976) asked subjects to volunteer to walk through a university cafeteria carrying a sign reading "Masturbation is fun." We can safely assume this task would **individuate** people — draw attention to them and make them quite self-conscious. Nonetheless, Mathes and Guess (1976) found that subjects were much more likely to volunteer when they could be anonymous — wear coveralls and a ski mask — than when they could not be anonymous.

Research on mob behavior, self-awareness, and deindividuation demonstrates that under certain circumstances, the presence of others induces people to behave irresponsibly. The research we now consider has produced similar results in a different context. At some point in life, virtually everyone encounters a stranger who needs help. Sometimes there are bystanders present, sometimes there are not. Are people more likely to intervene in emergencies when other people are present or when they are alone?

HELPING IN EMERGENCIES

In March of 1964, Kitty Genovese was attacked and murdered in New York City while 38 witnesses watched.

> For more than half an hour thirty-eight respectable, law-abiding citizens in Queens watched a killer stalk and stab a woman in three separate attacks in Kew Gardens. Twice the sound of their voices and the sudden glow of their bedroom lights interrupted him and frightened him off. Each time he returned, sought her out and stabbed her again. Not one person telephoned the police during the assault; one witness called after the woman was dead. (*New York Times,* March 27, 1964).

> An 18-year-old switchboard operator, working alone, is sexually assaulted. She momentarily escapes and runs naked and bleeding to the street, screaming for help. Forty pedestrians passively watch as the rapist tries to drag her back inside. Fortunately, two police officers happen by and arrest the assailant. (Myers, 1983, p. 382)

Why did no one intervene to help Kitty Genovese or the switchboard operator? In 1969, Latané and Rodin designed an experiment to investigate what has come to be called **bystander intervention.** They arranged for subjects working on a questionnaire to hear a crash, a scream, and the cry, "Oh, my god, my foot" coming from an adjacent room that a women had just entered. Some subjects were alone and some were in the presence of others. Seventy percent of the subjects who were alone went to help. Seventy percent of the subjects who were with two friends also helped. However, for subjects who were with two strangers, the number who helped fell to 40%. And for subjects who were with two colleagues of the experimenter who remained passive and acted like nothing had happened, the number of helpers plummeted to 7%.

In the years following Latané and Rodin's early study, social psychologists have conducted more than 50 studies on bystander intervention (see Latané, Nida, & Wilson, 1981). Researchers have arranged for accomplices to appear to fall off ladders, to collapse on subways, to be electrocuted, to faint, to undergo seizures, to be attacked, and even to get robbed. In almost all these studies experimenters have found a **bystander effect** — subjects are less likely to help in the presence of passive strangers than when alone. We can confidently conclude that the presence of passive strangers tends to inhibit people's tendency to help in emergencies. But why?

In their early work, Latané and Darley (1970) suggested three processes that might inhibit people from helping: fear of embarrassment, modeling the passiveness of others, and diffusion of responsibility. Research has indicated all three processes may be involved. Consider a study by Latané and Darley (1976). These investigators designed an experiment in which they varied the channels of communication between subjects and another bystander. The experiment contained the following conditions:

1. *Subject alone.*
2. *No communication* — subject and bystander could not see one another but subject was aware bystander was present.
3. *One-way communication* — subject could see bystander but not vice versa.
4. *One-way communication* — bystander could see subject but not vice versa.
5. *Full communication* — subject and bystander could see one another.

Latané and Darley reasoned that subjects should help most when *alone* because there would be no reason to fear embarrassment, no opportunity to diffuse responsibility, and no opportunity to model inaction. The investigators expected subjects to help somewhat less in the *no-communication condition.* Although there was no reason to fear embarrassment and no opportunity to model passiveness, the responsibility was not solely theirs because they knew another bystander was available. The investigators expected still less help in the two conditions involving one-way communication because, in addition to diffusion of responsibility, either fear of embarrassment (when the bystander could see the subject) or modeling passiveness (when the subject could see the passive bystander) were free to inhibit any help. Finally, Latané and Darley expected the least help in the full-communication condition, where all three processes could exert an inhibiting effect.

The cumulative percent who intervened to help in each of the conditions of the Latané and Darley study are displayed in Figure 11-3. The results reveal that, as so many other studies have found, bystanders are most likely to help when they are alone. More to the point, there was a systematic increase in inhibition (decrease in help) as the number of inhibitive processes increased. The inhibition was least in the no-communication condition, where only diffusion of responsibility was available as an excuse for not helping. More inhibition occurred when one channel of communication was opened and either modeling passiveness or fear of embarrassment was added to diffusion of responsibility. Finally, the least help occurred in the full-communication condition, where all three processes were free to inhibit intervention.

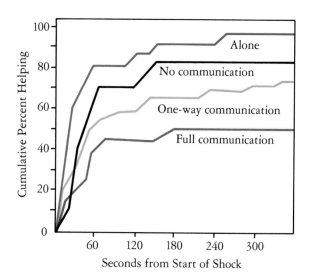

FIGURE 11-3
Bystander Intervention in the Latané and Darley Study More than 90% of the bystanders helped when alone, compared to approximately 50% in the full-communication mode — where diffusion of responsibility, modeling passiveness, and fear of embarrassment were free to inhibit intervention. *Source:* Latané, B., & Darley, J. M. (1976). *Help in a crisis: Bystander response to an emergency.* Morristown, NJ: General Learning Press.

The goal of the Latané and Darley (1976) experiment and of many other studies on bystander intervention was to explain why people are less likely to help in emergencies when they are alone than when they are with other bystanders. But there are many factors beside the presence of other bystanders that affect helping in emergencies. Piliavin, Dovidio, Gaertner, and Clark (1981) have developed a comprehensive model that organizes the many factors found to increase and decrease the probability that people will help in emergencies (see Figure 11-4). One way to understand the model in Figure 11-4 is to answer the following questions. Would you be more likely to help a victim who fell down in front of you or who asked you for help than a victim who fell down mutely a block away *(situational characteristics)?* Would you expect an impulsive, extroverted, uninhibited, and empathic person to be more likely to help than an inhibited introvert *(bystander characteristics)?* Would you be more likely to help a filthy drunk or a well-dressed fellow student *(victim characteristics)?* Would you be more likely to help some-

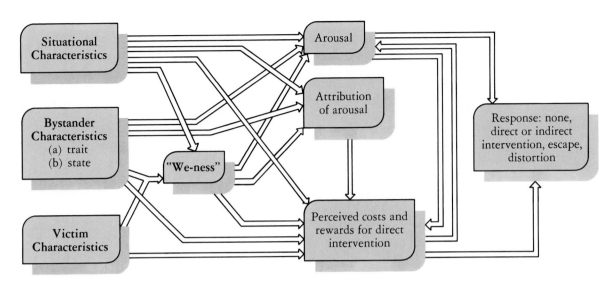

FIGURE 11-4

Piliavin's Model of Bystander Intervention   The model presents an analysis of the causes of helping in emergencies, emphasizing the interaction between (a) person and situation and (b) cognitive and affective reactions.   *Source:* Piliavin, J. A., Dovidio, J. F., Gaertner, S. L., & Clark, R. D., III (1981). *Emergency intervention* (p. 240). New York: Academic Press.

one who is similar to you or someone who is different *(we-ness)?*   Turning to the middle blocks of Figure 11-4, you next answer questions about the ways in which characteristics of situations, characteristics of bystanders, and characteristics of victims interact to produce various *levels of arousal.*   Whether arousal motivates helping or not depends, to a great extent, on how people interpret it.   If they *attribute* their arousal to the distress of the victim ("I feel bad because she feels bad"), they are more likely to help than if they attribute it to other factors (Batson & Coke, 1981).   And whether they help or not also depends on the perceived consequences of helping (and not helping).   Costs of helping include such factors as time, energy, fear of embarrassment, and harm.   Costs of not helping include such factors as public censure and distress caused by empathizing with someone who is suffering.   Studies reviewed by Piliavin et al. (1981) have examined the connection between all of the boxes in the model as they give rise individually or in various combinations to direct intervention, indirect intervention (for example, telephoning the police) or no intervention.

The results of studies on intervention in emergencies do not reflect well on human na-

ture.   In fact, they suggest that the principle that governs helping is a selfish one: when people encounter an emergency, they are motivated to minimize their costs and behave in a way that causes them the least displeasure.   Fortunately, however, the picture is not as bleak as it may appear.   Investigators have found that in certain types of emergency, almost everyone will intervene to assist people who need help, regardless of how many bystanders are present and without any apparent concern about the consequences to themselves.   Piliavin et al. have labeled this phenomenon **impulsive helping** (see Box 11-3).

We conclude our discussion of the unobtrusive forms of social influence with a summary. We opened by examining the effects of the mere presence of others on such nonsocial activities as winding fishing reels, and decided that increases in levels of arousal induce social facilitation and social inhibition.   We also saw that arousal plays an important role in mob behavior and deindividuation.   Extrapolating from research on social facilitation, we might expect the aggressive and sexual behaviors that occur in groups to be dominant responses.   Certainly Freud would have agreed.   Or perhaps the responses become dominant when deviant members of groups supply be-

Box 11-3
Impulsive Helping

Piliavin et al. (1981) suggest that bystanders weigh the costs and benefits of intervening, and that the result of this *hedonic calculus* determines whether they help or not. According to this idea, people should be least likely to help in life-threatening (high-cost) situations. In the early research on bystander intervention, studies generally supported the hedonic calculus model; however, later studies occasionally reported an anomalous result: bystanders would intervene almost reflexively, whether alone or in a crowd, apparently oblivious to personal costs and consequences. Indeed, in one study in which an individual appeared to have been electrocuted, bystanders behaved irrationally by grabbing the victim even though, had the emergency been real, they would have endangered their own lives (Clark & Word, 1974). In another study, subjects intervened to stop an "attempted rape" in which the attacker sounded very threatening (Anderson, 1974).

As the number of studies that found such *impulsive helping* grew, it became clear that such aid was evoked in situations involving clear, realistic, and imposing emergencies and that impulsive helping was facilitated when the intervener had prior involvement with the victim (see figure). Piliavin et al. note: "Not coincidentially, the same factors that facilitate impulsive helping —clarity, reality, involvement with the victim—have also been demonstrated to be related to greater levels of bystander arousal" (p. 238). These investigators conclude that the dynamics of impulsive helping are qualitatively different from the dynamics of other kinds of bystander intervention. They suggest that when individuals encounter an emergency they cannot avoid, they become flooded with intense arousal. This arousal produces a narrowing of attention (Easterbrook, 1959) directed toward the plight of the victim. "Cost considerations become peripheral and not attended to" (p. 239), and observers help reflexively. Piliavin et al. speculate that "there may be an evolutionary basis for . . . impulsive helping" (p. 180).

A Model of Impulsive Helping Individuals who encounter an event process information at a preconscious level and categorize the event as (a) nothing, (b) something interesting, or (c) an emergency. If the event is categorized as something interesting (b), the individual experiences a wait-and-see orienting response. If the event is categorized as an emergency (c), the individual experiences a *fight-or-flight* reaction that gives rise to an impulsive response. *Source:* From Piliavin, J. A., Dovidio, J. F., Gaertner, S. L., & Clark, R. D., III (1981). *Emergency intervention* (p. 244). New York: Academic Press.

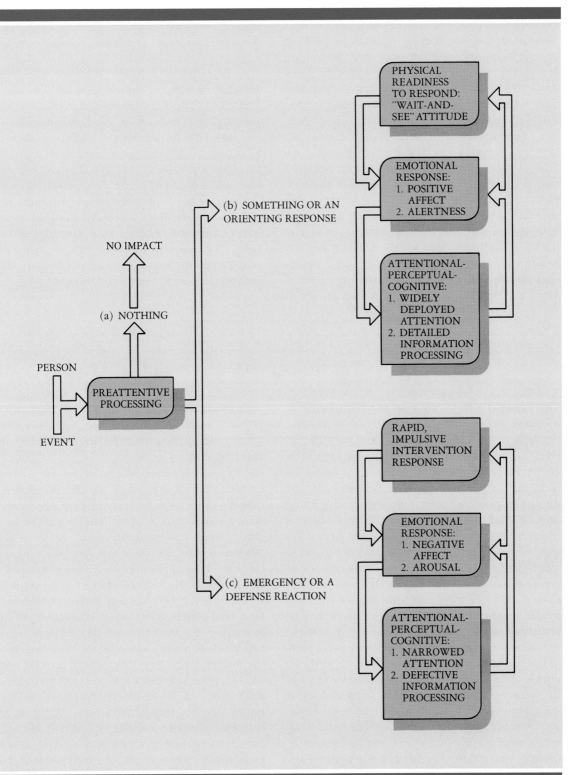

havioral cues by behaving in antisocial ways. According to Piliavin et al. (1981), arousal also plays an important role in emergency helping. Emergencies increase arousal, and bystanders search the circumstances of the event for guidance (behavioral cues) about what they should do. If the other bystanders remain passive, then doing nothing becomes the dominant response.

Recent analyses of social facilitation implicate self-presentation and embarrassment. Latané and Darley identify fear of embarrassment as one of the three main factors that inhibit people from helping in emergencies. We might expect public self-consciousness to increase fear of embarrassment but private self-consciousness and deindividuation to decrease it. In addition, diffusion of responsibility appears to play a significant role in mob behavior and helping in emergencies. Such feelings as "We're all in it together" and "I'm not the only one to blame" appear to supply a justification for engaging in antisocial behavior and failing to help people in need.

The forms of social influence considered thus far are minimal in the sense that no one intended to influence anyone's action. The audiences, members of mobs, and bystanders thus far discussed did not attempt to influence others deliberately. They did not attempt to set a standard or argue a position. Indeed, they did not even state their point of view. Yet people do try to influence other people. They advance their opinions, sometimes forcefully, and attempt to induce others to change their attitudes and beliefs. We now consider some of the more direct methods employed to persuade people, to induce compliance, and to instill conformity.

THE DEVELOPMENT OF GROUP NORMS

All social systems are governed by **norms** — standards of expected behavior — whether the norms are institutionalized as laws, formalized in books of etiquette, integrated within social roles, or popularized as fads. Norms exert a powerful influence on social behavior. If you doubt the power of their influence, try violating one. The next time you shop, try bargaining with the clerk over the listed price of some item ("I'll give you a dollar for this pen, and not a nickel more"). Failure to abide by the norm implicit in your role as customer is unlikely to be well received. Or try eating with your fingers, standing four inches from a friend when speaking to her, or refusing to shake an extended hand. All of these behaviors are perfectly acceptable in other parts of the world because they are consistent with the norms of those countries. You probably will not try violating the norms we have suggested; even imagining such violations may make you cringe.

We are born into societies that have well-established norms. How we come to internalize them or adopt them was discussed in Chapter 10. Here we raise a different question: How do norms originate? To investigate this issue, we start with a situation that is as free as possible from social norms. Early social psychologist Muzafer Sherif (1936) attempted to create such a context in a rather ingenious way.

From his experience with the study of perception, Sherif was aware of the **autokinetic effect** — the illusion (described in Chapter 4) in which a stationary spot of light appears to move when viewed in total darkness. Sherif placed subjects alone in dark rooms and asked them to estimate how many inches a stationary spot of light moved. He found that although initially the estimate given by a subject varied considerably from trial to trial, it eventually stabilized: the subject came to report that the spot of light moved approximately the same distance each time he or she made a judgment. Sherif believed this stabilization reflected the development of an **individual norm.** He found different people developed quite different individual norms. What would happen, wondered Sherif, if individuals were brought together in a group and asked to state their estimates aloud? Would each individual retain his or her original norm? Would individuals join with norms similar to theirs and develop shared norms? Or would the group develop one common norm?

The results of Sherif's experiments revealed that as the experiment progressed, each subject's estimate began to change until, ultimately, all subjects gave the same estimate; that is, a **group norm** developed (see Figure 11-5). Although the group norm that emerged was a compromise among the individual norms, it was not a simple average. Some individuals changed less than others; they were more influential in determining the group norm. Sherif found that once individuals adopted the group norm, they retained it when tested individually at a later date.

Although the results of Sherif's study are more a demonstration of how individual norms are transformed into group norms than a demonstration of how norms originate, they are nonetheless significant. They suggest that when people do not share an established frame of reference, they construct one, and that the norms of groups may well be different from the norms of individuals. The explanation given by Sherif for the emergence of a group norm was that people need to define reality and, in ambiguous situations, tend to rely on information from others. There are, however, two other possible explanations: individuals may have changed their estimates so as not to offend each other or in order to demonstrate group solidarity. Subsequent research has supported Sherif's explanation as well as the other two. In support of Sherif's original explanation, Alexander, Zucker, and Brody (1970) found that explaining the autokinetic effect to subjects (explaining that the light actually does not move) suppresses the formation of a group norm. Presumably there is no need to define real-

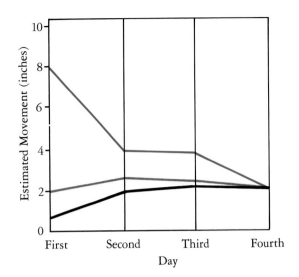

FIGURE 11-5

The Formation of Group Norms On the first day of the Sherif experiment, three subjects made individual estimates of the apparent movement of a stationary point of light in a darkened room. Beginning with the second day, the subjects made group estimates. By the fourth day, the estimates of three subjects converged. *Source:* Adapted from Sherif, M., & Sherif, C. W. (1969). *Social psychology.* New York: Harper & Row.

ity when it has been defined by the experimenter. In support of the other two explanations, studies have found that if you give subjects an incentive to abide by their own judgments (for example, saying they reflect their personality), they adhere to them or even become more extreme (Montmollin, 1977). According to Riecken (1952), "The consensus that is reached in many cases is nothing but an agreement not to disagree" (p. 252): there is no distortion of reality.

CONFORMITY AND DISSENT

A central conflict faced by all social animals involves the extent to which they assert their individuality and the extent to which they go along with others. On the one hand, people strive for autonomy and independence; on the other hand, they seek to live in harmony with others. Although a certain amount of conformity is necessary if society is to function effectively, too much robs people of their identities and stifles social change. Every individual must strike a balance between going along with the crowd and being his or her own person.

The research on the formation of group norms we have considered gives rise to one model of how some people resolve the conflict between autonomy and conformity—they meet in democratic contexts, state their opinions, listen to the opinions of others, and reach a compromise. The model is valid when the opinions of group members are fairly similar, an exchange of ideas is possible, and the goal is to achieve consensus. But what about situations in which an individual's point of view is markedly different from that of the majority and where the person is quite sure he or she is right? What would you do in such a situation? Would you adhere to your view even though no one else agreed with you or would you relinquish your position and conform to the judgment of the group? Four decades ago, social psychologist Solomon Asch set out to explore this very issue.

Perhaps the best way to appreciate Asch's research is to act as one of his subjects. As you enter the room, six subjects are seated already and you are asked to take the remaining seat—second from the end. The experimenter announces that the experiment concerns the ability to make visual judgments and explains that to study the judgments, a slide will be projected onto the screen at the front of the room (Asch actually used flash cards). Each slide contains a vertical line labeled R (reference line) and three other vertical lines labeled A, B, and C (see Figure 11-6). Your task is to determine which of the lines (A, B, or C) is the same length as the reference line (R). The experimenter instructs you to call out your answers so he can record them.

FIGURE 11-6

Asch's Lines Subjects in Asch's conformity experiment were asked to identify the line that is the same length as the reference line (R). *Source:* Asch, S. E. (1955, November). Opinions and social pressure. *Scientific American, 193,* pp. 31–35.

The first slide is projected. It is obvious which line is equal to R and, one at a time, everybody calls it out. The same is true for the second slide. Just as you begin to think the task is ridiculously simple, events take an unexpected turn. The third slide is flashed. Although B clearly is the correct answer, the first subject calls out "A." You are surprised she has made an error on such a simple task. Your surprise turns to astonishment when, one by one, the remaining subjects call out "A." You find yourself in a dilemma. B looks the same size as R, but five other people have claimed that A is the same size. You give your answer, and the experiment continues. On one-third of the trials, the other subjects select the line that seems correct to you; on two-thirds of the trials, all other subjects select a line that seems incorrect. What would you do in such a situation? Would you conform to the judgment of the group or would you report what you saw?

The results of Asch's early (1951) studies revealed that, on average, subjects repeated the *incorrect* responses of the other subjects on 36.8% of the critical slides—they conformed to the judgment of the majority more than one-third of the time. (Asch did not find that one-third of the subjects conformed; rather, on average, subjects conformed on approximately one-third of the critical slides.) Approximately 75% of the subjects conformed on at least one trial and four of fifty subjects conformed on nearly all the critical slides. Thirteen subjects did not conform at all (see Figure 11-7).

As you probably have guessed by now, the other subjects were accomplices of the experimenter and were instructed when to give incorrect responses. Under normal conditions, subjects made virtually no errors on the critical lines. Thus, we can safely assume that the subjects' mistakes were induced by the responses of the accomplices.

Asch's findings surprised him. He expected to show that individuals submit to group pressure only when there is, in effect, no right answer, such as in Sherif's research. Thus

The Asch experiment exemplifies an experiment whose value lies in the fact that it falsified what it set out to verify. . . . It serves . . . as one of the most dramatic illustrations of conformity, of blindly going along with the group, even when the

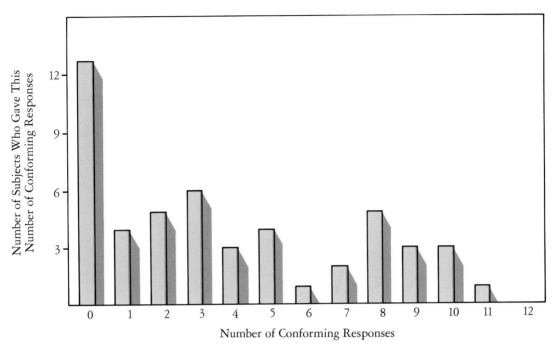

FIGURE 11-7

Asch's Conformity Study   Most subjects in Asch's experiment conformed on one or more trials.   Thirteen subjects did not conform on any trials.   *Source:* After Asch, S. E. (1951).   Effects of group pressure upon the modification and distortion of judgments.   In H. Guetzkow (Ed.), *Groups, leadership, and men.*   Pittsburgh, PA: Carnegie Press.

individual realizes that by doing so he turns his back on reality and truth.   (Moscovici, 1985, p. 349).

In the years following Asch's experiments, social psychologists conducted hundreds of studies on conformity.   The primary factors found to influence the amount of conformity in situations similar to the one created by Asch are summarized in Table 11-2.

When subjects in Asch's experiment heard all other subjects respond that a line that clearly differed from a comparison line was the same length, they faced a conflict between their perception of physical reality and the opinion of others.   Although the right answer seemed obvious to them, six people who saw things differently was quite strong evidence that something was wrong with their view of reality.   Subsequent research has found that factors that reduce subjects' confidence in their perception of reality (for example, ambiguous stimuli) and factors that increase the perceived competence of the group (for example, their expertise at the task) increase

informational social influence (see Table 11-2).   If only one other individual gives a nonconforming response — even if different from the response of the subject — the subject becomes much less likely to go along with the group (see Figure 11-8).   Although adding another dissenting view increases nonconformity even more, Asch found the influence of a minority peaks when its number reaches three.

In addition to the conflict associated with the discrepancy between the subjects' perception of reality and that of all others, subjects in experiments on conformity face another conflict — the conflict between being accepted by the group (fitting in, not rocking the boat, cooperating, and avoiding the others' wrath), on the one hand, and being honest about what they see, on the other hand.   Such factors as expectation of later interaction with members of the group, whether or not subjects' answers are anonymous, attractiveness of the group, and subjects' status in the group affect the degree to which they succumb to *normative social influence* (see Table 11-2).

TABLE 11-2
Factors Found to Influence Conformity

Factor	Effect	Supporting Evidence
Ambiguity of Stimulus	The less clear the correct answer, the greater the conformity.	When the comparison lines are similar to the reference line in the Asch situation, conformity increases (Asch, 1956). When subjects are required to make judgments about ambiguous stimuli (like the number of clicks produced by a fast metronome), conformity increases (Shaw, Rothschild, & Strickland, 1957).
Size of Group	Conformity will increase with group size.	Asch (1955) found that conformity is enhanced by group size to a maximum of three or four members and that additional members do not increase the degree of conformity. Wilder (1977), however, found that conformity continued to increase with larger groups when their members perceived their responses as independent from other members' responses.
Dissension in Group	When someone in a group disagrees with an otherwise unanimous majority, conformity will decrease. This reduction will be greatest when the dissenter gives the first response.	In the Asch experiment, conformity decreased substantially when a confederate broke the unanimity of the majority and gave the correct response (Asch, 1951). A reduction in conformity occurred in this situation even when the dissenting confederate gave an incorrect response (Allen & Levine, 1969; Asch, 1955; Wilder & Allen, 1977). However, when the task involves an opinion and not a perception of some physical stimulus, conformity will be reduced only when the dissenting response is correct (Allen & Levine, 1969; Wilder & Allen, 1977). Conformity is reduced most when the dissenter gives the first response, not when the dissent comes later (Morris & Miller 1975; Morris, Miller & Spangenberg, 1977).
Expectation of Later Interaction	If further interaction with a group is expected, conformity will increase.	(Lewis, Langan, & Hollander, 1972)
Attraction toward Group	Individuals will demonstrate greater conformity in groups to which they are attracted.	(Kelley & Shapiro, 1954; Wyer, 1966)
Low Status in Group	Within a group, low-status members will demonstrate greater conformity than high-status members.	Jones, Gergen, & Jones (1963) found that low-status ROTC cadets conformed more to the opinions of high-status cadets than the reverse.
Low Self-confidence of Subject	Individuals with low self-confidence will conform more than individuals with high self-confidence. Task competence, or expertise, will raise self-confidence and decrease conformity.	The more competent a person is when compared to others in the group, the less likely that person is to conform (Kelman, 1950; Snyder, Mischel, & Lott, 1960). The lower the self-esteem of a group member, the more likely that person is to conform (Stang, 1972).
Lack of Anonymity	Conformity is greater when individuals make their responses in public.	When subjects are required to make their judgments aloud, they conform more than when allowed to make their judgments privately (Deutsch & Gerard, 1955).

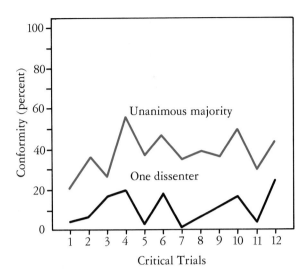

FIGURE 11-8

One Ally One individual who dissented caused a substantial decrease in group conformity. *Source:* Asch, S. E. (1955, November). Opinions and social pressure. *Scientific American, 193,* pp. 31–35.

The power of social influence and the costs of nonconformity are clearly revealed in studies that investigate the reaction of group members to dissenters. In an early study on the issue, Schachter (1951) found that people who refuse to go along with the opinion of a group (in this case a recommendation for dealing with a juvenile delinquent) eventually become rejected and ostracized. Following Schachter's study, other studies found that groups deal harshly with those who do not conform to their point of view.

For most people, the word *conformity* has a negative connotation. It suggests hordes of people blindly moving in the same direction (like a pack of lemmings) or row upon row of identical suburban houses (with a station wagon in the driveway and a family composed of mom, dad, and 2.3 children). But conformity does not necessarily carry these implications. Each individual has a limited and often biased store of information on which to base decisions. When making decisions, it seems reasonable to consider information from other people, especially from those with expertise in the area. Thus a *conforming response* may reflect the rational judgment of one who does not possess adequate information and who relies on others to fill the informational gap. Because in many social situations dissent can create unpleasantness, conformity may help preserve harmony. Nevertheless, there are obvious dangers to conformity. Failure to speak our minds against dangerous trends or attitudes (for example, racism) can easily be interpreted as support.

Minority Influence

If minority opinions were always rejected, all groups eventually would support the status quo and nothing would change. We know this is not the case. In some situations, nonconformists exert considerable influence on groups; in other situations, minority arguments prevail. What factors enhance the influence of dissenters and pave the way for innovative ideas? In a review of the literature, Tanford and Penrod (1984) concluded that two of the most important factors are size of the majority and size of the minority. According to these reviewers, minorities are most influential when the majority is small (six or fewer) and when two or more members of a minority advance a consistent position.

In addition to numbers, certain qualities of the individuals who argue minority positions are important. Hollander (1958) suggests that individuals who have a solid history of making contributions to groups acquire **idiosyncracy credits** that buy them the privilege of deviating from group norms. Moscovici (1985) suggests that the **behavioral style** of minority members af-

"All right, Bostock! Shape-up or ship out!"

Source: Drawing by Lorenz. © 1978 The New Yorker Magazine, Inc.

fects the amount of influence they exert. According to Moscovici, **consistency** is one of the most important aspects of behavioral style.

> When the majority of group members are faced with a consistent minority defending its position in terms that exclude all compromise — demonstrating thereby that uniformity will never be obtained by forcing it to give up its point of view — the majority will have no alternative but to change the group norm in the direction of the deviant position. (p. 391)

For example, consider the results of the following study.

Moscovici and Lange (1976) created groups of four naive subjects and two accomplices (a minority), and had them judge the color of slides. When both accomplices said "green" to all blue slides, they exerted a moderate influence on the majority (approximately one-third of the majority subjects increased their number of "green" responses). However, when the accomplices failed to maintain perfect consistency (for example, giving the correct "blue" response on one-third of the trials), they failed to influence the majority.

A second aspect of the behavioral style of minorities that increases their influence is perceived **autonomy.** Nemeth and Wachtler (1973) found that a single minority member who displayed autonomy and confidence by sitting at the head of a table and who consistently argued for his position influenced the majority (a group of four) in a mock jury trial. Conversely, a consistent accomplice seated beside the experimenter (and who, therefore, did not seem autonomous) did not influence the group.

A third influential aspect of the behavioral style of minorities is **rigidity.** To understand what happens when a minority rigidly advocates a position, we must distinguish between *direct* change (how much individuals publically change on an issue during or immediately following the exchange of opinions) and *indirect* change (how much individuals privately change on related issues in the days and weeks following the exchange of opinions). This difference sometimes is referred to in terms of **compliance** (publicly submitting to social pressure) and **conversion** (changing one's private attitudes and beliefs). Studies have shown that minorities that

rigidly argue their position fail to exert much direct influence on the majority; however, they do exert significant indirect influence (Papastamou, 1979). Indeed, some investigators have reported a tendency for majorities to induce compliance but not conversion, for minorities to induce conversion but not compliance, and a negative relationship between compliance and conversion (the greater the public compliance, the less the private conversion). Consider a study by Moscovici and Personnaz (1980).

Staring at a white screen after looking at a primary color (such as blue) produces a negative afterimage — you see the complementary color (in this case, yellow-orange; see Figure 11-9). Imagine taking part in an experiment on conformity. The experimenter flashes slides that appear blue (and are, in fact, blue), yet all other members of the group say they are green. You are not required to state your opinion publicly; rather, you are asked to look at a white screen privately and report the color of the afterimage. Moscovici and Personnaz (1980) found in this situation that most people reported what you would expect them to report — the afterimage of blue: yellow-orange. Apparently the tendency to conform (to say the slides are green) reflects only public compliance. They do not really see the slides as green; if they did, they would see the afterimage of green, not of blue.

Now imagine taking part in an experiment on minority influence. You are a member of a majority that says the color of the slide is blue, but are confronted by a consistent minority that says it

Stare at this star for about one minute. Then stare into the white box to the right.

Do you see the shape of the star? What color is it?

FIGURE 11-9
A Demonstration of Negative Afterimage

is green. It is, of course, unlikely you will change your judgment publicly. However, Moscovici and Personnaz (1980) found that significantly more subjects reported seeing the afterimage of green (red-purple) in private after being exposed to the influence of a consistent minority than after being exposed to the influence of a consistent majority. These investigators interpret the findings as support for the idea that although minorities may not be particularly successful in changing the public behavior of group members, they may be more successful in changing their private attitudes. Other researchers have replicated the findings of Moscovici and Personnaz (1980), but have concluded that the responses reveal changes in judgment, not in perception (see Sorrentino, King, & Leo, 1980).

The type of social influence involved in studies on conformity is more blatant and direct than the type of social influence involved in social facilitation, mob behavior, and bystander intervention. In studies on conformity, members of groups make their opinions clear and may even attempt to persuade dissenters to adopt them. However, majorities typically do not *impose* their views on minorities, at least in the groups studied by social psychologists. How successful can people be in imposing their will on others? Put another way, how submissive can the average person become? We now consider a series of studies that investigated probably the strongest pressure put on subjects in any social psychological experiment — Stanley Milgram's studies on obedience to authority.

OBEDIENCE TO AUTHORITY

Authority is a pervasive and integral aspect of our social system. Ordinarily, society functions smoothly when people obey legitimate authority; however, blind obedience to authority is rife with danger. If the prescriptions of authorities are immoral (for example, Hitler's Jewish "solution"), great numbers of people may suffer. Although obedience to authority just because it is authority sometimes works in the short run, blind obedience entails relinquishing control over one's own destiny and invites disaster. The conflict between obedience and defiance is pervasive in our lives and parallels the conflict between conformity and deviance.

The Milgram Obedience Studies

In 1963, Stanley Milgram advertised in local newspapers that he would pay $4.50 to males who participated in a certain experiment at Yale University. When potential subjects arrived at the laboratory, they were met by the experimenter and a middle-aged "subject" introduced as Mr. X, an accountant. The experimenter explained that the study required one subject to be a teacher and the other to be a learner. The accountant was "randomly" assigned the role of

(a)

(b)

(a) Shock generator panel; (b) accountant connected to electrodes by subject (left) and experimenter (right) *Source:* Copyright 1965 by Stanley Milgram. From the film *Obedience,* distributed by the New York University Film Division and the Pennsylvania State University, PCR.

learner. The experimenter then explained that the experiment concerned the effects of punishment on learning. Punishment consisted of an electric shock. The learner was seated in a chair, his left arm strapped down, and an electrode taped to his wrist (see illustration).

The teacher was led into an adjacent room where he was shown a shock generator. It was an impressive looking piece of machinery that contained a panel with 30 switches. The first switch was labeled "15 volts," and the label of each successive switch increased by 15 volts to a maximum of 450 volts. In addition, the following labels were visible: "Mild Shock (15 – 45 volts)," "Intense Shock (300 volts)," and "DANGER: Severe Shock (390 volts)." The last three switches (420 – 450 volts) were ominously labeled "XXX" (see illustration).

The experimenter explained that the learner would receive a list of paired associates (as examples, *dog - leaf, egg - book*), which he was instructed to memorize. The teacher would read the first word of each pair (for example, *dog*) and the learner would give the word with which it was paired *(leaf)*. If the learner made a mistake, the teacher was instructed to deliver a shock by activating the first switch on the shock panel and to increase the intensity by moving up one switch for each successive mistake until the learner made no mistakes. To demonstrate how painful the shocks were and to convince him of the authenticity of the shock generator, the experimenter gave the teacher a sample 75-volt shock.

The accountant was actually an accomplice of the experimenter; the experiment was rigged so that he was always chosen as the learner. Although he never actually received any shocks, the subjects did not know this. For each level of shock administered by the subjects, Milgram played a tape-recorded response of the learner — which seemed real to the teacher. At 45 volts the learner said "Ouch," at 75 volts he started to moan, at 150 volts he demanded to be released, at 180 volts he said he could not stand the shock anymore, and at 300 volts he refused to respond. If subjects demonstrated any reluctance to continue, the experimenter demanded they continue delivering shocks. He informed them that if the learner failed to respond, they should consider it an error and continue shocking him.

How many shocks would you deliver? Milgram described his experimental setup to Yale undergraduates and to several psychiatrists. Both groups felt that less than 3% of the subjects (teachers) would deliver the maximum shock. As it turned out, these estimates were drastically low. In the actual experiment, all 40 subjects individually delivered at least a 300-volt shock ("Intense Shock"—the point at which the learner refused to respond) and 26 of 40 subjects delivered the most extreme shock ("XXX"; see Figure 11-10).

Situational Pressures and Social Roles

What makes people so susceptible to the commands of authorities? Milgram accounted for his results in terms of the power of situational demands and social roles. In our daily lives we play

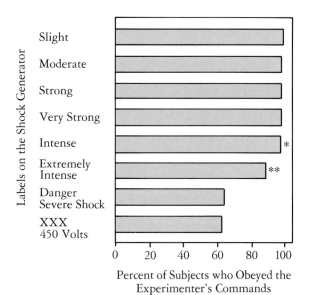

*Learner pounded on wall in protest.
**Learner pounded on wall again; following this he gave no further answers to learning task.

FIGURE 11-10
Results of Milgram's Original Study Sixty-five percent of the subjects continued to obey the experimenter throughout the entire series of shocks in spite of the victim's protests. *Source:* Milgram, S. (1963). Behavioral study of obedience. *Journal of Abnormal and Social Psychology, 67,* 371 – 78. In R. A. Baron & D. Byrne (1981). *Social psychology: Understanding human interactions* (3rd ed.). Boston, MA: Allyn and Bacon.

Box 11-4
Authority and Obedience in a Simulated Prison

The influence of social roles, situational pressures, and authority were demonstrated in a dramatic social psychological study by Philip Zimbardo and his colleagues (1973). Zimbardo created a "prison" in the basement of the Stanford University Psychology Department. It was made as much like a real prison as possible, so that the props (social setting) that support the roles of prisoner and guard would be realistic. Zimbardo chose 18 male college students, none of whom had any history of emotional problems, from a group of subjects who responded to an advertisement for participation in the study. These subjects were required to live in the simulated prison for two weeks. Half the subjects were randomly assigned to the role of prisoner, the other half to the role of guard.

The prisoners were unexpectedly "arrested" in their homes one evening by members of the Palo Alto police force. They were searched, handcuffed, and driven to "jail." On arriving at the basement prison, the guards fingerprinted them, stripped them, and deloused them; covered their hair with hair nets, and dressed them

in prison smocks. Prisoners were identified and referred to by the number imprinted on each smock and housed in six- by nine-foot cells, three to a cell. Guards were dressed in khaki shirts and trousers, wore large sunglasses, and carried a club and a set of keys. Guards were on duty 24 hours a day, in eight hour shifts, and had complete control over the prisoners.

Zimbardo's experiment ended dramatically. Within a few days he was forced to discontinue the experiment when both the guards and prisoners took their roles much more seriously than Zimbardo ever expected. The guards began to display unnecessary cruelty toward the prisoners. For example, they would have a roll call in the middle of the night simply to disrupt the prisoners' sleep. Prisoners became demoralized and apathetic; they even began to refer to themselves and others by their prison numbers. An outside observer with a long personal history of incarceration in federal penitentiaries reported that the Stanford set up was strikingly similar to real prisons, guards, and inmates.

You might object to the

conclusion that the subjects in Zimbardo's experiment were influenced in any real way by the roles they played. After all, you might protest, the prisoners and guards were not *enacting* the roles — behaving in accordance with roles they had internalized — they were only *playing* the roles. If the subjects were simply play acting, Zimbardo's study would show only that adults in our society are good at acting out stereotypic roles. On the other hand, if Zimbardo's subjects actually internalized their roles, the question arises as to why this happened so quickly and with so little incentive.

Several theorists have suggested the line that divides role-playing and role enactment is a faint one, and that role-playing can easily become role enactment. As we will learn, when people play roles (behave in certain ways), they sometimes adjust their attitudes to mirror the roles they play. The boundary between role-playing and role enactment is fuzzy. On a 24-hour-a-day basis and in a setting with highly realistic props (as in the prison study), role-playing may become role enactment.

many roles. A woman might be a mother, wife, and surgeon. Each role is related to a complementary role — daughter, husband, and patient. Attached to each role are sets of norms or expectations that prescribe appropriate behavior for people playing the role, especially in terms of behavior directed toward those in a complementary role. For example, students are expected to behave in certain ways when interacting with teachers and teachers are expected to behave in particular ways when interacting with students. Smooth interactions result when these expectations are mutually respected by the people playing each role. The mutual expectations present when one plays a role exert a powerful influence on behavior. To obtain a sense of the strength of this influence, imagine treating your teacher as if he or she were your best friend.

The situation created by Milgram made the roles of experimenter and subject dominant. Milgram suggested that once people play the role of subject, powerful pressures direct them to behave obediently toward the person in the complementary role, the role of experimenter. The role of subject implies cooperation with the experimenter. Pitted against the obedient subject role are other roles played by subjects who feel they are not the type to harm an innocent person. Milgram suggested that in his experiment the role of obedient subject was most prominent and, therefore, determined most subjects' behavior. Milgram did not view obedient subjects as sadistic people, but simply as normal people caught in a situation that required them to play a role that unintentionally led them to inflict harm on another (see Box 11-4 for another demonstration of the impact of social roles on antisocial behavior).

If Milgram's subjects behaved obediently because of the role they played vis-à-vis authority, then factors that decrease the salience or legitimacy of authority should decrease the amount of obedience. Milgram investigated this possibility by removing the experimenter from the room and having him give instructions over an intercom. In this situation, many subjects pretended to deliver the next shock and to increase the shock level, but actually did neither. Others refused to continue, but once the experimenter reentered the room tended to resume participation. Presumably, the physical presence of the experimenter made his authority more real. When the experiment was conducted in a rundown office building instead of a Yale University laboratory, subjects were less inclined to obey.

Milgram also varied the immediacy, or proximity, of the victim. He found that the maximum

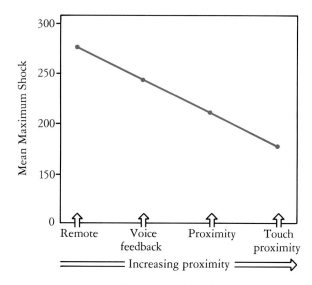

FIGURE 11-11

The Effect of Proximity in Milgram's Experiment Subjects administered increasingly fewer shocks as the proximity of the victim increased. *Source:* Milgram, S. (1974). *Obedience to authority: An experimental view.* New York: Harper & Row.

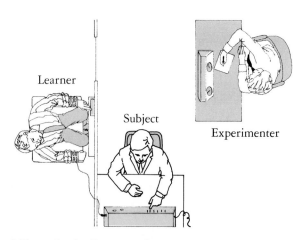

Milgram's obedience study *Source:* Adapted from Milgram, S. (1974). *Obedience to authority: An experimental view.* New York: Harper & Row.

amount of shock the teachers administered decreased when the learner was moved from a remote location and seated a foot and one-half away. Teachers were most resistant to commands of the experimenter when instructed to force the learner's hand down on a shock plate; however, some subjects even followed this command (see Figure 11-11 and the accompanying illustration).

Reactions to Milgrams's Studies of Obedience

Not surprisingly, Milgram's studies caused a great stir when they were published. Most reactions were negative. Some critics objected strongly to the ethics of conducting such an experiment, deceiving subjects, and exposing them to so much stress. Other critics argued the results were invalid. Some suggested that the teachers knew the experimental setup was fake and that the subjects did not believe the learner was really being shocked. Yet, according to Milgram, the teachers reported they believed the learner was being shocked—and anyone who has seen films of the study will attest to the agitation, anxiety, and conflict that at least some of the subjects appeared to experience.

Other critics have accepted the results of the experiment but have argued the results would not prevail in other, more natural situations. However, a study by Hofling et al. (1966) casts doubt on this criticism. Assisted by three nurses and a physician, Hofling, a psychiatrist, transmitted an irregular telephone order to nurses from an unfamiliar physician that instructed them to administer an overdose of an unauthorized drug to a patient (in violation of hospital policy), and found that over 95% of the nurses would have followed the order. The experimenters intervened before the harmful drug was actually administered, and informed the nurses about the study. When other nurses were presented with the same situation in hypothetical form, 31 of 33 maintained they would not have administered the drug. Although the Hofling et al. study was not in an experimental setting (the nurses did not know they were subjects in an experiment), the role relationship was nurse–doctor and the obedience request was different from Milgram's, subjects nonetheless showed blind obedience.

SOCIAL IMPACT

We have considered several kinds of social influence—ranging from the mere presence of one other individual to active attempts to induce people to obey. Social psychologists have tended to examine different forms of social influence as areas of research in themselves, as though the processes involved in each were independent from the processes involved in the others. Yet, as suggested earlier, similar processes may be involved in different forms of influence. Indeed, it seems probable that when the processes that underlie each form of influence are more fully understood, someone will develop a theory that ties them all together. A move in this direction has been made by Bibb Latané in his theory of *social impact.*

Latané defines **social impact** as

> any of the great variety of changes in physiological states and subjective feelings, motives, and emo-

tions, cognitions and beliefs, values and behavior, that occur in an individual, human or animal, as a result of the real, implied, or imagined presence or actions of other individuals. (1981, p. 303)

The social impact theory has three basic principles. The first is that the amount of social pressure an individual experiences in the presence of one or more other people depends on three factors—their strength, immediacy, and number (see Figure 11-12). **Strength** is determined by an individual's ability to affect the fate of others and is associated with such factors as social status, attractiveness, and power. **Immediacy** refers to closeness in space or time. **Number** defines how many people exert the influence. In general, social impact is greatest when individuals are confronted by a large number of powerful people who are close to them.

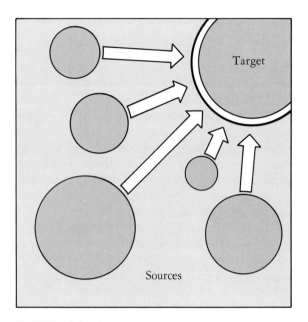

FIGURE 11-12

Social Impact The impact of a social group on a person is determined by three factors: the number of people in the group (represented as circles in this figure), their strength (size), and their immediacy to the target. *Source:* Deaux, K., & Wrightsman, L. S. (1984). *Social psychology in the eighties* (4th ed.). Monterey, CA: Brooks/Cole.

The second principle, which Latané calls a "psychosocial law," is really a law of diminishing returns. It states that the increments of social influence obtained from each individual added to a group become increasingly less. Thus, adding one person to a group of one produces a substantial increase in impact; adding one person to a group of 100 adds significantly less.

The third principle applies to the target of social impact. In parallel with the first principle, it suggests that the strength, immediacy, and number of targets in a situation (members of a minority or ingroup) cause a diminution of social impact. According to Latané, the second principle — the psychosocial law — also applies to targets of social impact. Adding one person to a minority of one diminishes social impact much more than adding one person to a minority of ten.

In support of his theory, Latané (1981) adduces the results of research from several different areas. For example, he shows that the amount

of anxiety students anticipate when they imagine reciting a poem increases, as predicted, in proportion to the number of people in the audience and their status (Latané & Harkins, 1976); the probability of an individual in an elevator helping a person pick up "accidentally dropped" pencils or coins decreases in proportion to the square root of the number of people in the elevator (Latané & Dabbs, 1975); and the percentage of a restaurant tab a waiter or waitress receives as a tip decreases systematically as the number in the party increases (from 19% when individuals dined alone at a certain restaurant in Columbus, Ohio, to 13% for a party of five or six).

Although Latané has not attempted to account explicitly for all types of social influence in terms of the principles of his theory, it is informative, by way of summary and integration, to consider some of the possible connections between principles of the theory and the types of social influence we have been discussing. The effect of *strength* — an influencer's authority — is demonstrated clearly in Milgram's experiments on obedience. Other studies have found the likelihood of a pedestrian violating a traffic signal is greater after observing a person of high status violating it than after observing a person of low status violating it (Lefkowitz, Blake, & Mouton, 1955) — a finding with obvious implications for collective behavior. Studies on bystander intervention have found people are less likely to help in emergencies when they believe other bystanders are of higher status or greater competence than they. For example, Schwartz and Clausen (1970) found females were much less likely to help someone who appeared to be having an epileptic fit when they believed another bystander was a premedical student than when they did not. The impact of the strength or authority of a dissenter is implied in Hollander's concept of idiosyncracy credits, as is the evidence that behavioral styles involving autonomy and rigidity increase the influence of minorities.

The effect of *immediacy* also was demonstrated in Milgram's studies: obedience increased when the experimenter stood close to the teacher and decreased when the victim was close in proximity. Studies on bystander intervention have found a positive relationship between helping and the physical proximity of victims to by-standers (Piliavin et al., 1981; Staub & Baer, 1974). Group density would be expected to contribute to the process of deindividuation and anonymity, and studies on conformity have found the influence of the group decreases when sub-jects are permitted to respond in private (see Table 11-2).

Mann's (1981) study on onlookers' reac-tions to people threatening suicide suggests a pos-itive relationship between *number* (group size), deindividuation, and anonymity. Latané's theory leads us to suspect that increases in influence would be greatest with the addition of the first few members to a group and would decrease sys-tematically with additional members. Research on bystander intervention and conformity has demonstrated that social influence increases dra-matically when one person is added to a group of one or two but tends to level off when other peo-ple are added. In his early studies, Asch (1951) found that increments in the size of the majority beyond three failed to exert any effect on con-formity; however, later studies (Gerard, Wil-helmy, & Conolley, 1968) found the type of di-minishing influence predicted by Latané (see Figure 11-13). Research on conformity also has shown that an individual's resistance to group pressure increases dramatically when one other person dissents (even, as we have mentioned, if the other individual does not agree with the sub-ject). Resistance increases further when other individuals join the minority, but not in propor-tion to their number.

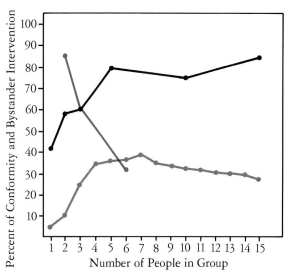

FIGURE 11-13

Effect of Group Size on Conformity and By-stander Intervention The black line represents the percent of passersby who looked up as a function of the number of people in a crowd looking up on a New York street in the Milgram experiment. The grey line represents the percent of people conforming in the Asch study on conformity. As demonstrated by these lines, as group size increases conformity increases — but only to a point. The blue line represents data on bystander intervention. This line shows that as group size increases, the likelihood that individuals will re-spond to an emergency decreases. *Sources:* Data from Asch, S. E. (1955, November). Opinions and social pres-sure. *Scientific American, 193,* pp. 31–35. Milgram, S., Bickman, L., & Berkowitz, L. (1969). Note on the drawing power of crowds of different size. *Journal of Personality and Social Psychology, 13,* 80, Figure 1. Latané, B., & Dar-ley, J. M. (1968). Group inhibition of bystander intervention in emergencies. *Journal of Personality and Social Psychol-ogy, 10,* 215–221.

ATTITUDE CHANGE, PROPAGANDA, AND PERSUASION

If you wanted to change people in a deep and enduring way, you probably would not just try to change their behavior in a particular situation. Let us say you have a friend who is prejudiced. Forcing the person to behave civilly toward the people against whom he is prejudiced would be of limited value if doing so did not alter his feel-ings toward them. If you wanted to change your friend, you would probably attempt to change his attitudes. When you change people's attitudes, you change something in them that you would expect to affect their behavior across a wide range of situations. Changing people's attitudes is a major enterprise in our society. It is part of the job of all parents, teachers, ministers, and psycho-therapists. It is the primary goal of advertisers, who spend over $50 billion annually in North America to extol the virtues of their products.

And it finds its most extreme forms in thought control, religious and political indoctrination, and brainwashing.

Although interest in attitudes has waxed and waned during the modest history of social psychology, the study of attitudes always has been an important area of research. Indeed, Gordon Allport (1968) wrote that attitudes are the "keystone in the edifice of American social psychology." McGuire (1985) estimates that over one thousand studies a year are conducted on attitude change.

What Is an Attitude?

Before considering the factors that induce changes in attitudes, we should define the term; however, the task is not as easy as it may seem — attitudes have been defined operationally in at least 500 different ways (Ajzen & Fishbein, 1972). It is generally accepted among psychologists that attitudes are evaluative judgments about people, things, and events and that they have three dimensions: cognitive (usually called a belief), affective (a positive or negative feeling), and behavioral [in Allport's (1935) words, "a preparation or readiness for response"] (see Figure 11-14). Your attitude toward abortion probably contains beliefs about the rights of women and fetuses, feelings about whether abortion is right or wrong, and a readiness to behave in particular ways toward issues that involve abortion (for example, by advocating or opposing abortion in arguments). The affective dimension is generally considered the most distinguishing feature of attitudes — some theorists define attitudes exclusively in evaluative terms. For example, Thurstone (1928, p. 39) defined attitudes as "the amount of affect for or against a psychological object" and Bem (1970, p. 14) defined attitudes succinctly as "likes and dislikes."

The Processes Involved in Attitude Change

A change in attitude seems like a relatively straightforward matter: "I used to believe in capital punishment, now I don't"; "I used to think professors were smart, now I think they are naive." In the 1920s and 1930s, psychologists put a great deal of effort into the construction of attitude scales, such as the one displayed in

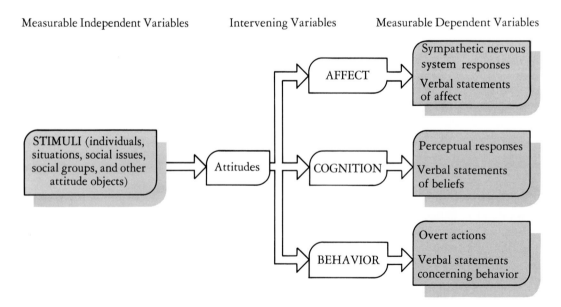

FIGURE 11-14

A Model of Attitudes Attitudes consist of affective, cognitive, and behavioral components. *Source:* Rosenberg, M. J., et al. (1960). *Attitude organization and change: An analysis of consistency among attitude components.* New Haven, CT: Yale University Press.

Box 11-5, and such scales were employed to assess changes in attitudes.

As research on attitude change blossomed in the 1950s and 1960s, contrary findings began to appear at a sometimes alarming rate. For example, one study would report it is easier to change the attitudes of intelligent people than unintelligent people, and other studies would report the opposite. One study would report that messages that arouse fear induce more attitude change than more rational appeals, but other studies would report that rational appeals are more effective. In an attempt to resolve such apparent contradictions, investigators were forced to take a closer look at the processes involved in attitude change.

As illustrated in Figure 11-15, the chain between a persuasive communication, such as "Buy a Cadillac," and executing a decision, such as actually buying a Cadillac, has at least eight links (see McGuire, 1985). First, an individual must attend to the message. Second, the individual must retain interest in the message long enough to perceive it. Third, the individual must understand the message. Fourth, the individual must think about it and integrate it with his or her other attitudes and beliefs. Fifth, the individual must take a stand on the relevant issue, agreeing or disagreeing with it (usually the measure of attitude change). Sixth, the individual must store the new information and sentiments in memory until he or she encounters a relevant situation (for example, enters a Cadillac showroom). Seventh, the individual must retrieve the information from memory. Finally, the individual must make a decision on the basis of the retrieved information.

Many of the inconsistent findings that plagued early research on attitude change were resolved when investigators recognized that variables affect different links in different ways in the chain of cognitive processes that lead to attitude change. For example, highly intelligent people tend to be more influenced than less intelligent people by complex messages because they are better at comprehending them (link three), storing them in memory (link six), and retrieving them (link seven). However, highly intelligent people also are more likely to generate counter-arguments (link four), which tends to diminish attitude change. Or, to consider another example, highly arousing messages facilitate attitude change by enhancing the first two links (they capture people's attention) but inhibit attitude change at the third and forth links (comprehending and integrating the message).

Mere Exposure and Forced Contact

The most obvious way to change an individual's attitude is to employ some method of persuasion. The majority of studies on attitude change have investigated the impact of persuasive communications. Before examining the factors that make communications persuasive, however, we point out that people's attitudes also are affected by mere exposure to people and things. Social psychologist Robert Zajonc has shown that the

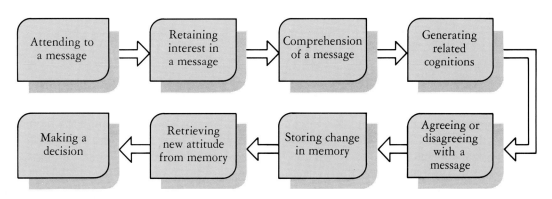

FIGURE 11-15

Chain of Cognitive Processes Leading to Attitude Change *Source:* McGuire, W. J. (1985). Attitudes and attitude change. In G. Lindzey & E. Aronson (Eds.) *Handbook of social psychology* (3rd ed.). New York: Random House.

Box 11-5
THE MEASUREMENT OF ATTITUDES ON THE LIKERT SCALE

One of the oldest—but still very popular—methods of assessing attitudes was developed by Rensis Likert in 1932. Likert obtained a substantial number of statements he thought might reflect the attitude he sought to assess, and divided them into clearly favorable and clearly unfavorable statements. Then he gave the statements to a group of subjects and asked them to indicate the extent to which they agreed or disagreed with them. For example, he might give subjects such statements as "Abortion is equivalent to murder" and "Every pregnant woman has the right to decide whether or not to give birth," and ask them to circle one of the following:

Agree strongly
Agree mildly
Disagree mildly
Disagree strongly

Likert gave each response a score ranging from 1–5

(reversed for unfavorable items) that reflected the degree of agreement. Following this, he determined the extent to which each item correlated with the total score and discarded those that did not correlate highly. By repeating this procedure with groups of subjects, Likert was able to produce an increasingly pure test of the atttitude in question. Typically, attitudes measured by the Likert method are assessed by tests that consist of 20–30 statements. The subject's score reflects the strength of the attitude. A current test based on a Likert scale follows. You are invited to take the test and to evaluate your attitude toward women. To score your results, apply the following scale for items 1, 4, 5, 10, 13, 14, 15, 16, 17, 19, 20, 22, and 23:

Agree strongly = 0
Agree mildly = 1
Disagree mildly = 2
Disagree strongly = 3

For items 2, 3, 6, 7, 8, 9, 11, 12, 18, 21, 24, and 25, the scale is reversed as follows:

Agree strongly = 3
Agree mildly = 2
Disagree mildly = 1
Disagree strongly = 0

To obtain a total, add the assigned values of all test items. The higher your score, the more liberal your attitude toward women. As a reference, here are the average scores of 241 female and 286 male college students who took the same test: males = 44.80, females = 50.26. Notice that female college students have a much more liberal attitude towards women than their male counterparts. In comparison, when this test was administered to 292 mothers and 232 fathers, the results were generally more conservative: fathers = 39.22, mothers = 41.86.

more often people see a stranger, the more they tend to like him or her. In one study, Zajonc (1968) found that students who were shown numerous photographs of strangers gave the highest evaluations to the photographs they saw most often. In another study, Grush, McKeough, and Ahlering (1978) found that 83% of the candidates who won political primaries in the United States received more exposure through the media than those who did not win. The findings of these studies and others suggest that if you want someone to develop an affection for you, the first step is to ensure that the person sees you often. In an interesting application of the principle that mere exposure enhances attraction, Mita, Derner, and Knight (1977) assessed people's preference for

Measuring Attitudes toward Women

Instructions: The statements below describe attitudes toward the role of women in society. There are no right or wrong answers, only opinions. Please express your feeling about each statement by indicating whether you (a) agree strongly, (b) agree mildly, (c) disagree mildly, or (d) disagree strongly. Please indicate your opinion by entering a, b, c, or d in the space next to each item.

_____ 1. Swearing and obscenity are more repulsive in the speech of a woman than of a man.

_____ 2. Women should take increasing responsibility for leadership in solving the intellectual and social problems of the day.

_____ 3. Both husband and wife should be allowed the same grounds for divorce.

_____ 4. Telling dirty jokes should be mostly a masculine prerogative.

_____ 5. Intoxication among women is worse than intoxication among men.

_____ 6. Under modern economic conditions, with women being active outside the home, men should share in household tasks such as washing dishes and doing the laundry.

_____ 7. It is insulting to women to have the "obey" clause remain in the marriage service.

_____ 8. There should be a strict merit system in job appointment and promotion without regard to sex.

_____ 9. A women should be as free as a man to propose marriage.

_____ 10. Women should worry less about their rights and more about becoming good wives and mothers.

_____ 11. Women earning as much as their dates should bear equally the expense when they go out together.

_____ 12. Women should assume their rightful place in business and all the professions along with men.

_____ 13. A women should not expect to go to exactly the same places or to have quite the same freedom of action as a man.

_____ 14. Sons in a family should be given more encouragement to go to college than daughters.

_____ 15. It is ridiculous for a woman to run a locomotive and for a man to darn socks.

_____ 16. In general, the father should have greater authority than the mother in the bringing up of children.

_____ 17. Women should be encouraged not to become sexually intimate with anyone before marriage, even their fiancés.

_____ 18. The husband should not be favored by law over the wife in the disposal of family property or income.

_____ 19. Women should be concerned with their duties of childbearing and house tending, rather than with desires for professional and business careers.

_____ 20. The intellectual leadership of a community should be largely in the hands of men.

_____ 21. Economic and social freedom are worth far more to women than acceptance of the ideal of femininity which has been set up by men.

_____ 22. On the average, women should be regarded as less capable of contributing to economic production than are men.

_____ 23. There are many jobs in which men should be given preferences over women in being hired or promoted.

_____ 24. Women should be given equal opportunity with men for apprenticeship in the various trades.

_____ 25. The modern girl is entitled to the same freedom from regulation and control that is given to the modern boy.

Source: Items for the Attitudes toward Women Scale. Reprinted by permission of J. T. Spence, R. Helmreich, and J. Stapp and the Psychonomic Society (1974). JSAS Catalog sel. doc. Psychol., *4*, 43.

---

photographs of their faces versus mirror images of photographs. These investigators found that people prefer mirror images of photographs of themselves, which, of course, is what they see most often. However, as predicted, their friends preferred the photographs. It is interesting that the face we see in the mirror every morning is not the same face others see throughout the day.

If exposure to people tends to enhance affection for them, we might be able to reduce prejudice by forcing contact between prejudiced people and the people whom they dislike. This possibility, of course, is relevant to such political issues as mandated busing and apartheid. Although the findings of studies on integration are mixed, they tend to show that forced contact in-

tensifies individuals' preexisting attitudes: prejudiced attitudes become more prejudiced; favorable attitudes become more favorable (Amir,
1976). Conditions found to work best in reducing prejudice (enhanced liking for members of
outgroups) include extended periods of integration that involve close and voluntary contact, the
discovery of similar beliefs and values, the ability
to reach desired outcomes by working together, a
cultural context that supports harmony, and
equality in status (Riordan, 1978).

Persuasive Communications

If you wanted to change someone's attitude, you
probably would begin by talking to the person.
Certainly that is what most teachers do. Unfortu-

nately most teachers are not particularly persuasive. What makes some people persuasive and
other people not? What characteristics enhance
the effect of persuasive communications? These
are important questions, whether one is seeking
to change someone's mind or whether one is the
object of a persuasive communication.

A persuasive communication involves delivering a message through a specific medium to
someone in a particular way. Therefore, in analyzing persuasive communication, we ask: ''Who
says what, via what medium, to whom . . . ?''
(McGuire, 1985, p. 258). The factors that constitute a persuasive communication consist of a
source (who), a **message** (what), a **channel**
(medium), and a **receiver** (whom) (see Figure
11-16). In Table 11-3 we outline the primary

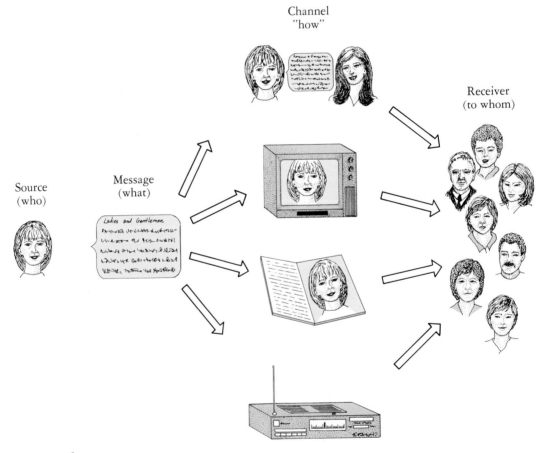

FIGURE 11-16
The Components of Persuasive Communications Persuasive communications consist of a source,
message, channel, and receiver.

characteristics of sources, messages, channels, and receivers that have been studied by researchers. In the text that follows, we present an overview of some interesting findings.

Source What kind of people are most persuasive? What characteristics enhance an individual's persuasiveness? An hour in front of the TV should suggest some answers to these questions. The three characteristics found to enhance people's persuasiveness most are their power, attractiveness, and credibility. Thus Mr. T is effective at selling cereal, Cheryl Tiegs at selling cosmetics, and John Houseman at selling financial services. Some research indicates that each characteristic appeals to a different attitudinal dimension and induces a different attitudinal change (Insko, Drenan, & Solomon, 1983). Power appeals to the behavioral component of attitudes and induces compliance. Attraction appeals to

the affective component of attitudes and induces identification. Credibility appeals to the cognitive component of attitudes and induces changes in beliefs.

A source's power may derive from such factors as control over people's fate, control over resources, status, physical strength, and degree of support from others. As shown by studies on conformity, power is effective for inducing compliance. Behavioral compliance may lead to attitude change under certain conditions, such as when it continues for a long time, but may interfere with attitude change under other conditions.

A source's attractiveness is influenced by such characteristics as beauty and similarity. In general, the better looking a person is, the more persuasive he or she tends to be (Dion & Stein, 1978). Perception of similarity is linked closely to liking. Investigators have compared and contrasted the power of different types of similarity,

TABLE 11-3
How Characteristics of Source, Message, Channel, and Receiver Affect Persuasive Communications

Characteristic	Effect on Audience
Source	
Power (control over fate, resources, status, physical strength, support)	Induces behavioral compliance; may lead to attitude change
Attractiveness (physical attractiveness, similarity)	Induces identification; increases behavioral acceptance
Credibility (trustworthiness)	Induces changes in beliefs
Message	
Rational Appeals	
one-sided communication (presents only one point of view)	Increases compliance when audience is unintelligent, uneducated, or ignorant
two-sided communication (presents both sides)	Increases compliance when audience is intelligent, educated, or informed
Emotional Appeals	
negative	Usually evoke fear; tend to produce more immediate compliance
positive	Produce less immediate compliance but more long-term effects
Channel	
Mass Media (TV, radio, newspaper)	Only a minimal effect on people's behavior; may induce some small changes in attitude (for example, materialistic); produce perceptual distortions and biases of underrepresented groups (the elderly, women, ethnic minorities)
Word of Mouth	Depending on the source, may be persuasive
Receiver	
Gender	Majority of studies show no difference between males and females; studies that report differences show females to be more influenceable
Self-esteem	People at intermediate levels of self-esteem are maximally persuasible

■ Social Psychology

focusing in particular on ethnic and ideologic (belief) similarities. Of these two types, ideologic similarity has been found to have the greater effect on abstract evaluations of people and ethnic similarity to have the greater effect on behavioral acceptance (Robinson & Insko, 1969). Recent studies indicate that ideologic similarity is gaining in persuasive power over ethnic similarity in the United States (Insko, Nacoste, & Moe, 1983).

It seems reasonable to assume the credibility of a source would be enhanced by the amount of knowledge he or she is believed to possess, but research has not supported this common-sense expectation (McGinnies & Ward, 1980). Credibility appears to be enhanced more by the source's trustworthiness, as reflected by such factors as lack of interest in the outcome of the communication, arguing against self-interest, and absence of awareness that an audience is present. Studies have found that scientists, physicians, and academics are perceived as highly credible; followed by military officers, police officers, and judges; with business leaders, media personalities, politicians, and labor-union officials at the bottom (Gallup, 1981).

Message If you want to persuade someone, how should you structure the persuasive communication? Suppose you want to persuade people to brush their teeth regularly. Would it be most effective to frighten them by, for example, showing pictures of diseased gums and decaying teeth? Or would it be most effective to emphasize such positive effects of dental hygiene as gleaming teeth and a beautiful smile? What works better — emotional appeals or rational appeals? Are you best off acknowledging the arguments against your position or should you present an entirely one-sided case? Should you present your best arguments first or save them for last? These are but some of the many questions asked about the structure of messages in persuasive communications.

The results of research on various aspects of messages are rarely straightforward. For example, studies have found that threatening and fear-arousing appeals tend to produce more immediate compliance than positive appeals (Weinmann, 1982) but that positive appeals appear to produce a stronger long-term effect (Beck,

1979). Threatening appeals tend to induce people to focus on their fear, which causes them to avoid thinking of the issue at hand; positive appeals appear to encourage people to focus on ways of dealing with the danger (Leventhal & Nerenz, 1983).

It is commonly believed that messages that forcefully present only one point of view are more persuasive than those that acknowledge another. Some evidence supports this expectation. Studies have found that one-sided communications are more effective than two-sided communications when people initially agree with the position being advocated (see Figure 11-17). However, when people initially oppose the position, two-sided communications appear to be more effective. In general, the evidence suggests it is better to acknowledge and refute opposition arguments before presenting your own (McGuire, 1964). The relatively recent tendency of advertisers to

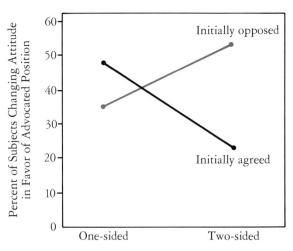

Argument in the Message

FIGURE 11-17

One-sided versus Two-sided Communications Hovland, Lumsdaine, and Sheffield presented U.S. World War II soldiers with either a one-sided or a two-sided argument that indicated the Japanese would not be defeated easily. Those soldiers who initially opposed the message were more persuaded by the two-sided argument. Those soldiers who initially agreed with the message became even more certain of their belief after hearing the one-sided argument. *Source:* Hovland, C. I., Lumsdaine, A. A., & Sheffield, F. D. (1949). *Experiments on mass communication. Studies in social psychology in World War II* (Vol. III). Princeton, NJ: Princeton University Press.

mention the names of competing brands (the Pepsi test; the Uncola) reflects such a strategy.

The results of research on the question of whether it is best to present strongest arguments first or last are mixed. Presenting strongest arguments last tends to create a crescendo effect and has the potential of keeping the most persuasive points fresh in the mind of the receiver. However, this tactic has such potential drawbacks as losing the audience at the beginning—unless measures are taken to retain their attention (Tetlock, 1983)—and creating early skepticism. Presenting strongest arguments first captures audience attention and creates a positive context for weaker arguments. Studies have found that once people commit themselves to a position, they are motivated to maintain it (Burger & Petty, 1981).

Finally, studies indicate that presenting extreme arguments moves people even further away from their original position than presenting more tempered positions—up to a point. If the message is too extreme, the source loses credibility; when that happens, people tend to disregard the entire communication (Lange & Fishbein, 1983).

Channel   Of the various channels employed to communicate messages, mass media, especially TV, have received the most attention in recent years. Considering the average American receives from three to four hours of mass-media messages each day and the average American high-school graduate spends more time watching TV than he or she spends in the classroom (Television Audience Assessment, 1983; Adler et al., 1980), it is not surprising social scientists have conducted in-depth studies on the effects of TV on attitudes, beliefs, and behavior.

It is difficult to imagine that TV does not affect people's attitudes and opinions; the billions of dollars spent on commercials seem ample evidence of the power of this medium. Surprisingly, years of research supply only modest support for the belief that TV commercials affect people's behavior. Studies find that the number of commercials for a given product has no appreciable effect on its sales (Assmus, Farley, & Lehmann, 1984), that political advertisements exert no clear influence on voting (Patterson, 1980), and that such public service announcements as those against smoking or in favor of seat belts have no appreciable effect on people's attitudes

and behavior (Robertson et al., 1974; Murphy, 1980).

One of the deepest concerns people have about mass media is how they affect general expectations and values. Scholars such as Sanford Fox (1984) have suggested that the vast amount of advertising on TV promotes materialistic and self-indulgent values; other critics have suggested that TV, radio, and newspaper messages indoctrinate people in the ideology of the elite who control such media. Although it is difficult to test such ideas, evidence from studies that evaluate the effects of large-scale media campaigns (for example, those that promote healthful life-styles) suggests that although they may induce some changes in people's attitudes, the changes are small (Maccoby & Alexander, 1980).

However, the case is stronger for the related accusation that mass media convey a distorted view of reality. Seniors, ethnic minorities, and, to some extent, women are greatly underrepresented on TV, appearing less frequently than their actual proportion of the population (Davis & Kubey, 1982; Gerbner et al., 1980; Greenberg et al., 1983). Moreover, portrayals of these groups are often stereotyped. Seniors often are portrayed as less competent, less sexually active, more dependent, less healthy, and more narrow-minded than they actually are (Gerbner et al., 1980). Women frequently are portrayed as passive, immature, and powerless (Downs, 1981). Research indicates that peoples' perceptions of such groups—indeed members of such groups' perceptions of themselves—are affected by biases inherent in media exposure and stereotyping (Berry & Mitchell-Kernan, 1982). For example, the public at large, especially devoted TV watchers, underestimate the number of seniors in the population and overestimate the prevalence of crime (Gerbner et al., 1980).

Receiver   We tend to think of susceptibility to influence as a negative trait; it conjures up images of mindless, wishy-washy conformists. However, the opposite condition is not much better. A person who is impervious to persuasion is rigid, fixed in his or her ways, and resistant to change. The ideal appears to lie somewhere between the two extremes—an openness to new points of view tempered by thoughtful discrimination between valid and invalid arguments.

We have seen that such characteristics as credibility, attractiveness, and power tend to enhance the persuasiveness of those who send messages. But what characteristics increase the susceptibility to persuasion of those who receive them? The two characteristics receiving the most attention from researchers are gender and self-esteem. More than 150 studies compared male and female susceptibility to persuasion (Block, 1976). The majority of studies failed to find any difference, and differences found by the minority are slight. However, among the studies that found differences, more than 90% found that females are more susceptible to influence than males (Maccoby & Jacklin, 1974; Block, 1976). Meta-analyses of studies on persuasion, group pressure, and conformity (see p. 527) confirm this trend (Becker, 1986; see Figure 11-18). In most cases, there is no difference between male and female susceptibility to persuasion; when there is, especially in pressure situations, females tend to accommodate more than males.

Two primary explanations have been advanced for the gender difference sometimes found in studies on susceptibility to persuasion. The first attributes the gender difference to methodological problems in studies reporting the effect: most of the communications in these studies involve masculine issues and most of the communicators are male. There is some evidence that women are more susceptible to influence on masculine issues and that males are more susceptible to influence on feminine issues (Karabenick, 1983; Eagly & Carli, 1981). Thus, the gender differences found may demonstrate a tendency for people to be most influenced on opposite-gender issues.

The second explanation treats the observed difference in susceptibility to persuasion as real, and attributes it to socialization. Some social scientists have suggested that our social system places greater pressure on females to obey authority, to foster harmony in interpersonal relations, and to conform (Eagly, 1978; Santee & Jackson, 1982; see Chapter 10).

More than 100 studies have investigated the relationship between self-esteem and susceptibility to persuasion; however, according to one

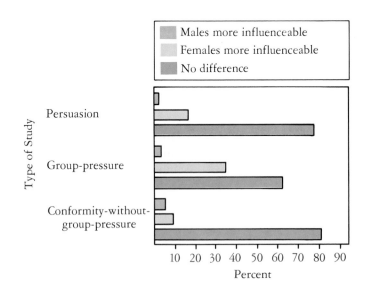

FIGURE 11-18

Gender and Influenceability Eagly gathered data from 62 persuasion studies, 61 group-pressure studies, and 22 conformity-without-group-pressure studies. Although most studies failed to report a gender difference, most of those that did report a difference found females to be more influenceable than males. *Source:* Eagly, A. H. (1978). Sex differences in influenceability. *Psychological Bulletin, 85,* 86–116. See also Becker, B. J. (1986). Influence again: Another look at studies of gender differences in social influence. In J. S. Hyde & M. C. Linn (Eds.), *The psychology of gender: Advances through meta-analysis* (pp. 178–209). Baltimore, MD: Johns Hopkins University Press.

major reviewer (Wylie, 1979), most of the studies are plagued by methodological flaws. Self-esteem is notoriously difficult to measure. As studies have grown more sophisticated, it has become apparent the relationship between self-esteem and susceptibility to persuasion is complex. Recent studies have found that people at intermediate levels of self-esteem are maximally persuasible. If you begin with a person chronically low in self-esteem and raise his or her self-esteem through successful experiences, you tend to increase that person's susceptibility to persuasion. However, successful experiences tend to lower susceptibility to persuasion in people with high self-esteem. Deaux (1972) found that people with chronically low self-esteem who were subjected to an esteem-lowering experience of failure were the most resistant to persuasion, and people with high self-esteem who were subjected to an esteem-lowering experience of failure were the easiest to persuade. One reason suggested for the relative imperviousness to persuasion of people chronically low in self-esteem is that they set up defenses to protect themselves from threatening information (Bennis & Peabody, 1962; see Chapter 12).

Brainwashing

No overview of persuasion, or indeed of social influence in general, would be complete without some mention of brainwashing. In Chapter 1 we alluded to the bizarre experience of Patty Hearst, and asked whether she had been brainwashed. The concept of brainwashing, originated during the Korean War, was used to explain why many American prisoners collaborated with their North Korean captors. F. Lee Bailey based his defense of Patty Hearst on the theory that she had been brainwashed, and he called Yale psychiatrist Robert Lifton, an expert on brainwashing, to testify she had been indoctrinated through "thought reform."

According to one of the first social scientists to scrutinize the processes involved in *coercive persuasion,* "There is a world of difference in the content of what is transmitted in religious orders, prisons, educational institutions, mental hospitals, and thought reform centers. But there are striking similarities in the manner in which the influence occurs . . ." (Schein, 1968, p. 285).

Accordingly, we should be able to explain brainwashing by means of the principles of social influence under consideration. To understand what happened to Patty Hearst, think back to earlier discussions and note the processes impinging on her. She was highly aroused and undoubtedly extremely fearful. She was blindfolded for several weeks and, thus, deindividuated. She was exposed to a majority that consistently pressured her to adopt their point of view. She was completely devoid of any social support and, like the subjects in Asch's experiments, exposed to a unanimous majority. To make matters worse, the issues at hand were matters of opinion, not matters of objective reality. The people who attempted to persuade her were powerful, attractive (she fell in love with one of her captors), and significantly more knowledgeable than her about political matters. They were, in effect, authorities. They formed a cohesive group with clearly defined norms and roles. The messages they put to her were extreme, repetitive, and forceful. Patty's capitalistic life-style was demeaned and she was subjected to humiliating, esteem-lowering experiences while, at the same time, implicitly offered the admiration of the group if she converted and conformed. These and other factors (see Zimbardo, Ebbensen, & Maslach, 1977, pp. 13–14) were sufficient to convert Patty Hearst to the cause of the Symbionese Liberation Army. Zimbardo et al. suggest they were more than enough to convert most of us, too.

Resistance to Persuasion

In closing our discussion of attitude change, it is worthwhile examining the factors found to increase people's resistance to persuasion. In many contexts, these factors are positive: they help us guard against indoctrination. In other contexts, however, they cause us to tune out information that could enhance our understanding of issues at hand.

McGuire (1985) outlines five factors found to increase people's resistance to persuasion. First, such negative emotional states as anger, anxiety, depression, and loneliness (all associated with low self-esteem) tend to lower people's susceptibility to persuasion. This generalization, however, must be qualified in certain contexts.

For example, although angry people tend to disagree with benevolent positions, they tend to agree with hostile positions (Berkowitz, 1974). Second, training in critical thinking has been found to increase people's resistance to persuasion in some situations (Huesmann et al., 1983). Third, inducing people to make a private, public, or behavioral commitment to an attitude tends to increase their resistance to discrepant information. Fourth, linking beliefs to other beliefs and values tends to increase resistance to change. Finally, inoculating people through exposure to weakened forms of a persuasive argument tends to increase their resistance to the argument in its entirety (see Figure 11-19; McGuire, 1964). There seem to be two reasons for the effectiveness of inoculation: it reduces the impact and credibility of subsequent attacks against the communication and it stimulates the cultivation of belief-supporting arguments. Studies have found that

> Just as biological inoculation requires the passage of an incubation period before resistance develops, threatening defenses also show delayed-action immunizing effects, conferring more resistance to attacks that come several days after the defence than to immediate attacks. (McGuire, 1985, p. 294)

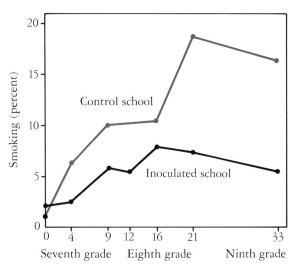

FIGURE 11-19

Inoculation Against Smoking   Telch et al. conducted an experiment involving the inoculation of high-school students against peer pressures to smoke. Compared to a control group that did not receive such training, the inoculated students were half as likely to begin smoking.   *Source:* Telch, M. J., Killen, J. D., McAlister, A. L., Perry, C. L., & Maccoby, N. (1982). Long-term follow-up of a pilot project on smoking prevention with adolescents. *Journal of Behavioral Medicine, 5,* 5.

THE RELATIONSHIP BETWEEN ATTITUDES AND BEHAVIOR

Changing attitudes is rarely an end in itself; it usually is a means to another end — changing behavior. It is reasonable to assume that if you change a person's attitude toward an object — whether an individual, a minority group, an issue, or a product — the person will behave differently toward it. Yet in what McGuire (1985) characterized as "the scandal of the field [of social psychology] for a half century" (p. 251), early studies failed to support this sensible assumption.

In the early 1930s, sociologist Richard La-Piere traveled through the West and Midwest of the United States for more than two years accompanied by a Chinese student and the student's wife. Anti-Asian feelings were strong in the United States at this time. LaPiere (1934) re-

corded the reactions of people who received the Chinese couple at restaurants and hotels. In his words, "We met definite rejection from those asked to serve us *just once.* We were received at 66 hotels, auto camps and 'Tourist Homes' . . . We were served in 184 restaurants and cafes . . . and treated with . . . more than ordinary consideration in 72 of them" (p. 232). Approximately six months after La-Piere returned home, he wrote letters to all of the establishments that had served his group, asking, among other things, "Will you accept members of the Chinese race as guests in your establishment?" Approximately 50% of the hotels and restaurants he contacted answered the letter; of those responding, approximately 90% said "No," the remainder saying "Uncertain." LaPiere concluded that the attitude of the people at the hotels and restaurants bore little relationship to their actual behavior.

Although critics have identified several methodological flaws in LaPiere's study (see Dillehay, 1973; and Box 11-6), later investigators also found little consistency between attitudes and behavior (Wicker, 1969). Faced with this evidence, some psychologists, such as Abelson (1972), have concluded that the relationship between attitudes and behavior is primarily in people's heads. Other psychologists, however, have concluded that there is a relationship between attitudes and behavior, but that it is more complex than early researchers assumed. Notable among the latter group are Fishbein and Ajzen, who have presented a theory of *reasoned action.*

Fishbein and Ajzen's Theory of Reasoned Action

Ajzen and Fishbein (1980) point out that most traditional studies on the relationship between attitudes and behavior assess general attitudes toward people or institutions, but evaluate their relationship to highly specific behaviors. For example, LaPiere attempted to assess a general attitude toward Chinese people, but examined its relationship to a highly specific behavior — admitting the particular Chinese couple accompanied by LaPiere to a restaurant or hotel. According to Fishbein and Ajzen, there is no reason to expect general attitudes to be related to each and every behavior relevant to them; rather, such attitudes should be related to the sum of all of the behaviors relevant to them. Thus, if you want to examine the relationship between an individual's *attitude* toward Chinese and that person's *behavior* toward them, you must obtain a representative sample of all that person's behaviors toward Chinese. Conversely, if you want to predict whether a woman will admit a Chinese couple to her hotel, you must determine her attitude toward engaging in this specific behavior — regardless of whether she has a positive or negative attitude toward Chinese people in general (see Figure 11-20). Fishbein and Ajzen (1975) show that when the level

BOX 11-6
METHODOLOGICAL PROBLEMS IN THE LaPIERE STUDY

LaPiere conducted his study early in the history of social psychology, and for many years it was cited as evidence that people's attitudes are inconsistent with their behavior. When contemporary psychologists examined the methods used by LaPiere, however, they discovered many problems with the study. For one thing, only one-half the establishments responded to LaPiere's follow-up questionnaire, creating a sample that was probably quite biased. Attitudes were measured by a *Yes* or *No* response only — a crude device. Even more problematical, it was unclear that those who answered the letters were the same people who made the behavioral decision. It also is unclear in LaPiere's study exactly what the attitudes in question were. Perhaps the people who admitted the Chinese couple into their establishment had a positive attitude toward that particular couple, or toward Chinese accompanied by a Caucasian; or perhaps their behavior reflected a negative attitude toward face-to-face rejection, or toward creating a scene. In conclusion, we have no idea whether LaPiere's findings revealed an inconsistency between attitudes and behavior because we do not know what the people's attitudes were or what determined their behavior.

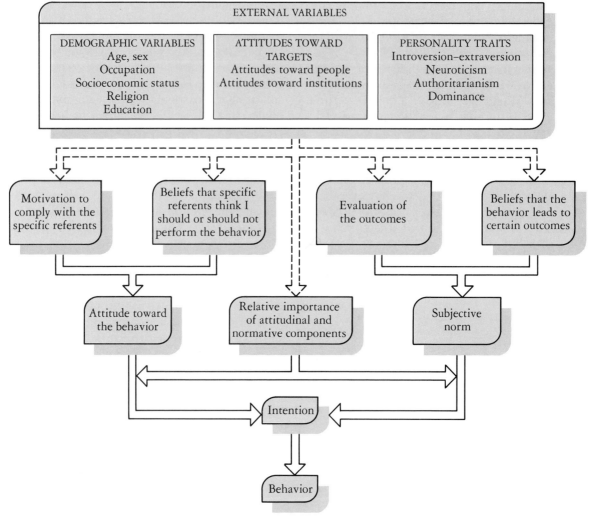

Possible explanations for observed relations between external variables and behavior

Stable theoretical relations linking beliefs to behavior

FIGURE 11-20

Ajzen and Fishbein's Model of the Relationship Between Attitudes and Behavior Broad variables such as age, general attitudes toward Chinese, and personality traits give rise to more specific beliefs that in turn, give rise to specific attitudes toward behaviors and subjective norms. These, in turn, give rise to intentions and behaviors. *Source:* Ajzen, I., & Fishbein, M. (1980). *Understanding attitudes and predicting social behavior.* Englewood Cliffs, NJ: Prentice-Hall.

of generality between attitudes and behavior is matched, the correlation between them is significantly higher than when they are not matched.

A second point made by Fishbein and Ajzen is that behaviors are influenced by factors other than attitudes, the most important of which are what they call subjective norms. **Subjective norms** represent the expectations of others. A

hotel clerk may be prejudiced against Chinese, but probably would admit a Chinese guest if the people with whom he worked liked the person.

The model outlined by Fishbein and Ajzen helps demonstrate the complexity of what initially may seem like a relatively straightforward issue—the relationship between attitudes and behavior—but even this model does not capture its full complexity. Several factors not explicitly addressed by Fishbein and Ajzen have been found to disrupt the relationship between attitudes and behavior, and several have been found to strengthen it. The relationship between attitudes and behavior is disrupted:

1. when other attitudes and values lead to competing behaviors (I like to smoke but I value good health)

2. when people are not able to control their behavior (I don't believe in drugs, but I'm addicted to cocaine)

3. when people have no choice (I hate Statistics 101, but it is a required course)

4. when such unforseen events as illnesses and accidents prevent people from engaging in a behavior

Conversely, the relationship between attitudes and behavior is strengthened when:

1. the attitude is clear, significant, and/or based on past behavior (Fazio & Zanna, 1981)

2. it is in people's vested interest to behave in a manner consistent with their attitudes (Regan & Fazio, 1977)

3. people possess personality traits that promote consistency (Snyder, 1979)

THE RELATIONSHIP BETWEEN BEHAVIOR AND ATTITUDES

It seems natural to expect that if you change people's attitudes, their behaviors also change: we expect people to maintain consistency between their attitudes and behaviors. However, changing a behavior to match an attitude is only one way to maintain consistency; another way is to change an attitude to match a behavior. Although this might appear to be putting the cart before the horse, social psychologists have found that people induced to behave in ways that are inconsistent with their attitudes—to engage in **counterattitudinal behavior**—often change their attitudes to match the behaviors. Consider a classic study by Leon Festinger and Merrill Carlsmith.

Festinger and Carlsmith (1959) arranged for subjects to work on an extremely dull task for an hour: putting twelve spools into a tray, emptying it, and refilling it. After they completed the task, the experimenter informed the subjects that his assistant had telephoned to say he could not work that day. Then the experimenter asked if they would fill in and remain on call in the future. The experimenter explained he was investigating the effects of people's expectation about how interesting a task would be on their actual performance of it and he needed someone to tell the next subjects that the task they had just com-

pleted was very "enjoyable," "interesting," "intriguing" and "exciting" (which, of course, it was not). The behavior in question, then, involved misleading subjects about the experimental task. The experimenter offered to pay the subjects for helping out. The independent variable of the study was the amount he offered. Half of the subjects were offered $1 for helping the experimenter (for lying); the other half were offered $20. Nearly all the subjects agreed to help. After the subjects completed the task, they were paid and then asked to indicate how interesting they actually thought the experimental task was. This indication of interest—a measure of their attitude toward the task they had performed—was the dependent variable.

Do you think inducing the subjects to say that a boring task was interesting (inducing subjects to behave in a manner inconsistent with their attitude) would cause them to change their attitude toward the task? It seems implausible that it would. After all, the subjects must have known how interesting they found the task; misrepresenting it to someone else should not have altered their own attitude toward it. In fact, this expectation is correct for one of the groups but incorrect for the other. The results of the study revealed that the subjects from one of the groups indeed changed their attitude toward the task, rating it as significantly more interesting than did the subjects in a control group. Which subjects changed their attitude — the subjects paid $20 or paid $1 for misrepresenting their view? Although it seems plausible to expect the subjects paid the most to change the most, just the opposite occurred: the subjects paid $1 rated the task as significantly more interesting than the subjects paid $20. The Festinger and Carlsmith experiment excited psychologists for two reasons. First, it showed that you can change people's attitudes by changing their behaviors; second, it showed that small incentives or rewards sometimes have a greater effect than large incentives or rewards.

Festinger's Theory of Cognitive Dissonance

The basic findings of the Festinger and Carlsmith study have been replicated many times; however, there has been considerable controversy about what they prove. Festinger and Carlsmith interpreted the results as support for Festinger's theory of cognitive dissonance. The theory of cognitive dissonance is the most influential of several cognitive consistency theories in social psychology — theories that assume people are motivated to maintain consistency among their cognitions. Indeed, the theory of cognitive dissonance has been characterized as "the most influential theory in social psychology" (Eisen, 1980, p. 132).

The central assumption of Festinger's theory is that people strive to maintain **consonance,** or consistency among their ideas, and that when they sense their ideas are inconsistent, they experience a state of unpleasant psychological tension called *cognitive dissonance.* Festinger (1957, p. 13) defined **cognitive dissonance** as "a negative drive-state occurring when an individual holds two cognitions which are psychologically inconsistent." Festinger and Carlsmith attempted to induce a state of dissonance in their subjects by getting them to behave in a manner inconsistent with their belief. Festinger (1957) suggested that people in a state of cognitive dissonance may attempt to reduce the tension in any of several ways, one of which is to deny responsibil-

ity for the counterattitudinal behavior and attribute it to an external source. For example, a person might say he or she was forced or enticed to act in a particular way. According to Festinger and Carlsmith, the subjects paid $20 resolved their dissonance by attributing their behavior to a strong external enticement — namely $20. In effect, they said to themselves "I can live with telling a small lie as long as there is a good reason for it." Because this specific option was not available to the subjects paid $1, according to the investigators they resolved their dissonance in another way — namely by changing their attitude toward the task (see Figure 11-21). In addition to these two methods, people reduce dissonance by reevaluating the dissonant cognition ("Telling small lies for the sake of science isn't bad"), creating supportive consonant ideas ("Think of all of the good things that happened because I helped the experimenter"), selectively recalling aspects of an idea ("There were parts of the task that were interesting"), and by qualifying the decision ("I did it once in these circumstances, but I won't do it again"). When social psychologists conduct studies on cognitive dissonance, they attempt to restrict the methods of reducing dissonance available to their subjects. For example, by indicating that the subjects might be asked to perform the same task again, Festinger and Carlsmith made it difficult for subjects to qualify their decision.

Festinger's theory of cognitive dissonance is based on a set of very simple assumptions; however, many of the predictions to which it has given rise are not obvious. Social psychologists have applied the theory to four main types of situation. The study we have just examined is an example of **induced compliance:** individuals are induced to behave inconsistently with one of their attitudes. The most common design for experiments on induced compliance is for subjects to write an essay or otherwise advocate a position different from the one they hold. The general finding of such studies is that people will change their attitudes if induced to behave in discrepant ways without strong external incentives or pressures.

The second type of situation also involves variations in external control; however, instead of such positive incentives and rewards as money,

Attitude-discrepant Behavior Performed for Small Rewards

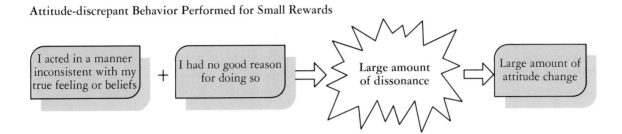

Attitude-discrepant Behavior Performed for Large Rewards

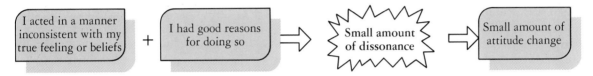

FIGURE 11-21

Attitude-discrepant Behavior When people do things that go against their true feelings or beliefs, they experience cognitive dissonance. However, if their behavior can be justified in some way, their dissonance can be reduced. *Source:* Baron, R. A., & Byrne, D. (1981). *Social psychology: Understanding human interaction* (3rd ed.). Boston, MA: Allyn and Bacon.

investigators use negative incentives and threats, and instead of inducing discrepant behavior, investigators prohibit individuals from engaging in a desirable behavior. For example, in some studies children are presented with a set of toys that includes one that is highly attractive but with which they are forbidden to play. Most children abide by the prohibition. Sometime later, the children are given an opportunity to play with the toys again, but this time they are not forbidden to play with the attractive toy (see Freedman, 1965). The independent variable in such experiments involves the degree of external control exerted on the children when they are forbidden to play with the attractive toy. Results reveal that children who are given strong external reasons (for example, severe threats) for not playing with a desired object subsequently are *more* likely to play with it than children who are subjected to less external control (such as, milder threats).

The explanation for the results of studies on **insufficient deterrence** is that when people are given strong external threats, they reduce the dissonance associated with behaving in a way that runs contrary to their attitude (not playing with an attractive toy) by reasoning "I had no choice"; so there is no need to change their attitude toward the toy. In contrast, those who feel they have a choice reduce their dissonance by devaluing the toy — in a sour grapes sort of way — reasoning "I could have played with the toy but I didn't because it's not that great anyway." Most people assume that if we want to induce someone to refrain from doing something he or she likes, the best way to do it is to "come on strong." However, the results of studies on insufficient deterrence suggest you will create a more enduring effect if you use the minimal amount of external control necessary to suppress the behavior.

The basic idea underlying the third type of situation investigated by dissonance theorists, **justification of effort,** is that people are motivated to maintain consistency between their investments and their outcomes. Consider a study by Aronson and Mills (1959). These researchers formed a group of female volunteers to take part in a discussion on the psychology of sex, which, the investigators said, would test their emotional maturity. Volunteers were divided into three groups. Two groups were told they were required to pass a screening test before taking part in the discussion. The first group was treated to an easy test: the subjects were called on to read a list of such relatively innocuous words as *virgin* and *prostitute*. The other group was subjected to a more severe test: they were required to read aloud to a male experimenter a list of 20 four-letter words and certain lurid passages from novels. The third group was not required to pass any screening test.

Following this first part of the study, the students were told they had been assigned to the group late and were asked to listen to a boring tape-recorded discussion of sexual behavior in nonhuman animals. The subjects then were asked to evaluate the tape-recorded discussion. The experimenters predicted the subjects who invested the greatest effort getting into the group would experience the greatest need to justify it and would therefore evaluate the boring discussion highest. The results supported this prediction, suggesting that such practices as subjecting people who want to join groups to severe initiation rites, charging high prices for merchandise, setting high standards of performance, and playing hard to get may enhance the attractiveness of objects, providing, of course, that the people ultimately obtain them.

The final situation studied by dissonance theorists is similar to those that involve invest-ment of time, effort, and money, but it involves investing in a choice between two attractive alternatives. We all have experienced the quandary involved in choosing between such material things as cars, such opportunities as colleges or jobs, or people ("You can only have one of us; which one do you choose?"). Dissonance theory predicts that once people make a decision (once they behave in a particular way), their attitude becomes more consistent with their choice—a process called **post-decision dissonance reduction** (see Figure 11-22). Studies have found that people elevate their evaluations of the alternatives they choose and lower their evaluations of those they reject. In a rather ingenious real-life study, Knox and Inkster (1968) approached bettors at a racetrack either before they placed a $2 bet or after they placed it, and asked them to estimate their chance of winning. These investigators found that bettors expressed significantly more confidence their horse would win the race after they placed their bet than before. Similarly, Rosenfeld, Giacalone, and Tedeschi (1983) found that students rated courses they selected for the upcoming semester as significantly more attractive after registration than before.

Chosen Alternative   Rejected Alternative

Positive features
Ten speeds
Several interchangeable blades
Powerful motor

Inconsistent { **Negative features**
with the { Color clashes with other appliances
decision { Blades are hard to clean

Inconsistent ⎰ **Positive Feature**
with the ⎱ Stainless steel construction
decision ⎱ Convenient light–dark toast switch

Negative features
Only toasts two slices
Cord is only nine inches long
Looks old-fashioned

FIGURE 11-22

Post-decision Dissonance Reduction After a decision has been made to purchase the hand mixer, the negative features of the toaster and the positive features of the hand mixer become emphasized in order to relieve post-decision dissonance and to strengthen the belief that the correct choice (decision) has been made. *Source:* Adapted from Kahn, A. S. (1984). *Social psychology.* Dubuque, IA: Wm. C. Brown.

Criticisms of Festinger's Theory of Cognitive Dissonance

In 1964, Chapanis and Chapanis published an influential critique of Festinger's theory of cognitive dissonance. These reviewers expressed concern about the failure of the theory to specify exactly what makes two cognitions dissonant, how to establish that subjects experience cognitive dissonance, and how to determine in advance which method subjects will employ to reduce it. In addition, Chapanis and Chapanis identified several methodological problems with the research purporting to test the theory, including the absence of appropriate control groups, the discarding of subjects, and dubious statistical procedures.

Although such criticisms dampened research on cognitive dissonance, after a brief fallow period supporters began to revise the theory in ways that accommodated to certain of the criticisms. It is interesting that such supporters of cognitive dissonance theory as Wicklund and Brehm (1976) characterize the revisions as "theoretical evolution," whereas such detractors as Forsyth, Riess, and Schlenker (1977) see them as "ad hoc modifications and interpretations."

Bem's Self-perception Theory

Most critiques of cognitive dissonance theory challenge the results of its supportive research. However, one influential critique accepts the basic findings of its supportive research but offers a radically different interpretation of them. We outline the assumptions of Daryl Bem's **theory of self-perception** and then examine research that has attempted to determine whether it is more valid than Festinger's theory of cognitive dissonance.

Cognitive dissonance theorists assume people harbor relatively stable attitudes and are sufficiently aware of them that when they behave in a manner inconsistent with their attitudes, it is quite obvious. Dissonance theorists also assume that subjects taking part in experiments change their attitudes in order to reduce an internal tension — cognitive dissonance. Daryl Bem (1965, 1967) questions these mentalistic assumptions. When you observe other people,

argues Bem, you infer their attitudes from their behavior — so why suggest a different process for yourself? According to Bem, people infer what their own attitudes are from how they behave. When they behave positively toward people and things, they infer they like them; when they behave negatively, they infer they dislike them.

Consider the subjects in the Festinger and Carlsmith study. What would you infer about the attitudes of subjects paid $20 to say a boring task was interesting? Most likely they did not find the task interesting, but wanted to make $20. However, if you were asked about subjects who said the task was interesting but were paid only $1, you might well infer these subjects did find the task interesting. In fact, Bem (1967) gave a group of subjects summary versions of the Festinger and Carlsmith study, and found exactly that. Bem suggested that subjects in studies on cognitive dissonance observe themselves in much the same manner they observe others, inferring their own attitudes on the basis of their own behaviors. Thus, the change in attitudes observed by Festinger and Carlsmith did not occur in order to reduce the tension of cognitive dissonance, argues Bem, but actually reflected inferences based on people's observations of their own behavior.

Dissonance or Self-perception?

In the Festinger and Carlsmith study, dissonance theory and self-perception theory give rise to identical predictions; consequently, the study does not provide a basis for distinguishing between the two theories. In an attempt to determine which theory offers the better explanation for the relationship between behavior and attitudes, other investigators have derived different predictions from each theory and then tested people to determine which predictions received greatest support. The findings from such studies are mixed, with some supporting Bem's theory and others supporting Festinger's. For example, if Bem's position is correct, then people should not infer their attitudes from their behaviors when they recognize their attitudes before engaging in behaviors. And if this is correct, then making people aware of their attitudes before they engage

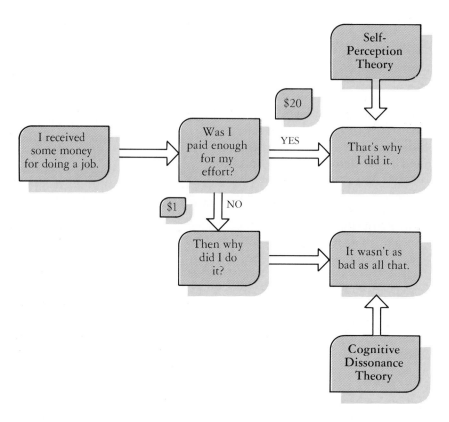

FIGURE 11-23

Self-perception versus Cognitive Dissonance Self-perception theory supplies a different explanation for attitude change, following counterattitudinal behavior from cognitive dissonance theory. *Source:* Adapted from Penrod, S. (1983). *Social psychology.* Englewood Cliffs, NJ: Prentice-Hall.

in a counterattitudinal behavior should reduce attitude change. In contrast, dissonance theorists predict greater change in attitudes that are conspicuous prior to engaging in inconsistent behaviors than attitudes that are not, because conspicuous attitudes evoke greater inconsistency. In support of Bem's position, Snyder and Ebbensen (1972) found that making people aware of their attitudes before they engaged in counterattitudinal behavior inhibited attitude change.

But other studies have supported Festinger's theory. In one rather ingenious study, Gonzalez and Cooper (1975) found that members of Princeton University's student dining clubs who agreed to write counterattitudinal essays advocating the abolition of such clubs indicated "new" lighting made them feel uneasy, when, in fact, the lighting had not been changed. The investigators interpreted these results as support for the assumption that counterattitudinal behavior produced an unpleasant tension (which was attributed to "new" lighting). Other studies have found a decrease in attitude change when arousal is low and an increase in attitude change when it is high (Kiesler & Pallak, 1976).

It appears that both cognitive dissonance and self-perception influence the relationship between behavior and attitudes. Fazio, Zanna, and Cooper (1977) suggest that self-perception theory is most applicable when people behave in ways consistent with, but more extreme than, their attitudes (see Box 11-7), and cognitive dissonance theory is most applicable when people behave in ways inconsistent with their attitudes and beliefs, especially important ones. Self-perception theory seems most applicable in mundane matters, when attitudes are weak or unclear, and when the discrepancy between attitudes and behavior is slight (see also Chaiken & Baldwin, 1981).

Box 11-7
Overjustification

A wise old man lived on a street where, every morning, a group of noisy boys gathered to play. The uproar was distressful to him, so, one day, when the boys were relatively subdued, he went out to talk to them. He told them that he loved the sound of children playing, and that he would pay them 50 cents each to play outside his house. The next day the boys came back and played with great vigor, collecting their reward at the end of the day. The old man promised them a reward if they would return the following day. The boys did return, and played vigorously, but when it came time to pay them, the old man explained that he didn't have much money, and gave them 25 cents each. The next day he explained that he could afford only 15 cents. He explained that he would be able to pay only 10 cents the next day, and beseeched them to return, but they never did. Who would do all that work for such a meagre wage? (Myers, 1983, p. 65)

The moral of this story can be found in Bem's theory of self-perception. If you offer people a large external incentive to behave in a particular way, they will infer they must not want to engage in the behavior. This principle, called the **over-justification effect,** has

been supported by a number of studies. Lepper and Greene (1979) have shown that promising children a reward or paying them to engage in an activity they already like (for example, playing with puzzles or crayons) produces a decrease in their desire to engage in the activity on subsequent occasions, especially if the children do not have a strong attitude toward the task beforehand (Fazio, 1981). Similarly, Benware and Deci (1975) found that paying students $7.50 to espouse a cause in which they already believed (that students should have some input to courses offered at their college) decreased their commitment to it.

The counterproductive consequences of rewarding individuals for doing things they like has important implications for such people as parents, teachers, and employers who are in a position to *overjustify* the behaviors they want others to perform. In one study, Greene, Sternberg, and Lepper (1976) demonstrated how injudiciously administered rewards can undermine fourth- and fifth-grade children's intrinsic motivation to learn. These investigators created a "math lab" that operated for approximately six weeks. During

the first two weeks, the researchers permitted children to select freely among four kinds of problems. During the second two weeks, they rewarded the children for working on two of the four problems. During the final two weeks, the children again were permitted to choose which problems they pursued, but without reward. The results of this study showed that the children's interest in the two problems accompanied by reward diminished after the reward was withdrawn (sound familiar?).

The moral of research on rewarding people for doing things they would do anyway is not that you should never reward people for doing things they like to do. Giving unanticipated rewards after people perform a task generally increases their desire to do it again and, in general, rewards that inform people about their performance tend to enhance that performance. It is rewards that people interpret as controlling their behavior that have the reverse effect. For example, Deci and Ryan (1980) found that teachers who use rewards to control students produce students with less intrinsic motivation to learn than teachers who use rewards to supply feedback about competence.

ATTRIBUTION

The model of human nature underlying Bem's theory of self-perception is significantly different from the one underlying Festinger's theory of cognitive dissonance. Festinger views people as consistency-seekers motivated to reduce the internal tension evoked by feelings of inconsistency. Bem views people in more exclusively rational terms, as naive scientists (indeed, as personality and social psychologists) searching for the causes of their behavior.

The portrait of people as naive scientists was first popularized in social psychology by Fritz Heider (1958), who suggested that people, like scientists, attempt to understand, predict, and control events that concern them by constructing theories of human behavior. Ross and Fletcher (1985) single out four of Heider's early ideas as particularly influential:

1. When people observe others, they tend to search for enduring, unchanging, and [in Heider's words] dispositional characteristics.

2. Observers distinguish between intentional and unintentional behavior (unintentional behavior is uninformative; it tells you little about the person in question).

3. Observers are inclined to attribute the behavior of others to one of two general sources: qualities within them (internal dispositions) and characteristics of the environment (external or situational sources).

4. People are inclined to attribute outcomes to events (causes) that are present when the outcome is present and absent when the outcome is absent (the covariation principle).

Heider's ideas concern **attribution**—the process through which people link effects to causes. Like the common-sense theories of the average person that he sought to explain, Heider (1958) did not formulate his own theory of attribution rigorously. Heider's primary contribution was to inspire other psychologists to follow up his original ideas. Less than a decade after

Heider published *The Psychology of Interpersonal Relations,* two extensions and refinements of his ideas were published (Jones & Davis, 1965; Kelley 1967). We consider Kelley's theory of attribution because it has been the more influential of the two (Ross & Fletcher, 1985).

Kelley's Covariation Theory of Attribution

Kelley's (1967) theory deals with the inferences observers make about people with whom they have repeated contact. Kelley suggests the average person makes judgments about others more or less out of habit. However, when others behave in unexpected ways, observers search for the cause of the unexpected behavior. Drawing from Heider, Kelley suggests people search for the causes of unexpected behavior in two main places—within the person whose behavior they are interpreting and in the environment (which often includes other people). In addition, suggests Kelley, observers may attribute causes to mitigating circumstances. Consider the following example. A good friend is late for a play. In the role of naive scientist, you ask yourself why. According to Kelley, you should consider three possibilities: (1) your friend is unreliable *(person attribution)*, (2) the play is being staged in an inaccessible place *(environmental attribution)*, and (3) something unexpected arose *mitigating circumstances*).

Faced with such questions, how do people answer them? Again drawing from Heider, Kelley suggests people search for **covariation:** attributing the behavior in question to the cause with which, over time, it is most closely associated. Kelley identifies three sources of information to which people appeal in making judgments based on covariation: information about *consensus, consistency,* and *distinctiveness*. Returning to our example, an observer might ask: (1) "How many people were late for the play?" (consensus), (2) "How often is my friend late for plays?" (consistency), and (3) "How often is my friend late?" (distinctiveness). Note that consensus refers to *other people* in the same situation;

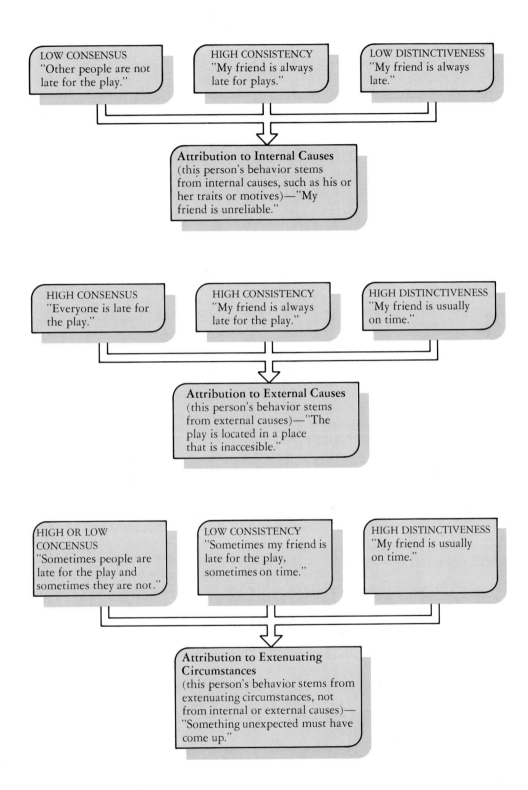

LOW CONSENSUS
"Other people are not late for the play."

HIGH CONSISTENCY
"My friend is always late for plays."

LOW DISTINCTIVENESS
"My friend is always late."

Attribution to Internal Causes
(this person's behavior stems from internal causes, such as his or her traits or motives)—"My friend is unreliable."

HIGH CONSENSUS
"Everyone is late for the play."

HIGH CONSISTENCY
"My friend is always late for the play."

HIGH DISTINCTIVENESS
"My friend is usually on time."

Attribution to External Causes
(this person's behavior stems from external causes)—"The play is located in a place that is inaccesible."

HIGH OR LOW CONCENSUS
"Sometimes people are late for the play and sometimes they are not."

LOW CONSISTENCY
"Sometimes my friend is late for the play, sometimes on time."

HIGH DISTINCTIVENESS
"My friend is usually on time."

Attribution to Extenuating Circumstances
(this person's behavior stems from extenuating circumstances, not from internal or external causes)—"Something unexpected must have come up."

FIGURE 11-24
Causal Schemata in Kelley's Covariation Theory of Attribution The three causal schemata in Kelley's theory are LHH, HHH, and L-HHH. (See text, p. 574.)

consistency refers to the person in question in the *same situation;* and distinctiveness refers to the person in question in *other situations.* The answers observers give to these questions determine whether they attribute the behavior in question to the person, to the environment, or to mitigating circumstances. Figure 11-24 outlines the types of attribution that follow from various combinations of information.

Causal Schemata   In his original theory, Kelley (1967) assumed people are quite thorough and scientific in their analyses of behavior — systematically processing information about consensus, distinctiveness, and consistency before reaching a conclusion. But this assumption proved untenable. In revisions of his theory, Kelley suggests people make attributions on the basis of limited information. In a sense, Kelley concludes people are not as scientific as he originally assumed; rather, their judgments are biased by preconceptions about which causes are associated with which effects. Kelley (1972) calls these preconceptions **causal schemata.** The three most significant causal schemata, outlined in Figure 11-24, state that people expect information to be arranged in terms of:

1. low consensus, high consistency, and low distinctiveness (**LHL**)
2. high consensus, high consistency, and high distinctiveness (**HHH**)
3. high or low consensus, low consistency, and high distinctiveness (**H-LLH**)

It follows, suggests Kelley, that if the only information you receive (or in some cases if the first information you receive) indicates high consensus ("Everyone is late for the play"), you make an external attribution (**HHH**) about the person's behavior (see Figure 11-24) and attribute it to something in the environment (the play). Information indicating low consensus is not as useful because low consensus can lead to an internal attribution (**LHL**) or to an attribution to extenuating circumstances (**L-HLH**; see Figure 11-24). Information indicating low consistency is more useful than information indicating high consistency because low consistency can lead only to an attribution to extenuating circumstances

(**L-HLH**). Thus, if your friend is sometimes late for the play and sometimes not, you should conclude that his or her behavior was due to extenuating circumstances (see Hanson, 1980). Finally, as shown in Figure 11-24, information indicating low distinctiveness is more useful than information indicating high distinctiveness because low distinctiveness can lead only to an internal attribution (**LHL**; the fact that "my friend is always late" shows that "my friend is unreliable").

The Fundamental Attributional Error

Heider (1958) suggested that when observers are faced with a choice between attributing another person's behavior to internal-personal versus external-situational causes, they tend to favor internal dispositional factors. Ross (1977, p. 184) labeled observers' "general tendency to overestimate the importance of personal . . . factors relevant to environmental influences" the **fundamental attributional error.** The fundamental attributional error is demonstrated in a study by Jones and Harris (1967) wherein subjects read debate speeches that either supported or attacked Fidel Castro. Some subjects were informed that speech writers selected the position they would debate and other subjects were informed that writers were assigned the position. Subjects were asked to predict how pro- or anti-Castro the speech writers' attitudes actually were. As expected, the results revealed that subjects predicted those writers who had chosen the position believed in it — the subjects made a dispositional attribution. However, subjects also predicted that those writers who were assigned their position also believed in it — they made a dispositional attribution, although a situational attribution seemed more appropriate. It would appear that the average person is more a personality theorist than a social psychologist at heart (social psychologists tend to focus on the effect of situational forces).

Although many studies have found that observers tend to attribute the behavior of others to internal dispositions, the fundamental attributional error does not always occur. In some situations, such as when observers have formed judg-

Box 11-8
"Quick and Easy" Inferences about Others

Kelley's revisions suggest people are somewhat impulsive when making attributions, that they jump to conclusions without adequate evidence. Research inspired by Kelley's theory tends to support this characterization. In a review of relevant literature, Nisbett and L. Ross (1980, p. 101) concluded that

> People's views of covariation in the social world . . . are not formed primarily on the basis of some computational procedures analogous to the statistician's procedures. Rather, the layperson's views of the data are greatly influenced by theories and expectations.

For example, Nisbett and Ross adduce evidence showing that people often expect causes to resemble effects. In one study, Henslin

(1967) found that crap-shooters believed the harder they threw the dice, the higher the number they would produce. Nisbett and Ross also found that people tend to attribute effects to perceptually conspicuous causes. If you see a person standing by a wrecked car crying, you are more likely to attribute the crying to the accident than to something less obvious, such as a toothache.

Other studies have found that consensus information about objects of attribution is ignored or downplayed in certain situations (see Kasin, 1979, for a review of the literature). For example, Nisbett and Borgida (1975) found that information about how a majority of hypothetical subjects responded in psychological experiments

involving shock and emergency intervention did not affect people's attributions of the causes of the subjects' behavior or predictions of how they themselves would respond. Similarly, Taylor (1980) found that people tend to disregard information about how others have responded to events with which they have had personal experience ("I don't care whether everyone else found the play dull, I thought it was good"). The evidence suggests that consensus information exerts an effect most often when people lack confidence in their opinions (Kulik & Taylor, 1980) and when the consensus information is perceived as representative of the population as a whole (Wells & Harvey, 1977).

ments about an individual's personality and the individual behaves inconsistently with these judgments, observers tend to attribute his or her behavior to situational factors (see Kulik, 1983).

The Attribution of Responsibility and Blame

An important implication of the tendency for observers to attribute the behavior of others to internal dispositions rather than to external factors relates to situations involving damage and misfor-

tune. Consider a study by Elaine Walster. Walster (1966) asked subjects to respond to a hypothetical accident. In one circumstance a car rolled down a hill and caused minor damage. In the other circumstance the car rolled down a hill and caused major damage. Although the initiating circumstances were identical, the subjects attributed significantly more responsibility to the owner of the runaway car when the damage was major than when the damage was minor. The tendency to attribute more responsibility (to make stronger dispositional attributions) when consequences are severe than when they are mild has been called **defensive attribution** (see Fiske & Taylor, 1984). Walster hypothesized that people make such attributions in order to defend against the idea that tragic things may happen to people (including themselves) for no reason.

Since Walster conducted her study, more than 20 studies have examined defensive attributions (see Burger, 1981), with inconsistent results. Burger (1981) suggests the inconsistent results can be resolved as follows. In situations where subjects do not identify with the perpetrator of damage (when they view themselves as dissimilar), they make defensive attributions and attribute more responsibility as the damage becomes greater. However, in situations where subjects identify with the perpetrator of damage, they attribute less responsibility as the damage becomes greater. Both biases tend to reduce the unpleasant implications of the conclusion for the subjects themselves.

The Need to Believe in a Just World An interesting implication of the tendency for people to hold others responsible for the damage they cause has been investigated by Melvin Lerner and his colleagues (Lerner, 1965; Lerner & Simmons, 1966). Consider a situation in which a woman is raped. It is not uncommon for people to blame the woman by, for example, accusing her of taking chances, giving mixed messages, or "asking for it." In fact, women who are raped and other victims of misfortune usually do not bring on their suffering by themselves. Why, then, do people tend to hold them responsible for it?

According to Melvin Lerner, people possess a need to believe in a just world—a world in which people get what they deserve and deserve what they get. Underlying this need is their fear of living in an irrational world in which there is no dependable relationship between what people do and what happens to them. According to Lerner, encountering a person who has suffered misfortune through no apparent fault of his or her own evokes considerable anxiety. Lerner suggests the anxiety is allayed by reinterpreting the situation as one in which the victim was not really innocent, thus preserving the belief that the world is just (see Lerner & Simons, 1966).

There is a great deal of experimental evidence in support of Lerner's theory. In an early study (Lerner, 1965), subjects observed two people working on a task. Subjects were told one of the workers would be paid but the other would not, and the paid worker would be picked at random by toss of a coin. The rationale given for this procedure was that the experimenter did not have enough money to pay both workers. Although the two workers (actually accomplices of the researcher) contributed equally to the task, when subjects were asked to rate the contribution of each, they rated the contribution of the paid worker higher than the contribution of the unpaid worker. According to Lerner, the subjects biased their perceptions in a manner that led them to view the paid worker as more deserving than the unpaid worker in order to maintain their belief in a just world.

Doubtless there are many people who do not believe the world is just and who, therefore, would be skeptical of Lerner's hypothesis. In particular, we might not expect victims of misfortune to believe they deserve to suffer; however, there is evidence that innocent victims sometimes blame themselves for their misfortunes. This view is exemplified by the guilt feelings experienced by survivors of the atomic bombing of Hiroshima toward the end of World War II (Lifton, 1963).

Differences in Self-Attributions and Attributions about Others

Try the following exercise taken from a study conducted by L. Goldberg in 1978 and discussed by Fiske & Taylor (1984) in their book on social cognition. Select a close friend of yours and rate this person according to the personality traits listed on the scale printed on the following page. Simply choose the appropriate numerical rating for each adjective and place the corresponding number in the column labeled "friend." (Note that the ratings pertain to the extent to which the personality characteristics distinguish the person being rated.) When you have finished, rate yourself on the same personality characteristics using the column labeled "self."

Rating Scale

−2	Definitely does not describe
−1	Usually does not describe
0	Sometimes describes, sometimes not
+1	Usually describes
+2	Definitely describes

	Friend	Self
Aggressive	_____	_____
Introverted	_____	_____
Thoughtful	_____	_____
Warm	_____	_____
Outgoing	_____	_____
Hard driving	_____	_____
Ambitious	_____	_____
Friendly	_____	_____
	Total _____	Total _____

Now count the number of qualified ratings in each column.

In this exercise, you attributed personality traits (internal dispositions) to another person (your friend) and to yourself. If you resemble most people tested, you assigned more qualified ratings to yourself than to your friend for personality traits (see Figure 11-25). Put another way, you made dispositional attributions for your friend and situational attributions for yourself. (When you say you are sometimes aggressive and sometimes not, you are, in effect, saying you behave aggressively in some situations but not in others). Whereas people are biased toward internal dispositional factors when making judgments about others, they are biased toward external situational factors when making judgments about themselves. This is called the **actor–observer difference** in attribution.

What causes people to prefer dispositional attributions for others and situational attributions for themselves? Social psychologists have offered two main explanations. The first is perceptual in nature, and suggests that people usually do not look at or perceive themselves (except in mirrors). Consequently, when motivated to explain their behavior, people heed things they can see or are most conspicuous—the external situation or

environment. When it comes to explaining the behavior of others, however, people heed the others—they are the most interesting objects in the environment. Heeding others evokes dispositional attributions. In support of this explanation, studies have found people make internal attributions about themselves when induced to view themselves as observers. Storms (1973) accomplished this by showing subjects a videotape of themselves from the perspective of an observer. Similarly, studies have found when subjects are induced to view others from the same perspective they view themselves (for example, empathizing with them), they attribute the behavior of others to situational factors (Regan & Totten, 1975).

The second explanation for the actor-observer difference relates to the difference between the amount of information actors have

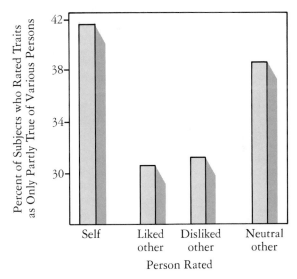

FIGURE 11-25

Actor–Observer Differences in Attribution
Subjects were asked to rate the extent to which a large number of traits were true of themselves and others. The results show that more subjects saw the traits "only partially true" of themselves than saw the traits "only partially true" of others. These results support the belief that people tend to view the behavior of others as stemming from such internal factors as traits and to view their own behavior as stemming from external or situational factors. *Source:* After Goldberg, L. R. (1978). Differential attribution of trait-descriptive terms to oneself as compared to well-liked, neutral, and disliked others: A psychometric analysis. *Journal of Personality and Social Psychology, 36,* 1012–28.

Box 11-9
Biases in Self-attribution

Self-attributions are susceptible to at least three biases: the *false consensus effect,* the *perception of uniqueness,* and the *self-serving bias.*

False Consensus Effect. The **false consensus effect** involves the tendency to assume that more people support your views than actually do. A study by Ross, Green, and House (1977) demonstrates this bias. Ross et al. (1977) asked college students if they would walk around campus wearing a sandwich board containing the message *Eat at Joe's.* After the students responded (agreeing or disagreeing), the experimenters asked how many other students they thought would agree to the same request. The students who accepted the request believed 62% of their fellow students also would accept it; those who rejected the request believed only 33% would accept it. The false consensus effect has been found to inflate people's estimates of the extent to which others agree with their political attitudes (Fields & Schuman, 1976), the causes of conflict in personal relationships (Harvey, Wells, & Alvarez, 1978), and

various other preferences (L. Ross, Greene, & House, 1977.)

Perception of Uniqueness. People appear to assume they are more unique than they actually are. For example, M. Ross (1981) found members of groups take more individual responsibility for group products than other members give them. Weinstein (1980) found people overestimate the probability they will be successful in life, (live past 80, own a house, and avoid divorce and heart attack).

Several explanations have been offered for the false concensus effect and the **perception of uniqueness.** Some investigators attribute these biases to such rational types of processes as interacting with people who are similar; other investigators attribute them to such irrational processes as the need to enhance self-esteem or justify beliefs (see L. Ross et al, 1977)

Self-serving Bias. Imagine you do unexpectedly well on a test. How would you explain it? If you resemble most people, you tend to attribute your success to yourself—perhaps to your intelligence—and take full

credit for it. But what if someone else does unexpectedly well? How would you explain his or her success? Research indicates people are inclined to attribute unexpected successes of others to such external factors as luck, unless they identify with the person experiencing the success. In addition, people tend to deny responsibility for their own failures—to attribute them to external factors ("The test was unfair")—but to attribute the failures of others to dispositional factors ("He isn't very smart"). Research has shown the self-enhancing side of the **self-serving bias** (people's tendency to take credit for their own successes) is stronger than the self-protective side (people's tendency to blame their own failures on external factors (see Miller & Ross, 1975).

Two explanations have been offered for self-serving biases. The most obvious is motivational in nature: people seek to elevate their self-esteem and to protect their egos. The other explanation is more subtle: it attributes the bias to such cognitive factors as expectation of success, the tendency to strive for success, and the

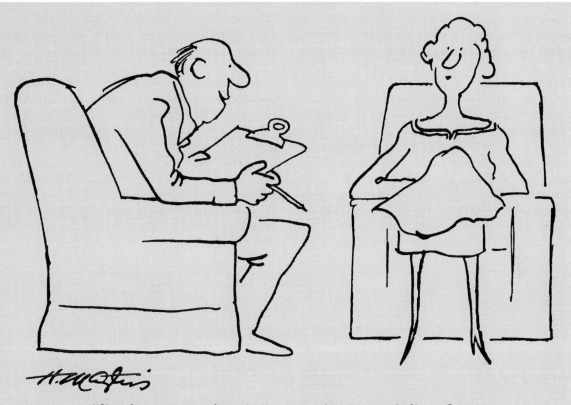

*"I'm drawing up a list of all my good points and all my flaws,
and so far my good points are running way, way ahead of my flaws."*

The self-serving bias   *Source: Better Homes and Gardens* magazine.   Meredith Corporation, 1975.

resulting sense of deserving success. For example, there tends to be a positive association between how hard you try and how well you do. Therefore, when you try hard, you expect to do well; and when you do well, you attribute it to such internal factors as trying hard. But people generally have much less information about such internal factors in others as how hard they try; therefore, they are less disposed to attribute the success of others to such factors. Several studies have attempted to assess the relative merits of these two explanations. In general, the motivational explanation has received greater support (see Weary, 1980); however, by no means have cognitive factors been ruled out (see Tetlock & Levi, 1982).

Although most research on self-serving biases has focused on the self (defined narrowly), some studies have found that self-serving biases also apply to individuals who are, in a sense, part of the self—such as one's spouse and children, close friends, reference groups, sports teams, and even political candidates (Burger, 1981). We tend to give people with whom we identify credit for their successes and tend to make excuses for their failures, much the same as we do for ourselves.

about themselves and the amount of information they have about observers. In essence, it assumes dispositional attributions are rather simplistic and situational attributions are more complex. People are not prone to attribute such dispositional qualities as altruism to themselves because they know they are sometimes altruistic and sometimes selfish — depending on the situation. In contrast, their judgments of others are based on much less experience.

In a review of studies on the difference between self-attributions and attributions about others, Monson and Snyder (1977) concluded there is substantial evidence the attributions of observers often differ from the attributions of actors, but not always in the ways we have discussed. These reviewers attempt to resolve inconsistencies in the research by suggesting that self-attributions generally are more valid than attributions about others because people know more about themselves. People tend to attribute their own behavior to aspects of situations because their own behavior usually is evoked by situational forces. However, when an individual's behavior does in fact reflect a disposition, the person will make an even stronger dispositional attribution than other people judging the same behavior.

The actor-observer difference suggests people may not always be objective in their role of naive scientist, especially when it comes to making attributions about themselves. Box 11-9 on page 578 describes three biases that affect the process of self-attribution.

SUMMARY

1. Performance on well-learned or simple tasks is improved by the mere presence of others — a phenomenon called social facilitation; performance on poorly-learned or complex tasks is impaired by the mere presence of others. There are four primary theories of social facilitation: Zajonc's drive theory; Cottrell's evaluation-apprehension theory; Sanders, Baron, and Moore's distraction-conflict theory; and Bond's self-image theory.

2. The behavior of people in mobs may be explained either by reduced accountability and lowered public self-awareness or by lowered private self-awareness and deindividuation. Deindividuation refers to a state in which individuals lose awareness of their identities. People behave in more ruthless and socially inappropriate ways when they are not easily identifiable and when they are caught up in highly emotional group activities.

3. The surprising finding that the chance of a victim receiving help decreases as the number of potential helpers increases follows naturally from a consideration of the social forces at work in the situation. Research has shown that at least three factors inhibit bystanders from intervening in emergencies: fear of embarrassment, modeling the inaction of others, and diffusion of responsibility. In immediate, severe, pressing emergencies almost all bystanders intervene impulsively, without apparent concern for their own well-being.

4. In ambiguous situations, individuals develop personal conceptions of reality — individual norms. Group norms, a convergence of individual norms, develop in ambiguous situations in which individuals report their individual norms.

5. Groups induce conformity by controlling information, setting an example, and regulating sanctions. In the Asch situation, the degree of conformity increases the more ambiguous the object of judgment, the greater the size of the group, the more unanimous

the judgments of group members, the greater the expectation of later interaction with group members, the greater the attraction of the group to the individual, the lower the individual's status in the group, the lower the individual's self-confidence, and the more public the individual's judgments. Failure to conform tends to result in rejection.

6. The influence of minorities and dissenters is greatest when the majority is small and when two or more members of a minority advance a consistent position. Three aspects of the behavioral style of minorities are important: consistency, autonomy, and rigidity.

7. Obedience to authority is one of the most powerful types of social influence. Studies by Milgram (1963) provide compelling examples. Situation pressures and social roles are central to an analysis of social behavior. People are more willing to behave in ways that correspond to the social roles they play than most of us expect. For example, Zimbardo's simulated prison experiment had to be terminated because subjects playing the roles of prisoners and guards became overly committed to their roles.

8. Latané's social impact theory is founded on three basic principles: (1) the amount of social impact experienced by an individual depends on the strength, immediacy, and number of others influencing him or her, (2) the increments in social influence obtained from each individual added to a group diminish accordingly, and (3) the strength, immediacy, and number of targets of social impact (for example, minority group members) lessen social impact.

9. Attitudes consist of affective, cognitive, and behavioral components. There are at least eight links in the chain between a persuasive communication and a behavioral decision: attending to a message, retaining interest in the message, comprehension of the message,

generating related cognitions, agreeing or disagreeing with the message, storing a change in memory, retrieving new attitudes from memory, and making a decision.

10. People's attitudes tend to become more favorable with repeated exposure to objects. The effects of persuasive communication depend on characteristics of the source, message, channel, and receiver of the communication.

11. Brainwashing may be understood in terms of the types of social influence and the aspects of persuasive communication considered in this chapter.

12. Five factors have been identified that strengthen the link between attitudes and behavior: (1) corresponding levels of specificity between attitudes and behavior, (2) subjective norms, (3) clarity of the attitude, (4) vested interest, and (5) personality traits that promote consistency.

13. The theory of cognitive dissonance, a major consistency theory, proposes that people will change their attitudes in order to maintain perceived consistency with their behavior. Studies on forced compliance, insufficient deterrence, justification of effort, and post-decision dissonance reduction have supplied support for cognitive dissonance theory.

14. An alternative explanation of people's tendency to make their attitudes consistent with their behavior is to assume that people make inferences about the attitudes they possess essentially in the same way they make inferences about the attitudes of others — by observing their own behavior. Research on Bem's self-perception theory has shown that forcing people to do things or giving them strong incentives to do things induces the people to perceive such things negatively.

15. Attribution is the process through which people link effects to causes. In general, actions

are explained when the cause of the action is located in the person (internal) or in the environment (external). Kelley's covariation theory of attribution holds that people appeal to three types of information when making attributions: information about consensus, consistency, and distinctiveness.

16. Two of the most common errors in attribution involve underestimating situational factors in judgments about others (the fundamental attributional error) and underestimating personal factors in judgments about self (actor–observer difference). People's need to believe the world is a just place where individuals get what they deserve may bias the attributions they make about others. The three biases of self-attribution are false consensus, perception of uniqueness, and self-serving bias.

KEY TERMS

Social Influence	Group Norm	Cognitive Dissonance
Social Cognition	Idiosyncracy Credit	Induced Compliance
Attribution	Behavioral Style	Insufficient Deterrence
Social Facilitation	Consistency	Justification of Effort
Social Inhibition	Autonomy	Post-decision Dissonance
Dominant Response	Rigidity	Reduction
Meta-analysis	Compliance	Theory of Self-perception
Deindividuation	Conversion	Overjustification Effect
Public Self-awareness	Social Impact	Attribution
Private Self-awareness	Strength	Covariation
Behavioral Cue	Immediacy	Causal Schemata
Objective Self-awareness	Number	Fundamental Attributional
Individuation	Source	Error
Bystander Intervention	Message	Defensive Attribution
Bystander Effect	Channel	Actor–Observer Difference
Impulsive Helping	Receiver	False Consensus Effect
Norm	Subjective Norm	Perception of Uniqueness
Autokinetic Effect	Counterattitudinal Behavior	Self-serving Bias
Individual Norm	Consonance	

RECOMMENDED READINGS

Aronson, E. (1984). *The social animal* (4th ed.). San Francisco, CA: W. H. Freeman. A very interesting overview of social psychology. Includes chapters on conformity, propaganda and persuasion, self-justification, aggression, and prejudice.

Fiske, S. T., & Taylor, S. E. (1984). *Social cognition.* Reading, MA: Addison-Wesley. A solid, encompassing introduction to attributions, attitudes, and other types of social cognition.

Krebs, D. L. (1981). *Readings in psychology: Contemporary perspectives* (2nd ed.). New York: Harper & Row. A collection of readings on the real-life effects of modeling, compliance, obedience to authority, deindividuation, and bystander intervention. Includes more elaborate reports of certain studies presented in this chapter.

Milgram, S. (1974). *Obedience to authority.* New York: Harper & Row. An effective discussion, oriented to the nonspecialist, of Milgram's provocative research on obedience to authority.

Piliavin, J. A., Dovidio, J. F., Gaertner, S. L., & Clark, R. D., III (1981). *Emergency intervention.* New York: Academic Press. A relatively high-level overview of research on bystander intervention.

Zimbardo, P. G., Ebbesen, E. B., & Maslach, C. (1977). *Influencing attitudes and changing behavior.* Reading, MA: Addison-Wesley. A readable introduction to the field, with a strong emphasis on practical applications.

12

PERSONALITY, INTELLIGENCE, AND PSYCHOLOGICAL TESTS

In the days of ancient Greece, actors wore masks during theatrical performances. The Latin word for such masks is *persona,* meaning to amplify or speak (*sona*) through (*per*). Over time, persona came to refer to the roles actors played. Our word *personality* derives from this root. In a sense, the linguistic association between personality and the images people project is appropriate. When we say people have a *good personality,* we mean, in part, that they have social poise: they make a good impression. Yet, in another sense this definition is inappropriate: there is more to personality than the roles we play and the masks we wear. Our personalities also include the person behind the mask—the actor as well as the act.

In psychology, the term **personality** refers both to the outer facades people display and to their inner qualities. Personality consists of a **periphery,** or outside, and a **core,** or inside (Maddi, 1976). The periphery of personality is what shows—for example, whether an individual smiles a lot, spends considerable time alone, or displays a quick temper. The core of personality consists of such inner characteristics as biological urges, intellectual capacities, and conscience.

In Chapter 11, we portrayed average people as amateur social psychologists; we open this chapter with an examination of average people as amateur personality theorists. People observe the periphery of others' personalities—aspects of appearance and behavior—and make inferences about their inner core, especially personality traits. For example, an observer might infer that someone wearing a beard, glasses, and tweed jacket is intellectual. But how good a personality theorist is the average person? How accurate are the impressions people form of others in their daily lives? How similar are the implicit theories of personality of different people? How do the implicit theories of personality of the average person compare to the more scientific theories of psychologists?

Following an examination of the average person as personality theorist, we outline several formal approaches to personality: the trait approaches of Hans Eysenck and Raymond Cattell, the psychoanalytic approaches of Sigmund Freud and Erik Erikson, the humanistic approach of Carl Rogers, and the cognitive approach of George Kelly. We then examine the person-situation controversy—Is behavior determined by inner characteristics or external constraints?—outlining the behavioristic position of B. F. Skinner and the social learning positions of Walter Mischel and Albert Bandura. Following this, we describe some of the most popular personality tests, examine the logic of their construction, and evaluate their credentials. Finally, we focus on the master trait of human personality—intelligence.

IMPLICIT PERSONALITY THEORIES OF ORDINARY PEOPLE

Person Perception

Researchers have found that people attribute a vast array of characteristics to others based on particular aspects of their appearance. For example, studies have shown that people assume:

1. Women with blond hair have more fun than women with brunette hair, but that women with brunette hair are more intelligent (Lawson, 1971).
2. People with low foreheads and short noses tend to be unhappy (Bradshaw, 1969).
3. People with thin lips are more conscientious than people with thicker lips (Secord, Dukes, & Bevan, 1954).
4. Chubby people (endomorphs) are unpopular, lazy, and talkative; skinny people are ambitious, tense, and suspicious; and well-built people are energetic, self-reliant, and well-adjusted (Dibiase & Hjelle, 1968).

It is interesting to note that the taller of the two candidates for the presidency of the United States has won almost every presidential election since 1900 and that tall male college graduates (6'2" and taller) tend to receive higher starting salaries than their shorter counterparts (Feldman, 1971). The average observer attributes more positive qualities to tall men than to short men, and vice versa. Wilson (1968) found that when a guest speaker was introduced as a professor, he was judged to be taller than when introduced as a student.

Although virtually any aspect of physical appearance may affect the impression an individual conveys, characteristics that relate to ethnic heritage, gender, and physical attractiveness are particularly important. Most people employ **stereotypes** in their judgments of others. They attribute to individual members the traits associated with the groups of which they are part. As shown in Table 12-1, ethnic stereotypes appear to

be growing more positive. We discussed stereotypes about women in Chapter 10 and consider stereotypes of physical attractiveness in Box 12-1.

How valid are the average person's inferences about personality: what can you tell about people from the way they look? Some aspects of appearance have been found to correlate with some aspects of personality. For example, college women who dress fashionably have been found to have different attitudes, values, and personality traits than women who do not (Reed, 1974). However, people have some control over this aspect of their appearance and, therefore,

TABLE 12-1
Percent of College Students Endorsing Ethnic Stereotypes*

Trait	Percent Checking Trait			Trait	Percent Checking Trait		
	1933	1951	1967		1933	1951	1967
Americans				***Italians***			
Industrious	48	30	23	Artistic	53	28	30
Intelligent	47	32	20	Impulsive	44	19	28
Materialistic	33	37	67	Passionate	37	25	44
Progressive	27	5	17	Musical	32	22	9
Aggressive	20	8	15	Imaginative	30	20	7
Sportsmanlike	19	—	9	Revengeful	17	—	0
Germans				***Japanese***			
Scientifically minded	78	62	47	Intelligent	45	11	20
Industrious	65	50	59	Industrious	43	12	57
Intelligent	32	32	19	Progressive	24	2	17
Methodical	31	20	21	Sly	20	21	3
Extremely nationalistic	24	50	43	Imitative	17	24	22
Efficient	16	—	46	Treacherous	13	17	1
Chinese				***Blacks***			
Superstitious	34	18	8	Superstitious	84	41	13
Sly	29	4	6	Lazy	75	31	26
Conservative	29	14	15	Happy-go-lucky	38	17	27
Tradition-loving	26	26	32	Ignorant	38	24	11
Loyal to family ties	22	35	50	Musical	26	33	47
Deceitful	14	—	5	Very religious	24	17	8
English				***Jews***			
Sportsmanlike	53	21	22	Shrewd	79	47	30
Intelligent	46	29	23	Mercenary	49	28	15
Tradition-loving	31	42	21	Industrious	48	29	33
Conservative	30	22	53	Grasping	34	17	17
Sophisticated	27	37	47	Intelligent	29	37	37
Courteous	21	17	17	Ambitious	21	28	48

* Note the general tendency for fewer college students to endorse unfavorable traits and for stereotypes to change over time. In 1967, Americans were seen as more materialistic, Germans as more efficient, Chinese as more loyal to family ties, English as more conservative and sophisticated, Italians as more passionate, Japanese as more industrious, Blacks as more musical, and Jews as more ambitious than in earlier decades.
Source: Karlins, M., Coffman, T. L., & Walters, G. (1969). On the fading of social stereotypes: Studies in three generations of college students. *Journal of Personality and Social Psychology, 13,* 4–5.

Box 12-1
The Effect of Physical Attractiveness on Inferences about Personality

Although you may believe that beauty is only skin deep, it certainly has proved otherwise so far as first impressions are concerned. Numerous studies have shown that observers infer that people in photographs who have been rated as physically attractive are more likeable, friendly, confident, sensitive, and flexible than people rated as physically unattractive (Miller, 1970). In addition, research has shown that people prefer interacting with others who are physically attractive. In a series of studies on blind dates, Ellen Berscheid and Elaine Walster (1974) found that no other measure was as powerful in predicting whether the partners sought out one another again as their physical attractiveness. Berscheid and Walster concluded that "Blind dates seem to be blind to everything but appearance."

The positive effect of physical attractiveness also has been found to apply to children. In one study, Karen Dion (1972) asked young women to examine reports of aggressive behavior by seven-year-old children. She attached a paper to each report giving the child's name and age, plus a photograph that other adults had judged either attractive or unattractive. The subjects — who were led to believe these reports came from teachers — were asked to describe the child and to characterize the child's behavior on a typical day. Dion found that the characterization of exactly the same report of aggressive behavior varied in accordance with the physical attractiveness of the child. A typical characterization of the misbehavior of an attractive child described a girl as "charming and well-mannered, but

having a bad day." Yet, an unattractive girl who had committed the same act typically was described as "bratty and a real problem." Another study, by Berscheid, Walster, and Clifford (reported in Berscheid & Walster, 1974), found that teachers asked to make judgments about children with exactly the same report cards judged children with physically attractive photos to have higher IQs, to be more likely to go to college, to have parents who were more interested in the children's education, and to relate better to classmates than children with unattractive photos. These and many other studies (see Berscheid & Walster, 1974) indicate that people base inferences about the inner qualities of others on such external characteristics as physical attractiveness.

---

may dress in ways consistent with their personalities. Inferences derived from other, less modifiable, aspects of appearance have not been found as valid. Krebs and Adinolfi (1975) found that although people who varied in physical attractiveness tended to have different personality profiles, observers were not accurate judges of them. For example, observers inferred that highly attractive people are friendly and affectionate, but actual ratings revealed that they tend

to be less friendly and affectionate than people of average attractiveness.

Impression Formation

Imagine that someone told you the instructor scheduled to teach your psychology course is a rather cold individual. What effect would such information have on your general impression of her or him? Early social psychologists attempted to determine the effect of specific information about the personality traits allegedly possessed by hypothetical people on the overall impression that others form of them (see Table 11-1). In 1946, Solomon Asch presented subjects with lists of traits (see Table 12-2) and asked them to write descriptions of the people whom the traits described. To determine the effect of specific traits on overall impressions, Asch systematically varied each trait on the list. For example, he compared the impressions his subjects formed of a person described as intelligent, skillful, industrious, *warm,* determined, practical, and cautious with their impressions of a person described as intelligent, skillful, industrious, *cold,* determined, practical, and cautious.

Asch found that certain traits, such as *warm* and *cold,* have a pronounced effect on people's overall impression; whereas other traits, such as *polite* and *blunt* are much less influential. For example, a subject might form the following impression of an intelligent, skillful, industrious, *warm,* determined, and practical person: a really nice person who is kind and friendly, a person on whom you can depend and trust; whereas a person described in the same terms, except now *cold,* might be seen as: an aloof person who thinks he is better than everyone else; a narrow, rigid, person who cares only about himself. Asch called such

TABLE 12-2
Asch's Trait Lists*

intelligent	intelligent	intelligent	intelligent
skillful	skillful	skillful	skillful
industrious	industrious	industrious	industrious
warm	*cold*	*polite*	*blunt*
determined	determined	determined	determined
practical	practical	practical	practical
cautious	cautious	cautious	cautious

* Asch (1946) presented subjects with one of four trait lists and asked them to write a description of the person whom the traits described. The lists were identical except for one trait (in italics here), which Asch varied. The results of Asch's research revealed that the traits *warm* and *cold* are more central in determining impressions of personality than the other traits.
Source: Asch, S. E. (1946). Forming impressions of personalities. *Journal of Abnormal and Social Psychology, 41,* 258–90.

traits as warm and cold **central traits** because they exert a strong effect on overall impressions.

When you evaluate other people, what qualities are most important to you? When Anderson (1968) asked college students to rate more than 500 personality traits in terms of how favorable they seemed, *sincere, honest,* and *understanding* topped the list; *liar, phony,* and *mean* were at the bottom (see Table 12-3). Apparently, moral qualities relating to trust are important to the

TABLE 12-3
Favorability Ratings of Personality Traits by College Students*

Rank	Term	Rank	Term	Rank	Term
1	sincere	80	ethical	531	loud-mouthed
2	honest	100	tolerant	540	greedy
3	understanding	150	modest	546	deceitful
4	loyal	200	soft-spoken	547	dishonorable
5	truthful	251	quiet	548	malicious
6	trustworthy	278	ordinary	549	obnoxious
7	intelligent	305	critical	550	untruthful
8	dependable	355	unhappy	551	dishonest
9	open-minded	405	unintelligent	552	cruel
10	thoughtful	465	disobedient	553	mean
20	kind-hearted	500	prejudiced	554	phony
30	trustful	520	ill-mannered	555	liar
40	clever				

* Anderson (1968) asked 100 college students to rate 555 personality traits on a seven-point scale that ranged from "least favorable or desirable" to "most favorable or desirable." This is a selection of their responses, in rank order. Note that *sincere* and *honest* are most highly valued, whereas *liar* and *phony* are the least desirable traits.
Source: Anderson, N. H. (1968). Ratings of likableness, meaningfulness, and likableness variances for 555 common personality traits arranged in order of decreasing likableness. *Journal of Personality and Social Psychology, 9,* 272–79.

average person. Other researchers (for example, Feldman, 1966) have found that negative traits exert a stronger effect on impressions than do positive traits.

As a Gestalt psychologist, Asch believed the "whole is greater than the sum of its parts" (see Chapter 1); he believed such central traits as warm and cold affect the meaning of other traits. For instance, when cautious is combined with warm, it might mean *calm and considerate,* but when combined with cold, it might mean *rigid.* Thus, according to Asch, the favorableness of an overall impression cannot be determined by adding up the favorableness of each trait.

Later theorists disagreed with Asch, arguing that the favorableness of people's impressions result directly from algebraic combinations of the favorableness of particular traits. Table 12-4

TABLE 12-4
Models of Impression Formation*

Adding Model

First Person		Second Person	
Traits	**Value**	**Traits**	**Value**
tidy	+1	humorous	+3
stern	−1	studious	+1
musical	+3	messy	−2
		talkative	+1
Total	+3		
		Total	+3

First person and second person viewed equally favorably

Averaging Model

First Person		Second Person	
Traits	**Value**	**Traits**	**Value**
tidy	+1	humorous	+3
stern	−1	studious	+1
musical	+3	messy	−2
		talkative	+1
Total	+3		
+3 ÷ 3 = +1		Total	+3
		+3 ÷ 4 = +0.75	

First person viewed more favorably than second person

Weighted Averaging Model

First Person		Second Person	
Traits	**Value × Weight**	**Traits**	**Value × Weight**
tidy	+1 × 1 = +1	humorous	+3 × 3 = +9
stern	−1 × 3 = −3	studious	+1 × 1 = +1
musical	+3 × 1 = +3	messy	−2 × 1 = −2
		talkative	+1 × 1 = +1
Total	+1		
+1 ÷ 3 = +0.33		Total	+9
		+9 ÷ 4 = +2.25	

Second person viewed more favorably than first person

* The favorableness of an overall impression of two hypothetical people may differ when computed by different models of impression formation. In the *adding model,* adding favorable traits increases the favorableness of a rating. In the *averaging model,* adding more positive traits than the average of the existing traits increases the favorableness of a rating. In the *weighted averaging model,* adding traits that are important (to a person), here sterness and humor, exert a much greater effect on the overall impression than do unimportant traits.

outlines three algebraic models of impression formation—the **adding model**, the **averaging model**, and the **weighted averaging model.** Although the weighted averaging model is the closest to Asch's Gestalt model because it acknowledges that some traits have more influence on impressions than others, it differs because it assumes that the meaning of traits does not change when traits are combined with other traits.

Implicit Personality Theories

According to some theorists, people harbor **implicit theories of personality** that consist of assumptions about the association among a wide array of personality traits. For example, if I tell you someone is *sly*, you might assume the person also is *dishonest* and *private*. In your implicit theory, dishonesty and privacy are associated with *sly*. In someone else's implicit theory, such other traits as *clever* and *enterprising* might be associated with *sly*. How are people's assumptions about the association among traits mentally organized?

In a study designed to answer this question, Rosenberg, Nelson, and Vivekananthan (1968) asked college students to rate people they knew on a large number of personality traits, and computed the correlation between each trait and every other one on the list. The results of this study are displayed in Figure 12-1.

Although the implicit theories of personality harbored by the college students tested by Rosenberg and colleagues were quite similar, people's implicit theories may differ in significant ways. In an interesting study, Rosenberg and Jones (1972) analyzed the traits used by novelist Theodore Drieiser in *A Gallery of Women* and found that certain traits appeared significantly

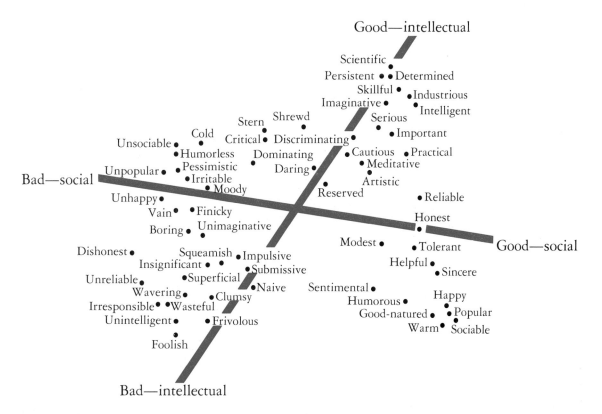

FIGURE 12-1

The Implicit Personality Theory of College Students   Rosenberg et al. (1968) found that college students tend to view one another in terms of three dimensions: good/bad, social/unsocial, and intellectual/nonintellectual. *Source:* Rosenberg, S., Nelson, C., & Vivekananthan, P. J. (1968). A multidimensional approach to the structure of personality impressions. *Journal of Personality and Social Psychology, 9,* 290.

TABLE 12-5

The 99 Most-frequently Used Personality Traits in Drieiser's *A Gallery of Women*

Trait Category	Frequency	Trait Category	Frequency
Young	100	Fool, good-looking, literary, pagan	14
Beautiful	67	Aspirant, determined, good, had means, sad, society person, not strong, tasteful	13
Attractive	44		
Charming, dreamer	41		
Poetic	39	Ambitious, careful, defiant, different, erratic, genial, happy, lonely, man, varietistic	12
Interesting, worker	32		
Artistic	29		
Gay	26	Clever, genius, indifferent, Irish, manager, nice, old, pale, quiet, restless, serious, shrewd, sincere, successful, suffering, sympathetic, thin, understanding	11
Practical, romantic, writer	25		
Conventional, girl	24		
Free, strong	23		
Woman	22		
Unhappy	20		
Intellectual, radical, sensitive, sensual	19	American, communist, crazy, critical, emotional, enthusiastic, fearful, fighter, forceful, great, handsome, hard, lovely, had money, painter, physically alluring, playful, repressed, reserved, skilled, sophisticated	10
Kind, cold	18		
Vigorous	17		
Able, drinker, generous, troubled	16		
Colorful, graceful, intelligent, poor, reads, religious, studies, tall	15		

Source: Rosenberg, S., & Jones, R (1972). A method for investigating and representing a person's implicit theory of personality. *Journal of Personality and Social Psychology, 22,* 372–86.

more frequently than others. According to Rosenberg and Jones (1972), the traits *young* and *beautiful* were central in Drieiser's implicit theory of women (see Table 12-5).

What causes people to assume that certain personality traits go together? There are two possibilities: the traits are, in fact, associated—for example, sly people are, in fact, dishonest; or the traits overlap in meaning—both sly and dishonest are unfavorable attributes whose definitions involve violations of trust. The first position, *realist,* assumes the association between traits is real; the second position, *idealist,* assumes the association exists primarily in people's heads and may be based on false assumptions, stereotypes, and other kinds of cognitive bias. Research comparing these two sources of influence has found that although each exerts an influence on people's implicit theories of personality, much of the consistency we perceive exists in our heads (see Dornbush, Hastorf, Richardson, Muzzy, & Vreeland, 1965; Fiske & Taylor, 1984). Note, however, that people's behavior follows from inferences they make, not from objective facts. If individuals think fat people are jolly, they react to them in such terms whether or not the theory is correct. Ironically, behaving in accordance with a false assumption or stereotype may cause it to be confirmed. Thus behaving frivolously toward fat people may evoke jolly behavior from them—a phenomenon in social science called the **self-fulfilling prophesy.**

THEORIES OF PERSONALITY

The Trait Approaches of Hans Eysenck and Raymond Cattell

As demonstrated in Chapter 1, psychologists attempt to improve on the common-sense theories of the average person. Nowhere is this better exemplified than in the trait approach to personality. Like most of us, trait theorists assume personality is composed of a constellation of inner traits associated in particular ways. However, unlike most of us, trait theorists obtain representative samples of behavior from large numbers of subjects and determine scientifically which traits the samples represent. Consider the theories of Hans Eysenck and Raymond Cattell.

The Type Theory of Hans Eysenck Eysenck's theory of personality is outlined in Figures 12-2 and 12-3. As shown in Figure 12-2, Eysenck believed people's behavior is organized in a hierarchy. Specific responses group together to form habitual responses that, in turn, group together to form personality traits; personality traits group together to form personality types. Impressed with the wisdom of early Greek philosophers and later scholars who suggested the human body contains four *humors* that generate four basic temperaments (sanguine, melancholic, choleric, and phlegmatic; see Figure 12-3 and Chapter 13), Eysenck hypothesized there are four basic **personality types** — *introverted, extroverted, stable,* and *unstable.* The introverted type is exemplified in Figure 12-2. Eysenck suggests only a few people are pure types, but that everyone's personality can be located somewhere on intersecting *dimensions* of introversion–extroversion and stability–instability (see Figure 12-3). Thus, in contrast to the college students

studied by Rosenberg (whose personality theories consisted of such traits as unhappy, vain, irritable, and unsocial that formed such types as bad-social), Eysenck claims that such traits as moodiness should go with touchiness, restlessness, and anxiety to form the *unstable* personality type. Recently, Eysenck has added another dimension — *psychoticism,* which characterizes abnormally solitary, uncaring, and insensitive people.

Eysenck (1973) reports that introversion and extroversion are associated with occupational choice — salespeople and business executives are more likely to be extroverted than scientific researchers, who tend to be introverted. Eysenck also has found that extroverts are more likely than introverts to be involved in accidents, to engage in sexual activities, and to run afoul of the law.

According to Eysenck, people's personality is shaped by genes that influence the growth of the central nervous system. Introverts have an active nervous system and avoid external stimulation; extroverts have a relatively inactive nervous system and seek to elevate their level of arousal. If you place a drop of lemon juice on the tongue of

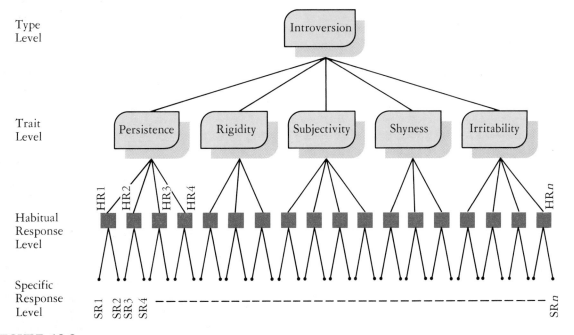

FIGURE 12-2

Eysenck's Structural Model of Personality According to Eysenck, such personality types as introversion are made up of personality traits (like persistence and rigidity). In turn, personality traits are made up of such habitual responses as not giving up easily and sticking to one's way of thinking. In turn, the latter are made up of such specific responses as studying hard for a psychology exam and refusing to take a different route to work. *Source:* Adapted from Eysenck, H. J. (1953). *The structure of human personality.* London: Methuen.

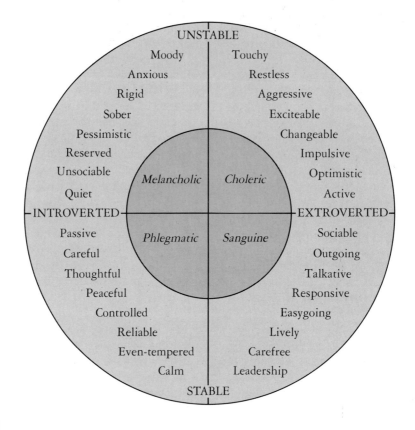

FIGURE 12-3

Eysenck's Personality Dimensions   Eysenck's factor analysis revealed two basic personality dimensions: introversion/extroversion and stability/instability.   Such specific personality traits as quiet and passive lie close to primary dimensions (like introverted).   Such other personality traits as sober and excitable lie midway between primary dimensions.   The four personality types in the center circle were described by the Greek physician and historical "Father of Medicine," Hippocrates.   *Source:* Eysenck, H. J., & Rachman S. (1965).   *The causes and cures of neurosis.*   San Diego, CA: EdITS.

an introvert, would you expect him or her to excrete more or less saliva than an extrovert? Eysenck (1973) found, as expected, that the active systems of introverts produce significantly more saliva than the inactive systems of extroverts.

   To what extent is personality determined by heredity? We examine this controversial question in Box 12-2.

The Trait Theory of Raymond Cattell A significant difference between the scientist and the average person is exemplified in the work of Raymond Cattell.   Originally, Cattell was a chemist. A fundamental goal of chemistry is to discover the basic elements of matter; when Cattell switched his interest to psychology, he undertook a comparable task: to discover the basic elements of personality.   His approach is exemplified by consid-

ering one aspect of his voluminous research program.

   In 1937, psychologist Gordon Allport combed the dictionary for every word that could be used to describe a person.   He found 18,000! Nevertheless, it makes no sense to conclude there are 18,000 *elements* of personality — compared to the slightly more than 100 elements of matter known to chemists — because many of the words Allport found were synonyms and others (such as *breathing*) do not distinguish one person from another.   Cattell analyzed Allport's list and distilled 171 *trait-elements,* as Cattell called them. The question asked by Cattell was whether each trait-element is sufficiently different from the others to justify concluding it is a basic element of personality.   To answer this question, Cattell gave the list of 171 trait-elements to a sample of

Box 12-2
Temperament — The Inheritance of Personality Traits

To what extent are personality differences passed on genetically? And to what extent are they acquired through experience? As discussed in Chaper 2, personality characteristics result from the interaction between genes and environment; however, research may still supply estimates of the extent to which differences between people result from genetic inheritance.

In a study that assessed Eysenck's contention that introversion – extroversion and neuroticism are highly heritable, Floderus-Myrhed, Pedersen, and Ramuson (1980) administered Eysenck's test to 12,898 pairs of twins selected from the Swedish Twin Registry. The heritability index for introversion – extroversion was .54 for males and .66 for females; the heritability index for neuroticism was .50 for men and .58 for women.

Other studies, using different methods, have shown the following nine aspects of infant temperament to be quite stable throughout development.

1. *Activity Level:* the motor component present in a given child's functioning and diurnal proportion of active and inactive periods. Protocol data on mobility during bathing,

eating, playing, dressing, and handling, as well as information concerning the sleep – wake cycle, reaching, crawling, and walking, are used in scoring this category.

2. *Rhythmicity (regularity):* the predictability and/or unpredictability in time of any function. It can be analyzed in relation to the sleep – wake cycle, hunger, feeding pattern, and elimination schedule.

3. *Approach or Withdrawal:* the nature of the initial response to a new stimulus, be it a new food, new toy, or new person. Approach responses are positive, whether displayed by mood expression (smiling, verbalizations, etc.) or motor activity (swallowing a new food, reaching for a new toy, active play, etc.). Withdrawal reactions are negative, whether displayed by mood expression (crying, fussing, grimacing, verbalization, etc.) or motor activity (moving away, spitting out new food, pushing away new toy, etc.).

4. *Adaptability:* response to new or altered situations. One is not concerned with the nature of the initial responses, but with the ease with which they are modified in desired directions.

5. *Threshold of Responsiveness:* the intensity of

stimulation that is necessary to evoke a discernible response, irrespective of the specific form that the response may take or the sensory modality affected. The behaviors utilized are those concerning reactions to sensory stimuli, environmental objects, and social contacts.

6. *Intensity of Reaction:* the energy level of response irrespective of its quality or direction.

7. *Quality of Mood:* the amount of pleasant, joyful, and friendly behavior as contrasted with unpleasant, crying, and unfriendly behavior.

8. *Distractibility:* the effectiveness of extraneous environmental stimuli in interfering with or in altering the direction of the ongoing behavior.

9. *Attention Span and Persistence:* two categories that are related. Attention span concerns the length of time a particular activity is pursued by the child. Persistence refers to the continuation of an activity in the face of obstacles to the maintenance of the activity direction.

Source: Thomas, A., & Chess, S. (1981). The role of temperament in the contributions of individuals to their development. In R. M. Lerner & N. A. Busch-Rossnagel (Eds.), *Individuals as producers of their development* (p. 236). New York: Academic Press.

people and asked them to rate several acquaintances on a 1- to 7-point scale; he then computed the correlation between the ratings acquaintances received on each pair of adjectives. Regarding the trait-elements *sensitive* and *considerate,* for example, he might have found the following:

Acquaintance	Rater's rating on *sensitive*	Rater's rating on *considerate*
Jane	6	5
Sally	2	3
Sue	1	2
Tom	5	5
Bill	3	2

As you see, acquaintances rated high on *sensitive* also were rated high on *considerate:* the correlation between sensitive and considerate is +0.9. Cattell computed the correlations between each pair in his set of 171 adjectives, a total of 14,535 correlations. He selected a cutoff point—a degree of association he considered significant—and formed groups of traits whose correlations exceeded the cutoff point. How many clusters of adjectives were generated by this process? Forty. Cattell called these 40 clusters **surface traits.** In essence, Cattell concluded there were 40 *molecules* of personality.

But Cattell "had still not smashed the atom" (Scrogg, 1985, p. 166). In examining the 40 surface traits, Cattell sensed there were clusters of similar traits that stemmed from even more

TABLE 12-6
The 16 Personality Traits Identified by Cattell (1973)

FACTOR	LOW SCORE DESCRIPTION	HIGH SCORE DESCRIPTION
A	RESERVED, DETACHED, CRITICAL, ALOOF, STIFF (Sizothymia)	OUTGOING, WARMHEARTED, EASY-GOING, PARTICIPATING (Affectothymia)
B	LESS INTELLIGENT, CONCRETE-THINKING (Lower scholastic mental capacity)	MORE INTELLIGENT, ABSTRACT-THINKING, BRIGHT (Higher scholastic mental capacity)
C	AFFECTED BY FEELINGS, EMOTIONALLY LESS STABLE, EASILY UPSET CHANGEABLE (Lower ego strength)	EMOTIONALLY STABLE, MATURE, FACES REALITY, CALM (Higher ego strength)
E	HUMBLE, MILD, EASILY LED, DOCILE, ACCOMMODATING (Submissiveness)	ASSERTIVE, AGGRESSIVE, STUBBORN, COMPETITIVE (Dominance)
F	SOBER, TACITURN, SERIOUS (Desurgency)	HAPPY-GO-LUCKY, ENTHUSIASTIC (Surgency)
G	EXPEDIENT, DISREGARDS RULES (Weaker superego strength)	CONSCIENTIOUS, PERSISTENT, MORALISTIC, STAID (Stronger superego strength)
H	SHY, TIMID, THREAT-SENSITIVE (Threctia)	VENTURESOME, UNINHIBITED, SOCIALLY BOLD (Parmia)
I	TOUGH-MINDED, SELF-RELIANT, REALISTIC (Harria)	TENDER-MINDED, SENSITIVE, CLINGING, OVERPROTECTED (Premsia)
L	TRUSTING, ACCEPTING CONDITIONS (Alaxia)	SUSPICIOUS, HARD TO FOOL (Protension)
M	PRACTICAL, "DOWN-TO-EARTH" CONCERNS (Praxernia)	IMAGINATIVE, BOHEMIAN, ABSENT-MINDED (Autia)
N	FORTHRIGHT, UNPRETENTIOUS, GENUINE BUT SOCIALLY CLUMSY (Artlessness)	ASTUTE, POLISHED, SOCIALLY AWARE (Shrewdness)
O	SELF-ASSURED, PLACID, SECURE, COMPLACENT, SERENE (Untroubled adequacy)	APPREHENSIVE, SELF-REPROACHING, INSECURE, WORRYING, TROUBLED (Guilt proneness)
Q_1	CONSERVATIVE, RESPECTING TRADITIONAL IDEAS (Conservatism of temperament)	EXPERIMENTING, LIBERAL, FREE-THINKING (Radicalism)
Q_2	GROUP-DEPENDENT, A "JOINER" AND SOUND FOLLOWER (Group adherence)	SELF-SUFFICIENT, RESOURCEFUL, PREFERS OWN DECISIONS (Self-sufficiency)
Q_3	UNDISCIPLINED SELF-CONFLICT, LAX, FOLLOWS OWN URGES, CARELESS OF SOCIAL RULES (Low integration)	CONTROLLED, EXACTING WILL POWER, SOCIALLY PRECISE, COMPULSIVE (High strength of self-sentiment)
Q_4	RELAXED, TRANQUIL, UNFRUSTRATED, COMPOSED (Low ergic tension)	TENSE, FRUSTRATED, DRIVEN, OVERWROUGHT (High ergic tension)

ipat   **16 PF TEST PROFILE**

STANDARD TEN SCORE (STEN) → Average ← 1 2 3 4 5 6 7 8 9 10

A sten of   1   2   3   4   5   6   7   8   9   10   is obtained
by about   2.3% 4.4% 9.2% 15.0% 19.1% 19.1% 15.0% 9.2% 4.4% 2.3% of adults

basic traits. Employing the method of *factor analysis*—a statistical device that, in effect, computes the correlation among clusters of correlations—Cattell discovered that surface traits form 15 factors. He named the 15 factors **source traits**: the fundamental building blocks of personality.

Although the thoroughness and sophistication of Cattell's methods sharply contrast with those of the average person, you might reasonably argue that his findings are, nonetheless, based on a synthesis of his raters' implicit theories of personality. Perhaps the associations among traits were in his raters' minds and not in the behavior of the people they rated. To evaluate this possibility, Cattell repeated essentially the same procedure we have described, but employed two other kinds of data: self-ratings by individuals (called **Q-data** by Cattell, *Q* for *questionnaire*) and a vast array of objective psychological tests (called **T-data**). (Cattell called the ratings people made of acquaintances **L-data**, *L* for *life*, because he obtained the data from people in such everyday-life situations as work.)

It would have been wonderful if Cattell had obtained exactly the same results from Q- and T-data as he had from L-data, but this was not quite the case: he obtained 20 source traits from Q-data and 18 source traits from T-data. Yet, there was considerable overlap between most of the traits. Cattell's ultimate conclusion—his best estimate of how many basic personality elements there are—is 16 bipolar traits. The 16 fundamental source traits identified by Cattell are described in Table 12-6. It is interesting to note the first one parallels Asch's central trait of warm versus cold and several are similar to the traits that constitute Eysenck's four basic personality types. According to Cattell, people's behavior in particular situations derives from the combined strength of all the source traits relevant to the situation.

The trait theories of Eysenck and Cattell are most similar to the implicit theories of the average person. There are many trait theories in psychology, and trait theories are only one of many types of personality theory. We now examine four other approaches to personality. We begin with those that, like the trait approach, view personality in terms of hypothetical, inner, core characteristics; we end with those that insist personality is

nothing more than patterns of overt and observable behaviors.

The Psychoanalytic Approach of Sigmund Freud

Freud's psychoanalytic theory was introduced in Chapter 1 and discussed further in several other chapters, especially Chapter 10. Freud's theory is a theory of the mind; he likened the mind to an iceberg—the tip showing and the remainder submerged (see Figure 12-4). Freud called the tip of the mind the **conscious**, a level that includes everything we are aware of experiencing at a given moment—thoughts, sensations, visual images, and so on. The next, intermediate level, called the **preconscious**, is not in our awareness but is accessible to us. For example, you may not be conscious of what you did last night but, if asked, you could remember easily. Freud called the third, submerged level, the **unconscious**. Freud differed from virtually all theorists before him in insisting the unconscious is the largest and most important part of the mind. It lies outside

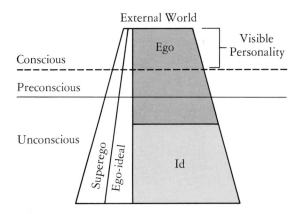

FIGURE 12-4

Freud's Tripartite Structure of the Mind. According to Freud, the mind—like an iceberg—lies largely beneath the surface; only the tip—the conscious—is visible, or available, to conscious awareness. Between the conscious and unconscious parts of the mind is the preconscious, which contains material that can become conscious when attention is directed to it. The largest part of the mind—the unconscious—lies below the surface and is normally inaccessible. The ego and the superego operate on all three levels of awareness; however, the id does not rise above the unconscious level.

awareness and ordinarily is not accessible. Indeed, according to Freud, we actively resist becoming aware of what goes on in the unconscious part of our mind.

The Structure of Personality

Within the unconscious, preconscious, and conscious levels of awareness are, according to Freud, three systems — the *id, ego,* and *superego.* Together, these systems constitute the basic structures of personality. They may be thought of as the instinctual, intellectual, and moral aspects of human nature respectively.

The Id

Writing in German, Freud called the most primitive component of personality the *es.* Although *es* translates directly to *it,* this aspect of our nature has come to be called the *id.* The **id** is located entirely in the unconscious level of awareness and consists of everything that is inherited, particularly instincts. You gain good insight into Freud's concept of the id by observing infants' behavior. When newborns are hungry, they wail without consideration for whether or not it is convenient for their parents to feed them. If they feel like defecating or urinating, they do so, regardless of the circumstances. Like the infant, the id is directed by the **pleasure principle:** the id seeks to reduce unpleasant tensions and to maintain a pleasurable state, notwithstanding circumstances and consequences.

The Instincts Freud referred to the various biological needs, urges, and tensions that reside in the id as drives or instincts, emphasizing their inherited nature. According to Freud, all **instincts** have a *source* (the body area where tension arises), an *aim* (the reduction of tension), a *pressure level* (the intensity with which the instinctual need is felt), and an *object* (the person or object in the environment that will relieve the instinctual tension).

In his early work, Freud talked only about one class of instincts: the **preservation instincts** (which he called *Eros,* Greek for life). However, toward the end of Freud's life he posited a second class: the **death instincts** (which he called *Thanatos,* Greek for death). The preservation instincts include the needs that must be met to ensure survival. Freud gave the energy associated with the life instincts a special name — *libido.* Although the need for food, water, air, and protection from the elements are all preservation instincts, Freud attached little psychological significance to them. Rather, he devoted almost all of his thinking and theorizing to the preservation instinct that ensures the survival of the species — *sexual instinct.*

It might be argued that the instincts that ensure the survival of individuals are more important than the instinct that ensures the survival of the species. Why, then, did Freud emphasize the sexual instinct? Freud's answer is founded on the fact that sex involves a great deal more social conflict than other instincts (especially in Freud's Victorian era) — and Freud believed our personalities are shaped by conflict. According to Freud, infants are born with sexual instincts that express themselves in immature forms from birth on.

As a psychotherapist, Freud treated a variety of patients. He noted that neurotics often engage in self-abusive acts; indeed, some neurotics even commit suicide. Since self-abusive behavior seemed inconsistent with the pleasure principle and self-preservation instincts, Freud reasoned there must be another kind of instinct, a death instinct, that is antagonistic to the preservation instincts. Death instincts push humans toward the ultimate tensionless state of peace and quiescence — death. Freud suggested the conflict between the preservation instincts and the death instincts is one of life's most basic conflicts, but did not work out the implications of this idea before his own death.

To this point in our discussion, we have more or less equated instincts with biological needs, but Freud did not view them in this way. Freud's theory is a psychological theory; a theory of the mind, not the body. According to Freud, instincts are mental representations of bodily processes and emotions; they serve as a link between body and mind. The instincts originate from the body, but their messages are translated into thought processes. Thus, a dry mouth, a distended bladder, or a constricted stomach are not instincts; the desire for water, the need to urinate and the wish for food are.

As mental representations, instincts may affect individuals long after the bodily tension that produced them has gone: instincts endure as unconscious memories. Thus, unfulfilled needs during childhood may continue to affect people throughout their adult lives. According to Freud, many adult psychological problems stem from unfulfilled childhood needs, especially sexual desires. For this reason, Freud believed that psychoanalytic therapy must delve into clients' childhood conflicts (see Chapter 14).

Primary Process Thinking If our instincts indeed are mental, it seems reasonable to satisfy them by mental operations. Freud believed the primary way in which infants attempt to satisfy their instinctual demands is through a thought process called *primary process thinking*. **Primary process thinking** is not bound by logical or realistic constraints. There is no awareness of changes in time, progression, and sequence of events. There are no distinctions between past, present, and future. Incompatible concepts may exist side by side. Although this type of thinking may seem incomprehensible, it should be easy to recognize as the type of thinking that occurs in dreams. It also bears a close resemblance to the type of thinking displayed by people with schizophrenia (see Chapter 13). Freud suggested the id attempts to satisfy biological needs through the wishes, fantasies, and hallucinations of primary process thinking. For example, infants attempt to satisfy their hunger by imagining or hallucinating their mother's breast.

The Ego

As you might suspect, the id is hopelessly ineffective in coping with reality. To survive, infants must obtain knowledge of the real world (especially about objects that satisfy their needs) and must develop the capacity to act on that knowledge. Infants must develop perceptual processes (to perceive sources of satisfaction), cognitive processes (to develop a plan with which to obtain satisfaction), and memory (to recall previously successful and unsuccessful plans). Freud referred to such abilities as **secondary process thinking** and hypothesized such abilities develop through the formation of a structure called the *ego*. According to Freud, although the **ego** develops in order to serve the id (to help people satisfy their instinctual needs), the ego and the id inevitably come into conflict (over the compromises with reality necessary to satisfy the needs of the id).

The Superego

A person who possessed only an id and an ego would get along fairly well in the physical world, because he or she could meet all basic biological needs. However, such a person would be poorly equipped to live in the social world. He or she would pursue personal goals without concern for others and would not feel bound by society's rules, except when necessary for the satisfaction of biological needs. In short, such a person would lack a moral agency, or conscience. Psychopaths (see Chapter 13) may exemplify such a personality. Freud recognized that most people develop a conscience and hypothesized that it grows out of the ego, forming one part of a two-part structure he called the **superego**. Freud called the other part of the superego the **ego-ideal**. Our conscience judges us when we are not good; our ego-ideal urges us to improve.

What causes the superego to develop? Why do some people have a stronger superego than other people? We outlined Freud's answers to these questions in Chapter 10, where we discussed theories of moral development. For now, it is sufficient to say that Freud believed children introject codes of acceptable behavior from their parents at a critical stage of development. Freud's structure of personality is outlined in Table 12-7.

The Defense Mechanisms

According to Freud, the ego must serve the often-incompatible desires of three stern masters: the id, the superego, and the constraints of reality. The id demands immediate gratification; the superego attempts to prevent such gratification when it countermands the rules of society; and the means for obtaining gratification may not be available. The conflicts that result give rise to feelings of anxiety. The ego deals with anxiety by developing what Freud called **ego defense mechanisms**. The function of defense mechanisms is to reduce anxiety by distorting reality.

TABLE 12-7
Summary of Freud's Structure of Personality

Structure	Basis	Level of Consciousness	Principle Followed	Process used
Id	Instincts for sex and aggression	Unconscious	Pleasure principle	Primary process thinking
Ego	Learned behaviors in response to reality	Mostly conscious	Reality principle	Secondary process thinking
Superego and Ego-ideal	Social inhibitions and ideals introjected from parents	Partly conscious	—	—

Source: Adapted from Ruch, J. C. (1984). *Psychology: The personal science.* Belmont, CA: Wadsworth.

Defense mechanisms are like painkillers: they reduce pain (anxiety) by masking the source of the pain (often unsatisfied instinctual needs), but they do nothing to eliminate the cause of the distress. At best, defense mechanisms provide people with time to develop resources to cope with their problems. At worst, defense mechanisms consume people's psychological energy, rendering them overly vigilant and guarded (*defensive*), with little time or energy for more constructive activities.

Freud believed people rarely rely upon only one defense mechanism, but usually employ several. Freud and other psychoanalysts have identified at least 15 defense mechanisms (see Table 12-8).

Stages of Personality Development

We have been discussing Freud's ideas about the *core* of personality—structures and processes common to all people. Obviously, all people are not the same—different people develop different *peripheries*. Some people are outgoing, others are shy; some are assertive, others submissive; and so on. How can we explain different types of personality?

Freud accounted for individual differences primarily in terms of personality development and analyzed personality development primarily in terms of the ways in which children relieve tensions associated with their sexual needs. According to Freud, personality is virtually fixed by

the fifth year of life. Freud hypothesized that children go through five stages of psychosexual development—oral, anal, phallic, latency, and genital—and suggested that the manner in which children resolve the inevitable conflicts at each of these stages plays a central role in determining the type of personality they acquire. Freud suggested that children seek satisfaction of their sexual instincts through specific behaviors associated with the **erogenous zones** of their bodies—particularly the mouth, anus, and genital organs—and that these behaviors elicit certain parental responses that, in turn, activate particular defense mechanisms. How all this is resolved determines the type of person the child becomes.

The Oral Stage   Freud's first stage of psychosexual development, the **oral stage,** begins at birth and lasts until about age one and one-half. The ego develops during the oral stage. According to Freud, infants relieve their sexual tension primarily through the mouth. Sucking is the first source of nourishment and pleasure. Later, when children develop teeth, they may satisfy their oral needs more actively and aggressively. Freud suggested that if children are weaned too soon or too severely, or if they are punished for biting, they may become fixated at the oral stage. (**Fixations** refer to excessive charges of sexual energy focused at a particular stage of development.) Freud believed people fixated at the oral stage develop an **oral character.** People with oral

TABLE 12-8
Ego Defense Mechanisms

Defense Mechanism	Description	Example
Compensation	Covering up weaknesses by emphasizing desirable traits or making up for frustration in one area by overgratification in another.	"It doesn't matter that I keep a messy house because I am enhancing my education by reading books all day."
Denial of Reality	Protecting self from unpleasant reality by refusal to perceive it.	"Of course he is not an alcoholic; he has to drink everyday because he has business lunches."
Displacement	Discharging pent-up feelings, usually of hostility, on objects less dangerous than those that initially aroused the emotion.	"I'm kicking the dog because it annoys me when he sits there scratching at fleas."
Emotional Insulation	Withdrawing into passivity to protect self from being emotionally hurt.	"I don't want to go out; I'm fine by myself."
Fantasy	Gratifying frustrated desires in imaginary achievements (daydreaming is a common form).	"I'm rich and famous; Robert Redford is pursuing me. . . ."
Identification	Increasing feelings of worth by identifying self with person or institution of illustrious standing.	"I know Robert Redford; he's a friend of mine."
Introjection	Incorporating external values and standards into ego structure so individual is not at their mercy as external threats.	"The reason I don't smoke is because I don't want to. I don't care whether my parents threaten to punish me for smoking. It's just stupid to smoke."
Compartmentalization	Cutting off emotional charge from hurtful situations or separating incompatible attitudes in logic-tight compartments (holding conflicting attitudes which are never thought of simultaneously or in relation to each other).	"I love everyone." "I can't stand my mother."
Projection	Placing blame for one's difficulties upon others or attributing one's own "forbidden" desires to others.	"Why don't you admit it: you want to have an affair."
Rationalization	Attempting to prove that one's behavior is "rational" and justifiable, thus worthy of the approval of self and others.	"I know I said I would call but I couldn't. I was in a rush and I couldn't find a telephone. Anyway, I would have missed my bus if I had called."
Reaction Formation	Preventing dangerous desires from being expressed by endorsing opposing attitudes and types of behavior and using them as "barriers."	"How can you say that! I'm not interested in him. I study with him because I feel sorry for him."
Regression	Retreating to earlier developmental level involving more childish responses and usually a lower level of aspiration	"School is getting so competitive. What's the point anyway? I think I'll have a drink of hot milk and go to bed."
Repression	Preventing painful or dangerous thoughts from entering consciousness; keeping them unconscious (considered the most basic of defense mechanisms).	"I don't remember feeling like that."
Sublimation	Gratifying or working off frustrated sexual desires in substitutive nonsexual activities socially accepted by one's culture.	"I love to paint. It is totally gratifying."
Undoing	Atoning for, and thus counteracting, immoral desires or acts.	"I always feel better after going to confession."

characters are either excessively dependent on others, passive, immature, and insecure (oral passive) or sarcastic, biting, and passively hostile (oral aggressive). Adults fixated at the oral stage may seek oral gratification by sucking, smoking, and other oral activities.

The Anal Stage The **anal stage** of psychosexual development typically occurs during the second year of life. According to Freud, the primary source of pleasure in this stage shifts from the mouth to the anus. Early in the anal stage, children obtain gratification through defecation. Adults fixated early in the anal stage of psychosexual development are messy, destructive, and impulsive *(anal expulsive)*. Late in the anal stage, children begin to assert their independence. One method they use is to resist toilet training. Retaining feces entails a certain orderliness and cleanliness. Refusing to cooperate involves stubborness and obstinacy. Freud suggested children at this stage value and "hoard" their feces (both because they obtain sexual pleasure from retaining feces and to exert their independence). Adults fixated late in the anal stage *(anal retentive)* possess the classic **anal character** referred to by Freud: they are orderly, obstinate, punctual, and stingy.

The Phallic Stage The **phallic stage** of psychosexual development extends from the third to the sixth year of life. According to Freud, the penis becomes the young boy's major source of pleasure at this stage. (Freud based his theory primarily on development of males.) Early in the phallic stage, young boys take great pride in their penis and often exhibit it. Thus, the **phallic character** involves the traits of pride, vanity, self-assurance, and recklessness. In Freud's theory, the phallic stage of psychosexual development is crucial: it is at the phallic stage that children acquire a sex identity and develop a superego (see Chapter 10).

The Latency Period Following resolution of the conflicts of the phallic stage, children enter a **latency period** considered by some psychologists a separate stage of psychosexual development. During the latency period, sexual and aggressive urges become subdued. Boys and girls tend to interact in same-sex groups or *packs.*

Latency continues until puberty, at which time chidren enter the genital stage.

The Genital Stage The primary source of sexual energy at the **genital stage** remains *genitalia.* However, although children in the phallic stage relate to others solely to provide bodily pleasure for themselves, young adults in the genital stage pursue mutual pleasure and express altruism in relationships. Freud did not describe a *genital character.* Consistent with his pessimistic view of human nature, Freud did not believe that people ever achieve the complete integration characteristic of the genital stage. Rather, he believed that because of overindulgence or frustration, all adults are burdened by fixations at earlier stages. Freud's theory of psychosexual development and associated individual differences are outlined in Table 12-9.

To conclude, Freud believed humans are driven by sexual and aggressive instincts; are self-centered, defensive, irrational, conflicted; and, all the while, are oblivious to their true nature. The notion that human beings are rational, principled, altruistic, and kind was viewed by Freud as an illusion developed to protect people from the anxiety and guilt they would feel if aware of their basic (and base) nature.

Not surprisingly, some of Freud's students and followers objected to his pessimistic view of human nature. The central thesis of one group of theorists, called the **ego analysts,** was that Freud placed too much emphasis on the id-based sexual instinct and its conflicts. Retaining Freud's conception of personality structure and defense mechanisms and considering themselves psychoanalysts, these theorists argued that some processes of the ego, especially cognitive processes, are conflict-free, have their own source of energy, and therefore do not stem from or serve the id and its instincts. According to ego analysts, thinking is energized by forces other than suppressed or displaced sexual energy: the ego contains an energy of its own.

Erik Erikson's Psychosocial Theory of Personality

One of the most influential ego analysts is Erik Erikson, who presented a *psychosocial* theory of

TABLE 12-9
The Psychosexual Stages of Development

Approximate Age	Stage Name	Focus of Sexual Instincts	Gratifying Behaviors	Gratification Results In:	Frustration Results In:
0 – 1½	**ORAL**	Mouth	Sucking, swallowing; biting.	Trust, independence.	Passivity; gullibility, immaturity; unrealistic optimism; manipulative personality.
1½ – 3	**ANAL**	Anal Region	Retention and expulsion of feces.	Self-control, mastery.	Obstinacy; stinginess; conscientiousness; orderliness; punctuality; cleanliness or messiness.
3 – 6	**PHALLIC**	Genital Organs	Examining genitals; self-manipulation; sexual curiosity.	Sexual identity (through identification with same-sex parent); healthy conscience.	Men: ambition; recklessness; vanity; exhibitionism; Don Juanism; Women: striving for superiority over men; flirtatiousness; seductiveness; promiscuity.
6 – 12	**LATENCY**	None (instincts are sublimated)			
puberty onward	**GENITAL**	Genital Organs and Sublimations	Intercourse; intimacy; loving and being loved; sublimation of instincts in creative work.	Ability to love unselfishly; ability to find fulfillment in work; responsibility; ability to delay gratification.	Narcissism; aimlessness; lack of ego integration; stagnation.

Source: Scroggs, J. R. (1985). *Key ideas in personality theory.* St. Paul, MN: West.

personality development. Like Freud, Erikson believes personality evolves through a series of developmental stages, each stage marked by a particular crisis or conflict. Further, like Freud, Erikson holds that the way in which the crisis is resolved influences the overall direction of personality growth. Although Erikson's first four stages of psychosocial development parallel Freud's stages of psychosexual development, Erikson defines the crises that occur at each stage more broadly than Freud — placing less emphasis on sexual conflicts and more on social relations. In addition, Erikson extends personality development beyond the four stages of development outlined by Freud. For Freud, personality growth ends at young adulthood; Erikson added four additional stages that extend into maturity and old age. Erikson defines each of his eight stages in terms of a particular crisis, yet believes the crises characteristic of early stages may recur at later stages, especially if they remain unresolved. Erikson's eight stages of psychosocial development are outlined in Table 12-10. We discussed Erikson's adult stages of psychosocial development more fully in Chapter 10.

Rooted in psychoanalysis, Erikson's theory is most appropriately considered a conflict theory. Crises involve conflict, and Erikson's theory is structured around what he considers to be the eight great crises of life. Yet, Erikson's theory also is an appropriate bridge to humanistic theories of personality that emphasize self-actualization. Erikson's stages form a hierarchy of increasingly broad and encompassing stages that, in effect, constitute an eight-rung ladder to self-fulfillment. From Erikson's perspective, people can reach fulfillment, but not without some difficulty. In the theory to which we now turn, the ladder to self-fulfillment is somewhat easier to climb.

TABLE 12-10
Erikson's Stages of Psychosocial Development

Age	Stage	Description	Successful Resolution	Unsuccessful Resolution
Infancy	Basic trust versus mistrust	Parents must maintain an adequate environment – supportive, nurturing, and loving – so that the child develops basic trust.	Trust	Wariness
Years 1–3	Autonomy versus shame or doubt	As the child develops bowel and bladder control, he or she should also develop a healthy attitude toward being independent and somewhat self-sufficient. If the child is made to feel that independent efforts are wrong, then shame and self-doubt develop instead of autonomy.	Willpower and independence	Self-doubt
Years 3–5½	Initiative versus guilt	The child must discover ways to initiate actions on his or her own. If such initiatives are successful, guilt will be avoided.	Purpose	Unworthiness
Years 5½–12	Industry versus inferiority	The child must learn to feel competent, especially when competing with peers. Failure results in feelings of inferiority.	Competency	Incompetency
Adolescence	Identity versus role confusion	A sense of role identity must develop, especially in terms of selecting a vocation and future career.	Sense of self	Aimlessness
Early adulthood	Intimacy versus isolation	The formation of close friendships and relationships with the opposite sex is vital to healthy development.	Love	Loneliness
Middle adulthood	Generativity versus stagnation	Adults develop useful lives by helping and guiding children and by other productive activities.	Productiveness	Sterility
Late adulthood	Ego integrity versus despair	An adult will eventually review his or her life. A life well spent will result in a sense of well-being and integrity.	Wisdom	Meaninglessness and despair

Source: Adapted from Dworetzsky, J. (1982). *Psychology.* St. Paul, MN: West.

The Humanistic Approach of Carl Rogers

There are several humanistic theories of personality. Maslow's theory of self-actualization, outlined in Chapter 7, is humanistic in approach. Here we consider the best-known and most-influential humanistic theory, that of Carl Rogers.

In his book, *Freedom to Learn,* Carl Rogers writes:

> I have little sympathy with the rather prevalent concept that man is basically irrational, and thus his impulses, if not controlled, would lead to destruction of others and self. Man's behavior is exquisitely rational, moving with subtle and ordered complexity toward the goals his organism is endeavoring to achieve. The tragedy for most of us is that our defenses keep us from being aware of this rationality, so that consciously we are moving in one direction, while organismically we are moving in another. (1969, p. 29)

The difference between the approaches of Rogers and Freud is profound. According to Freud (and many other personality theorists), people are motivated to obtain a state of quiescence and homeostasis. According to Rogers, people are motivated to improve themselves, which often involves an increase in tension. Phrases used by Rogers such as the "forward thrust of life" exemplify this view.

The Actualizing Tendency and Self-actualization

Rogers believes all individuals are born with an **actualizing tendency:** a natural tendency to maintain and enhance themselves, to grow. The actualizing tendency reveals itself from the moment of conception, when the ovum divides and differentiates. It is not limited to humans, but is characteristic of all life — human, animal, and plant. What is unique to humans is the disposition toward **self-actualization** (see Box 12-3). As children grow, they develop an ever-increasing capacity to distinguish between things that are a part of them and things that are not. This ability to differentiate, expressed through language and other symbols, leads to the development of self-concepts (*me-not me*). Like Freud, Rogers believes parents exert a major influence on the development of children's self-concepts. The way parents talk to their children, what they say to them, the positive and negative statements they make about them, help shape children's conceptions of themselves. In Rogers'

theory, the actualizing tendency is inherited but the course of self-actualization is directed primarily by learning, particularly through the influence of parents.

Conditions of Worth

The inherited actualizing tendency and the socially learned tendency toward self-actualization may work either with or against one another. Rogers believes that initially the quality of the parent-child relationship determines how the actualizing and self-actualizing tendencies interact. The way in which parents demonstrate their love for their children is crucial. Parents may love their children only when they fulfill certain **conditions of worth** — a phenomenon Rogers calls *conditional positive regard.* Children who experience conditional positive regard incorporate their parents' conditions of worth into their self-concepts and begin to view themselves in terms originally designed to please or to placate their parents. In doing so they attempt to gain love or approval in ways that violate their natural actualizing tendency. For example, an overly socialized, quiet, well-mannered child may stifle his or her natural exuberance because his or her parents frown upon it.

Defensive Functioning

Once conditions of worth are incorporated into the self-concept of a child, such conditions create a distance between the experiences of the organism and the experiences of the self. Experiences consistent with conditions of worth are valued, allowed to enter awareness, and perceived accurately. Experiences inconsistent with conditions of worth are devalued, prevented from entering awareness, and perceived inaccurately.

Psychological problems may occur when individuals develop defenses to guard against evidence suggesting that they are not meeting conditions of worth. When people feel they are not fulfilling conditions of worth, they experience anxiety. They attempt to reduce anxiety by denying or distorting experiences inconsistent with their self-concept. Defensiveness feeds on itself. The more that information is denied and distorted, the greater the discrepancy becomes between what a person thinks he or she is and what the person really is. The greater this discrepancy, the greater the anxiety.

Box 12-3
SELF-ACTUALIZATION

Abraham Maslow examined people he considered self-actualized and noted their distinguishing characteristics. These characteristics are listed on the right, together with behaviors Maslow recommends that you practice in order to further develop the characteristics of self-actualizers.

Characteristics of Self-Actualizers

Perceive reality efficiently and tolerate uncertainty

Accept themselves and others for what they are

Spontaneity in thought and behavior

Problem-centered rather than self-centered

Possess good sense of humor; never joke at expense of others

Highly creative

Free from dependence on external authority or other people; resourceful, independent

Broad identification with others and concern for the welfare of humanity

Constantly renew appreciation of basic life experiences

Establish deeply satisfying interpersonal relations with a few, rather than many, people

Able to look at life objectively

Behaviors Leading to Self-actualization

Experience life as does a child: with full absorption and concentration

Try something new rather than maintaining secure and safe ways

Listen to personal feelings in evaluating experiences rather than the voice of tradition, authority, or the majority

Be honest; avoid pretenses of *game playing*

Be prepared to be unpopular if personal views conflict with those of majority

Assume responsibility

Work hard at whatever you do

Try to identify personal defenses and have the courage to drop them

Sources: Adapted from Maslow, A. H. (1954). *Motivation and personality.* New York: Harper & Row. Maslow, A. H. (1967). Self-actualization and beyond. In J. F. T. Bugental (Ed.), *Challenges of humanistic psychology.* New York: McGraw-Hill.

Although both Freud and Rogers postulate defenses, there is considerable difference in the role defense mechanisms play in their theories. According to Freud, defenses are a necessary part of living, with mature defenses (those that distort reality as little as possible) characteristic of even the healthiest individuals. According to Rogers, the truly healthy individual — the fully functioning person — is completely defense-free.

The Fully Functioning Person The **fully functioning person** develops in a family atmosphere of **unconditional positive regard:** parents set no conditions for loving their children, demonstrate they are loved and accepted for what they are, and instill in them the confidence they will be loved and respected whatever they do. Unconditional positive regard does not mean approving of everything a child does regardless of its consequences. Parents can show unconditional positive regard by making it clear they are evaluating their children's actions and not their children themselves. For example, instead of saying, "You are bad for playing with matches," parents simply take away the matches and say, "I don't want you to play with matches because you might burn yourself."

Rogers outlines five characteristics of the ideal fully functioning person:

1. *Openness to Experience* allowing all experiences to enter awareness without distorting or denying them, whether they are positive or negative

2. *Living Existentially* living for the moment; not basing actions on preconceived ideas of how things should be but rather on how each situation is experienced

3. *Organismic Trusting* openness; faith in personal reactions to events and people, and willingness to act on them

4. *Experiential Freedom* feeling of being in charge of one's life, of freely choosing between alternatives

5. *Creativity* tendency toward imaginative thoughts and actions

According to Rogers, fully functioning people lead a special kind of life, called *the good life*. It is a life of richness and vitality in which the individual experiences feelings intensely, is capable of intimacy in relationships, and finds meaning in existence.

At an opposite pole from the fully functioning person is the **incongruent person** upon whom, as a child, conditions of worth were imposed. Incongruent people experience an inconsistency between their natural selves and their self-images. They are motivated to maintain the status quo rather than to enhance their lives. They are defensive rather than open; they live according to preconceived plans rather than spontaneously and existentially; they disregard their natural feelings rather than trusting them; they feel manipulated rather than free to assert themselves; and they conform rather than chancing creative solutions to life's problems.

Rogers summarizes his philosophical position with the following quote from Lao-Tse.

> If I keep from meddling with people, they take care of themselves,
> If I keep from commanding people, they behave themselves,
> If I keep from preaching at people, they improve themselves,
> If I keep from imposing on people, they become themselves. (1973, p. 13)

Embedded within the approaches to personality we have examined is the assumption that how people think affects the development of their personalities. Freud distinguished between two forms of thought — primary- and secondary-process thinking — and Rogers believes that language and thinking are integral in personality development. The next approach we consider, the cognitive approach of George Kelly, places almost exclusive emphasis on the effect of thought on personality development.

The Cognitive Approach of George Kelly

Near the beginning of his book *The Psychology of Personal Constructs,* George Kelly writes:

> It is customary to say that the scientist's ultimate aim is to predict and control. This is a summary statement that psychologists frequently like to quote in characterizing their own aspirations. Yet curiously enough, psychologists rarely credit the human subjects in their experiments with having similar aspirations. It is as though the psychologist were saying to himself, "I, being a psychologist, and therefore a scientist, am performing this experiment in order to improve the prediction and control of certain human phenomena; but my subject, being merely a human organism is obviously propelled by inexorable drives welling up within him, or else he is in gluttonous pursuit of sustenance and shelter. (Kelly, 1955, p. 5)

Kelly's theory of personality is based on the idea that all people are scientists, attempting to understand, organize, predict, and control the events in their lives. A girl who refrains from calling her boyfriend after he has neglected her may be viewed as a scientist testing the theory "If he loves me, he will call me." If the boyfriend calls, the hypothesis is confirmed and the implicit theory from which it was derived is supported. If not . . . well, back to the drawing board.

Construing and Constructs   Kelly employs a special word to refer to the process people employ to interpret the events in their lives — **construing.** He argues there is no meaningful reality beyond people's construction of events, and people's constructions of reality determine their behavior. According to Kelly, people employ two cognitive processes to construe events: *abstraction* and *generalization.* When confronted by a completely novel situation, a person attempts to abstract general features of the events and construct a pattern that accounts for them. (This process is apparent in person perception and impression formation, through which people form elaborate inferences about others on the basis of sparse information.) After a pattern is abstracted, it is generalized, or applied to similar events.

It is important to recognize there are many ways of construing events, and different people may emphasize different features. Kelly refers to the tendency for people to construe the world in different ways as the principle of **constructive alternativism.** This tendency enables people to alter the way they view the world, including themselves, by changing the way they think about things. The freedom of thought accorded humans by Kelly is quite different from the freedom accorded humans by Freud. Freud believed people are victims of their biological endowment. Kelly believes people have the capacity to construct and change their personalities because they have the capability to construe the world in different ways.

Kelly refers to the hypotheses or interpretations people make about their worlds as **constructs.** In Kelly's words, constructs are "transparent realities of which the world is composed" (Kelly, 1955, pp. 8–9). Examples of constructs are *good versus bad, happy versus sad, black versus white,* and *beautiful versus ugly.* Note that constructs consist of two poles. Kelly believes he mirrors the nature of thought by defining constructs in this way. He believes a person must recognize that two events are similar to each other and different from a third in order to develop a construct (see Box 12-4). If we think two individuals are similar because they are happy, we must also assume other individuals are different because they are sad. Once a construct is formed, it is used to anticipate future events. If predictions based on the construct are confirmed, the construct is supported and retained. If predictions are not confirmed, the construct is revised or discarded.

People's constructs do not exist in isolation; rather, they are organized hierarchically: some are subordinate, some are superordinate. For example, a moralizer may have a superordinate *good-versus-bad* construct that encompasses many other concepts. For this individual, a *good* person might be punctual, temperate, kind, sincere; a *bad* person might be unreliable, selfish, cruel, and insincere (Figure 12-5, page 612).

Behavioristic and Social Learning Approaches — The Person-situation Controversy

The theories of personality considered thus far assume people's behavior is governed by internal factors — whether called personality traits, instincts, ego, actualizing tendencies, or personal constructs — but some psychologists argue it is misleading to attribute behavior to hypothetical, unobservable, internal factors when behavior can be explained perfectly well by observable aspects of the environment. Social psychologists adduce evidence from such studies as Milgram's experiments on obedience to authority, Asch's experiments on conformity, and Zimbardo's prison study to show that people's behavior is controlled by external pressures (see Chapter 11). Learning theorists adduce evidence to show that people's behavior is controlled by reinforcers in the environment (Chapter 5). If you reward a person for helping others, the person will acquire an altruistic behavioral style (an altruistic *personality*); if you reward a person for behaving aggressively, the person will acquire an aggressive personality (see Krebs & Miller, 1985).

The Behavioristic Position of B. F. Skinner

Behaviorist B. F. Skinner — whose general philosophy is outlined in Chapter 1 and whose operant

Box 12-4
Assessing Your Personal Constructs

Kelly created the *Role Construct Repertory Test* to assess personal constructs. To learn about your constructs, follow the directions below.

Turn the grid so the word *Figure* appears at the top. For each numbered space write the name of the person described below

1. Write your own name in the first blank here.

2. Write your mother's first name here. If you grew up with a stepmother, write her name instead.

3. Write your father's first name here. If you grew up with a stepfather, write his name instead.

4. Write the name of your brother who is nearest your own age. If you had no brother, write the name of a boy near your own age who was most like a brother to you during your early teens.

5. Write the name of your sister who is nearest your own age. If you had no sister, write the name of a girl near your own age who was most like a sister to

you during your early teens.

FROM THIS POINT ON DO NOT REPEAT ANY NAMES. IF A PERSON HAS ALREADY BEEN LISTED, SIMPLY MAKE A SECOND CHOICE.

6. Your wife (or husband) or, if you are not married, your closest present girl (boy) friend.

7. Your closest girl (boy) friend immediately preceding the person mentioned above.

8. Your closest present friend of the same sex as yourself.

9. A person of the same sex as yourself whom you once thought was a close friend but in whom you were badly disappointed later.

10. The minister, priest, or rabbi with whom you would be most willing to talk over your personal feelings about religion.

11. Your physician.

12. The present neighbor whom you know best.

13. A person with whom you have been associated who, for some unexplained reason, appeared to dislike you.

14. A person whom you would most like to help or for whom you feel sorry.

15. A person with whom you usually feel most uncomfortable.

16. A person whom you have recently met whom you would like to know better.

17. The teacher whom you have recently met whom you would like to know better.

18. The teacher whose point of view you have found most objectionable.

19. An employer, supervisor, or officer under whom you served during a period of great stress.

20. The most successful person whom you know personally.

21. The happiest person whom you know personally.

22. The person known to you personally who appears to meet the highest ethical standards.

Instructions for Figure List (from Kelly, 1955, p. 270)

The Rep Test: Grid Form

Figure 1	2	3	4	5	6	7	8	9	10	11	12	13	14	15	16	17	18	19	20	21	22	Sort No.	CONSTRUCT	CONTRAST
																			0	0	0	1		
																0	0	0				2		
												0	0		0							3		
			0	0	0																	4		
	0	0	0																			5		
			0												0			0				6		
	0							0							0							7		
		0															0	0				8		
			0									0			0							9		
			0									0			0							10		
			0										0								0	11		
		0						0					0									12		
				0									0							0		13		
	0				0	0																14		
		0			0	0																15		
							0	0							0							16		
0			0	0																		17		
																	0	0			0	18		
	0	0											0									19		
0												0		0								20		
					0							0	0									21		
0				0		0																22		

After writing names in all the spaces, turn the grid so the words *Construct* and *Contrast* are at the top. Note that immediately left of the number 1 in the column entitled *Sort No.* there are three circles, one under the 20, one under the 21, and one under the 22. "This means that you are first to consider the three people whose name appears" (Kelly, 1955, p. 273) above these numbers in the *Figure* column: the people you named as most successful, happy, and ethical.

Think about these three people. Are two of them *alike in some important way that distinguishes them from the third person?* Keep thinking about them until you remember the important way in which two of them are alike and which sets them off from the third person.

When you have decided which two it is, and the important way in which they are alike, put an "X" in the two circles corresponding to the two who are alike. Do not put any mark in the third circle.

Now write in the blank under "Construct" the word or short phrase that tells how these two are alike.

Next write in the blank under "Contrast" what you consider to be the opposite of this characteristic.

Now consider each of the other nineteen persons whose names appear at the heads of columns 1 to 19. In addition to the persons whom you have marked with an "X," which ones also have this important characteristic? Put a check Mark (✓)—not an "X"—under the name of each other person who has this important characteristic . . . .

[Now proceed to Sort No. 2.] Think about persons number 17, 18, and 19—the three who have circles under their names. In what important way are two of these distinguished from the third? Put "X's" in the circles to show which two are alike. Write the "Construct" and the "Contrast" in the blanks at the right just as you did before. Then consider the other sixteen persons. Check (✓) the ones who also have the characteristic you have noted.

Complete the test in the way you have done the first two rows. (Kelly, 1955, p. 273)

Your constructs are easily identifiable in the grid; they are listed below the heading *Construct*. The *Contrast* column provides the opposite pole. Together, these 22 pairs of words represent your personal constructs. Of course, this is not a complete set of your constructs—you have many more not assessed by the test. Nonetheless, the set assessed by Kelly's test should be among your most important constructs.

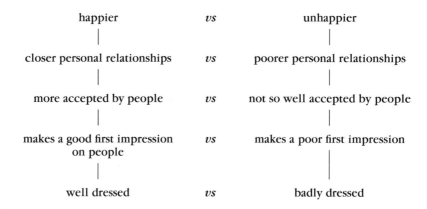

happier	*vs*	unhappier
closer personal relationships	*vs*	poorer personal relationships
more accepted by people	*vs*	not so well accepted by people
makes a good first impression on people	*vs*	makes a poor first impression
well dressed	*vs*	badly dressed

FIGURE 12-5

The Hierarchical Organization of Constructs   By asking a male subject whether he would prefer to be viewed by others as well dressed or badly dressed, Bannister (1970) demonstrated that constructs are organized in hierarchies.   After the subject replied, Bannister asked "Why?"   The subject replied, and again was asked "Why?"   This procedure continued until the subject could no longer provide an answer to Bannister's "Why?"   The subject's final answer — that being well dressed made him happy and that being poorly dressed made him unhappy — revealed that the organizing construct was *happiness.   Source:* Phares, J. E. (1984).   *Introduction to Personality* (p.178).   Columbus, OH: Charles Merrill.

theory of learning is outlined in Chapter 5 — is perhaps strongest in his rejection of the idea that behavior is determined by internal factors.   In Skinner's words, "The inside of the organism is irrelevant either as the site of physiological processes or as the focus of mentalistic activities."   According to Skinner, the reason why different people behave differently is because they grow up in different environments and have different histories of reinforcement.   Skinner argues that the reasoning of personality theorists is circular: they observe a person engaging in a behavior (looking in the mirror), invent a word to describe it (*narcissism*), then use the word to explain the cause of the original behavior (the personality trait of narcissism).

Skinner shuns use of the term *personality* but allows that people may have different repertoires of behavior, which "like the repertoire of a musician . . . is what a person . . . is capable of doing, given the right circumstances" (Skinner, 1974, p. 138).   Thus, the closest Skinner comes to endowing people with personalities is to endow them with *repertoires* of behavior.

The Social Learning Position of Walter Mischel

In 1968, social-learning theorist Walter Mischel published an influential attack on the idea that

behavior stems from personality traits.   Mischel argued that if behavior stems from personality traits, people should behave consistently across situations.   For example, if an individual has an aggressive personality, he or she should behave aggressively at home, at work, and at social events.   Mischel (1968) reviewed a mass of social psychological research on the consistency of various kinds of behavior across situations and found a low average correlation (.30) between such behaviors.   Mischel (1968) concluded:

> With the possible exception of intelligence, highly generalized behavioral consistencies have not been demonstrated, and the concept of personality traits as broad predispositions is thus untenable.   (p. 146)

Mischel argued that the reason why people attribute personality traits to others is either because people have a need to believe others are predictable or because people are exposed to others in only a select sample of situations.   Although Mischel was correct in showing people do not always behave consistently, subsequent research has shown he overstated his case.

In Defense of Personality Traits

Following the publication of Mischel's 1968 book, several investigators attacked his conclusions; they based their defense of personality traits on four main points. First, when Mischel concluded that people's behavior is inconsistent, he used a behavioral definition of consistency. Although inconsistent on one level, people's behavior might be consistent on another. A person with a high need for approval might behave aggressively in an aggressive group and helpfully in a helpful group. Second, most of the studies from which Mischel drew his conclusions assessed behavior in only two situations. Critics such as Epstein (1979) argue we should not expect people to behave the same way in all situations. For example, we would not expect an aggressive person to behave aggressively in church. To evaluate consistency fairly, we must assess people's behavior over a large number of situations and *aggregate* their behaviors. Epstein (1979) showed that although personality traits related to sociability and to impulsivity may be inconsistent when assessed on two occasions, they are highly consistent when assessed over several occasions. Moskowitz (1982) reported similar findings for dominance and dependency.

Third, Bem and Allen (1974) showed that the degree of consistency depends on the importance of the personality trait in question to the person whose behavior is being assessed. These investigators found that students who viewed themselves as reasonably conscientious and friendly were rated as consistently conscientious and friendly by parents and a close friend; those who did not view themselves in these terms were not so rated. Finally, Snyder and Kendzierski (1982) point out that most research showing situational specificity of behavior has been conducted in the laboratory, which constrains people's options. People's behavior is much more consistent in the natural world, where they are free to choose the situations they encouter. For example, extroverts tend to seek out social occasions; introverts choose to spend time alone.

The Interaction between People and Situations

Given the evidence that both situations and personality characteristics channel behavior, the obvious conclusion is that the either-or approach is inadequate: both factors play a role. Although some situations support aggression and others support altruism (Krebs & Miller, 1985), some

people are more likely than others to behave aggressively in aggressive situations (Olweus, 1977) and other people are more likely to behave altruistically in altruistic situations (Rushton, 1980). In a review of relevant studies, Bowers (1973) found the critical element was the *interaction* between personality and situational factors.

Endler and Magnusson (1976, p. 12) name four assumptions of modern or *organic* forms of **interactionism:**

1. Behavior is determined by a continuous process of interaction between the individual and the situation he or she encounters (feedback).
2. The individual is an intentional, active agent in this interaction process.
3. Cognitive factors are important in interaction.
4. The psychological meaning of the situation to the individual is an essential determinant of behavior.

Interactionist theorists view individuals as active selectors of situations and processors of (situational) information. Different individuals behave differently both because they seek out different situations and process the information involved in the same situations differently. As a result, the same physical situation is psychologically different to different people because it has a different meaning to them: "The spectacle seen depends upon the methodological and conceptual spectacles worn; what is known depends as much upon schemes inside the knower as it does upon the world outside him" (Bowers, 1973, p. 153). The outside world—external events — exerts some influence on how situations are perceived. In Piagetian terms, however, individuals both assimilate information to existing schemes and accommodate to the objects of understanding.

In 1981, Mischel revised his original situational position and developed a more interactional account of personality. In his new position, Mischel (1981) suggests that situations provide information and that people—who may differ in such personality traits as styles of information processing, expectancies about outcomes, values, and competencies—process the information. When situational factors are strong (such as in many situations studied by social psychologists) and when people are exposed to situations frequently enough to develop habitual or entrenched reactions, personality factors exert little influence and most people behave similarly. However, in weak or ambiguous situations, different people react differently depending on their personality.

Albert Bandura's Social Learning Approach to Personality

The social learning theory of Albert Bandura, considered in Chapters 5 and 10, is interactional in nature. Bandura agrees with Skinner and other behaviorists that reinforcement is a powerful determinant of behavior. In addition, Bandura suggests people learn by watching others — a process called *observational learning,* or modeling. Bandura points out that people often learn more

than may be apparent. Although people may not copy the behavior of models at the time they observe them, people may copy such behavior (stored in their memories) at some future time in similar situations. According to Bandura, the most importat factor in the development of personality is modeling.

Bandura also emphasizes the significance of **vicarious reinforcement** (reinforcement experienced by observing others being rewarded and punished), **self-reinforcement,** and **self-efficacy** (the sense of control over outcomes in one's life.) As shown in Figure 12-6, Bandura attends to the interaction between environmental stimuli (such as the distinctiveness of a model) and characteristics of observers (such as their cognitive organization). In addition, Bandura emphasizes the reciprocal nature of social interactions and their effect on personality: the behavior of one individual affects the behavior of another, which

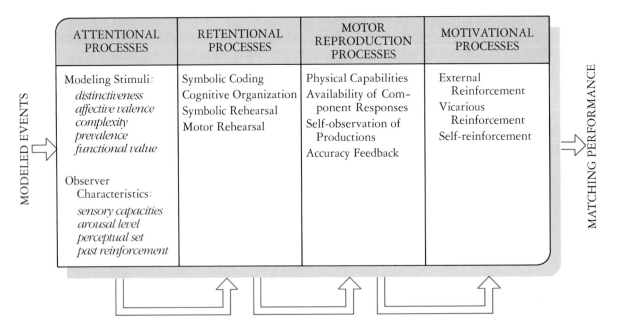

FIGURE 12-6

Bandura's Social Learning Theory In Bandura's theory, characteristics of models (such as their distinctiveness) interact with characteristics of observers (such as their sensory capacities) to give rise to information that is coded, organized, and rehearsed. Factors within observers (such as their physical capabilities) are channeled into modeled behavior by external and internal reinforcement. *Source:* Bandura, A. (1977). *Social learning theory* (p. 23). Englewood Cliffs, NJ: Prentice-Hall.

feeds back on the behavior of the first, and so on.

Yet, in agreement with behaviorists, Bandura does not believe it is useful to assume personality structures exist in people, because no one has ever observed them. He defines personality in terms of patterns of behavior and believes personality differs in different situations (a person might be shy in a group of strangers but talkative with friends). According to Bandura, the general patterns of behavior that define personality are acquired through experiences with the environment, especially other people. For example, children develop aggressive personalities when exposed to people who behave aggressively—even television actors—and when, for whatever reason, they expect aggression to

pay off for them (see Bandura, 1977).

In conclusion, it is clear a full account of personality must attend to characteristics of people, characteristics of situations, and, especially, the interaction between them. It is inadequate to say a person is extroverted or anxious, and it is inadequate to assume people react to situations like automatons. Personal inner characteristics determine how people interpret, perceive, analyze, and react to situations. Interaction between personality and situations is a two-way process: situations affect the development of personality, especially through social learning, as much as personality affects people's response to situations.

PERSONALITY THEORIES—COMPARISON AND EVALUATION

The variety and range of perspectives adopted by different personality theorists may seem overwhelming. Freud outlined five discontinuous stages of development; Erikson outlined eight; Rogers and Bandura view personality development as a continuous process. Freud assumes we are motivated by sexual and aggressive instincts; Rogers assumes our basic motive is to actualize our potential. Freud emphasizes the irrational aspects of human nature; Kelly emphasizes the rational. Skinner and Bandura focus on social-environmental influences on behavior; other theorists emphasize inner characteristics. And on it goes. The position on ten essential issues of each major approach to personality we have discussed is summarized in Table 12-11.

If different approaches to personality take different positions on essential issues, which one is right? Which theory supplies the most valid account of personality? These are contentious questions that have been debated for many decades, and we can safely assume they will be de-

bated for many more. Although we have no final answers to these questions, we offer seven criteria on which theories of personality can be evaluated (Table 12-12).

All theories of personality considered thus far have been evaluated by supporters and critics. Although different evaluators sometimes reach different conclusions, there is general consensus on many issues. We interpret this consensus in Table 12-13 (page 620) and elaborate on certain major points in Box 12-5.

In general, we can conclude that the value of a theory of personality depends on what it is used to explain. Theories that focus on the core of personality attempt to supply broad sketches of human nature. These sketches tend to be abstract and difficult to test. Theories that focus on the periphery of personality tend to supply detailed etchings of the behavior of people in specific situations. These etchings tend to be precise and scientifically respectable, but provide a reduced sense of the structure of personality as a whole.

TABLE 12-11   Approaches to Personality — A Comparison

Point of Comparison	Approach			
	Psychoanalytic	*Humanistic*	*Cognitive*	*Behavioral/ Social-learning*
View of human nature	negative	positive	positive	neutral
Is behavior free or determined?	determined	free	free	determined
Principal motives	sex and aggression	self-actualization	understanding of self and others	learning goals
Personality structure	id, ego, superego	self	constructs	habits
Developmental emphasis	psychosexual stages	self-actualization	neglected	critical learning situations; identification and imitation
Barriers to personal growth	unconscious conflicts; fixations; defenses	conditions of worth; incongruence	invalid, inconsistent, and narrow constructs	maladaptive habits; pathological environment
Are people rational or irrational?	irrational	rational	rational	rational
Emphasis on heredity and environment	interaction	interaction	environment	environment
Emphasis on internal structures and processes versus behavior	internal processes	internal processes	internal structures	observable behavior
Basic question	How do people deal with their basic instincts?	How can people realize their potential?	How do people anticipate events?	How is behavior shaped by its consequences and by modeling?
Emphasis on normal or abnormal behavior	abnormal	normal	normal	normal

Source: Adapted from Coon, D. (1985). *Essentials of psychology* (3rd ed.). St. Paul, MN: West.

TABLE 12-12   Criteria for the Evaluation of Personality Theories

Comprehensiveness
The breadth of explanation of a theory: how many aspects of human nature it aspires to explain.

Parsimony
The economy with which concepts are used. A parsimonious theory contains only the assumptions it requires to make its point — no more and no less.

Logical consistency
The constructs of the theory should be organized coherently and be free of contradiction.

Testability
The primary criterion of a theory's scientific status: a testable theory is one that specifies the conditions under which particular events should occur and does so in a way that permits such predictions to be confirmed or disconfirmed.

Empirical support
The extent to which a theory has been confirmed through research.

Heuristic value
The ability to organize information from associated areas and to stimulate scholars to conduct research.

Applied value
The applicability to real-life problems.

Box 12-5
Evaluating Theories of Personality

A sound theory of personality should be comprehensive, parsimonious, logically consistent, and testable; it should be supported by empirical research and have heuristic and applied value. In Table 12-13 we summarize the extent to which each theory we have considered meets these criteria. Here we elaborate on some of the most significant points.

Comprehensiveness

Theories that fare best on breadth of explanation tend to fare worst on scientific status. Critics of behavioristic and social learning approaches argue the theories are not comprehensive and neglect most of what is important about personality—the internal, unobservable, core aspects of human nature. Freud's psychoanalytic theory is the most comprehensive. The magnitude of Freud's concerns is reflected in his writings; his collected works constitute some 24 volumes!

Parsimony

What the behavioristic approaches lose in comprehensiveness, they gain in parsimony—principles of operant conditioning are few but far-reaching. Although Skinner criticizes Bandura for including unnecessary constructs in his theory, the range of phenomena accounted for by Bandura is significantly greater than that accounted for by Skinner. What Freud gains in comprehensiveness, he losses in parsimony. Freud attempts to account for a broad range of phenomena through a small number of constructs—especially sexual and aggressive instincts, the unconscious, the three-level structure of personality, and defense mechanisms—but his theorizing seems convoluted and implausible to many reviewers.

Logical Consistency

Because such theories as those of Skinner and, to a lesser extent, Bandura are based on a small number of relatively straightforward propositions, they tend to fare well on the criterion of internal consistency. In its elaborateness, Freud's theory is susceptible to inconsistency. Freud has been criticized severely on this basis.

One of the central sources of logical inconsistency and implausibility in Freud's theory lies in his attempts to account for the development of personality in women. Freud floundered in his attempt to find parallel events to the Oedipus conflict of young boys, settling for the questionable conclusion that females never really develop an adequate conscience. By and large, psychoanalysis is a theory of male personality. Its view of women—whom it portrays as unconsciously envious of the male's anatomical mark of superiority (*penis envy*) and therefore as unconsciously inferior—is unacceptable to most reviewers.

Testability

Theories that focus on the periphery of personality and on observable behavior are the most testable. Indeed, they are based on the results of experimental research. Theories that focus on inner qualities and the core of personality are more difficult to test. In addition, the terms employed by many core theories are vague and difficult to quantify. What exactly is an *id, basic trust, libido, actualizing tendency, condition of worth,* or *elaborative choice*? Under what conditions can these *things* be observed and measured?

To test the postulates of a theory, you must be able to disconfirm them. The postulates of some theories are stated in such a way that two contradictory examples of behavior can be interpreted as support for the theory. For example, Freud postulated that young boys become sexually attracted to their mothers. If, on questioning, a boy were to admit to such an attraction, it would appear to confirm the postulate. However, if the boy were to deny the attraction, Freud also could consider the postulate confirmed—arguing the boy was employing the defense mechanism of denial.

Psychoanalytic theory forms the basis of psychoanalysis—a form of treatment for psychological disorder (see Chapter 14). To undergo successful psychoanalysis, people must accept the assumption that they repress wishes and desires. When individuals object to interpretations made during treatment by their psychoanalyst, the psychoanalyst may claim they are denying or resisting. Critics of psychoanalysis have suggested that vulnerable people in psychoanalysis often become *converted* to Freud's *mythology*, believing they are abnormal when they are not.

Empirical Support

As you might expect, the most testable approaches are those that have received the most support through experimental investigations. Again as you might expect, such approaches tend to focus on the periphery of personality and observable behavior. For example, there have been numerous empirical tests of Bandura's theory, and most results have been supportive.

Kelly's theory also fares quite well on the criterion of empirical support. Studies have found Kelly's Rep Test (RCRT) moderately reliable (see Hunt, 1951; Mitsos, 1958).

As far as Freud was concerned, clinical observations were adequate to verify his ideas. When American psychologist Saul Rosenzweig sent Freud reports of his research of repression, Freud answered, "I cannot value these confirmations very highly since the abundance of reliable observations upon which these propositions rest makes them independent of experimental verification" (quoted by Bavelas, 1978, p. 32). However, in the words of modern Freudian

scholar David Rappaport, "Clinical evidence . . . fails to be conclusive . . . because there is no established *canon for the interpretation of clinical observations*" (1959, pp. 141–42).

In spite of Freud's attitude toward experimental verification, many of his ideas have been tested experimentally. Some have been supported, some have not. For example, evidence from developmental psychology suggests it is unlikely that infants' perceptual and cognitive systems are developed sufficiently to enable them to hallucinate an image of their mother or her breast and suggests that the latency period is more significant than Freud believed, that it is a time of impressive intellectual and social growth. However, Freud's assertion that the events of childhood are important for future adult functioning has been accepted widely. Perhaps Freud's greatest legacy to psychology is not the correctness of his views but the ability of his theory to stimulate new intellectual exploration (see Kline, 1972).

Relatively little scientific research has been conducted on Carl Rogers' theory. Rogers himself has acknowledged some aspects of his theory "contain some logical and systematic gaps and flaws, and still others [not presented] exist as highly personal and subjective hunches" (Rogers, 1959, p. 244). In addition, referring to the "translation" of his theory into scientifically testable form, Rogers has admitted "there is still a woefully long distance to go." Perhaps Rogers' theory (and other humanistic theories) is better considered a philosophical theory of personality than a psychological theory — and should be evaluated accordingly.

Heuristic Value

Freud's psychoanalysis is the most influential theory of personality. Many of Freud's concepts have become part of everyday language. Such words as *ego-trip, Freudian slip, projection, rationalization,* and *the unconscious* are drawn from psychoanalytic theory. Freud is indisputably the most widely cited psychologist (see Chapter 1).

Erikson's theory has influenced anthropologists and historians. Rogers' theory has impacted on education and encounter groups. Skinner's approach has spawned behavior modification, inspired economic theories of exchange, stimulated philosophers, and formed the basis of utopian communities. Bandura's theory has been restricted primarily to social and developmental psychology. Of the theories we have considered, Kelly's has had the least impact on areas outside psychology.

Applied Value

Psychoanalysis has had the greatest impact on psychiatry and clinical psychology. Skinner's approach, through behavior modification, and Rogers, through client-centered therapy, also have spawned schools of therapy (see Chapter 14). The approaches of Skinner and Rogers also have impacted on education. Erikson's theory has influenced child psychologists, psychiatrists, and marriage and vocational counselors. Many adults who have undergone per-

sonal crises have been helped by books based on Erikson's theory (see Chapter 10).

The applied value of Bandura's approach is mixed. Educators and clinicians have employed principles of social learning; however, with principles of operant conditioning, the changes in behavior they induce often are transient and specific to the experimental situation. For example, it is relatively easy to reduce the incidence of aggression in an aggressive child in a laboratory or controlled environment; but it is difficult to maintain this effect over time or in different contexts without repeated exposure to the learning experience.

TABLE 12-13
Evaluation of Six Personality Theories

	Criterion of Evaluation		
Theory	**Comprehensiveness**	**Parsimony**	**Logical Consistency**
Cattell	Good to very good: addresses a wide range of phenomena; considers both biological and sociocultural factors	Good: economical but not overly simplistic	Excellent: relationships based on the results of empirical research
Freud	Excellent: covers virtually all human behavior (for example, humor, marriage, war, death, incest, dreams, and so on)	Poor: essentially a *nothing-but* theory; sex and aggression are sole determinants of behavior	Poor: theorizing in one area sometimes is inconsistent with theorizing in another area
Erikson	Very good: seeks to account for biological, social, cultural, and instinctual factors	Fair: explanatory base is limited	Good: logical developmental matrix
Rogers	Fair: theory newly extended to explain several phenomena (for example, family life, education, politics) but neglects development	Fair: relies on limited number of concepts and assumptions	Fair: some connections are difficult to understand
Kelly	Poor: primarily cognitive; deemphasizes role of situation/environment; says little about growth and development	Fair: limited number of concepts	Good: theory presented in postulates and corollaries
Bandura	Fair: limited in range and diversity of phenomena	Good: relatively limited number of assumptions but considers biological, social, and cultural phenomena	Good: based on learning theory and modeling

PERSONALITY ASSESSMENT

Since at least the time of Sir Francis Galton (1822–1911; Chapter 1), social scientists have been developing tests to assess personality. Today, thousands of personality tests are available to psychologists and to other professionals. There is a rough association between the types of test employed by psychologists and their theoretical orientation. If, with psychoanalysts, you believe the most important aspects of personality are unconscious needs and desires, it follows you would prefer tests that measure these constructs. If, on the other hand, you believe personality is best defined as patterns of observable behavior, you should prefer tests that assess behavior. Because most psychologists are eclectic — they recognize, for example, the significance of both unconscious needs and observable behaviors — most psychologists employ a battery of tests, some of which are associated with a theory of personality and some of which are atheoretical.

Imagine finding yourself in a dispute with a friend about the personality characteristics possessed by a mutual acquaintance: you say she is friendly, generous, and trusting; your friend says

Criterion of Evaluation			
Testability	**Empirical Support**	**Heuristic Value**	**Applied Value**
Very good: precisely defined concepts	Good: considerable support for basic concepts	Good: but little impact on other investigations	Good to very good
Poor: concepts are vague and ambiguous; much of the theory is presented in metaphors (for example, instincts, ego, id)	Fair: good support for some concepts, very modest for others	Excellent: has stimulated interest in many disciplines (for example, sociology, history, religion)	Excellent: theory has been employed by many disciplines
Poor: highly abstract and complex concepts (for example, integrity)	Fair to good: difficult and costly to conduct longitudinal studies; research on identity generally consistent	Very good: has generated interest in a variety of disciplines	Very good: impact on many different areas (for example, child psychology)
Poor: vague and ambiguous key concepts (for example, empathy, genuineness)	Poor: limited research, primarily on empathy and self-actualization	Very good: has provoked continued vigorous debate	Very good: has been applied to such areas as education, politics, family life, and counseling
Very good: clear and explicit framework; the RCRT is a precise and reliable measure of basic theoretical ideas	Fair to good: solid support of the RCRT; needs more sophisticated experimental work	Fair to good: primarily the RCRT; needs more experimental research	Poor: little impact outside psychology; sparse contribution to solution of social problems
Very good: considerable degree of conceptual clarity; systematic	Very good to excellent: impressive evidence from empirical tests	Very good: great impact on clinical and social psychology	Very good: especially in the area of psychopathology

she is unfriendly, selfish, and suspicious. How would you resolve this difference? How could you determine the accuracy of your assessment?

Direct Ratings of Personality Traits

Perhaps the most common way of resolving disputes about what people are like is to appeal to another person who knows them. You might ask someone who knows the person to describe her or, if you wanted to be a little more precise, you might ask the person to rate the woman on a scale of, say, 1–10. Although psychologists sometimes use a **trait-rating approach** to personal-

ity, they typically guard against *response biases* that plague ratings of the average person.

Response Biases One of the most common **response biases** is the **halo effect**: the tendency to rate people who possess one desirable characteristic high on other desirable characteristics. For example, if a rater rates a person as *friendly,* he or she is more likely to rate the person as *generous* than as *selfish.* A comparable response bias is the **horns effect**: the tendency to attribute undesirable characteristics to people who possess other undesirable characteristics.

Another response bias is **yea-saying/nay-saying**: the tendency for people to agree (or to disagree) with whatever question you ask them. If you asked a yea-sayer whether he or she thinks someone is friendly, the yea-sayer probably would say yes. But if you had asked the yea-sayer the opposite question (whether he or she thinks someone is unfriendly), he or she probably would still say yes. Personality ratings in a true/false, agree/disagree format are susceptible to this bias.

Another response bias occurs when people rate others on scales: people may use different parts of scales. For example, one judge might give a person a 7 on a 1- to 9-point scale of emotional stability; a second judge might give the same person a 5. Although these rating seem different, the first judge might rate almost everybody between 5 and 9 on the scale, whereas the second judge might rate almost everybody between 3 and 7. Considered in relation to each rating distribution, the 7 and 5 mean the same thing: that the target person was average on each judge's scale of emotional stability.

Psychologists attempt to minimize response biases; consider two popular variations of the trait-rating method of personality assessment.

The Adjective Check List and the Q-sort The **Adjective Check List** (Gough, 1965) contains 300 adjectives that describe personality characteristics, listed in alphabetical order (see Table 12-14). Raters are asked to check the adjectives characteristic of the person being assessed.

TABLE 12-14
The Adjective Check List

The First 17 Adjectives on One Version of the Adjective Check List	
absent minded	ambitious
active	anxious
adaptable	apathetic
adventurous	appreciative
affected	argumentative
affectionate	arrogant
aggressive	artistic
alert	assertive
aloof	

Source: Gough, H. G. (1965). *The adjective check list manual.* Palo Alto, CA: Consulting Psychologist Press.

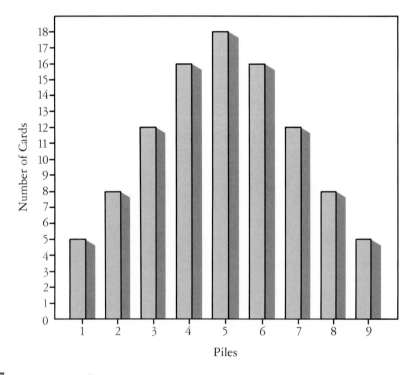

FIGURE 12-7

Q-sort Pattern Cards that contain personality characteristics are sorted into piles that range from the least characteristic (1) to the most characteristic (9). The number of cards required for each pile conforms to a normal distribution.

A **Q-sort** is a stack of cards (usually 100), each card containing a description of a personality characteristic. Raters are required to place the cards in, say, ten stacks of ten, ranging from cards *least characteristic* of the person being assessed to cards *most characteristic*. After raters complete this task, they may be asked to rank-order the cards within each of the ten stacks, producing up to 100 items ranked in terms of how characteristic they are of the person being assessed. Alternatively, raters may be asked to place cards in nine stacks that represent a normal distribution or bell-shaped curve (see Figure 12-7 and the Appendix).

The Adjective Check List (ACL) and Q-sort methods contain safeguards against response biases. They ensure that raters consider a large number of traits, rather than one or a few. The traits have been selected carefully to complement one another and to supply a full assessment of personality. The ACL controls for people's tendency to employ different parts of a scale by forc-ing raters to use a 0–1 scale (to say whether the person being assessed possesses the characteristic or not). The Q-sort controls for this response bias by forcing judges to rank-order their responses. The ACL and Q-sort control for the halo and horns effects by including numerous favorable and unfavorable items: we would expect fewer people to give a person they liked positive ratings on 100 out of 100 socially desirable characteristics than on 5 out of 5. The Q-sort is not susceptible to yea-saying or nay-saying because it requires people to rank-order the characteristics they impute to others. Finally, because both tests contain so many items, the test-giver can check for response biases and remove them statistically.

Self-rating In practice, psychologists are more likely to ask people to rate themselves on the ACL and the Q-sort than they are to ask them to rate others. Q-sorts often are used to obtain a measure of self-concept and self-esteem. In one version, people are asked to sort the cards first in terms of their actual self and then in terms of their ideal

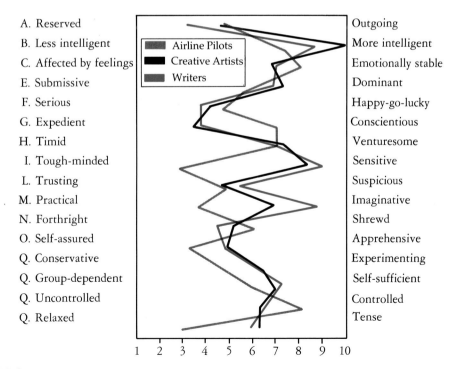

A. Reserved	Outgoing
B. Less intelligent	More intelligent
C. Affected by feelings	Emotionally stable
E. Submissive	Dominant
F. Serious	Happy-go-lucky
G. Expedient	Conscientious
H. Timid	Venturesome
I. Tough-minded	Sensitive
L. Trusting	Suspicious
M. Practical	Imaginative
N. Forthright	Shrewd
O. Self-assured	Apprehensive
Q. Conservative	Experimenting
Q. Group-dependent	Self-sufficient
Q. Uncontrolled	Controlled
Q. Relaxed	Tense

Legend: Airline Pilots, Creative Artists, Writers

Scale: 1 2 3 4 5 6 7 8 9 10

FIGURE 12-8

Personality Profiles from Cattell's 16PF Test The traits listed along the left side of the figure are the opposite of the traits listed along the right side of the figure. Extreme scores (represented by low and high numbers) cause the jagged lines to point to the traits that characterize the personality of the person taking the test. Average scores cluster around the center. *Source:* Adapted from Cattell, R. B. (1973, July). Personality pinned down. *Psychology Today,* pp. 40–46.

self. Sometimes therapists employ changes in the discrepancy between actual and ideal self-ratings as a measure of progress in psychotherapy.

Assessing personality by having people rate themselves may seem foolhardy. Certainly, it would be absurd to resolve a dispute about whether a person possessed desirable or undesirable personality characteristics by asking the person being assessed to deliver the verdict. This consideration raises an interesting quandary. The better we know someone — including ourselves — the more biased we might be in our evaluations (see Chapter 11); the less well we know someone, the less informed we are about him or her. How can we resolve this quandary?

The general strategy adopted by psychologists is to ask people to supply raw information about themselves, but to rely on their own psychological expertise to interpret the information. Although test-takers are treated as experts on how they think, feel, and behave in various situations, the psychologist reserves the right to interpret this information — to decide what personality traits people's self-reports reflect.

Personality Inventories

The type of test psychologists most frequently use to assess personality is a *personality inventory*. **Personality inventories** contain statements about attitudes, beliefs, opinions, feelings, and typical behaviors to which test-takers respond, usually by indicating the extent to which the statements pertain to them. Let us consider three of the most widely used personality inventories: Cattell's 16 Personality Factor Questionnaire (16PF), the California Psychological Inventory (CPI), and the Minnesota Multiphasic Personality Inventory (MMPI).

The 16PF Raymond Cattell, whose trait theory of personality we considered earlier, developed the **16PF.** The test consists of 100 items — such as *I like parties* — to which people respond *yes* or *no* (approximately 6 items for each of Cattell's 16 personality traits). Cattell selected the 100 items by factor analyzing a large number of candidates. In addition to providing a score for each trait, the total 16PF forms a personality profile (see Figure 12-8, page 623).

The CPI The **CPI** (Gough, 1975) measures such personality characteristics as dominance, socia-

bility, self-acceptance, responsibility, and socialization (see Table 12-15). In creating the test, its originators asked high school and college students to name classmates who were most dominant and least dominant, most sociable and least sociable (and so on) and then asked those nominated to respond to numerous items, such as the illustrative items in Table 12-15. Items responded to differently by students whose classmates had rated them high and low on the traits were retained; items responded to similarly were rejected. Through a process of refinement, items that supplied the best basis for predicting how, in fact, these students had been rated by their classmates won a place on the test (see Figure 12-9). This method of constructing a personality test employs an **empirical strategy.**

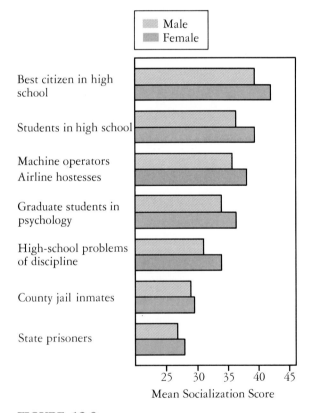

FIGURE 12-9
Validity of the Socialization Scale of the CPI
The CPI socialization scale is a good predictor of educational achievement and career success among people in the armed forces, law enforcement, medicine, dentistry, nursing, and teaching; it is also a predictor of social behaviors. *Source:* Adapted from Gough, H. G. (1960). *Manual for the California psychological inventory* (rev. ed.). Palo Alto, CA: Consulting Psychologists Press.

The MMPI The **MMPI** (Hathaway & McKinley, 1961) is similar to the CPI, except it assesses types of psychopathology. The MMPI also was developed empirically: by selecting items responded to differently by normal people and by people with various psychiatric diagnoses. For example, a group of patients diagnosed as psychopathic was asked how much they agreed or disagreed with such statements as: "I don't blame anyone for trying to grab everything he can get in the world" and "When someone wrongs me, I believe I should get even, just for the principle." The responses of those diagnosed as psychopathic were compared to the responses of a group of normal people, and those items answered differently by psychopaths formed the *Psychopathic-deviate Scale* of the MMPI. The MMPI contains 14 scales (see Table 12-16, page 628), 550 statements (total), and provides profiles such as the one displayed in Figure 12-10. Researchers have found that patterns of scores form a better basis for predicting behavior than scores on individual scales. Today, elaborate computer programs help analyze patterns of MMPI scores (Figure 12-10).

Personality Inventories — Strengths and Weaknesses Personality inventories have several advantages over other kinds of psychological tests: they are economical, easy to administer, and easy to score (in many cases by computer). Because such tests do not rely on the interpretive skill of the scorer, they tend to be highly reliable (discussion follows). However, personality inventories are susceptible to several problems:

1. They are dependent on people's accurate knowledge of their own attitudes, beliefs, feelings, and behavior.

2. They are dependent on people's willingness to disclose this knowledge.

3. They do not permit people to expand or refine their responses (*yes* or *no* may not capture a person's true response).

4. They rarely assess the reasons behind statements.

5. People who endorse the same number of

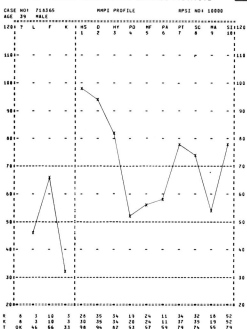

FIGURE 12-10

Computer-scored MMPI Profile (a) A Minnesota Multiphasic Personality Inventory (MMPI) profile of scores for a 39-year-old male. (b) The first page of a computerized interpretation of his profile. The client scored highest on hypochondria and neuroticism; he scored lowest on psychopathic deviancy and masculinity. *Source: Minnesota multiphasic personality inventory.* Copyright the University of Minnesota 1943. Renewed 1970. All rights reserved. Scored and distributed exclusively by NCS Interpretive Scoring Systems under license from the University of Minnesota.

TABLE 12-15   Scales, Psychological Significance, and Illustrative Items of the CPI

High Scorers	Scale and Purpose	Low Scorers
Tend to be seen as:		*Tend to be seen as:*
Class I. Measures of Poise, Ascendancy, Self-Assurance and Interpersonal Adequacy		
Aggressive, confident, persistent, and planful; as being persuasive and verbally fluent; as self-reliant and independent; and as having leadership potential and initiative.	1. Do (dominance) To assess factors of leadership ability, dominance, persistence, and social initiative.	Retiring, inhibited, commonplace, indifferent, silent and unassuming; as being slow in thought and action; as avoiding of situations of tension and decision; and as lacking in self-confidence.
Ambitious, active, forceful, insightful, resourceful, and versatile; as being ascendant and self-seeking; effective in communication; and as having personal scope and breadth of interests.	2. Cs (capacity for status) To serve as an index of an individual's capacity for status (not his actual or achieved status). The scale attempts to measure the personal qualities and attributes which underlie and lead to status.	Apathetic, shy, conventional dull, mild, simple, and slow; as being stereotyped in thinking; restricted in outlook and interests; and as being uneasy and awkard in new or unfamiliar social situations.
Outgoing, enterprising, and ingenious; as being competitive and forward; and as original and fluent in thought.	3. Sy (sociability) To identify persons of outgoing, sociable, participative temperament.	Awkard, conventional, quiet, submissive, and unassuming; as being detached and passive in attitude; and as being suggestible and overly influenced by others' reactions and opinions.
Clever, enthusiastic, imaginative, quick, informal, spontaneous, and talkative; as being active and vigorous; and as having an expressive, ebullient nature.	4. Sp (social presence) To assess factors such as poise, spontaneity, and self-confidence in personal and social interaction.	Deliberate, moderate, patient, self-restrained, and simple; as vacillating and uncertain in decision; and as being literal and unoriginal in thinking and judging.
Intelligent, outspoken, sharp-witted, demanding, aggressive, and self-centered; as being persuasive and verbally fluent; and as possessing self-confidence and self-assurance.	5. Sa (self-acceptance) To assess factors such as sense of personal worth, self-acceptance, and capacity foe independent thinking and action.	Methodical, conservative, dependable, conventional, easygoing, and quiet; as self-abasing and given to feelings of guilt and self-blame; and as being passive in action and narrow in interests.
Energetic, enterprising, alert, ambitious, and versatile; as being productive and active; and as valuing work and effort for its own sake.	6. Wb (sense of well-being) To identify persons who minimize their worries and complaints, and who are relatively free from self-doubt and disillusionment.	Unambitious, leisurely, ackward, cautious, apathetic, and conventional; as being self-defensive and apologetic; and as constricted in thought and action.
Class II. Measures of Socialization, Maturity, Responsibility, and Intrapersonal Structuring of Values		
Painful, responsible, thorough, progressive, capable, dignified, and independent; as being conscientious and dependable; resourceful and efficient; and as being alert to ethical and moral issues.	7. Re (responsibility) To identify persons of conscientious, responsible, and dependable disposition and temperament.	Immature, moody, lazy, awkward, changeable, and disbelieving; as being influenced by personal bias, spite, and dogmatism; and as undercontrolled and impulsive in behavior.
Serious, honest, industrious, modest, obliging, sincere, and steady; as being conscientious and responsible; and as being self-denying and conforming.	8. So (socialization) To indicate the degree of social maturity, integrity, and rectitude which the individual has attained.	Defensive, demanding, opinionated, resentful, stubborn, headstrong, rebellious, and undependable; as being guileful and deceitful in dealing with others; and as given to excess, exhibition, and ostentation in their behavior.
Calm, patient, practical, slow, self-denying, inhibited, thoughtful, and deliberate; as being strict and thorough in their own work and in their expectations for othrs; and as being honest and conscientious.	9. Sc (self-control) To assess the degree and adequacy of self-regulation and self-control and freedom from impulsivity and self-centeredness.	Impulsive, shrewd, excitable, irritable, self-centered, and uninhibited; as bing aggressive and assertive; and as overemphasizing personal pleasure and self-gain.
Enterprising, informal, quick, tolerant, clear-thinking, and resourceful; as being intellectually able and verbally fluent; and as having broad and varied interests.	10. To (tolerance) To identify persons with permissive, accepting, and non-judgmental social beliefs and attitude.	Suspicious, narrow, aloof, wary, and retiring; as being passive and overly judgmental in attitude; and as disbelieving and distrustful in personal and social outlook.

statements on a scale may receive the same score even though the statements they endorse are different.

One remedy to these problems is to select items for tests empirically, as with the CPI and MMPI. It is unclear which attributes some empirically derived questions assess; however, even if people give dishonest and guarded answers, their answers still provide information about their personality (as long as most people of their personality type answer in the same way).

Another way to remedy invalid responses is to include scales that assess test-takers' honesty and biases. For example, the MMPI contains an L (lie) scale, a K (correction) scale, and an F (frequency) scale. The L scale consists of such statements as: "I never get angry" and "I love every-

High Scorers	Scale and Purpose	Low Scorers
Tend to be seen as:		*Tend to be seen as:*

Class II. Measures of Socialization, Maturity, Responsibility, and Intrapersonal Structuring of Values

High Scorers	Scale and Purpose	Low Scorers
Co-operative, enterprising, outgoing, sociable warm, and helpful; as being concerned with making a good impression; and as being diligent and persistent.	11. Gi (good impression) To identify persons capable of creating a favorable impression, and who are concerned about how others react to them.	Inhibited, cautious, shrewd, wary, loof, and resentful; as being cool and distant in their relationships with others; and as being self-centered and too little concerned with the needs and wants of others.
Dependable, moderate, tactful, reliable, sincere, patient, steady, and realistic; as being honest and conscientious; and as having common sense and good judgment.	12. Cm (communality) To indicate the degree to which an individual's reactions and responses correspond to the model ("common") pattern estblished for the inventory.	Impatient, changeable, complicated, imaginative, disorderly, nervous, restless, and confused; as being guileful and deceitful; inattentive and forgetful; and as having internal conflicts and problems.

Class III. Measures of Achievement Potential and Intellectual Efficiency

High Scorers	Scale and Purpose	Low Scorers
Capable, co-operative, efficient, organized, responsible, stable, and sincere; as being persistent and industrious; and as valuing intellectual activity and intellectual achievement.	13. Ac (achievement via conformance) To identify those factors of interest and motivation which facilitate achievement in any setting where conformance is a positive behavior.	Coarse, stubborn, aloof, awkward, insecure, and opinionated; as easily disorganized under stress or pressures to conform; and as pessimistic about their occupational futures.
Mature, forceful, strong, dominant, demanding, and foresighted; as being independent and self-reliant; and as having superior intellectual ability and judgment.	14. Ai (achievement via independence) To identify those factors of interest and motivation which facilitate achievement in any setting where autonomy and inderpendence are positive behvior.	Inhibited, anxious, cautious, dissatisfied, dull, and wary; as being submissive and compliant before authority; and as lacking in self-insight and self-understanding.
Efficient, clear-thinking, capable, intelligent, progressive, planful, thorough, and resourceful; as being alert and well-informed; and as placing a high value on cognitive and intellectual matters.	15. Ie (intellectual efficiency) To indicate the degree of personal and intellectual efficiency which the individual has attained.	Cautious, confused, easygoing, defensive, shallow, and unambitious; as being conventional and stereotyped in thinking; and as lacking in self-direction and self-discipline.

Class IV. Measures of Intellectual and Interest Modes

High Scorers	Scale and Purpose	Low Scorers
Observant, spontaneous, quick, perceptive, talkative, resourcefoul, and changeable; as being verbally fluent and socially ascendant; and as being rebellious toward rules, restrictions, and constraints.	16. Py (psychological-mindedness) To measure the degree to which the individual is interested in, and responsive to, the inner needs, motives, and experiences of others.	Apathetic, peaceable, serious, cautious, and unassuming; as being slow and deliberate in tempo; and as being overly conforming and conventional.
Insightful, informal, adventurous, confident, humorous, rebellious, idealistic, assertive, and egoistic; as being sarcastic and cynical; and as highly concerned with personal pleasure and diversion.	17. Fx (flexibility) To indicate the degree of flexibility and adaptability of a person's thinking and social behavior.	Deliberate, cautious, worrying, industrious, guarded, mannerly, methodical, and rigid; as being formal and pedantic in thought; and as being overly deferential to authority, custom, and tradition.
Appreciative, patient, helpful, gentle, moderate, persevering, and sincere; as being respectful and accepting of others; and as behaving in a conscientious and sympathetic way.	18. Fe (femininity) To access the masculinity of femininity of interests. (High scores indicate more feminine interests, low scores more masculine.)	Outgoing, hard-headed, ambitious, masculine, active, robust, and restless; as being manipulative and opportunistic in dealing with others; blunt and direct in thinking and action; and impatient with delay, indecision, and reflection.

Source: Gough, H. G. (1975). *Manual for the California psychological inventory* (revised 1964, 1969, 1975). Palo Alto, CA: Consulting Psychologists Press, pp. 10 and 11.

body all the time"; though socially desirable, all could not possibly be true. The K scale assesses defensiveness and reluctance to admit faults. The F scale indicates infrequent and improbable responses (the scores of those who score high on this scale are considered invalid).

We have mentioned reliability and validity — the primary criteria for evaluating psychological tests — but we have not defined the terms. Before continuing with our discussion of psychological assessment, we should discuss the formal criteria psychologists employ to evaluate psychological tests.

Standardization and Norms

Scores on tests make little sense when considered out of context. A score of 75/100 on a test of introversion appears to indicate the person is an introvert — but what if the average person scored 80 on the test? Individual scores on psychological tests make sense relative only to scores achieved by others. **Standardizing** a test in-

TABLE 12-16   MMPI Scales; Sample Items and Interpretations

Scale	Sample Item	Interpretation
?	No sample. It is merely the number of items marked in the "cannot say" category.	This is one of four validity scales, and a high score indicates evasiveness.
L	I never have had bad dreams (FALSE).*	This is the second validity scale. Persons trying to present themselves in a favorable light (e.g., good, wholesome, honest) obtain high *L* Scale elevations.
F	Everything sounds the same (TRUE).	*F* is the third validity scale. High scores suggest carelessness, confusion, or "fake bad."
K	I have very few nightmares compared with my friends (FALSE).	An elevation on the last validity scale, *K*, suggests a defensive test-taking attitude. Exceedingly low scores may indicate a lack of ability to deny symptomatology.
Hs	I wake up tired most mornings (TRUE).	High scorers have been described as cynical, defeatist, and crabbed.
D	At times I am full of hope (FALSE).	High scorers usually are shy, despondent, and distressed.
Hy	I have never had a dizzy spell (FALSE).	High scorers tend to complain of multiple symptoms.
Pd	I like authority (FALSE)	Adjectives used to describe some high scorers are adventurous, courageous, and generous.
Mf	I like sports (FALSE).	High-scoring men have been described as aesthetic and sensitive. High-scoring women have been described as rebellious, unrealistic, and indecisive.
Pa	I am agreeable most of the time (FALSE).	High scorers on this scale have been characterized as shrewd, guarded, and worrisome.
Pt	I am certainly full of self-confidence (FALSE).	Fearful, rigid, anxious, and worrisome are some of the adjectives used to describe high *Pt* scorers.
Sc	I believe I am someone else (TRUE).	Adjectives such as withdrawn and unusual describe *Sc* high scorers.
Ma	I am important (TRUE).	High scorers are called energetic and impulsive.
Si	I avoid social gatherings (TRUE).	High scorers are described as modest, shy, and self-effacing. Low scorers are seen as sociable, colorful, and ambitious.

* The (TRUE) or (FALSE) response indicates the scored direction of the item.
Source: Kleinmuntz, B. (1982). *Personality and psychological assessment.* New York: St. Martin's Press.

volves testing a representative sample of people and determining the distribution of their scores. Problems involved in selecting a representative sample are discussed in Chapter 1. Suffice it to say the sample must include a sufficient number of people from all groups who will take the test — people of different age, sex, social class, race, education, and so forth — to enable a test-maker to determine the norms for each group.

Colligan, Osborne, Swenson, and Offord (1983) question the norms for normal behavior on the MMPI: they point out the test was standardized in the 1930s on an unrepresentative sample of people. These investigators gave the test to a random sample of 1,400 people and found the norms on most scales were significantly higher than those from the original sample. Does this mean people are becoming more abnormal? Colligan and colleagues think not, suggesting instead that people are simply more open about their behavior.

Although it is important to standardize a test, standardization does not guarantee a good test. The *goodness* or accuracy of a psychological test is defined in terms of two constructs — *reliability* and *validity*.

Reliability   We term people reliable when we

can depend on them. So too with psychological tests. **Reliability** refers to the extent to which a test produces the same result when given at different times, in different forms, and scored by different people. There are three basic ways to determine test reliability: giving it to the same people more than once, comparing test-taker scores on two halves of the test, and having different people score it. **Test-retest reliability** refers to the extent to which the same test produces the same pattern of scores on two different occasions. **Split-half reliability** refers to comparability between the two sets of scores produced when the test is divided in half (say, odd-numbered and even-numbered items). **Alternate-form reliability** is similar to split-half reliability, except that it refers to similarity of scores on alternate forms of the same test. **Inter-rater reliability** refers to agreement between two or more raters on the scores assigned people who have taken the test.

Of course, any test of a personality trait will be only as reliable as the trait it assesses and the people who score the test. Although you may have an entirely accurate measure of, say, self-esteem, if a person underwent an uplifting experience between the first and second time he or she took the test, you would expect the scores to differ. Similarly, a good rater would be expected to obtain a different result than a poor rater, thus producing a low reliability figure. When we fail to find a test reliable, we know *something* is wrong, but it need not necessarily be the test itself.

Validity If the reliability of a test is like a person's dependability, the **validity** of a test is like a person's authenticity—being what he or she claims to be. Just as it is easier to determine whether a person is dependable than whether a person is authentic, it is easier to assess whether a test is reliable than whether it is valid. For a test to be valid, it must measure what it claims to measure. A test may be perfectly reliable, yet totally invalid. For example, you might find that individuals receive the same score on a test of shyness regardless of when they take the test or who scores it—yet some people who score high on it will talk to anyone who listens. To establish that the reliable characteristic you measured was shyness, you must show it relates to some other criterion of shyness. We have no known objective device

with which to measure qualities like shyness; consequently, the process of establishing the validity of a personality test is always a relative, judgmental one. The process involves marshaling as much evidence as possible that scores on the test relate to types of characteristics we would expect to be possessed by people who score high or low on the test. The five primary strategies psychologists employ to evaluate the validity of tests are outlined in Table 12-17.

As you examine Table 12-17, it should occur to you that not all types of validity are appropriate for all psychological tests. For example, content validity is irrelevant to empirically derived tests and construct validity is irrelevant to tests that have no theoretical basis. There are no absolute tests of the validity of any psychological trait. The best anyone can do is demonstrate that a test relates to other events in the way we would expect it to if it were measuring what it purports to measure. With the criteria of reliability and validity in mind, we now turn to a discussion of projective tests.

Projective Tests

In movies, psychiatrists are sometimes portrayed administering a *projective test*. Usually involving sentence completions or inkblots, such tests are cast as instruments having the power to root out secret desires and motives—the power to uncover patients' psychological hangups and psychoanalyze them. This portrayal is misleading in three respects. First, psychiatrists rarely give personality tests: psychologists virtually always administer and score them. Second, projective tests, such as the inkblot test, are given much less frequently than other kinds of psychological tests. Third, projective tests cannot be relied upon to uncover hidden hangups and secret desires.

Projective tests are based on the assumption that most people are motivated to avoid acknowledging unfavorable aspects of themselves, and that one of the methods they employ to avoid acknowledging unacceptable characteristics is to *project* them into other people or things. This assumption derives from Freud's psychoanalytic theory of personality. In contrast to tests that assess traits, projective tests seek to assess more deep-rooted, unconscious desires, needs, and motives.

TABLE 12-17   Six Types of Validity

Type	Strategy	Example
Content or face validity	Examine test items to determine their relevance to the concept to be measured.	A test of your knowledge of the material in this chapter would have face validity if the test items actually covered material presented in the chapter.
Predictive validity	Compare scores on a test to some future criterion.	Success in law school would be the criterion for an entrance test given to law-school applicants.
Convergent validity	Compare subjects' responses on the test with their responses on another measure of the same characteristic taken at approximately the same time and determine their similarity.	Compute the correlation between subjects' scores on the psychopathic-deviate scale of the MMPI with their scores on Cleckly's rating scale of psychopathy.
Concurrent validity	Compare scores of groups that should obtain different scores on the test.	A test to measure potential child abuse would be given to known abusers and known nonabusers. The test would be valid if it correctly sorted the test-takers into the two groups.
Discriminant validity	Compare subjects' scores on one test to their responses on a test that measures a different characteristic and determine their dissimilarity.	Compute the correlation between scores on a test of shyness and on a test of intelligence.
Construct validity	Examine the relationship between your measure and other scores (or measures) to determine if the relationships make sense theoretically.	If a measure of warmth in parents proves to be related to other theoretically relevant measures of personality in the parents or to behavior in the child, the measure of warmth would have some validity.

Source: Adapted from Houston, J. P., Bee, H., & Rimm, D. (1985). *Essentials of psychology.* New York: Academic Press.

Lawrence Frank popularized the term *projective test* in 1939. He likened projective tests to X rays, suggesting they enable investigators to examine the internal psychological characteristics of people without disturbing their exteriors. The three most popular projective tests are the sentence completion test, the Thematic Apperception Test, and the Rorschach Inkblot Test.

Sentence Completion Tests **Sentence completion tests** are simple in design; they consist of several incomplete sentences such as:

My mother . . .
My father . . .
The future . . .
My happiest time . . .
My greatest fear . . .

People are asked to complete each sentence with the first answer that comes to mind. Responses to such incomplete sentences sometimes are relatively straightforward. For example, an individual who completed the preceding incomplete sentences —

. . . is a bag.
. . . never was any good.
. . . will be full of wars.
. . . was when I told off my teacher.
. . . is losing a fight.

— might safely be said to harbor hostility. But try giving these incomplete sentences to a couple of your friends. Responses are often difficult to interpret and their significance quite elusive.

Manuals and other scoring aids are available to guide psychologists in interpreting sentence completion tests. Scoring manuals classify responses people make most often to incomplete sentences under such headings as hostile, anxious, erotic, and so on. However, because the range of responses and the variety of meanings attached to them are so great, all manuals are necessarily incomplete.

The Thematic Apperception Test   The **Thematic Apperception Test** (TAT) was developed originally by Henry Murray (in conjunction with Christiana Morgan) in 1935.   It consists of 20 black-and-white pictures, such as the one in Box 12-6.   People are shown the pictures one at a time and asked to create a story about each one.   In doing so, they are asked to imagine:

1. the events that led up to the scene
2. what is happening at the moment
3. what the characters are thinking and feeling
4. how the situation ends

The assumption underlying the TAT is implicit in the definition of apperception: a predis-

---

Box 12-6
RESPONSES TO THE TAT AND INTERPRETATION

A 42-year-old woman gave the following responses to cards on the TAT.

- Looks like a little boy crying for something he can't have. (Why is he crying?) Probably because he can't go somewhere. (How will it turn out?) Probably sit there and sob hisself (sic) to sleep.

- Looks like her boyfriend might have let her down. She hurt his feelings. He's closed the door on her. (What did he say?) I don't know.

- Girl looks like somebody's run off and left her. She's ready for a dance. Maid is watching to see where she goes. (Why run off?) Probably because she wasn't ready in time.

- Looks like there's sorrow here. Grieving about something. (About what?) Looks like maybe one of the children's passed away.

- Looks like his wife might have passed away and he feels there's nothing more to do.

- Looks like a man that's ready to rob something. Hiding behind a high fence of some kind. Has his hand in his pocket with a gun ready to shoot if anybody comes out.

Example of a picture used in conjunction with TAT

The TAT produced responses that were uniformly indicative of unhappiness, threat, misfortune, or lack of control over environmental forces. None of the test responses were indicative of satisfaction, happy endings, etc. In this test, as in the Rorschach, impoverished and constricted responses are evident which probably indicate anxiety and depression. . . . In summary, the test results point to an individual who is anxious and, at the same time, depressed. Feelings of insecurity, inadequacy, and lack of control over environmental forces are apparent, as are unhappiness and apprehension. These factors result in a constriction of performance that is largely oriented toward avoiding threat and that hampers sufficient mobilization of energy to perform at an optimal level.

Source: Phares, E. J. (1984). *Clinical psychology: Concepts, methods, and profession* (2nd ed.; p. 296). Homewood, IL: Dorsey.

position to perceive things in a particular way as a result of one's prior experience. The stories people tell are scored for such structural characteristics as length, intensity, creativity, and repetitiveness as well as for content. Typically, psychologists assume that central characters in the stories represent either the storytellers or people important to them. When analyzing stories, psychologists search for consistent themes that relate to needs, sensitivities, ambitions, defenses, characteristic behavior patterns, motives, and unconscious concerns. Responses of a 42-year-old woman to a TAT are presented in Box 12-6, with the testing clinician's interpretation.

The TAT may be adapted to special purposes. For example, personality psychologists David McClelland and John Atkinson created an adaptation of the TAT to measure *need for achievement*. Although their test is similar to the TAT — subjects are required to create stories about pictures — scoring subjects' need for achievement is more highly standardized. Scorers read the stories and analyze their content

in terms of *achievement imagery*: references to competition with a standard of excellence. Such achievement imagery might involve defeating someone, winning a game, doing well, or accomplishing some goal.

The Rorschach Inkblot Test The **Rorschach Inkblot Test** is the oldest and perhaps most widely used projective test. It was developed by Herman Rorschach in the 1920s. Rorschach originally developed the test to investigate the relationship between perception and personality; he later discovered it could be used as an aid in psychiatric diagnosis (its principal use today).

Rorschach test materials consist of ten 17-×24-cm cards that contain bilaterally symmetrical inkblots similar to those shown in Figure 12-11. Half the Rorschach inkblots are black and gray; two are black, gray, and red; and the rest are multicolored. Administering the test is relatively straightforward: the tester holds up a card, says "Tell me what this might be?" writes down the subject's responses and times them. After the

Response	Inkblots	Nature of Interpretation
This is a butterfly. Here are the wings, feelers and legs.		Using the whole blot in this way is considered to reflect the subject's ability to organize and relate materials.
This is part of a chicken's leg.		Referring to only a part of this inkblot is interpreted usually as indicative of an interest in the concrete.
This could be a face.		The use of an unusual or tiny portion of this blot may suggest pedantic trends.
Looks somewhat like a spinning top.		Persons who reverse figure and ground in this manner often are observed as oppositional, negative, and stubborn.

FIGURE 12-11

Inkblots with Sample Rorschach Responses and Interpretations *Source:* Kleinmuntz, B. (1974). *Essentials of abnormal psychology.* New York: Harper & Row.

subject discloses what he or she has seen in each of the ten cards, the tester returns to each card and asks more precisely what elicited each percept.

Scoring the test is more difficult. Responses are evaluated in terms of:

1. the part of the inkblot attended to
2. whether color or shading is important
3. how typical the response is
4. what the person sees in the inkblot
5. correspondence between the percept and inkblot

Manuals are available to aid in scoring.

Interpreting responses to inkblots is the most difficult task of all. Most psychologists analyze the content impressionistically: in terms of themes and response styles they believe supply insights into the inner thoughts, feelings, and needs of the people being tested. In addition, scoring manuals outline patterns of responses that indicate certain personality traits and psychiatric problems. For example, the ratio of human movement responses to color responses is taken as a measure of introversion. Color is assumed to reveal an orientation toward emotion. Viewing an inkblot as a whole is believed to indicate organizational, theoretical, and abstraction skill. Viewing an inkblot in terms of its parts reflects a more concrete, practical orientation and, in some cases, obsessiveness (see Figure 12-11).

Projective Tests — An Evaluation Most people find projective tests mysterious and fascinating; however, many professionals are skeptical about their usefulness. Consider, for example, the conclusion reached by Nunnally (1967).

> Most projective techniques do a rather poor job of measuring personality traits. . . . In applied settings, the evidence is clear that projective techniques have, at most, only a low level of validity. . . . They do a poor job of differentiating normal people from people who are diagnosed as neurotic and they do a poor job of differentiating various types of mentally ill persons. (p. 497)

The test-retest reliability of the TAT is poor: people tend to create different stories during a second testing (even though some of the themes may be the same as during the first testing). Faced with the task of matching one half a subject's responses with the other half, trained experts have fared

poorly. Furthermore, psychologists with different theoretical orientations tend to interpret the same TAT responses differently (Davison & Neale, 1986).

Similar difficulties plague the Rorschach and other projective tests (Jensen, 1964): trained scorers often disagree on interpretations of responses. Because responses to projective tests often are analyzed in terms of Freud's psychoanalytic theory, it is not surprising that critics of psychoanalytic theory tend to be skeptical of projective tests, whereas advocates of the theory find the tests useful.

When projective tests are used to assess such specific personality needs as the need for achievement, they fare better. Working from scoring manuals, trained raters are able to make highly reliable ratings, and resulting scores have been found to predict a wide array of behaviors (see Chapter 7).

In view of the failure of projective tests to meet traditional standards of reliability and validity, you might wonder why psychologists continue to use them. The primary reason is because the information supplied by projective tests is useful to skilled clinicians privy to other background information on clients.

To conclude, what projective tests gain in counteracting the problems of transparent questions and forced alternatives that characterize many personality inventories, they lose in interpretability. The advantage of straightforward questions is that answers to them are relatively easy to interpret. Although in projective tests people are given considerable freedom to respond, it is often unclear what their responses mean. Some critics even argue that assessments derived from projective tests reveal more about the psychologists who make them than about the people who take the tests!

Behavioral Assessment

We have seen that behavioristic psychologists really do not believe in personality, suggesting personality traits are common illusions — the products of unscientific thinking. It is not surprising that, when it comes to assessment, behaviorists insist we are better off measuring observable behaviors then trying to measure imaginary

Box 12-7
The Barnum Effect

Imagine you have taken a personality test and receive the following profile:

You have a strong need for other people to like you and for them to admire you. You have a tendency to be critical of yourself. You have a great deal of unused capacity which you have not turned to your advantage. While you have some personality weaknesses, you are generally able to compensate for them. Your sexual adjustment has presented some problems for you. Disciplined and controlled on the outside, you tend to be worrisome and insecure inside. At times you have serious doubts as to whether you have made the right decision or done the right thing. You prefer a certain amount of change and variety and become dissatisfied when hemmed in by restrictions and limitations. You pride yourself as being an independent thinker and do not accept others' opinions without satisfactory proof. You have found it unwise to be too frank in revealing yourself to others. At times you are extroverted, affable, sociable, while at other times you are introverted, wary, and reserved. Some of your aspirations tend to be pretty unrealistic.

Not a bad test! Ulrich, Stachnik, and Stainton (1963) gave 136 students a battery of personality tests and the profile you just read. Eighty-two percent of the students said it supplied an excellent or very good description of them. This study shows that abstract descriptions of personality tend to be interpreted to fit people's conceptions of themselves — a tendency exploited by fortune-tellers and astrologers. As voiced by P. T. Barnum (Barnum and Bailey Circus), "There's a sucker born every minute." Snyder, Shenkel, and Lowery (1977) discuss the significance of the "Barnum Effect."

dispositions that may not even exist. Say you believe someone is sympathetic; a behaviorist might ask, "How do you know?" You would probably justify your belief in terms of the person's behavior, saying, for example, that the person typically looked sad when others were sad, cried at the movies, and comforted people in need. A behaviorist would insist that you really are interested in these behaviors and should measure them directly.

Behavioristic psychologists have developed methods to assess *personality* (see Table 12-18). Although some behavioral tests are similar to personality inventories, behavioristic psychologists interpret them differently. For example, psychiatrist John Wolpe, famed for his techniques of behavior therapy (see Chapter 14), developed a *Fear Survey Schedule* (Wolpe, 1973). People are asked to rate such behaviors as

fear of worms, fear of snakes, and fear of losing control on 5- or 7-point scales. However, instead of employing self-ratings as a measure of an underlying personality trait such as anxiety, Wolpe interprets fears at face value, in terms of each behavior in question.

In addition to self-ratings, information about behaviors that constitute personality may be obtained from trained raters, psychologists, teachers, supervisors, parents, and peers. Although directly-observable, specific behaviors are usually rated, some scales contain such general categories of behavior as aggressiveness or withdrawal. In such cases, **behavioral ratings** are much the same as trait ratings and suffer from the same problems.

A study by Barlow (1977) provides a good example of the behavioral strategy. Barlow arranged for aides to observe ten patients in a mental

TABLE 12-18
Five Types of Behavioral Assessment

Behavioral interview	Used by therapists and others to obtain information about a specific behavior problem and the circumstances surrounding it.
Self-report questionnaires	Ask specific questions about behavior; for example, fearful responses toward particular objects or events.
Self-monitoring	The subject is asked to keep track of her or his own behavior in specific categories, such as the foods eaten, or the hours spent studying, or the responses to a child's tantrums. Records may be kept on paper, or mechanical counters may be used.
Direct observation in natural settings	Most often used with children or in institutions like mental hospitals where the subjects are in confined areas and easy to observe.
Direct observation in artificial situations	Subjects may be shown scenes on videotape, and their reactions observed; particular kinds of social encounters may be simulated; generally the experimenter can create a situation that permits her or him to observe a subject responding to carefully defined stimuli.

Source: Houston, J., Bee, H., & Rimm, D. (1985). *Essentials of psychology.* New York: Academic Press.

hospital every half-hour for eight hours a day and to rate them on four types of behavior: talking, social interaction, smiling, and physical movement. He found that patients who displayed an increase in these behaviors over the month in which they were observed were more likely not to return following release than patients who did not display an increase. He also found that this method of behavioral assessment was a better predictor of remission than other self-report methods.

To conclude, different psychologists employ different methods to assess personality. In part, the tests used by psychologists stem from their theoretical orientations. Psychologists who, like the average person, believe personality is composed of traits employ tests that assess these hypothetical constructs. Psychologists who believe the most important aspects of personality are cognitive in nature direct their energies toward measurement of thought processes. Psychoanalytically oriented psychologists attempt to assess unconscious needs, desires, and defenses. And behavioristic psychologists assess observable behavior.

ASSESSMENT OF INTELLIGENCE

Of all the aspects of personality assessed by psychologists, intelligence has received the greatest attention by far. There are historical, practical, and theoretical reasons why this is so. Historically, intelligence testing was associated closely with academic curriculum development. Indeed, the first formal intelligence test was created in an attempt to identify slow learners and to develop special programs for them. Intelligence also has considerable practical value. As Herrnstein (1973) documents, measured IQ positively correlates with academic achievement, oc-

cupational success, income, and social status (see Table 12-19). Finally, intelligence is a core, or *executive,* aspect of personality. For example, in Freud's psychoanalytic theory, the intellectual functions are performed by the structure that gives us our identity—the *I,* or ego. In Kelly's role-construct theory, the major force in personality development is people's ability to understand their world. Even such social learning theorists as Walter Mischel and Albert Bandura acknowledge the significance of this internal construct. Although intelligence is so integral to our identity

TABLE 12-19
Correlates of IQ Scores

Correlate	Correlation Coefficient
IQ × mental retardation	−.90
IQ × educational attainment (years)	.70
IQ × academic success (grade point)	.50
IQ × occupational attainment	.50
IQ × socioeconomic status	.40
IQ × success on the job	.20

Source: Matarazzo, J. D. (1972). *Wechsler's measurement and appraisal of adult intelligence* (5th ed.). Oxford, Eng.: Oxford University Press.

that it is easy to take for granted, we can appreciate the value of intelligence by comparing it to other personality traits. Consider the first sixteen source traits identified by Cattell (see Table 12-6). If required to give up the outgoing, intelligent, emotionally stable, or assertive aspects of your personality, intelligence probably would be the last to go.

Issues in Intelligence Testing

The enterprise of intelligence assessment is embroiled in controversy; because of the strong feelings associated with it, it is particularly important to keep the issues clear. Two of the central questions raised by intelligence testing are similar to the questions raised by other types of psychological assessment: what is **intelligence**? and what are the behaviors that represent or reveal it? In spite of the fact that we use the word *intelligent* with its synonyms (*smart, bright, brilliant, clever,* and so forth) and antonyms (*dumb, dull, stupid, slow*) in our daily conversation, many of us have no precise idea of what intelligent means. Is intelligence good memory, knowledge of facts, ability to do math mentally, ability to solve logical problems, ability to propose alternatives not thought of by others, all these abilities, some, or just one? To assess intelligence, we must select a group of behaviors that reveal it — we must *operationalize* it. Intelligence tests must meet the standards of validity we use to evaluate other types of tests — they must measure

what it is claimed they are measuring.

Another issue in intelligence testing — one that closely relates to the issue of validity — concerns whether intelligence is a unitary or multidimensional ability. On the one hand, we tend to expect people who, for example, have a good memory also to know a lot, to think logically, and to be good at math. On the other hand, we may know people who can figure out how almost any machine works but cannot write well and take ages to read a simple novel. In fact, it sometimes seems that people good with numbers are poor with words, and vice versa. Because the question of the extent to which the abilities that constitute intelligence go together is similar to the question of how personality traits correlate with one another, it can be examined in the same way.

Another controversial issue in intelligence testing — the issue that has generated the most heated debate — concerns the ability of intelligence tests to assess the intelligence of people from different cultures, social classes, and ethnic groups. Is it fair to give the same intelligence test to a black person and a white person? Do higher scores indicate more intelligence or a different background? This sensitive question has supplied the impetus for considerable scientific research. The question of the extent to which intelligence is determined by heredity and environment is related closely to the problems of measuring intelligence. To assess the relative influence of nature and nurture on intelligence, scientists require a culture-fair test.

In recognition of the complexity and social significance of the controversy surrounding genetic determination of intelligence, we subjected it to special consideration in Chapter 2. Here we consider what intelligence is, proceed to examine how the first intelligence tests were developed, turn to a discussion of whether intelligence tests really measure intelligence, and conclude by discussing biases in intelligence tests and racial differences in IQ.

Definitions of Intelligence In 1926 the *Journal of Educational Psychology* asked leading scholars to define intelligence; they were unable to reach a consensus. This led psychologist-historian Edwin Boring to remark that intelligence is "the capacity to do well on an intelligence test (1923, p. 35)." More recently, science writer

Berkely Rice (1973) interviewed experts in the area and reported, "When I asked researchers in the field to tell me about new tests of intelligence, they often replied, 'What do you mean by intelligence?' "

Although not necessarily agreeing with Boring that intelligence is what intelligence tests measure, we feel an examination of what intelligence tests measure is a sound way to launch an examination of the construct. We first determine how this hypothetical construct has been operationalized, then evaluate the result.

The Development of Intelligence Tests — A Historical Account

Sir Francis Galton is commonly credited with developing the precursor of modern intelligence tests. Galton assumed that because people receive all information through their senses, intelligent people should possess superior sensory-perceptual skills. Thus, he believed that such measures as reaction time should supply an indication of mental power and that there should be a positive association between mental and physical superiority.

Galton evaluated his ideas by developing a battery of tests consisting of such physical measures as head size, breathing capacity, and strength of hand grip and such measures of mental ability as memory for visual forms. He gave this battery of tests to some 9,000 visitors to the 1884 London Exhibition. The results did not confirm Galton's expectations. The most prominent British scientists of his day did not obtain superior scores on most of his measures. If they had bigger heads than other Englishmen, they went unnoticed in Galton's tests!

Binet's Intelligence Test The first intelligence test was developed by French psychologist Alfred Binet (1857–1911). A revised version of his test, the Stanford-Binet, is still used today. In contrast to Galton — who attempted to develop a measure of intelligence to test his ideas about heredity — Binet developed his test in response to a practical educational problem. In 1881, the French government made school attendance compulsory; in 1904, it asked Binet to head a committee charged with determining why some children could not keep up with their peers.

Binet assumed the difference between normal students and slow learners was quantitative rather than qualitative: although normal students know more than their slower peers, normal students do not think differently. Thus, Binet expected a slow ten-year-old to possess the same intellectual skills as, say, a normal eight-year-old. Working with psychologist Theodore Simon, Binet developed tests to assess such mental abilities as memory, imagination, and attention — which he believed to constitute intelligence. Binet gave his tests to children of different ages, and then selected the tests that discriminated best among them. Binet's final test, the Binet-Simon Intelligence Test, was published in 1905 and revised in 1908 and 1911.

The assumptions Binet made about the nature of intelligence determined the way he scored his test. He employed the concept of **mental age** to refer to the age level of a child's test performance. If a child (of any age) performed at the average level of a nine-year-old child, the child was given a mental age of nine. If the chronological age of the child was eight, this score indicated intellectual precociousness. If

the child was ten years old, the child was considered *slow*. The Binet-Simon test fulfilled its purpose well—it identified students named by teachers as slow learners.

It remained for psychologist Lewis Terman of Stanford University to take the next logical step and produce a single score based on a comparison of mental and chronological age. Guided by the ideas of German psychologist William Stern, Terman developed the following formula for what he called an **intelligence quotient, or IQ:**

$$IQ = \frac{MA}{CA} \times 100$$

A ten-year-old child who achieved a score (a mental age) on Binet's test characteristic of ten-year-old children received an IQ score of 100:

$$\left(\frac{10}{10} \times 100\right)$$

A nine-year-old child who achieved the same mental-age score received an IQ score of 111:

$$\left(\frac{10}{9} \times 100\right)$$

In 1916, Terman revised the Binet-Simon test for use in America. The resulting **Stanford-Binet Intelligence Scale** underwent revisions in 1937, 1960, and 1985. The format of the new Stanford-Binet scale and the age ranges associated with each test are displayed in Table 12-20. The major change Terman made in the early Binet test related to the assumption that IQ consists of a ratio of mental to chronological age. Terman questioned whether a 10-year-old child who obtains the same mental-age score as the average 15-year-old child should receive the same IQ score (150) as a 40-year-old adult who obtains the same mental-age score as the average 60-year-old adult. Perhaps mental abilities develop faster during childhood than during adulthood.

Terman devised a new scoring method that assigned as the mean score for each age group an IQ value of 100 and that set the standard deviation of IQ scores at 16 (see Appendix 1). The scoring manual for the Stanford-Binet contains these norms. Thus, the IQ score produced by the modern Stanford-Binet test is really no longer a *quotient* at all.

TABLE 12-20

The *Stanford-Binet Intelligence Scale*

I. Crystallized Abilities
   A. Verbal Reasoning Area
     1. Vocabulary: ages 2–18+
     2. Comprehension: ages 2–18+
     3. Absurdities: ages 2–14
     4. Verbal Relations: ages 12–18+
   B. Quantitative Reasoning Area
     1. Quantitative: ages 2–18+
     2. Number Series: ages 7–18+
     3. Equation Building: ages 12–18+

II. Fluid–Analytic Abilities
   C. Abstract/Visual Reasoning Area
     1. Pattern Analysis: ages 2–18+
     2. Copying: ages 2–13
     3. Matrices: ages 7–18+
     4. Paper Folding and Cutting: ages 12–18+

III. Short-term Memory
   D. Short-term Memory
     1. Bead Memory: ages 2–18+
     2. Memory for Sentences: ages 2–18+
     3. Memory for Digits: ages 7–18+
     4. Memory for Objects: ages 7–18+

Source: Thorndike, R. L., Hagan, E., & Sattler, J. (1985). *Stanford-Binet intelligence scale: Fourth edition.* Chicago, IL: Riverside.

There are two points worth emphasizing about IQ scores as defined by Binet and Terman. First, as long as you are referring to IQ, it is futile to question whether the Stanford-Binet test yields a valid measure of it—it does, by definition. However, it is quite legitimate to ask whether IQ scores supply a valid measure of *intelligence*. (We discuss this issue at the end of the chapter.) Second, individuals may acquire more knowledge, or even lose the knowledge they possess, yet retain the same IQ. Indeed, to maintain the same IQ, a child *must* be able to answer more and more questions correctly as he or she grows older.

Wechsler's Intelligence Tests Although the Stanford-Binet is used by many psychologists today, it is not the most widely used intelligence test; the **Wechsler Adult Intelligence Scale (WAIS-R,** *R* for *revised*) and the **Wechsler Intelligence Scale for Children (WISC-R)** are. Wechsler's intelligence tests (Wechsler, 1974, 1981) consist of eleven or twelve subtests, six of which assess verbal abilities and five of which assess nonverbal abilities (see Table 12-21). If you were taking the WAIS-R, you would begin by

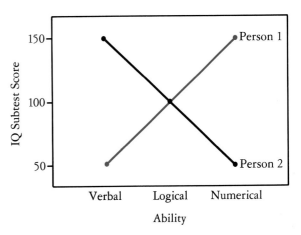

FIGURE 12-12
Hypothetical Profile of Two Persons, Each with an IQ of 100 The IQ scores of both people are 100, yet the intellectual abilities that comprise them are quite different.

answering the easiest questions on the *Information* test, such as "Name the four seasons," go on to more difficult questions, such as "How many zeros are there in one billion?" and continue until you failed to answer several questions in a row. Following that, you would be given the easiest questions on the next subtest, and continue until you completed all verbal and performance subtests.

The Wechsler tests are scored in accordance with age norms similar to the Stanford-Binet. When people score the same as the average person their age, they receive an IQ score of 100. When people achieve a score higher than 66% of the people their age, they receive an IQ score of 115, and so on.

There are two primary differences between the Stanford-Binet and Wechsler tests. First, the Wechsler tests yield scores for eleven or twelve separate abilities whereas the Stanford-Binet test yields scores for four separate areas — verbal,

quantitative, abstract/visual reasoning, and short-term memory. Second, the Wechsler test is less exclusively verbal than the Stanford-Binet.

The value of obtaining measures for separate abilities and the danger of characterizing people only in terms of their IQ can be seen by examining the hypothetical profiles of two people in Figure 12-12. Although both people would receive the same IQ score, they obviously do not possess the same mental abilities.

Group Intelligence Tests Because intelligence tests such as the Stanford-Binet and Wechsler must be administered individually, they are time-consuming and costly. In response to this problem, psychologists have devised **group-administered tests.** Group tests are quick and easy pencil-and-paper versions of individual intelligence tests. They are more practical than individual tests, but, as you might expect, somewhat less accurate.

The first major group-intelligence tests were developed by the U.S. Army during World War I in an attempt to classify more than 1.5 million recruits. The primary tests were called the Army Alpha (for readers) and Army Beta (for nonreaders). In the ensuing years, the U.S. military developed other tests, such as the Army General Classification Test and the Armed Forces Qualification Test (used during World War II), that pro-

TABLE 12-21
Subtests of the Wechsler Adult Intelligence Scale (WAIS-R, 1981)

Verbal Scale

1. **INFORMATION**   Questions covering a wide range of general knowledge that people have presumably had an opportunity to gain simply by being exposed to the
culture.

    EXAMPLE   "What is the distance (in miles) between San Francisco, California and
London, England?"

2. **DIGIT SPAN**   Groups of from two to nine digits presented orally, one group at a
time. After hearing a group, subjects must repeat it from memory. Some exercises require repetition forward, others backward.

3. **VOCABULARY**   Vocabulary words of increasing difficulty presented visually and
orally. Subjects must define each word.

    EXAMPLE   "What does *ruminate* mean?"

4. **ARITHMETIC**   Problems similar to those encountered in elementary school. The
problems must be solved without paper or pencil.

    EXAMPLE   "How much would three cigars cost if each cigar was $1.80 and the store
was offering a ten percent discount on all purchases?"

5. **COMPREHENSION**   Questions that ask subjects to indicate the correct thing to do
under varied circumstances, what certain proverbs mean, or why certain practices
are followed.

    EXAMPLE   "What is meant by 'too many cooks spoil the broth'?"

6. **SIMILARITIES**   Items requiring that subjects explain the similarity between two
things.

    EXAMPLE   "In what way are red and hot alike?" (ANS. Both can be sensed; both are
stimuli.)

Performance Scale

7. **PICTURE COMPLETION**   Pictures. In each picture something is missing. Subjects must identify the missing part.

    EXAMPLE

8. **PICTURE ARRANGEMENT**   Sets of cards. Each set contains cartoon characters
performing an action. If the set of cards is placed in the proper sequence, it will
depict a sensible story. Subjects must place cards from each set in the proper
order.

    EXAMPLE   "Place the cards in the proper sequence so that they depict a sensible
story."

(ANS. Correct order is: 4, 3, 1, 2.)

9. **BLOCK DESIGN**   Designs of increasing complexity must be made using four to nine blocks having sides that are white, red, or half white and half red.

EXAMPLE

10. **OBJECT ASSEMBLY**   Subjects are provided with pieces of a puzzle. The pieces are made of hardened cardboard. Subjects must decide what the pieces represent and assemble them correctly.

EXAMPLE

11. **DIGIT SYMBOL**   Symbols paired with digits are shown. Subjects must then pair the appropriate symbols with the correct digit in a long list of digits. The test is timed. Subjects who forget and have to look back at the pairings take longer to complete the test.

EXAMPLE

1	2	3	4	5	6	7	8	9
//	△	□	○	◇	☆	⚊	⊙	∿

5 3 8 6 7 2 9 4 1 6 9 5 7 8 4

_ _ _ _ _ _ _ _ _ _ _ _ _ _ _

vide fast and relatively accurate estimates of basic intellectual ability. These tests were given to all draftees and became the basis for deciding where to assign military personnel.

Aptitude Tests **Aptitude tests** are designed to predict success in specific domains; *scholastic aptitude tests* are designed to predict success in school. The **Scholastic Aptitude Test (SAT)** is a direct descendant of the Army Alpha test and is indistinguishable from a group-intelligence test. The SAT focuses on academic subject matter, especially vocabulary, mathematics, general information, and problems (see Table 12-22). Almost everyone who attends a North American high

school or college takes a test of this type at one time or another.

Although statistics show that SAT scores of North American high-school students declined between 1965 and 1980 (see Figure 12-13), there is some evidence they may be on the rise again. The reason for the decline in the 1960s and 1970s is controversial. Some analysts blame permissive parents and schools; others attribute the decline to increased numbers of disadvantaged students taking the tests. In 1976, social psychologist Robert Zajonc offered an interesting theory. Zajonc suggested that in the early 1960s the effects of the postwar baby-boom began to be felt, with most high-school students coming from

TABLE 12-22
Selected Items from the November 6, 1982 SAT

Verbal	Choose the word or phrase that is most nearly *opposite* in meaning to the word in capital letters.
	WILT: (a) prevent (b) drain (c) expose (d) revive (e) stick
	(93 percent correctly answered d)
	GARNER: (a) disfigure (b) hedge (c) connect (d) forget (e) disperse
	(26 percent correctly answered e)
	Each question below consists of a related pair of words or phrases, followed by five lettered pairs of words or phrases. Select the lettered pair that <u>best</u> expresses a relationship similar to that expressed in the original pair.
	PAINTING : CANVAS (a) drawing : lottery (b) fishing : pond (c) writing : paper (d) shading : crayon (e) sculpting : design
	(92 percent correctly answered c)
	SCOFF : DERISION (a) soothe : mollification (b) slander : repression (c) swear : precision (d) stimulate : appearance (e) startle : speediness
	(21 percent correctly answered a)
Mathematical	If $x^3 + y = x^3 + 5$, then $y =$
	(a) -5 (b) $-\sqrt[3]{5}$ (c) $\sqrt[3]{5}$ (d) 5 (e) 5^3
	(93 percent correctly answered d)
	In a race, if Bob's running speed was $\frac{4}{5}$ Alice's, and Chris's speed was $\frac{3}{4}$ Bob's, then Alice's speed was how many times the average (arithmetic mean) of the other two runners' speeds?
	(a) $\frac{3}{5}$ (b) $\frac{7}{10}$ (c) $\frac{40}{31}$ (d) $\frac{10}{7}$ (e) $\frac{5}{3}$
	(10 percent correctly answered d)

In the figure above, one side of the square is a diameter of the circle. If the area of the circle is p and the area of the square is s, which of the following must be true?

I. $s > p$
II. $s \geqq 2p$
III. $s < p$
(a) none (b) I only (c) II only (d) III only (e) I and II
(45 percent correctly answered b)

Source: SAT questions selected from *10 SATs*. College Entrance Examination Board, 1983. Reprinted by permission of Educational Testing Service, the copyright owner of the sample questions.

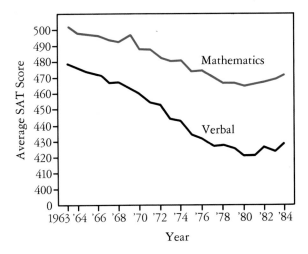

FIGURE 12-13

Declining SAT Although average SAT scores declined dramatically between 1963 and 1980, they now appear to be recovering. The reason why is controversial. *Source:* Astin, G. R., & Garber, H. (1982). *The rise and fall of national test scores.* New York: Academic Press.

larger families whose later-born children were at a disadvantage intellectually (because their principal models were siblings whose vocabularies and intellectual skills were less mature than those of their parents). Zajonc has shown that intellectual performance does indeed decline with birth order (firstborns, on average, score higher than later borns). Zajonc (1986) predicts now that the effects of the postwar baby-boom are over, SAT scores will continue to rise.

The Structure of Intelligence

Intelligence tests define intelligence operationally in terms of vocabulary, the amount of information people possess, the ability to solve puzzles, to build block designs, and so on. How do these abilities relate to one another? On this issue, psychologists have taken two opposing positions: (1) intelligence is a general capacity that gives rise to the specific abilities assessed on intelligence tests and (2) intelligence consists of a set of independent, qualitatively different types of abilities. Both Binet and Wechsler held that intelligence is a unitary quality; in Wechsler's (1958) words, "Intelligence is [an] aggregate or global capacity." Other psychologists, however, disagree.

Spearman's Position Charles Spearman, inventor of factor analysis, attempted to determine mathematically the extent to which the specific intellectual abilities people possess go together — whether, for example, people with good vocabularies also are good at solving puzzles, constructing block designs, and repeating series of numbers. Spearman concluded that people possess a general intelligence — which he called **general mental facility (g)** — that determines how people perform on intelligence tests and whether they are *bright or dull;* but people also possess more specific abilities — which he called **specific mental capabilities (s)** — that cause people to perform better on some tasks than on others.

Thurstone's Position In 1938, psychologist Lewis Thurstone reexamined Spearman's position and reached a different conclusion. Thurstone gave people a larger battery of tests, factor analyzed the results, selected the tests that best represented the factors, gave them to more people, reanalyzed them, and so on. Thurstone attempted to determine (1) the extent to which the final factors (composed of scores from groups of related tests) were associated — whether people who score high on one test also score high on the others — and (2) if there are independent factors, how many separate abilities there are. Thurstone concluded there are seven **primary mental abilities,** those outlined in Table 12-23.

To establish that intelligence consists of separate abilities, one must show that no one ability is associated significantly with any other. Perhaps to Thurstone's dismay, his results never met this criterion; he was unable completely to reject the notion that people possess a *general intelligence,* or *g.*

Guilford's Position The number of factors produced by factor analysis depends on the number and kind of variables (test scores) the investigator analyses and on the cutoff points he or she decides to employ. J. P. Guilford (1967) employed a multitude of tests, and drew the line very finely. Guilford views intelligence as an interaction among four *content factors,* five *operation factors,* and six *product factors* (see Figure 12-14). The interaction of $4 \times 5 \times 6$ factors produces

TABLE 12-23
Thurstone's Primary Abilities

Primary Ability	Ability Indicated by
Verbal comprehension	Understanding word meanings, as in a vocabulary test
Word fluency	Using words rapidly and flexibly, as in solving verbal problems
Number	Using numbers, as in solving arithmetic problems
Space	Creating and manipulating mental representations of objects, as in deciding what an object would look like from another angle
Memory	Remembering previously presented information, such as word lists
Perceptual speed	Discriminating the details of a complex presentation rapidly and accurately, as in deciding if two drawings are identical or not
Reasoning	Discovering a general rule, based on a series of examples, as in deciding what the next number will be in a series such as 2, 4, 8 . . .

Source: Thurstone, L. L., & Thurstone, T. G. (1963). *SRA primary abilities.* Chicago: Science Research Associates.

120 theoretical components of intelligence. According to Guilford, this set of components supplies the most adequate model of the structure of the intellect. To date, evidence exists for more than 100 of the factors identified by Guilford. However, as we might expect from the work of Thurstone, many factors correlate with others.

Gardner's Position   Recently, in a book titled *Frames of Mind,* Howard Gardner (1983) adduced evidence of seven qualitatively distinct types of intelligence: language, logic and mathematics, visual and spatial thinking, music, bodily kinethetic skills (such as dance or athletics), intrapersonal skills (self-knowledge), and interpersonal skills (leadership, social abilities). Gardner argues these kinds of intelligence are largely independent and are mediated by different areas in the brain (some, for example, originate primarily in the left hemisphere, others in the right; see Chapter 3). Gardner suggests the reason why such researchers as Spearman and Thurstone did not discover all seven types of intelligence is because their implicit definition of the construct led them to employ a narrow range of tests.

What can we conclude about the structure of intelligence? The fairest conclusion appears to be that people possess a general intellectual ability — as evidenced by people's tendency to score in the same range on most mental tests — but that those with the same general intellectual ability have strengths and weaknesses in different

areas. Whether you focus on people's general intelligence or on their specific abilities depends on your purpose.

The Distribution of IQ Scores in the Population

Like so many characteristics of people — height, weight, running speed, strength — IQ scores array themselves in the *bell-shaped curve* that defines a *normal distribution* (see Figure 12-15 and Appendix). Most people obtain average IQ scores and about the same proportion are slightly above and slightly below average, very bright and very dull, gifted and mentally retarded, and so on. The distribution of IQ scores was computed as part of the standardization procedure for the Wechsler intelligence tests and corresponded exceptionally well to the ideal outline of a normal distribution (see Table 12-24).

Mental Retardation and Genius   About 2% of the population have an IQ of 69 or below (Isaacson, 1970) and about 2% have an IQ of 130 or above. We commonly call people with IQs of 70 or below *mentally retarded* and people with IQs of 130 or above *gifted*. **Primary retardation** refers to genetically determined mental retardation; **secondary retardation** refers to retardation produced by brain injury. Although there is little that can be done to prevent primary retardation, increasingly sophisticated childbirth methods, better prenatal care, proper diet, and

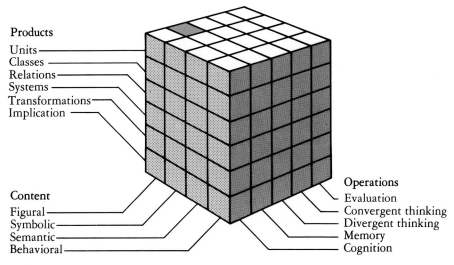

FIGURE 12-14

Guilford's Structure-of-intellect Model Guilford's structure-of-intellect model of intelligence suggests that a total of 120 different special abilities can be distinguished. Each represents the intersection of three dimensions, or one small block in the diagram. The accented block, for example, represents a memory operation for a figural content to produce a unit product; it might be shown in the ability to remember a particular shape. *Source:* Guilford, J. P. (1966). Intelligence: 1965 model. *American Psychologist, 21,* 20–26.

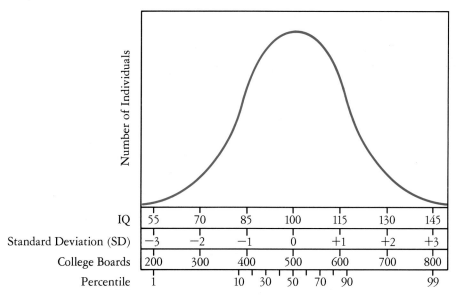

FIGURE 12-15

Distribution of IQ Scores The correspondence between IQ scores, standard-deviation scores, college boards, and percentile rankings is shown below the graph. Note that one standard deviation from the mean—from 0 to 1 on the SD axis—is equivalent to the range from 100 to 115 in IQ, from 500 to 600 in college boards, and from 50 to 84 in percentile rankings. The percents under the curve point out that 68% of the population falls within standard deviations of −1 to +1, about 95% within −2 to +2, and about 99% within −3 to +3. *Source:* Adapted from Lindzey, G., Hall, C. S., & Thompson, R. F. (1978). *Psychology* (2nd ed., p. 361). New York: Worth Publishers.

TABLE 12-24
Intelligence Distribution — Real and Ideal

		Percent of People Included	
IQ	Classification	Theoretical Normal Curve	Actual Sample[a]
130 and above	Very Superior	2.2	2.3
120–129	Superior	6.7	7.4
110–119	High Average (Bright)[b]	16.1	16.5
90–109	Average	50.0	49.4
80–89	Low Average (Dull)[b]	16.1	16.2
70–79	Borderline	6.7	6.0
69 and below	Mentally Deficient[b]	2.2	2.2

[a] The percents shown are for Full Scale IQ and are based on the total standardization sample (N = 2200). The percents obtained for Verbal IQ and Performance IQ are essentially the same.

[b] The terms *High Average (Bright)*, *Low Average (Dull)*, and *Mentally Deficient* correspond to the terms *Bright Normal*, *Dull Normal*, and *Mental Defective*, respectively, used in the WPPSI, WAIS, and 1949 WISC manuals.

Source: Wechsler, D. (1981). *Manual for the Wechsler adult intelligence scale* (rev.). New York: Psychology Corporation.

early treatment of brain-destroying diseases reduce the incidence of secondary retardation.

Most mentally retarded individuals possess IQs that fall in the 50–70 range. As young children, such individuals are virtually indistinguishable from average children (see Table 12-25). However, during school-age years, they cannot keep up with classmates. Without special treatment, they typically reach only the sixth grade by the time their peers graduate from high school. In the past, moderately retarded children were considered untrainable and often were institutionalized. However, it is increasingly apparent that moderately retarded children benefit from special training and can perform well at many tasks (Zucker & Altman, 1973).

Most people are fascinated by the idea of genius. The esteem in which Albert Einstein is held and the mythology that has developed around him exemplify the point. What are people like who have IQs in the genius range? In an attempt to answer this question, psychologist Terman and Merrill (1959) observed some 1,000 children with an average IQ of 150. Terman tested the children in 1922 and contacted them repeatedly over the ensuing four decades.

Terman found that 90% of the gifted children he studied had professional or managerial parents. Of the 800 males in the study, about 16% obtained M.D. or Ph.D. degrees, about 10% earned law degrees, and about 12% held engineering degrees. When tested in 1959, these gifted individuals had published more than 2,000 scientific papers, 350 short stories and plays, 60 nonfiction books, and 30 novels and had obtained more than 230 patents.

The stereotype of genius portrays a bookworm, physically weak, socially meek, and, perhaps, slightly strange. Terman's research belies this stereotype. Most people in his group were excellent athletes, healthier than average, leaders of a wide variety of groups, and unlikely to suffer mental disorders. Recently, Sears (1977) conducted a follow-up of Terman's geniuses. Notable among his findings was that with advancing age, these subjects reported feeling most satisfaction from their family lives.

Although the abilities that cause people to score high on intelligence tests are associated strongly with success in the Western world, they are not a guarantee. Some of Terman's subjects flunked out of college, others proved unable to hold a job, and some resided in prison.

When large numbers of people are given intelligence tests, someone inevitably asks which groups obtain the highest scores. Investigators have compared the IQ scores of groups of people who differ in occupation, social class, and ethnic heritage. As we might expect, the results have proven controversial, especially as they reflect

TABLE 12-25
Behavioral Characteristics of Mentally Retarded People

Retardation Type	Characteristics from Birth to Adulthood		
	Birth through Five	**Six through Twenty**	**Twenty-one and Over**
Mild (IQ 53–69)	Often not noticed as retarded by casual observer but is slower to walk, feed himself, and talk than most children.	Can acquire practical skills and useful reading and arithmetic to a third- to sixth-grade level with special education. Can be guided toward social conformity.	Can usually achieve social and vocational skills adequate to self-maintenance; may need occasional guidance and support when under unusual social or economic stress.
Moderate (36–52)	Noticeable delays in motor development, especially in speech; responds to training in various self-help activities.	Can learn simple communication, elementary health and safety habits, and simple manual skills; does not progress in functional reading or arithmetic.	Can perform simple tasks under sheltered conditions; participates in simple recreation; travels alone in familiar places; usually incapable of self-maintenance.
Severe (20–35)	Marked delay in motor development; little or no communication skill; may respond to training in elementary self-help — for example, self-feeding.	Usually walks barring specific disability; has some understanding of speech and some response; can profit from systematic habit training.	Can conform to daily routines and repetitive activities; needs continuing direction and supervision in protective environment.
Profound (below 20)	Gross retardation; minimal capacity for functioning in sensorimotor areas; needs nursing care.	Obvious delays in all areas of development; shows basic emotional responses; may respond to skillful training in use of legs, hands, and jaws; needs close supervision.	May walk, need nursing care, have primitive speech; usually benefits from regular physical activity; incapable of self-maintenance.

Source: Kagan, J., & Haveman, E. (1972). *Psychology: An introduction* (2nd ed.). New York: Harcourt Brace Jovanovich.

differences among ethnic groups. This controversy was examined in Chapter 2 in terms of the relative contributions of heredity and environment. We now consider the role played by **cultural bias** in tests of intelligence.

Cultural Bias in IQ Tests   If you gave an intelligence test to a person who grew up in a foreign culture and who had just learned to speak English, you would hardly expect him or her to achieve a high score on a standard vocabulary test or to correctly answer questions about U.S. history. Yet, the person might be exceptionally intelligent. And you would hardly accept as valid the IQ score of a psychologist familiar with the questions on intelligence tests. These examples show how differential exposure to the questions on intelligence tests may affect the IQ scores people obtain

and, therefore, that IQ scores do not always supply a valid index of intelligence. Sociologist Adrian Dove (1968) demonstrated this point by giving white people the culturally biased (black) Dove Counterbalance Intelligence Test, or Chitlin Test (see Box 12-9, page 650).

Many of the verbal items on traditional intelligence tests are biased in favor of white middle-class Americans. However, defenders of intelligence tests point out that, compared to whites, blacks tend to achieve lower average scores on the *performance* subtests of the WAIS than on the verbal subtests. In response, critics of intelligence tests argue that the scores of blacks on performance tests may be affected by cultural differences in pace of life (most performance tests have time deadlines), degree of inhibition about the test situation, and motivation.

Box 12-8
Assessing Your IQ

Mensa is an elite international society for people with IQs of at least 130 (higher than 98% of the population). Dr. Abbie F. Salny, Mensa's Director of Science and Education, created this sample Mensa quiz for "PD," the *St. Louis Post-Dispatch* Sunday magazine published May 6, 1984. The questions are of the sort used on Mensa admission tests.

Questions

1. The same nine letters, if rearranged, will form two different words that can fill in the blanks of the following sentence sensibly:

   The musician's mother said that her son and her brother both played many instruments. "My _____ are indeed very _____."

2. Three sacks of flour and two sacks of sugar weighed 34 pounds. Three sacks of sugar and two sacks of flour weighed 31 pounds. How much did a sack of flour weigh?

3. What word of five letters means (a) cylindrical and (b) free from fractions?

4. You have a pocketful of change. You find you have the same number of nickels, dimes and quarters. The total amount is $2.40. How many of each coin do you have?

5. Five words are shown below. Two of them are ap-proximately opposite to each other in meaning. Which two?
(a) arid (b) moist
(c) helpful (d) penniless
(e) happy

6. In an auto race, the Delta car scored more points than the Gamma. The Gamma car scored fewer points than the Alpha. The Beta car scored more points than the Alpha, but fewer than the Delta. Which car came in last?

7. What is the following scrambled word? (or words?)
   SSTILUO

8. Complete the following visual analogy. Select the proper lettered answer from the line below the illustrations:

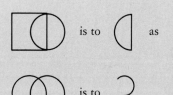

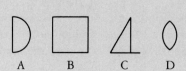

9. What numbers could logically come next in the following sequence? Pick your answer from the lettered choices.

1 9 3 8 5 7 7 6 9
5 11 4 13 3 15
(a) 17 4   (b) 17 2
(c) 2 17   (d) 2 21
(e) 2 13

10. In the square below, a rule of arithmetic has been followed that applies both across and down. Find the rule and insert the missing number in the second square:

21 3 7   32 4 8
 7 1 7   8 2 4
 3 3 1   4 2 ?

11. A man walks to his friend's house at 4 miles an hour. It takes him 2 hours, and he spends an hour there. Then his friend drives him home through traffic at 24 mph. What was the total elapsed time for the whole trip?

12. Which of the lettered proverbs below means almost the same as:

   An ounce of prevention is worth a pound of cure.

(a) Don't count your chickens until they are hatched.
(b) People who live in glass houses shouldn't throw stones.
(c) All that glitters is not gold.
(d) A Stitch in time saves nine.

13. The following crypto-gram is a simple substitution. What does it say?

1 18 5 14 20   25 15 21
    19 13 1 18 20

14.

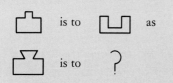

is to   as

is to   ?

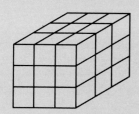

(a)   (b)   (c)   (d)

15. There is a block, 3
inches by 3 inches by 3
inches, cut as shown below,
after it was painted on all
outside surfaces. How many
blocks in the cube have no
paint on any of their sides?

16. All blaphles are blue. All
glorphs are blaphles. Some
roffles are blaphles. Some
roffles are red. Can a glorph
be red?

(a) yes (b) no (c) cannot
tell from information given

17. Choose the lettered
group of numbers that would
best complete the sequence
below:

98 96 99 97 100 98
101 — — 100 103
101 104

(a) 99 100 (b) 99 102
(c) 99 101 (d) 98 100

18. Flower is to plant and
garden as leaf is to tree and
_____.

(a) plant (b) forest
(c) city (d) street

19. The same four-letter
word can be inserted in the
blanks below to make two
new words from the words
shown below.

Example:
HEAD   (LAND)   FALL
CARE   _____   HAND

20. Two children were
comparing the money they
had. Sally said to John, "If
you give me one penny, I'll
have as many as you." John
said, "But if you give me one
penny, I'll have three times
as many pennies as you do."
How many pennies did each
one have?

etc. The other sequence goes
down one number at a time,
i.e., 9,8,7 etc.)
10. 2
11. 3 hours and 20 minutes
12. (d)
13. ARENT YOU SMART
    Each number was used in
place of the letter it represents in numerical sequence
in the alphabet; i.e., A = 1,
Z = 26.
14. (b)
15. Only one — exactly in
the center of the cube.
16. (b) no
17. (b) 99 102. There are
two alternating sequences,
each going up one number at
a time.
18. (b) forest
19. FREE
20. They had 3¢ and 5¢,
respectively.

Source: Dr. Abbie F. Salny.
Copyright © 1984 by American
Mensa, Ltd., Department HB88,
2626 East 14th Street, Brooklyn, NY
11235-3992.

Answers

1. RELATIVES   VERSATILE
2. 8 pounds
3. ROUND
4. 6 of each
5. (a) and (b)
6. GAMMA
7. ST. LOUIS
8. D (the area that overlaps
where the two figures
coincide)
9. (c) (There are two
alternating sequences. One
starts with 1 and goes up two
numbers at a time, i.e., 3,5,7

Box 12-9
The Dove Counterbalance Intelligence Test

Intelligence in Perspective — Are Intelligence Tests Intelligent?

Almost everyone has some curiosity about how they would score on an intelligence test. It you would like to get a rough estimate of your IQ, take the following self-administered test.

Time limit: 5 minutes   Circle the correct answer.

1. T-bone Walker got famous for playing what?
   a. trombone *c.* T-flute *e.* "hambone"
   b. piano *d.* guitar

2. A "gas head" is a person who has a _____.
   a. fast-moving car *d.* habit of stealing
   b. stable of "lace"   cars.
   c. "process" *e.* long jail record
                                       for arson

3. If you throw the dice and 7 is showing on the top, what is facing down?
   a. 7 *c.* boxcars *e.* 11
   b. snake eyes *d.* little joes

4. Cheap chitlings (not the kind you purchase at a frozen-food counter) will taste rubbery unless they are cooked long enough. How soon can you quit cooking them to eat and enjoy them?
   a. 45 minutes *d.* one week (on a low
   b. two hours   flame)
   c. 24 hours *e.* one hour

5. Bird or Yardbird was the jacket jazz lovers from coast to coast hung on _____?
   a. Lester Young *d.* Charlie Parker
   b. Peggy Lee *e.* Birdman of
   c. Benny Goodman   Alcatraz

6. A "handkerchief head" is:
   a. a cool cat *d.* a hoddi
   b. porter *e.* a preacher
   c. an Uncle Tom

7. Jet is _____.
   a. an East Oakland motorcycle club
   b. one of the gangs in *West Side Story*
   c. a news and gossip magazine
   d. a way of life for the very rich

Answers: 1. d 2. c 3. a 4. c 5. d 6. c 7. c 8. c 9. c 10. c 11. c 12. b 13. c 14. c 15. d

Source: Dove, A. (1968, July). Taking the chitling test. *Newsweek,* pp. 51–52.

Formal Evaluation of Intelligence Tests

When considering the controversy surrounding ethnic differences in intelligence, you must keep the distinction between IQ and intelligence clear. Few critics question that different ethnic groups obtain different average IQ scores (see Chapter 2). Rather, they argue that IQ scores do not represent intelligence accurately because IQ scores are affected by factors irrelevant to the hypothetical construct. This is one way of saying that intelligence tests are invalid. In spite of their special problems, intelligence tests are basically the same as other types of personality tests, and as

such evaluated by the same criteria. How well then do intelligence tests fare on traditional tests of reliability and validity?

Reliability   Most experts agree that conventional intelligence tests such as the Stanford-Binet and WAIS-R fare very well on measures of inter-rater and split-half reliability: the typical reliability coefficient is +.90 or more. Test-retest reliability also has been found to be relatively high, but decreases as the length of time between testing increases (see Jensen, 1963; Bayley, 1970). Other studies have found that conditions under which individuals are tested affect IQ scores—a finding that may help explain some of the re-

8. "Bo Diddly" is a _____ .
   a. game for children   d. new dance
   b. down-home cheap wine   e. Moejoe call
   c. down-home singer
9. Which word is most out of place here?
   a. splib   c. gray   e. black
   b. blood   d. spook
10. If a pimp is uptight with a woman who gets state aid, what does he mean when he talks about "Mother's Day"?
    a. second Sunday in May
    b. third Sunday in June
    c. first of every month
    d. none of these
    e. first and fifteenth of every month
11. How much does a "short dog" cost?
    a. 15¢   c. 35¢   e. 86¢ plus tax
    b. $2   d. 5¢
12. Many people say that "Juneteenth" (June 10th) should be made a legal holiday because this was the day when:
    a. the slaves were freed in the United States
    b. the slaves were freed in Texas
    c. the slaves were freed in Jamaica
    d. the slaves were freed in California
    e. Martin Luther King was born
    f. Booker T. Washington died
13. If a man is called a "blood," then he is a _____ .
    a. fighter   d. hungry hemophile
    b. Mexican-American   e. red man or Indian
    c. Negro
14. What are the Dixie Hummingbirds?
    a. a part of the KKK
    b. a swamp disease
    c. a modern gospel group
    d. a Mississippi Negro paramilitary strike force
    e. deacons
15. The opposite of square is _____ .
    a. round   c. down   e. lame
    b. up   d. hip

ported racial differences in IQ. For example, Zigler and Butterfield (1968) found that children gained an average of more than ten IQ points on the Stanford-Binet after a second testing in which they were encouraged to do well, to try difficult items, and so on.

Validity Whether intelligence tests have content validity is a question each assessor must answer independently. According to Wechsler:

Intelligence exists — it exists for the layman as well as for the scientist. An average adult and a normal 12-year-old will understand the word *intelligent* if used in a meaningful context. What we measure with tests is not what tests measure — not information, not spatial perception, not reasoning ability. These are only means to an end. What intelligence tests measure, what we hope they measure, is something much more important: the capacity of an individual to understand the world about him and his resourcefulness to cope with its challenges. (1975, p. 139)

Yet, as we have seen, experts have not reached agreement on precisely what abilities constitute intelligence.

Intelligence tests fare relatively well on measures of predictive validity (Table 12-19), discriminant validity, and convergent validity. Scores of different intelligence tests tend to correlate highly with one another (although these correlations tend to vary with the time that elapses between testing; Honzik, MacFarland, & Allen, 1948). Also, scores of intelligence tests tend not to correlate positively with scores of most personality tests (personality test-makers customarily eliminate items that correlate with IQ).

As for the construct validity of intelligence tests, the work of Spearman, Thurstone and Guilford indicates there is considerable disagreement on the question of the number and nature of abilities that comprise intelligence and whether it is a unitary or multidimensional construct.

Intelligence Testing — Some Important Distinctions

The late Canadian psychologist, Donald Hebb, suggested it is useful to distinguish between two types of intelligence, which he called Intelligence A and Intelligence B (Hebb, 1966). *Intelligence A,* with which we are born, places an upper limit on our intellectual potential. Intelligence A is determined principally by our genetic endowment, and is affected by prenatal and birth-related events. But people may fulfill their genetic potential in different ways. Differences in opportunities, tutoring, motivation, and other

factors may affect the extent to which individuals develop their intellectual capacity. *Intelligence B* is the intelligence people display in their daily lives. Hebb points out that many people mistakenly equate a person's cleverness (Intelligence B) with his or her innate potential (Intelligence A). Note the similarity between Hebb's two types of intelligence and the crystallized and fluid types described in Chapter 9.

Psychologist Phillip Vernon (1965) has taken Hebb's argument one step further. Vernon suggests we should make a third distinction — between the two types of intelligence Hebb outlined and *Intelligence C* — defined as scores on intelligence tests. Making such distinctions draws attention to the potential fallacy of inferring that scores on intelligence tests reflect either real-life cleverness or innate potential. Such distinctions also sharpen the task faced by those who evaluate the validity of intelligence tests. To establish that intelligence tests assess Intelligence A and B, we must develop measures for evaluating daily cleverness and innate potential. As to the latter, several psychologists have been developing neurological methods — capable of evaluating electrical activity in the brain — that might someday lead to a measure of innate intellectual potential (see Rice, 1973).

SUMMARY

1. People typically make inferences about the personality of others on the basis of such aspects of their appearance as hair color, body type, skin color, and physical attractiveness. Given information about one personality trait, people make elaborate inferences about other traits possessed by people.

2. Eysenck and Cattell have attempted to determine which traits constitute personality as a whole. Although there is considerable overlap in the traits identified by different investigators, as yet there is no agreement on which combination of traits best describes personality.

3. The basic elements of personality according to Freud's psychoanalytic theory are the id

(instinct), ego (intellect), and superego (morality). These elements operate within the unconscious, preconscious, and conscious levels of awareness. Freud's theory focuses on the conflicts that emerge as children go through five stages of psychosexual development: the oral, anal, phallic, latency, and genital stages. The resolution of these conflicts plays a central role in determining the type of personality people develop.

4. Erikson's psychosocial theory of personality extends and elaborates on the five stages described by Freud. For Erikson, personality development is determined by the ways in which people resolve psychosocial crises during the eight stages of life from infancy to old age.

5. Roger's theory of self-actualization is based on the idea that the driving force of life is to fulfill one's potential. Rogers maintains that all individuals are born with an actualizing tendency: the natural tendency to maintain themselves, to enhance themselves, and to grow. The actualizing tendency and the socially learned tendency toward self-actualization are involved in the development of self-concepts and personality.

6. Kelly's psychology of personal constructs emphasizes the cognitive aspect of personality: the way people think. Kelly assumes that all people are scientists, construing the events in their lives through abstraction and generalization.

7. Behavioristic theories focus on the periphery of personality: observable behavior. According to B. F. Skinner, the environment structures people's behaviors: people learn to behave in certain ways because the behavior has paid off in the past. Walter Mischel offers a social-learning theory that proposes behavior stems from an interaction between environmental factors and such internal forces as styles of information processing and values. Albert Bandura emphasizes the effect of modeling, vicarious reinforcement, self-reinforcement, and self-efficacy on personality development.

8. Theories of personality can be evaluated on the basis of seven principal criteria: comprehensiveness, parsimony, logical consistency, testability, empirical support, heuristic value, and applied value.

9. To assess personality, psychologists sometimes ask others to rate individuals on various personality traits or ask individuals to rate themselves. Statistical and methodological techniques are used to minimize response biases. The *Adjective Checklist* and the *Q-sort* are examples of rating tests that control for response biases.

10. The most common means for assessing personality is the personality inventory, in which respondants indicate the extent to which various statements are or are not characteristic of them. Three popular personality inventories are the 16PF, the CPI, and the MMPI.

11. To determine the significance or meaning of a test score, tests must be standardized. In addition, standardized tests must supply reliable and valid measures of personality. There are six standards of validity: content, predictive, concurrent, convergent, discriminant, and construct.

12. Projective tests are based on the assumption that most people project unfavorable aspects of their own personality onto other people or things. The Sentence Completion Test, the Thematic Apperception Test, and the Rorschach Inkblot Test are examples of projective tests. Projective tests do not fare well on traditional standards of reliability and validity.

13. Behavioristic psychologists assess behavior rather than hypothetical personality traits that underlie behavior.

14. Intelligence can be considered the master trait of personality. The first intelligence test was created by Binet. Revised by Terman and still used today, it has become the Stanford-Binet Intelligence Test. Wechsler's WAIS-R and WISC-R, with performance and verbal scales, are currently the most popular individual intelligence tests. The SAT is similar to a group-intelligence test.

15. Early psychologist Spearman believed there is one overriding ability, g, that constitutes intelligence, but that it is composed of specific abilities, s. Thurstone held that intelligence consists of seven primary mental abilities; Guilford identified 120 theoretical possibile factors. Recently Howard Gardner has argued there are at least seven qualitatively different kinds of intelligence, including athletic, social, and artistic abilities.

16. There is evidence that at least some of the difference between the average IQ scores of different ethnic groups arises from cultural biases in intelligence tests.

KEY TERMS

Personality
Periphery
Core
Stereotype
Central Trait
Adding Model
Averaging Model
Weighted Averaging Model
Implicit Theory of
    Personality
Self-fulfilling Prophesy
Personality Type
Surface Trait
Source Trait
Q-data
T-data
L-data
Conscious
Preconscious
Unconscious
Pleasure Principle
Instinct
Preservation Instinct
Death Instinct
Primary Process Thinking
Secondary Process Thinking
Ego
Superego
Ego-ideal
Ego Defense Mechanism
Erogenous Zone
Oral Stage
Fixation
Oral Character

Anal Stage
Anal Character
Phallic Stage
Phallic Character
Latency Period
Genital Stage
Ego Analyst
Actualizing Tendency
Self-actualization
Conditions of Worth
Fully Functioning Person
Unconditional Positive
    Regard
Incongruent Person
Construing
Constructive Alternativism
Construct
Interactionism
Vicarious Reinforcement
Self-reinforcement
Self-efficacy
Trait-rating Approach
Response Bias
Halo Effect
Horns Effect
Yea-saying/Nay-saying
Adjective Check List
Q-sort
Personality Inventory
16PF
CPI
Empirical Strategy
MMPI
Standardize

Reliability
Test-retest Reliability
Split-half Reliability
Alternate-form Reliability
Inter-rater Reliability
Validity
Projective Test
Sentence Completion Test
Thematic Apperception Test
    (TAT)
Rorschach Inkblot Test
Behavioral Rating
Intelligence
Mental Age
Intelligence Quotient (IQ)
Stanford-Binet Intelligence
    Scale
Wechsler Adult Intelligence
    Scale (WAIS-R)
Wechsler Intelligence Scale
    for Children (WISC-R)
Group-administered Test
Aptitude Test
Scholastic Aptitude Test
    (SAT)
General Mental Facility (g)
Specific Mental Capability (s)
Primary Mental Ability
Primary Retardation
Secondary Retardation
Cultural Bias

RECOMMENDED READINGS

Anastasi, A. (1982). *Psychological testing* (4th ed.). New York: Macmillan. A comprehensive text that covers reliability, validity, and surveys of intelligence and personality tests.

Eysenck, H. J. (1981). *The intelligence controversy: H. J. Eysenck vs. Leon Kamin.* New York: Wiley. A spirited exchange between Eysenck, de-fending the *nature* side of the IQ controversy, and Kamin, defending the *nurture* side.

Fisher, S., & Greenberg, R. P. (1977). *The scientific credibility of Freud's theories and therapy.* New York: Basic Books. A review of research on psychoanalytic theory.

Gould, S. J. (1981). *The mismeasure of man*. New York: Norton. A provocative and critical look at the history of the intelligence testing movement, with an emphasis on abuse.

Hall, C. S., Lindzey, G., Loehlin, J. C., & Manosevitz, M. (1985). *Introduction to theories of personality*. New York: Wiley. A revision of the classic Hall and Lindzey text that outlines and evaluates personality theories from Freud to modern social-cognitive theorists.

Phares, J. E. (1984). *Introduction to personality*. Columbus, OH: Charles E. Merrill. Well-illustrated text on personality, beginning with traditional approaches and ending with a consideration of such personality processes as intelligence, anxiety and stress, control, aggression, and altruism.

13

ABNORMAL PSYCHOLOGY

Spain has a king. They've found him. I am the King. I discovered it today. It all came to me in a flash. It's incredible to me now that I could have imagined that I was a civil-service clerk. . . . But what was happening to me before? Then things loomed at me out of a fog. Now, I believe that all troubles stem from the misconception that human brains are located in the head. They are not: human brains are blown in by the winds from somewhere around the Caspian sea. . . . Marva was the first to whom I revealed my identity. When she heard that she was facing the King of Spain she flung up her hands in awe. She almost died of terror. The silly woman had never seen a King of Spain before. However, I tried to calm her and, speaking graciously, did my best to assure her of my royal favor. I was not going to hold against her all the times she had failed to shine my boots properly. The masses are so ignorant. One can't talk to them on lofty subjects.*

Nicolai Gogol writes of a clerk who believes he is the King of Spain. If we met the clerk on the street, we might well react like his friend Marva and fling up our hands in terror. Like Gogol, we might conclude that he was mad. Lawrence Durrell also writes of a person who behaves in a bizarre manner. In Durrell's book *Balthazar,* we join an old sea captain named Scobie toward the end of a visit with a friend.

"Before you go, there's a small confession I'd like to make to you, old man. Right?" I sat down on the uncomfortable chair and nodded. "Right," he said emphatically and drew a breath. "Well then: sometimes at the full moon, I'm Took. I come under An Influence." . . . This was on the face of it a somewhat puzzling departure from accepted form, for the old man looked quite disturbed by his own revelation. He gobbled for a moment and then went on in a small humbled voice devoid of his customary swagger. "I don't know what comes over me." I did not quite understand all this. "Do you mean you walk in your sleep or what?" He shook his head and gulped again. "Do you turn into a werewolf, Scobie?" Once more he shook his head like a child upon the point of tears. "I slip on female duds and my Dolly Varden," he said, and opened his eyes fully to stare pathetically at me. "You what?" I said. . . . To my surprise he rose now and walked stiffly to a cupboard which he unlocked. Inside, hanging up, moth-eaten and unbrushed, was a suit of female clothes of ancient cut, and on a nail beside it a greasy old cloth hat which I took to be the so-called "Dolly Varden." A pair of pointed toes completed this staggering outfit. He did not know how quite to respond to the laugh which I was now compelled to utter. He gave a weak giggle. "It's silly, isn't it?" he said, still hovering somewhere on the edge of tears despite his smiling face, and still by his tone inviting sympathy in misfortune. "I don't know what comes over me. And yet, you know, its always the old thrill. . . ."†

When old Scobie becomes "Took," he engages in behavior most of us would consider abnormal. If we encountered Scobie when he was in that state, we might conclude that, like Gogol's madman, he was disturbed psychologically. We make judgments about normality and abnormality every day of our lives; in most cases we make these judgments quickly and without much thought. We possess an implicit knowledge of these phenomena, accumulated throughout our lives on the basis of countless experiences. But what exactly is abnormal behavior; what are the defining conditions of psychological disturbance? If the behavior of Gogol's clerk and Durrell's old Scobie are both abnormal, what do they have in common? On what bases do we conclude that someone is disturbed psychologically? To establish a context for answering these questions, it is useful to go back in history and trace the ways in which people have defined psychological disorders and dealt with the people afflicted with them.

---

* From *The Diary of a Madman and Other Stories* by Nicolai Gogol, translated by Andrew R. MacAndrew. Copyright © 1961 by Andrew R. MacAndrew. Published by arrangement with the New American Library of World Literature, Inc., New York.

† From *Balthazar* by Lawrence Durrell. Copyright © 1958 by Lawrence Durrell. Reprinted by permission of E. P. Dutton & Co., Inc.

CONCEPTIONS OF ABNORMALITY —A HISTORICAL ACCOUNT

DEMONOLOGY

For most of the history of the human species, *madness* was considered to be the work of the devil, and disturbed people were thought to be *possessed* by evil spirits or demons. If posses-

Archaeologists have found the skulls of humans who had been subjected to trephining, skulls that date back to the Stone Age. In some cases (right skull), holes in the skull had begun to grow over, suggesting that the individuals may have survived the treatment. As depicted in the illustrations from a sixteenth century medical text, trephining was common then and in the seventeenth century as well. *Sources:* (above) Department of Library Services, American Museum of Natural History. (below) National Library of Medicine.

sion is the problem, it follows that **exorcism** is the cure. In some cultures exorcisms were mild: spirits were calmed by music or chased away by prayers and religious rites. However, such benign procedures were by no means the most common. Archaeological evidence suggests that during the Stone Age, demons were released through **trephining:** cutting or drilling a large hole in the afflicted individual's skull. During the Middle Ages, religious authorities attempted to drive out demons by immersing the "possessed" in boiling-hot or ice-cold water, starving them, or flogging them. Not surprisingly, the "cure" was often more harmful than the affliction. The demonological explanation of mental disorders reached its peak during the witch hunts of the sixteenth and seventeenth centuries. Individuals judged to be "possessed" were burned, strangled, or beheaded. Estimates of the number of lives lost during this period range from 100,000 to 500,000 (see Chapter 14 for illustrations of the forms of treatment used).

The idea that certain disorders are the work of the devil still exists in some places. For example, a 1978 newspaper report from Germany described a murder trial that involved two rural priests and the parents of a girl who died of starvation while undergoing a modern exorcism. The priests explained they had successfully starved the devil out of the girl but, unfortunately, at the very moment the devil left, the girl died.

MEDICAL MODEL OF MENTAL ILLNESS

During the golden days of Greece, the father of medicine, Hippocrates (*ca.* 460 – *ca.* 377 B.C.) suggested that mental disorders were caused by imbalances in the four humors of the body. This widsom was lost until the eighteenth and nineteenth centuries when certain courageous reformers — most notably Philippe Pinel

Pinel is shown overseeing the removal of shackles from inmates in the courtyard of the mental asylum Salpêtrière.
Source: National Library of Medicine.

Dorothea Dix, a Massachusetts school teacher, spear-headed reforms in women's prisons and mental institutions. She is credited with establishing 32 hospitals.
Source: Reproduced from the collection of the Library of Congress.

(1745 – 1826) and Dorothea Dix (1802 – 1887) — objected to the medieval assumption that insanity is caused by demonic possession. Significant medical advances were being made during these eras, and it occurred to such reformers as Pinel and Dix that the symptoms of madness displayed by some poor souls were caused by physical maladies, not by evil spirits. As specific causes of many physical disorders began to be isolated (for example, bacteria), hopes were raised that similar causes also would be found for mental disorders. Such hopes were fed by the discovery that one of the most dramatic and mystifying forms of mental derangement, **general paresis of the insane** (GPI), was caused by syphilis (see Box 13-1).

The crusades of reformers who believed in and preached the **medical model of mental illness** played a significant role in ushering in humane treatment for people who hitherto had been persecuted as the agents of the devil. Their work had a profound impact on the way in which we conceive of abnormal behavior. Today most peo-

Box 13-1
The Search for and Discovery of a Cure for General Paresis of the Insane (GPI)

Before the twentieth century, ten percent of all admissions to mental hospitals were believed to be afflicted by general paresis of the insane (GPI) — first identified in 1798 by John Haslam, superintendent of the Bethlehem Mental Asylum (''Bedlam''). GPI was marked by a deterioration in thought processes and memory, delusions, agitation, and a variety of physical symptoms.

In Victorian England, physicians observed that both upper-class gentlemen and lower-class ladies suffered an unusually high incidence of GPI and speculated about the factors that might link the two afflicted groups. One theory suggested that because both groups were regular users of the railway, railway carriages might somehow be implicated in

the disorder. Other theories attributed the disease variously to alcohol, coffee, tea, or to moral offenses (Landis & Bolles, 1950).

The first step in explaining the correlation occurred in 1857 when German surgeon Johannes von Esmarch and a colleague reported cases of paresis that were known to have syphilis. On the basis of this evidence, they proposed that syphilis was the cause of paresis — offering a telling explanation for the connection between upper-class gentlemen and lower-class ladies.

The idea that syphilis was the cause of GPI was disputed for a half century until 1906, when August von Wassermann, a German professor of medicine, developed a blood test for syphilis. Studies found that the

overwhelming majority of paretics reacted positively to the Wassermann test, providing strong evidence that paresis and syphilis were connected. In 1913 a Japanese bacteriologist, Hideyo Hoguchi, found syphilitic spirochetes in the brains of people suffering from GPI; however, it wasn't until 1917 that a means was found to kill these microorganisms. The first method was crude: people suffering from GPI were inoculated with malaria because observers had noted that the symptoms seemed to abate in patients who had high fevers. A decade later, Sir Alexander Fleming discovered penicillin; a decade later than that, in 1940, penicillin was applied directly to a syphilis spirochete and destroyed it. Today virtually no one suffers from GPI.

ple implicitly view psychological disturbances in medical terms. We send mentally *ill* people to *doctors* who put them in *hospitals* where they become *patients;* their conditions are *diagnosed* and they are given *treatments* designed to *cure* their disorders. This conception is, of course, appropriate in some instances; as we will see, there is evidence that schizophrenia and other severe disorders are caused by biochemical imbalances in the body, at least in part. But does it make sense to view all psychological disorders in medical terms? Was old Scobie's ''affliction''

caused by a physical dysfunction? Are people ''sick'' who fear snakes, feel a compulsion to stay clean, or drink to excess?

Psychoanalytic Model of Mental Illness

The assumption that certain disorders stem from physical causes was challenged in the nineteenth century by the founder of psychoanalysis, Sigmund Freud. During the nineteenth century a group of disturbances called **hysteria** was receiving considerable attention from the medical profession. Hysteria involved such physical dysfunctions as blindness, loss of hearing, and paralysis of limbs. Freud shocked his medical colleagues by suggesting that the cause of hysteria was psychological — namely, unresolved sexual conflicts from childhood.

Freud's **psychoanalytic model of psychological disorder** is similar to the medical model in that it assumes disturbances are caused by internal malignant factors. However, unlike the medical model, psychoanalysis assumes the malignant factors are psychological, not physical. People become "mentally ill" when they cannot deal with psychological problems, especially, in Freud's view, those problems that pertain to unconscious sexual conflicts. Freud believed that psychological problems require psychological treatment — namely psychoanalysis (see Chapter 14).

Critiques of the Medical Model of Mental Illness and Alternatives

The tremendous advances introduced by the medical model of mental illness notwithstanding, the idea that psychological disorders have specific, identifiable physical or psychological causes has not gone uncriticized. We now consider three of the alternatives offered by critics of the medical conception of psychological disorder.

Problems in Living Psychiatrist Thomas Szasz may be the leading North American critic of the medical model. Szasz objects to the assumption that psychological disorders are similar to physical disorders, and argues it is unfortunate that medical doctors (psychiatrists) treat them. Rather, suggests Szasz, psychological disorders should be thought of as **problems in living** because they are interpersonal in nature — they stem from people's inability to adapt to the demands of society. Szasz believes it is unfortunate that people with problems in living are labeled "mentally ill"; such labels limit what they are permitted to do, induce them to adopt the social role of a "patient," and encourage them to evade responsibility for their behavior. Ironically, in view of the role it played in freeing institutionalized victims, Szasz suggests the medical model is now responsible for the involuntary incarceration of three quarters of a million patients. Szasz (1970) argues that involuntary confinement entails "punishment without trial, imprisonment without limit, and stigmatization without hope of redress." In his famous essay *The Myth of Mental Illness* (1961), Szasz outlines the implications of this view in some detail. Although many have found Szasz's critique stimulating, his model has met with only limited acceptance in the field.

Social Deviation Another critique of the medical model suggests the names we give to psychological disorders are labels for behaviors that violate the social norms of our society (see Figure 13-1). Advocates of the **social-deviation model** point out that behaviors considered abnormal in one society may be considered perfectly normal in others and that definitions of abnormality change from one historical period to another within the same society. Extreme advocates of the social-deviation model of psychological disorder suggest that societies use psychiatric diagnosis as a way of forcing people to conform and as a means of controlling individuals whose nonconformity is seen as dangerous to the society. Ken Kesey's novel, *One Flew Over the Cuckoo's Nest,* is an account of how psychiatric treatment may be used in this way. Alexander Solzhenitsyn's novels supply similar accounts from Russia, where political dissenters are placed in psychiatric institutions.

As exemplified by the clerk who fancied himself the King of Spain and by old Scobie, people we consider to be disturbed psychologically generally behave in ways that violate social norms. *Abnormal* means, literally, "away from the norm." Yet behaviors we consider abnormal may be acceptable in other cultures. For example, cross-sex dressing, alcohol and drug addiction, compulsiveness, public nudity, and speaking with "voices" are perfectly acceptable in some places in the world. Even in our society, norms related to drinking, drugs, sexual behavior, and traditional dress have changed radically over the years.

How far can we take the idea that there is no such thing as mental disorder (only labels for nonconformist behaviors)? What about hallucinations, delusions of persecution, and nonsensi-

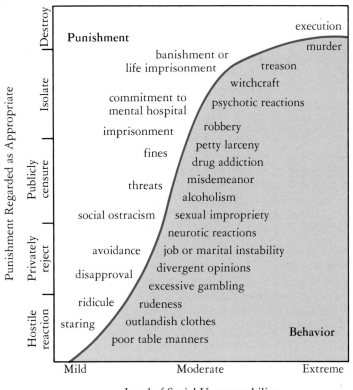

FIGURE 13-1

Violations of Social Standards and Associated Punishments   At the mildest end of the continuum, poor table manners are punished by a fixed stare.   At the extreme end of the continuum, murder is punished by execution.   *Source:* Hass, K. (1965).   Direction of hostility and psychiatric symptoms.   *Psychological Reports, 16,* 555–56.

cal speech?   Extreme advocates of the social-deviation model of psychological disorder have suggested that judgments about even the most deviant behaviors reflect the views of a particular culture at a particular time.   They claim that a person whom we would diagnose as *schizophrenic* would be regarded as a medicine man or healer in some primitive tribes and that trances practiced as part of religious and healing rituals in some cultures would be considered a sign of mental disorder in our culture.   However, anthropologists who have examined other cultures have not supported these claims; people from preliterate societies make clear distinctions between religious trances and thought disorders.   Thought disorders are usually viewed as possession by evil spirits and as a sign of abnormality.   There appears to be only one exception: people who have suffered a syndrome we might label schizo-

phrenic occasionally become Siberian *shamans* (holy men), but only if they successfully recover from the disturbance (see Draguns & Phillips, 1972).

Thus, although there are some differences among different cultural groups in what they consider normal and abnormal, all people appear to consider severe forms of psychological disturbance abnormal.   In addition, people of virtually all cultures appear to interpret anxiety and depression and their accompanying signs (for example, insomnia and lack of interest in the social environment) as evidence of a physical or psychological disorder (Draguns & Phillips, 1972). There is less consensus about personality disorders (Ackerknecht, 1968).   It seems reasonable to conclude that although psychological disorders often involve the violation of social norms, such a violation in itself is not a sufficient basis on which to define psychological disorders. Behaviors that deviate from social norms and are defined as abnormal by the majority of people in a particular society — homosexuality, for example — need not necessarily be psychologically maladaptive (see Chapter 8).

Problems with Learning   In the medical and psychoanalytic models, psychological disorders are attributed to internal problems: something goes wrong with the physical or psychological makeup of people that causes them to behave in abnormal ways. In the **behavioristic model,** psychological disorders are attributed to external factors. According to behaviorists, maladaptive behavior is learned and maintained in the same way as adaptive behavior.

The behavioristic model advocates a careful investigation of the environmental conditions in which people display abnormal behavior. Special attention is given to situational stimuli, or *triggers,* that elicit the behavior and to the typical consequences that follow it. Behaviorists search for factors that reinforce or encourage the repetition of abnormal behaviors. As we will learn, this model supplies a plausible explanation for some, but certainly not all, abnormal behaviors.

In conclusion, the phenomenon we now call psychological or mental disorder may be viewed in a variety of ways (see Table 13-1). Faced with a person who behaves like Gogol's clerk or Durrell's old Scobie, we may label the person "possessed," "mentally ill," "emotionally disturbed," "socially deviant," or the victim of an unfortunate history of learning. Why are there so many ways of categorizing abnormal behavior, and which conception is most valid? The many models of abnormality probably stem from the fact that most abnormal behaviors are determined by a complex interaction between factors. We define abnormal behavior largely in terms of its causes. In the case of GPI, the discovery of a physical cause established it as a physical disorder. Similarly, the ability of behaviorists to induce phobias through conditioning (see Chapter 5) supports their contention that some phobias are disorders of learning. Unfortunately, it is increasingly apparent that most "mental disorders" are caused by many factors working together. Thus, the best answer to the second question — which conception is most valid — appears to be that parts of all of them, except demonic possession, with some models more appropriate to some disorders and others to others. To summarize the discussion, most psychological disorders originate from complex interactions among physical, social, and psychological factors that include but exceed all single and simplistic conceptions.

TABLE 13-1
Models of Psychopathology

Model	Assumed Cause(s) of Disorder	Treatment
Demonic	Possession by evil spirits, moral corruption	Exorcism, torture, imprisonment, death
Medical	Physical agents, diseases of the nervous system	Medicine, drugs, psychosurgery, electroconvulsive therapy
Psychoanalytic	Unconscious psychological conflicts, especially stemming from pent-up sexual and aggressive urges and repressed childhood memories	Psychoanalysis
Problems in Living	Failure to adapt to other people in a constructive way	Change in interpersonal habits
Social Deviation	Factors that cause people to violate social norms	Tolerance: leave nonconformists alone; change society
Problems with Learning	Maladaptive learning	Extinction of bad habits; learning of new habits through conditioning and modeling

THE CLASSIFICATION OF PSYCHOLOGICAL DISORDERS

The behaviors displayed by the clerk who thought he was the King of Spain and by old Scobie are similar because they seem abnormal, yet they are different in several respects. And the same can be said about a vast array of other abnormal behaviors. When people see things that seem different in some respects, yet similar in others, they are disposed to classify or categorize them (Bruner, Goodnow, & Austin, 1956). Throughout the ages, physicians and scholars have classified psychological disorders in a variety of ways. We examine the earliest classification schemes and then outline those employed by psychologists and psychiatrists today.

Early Classification Schemes

One of the earliest classification schemes was proposed by the Greek physician Hippocrates. Extending Empedocles' idea that the world is composed of four elements — air, earth, fire, and water, Hippocrates suggested that the human body is composed of four basic humors (fluids) — blood, black bile, yellow bile, and phlegm. According to Hippocrates, imbalances among these humors give rise to both personality traits and abnormal behaviors. For example, when the level of blood becomes high, people become sanguine, or cheerful; when black bile dominates, they become gloomy (see Figure 13-2). Although primitive, Hippocrates' classification scheme supplied a model for subsequent attempts to classify psychological disorders.

The wisdom of the Greeks was lost for many centuries until Philippe Pinel and other reformers freed the psychologically disturbed from their chains. Pinel, also a physician, grouped the dis-

orders he believed psychological or mental in nature in a category he called **neurosis** — defined as functional diseases of the nervous system — and divided them into several types.

At the end of the nineteenth century, physician Emil Kraepelin (1856 – 1926) published a classification scheme that synthesized earlier systems and elaborated on them in significant ways. Kraepelin based his classification on an extensive review of hospital records and on careful observations of patients. He suggested there are 18 types of mental disorder, each with a characteristic pattern of symptoms (called a **syndrome**), a distinct course of development, particular causes, and a characteristic outcome. Kraepelin supplied the foundation for classification schemes used today.

Modern Classification Schemes

Soon after the World Health Organization was created (1948), it published the *International Statistical Classification of Diseases, Injuries, and Causes of Death (ICD)*, a manual that supplied a classification of all diseases, including those considered *mental* in nature. It has undergone nine revisions since its publication, and continues to guide psychiatric and psychological diagnosis in most countries of the world.

Independently, the American Psychiatric Association sponsored the preparation and publication of a *Diagnostic and Statistical Manual (DSM)* that contained a classification of mental disorders (1952). Because earlier versions of the *ICD* and *DSM* were incompatible, in the mid-1960s a committee of the American Psychiatric Association made the *DSM* more compatible

Empedocles	air	earth	fire	water
Hippocrates	blood	black bile	yellow bile	phlegm
	sanguine	melancholic	choleric	phlegmatic
	/	/	/	/
	naturally hopeful and cheerful	gloomy	easily made angry, irritable	sluggish, indifferent, cool and calm

FIGURE 13-2

Hippocrates' Extension of Empedocles' Classification of the Elements of Nature   *Source:* Coles, E. M. (1982). *Clinical psychopathology: An introduction.* London: Routledge & Kegan Paul.

with the revised *ICD* in an attempt to promote improved international communications. The resulting manual, published in 1968, was called the *DSM-II,* and until the 1980s was the primary guide for psychiatric diagnosis in North America.

There were several problems with the classification scheme contained in the *DSM-II.* For example, different criteria were employed to define the disorders in different categories, making the manual more a collection of classification schemes than a single scheme organized around a consistent set of principles. Mental disorders were viewed from a medical perspective, as diseases rather than as psychological reactions. And diagnoses based on the manual did not fare well when tested for reliability and validity. Because of these and other problems, the American Psychiatric Association formed a task force to revise the

TABLE 13-2
A Classification of Mental Disorders

Axis I	*Disorders usually first evident in infancy, childhood, or adolescence* A variety of intellectual, emotional, physical and developmental disorders, including attention deficit, hyperactivity, eating disorders (such as anorexia nervosa and bulimia), autistic disorder, childhood anxieties, and gender identity disorders.
	Organic mental disorders Disorders in which the psychological symptoms are directly related to injury to the brain or abnormality of its biochemical environment; may be the result of aging or the ingestion of toxic substances (for example, lead poisoning or extreme alcoholism).
	Psychoactive Substance-use disorders Includes excessive use of alcohol, barbiturates, amphetamines, opiates, cocaine, and other drugs that alter behavior. Marijuana and tobacco are also included in this category.
	Schizophrenia A group of disorders characterized by loss of contact with reality, marked disturbances of thought and perception, especially hallucinations and delusions, blunted or inappropriate emotions, and bizarre behavior.
	Delusional (paranoid) disorders Disorders characterized by such delusions as those that involve feelings of being persecuted; reality contact in other areas is satisfactory.
	Mood disorders Disturbances of normal mood; involving extreme depression, abnormal elation and excitement, or alternating periods of elation and depression.
	Anxiety disorders Includes disorders in which anxiety is the main symptom (generalized anxiety or panic disorders) or anxiety is experienced unless the individual avoids certain feared situations (phobic disorders), performs certain rituals or thinks persistent thoughts (obsessive-compulsive disorders).
	Somatoform disorders The symptoms of these disorders are physical, but have no known organic basis. Psychological factors appear to play the major role. Included are hypochondriasis and conversion disorders.
	Dissociative disorders Temporary alterations in the functions of consciousness, memory, or identity due to emotional problems. Included are psychogenic amnesia, fugue, depersonalization, and multiple personality.
	Sexual disorders Includes problems of sexual aim (for example, sexual interest in children) and sexual performance (for example, impotence, premature ejaculation, and frigidity). Homosexuality is considered a disorder only when the individual is unhappy with his or her sexual orientation and wishes to change it.
Axis II	*Developmental disorders and personality disorders* Long-standing patterns of inflexible and maladaptive behavior that constitute immature and inappropriate ways of coping with stress, solving problems, and dealing with others and such developmental disorders as mental retardation, autism, and learning disorders.
Axis III	Any medical or physical disorder that may also be present.
Axis IV	A 6-point scale ranging from 1 (none) to 6 (catastrophic) that rates the severity of psychological and social factors that may have placed the individual under stress.
Axis V	An imaginary continuum ranging from minimal symptoms to persistent danger of hurting self.

Source: Adapted from *Diagnostic and statistical manual of mental disorders* (3rd ed., revised). American Psychiatric Association, 1987.

DSM-II; in 1980, a new manual called the *DMS-III* was produced. In 1983, a work group was appointed to revise the *DSM-III;* in 1987, the manual in current use — the *DSM-III-R* — was published.

The *DSM-III-R* contains more than twice as many diagnostic categories as the *DSM-II* and describes each disorder more elaborately and precisely than the *DSM-II.* As a result, the manual expanded from 37 pages to 567 pages. The *DSM-III-R* does not employ the category of neurosis or psychophysiological disorder, and it does not consider homosexuality a psychological disorder unless the person who practices it finds it unacceptable. In addition, the *DSM-III-R* employs a quite different approach to classification from the *DSM-II:* it requires clinicians who use it to make five judgments about each individual they diagnose, which represent five dimensions or **axes of classification.**

The major change in classification involves a separation between such clinical-psychiatric syndromes as schizophrenia (Axis I) and personality styles or developmental disorders like dependency (Axis II) (see Table 13-2). Instead of the single diagnosis required by the *DSM-II,* clinicians are encouraged to make two diagnoses. Thus, for example, one patient might be classified as schizophrenic and dependent, while another might be classified as schizophrenic and passive-aggressive. In addition, clinicians are asked to make judgments about patients' physical condition (Axis III), to rate the degree of psychosocial stress using a list similar to the one in Table 13-3 (Axis IV) (see Box 13-2), and to provide an assessment of overall global functioning (Axis V).

In addition to the **multiaxial approach,** the *DSM-III-R* (with the *DSM-III*) departs from earlier versions by supplying descriptions of behaviors that characterize the disorders it lists. The manual indicates the ways in which disorders that seem similar differ from one another and describes typical cases, including information about usual age of onset, usual course of development, degree of impairment, factors that increase susceptibility, prevalence, and familial pattern. When appropriate, the manual mentions what is known about the cause of the disorder, but does not include as much speculation about causes as

TABLE 13-3
Sources of Stress — *DSM-III*

Source	Examples
Conjugal	Engagement, marriage, divorce, death of a spouse
Parenting	Becoming a parent, illness or death of a child, problems with a child
General interpersonal	Problems with friends, neighbors, fellow employees
Occupational	Problems at work, school, home, retirement
Living circumstances	Changes in residence, immigration
Financial	Inadequate finances, changes in financial circumstances
Legal	Arrest, involvement in a lawsuit, imprisonment
Developmental	Phase of life cycle: puberty, midlife crisis, menopause
Physical illness or injury	Illness, accident, surgery, abortion
Other psychological stressors	Natural disasters, war, persecution, rape

Source: Adapted from *Diagnostic and statistical manual of mental disorders* (3rd ed., revised). American Psychiatric Association, 1987, pp. 19–20.

did the *DSM-II* (see Box 13-3). Finally, the *DSM-III-R* makes a subtle but potentially significant distinction. It does not employ diagnostic categories to refer to types of people; rather, it uses diagnostic categories to refer to the types of disorder from which people suffer. Thus, for example, it does not refer to individuals as *schizophrenic;* rather, it refers to them as *people with schizophrenia.*

Although the *DSM-III* contained significant improvements over its predecessors, it was revised because it did not solve all the problems associated with the classification of psychological disorders. Among the criticisms of the *DSM-III,* four stand out. First, some critics have questioned the practice of deleting disorders from the classification system, arguing, for example, that it

Box 13-2
STRESS ASSOCIATED WITH SIGNIFICANT LIFE EVENTS

In recent years, the role of psychological stress in the development of physical disorders found in studies on animals has been extended to humans. In a series of studies based on the notion that life changes are in themselves stressful to all persons, Holmes and Rahe (1967) constructed a table of significant life events (or changes) and developed a pathology-weight for each item (see table). They demonstrated that people who score above a certain level on this scale often develop a physical illness within one year. Although the model attempts to predict whether any individual will develop some disorder, it does not attempt to specify which individuals are particularly susceptible or which specific disorder will develop.

Social Readjustment Rating Scale

Rank	Life Event	Mean Value
1	Death of spouse	100
2	Divorce	73
3	Marital separation	65
4	Jail term	63
5	Death of close family member	63
6	Personal injury or illness	53
7	Marriage	50
8	Fired from work	47
9	Marital reconciliation	45
10	Retirement	45
11	Change in health of family member	44
12	Pregnancy	40
13	Sex difficulties	39
14	Gain of new family member	39
15	Business readjustment	39
16	Change in financial state	38
17	Death of close friend	37
18	Change to different line of work	36
19	Change in number of arguments with spouse	35
20	Expensive mortgage or loan	31
21	Foreclosure of mortgage or loan	30
22	Change in responsibilities at work	29
23	Son or daughter leaving home	29
24	Trouble with in-laws	29
25	Outstanding personal achievement	28
26	Wife begins or stops working	26
27	Begin or end school	26
28	Change in living conditions	25
29	Revision of personal habits	24
30	Trouble with boss	23
31	Change in work hours or conditions	20
32	Change in residence	20
33	Change in schools	20
34	Change in recreation	19
35	Change in church activities	19
36	Change in social activities	18
37	Inexpensive mortgage or loan	17
38	Change in sleeping habits	16
39	Change in number of family get-togethers	15
40	Change in eating habits	15
41	Vacation	13
42	Christmas	12
43	Minor violations of the law	11

Source: Adapted from Holmes, T. H., & Rahe, R. H. (1967). The social readjustment rating scale. *Journal of Psychosomatic Research, 11,* 213–18.

Box 13-3
Diagnosing Depression—*DSM-II* versus *DSM-III*

For three years, Christine had been miserable. Since leaving home in Ohio and coming to New York, she had been suffering from periods of listlessness. Employed as a secretary in an advertising agency, she was barely able to go to the office in the morning. In the evening she would come straight home, watch TV, and fall asleep by eight P.M. She hardly knew anyone outside her office and had no interest in meeting friends. When she brooded about her life, which was often, she usually cried. She sometimes wished she were dead.

At last she went to see a therapist at the outpatient clinic of a nearby hospital. It seemed clear to him after the first interview that Christine's depression had been triggered by moving away from home. He therefore entered beside her name in the hospital case record the notation "300.4 Depressive Neurosis." The diagnosis was based on the then current edition of the *Diagnostic and Statistical Manual of Mental Disorders,* referred to as *DSM-II,* which defines it

300.4 Depressive neurosis. This disorder is manifested by an excessive reaction of depression due to an internal conflict or to an identifiable event such as the loss of a love object or cherished possession. It is to be distinguished from *Involutional melancholia* (q.v.) and *Manic-depressive* illness (q.v.). *Reactive depressions* or *Depressive reactions* are to be classified here.

In the manual revision, Christine's problem comes under "301.11 Intermittent Depressive Disorder," which contains two full pages of detail and illustrates the range of information covered in *DSM-III* for every kind of disorder. For "Intermittent Depressive Disorder," the manual describes its essential features ("periods of depressed mood"), occasionally associated features ("crying, a pessimistic attitude, brooding"), type of impairment or complications that can occur ("hospitalization is rarely required"), age at onset and course ("chronic, and usually begins early in adult life"), predisposing factors ("chronic medical disorder, chronic life stresses, or another psychiatric disorder"), and prevalence, sex ratio, and familial pattern

("common among outpatients, . . . probably more common in females, . . . familial pattern not known").

Two final sections are especially important in establishing the reliability of diagnosis. One is called "differential diagnosis" and spells out how intermittent depressive disorder can be differentiated from other, similar conditions ("This disorder is distinguished from normal fluctuations of mood by the greater frequency and severity"). The other provides "operational criteria," or specific symptoms that must be present before the diagnosis can be made, including: "sleep difficulty or sleeping too much, low energy or chronic tiredness, loss of interest or pleasure in usual activities, recurrent thoughts of death or suicide."

According to the task force that revised the manual, *DSM-III's* more complete guidelines and greater specificity will enhance its reliability.

Source: Adapted from Goleman, D. (1978). Who's mentally ill? *Psychology Today, 11*(8), pp. 34–41.

makes no sense to assume that people who practiced homosexuality in 1979 were suffering from a mental disorder but were not in 1980. (This objection has captured little support among psychologists.) Second, critics have been troubled by the addition of some disorders, especially such developmental disorders as *specific reading disorder* and *specific shyness disorder* (Garmezy, 1978); they are concerned that children with such problems will be labeled psychiatric cases. Characterizing the behavior of an individual as a psychiatric disorder may stigmatize him or her. Third, critics have regretted that the *DSM-III* continued to employ an implicit disease model of psychological disorder in its main classification scheme (Axis I), arguing that it neglects social and interpersonal factors. McLemore and Benjamin (1979) suggest that in actual practice, clinicians base diagnoses of psychological disorders more on problems in interpersonal relations than on the medical criteria emphasized in the *DSM-III*. Finally, the *DSM-III* has been criticized for failing to classify mental disorders in terms of a consistent set of overriding principles. Whether these criticisms will be leveled at the *DMS-III-R* remains to be seen.

In addition to supplying a system of classification organizing disorders in categories, the *DSM-III-R* supplies a basis for determining whether an individual has a disorder; indeed, the primary purpose of the manual is to guide psychiatric diagnosis. We shall evaluate the ability of psychiatrists and psychologists to make reliable and valid diagnoses, but first we examine the primary disorders outlined in the *DSM-III-R*.

A SURVEY OF PSYCHOLOGICAL DISORDERS

As we begin an examination of the psychological disorders outlined in the *DSM-III-R*, a caution is appropriate. Medical students often are surprised to discover in themselves symptoms of the various disorders they are studying. When they review neurological diseases, they become aware of feelings of faintness, difficulties in sleeping, and memory blanks. As they progress to gastrointestinal disorders, their bowels start to behave in suspicious ways, and so on. Similarly, descriptions of symptoms of various mental disorders often seem uncomfortably familiar to beginning students of psychology. And this is all quite understandable; abnormal behaviors often represent extremes of normal behaviors.

The Prevalence of Psychological Disorders

Epidemiology is the study of the prevalence of disorders (number of cases in a population) and the incidence (number of new cases) of disorders. Such figures often are broken down by age, sex, social class, geographic area, and other demographic variables. The prevalence of many psychological disorders is difficult to determine because there are no absolute criteria for them and because many (if not most) cases go unreported. Consequently, epidemiological studies often provide vastly different estimates. A notable example of an epidemiological study is the ongoing study by Robins et al. (1984) funded by a $15 million grant that has underwritten 17,000 door-to-door interviews. Selected preliminary findings from this study are displayed in Figure 13-3.

DISORDERS USUALLY FIRST EVIDENT IN INFANCY, CHILDHOOD, OR ADOLESCENCE

The disorders in this category typically originate in the early years of life, but in some cases appear in adulthood for the first time. Disorders usually first evident in infancy, childhood, or adolescence can be divided into eleven types:

1. *mental retardation*
2. *pervasive disorders*
3. *specific disorders*
4. *disruptive disorders*
5. *anxiety disorders*

6. *eating disorder*
7. *gender identity disorders*
8. *tic disorders*
9. *elimination disorders*
10. *speech disorders*
11. *other disorders*

We discuss three disorders from this category: two eating disorders — anorexia nervosa and bulimia nervosa — and the "pervasive developmental disorder" autism.

Anorexia Nervosa and Bulimia Nervosa

People with **anorexia nervosa** are abnormally concerned about their weight and body image. They fear getting fat and take extreme measures to

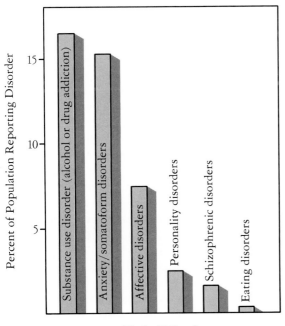

FIGURE 13-3
The Percent of the Population Reporting Six Psychological Disorders Alcohol and drug addiction are the most frequently reported disorders. Note that most disorders are reported by fewer than one percent of the population. *Source:* Robins, L. N., Helzer, J. E., Weissman, M. M., Orvaschel, H., Gruenberg, E., Burke, J. D., & Regier, D. A. (1984). Lifetime prevalence of specific psychiatric disorders in three sites. *Archives of General Psychiatry, 41,* 949 – 58.

lose weight — dieting, exercising, vomiting, and using laxatives. They regularly lose up to 25% of their body weight, and often much more. Anorexia nervosa occurs mainly in females, afflicting as many as one in 250 between the ages of 12 and 18. The loss in body weight is often accompanied by the cessation of menstruation (amenorrhea). People suffering from this disorder say that they feel fat when their weight is normal or even when their body is emaciated (Bruch, 1980). They usually come to the attention of physicians when their weight loss becomes so extreme that they become ill (see Case 13-1).

Bulimia nervosa is an eating disorder that, unlike anorexia, involves binges of excessive eating, usually followed by attempts to purge the body of the food through vomiting or taking laxatives. Like people with anorexia, people with bulimia have a morbid fear of getting fat; unlike people with anorexia, they fluctuate between weight gain and weight loss (Schlesier-Stropp, 1984). When people with bulimia go on eating binges, they may consume extremely high quantities of food. They generally eat sweet foods, like ice cream, with a high caloric content and a texture that facilitates rapid consumption. They typically wolf down food without chewing it properly and, once they start, appear unable to stop until forced to do so by abdominal pain. Bulimic people usually are quite secretive about their eating, and feel very depressed and self-critical following an eating binge. Bulimia is more difficult to detect than anorexia because bulimia does not involve a consistent loss of weight and because the eating habits of bulimic people may appear normal in public (Fairburn & Cooper, 1982). As a result, the prevalence of bulimia is not known, although some experts have suggested it is quite common among females (Pyle et al., 1981).

What Causes Anorexia Nervosa? Because anorexic people come to the attention of clinicians more frequently than those with bulimia, anorexia nervosa has received more attention from researchers. Several theories have been advanced (Hsu, 1983). First, there is evidence that supports a genetic basis to the disorder. For example, studies have found a 50% **concordance rate** for identical twins (see Askevold & Heiberg,

CASE 13-1
ANOREXIA NERVOSA

Frieda had always been a shy, sensitive girl who gave little cause for concern at home or in school. She was bright and did well academically, although she had few friends. In early adolescence, she had been somewhat overweight and had been teased by her family that she would never get a boyfriend unless she lost some weight. She reacted to this teasing by withdrawing and becoming very touchy. Her parents had to be careful about what they said. If offended, Frieda would throw a tan-

trum and march off to her room — hardly the behavior they expected from their bright and sensitive 15-year-old.

Frieda began dieting. Initially her family was pleased, but gradually her parents sensed that all was not well. Mealtimes became battle times. Frieda hardly ate at all. Under pressure, she would take her meals to her room and later, having said that she had eaten everything, her mother would find food hidden away untouched. When her mother caught her deliber-

ately inducing vomiting after a meal, she insisted they go to the family physician. He found that Frieda had stopped menstruating a few months earlier. Not fooled by the loose, floppy clothes that Frieda was wearing, he insisted on carrying out a full physical examination. Her emaciated body told him as much as he needed to know, and he arranged for Frieda's immediate hospitalization.

Source: From Rosenhan, D. L., & Seligman, M. E. (1984). *Abnormal psychology* (p. 526). New York: W. W. Norton.

1979). (A 50% concordance rate means half the twins of people with anorexia also have anorexia; put another way, the probability is 0.5 that the twin of a person with anorexia will also have anorexia.) Unfortunately, however, there are no studies that have investigated the concordance rate for fraternal twins or for twins reared apart.

Investigators searching for a biological basis of anorexia have tended to focus on dysfunctions of the hypothalamus (Russell, 1977). It is well established that the hypothalamus plays a significant role in the regulation of eating and menstruation (see Chapter 7). Although there is evidence that dysfunctions of the hypothalamus accompany anorexia nervosa, it is unclear whether they are a cause, correlate, or effect (Hsu, 1983).

In addition to biological theories, several psychological theories of anorexia have been advanced. Psychoanalytically oriented theorists have suggested that anorexia reflects an attempt on the part of adolescents to separate themselves from their parents and to establish an identity of

their own (Bemis, 1978). Such theorists also suggest that the parents of people with anorexia are domineering, and that anorexic people attempt to exert individuality and to achieve independence from their parents by assuming control over what is most concretely themselves — their bodies. In this view, thinness and starvation are signs of self-control and independence.

More developmentally oriented psychologists have attributed anorexia to a fear of growing up, or to a phobia of adolescence and all the responsibilities it entails (Crisp, 1977). Associated with this view is the idea that anorexic females are motivated to avoid sexual maturity. In support of the view that the purpose of anorexic eating is to delay puberty, researchers have found that individuals must obtain a certain level of body fat before they can achieve puberty and that anorexic people will eat as long as they do not gain weight. However, the developmental approach does not explain why some individuals become anorexic after they have reached puberty.

Other psychologists have searched for the roots of anorexia in the family. Although early studies failed to find a typical *anorexic mother* or *anorexic father,* later studies reported abnormalities in the families of anorexics (see Bruch, 1977). Unfortunately, however, the family portraits painted by different investigators differ significantly from one another. Although it appears there is more pathology than usual in the families of anorexic people, no distinguishing pattern has been found and we do not know whether family pathology is a cause or effect of anorexia.

Finally, some investigators have emphasized the impact of social norms, values, and roles. They have, for example, pointed out a consistent tendency for ideal models of female beauty to emphasize increasing degrees of thinness during the past several decades. Garner et al. (1980) found that *Playboy* centerfolds and winners of Miss America contests are considerably below the average weight and have become significantly more so over the past two decades (from 91% of the average in 1959 to 83% in 1978 for Playboy Playmates). There is considerable cultural pressure on women to be thin. This pressure is particularly intense on women dancers (for example, ballerinas), models, and athletes; in fact, the incidence of anorexia is much higher among these women than among others (Garner & Garfinkel, 1980). Even more direct support for the idea that tendencies toward anorexia are reinforced by the culture was reported by Branch and Eurman (1980), who found that the friends and relatives of people with anorexia admired their slimness and self-control.

In conclusion, investigators have advanced several theories of anorexia nervosa, which is not unusual in the field of abnormal psychology. How do we decide which theory to accept? Although some theories seem more plausible and are supported by more evidence than others, it has become increasingly evident that many, if not most, psychological disorders are caused by several interacting factors. In the words of one expert in the area, "The very idea of 'cause' has become meaningless, other than as a convenient designation for the point in the chain of event sequences at which intervention is most practicable" (Kendell, 1975, p. 64). Concerning anorexia nervosa, the conclusion reached by Hsu (1983) seems most appropriate: "While it is possible that anorexia nervosa has a single discrete cause, it is equally possible that complex chains of events interact to precipitate the illness" (p. 235).

Autistic Disorder

In 1943 psychiatrist Leo Kanner studied eleven withdrawn children who appeared to shut other people out of their world almost from the day they were born. These children were unresponsive to other people; indeed, the children often seemed oblivious to their presence — a phenomenon called **autistic aloneness** — and showed a clear preference for nonsocial objects. The children either did not talk or they repeated phrases, words, and noises in parrot-like fashion. The children became upset when the objects in their world, typically arranged in a special order, were moved or changed, and they displayed an extraordinary rote memory, especially as it related to the arrangement of objects. In addition, these children regularly engaged in such self-stimulating repetitive behaviors as hand flapping and rocking and such self-destructive behaviors as head banging and self-biting — often for hours on end.

Kanner believed the disorder from which these children suffered, now called **autistic disorder** (from the Greek word for self, or self-absorption), was present at birth or shortly thereafter, and he believed autistic children were of average or above-average intelligence. Although Kanner's description of autism was based on a very small sample, it has stood up well over the years. However, subsequent research has established that children may acquire the disorder at any time during the first two and one-half years of their lives and that most autistic children are below average in intelligence (even though they may possess exceptionally good rote memories). The differences between infantile autism and another debilitating disorder, childhood schizophrenia, are outlined in Table 13-4.

Fortunately, the incidence of autism is low; Kessler (1966) estimates it at fewer than one percent of people with psychiatric disorders. However, the prognosis for autism is poor. Lotter (1978) reviewed eight follow-up studies of infantile autism, reporting that from 61 – 74% of the

TABLE 13-4
Autistic Disorder and Childhood Schizophrenia — A Comparison

Symptom	Autistic Disorder	Childhood Schizophrenia
Onset	Gradually apparent, but may have been present from birth	Gradual, between age two to eleven, after period of normal development
Social and Interpersonal	Failure to show anticipatory postural movements; insistence on sameness; seems to be off in own world, even when around others	Decreased interest in external world; withdrawal; loss of contact; impaired relations with others
Intellectual and Cognitive	High spatial ability; good memory; low IQ but seems to have intellectual potential	Thought disturbance; perceptual problems; distorted time and space orientation; below-average IQ
Language	Disturbances in speech; mutism or speech is not used for communication; very literal; delayed echolalia; pronoun reversal; *I* and *yes* absent until age six	Disturbances in speech; mutism or speech is not used for communication; bizarre associations
Affect	Inaccessible and emotionally unresponsive to people	Defect in emotional responsiveness and rapport; decreased, distorted, and/or inappropriate affect
Motor	Head banging and body rocking; remarkable agility and dexterity; preoccupation with mechanical objects; spinning, repetitive movements	Bizarre body movements; repetitive and stereotyped motions; motor awkwardness; distortion in mobility
Physical and Developmental Patterns	Peculiar eating habits and food preferences; normal EEG	Unevenness of somatic growth; disturbances of normal rhythmic patterns; abnormal EEG
Family	High intelligence and educational and occupational levels; low divorce rate and incidence of mental illness	High incidence of mental illness

Sources: Adapted from Rimland, B. (1964). *Infantile autism* (pp. 67–76). New York: Appleton-Century-Crofts. Knopf, I. J. (1979). *Childhood psychopathology: A developmental approach* (p. 246). Englewood Cliffs, NJ: Prentice-Hall.

children had not recovered by adulthood and that half the subjects were in institutions. The prognosis appears best for autistic children who develop useful speech by age five (Kanner, Rodriquez, & Alexander, 1972).

What Causes Autistic Disorders? Because of the early onset of most cases of autism, theories have tended to focus on abnormalities of the brain caused either by heredity or by brain damage during pregnancy and childbirth. A study of twins found a concordance rate of 36% for identical twins compared to 0.0% for fraternal twins (Fol-

stein & Rutter, 1978). The concordance rate jumped to 86% for identical twins, compared to 10% for fraternal twins, when the degree of cognitive impairment or speech deficiency was assessed instead of the autistic syndrome as a whole. Folstein and Rutter suggest that an inherited cognitive deficiency especially related to language may lie at the core of autism and that the other symptoms may be offshoots of this deficiency.

There is evidence of more complications during pregnancy and childbirth among autistic than nonautistic children (Piggott, 1979); however, these complications do not appear sufficiently severe to account for the disorder. And although there is some evidence that autistic children suffer from abnormalities of the brain, no one as yet has discovered exactly what they are (Delong, 1978).

In addition to biological theories of autism, some psychological theories have been advanced, the best known of which is that of psychoanalyst Bruno Bettelheim. Bettelheim attributes autism to a rejecting attitude on the part of the parents that causes the children to withdraw from the world; however, research has not supported Bettelheim's position (Cantwell, Baker, & Rutter, 1978).

ORGANIC MENTAL DISORDERS

As exemplified by GPI, disorders with physical or organic causes may seriously disrupt people's psychological functioning. Disorders that originate from destruction of brain tissue or from chemical imbalances in the brain are classified as **organic mental disorders** in the *DSM-III-R,* and include disorders caused by:

1. old age
2. alcohol
3. sedatives
4. opiates
5. cocaine
6. amphetamines
7. other drugs and physical factors

Although the symptoms of organic brain disorders are variable, they usually include disorientation, impaired memory, impairment of such intellectual functions as comprehension and logic, impaired judgment, and inappropriate affect.

As we shall see, most of these symptoms also are characteristic of such other severe psychological disorders as schizophrenia. The diagnosis of organic brain syndrome depends on the ability of a practitioner to establish that an organic cause underlies the symptoms.

PSYCHOACTIVE SUBSTANCE-USE DISORDERS

Most people have had experience with such drugs as caffeine, nicotine, and alcohol; many also have taken such prescription drugs as Valium, Dexedrine, and Seconal; some also have tried such illegal drugs as marijuana, LSD, and heroin. When people develop a dependence on drugs and when their lives are seriously disrupted by such use, they are said to have a **substance-use disorder.** Table 13-5 lists the most commonly abused drugs and their effects; Figure 13-4 (page 678) indicates the prevalence of drug use among high school students. Topping the list is alcohol.

Alcohol Abuse and Alcohol Dependence

Psychologists distinguishes between **alcohol abuse** and **alcohol dependence.** To receive a diagnosis of alcohol abuse, an individual must abuse alcohol for at least one month (or repeatedly over a longer period) and either use alcohol on an ongoing basis "despite knowledge of having a persistent or recurrent social, occupational, psychological, or physical problem that is caused or exacerbated by use" or "use alcohol in situations in which use is physically hazardous" (*DMS-III-R,* p. 169).

People diagnosed as alcohol dependent must display at least three of the following symptoms:

1. substance often taken in larger amounts or over a longer period than the person intended
2. persistent desire or one or more unsuccessful efforts to cut down or control substance use
3. a great deal of time spent in activities necessary to get the substance
4. frequent intoxication or withdrawal symptoms when expected to fulfill major role obligations at work, school, or home
5. important social, occupational, or recreational activities given up or reduced because of substance use

TABLE 13-5
Commonly Abused Drugs

Group	Drug	Short-term Effects	Duration of Effects (in hours)	Long-term Effects of Extensive Use	Physiological Withdrawal
Depressants	Narcotics Opium Morphine Heroin Methadone	Depression of the central nervous system, pain relief, sedation, general feelings of disorientation and well-being (euphoria)	3–6	Physiological and psychological dependence, increased tolerance, loss of appetite (and possible malnutrition), constipation, temporary impotence or sterility	Yes; may be severe muscle and joint pain, insomnia, anxiety, perspiration, crying and craving for drug, nausea, weight loss, and muscle spasms
	Barbiturates Phenobarbital Nembutal Seconal	Relaxation, euphoria, impaired alertness, slowed speech, poor coordination, anesthesia	1–16	Physiological and psychological dependence, increased tolerance, weight loss, irritability	Yes; with tremors, anxiety, insomnia, muscle weakness, and possible convulsions
	Alcohol	Same as for barbiturates		Same as for barbituates, plus malnutrition, liver damage, and possible brain damage	Yes; delirium tremens (DTs)
	Minor tranquilizers Meprobamate (Miltown, Equanil) Diazepam (Valium) Chlordiazepoxide (Librium)	Anxiety reduction, sedation in large quantities, relaxation	4–8	Possible psychological dependence, with a few reported instances of physical dependence after prolonged excessive use	Rare
	Cannabis Marijuana Hashish	Effects depend somewhat on person's expectancies and context, but generally include relaxation, euphoria, distorted time perception, decreased efficiency, increased sensory sensitivity, disorientation.	2–4	Initially decreased tolerance (takes less to "get high") but later increased tolerance; possible psychological dependence and impairment of immunological system and testosterone production	No

Source: Adapted from Mahoney, M. J. (1980). *Abnormal psychology: Perspectives on human variance* (pp. 379–80). San Francisco, CA: Harper & Row.

Group	Drug	Short-term Effects	Duration of Effects (in hours)	Long-term Effects of Extensive Use	Physiological Withdrawal
Depressants (*continued*)	Nicotine	Effects depend on person's expectancy, but generally include slowing of digestion, loss of appetite, increase in blood pressure, and arousal of the central nervous system simultaneous with relaxation of the skeletal muscles	1–2	Physiological and psychological dependence, increased tolerance, and much higher likelihood of lung cancer, heart disease, emphysema, and (in women) childbirth abnormalities	Yes
Stimulants	Cocaine Amphetamines Benzedrine Dexedrine Methedrine	Stimulation of the central nervous system, loss of fatigue, alertness, feelings of increased energy, overdose can produce hallucinations and delusions	2–4	Possible psychological dependence and increased tolerance, irritability, weight loss, occasional psychotic episodes with hallucinations and delusions	Yes
	Caffeine	Same as above except that overdose is more likely to cause nausea and tremors		Possible psychological dependence and increased tolerance	Yes
	Nicotine (see above)	(see above)		(see above)	
Hallucinogens	Mescaline LSD Psilocybin	Perceptual distortions with bizarre imagery, loss of reality contact, lack of coordination, possible panic	1–8	Research to date has failed to indicate any physical or psychological harm attributable to LSD use	No

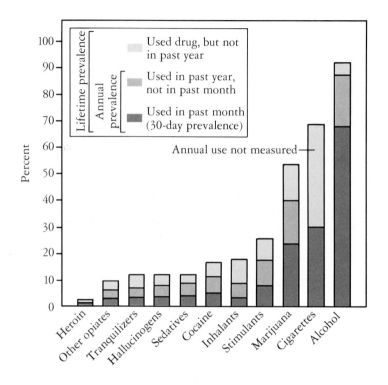

FIGURE 13-4

Lifetime, Annual, and Monthly Use of Eleven Drug Types: Class of '85   *Source:* Adapted from Drug use among American high school students, college students, and other young adults. National trends through 1985.   *U.S. Department of Health and Human Services,* Washington, D.C.: National Institute on Drug Abuse.   DHHS Publication No. ADM 86-1450.

6. continued substance use despite knowledge of having a persistent or recurrent social, psychological, or physical problem that is caused or exacerbated by the use of the substance

7. marked tolerance: need for markedly increased amounts of the substance (at least a 50% increase) to achieve intoxication or desired effect, or markedly diminished effect with continued use of the same amount

8. characteristic withdrawal symptoms

9. substance often taken to relieve or avoid withdrawal symptoms
    (*DSM-III-R,* 1987, pp. 167–168)

Alcohol abuse and dependence are prevalent in the Western world; approximately ten percent of adult American males and two to four percent of adult American females are problem drinkers (Miller, 1979). A recent Gallup poll indicated one-third of all American families have experienced alcohol-related problems (Saxe et al., 1983) and the American Hospital Association estimates that almost half of all occupied beds in American hospitals are filled by people with alcohol-related problems. Alcohol is involved in as many as 66% of all single-vehicle fatalities (Niven, 1979), 50% of all suicides (Coleman, Butcher, & Carson, 1984), and 40% of all family-court litigation.

Although alcohol is a depressant, it also may have an energizing effect. The energizing effect, which usually takes place during the first couple of drinks, appears to occur because the first components of the central nervous system to be depressed are inhibitory centers. Suppressing inhibitions gives people a lift. Before long, however—especially with increased consumption—alcohol exerts a depressive effect, slowing down reaction time, disrupting motor coordination, and interfering with speech. In the final stages of drunkenness, individuals fall asleep or pass out; extreme intoxication may result in death from alcohol poisoning.

Because some people metabolize alcohol more quickly than others, the degree of drunkenness people experience is only moderately correlated with the number of drinks they consume. Drunkenness is more highly correlated with the level of alcohol in the blood, and the level of alcohol in the blood is affected by body weight, amount of food in the stomach, and other physiological factors. A blood alcohol level of from 0.08 to 0.10% (induced in a person weighing 100 pounds by two to three drinks and in a person weighing 200 pounds by four to five drinks consumed in an hour and one-half) is the legal level set for intoxication by the statutes of most English-speaking nations.

What Causes Alcoholism?

Genetic Factors According to one expert (Goodwin, 1979), "Every family study of alcoholism, irrespective of country of origin, has shown much higher rates of alcoholism among the relatives of alcoholics than in the general population." This finding is consistent both with the assumption that people inherit a disposition for alcoholism and the assumption that people become alcoholic because they grow up in alcoholic environments. Studies of twins help sort out the relative effects of heredity and environment. The concordance rate for alcoholism in identical twins is approximately 50–60%; the concordance rate for fraternal twins is approximately 20–30%, half as high (Kaij, 1960). In a recent study, Goodwin (1979) compared the concordance rate for alcoholism in males adopted at an early age to the rate for alcoholism in their biological parents. The results revealed that 18% of the males whose biological parents were alcoholic had become alcoholic by their late twenties, compared to 5% of the males whose parents were not alcoholic. These relationships did not hold for females. Despite these findings, decades of research have failed to find any genetically mediated mechanism or any physical differences between alcoholics and nonalcoholics that would explain the origin of the disorder.

Learning Drinking alcohol induces a pleasurable sensation in most people that reinforces drinking behaviors. It is commonly believed that one of the functions drinking serves is to reduce anxiety and tension. Several studies have induced stress in subjects and then observed whether the stress leads to increased consumption of alcoholic beverages; the findings from these studies are mixed. For example, Higgins and Marlatt (1973) found that the threat of electric shock did not lead to an increase in alcohol consumption; however, Tucker, Vuchinich, Sobell, and Maisto (1980) found that the stress associated with solving a difficult problem led to a notable increase in drinking. A study by Nathan and O'Brien (1971) found that although alcohol decreases anxiety during the first 12 to 24 hours of drinking, it induces an increase in tension and anxiety following that. Learning theory leads us to expect the aversive effects of heavy drinking (such as hangovers) to serve as punishment and cause a decrease in drinking behavior, yet hangovers do not appear to be the deterrent we might expect, especially in people who have developed a high tolerance for alcohol. One reason might be that the immediate effect of alcohol appears to be rewarding, with the punishment quite removed in time.

The rewards and punishments associated with drinking are complex. In addition to the positive and negative physical effects of alcohol consumption, there are a variety of positive and negative social rewards and punishments. Although moderate drinking is often approved of, the social costs of drunkenness and alcoholism seem to far outweigh the rewards.

Social Learning Social learning and sociologically oriented theorists emphasize modeling and social roles. Studies have found that people are more likely to drink and to consume more alcohol when in the presence of models who drink than when in the presence of nondrinking models (Tomaszewski et al., 1980). Such findings are consistent with the observation that drinking tends to run in families. Interestingly, there is some evidence that the behavior of parents and peers has a greater effect on females than on males (Margulies, Kessler, & Kandel, 1977). The social learning approach does not account, however, for solitary drinking.

Psychodynamic Factors Psychoanalysts view drinking as a means of obtaining oral gratification and see heavy drinkers as people fixated at the oral-dependent stage of development.   Consistent with Freud's theory, there is some evidence that alcoholics are more dependent than the average person and engage in many more *oral* behaviors, such as smoking (Maletzky & Klotter, 1974).   However, psychoanalytic theory leads us to expect that alcoholics develop oral characters before they become alcoholic; yet the evidence in support of this prediction is not strong (Saxe et al., 1983).

SCHIZOPHRENIA

Schizophrenia is probably the best known of the serious psychological disorders.   Although the name implies that schizophrenia is one disorder, it is possible that schizophrenia is actually a group of disorders similar in certain respects, but different in others.   Schizophrenic disorders are characterized by serious disruptions in normal functioning, a severe deterioration in personality, and a loss of contact with reality.   Historical records from ancient India (1400 B.C.) indicate that schizophrenia has afflicted people for centuries. In 1911 Swiss psychiatrist Eugen Bleuler published *Dementia Praecox or the Group of Schizophrenias,* in which he introduced the term schizophrenia, referred to a splitting (from the Greek *schizein*) of various functions of the mind (from the Greek *phren*).   However, this choice of name is somewhat unfortunate: people tend to confuse it with the splitting of personality into two or more identities characteristic of multiple personality, a dissociative disorder we describe later in the chapter.

Approximately one-fourth of the people initially admitted to mental hospitals and from 40–50% of long-term patients have been diagnosed as schizophrenic (Kramer, 1977).   Estimates of the prevalance of this disorder suggest that up to one person in every one hundred will suffer from it in his or her life (Rimm & Somerville, 1977). Schizophrenic disorder is most prevalent among people from 25–35 years of age.

The Symptoms of Schizophrenia

The symptoms displayed by people with **schizophrenia** are quite variable; however, in most cases schizophrenic disorders involve abnormalities in attention, thinking, perception, emotional reactions, motor behavior, and social relations.

Abnormalities in Attention   Countless stimuli bombard our senses every waking minute of the day; to function in the world, we must block out vast amounts of information and focus on selected aspects of the environment.   Imagine what it would be like if you were unable to attend to the things that interest you.   You would be overwhelmed by unintegrated sensations and ideas, unable to concentrate, and unable to maintain a coherent line of thought.   This is exactly what appears to happen to some people with schizophrenia.

Abnormalities in Thought and Language The inability to maintain a focus of attention is reflected in the inability to maintain a focus of thought that, in turn, is reflected in the inability to maintain a focus in language.   Consider the following sample of schizophrenic speech.

> Speeds up your metabolism.   Makes your life shorter.   Makes your heart bong.   Tranquilizes you if you've got the metabolism I have.   I have distemper just like cats do, 'cause that's what we all are, felines.   Siamese cat balls.   They stand out.   I had a cat, a Manx, still around somewhere. His name is GI Joe: he's black and white.   I had a little goldfish too like a clown.   Happy Halloween down.   (Chaika, 1982, pp. 34–35)

There is neither coherence nor integration to the ideas expressed.   One thought seems to key a loosely related association that keys another, and so on, with no common theme.   The language of people with schizophrenia is often rambling and disjointed; ideas appear to be split off from overriding concepts or trains of thought.   In some cases, the sound of one word appears to key an association with a similar-sounding word: "The King of Spain feels no pain in the drain of the crane.   I'm lame, you're tame; with fame, I'll be the same."   This is called a **clang association.** In other cases, people with schizophrenia invent words, called **neologisms,** such as *flump* (combination of *flop* and *grumpy?*) to express bizarre ideas.

However, the thinking processes of people with schizophrenia are not always scrambled and disjointed.   For example, people with schizophrenia may experience **delusions:** highly systematic but irrational beliefs about themselves, others, and their worlds. The most common type of delusion involves the belief that some external force, such as the FBI or God, is controlling the individual's thoughts and behavior. People suffering from schizophrenia may also harbor delusions of persecution—for example, that creatures from outer space are plotting to kill them. Or, like the clerk who thought he was the King of Spain, they may experience delusions of grandeur. In a particularly interesting experiment, psychologist Milton Rokeach brought three people together who suffered from the delusion they were Jesus Christ in an attempt to work out the discrepancy (see Box 13-4).

Abnormalities in Perception and Sensation
Closely associated with abnormalities in attention and thought are abnormalities in perception and sensation. Schizophrenic people sometimes are unable to perceive objects in their entirety; they sometimes perceive parts of their bodies as larger, smaller, transparent, inside out, or in positions other than normal. They also may have an exaggerated sensitivity to certain sights, sounds, smells, or tactile sensations. In addition, people with schizophrenia often experience **hallucinations.** When we think of hallucinations, we tend to think of people seeing things. Although people with schizophrenia sometimes have visual hallucinations, they are much less frequent than auditory hallucinations. People with schizophrenia often think they hear people talking about them or they hear voices accusing them or directing them to do certain things. David Berkowitz, the "Son of Sam" killer who claimed he was directed to murder people by his neighbor's dog, Sam, exemplifies this tendency. People with schizophrenia also may experience hallucinations of other senses such as the feeling that animals or microbes are crawling on them or are inside of them (see Figure 13-5).

Abnormalities in Emotion There are two ways in which the affective reactions of people with

Paintings by the cat artist, Louis Wain (1860–1939), who suffered from schizophrenia. Note the increasing bizarreness of the style.

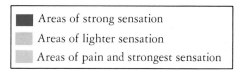

- Areas of strong sensation
- Areas of lighter sensation
- Areas of pain and strongest sensation

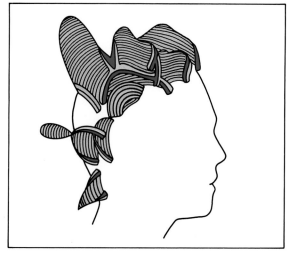

FIGURE 13-5
Drawing by a Schizophrenic Woman Reflecting Her Tactile Hallucinations *Source:* Pfeifer, L. (1970). A subjective report of tactile hallucination in schizophrenia. *Journal of Clinical Psychology, 26,* 57–60.

BOX 13-4   THE THREE CHRISTS OF YPSILANTI

What would happen if three men, each claiming to be God, were brought together? This is precisely what Milton Rokeach, a Michigan State University psychology professor, wanted to find out when he introduced Joseph Cassel, Clyde Benson, and Leon Gabor—all patients of Ypsilanti State Hospital and all diagnosed schizophrenic/paranoid type.

Joseph Cassel was 58 at the time and had been hospitalized for nearly 20 years. There was no history of mental illness in Joseph's family. Joseph described his mother as both a good woman and mother; he described his father as independent, quick-tempered, and cruel to his wife. Neither parent was particularly religious; however, his grandmother, with whom he lived after the death of his mother (Joseph was 16 at the time), was very religious—often appealing to God for personal favors. As a young man, Joseph was a voracious reader and preferred books to an active social life. At age 24 he married. Finding no intellectual equals among his wife and friends, Joseph complained of a lack of companionship, and withdrew into himself and his reading.

Joseph's wife remembers a car accident as the time his problems started. Rather than trying to avoid an accident, Joseph—out of fear of fire—turned off the ignition, hitting another car and injuring everyone except himself. This caused a tremendous strain on Joseph. Shortly after the accident, Joseph quit his job (he said it made him ill) and moved his family to a farm, where he planned to spend his time writing. But Joseph's in-laws put pressure on him to get another job. He became suspicious of them—accusing them of poisoning his food and tobacco. His wife was also the target of his suspicions; he accused her of purposely doing things to avoid having sex with him, of causing his hair to fall out, of being unfaithful, and of making him suffer. Eventually, she had him committed. It was not until ten years after his hospitalization that Joseph began believing he was God.

Clyde Benson had been hospitalized for 17 years. He came from a religious family. As a child he was very close to his mother, was overprotected by her, and was dependent on both his parents. Clyde married at age 24. Eight years later his wife died, leaving him with three daughters to raise. Shortly after his wife's death, Clyde's father, mother, and father-in-law died, and his eldest daughter married and moved away. This was too much for Clyde—he began to drink heavily.

Clyde continued to drink heavily even after he remarried in 1934; he stated that he drank to drown his sorrows. Eventually his drinking led to financial disaster. Clyde left the farm and his wife, and moved into a room in town. His wife divorced him in 1941. Soon after the divorce Clyde was jailed for drunkenness. In jail he became violent, tearing up his clothing and bedding and trying to break the window of his cell. Clyde began ranting, swearing, and claiming to be God and Christ. Following this episode, he was committed to a mental hospital.

Leon Gabor had been hospitalized for only five years. Prior to his hospitalization, Leon lived with his mother—a religious fanatic. Leon's father had divorced Leon's mother soon after Leon was born—on the grounds of cruelty. Leon's mother was described by her priest as having "too much religion, not healthy religion." She was consumed with prayer and reported hearing voices. This preoccupation with religion prevented her from leading a productive life; as a result, Leon was forced at an early age to provide for himself and his mother.

Although Leon expressed an interest in several careers

(medicine, radio operator or repairman, social worker, psychologist) and was successful in the military, his work habits were poor at college and on the job. Leon quit college and, due to absenteeism, was unable to hold a job. He complained of chronic exhaustion and thoracic spine pain that prevented him from working. Ultimately Leon was committed to a psychiatric hospital, where he began to hear God speaking to him. According to Leon, God told him that he, Leon, was Jesus. He was released after two months; however, a short time later he became violent, destroying all his mother's religious icons and demanding that she worship him. He has been hospitalized since.

When the three Christs met, Joseph Cassel was the first to introduce himself.

"My name is Joseph Cassel."
—Joseph, is there anything else you want to tell us?—
"Yes, I'm God."
(Clyde Benson introduces himself next.)
"My name is Clyde Benson. That is my name straight."
—Do you have any other names?—
"Well, I have other names, but that's my vital side and I made God five and Jesus six."
—Does that mean you're God?—
"I made God, yes. I made it 70 years old a year ago. Hell! I passed 70 years old."

(Leon was the last to introduce himself.)
"Sir," Leon began, "it so happens that my birth certificate says that I am Dr. Domino Dominorum et Rex Rexarum, Simplis Christainus Pueris Mentalis Doktor. It also states on my birth certificate that I am the reincarnation of Jesus Christ of Nazareth, and I also salute the manliness in Jesus Christ also, because the vine is Jesus and the rock is Christ, pertaining to the penis and testicles; and it so happens that I was railroaded into this place because of prejudice and jealousy and duping that started before I was born, and that is the main issue why I am here. I want to be myself. I do not consent to their misuse of the frequency of my life."
(Joseph could not accept Leon's claim to be Christ.)
"He says he is the reincarnation of Jesus Christ . . . I can't get it. I know who I am. I'm God, Christ, the Holy Ghost, and if I wasn't, gosh, I wouldn't lay claim to anything of the sort. I'm Christ. I don't want to say I'm Christ, God, the Holy Ghost, Spirit. I know this is an insane house and you have to be very careful."

The first meeting of these three Ypsilanti State Hospital patients involved a great deal of conflict regarding their delusional identities. Toward the end of the discussion, the three men—each of whom reported he had been resurrected—was asked:
—How many Christs have been resurrected?—

"Only one. Just myself," Joseph said.
"I'm one—not you," said Clyde. "There's something wrong with you."
"I am the reincarnation of Jesus Christ of Nazareth," Leon said, "My birth certificate says so; my habeas corpus says so."

These meetings were held regularly for just over two years. During this time there were many outbursts of emotion, expressed through name calling and, at times, physical attacks. Each patient, in turn, assumed responsibility for chairing the sessions—directing conversation, reading and discussing correspondence. Over time, the degree of conflict diminished; when disagreement arose, the men overlooked it or responded with such statements as "That's your belief, sir." However, the exercise did not recover the sanity of these men. Instead, Joseph and Clyde engaged in denial—believing the others not to be Christ because they did not exist. For example, Clyde believed the other two men were corpses with machines inside them. Leon, however, did not deny the existence of the others; indeed, he did not deny the others were Christ. He simply asserted the others were different types of Christ.

Source: Adapted from Rokeach, M. (1964). *The three christs of ypsilanti* (pp. 4–6, and 13). New York: Vintage Books.

schizophrenia deviate from normal—they are flat and they are inappropriate. Many people with schizophrenia become withdrawn, apathetic, and unresponsive; they tend to maintain a deadpan facial expression and appear not to experience the types of emotions that color the lives of the average person. Other schizophrenic people display highly inappropriate emotional reactions—giggling and laughing for no apparent reason, smiling slyly when told of a tragedy, or becoming agitated and violent. As indicated by the following testimonial, the inappropriate affective reactions of people with schizophrenia may stem from the bizarre thoughts they harbor.

> Half the time I am talking about one thing and thinking about half a dozen other things at the same time. It must look queer to people when I laugh about something that has got nothing to do with what I am talking about, but they don't know what's going on inside and how much of it is running around in my head. You see I might be talking about something quite serious to you and other things come in to my head at the same time that are funny and this makes me laugh. If I could only concentrate on one thing at the one time I wouldn't look half so silly. (McGhie & Chapman, 1961, p. 104)

Abnormalities in Motor Behavior As the following illustrations show, people with schizophrenia assume unusual postures, which they sometimes maintain for hours, or even days. They frequently show little interest in grooming or self-presentation and may engage in such highly repetitive, ritual behaviors as saluting a picture or weaving an imaginary sweater.

Abnormalities in Social Relations Schizophrenic people appear to be in a world of their own. In minor cases they live asocial and secluded lives; in more serious cases, they seem oblivious to the presence of others and completely unresponsive to social overtures.

Recounting the symptoms of schizophrenia is informative, but somewhat misleading because people afflicted with the disorder usually display only some of the symptoms, and they do so in many different combinations. Five of the most common combinations are outlined in Table 13-6; however, even these patterns are overgeneralized. The best way to gain a sense of the symptoms of schizophrenia is to examine the case histories that accompany this discussion.

In the "waxy flexibility" of catatonic schizophrenia, bizarre postures are often maintained for long periods of time. If the posture of people in this state is changed, they often maintain the changed posture—much like a mannequin.

The Course of Schizophrenia

Whatever the type, schizophrenia rarely appears full-blown; instead, it usually develops in three phases. In the first phase, the **prodromal phase,** the person developing schizophrenia becomes increasingly withdrawn, eccentric, emotionally flat, bizarre, and ineffective. This phase may extend anywhere from a few weeks to several years. The next phase, the **active phase,** is usually brought on by some type of stress. In this phase, the individual displays the classic symptoms of schizophrenia. Following the active phase, people with schizophrenia usually enter a **residual phase** in which they behave in much the same way they did in the prodromal phase.

TABLE 13-6
Five Subtypes of Schizophrenia

Subtype	Symptoms
Disorganized Schizophrenia (hebephrenic)	Most severe disintegration of personality. Common symptoms are frequent incoherent speech and incongruous affect, such as crying or laughing at inappropriate times. Disorganized and fragmentary delusions and hallucinations may be present.
Catatonic Schizophrenia	Characterized by marked psychomotor disturbance, which may involve stupor, rigidity, posturing, or violent motor activity. Sometimes there is a rapid alteration between extremes of excitement and stupor, but often one or the other behavior pattern predominates.
Paranoid Schizophrenia	Characterized by one or more systematic delusions or auditory hallucinations. Associated features include unfocused anxiety, anger, argumentativeness, and violence. Typically there is no incoherence, loosening of associations, flat or inappropriate affect, catatonic behavior, or gross disorganization.
Undifferentiated Schizophrenia	Characterized by hallucinations, delusions, and incoherence without meeting the criteria for the other types of schizophrenia or showing symptoms characteristic of more than one type.
Residual Schizophrenia	Individuals not in active phase of schizophrenia but show such residual symptoms as emotional blunting, social withdrawal, eccentric behavior, illogical thinking and/or loosening of associations.

Although they may experience occasional weak hallucinations and delusions and although they may still be withdrawn, devoid of normal emotional responses, and socially ineffectual, their behavior is significantly less bizarre than it was in the active phase. A long-term study of more than 1,000 schizophrenics indicated that 10% remained permanently in the active phase, 25% regained the capacity to function normally, and 50–65% alternated between the residual and active phases (Bleuler, 1978).

The Process–Reactive Distinction

Some investigators (see Chapman & Chapman, 1973) have distinguished between types of schizophrenia on the basis of the length of time people spend in the prodromal phase. In **process schizophrenia,** behavior typically begins to deteriorate gradually in early adolescence, with the individual becoming increasingly less effective at school, at work, and in social settings. Eventually the individual must be hospitalized. In contrast, **reactive schizophrenia** usually

TABLE 13-7
Signs of Early Recovery from Schizophrenia

1. Sexual–marital status: married, or at least a prior history of stable sexual-social adjustment
2. A family history of affective rather than schizophrenic disorder
3. Presence of an affective response (elation or depression) in the acute stage of the disorder
4. Abrupt onset of the disorder; reactive rather than process schizophrenia
5. Onset later than early childhood
6. Minor or no paranoid trends in the disorder
7. Higher socioeconomic status
8. Adequate pre-disorder vocational adjustment
9. Pre-disorder competence in interpersonal relationships
10. Short length of stay in hospital
11. No history of electroconvulsive shock therapy
12. Tendency to be stimulation-receptive rather than stimulation-avoidant
13. Clear precipitating factors at the onset of disturbance

Source: Adapted from Meyer, R. G., & Salmon, P. (1984). *Abnormal psychology* (p. 205). Boston, MA: Allyn and Bacon.

CASE 13-2
PARANOID SCHIZOPHRENIA

Laura was a 40-year-old married woman. A few weeks prior to her first examination, her husband had noted restlessness and agitation, which he interpreted as being due to some physical disorder.

A physician who was consulted prescribed a tonic. Later Laura started to complain about the neighbors. A woman who lived on the floor beneath them was knocking on the wall to irritate her. According to the husband, this woman had really knocked on the wall a few times; he had heard the noises. However, Laura became more and more concerned about it. She would wake up in the middle of the night under the impression that she was hearing noises from the apartment downstairs. She would become upset and angry at the neighbors. Once she was awake, she could not sleep for the rest of the night. The husband would vainly try to calm her. Later she became more disturbed. She started to feel that the neighbors were now recording everything she said; maybe they had hidden wires in the apartment. She starting to feel "funny" sensations. There were many strange things happening, which she did not know how to explain; people were looking at her in a funny way in the street; in the butcher shop, the butcher had purposely served her last, although she was in the middle of the line. During the next few days she felt that people were planning to harm either her or her husband. In the neighborhood she saw a German woman whom she had not seen for several years. Now the woman had suddenly reappeared, probably to testify that the patient and her husband were involved in some sort of crime.

Laura was distressed and agitated. She felt unjustly accused, because she had committed no crime. Maybe these people were really not after her, but after her husband. In the evening when she looked at television, it became obvious to her that the programs referred to her life. Often the people on the programs were just repeating what she had thought. They were stealing her ideas. She want to go to the police and report them.

Source: Arieti, S. (1974). *Interpretation of schizophrenia* (pp. 165–66). New York: Basic Books.

---

strikes relatively well-adjusted people later in life, in early adulthood. Reactive schizophrenics tend to recover relatively fast; the prognosis for process schizophrenia is poorer. Thirteen factors correlated with early recovery from schizophrenia are listed in Table 13-7.

What Causes Schizophrenia?

There has been more research on schizophrenic disorders than on any other severe psychological disorder. In view of the broad array of symptoms that characterize schizophrenia, it is not surprising that a broad array of theories have been advanced to explain it. Some theories focus on the genetic background of people with schizophrenia and some focus on possible biochemical abnormalities. Others, more psychological in nature, focus on learning and social relations. Still others focus on what they consider to be the basic defect in schizophrenia—defects in attention, perception, thought, and language. Even humanistic psychologists have gotten into the picture, attributing schizophrenia to an inner search

CASE 13-3
CATATONIC SCHIZOPHRENIA

Sally was a 23-year-old Jewish married woman who lived in a small town in the vicinity of New York City. . . . The first time she came, she was accompanied by her parents, who gave the following history: The apparent beginning of the illness occurred a few days after her marriage, when the patient was 22. During the honeymoon the patient had been anxious and disturbed, and had wanted to go back to her parents' home. When she returned to her new apartment, she became increasingly distressed by obsessions. She gradually became slower in her motions and finally lapsed into a catatonic stupor. She had to be dressed, undressed, and spoon fed, and she defecated and urinated in bed. She was unable to move and hardly answered questions; often she answered in monosyllables.

. . . When she was not in a catatonic state, she had the impression that small pieces or corpuscles were falling down on her body or from her body. She preferred not to move, because she was afraid that her movements would cause small pieces to fall. She had to reassure herself constantly that pieces were not falling down, and she had to check herself constantly in an obsessive way. If she moved, even if she made the smallest movement, she had to think about the movement, dividing it into small parts to reassure herself that each part of the movement had not been accompanied by the falling of small bodies. This task was terrific; it kept her in mortal fear of any movement and compelled obsessive thinking from which she could not escape. She used to ask her relatives to help her do the researching for her, to reassure her that no bodies were falling down.

Source: Arieti, S. (1974). *Interpretation of schizophrenia* (pp. 147–48). New York: Basic Books.

for a sense of identity and wholeness. Let us sample some of the most influential theories.

Genetic Factors The chance of any randomly selected individual becoming schizophrenic is about 1 in 100. However, if the individual has a brother or sister who is schizophrenic, the odds increase quite dramatically to about 1 in 10. If, in addition, one of the individual's parents has schizophrenia, the odds jump to about 1 in 5. And if both parents are schizophrenic, the odds escalate to 1 in 2 or 3. Although these statistics are compelling, they do not establish that the disposition to develop a schizophrenic disorder is inherited because the people who become schizophrenic and their relatives come from similar environments (see Box 13-5, page 690). To assess the effect of heredity, an investigator must somehow control for the effect of the environ-

ment. Research on schizophrenia has accomplished this in three ways:

1. by studying children who had schizophrenic mothers and who were brought up in foster homes
2. by comparing the incidence of schizophrenia in the biological and adoptive parents of adopted children with schizophrenia
3. by comparing the concordance rate for schizophrenia in identical and fraternal twins (see Chapter 2)

In 1966 an investigator, Leonard Heston, discovered that newborn children of schizophrenic mothers confined in a state hospital in Oregon had been sent routinely to a particular foundling home between the years 1915 and

CASE 13-4
HEBEPHRENIC SCHIZOPHRENIA

Ann's illness began a week and a half prior to admission. The patient had been going dancing frequently with her sister. About this time she had met a young man, Charles, at the dance hall, and they had danced together. One evening she came home from dancing and told her mother that she was going to give up her husband Henry, marry Charles, go to Brazil with him, and have twenty babies. She was talking very fast and saying many things, several of which were incomprehensible. At the same time she also told her mother that she was seeing the Virgin Mary in visions. She then went to her mother-in-law and told her to take back her son Henry, because he was too immature. The following day Ann went to work and tried to get the entire office down on their knees with her to recite the rosary. A few days later, her mother took her to a priest, whom she "told off" in no uncertain terms. She finally spit at him. A psychiatrist was consulted, and he recommended hospitalization. . . .

When the patient was first seen in the ward by the examiner, she was dashing around the room, singing and laughing. She was markedly agitated; frequently she would cry one minute and then laugh in a silly, impulsive manner, or suddenly slump over and become mute. Her speech would be incoherent at one time because she mumbled and at another time she would shriek very loudly.

Source: Arieti, S. (1974). *Interpretation of schizophrenia* (pp. 173–74, and 177). New York: Basic Books.

1945, where they were put up for adoption or placed in foster homes. Heston set out in search of these people in order to compare them to a matched group of children from the same foundling home whose mothers did not have schizophrenia. He managed to find approximately 50 people from each group, whose average age was about 36. Heston found that the children of schizophrenic mothers fared much worse in life than the children of mothers who did not have schizophrenia; more than ten percent of them also had schizophrenia (compared to zero percent for the comparison group). In addition, the children of schizophrenic mothers were more likely than the children of nonschizophrenic mothers to be mentally defective, sociopathic, neurotic, criminal, and to have been discharged from the armed forces on psychiatric grounds.

Approximately a dozen studies conducted in several different countries have compared the concordance rate for schizophrenic disorders in identical and fraternal twins (see Gottesman &

Shields, 1972). As shown in Figure 13-6 (p. 691), these studies reveal that the average concordance rate for identical twins is from 40–50%, compared to approximately 15% for fraternal twins. It is important to note, however, that these figures underestimate the similarity between identical twins and their siblings. If an identical twin has a schizophrenic disorder, the chances are almost 90% the other twin will have some sort of psychological disorder (Heston, 1970) and possess minor schizophrenic or schizoid characteristics.

Seymour Kety and his coworkers studied a group of adopted children who became schizophrenic, comparing the incidence of schizophrenic disorders in their biological versus adoptive relatives (Kety et al., 1968, 1975). If the disposition toward schizophrenia is transmitted through heredity, we would expect its incidence to be higher in biological than in adoptive relatives. If, on the other hand, the environment is the more important factor, we would expect its

CASE 13-5
SIMPLE SCHIZOPHRENIA

Edwin W. is a 49-year-old man who has been in the psychiatric hospital for more than thirty years. He was a physically healthy and mentally alert youngster until the third year of high school when he failed Latin. He became discouraged, and refused to return to school for his senior year. He took a job as a bank messenger, but after nine months' employment decided to return to a military academy where he did well in his academic subjects. He also won several athletic medals. However, he complained that he could not concentrate, and felt that he did not have enough intelligence to go to college. He returned to work, but soon lost his job because he remained in bed until late morning. He refused to mix with his friends, and became exceptionally quiet. He lost interest in everything around

him, and would not leave the house unless coaxed by his family. Occasionally he would go to his room and cry. He would shrug his shoulders frequently, saying, "What's the use!" The patient often talked of going away, insisting that his family did not care for him. He was sent to a private sanitarium, and later transferred to the state psychiatric hospital. When first seen at the hospital, the patient was well oriented, and his memory was intact. Speech was slow, and the patient would reply to questions only after much prompting. There were no delusions, hallucinations, or other signs of severe mental illness.

During the thirty years of hospitalization, the patient has remained withdrawn and apathetic. His speech is slow and soft, and he speaks in a low monotone. He does not mingle with other

patients, and sits by himself most of the time. He is generally well behaved, and seldom causes a disturbance on the ward. He shows no interest in his surroundings or in ward activities. Although the patient was well oriented when he first came to the hospital, there has been a certain amount of deterioration over the years. He is no longer certain about the date or his age. When asked how long he has been in the hospital, he replies, "about two or three months." When questioned about how he likes it at the hospital, he replies, "pretty good." He presents the classic picture of the long-term hospitalized simple schizophrenic patient.

Source: Kisker, G. W. (1964). *The disorganized personality* (p. 350). New York: McGraw-Hill.

incidence to be higher in the adoptive relatives with whom the schizophrenic children shared a similar environment. The results of Kety's research revealed that 21% of the biological relatives of his subjects possessed schizophrenic qualities, compared to 5% of the adoptive relatives.

Considered as a whole, studies on the heritability of schizophrenic disorders suggest that the disposition to become schizophrenic is inherited, but that other factors are involved. The weight of

the evidence suggests schizophrenic disorders are caused by a complex interaction between inherited dispositions and environmental events.

Biochemical Factors One of the most direct means by which genes influence behavior is through biochemical agents in the brain. Many researchers have looked for biochemical abnormalities, which may cause the bizarre symptoms of the disorder, in the brains of people with schizophrenia. During the past two decades, sev-

Box 13-5
The Genain Quadruplets

The odds of all four identical quadruplets being diagnosed schizophrenic is one in two billion, but Nora, Iris, Myra, and Hester Genain (shown in the photograph on their 51st birthday) were diagnosed schizophrenic before their 25th birthday. Hester broke light bulbs and tore off buttons from her clothes. Nora complained that the bones in her neck were slipping. Iris screamed and drooled at meals and said that she heard voices. Myra was the last to break down, at age 24. All four have been in and out of mental hospitals for more than 20 years.

Do these cases establish that schizophrenia is inherited? Although they are consistent with this assump-

tion, these cases do not establish that schizophrenia is inherited because the Genain quadruplets shared both heredity and environment. Indeed, the environment in which the quadruplets grew up was tragic. Their father was an alcoholic who terrorized and sexually molested the girls. Their

mother was ineffectual, bizarre, and preoccupied with sex. Coleman, Butcher, and Carson (1984) concluded that the sisters' disorder was due both to adverse heredity and environment, noting that Myra, the best off of the four, was the mother's favorite and the least molested by the father.

eral "breakthroughs" have been announced, but none has survived the critical appraisal that followed. A particularly dramatic case in point involved the idea that schizophrenia is caused by hallucinogens in the brain similar to such synthetic hallucinogens as mescaline and LSD. Researchers noted the similarities between the experiences of people under the influence of hallucinogenic drugs and the experiences of people with schizophrenia, and showed that the chemical structure of hallucinogenic drugs and certain chemicals in the brain is similar (Hoffer & Osmond, 1968). Although the parallel between hallucinogenic drugs and chemicals in the brains

of people with schizophrenia seemed promising, later research revealed significant differences between the effects of such drugs and the symptoms of schizophrenia.

It is perhaps ironic that the biochemical theory of schizophrenia that has gained most favor is supported by research on the effects of a drug quite different from hallucinogenic drugs, namely amphetamine, or "speed." Clinicians have observed that people who consume large quantities of amphetamines develop symptoms similar to the symptoms of schizophrenia, especially paranoid schizophrenia. Further, the symptoms of schizophrenic people become more

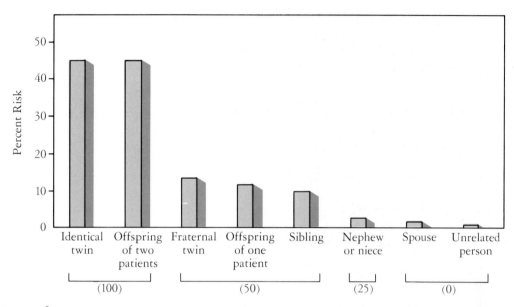

FIGURE 13-6

The Risk of Schizophrenia and Genetic Relatedness (percent genetic relatedness in parentheses)   *Source:* Adapted from Gottesman, I. I., Shields, J., & Hanson, D. R. (1982). *Schizophrenia: The epigenetic puzzle.* New York: Cambridge University Press.

extreme after they are given amphetamines. Biochemical research has revealed that one of the effects of amphetamine is to induce the release of the neurotransmitter **dopamine** (Snyder, 1976). Dopamine affects attention, perception, and the ability to integrate information; it has been suggested that it helps people link sensations such as sounds, smells, and colors with appropriate memories and emotions. An excess of dopamine could cause an individual to be bombarded by unintegrated sensations, memories, and emotions — which is what appears to happen in some forms of schizophrenia. Therefore, it is possible that schizophrenic disorders are caused by excess dopamine in the brain or by overly sensitive postsynaptic receptors for dopamine (Snyder, 1980).

The **dopamine theory** is supported by three other lines of evidence. First, animals who have been injected with chemicals that increase the concentration of dopamine in their brains display symptoms similar to catatonic schizophrenia. Second, researchers have found that drugs that relieve the symptoms of schizophrenia also block dopamine receptors in the brain (Snyder,

1980; see Chapter 14). And third, postmortems of people diagnosed schizophrenic have revealed excessive amounts of dopamine in their brains and a surplus of dopamine receptors (Mackay et al., 1982). Although the dopamine theory seems quite promising, evidence suggests that other biochemical agents are involved in schizophrenia and that the interaction between them and other factors is more complex than the present dopamine theory indicates.

Problems with Research   One reason why scientists have not yet unearthed the biochemical roots of schizophrenia is because research on biochemical processes is so fraught with difficulty. As we have seen, schizophrenia may consist of a group of disorders with different determinants; as we shall see, clinicians have been unable to diagnose the disorder accurately, especially prior to publication of the *DSM-III.* As a result, investigators who assumed they were studying the same disorder may have been studying qualitatively different disorders with quite different causes. Another problem relates to the fact that most schizophrenic people studied by scientists are institutionalized: they follow unusual diets, take a wide variety of drugs, and may be exposed to such unusual experiences as electroconvulsive therapy.

Because of these factors, many of the differences reported by early researchers between schizophrenic and normal people turned out to be effects of the disorder, not causes (see Kety, 1959). When institutionalized schizophrenics were compared to other institutionalized patients, the differences disappeared. Lack of knowledge about the nature of psychological disorders, problems with diagnosis, and the difficulty of determining whether differences between people with and without a disorder are causes or effects plague most research on psychopathology. Fortunately, contemporary researchers are sensitive to these problems and have developed increasingly effective controls for them.

Basic Defects **Experimental psychopathologists** (psychologists who conduct research on psychological disorders) have tested people with schizophrenia in an attempt to discover whether schizophrenic people possess a basic defect in a major psychological process — for example, sensation, perception, language, thought, memory, or motor responsivity — that would account for their defects in other processes. Evidence from such studies has revealed schizophrenic people cannot filter out external sensory stimuli normally and, therefore, experience sensory overload (Broen & Nakamura, 1972). As a result, schizophrenic people may take measures to reduce sensory input and brain excitation by withdrawing, isolating themselves, and learning to block out stimuli from the external world (Mialet & Pichot, 1981). Other studies have suggested that schizophrenic disorders originate from such other types of basic defects as a deficiency in attention, reaction time, conditionability, the ability to discriminate among ideas, thinking, and motivation (see Maher, 1966). Of particular interest is recent evidence that people with schizophrenia have difficulty dealing with high levels of emotion (Leff & Vaughn, 1985).

Learning Learning theorists have shown that certain symptoms of schizophrenia can be modified through conditioning. For example, Meich-enbaum and Goodman (1969) found that the speech of people with schizophrenia became more normal when they were rewarded for speaking normally; other researchers have induced changes in motor behavior by the same means (Salzinger, 1980). Such findings have led some learning theorists to suggest schizophrenic disorders are caused either by the unintentional reinforcement of schizophrenic behavior or by the absence of reinforcement for attending to appropriate objects (Ullman & Krasner, 1969). These theories, however, have received only weak support.

Psychodynamic Factors Psychoanalytic theorists attribute schizophrenic behavior to a regression to the oral stage of development. They suggest that people who fail to develop strong egos (the structure in the mind that deals with reality) early in their lives are susceptible to schizophrenia (Lehmann, 1975). Thus, schizophrenic thought is viewed as **id-dominated primary process thinking.** As eminent psychologist Roger Brown pointed out, the incoherent ramblings, hallucinations, delusions, and other aspects of schizophrenic thought make perfect sense when preceded by the phrase "I dreamed . . . ."

Social Factors Psychoanalyst Harry Stack Sullivan stressed the role of social and family relations in the development of disturbed behavior. One of his students, Frieda Fromm-Reichman, was particularly interested in the role of mothers in the families of schizophrenic children. (Fromm-Reichman was the real-life therapist described in Hanna Green's autobiographical novel *I Never Promised You a Rose Garden.*) She described **schizophrenogenic** mothers (mothers who generate schizophrenic children) as domineering, cold, rejecting, and guilt-producing; she proposed that in combination with passive, ineffectual fathers, such mothers drive their children into schizophrenia. Subsequent research on schizophrenic families, however, has shown that this view is too simple.

Another psychoanalyst (Lidz, 1973) found that families of schizophrenics were frequently marked by either **marital schism** or **marital skew.** Marital schism occurs when both parents are preoccupied with their own severe problems that threaten the continuity of the household; marital skew occurs in homes where one severely disturbed parent dominates the household. A somewhat different point of view has been advanced by Bateson and his colleagues (1956), who suggest parents dispose children to schizophrenia by communicating with them in ways that put them in a *no-win* quandry. For example, a father may complain about his daughter's lack of affection at the very moment he is pushing her away from him. Such contradictory verbal and nonverbal messages are examples of what Bateson and others call **double-bind communication.**

There have been numerous problems with research on the families of people with schizophrenia. Some studies have failed to include appropriate control groups; others have failed to determine whether the differences they found were causes or effects of the disorder. It is possible that family patterns found to be correlated with schizophrenia constitute a reasonable response to an unusual child. Klebanoff (1959) found that mothers of schizophrenic, brain-injured, and retarded children tended to be more possessive and controlling than mothers of normal children. Most studies use methods that rely primarily on verbal reports from parents in the afflicted families, but these reports are subject to a variety of biases. And most family studies also have failed to explain why the abnormal patterns affect only some of the children in the family. Because of such problems as these, a review by Jacob (1975) concluded it is not yet possible to identify the specific family processes that may contribute to the development of schizophrenia.

Sociocultural Factors It is well established that the incidence of schizophrenia is highest among people from the lower socioeconomic strata (Strauss, 1979). Three explanations have been offered for this trend:

1. Clinicians are unlikely to diagnose people from the high socioeconomic strata as schizophrenic.
2. People with schizophrenia "drift downward" to the lower socioeconomic strata because they fail to develop the skills necessary to maintain positions in the high socioeconomic strata.
3. People from the low socioeconomic strata are subjected to significantly more stress than people from the high socioeconomic strata.

TABLE 13-8
Interacting Factors that Contribute to Schizophrenia

Heredity	Biological Mechanisms	Psychological Characteristics	Stress and Skill Factors	Probable Adjustment
		Heightened sensitivity to punishment	Low stress and/or good coping-skills	⟶ Normal adjustment
		Lower threshold for perceptual/ intellectual variance	Moderate stress and/or minimal coping-skills	⟶ Marginal adjustment
Genetic Predisposition	Biochemical Irregularities	Higher likelihood of attentional problems	Excessive stress and inadequate coping-skills	⟶ Schizophrenic reaction
		Higher likelihood of thought disorder		
		Higher likelihood of communication problems		

Source: Adapted from Mahoney, M. J. (1980). *Abnormal psychology: Perspectives on human variance* (p. 454). Cambridge, MA: Harper & Row.

The Humanistic Approach Humanistic psychologist R. D. Laing (1964) suggests most people who investigate schizophrenia have it all wrong. Researchers assume something is wrong with people who have schizophrenia, when actually schizophrenic people are courageous pioneers in search of a better world. It is the social environment of schizophrenics that is crazy, suggests Laing, not the people who withdraw from it into themselves. Laing (1964) reports that parents of disturbed children persistently refuse to acknowledge reality, preferring to create more comfortable family myths or lies. In forcing the children to accept these false versions of reality, they force them into greater confusion and further misinterpretation of reality.

Integrative Approaches — Complex Interactions One model attentive to the interaction between biological and genetic factors is called the **diathesis-stress model.** Diathesis refers to such constitutional factors as an individual's genetic predisposition or temperament; stress refers to such environmental factors as loss of a loved one, going to college, failing a course, and being fired (see Box 13-2). Meehl (1962) suggested people may inherit a disposition toward schizophrenia (which he called **schizotaxia**). People with this disposition who undergo healthful social experiences develop normally; people who undergo unhealthful social experiences develop schizoid personalities (called **schizotypy** by Meehl). Of the people with schizoid personalities, only those who experience environmental stress develop schizophrenia. A somewhat more elaborate integrative model is outlined in Table 13-8 (page 693).

DELUSIONAL (PARANOID) DISORDERS

We have discussed paranoid schizophrenia and we will touch on the paranoid personality disorder; somewhere between these types of paranoia lie **delusional disorders.** Delusional disorders do not involve the kind of personality disintegration found in paranoid schizophrenia, yet they are more debilitating than the deeply in-grained paranoid traits of the personality disorder. The primary symptom of delusional disorders is a persistent **delusion** (false belief) that dominates an individual's life: *delusions of persecution* and delusions that evolve around jealousy are the most common, with *delusions of grandeur* less common. Unlike people suffering from paranoid schizophrenia, people with paranoia may seem entirely normal until they disclose their irrational beliefs. Once disclosed, however, it becomes apparent these beliefs are at the core of their lives. Often it is only the basic assumption of the delusional system that is wrong (for example, the communists are spying on me); once the assumption is accepted, everything else fits together in a logical way. People with paranoia are generally hypervigilant, inflexible, distrustful, and their thinking is very rigid. Although some people with paranoia are passive and benign, engulfed in a world dominated by their delusions, others may be extremely dangerous because they may strike out aggressively against their imagined tormentors. It has been suggested that several assassins and demagogues, such as Adolph Hitler, have suffered from paranoia. Occasionally two or more people collaborate in a system of delusions. Psychiatrist Robert Lindner describes in *The Fifty Minute Hour* how he almost became engulfed in an elaborate delusional system of one of his patients who believed he could communicate with people from other planets.

MOOD DISORDERS

Minor fluctuations in mood are part of life: some days we feel marvelous, some days we feel miserable. In addition to minor fluctuations in mood, most people experience more prolonged periods of elation and depression. They may experience elation for weeks or even months when things are going their way and they may experience periods of depression in reaction to such crises as the death of a loved one, the breakup of a relationship, the loss of a job, illness, injury, or a major failure. As uplifting or deflating as these experiences may be, they pale in the shadow of moods experienced by people with mood disorders.

People who experience normal highs and lows can hold their lives together in a reasonable way; people with manic and depressive disorders become incapacitated and, in some cases, must be institutionalized.

There are three primary types of **mood disorder** — mania, depression, and manic–depressive, or bipolar disorder (see Figure 13-7). Depressive disorders are by far the most frequent; indeed, they are the most prevalent of all psychological disorders. The Surgeon General (1979) estimated that from 45 to 55 million Americans suffer from mild to moderate depression and that 2 million suffer from severe depression. Manic disorders occur significantly less frequently than depressive disorders and manic–depressive disorders are rarest of all, affecting only about one percent of the population. Although depressive disorders are twice as prevalent among women as they are among men, males and females are equally likely to suffer from manic–depressive disorders.

Manic Disorders

Manic states are somewhat similar to the "high" some people experience after taking amphetamines, or "speed," except they are much more extreme. People in a **manic state** are full of energy but easily distracted, finding it difficult to maintain a focus on any one task. They talk incessantly, loudly, and rapidly, changing from topic to topic in midstream. People in a manic state often experience an inflated sense of self-importance: they view themselves as experts on everything and take it upon themselves to tutor anyone who will listen. They often hatch quite grandiose schemes: making a million dollars, developing a cure for cancer, and the like. They lose perspective on themselves and others, typically borrowing and spending money willy-nilly. In a manic state, people find it difficult to relax enough to sleep and may go days on end with little or no rest. Although in the early stages of a manic reaction people seem to feel great, as the high intensifies it seems to overwhelm them (see Case 13-6). When people in a manic state are contradicted or restrained, as eventually they must be, they may become hostile and abusive. There is a driven, agitated quality to mania that is not present in normal euphoria. When manic states become extreme, individuals may behave like "maniacs" ranting, raving, singing, pounding walls, and throwing things.

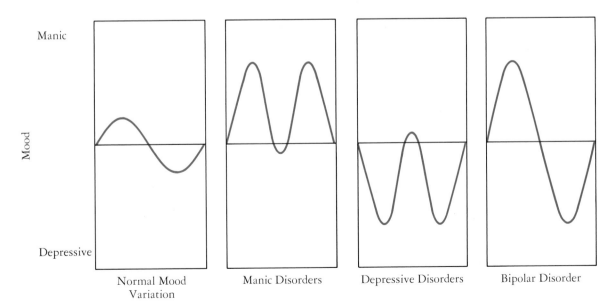

FIGURE 13-7
Patterns of Mood Variation — Manic Disorders, Depressive Disorders, and Manic–Depressive or Bipolar Disorders

CASE 13-6
FROM HIGH TO OUT OF CONTROL

At first, when they begin to grow, manic reactions induce a high. As demonstrated by the following account, however, the high typically gets out of control.

[Hypomania] At first when I'm high it's tremendous . . . ideas are fast . . . like shooting stars you follow 'til brighter ones appear . . . all shyness disappears, the right words and gestures are suddenly all there . . . uninteresting

people, things become intensely interesting. Sensuality is pervasive, the desire to seduce and be seduced is irresistible. Your marrow is infused with unbelievable feelings of ease, power, well-being, omnipotence, euphoria . . . you can do anything . . . But somewhere this changes. . . .

[Mania] The fast ideas become too fast and there are far too many . . . overwhelming confusion replaces clarity . . . you stop keeping up with it — memory

goes. Infectious humor ceases to amuse — your friends become frightened . . . everything is now against the grain . . . you are irritable, angry, frightened, uncontrollable and trapped in the blackest caves of the mind — caves you never knew were there. It will never end.

Source: Goldstein, M. J., Baker, B. C., & Jamison, K. R. (1980). *Abnormal psychology: Experience, origins, and interventions* (p. 201). Boston, MA: Little, Brown.

Depressive Disorders

When normal people become depressed, they experience all or some of the following symptoms: lack of energy and motivation, feelings of worthlessness, pessimism about their future, difficulty in concentrating and making decisions, fits of crying, poor appetite, and abnormal patterns of sleep. Severe depression involves all of these symptoms and more. When people succumb to severe depression, their faces tend to lack muscle tone; they slump over, find it difficult to talk, and feel overwhelmed with despair. The psychological pain they experience seems almost physical in nature. In some cases, called **agitated depression,** people become restless and fidgety, have difficulty sitting still, and appear to be trying to escape the pain they feel by moving away from it. For a diagnosis of **major depressive syndrome,** a person must display at least five of the following symptoms in an extreme form:

1. depressed mood (most of the day, nearly every day)
2. markedly diminished interest or pleasure in all, or almost all, activities (most of the day, nearly every day)
3. significant weight loss or weight gain when not dieting, or decrease or increase in appetite (nearly every day)
4. insomnia or hypersomnia (nearly every day)
5. psychomotor agitation or retardation (nearly every day)
6. fatigue or loss of energy (nearly every day)
7. feelings of worthlessness or excessive or inappropriate guilt (nearly every day)
8. diminished ability to think or concentrate, or indecisiveness (nearly every day)
9. recurrent thoughts of death (not just fear of dying), recurrent suicidal ideation without a specific plan, or a suicide attempt or a specific plan for committing suicide

Research has indicated that 40% of people who experience severe depression remain depressed after six months and that 24% have not recovered after a year; the median duration is about seven months (Keller & Shapiro, 1981). One of ten severely depressed people attempts suicide (see Box 13-6, page 698).

CASE 13-7
MANIC–DEPRESSIVE, OR BIPOLAR DISORDER

Mrs. M. was first admitted to a state hospital at the age of 38. She had experienced mood swings since childhood, some of which had been extreme enough to be characterized as psychotic. At 33, shortly before the birth of her first child, the patient was greatly depressed. For a period of four days she appeared to be in a coma. About a month after the birth of the baby she became "excited" and was entered as a patient in an institution for neurotic and mildly psychotic patients. As she began to improve, she was sent to a shore hotel for a brief vacation. The patient remained at the hotel for one night and on the following day signed a year's lease on an apartment, bought furniture, and became heavily involved in debt. Shortly thereafter Mrs. M. became depressed and returned to the hospital in which she previously had been a patient. After several months she recovered, and except for relatively mild fluctuations of mood, remained well for approximately two years.

She then became overactive and exuberant in spirits and, visiting friends, outlined her plans for reestablishing different forms of lucrative businesses. She purchased many clothes, bought furniture, pawned her rings, and wrote checks without funds. She was returned to a hospital. Gradually her manic symptoms subsided, and after four months she was discharged. For a period thereafter she was mildly depressed. In a little less than a year Mrs. M. again became overactive, played her radio until late in the night, smoked excessively, and took out insurance on a car that she had not yet bought. Contrary to her usual habits, she swore frequently and loudly, created a disturbance in a club to which she did not belong, and instituted divorce proceedings. On the day prior to her second admission to the hospital, she purchased 57 hats.

During the past 18 years this patient has been admitted and dismissed from the hospital on many occasions.

At times, with the onset of a depressed period, she has returned to the hospital seeking admission. At such times she complained that her "brain just won't work." She would say, "I have no energy, am unable to do my housework; I have let my family down; I am living from day to day. There is no one to blame but myself." During one of her manic periods, she sent the following telegram to a physician of whom she had become much enamored.

"To: You; Street and No.: Everywhere; Place: the remains at peace! We did our best, but God's will be done! I am so very sorry for all of us. To brave it through thus far. Yes, Darling— from Hello Handsome. Handsome is as Handsome does, thinks, lives and breathes. It takes clear air, Brother of Mine, in a girl's hour of need. All my love to the Best Inspiration one ever had."

Source: From Kolb, L. C. (1973). *Modern clinical psychiatry* (8th ed., pp. 376–77). Philadelphia, PA: Saunders.

Manic–Depressive, or Bipolar Disorder

As though mania and depression were not enough in themselves, some people suffer from a disorder that involves both. They may experience several bouts of depression interspersed with periods of mania or several episodes of mania interspersed with periods of depression. In some (relatively rare) cases, manic episodes are followed by severe depression from which the person recovers and is relatively normal until the cycle starts

BOX 13-6 SUICIDE

It has been estimated that people who are depressed are approximately ten times more likely to commit suicide than people who are not depressed. However, it would not be correct to say that depression causes suicide: most depressed people do not commit suicide and many people who commit suicide are not depressed. Suicide is a complex phenomenon that at present is poorly understood (Colt, 1983). In a review of the evidence on suicide, Davison and Neale (1986) identify 14 misconceptions and 17 facts.

Fourteen Myths about Suicide

1. *People who discuss suicide will not commit the act* The fact is that up to three-fourths of those who take their lives have communicated the intent beforehand, perhaps as a cry for help, perhaps to taunt. On the other hand, the vast majority of people who contemplate suicide do not actually attempt to kill themselves.

2. *Suicide is committed without warning* The falseness of this belief is readily indicated by the preceding myth. The person usually gives many warnings, such as saying that the world would be better off without him or making unexpected and inexplicable gifts to others, often of his most valued possessions.

3. *Only people of a certain class commit suicide* Suicide is actually neither the curse of the poor nor the disease of the rich: people in all classes commit suicide.

4. *Membership in a particular religious group is a good predictor that a person will not consider suicide* It is mistakenly thought that the strong Catholic prohibition against suicide makes the risk that Catholics will take their lives much lower. This is not supported by the evidence, perhaps because an individual's formal religious identification is not always an accurate index of true beliefs.

5. *The motives for suicide are easily established* The truth is that we do not fully understand why people commit suicide. For example, the fact that a severe reverse in finances precedes a suicide does not mean that the reversal adequately explains the suicide.

6. *All who commit suicide are depressed* This fallacy may account for the tragic fact that signs of impending suicide are overlooked because the person does not act despondently. Many of the people who take their lives are *not* depressed; in fact, some people appear calm and at peace with themselves after having decided to kill themselves.

7. *A person with a terminal physical illness is unlikely to commit suicide* A person's awareness of impending death does not preclude suicide. Perhaps the wish to end their own suffering or that of their loved ones impels many to choose the time of their death.

8. *To commit suicide is insane* Although most suicidal persons are very unhappy, most appear to be completely rational and in touch with reality.

9. *A tendency to commit suicide is inherited* Since suicides often run in families, the assumption is made that the tendency to think in terms of self-annihilation is inherited. There is no evidence for this.

10. *Suicide is influenced by seasons, latitude, weather fronts, barometric pressure, humidity, precipitation, cloudiness, wind speed, temperature, and days of the week* There are no good data to substantiate any of these myths.

11. *Suicide is influenced by such cosmic factors as sunspots and phases of the moon* No evidence confirms this.

12. *Improvement in emotional state means lessened risk of suicide* The fact is that people often commit the act after their spirits begin to rise and their energy level improves; this appears to be especially true of depressed patients.

13. *Suicide is a lonely event* Although the debate whether to commit suicide is

waged within the individual's head, deep immersion in a frustrating and hurtful relationship with another person—a spouse, a child, a lover, a colleague—may be a principal cause.

14. *Suicidal people clearly want to die* Most people who commit suicide appear to be ambivalent about their own deaths.

Seventeen Facts about Suicide

1. *Every 30 minutes someone in the United States kills himself or herself* This rate—over 25,000 a year—is probably a gross underestimate.

2. *As many as 200,000 in this country attempt suicide each year* There is one suicide for every eight attempts.

3. *About half of those who commit suicide have made at least one previous attempt.*

4. *Three times as many men kill themselves as women* The ratio may be approaching twice as many men as women, for women are becoming a higher-risk group.

5. *Three times as many women as men attempt to kill themselves but do not die.*

6. *Divorced men are three times more likely to kill themselves than are married men.*

7. *Suicide is found in both the very old and the very young* Even in those older than 90 years and younger than 10 years.

8. *Suicide is found at all socioeconomic levels* It is especially frequent among psychiatrists, physicians, lawyers, and psychologists.

9. *No other kind of death leaves in friends and relatives such long-lasting feelings of distress, shame, guilt, puzzlement, and general disturbance* Indeed, these survivors are themselves victims, having an especially high mortality rate in the year following the suicide of their loved one.

10. *Guns are the most common means of suicide in the United States* Men usually choose to shoot or hang themselves; women are more likely to use sleeping pills. Elsewhere in the world methods vary by country. For example, coal gas is often chosen in England; gas and hanging are common means in Austria; pills and poisons are used in the Scandinavian countries.

11. *Suicide ranks tenth as a leading cause of death among adults* And second, after accidents, among college students.

12. *Most of the people who kill themselves in the United States are native-born Caucasian males between 45 and 60 years of age.*

13. *It is estimated that each year upwards of 10,000 American college men and* women attempt to kill themselves.

14. *Suicide rates among whites and native American youths are more than twice those for blacks* Indeed, between 1970 and 1980 the rates for young white men increased by 50 percent for ages 15–24, and by nearly 30 percent for ages 25–34.

15. *Suicide rates for adolescents and children in the United States are increasing* As many as 1,600 young people between the ages of 15 and 19 are believed to kill themselves each year and attempts are made by children as young as 6—but the rates are far below those of adults.

16. *Hungary has the highest suicide rate in the world* Czechoslovakia, Finland, Sweden, and Austria also have high incidences.

17. *Suicide rates increase during depression years, remain stable during prosperity years, and decrease during war years.*

Source: From Davison, G. C., & Neale, J. M. (1986). *Abnormal psychology* (4th ed., pp. 220–21). New York: Wiley & Sons.

again.   Or, even rarer, patients appear to experience manic and depressive reactions simultaneously—a reaction similar to agitated depression.   Unlike the other mood disorders, **manic–depressive disorders** tend to run in families, abate in response to particular types of medication, and recur unless controlled through treatment.   (See Case 13-7, page 697.)

What Causes Mood Disorders?

Psychologists have invested much more time and energy searching for the determinants of depression than they have searching for the determinants of manic reactions, probably because depression is so much more prevalent.   We consider the most influential of five approaches to understanding depression—those that are genetic, biochemical, learning, cognitive, and psychoanalytic in nature.

Genetic and Biochemical Factors   The evidence is strong that the tendency to develop a manic-depressive disorder is inherited.   Studies have found that concordance rates for identical twins range from 50–93%, with an average of about 75%; the comparable range for fraternal twins is 3–38%, with an average of about 15% (Rosenthal, 1970).   Concordance rates for manic-depressive disorders are higher than those for any other psychological disorder.   And the concordance rate for depression is higher in identical twins than in fraternal twins (40% compared to 10%; Allen, 1976), but significantly lower than concordance rates for manic-depressive disorders.   These statistics suggest that manic-depressive disorders may be caused by different factors from those that cause depressive disorders (Bertelsen, Harvald, & Hauge, 1977).

Research suggests the genetic mechanism that disposes people to manic-depressive disorders may involve a biochemical deficiency.   Over the past decade or so, evidence has been accumulating in support of the idea that a group of chemicals found in the brain called **neurotransmitters** play an important role in the regulation of moods.   As described in Chapter 3, neurotransmitters are chemicals that mediate the transmission of nerve impulses across synapses.   Two of the most important neurotransmitters are **norepinephrine** and **serotonin.**   The results of

several studies have supplied indirect evidence that a deficiency in either or both these chemicals is associated with depression and that an excess of either or both is associated with mania.   Studies have found that amphetamines and antidepressants produce an increase in both norepinephrine and serotonin (Snyder, 1980).   Because these drugs affect both neurotransmitters, it is difficult to isolate the relative effects of each (and, for that matter, their effect on other neurotransmitters not yet studied).   Some studies indicate norepinephrine plays the greater role; some studies indicate serotonin is the more important; other studies indicate it is the balance between these two chemicals that affects mood, with serotonin serving as a regulator of other neurotransmitters (see Snyder, 1980).   Still other studies suggest each neurotransmitter plays a different role in different types of depression and mania (see Kety, 1980; Martin, 1981).   Although the final word is by no means in, research in this area is progressing rapidly; thus far the results have made many professionals hopeful that a biochemical basis for mood fluctuations and affective disorders soon will be found (see Chapter 14).

Learning   Learning theorists have adopted two primary approaches to depression, and they apply to both moderate and severe depression.   The first approach emphasizes the rewards or reinforcements that people experience.   Lewinsohn et al. (1980) suggest that people become depressed when there is a significant reduction in the rewards in their lives.   Such events as the loss of a loved one, being fired from one's job (with the associated depletion of financial resources), illness, and injuries induce depression because they cause a reduction in positive reinforcement.   Depression may become part of a vicious circle.   When people become depressed, they tend to mope and complain.   After an initial period of support from friends (which reinforces the complaining and moping), their friends avoid them, which causes a further reduction in their rewards.   This reduction exacerbates their feelings of depression, which makes them complain even more, which evokes more rejection, and so on (see Figure 13-8).   It follows that the way to break the cycle is to induce depressed people to become involved in rewarding activities.

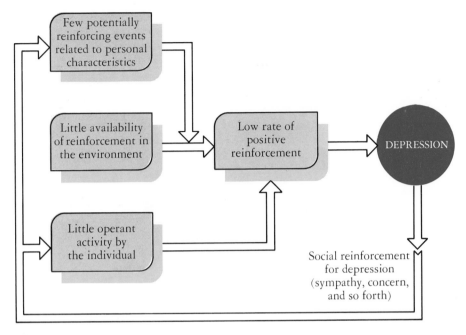

FIGURE 13-8
Lewinsohn's Learning Theory of Depression Personal characteristics, environmental inputs, and lethargy combine to produce a low level of positive reinforcement—which leads to depression. Depression is reinforced by other people. *Source:* Davison, G. C., & Neale, J. M. (1986). *Abnormal psychology* (4th ed.). New York: Wiley and Sons.

The second learning approach emphasizes **learned helplessness.** This approach originated from experiments on animals that showed if an animal is restrained over a series of trials so it cannot escape electric shocks, it will learn to be helpless and give up trying to escape when released from its restraints (Seligman & Maier, 1967). Seligman and his colleagues noted that dogs exposed to this experience displayed some of the classic symptoms of depression—they were lethargic and sluggish; they lost their appetites; and they showed little interest in sexual activity. Seligman suggested that when people become depressed, they undergo an experience similar to the experience of his experimental dogs—at first they try to avoid adversities, but when they fail, they learn to become helpless.

Following its publication, Seligman's learned helplessness theory of depression was roundly criticized by cognitively oriented theorists. Why, they asked, do some depressed people blame themselves for their depression and other depressed people blame the world? And why do

depressed people tend to minimize their successes and attribute them to luck (Rizley, 1978)? In response to such criticisms as these, Seligman and his colleagues revised their theory, making it more cognitive in nature.

Cognitive Factors In Seligman's revised theory (Abramson, Seligman, & Teasdale, 1978), bad experiences over which people have no control are less important than people's interpretation or attribution of their experiences (see Chapter 11). People who make external attributions—for example, blaming their miseries on bad luck—tend to become less depressed than people who make internal attributions and blame themselves. And, of the people who make internal attributions, those who attribute the bad things that happen to enduring internal deficiencies (such as a lack of intelligence) become more depressed and stay depressed longer than those who attribute them to more transient characteristics, such as a bad mood. A questionnaire developed by Seligman and his colleagues to assess how people interpret

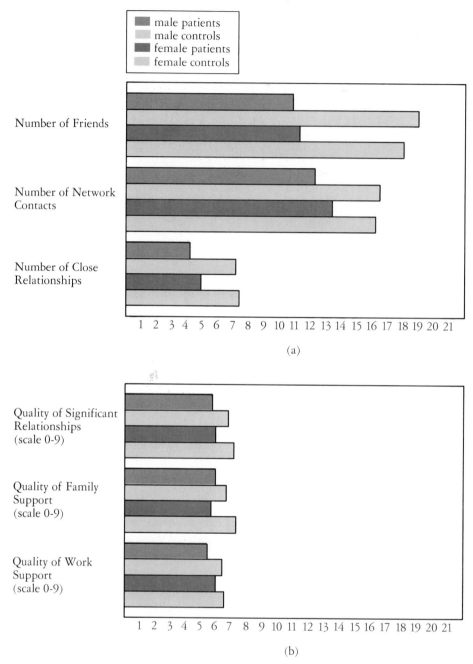

FIGURE 13-9

The Support Networks of Depressed and Nondepressed Individuals *Source:* Adapted from Billings, A. G., Cronkite, R. C., & Moos, R. H. (1983). Social-environmental factors in unipolar depression. *Journal of Abnormal Psychology, 92,* 119–33.

the adversities in their lives has been found to predict their susceptibility to depression. For example, in one study pregnant women prone to making dispositional attributions (attributing their experiences to enduring internal characteristics) were found to be more susceptible to postpartum depression than pregnant women not so prone. Seligman suggests the basis for the differences in the way people interpret negative experiences lies in their learning histories, especially in the family and at school.

Aaron Beck (1974) has advanced a cognitive theory of depression somewhat similar to that of Seligman et al., but broader in scope. Beck focuses on the self-talk of people prone to depression, noting that they engage in all-or-nothing and overgeneralized thinking and tend to blow up problems to catastrophic proportions ("Everything went wrong; nothing will ever be the same"). Beck suggests depressive people interpret things that happen to them in terms of their personal inadequacies; it is as though they have made up their minds they are inadequate and search for evidence to support the conclusion. In some cases this tendency can become extreme — for example, some people blame themselves for the fate of victims of a natural disaster. As you can imagine, people who are convinced they are inadequate have little difficulty finding evidence to support the belief. Everyone experiences failures and disappointments — they are part of life. If you blame yourself for every failure you experience and if you attribute your successes to luck rather than to your efforts, it is easy to see why you would be unhappy.

Psychodynamic Factors   Psychoanalytically oriented psychologists view depression as a reaction to loss that evokes feelings associated with losses of parental affection experienced during earlier stages of development. When adults lose a loved one, or even when they suffer a loss such as the loss of a job or money, they reexperience childhood feelings of when they were separated from their parents or when their parents withdrew their love. For this reason depressed adults become dependent and clinging or, in extreme cases, regress to a childlike state. The greater the experiences of loss in childhood, the greater the regression experienced during adulthood. Support for this idea comes from studies that have found that depression often is evoked by loss (Paykel, 1979) and that children who have lost a parent are particularly susceptible to depression later on (Roy, 1981). Other studies, however, have failed to support this view (see Lewinsohn & Hoberman, 1982).

Some psychoanalysts also view depression as anger and hostility toward a loved one turned inward. According to this view, when people experience a loss, they experience anger toward the person whom they have lost or toward the people in their past whom they were unable to possess (their parents); however, because such hostility is unacceptable to the ego, people in this state displace the anger onto themselves. Although this explanation is consistent with the observed association between anger and depression, it has received little empirical support. The evidence suggests that whatever the early experiences of people who become depressed, depressed patients suffer from a distinct lack of social support in their current lives (see Figure 13-9).

A Multifactor Approach to Depression   In recent years investigators have advanced integrated approaches that outline the ways in which biological, learned, cognitive, and social dispositions interact to give rise to depression (Akiskal, 1979). Consider two studies that supply examples of the way in which biological and psychological factors interact. Weiss and Cerreto (1980) found that rats exposed to shocks from which they could not escape learned to become helpless and, in addition, produced less norepinephrine in their brains. Simons et al. (1984) found that two different treatments — one involving antidepressant drugs and one involving psychotherapy — were equally effective in alleviating depression. Results of the Simons et al. study revealed that patients who received drugs engaged in more positive thinking than before they received the drugs. The emotions people feel, whether induced through drugs or through personal experiences, affect the way people think; the way they think affects the way they feel. Ultimately these factors are inseparable, and a full understanding of depression must take them both into account.

NEUROSIS

In the classification system that guided psychiatric diagnosis until recently, most disorders were classified under two broad headings — **neurosis** and **psychosis.** William Cullen introduced the word *neurosis,* derived from the Greek words for "nerve disorder," in 1769 in his book *System of Nosology*. The introduction of this term marked an advance in conceptions of pathology because it implied that the disorders it categorized stemmed from problems in the nervous system rather than from an imbalance in body humors. In the early twentieth century, as the influence of psychoanalytic theory grew, the meaning of the term *neurosis* underwent a change, coming to refer to disorders believed to stem from high levels of anxiety and from the defenses employed to control them (see Chapter 12). In the *DSM-II, neuroses* referred to moderate disorders in which contact with reality was unimpaired; *psychoses* referred to severe disorders that involved a loss of contact with reality. In 1980 the category *neurosis* was deleted from the new classification system, the *DSM-III*. The disorders formerly classified under this label — anxiety, dissociation, and somatoform are categorized independently as unrelated disorders in the *DSM-III-R*.

ANXIETY DISORDERS

The category **anxiety disorders** includes five primary types: generalized anxiety, panic attacks, phobias, obsessive-compulsiveness, and post-traumatic stress. People with generalized anxiety and panic attacks experience unusually high levels of anxiety. People with phobias and obsessive-compulsiveness experience high levels of anxiety unless they avoid certain situations or objects (phobias), entertain certain thoughts (obsessions), or engage in certain behaviors (compulsions). People with post-traumatic stress suffer a belated reaction to an exceptionally high level of anxiety. We now consider each type of anxiety disorder.

Generalized Anxiety and Panic Attacks

> Mr. Wright, a man of 35, was referred to [the] hospital because of a "dizzy turn" which he had experienced during his work as a laborer. He had similar attacks in the past but, with each one, the associated feelings of panic became more acute. . . .
> As the attacks developed, he began to sleep badly. He had difficulty in getting off to sleep because of

worrisome thoughts that raced through his mind; frequently his dreams had a menacing content and more and more they were only resolved by his awakening in a cold sweat, accompanied by frequent headaches. . . .
> [Later] he began to complain of pressure in the front of his head and uncontrollable trembling and palpitations. He became more and more dependent on his wife and would go nowhere without her. . . . This meant of course [he] had to give up work. . . . The worries about his failure to support his family caused his anxiety to "spiral." (McCullogh & Prins, 1978, p. 54)

Mr. Wright displays some of the symptoms of **generalized anxiety.** People who suffer from this disorder experience such physical symptoms as high levels of muscle tension (shakiness, trembling, inability to relax) and heightened autonomic activity (sweating, pounding heart, diarrhea); they feel apprehensive, worried, nervous, and full of dread; and they have trouble concentrating, making up their minds, and sleeping. People in this state typically do not feel in control of their lives and experience what Freud called **free-floating anxiety** — a diffuse, unfocused sense of apprehension without any apparent basis. Because of these physical, cognitive, and emotional problems, people with generalized anxiety often become irritable, fatigued, socially inept, and ineffective at school or work (see Table 13-9).

People who suffer from generalized anxiety also may suffer from **panic attacks** — sudden episodes of intense and overwhelming terror and dread. During panic attacks the sympathetic nervous system races, producing heart palpitations, difficult in breathing, perspiration, dizziness, faintness, and nausea. Although the attacks usually last only a few minutes, they sometimes last an hour or more. People experiencing panic attacks may feel they are having a heart attack, and in many cases are rushed to a hospital for treatment.

Phobias

A **phobia** is an intense, persistent, irrational fear of and desire to avoid a particular object or situation. Although the fear may relate to things that contain a moderate element of risk associated with them, such as dogs or germs, phobic re-

TABLE 13-9
Symptoms of Anxiety

Type of Symptom	Maladaptive Behaviors
Affective	Experience of ''hyperness,'' dread, fear, irritability, subjective discomfort, depression
Cognitive	Sense that something bad will happen, lack of sense of control, negative beliefs about self, expectation of negative evaluations from others, inability to concentrate
Motivational	Avoidance, reduction of anxiety
Interpersonal	Problems in social relations common, deficits in social skills, avoidance of social occasions
Physical	Inadequate or excessive eating, insomnia, reduction in sexual desire, use of drugs (including alcohol), high level of sympathetic arousal
Motor	Stiffness of posture, scratching and rubbing of parts of the body, pacing, trembling, handwringing

Source: Adapted from Lahey, B. B., & Ciminero, A. R. (1980). *Maladaptive behavior: An introduction to abnormal psychology* (p. 191). Chicago, IL: Dorsey Press.

sponses involve extreme overreactions to the dangers. Fear of snakes, heights, storms, doctors, sickness, injury, and death constitute the seven most common fears reported by normal adults (Agras, 1967). However, these fears are regarded as phobias only when they are so severe that they interfere with the normal pattern of people's lives.

Psychologists distinguish between simple phobias and complex phobias. **Simple phobias** refer to fears of specific objects or situations; Figure 13-10 illustrates the objects and situations most commonly feared by Americans in a 1984 survey. However, *what* people fear is less important than the fact that they experience fear; in fact, the object that evokes the fear may be arbitrary. Further, phobic people often fear several objects.

There are two **complex phobias**—agoraphobia and social phobias. Although **agoraphobia** is defined as the fear of open spaces, it typically involves the fear of being in situations from which escape may be difficult or help may be unavoidable. It has been estimated that one in every 100 people suffer from agoraphobia (Hardy, 1976). The disorder is most often found in housewives and other people who have been confined to their homes for long periods and often appears to follow a stressful event or crisis (Last, Barlow, & O'Brian, 1984). **Social phobias** involve a persistent fear of situations in which the individual is exposed to possible scrutiny by

others and may embarrass himself or herself. Although social phobias are not as incapacitating as agoraphobia, complex phobias interfere with people's lives more than simple phobias. People suffering from them tend to experience considerable anxiety and are likely to seek professional help. As you might expect, complex phobias are more resistant to treatment than simple phobias.

Obsessive–Compulsive Disorders

Obsessions are persistent, recurring thoughts; **compulsions** are irresistible urges to engage in particular behaviors. People may suffer from obsessions and compulsions separately or in concert. Everyone has been plagued by obsessive thoughts (a song that keeps playing in our heads, for example) and all of us are sometimes compulsive (double checking to ensure that doors are locked or stoves are turned off). Indeed, success in certain professions is fostered by an obsessive-compulsive style. For instance, surgeons traditionally are compulsive about cleanliness before operating, and academics develop compulsive habits of orderliness and concern for deadlines. However, the recurring thoughts entertained by those who suffer from obsessive-compulsive disorders are more bizarre than the ideas of the average person; people with the disorder carry compulsive behaviors to the extreme. Indeed, some people turn normal concerns for cleanliness into rituals: they wash their hands from 50 to 100

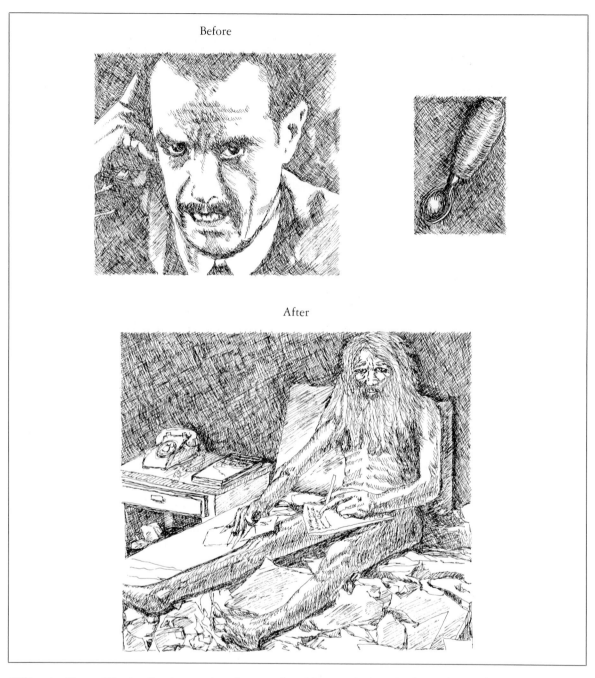

Before

After

Billionaire Howard Hughes lived as a recluse for more than 20 years, during which time he indulged an extreme fear of contamination. Among the many precautions against contamination taken by Hughes was the practice of having his silverware wrapped in tissue paper, sealed, and then wrapped again.

times a day, often until their hands are raw. It is only when obsessions and/or compulsions seriously interfere with people's lives that they qualify as a psychological disorder.

The three most common themes in obsessions are (1) harming oneself or others, (2) becoming contaminated, and (3) repetitive doubting (Sturgis & Meyer, 1981). Obsessions of the

Question: Everybody has fears about different things. But some are more afraid of certain things than others. Sometimes people fear things more than perhaps they should logically. I'm going to read a list of some of these fears. For each one, would you say whether you're afraid of it, whether it bothers you slightly, or whether you're not at all afraid of it.

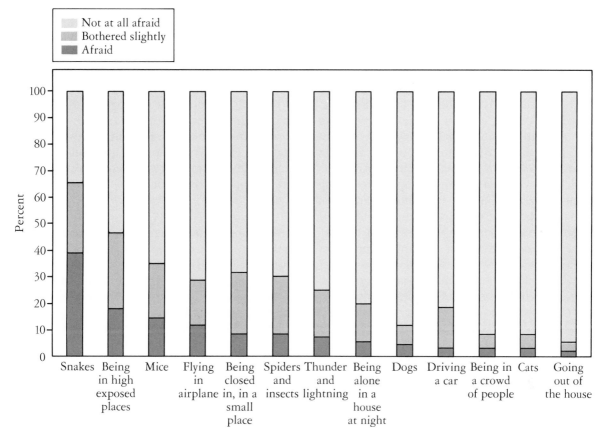

FIGURE 13-10

Survey of Objects and Situations Most Frequently Feared in the United States (1984) *Survey Question* "Everybody has fears about different things. But some are more afraid of certain things than others. Sometimes people fear things more than perhaps they should logically. I'm going to read a list of some of these fears. For each one, would you say whether you're afraid of it, whether it bothers you slightly, or whether you're not at all afraid of it." *Source:* Adapted from Roper report 84-3, February 11–25. *Public Opinion,* August/September 1984, p. 32. Used with permission of American Enterprise Institute.

first type often occur in parents, especially new mothers, and involve hurting or killing their children. Fortunately, few people ever carry out such obsessions. In contrast, people obsessed with germs and contamination often engage in compulsive cleaning rituals. Eccentric billionaire Howard Hughes is a dramatic case in point: he wore gloves, walked on clean paper, bathed repeatedly, and refused to see people. People who engage in compulsive behavior report they experience considerable reduction in anxiety when they carry out such compulsive rituals as handwashing (Hodgson & Rachman, 1972) and checking (Roper, Rachman, & Hodgson, 1973).

Post-traumatic Stress Disorder

It is not unusual for people to experience "mental breakdowns" during times of severe stress. For example, during World War I many combat soldiers suffered from **shell shock**—a condition involving a dazed or shock-like state. In World War II soldiers experienced a related reaction, **combat exhaustion,** characterized by fatigue, inability to sleep, feelings of terror, extreme jumpiness, and either extreme apathy or extreme agitation. In most cases, soldiers experienced shell shock and combat exhaustion while actively involved in fighting and under highly stressful conditions.

During the Vietnam War there were relatively few cases of shell shock or combat fatigue, probably because soldiers generally were flown into and out of fighting zones, given periods of rest, treated by skilled battalion physicians, and required to serve in combat for only a year. Nevertheless, Vietnam veterans, upon returning home, generally found it more difficult to adjust than the soliders of World War I and World War II (Horowitz & Solomon, 1975); as many as one-third experienced fatigue, apathy, depression, nightmares, social withdrawal, jumpiness, and recurring memories of traumatic war experiences. Largely on the basis of such cases as these, the *DSM-III* introduced a new category entitled **post-traumatic stress disorder.** Investigators attribute the high incidence of this disorder in Vietnam veterans to five factors (Lyons, 1984):

1. inability to form cohesive groups while in Vietnam
2. public opposition to the war
3. high rates of drug use
4. suddenness with which soldiers were shipped home
5. relative youthfulness (average 19.2 years)

As the name implies, post-traumatic stress disorder occurs after such traumatic experiences as those induced by war, natural disasters, automobile and airplane crashes, rape, torture, and detention in concentration camps. The disorder may occur immediately following a traumatic experience or weeks, months, and even years later. Although post-traumatic stress disorders have been observed most often in war veterans (Pearce et al., 1985), they also have been observed in people who have witnessed the murder of a loved one (Rynearson, 1984; Terr, 1983), in policemen who have killed in the line of duty (Stratton, Parker, & Snibbe, 1984), and in the children bur-

ied alive in a bus and held for ransom in Chowchilla, California (Terr, 1983).

What Causes Anxiety Disorders?

The prevalence of anxiety disorders is difficult to determine because most people who suffer from them are not hospitalized and because many (if not most) cases are not reported. Nevertheless, it is generally agreed that anxiety disorders affect the single largest group of people receiving treatment — two to four percent of the total population. Of the six theoretical approaches to anxiety we consider, five attribute it to psychological, as opposed to biological, sources.

Genetic and Biological Factors

The most salient symptoms of anxiety involve such activities of the autonomic nervous system as heart rate and sweating. British psychologist Hans Eysenck (1967) suggests that people inherit autonomic nervous systems that vary in reactiveness; consequently, people who inherit autonomic nervous systems that react strongly to stimuli tend to be anxious. Indeed, according to Eysenck, anxiety is one of the three fundamental traits that distinguish people from one another (introversion – extroversion and psychoticism being the other two: see Chapter 12). In support of Eysenck's theory, studies of twins have found the concordance rate for anxiety is approximately four times as great for monozygotic as for dizygotic twins (Scarr, 1966). Similarly, studies have found higher concordance rates for anxiety disorder among monozygotic than among dizygotic twins (Tiernari, 1963). Other studies have found that patients with anxiety disorder have significantly higher levels of such autonomic activity as galvanic skin response (Lader, 1975; Lader & Wing, 1966).

Psychodynamic Factors

The psychoanalytic view of phobias is exemplified by the case of little Hans discussed in Chapter 1. Psychoanalytic theorists believe anxiety is the root cause of many disorders. Anxiety is believed to develop when sexual and aggressive urges from the id and/or moralistic demands from the superego threaten to overwhelm the ego. The ego employs various defense mechanisms to help control anxiety that, when they become extreme, may give rise to anxiety disorders. Consider the following example.

A woman develops aggressive urges toward her husband, but her ego cannot accept these urges—they are inconsistent with her self-concept and socially unacceptable. So the ego employs such defense mechanisms as repression, denial, projection, and displacement to control them and to keep them from consciousness (see Chapter 12). However, the unconscious tension associated with the forbidden impulses gives rise to anxiety. The woman may relieve some of the tension by displacing her anxiety onto an object, such as germs, that can be avoided legitimately. Alternatively, she may develop an obsession about her husband dying in a car accident or a compulsion to sharpen knives in the kitchen. In cases where the pressures are particularly intense, the anxiety associated with her repressed urges may explode in a panic attack.

Learning In Chapter 5 we described how phobias can be induced through classical conditioning. Watson (the original *behaviorist*) and Rayner slammed a hammer against a steel bar, producing a loud noise that frightened young Albert who was playing with a white rat. Through classical conditioning, the child developed a phobia of rats and other objects that resembled them. Learning theorists argue that phobias are acquired accidentally through classical conditioning.

Phobias are often very resilient. The natural response of people who fear something is to avoid it, and every time a person avoids a feared object he or she obtains relief from anxiety, thereby reinforcing the avoidance response. This phenomenon is called the **neurotic paradox.** To extinguish a phobia, you must induce the person suffering from it to encounter the feared object; we describe the methods that learning theorists employ to accomplish this in Chapter 14.

The principles of conditioning also supply an explanation for the maintenance of obsessions and compulsions: thinking certain thoughts and performing certain actions are reinforced through the reduction of anxiety. However, learning theorists do not explain why particular, often bi-

zarre, thoughts and behaviors acquire the power to relieve anxiety—nor from where the anxiety originates. In addition, learning theorists have not been successful in extinguishing complex phobias.

Social Learning Social learning theorists propose that although anxiety disorders may be acquired through classical and operant conditioning, they also may be learned by imitating others and through vicarious reinforcement (see Chapters 5 and 12). In this perspective, a child could learn to fear snakes simply by imitating the behavior of someone who was afraid of snakes. Such social learning theorists as Bandura (1977) also emphasize the significance of people's sense of control over their fate (the rewards and punishments they experience) and that generalized anxiety results when people feel no control over the outcomes in their lives. Not surprisingly, compulsive rituals provide a sense of control over a threatening world and, in addition, supply a way of avoiding problems that seem overwhelming.

Social Stress Social stress theorists assume that when people encounter numerous unpleasant events or a great many changes in their lives, they become vulnerable to psychological disorder. Although the idea that physical disorders result from *stress* has received considerable press of late, there also is evidence that links psychological disorders to social stress. For example, some studies suggest that the expectations built into women's roles may induce psychological breakdown.

While the social stress model is intuitively attractive, many psychologists feel it neglects cognitive and phenomenological aspects of behavior. Different people interpret identical situations in different ways—which brings us to a final explanation of anxiety disorders.

Cognitive Factors Cognitive theorists suggest the ways in which people view their circumstances is the crucial factor that determines their psychological well-being. Viewing a situation as full of uncertainty may cause feelings of anxiety; cognitively oriented therapists help clients interpret such circumstances in ways that emphasize their ability to surmount difficulties.

In conclusion, several factors may be implicated in the determination of anxiety disorders. There may be genetic differences in nervous-system responsiveness that make people unusually vulnerable to anxiety. Early childhood experiences may create conflicts that dispose people toward anxiety. As people develop, they may undergo learning experiences that induce fears. Periods of social stress may elevate people's levels of anxiety. The way people think about themselves and their environment may affect the way they feel. Singly, or in combination, these factors may lead to the development of an anxiety disorder.

SOMATOFORM DISORDERS

Soma is Greek for *body*. People with **somatoform disorders** believe they have a physical ailment when, in fact, they do not. Somatoform disorders are different from the psychophysiologic or psychosomatic disorders described in the *DSM-II;* the latter conditions are genuine physical disorders caused by emotional stress. As we better understand the inextricable connection between mind and body, the clearer it becomes that prolonged states of stress and high emotional arousal always exact some physical toll — making it misleading to single out such particular physical disorders as ulcers, migraine headaches, and asthma as psychologically induced.

Hypochondriasis

Have you ever met a person abnormally preoccupied with his or her health — a person who constantly checks himself or herself, takes his or her pulse and temperature, visits doctors, swallows pills, and complains about his or her health? Every palpitation, bruise, dizzy spell, or upset stomach is viewed by such a person as evidence that he or she is seriously ill: a headache is evidence of a brain tumor, a cough indicates lung cancer. People suffering from **hypochondriasis** seem to need to believe they have medical problems. And although you might expect them to feel reassured when doctors fail to find evidence of any illness, negative results only intensify their concerns. Hypochondriacs often go from doctor to doctor in search of support for their suspicions.

Psychoanalysts believe that hypochondriasis involves the displacement of anxiety from its real source to a more acceptable source: it is easier to complain about headaches than to face the fact you are sexually frustrated. Behaviorists, on the other hand, emphasize the reinforcing effect of the attention people receive when they are sick — especially as young children. It is often during these times that they receive the most love, reassurance, and comfort.

Conversion Disorder

As we discussed in Chapter 1, the disorders formerly called *hysteria* played an important role in the founding of psychoanalysis. In fact, Freud's first book, with Joseph Breuer, was titled *Studies in Hysteria.* Hysteria, or what is now called **conversion disorder,** does not involve such "hysterical" behavior as ranting and raving; rather it involves such genuine physical dysfunctions as paralysis of a limb, blindness, or deafness that have no organic basis. Ancient Greeks named the disorder after the Greek word for uterus; they believed (incorrectly) it was caused by a "wandering uterus" and afflicted only women. Freud believed women developed hysteria when psychological tension or anxiety associated with forbidden unconscious desires was *converted* to physical symptoms (thus the name *conversion hysteria* or *conversion disorder*).

Glove anesthesia supplies a good example of conversion hysteria. People with glove anesthesia lose feeling in their hand (from the wrist down), but this is impossible neurologically because the nerves that serve the hand continue up the arm (see Figure 13-11).

Robert Malmo (1970) describes a case of conversion hysteria involving a 19-year-old girl named Anne. Anne awoke one morning to find herself totally deaf. No physical cause could be found, and the sudden onset of the disorder was typical of conversion hysteria. That the disorder did not involve *malingering,* or faking, was demonstrated by the fact that Anne did not show a

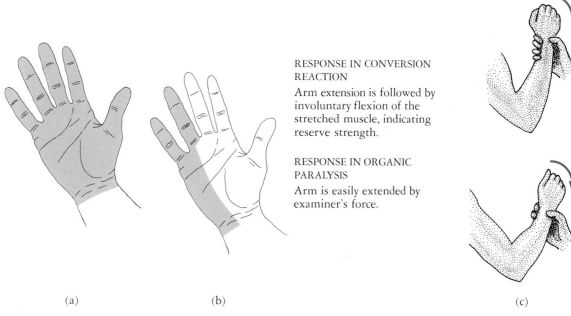

RESPONSE IN CONVERSION REACTION

Arm extension is followed by involuntary flexion of the stretched muscle, indicating reserve strength.

RESPONSE IN ORGANIC PARALYSIS

Arm is easily extended by examiner's force.

(a)   (b)   (c)

FIGURE 13-11

Glove Anesthesia and Paralysis of the Arm   (a) An individual reports that his or her hand has become numb from the wrist down.   (b) The pattern of numbness that would be experienced if the anesthesia were caused by damage to the nerves that serve the hand.   (c) Simple tests can reveal whether paralysis of the arm is due to organic factors or is a conversion reaction.   *Source:* Weintraub, M. I. (1983).   *Hysterical conversion reactions.*   New York: SP Medical and Scientific Books.

startle response to a loud clap behind her back. However, electronic sensors attached to her body indicated that at some unconscious level she could hear the sound because she made appropriate psychophysiological responses to it. (Interestingly, this psychophysiological recognition occurred only for the first clap.)   Malmo set up a classical conditioning situation in which a sound (that Anne's brain but not her conscious mind could hear) signaled the onset of a shock.   After repeated pairing of the sound (CS) and shock (US), the sound alone evoked the kinds of psychophysiological reactions associated with the anticipation of shocks.   The morning following the treatment, Anne's hearing returned, and remained intact thereafter.   The sudden disappearance of such symptoms is also common in conversion hysteria.

Some investigators have speculated that "miracle cures" may involve the cure of conversion hysteria rather than the cure of genuine physical disorders.   The most common context in which conversion hysteria occurs today is the military service and the most frequent victims are men (see Martin, 1981).

Most psychologists believe that conversion disorders are brought on by psychological stress and that they supply a way of relieving the stress, avoiding responsibility, and obtaining care and attention.   For example, it is more acceptable for a soldier to be relieved from duties because he is blind than because he is afraid.   It must be emphasized, though, that the blindness is real to the soldier.   The mechanisms through which psychological stress produces conversion disorders are not known.

CASE 13-8
FUGUE STATE

On September 13, 1980, a woman—naked, starving, filthy—was discovered by a park ranger; she was lying in the brush of Birch State Park in Florida. She could not remember her name, anything from her past, or how she came to be in the park.

The authorities named her *Jane Doe,* and launched a search to discover her identity. In time, with the help of hypnosis and sedatives, she recalled events from her past. Her fugue was precipitated by difficulties with her boyfriend.

"Jane Doe"

DISSOCIATIVE DISORDERS

People who experience **dissociative disorders** become cut off in some way from knowledge about themselves and their pasts while continuing to behave in a relatively normal manner. There are four types of dissociative disorder: psychogenic amnesia, depersonalization, fugue, and multiple personality. All are extremely rare.

Psychogenic Amnesia

As we explained in Chapter 3, amnesia may be caused by a blow to the head or by other physical assaults on the brain. **Psychogenic amnesia** involves a partial or total relapse in memory for which no physical cause can be found. It typically occurs during periods of extreme psychological stress. The memory lapses associated with dissociative amnesia are selective and sometimes may be recovered through hypnosis or following injections of sodium amytal ("truth serum").

Fugue and Depersonalization

Fugue (from the Latin "to flee") involves a loss of memory of one's past that may last from a few

hours to a few years; people in this state do not know who they are or where they came from. For example, in September 1980 a 34-year-old woman who was unable to identify herself was found in a park in Florida. Through a nationwide publicity campaign and injections of sodium amytal, her parents were located. She had been missing for seven years (see Case 13-8). Holden Caufield, the hero of J. D. Salinger's *Catcher in the Rye,* experiences a fugue. **Depersonalization** involves either a feeling of detachment from one's mental processes or body (as if one were an outside observer), or a feeling of automation (as if one were an automaton).

Multiple Personality

All of us play many roles. For example, we behave differently in a church than we do in a bar. Some people, however, appear to develop several entirely different personalities—for which they may even create different names. The fundamental difference between role playing and multiple personality is that when we play roles, we maintain our sense of self (the *I* who plays the role); people with **multiple personalities** adopt different senses of self. Indeed, the different personalities in this dissociative disorder may not

CASE 13-9
MULTIPLE PERSONALITIES

In 1978 Billy Milligan, age 23, was acquitted of raping four women on the Ohio State University campus on the grounds "he" did not commit the crimes for which he was accused. Who did? According to Billy's defense attorney, Adelena—a young lesbian living in Billy as one of his ten personalities—committed the rapes. And one of Billy's other personalities turned her in.

In addition to Adelena, Billy Milligan harbors Christine, a warm-hearted three-year-old who loves to draw; David; a withdrawn child who bangs his head against the wall when he becomes upset; Arthur, an intellectual who speaks with a British accent; Ragan, the "protector" of the other personalities, who speaks with a slavic accent; Allen, who plays the drums and smokes; Tommy, who was dishonorably discharged from the navy; and Danny and Christopher, two timid adolescents (Footlick & Lowell, 1978).

Psychiatrist Eugene Bliss suggests that people develop alternate personalities when confronted with intolerable events in their lives. The purpose of these personalities is to express unaccept-

Billy Milligan

able urges, especially those that are sexual and aggressive in nature. Consider, for example, the following statements by women treated by Bliss.

> I [one of the personalities] came to help when she was raped. She needed someone to take over. I don't like sex but I can manage it, I'm a whore and a prostitute but she [the patient] is very moral and proper. I'm a tramp, just dirt and filth, but I take over the sexual part of life which she can't tolerate.

> I want her dead. She hasn't enough guts to commit suicide for herself but I'm going to get those pills and do it for her.

Joan [a personality] went out for a walk, Rebecca [another personality] ran into the middle of the road to commit suicide, but a policeman drove up and stopped her. So Joan took over again. When the cop tried to touch her she told him to stay away. He didn't, so she threatened to wrap his balls around his neck. Then she punched him, so he put her in handcuffs and shoved her into the patrol car. I [Lois] then took over and gave the body to [the patient] who started to cry. At the police station they telephoned Jan [a friend] who said there were 18 different personalities. I [Lois] told the police that we were making splendid progress in therapy. When he said that I was plenty cool and composed for such a problem, I told him it was not my problem and furthermore the body didn't belong to me.

Most people who develop multiple personalities are women who have a history of physical or sexual abuse in childhood.

even be aware of one another (see Case 13-9). For example, in 1978 the California Supreme Court reversed a guilty verdict against a woman convicted of forgery and check fraud on the basis of testimony given by psychologists and psychiatrists that the criminal acts had been committed by her alternate personality. This personality was eventually eliminated when the patient placed "it" in a bottle and threw "it" away during a hypnotic trance.

Many people think that "split personality" is the informal term for schizophrenia and that the famous cases of multiple personality reported in *Three Faces of Eve* (Thigpen & Cleckley, 1954) and *Sybil* (Schreiber, 1974) are cases of schizophrenia — they are not. The people in these accounts suffered from multiple personality. Cases of multiple personality are extremely rare; Coleman, Butcher, and Carson (1980) could find only 100 cases in the psychological and psychiatric literature, virtually all of whom were female. The number of personalities often increases markedly if patients receive a lot of attention. Perhaps encouraged by the interest of the therapist, cases of multiple personality have been reported where more than ten personalities have emerged.

capacity for affectionate sexual activity between adult human partners." The *DSM-III-R* contains two groups of **sexual disorders** (see Table 13-10). Another group was previously classified as psychosexual disorders in *DSM-III* but was reclassified in the group of disorders usually first evident in infancy, childhood, or adolescence in the *DSM-III-R*. This group, called **gender-identity** (or role) **disorders,** involves feelings of discomfort or lack of identification with one's anatomical sex and the desire to behave like or be a member of the opposite sex. We considered a major gender-identity disorder, *transsexualism,* in Chapter 2.

Behaviors commonly called "sexual perversions" are contained in the second group, **paraphilias.** This group of disorders is characterized by arousal in response to objects or situations that normally do not evoke arousal and that are inconsistent with mutually affectionate sexual activity. We discussed the origins and treatments of such sexual deviations in Chapter 8. The second group of disorders, **sexual dysfunctions,** is characterized by sexual inhibitions and deficiencies in the responses that normally occur during sexual arousal and intercourse; reactions commonly called *impotence, frigidity,* and *premature ejaculation* are contained in this category.

SEXUAL DISORDERS

The criteria for sexual disorders have changed significantly over the past decade or two, a fact which demonstrates the influence of social norms on assumptions about abnormality. In 1968, with the publication of the *DSM-II,* people were believed to suffer from a *psychosexual disorder* if their "sexual interests [were] directed primarily toward objects other than people of the opposite sex, toward sexual acts not usually associated with coitus, or with sexual acts performed under bizarre circumstances" (p. 44). However, with the revision of the *DSM-II* in 1980, people who met those conditions were treated more generously. In the *DSM-III,* sexual disorders are described as "those deviations from standard sexual behavior that involve gross impairments in the

PERSONALITY DISORDERS

Many people display life-long patterns of behavior that seem maladaptive and certainly are annoying or unacceptable to their friends, family, and community — yet are not problematic enough to lead them to seek treatment. Typically, such people do not regard their behavior as a problem; it is so deep-seated it seems second nature to them, an integral aspect of their personality. Occasionally such people are admitted to hospitals for other reasons, where their inflexible and maladaptive behavior is recognized as abnormal. Table 13-11 outlines the eleven major categories of **personality** (or character) **disorders** that fall on Axis II in the *DSM-III-R.* The central feature they share is immature and inflexible styles of

TABLE 13-10
Sexual Disorders

Category of Sexual Disorder	Example
Paraphilias (sexual deviations)	
Fetishism	Sexual arousal to inanimate object, usually clothing (for example, rubber boots, underclothes)
Frotteurism	Sexual urges related to touching and rubbing against a nonconsenting person
Pedophilia	The use of a young child as the choice of sexual excitement
Exhibitionism	Gaining sexual excitement by fantasizing about and/or exposing the genitals to an unsuspecting stranger
Voyeurism	Spying on a member of the opposite sex while that person undresses, is nude, or engages in sexual activity
Sexual masochism	Deriving sexual excitement from being humiliated, beaten, bound, or made to suffer in other ways
Sexual sadism	Deriving sexual excitement from inflicting pain or suffering on another.
Sexual Dysfunctions	
Sexual desire disorders	Lack of sexual desire, sexual aversion
Sexual arousal disorders	Lack of lubrication in females and failure to attain or maintain erection in males
Orgasm disorders	Inability to achieve orgasm, premature ejaculation
Sexual pain disorders	Recurrent genital pain during or after intercourse, muscle spasms in the vagina

Source: Adapted from American Psychiatric Association. (1987). *Diagnostic and statistical manual of mental disorders* (3rd ed., revised).

coping. We consider one of the most extensively studied of all personality disorders, *antisocial personality,* also known as *psychopathic* and *sociopathic* personality; individuals who manifest the symptoms are commonly called psychopaths.

Antisocial Personality

The term **antisocial personality** is used to describe people who have shown major signs of antisocial behavior (such as habitual truancy, poor school performance) before the age of 15 and who, as adults, display at least three of the following characteristics:

1. aggressiveness
2. absence of remorse
3. recklessness
4. deceptiveness
5. involvement in criminal activities
6. inability to maintain a job
7. inability to maintain a lasting sexual attachment
8. failure to act as a responsible parent
9. failure to honor financial obligations

Most people with this personality disorder are male.

Repeated violation of the rights of others, "lovelessness," and "guiltlessness" are the distinguishing features of this disorder. People with antisocial personalities feel no loyalty or commitment to family, friends, or commonly accepted social values. Their frustration tolerance is low; they become bored easily, seek thrills, fail to mend their ways after bad experiences, and care little about the impact of their behavior on others. They usually are gifted in providing plausible explanations for their transgressions that are accompanied by unfulfilled promises to use their newly gained insights in the future. People with antisocial personalities are often charming and intelligent (see Case 13-10, page 718).

TABLE 13-11
Personality Disorders — *DSM-III-R*

Label	Signs
Paranoid	Pervasive and unwarranted tendency to interpret the actions of others as demeaning or threatening
Schizoid	A pervasive pattern of indifference to social relationships and a restricted range of emotional expression; defect in capacity to form friendships
Schizotypal	Such various oddities of thought, perception, speech, and behavior as magical thinking, recurrent illusions, suspiciousness, and social anxiety that is not severe enough to meet the criteria for schizophrenia; poor rapport with others
Antisocial	History of continuous and chronic violations of the rights of others; irresponsibility; inability to hold a job, fulfill responsibilities to others, or abide by social norms
Borderline	Instability in interpersonal relations, mood, and self-image; impulsive and unpredictable behavior; uncertainty about long-term goals and values; unstable moods; chronic feelings of emptiness or boredom
Histrionic	A pervasive pattern of excessive emotionality; problems in interpersonal relations due to superficiality, egocentricity, vanity, dependency, and affectedness
Narcissistic	Grandiose sense of self-importance or uniqueness; focus on special nature of one's problems; preoccupation with fantasies of success, power, brilliance, beauty or love; exhibitionism; indifference or anger in response to criticism; exploitativeness, selfishness, and lack of empathy in interpersonal relations
Avoidant	Hypersensitivity to rejection, criticism, or shame; unwillingness to enter into relationships unless guaranteed uncritical acceptance; withdrawal in spite of need for affection; timid
Dependent	Passive tendency to induce others to assume responsibility for major obligations; inability to function independently; difficulty making decisions; fears abandonment
Obsessive-compulsive	A pervasive pattern of perfectionism and inflexibility; preoccupation with details; excessive devotion to work; overconscientiousness
Passive-aggressive	Resistance to demands for adequate performance in both occupational and social areas expressed through procrastination, stubbornness, dawdling, "forgetfulness," or intentional inefficiency

Source: Adapted from American Psychiatric Association. (1987). *Diagnostic and statistical manual of mental disorders* (3rd ed., revised).

Psychiatrist Harvey Cleckley has written a fascinating book about *psychopaths.* Now in its fifth edition, *The Mask of Sanity* (1976) presents theoretical discussions of the condition, together with interesting case studies of these high-flying, self-interested people. Although Marshall seems quite tame in comparison with some of Cleckley's cases, he shares with them a lack of concern for the feelings of others.

What Causes People to Develop Antisocial Personalities?
Extensive research has been carried out on people with antisocial personalities (Martin, 1981).

There is some evidence that dispositions for this personality disorder are inherited. Biologically oriented researchers have supplied evidence that people with antisocial personalities have underreactive autonomic nervous systems (Hare, 1970, 1981); because of this deficiency, they do not experience as much anxiety as the average person and require more excitement to experience emotion. The inability of people with antisocial personalities to learn from experience may stem from this deficiency. Actually, it is not that such people are unable to learn — most are of average intelligence — it is that they do not learn to avoid aversive experiences as easily as the average person (Hare, 1970). This deficiency in avoidance learning (see Chapter 5) may occur because they do not experience the same degree of anxiety or pain as the average person; or they may experience normal levels of anxiety and pain, but suppress their reactions in order to foster a *macho* image.

Research also indicates that people with antisocial personalities have problematic family histories. Their parents often possess antisocial personalities or other problems that cause them either to neglect their children, pamper them, or treat them inconsistently (Robbins, 1978). Evidence suggests that children who develop antisocial personalities become adept early in their lives at manipulating others and at avoiding punishment, often through the use of charming maneuvers.

In Chapter 10 we described theories of moral development, and these theories are relevant to the study of antisocial personality. Research has found that people with antisocial personalities score lower than comparison groups on Kohlberg's test of moral judgment (see Blasi, 1980); studies also have found that such people have adverse social learning histories, especially exposure to antisocial models. As explained in Chapter 10, Freud suggests that the conscience is formed in a male when he identifies with his father in order to be like him and to maintain his love. According to psychoanalysts, males who develop antisocial personalities fail to form an adequate superego because they neither identify with their father nor fear the loss of his love.

In closing, we emphasize an important sense in which the categories and descriptions of mental disorders we have considered are misleading: they seem to imply that certain distinct disorders exist (for example, schizophrenia, obsessive-compulsive disorder, antisocial personality), that people become afflicted with these disorders, and that psychologists and psychiatrists can diagnose them with considerable accuracy. However, if you were to sit in on a diagnostic interview or were to observe actual patients, you would soon see that the process of identifying the disorder from which they are suffering is riddled with problems. One problem relates to the implicit assumptions in the classification system about the nature of mental disorder; another problem relates to the ability of professionals to make accurate diagnoses. We now review the process of psychiatric diagnosis, and then examine the problems related to it.

Figure 13-12 outlines the process of psychiatric diagnosis. The major steps are interviewing

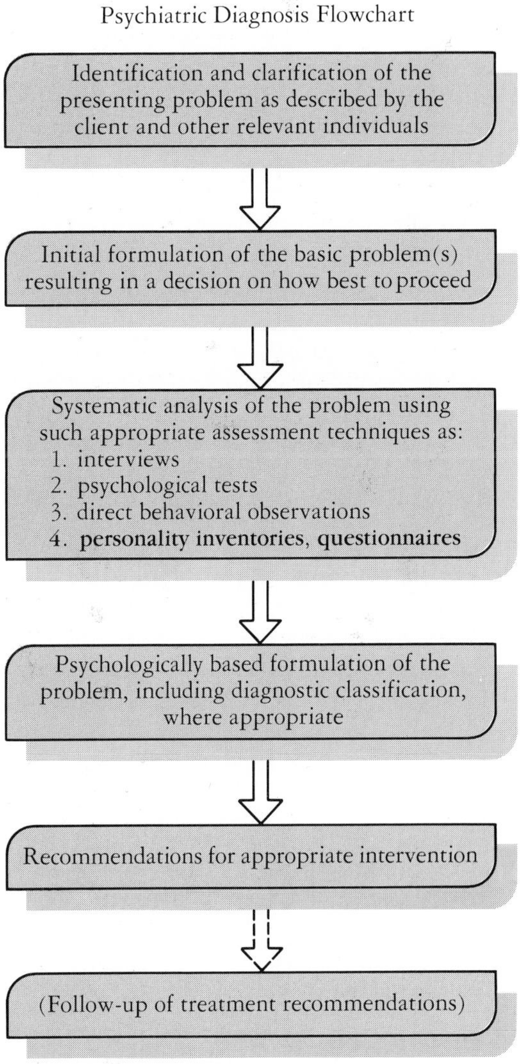

Psychiatric Diagnosis Flowchart

FIGURE 13-12

The Major Steps in the Diagnosis of Psychological Disorder *Source:* Meyer, R. G., & Salmon, P. (1984). *Abnormal psychology* (p. 56). Boston, MA: Allyn and Bacon.

CASE 13-10
ANTISOCIAL PERSONALITY

By the time Marshall was 37, he had been a "con man" for most of his life. Whether he was selling used cars to unsuspecting poor people without mentioning the faulty brake systems, or selling real estate without bothering to mention the house was directly in the path of a planned freeway, or borrowing several thousand dollars from his retired parents for a "sure" investment (although really planning to use the money to pay off a gambling debt), Marshall enjoyed the fun and excitement of putting something over on a "sucker." When his victims confronted him with the consequences of his misdeeds, he felt no remorse. On the contrary, he considered them stupid for being so trusting, or perhaps for being so greedy for a bargain that they didn't fully investigate; in either case, he rationalized that they had deserved it and that they would have done the same to him had they had the opportunity or the brains.

Most people meeting Marshall for the first time found him to be poised, bright, and charming. Because he was tanned, handsome, trim, and smartly dressed, people naturally trusted him and wanted to believe him. Marshall had learned in childhood that he could "get away with murder"—that he could ask outrageous things of people and they would comply. When caught shoplifting at the age of seven, he explained he was actually returning an item his friend had taken the previous day; apparently he looked so innocent and convincing that the shopkeeper believed him. When Marshall vandalized the school one weekend at the age of eleven, he was the student most "shocked" at this behavior on Monday morning; he comforted the distressed teacher, accompanied her home, and accepted her gratitude for his helpfulness and understanding. By the time he was 15 and in high school, he was regularly stealing school supplies from the storeroom and selling them after school to other children; Marshall told them that his father had opened a stationary store and was selling these items at reduced costs as a goodwill gesture (this incident illustrates his tendency to be a pathological liar).

TABLE 13-12
Example of Diagnostic Evaluation Based on *DSM-III*

A 32-year-old computer programmer, depressed by a recent failure to secure a job promotion (though competent enough when working with computers), has a history of poor social relationships dating from childhood. Promotions of workers within the company, however, are awarded only to those who show managerial potential by exhibiting good interpersonal skills.

Axis I	Dysthymic disorder (depressive neurosis)
Axis II	Avoidant personality disorder
Axis III	Deferred (no known contributory physical disorder)
Axis IV	Severity of psychological stressors: moderate a. job promotion denied in favor of younger colleague b. forced by economic factors to move into an apartment with two roommates
Axis V	Highest level of adaptive functioning past year: fair

Source: Meyer, R. G., & Salmon, P. (1984). *Abnormal psychology* (p. 61). Boston, MA: Allyn and Bacon.

Marshall had never been in trouble with the law directly; as an adult, he engaged in various petty thefts from employers, but always seemed able to talk his way out of being prosecuted. Most of his sexual contacts had been with prostitutes. However, at the age of 30 he married Arlene — after learning her parents were wealthy and might set him up in business. Restless, impulsive, and impatient, he moved from one business to another until he developed the plan to start the Church of Purity. His trusting wife, who believed that he had found God, never realized this was another "hype."

Marshall came to the attention of a psychologist when his wife, from whom he was separated, was referred for psychotherapy by her minister. She was a deeply religious woman, the mother of four children, and totally unprepared for Marshall's abrupt departure six months earlier. At that time he had simple announced that he was fed up with her, that she was sexually an "iceberg," that he laughed at her belief in God, that he had emptied their small bank account, and that he planned to marry a go-go dancer employed in a topless bar. Although he lived only four blocks away, once Marshall left the house he never contacted Arlene or the children. Despite his huge income from the "church" he founded — to which hundreds of believers were sending contributions — he sent them no money. To make matters worse, Marshall's wife was receiving bills amounting to thousands of dollars from stores, finance companies, and a variety of creditors who had loaned Marshall money. His wife — who had moved in with her parents — was unable to cope with the situation and was near a serious breakdown that ultimately necessitated her hospitalization.

The psychologist saw Marshall for six sessions, during which he told his story. Then he suddenly disappeared and never contacted the psychologist again. Needless to say, he never bothered to pay the bill.

Source: Adapted from Goldenberg, H. (1977). *Abnormal psychology* (pp. 567–68). Monterey, CA: Brooks/Cole.

---

a client, talking to his or her relatives or friends, making a preliminary judgment about whether further examination is warranted, obtaining information more systematically where necessary, then making a diagnosis. Table 13-12 supplies an example of a diagnosis based on the *DSM-III.*

DIAGNOSIS — ISSUES AND PROBLEMS

In view of the pervasiveness of the medical model of mental illness, we might expect that psychiatric diagnosis would be patterned closely after the diagnosis of physical disorders. In medicine, diseases typically have a specific cause, a natural history or pattern of development, a particular outcome, and an established array of treatments. Consider pulmonary tuberculosis, for example. The signs include coughing, afternoon and evening fevers, bacilli in sputum or stomach juices, positive reactions to skin tests, and visible evidence of infection on an X ray of the lungs; symptoms may include fatigue or general malaise. Once the bacillus is identified, all the signs and symptoms make sense and the treatment is established. However, such tidy correlates as these do not exist for most psychological disorders. In a classic article, Zigler and Phillips (1961) pointed out that the diagnostic system employed by psychologists and psychiatrists does not provide information about causes, signs, symptoms, background factors, and amenability to treatment for all disorders in a systematic way, thereby making accurate diagnosis difficult. Fur-

thermore, few people fit the descriptions of the disorders described in the *Diagnostic and Statistical Manual;* most patients display symptoms characteristic of several disorders (see Table 13-13).

The developers of *DSM-III-R* attempt to counter the criticisms of earlier diagnostic and statistical manuals by providing detailed descriptions of the behaviors associated with each disorder and as much background information as possible. They argue it may be quite appropriate to employ different kinds of criteria to diagnose different disorders. For example, although anomalies in behavior may supply the most appro-

TABLE 13-13
Symptomatic Overlap across Diagnostic Categories

	Manic-depressive	Neurotic	Personality Disorder	Schizophrenia
Symptoms that tend to occur	Suicidal attempts Suicidal ideas Euphoria Depression Insomnia Obsessions Does not eat	Suicidal ideas Bodily complaints Tension Headaches Depression Fears own hostile impulses Phobias	Perversions Drinking Robbery Assaultiveness Threatens assault Emotional outbursts Lying Rape	Suspiciousness Perplexity Bizarre ideas Hallucinations Sexual preoccupation Apathy Withdrawal Depersonalization Feels perverted Maniacal outbursts Bodily complaints
Symptoms that tend not to occur	Withdrawal Robbery	Suspiciousness Perplexity Bizarre ideas Hallucinations Robbery Assaultiveness	Suspiciousness Perplexity Bizarre ideas Hallucinations Sexual preoccupation Apathy Withdrawal Depersonalization Feels perverted Euphoria Bodily complaints Self-depreciation Depression Phobias Obsessions	Perversions Drinking Threatens assault Emotional outbursts Lying Rape Suicidal attempts Suicidal ideas Depression Fears own hostile impulses

Source: Adapted from Zigler, E., & Phillips, L. (1961). Psychiatric diagnosis and symptomatology. *Journal of Abnormal Psychology, 63;* 69–75. American Psychological Association.

priate basis for diagnosing a disorder characterized by frequent stuttering, information about the cause of an affective disorder or its responsiveness to particular drugs may be more useful.

It would be simple to diagnose mental disorder if specific symptoms were related to one and only one disorder, but this is rarely the case. In the same way that fever and vomiting may stem from a wide array of physical disorders, such symptoms as anxiety and disorganized thought accompany many psychological disorders. In some cases, the same observable characteristics have different origins; in other cases, different observable characteristics have the same origin. For instance, a patient with no known or available history may answer questions with one syllable words. From what disorder is this person suffering: mental retardation, schizophrenia, an acute fear response, severe depression, or an aphasic (language-impaired) condition caused by a modest stroke? Such problems make psychiatric diagnosis a difficult task. Let us examine the evidence in an attempt to determine how well psychologists and psychiatrists have done.

Reliability of Psychiatric Diagnosis

In the 1950s several studies challenged the reliability of psychiatric diagnosis. Follow-up research found that when broad classificatory groups were used (such as the old categories of neurosis and psychosis), there was a fairly high level of inter-judge agreement. One study reported 70% agreement; other studies reported agreement ranging from 54–84% (Zigler & Phillips, 1961). However, when a larger array of more differentiated categories was used (for example, specific types of anxiety), agreement dropped to a range of from 32–57%. (Kendell, 1975). Although these figures are not reassuring, they may not be as bad as they seem when compared to medical diagnosis. McGuire (1974) points out that a study of the reliability of the diagnosis of "cause of death" revealed only 66% agreement when the death certificate was compared to the autopsy report.

Improving Diagnostic Reliability Two decades ago observers noted that there appeared to be many more schizophrenic than manic-depressive

patients in the United States and that the reverse was true in England. A series of studies called the *US/UK Project* was conducted over a period of ten years to investigate the apparent differences in the incidence rates for first admissions to mental hospitals in the United States and the United Kingdom. The project ultimately showed that when specific criteria were established for the diagnosis of schizophrenic and manic-depressive psychosis and when judges in the two countries were trained to use these critera, they obtained very similar incidence levels (Cooper, Kendell, Gurland, Sharpe, Copeland, & Simon, 1972).

One of the goals in revising the *DSM-II* was to enhance the reliability of psychiatric diagnosis by supplying detailed descriptions of disorders and by ensuring that clinicians employ the same criteria. Although still not as high as psychologists would like (see Table 13-14), the evidence suggests that reliability was enhanced (Spitzer et al., 1979). With improvements in criterion-specification in the *DSM-III-R*, reliability may be improved even further.

TABLE 13-14
Reliability Coefficients Achieved in Field Trials with *DSM-III*[*]

Diagnostic Category	Reliability[†]
Disorders usually first evident in infancy, childhood, or adolescence	0.65
Organic mental disorders	0.79
Substance-use disorders	0.86
Schizophrenic disorders	0.81
Paranoid disorders	0.66
Affective disorders	0.69
Anxiety disorders	0.63
Somatoform disorders	0.54
Dissociative disorders	0.80
Psychosexual disorders	0.92
Psychological factors affecting physical condition	0.62
Personality disorders	0.56

[*] Data shown from phase I of field trial; number of patients, 339.
[†] Reliabilities use a statistic called *kappa* that reflects percent agreement corrected for chance agreements.
Source: Adapted from Davison, G. C., & Neale, J. M. (1986). *Abnormal psychology: An experimental clinical approach* (4th ed., p. 66). New York: Wiley & Sons.

Validity of Psychiatric Diagnosis

It is possible for several experts to agree that a patient has a disorder such as schizophrenia yet still be wrong. A study by social psychologist David Rosenhan (1973) exemplifies this point and explores its implications.

Rosenhan presented himself and eight other "sane" people for admission to different psychiatric hospitals in the United States. These individuals, as normal as you and me, fabricated the claim that they had heard voices saying "empty," "hollow," and "thud." This was the only symptom they presented, and during all diagnostic questioning they described themselves with complete accuracy. All patients were diagnosed as having a mental disorder, primarily schizophrenia; none was detected as being a pseudopatient. After the initial complaint of "voices," the pseudopatients behaved in an entirely normal manner. Although other patients often voiced suspicions about the legitimacy of these people (accusing them of being journalists or academic researchers), the staff never questioned their status. The "patients" were hospitalized an average of 19 days before discharge, some being retained for almost two months. The diagnosis given all these patients at the time of discharge was "schizophrenia in remission" (schizophrenic, but not actively so).

When the staff of one hospital heard the results of Rosenhan's study, they were skeptical and challenged him to try the same thing with them. In response, Rosenhan asked them to rate all new admissions to their hospital over a three-month period on a scale that described the likelihood each patient was a pseudopatient. At the end of three months, judgments were available for 193 admitted patients: 41 were suspected of being pretenders by at least one staff member; 19 were labeled "suspicious." In fact, Rosenhan never sent even one pseudopatient to the hospital in question!

When Rosenhan studied the hospital case records of his pseudopatients, he noticed that normal incidents were described with a pathological twist and that doctors interacted with patients as though the patients were abnormal. For example, if a pseudopatient asked a simple question such as "Pardon me, Dr. X, could you tell me when I am eligible for grounds privileges?", a typical response would be "Good morning Dave. How are you today?" Then the doctor would walk away without waiting for a response. Rosenhan concluded that hospital environments structure the meaning of behavior in ways that maximize the perception of pathology and minimize the awareness of normal behavior. However, Rosenhan's study has not gone without criticism. Yale University pychiatrist Paul Fleischman wrote a critical analysis of the study, part of which is reprinted in Box 13-7.

Reliability and validity are important issues in psychological diagnosis because the consequences of making errors can be serious: individuals may receive inappropriate treatment or may be shackled with stigmatizing labels for the rest of their lives. As explained in Chapter 12, people often form general judgments about others on the basis of scant information. Imagine that you discover someone has been a "mental patient" or has suffered from a mental illness. What traits would you automatically attribute to the person? Numerous studies have found that people attribute an array of negative qualities to those whom they (incorrectly) believe are former mental patients (see Farina & Hagelauer, 1975); other studies have found a pervasive tendency in the general population to view mental patients with apprehension and distrust. Indeed, one study found that college students have more favorable opinions of ex-convicts than of ex-mental patients (Lamy, 1966): they would rather have an ex-convict care for their child, would rather hire an ex-convict for a permanent position, and would rather be an ex-convict than an ex-mental patient. And, as revealed by the case of Senator Thomas Eagleton of Missouri, (Senator George McGovern's vice-presidential running mate — who was asked to withdraw his candidacy for that office in the 1972 presidential election when it became publically known that he had undergone psychiatric treatment for depression) people do not want ex-mental patients for their political leaders. Social psychological research also has found that people tend to live up (or down) to the labels given them (see Chapter 12), thus creating a self-fulfilling prophesy. People labeled

Box 13-7
CRITICAL REACTIONS TO ROSENHAN'S STUDY *ON BEING SANE IN INSANE PLACES*

In one of several critical letters to the editor of *Science,* Yale psychiatrist Paul R. Fleischman (1973) writes:

D. L. Rosenhan's article "On being sane in insane places" . . . while full of important observations, is seriously flawed by methodological inadequacies and by conclusions that are inconsistent with—indeed, that directly contradict—the data he presents. . . . When Rosenhan's pseudopatients faked a history and were subsequently "misdiagnosed" by physicians at the psychiatric hospitals where they presented themselves, they established nothing about the accuracy of diagnosis per se, but merely reaffirmed the critical role of history-taking in medicine. Most physicians do not assume that patients who seek help are liars; they can therefore, of course, be misled. It would be quite possible to conduct a study in which patients trained to simulate histories of myocardial infarction would receive treatment on the basis of history alone (since a negative electrocardiogram is not diagnostic), but it would be preposterous to conclude from such a study that

physical illness does not exist, that medical diagnoses are fallacious labels, and that "illness" and "health" reside only in doctors' heads.

Most shocking, however, is Rosenhan's conclusion that "the normal are not detectably sane," by which he evidently means "not detectably nonpsychotic." In fact, all the pseudopatients were discharged with the diagnosis of "schizophrenia in remission," which means that they were clearly seen by the doctors to be nonpsychotic in the hospitals where they were observed but had been psychotic during the period described by their "history." Thus, Rosenhan's study demonstrates that despite false historical data and the set of the hospital environment, twelve nonpsychotics were observed by their psychiatrists to be nonpsychotic—a record of 100-percent accuracy.

Other critics have pointed out that psychotics are not bizarre all the time and generally respond well to treatment procedures, making them relatively similar to "sane" people in the ward setting. Rosenhan was challenged to conduct a reverse experiment: remove obviously psychotic patients

from a hospital to a new community and try to pass them off successfully as normal.

Critics noted that Rosenhan's use of the term "insane," while catchy as a headline, was inaccurate considering the term is not a psychiatric diagnostic category but a legal term decided in a court of law—and as such incorrectly used in his study.

Generally the critics agreed there are reliability problems in diagnosis in psychiatry, but felt the methodological problems and the unusual data interpretations in Rosenhan's report raised serious questions about the value of his findings.

Source: Adapted and selections taken from Fleischman, P. R. (1973, April). *Science, 180,* No. 4084, p. 356.

"crazy" or "mentally ill" are avoided and are treated in ways that evoke behaviors believed to be characteristic of the mentally ill. Behaviors that would be considered normal in someone not diagnosed mentally ill take on special meaning — even to the person displaying them — creating further confusion and self-doubt in an already disturbed person. "Why do I have these strange thoughts; why do I feel confused?" Eventually, many people accept the labels given them and incorporate the labels into their identities, often in self-defeating ways. "I'm mentally ill, so I don't have to take responsibility for my behavior."

In a broader perspective, misdiagnoses give rise to inaccurate estimates of the incidence and prevalence of psychological disorders, as well as misleading information about their causes and correlates. The primary reason why psychiatrists and psychologists make mistakes in diagnosis is because so little is known about the various psychological disorders. If more were known about their causes and their natural history, fewer mistakes would be made.

SUMMARY

1. Historically, individuals suffering from mental disorders have been characterized as "possessed," "mentally ill," "emotionally disturbed," "socially deviant," or victims of unfortunate histories of learning. These labels derive from models of psychopathology based on assumptions about the causes of abnormal behavior. Although some psychological disorders have been found to stem from single causes, most appear to originate from complex interactions among physical, social, and psychological factors.

2. The *Diagnostic and Statistical Manual of Mental Disorders* of the American Psychiatric Association *(DSM-III-R)* classifies mental disorders, listing behavior associated with each disorder together with an example of a typical case. Such information as age of onset, usual course of development, degree of impairment, factors that increase susceptibility, prevalence, and genetic risk also is included. The *DSM-III-R* contains five axes: Axis I (clinical syndromes and other conditions), Axis II (personality disorders and specific developmental disorders), Axis III (physical disorders and conditions), Axis IV (severity of psychosocial stressors), and Axis V (global assessment of functioning).

3. Anorexia nervosa and bulimia are examples of disorders usually first evident in infancy, childhood, or adolescence. Individuals who suffer from these disorders (usually females) are abnormally concerned with body weight; they fear getting fat. It appears these disorders are caused by several interacting factors.

4. Another developmental disorder, autistic disorder, is characterized by unresponsiveness to other people and a preference for nonsocial objects. This disorder may strike children at any time during their first two and one-half years. Most theories of autism attribute the disorder to such biological factors as abnormalities of the brain. Although psychological theories — such as those that attribute the disorder to a rejecting attitude on the part of the parent — have been offered, they lack empirical support.

5. Disorders that originate from destruction of brain tissue or chemical imbalances in the brain are classified as organic brain syndromes.

6. Alcoholism is the most prevalent substance-use disorder. Although the tendency to alcoholism runs in families and appears, in part, to be inherited, learning experiences and social factors also play a part.

7. The schizophrenias are a group of disorders characterized by serious disruptions in functioning, a severe deterioration in personality, and a loss of contact with reality. People with schizophrenia typically display abnormalities in attention, thinking, perception,

emotional reactions, motor behavior, and social relations. Genetic research indicates the disposition to become schizophrenic is inherited. Biochemical research suggests schizophrenic disorders may be caused by an excess of the neurotransmitter dopamine or by overly sensitive dopamine receptors. Social psychological research suggests social experiences, especially concerning family relations, may induce schizophrenic reactions.

8. Mood disorders are characterized by extreme disturbances of emotional states. There are three primary mood disorders: mania (extreme elation and agitation); depression; and manic-depressive, or bipolar disorder (characterized by fluctuations between manic and depressive states). Of the three types, depression is the most prevalent. Concordance rates for manic-depressive disorders are the highest of all psychological disorders. Deficiencies in the neurotransmitters norepinephrine and serotonin have been implicated in the development of affective disorders. Learning theorists attribute depression to a decrease in life's rewards and to learned helplessness. Cognitive theorists attribute depression to self-defeating styles of thinking. The evidence suggests depression is determined by several interacting factors.

9. There are five primary types of anxiety disorder: generalized anxiety, panic attacks, phobias, obsessive-compulsiveness, and post-traumatic stress disorder. The first two are characterized by high levels of anxiety, the next two by defenses against anxiety, and the last by a belated reaction to prolonged periods of high anxiety. Most theories of anxiety emphasize such psychological factors as the breakdown of ego defenses, the conditioning of fear, our sense of control over the outcomes in our lives, and the ways in which we view ourselves and our circumstances.

10. Somatoform disorders involve the belief that one has a physical ailment that does not, in fact, exist. Hypochondriasis (preoccupation with bodily symptoms) and conversion disorder (development of a physical dysfunction that has no physical basis) are two

types. Most psychologists believe somatoform disorders are induced by psychological stress and supply a means of relieving the stress, avoiding responsibility, and obtaining care and attention.

11. Dissociative disorders involve blocking information about the self from consciousness. Such dissociative disorders as amnesia, fugue, and multiple personality are extremely rare, and appear to be induced by extreme psychological stress.

12. Sexual disorders are deviations in normal sexual behavior that involve gross impairments in people's capacity for affectionate sexual activity. There are two types of sexual disorders: paraphilias and sexual dysfunctions. Paraphilia disorders involve arousal evoked by objects or situations other than those that normally evoke sexual arousal. Sexual dysfunctions involve sexual inhibition and deficiencies in the responses that normally occur during sexual intercourse. Included among sexual dysfunctions are inhibited desire, inability to sustain an erection, and inability to achieve organism.

13. Personality disorders involve life-long, deep-seated patterns of inflexible and maladaptive behavior. Antisocial personality, also called sociopathic and psychopathic personality, has received the most attention from researchers. Studies have found that antisocial personalities tend to run in families and that people with antisocial personalities tend to have underreactive nervous systems, deficiencies in avoidance learning, and inadequate parents.

14. There is a long history of controversy over psychiatric diagnosis. In the old versions of the *Diagnostic and Statistical Manual of Mental Disorders,* reliability of diagnoses for specific disorders was low; however, detailed descriptions of disorders in the *DSM-III* have led to improved reliability of diagnoses for most disorders. Critics still question the validity of psychiatric diagnosis; valid diagnoses await discovery of the causes and natural histories of psychological disorders.

KEY TERMS

Exorcism
Trephining
General Paresis of the Insane (GPI)
Medical Model of Mental Illness
Hysteria
Psychoanalytic Model of Psychological Disorder
Problems in Living
Social-deviation Model of Psychological Disorder
Behavioristic Model
Neurosis
Syndrome
Axes of Classification
Multiaxial Approach
Epidemiology
Anorexia Nervosa
Bulimia Nervosa
Concordance Rate
Autistic Aloneness
Autistic Disorder
Organic Mental Disorder
Psychoactive Substance-use Disorder
Alcohol Abuse
Alcohol Dependence
Schizophrenia
Clang Association
Neologism
Delusion

Hallucination
Prodromal Phase
Active Phase
Residual Phase
Process Schizophrenia
Reactive Schizophrenia
Dopamine
Dopamine Theory
Experimental Psychopathologist
Id-dominated Primary Process Thinking
Schizophrenogenic
Marital Schism
Marital Skew
Double-bind Communication
Diathesis-stress Model
Schizotaxia
Schizotypy
Delusional (Paranoid) Disorder
Delusion
Mood Disorder
Manic State
Agitated Depression
Major Depressive Syndrome
Manic–Depressive Disorder
Neurotransmitter
Norepinephrine
Serotonin
Learned Helplessness
Neurosis

Psychosis
Anxiety Disorder
Generalized Anxiety
Free-floating Anxiety
Panic Attack
Phobia
Simple Phobia
Complex Phobia
Agoraphobia
Social Phobia
Obsession
Compulsion
Shell Shock
Combat Exhaustion
Post-traumatic Stress Disorder
Neurotic Paradox
Somatoform Disorder
Hypochondriasis
Conversion Disorder
Glove Anesthesia
Dissociative Disorder
Psychogenic Amnesia
Fugue
Depersonalization
Multiple Personality
Sexual Disorder
Gender-identity Disorder
Paraphilias
Psychosexual Dysfunction
Personality (or character) Disorder
Antisocial Personality

RECOMMENDED READINGS

Kesey, K. (1962). *One flew over the cuckoo's nest.* New York: Viking. This popular novel and movie make the point that psychiatric diagnosis and treatment can be used to control behavior considered undesirable in a hospital yet healthy and appropriate from other perspectives.

Lowinson, V., & Ruiz, P. (Eds.) (1981). *Substance abuse.* Baltimore, MD: Williams and Wilkins. A collection of articles contributed by leading scientists and clinicians on all aspects of substance abuse.

Meyer, R. G., & Salmon, P. (1984). *Abnormal psychology.* Boston, MA: Allyn and Bacon. An up-to-date and thorough overview of the field of abnormal psychology.

Millon, T. (1981). *Disorders of personality.* New York: John Wiley and Sons. A thorough overview of personality disorders.

Shapiro, S. (1981). *Contemporary theories of schizophrenia: Review and synthesis.* New York: McGraw-Hill. An overview of the various theories of schizophrenic behavior.

Stone, A. A., & Stone, S. S. (1966). *The abnormal personality through literature.* New Jersey: Prentice Hall. A selection of excerpts from major fictional works of Western literature that deal with pathological behavior.

Triandis, H., & Draguns, J. (Eds.) (1980). *Handbook of cross-cultural psychology: Psychopathology.* Boston, MA: Allyn and Bacon. A recent cross-cultural perspective on psychopathology.

Weiner, I. B. (1982). *Child and adolescent psychopathology.* New York: John Wiley and Sons. A look at various developmental problems as they occur from early childhood through late adolescence.

Zilboorg, G., & Henry, G. (1941). *A history of medical psychology.* New York: Norton. An excellent historical account of conceptions and treatments of mental disorder.

14

THE TREATMENT OF PSYCHOLOGICAL DISORDERS

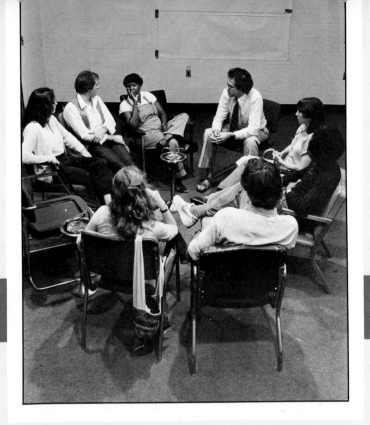

The attendants should enter into a few of his delusions but should reject others. If insufficient attendants are available, the patient should be carefully fettered in order to keep him quiet. [Patients should have] warm poultices of oil, to be applied particularly to the head, and also careful blood-letting. On the third or fourth day the head should be shaved and treated with cupping [bleeding], leeches, and scarification. Passive exercises such as rocking and a careful diet are indicated. . . . one should maintain a serious attitude towards abnormally cheerful patients and a friendly one to those who are downcast. (Ackerknecht, 1968, p. 13)

This is how, in A.D. 100, Roman physician Soranus described treatment for mentally deranged people. Soranus also recommended that patients participate in discussions with philosophers, which, he believed, would relieve their fears and feelings of distress. In Chapter 13 we described the models that have guided conceptions of abnormality and psychological disorder over the centuries and referred to the forms of treatment associated with each model. For example, if you believe that abnormal behavior is caused by possession of evil spirits, it follows that the way to change such behavior is to exorcise those evil spirits. Exorcism and other methods of driving out evil spirits from people's bodies were the preferred forms of treatment for most of the history of the human species (see illustrations) and, as noted, are still employed in some parts of the world today. If, however, you believe that mental illness is a type of disease, it follows that you would employ some form of physical treatment. Or if you assume that mental illness is caused by such psychological factors as repressed memories, then it makes sense to adopt a psychological approach. As primitive as Soranus' methods may seem to us today, they constituted a significant improvement over exorcism.

Today, a wide array of techniques is available to professionals who specialize in the treatment of psychological disorder, each with its own assumptions about the nature, cause, and appropriate way of responding to abnormal behavior. Some professionals employ such medical treatments as psychosurgery and drug therapy. Some provide such psychological treatment as psychoanalysis. Some treat psychological disorders with techniques based on the principles of learning. Some employ cognitive techniques, attempting to change the way clients think about themselves. Others attend to the patterns of interaction between groups of people, especially families. Still others attempt to change the social system instead of the people affected by it. In this chapter, we describe the major approaches to treatment employed by psychologists and other practitioners, examine their commonalities and differences, and explore the critically important question: How well do they work?

CONTEMPORARY PSYCHOTHERAPY — AN OVERVIEW

In North America, more people are hospitalized for mental disorders than for any other ailment. The odds of an individual in the United States receiving some form of psychotherapy are about three in one hundred. According to the U.S. Department of Health and Human Services, each year more than seven million Americans seek professional help for a psychological problem. Virtually anyone is a candidate for treatment at sometime in his or her life. Among the people with whom we went to high school, one has been diagnosed manic depressive, two have had acute schizophrenic breakdowns, several have suffered through intense periods of depression, and many

would be considered neurotic. Frank (1973) suggests that most people who receive psychological treatment fall in the six categories outlined in Table 14-1.

WHO SUPPLIES TREATMENT?

If you lived in certain parts of the world and you developed a physical or mental problem, you would see a witchdoctor and take your chances. If you had lived during the Middle Ages, you

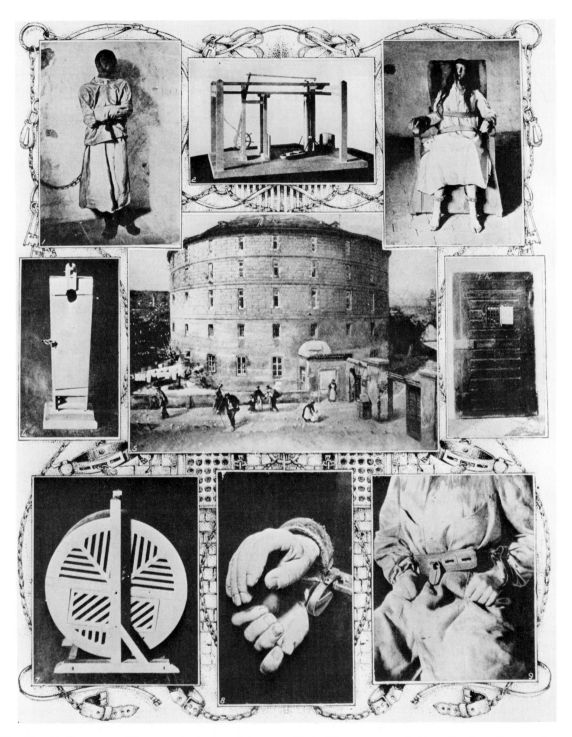

The Fool's Tower — Vienna   At the lunatic's tower (5) in Vienna, a remarkable collection of strange instruments and fetters were employed in the treatment of the insane.   (1) A lunatic in hood and straitjacket, padlocked to a cell wall.   (2) The machine in which lunatics were swung until they were in a state of stupefaction and therefore remained quiet.   (3) A patient strapped in a chair, in a position sometimes held for weeks.   (4) The "English coffin," in which the lunatic was kept, face at the hole, for discipline.   The face and the box together resembled a standing clock.   (6) A cell door with its iron "spy-hole."   (7) An enormous wheel that turned each time the lunatic inside it moved.   (8) A patient's hands in padlocked handcuffs.   (9) Another straitjacketed lunatic.

TABLE 14-1
Types of People Who Receive Psychological Treatment

Psychotics	People who have lost contact with reality; most likely diagnosed as schizophrenic or suffering from serious depression; probably receiving antipsychotic drugs or institutionalized
Neurotics	People who have some difficulty functioning; most receive psychotherapy and do not require hospitalization
The Psychologically Shaken	People who are temporarily overwhelmed by a stressful event or a crisis, such as illness, death of a loved one, or divorce; usually need temporary support to get them through the crisis
The Unruly	Acting-out children, alcoholics, antisocial personalities, and gamblers are examples of the unruly; usually do not seek help voluntarily but brought to therapy by concerned others
The Discontented	People who seek to make their lives more fulfilling; respond well to human potential programs directed toward self-enhancement

would have gone (or likely would have been dragged) to a priest. If you had lived in the early twentieth century, you probably would have seen a medical doctor. Today you have many more options.

For most people, the first person who comes to mind when they think of mental disorder is a **psychiatrist**. Psychiatrists are medical doctors who undergo postgraduate training (called a *residency*) in the treatment of mental disorder. Because they are medical doctors, they may serve as physicians; most often, however, the only medicine they practice is prescribing drugs. In the main, psychiatrists provide **psychotherapy**: treating mental disorders by means of psychological techniques. Although historically the methods used by psychiatrists have tended to be based on psychoanalysis, during the past decade psychiatrists have begun to use a wider variety of techniques.

Even though psychiatrists may employ techniques based on psychoanalysis, the term **psychoanalyst** is applied most appropriately to those trained in a psychoanalytic institute who have undergone psychoanalysis. In Canada, Europe, and some states, any suitable, well-educated person can apply for psychoanalytic *lay* training and eventually become a fully accredited psychoanalyst.

A **clinical psychologist** has taken a program leading to a Ph.D. degree in psychology, with an emphasis on the application of psycholog-

ical principles to the assessment and treatment of psychological disorders. Clinical psychologists are trained to work with people who have psychological problems—typically during a year's residency in an institutional setting. Clinical psychologists are trained to conduct psychological research, make psychological assessments, and practice psychotherapy. Because clinical psychologists are not medical doctors, they are not permitted to prescribe drugs or supply other forms of medical treatment. **Counseling psychologists** are similar to clinical psychologists, but undergo less training in research and diagnosis. Counseling psychologists usually work within such large institutional systems as schools, industry, social welfare services, and drug and alcohol treatment centers, where typically they deal with people who display problems of adjustment.

Psychiatric social workers possess a Master of Social Work degree, typically focusing on psychological problems related to the family and the community. Psychiatric social workers gather information about problems in the home and participate in family therapy. Their training often incorporates psychoanalytic concepts similar to those employed in the training of psychiatrists. **Psychiatric nurses** possess a nursing degree and undergo special training in the care of mental patients. They work in such treatment facilities as mental hospitals and community mental health centers.

TABLE 14-2
People Who Provide Psychological Treatment Today

Treatment Provider	Training	Where and With Whom
Clinical Psychologist	Doctoral degree in psychology and specialized clinical training	Not restricted—may provide treatment in private practice or be associated with such institutions as schools and hospitals
Psychiatrist	Medical degree and advanced training in psychiatry	Not restricted—may provide treatment in private practice or through association with hospitals; only treatment provider permitted to prescribe medication
Counseling Psychologist	Master's or doctoral degree in education with focus on counseling	Not restricted—although private practice is possible, most often associated with educational settings
Social Worker	Master's degree in social work and some advanced clinical training	Not restricted—although private practice is possible, most often associated with government agency/department; primary work with families
Psychoanalyst	Any of the above and advanced training in psychoanalysis	Most often private practice
Psychiatric Nurse	R.N. and advanced training in psychiatry	Privately and publically administered institutions
Paraprofessionals	Individuals who receive basic training in area of focus	Always associated with a community agency: crisis intervention centers, rape relief, and the like
Self-help Groups	No formal training—individuals who have undergone prior group experience	Associated with self-help groups: Alcoholics Anonymous, drugs, victims of crime, and the like

In recent years it has become apparent that there are too few trained professionals to meet the needs of all troubled people. Moreover, trained professionals tend to be middle-class individuals to whom those of other social classes sometimes find it difficult to relate. Consequently, nonprofessionals or **paraprofessionals** have begun to play an increasingly prevalent role in the treatment of psychological disorder. For example, former drug users work in some drug treatment programs and members of minority groups have been trained to assist the professional mental health staff in their communities. Although some professionals have resisted the use of lay people (partly because of professional protectionism and partly because of legitimate concerns about their lack of training), more and more the two groups are reaching satisfactory working compromises that take advantage of the skills of each. Table 14-2 supplies a summary description of the types of people who provide treatment in North America today.

WHERE DO PEOPLE GO TO OBTAIN HELP?

Assume you wanted to talk to a therapist; how could you go about finding one? The two settings that often spring to mind when we think of psychotherapy are the private office of a psychiatrist or psychoanalyst and the psychiatric ward of a mental hospital. People suffering from relatively mild disorders usually see therapists in private practice. Although it is best to obtain a reference from someone who has had experience with a therapist, psychologists are listed in telephone directories under *psychologists* and *counseling services*; psychiatrists usually are listed under *physicians*. The choice between psychologist and psychiatrist is somewhat arbitrary. Average fees for psychiatrists generally are higher ($80 an hour) than for psychologists ($40 – $60 an hour); however, many therapists employ a sliding scale on an ability-to-pay basis for clients who cannot afford regular rates. Group therapy provides a less-expensive means of treatment because the therapist's fee is divided among several clients.

Academic preparation and specialized training of therapists usually can be learned simply by asking. However, if you have any doubt, credentials may be checked and helpful information obtained by contacting such organizations as The National Association for Mental Health (1800 North Kent Street, Rosslyn, VA 22209), The American Psychiatric Association (1700 18th Street NW, Washington, D.C. 20009), and The American Psychological Association (1200 17th Street NW, Washington, D.C. 20036).

Until the 1960s, people suffering from severe disorders were confined in mental hospitals. More recently, however, there has been a major trend away from treatment in large mental hospitals toward more accessible, community-based settings (see Figure 14-1). Several reasons underlie this trend. The traditional location of the mental hospital in a relatively isolated area (often in the country) led to problems in the quality of staff: few professionals wanted to isolate themselves from major centers of research and from opportunities for advancement. The remote location also made it difficult for the patient's family to provide emotional support. In addition, patients often lost the ability to function in normal social roles; once treatment ended, they found it difficult to return to life on the "outside."

Today most cities have **community mental-health centers** for people who need psychological assistance. People who do not require hospitalization can receive treatment in an outpatient clinic without having to leave family and friends or sacrifice jobs or schooling. More seriously disturbed people who require short-term hospitalization usually are placed in a general hospital in their community. Community mental-health programs provide three types of service. First, they encourage efforts to change the social system in order to reduce the stresses associated with poverty, disease, discrimination, injustice, and social isolation. Second, they offer services to people in immediate need. For example, many communities have 24-hour walk-in **crisis intervention centers** or **telephone hotlines** for people experiencing an acute crisis so they may make immediate contact with someone, usually a volunteer, who will listen supportively to their problem, give advice when appropriate, and apprise them of available resources. Third, community mental-health programs help people with past problems reintegrate in their community. They may supply job training, counseling on how to seek employment, and social skills training.

Halfway houses are residences for people who have been hospitalized, imprisoned, or who believe they may require hospitalization. Halfway houses usually accommodate a dozen or fewer residents who live in a family-like atmosphere. Residents leave the house during the day for school or work, to seek a job, or to engage in some other activity. Half-way houses usually are run by nonprofessionals who consult with mental health authorities; they provide transitional support in readjusting to community life.

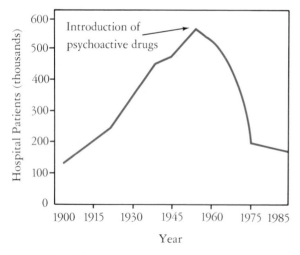

FIGURE 14-1
The Number of Mental Hospital Residents (1900–1985) Note the dramatic decrease beginning in 1960 following the introduction of psychoactive drugs. *Source:* Adapted from Bassuk, E. L., & Gerson, S. (1978). Deinstitutionalization and mental health services. *Scientific American, 238,* 46–53.

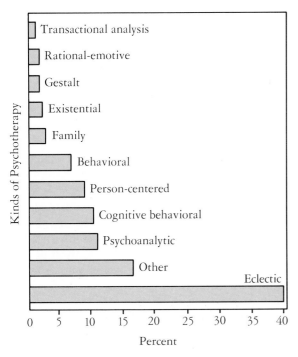

FIGURE 14-2

Therapists' Preferences for Types of Psychotherapy Most therapists are eclectic. *Source:* Adapted from Smith, D. (1982). Trends in counseling psychotherapy. *American Psychologist, 37,* 802–809.

"In time the dog world will undoubtedly have its Freuds and Jungs."

JAMES THURBER

WHAT KINDS OF TREATMENT ARE AVAILABLE?

One consideration in selecting a psychotherapist is the type of psychotherapy he or she gives. There are more than one hundred different types of treatment, each with implicit assumptions about the nature, causes, and ways of altering psychological disorder. Most of this chapter is devoted to describing different forms of treatment; however, before beginning we must emphasize this proviso: Although different types of treatment focus on different techniques, experienced clinicians usually employ more than one technique. In a survey of more than 400 counseling and clinical psychologists, Smith (1982) found nearly 41% viewed themselves as eclectic — drawing from the techniques of two or more orientations (see Figure 14-2). Quoting Ricks, Wanderman, and Popper (1976, p. 401):

> So long as we stay out of the day to day work of psychotherapy, in the quiet of the study or library, it is easy to think of psychotherapists as exponents of competing thoughts. When we actually participate in psychotherapy, or observe its complexities, it loses this specious simplicity.

Armed with this proviso, let us consider the most popular forms of treatment for psychological disorder. We begin with three types of treatment primarily physical in nature: psychosurgery, electro-convulsive therapy, and drug therapy; then we examine various forms of psychotherapy.

THE PHYSICAL TREATMENT OF PSYCHOLOGICAL DISORDERS

If you suspected that a psychological disorder originated from a physical source — or at least that it might respond to medical treatment — where would you look? The physical organ most closely associated with psychological experience is, of course, the brain. We know that two primary factors mediate functioning of the brain: chemical reactions and electrical currents (Chapter 3). It follows that if something is wrong with the brain, we should change its chemical balance and/or alter its electrical connections. Researchers and therapists have accomplished this in three basic ways — by surgically severing connections between parts of the brain, by administering electric shocks, and by prescribing drugs.

PSYCHOSURGERY

Psychosurgery is the most controversial physical treatment of psychological disorder. It involves the destruction of brain tissues — not themselves necessarily diseased — with the intent of blunting severely disturbed thoughts, behaviors, or emotions. Because the effects of psychosurgery may be profound and because they are irreversible, it is not surprising that this form of treatment has evoked considerable misgiving.

The first, and best known, psychosurgical procedure was introduced in the 1930s by Portuguese psychiatrist Egaz Moniz. The **prefrontal lobotomy** (see Figure 14-3) was a bold extension of earlier animal research conducted in the U.S. that revealed extremely agitated monkeys could be calmed by severing the nerve tracts that connect the frontal lobes of their brains to brain structures responsible for emotions. Moniz's application of this technique to human psychiatric patients elicited reaction from the scientific community that ranged from extreme enthusiasm (Moniz received the Nobel Prize in 1949) to abject denunciation.

During the 1940s and 1950s, more than 50,000 prefrontal lobotomies were performed in the United States — many in physicians' offices. The techniques were crude, and follow-ups indicated that although some patients improved dramatically, others suffered such severe side effects as inability to plan or concentrate, personal slovenliness, whimsical personality changes, and lethargy. Even though such depictions of prefrontal lobotomy as that popularized by Ken Kesey in *One Flew Over the Cuckoo's Nest* were not representative of most operations, the undesirable side effects were sufficiently serious to cause most surgeons to halt the practice, espe-

cially as the benefits of antipsychotic drugs become increasingly apparent.

Recent research has indicated it may be possible to improve the trade-off between the therapeutic effects and the undesirable side effects of psychosurgery. Harry Crow and his colleagues at the Burden Neurological Hospital in England examined a large number of postsurgical reports of lobotomy performed in many different clinics and found the operation had a beneficial effect on only certain types of disorder. For example, it seemed to help patients so fearful or obsessive-compulsive that they could not function outside a hospital, but to be considerably less helpful to patients suffering from schizophrenia. In addition, the effects of prefrontal lobotomy appeared to differ depending on exactly which fibers in the brain were destroyed.

Discovering these facts, the Burden group selected the types of patients who responded best to psychosurgery and then refined the techniques used to sever brain fibers (See Figure 14-3). They inserted several tiny gold wires into the region of the brain that produced relief with the fewest side effects, then passed an electrical current through the wires in order to destroy only the brain tissue in a small area around the tips of the wires. By planting many small electrodes, the Burden procedure enables the surgeon slowly to increase the amount of tissue destroyed and to assess the effects following each increment. Thus, the lesion (destruction of brain tissue) is made only as large as is necessary to relieve the psychiatric symptoms. This surgical precision was not possible with earlier methods in which frontal-nerve pathways were cut with surgical knives.

Today psychosurgery is not used until all other forms of psychotherapy have proven futile. Patients at the Burden Neurological Hospital on whom psychosurgery was performed had been in that or other institutions for an average of more than ten years. Following surgery, the vast majority were able to return to their families and to find productive work in the community. Psychosurgery appears most appropriate for patients who are experiencing a great amount of physical pain, who are severely depressed and suicidal, who display uncontrollable bouts of aggression, and who suffer from obsessive-compulsive neurosis (Valenstein, 1980).

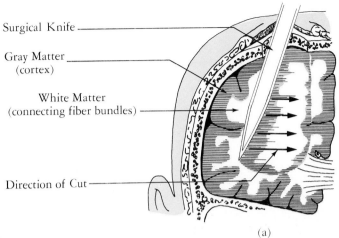

Surgical Knife

Gray Matter
(cortex)

White Matter
(connecting fiber bundles)

Direction of Cut

(a)

(b)

Old prefrontal lobotomy: a surgical knife was used to sever most of the white matter fiber bundles in the frontal lobe. The operation often relieved extreme anxiety and fearfulness, but at a cost of many undesirable side effects (general blunting of other emotions, socially inappropriate behaviors, attentional problems, and so forth).

Comparison of post-operative surgical reports concerning different methods used to cut the white matter fiber bundles indicated that by limiting destruction to fibers in the crosshatched area, relief from extreme anxiety could be achieved with far fewer negative side effects. Operations that destroyed fibers in the stippled area also provided relief, but produced more of the side effects listed in (a).

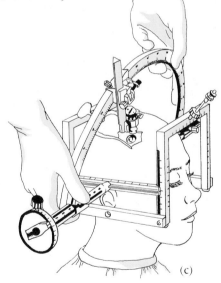

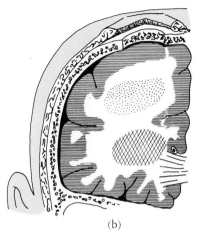

Fine gold wire electrodes

(c)

(d)

The Burden focal leucotomy: using a stereotaxic implant device such as the one shown here, fine gold wire electrodes can be placed accurately in specific sites in the brain. When electric currents of sufficient strength are passed through the electrodes, small areas of cells around the electrode tips are destroyed. This allows cells to be removed in areas where relief from the psychological symptoms can be obtained with miminal effects on areas where side effects will be produced.

In the Burden multistage surgical procedure, the electrodes are implanted under general anaesthesia. After the patient recovers from the operation, lesions (destroyed cells) are effected at the tips of the electrodes —one at a time—over a period of weeks or months. By this means, cells in the crosshatched area in (b) are eliminated in tiny increments. After each individual lesion is effected, the patient is evaluated for relief of the symptoms. Side effects are also minimal. The electrodes are withdrawn after the last lesion is made.

FIGURE 14-3
Old and New Methods of Psychosurgery   *Source:* Information from Valenstein, E. S. (1986).   *Great and Desperate Cures: The Rise and Decline of Psychosurgery and Other Radical Treatments for Mental Illness.*   New York: Basic Books.

BOX 14-1
PSYCHOSURGERY AND THE CONTROL OF EXTREME VIOLENCE

In Chapter 3 we discussed evidence indicating that in some people dysfunctions in certain parts of the brain are associated with unprovoked, extreme, uncontrollable outbursts of violence. In 1970, Mark and Ervin wrote a book describing several people who displayed this syndrome. The cases are relatively straightforward because the patients clearly were pathologically violent, not merely belligerent or troublesome, and there was evidence of abnormal brain activity. According to Mark and Ervin, many patients were frightened by their loss of control and, therefore, sought treatment.

These investigators also described the operations performed on the pathologically violent individuals.

Doctors inserted fine wire electrodes into suspected trigger zones deep in patients' temporal lobes. Experimenters found that spontaneous epileptic activity could be recorded through these electrodes and that violent outbursts could be elicited by sending an electric current into the areas of the brain in which the electrodes were planted. When the brain tissue around the electrodes was destroyed, the rage attacks ended in many patients. The operative target was the amygdala, a part of the limbic system in the temporal lobe of the brain.

Although Mark and Ervin tended to discount the negative side effects that accompanied relief from violent episodes, other researchers found evidence

of weight gain, sexual dysfunction, general blunting of emotional responses, and attentional deficits in patients subjected to **amygdalectomy** (Valenstein, 1973). Such negative side effects should not be surprising: the amygdala is part of a complex brain circuit implicated in the control of eating, sexual behavior, emotional response to visual stimuli, and general arousal, as well as certain kinds of aggressive behavior. These side effects are a problem for psychosurgery because, although there is specialization of function in different parts of the brain, there is rarely a discrete area devoted exclusively to the control of a single complex behavior like aggression. Thus, surgical destruction of a

From time to time, extremists have suggested psychosurgery be performed on people convicted of violent crimes and on other social deviants (see Box 14-1). Fears of such abuse led to the creation of a congressional committee — the *National Commission for the Protection of Human Subjects of Biomedical and Behavioral Research* — in 1977, charged with determining whether psychosurgery should be banned. Committee chairman Kenneth Ryan summarized the conclusion reached as follows.

> We saw that some very sick people had been helped by [psychosurgery], and that it did not destroy their intelligence or rob them of feelings. Their marriages were intact. They were able to work. The operation shouldn't be banned.

However, the committee recommended that psychosurgery be employed only on selected patients for whom all other methods of treatment had failed, that procedures be tightened to prevent coercion of patients and other abuses, and called for additional research on the effects of increasingly finely tuned operations.

ELECTRO-CONVULSIVE THERAPY

In **electro-convulsive therapy (ECT),** an alternating electrical current with a frequency of 50–60 cycles per second and ranging from 70–150

brain area may cause a troublesome behavior to diminish, but virtually always at the cost of other functions that share overlapping brain circuitry. Notwithstanding the great debate over both the scientific rationale and the cost-benefit ratio of psychosurgery (see Smith & Kling, 1976; Valenstein, 1980), many patients consider the side effects a tolerable risk in return for ending the fear of "going berserk." Clearly some people have been helped by such operations; yet the potential for abuse remains a serious concern.

Between the textbook cases described by Mark and Ervin and aggressive behaviors that stem from social causes, there is a large gray area. Civil libertarians were alarmed when Mark and Ervin appeared to overestimate the proportion of

serious violence in society due to brain malfunction (Valenstein, 1976) and when these investigators argued that the magnitude of the social problem justified extension of their "treatment" to violent individuals for whom no evidence of neurological disorder could be adduced. Because surgery in the limbic system can pacify people who do not suffer any brain pathology, critics of psychosurgery worried the operation would be used against various minority groups, especially prisoners, as a means of social control. Pronouncements of certain prominent physicians, politicians, and bureaucrats that this would be socially desirable aroused broad-based opposition in the early 1970s to plans for increasing the amount of psychosurgery performed on prisoners. A thorough

review of the scientific status and the ethical issues surrounding the surgical control of violence was instituted by the U.S. Congress' National Commission for the Protection of Human Subjects of Biomedical and Behavioral Research (1977). As a result of their findings and the public controversies they aroused, laws were passed in several states that curtailed psychosurgery in general and surgery on incarcerated persons in particular. A thoughtful review of the many scientific and moral concerns surrounding this treatment is contained in a volume edited by noted brain researcher Elliot Valenstein (1980). It shows that in this, as in many other areas of technological application, the only sure defense against abuses of technology lies in an informed and vigilant citizenry.

volts is administered to a patient's head for a fraction of a second. Typically this electrical shock produces convulsions similar to the **grand-mal seizures** of epileptics. When ECT was first used, patients sometimes suffered dislocated joints and fractured bones because of the intensity of the seizure. Since 1940, ECT patients have been given muscle relaxants and sedatives to ease their discomfort and to reduce the risk of injury.

The use of electric shock to treat physical disorders has a long history. In early Greek and Roman times, both the electric catfish of the Nile and the electric ray fish were used to alleviate headaches (Kellaway, 1946). In the nineteenth century, some physicians (including Charcot, who inspired Freud) employed mild electrical

currents as an adjunct to hypnosis in the treatment of hysteria. However, it was not until 1938 that ECT per se was used.

During the first half of the twentieth century, some doctors claimed that epileptics were less likely than others to have schizophrenia; moreover, the relatively few epileptics with schizophrenia seemed to improve (in medical jargon, to be in **temporary remission**) following an epileptic seizure. It occurred to some doctors that schizophrenia could be alleviated by inducing epileptic-like seizures. At first seizures were induced by drugs; however, in 1938 Italian scientists Cerletti and Bini used electricity to induce seizures in a male schizophrenic. Although Cerletti and Bini's patient improved, subsequent re-

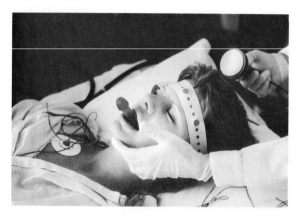

In electroconvulsive therapy, brief electrical currents are applied to the brain and produce convulsions. This treatment is often effective in relieving the symptoms of severe depression.

search has failed to confirm the hypothesized relationship between epilepsy and schizophrenia and has failed to support the idea that ECT helps people suffering from schizophrenia.

Today ECT is used primarily to treat severe depression. It is known to alleviate depression in many suicidal patients (Scovern & Kilmann, 1980). As with many medical treatments, however, there are side effects. Immediately following ECT, patients report temporary confusion and loss of memory. Further, progressive damage to the capacity for new learning may develop with repeated use. Some patients are afraid of the treatment; other patients request it because the horrors of deep depression outweigh their fear of shock. Psychologists tend to be critical of ECT due to the aversiveness of electric shock and the potential for memory damage. Although there are at least 50 theories of how ECT exerts its effect, none has received consistent support (Kalinowsky, 1975).

PSYCHOACTIVE DRUGS — CHEMOTHERAPY

The development of **psychoactive drugs** — drugs that affect people's psychological state — has profoundly affected the physical treatment of mental disorder. Psychoactive drugs have made it possible for disturbed people to continue functioning in their communities during treatment rather than being hospitalized (see Figure 14-1, p. 734), have facilitated the early release of hospitalized patients, and have reduced significantly the need for such traditional restraints as straitjackets and locked wards. Some drugs have even been described as "miracle cures"; however, none as yet has fulfilled the promise of this label. Although psychoactive drugs may reduce symptoms of disorders, they do not "cure" them; if the patients stop taking the drugs, their symptoms return. The three major groups of psychoactive drugs in use today are *antipsychotic drugs, antidepressant and antimanic drugs,* and *antianxiety drugs.*

Drugs may be referred to by their chemical name (for example, acetylsalicylic acid), by their generic name (aspirin), and by their brand name (Bayer). Table 14-3 displays the primary drugs used in the treatment of psychological disorders.

Antipsychotic Drugs (major tranquilizers)

Until the early 1950s, the drugs used most often to calm excited or aggressive patients were narcotic sedatives — such opiate derivatives as morphine and codeine — but these drugs had at least two serious side effects: they caused physical dependence and severe withdrawal when discontinued and most of them induced a stuporous state. In the 1950s, *reserpine* (derived from the rauwolfia plant used for centuries in India to treat mental disorders) was introduced into North America. Reserpine was found to have calming effects without the disadvantages of the narcotic sedatives; however, because reserpine also produced undesirable side effects, it has been largely replaced by another family of synthetic drugs, the *phenothiazines.*

The phenothiazines are the most widely used **antipsychotic drugs;** *Thorazine* and *Stelazine* are the most popular of the phenothiazine family. Antipsychotic drugs are sometimes called **major tranquilizers;** however, the term is misleading. Although antipsychotic drugs do tranquilize agitated people, they also affect their thought processes by, for example, reducing hallucinations and delusions. And, of equal importance, they help many patients become less emo-

TABLE 14-3
Psychoactive Drugs

Class	Generic Name	Trade Name	Used to Treat	Effects
Antipsychotic (major tranquilizers) phenothiazines	chlorpromazine trifluoperazine	Thorazine Stelazine	Such psychotic (especially schizophrenic) symptoms as extreme agitation, delusions, and hallucinations; aggressive or violent behavior	Somewhat variable in suppressing psychotic symptoms; side effects, such as dry mouth, are often uncomfortable; in long-term use may produce such motor disturbances as tardive dyskinesia
butyrophenones	haloperidol	Haldol	(same as above)	(same as above)
thioxanthenes	thiothixine chlorprothixene	Navane Taractan	(same as above)	(same as above)
Antidepressant tricyclics	imipramine amitriptyline nortriptyline	Tofranil Elavil Aventyl	Relatively severe depressive symptoms, especially of psychotic severity and unipolar type	Somewhat variable in alleviating depression and effects may be delayed up to three weeks; multiple side effects, some dangerous; use of MAO inhibitors requires dietary restrictions
monoamine oxidase (MAO) inhibitors	isocarboxazid phenelzine	Marplan Nardil	(same as above)	(same as above)
inorganic salt	lithium carbonate	Eskalith Lithane Lithonate	Manic episodes and some severe depressions, particularly recurrent ones or those alternating with mania	Usually effective in resolving manic episodes, but highly variable in effects on depression; multiple side effects unless carefully monitored; high toxicity potential
Antianxiety (minor tranquilizers)	diazepam chlordiazepoxide meprobamate	Valium Librium Miltown	Nonpsychotic problems in which anxiety and tension are prominent features; also used as anticonvulsants and sleep inducers	Somewhat variable in achieving tension reduction; side effects include drowsiness and lethargy; dependence and toxicity are dangers

Source: Adapted from Coleman, J. C., et al. (1980). *Abnormal psychology and modern life* (6th ed.). Glenview, IL: Scott, Foresman.

tionally withdrawn, thus making them more amenable to psychotherapeutic treatment. Antipsychotic drugs are given almost exclusively to people suspected of having schizophrenia. Their success has resulted in a significant reduction in the use of electro-convulsive therapy and psychosurgery in the treatment of severe mental disorder.

Although antipsychotic drugs have helped to improve the functioning of many people affected by schizophrenia, they are not without their drawbacks. Side effects may include a dry mouth, blurred vision, flushing, constipation, grotesque postures, restlessness, seizures, impotence, and menstrual problems. Further, their extended use in high dosages may result in a disorder that affects muscular coordination (see Box 14-2). And when used with alcohol, these drugs can be fatal. The potential for abuse by the general public is relatively low because of such unpleasant effects.

Antidepressant (and antimanic) Drugs

Antidepressant drugs are considered the treatment of choice in cases of mild or moderate depression. As the name implies, they elevate depressed moods—but without inducing overactivity and without heightening anxiety. There are several kinds of antidepressant drugs and each affects the nervous system differently. *Nardil, Marplan,* and *Elavil* are among the best known.

The drug coming closest to the ideal of a "wonder drug" is the mineral salt **lithium carbonate.** Lithium carbonate can be classified as an antipsychotic, antidepressant, or **antimanic drug** because it reduces psychotic behavior, re-

BOX 14-2
THE RIGHT TO REFUSE TREATMENT

Rubie Rogers, a mental-health patient at Boston State Hospital, was forced to take an antipsychotic drug. The drug, Haldol, is prescribed to relieve such psychotic symptoms as extreme agitation, delusions, hallucinations, aggression, and violent behavior. Rubie Rogers dreaded the side effect of the drug—her muscles would tighten, causing her extreme pain. In a desperate attempt to be transferred to a hospital where she would not be forced to take the pain-inducing drug, Rubie Rogers set herself on fire.

Shortly after Rogers' dramatic effort to resist treatment, a patients'-rights lawyer filed suit on behalf of Rogers and six other patients

to prevent hospitals from forcing patients to take drugs. In a 1975 decision, the U.S. Supreme Court upheld the right of patients to refuse antipsychotic treatment. Since this decision, considerable progress has been made toward increasing the legal rights of mental-health patients. Indeed, at present those who are "legally competent" have the right to refuse treatment, except in emergencies (Appelbaum, 1982).

Many mental-health professionals are displeased with the right of patients to refuse treatment; patients who refuse treatment— especially those harmful to themselves or others—may be more difficult to handle. The drugs help to calm them

and to ensure their safety. Nevertheless, many patients feel the side effects of drugs are too high a price to pay for the tractability of their behavior. Furthermore, formation of patients'-rights groups has drawn attention to their concerns and the groups have gained the support of an increasing number of psychologists and psychiatrists.

While the right to refuse treatment leaves many unresolved issues— especially those relating to when patients are "legally competent" to make such a choice—the Rogers case has established firmly that mental-health patients have civil rights and that these rights must be respected.

lieves depression, and calms the agitation associated with manic reactions. Not surprisingly, it works best on people suffering from bipolar, or manic–depressive, disorders. Lithium carbonate has been found to reduce the symptoms of bipolar disorders in 70–80% of the cases within fourteen days (Davis, 1980).

Lithium carbonate has enabled many people suffering from manic-depressive disorder to leave mental hospitals and to function with reasonable normalcy in everyday life. Although it does not cure the disorder, it reduces the intensity of the symptoms. The major disadvantages of lithium carbonate are the length of time it requires to take effect (up to two weeks) and the fine line between therapeutic and toxic doses. Because of the latter, the level of lithium carbonate in the blood must be monitored carefully; even small excesses may produce such side effects as diarrhea, nausea, fatigue, weight gain, difficulties in concentrating, frequent urination, thirst, and, if not checked, uncoordinated movements, hallucinations and delusions, seizures, coma, and death.

Antianxiety Drugs (minor tranquilizers)

As the name suggests, **antianxiety drugs** reduce anxiety and tension, and produce a state of calmness and well-being. The trade names of *Miltown*, *Valium* and *Librium* are household words for many. Antianxiety drugs are popularly referred to as **minor tranquilizers;** however, the term *minor* is misleading. Each year many people die from overdoses of "minor" tranquilizers.

Antianxiety drugs are widely prescribed — during 1974–1975, over 80 million prescriptions for minor tranquilizers were written in the United States — and Valium is the most frequently prescribed drug in the world (Roy, 1983). They are prescribed commonly for normal people experiencing an unusual level of stress and approximately 30% of all medical patients receive minor tranquilizers in addition to other prescribed medications (D'Andrea, 1977). Antianxiety drugs also are used in the treatment of neurotic disorders, psychosomatic ailments, as part of treatment programs for withdrawal from drugs or alcohol, and as sleeping aids. Although the side effects of antianxiety drugs are minimal — usually involving sleepiness — long-term use tends to produce dependence and abrupt withdrawal can have deleterious physical effects.

The relaxed, pleasant states induced by the minor tranquilizers make them prime candidates for abuse; however, because they are most often obtained legally through prescriptions, the extent of abuse is difficult to estimate. As with antidepressant drugs, minor tranquilizers should never be used in combination with alcohol or barbiturates.

How Do Drugs Exert Their Effect on Psychological Disorders?

We have said little about how or why certain drugs alleviate the symptoms of various disorders. Al-

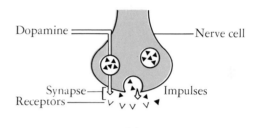

(a)

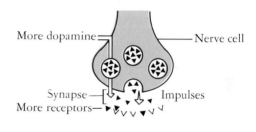

(b)

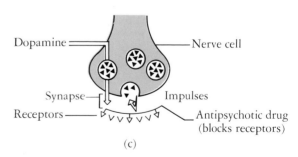

(c)

FIGURE 14-4

How Antipsychotic Drugs May Work (a) In the normal physiological state, the neurotransmitter dopamine aids the transmission of neural impulses across synapses to receptors. (b) In schizophrenics, the levels of dopamine may be abnormally high or receptor sites abnormally abundant, causing disruption of thought and mood. (c) Antipsychotic drugs may block the receptor sites on neurons, preventing them from accepting the excess dopamine.

though we know drugs exert their effect through such neurotransmitters as norepinephrine and dopamine (see Chapters 3 and 13), we do not as yet know precisely how. One possibility is diagrammed in Figure 14-4. Chemical activity in the brain is exceedingly complex and research on how drugs affect psychological disorders has progressed primarily through fortunate coincidences and educated guesses. For example, the first antidepressant drug was discovered by accident in 1952 when a group of researchers treating tuberculosis noticed the drug they were using produced an elevation in the mood of the patients (Selikof et al., 1952). The possibility a particular chemical is involved in a disorder may suggest itself by a correlation between the incidence of the disorder and such characteristics as age, sex, type of preferred food, drug use, or physical disorder (for instance, the early misguided observation that epilepsy and schizophrenia are not compatible). Hypotheses about the effects of drugs also originate from biochemical research on the brains of nonhuman animals.

How Effective Are Psychoactive Drugs?

As noted, the use of drugs has revolutionized both the treatment of psychological disorder and the operation of modern mental hospitals. Although the early hopes that drugs would cure all psychological disorder have not been realized, many drugs relieve a variety of symptoms and help improve functioning — but only conditionally. In many instances, the patient must continue to take the drug for a long time. For drugs such as phenothiazines and lithium carbonate, it has been found that discharged patients who stop taking their medication show a relapse rate based directly on the time of abandoning their medication. In many cases psychological treatments are used in conjunction with drugs, which appears to enhance considerably the long-term effectiveness of both.

PSYCHOLOGICAL FORMS OF TREATMENT

When people feel disturbed, they often tell their troubles to a friend. Psychological forms of treatment are based on the idea that many problems can be treated successfully by talking about them and that medication, shock, and psychosurgery are unnecessary. Most types of psychotherapy consist entirely of talking, although some emphasize behavior modification. There are numerous theories about the causes of psychological disturbance and many associated treatments; nevertheless, it is possible to classify most psychological forms of treatment under six headings: psychoanalytic, humanistic, behavioral, social-learning, cognitive, and interpersonal.

PSYCHOANALYTIC APPROACHES

We introduced Freud in Chapter 1, discussed his views on social development in Chapter 10, outlined his theory of personality in Chapter 12, and presented his explanations of various psychological disorders in Chapter 13. We now outline Freud's methods of treatment — described by the same name as his theory, **psychoanalysis** — and examine some modifications made by those who followed in his path.

Psychoanalysis, the Psychotherapy

As noted in Chapter 1, Freud contended that such physical symptoms as those characteristic of hysteria stem from psychological forces. Freud believed children experience conflicts at early stages of development — usually involving sexual and aggressive desires — that they repress from consciousness. The energy attached to these conflicts, buried in the unconscious, presses for release. It is the task of the ego to keep illicit urges in check, to negotiate compromises that permit the release of pent-up wishes and desires in socially acceptable ways, and to protect people from the truth of their nature. The ego employs defense mechanisms to help it control the anxiety associated with threats to its integrity; most symptoms of psychological disorder are caused by the tension associated with conflicts between the id and the ego. In some cases, such as obsessive compulsiveness, the symptoms reflect rigid defense mechanisms. In other cases, such as psychosis, the symptoms reflect regressions to earlier stages of development.

The goal of psychoanalysis is to uncover the unconscious conflicts that give rise to neurotic symptoms; in Freud's words, this involves "draining the psychic abscess," and "making the unconscious conscious." The central assumption of psychoanalytic therapy is that discovering and "working through" the unconscious conflicts causing the patient's problems will make the patient well. This may seem straightforward enough — you simply ask patients about their childhood and explain what happened — but it does not work that way. For many years the ego has been at work defending against threatening memories and developing mechanisms to cope with anxiety; it is not about to relinquish its defenses without a fight. In a very real sense, the psychoanalyst is like a detective attempting to catch a criminal (repressed memories) in hiding, and the ego is the experienced harborer.

The basic goal of psychoanalysis is to evoke information from patients that supplies a window into their unconscious minds. This is accomplished by creating a context that disinhibits patients and encourages them to reveal information about themselves: external distractions are minimized; the patient lies on a couch and looks at the ceiling; the therapist sits behind the patient, out of view. At first Freud hypnotized his patients because he believed they would be less defensive in a hypnotic state. Later he simply asked patients to talk about whatever came to their minds and to recount their dreams. The four basic techniques employed by psychoanalysts are:

1. interpretation of material reported during *free association*
2. interpretation of dreams
3. analysis of patient's responses to these interpretations (often involving *resistance*)
4. analysis of patient's emotional responses to therapist (*transference*)

The technique of **free association** is the cornerstone of psychoanalytic treatment. The patient is directed to talk about whatever comes to mind without censoring thoughts that seem irrelevant, irrational, or shameful, and without trying to impress the analyst. The idea behind the technique is that if patients let their thoughts flow freely, they will talk in a fragmented way about apparently unconnected ideas that will reveal unconscious conflicts. The therapist attempts to guide the patient in interpreting what he or she says in terms of psychoanalytic theory.

Patients are encouraged to remember their dreams and describe them during psychoanalysis. Freud believed that during sleep a person's defenses are lowered and that repressed material seeps out in dreams; events of the day, he believed, evoke repressed childhood memories and desires. Because some wishes are too disturbing for the patient to face even during sleep, they are expressed in symbolic form. Thus a dream has both **manifest content**, actual events of the dream as the patient describes them, and **latent content**, underlying wishes seeking an outlet with which the patient is unable to deal directly (see Figure 14-5). A process in the unconscious mind, called the **censor**, employs such devices as **displacement** (for example, attributing urges to the wrong person) and **condensation** (for example, making two people one animal) to restructure the content of the dream. It is the analyst's task to expose the latent content of the dreams by interpreting the symbols in the manifest content (see Table 14-4). Consider, for example, the following interpretation of a patient's dream reported by Freud.

A scene at the customs-house: Another traveler opened his box, and coolly smoking a cigarette, said: "There's nothing in it." The customs officer seemed to believe him, but felt about once more inside it, and found something quite particularly prohibited. The traveler said in a resigned voice: "There's nothing to be done about it."

Freud's patient in this example, was "a foreigner of a highly polygamous disposition." Freud assumed that the trunks were symbols of women and gave the following interpretation of the dream: "He himself (the patient) was the traveler; I was the customs officer. As a rule he was very straightforward in making admissions; but he had intended to keep silent to me about a new connection he had formed with a lady, because he rightly supposed that she was not unknown to me.

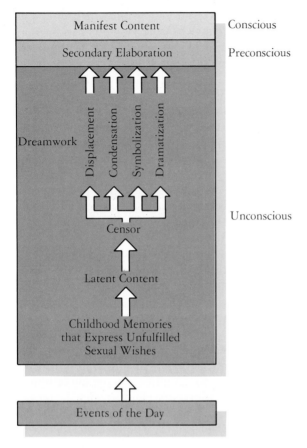

FIGURE 14-5
Freud's Theory of the Meaning of Dreams
Events of the day trigger repressed childhood memories
and wishes that are transformed by the censor into the
content of the dream that is remembered. As patients
report their dreams, they modify them through secondary elaboration. *Source:* Adapted from Ellenberger, H. F.
(1970). *The discovery of the unconscious.* New York:
Basic Books.

He displaced the distressing situation of being
detected onto a stranger, so that he himself did
not seem to appear in the dream.'' (Freud, in
Strachey, 1976, p. 195–96).

In this interpretation, the patient is identified as one of the characters in the dream. The
analyst infers that the therapist was involved in
the dream in the form of the customs officer and
he identifies a new secret liaison with a woman,
symbolically shown as the trunk containing forbidden treasures. Freud's patient confirmed to
him the accuracy of this interpretation. This ex-

ample is typical in the sense that a new meaning is
revealed beneath the superficial dream content.
And, of course, the interpretation focuses on sexual desire. Freud identified sex and death as most
frequently underlying the superficial content of
dreams and free association.

Because the prospect of facing the deep-
rooted conflicts one fears most is painful, patients
typically develop **resistance** to the analyst's interpretations, creating defenses that enable them
to avoid dealing with threatening material. Resistance may be expressed in several ways: patients may change the subject when they are close
to revealing something important; they may joke
or suddenly "forget" a crucial element in an episode; they may arrive late for appointments with
their analyst or not arrive at all. When resistance
occurs, the therapist points it out to the patient
and analyzes its source so the resistance may be
overcome. Here is how Freud describes resistance.

> . . . The patient endeavors in every sort of way to
> extricate himself from [the rule of free associa-
> tion]. At one moment he declares that nothing
> occurs to him, at the next that so many things are
> crowding in on him that he cannot get hold of
> anything. Presently we observe with pained as-
> tonishment that he has given way first to one and
> then to another critical objection; he betrays this to
> us by the long pauses that he introduces into his
> remarks. He then admits that there is something
> he really cannot say—he would be ashamed to;
> and he allows this reason to prevail against his
> promise. Or he says that something has occurred
> to him, but it concerns another person and not
> himself and is therefore exempt from being re-
> ported. Or, what has now occurred to him is
> really too unimportant, too silly and senseless; I
> cannot possibly have meant him to enter into
> thoughts like that. So it goes on in innumerable
> variations . . . . (Freud, in Strachey, 1976,
> p. 288)

Resistance is common in psychotherapy; psychoanalysts view it as an indication that an important
theme or conflict is on the verge of discovery.

During the analytic process, the patient
shares with the therapist thoughts and feelings
that often have never been revealed to any other
individual. So it is not surprising that the pa-
tient-therapist relationship becomes laden with
emotion. However, because psychoanalysts

TABLE 14-4
The Contents of Dreams and Their Symbols

Object(s)	Symbolic for
Emperors, empresses, kings, queens	Parents
Small animals	Children, especially brothers and sisters
Water	Birth
Journey	Death
Clothes, uniforms	Nakedness
Sticks, umbrellas, poles, trees, anything elongated, pointed weapons of all sorts	Male genitals
Balloons, airplanes, zeppelins, dreamer himself flying	Erection
Reptiles, fish, serpent, hand or foot	Male sexual symbols
Pits, hollow caves, jars, bottles, doors, ships, chests	Female genitals
Apples, peaches, other fruit	Breasts
Mounting a ladder or stairs, entering a room, walking down a hall or into a tunnel, horseback riding, and so forth	Intercourse

Source: Adapted from Coon, D. (1986). *Introduction to psychology: Exploration and application* (4th ed., p. 174). New York: West Publishing.

make it a point not to respond personally to the emotional reactions of the patient, the patient often projects onto the analyst qualities the analyst may not really possess, and then responds to these projected qualities with strong emotions. Freud believed these projected qualities were possessed by important individuals in the patient's life, especially the parents. During this process, called **transference,** the therapist helps the patient interpret these emotional responses as repetitions of childhood emotions involving conflict with the patient's parents. With the aid of the analyst, the patient attempts to work through the emotions rooted in these early conflicts and thereby gain insights that, it is assumed, will promote emotionally healthy behavior. A transcript of psychoanalytic psychotherapy is presented in Box 14-3.

Evaluation of Psychoanalytic Therapy Many people who have undergone psychoanalysis feel it helped them achieve insight into their problems and provided them with relief from long-repressed feelings that interfered with healthy functioning. Critics of psychoanalysis focus on the fact that insights obtained through psychotherapy do not necessarily affect behavior in everyday life. They argue that although many patients develop significant insights while in therapy, they continue to behave in neurotic, ineffective ways.

Psychoanalysis also has been criticized for some of the same reasons as has Freud's psychoanalytic theory of personality: it is based on unsystematically recorded case studies; there is little experimental support for its effectiveness; it is difficult to disprove; and it is based on a rather pessimistic and perhaps inaccurate conception of human nature. Further, critics point out that because psychoanalysis is usually an extremely long-term and expensive process, it is available only to a privileged few. Moreover, inasmuch as insight is required, psychoanalysis is not applicable to all disorders; is useful primarily for relatively bright people suffering from mild, neurotic disorders; and has rarely proved useful in treating individuals out of touch with reality.

Psychoanalytic Therapy Today

Although there are still some orthodox Freudian analysts in practice today, most psychoanalysts practice a modified version of Freud's ideas. In general, they place greater emphasis than Freud on current problems and current environmental pressures in the patient's life and less emphasis on repressed sexual and aggressive impulses. The general goals of contemporary psychoanalysis are to give the patient more insight into his or her behavior, to give the patient's intellect (ego) more power to deal with the id (emotions), to relieve tension and anxiety, and to free up the energy invested in defenses for more constructive and creative purposes.

Transactional Analysis (TA) TA has become a popular technique in nursing, social work, and school guidance settings. Although it is derived from Freudian psychoanalysis and thus focuses on conflict, it is more interpersonally oriented than psychoanalysis. In **transactional analysis,**

Box 14-3
Psychoanalysis — A Transcript of Therapy

THERAPIST It sounds as if you would like to let loose with me, but you are afraid of what my response would be *(summarizing and restating).*

PATIENT I get so excited by what is happening here. I feel I'm being held back by needing to be nice. I'd like to blast loose sometimes, but I don't dare.

THERAPIST Because you fear my reaction?

PATIENT The worst thing would be that you wouldn't like me. You wouldn't speak to me friendly; you wouldn't smile; you'd feel you can't treat me and discharge me from treatment. But I know this isn't so, I know it.

THERAPIST Where do you think these attitudes come from?

PATIENT When I was nine years old, I read a lot about great men in history. I'd quote them and be dramatic. I'd want a sword at my side; I'd dress like an Indian. Mother would scold me. Don't frown, don't talk so much. Sit on your hands, over and over again. I did all kinds of things. I was a naughty child. She told me I'd be hurt. Then at 14 I fell off a horse and broke my back. I had to

be in bed. Mother then told me on the day I went riding not to, that I'd get hurt because the ground was frozen. I was a stubborn, self-willed child. Then I went against her will and suffered an accident that changed my life, a fractured back. Her attitude was, "I told you so." I was put in a cast and kept in bed for months.

THERAPIST You were punished, so to speak, by this accident.

PATIENT But I gained attention and love from my mother for the first time. I felt so good. I'm ashamed to tell you this. Before I healed I opened the cast and tried to walk to make myself sick again so I could stay in bed longer.

THERAPIST How does that connect up with your impulse to be sick now and stay in bed so much? *(The patient has these tendencies, of which she is ashamed.)*

PATIENT Oh . . . *(pause)*

THERAPIST What do you think?

PATIENT Oh, my God, how infantile, how ungrown-up *(pause).* It must be so. I want people to love me and be sorry for me. Oh,

my God. How completely childish. It is, *is* that. My mother must have ignored me when I was little, and I wanted so to be loved. *(This sounds like insight.)*

THERAPIST So that it may have been threatening to go back to being self-willed and unloved after you got out of the cast *(interpretation).*

PATIENT It did. My life changed. I became meek and controlled. I couldn't get angry or stubborn afterward.

THERAPIST Perhaps if you go back to being stubborn with *me*, you would be returning to how you were before; that is, active, stubborn but unloved.

PATIENT *(excitedly)* And, therefore, losing your love. I need you, but after all you aren't going to reject me. But the pattern is so established now that the threat of the loss of love is too overwhelming with everybody, and I've got to keep myself from acting selfish or angry.

Source: Wolberg, L. R. (1977). *The technique of psychotherapy* (3rd ed., pp. 560–61). New York: Grune & Stratton.

conflicts are explained in terms of three aspects of each individual's personality: the *parent* (Freud's superego), the *adult* (ego), and the *child* (id). People who have difficulties in their relationships with others are encouraged to look at their own behavior as being an expression of one or another of these aspects. For example, a *parent* behavior (issuing reprimands, judgments, orders) often causes the person at whom this behavior is directed to act like a *child* (complaining, resisting, behaving irresponsibly). This basic view has been popularized in the interesting and entertaining book *Games People Play* (Berne, 1964), which describes how people develop manipulative and neurotic interactions ("games") with others when unaware of the different parent-adult-child roles they play at different times. TA therapy usually takes place in a group setting, where the transactions of the participants are analyzed with the goal of increasing their awareness of the unproductive ways (child–child, child–parent) in which they communicate with each other. Group members learn to give up psychological "games" and to deal with each other in supportive, healthy (adult-adult), ways (see Figure 14-6).

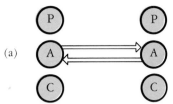

Complementary Interaction

(a)

"I don't feel like studying."
"Neither do I."

Crossed Interaction

(b)

"I don't feel like studying."

"You are going to have to learn to take responsibility
if you expect to amount to anything."

Ulterior Interaction

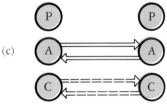

(c)

"I don't feel like studying."
"Neither do I; so let's forget it and party."

FIGURE 14-6

Transactions (a) The first interaction is *complementary:* two adults respond to one another in a mature manner. (b) The second interaction is *crossed:* respondent behaves like a parent to a child. (c). The third interaction is *ulterior:* people appear to be behaving like adults but in fact are involved in a childish exchange. *Source:* Adapted from Berne, E. (1964). *Games people play.* New York: Grove Press.

HUMANISTIC APPROACHES

Humanistic, or person-centered, forms of treatment originate from the humanistic school of psychology (see Chapter 1) and emphasize individual integrity, personal growth, authenticity, self-actualization, trust, empathy, caring, warmth, openness, self-disclosure, and interpersonal honesty. The most popular **humanistic approach** to therapy is Carl Roger's client-centered, or person-centered, therapy.

Client-centered/Person-centered Therapy

In the same way that psychoanalytic therapy follows from Freud's psychoanalytic theory of personality, **client-centered therapy** follows from Carl Roger's humanistic theory of personality

(Chapter 12). Indeed, Rogers developed his theory and therapy largely as a reaction against Freud's pessimistic view of human nature and against Freud's analytic, conflict-centered techniques of therapy. Because Rogers believes the way people feel about themselves determines how they function, we can assume that client-centered therapy focuses on the "here and now" rather than on the past, on the conscious rather than on the unconscious, and on feelings rather than on insight. Similarly, because Rogers believes people inherit a natural tendency to actualize themselves, it follows that client-centered therapy focuses on the forward-looking and optimistic process of self-actualization rather than on the backward-looking and pessimistic process of resolving past conflicts. Finally, because Rogers believes people develop defenses when others impose conditions of worth on them, we can assume that the therapist attempts to treat the client with **unconditional positive regard.** The client, or person (note the rejection of the medical model intrinsic to the label *patient*), is encouraged to take responsibility for his or her problems in client-centered therapy. Unlike the psychoanalyst — playing the role of an authority who possesses esoteric knowledge, who probes, and who provides interpretations — the client-centered therapist adopts a more receptive attitude.

Consider the following exchange between a client-centered therapist and his client.

Alice   I was thinking about this business of standards. I somehow developed a sort of a knack, I guess, of — well — habit — of trying to make people feel at ease around me, or to make things go along smoothly . . .

Counselor   In other words, what you did was always in the direction of trying to keep things smooth and to make other people feel better and to smooth the situation.

Alice   Yes. I think that's what it was. Now the reason why I did it probably was — I mean, not that I was a good little Samaritan going around making other people happy, but that was probably the role that felt easiest for me to play. I'd been doing it around home so much. I just didn't stand up for my own convictions, until I don't know whether I have any convictions to stand up for.

Counselor   You feel that for a long time you've been playing the role of kind of smoothing out the frictions or differences or whatnot . . .

Alice   M-hm.

Counselor   Rather than having any opinion or reaction of your own in the situation. Is that it?

Alice   That's it. Or that I haven't been really honestly being myself, or actually knowing what my real self is, and that I've been just playing a sort of false role. Whatever role no one else was playing, and that needed to be played at the time, I'd try to fill it in. (Rogers, 1951, pp. 152–53)

How different from psychoanalysis! Who is guiding the conversation? The client is, in effect, resolving her own problems. And note that the issues under discussion are current, conscious, and concerned with feelings about the self.

If the client guides the therapeutic exchange, what is the role of the therapist? Whereas the psychoanalyst attempts to be objective and unemotional, the client-centered therapist openly expresses empathy, emotional acceptance of the client as a worthwhile person, and genuineness or honesty. As the reactions of the counselor to Alice's statements suggest, the therapist attempts to view the problems from the client's perspective and to take a genuine interest in the client as a person. People are much more likely to open up to those concerned about them as *people* than they are to those who think of them simply as a *patient.*

One of the techniques used in client-centered therapy, **reflection,** is exemplified in the preceding exchange. The therapist reveals an understanding of what the client is feeling by restating what was said or the emotional meanings behind it. It is as though the therapist presents a mirror to the client. By clarifying clients' statements, helping them reflect on their current feelings, and making them aware of the emotional responses they arouse in the therapist, it is expected that clients will gain the necessary insights and self-awareness to resolve their own problems.

As is true of psychoanalysis, few of the clients traditionally treated in client-centered therapy were seriously disturbed. Client-centered therapy is used commonly in university counseling services; indeed, the approach was developed at the University of Chicago Student Counseling Center. Client-centered techniques have been studied extensively. In general, the findings suggest that middle-class people suffering from neurotic disorders gain self-acceptance through this form of psychotherapy; however, it is unclear just how much this change affects their everyday behavior. People suffering from such other kinds of disorders as schizophrenia do not appear to profit as much from client-centered therapy.

Gestalt Therapy

Gestalt therapy can be viewed as a hybrid between psychoanalytic and humanistic approaches, with the major emphasis on the latter. It grew from the work of psychoanalyst Frederick (Fritz) Perls, who rejected many of Freud's ideas in favor of more humanistic ones. Perls shared with Freud the idea that troubled behavior results from unresolved unconscious conflicts and, like Freud, stressed the importance of dream analysis. However, differing from Freud, Perls focused on current problems and stressed individual responsibility for controlling the direction of one's life. As its definition implies, the goal of Gestalt therapy is to help people achieve a sense of wholeness (**organismic self-regulation**) so they can relate more fully to others and can live more spontaneous lives. Therapy is usually conducted in a group setting, with the focus on one individual at a time.

Gestalt therapists behave like psychoanalysts in some ways—for example, by directing their clients' attention to conflicts and dreams.

Table 14-5
The Moral Injunctions of Gestalt Therapy

Live now. Be concerned with the present rather than the past or future.

Live here. Deal with what is present rather than what is absent.

Stop imagining. Experience the real.

Stop unnecessary thinking. Rather, taste and see.

Express rather than manipulate, explain, justify, or judge.

Give in to unpleasantness and pain just as to pleasure. Do not restrict your awareness.

Accept no "should" or "ought" other than your own. Adore no graven image.

Take full responsibility for your actions, feelings, and thoughts.

Surrender to being as you are.

Source: Naranjo, C. (1971). Contributions of Gestalt therapy. In H. Otto & J. Mann (Eds.), *Ways of growth: Approaches to expanding awareness.* New York: Pocket Books.

However, Gestalt therapists interpret dreams differently: they view fragments of dreams (including objects that appear to have symbolic significance) as aspects of personality. They help their clients piece together dream fragments as they relate to current problems, hoping to integrate the alienated parts of the personalities and to achieve unity of thought, feeling, and action. Gestalt therapists behave more like humanistic therapists, however, in their emphasis on the unfolding of potential, the increase in awareness, the expression of feelings, and the here and now. Gestalt therapists encourage clients to treat them as equals, to express themselves in the first person singular ("I feel angry" rather than "You made me angry"), and to take responsibility for their actions. Consider the following exchange.

Client Every day I just sit there and feel like a stooge. I just can't speak up in that class.

Therapist You say you can't.

Client That's right. I've tried and I know I should, I mean I know the stuff, that's not the problem. I just can't get the words out.

Therapist Try saying "I won't talk" instead of "I can't talk."

Client I won't talk in that class.

Therapist Let yourself feel how you are refusing to talk.

Client I guess I am holding myself back a little.

Therapist What are your objections to speaking up?

Client Well, everyone else in there seems to be talking just to talk. I don't like doing that. (Passons, 1975, p. 82)

Clients are encouraged to act out unresolved conflicts by assuming different aspects of their personalities and to heighten awareness of their bodies, physical movements, tone of voice, and feelings. Table 14-5 outlines the *moral injunctions* of Gestalt therapy.

BEHAVIOR THERAPY

The goal of psychoanalytic and humanistic therapies is to change the structure of an individual's personality. Although different in many ways, both therapies assume that if you change the way people think and feel, you change the way they behave; behavior is of secondary significance, inasmuch as changes in behavior follow from changes in personality. Indeed, in some cases therapists encourage clients to accept the behaviors they display and not to change them. The therapists to whom we now turn adopt the opposite point of view — for them the goal of therapy is to change behavior.

Although there are many kinds of **behavior therapy,** they all share at least six features. First, determination of the success or failure of treatment is based on changes in specific and observable behavioral responses. Second, behavior therapies are based on the assumption that maladaptive behaviors are acquired in the same way as other learned responses and that they can be changed through the principles of learning. Third, they assume that events in the environment, especially reinforcers, maintain problematic behaviors. Fourth, they focus on current behavior rather than on past problems. Fifth, they typically focus more on the techniques of therapy than on the therapeutic relationship between therapist and patient (although this is not invariably the case). Finally, behaviorally oriented therapists are committed to the idea that the value claimed for any treatment must be documented by evidence from controlled experimental studies. In the past, *behavior modification* (or "behavior mod," as it is popularly known) referred to the use of operant conditioning techniques based on Skinner's theory of learning (see Chapter 5); currently it is used interchangeably with *behavior therapy* (Eysenck & Skinner, 1980).

BEHAVIOR THERAPIES BASED ON CLASSICAL CONDITIONING

In Chapter 5, we discussed the early experiment of Watson and Rayner in which little Albert was classically conditioned to fear a white rat. The experiment supplies a model of how neurotic behavior may be acquired through conditioning. People experience emotional reactions, especially fear, in the presence of previously neutral stimuli (a white rat), and through this association the neutral stimulus comes to evoke the fear re-

sponse. When you fear something you tend to avoid it, and avoiding it tends to reduce your fear. This, according to behavior therapists, is how neurotic behaviors are maintained.

Extinction — Flooding/Implosion Therapy

When someone learns a neurotic behavior (little Albert's avoidance of the white rat), the obvious antidote is to induce the person to "unlearn" it: to extinguish the fear response and avoidance behavior. The basic principle underlying this idea is that by repeatedly presenting the object that evokes a conditioned response (for example, white rat) without any reinforcement, it loses its power to evoke the response. There are, however, three major problems with the use of extinction to eliminate neurotic behaviors. First, in cases where the emotional response involves intense fear, people may refuse to expose themselves to the feared object. Second, many (neu-

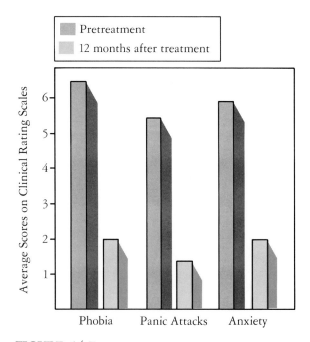

FIGURE 14-7

Extinction of Agoraphobia One year after completing twelve hours of treatment for agoraphobia, the fear response was still extinguished. *Source:* Hafner, R. J. (1983). Behavior therapy for agoraphobic men. *Behaviour Research and Therapy, 21,* 51 – 56.

rotic) emotional responses are deeply ingrained and difficult to extinguish. Third, when people are exposed to an object that evokes an unpleasant emotional response, the response may be reinforced when they avoid the object.

One means by which the first problem may be overcome is, in effect, to force people to confront the objects of their fear. In one version of this technique, **implosion therapy** (Stampfl & Lewis, 1967), the therapist repeatedly exposes the patient to vivid mental images of the feared stimulus in the safety of the therapist's office. The reasoning behind this procedure is that the stimulus will lose its anxiety-producing power and the anxiety will extinguish (implode) because no harm will come to the patient in this safe situation.

Flooding, or implosion, therapy is sometimes used in real-life settings. In treating a patient suffering from agoraphobia (fear of open spaces), for example, the therapist might insist that the patient leave home (the only place the patient feels safe) and visit a grocery store for a certain period of time. Repeatedly confronting the anxiety-producing situation causes the fear response to extinguish (see Figure 14-7). Although implosion therapy appears to produce favorable results in some cases, in others it appears to lead to increased anxiety. For this reason, the treatment is used with considerable caution.

Counterconditioning

One way to counteract the limitations of techniques based on extinction is to sweeten the pot a little by substituting a desirable response for the one to be extinguished. In fact, this was how a colleague of J. B. Watson treated the fear response conditioned in little Albert. Mary Jones (1925) conducted studies involving some 70 children in which she eliminated fear responses by giving children candy and other incentives in the presence of a feared object (a white rabbit). At first Jones put the rabbit far away, in the corner of the room; then she moved it closer, step by step, until finally it was touching the children. Jones' work remained unrecognized for several decades, until popularized and refined by American psychiatrist John Wolpe under the name *systematic desensitization*.

Systematic Desensitization **Systematic desensitization** is based on the idea that to extinguish a maladaptive response, an individual must be trained to perform an *adaptive substitute response* in the presence of the stimulus that elicits the maladaptive response. The substitute response used by most modern behavior therapists is relaxation. During early treatment sessions, patients are trained in muscle relaxation and asked to rank several situations that cause anxiety, creating an **anxiety hierarchy** that ranges from those situations that produce the least anxiety to those that produce the most (see Table 14-6).

After relaxation training and creation of an anxiety hierarchy, the therapist selects the least anxiety-arousing item in the patient's anxiety hierarchy and asks the patient to think of it while remaining calm and relaxed. If the patient reports an increase in anxiety or if the patient becomes aroused psychophysiologically, the image is terminated and the patient is helped to regain a state of relaxation. When thinking about the item no longer evokes anxiety, the therapist presents the next item in the hierarchy. This process continues until the patient can imagine each item in the hierarchy wthout anxiety or discomfort. Once the patient can control his or her reaction to anxiety-provoking situations in the therapeutic

TABLE 14-6
An Anxiety Hierarchy

Ratings	Items
5	Seeing an ambulance
10	Seeing a hospital
20	Being inside a hospital
25	Reading the obituary notice of an old person
30–40	Passing a funeral home (the nearer, the worse)
40–55	Seeing a funeral (the nearer, the worse)
55–65	Driving past a cemetery (the nearer, the worse)
70	Reading the obituary notice of a young person who died of a heart attack
80	Seeing a burial assemblage from a distance
90	Being at a burial
100	Seeing a dead man in a coffin

Source: Wolpe, J., & Wolpe, D. (1981). *Our useless fears.* Boston, MA: Houghton Mifflin.

setting, the patient is ready to confront them in real life.

Freeling and Shemberg (1970) examined the effects of systematic desensitization on test anxiety. They convened a number of students who experienced test anxiety and divided them into three groups. They gave the first group training in relaxation and asked the students to imagine neutral scenes. They had the second group construct an anxiety hierarchy consisting of 15 items — ranging from "You are sitting in a classroom of 100 students listening to a lecture" to "The test papers are being passed out and you are sitting in your seat waiting to receive your paper" — but did not give them relaxation training. They gave the third group training in relaxation and in imagining scenes from the anxiety hierarchy. In accordance with the principles of systematic desensitization, the students imagined the least-arousing scene from the anxiety hierarchy and then, when they no longer felt anxious, went on to the next scene, and so on. Each group met once a week for six weeks. The results of this study showed that students who received systematic desensitization felt generally less anxious following treatment than students in the other groups and felt less anxious while actually writing a test (see Figure 14-8).

Systematic desensitization has been used successfully in the treatment of frigidity and impotence, extreme jealousy, phobias, obsessions and compulsions; such psychophysiological disorders as ulcers and test anxiety; and such complex interpersonal problems as fear of rejection and criticism (Rimm & Lefebvre, 1981).

Aversion Therapy   Systematic desensitization is appropriate for people who want to extinguish such unpleasant emotions as anxiety or jealousy. **Aversion therapy** is appropriate for people who, in effect, want the opposite: they seek to extinguish pleasant emotions associated with such socially undesirable behaviors as gambling, drinking, smoking, overeating, and sexual aberrations. Instead of substituting a pleasurable response for an aversive one, aversion therapy reverses the procedure: an unpleasant event — for example, nausea, shock, or a disgusting picture — is paired with a desired but socially undesirable behavior. With repeated pairings, previously desired stimuli come to elicit negative

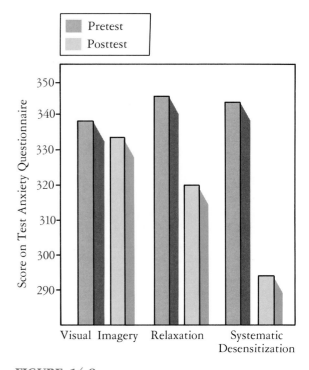

FIGURE 14-8

Changes in Test Anxiety Following Three Kinds of Treatment   Systematic desensitization was superior to relaxation and visual imagery in reducing test anxiety.   *Source:* Adapted from Freeling, N. W., & Shemberg, K. M. (1970). The alleviation of test anxiety by systematic desensitization. *Behaviour Research and Therapy, 8,* 293–99.

responses. Male homosexuals who wish to change their sexual orientation have been treated by pairing electric shocks with photos of male nudes, often in conjunction with systematic desensitization focused on heterosexual stimuli (Adams, Tollison, & Carson, 1981).

Covert Sensitization   In **covert sensitization** (a mild form of aversion therapy), patients are trained to punish themselves by using their imaginations. For example, a heavy drinker might be asked to imagine himself feeling nauseous as soon as he walks into a bar, vomiting all over himself, and feeling better only when he leaves the bar and walks out into the fresh air. Although more experimental work is needed to verify their reports, some clinicians have reported that covert sensitization is helpful in controlling excessive drinking, overeating, and cigarette smoking (Cautela, 1967).

Aversive procedures are vulnerable to criticism on both ethical and practical grounds. The idea of inflicting pain as a means of eliminating maladaptive behavior offends many people. Nevertheless, there is evidence that aversive conditioning has worked where other procedures have failed (Brady, 1980). Some critics have argued that although aversive techniques suppress maladaptive behavior, there is no cure until the patient learns an adaptive alternative. For example, a man who has learned not to respond sexually to leather shoes must also be taught how to respond sexually to women. For such reasons, most behavior therapists try to shape new adaptive behaviors in the patient at the same time they try to reduce old maladaptive ones through aversive procedures.

BEHAVIOR THERAPIES BASED ON OPERANT CONDITIONING

The responses modified during classical conditioning usually involve such emotional reactions as anxiety, although such observable behaviors as approaching a feared object may be modified as well. Techniques based on operant conditioning aim directly at observable voluntary behaviors (see Chapter 5). The basic principle of operant conditioning is simple: people tend to do things that are followed by rewards and stop doing things that are not rewarded or punished. According to learning theorists, children learn to behave in abnormal ways when they are rewarded unintentionally by parents, teachers, or peers for behaving abnormally. In reality, everyone is rewarded for behaving abnormally some of the time—especially when it concerns avoiding responsibility and satisfying basic needs. According to learning theorists, abnormal behaviors can be unlearned in the same way they were learned: through operant conditioning.

The first step in operant conditioning is to identify the behavior to be modified. We choose an example that all parents encounter—temper tantrums. Next, the therapist must identify the events that reinforce the behavior. The reinforcer for temper tantrums (and many other behaviors) is often attention. It is important to note that reinforcers originate from the environment. Next, the therapist attempts to restructure the environment so the problematic behavior is no longer reinforced, which in most cases involves withdrawing the reinforcer. For example, parents may be instructed to ignore the child (withdraw attention) when the child runs around screaming. Sometimes restructuring the environment involves *time-out from positive reinforcement* ("Go to your room"); in extreme cases it may involve administering some form of punishment. When applied consistently, such techniques regularly produce dramatic results. Although at first people characteristically increase the frequency of the problematic behavior, they quickly give it up after they learn it no longer pays off (see Figure 14-9).

In addition to eliminating undesirable behaviors, operant conditioning may be used to increase desirable behaviors. Because people usually emit some behaviors the therapist wants to strengthen, the therapist simply ensures they are reinforced. In cases where a person presents no desired behaviors, the technique of **shaping** must be used. In Chapter 5 we described how

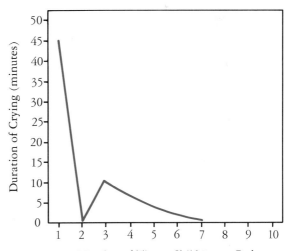

FIGURE 14-9

Duration of Crying Each Time the Child Was Put to Bed during a Week When first ignored, the child cried for 45 minutes. Within a week, crying was extinguished. *Source:* Adapted from Williams, C. D. (1959). The elimination of tantrum behavior by extinction procedures. *Journal of Abnormal Psychology, 59,* 269.

novel behaviors not part of an organism's repertoire can be developed by reinforcing behaviors that are increasingly similar to the desired behavior. Shaping techniques have proven useful in instilling adaptive behaviors in disturbed or retarded individuals, especially children. Wolf, Risley, and Mees (1964) report the case of an autistic boy who refused to wear his eyeglasses and was taught to wear them through the technique of shaping. The child was reinforced with candy or fruit for picking up the eyeglasses, carrying them around, putting them near his face, putting them on his head, and so on until, eventually, he learned to wear them for extended periods of time.

Operant procedures have been adopted widely in institutional settings, particularly in mental hospitals, prisons, and institutions for retarded people and juvenile delinquents. This is explained in part because the effectiveness of operant techniques depends on behavioral therapists acquiring complete control over the environment in order to apply the principles of learning as systematically and consistently as possible.

Token Economies and Contingency Management

An operant conditioning application called **token economy** has been used in such institutions as mental hospitals and reform schools. The technique involves giving patients tokens or "funny money" that can be exchanged for privileges or desired goods when they behave in desirable ways. Ayllon and Azrin (1968) were the first to institute a token economy in a psychiatric ward. They began by observing patients in order to identify what they liked. They found that such privileges as selecting a dining companion; talking to a physician, psychologist, or chaplain; watching TV; and obtaining candy or cigarettes were reinforcing to patients. So the investigators gave the patients tokens that could be exchanged for these rewards when the patients engaged in such desirable behaviors as serving meals, grooming themselves, and helping with housekeeping tasks. In a series of six experiments, Ayllon and Azrin showed that the rewards were effective in eliciting and maintaining the desired behaviors (see Figure 14-10). Later studies confirmed the

findings in other settings (Salzinger, 1981). A by-product of the token economy was an elevation in both patient and staff morale: patients were less apathetic and less irresponsible; staff were increasingly enthusiastic about the patients and the technique.

Whereas token economies are based on the principle of positive reinforcement, **contingency management** techniques employ withdrawal of reinforcement or mild punishment to

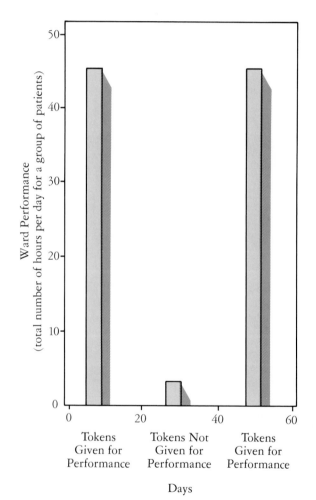

FIGURE 14-10

Total Ward Hours of Self-grooming and Work Performed by a Group of Patients Each Day Note the marked decrease when behavior was not reinforced with tokens. *Source:* Adapted from Ayllon, T., & Azrin, N. H. (1968). *The token economy: A motivational system for therapy and rehabilitation.* New York: Appleton-Century-Crofts.

extinguish maladaptive responses. For example, a child who engages in aggressive behavior might be removed from the situation and placed in an empty room. (Note this is not the same as sending a child to his or her room for behaving badly inasmuch as the child might find rewarding things to do in the room.) Withdrawal of reinforcement has been used successfully to prevent self-mutilation and to reduce excessive aggression and temper tantrums in severely disturbed children, and to treat anorexia nervosa. Consider a study by Halmi, Powers, and Cunningham (1975), who monitored the activities of eight anorexic patients (see Chapter 13) and made such privileges as being in the company of other patients, receiving mail, and watching television contingent upon increased food intake and actual weight gain. Over an average hospitalization of six weeks, the patients each gained an average of 19 pounds. Upon discharge, the patients' families were taught to use the behavior modification techniques employed in the hospital setting. If a patient lost more than two pounds in any week, the patient was readmitted immediately for tube feeding, a distinctly unpleasant procedure. The experimenters followed up on the progress of the patients seven months after discharge and found they continued to show moderate weight gain and no relapse that required hospitalization. Although this study did not use a control group, the results are nevertheless encouraging—particularly in view of the fact that anorexia nervosa is notably unresponsive to most forms of treatment (see Chapter 13).

Sex Therapy

Traditionally, people have seen physicians for sexual problems. However, for the two major sexual dysfunctions—in men, premature ejaculation; in women, lack of orgasm—there is usually no physical problem involved. Prior to the pioneering work of Masters and Johnson (1966, 1970), psychologically based treatment focused on conflicts within a couple's relationship and on how those conflicts expressed themselves in the sexual situation. In concert with the growing popularity of behavior therapy, the work of Masters and Johnson has led to the increased use of behaviorally oriented sex therapy.

Behavioral methods of sex therapy possess several characteristic features: goals are directed exclusively at the sexual problems of clients; specific behavioral instructions are given to couples, which they are asked to practice in private; couples participate in psychotherapy sessions in the therapist's office; duration of treatment is limited, for example, to a period of two weeks; there are ordinarily two therapists (male and female); and initial assessment of the problem is combined with appropriate instruction, to ensure that both partners understand the nature of sexual functioning.

Treatment often requires an initial period of sexual abstinence, during which couples are systematically trained to give each other pleasurable feelings by using tactile stimulation—but without seeking orgasm. As the couple begins to relax and share in giving and receiving this mutual pleasure, treatment focuses more on their specific problems. Men who suffer premature ejaculation may be trained in the use of the *squeeze* or the *stop-start* technique. In both these techniques the man and woman are trained to arouse the man, then to control and reduce the arousal, and then to arouse the man again (and so on) until he can sustain an erection for a reasonable period of time without ejaculating. The success rate for different versions of the squeeze technique is impressively high; Masters and Johnson report 98% success following two weeks of treatment.

Now that research has clearly established that orgasm requires appropriate stimulation of the clitoris (see Chapter 8), treatment is substantially more focused and effective. The woman is trained in self-stimulation (sometimes with the aid of a vibrator) so she will experience orgasm, learn to recognize the signs and levels of excitement that lead up to it, and be reassured she is capable of achieving orgasm. Orgasm is treated as a psychological reflex that automatically occurs with proper stimulation. Accordingly, the woman's partner is taught how to provide effective clitoral stimulation. The partners practice together and participate in psychotherapeutic discussions that attempt to keep the facts clear, relieve anxieties, and remove possible interpersonal conflicts relating to their sexual relationship.

Self-management

In the techniques under discussion, therapists control the reinforcers. When patients are not institutionalized, however, therapists are not present to insure that reinforcers are given appropriately in all situations. In addition, many people are wary of the external control involved in behavior modification. One way to solve both the practical and ethical problems is to teach troubled people how to control their own reinforcement and to give them that responsibility. In recent years, **self-control programs** based on principles of operant conditioning have helped people improve study habits, reduce overeating, stop smoking, stop stuttering, and decrease excessive drinking (see Rimm & Masters, 1979). Such programs involve removing undesirable sources of reinforcement from the environment (for example, removing all alcohol from the house and avoiding bars), constraining environments in which the undesirable behaviors occur (for example, eating only in one's own kitchen), and delivering self-rewards for engaging in desirable behaviors (for example, watching a movie after studying for three hours). Techniques you might consider using to manage certain of your problems are described in Box 14-4, page 760.

Biofeedback

The basic idea underlying **biofeedback** is to provide feedback about increases and decreases in biological or psychophysiological responses, usually those not directly observable. This usually is accomplished by sounding a tone or flashing a light in synchronization with a psychological response that is recorded by electronic sensors. For example, a person suffering from hypertension (high blood pressure) might listen to a series of tones whose pitch grows higher whenever his or her blood pressure increases and becomes lower whenever it decreases. Aided by this feedback, the person is encouraged to lower the pitch of the tone, and thus lower his or her blood pressure. Experimenters usually do not tell subjects how to modify the responses being monitored; they simply encourage them to try various means they think might affect the feedback signal. Ultimately, it is hoped the methods the subjects develop will work outside the laboratory in their everyday lives.

Researchers have employed biofeedback in the treatment of such disorders as tension headache, peptic ulcer, and hypertension. The procedures used often include some form of reinforcement for success in reaching goals, thus combining operant principles with practice in self-control. Thus far, efforts to relieve hypertension through biofeedback have been less promising than originally hoped; more encouraging results have been obtained in controlling tension headaches by using a combination of at-home relaxation techniques and biofeedback (Budzynski, Stoyva, Adler & Mullaney, 1973). In addition, biofeedback has been used to enhance muscle relaxation and to promote a mental state of alert, relaxed consciousness (Blanchard & Epstein, 1978).

EVALUATION OF BEHAVIOR THERAPY

Because of its reliance on principles of learning, environmental influence, and observable responses, behavior therapy lends itself neatly to experimental research. There are more than one thousand operant-conditioning studies on humans, hundred of studies on modeling, and more than 200 studies on systematic desensitization. And most have found that the problematic behaviors in question were modified through the methods of behavior therapy employed. Proponents of behavior therapy point out that it is relatively inexpensive, quick, and easy to evaluate.

However, behavior therapy has not gone without criticism; indeed, it is one of the most criticized of all approaches to psychotherapy. Five major criticisms have been leveled against behavior therapy:

1. It is unethical to manipulate people, and behavioral techniques are dehumanizing.

2. Although behavior therapy may modify the symptoms of psychological disorders, it does not cure their underlying causes.

3. The effects of behavior therapy are temporary and specific to the situations experienced during treatment.

4. Behavior therapy ignores the client-therapist relationship.

5. Behavior therapy works only with simple disorders.

Manipulation and Dehumanization

Some critics have accused behavior therapists — more particularly behavior modifiers — of authoritarian control, dehumanization of clients, brainwashing, and fascism. Other critics have argued that behavior therapists manipulate people and deprive them of freedom. The bases for these accusations lie in three primary features of behavior therapy: therapists, not clients, control reinforcers; therapists sometimes use punishment; and therapists do not encourage clients to obtain insight about their conflicts or to seek a better understanding of themselves. Behavior therapists argue first that because all (learned) behavior is under external control, the techniques they employ are essentially the same techniques used by all people in their everyday lives. (Both the boss who criticizes an employee's performance and the mother who hugs her child for picking up her toys are employing behavior modification.) In effect, everyone is a naive behavior therapist; the only difference is that behavior therapists employ the techniques more consistently and systematically. Second, behavior therapists point out that they do not modify behavior without client consent. Although they may employ aversive techniques, their clients agree to such treatments because their problems (phobias, addictions, sexual perversions) are more aversive than the techniques. According to behavior therapists, the goal is not to control clients but to help them regain control of their behavior.

The Modification of Behavior versus the Restructuring of Personality

Because behavior therapists consider the maladaptive behaviors they modify to be the disorder, they assume the disorder is "cured" when the behaviors are modified. Critics argue that the behavioristic model of psychological disorder is wrong and that maladaptive behaviors are only symptoms of underlying disorders. Most critics grant that behavior therapists can modify behavior, but these same critics suggest they fail to modify the internal causes that produce the behavior. One consequence of this "Band-Aid approach" to treatment, argue critics, is that symptoms (maladaptive behaviors) reappear in other forms **(symptom substitution).** However, the evidence on symptom substitution is mixed: it appears to occur for some disorders but not for others. For example, the evidence suggests that hysteria may originate from deep-seated conflicts and, therefore, that the symptoms of hysteria may reappear in many forms. On the other hand, the symptoms of single phobias seem to disappear when extinguished, and successful treatment of some symptoms appears to generalize to others (Bandura, 1969).

Specific and Temporary Effects

When critics question the generality and endurance of the effects of behavior therapy, they challenge behavior therapy on its own ground. Because behavior therapists believe behavior is controlled by the environment, there should be no surprise when behaviors modified in the laboratory fail to endure in other contexts. Indeed, studies have found that specificity of changes is among the major limitations of behavior therapy (Rimm, 1976). There are four primary ways to extend the generality of modified behaviors: modifying them in environments representative of those in real life, encouraging clients to avoid environments that elicit maladaptive behaviors, encouraging clients to return for follow-up treatments, and teaching clients how to modify their behavior on a continuing basis.

Therapist – Client Relationship

Behavior therapists have been criticized for being detached and impersonal. In point of fact, however, although behavior therapists disagree with the psychoanalytic view that the patient's emotional response to the therapist (embodied in *transference*) is a key factor in the success of therapy, many behavior therapists believe that a positive therapist – client relationship helps foster an atmosphere in which therapy has the best chances of success.

Disorder of Choice

As noted, behavior therapy appears to work well with disorders that involve anxiety, especially simple phobias, and such disorders as alcoholism,

BOX 14-4
CONTROLLING YOUR OWN BEHAVIOR

If you believe you have a severe psychological problem, you should seek professional help. But if you believe you have a modest problem, you may be able to "treat" yourself with one or more of the techniques employed by behavior therapists. Four are especially adaptable to everyday use.

Desensitization

Many people suffer from moderate anxieties and mild fears. For example, students often feel anxious about taking tests and speaking in class; many people feel anxious about talking with people they don't know, interacting with members of the opposite sex, applying for a job, flying, and so on. Following the procedure popularized by Wolpe (1973), you can control fears and anxieties by learning how to induce deep muscle relaxation, constructing an anxiety hierarchy, and by substituting relaxation for anxiety through systematic desensitization. Assume you are terrified to make a presentation before a class. You would begin by learning how to relax your muscles. One method involves tensing the muscles in a particular part of your body (perhaps your right arm) until they

tremble (for about five seconds), then allowing them to go as limp as possible, and repeating the process two or three times until the muscles are relaxed. Following this, the muscles in another part of the body (perhaps your left arm) are tensed and then released until relaxed. After the second part of your body is relaxed, turn to another part (perhaps your right leg), and so on until all of your body is relaxed. And don't forget your forehead, neck, chin, mouth, scalp, nose, eyelids, cheeks, and the like. You must practice this relaxation technique at least once a day for one or two weeks. Some people find it helpful to imagine a soothing scene while relaxing muscles.

The next step is to make an anxiety hierarchy (perhaps on ten index cards). The first (least frightening) item might involve thinking about someone else giving a speech. The fourth item might involve assembling the materials to start writing a speech. The last (most frightening) item might involve standing before a class and delivering your opening line.

The final step is to countercondition the fear. Begin with the least frighten-

ing item on your anxiety hierarchy, imagine it vividly, and then relax. Continue the process until you can relax completely while imagining the first item on your hierarchy, then the second item, and so on until you can imagine standing before a class and delivering your opening line without being anxious. You should engage in this technique at least once a day, going back over one or two items each time to extinguish the spontaneous recovery that is bound to occur.

Covert Sensitization

Whereas in systematic desensitization positive reactions (relaxation) are substituted for negative reactions (fears and anxieties), in covert sensitization negative reactions are substituted for such problematic positive reactions as the pleasure derived from smoking, drinking, and eating. Assume you want to stop smoking. Your goal is to endow the cues associated with smoking with the power to evoke in you a negative response sufficiently strong to overwhelm the desire to indulge in the habit. One approach is to construct a personal list of the most disgusting factors associated with smoking. For example, one such factor might involve you slowly dying of lung cancer, barely able to breathe, with distraught relatives gathered around your bed arguing about who should get what from your estate. You may want to write out such scenes on index cards for easy future reference and, if you are really serious, you may want to obtain graphic pictures of lung surgery, blackened lungs, victims of cancer, and so forth. For the technique to work, the stimuli must evoke strong negative reactions in you.

The next step is to repeatedly pair your aversive reactions with cues to smoking throughout the day. For example, you might look at a package of cigarettes and then imagine each scene, starting with the least aversive and ending with the most disgusting. If the scenes you imagine lose their power to evoke disgust in you, you must create a new set. Over time, the cues to smoking should evoke a negative reaction sufficiently strong to overwhelm the previous desire.

Reinforcement — Overt and Covert

In addition to evoking negative feelings about stimuli associated with bad habits, it is helpful to reward yourself for not indulging in them. Assume you want to reduce your sugar intake. In addition to imagining yourself in a disgusting state of gross obesity, you might also treat yourself to some tangible reward each time (or every day or week) you resist the temptation to eat sweets. Or you may employ such covert, or imaginary, reinforcement as receiving profuse compliments on your trim figure. Although tangible reinforcers tend to be most powerful when appropriately chosen (when they are rewarding), imaginary reinforcers are more adaptable and convenient. Indeed, the entire process of behavioral change can be accomplished mentally by people who take it seriously enough to create vivid images and evoke them regularly.

Changing Self-defeating Thoughts

Covert sensitization and covert reinforcement are based on the idea that emotions associated with thoughts about behaviors may be as powerful as emotions associated with actual performance of the behavior. The power of thoughts also is revealed in the ways people think about themselves and others. Cognitive-behavior therapists believe people who feel bad about themselves will feel a lot better if they substitute positive thoughts for negative thoughts.

The first step is to identify the negative thoughts. Although reflecting on your own behavior is the most convenient method, you also might seek feedback from someone who listens to you frequently. The second step is to punish yourself when you engage in negative thinking. Various forms are available. Some people place a rubber band around their wrist and give themselves a quick slap, more as a reminder of their negative thoughts than as a physical punishment. Other people deliberately engage in negative thinking and then mentally chastise themselves, sometimes in such dramatic ways as thinking (and even shouting) "Stop!" The third step is to substitute a positive idea for the negative one (for example, "Although I have my faults, I'm as good as most people, and better than many."). As with the other techniques, the key to success is to determine appropriate reinforcers and to pair them with problematic behaviors and thoughts in a systematic way. It is recommended that specific times be set aside throughout the day to engage in the techniques of self-control.

overeating, stuttering, enuresis, and sexual perversions involving highly specific maladaptive responses. Behavior modification also has been employed successfully in the treatment of autism and schizophrenia. It has not, however, proven as effective in the treatment of more complex phobias and other disorders that appear to reflect deep-seated and well-entrenched personality problems (Mahoney, 1980).

TREATMENTS BASED ON SOCIAL LEARNING

As discussed in Chapters 5, 10, and 12, social learning theory accepts the principles of conditioning and emphasizes observational learning, or modeling. The central idea underlying social learning therapy is that people can correct maladaptive behaviors by watching others perform adaptive behaviors. In one study Bandura, Grusec, and Menlove (1967) reduced children's fear of dogs by having them watch a "fearless peer" approach, then pet, and eventually play with a dog. After observing the model over a series of trials, 67% of the children could climb into a playpen with the dog and pet it. In another study Bandura, Blanchard, and Ritter (1969) divided subjects who feared snakes into three matched groups, giving each group a different type of behavior therapy. The people in the first group were treated with *systematic desensitization*—they were taught to relax while imagining scenes of snakes. The subjects in the second group were exposed to *symbolic models*—they watched a film in which a child and an adult played with a large king snake in progressively more frightening ways. Those in the third group engaged in *participant modeling*—they observed a live model interact with a snake and slowly, step-by-step, imitated the model's behavior. The results of the study, displayed in Figure 14-11, reflect that all types of behavior therapy were better than no therapy and that participant modeling was most effective.

Assertiveness Training

Modeling is a major component of **assertiveness training,** which aims at helping people who experience difficulty asserting themselves in interpersonal situations. Although assertiveness training may be conducted individually with a therapist, it usually takes place in a group setting. Assertiveness training begins by identifying situations in which people feel unable to assert themselves. For example, if you had difficulty standing up to an overbearing boss, you might select an incident involving the boss and act it out, with another member of the group or with the therapist playing the role of boss. The therapist (and perhaps other members of the group) would supply feedback about your "performance," pointing out, for example, that you avoided eye contact, were barely audible, and in general behaved like a wimp. The therapist would then take your role, someone else playing the boss, and

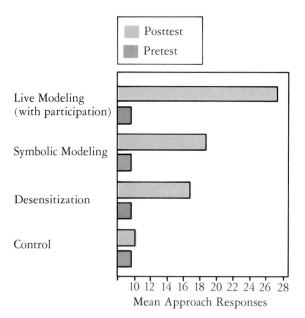

FIGURE 14-11
Treating Snake Phobias Behaviorally The mean number of approach responses made by subjects before and after receiving different kinds of behavior therapy reflects that participant modeling was most effective. *Source:* Adapted from Bandura, A., Blanchard, E. B., & Ritter, B. (1969). The relative efficacy of desensitization and modeling approaches for reducing behavioral, effective, and attitudinal changes. *Journal of Personality and Social Psychology, 13,* 173–99.

model appropriately assertive behavior. You would then try again, imitating the therapist as best you could. This alternating between modeling and **behavioral rehearsal** would continue until you had mastered the assertive role. After developing appropriate skills in the context of therapy, you would be ready to try them in real life. Although the process seems simple, modeling assertive behavior is, in fact, extremely difficult for people who have developed a life-long habit of deference.

Although assertiveness training usually is undertaken by people who consider themselves unassertive, it also may benefit people who consider themselves overassertive and aggressive (Arglye, Furnham, & Graham, 1981). The evidence suggests that assertiveness training is effective in helping people behave more assertively in the situations they have modeled and rehearsed; however, the training often fails to generalize to other situations (Rimm & Masters, 1979).

Social learning techniques are used most commonly to treat neurotic disorders and interpersonal difficulties; nevertheless, they also have been employed to treat more severe disorders. For example, Bellack, Hersen, and Turner (1976) found that a combination of role playing, modeling, and positive reinforcement significantly improved the social skills of three schizophrenic patients and that the newly developed skills generalized to social interactions not covered in therapy.

Self-efficacy

In an extension of early social learning theory, Albert Bandura emphasizes the significance of believing that one is the master of his or her outcomes and is able to deal effectively with difficult situations. Bandura (1977) calls this belief and associated behavior **self-efficacy.** Bandura, Adams, Hardy, and Howells (1980) describe the ways in which people's beliefs about their ability to cope interfere with or facilitate various behaviors. One implication of this more cognitive approach to therapy is to place less emphasis on observational learning and more emphasis on participant modeling—a technique that encourages clients to feel that the gains they make belong to them and not to the therapist.

COGNITIVE APPROACHES

Whereas behavior therapists attempt to modify maladaptive behavior, cognitive therapists attempt to modify maladaptive thoughts. As noted in Chapter 13, Beck attributes depression to implicit assumptions people make about themselves—such assumptions as "If I don't get everything right, I'm a failure" and "When good things happen to me, it's because I'm lucky." According to cognitive therapists, events in people's lives (failing an exam) are less important than the meaning people attach to them ("I am stupid; I'll never succeed"). Treatments based on Beck's cognitive theory of depression help people identify the implicit, self-defeating assumptions they make about themselves, challenge their validity, and encourage them to substitute those that are more positive. Consider, for example, the following exchange between a therapist and client.

Therapist Why do you want to end your life?

Client Without Raymond, I am nothing. . . . I can't be happy without Raymond. . . . But I can't save our marriage.

Therapist What has your marriage been like?

Client It has been miserable from the very beginning. . . . Raymond has always been unfaithful. . . . I have hardly seen him in the past five years.

Therapist You say that you can't be happy without Raymond. . . . Have you found yourself happy when you are with Raymond?

Client No, we fight all the time and I feel worse.

Therapist You say you are nothing without Raymond. Before you met Raymond, did you feel you were nothing?

Client No, I felt I was somebody.

Therapist If you were somebody before you knew Raymond, why do you need him to be somebody now?

Client (puzzled) Hmm. . . .

Therapist If you were free of the marriage, do you think that men might be interested in you—knowing that you were available?

Client I guess that maybe they would be.

Therapist Is it possible that you might find a man who would be more constant then Raymond?

Client I don't know. . . . I guess it's possible. . . .

Therapist   Then what have you actually lost if you break up the marriage?

Client   I don't know.

Therapist   Is it possible that you'll get along better if you end the marriage?

Client   There is no guarantee of that.

Therapist   Do you have a real marriage?

Client   I guess not.

Therapist   If you don't have a real marriage, what do you actually lose if you decide to end the marriage?

Client   (long pause) Nothing, I guess.

(Beck, 1976, pp. 289–91)

Rational–Emotive Therapy

The cognitive therapy approach that has received the most attention is the rational-emotive therapy of Albert Ellis. Ellis, originally a psychoanalyst, disagreed with two basic assumptions of Freud's approach — that childhood events are the primary source of psychological disorder and that the id is the most powerful component of personality. Ellis insisted that the primary source of psychological disorder lies in the ego, or rational processes, and involves fallacious assumptions people make about themselves. The goal of **rational-emotive therapy** is to reduce feelings of anxiety and hostility through the rational processes of self-observation and self-assessment.

Examine the beliefs in Table 14-7. How many do you endorse? According to Ellis, neurotic behavior occurs because people develop such irrational beliefs about themselves as those displayed in Table 14-7 and reinforce them by repeating them to themselves. People who believe (and frequently tell themselves) such things as "I must be loved and approved of by everyone I meet" or "I must be perfectly competent at everything I try, otherwise I'm worthless" make impossible demands of themselves that inevitably lead to feelings of anxiety and hostility, failure, and frequently, abnormal behavior. For example, consider the following description by Ellis (1984, p. 198) of a woman in therapy.

> She does not merely believe it is undesirable if her love partner is rejecting. She tends to believe, also, that (1) it is awful; (2) she cannot stand it; (3) she should not, must not be rejected; (4) she will never be accepted by any desirable partner;

(5) she is a worthless person because one lover has rejected her; and (6) she deserves to be damned for being so worthless. Such common covert hypotheses are nonsensical. . . . They can be easily elicited and demolished by any scientist worth his or her salt; and the rational-emotive therapist is exactly that: an exposing and nonsense-annihilating scientist.

The role of the therapist in rational-emotive therapy is opposite the role of the therapist in client-centered therapy in two senses: rational-emotive therapists focus on thinking rather than on feeling and rational-emotive therapy is therapist-centered. Rational-emotive therapists seek to expose and challenge the client's faulty assumptions in order to diminish the emotional impact of the faulty assumptions and to help the patient learn to substitute more realistic ideas and expectations. According to Ellis (1977, p. 20) "Rational-emotive therapy largely consists of the use of the logico-empirical method of scientific questioning, challenging, and debating." In many cases, the emphases are on challenging, debating, and "disrupting" — exposing the irrational assumptions that people make about themselves, in an aggressive manner if necessary.

TABLE 14-7
Irrational Beliefs

I must be loved and approved of by almost every significant person in my life.

I should be completely competent and achieving in all ways to be a worthwhile person.

Certain people I must deal with are thoroughly bad and should be severely blamed and punished for it.

It is awful and upsetting when things are not the way I would very much like them to be.

My unhappiness is always caused by external events; I cannot control my emotional reactions.

If something unpleasant might happen, I should keep dwelling on it.

It is easier to avoid difficulties and responsibilities than to face them.

I should depend on others who are stronger than I am.

Because something once strongly affected my life, it will do so indefinitely.

There is always a perfect solution to human problems, and it is awful if this solution is not found.

Source: Rohsenow, D. J., & Smith, R. E. (1982). Irrational beliefs as predictors of negative affective states. *Motivation and Emotion, 6,* 299–301.

Consider the following exchange between Ellis, a rational-emotive therapist, and a patient.

Ellis The same crap! It's always the same crap. Now if you would look at the crap—instead of "Oh, how stupid I am! He hates me! I think I'll kill myself"—then you'd get better right away.

Client You've been listening! (laughs)

Ellis Listening to what?

Client (laughs) Those wild statements in my mind, like that, that I make.

Ellis That's right! Because I know that you have to make those statements—because I have a good theory. And according to my theory, people couldn't get upset unless they made those nutty statements to themselves. . . . Even if I loved you madly, the next person you talk to is likely to hate you. So I like brown eyes and he likes blue eyes, or something. So you're then dead! Because you really think: "I've got to be accepted! I've got to act intelligently!" Well, why?

Client (very soberly and reflectively) True.

Ellis You see?

Client Yes.

Ellis Now, if you will learn that lesson, then you've had a very valuable session. Because you don't have to upset yourself. As I said before: if I thought you were the worst [expletive] who ever existed, well that's my opinion. And I'm entitled to it. But does it make you a turd?

Client (reflective silence)

Ellis Does it?

Client No.

Ellis What makes you a turd?

Client Think that you are.

Ellis That's right! Your belief that you are. That's the only thing that could ever do it. And you never have to believe that. See? You control your thinking. I control my thinking—my belief about you. But you don't have to be affected by that. You always control what you think. (Ellis, 1982, p. 219)

Rational-emotive therapists question the value of building the close, caring, and supportive relationship with their clients that characterizes client-centered therapy.

> If you give clients a lot of warmth, support, attention, and caring, you may be reinforcing their dire needs for love, which frequently and even usually are the central core of their disturbances. You also run the risk of making the client dependent on you and therapy instead of helping him or her cope with life's difficulties directly. (Saltzberg & Elkins, 1980, p. 326)

Cognitive-behavior Therapy

We stated earlier that the goal of behavior therapy is to modify behavior and the goal of cognitive therapy is to modify thoughts. It follows that the goal of **cognitive-behavior therapy** is to modify both thoughts and behavior, or more precisely, to alter behavior by modifying the way people think. Some of the treatments practiced by behavior therapists, such as systematic desensitization, involve cognitive-behavior modification. Clients are asked to imagine anxiety-producing stimuli and to think about them while relaxing. Similarly, social-learning therapy, especially techniques that involve self-efficacy, are quite cognitive in orientation. The dividing line between these types of behavior therapy and cognitive-behavior therapy is thin, and in some cases arbitrary. In practice, therapists who identify their primary orientation as behavioral, social learning, and cognitive behavioral may be doing much the same thing. The basic difference lies in the extent to which they identify changing thoughts or changing behavior as their goal.

When we discussed the causes of depression in Chapter 13, we noted that Seligman, who originally emphasized the learning of helplessness, revised his theory to make it more cognitive. Seligman and his colleagues came to believe that people seldom find themselves in aversive situations over which they have no control; what frequently happens is that people interpret situations in ways that make them feel helpless. In general, cognitive-behavior therapists assume that ideas are learned in the same way that behavior is learned and, therefore, can be modified through principles of learning. Certain thoughts ("No one will listen to my speech") evoke certain feelings (anxiety, depression) that affect behavior (making a poor speech) in a circular way ("I knew no one would like it"). In cognitive-behavior therapy, therapists begin by helping clients identify self-defeating thoughts. They encourage clients to listen to their internal monologues—to get in touch with the statements clients make to themselves and to heed the emotional reactions these thoughts evoke (Meichenbaum, 1977). After the self-defeating thoughts have been identified, therapists encourage clients to give themselves more positive and constructive types of self-instruction ("I know that some people in the audience will appreciate my speech, so I'll direct it toward them") and to follow it up by engaging in adaptive behaviors. The evidence is accumulating that such "power-of-positive-thinking" approaches used in conjunction with reinforcement and modeling are quite successful in the treatment of anxiety and depression (Meichenbaum, Henshaw, & Himmel, 1982).

INTERPERSONAL APPROACHES — GROUP THERAPY

People often seek therapy because of interpersonal problems, especially those involving feelings of loneliness and isolation and difficulties forming meaningful relationships. Although individual therapists may help people sort out their feelings and trace the origins of their problems, and although the relationship formed between a client and therapist may be significant (Schofield, 1964), **group therapy** provides a fuller social context in which people can work out their social problems. Clients help one another in group therapy. They become, in effect, both client and therapist — or at least they are encouraged to play both roles. Group therapy affords a unique laboratory for working out interpersonal relationships. Troubled individuals quickly recognize they are not the only ones who feel the way they do. They have an opportunity to see themselves as others see them and to obtain more honest feedback about their behavior than elsewhere in everyday life. They also have an opportunity to try alternative responses when old ones prove ineffective (Sadock, 1980).

Group therapy usually includes from six to twelve clients and may last from 24 hours (continuous marathon encounter session) to several months (repeated sessions). One advantage of group therapy over individual therapy is that clients interact in a setting more representative of real life. Members of groups must express themselves "in public," listen as well as talk, play the role of others as well as make themselves understood, and help as well as be helped. Consequently, members of groups receive multiple feedback, learning that some of what they do offends everyone, some offends only a few, and much of what they do offends no one at all. Clients in groups learn they are not alone in many of their insecurities and fears. Group interactions afford an opportunity to try various social skills, provide exposure to a variety of models, and supply generous opportunity for vicarious learning. In addition, the feeling of being part of a group, of getting to know new people, of expressing a point of view, of belonging, and of intimacy may be therapeutic in themselves. And last, but not least, group therapy is less expensive than individual therapy.

Although group therapy has existed for a long time, in recent decades it has undergone a change in orientation and has expanded considerably in scope. One of the first forms of group therapy, **psychodrama,** (Moreno, 1934) was based on psychoanalysis. In psychodrama, group members act out scenes from their lives with the goal of expressing their feelings more openly. For example, a client might be asked to act out an emotionally painful childhood episode with another member of the group playing the role of the client's father. The therapist sometimes acts as "director," urging clients to develop the scene in a way that will help them confront previously repressed feelings. When the scene concludes, the therapist discusses the interaction with the clients, interpreting the exchanges in an attempt to help the participants gain insight into the unconscious roots and motivations of their feelings.

As individual therapy became more prevalent in the 1950s and 1960s, so also did group therapy. Various types emerged, most of which were influenced by psychoanalytic, behavioristic, and humanistic schools of thought. We have discussed one behavioral type of group therapy, assertiveness training, that is popular today. However, the humanistic school of thought — especially in the form of the "human potential movement" — has had the greatest impact on group therapy. In America during the 1960s and 1970s, thousands of groups sprang up and hundreds of thousands of people took part in them. Most people who joined were not suffering from any disorder; their goals were to improve their social skills and to pursue self-actualization. According to Lubin and Lubin (1980), the group movement has been the most significant development in psychotherapy during the past 30 years. Table 14-8 summarizes the advantages and disadvantages of group therapy and individual therapy.

Encounter Groups

What came to be called **encounter groups,** or sensitivity-training groups, evolved from human-relations training groups, or **T-groups** (the T stands for training), created by the students of early social psychologist Kurt Lewin. Although the original function of these groups was academic — to study group processes — members quickly discovered their potential therapeutic gains. At the heart of encounter groups is the idea that to achieve personal growth and to improve interpersonal relationships, people must learn to express their feelings in an open and honest manner. In addition to positive feelings, these feelings include those that people hide for fear others will dislike or reject them. Group members are encouraged to drop their public face and to say what they really feel — to *tell it like it is.* In turn, other members are encouraged to respond candidly to these expressions. Such exchanges give participants an opportunity to practice frankness, openness, and honesty; of equal importance, they give members immediate feedback on how others react to them. The desired result is that each individual will gain insights that lead to new patterns of behavior.

The term **facilitator** is used frequently to describe the role of the leader of an encounter group. It is an apt choice. In most instances the leader does not direct the interactions of the group but helps establish an atmosphere in which spontaneous, uncensored communication can take place. In many encounter groups, facilitators are also group members, and their feelings

TABLE 14-8
Group Therapy versus Individual Therapy — Advantages and Disadvantages

Group Therapy	Individual Therapy
Extra people provide a fuller range of feedback.	Continuous one-on-one relationship allows more in-depth exploration of problems.
Some problems are especially responsive to the group process (through multiple feedback and/or confrontation), such as postdivorce adjustment problems and hypochondriasis.	Some problems are too embarrassing to the client to share with others or are upsetting to effective group process, such as sexual deviations or antisocial or paranoid disorders.
Group therapy is usually less costly per hour.	Individual therapy is less costly in terms of cost per unit of time spent on a single individual's problems.
Everyone has a chance to help as well as to receive help.	There is greater opportunity to know the therapist as a person who has also experienced problems.
Group response is well suited to *interpersonal* aspects of problems.	Individual response allows fuller disclosure of *intrapsychic* aspects of problems.
There is a chance to break into new social systems and make new friends.	Confidentiality is more likely to be maintained.
If a therapist somehow gets on the wrong track or responds to a personal bias, at least one group member can often make a corrective comment.	Feedback from fellow group members who are biased or ignorant is not particularly valuable and wastes time.

Source: Meyer, R. G., & Salmon, P. (1984). *Abnormal psychology* (p. 110). Boston, MA: Allyn and Bacon.

and reactions are open to discussion. Effective group leaders try to serve as models for other participants, openly sharing their feelings and accepting criticism. They teach group members to describe their feelings with precision, and not to make judgmental and evaluative statements about others. For example, a member might be encouraged to tell another, "Your tone of voice makes me feel impatient with you" and not "You sure have a negative attitude." This technique is intended to reduce defensive reactions and to enhance the likelihood that group members will consider the feelings expressed by others. Inasmuch as it involves stripping away social masks and exposing innermost feelings, the encounter group is often an extremely intense experience. Typically, however, when members realize they will not be rejected for their feelings, a climate of trust and mutual support develops.

Evaluation of Encounter Groups Although getting in touch with inner feelings and learning to be open help some people take a new, more positive direction, experiences in encounter groups cause other people problems. Most people are unaccustomed to expressing their feelings openly and freely; indeed, they may explicitly reject the value of such behaviors. In an ambitious study involving more than 200 subjects, Lieberman, Yalom, and Miles (1973) compared the effects of 17 encounter groups. The results revealed that about one-third of the participants benefitted from the encounter group (as revealed by self-ratings and ratings of friends), about one-third experienced no significant change, and about one-third had a negative experience. Ten percent of the participants were judged to be "casualties"—to have suffered a severe psychological disturbance that endured up to six months after the group experience. Lieberman et al. identified the group leader as particularly important to the outcome, and warned against the danger of entering a group with an unqualified or disturbed leader. Other studies have found that the gains experienced by participants in encounter groups are temporary (Bednar & Kaul, 1978) and that the emphasis on "free expression of emotion" may prove harmful to individuals with low self-esteem (Kirsch & Glass, 1977). Pruyser (1973) points out an additional problem, questioning the assumption that pathology results

from repression and restriction of underlying emotions. According to Pruyser, our culture is characterized by "weakness of impulse control, narcissistic self-indulgence, loose thought organization, and externalization of conflicts." For this reason, psychological treatment should emphasize the development of self-control and not the freeing of impulse.

Family and Marital Therapies

Family and marital therapies share with other forms of group therapy the belief that faulty interpersonal relations lie at the heart of many human problems. Marital and family therapy focus on the couple or family as a unit or system. Couples and families usually attend therapy together, but sometimes attend separately as well. Sessions are generally led by both a male and a female therapist. The overall goal is to help family members recognize and correct maladaptive ways of interacting with one another, most of which are unconscious and habitual. Two of the most common problems faced by couples and families relate to the expression of feelings and expectations about roles. Unfulfilled couples tend to communicate less or to communicate less effectively than more fulfilled couples and to show less sensitivity to each other's needs. Consider the following exchange.

Therapist As far as you know, have you ever been in that same spot before, that is, were you puzzled by something Alice said or did?

Husband Hell, yes, lots of times

Therapist Have you ever told Alice you were puzzled when you were?

Wife He never says anything.

Therapist (smiling, to Alice) Just a minute, Alice, let me hear what Ralph's idea is of what he does. Ralph, how do you think you have let Alice know when you are puzzled?

Husband I think she knows.

Therapist Well, let's see. Suppose you ask Alice if she knows.

Husband This is silly.

Therapist (smiling) I suppose it might seem so in this situation, because Alice is right here and certainly has heard what your question is. She knows what it is. I have the suspicion, though, that neither you nor Alice are very sure about what the other expects, and I think you have not developed ways to find out. Alice, let's go back to when I commented on Ralph's wrinkled brow. Did you happen to notice it, too?

Wife   (complaining) Yes, he always looks like that.

Therapist   What kind of message did you get from that wrinkled brow?

Wife   He don't want to be here. He don't care. He never talks. Just looks at television or he isn't home.

Therapist   I'm curious. Do you mean that when Ralph has a wrinkled brow that you take this as Ralph's way of saying, "I don't love you, Alice. I don't care about you Alice?"

Wife   (exasperated and tearfully) I don't know.

Therapist   Well, maybe the two of you have not yet worked out crystal-clear ways of giving your love and value messages to each other. Everyone needs crystal-clear ways of giving their value messages. (to son) What do you know, Jim, about how you give your value messages to your parents?

Son   I do what she tells me to do. Work and stuff. . . .

Therapist   Let's check this out and see if you are perceiving clearly. Do you, Alice, get a love message from Jim when he works around the house?

Wife   I s'pose — he doesn't do very much.

Therapist   So from where you sit, Alice, you don't get many love messages from Jim. Tell me, Alice, does Jim have any other ways. . . . that say to you he is glad you are around?

Wife   (softly) The other day he told me I looked nice. (Satir, 1967, pp. 98–100)

"Clifford and I love New York, but all we seem to have for each other is mutual respect."

Drawing by Weber, © 1986 *The New Yorker*, Inc.

Unfulfilling relationships are usually not balanced. Two of the most typical patterns involve the husband trying to dominate and control his wife rather than listening to her concerns and the wife constantly nagging and criticizing her husband, with the husband responding passively and withdrawing from interactions with her.

Several techniques have been employed to treat marital and family problems. Transactional therapy is used frequently with couples. Client-centered therapy has helped couples improve their understanding of what they and their children are feeling. Behavior therapy guides members of families in reinforcing desirable behaviors through verbal praise, smiles, and demonstrations of affection, and in withdrawing reinforcement for undesirable behaviors by not responding to them.

The **systems approach** to family therapy has gained popularity recently. It focuses on the family as a system — each member influencing the behavior of all other members — and on the mutually interacting and supporting roles that family members develop (Minuchin, 1974). For example, some of the roles that characterize families include "boss," "helper," "scapegoat," "black sheep," and "good daughter." System therapists look beyond the presenting problem to uncover the role that each member plays in the life of every other member.

A recent innovation in marital and family therapy involves videotaping therapy sessions. Most people find it easier to pinpoint the faults of others than to recognize their own. Videotape provides an instant replay of interactions that helps couples or the members of a family view themselves more objectively. By viewing herself, a daughter might see the disapproving look on her face and hear the sarcastic tone she uses with her parents.

It is obvious from our consideration of psychological forms of treatment that they are many and varied, each with its characteristic techniques. To summarize and integrate our overview, the central features of the major approaches are outlined in Table 14-9.

TABLE 14-9

A Comparison of Types of Psychotherapy

Type of Psychotherapy	Primary Founders	Origin of Disorder	Main Goals	Main Techniques
Psychoanalysis	Freud	Unconscious conflicts between repressed sexual urges and memories, and constraints from the ego and superego	Insight gained by bringing unconscious conflicts into consciousness where they can be worked through; personality reorganization	Interpretation, free association, dream analysis, working through resistance and transference
Client-centered	Rogers	Socially induced thwarting of natural drive toward self-actualization	To help the client understand and accept his or her true self; to cultivate personal growth	Unconditional positive regard, active listening, empathy, reflection, openness, honesty
Behavioral	Watson, Skinner, Wolpe	Maladaptive learning experiences	Learning adaptive behaviors	Classical and operant conditioning: extinction, systematic desensitization, shaping, reinforcement, punishment
Social Learning and Cognitive-Behavioral	Bandura, Meichenbaum	Maladaptive social learning, especially modeling; distorted assumptions about the self's ability to cope	Learning adaptive behaviors, especially through modeling; restructuring maladaptive ways of processing information	Conditioning, vicarious learning, and modeling; cognitive restructuring, especially self-statements
Cognitive	Beck, Ellis	Invalid, illogical, and self-defeating assumptions about the self and events relating to the self	Discovering self-defeating assumptions about the self and substituting more realistic ways of thinking	Encouraging client to think realistically, exposing irrational beliefs, challenging self-defeating assumptions, substituting appropriate thoughts
Interpersonal	Moreno, Lewin	Mutually defeating interpersonal relations; distorted communication	Understanding maladaptive roles, modes of interaction, communication, and correcting them	Role-taking/role-playing encounters; feedback to and from others

THE ROLE OF SOCIETY IN MENTAL HEALTH

Before concluding our discussion of psychotherapy, we raise an important issue. Living in a supportive family, maintaining gainful employment, having friends, and feeling part of a community are important to one's psychological well-being. Unfortunately, complex technological societies increasingly inhibit satisfaction of these basic needs. Today the family is in a dangerous state:

Directiveness	Time Orientation	Disorders of Choice	Individual or Group	Duration of Treatment
Directive: the psychoanalyst interprets free association, dreams, and so forth	Mainly past: childhood experiences	Hysteria, complex neuroses	Individual	Long-term
Nondirective	Past and present	Neuroses	Individual	Variable
Directive: therapist directs relearning systematically, often in laboratory	Present and future	Phobias, stuttering, tics, obsessive-compulsions, autism, addictions, sexual dysfunction	Mainly individual, sometimes group (token economies)	Short-term
Directive: therapist structures cognitive and behavioral experiences	Present and future	Phobias, depression, lack of assertiveness	Individual	Short-term
Directive: therapist exposes irrational beliefs and directs client's identification of self-defeating thoughts	Mainly present	Depression	Individual	Short-term
Directive: therapist draws attention to roles and patterns of communication	Mainly present	Marital/family problems	Group	Short-term

unemployment is high, large cities generate feelings of isolation and alienation, shopping centers substitute for neighborhood community centers, and the tendency to move from place to place makes it difficult for people to maintain long-term friendships.

Although some people believe that distress, poverty, disappointment, and "hard knocks" are an inevitable part of human life, most industrialized countries invest considerable resources in social planning, with the goal of improving the quality of life for their citizens. Programs designed to ensure nutritious diets, enhance infant survival, increase social and educational benefits, and provide full-employment opportunities play an essential role in helping reduce social stresses that generate psychological disorders. When such programs fail, some people inevitably become maladapted, and reformers press for change.

Whether or not the utopian dream of creative-but-stressless existence is possible remains an open question. Years ago, Schofield (1964) suggested that psychotherapy involved the "purchase of friendship"; while obviously not a complete description of psychological treatment, it is a telling reminder of the importance of close personal relationships to our psychological well-being (see Box 14-5). It is when friends are inca-

pable of meeting an individual's needs that he or she may require professional help.

COMMON FACTORS IN PSYCHOTHERAPY

The different treatments we have described are ideal types in the sense that few therapists subscribe exclusively to their exact form. As noted earlier, most psychotherapists are eclectic: they draw from various schools of therapy those techniques they consider most useful. In response to the myriad debates over which therapy is "best," some evaluators suggest it doesn't really matter which techniques are employed: the features of therapy that help clients are common to all thera-

---

Box 14-5
TIPS ON HOW TO HELP FRIENDS WHO FEEL TROUBLED

At some point in your life, a friend will turn to you for help. If your friend is in serious trouble, it is best to refer him or her to a professional. In some cases, however, your support may be enough. How can you be most helpful? Here are some tips from the experts:

Communicate Positive Regard Make it clear that you have an unshakable acceptance of the troubled person as an individual and that the person can depend on you as a friend.

Avoid Giving Advice Giving advice to a friend is dangerous because you may

not know all the details. Let friends make their own decisions; after all, they have all the facts at hand—you don't. However, if you must advise a friend, understand that troubled people often seek advice but rarely take it, offering numerous reasons why it won't work.

Once your friend believes in your support, he or she may want to talk with you about the specifics of the problem. Here are several points to keep in mind.

Listen Actively When people are upset, they often need to talk to someone. Be a good listener. They may

just need to "let out steam." Let them. But show you are listening through your tone of voice, replies, posture, and eye contact. According to Stevens (1971):

> The way to really help someone is not to help him do anything but become more aware of his own experience—his feelings, his actions, his fantasies—and insist that he explore his own experience more deeply and take responsibility for it, no matter what that experience is.

Focus on Feelings Crises are emotional, and it is important that people

pies (Frank, 1982). Six of the most important features are:

1. client expectation of improvement
2. involvement in new experience
3. reinforcement and punishment
4. relationship between client and therapist
5. new perspectives
6. desensitization

Expectation of Improvement

Most people who enter therapy expect to improve. Investigators from several areas of psychology have found that the expectation an individual will succeed may increase the probability of success (Rosenthal, 1966). Frank (1973, 1982) and others (Aronoff & Lesse, 1983) have suggested that a similar process occurs when people enter therapy. In his classic work, *Persuasion and Healing,* Frank (1973) showed how the placebo effect (see Chapter 1) applies to psychotherapy. Frank suggests that virtually all people who seek therapy share feelings of demoralization, incompetence, low self-esteem, alienation, hopelessness and/or helplessness. The promise of relief and the hope supplied by entering therapy, argues Frank, produce an improvement in morale that — more than any of the techniques involved — is therapeutic.

Involvement in a New Experience

Entering therapy, especially for the first time, is a new and sometimes exciting experience. Many

release the emotions they feel. Ask your friend how he or she feels about the crisis or comment on how you think he or she must be feeling. And direct your attention to your friend's emotions, not the issues. For example, if a friend is fired, ask "How do you feel about it?", not "Was it because you were always late?"

Accept the Person's Point of View Let your friend tell his or her side of the story. Even if you know another side of the story, resist contradicting your friend. Your friend's view is correct as far as he or she is concerned; opposing it will only make your friend defensive. If your friend feels that his or her view is accepted, he or she will be less inclined to form a narrow view of the situation.

Reflect on Thoughts and Feelings One useful technique when counseling is to reflect on what has just been said. This is effective in getting people to talk more and, in addition, it tells them you are listening. For example:

Friend It's not fair. I really tried hard at that job. I worked much more than the other clerks.

You So you feel you've been treated unjustly.

Friend Yeah, none of them were fired. The boss was picking on me. I didn't deserve to be singled out.

You You feel that he was picking on you?

This simple technique is especially helpful when the person being counseled is at a loss for words or has trouble understanding the reason for his or her emotions.

Don't Gossip When a friend confides in you, it is important that you respect his or her privacy.

These guidelines are meant to help you help others more effectively; they are not meant to create counselors. It cannot be stressed enough: people experiencing a crisis need a friend who understands and whom they can trust. Such qualities are the most valuable resource you can offer someone; professional counseling can be purchased.

people suffer from loneliness, boredom, and habit. Therapy is something different, something novel; it breaks routine and provides something new to think about. Therapists of many different orientations have underscored the significance of giving clients new, "corrective" experiences (Brady et al., 1980).

Positive Reinforcement and Punishment

The positive reinforcement and punishment given by behavior-oriented therapists is concrete and easy to identify; however, all forms of therapy involve reinforcement. It is impossible to supply feedback to clients without evoking positive and negative feelings in them and without communicating approval and disapproval of various courses of action, even in the most nondirective of therapies. In a careful analysis of a recording made by Carl Rogers of the "reflective" responses during a session with a client, Truax (1966) found that Rogers in fact reinforced certain types of response by positive reactions.

The Relationship between Client and Therapist

All forms of psychotherapy involve a relationship between client and therapist. Psychologists such as Aronoff and Lesse (1983), Frank (1982), and Strupp (1976) have suggested that, whatever its form, establishing a new relationship makes people feel better. The relationship between client and therapist is a unique one: it involves two reciprocal, socially sanctioned roles—helper and person in need of help. The role of the client is always the more dependent of the two; the role of therapist involves expertise and authority. Research has shown that whatever the orientation of the therapist, he or she must inspire trust and respect to be effective. Clients must be comfortable enough with a therapist to disclose information about themselves. And they must believe the therapist is competent, has no ulterior motives, and cares about them. Although behavior therapy may appear cold and impersonal, studies have found that behavior therapists display as much empathy and interpersonal understanding as psychoanalytically oriented therapists (Sloan et al., 1975).

New Perspectives, Reality-testing, and New Ways of Thinking

People often seek help from a therapist because they are confused. They have a problem, they have tried to solve it, and they have failed. Individuals with psychological problems commonly distort and deny reality. Two things people expect from psychotherapists are insight about what is wrong with them — a new view of reality — and advice about what to do. Most therapists offer clients a new perspective (Aronoff & Lesse, 1983); some, such as psychoanalysts, offer elaborate theoretical frameworks; others, such as client-centered therapists, help clients clarify their own feelings. Frank (1982) has suggested it is not the validity of the alternative perspective per se that helps people (different therapists offer different perspectives) but the new way of thinking about problems and the encouragement to test reality.

Marmor (1976) argues that all types of therapy involve cognitive learning; what differs across theoretical orientations is how this process is conceptualized or labeled. In the psychoanalytic perspective, cognitive learning is known as *insight;* in the cognitive behavioral and rational-emotive approaches it is called *cognitive restructuring* or *changing belief systems;* in the humanistic approach it is referred to as *self-actualizing.*

Desensitization

Most people who seek therapy engage in some form of avoidance, whether it relates to physical objects or to thoughts; most therapists encourage clients to confront the issues they avoid. In behavior therapy, this may entail physically confronting a feared object; in other forms of therapy, it may entail talking about painful issues. The troublesome objects or thoughts tend to lose their threatening power when discussed with someone who accepts and understands them. From the learning-theory perspective, repeated discussion in a relaxed context of issues that evoke anxiety causes the anxiety to extinguish. From more cognitive perspectives, putting into words one's fears and insecurities helps provide a means for dealing with them. In addition, the very process of self-disclosure may make people feel better.

EVALUATION OF PSYCHOTHERAPY

Millions of people have undergone psychotherapy. What happens to them? Do they improve? Does psychotherapy work? Do some types of psychotherapy work better than others? Are certain types of psychotherapy effective for certain disorders and other types effective for other disorders? These are fundamentally important and extremely complex questions.

To evaluate the effectiveness of a form of treatment, you must have some measure of outcome or change. But what measure is most appropriate? Behavior therapists insist the most appropriate measure of success in psychotherapy is an observable change in behavior. Psychoanalysts disagree, arguing that to be successful, psychotherapy must resolve unconscious conflicts and produce a restructuring of personality. Humanistic therapists adopt a different orientation, setting as their goal the actualization of client potential. And so it goes. Of course, some measures of outcome are easier to assess than others. If a client's problem involves a fear of snakes, it is easy to determine whether the problem is solved. But how can we assess the resolution of unconscious conflicts or the actualization of potential?

Linked to the issue of what qualifies as a beneficial change or an improvement is the issue of who determines whether a change has occurred? It might seem obvious that the person who should make such a judgment is the client; however, as demonstrated in our discussion of social cognition (Chapter 11), people aren't very good judges of their own behavior. Because the therapist is the expert, he or she is the likely person to evaluate the outcome. Yet, you would hardly expect a therapist who has seen a client for months or even years to conclude that treatment was ineffective. Perhaps, then, members of the client's family and friends of the client should judge whether the person has changed. In some cases such people are objective, but as noted in our discussion of family therapy, relatives and friends may be part of a client's problem. We would not, for example, expect an overbearing husband to approve of the increased assertiveness of a submissive wife. Perhaps, then, we should

rely on the kinds of psychological tests we discussed in Chapter 12 — tests designed to assess personality and psychopathology. Yet, as we pointed out in Chapter 12, such tests have their problems too.

One means of circumventing the problems associated with selecting an outcome measure is to match the measure with the presenting problem. For example, if a client seeks psychotherapy because he is impotent, an appropriate measure of success would be improved sexual performance. Or if a client seeks psychotherapy because she is depressed, an appropriate measure of success would be how she feels about herself. Another way around the problem is to use several different measures and seek concurrent validity (see Chapter 12).

Assume you find an appropriate measure of outcome, provide psychotherapy, and establish that the client has changed. You are still a long way from establishing that the psychotherapy worked — that it caused the change. Perhaps the client would have changed anyway. Perhaps the change was a placebo effect. Numerous studies have documented the strength of the placebo effect: People who believe they are receiving a treatment but who in fact are not conclude they have been helped and show signs of improvement. The strength of this phenomenon has led a leading researcher to warn in a particularly pessimistic mood:

> Whatever is new and enthusiastically introduced and pursued seems, for the time, to work better than what previously did, whether or not it is more valid scientifically. Eventually, these novelties too join the Establishment of Techniques and turn out nothing more than whatever went before. (London, 1964, p. 118)

The assessment of psychotherapy has a long and stormy history in psychology. Hundreds of studies have been conducted on the success of psychotherapy and several reviews of the literature have been published. One of the earliest and most controversial was that of Hans Eysenck. Eysenck (1952) examined the existing research on psychotherapy and concluded that approximately two-thirds of all neurotics improve over a two-year period whether they receive psychotherapy or not—a phenomenon called **spontaneous recovery**—and that those who receive psychotherapy are not significantly more likely to improve than those who do not. In a 1965 update of his conclusions, Eysenck wrote that "Current psychotherapeutic procedures have not lived up to the hopes which greeted their emergence 50 years ago" (1965, p. 136). The only form of therapy for which Eysenck found evidence of success was behavior therapy.

Needless to say, Eysenck's conclusions caused quite an uproar among psychotherapists. Practicing therapists were not pleased to hear that their treatment was no better than no treatment at all. Following the publication of Eysenck's review, numerous researchers published critiques of his conclusions and supplied additional evidence on the effectiveness of psychotherapy. For example, Bergin (1971) reviewed Eysenck's work and found it flawed by errors in computation and judgment. Bergin reviewed a number of other studies and reported a median spontaneous recovery rate of about 30%, far lower than Eysenck's 66%. Malan, Heath, Bacal, and Balfour (1975) studied "untreated" neurotics who had received only one assessment interview yet had recovered "spontaneously", and discovered that the single interview was perceived by these subjects as a powerful impetus for self-initiated change. Research also has revealed that spontaneous recovery from certain disorders is much less likely than from others. For example, psychopathic and psychosomatic conditions show little spontaneous recovery, whereas anxiety and depression tend to show more.

Smith, Glass, and Miller (1980) provided the strongest support for the effectiveness of psychotherapy. These investigators reviewed 475 studies (using a total of 1,776 outcome measures) that compared people who received psychotherapy and people in some type of control group. After examining this massive body of data, Smith, Glass, and Miller (1980) reached the following conclusion.

> Psychotherapy benefits people of all ages as reliably as schooling educates them, medicine cures them, or business turns a profit . . . The average person who receives therapy is better off at the end of it than 80% of the persons who do not. This does not, however, mean that everyone who receives psychotherapy improves. The evidence suggests that some people do not improve, and a small number get worse. (p. 87)

Although the results of the Smith et al. study seem impressive, they are limited in three major ways. First, almost half the subjects in the studies reviewed by Smith et al. were college students. Second, most problems treated—such as smoking, overeating, and performance anxieties—were not serious. Finally, most studies involved either behavior therapy or cognitive-behavior modification (Shapiro & Shapiro, 1983).

Which Type of Psychotherapy Is Best?

An issue interwoven with the evaluation of psychotherapy involves the comparison between different types of therapy. Consider one of the most careful studies on this issue.

Sloan, Staples, Cristal, Yorkston, and Whipple (1975) randomly assigned clients suffering from moderately severe neurotic or personality disorders to a psychoanalytic therapist, a behavior therapist, or a waiting-list control group. Clients were treated individually by one of six experienced therapists—three behavior and three psychoanalytic. Investigators used a wide range of techniques to assess each patient's condition before treatment, after four months in treatment, and one and two years following treatment. Their measures included psychological tests, structured interviews to determine work and social adjustment, observer ratings of the severity of target symptoms, ratings by "significant others" (usually family members) of work and social adjustment, severity-of-illness ratings, and other relevant measures.

The findings of this study revealed that after four months of treatment, the patients in the two active-treatment groups were significantly better off than the patients in the waiting-list control group, but that there were no differences between behavior therapy and psychoanalytic therapy. When patients were followed up after a year, it was found that those who received psychotherapy maintained their improvement and that the people from the waiting-list control group made small but steady gains toward the levels of the two treatment groups. This study suggests that people who do not receive psychotherapy may show some spontaneous recovery, but that skilled treatment using either behavior or psychoanalytic techniques is more effective than this natural process.

The results of the Sloan et al. study are consistent with the results of the Smith et al. (1980) study. Glass (1983) compared behavior modification, client-centered, rational-emotive, cognitive-behavioral, cognitive, and other types of therapy. Although Glass found cognitive therapy to be superior, most of the other types produced quite similar effects, with the similarities between types of therapy more important than the differences (see Figure 14-12).

The conclusion that all types of psychotherapy are equally effective has not gone unchallenged. Behavior therapists, in particular, have objected to it, adducing evidence that even within the domain of behavior therapy some types of treatment are better than others. For example, modeling has been found more effective in the treatment of dog and snake phobias than systematic desensitization (Rosenthal & Bandura, 1978). The differences in the conclusions reached by different investigators are generated in part by the measures they employ to evaluate the outcome of therapy. Behavior therapists, of course, insist on observable changes in behavior. And when this criterion is used, the evidence suggests that behavior therapies are more effective than humanistic or psychoanalytic therapies, with cognitive approaches in between (Rachman & Wilson, 1980; Shapiro & Shapiro, 1982). Concerning serious disorders, the Commission on Psychiatric Therapies of the American Psychiatric Association concluded in its first report that the use of drugs is essential in the treatment of schizophrenia and that psychoanalytically based forms of therapy "contribute little additional benefit" (Pines, 1982). However, the Commission concluded that both drugs and psychotherapy are useful in the treatment of depression. In a subsequent article, Garfield (1983) called for more research on the specific effects on particular disorders of different kinds of therapy.

The success of psychotherapy appears to depend more on the qualities of therapists and clients than on the types of therapy. Therapists who have warm, nonpossessive, open, and empathic concern for clients are more successful than those who do not. Indeed, a lack of such qualities tends to be associated with client deterioration. Training in psychotherapy and experience in giving treatment tend to be correlated positively with success — but not always. Strupp and Hadley (1979) compared the outcome of therapy with highly experienced psychologists and psychiatrists and college professors noted for forming understanding and supportive relationships with students, and failed to find any difference, on average, between the two groups.

Research also has revealed that client characteristics correlate with success in psychotherapy. For example, investigators have found that relatively healthy clients improve more than seriously troubled clients. The prognosis is better for people from high socioeconomic strata than for people from low socioeconomic strata. Verbal therapies work better with bright clients than with less-intelligent clients. Highly motivated and confident clients seem to benefit from ther-

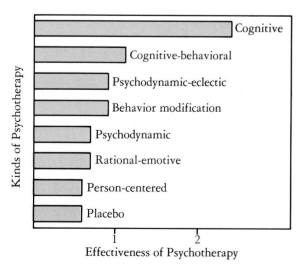

FIGURE 14-12

The Effectiveness of Various Types of Psychotherapy A review of more than 400 studies revealed cognitive types of therapy were the most effective and that person-centered therapy was no more effective than a placebo. *Source:* Adapted from Glass, G. (1983). Effectiveness of different psychotherapies. *Journal of Consulting and Clinical Psychology, 31,* 28–41.

apy. And patients with social backgrounds and interests similar to those of their therapists have better success in treatment (see Garfield, 1980, for a review).

In summary, the weight of evidence suggests that the unique personality of client and therapist may affect whether a client will improve under one therapist but not another. Also relevant is the interaction among type of therapist, type of therapy, and type of client. While all types of therapy appear to help most clients, some have proven particularly successful for particular

TABLE 14-10

Comparing the Success of Four Therapeutic Approaches to the Treatment of Eight Types of Distress or Deviance

Form of Distress Or Deviance	Biomedical Therapy
1. Physiological (psychosomatic) disorders	Depending on the disorder, drug therapy may be very helpful in controlling symptoms but may be insufficient to deal with contributory psychological causes.
2. Anxiety	Drug therapy may be helpful in controlling anxiety, but many tranquilizers have side effects and can lead to psychological dependence.
3. Depression	Tricyclic drugs may be very helpful in the treatment of chronic depression; in severe cases, electroconvulsive therapy (ECT) has been shown to relieve depressive symptoms for moderate periods of time.
4. Aggression	No direct therapeutic methods have been applied.
5. Addiction	The three most popular treatments — detoxification, substitution, and motivated avoidance — have been generally unsuccessful in producing long-term improvement.
6. Relationships and Sexuality	Limited applicability except where organic problems are known to be a contributing factor.
7. Schizophrenia	Phenothiazines are clearly effective in "managing" some of these disorders and in reducing the distress associated with them; they are seldom sufficient to produce recovery, however, and the patient may relapse after being taken off medication. Institutions — which are most closely associated with biomedical treatment — appear to be ineffective and may even contribute to further problems.
8. Developmental and Organic Disorders	Some drugs may be helpful in reducing specific symptoms, but they are seldom sufficient to produce recovery. Other biomedical treatments, including eugenic sterilization, have been criticized on ethical grounds.

Source: From Mahoney, M. J. (1980). *Abnormal psychology* (p. 67). San Francisco, CA: Harper & Row.

disorders. Table 14-10 summarizes the evidence on the effectiveness of physical, psychodynamic, behavior, and cognitive treatments for eight disorders.

In conclusion, we note that psychotherapy is a delicate process—often involving the inner-most core of personality—that has proven helpful to many but harmful to some. Psychotherapy must be conducted in accord with strict ethical standards, an important aspect of which is informed consent (see Box 14-6).

Psychodynamic Therapy	Behavior Modification	Cognitive Social Learning Therapy
Existing research has been poor in quality and generally modest in terms of results.	Moderate success with some disorders (for example, obesity); poor with others (for example, smoking). Biofeedback has some limited but valuable applications.	Insufficient research to warrant a confident evaluation.
When physiological and behavioral measures are the criteria of improvement, these therapies are not consistently superior to no treatment.	Very successful and consistently more effective than no treatment; success rates may vary but average around 80%.	Very successful and consistently more effective than no treatment; success rates may vary but average around 80–90%.
Insufficient research to warrant a confident evaluation.	Insufficient research to warrant a confident evaluation.	Research findings are still preliminary but very positive.
Insufficient research to warrant a confident conclusion	Moderately good results with delinquents in noninstitutional settings; less promising results with adult prison inmates.	Research is still very preliminary but moderately promising.
Available research has been sparse, poor in quality, and generally pessimistic in its findings.	Research is still very preliminary and only mildly promising; aversion techniques appear to be least effective.	Research is still very preliminary and only mildly promising except in the area of alcoholism, where "controlling drinking" appears to be moderately effective.
Orthodox psychodynamic methods have not been evaluated experimentally, but their limited effectiveness is suggested by the trend toward supplementing these methods with some of the newer techniques of "sex therapy."	Very successful, particularly with the disorders of premature ejaculation, vaginismus, and orgasmic dysfunction. Success rates are slightly lower, but hardly modest, in the treatment of impotence.	
Available research has been sparse owing, in part, to the presumed unresponsiveness of persons with these disorders to psychodynamic therapy. Results to date have not suggested much promise in this approach to perceptual and intellectual disorders.	Very effective when the criterion is behavior change *within* an institution; more modest results have been obtained in efforts to return the patient to self-sufficiency in the community.	Insufficient research to warrant a confident evaluation.
Psychodynamic treatment of severe developmental and organic disorders is rare and poorly evaluated; thus its effectiveness is unknown.	Very effective in mental retardation and moderately effective with some of the patterns labeled *childhood psychosis*.	Insufficient research to warrant a confident evaluation.

Box 14-6
Informed Consent in Psychotherapy

Informed consent is now an issue not just for research and for treatment in mental institutions but also for private therapy which individuals seek on their own initiative. Traditionally a person who consults a therapist, in essence hiring the therapist to perform expert services, consents to be treated in a certain way and for a certain purpose. In the past the client's informed consent to be treated was seldom obtained in any explicit or formal way.

The spirit of consumerism and a desire to be open and accountable, along with dramatic increases in malpractice suits, may prompt therapists to consider whether more explicit arrangements might not be in their own and in their client's best interests. Richard Stuart, a leading behavior therapist, has suggested an intervention contract. The proposed contract would place great demands on the therapist and the fields of clinical psychology and psychiatry to provide evidence that particular techniques are effective, and on the client as well. Although not yet widely adopted, this kind of contract might become common in the future, requiring documentation on how and why a particular program of treatment was undertaken.

Name of Client: _____   Name of Therapist: _____

Address: _____   Title: _____

Phone: _____   Organization: _____

Highest academic degree: _____

License: _____

1. I, the above named therapist, certify that I am (circle one) duly licensed to offer the services described below *or* under the supervision of _____ who is so licensed. (Address) _____

2. I have assessed the client's behavior change objective(s) in the following manner:

_____

_____

3. I propose to use the following intervention technique(s) in my effort to assist the client to achieve the above objective(s): _____

a. This (these) technique(s) have been fully described in the following standard professional reference: _____

_____

b. The most recent comprehensive account of the clinical results achieved with this (these) technique(s) may be found in the following source(s): _____

4. It is expected that this (these) intervention technique(s) will have the following beneficial effects for the client by the dates specified: ___

_____

5. It is also noted that this (these) intervention technique(s) may be associated with the following undesirable side effect(s): _____

_____

6. Both the progress toward achieving the specified objectives and the potential side effects will be monitored continuously in the following manner(s): _____

_____

_____

(Date)   (Signature of Therapist)

A. I, the above named client, assert that I have discussed the above named objectives for the change of my behavior and that I consent to work toward the achievement of those objectives.

B. I further assert that I have discussed the above named intervention technique(s) with the therapist and that I consent to apply these techniques.

C. I further assert that I shall provide the above named data in order to determine the effectiveness of the use of the intervention technique(s).

D. I further assert that I shall provide the therapist with the following compensation for his or her efforts in my behalf: _____

E. I further assert that I have freely entered into this contract knowing the therapeutic objectives and both the positive and negative potential effects of the intervention technique(s).

F. I further assert that I have been assured of my right to terminate my participation in treatment at any time, for any reason, and without the need to offer an explanation.

G. I further specifically limit the above named therapist's use of any information which can in any way identify me to others unless I have offered my specific, written permission.

_____

(Date)   (Signature of Client)   (Signature of Witness)

Source: Stuart, R. B. (1978). Protection of the right to informed consent to participate in research. *Behavior Therapy, 9,* 73–82. Copyright © 1975 by Richard B. Stuart, Behavior Change Systems.

SUMMARY

1. People suffering from psychological disorders may be treated by psychiatrists — medical doctors who specialize in the treatment of mental disorder, psychoanalysts — usually psychiatrists trained in psychoanalysis, clinical psychologists — Ph.D.s in psychology who have completed a clinical internship, counseling psychologists — who usually work in institutional settings with people having adjustment problems, psychiatric social workers — who focus on problems related to the family and community, psychiatric nurses — registered nurses who have completed special training in the care of mental patients, or paraprofessionals — people with no formal training as therapists but with special experience in certain types of problems. The introduction of antipsychotic drugs helped promote an exodus of patients from mental hospitals.

2. Abnormalities of the brain may contribute to certain kinds of psychological disorder and, therefore, treatments that alter the chemical balance of the brain or alter its electrical connections may contribute to their cure. The three primary forms of physical treatment for psychological disorder are psychosurgery, electro-convulsive therapy, and chemotherapy. Of the three, chemotherapy is used most frequently. The three major types of psychoactive drugs are antipsychotics, antidepressants, and antianxiety drugs. It is important to note that such drugs do not "cure" psychological disorders but serve only to relieve a variety of symptoms and improve functioning.

3. Psychological forms of treatment are based on the belief that many disorders may be treated successfully through psychological and behavioral means. Psychological treatments may be classified as: psychoanalytic, humanistic, behavioral, social learning, cognitive, and interpersonal.

4. Developed by Freud, the goal of psychoanalysis is to identify patients' unconscious conflicts and to help patients work through them. The methods employed in psychoanalysis include: interpretation of material reported during free association; interpretation of dreams; analysis of client's response to dream interpretations; and analysis of client's emotional responses to therapist, called transference. Psychoanalysis has been criticized widely. It seems primarily suited to relatively bright people suffering from mild neurotic disorders.

5. The most popular humanistic, or person-centered, approach to psychotherapy is client-centered therapy, which asserts that the way people feel about themselves determines how they function. Accordingly, client-centered therapy emphasizes growth, authenticity, self-actualization, trust, empathy, caring, warmth, openness, self-disclosure, and interpersonal honesty. The client is responsible for solving his or her own problems. Humanistic approaches are most appropriate for people suffering from mild, neurotic disorders.

6. The goal of behavior therapy is to help people extinguish maladaptive behaviors and relearn adaptive behaviors. Techniques based on classical conditioning include extinction and flooding, or implosion therapy; systematic desensitization; aversion therapy; and covert sensitization. Techniques based on operant conditioning include time out from positive reinforcement, shaping, token economies, contingency management, self-management, and biofeedback. Behavior therapy has been criticized for manipulating and dehumanizing people, modifying behavior rather than changing personality, instilling only specific and temporary changes in people, failing to promote a close therapist-client relationship, and working only on certain disorders. Behavior therapy appears to work best with disorders involving anxiety and such disorders as alcoholism, overeating, stuttering, enuresis, and some sexual perversions. It appears less effective for the treatment of deep-seated and well-entrenched personality problems.

7. Treatments based on social learning are guided by the assumption that people can correct maladaptive behaviors by watching others perform adaptive behaviors. Assertiveness training is based on social learning. Social-learning techniques are used primarily with people suffering from neurotic disorders or experiencing interpersonal difficulties.

8. Cognitive approaches focus on modifying maladaptive thoughts. The most prominent cognitive approach, developed by Albert Ellis, is rational-emotive therapy. Its purpose is to expose the irrational beliefs that people form and to help them substitute more realistic ideas and expectations. The focus is on thinking rather than feeling, and the therapist, not the client, plays the dominant role. Cognitive approaches are quite successful in the treatment of anxiety and depression, especially when used in conjunction with reinforcement and modeling.

9. Interpersonal approaches, or group therapy, provide a social context in which people can work out their social problems. The participants in group therapy are encouraged to act as both client and therapist — to help and to be helped. In some forms of group therapy, for example encounter groups, the professional merely facilitates discussion. In other types of group therapy, for example family and marital therapy, the therapist may play a more prominent role.

10. Most therapists are eclectic — they use whichever treatment techniques they feel are most appropriate for their clients' needs. Research indicates that the type of therapy employed by a psychotherapist may be less important than the therapeutic relationship and match between client and therapist. The expectation that therapy will help is often therapeutic, as are the involvement in a new experience and the positive reinforcement and punishment, and the new perspectives, reality testing, and desensitization that constitute most types of therapy. To be effective, a therapist must demonstrate competence and inspire trust and respect in his or her clients.

11. Evaluating psychotherapy is a very difficult task. The basis of this difficulty lies in finding a measure of success. One approach is to match the measure with the presenting problem; another approach is to use several different measures and seek concurrent validity.

12. Some psychologists take the position that all types of psychotherapy produce quite similar effects; others maintain that some types of treatment are better than other types of treatment, especially for particular disorders; still others assert that success of psychotherapy appears to depend more on qualities of therapists and patients than on types of therapy.

KEY TERMS

Psychiatrist
Psychotherapy
Psychoanalyst
Clinical Psychologist
Counseling Psychologist
Psychiatric Social Worker
Psychiatric Nurse
Paraprofessional
Community Mental-health
   Center
Crisis Intervention Center

Telephone Hotline
Halfway House
Psychosurgery
Prefrontal Lobotomy
Amygdalectomy
Electro-convulsive Therapy
   (ECT)
Grand-mal Seizure
Temporary Remission
Psychoactive Drug
Antipsychotic Drug

Major Tranquilizer
Antidepressant Drug
Lithium Carbonate
Antimanic Drug
Antianxiety Drug
Minor Tranquilizer
Psychoanalysis
Free Association
Manifest Content
Latent Content
Censor

Displacement
Condensation
Resistance
Transference
Transactional Analysis
Humanistic Approach
Client-centered Therapy
Unconditional Positive
  Regard
Reflection
Gestalt Therapy
Organismic Self-regulation
Behavior Therapy

Implosion Therapy
Systematic Desensitization
Anxiety Hierarchy
Aversion Therapy
Covert Sensitization
Shaping
Token Economy
Contingency Management
Self-control Program
Biofeedback
Symptom Substitution
Assertiveness Training
Behavioral Rehearsal

Self-efficacy
Rational-emotive Therapy
Cognitive-behavior Therapy
Group Therapy
Psychodrama
Encounter Group
T-group
Facilitator
Family/Marital Therapy
Systems Approach
Spontaneous Recovery

RECOMMENDED READINGS

Corsini, R. J. (Ed.) (1984). *Current psychotherapies* (3rd ed.). Itasca, IL: Peacock. A collection of psychotherapeutic techniques described by prominent therapists.

Garfield, S. L., & Bergin, A. E. (Eds.) (1986). *Handbook of psychotherapy and behavior change* (3rd ed.). New York: Wiley. An informative and well-written account of every major therapeutic approach.

Menninger, K., & Holzman, P. S. (1973). *Theory of psychoanalytic technique* (2nd ed.). New York: Basic Books. An introduction to the techniques of psychoanalysis.

Rogers, C. R. (1970). *On becoming a person: A therapist's view of psychotherapy.* Boston, MA: Houghton Mifflin. An engaging account of client-centered therapy from the perspective of a therapist.

Valenstein, E. S. (Ed.) (1980). *The psychosurgery debate: Scientific, legal, and ethical perspectives.* San Francisco, CA: W. H. Freeman. An easy-to-read discussion of psychosurgery: its history, current practices, and controversies.

Watson, D. L., & Tharp, R. G. (1981). *Self-directed behavior: Self-modification for personal adjustment* (3rd ed.). Belmont, CA: Wadsworth. A user's guide to self-modification of behavior.

Wilson, G. T., & O'Leary, K. D. (1980). *Principles of behavior theory.* Englewood Cliffs, N.J.: Prentice-Hall. A collection of current techniques from behavioral social learning theory.

APPENDIX

STATISTICS IN BEHAVIORAL RESEARCH

DESCRIBING THE EVIDENCE

Central Tendency
Dispersion
Correlation

DRAWING INFERENCES FROM THE EVIDENCE

Hypothesis Testing — A Taste Test

The measurements obtained in psychological research are referred to as *raw data*. Like raw food, such measurements must be treated in certain ways to make them digestible. The various procedures used to treat raw data are called *statistics*. The sight of this word makes many people groan; they feel their lack of mathematical sophistication puts statistics beyond their grasp. But we believe that if people are willing to set aside preconceptions about the difficulty of the subject, most will come to appreciate the necessity of using statistics and will understand their logical basis. If your arithmetical skills are rusty from disuse, don't worry. You will encounter only a few formulae in this section and, in our opinion, none that should be committed to memory. For present purposes, then, you don't have to know how to cook but only how to find the right recipe, recognize the ingredients, and know what to do with the dish when it is served.

There are two types of statistics: the first is called *descriptive,* the second *inferential.* The purpose of **descriptive statistics** is to reduce the complexity of a group of observations or measurements by summarizing the information they contain. The purpose of **inferential statistics** is to draw conclusions about all members of a population from information collected from a sample of them. For example, if we gave a sociability test to a group of males and to a group of females, we could compute the average test score for each group. These average scores are descriptive statistics. If the average scores for these two groups were different, we might want to know whether this *sample* difference could be taken as convincing evidence of a *population* difference—a difference in sociability between males and females *in general*. We would use inferential statistics to guide our answer to this question.

DESCRIBING THE EVIDENCE

Imagine trying a new method of teaching spelling to a class of third-grade students. You are convinced the new method is better than the old method used by a fellow teacher. You tell him so. He disagrees and challenges you to a contest. He will teach spelling to his class using the old method, and you will teach spelling to your class using the new method. At the end of the term, both classes will take a spelling test to determine which class performs better. Although this is a weak research design (for reasons which should be obvious), assume, for the sake of discussion, that you accept the challenge. At the end of the term, the spelling test is given. The scores of the students in the two classes are given in Table A-1.

You want to compare the two sets of scores, but find it difficult to do in such raw form. You need a way to organize and summarize them. First, arrange the scores so you can visualize their overall pattern; a good way is to display them graphically in what is called a frequency distribution. A **frequency distribution** indicates how frequently each score occurs. Figure A-1 shows a type of frequency distribution called **frequency histogram.** Values for the variable being measured (spelling test score) are shown along the bottom on the horizontal axis. The number of people receiving each score is represented by the height of the bar over that score, and this height is measured along the vertical axis labeled "Frequency of Score."

Although displaying the scores graphically enables us to obtain a better sense of how the students did in both classes, it offers little help when it comes to making a precise comparison

TABLE A-1
Spelling Test Scores (maximum score = 20)

Your Class (new method)		His Class (old method)	
Student #	Score	Student #	Score
1	6	1	3
2	7	2	5
3	8	3	5
4	8	4	6
5	8	5	6
6	9	6	8
7	9	7	8
8	9	8	10
9	9	9	10
10	9	10	10
11	9	11	10
12	10	12	10
13	10	13	10
14	10	14	11
15	11	15	<u>11</u>
16	<u>11</u>	16	<u>12</u>
17	11	17	12
18	11	18	12
19	12	19	12
20	12	20	13
21	12	21	13
22	12	22	13
23	12	23	13
24	12	24	13
25	12	25	14
26	13	26	14
27	13	27	14
28	14	28	14
29	17	29	15
30	18	30	18
31	18		

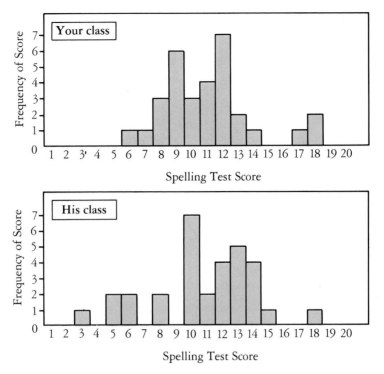

FIGURE A-1
Frequency Histograms of Student Spelling-Test Scores

between the classes — our ultimate goal. How then can we compare the two classes? One way is to compare the scores that occur most frequently in each class. Look at the two distributions of scores in Figure A-1 and find the peak score (highest point) of each distribution: 12 for your class and 10 for his class. Compared in this way, your class performed better than your colleague's. Finding the score that occurs most frequently entails computing a descriptive statistic — in this case a measure of the **central tendency** of the distributions of the scores. Let us consider central tendency in greater detail.

Central Tendency

The statistic just computed is called the **mode:** the most frequently occurring score in a distribution. Although you might favor basing the comparison of the two classes on the mode — doing so makes your class appear better than your colleague's class — you probably are willing to admit it is not a good way of summarizing the two

sets of scores. The mode is simple to compute, but does a poor job of describing the entire distribution. Because it fails to represent most of the scores, it is totally insensitive to changes in the outline of the distribution unless such changes match or exceed the peak of the frequency distribution.

If the mode is deficient, are there other measures of central tendency that more efficiently represent the scores in a distribution? There are, and one your fellow teacher might prefer to use is the **median:** the score that is larger than half the scores in the distribution and also smaller than half the scores in the distribution. Since it is simpler to compute the median from a list of raw scores than from a frequency distribution, let us return to Table A-1. Scores should be listed in order from smallest to largest (which we have done in the table). Now consider the 31 scores from your class. The score that divides these values into two equal-size groups is 11 and is, therefore, the median score (underlined in Table A-1). When you calculate the scores obtained by your adversary, you run into a problem. Because there are an even number of students in his class, there is no single score which has an equal number of scores larger and smaller than itself. Nevertheless, just take the halfway point between the *two* middle scores (both underlined in Table A-1). Thus, the median score for his class is 11.5.

Using the median as a measure of central tendency, your adversary's students performed slightly better than yours. So which measure should we use—the mode or the median? The median, at least, takes into account all scores in the distribution. If you add a score to the distribution, the median is more likely than the mode to reflect this change; however, the median does not take full account of the *size* of scores. If the added score is less than the median value, the median is simply shifted down a notch regardless of how small the added score is. In this regard, the mode is no better. In fact, it is worse: the mode would probably not change at all.

Consequently, neither the mode nor the median is fully satisfactory as a measure of central tendency. A better statistic for describing the central tendency of a set of numbers is the *arithmetic mean,* the most commonly used measure of central tendency. The **arithmetic mean**—often shortened to *mean* and also referred to simply as the *average*—is a better representative of the entire distribution of scores than the median or the mode because it is sensitive to the value of each score. To compute the mean of a group of scores, obtain the sum of all scores and divide the sum by the total number of scores. The sum of the 31 scores for your class is 342. Thus, your mean score is 342 divided by 31, or 11.03. A similar calculation shows the mean for the other class is 10.83—a victory for your teaching method, it would appear.

Your fellow teacher would probably refuse to accept the small difference between the average spelling-test scores as convincing evidence that your method of teaching is better. For reasons we will consider when we discuss inferential statistics, he would be right. For now, we note that even the best measure of central tendency, the mean, does not supply a completely adequate way of summarizing or describing *all* information in the distribution of scores. For example, the same means can represent very different distribu-

tions of scores. Thus, the mean of the scores 10, 10, 10, 10, and 10, is 10. The mean of the scores 0, 0, 10, 20, and 20, is also 10. But the two sets of scores are obviously quite different: they differ in their variability, or *dispersion*.

Dispersion

The frequency distribution of scores obtained by your class, shown in Figure A-1, is jagged and irregular. If the class had been larger, the curve would probably have been smoother. The following discussion is simpler if we deal with perfectly smooth distributions. Two such idealized frequency distributions are shown in Figure A-2.

Assume these two distributions contain an equal number of scores and that their mean scores are identical. Despite having the same central tendency, the two distributions are quite different: they differ in how closely the scores cluster around the mean, or in their **dispersion.** If we want to make precise comparisons of the two sets of scores represented by these distributions, we need a way to measure their dispersion.

One way to measure dispersion is simply to note the distance between the smallest and largest observations. Such a measure, called the *range,* is obviously crude; for example, it would change dramatically if a single exceptionally small or large observation was added to the distribution. A better measure of dispersion is provided by the **standard deviation,** discussed in Box A-1. Simply knowing the formula for the standard devia-

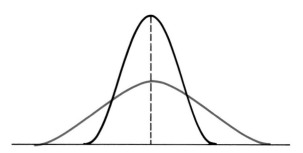

FIGURE A-2
Two Idealized Frequency Distributions Although each distribution contains the same number of observations and has the same central tendency, each has a different degree of dispersion.

tion is little help in understanding how dispersion is measured. Our intention in Box A-1 is to provide an intuitive appreciation of this index of dispersion and to help you understand that the standard deviation is a number whose size is proportional to the degree of dispersion of scores in a distribution.

Taken together, the mean and the standard deviation supply an adequate way of summarizing and representing a set of scores. The larger the

---

Box A-1
The Standard Deviation

The dispersion of a distribution of scores is measured by a descriptive statistic called the *standard deviation*. The defining formula of the standard deviation (s.d.) appears complex:

$$s.d. = \sqrt{\frac{\Sigma(X-M)^2}{N}}$$

Rather than accepting on faith that the formula measures dispersion or deriving dispersion from mathematical principles, let us attempt to obtain an intuitive understanding of the formula itself.

If we want to measure the dispersion of a set of scores, a good starting point is the distance of each score (which we call X) from the center of the distribution, the mean (M). In symbolic terms, this distance is ($X-M$). Thus, if the mean height of males is 69 inches, a person 72 inches tall is $72-69=3$ inches above the mean of the distribution. Because we want our measure of dispersion to take into account *all* scores, we take the sum (symbolized by Σ) of the deviations of all scores in the distribution: $\Sigma(X-M)$. However, this causes a problem: roughly half the deviations will be positive (X will be larger than M) and half negative (X will be smaller than M). Consequently, adding them together results in the positive values canceling the negative values. In fact, because of the way the mean is defined, $\Sigma(X-M)$ *always* equals zero. How can we avoid this problem? One way is to square each deviation value before summing it. Squaring gets rid of the negative values.

So far, so good; our formula is now $\Sigma(X-M)^2$. This measure of dispersion would be fine if all distributions we wanted to compare contained an equal number of scores. Since they do not, distributions with larger numbers of scores would likely yield larger measures of dispersion: there are more deviations to sum. What we need is not a total but an *average* measure of dispersion:

$$\frac{\Sigma(X-M)^2}{N}$$

This formula supplies a measure of dispersion called the **variance.** But remember that we squared the deviation scores. So it makes sense to return to the original unit of measurement by taking the square root of the variance:

$$\sqrt{\frac{\Sigma(X-M)^2}{N}}$$

We have now arrived at the formula used to define the standard deviation of a set of scores.

If you need to calculate the standard deviation of a distribution of numbers, you should consult a statistics textbook and find the computational formula for s.d. The computational formula is mathematically equivalent but is easier to use than the foregoing formula.

BOX A-2
THE NORMAL DISTRIBUTION

The curve in the illustration—called the *normal distribution,* or bell-curve—is an idealized distribution of scores of particular interest to researchers and statisticians. This bell-shaped distribution has very useful characteristics. For one thing, it is symmetrical around its point of central tendency. Thus the mode, median, and mean of a normal distribution have the same value.

Another characteristic concerns the dispersion of scores. The distribution is shown cut into sections by vertical lines. These lines are placed at the mean and at points that are whole standard deviations above and below the mean. Because the distribution is symmetrical, the vertical line at the mean cuts the distribution exactly in half; each half contains 50 percent of the scores. In addition, the section between the mean and 1 standard deviation above the mean contains nearly 34 percent of the scores, and the section between 1 and 2 standard deviations above the mean contains approximately 14 percent of the scores. This leaves about 2 percent in the extreme tail of the distribution (more than 2 standard deviations above the mean). These same values apply to the half of the distribution lying below the mean.

There is no easy way to explain how these figures were derived. For now, simply accept them as important characteristics of the normal distribution. They are important because they give you a frame of reference for locating individual scores within the distribution. For example, if your score on an exam is 1 standard deviation above the mean, you performed better than roughly 84 percent of those who took the exam (the 50 percent below the mean plus the 34 percent within one standard deviation above it).

Note the two scales under the normal distribution curve. One is in standard deviation units; the other is an IQ scale. The developers of early IQ tests devised a scoring system that gives a value of 100 to the mean IQ in the population and a standard deviation equal to 15 IQ points. Knowing this, you can locate an individual IQ score within the population of IQ scores and estimate the percent of the population above or below it.

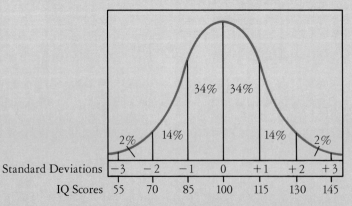

The Normal Distribution An idealized symmetrical distribution that shows the proportion of observations lying within 1, 2, and 3 standard deviations from the mean. A scale for IQ scores is also shown.

standard deviation, the less representative the mean is of each individual score in the set. It follows that you should place questionable reliance on a mean if you don't know the standard deviation of the scores it represents. In psychological research, reports of mean scores are usually accompanied by standard deviation values.

If you felt uneasy about the jump we made at the start of this section from an actual to an idealized distribution, the discussion in Box A-2 may help. The box describes a type of idealized distribution (the **normal distribution**), tells why it is of importance in psychological research, and provides more information about the standard deviation measure of dispersion.

All the descriptive statistics considered thus far have described characteristics of scores distributed on a single variable. Correlational research, however, provides information about the relationship between two variables. To describe this relationship, we need statistical procedures that measure the degree of association or correlation between two distributions of scores. These *bivariate* (two-variable) descriptive statistics are discussed in the following section.

Correlation

Do women drivers have more accidents than men drivers? Is a person's level of education related to his or her social class? Is there an association between students' level of anxiety and their examination performance? An investigator conducting research on any of these questions would probably use a correlational approach. In each case, the data collected would be in the form of paired observations or measurements. Every subject would provide one value for each of the two variables being studied. The questions just posed take the following general form: Are large values on one variable typically paired with large (or with small) values on the other variable? More simply: Do the values on the two variables go together?

First consider the hypothetical evidence in Table A-2 showing the frequency of accidents reported by a sample of male and female drivers. If the percent of male drivers reporting accidents is

TABLE A-2

Accident Record of Sample of Male and Female Drivers (hypothetical data)

		Accident Involvement		
		Yes	No	Total
Driver's Sex	Male	60	120	180
	Female	30	60	90
	Total	90	180	270

different from the percent of female drivers, the evidence suggests a correlation between sex and accidents. If accidents are unrelated to sex of the driver, however, we would expect the percentages to be the same—as they are in Table A-2. The hypothetical data show the percent of male drivers involved in an accident to be $(60/180) \times 100$ whereas the percent of female drivers is $(30/90) \times 100$, or 33 1/3% in both cases. Although percentages are not difficult to calculate, it is surprising how often people fail to compute them when they should. If the conclusion is based on *numbers* rather than *percentages* of male and female drivers having accidents, the conclusion may be wrong (see Box A-3, page 792).

Now consider the problem of describing the results of the correlational study discussed earlier: anxiety level versus exam performance. We wanted to determine whether the more anxious students typically had different exam scores than the less anxious students. The answer is revealed by the hypothetical results displayed in Figure A-3. The pair of values for each student is plotted on a graph in which the two axes represent the two variables in the correlation. The clustering of points on this **scattergram** shows the manner in which the two sets of values go together.

Statistical procedures—called **correlation coefficients**—have been developed to measure the correlation between two variables. It would not be particularly helpful to describe how these coefficients are computed; nevertheless, we note that the most commonly used coefficient is named after an important figure in the

BOX A-3
INSUFFICIENT EVIDENCE

The hypothetical data in Table A-2 show no evidence of a correlation between sex and accidents: the percentage of male and female drivers who had accidents is the same — 33 1/3%. This conclusion is based on the data in the four cells in the core of the table. To draw such a conclusion from less evidence would have been wrong. Suppose all you knew was the *number* of drivers of each sex who had accidents. Would the fact that 60 drivers were male and 30 were female lead you to conclude that female drivers were less prone to accidents than male drivers? Probably not, because you might

suspect there are more male than female drivers in the *non*accident group as well. But let us look at more seductive examples.

Neilson (1965) found that nearly half the drivers involved in fatal accidents had a blood-alcohol concentration of at least 0.05 percent. Many people would accept this as evidence of an association between alcohol and accidents. But what if it were also found that nearly half the drivers *not* involved in fatal accidents had blood-alcohol levels in the same range? Very unlikely, perhaps, but possible. If that were the case, Neilson's findings would not be

evidence of a correlation between drinking and accidents.

Consider how often you are invited to accept as evidence of a correlation such information as "A large number of crimes are committed when the moon is full" or "Most marriages between teenagers end in divorce." Unless you are also told how many crimes are committed when the moon is *not* full and are given the divorce rate for couples who married when they were older, you have no way of knowing whether or not the variables in question are actually correlated.

theory of measurement, Karl Pearson, and is represented symbolically by *r*. Values of *r* can range from -1.00 to $+1.00$, where the algebraic sign shows the *direction* of correlation (positive or negative) and the numerical value reflects the *strength* of the correlation.

The scores in Figure A-3 cluster around a line drawn diagonally from the upper left to the lower right of the scattergram. The line has been positioned to provide the best "fit" with the evidence — in the sense that it is the line that minimizes the overall distance of points from the line. Because in this example higher anxiety levels appear to be associated generally with lower exam scores, the direction of their correlation is described as *negative*. If the scores all fell

exactly on the line, we would have a perfect negative correlation and the value of Pearson's correlation coefficient would be -1.00. As scores deviate farther from the line, strength of the correlation decreases and the correlation coefficient approaches zero. We have computed a value of Pearson's *r* for the scores in Figure A-3: $r = -.54$.

Suppose the same two sets of score values were paired differently; the correlation between the variables would change. Figures A-4 to A-6 show different directions and strengths of correlation between the same sets (but differently paired) of anxiety level values and exam scores. A zero correlation (the absence of association) is evident in Figure A-4: there is no general tendency

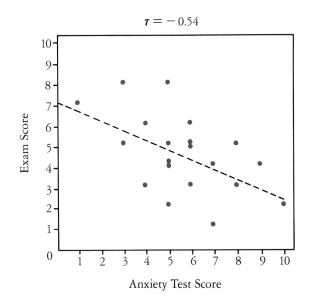

FIGURE A-3
Scattergram of Exam Scores and Anxiety Test Scores that Show a Moderately Strong Negative Correlation

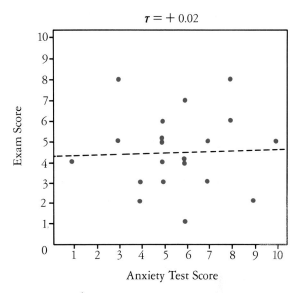

FIGURE A-4
Scattergram of Exam Scores and Anxiety Test Scores that Show an Absence of Correlation

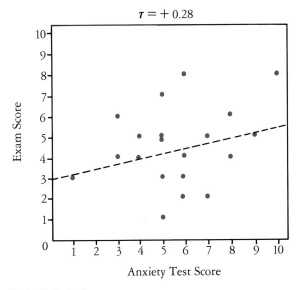

FIGURE A-5
Scattergram of Exam Scores and Anxiety Test Scores that Show a Weak Positive Correlation

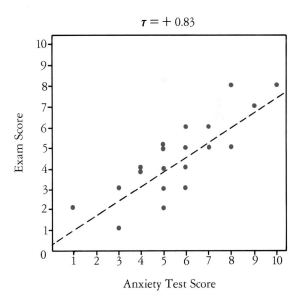

FIGURE A-6
Scattergram of Exam Scores and Anxiety Test Scores that Show a Strong Positive Correlation

for students with a particular anxiety level to do either poorly or well on the exam. Figures A-5 and A-6 both show positive correlations: high anxiety is associated with high exam scores and low anxiety is associated with low exam scores. These two correlations differ only in the strength of association between the variables: Figure A-5 shows a weak positive correlation; Figure A-6 shows a strong positive correlation. We have computed the values of Pearson's correlation coefficient *r* for the four sets of scores under consideration and they appear in the figures.

With the preceding background in mind, we now consider the statistics used to draw inferences from the evidence collected in psychological research.

DRAWING INFERENCES FROM THE EVIDENCE

There is a natural tendency to think of scientific research as a methodology designed to determine whether certain events cause other events — as opposed to determining whether certain events *fail* to cause other events. However, the logic of scientific thinking (especially in psychological research) is slanted toward drawing conclusions from negative rather than positive outcomes: psychological research is better at *dis*confirming hypotheses than at confirming them. Instead of testing a hypothesis that corresponds to their prediction (that a particular relationship in fact *does* exist), psychologists reverse the logic and test the hypothesis that *no* relationship exists between the variables they measure. Let us learn why.

If you wanted to predict how people would vote in an upcoming election, you would probably poll a relatively small number of carefully selected voters (a representative sample). If you wanted to examine the effectiveness of a new instructional program, you would probably test the pupils in a limited number of classes from one or two conveniently located schools. In psychology, most laboratory experiments are conducted on groups of volunteers from undergraduate psychology courses. In all such cases, the researchers' ultimate interest is not the behavior of the particular people whom they actually test but the conclusions they can draw about the behavior of all people like them (voters, students, people in general). Researchers test *samples* of people to obtain information about the *population* from which the people were drawn. In situations where researchers can test all the people in a population, there is no need for inferential statistics. When limited to testing a sample of people, however, researchers can only *infer* that the behavior of the sample is representative of the behavior of the population. Inferential statistics supply an indication of the likelihood that such an inference is mistaken.

Hypothesis Testing — A Taste Test

Consider this example. Imagine you and some friends are debating the difference between two brands of soft drink (we shall call them colas). Some say that one cola tastes better; some favor the other. You are skeptical and argue that there really is no difference in taste. To test your friends' contention that they taste a difference between the two colas, you suggest a blind test. You disguise the identity of the two colas, have eight of your friends take a sip of each (in random order), and ask them to say which drink is which brand. Assume five of your friends identify the colas correctly and three fail the test. What might you conclude? You can say with absolute certainty that a majority of your eight friends (about 63 percent) identified the drinks correctly. But what you really want to know is whether a majority of *people in general* can tell the two drinks apart. Would you confidently expect to find that five people in every eight (about 63 percent) would identify the two colas correctly if you tested a group of 20 people, or 200, or 2,000, chosen at random? Perhaps not. The pattern you observed in your sample of eight friends could have occurred by chance. As we have seen, chance variations *average out* only if given sufficient opportunity — and eight judgments are hardly sufficient. What you need is a larger sample.

Imagine you repeated the taste test with 30 randomly chosen people. How many must make a correct identification before you would conclude they were not simply guessing? Surely you would accept a 30/0 correct/incorrect split as evidence that more was involved than guessing. But what about a 23/7 or a 20/10 split? The purpose of inferential statistics is to guide your answers to questions such as these. This is how it works. First we ask the question: "What is the probability the split in the sample (say 23/7) could occur by chance?" In other words, what is the probability of randomly selecting a sample of 30 people and finding that 23 of them identify the colas correctly simply by chance (the actual split in the population at large being *fifty-fifty*)? We answer the question by appealing to the basic logic of probability.

If you tossed a set of 30 unbiased coins a very large number of times (say 10,000), you would almost certainly find that a fifty-fifty or 15/15 split between heads and tails was the most frequent outcome. Splits of 16/14 and 14/16 would probably tie for second, then 17/13 and 13/17, and so on. The law of averages tells us the

most likely distribution of outcomes would be as indicated in Table A-3, page 798. Note that very unbalanced outcomes, while extremely unlikely, can occur. For example, if you tossed 30 coins 10,000 times, you would expect a 23/7 split about 19 times.

The distribution of chance outcomes shown in Table A-3 can be interpreted conveniently as either odds or probabilities. The odds of a 15/15 split are approximately 1 in 7, or roughly 14 in 100, which is equivalent to a probability of 0.14. The probability of a 23/7 split is 0.0019 (odds of 19 in 10,000). Returning to the cola test, think of heads as a correct identification of the colas and tails as an incorrect identification. How likely is it that a 23/7 split would occur simply as a result of guessing? As we have seen, the probability of a 23/7 split when the odds are fifty-fifty (the coins are unbiased; the colas taste the same) is 0.0019. If we add the probabilities of even less likely outcomes in the same direction

Box A-4
Hypothesis Testing — The Underlying Logic

In the experiment described in text on the two methods of teaching spelling, your prediction was that spelling test scores of your class would, on average, be higher than those of your colleague's class. You were right — but only just. The average score for your class was 11.03 compared to 10.83 for the other class. Is this difference too small to supply convincing evidence that your method of teaching is really better? Psychologists answer such questions as this by determining the probability that the observed difference could have occurred by chance alone. For the sake of discussion, we shall assume no confounding variables biased the results: that teaching method was the only variable that could have *systematically* influenced the test scores. Let us go step-by-step through the process of testing the inference that a similar difference in average test scores would have been found had the entire population of school-children been tested.

Step 1 First, we make the assumption that the difference between the two mean scores was due entirely to chance: to the failure of the chance variation in scores to average out. This assumption is called the **null hypothesis.** The null hypothesis states that *none* of the differences we observed between the scores in the two groups is due to a systematic influence (in our case, the difference in teaching method). It may seem odd to make the assumption that there is no systematic difference between the performance of the groups: this is just the opposite of the prediction that led to the experiment. But there is a good reason for doing so: the null hypothesis is precise. Although you were willing to predict that your class would score higher, you had no way of knowing how much higher. Therefore, your **experimen-**tal hypothesis was not precise. In contrast, the null hypothesis is exact: it says that the difference in mean test scores is *entirely* due to chance variations (or **random error,** as it is called). The null hypothesis thus denies the existence of any systematic effect on performance. You can think of the null hypothesis as a statistical straw man the investigator sets up and attempts to shoot down, using the experimental results as ammunition. To confirm a prediction in an experiment, a psychologist generally must *disconfirm* the hypothesis that says the prediction is wrong: the null hypothesis.

Step 2 We test the null hypothesis by determining how probable it is the difference in mean test scores (11.03 – 10.83) was entirely due to chance. Although we cannot use the coin-tossing analogy in this case because we do not have a simple heads/tails outcome, we do have a basis for estimating

(24/6, 25/5 . . . 30/0), we can say the probability of a split *at least as extreme as* 23/7 — when only chance determines the outcome — is 0.0026 (0.0019 + 0.0006 + . . . + 0.0000; see Table A-3). Put another way, the odds are roughly 1 in 385 (1/385 = 0.0026) that 23 or more people in 30 will identify the colas correctly if their judgments are really guesses.

For the cola test results, the question you must answer comes down to this: Does the 23/7

the influence of chance factors on the test scores: the variability of scores *within* each class. All students within each class were taught by the same method. If we assume that method was the only variable permitted to vary systematically, it follows that *all* within-group variability in scores must have been caused by chance factors. In other words, it is random error.

Once we have computed average within-group variability, we can calculate the probability that this amount of random error could have caused the observed *between-group* difference in average scores. It should be apparent that the greater the amount of random error, the more likely a mean difference of a given size was the result of the failure of chance to average out. We have calculated the probability that the observed difference of 0.20 points between the mean scores of the two classes (11.03 − 10.83) was entirely due to random error: the probability is approximately 0.8. In other words, if you were to repeat this experiment many times

under the same conditions and only chance was determining the differences in scores within and between classes, you would find a mean difference *at least* as big as 0.20 in 80% of the experiments. Clearly, the difference is too small to knock down our straw-man null hypothesis. These results fail to confirm our prediction that there would be a *statistically significant* (beyond chance) difference between the average scores of the two classes.

Step 3 Inferential statistics have now served their purpose. When the outcome is *not* statistically significant —as in the case of the spelling test scores — you should conclude that the evidence failed to support the experimental hypothesis. Now consider what conclusion you should draw if the difference *is* statistically significant: if the null hypothesis is rejected as being too improbable. In such an event, one final step remains: a decision must be made about your experimental hypothesis, your prediction that manipulating the

independent variable (teaching method) would cause a systematic difference on the dependent variable (spelling test score).

You might think that the experimental hypothesis is confirmed automatically when the null hypothesis is rejected. But there are really two components here: rejecting the null hypothesis signifies you have identified a systematic effect; however, inferential statistics do not tell us what caused the systematic effect. Naturally, you want to believe the cause is the manipulation of the independent variable. But a confounding variable also could have had a systematic effect. So you must demonstrate you have controlled all potential confounding variables before you can finally claim you have confirmed your experimental hypothesis. Unfortunately, there are many examples in psychological research of statistically significant differences later discovered to have been due to the systematic effect of an overlooked confounding variable.

split merely reflect the failure of the law of averages to exert its balancing effect over choices that are simply guesses — or does the split reflect that a substantial majority of the population can correctly identify the colas? Simply put, your decision or inference is a matter of *playing the odds.* Again, you can never know for sure what the population split is unless you test the entire population. Your best estimate is usually that the split you observe in your sample represents the split

TABLE A-3
Frequency, Probability, and Odds*

Outcome (heads/tails)	Frequency (F)	Probability (P) (P = F/10,000)	Odds (O) (O = 1 in 10,000/F)
30/0	Less than once	.000 000 000 9	1 in 1 billion
29/1	Less than once	.000 000 03	1 in 36 million
28/2	Less than once	.000 000 4	1 in 2.5 million
27/3	Less than once	.000 004	1 in 264,468
26/4	Less than once	.000 03	1 in 39,181
25/5	1	.0001	1 in 7,535
24/6	6	.0006	1 in 1,808
23/7	19	.0019	1 in 527
·	·	·	·
·	·	·	·
·	·	·	·
17/13	1,115	.1115	1 in 9
16/14	1,354	.1354	1 in 7
15/15	1,445	.1445	1 in 7
14/16	1,354	.1354	1 in 7
13/17	1,115	.1115	1 in 9
·	·	·	·
·	·	·	·
·	·	·	·
1/29	Less than once	.000 000 03	1 in 36 million
0/30	Less than once	.000 000 000 9	1 in 1 billion
Total (all possible outcomes)	10,000	1.000	1 in $\dfrac{10,000}{10,000}$ (1 in 1)

* For selected outcomes expected to occur when a set of 30 unbiased coins is tossed 10,000 times.

you would observe in the population. The question that inferential statistics help answer is how confident you should be in your best estimate. If the 30 people tested *were* only guessing, the odds of 23 or more guessing correctly are roughly 1 in 385. You would be a poor gambler indeed to bet on such odds. Obviously, the bet of choice is on the opposite hypothesis: the difference you observed did *not* occur by chance and if you tested the entire population, a similar pattern of results would be found. You *could* be wrong, but it is highly unlikely.

This, basically, is what inferential statistics are all about. We have shown how they can be applied in a fairly simple situation. However, psychological experiments are usually more complicated than the cola-taste study. For example, in the study of spelling methods considered earlier, the evidence consisted of two sets of

scores with different means. When the evidence assumes this form, the inference evaluated is that a similar difference would be found if the two methods of teaching were applied to all school children — to the entire population from which the samples were drawn. Box A-4 on page 796 contains the steps involved in testing such inferences as these.

By now it should be clear that inferential statistics provide only a guide for deciding whether or not to reject the hypothesis that chance alone caused the difference. Investigators must decide where to draw the line. In psychological research, a tradition has been established that the line should be drawn at odds of 1 in 20. Researchers are generally willing to conclude that an observed difference is reliable (due to a systematic, nonchance influence) if the odds are 1 in 20 or longer that the difference was entirely due to chance. By convention, these odds are usually stated as a *probability value.* Odds of 1 in 20 (5 in 100) correspond to a probability value of .05. If you read the phrase "The difference is **statistically significant** ($p < .05$)" in a research report, it simply means that inferential statistics show that the probability (p) of the difference being due solely to chance is less than ($<$) or equal to .05. Alternatively, when the evidence is not strong enough to rule out a chance explanation, the difference in question is referred to as "not statistically significant ($p > .05$)," where $>$ means *greater than.* In both cases, .05 is referred to as the **level of significance.**

KEY TERMS

Descriptive Statistics	Arithmetic Mean	Correlation Coefficient
Inferential Statistics	Dispersion	Statistically Significant
Frequency Distribution	Standard Deviation	Level of Significance
Frequency Histogram	Variance	Null Hypothesis
Central Tendency	Normal Distribution	Experimental Hypothesis
Mode	Scattergram	Random Error
Median		

GLOSSARY

Glossary entries are not dictionary definitions; they are intended to capture the meaning of significant terms as they are used in this book. The number or letter in parentheses indicates the chapter or appendix in which the entry occurs as a **Key Term.**

ablation: (3) Surgical removal of brain tissue for treatment of brain disease or as a means of studying brain function in nonhumans. *See also* lesion.

accommodation: (4, 9) In sensation and perception, an increase or decrease in curvature of the lens of the eye that occurs with a change in distance of the fixation point; a depth cue. In Jean Piaget's theory, a form of adaptation in which existing ways of thinking change in order to incorporate new forms of knowledge.

acquired immune deficiency syndrome (AIDS): (8) A potentially fatal pattern of symptoms caused by a virus that breaks down the human immune system; the virus is transmitted sexually or intravenously by contaminated needles.

action potential: (3) The all-or-none transmission of a nerve impulse along the axon of a nerve cell.

action unit: (7) Any of several facial muscles identifed by Paul Ekman and Wallace Friesen as capable of independent action in the expression of emotion. *See also* facial action coding system.

active phase: (13) The second phase in the development of schizophrenia, usually brought on by some type of stress.

actor–observer difference: (11) The tendency of individuals to make dispositional attributions about others and situational attributions about themselves.

actualizing tendency: (12) Carl Rogers' term for the natural tendency of people to maintain and enhance themselves.

adaptation: (4, 9) In sensation, the reduction in output of a sensory receptor cell through continual stimulation. In Jean Piaget's theory, one of the *invariant functions* of existence — the tendency to change in ways that foster growth.

adding model: (12) A model of impression formation in which overall impressions are based on the sum of an individual's traits.

additive color mixture: (4) The principle governing the mixing of lights: when lights of complementary color are added, the resultant light is white. *See also* subtractive color mixture.

adjective check list: (12) A list of up to 300 adjectives that describe personality characteristics. Raters are asked to check the adjectives characteristic of the person being assessed.

adolescent growth spurt: (9) The rapid increase in height and weight that occurs during adolescence.

adoption study: (2) A study of the characteristics of children, their birth, and adoptive parents designed to compare genetic and environmental influences on the measured characteristics. *See also* twin study.

afterimage: (4) A continuing sensory impression in complementary colors that follows prolonged inspection of a brightly illuminated figure.

agitated depression: (13) A state of severe depression in which people become restless and fidgety, have difficulty sitting still, and appear to be trying to escape the pain they feel by moving away from it.

agoraphobia: (13) The fear of being in places or situations from which escape is seen to be difficult and help is unavailable.

alcohol abuse: (13) The abuse of alcohol for at least one month, despite knowledge of problems caused by it, and the recurrent use of alcohol in situations in which such use is hazardous.

alcohol dependence: (13) A psychoactive substance-use disorder characterized by increased tolerance to alcohol, withdrawal symptoms, alcohol-related social and physical problems, and other symptoms.

algorithm: (6) Any well-specified set of procedures for attempting to solve a problem. *See also* heuristic.

alpha rhythm: (3) Electrical waves from the visual area of the brain that have a frequency of 8–12 cycles per second; prominent when relaxing and not attending to visual input. *See also* beta rhythm, theta rhythm.

alternate-form reliability: (12) The similarity of scores on alternate forms of the same test.

altruism: (2) In sociobiology, behavior that occurs when an individual sacrifices personal fitness in order to enhance the fitness of another member of the species.

amphetamine: (3, 8) A drug that stimulates the central nervous system.

amplitude: (4) In audition, the height of a sound wave; determines the loudness of the sound.

amygdala: (3) A structure in the limbic system of the brain that is involved in the control of aggression and eating behavior.

amygdalectomy: (14) The destruction of the amygdala, a part of the limbic system of the brain, with the intention of relieving unprovoked, extreme, uncontrollable outbursts of violence.

amyl nitrate: (8) A drug that causes blood vessels to expand, producing a sudden drop in blood pressure; reputed to affect sexual arousal and performance.

anal character: (12) According to Sigmund Freud, the type of character developed by an adult who fixates at the anal stage: one who is orderly, obstinate, punctual, and stingy.

anal stage: (12) Sigmund Freud's second stage of psychosexual development in which the primary source of pleasure shifts from the mouth to the anus.

analytic cognition: A term used by Ross Buck (in a speculative manner) to label types of cognitive activity that are linear, sequential, verbal, conscious, intentional, indirect, and based in the left hemisphere. *See also* syncretic cognition.

androgen: (9) The male sex hormone.

anger rape: (8) Rape in which the goal of the rapist is to humiliate, degrade, and physically hurt the victim.

annual monogamy: (8) A reproductive system in which a male pairs with a female for the duration of a mating season. *See also* perennial monogamy.

anorexia nervosa: (13) An eating disorder, occurring mostly in females, in which individuals are abnormally concerned about their weight and body image, fear getting fat, and take extreme measures to lose weight. *See also* bulimia nervosa.

antianxiety drug: (14) A psychoactive drug that reduces anxiety and tension, and produces a state of calmness and well being; examples include: Miltown®, Valium®, Librium®, popularly called minor tranquilizers. *See also* brain depressant.

antidepressant drug: (14) A psychoactive drug used to treat mild or moderate depression.

antimanic drug: (14) A psychoactive drug that calms the agitation associated with manic reactions; lithium carbonate is an example.

antipsychotic drug: (14) A psychoactive drug used to treat such psychotic symptoms as extreme agitation, delusions, hallucinations, and aggressive or violent behavior; sometimes called major tranquilizers.

antisocial personality: (13) A type of personality disorder marked by impulsiveness, recklessness, deceptiveness, involvement in criminal activities, inability to maintain a job or a lasting sexual attachment, repeated violations of rights of others, and an absence of remorse.

anxiety disorder: (13) A group of mental disorders involving anxiety; includes generalized anxiety, panic attacks, phobias, obsessive-compulsiveness, and post-traumatic stress.

anxiety hierarchy: (14) A list of situations whose contemplation produces anxiety, ranked from those that evoke the least anxiety to those that evoke the most.

aphrodisiac: (8) A substance that creates or increases sexual desire.

apparent movement: (4) The impression of movement that results from exposure to successive stationary visual patterns, as in the perception of a movie film. Also referred to as the phi phenomenon and as stroboscopic movement.

aptitude test: (12) A test designed to predict success in a specific domain of activity.

arithmetic mean: (A) A descriptive statistic that measures central tendency, often referred to simply as mean or average; defined by the formula $\Sigma x/n,$ where Σx is the sum of the n values of variable x. *See also* median, mode.

ascending reticular activating system: (3) The part of the brain's central core involved in the control of wakefulness. *See also* reticular formation.

asexual reproduction: (8) A reproductive process, not involving the union of male and female sex cells (gametes), in which 100% of the genetic material from the parent is transmitted to the offspring. *See also* sexual reproduction.

assertiveness training: (14) A social-learning technique designed to help people who experience difficulty asserting themselves in interpersonal situations.

assimilation: (9) In Jean Piaget's theory, a form of adaptation in which environmental features are incorporated into already existing ways of thinking.

association cortex: (3) The most recently evolved area of the brain's cortex; involved in the integration of sensory and motor processes and in such cognitive activities as learning, remembering, and thinking. *See also* motor cortex, sensory cortex.

attachment: (2, 10) The social and emotional bond that infants form with primary caretakers, especially their mothers. *See also* bonding.

attachment behavior: (2, 10) Reciprocal patterns of social interaction between infant and caregiver that reflect attachment.

attend: (9) In information-processing theory, the focus on a specific aspect of the environment.

attention: (6) The process that selects sensory input for representation in conscious awareness and for further processing.

attribution: (11) The cognitive process by which individuals reach conclusions about the causes of behavior.

auditory canal: (4) The passage leading from the outer ear to the eardrum.

authoritarian parenting: (10) A parenting style based mainly on the assertion of power. *See also* authoritative parenting, permissive parenting.

authoritative parenting: (10) A parenting style in which limits are set and rules are reinforced through warmth and respect. *See also* authoritarian parenting, permissive parenting.

autistic aloneness: (13) Being unresponsive to other people and seemingly oblivious of their presence.

autistic disorder: (13) A disorder acquired early in a child's life, characterized by unresponsiveness to other people and preference for nonsocial objects.

autokinetic effect: (4, 11) The illusory impression of the movement of a stationary spot of light viewed in otherwise dark surroundings.

autonomic nervous system (ANS): (3, 7) The set of sensory and motor nerves that controls such internal bodily functions as heart rate, blood pressure, respiration, digestion, and perspiration. *See also* central nervous system.

autonomy: (11) A behavioral style characterized by independent functioning.

averaging model: (12) A model of impression formation in which overall impressions are based on the average of an individual's traits.

aversion therapy: (14) Pairing an unpleasant event with a desired but socially undesirable behavior—such as smoking, overeating, and sexual aberrations—in order to extinguish the desire.

avoidance learning: (5) A form of instrumental conditioning in which an animal learns to react to a warning signal by making a response that prevents occurrence of an otherwise unavoidable aversive stimulus.

axes of classification: (13) The five dimensions in the *DSM-III-R* used by clinicians to diagnose mental disorder.

axon: (3) The outgrowth of a neuron that conducts all-or-none nerve action potentials away from the cell body to other neurons.

backward conditioning: (5) In learning, a classical conditioning procedure in which onset and offset of the unconditioned stimulus precede onset of the conditioned stimulus.

bait shyness: (5) A quickly learned and long-lasting aversion to novel foods that develops when acute illness follows ingestion of the food.

basal ganglia: (3) A group of nerve centers, located between the limbic system and the cerebral cortex, involved in the control of movement.

basilar membrane: (4) A band of fibrous material in the cochlea of the inner ear. Wave action in the cochlear fluid causes bending of the hair cells seated on the basilar membrane.

behavior therapy: (14) A form of psychological treatment used to effect behavior change and based on principles of learning.

behavioral cue: (11) An environmental prompt that "pulls" for a particular type of behavior.

behavioral ratings: (12) Information about an individual's behavior obtained from trained raters, psychologists, teachers, supervisors, parents, peers, and others for the purpose of assessing personality.

behavioral rehearsal: (14) Practicing adaptive behaviors in safe situations.

behavioral style: (11) Distinctive and consistent behavior thought to be effective in convincing a majority to adopt a minority point of view.

behavioristic model: (13) A model of psychological disorders that assumes maladaptive behavior is learned and maintained in the same way as adaptive behavior.

beta rhythm: (3) Electrical brain activity of high frequency (greater than 15 cycles per second); prominent when alert and attending to the environment. *See also* alpha rhythm, theta rhythm.

binocular disparity: (4) The difference in the images received by each eye; a cue to the relative distance of objects.

biofeedback: (14) Information about increases and decreases in such psychophysical responses as heart rate.

biological evolution: (2) The process of change in a species caused by natural selection operating on random genetic variation.

biologically based sexual disposition: (8) An inherited sexual disposition resulting from an individual's biological makeup.

bisexual: (8) Preference for both male and female sexual partners.

bleaching: (4) A chemical change in the pigment of rod cells that occurs when light strikes the retina, making the rods temporarily insensitive to light.

blood-brain barrier: (3) The reduced permeability of blood vessels in the brain compared with blood vessels in the rest of the body; protects the brain from the possibly harmful effects of substances circulating in the blood.

bonding: (10) In animals, the formation of a bond in the mother for her newborn infant that occurs during a critical postnatal period; evidence suggests it does not occur in humans. *See also* attachment.

brain depressant: (3) A drug such as an opiate, barbiturate, tranquilizer, or alcohol that depresses brain activity and induces relaxation, reduced sensory-motor performance, unconsciousness and—in sufficiently large doses—death.

brain stimulant: (3) A drug such as amphetamine, cocaine, caffeine, or nicotine that increases activity in certain parts of the brain; prolonged heavy use can induce severe personality changes.

Broca's area: (3) An area in the frontal lobe of the brain, usually in the left hemisphere, involved in the production of speech.

bulimia nervosa: (13) An eating disorder that involves binges of excessive eating, often followed by attempts to purge the body of the food through vomiting or laxatives. *See also* anorexia nervosa.

bystander effect: (11) The tendency of individuals not to intervene or to help less quickly in the presence of passive strangers.

bystander intervention: (11) A prosocial or helping response to an individual in distress.

California Personality Inventory (CPI): (12) A personality inventory that measures such personality characteristics as dominance, sociability, self-acceptance, responsibility, and socialization.

calpain: (3) A chemical produced in the brain that is believed to play a role in establishing memories.

capacity: (6) In cognition, the size and duration of short-term and long-term memory.

case study: (1) A research approach in which an in-depth investigation is made of a single case, typically a person but sometimes a single school, community, event, or the like.

castration: (8) The surgical removal of the testes.

cataract: (3) A clouding of the lens of the eye that diminishes and may eventually eliminate vision.

causal schemata: (11) In Harold Kelley's theory, preconceptions about the relationship between such events as the consistency and distinctiveness of individuals' behavior and the attributions made about the causes of such behavior.

cell body: (3) The part of a neuron containing the cell nucleus that, with the dendrite, receives input from other neurons.

censor: (14) According to Sigmund Freud, a process in the unconscious mind that employs such devices as displacement and condensation to restructure the content of dreams.

central core: (3) The oldest part of the brain, comprised of six structures: medulla, pons, cerebellum, reticular formation, hypothalamus, and thalamus.

central nervous system (CNS): (3) The brain and spinal chord. *See also* autonomic nervous system.

central tendency: (A) The average value in a set or distribution of values; measured by the descriptive statistics mode, median, and mean.

central trait: (12) Solomon Asch's term for traits that strongly affect overall impressions of personality; examples are warmth and coldness.

cerebellum: (3) A brain structure lying behind and below the occipital lobe and attached to the central core at the level of the pons; involved in the control of movement.

cerebral cortex: (3) The outermost layers of neurons on the surface of the cerebral hemispheres; also called *gray matter*; involved in higher mental processing.

cerebral hemispheres: (3) Two halves of the most recently evolved part of the brain; lies in a mantle over the brain stem.

chancre: (8) A painless sore indicating syphilis. On the glans of the penis, a chancre may resemble a pimple or a small crater; in women, it is not usually visible because it develops on the vaginal walls or on the cervix.

channel: (11) A vehicle of communication such as the mass media.

chemical senses: (4) The senses of taste and smell; so named because they are activated by chemicals in the saliva and air, respectively.

chlamydia: (8) A nongonococcal type of urethritis (NGU)—inflammation of the urethra not caused by gonococcal bacteria—usually sexually transmitted.

choroid coat: (4) The layer between the retina and the outer covering of the eyeball, consisting mostly of blood vessels.

chunk: (6) A loosely defined unit of capacity in short-term memory; a meaningful grouping of such material as a letter, syllable, word, or phrase.

clang association: (13) In schizophrenia, the stringing together of words that rhyme but make no sense; for example, "The King of Spain feels no pain in the drain of the crane."

class inclusion: (9) In Jean Piaget's theory, understanding that a set or class of objects (for example, flowers) has subsets (for instance, roses).

classical conditioning: (5) In learning, the procedure of pairing a conditioned stimulus (CS) with an unconditioned stimulus (US); also, the learned production of a conditioned response to a conditioned stimulus that results from such pairing.

classification: (9) In Jean Piaget's theory, a schema that allows the child to organize things coherently according to some rule or principle.

client-centered therapy: (14) A humanistic form of psychotherapy developed by Carl Rogers that is nondirective in orientation, forward-looking, and optimistic.

climacteric: (9) The period during which reproductive capacity declines for both men and women, culminating in menopause for women.

clinical method: (9) An unstructured, flexible, nondirective method of study used by Jean Piaget to explore children's thinking that involves small samples, sophisticated observation, and interviewing skills on the part of the researcher.

clinical psychologist: (14) One who has pursued an academic program of study and research leading to a Ph.D. in psychology, with an emphasis on the application of psychological principles to the assessment and treatment of psychological disorders.

cocaine: (8) A drug that stimulates the nervous system. *See also* brain stimulant.

cochlea: (4) A coiled, fluid-filled tube in the inner ear that contains the auditory receptor (hair) cells.

coding: (6) The translation of information processed by the perceptual and cognitive systems into different representational forms.

cognition: (6) Such mental activities as remembering, thinking, and problem solving that follow from (or occur in the absence of) perception.

cognitive appraisal: (7) In cognitive theories of emotion, the evaluation of circumstances that determines the type of emotion experienced in response to a stimulus.

cognitive dissonance: (11) A state of unpleasant psychological tension created when two inconsistent cognitions exist simultaneously.

cognitive learning: (5) Learning involving the formation of expectations without behavior or reinforcement; requires only that the organism pays attention to events in the environment.

cognitive psychology: (1, 6) The study of thought processes, including those involved in memory, language, and reasoning.

cognitive-aesthetic need: (7) In Abraham Maslow's view, the need to understand and appreciate events in one's life.

cognitive-behavior therapy: (14) A form of psychotherapy that attempts to alter behavior by modifying the way people think.

cognitive-developmental theory: (1, 9) Jean Piaget's theory concerned with the growth of thinking; Jean Piaget believed that children's knowledge of the world develops in several distinct stages.

coitus: (8) Sexual intercourse.

combat exhaustion: (13) A condition suffered by combat soldiers characterized by fatigue, inability to sleep, feelings of terror, extreme jumpiness, and either apathy or extreme agitation.

community mental health center: (14) An outpatient clinic for people in need of psychological assistance but not hospitalization/institutionalization.

complementary hue: (4) Two hues or colors that, when mixed in appropriate proportions, produce gray or white; any two colors lying opposite each other on the color circle.

complex phobia: (13) An irrational fear; differs from a simple phobia in that the fear is not confined to specific objects or situations. *See also* simple phobia.

compliance: (11) A public yielding to social pressure not necessarily accompanied by an inward change; induced by majority pressure.

compulsion: (13) An irresistible urge to engage in a particular behavior.

computer simulation: (6) Programming a computer to produce output that matches or simulates the output of a different system; used by cognitive psychologists to develop and test theories of how the human mind works.

computerized axial tomography (CAT): (3) A procedure that employs differential absorption of X rays to provide an image of bodily structures; also referred to as computer-assisted tomography and computed tomography (CT).

concordance rate: (13) The degree of association between characteristics such as psychological disorders in individuals, especially relatives.

concrete operation: (9) In Jean Piaget's theory, a reversible mental action performed on a real object.

concrete operations stage: (9) In Jean Piaget's theory, the stage of development following preoperational thinking, lasting from approximately seven to eleven years of age, marked by an ability to employ reversible thinking.

condensation: (14) Sigmund Freud's term for the unconscious combination of symbols or words into a single entity with many meanings, especially in dreams.

conditioned punisher: (5) In learning, an originally neutral stimulus that has acquired punishing power by virtue of having been paired with an aversive stimulus during classical conditioning.

conditioned (secondary) reinforcer: (5) In learning, an originally neutral stimulus that has acquired reinforcing power by virtue of having been paired with a primary reinforcer during classical conditioning. *See also* primary reinforcer.

conditioned response (CR): (5) In learning, the response elicited by a conditioned stimulus. The conditioned response is similar to, but not necessarily identical to, the unconditioned response.

conditioned stimulus (CS): (5) In learning, a stimulus that is initially neutral with respect to a particular unconditioned response. After repeated pairings with the unconditioned stimulus, the conditioned stimulus elicits a conditioned response.

conditions of worth: (12) In Carl Rogers' theory, the conditions that children must fulfill in order to earn their parents' love.

cone: (4) A receptor cell in the visual system responsible for color vision and for perception of focal detail in medium to strong light. The density of cones is greatest in the foveal area of the retina. *See also* rod, retina.

confirmation: (1) Support for a prediction from evidence consistent with such prediction; a prediction that is probably but not certainly correct. *See also* proof.

confounding variable: (1) In an experiment, any variable other than the dependent variable that is related systematically to the differences produced on the independent variable. The presence of a confounding variable makes the interpretation of experimental results uncertain. *See also* third factor.

conscious: (12) In Sigmund Freud's psychoanalytic theory, the relatively small part of the mind that includes everything we are aware of experiencing at the moment.

consciousness: (3) The momentary awareness of sensations, perceptions, thoughts, memories, or feelings.

conservation: (9) In Jean Piaget's theory, an understanding that certain properties, such as amounts, remain constant when other properties, such as shape, change.

consistency: (11) A behavioral style in which individuals remain constant in the position they advance.

consonance: (11) Consistency among cognitions.

constructive alternativism: (12) According to George Kelly, the tendency of people to select from among available constructs those that enable them best to anticipate events. *See also* constructs, construing.

constructs: (12) George Kelly's term for the hypotheses or interpretations that people make about their worlds; bipolar in nature (for example, good/bad).

construing: (12) George Kelly's term for the process that people employ to interpret events in their lives.

contact comfort: (10) Comfort that an infant derives from physical contact with his or her mother (or substitute caretaker).

context-dependent recall: (6) Recall under conditions similar to those in which the memories were established originally; typically superior to recall under dissimilar conditions. *See also* state-dependent recall.

contingency management: (14) A technique employing withdrawal of reinforcement or application of mild punishment to extinguish maladaptive responses.

continuation: (4) A Gestalt principle of perceptual organization that describes the tendency to group elements of a figure with intersecting contours according to abruptness of transition between contours.

continuous reinforcement schedule: (5) In learning, a reinforcement schedule in which every target response is reinforced.

control group: (1) The subjects in an experiment who are exposed to the normal, standard, or zero value of an independent variable. *See also* experimental group.

conventional level: (10) The second level of moral

development described by Lawrence Kohlberg, consisting of stages three and four. Individuals at this level — mostly adolescents and adults — view morality in terms of laws, social order, and rules.

convergence: (4) The natural tendency of both eyes to converge on a fixation point; a cue to the distance of the fixation point provided by the muscular action controlling convergence of the eyes.

conversion: (11) Changing one's private attitudes and beliefs; typically induced through minority influence.

conversion disorder: (13) A psychological disorder characterized by such genuine physical dysfunctions as paralysis of a limb, blindness, or deafness with no organic basis.

copulation: (8) Sexual intercourse; coitus.

core: (12) Such inner components of personality as biological urges, intellectual capacities, and conscience.

cornea: (4) The bulging circular area of the outer coating of the eyeball that forms a transparent window at the front of the eye.

corpus callosum: (3) A large bundle of nerve fibers connecting the left and right cerebral hemispheres.

correlational approach: (1) A research approach that examines the existing association among variables, as distinguished from the experimental approach in which different values are produced by manipulating an independent variable.

correlation coefficient: (A) A descriptive statistic that measures the association between two variables; the algebraic sign of the coefficient indicates direction of association and its numerical size reflects strength of association.

counseling psychologist: (14) One who has credentials similar to those of a clinical psychologist but with less training in research and diagnosis.

counterattitudinal behavior: (11) Behavior inconsistent with one's attitudes.

covariation: (11) In Harold Kelley's theory, attributing behavior to the cause with which it is most closely associated over time.

covert sensitization: (14) A mild form of aversion therapy in which clients imagine anxiety-evoking events and learn to relax while thinking about them.

creativity: (6) Synthesis of a novel combination of ideas.

crisis intervention center: (14) A service for people experiencing an acute crisis, usually staffed by volunteers who listen supportively to problems, give advice when appropriate, and explain available services.

criterion images: (10) Cognitive templates used to evaluate various types of behavior.

critical period: (2) A relatively short time during development when the presence or absence of an environmental event has a marked effect (usually irreversible) on the behavior of an animal. *See also* sensitive period.

cross-sectional method: (9) A research method in which different age groups are compared on a specific behavior at approximately the same time. *See also* longitudinal method.

crystallized intelligence: (9) In John Horn and Raymond Cattell's theory, the type of intelligence that depends on systematic schooling and cultural experiences and that increases over the life span. *See also* fluid intelligence.

cultural bias: (12) A deficiency in a test that gives individuals from one culture an unfair advantage over individuals from another culture.

cultural evolution: (2) Growth and change in culture over generations, determined by selective retention of particular forms.

cumulative recorder: (5) A device that records the responses of animals experiencing various schedules of reinforcement in a Skinner box. Each response registers as an elevation above an inked line on a strip of moving paper.

cutaneous sensory system: (4) The skin-based sensory system responsible for perceptions of touch, pressure, pain, and warmth and cold.

dark adaptation: (4) With the onset of darkness, the gradually increasing light sensitivity of the rods in the periphery of the retina. Elapsed time to maximum sensitivity after exposure to strong illumination is approximately 30 minutes.

death instinct: (12) According to Sigmund Freud, the instinct that pushes humans toward the ultimate tensionless state of peace and quiescence — death; also called thanatos.

deductive reasoning: (6) Drawing a conclusion from premises according to the rules of logic. *See also* inductive reasoning.

deep structure: (9) The abstract structures of events such as language that give rise to the particular forms in which they appear, such as in grammar.

defensive attribution: (11) The tendency to attribute more responsibility (make stronger dispositional attributions) when consequences are severe than when they are mild.

deferred imitation: (9) Sequences of imitative behavior stored in memory for some time before use. *See also* delayed imitation.

deficiency need: (7) In Abraham Maslow's theory, basic physical and social motives evoked by the absence of resources necessary for survival.

deindividuation: (11) A psychological state characterized by a decrease in private self-awareness and often accompanied by a diffusion of responsibility and irresponsible behavior.

delayed conditioning: (5) In learning, a classical conditioning procedure in which the onset of the unconditioned stimulus occurs after the onset of the conditioned stimulus (the two stimuli terminate together).

delayed imitation: (9) Imitation of a behavior sometime after it has occurred. *See also* deferred imitation.

delusion: (13) A systematic but irrational belief about oneself, others, or one's world.

delusional (paranoid) disorder: (13) A psychological disorder characterized by a systematic delusion that dominates an individual's life, especially a delusion of persecution or grandeur.

dendrite: (3) The section of a neuron that, with the cell body, receives neural messages from other neurons; specialized for comparing excitatory and inhibitory responses to input from other neurons.

deontic choice: (10) A moral judgment concerning which course of action is right.

dependent variable: (1) The behavior of subjects measured in an experiment to reveal differences caused by manipulation of the independent variable.

depersonalization: (13) A disorder characterized by feelings of detachment from one's mental process or body; feeling like an automaton or as if in a dream.

depth of processing: (6) The extent of active consideration a person gives to an item being committed to memory. The deeper the consideration, the more likely the item can be recalled.

depth reversal: (4) The spontaneous reversal in apparent object depth represented in a drawing that contains ambiguous or contradictory depth cues.

descriptive statistic: (A) A summary measure that characterizes important information about a set or distribution of values or about the association between two such distributions. *See also* inferential statistics.

despair: (10) In Erik Erikson's theory, the feeling that one's life has been in vain, which may occur during the final stage of psychosocial development.

determinism: (3) The doctrine that acts of will or choice result from specifiable causes in accordance with natural laws.

diathesis-stress model: (13) A developmental model of schizophrenia that focuses on the interaction between genetic and environmental factors.

differential psychology: (1) The study of individual differences.

differentiation: (9, 10) The processs of increasing specialization of function, complexity, and organization that occurs in both physical and psychological development.

direct perception theory: (4) The perceptual theory, championed by James Gibson, that there is sufficient information in sensory stimulation to account for the richness of the perceptual world; no process of perceptual inference is needed. *See also* indirect perception theory.

directed thinking: (6) Thinking directed to some purpose, such as deductive or inductive reasoning. *See also* problem solving.

discrimination: (5) The ability to respond in different ways to similar stimuli; the procedure for teaching an organism to respond differently to two similar stimuli. *See also* generalization.

discriminative stimulus: (5) In learning, a stimulus in the presence of which reinforcement is (or is not) available. The discriminative stimulus is called S+ when reinforcement is given in its presence and S− when reinforcement is withheld in its presence. *See also* stimulus control, stimulus generalization.

dispersion: (A) The variability in a set or distribution of values, measured by descriptive statistics, standard deviation, and variance.

displacement: (14) Sigmund Freud's term for an unconscious change in emphasis—especially concerning dreams—of important events to unimportant events and for relieving instinctual urges through inappropriate objects.

display rule: (7) Conventional constraints that determine which emotional responses can be displayed in certain situations.

disruptive selection: (8) A type of natural selection in which variations at both ends of a continuum are selected but the more usual types in the middle are not.

dissociative disorder: (13) A psychological disorder in which people become cut off in some way from knowledge about themselves and their pasts while continuing to behave in a relatively normal manner. The four main types of dissociative disorder are dissociative amnesia, fugue, dissociation, and multiple personality.

distance/depth cue: (4) A source of information in the form of visual input or observer responses to it that indicates relative or absolute distances of parts in a visual scene.

dominance hierarchy: (10) A type of group power relationship that permits individuals at the top to have first access to resources (for example, food, play materials, choice of territories) and thus helps reduce group conflict.

dominant response: (11) A response that is habitual, well-learned, or innate, and therefore most likely to occur in a relevant situation (for example, the tendency to smile when smiled at).

dopamine: (13) A neurotransmitter produced in the brain that, in excess, is believed to induce symptoms of schizophrenia.

dopamine theory: (13) The theory that schizophrenic disorders are caused by excess dopamine in the brain or by overly sensitive postsynaptic receptors for dopamine.

double-bind communication: (13) Contradictory verbal and nonverbal messages that place children in a no-win situation.

double-blind procedure: (1) The withholding of information about experimental conditions from both subjects and experimenters in order to prevent their expectations from biasing the outcome of the study.

double standard: (8) Two sets of standards, typically discriminatory, that vary according to cultural norms; for example, premarital sex is acceptable for men but not for women.

drive: (7) A state of arousal and tension resulting from deprivation of a biological necessity that directs the behavior of an organism toward a specific goal.

drive reduction: (7) In learning theory, the axiom that a primary need must be relieved before reinforcement and learning can occur.

dual-code theory: (6) The theory that there are two semi-independent storage systems in long-term memory, one verbal and one visual. *See also* propositional memory.

dualist: (3) One who adheres to the doctrine that mind and body are essentially separate entities and need not obey the same natural laws. *See also* monist.

eardrum: (4) The thin, flexible membrane separating the outer and middle ears that vibrates in synchrony with the pressure changes of sound waves.

echoic memory: (6) The initial sensory representation of auditory input; relatively unselective and brief. *See also* iconic memory, sensory memory.

ecological validity: (1) The extent to which conclusions drawn from experiments conducted in the artificial environment of a psychological laboratory can be applied to naturally occurring behavior.

edge detector: (4) A specialized neuron in the brain that responds to edges in the visual scene.

ego: (10, 12) According to Sigmund Freud, the part of the psyche that developed in order to negotiate necessary compromises between the need to relieve instinctual tension and the need to conform to social rules and conventions; the intellectual aspect of personality.

ego analyst: (12) One of a group of theorists who objected to the emphasis Sigmund Freud placed on the id-based sexual instinct and its conflicts. According to such theorists, thinking is energized by forces other than suppressed or displaced sexual energy; the ego contains an energy of its own.

egocentricity: (10) The tendency in young children (and some adults) to assume that everyone else sees things the same as they do.

egocentrism: (9) In Jean Piaget's theory, an inability to distinguish between one's own perspective and another person's perspective.

ego defense mechanism: (12) In Freudian theory, a device employed by the ego to reduce anxiety by distorting reality.

ego-ideal: (12) In Freudian theory, the part of our superego that urges us to actualize potential and strive for perfection.

ego-integrity: (10) A property of Erik Erikson's last stage of psychosocial development: acceptance of one's life, whether or not one has achieved all personal goals, and belief that one's life has had meaning.

ejaculation: (8) The muscular contraction of bodily tissues that transports semen; the expulsion of semen from the penis during orgasm.

elaborative rehearsal: (6) A manner of processing items being committed to memory that seeks to relate such items to information already stored in long-term memory. *See also* maintenance rehearsal.

Electra complex: (10) During Sigmund Freud's phallic stage of development, the conflict experienced by young girls who resent their mothers and desire their fathers. *See also* Oedipus conflict.

electroconvulsive therapy (ECT): (14) A treatment of severe depression in which an alternating electric current (70–150 volts, 50–60 cycles per second) is administered to a patient's head for a fraction of a second, typically producing convulsions similar to the grand-mal seizures of epilepsy.

electromagnetic radiation: (4) Radiant energy that has magnetic and electric properties; includes visible light.

electroencephalogram (EEG): (3) A printout of the electrical activity of the brain.

electroencephalograph: (3) An electronic amplifier and printer used to record and print the electrical activity of the brain.

embryo: (9) A fetus between the second and eighth weeks of prenatal development.

emotion: (7) An aroused state characterized by specific physiological responses, facial expressions, subjective feelings, and dispositions to certain behaviors.

empirical strategy: (12) The strategy of personality test development based on selecting items responded to similarly by people who share a specific characteristic.

encode: (9) *See* coding.

encounter group: (14) A form of group therapy and a technique for interpersonal growth in which members express their feelings openly and challenge artificial behaviors.

endorphin: (4) A naturally occurring neurotransmitter in the brain, the effects of which are mimicked by opiate drugs; believed to relieve pain.

environment: (2) All experiential (nongenetic) factors that influence physical development and behavior; the nurture side of the nature/nurture dichotomy.

environmental determinism: (2) The theory that characteristics and behaviors are determined by previous experiences. *See also* genetic determinism.

epidemiology: (13) The study of the prevalence (number of cases in a population) and incidence (number of new cases) of disorders or diseases.

epinephrine: (7) A hormone secreted by the adrenal

gland that produces the type of autonomic arousal characteristic of emotion.

equilibration: (9) In Jean Piaget's theory, the process of balancing information in cognitive systems through assimilation and accommodation.

equilibrium: (9) In Jean Piaget's theory, a state of thinking in which there is a balance between mental activity and the environment.

erogenous zone: (8, 12) A sexually sensitive area of the body; in psychoanalytic theory, the mouth, anus, and genital organs especially.

escape learning: (5) An experimental situation used to study animal learning in which an unpleasant stimulus is activated without prior warning, requiring the animal to make a target response in order to terminate the stimulus.

esteem need: (7) Generally, the need to be liked; specifically, needs for approval and self-esteem.

estrogen: (8, 9) The primary female sex hormone; also produced in small quantities in males.

estrus: (8) The period of sexual receptivity in female mammals induced by hormonal changes associated with ovulation.

ethologist: (10) A researcher, often a biologist, who observes animals in their natural environment.

ethology: (1) The field of inquiry concerned with observation of animal behavior in natural environments; often guided by evolutionary theory.

eugenics: (2) The improvement of the qualities of a breed or species, especially the human race, through artificial parental selection.

eustachian tube: (4) The passage that connects the middle ear to the throat and that equalizes air pressure on either side of the eardrum.

excitement phase: (8) A phase in the sexual response cycle marked by engorgement of blood vessels and muscle tension.

exhibitionism: (8) Indecent exposure of one's genitals to others.

exorcism: (13) The process of expelling an evil spirit or demon believed to possess an individual.

expanded imitation: (9) A sequence of imitative behavior that includes components not present in the behavior originally observed and stored in memory.

expansion pattern: (4) The radiating movement across the retina of the image of a visual scene as an observer approaches it.

expectancy: (5) In learning theory, the idea or knowledge that a particular unconditioned stimulus always follows a particular conditioned stimulus; a central concept in the cognitive view of classical conditioning. *See also* stimulus substitution.

experimental approach: (1) A type of research in which differences in an independent variable are produced by manipulation and their effects on a dependent variable are measured; best suited for identifying casual relationships. *See also* correlational approach.

experimental group: (1) Subjects in an experiment exposed to a new, different, or nonzero value of an independent variable. *See also* control group.

experimental hypothesis: (A) The hypothesis tested by experiment—typically a determination of whether the independent and dependent variables are causally related. *See also* null hypothesis.

experimental method: (1) See experimental approach.

experimental psychopathologist: (13) One who conducts experimental research on psychological disorders.

experimenter expectancy effect: (1) Bias in the experimenter's measurement or evaluation of subjects' behavior that makes the outcome of the research more likely to fit the experimenter's expectations.

extinction: (5) In learning, the weakening and eventual elimination of a previously reinforced response by withholding reinforcement; used as a measure of the strength of learning.

extramarital sex: (8) Sexual relations between a married person and someone to whom he or she is not married.

eye: (4) The receptor organ in the visual sensory system; the mechanism that translates differences in light energy into patterns of nerve impulses.

facial action coding system (FACS): (7) A method developed by Paul Ekman and Wallace Friesen for classifying and objectively scoring the facial components of emotional expression. *See also* action unit.

facilitator: (14) The leader of an encounter group.

fairweather cooperation: (10) Robert Selman's third stage of friendship formation—characteristic of the later school years—in which there is an awareness of its reciprocal nature and a willingness to adjust to the likes and dislikes of others.

false consensus effect: (1, 11) The tendency for individuals to believe that more people share their opinions than actually do.

familiar size: (4) A pictorial cue to the distance of objects based on the viewer's knowledge of the object's size.

family/marital therapy: (14) A therapy for families and couples based on the belief that faulty interpersonal relations lie at the heart of many psychological problems.

Fechner's law: (1) A formula proposed by Gustav Fechner that outlines the relationship between physical qualities and psychological experiences; for example, the sensation of heaviness varies with the logarithm of weight.

fetishism: (8) A sexual deviation in which the object of sexual desire is a particular body part or a particular physical object.

field dependent: (9) A cognitive style characterized by dependence on the surrounding perceptual field for contextual cues.

field independent: (9) A cognitive style characterized by an ability to ignore misleading perceptual cues and to function independently from the surrounding perceptual field.

figure–ground reversal: (4) The spontaneous reversal of foreground (figure) and background in patterns ambiguous in this regard. *See also* object reversal.

figure–ground separation: (4) The tendency to perceive certain regions of a visual scene or pattern as foreground (figure) and adjacent regions as background.

fine motor skills: (9) The abilities involved in coordinating the thumb and fingers in order to execute specific manual tasks.

fixation: (12) In Freudian theory, an excessive charge of sexual energy trapped at a particular stage of psychosexual development.

fixed schedule: (5) In learning, a reinforcement schedule in which reinforcement is delivered after either a fixed time interval or a fixed number of responses following the last reinforced response. *See also* variable schedule.

flashbulb memory: (6) Memory for the circumstances when one first learned a very surprising or emotionally arousing event; typically a very vivid and long-lasting memory.

fluid intelligence: (9) In John Horn and Raymond Cattell's theory, a type of intelligence that is relatively independent of schooling and cultural experiences and that increases through adolescence and declines in adulthood. *See also* crystallized intelligence.

foreclosure: (10) In James Marcia's theory, adopting an identity from one's parents without a reexamination of values and goals.

form perception: (4) The organization of sensory elements into the perception of discrete objects and events.

formal operations stage: (9) In Jean Piaget's theory, the most advanced stage of thinking that emerges during adolescence; characterized by abstract thought.

fovea: (4) The small, central area of the retina responsible for focal vision.

free association: (14) A psychoanalytic technique, developed by Sigmund Freud to expose unconscious processes, in which the patient is encouraged to say whatever comes into his or her mind.

free-floating anxiety: (13) Sigmund Freud's term for a diffuse, unfocused sense of apprehension without any apparent basis.

free nerve endings: (4) Receptor cells widely distributed over the body surface. Once thought to be involved exclusively in pain perception, they are now considered also to play a role in the perception of pressure and temperature.

free recall: (6) A procedure in which subjects are asked to recall items from memory without regard to the order in which they were learned.

frequency: (4) The distance between successive wave peaks or the number of wave cycles that pass a given point each second; in audition, the characteristic of a sound wave that determines pitch. *See also* wavelength.

frequency distribution: (A) A graphic means of displaying the frequency of occurrence of different values in a set or distribution of values. *See also* frequency histogram.

frequency histogram: (A) A type of frequency distribution in which the frequency of occurrence of each value is represented graphically by the height of a vertical bar.

frequency theory: (4) The theory of how sound-wave frequency is translated into the perception of pitch, which asserts that the entire basilar membrane vibrates at the frequency of the sound wave. *See also* place theory, volley principle.

fugue: (13) A dissociative disorder involving a loss of memory of one's past that can last from a few hours to a few years; characterized by the sense that one does not know who one is or from where one came.

fully functioning person: (12) Carl Rogers' term for an individual whose parents set no conditions for love, and who actualizes his or her potential.

function fixedness: (6) A problem-solving block involving the use of the strategy that usually works, but which is inappropriate for the present problem.

functionalism: (1) The second major early school of psychology, which focused on how the mind functions rather than on its structure.

fundamental attribution error: (11) An individual's tendency to underestimate the influence of environmental factors on the behavior of others.

gamete: (8) A sex cell (ovum and sperm) specialized to achieve sexual reproduction.

ganglion: (3) A mass of nerve tissue containing the cell bodies of many neurons; an identifiable collection of nerve cells in the brain, spinal cord, or autonomic nervous system. *See also* nucleus.

gate control theory: (4) The theory that the perceived painfulness of a stimulus is controlled by the position of a *gate* in the spinal cord. Positioning of the gate, a neurophysiological mechanism, is determined by both the intensity and pattern of stimulation and by the perceiver's state of mind.

gender identity: (2) An individual's sense of being male or female; normally consistent with one's genetic makeup and the way one is treated by parents; may be inconsistent in extreme cases. *See also* sex identity.

gender identity disorder: (13) A sexual disorder that involves intense and persistent distress about one's assigned sex and the desire to be of the opposite sex.

gender permanence: (2, 10) The belief that one is, and always will be, male or female.

general mental facility (g): (12) Charles Spearman's term for the general intelligence that determines how well people do on intelligence tests.

general paresis of the insane (GPI): (13) A mental derangement caused by syphilis.

generalized anxiety: (13) An anxiety disorder characterized by such physical symptoms as high levels of muscle tension (shakiness, trembling, inability to relax) and heightened autonomic activity (sweating, pounding heart, diarrhea); sufferers feel nervous, apprehensive, and have difficulty sleeping and concentrating.

generativity: (10) An attribute of Erik Erikson's seventh stage of psychosocial development; the sense of making a lasting contribution to future generations.

gene: (2) A complex protein structure constituting basic genetic material.

genetic determinism: (2) The belief that individual differences in characteristics are due to genetic variation rather than to environmental influences. *See also* environmental determinism.

genetic epistemology: (9) The name Jean Piaget gave to his theory of development; the study of the growth of knowledge.

genetic transmission: (2) The passage of inherited characteristics from parent to offspring through the genetic material contained in the sex cells. *See also* sexual recombination.

genetic variability: (2) The differential distribution of genes in the individuals of populations.

genital stage: (12) The final stage in Sigmund Freud's theory of psychosexual development. Although at this stage the primary source of sexual energy remains genital, young adults pursue mutual pleasure and express altruism in relationships.

genitourinary tract: (8) The tube through which ejaculate and urine in males and urine in females are transmitted.

genotype: (2) The internal genetic makeup of an organism. *See also* phenotype.

geometric illusion: (4) A line drawing perceived differently from actual shape, size, or orientation.

gerontology: (9) The scientific study of psychological and biological changes that occur with age and the factors that influence the aging process.

Gestalt psychology: (1) An early school of psychology whose motto was "The whole is greater than the sum of its parts."

Gestalt therapy: (14) A therapy developed by psychoanalyst Frederick (Fritz) Perls in reaction against psychoanaylsis; encourages patients to express their feelings honestly and emphasizes the positive aspects of human potential.

gestation period: (8) In pregnancy, the time from conception to birth.

glial cell: (3) A cell of the central nervous system that supports neurons and provides their myelin sheath.

glove anesthesia: (13) A type of conversion hysteria characterized by loss of feeling in the hand not caused by neurological dysfunction.

gonococcus: (8) A contagious bacterium that causes gonorrhea. *See also* gonorrhea.

gonorrhea: (8) The oldest recorded sexually transmitted disease; caused by a contagious bacterium.

grammar: (9) The structure of language by which meaning is conveyed through word order and inflection.

grand-mal seizure: (14) A major seizure involving strong bursts of electrical activity in the brain produced during an epileptic fit or induced by electroconvulsive shock.

group-administered test: (12) A pencil-and-paper version of an intelligence test; usually administered in group sittings.

group norm: (11) The consensus of norms, or standard performances, in a group of individuals. *See also* norm.

group therapy: (14) A form of psychotherapy in which individuals discuss their problems in groups.

growth need: (7) The human motives concerned with maximizing personal potential; includes aesthetic, spiritual, and intellectual motives.

habituation: (5) A primitive form of learning in which the strength or readiness of an unconditioned response decreases with repeated stimulation.

hair cell: (4) The auditory receptor cell, located in the cochlea of the inner ear, that translates the frequency and intensity of sound waves into nerve impulse patterns responsible for the perception of pitch and loudness.

halfway house: (14) A residence for those just released from a prison or a hospital or for those who believe they may require hospitalization, that provides transitional support in adjusting to community life.

hallucination: (13) The illusory perception of objects or events in the absence of the sensory stimulation responsible for their normal perception.

hallucinogen/psychedelic: (3) A drug that dramatically alters thinking, mood, or perception; examples are marijuana, hashish, and mescaline.

halo effect: (12) The tendency to rate people who possess one desirable characteristic high on other desirable characteristics. *See also* horns effect.

head ganglion: (3) The ganglion in the head of a segmented organism that directs the semiautonomous activity of ganglia in other body segments.

heredity: (2) The genetic characteristics transmitted from parents to offspring.

herpes: (8) An incurable virus that produces skin sores; of the five types, Genital Herpes Type II is sexually transmitted.

heterosexuality: (8) Sexual attraction to and/or sexual behavior toward a person of the opposite gender. *See also* homosexuality.

heuristic: (6) A rule-of-thumb approach to problem-solving; examples are means–end analysis and working backward from goal to problem. *See also* algorithm.

hippocampus: (3) A structure in the temporal lobe of the brain; a part of the limbic system involved in learning and memory.

homosexuality: (8) Sexual attraction to and/or sexual behavior toward a person of the same gender. *See also* heterosexuality.

horns effect: (1) The tendency to attribute undesirable characteristics to people who possess other undesirable characteristics. *See also* halo effect.

hue: (4) The characteristic color determined by the wavelength of light.

humanistic approach: (14) A person-centered form of psychotherapy originating from the humanistic school of psychology; emphasizes individual integrity, personal growth, authenticity, self-actualization, trust, empathy, caring, warmth, openness, self-disclosure, and interpersonal honesty.

humanistic psychology: (1) The school of psychology that insists people should be respected as individuals, that society should foster trust, and that the honest communication of feelings can contribute to self-actualization.

Hunt survey: (8) The most comprehensive investigation of the sexual attitudes and behaviors of a large sample of subjects since Alfred Kinsey's reports.

homeostasis: (7) The process of maintaining a stable environment within the body so that biochemical balances can be achieved and biological and social needs can be satisfied.

hypnosis: (3) A technique that induces a temporarily altered state of consciousness characterized by increased suggestibility.

hypochondriasis: (13) A psychological disorder characterized by the persistent belief that one is suffering from a variety of physical disorders when, in fact, one is not.

hypothalamus: (3) A part of the brain's core structure that plays a major role in eating, drinking, sexual activity, the expression of emotion, and the regulation of homeostasis.

hysteria: (1, 13) A conversion disorder that involves such physical symptoms as paralysis and blindness but which has no identifiable organic origin; believed to stem from psychological problems.

iconic memory: (6) A representation of visual input that is relatively unselective and brief. *See also* echoic memory, sensory memory.

id: (12) In Sigmund Freud's theory, the most primitive part of the mind, located entirely in the unconscious; consists of everything that is inherited, particularly instincts, and seeks immediate gratification.

id-dominated primary process thinking: A type of thinking that involves imagining desired objects; characteristically childish, dreamlike, and not oriented to reality.

identity achievement: (10) In James Marcia's theory, the resolution of an identity crisis through reappraisal of values and choices and commitment to self-established goals.

identity diffusion: (10) In James Marcia's theory, the identity status defined by failure to explore choices or to make a commitment. Individuals in this state seem to be "just drifting."

idiosyncracy credits: (11) The credits gained from previous contributions and conformity to group norms that earn the privilege of deviation from group norms without fear of punishment or rejection.

illumination: (6) Graham Wallas' third stage of creativity, in which the creative idea is realized; supposedly preceded by incubation and followed by verification. *See also* incubation, preparation, and verification.

immediacy: (11) In Bibb Latané's theory, the notion that social pressure is more effective the closer it is in space or time.

immediate (proximate) cause: (2) The precipitating factor, as distinct from earlier or prior causes; the cause of behavior typically investigated by psychologists. *See also* ultimate (distal) cause.

implicit theories of personality: (12) Assumptions that people harbor about the degree of association among personality traits.

implosion therapy: (14) A form of therapy in which the therapist repeatedly exposes the client to vivid mental images of a feared stimulus in the safety of the therapist's office until the stimulus loses it's anxiety-producing power and the anxiety is extinguished (implodes).

impossible figure: (4) A figure or object that cannot physically exist in the form it is visually perceived.

imprinting: (6, 10) An organism's rapid attachment to an object, usually its primary caretaker, that typically occurs shortly after birth.

improbable object: (4) A figure or object perceived in a manner unlikely to correspond to reality.

impulsive helping: (11) The spontaneous tendency of bystanders to intervene in emergencies regardless of personal consequences or whether others are present.

incentive: (7) An environmental goal/object that motivates behavior.

incest: (8) A sexual deviation in which the object of sexual desire is a close relative.

inclusive fitness: (2, 10) The sum of an individual's fitness as measured by the total representation of replicas of one's genes in future generations that is promoted both by reproducing and helping kin.

incongruent person: (12) In personality, Carl Roger's term for the opposite of a fully functioning person; a person whose parents set conditions for love.

incubation: (6) Graham Wallas' second stage of creativity; a period during which the creative solution is not pursued consciously. *See also* illumination, preparation, and verification.

independent variable: (1) A variable systematically manipulated during an experiment to reveal its effect on a dependent variable.

indirect perception theory: (4) The traditional and commonly accepted theory that perception is an indirect achievement requiring interpretation of inherently ambiguous stimuli. *See also* direct perception theory.

indirect reciprocity: (10) A system in which individuals who help others are likely to receive help from individuals other than those they help.

indiscriminate social investment: (10) Risking a relatively small amount to help people even when help is not reciprocated.

individual fitness: (2) An individual's reproductive success as measured by the number of offspring who reach maturity.

individual norm: (11) The standard adopted by one who makes a judgment.

individuate: (11) To draw attention to the self; to make self-conscious.

induced compliance: (11) Inducing individuals to behave in ways inconsistent with their attitudes.

induced movement: (4) The mistaken impression of

an object moving across a stationary background that sometimes occurs when an observer views a stationary object against a moving background.

induction: (10) A disciplinary method that involves explaining to children the reasons why their behavior is unacceptable, usually by pointing out how it violates a rule or principle.

inductive reasoning: (6) The drawing of inferences (from knowledge or observation) that go beyond the available evidence. *See also* deductive reasoning.

inferential statistic: (A) An estimate of the likelihood that an error has been made in concluding that the pattern of results observed in a sample reflects the pattern in the population from which the sample was drawn. *See also* descriptive statistic.

inner ear: (4) A recess beyond the middle ear that contains the cochlea and the vestibular mechanism.

insight: (5, 6) The name given by Gestalt psychologists to the sudden understanding of the solution to a problem.

instinct: (12) According to Sigmund Freud, a biological need, urge, or tension that resides in the id and has a source, aim, pressure level, and object.

instinctive drift: (2) The overriding of a conditioned behavior by an innately determined behavioral disposition.

instrumental competence: (10) A cluster of traits consisting of social responsibility, independence, achievement orientation, and vitality that Diana Baumrind has described as the optimal outcome of child rearing.

instrumental conditioning: (5) A form of learning in which a target response is reinforced whenever an organism voluntarily emits it. Unlike operant conditioning, instrumental conditioning focuses on single responses, not on a series of responses.

insufficient deterrence: (11) In the presence of weak external threats, the tendency of individuals to change their attitudes to correspond with their behaviors.

integration: (9, 10) The coordination of functioning; joining units coherently; on a social level, a sense of cohesiveness with others.

intelligence quotient (IQ): (12) Defined as mental age divided by chronological age multiplied by 100; developed by Lewis Terman as a means of reporting intelligence test results with a single score.

intelligence: (12) A concept whose elusive defini-

tions are legion, most of which involve the ability to adapt to the environment, to learn, and to solve problems.

intensity: (4) In vision, the density of photons in a light wave; the primary determinant of perceived brightness. In audition, the pressure exerted by a sound wave; the primary determinant of perceived loudness.

interactionism: (12) The position in social and personality psychology that assumes human behavior results from an interaction between personality traits and situational pressures.

inter-rater reliability: (12) The degree of agreement between two or more raters on the scores they assign to people who have taken the same test.

interaural intensity: (4) The difference in sound-wave intensity reaching the two ears; a cue for sound localization.

interaural time: (4) The difference in arrival time of sound waves reaching the two ears; a cue for sound localization.

interposition: (4) A pictorial cue to relative object depth available when one object partially obscures another in the observer's view.

interval schedule: (5) In learning, a schedule of reinforcement in which a response is reinforced only following a specified delay after the last reinforced response. *See also* ratio schedule.

intimacy: (10) Erik Erikson's sixth stage of psychosocial development, involving the ability to make an emotional commitment to another person in a sharing and loving relationship.

intimate and mutually shared friendship: (10) Robert Selman's final stage in friendship formation, characteristic of late childhood and early adolescence, in which friendship is seen as a means of developing intimacy and mutual support.

intonation: (9) The patterns of rising and falling pitch in spoken language, particularly within sentences.

introjection: (10) The internalization of parental values.

introspection: (1) A psychological technique advocated by early structuralists involving direct perception of conscious mental experience.

invariant sequence: (10) A sequence of stages through which an individual progresses without any reversals or stage-skipping (although it is possible to fixate at one stage).

invertebrate: (2) An animal lacking a spinal column or backbone.

iris: (4) The circular muscle in front of the eye's lens that contracts and expands to accommodate pupillary response; the opening through which light enters the eye.

isolation: (10) Erik Erikson's sixth stage of psychosocial development, involving a sense of being cut off from others caused by inability to develop a loving and sharing relationship.

judgment of responsibility: (10) A judgment about whether an individual is obliged to carry out a moral action.

justification of effort: (11) Motivation to maintain consistency between input and outcome.

kinesics: (2) In nonverbal communication: gestures; postures; movements of the body, limbs, and head; facial expressions; and eye movements.

kinesthetic sense: (4) The sensory system in which receptors in the muscles, tendons, and joints detect the relationship of body parts to one another.

Kinsey reports: (8) Publications of the first large-scale surveys of the sexual attitudes and practices of American men and women, conducted by Alfred Kinsey.

lactation period: (8) The period following birth during which a mother secretes milk from her breasts.

language: (9) A mode of communication that employs symbols to convey meaning.

latent learning: (5) Learning that occurs in the absence of reinforcement and is not evident (is latent) until reinforcement becomes available.

latency period: (12) In Freudian theory, the period following the phallic stage, in which sexual and aggressive urges are subdued.

latent content: (14) Sigmund Freud's term for the wishes underlying the actual events of a dream that are expressed in covert form.

lateral geniculate nucleus (LGN): (3) A grouping of cell bodies in the thalamus that relays information along the main visual pathway.

law of effect: (5) The apparently universal phenomenon wherein responses followed by reinforcement are strengthened and are more likely to occur, and responses not followed by reinforcement are weakened and are less likely to occur. *See also* reinforcement.

L-data: (12) Raymond Cattell's term for the ratings people make of acquaintances.

learned helplessness: (5, 13) An animal's tendency to give up (stop responding) following a series of inescapable and unavoidable shocks or other such aversive stimuli.

learning: (5) A relatively enduring change in behavioral potential as a result of experience or practice.

learning set: (5) Harry Harlow's name for the observation that an organism's ability to solve specific problems improves as more of the same kind of problems are solved; also referred to as learning-to-learn.

lens: (4) The translucent, crystalline body that focuses light entering the eye onto the retina.

lesion: (3) The accidental or disease-related destruction of living tissue; tissue destruction carried out during experimental research or therapy.

level of significance: (A) In inferential statistics, the probability of the null hypothesis being correct; the level established by a psychological researcher is typically .05. *See also* statistically significant.

light: (4) The information carrier that specifies the world's visual properties. *See also* electromagnetic radiation.

light wave: (4) A stream of oscillating energy particles called photons.

limbic system: (3) Brain structures — including the hippocampus, amygdala, and septal area — involved in motivation, emotion, learning, and memory.

lithium carbonate: (14) A psychoactive drug that can be classified as an antipsychotic, antidepressant, or antimanic drug because it reduces psychotic behavior, relieves depression, and calms the agitation associated with manic reactions; works best on people suffering from bipolar or manic-depressive disorders.

lobes: (3) Four areas of the brain's cerebral cortex: frontal, parietal, temporal, and occipital.

longitudinal approach: (9) A research approach in which behavioral changes within a single age group are studied repeatedly over a significant period of time.

long-term memory: (6) A system for storing information and experiences acquired during a lifetime; seemingly unlimited capacity and relatively long-lasting.

long-term potentiation: (3) The relatively long-lasting increased sensitivity of hippocampal neurons following a short burst of electrical stimulation of nearby cells; a process that may be involved in learning and memory.

loudness: (4) The characteristic of sound determined by amplitude of the sound wave.

love-withdrawal: (10) A disciplinary method that involves the explicit or implicit message: "If you do (or do not do) this, I will not love you anymore."

macroneuron: (3) A type of brain cell with relatively long axon and dendrites for transmitting information over long distances. *See also* microneuron, neuron.

magnetic resonance imaging (MRI): (3) A method of imaging any part of the body based on differential magnetization of tissue when the subject part is placed in a weak magnetic field; previously known as nuclear magnetic resonance (NMR).

magnetoencephalogram (MEG): (3) The very weak magnetic field created by the brain's electrical activity. *See also* electroencephalogram (EEG).

maintenance rehearsal: (6) The simple repetition of items being memorized, with no attempt made to relate items to existing information in memory. *See also* elaborative rehearsal.

major depressive syndrome: (13) A state of depression that involves such symptoms as depressed mood, loss of interest and pleasure in activities, loss of energy, slowing of behavior, difficulties in thinking, loss of appetite, problems in sleeping, feelings of worthlessness, and thoughts of death and suicide.

major tranquilizer: (14) See antipsychotic drug.

make-believe play: (9) A type of play in which children transform the physical environment into symbols by engaging in pretend activities and by playing different roles.

manic–depressive disorder: (13) An affective disorder characterized by alternating moods of excitement and elation (manic phase), and despondency and sadness (depressive phase).

manic state: (13) A state of prolonged excitement and high energy in which people talk incessantly, loudly, and rapidly, change topics in midstream, and experience an inflated sense of self-importance.

manifest content: (14) Sigmund Freud's term for the actual events of a dream as described by the patient. *See also* latent content.

marital schism: (13) A marriage state in which both partners are preoccupied with their own severe problems.

marital skew: (13) A marriage state in which one severely disturbed partner dominates the relationship.

masochism: (8) Sexual gratification obtained through subjugation and pain. *See also* sadism.

masturbation: (8) Stimulation of one's own genitals.

means–end analysis: (6) A problem-solving strategy in which the current problem-state is compared with the desired end-state to identify differences that can be eliminated and the means that can be employed to eliminate them.

median: (A) A descriptive statistic measuring central tendency; the value that is both larger and smaller than half the values in a set or distribution of values. *See also* arithmetic mean, mode.

medical model of mental illness: (13) A model of mental disorder that assumes mental disorders are caused by internal, physical, malignant factors.

meditation: (3) A state of extreme relaxation of both mind and body—often achieved by rituals involving muscular control and focused attention—that may involve a diffusion of awareness.

medulla: (3) A central core structure of the brain located at the top of the spinal cord; involved in the control of skeletal muscles and of such internal functions as heart rate, respiration, blood pressure, and body temperature.

memory span: (6) The greatest number of items (numbers, letters, or, more generally, chunks) that can be held in short-term memory without rehearsal for a few seconds at least; typically about seven chunks.

menarche: (9) The first menstrual period.

menopause: (9) The cessation of menstruation in women.

menstrual cycle: (8) The female reproductive cycle that begins (and ends) with discharge (from the body) of the uterine lining that protects unfertilized eggs; the average length in women is 28 days.

menstruation: (8) Cyclical shedding of the uterine lining; in women, approximately every 28 days (except during pregnancy).

mental age: (12) Alfred Binet's concept that refers to the level to which an individual has advanced intellectually, measured by performance typical of a particular age. *See also* intelligence quotient (IQ).

message: (11) The content of a persuasive communication.

meta-analysis: (11) A quantitative synthesis of the results of all research conducted on a specific issue.

metazoa: (2) Multicell animals. *See also* protozoa.

microneuron: (3) A small, later-maturing brain cell more responsive than macroneurons to environmental effects during maturation.

middle ear: (4) A cavity beyond the eardrum that contains the ossicles and one end of the eustachian tube.

mind–body problem: (3) A philosophical issue concerning whether mental activities are necessarily linked to physical activities in the brain.

Minnesota Multiphasic Personality Inventory (MMPI): (12) An objective pencil-and-paper personality inventory employed to assess types of psychopathology.

minor tranquilizers: (14)   *See* antianxiety drugs.

misattribution therapy: (7) A method of treating people who exhibit strong irrational fears that is based on Stanley Schachter's theory of emotion: sufferers are induced to misattribute arousal to sources other than those that trouble them.

mnemonic: (6) A method of improving memory, typically by organizing and associating new information with old information stored in long-term memory.

mode: (A) A descriptive statistic measuring central tendency; the most frequently occurring value in a set or distribution of values. *See also* arithmetic mean, median.

modeling: (5) Learning by imitating the behavior of others.

monist: (3) One who believes there is only one kind of substance or ultimate reality: mind or matter. Material monism asserts that mind is reducible to brain function. *See also* dualist.

monogamy: (8) The reproductive relationship in which one male pairs with one female. *See also* polyandry, polygamy, polygyny.

mood disorder: (13) A psychological disorder characterized by disturbances of mood or affect. The three major mood disorders are mania, depression, and manic–depressive or bipolar disorder.

moon illusion: (4) The mistaken impression that the moon seen on the horizon is larger than the moon seen overhead; possibly due to the influence of distance cues that operate in the former situation but not the latter.

moratorium: (10) In James Marcia's theory, the identity status defined by a rethinking of values and goals with no definite commitment.

motion aftereffect: (4) The mistaken impression that a stationary object is moving that occurs after sustained viewing of motion in the opposite direction; probably due to the satiation of motion detector cells in the visual system.

motion parallax: (4) A distance cue available to a moving observer based on differences in the displacement rate of parts of the retinal image.

motivation: (7) The process of initiating, sustaining, and directing behavior.

motor cortex: (3) A functional division of the cerebral cortex, lying in front of the central fissure, responsible for controlling muscular activity. *See also* association cortex, sensory cortex.

motor skill: (9) An ability or task requiring coordinated bodily movements.

motor system: (3) Components of the central nervous system involved in regulation and coordination of muscular activity. *See also* sensory system.

multiaxial approach: (13) The approach used in the *DSM-III-R* on which clinicians make five kinds of judgment in diagnosing mental disorders.

multiple personality: (13) A dissociative disorder characterized by the existence of two or more well-developed personalities within the same individual.

mutation: (2) A change in the chemical composition of a gene.

mutual respect: (10) As described by Jean Piaget, the moral orientation of older children characterized by reciprocity and cooperation.

myelin sheath: (3) A layer of glial cells that provides a fatty protective covering around the axon of neurons.

nanometer: (4) One-billionth of a meter.

natural selection: (2) The process by which natural environments select those individuals of a species most fit to live in them.

naturalistic observation: (1) A research approach in which naturally occurring behavior is observed, generally in an unobtrusive manner.

need for affiliation: (7) The motivation to be with others.

need for approval: (7) The desire to have the respect and approval of others.

negative reinforcer: (5) In learning, an aversive event (such as an electric shock) whose termination increases the likelihood of occurrence of the response that caused the aversive event to be terminated. *See also* positive reinforcer.

neologism: (13) An invented word.

nerve: (3) A bundle of neural axons forming a tract in the peripheral nervous system.

nervous system: (3, 7) A general term labeling collections of neurons involved in various aspects of the functioning of organisms. *See also* autonomic nervous system (ANS), central nervous system (CNS), peripheral nervous system (PNS).

neural desynchrony: (3) The irregular pattern of the brain's electrical activity in its normal waking state. *See also* neural synchrony.

neural processing: (3) The transmission of electrical signals between neurons during reception and coding of sensory information, cognitive activity, and channeling of commands to muscles and glands.

neural synchrony: (3) The regular pattern of the brain's electrical activity, particularly characteristic of slow-wave sleep. *See also* neural desynchrony.

neuron: (3) One of 100 billion or more nerve cells in the human brain; the basic functional unit of a nervous system with the capacity to propagate electrical impulses.

neurosis: (13) In the former psychiatric diagnostic system *(DSM-II)*, disorders characterized by reasonable contact with reality and high levels of anxiety. *See also* psychosis.

neurotic paradox: (13) The tendency of a phobic reaction to be reinforced when an individual avoids a feared object to reduce fear or anxiety.

neurotransmitter: (3, 13) One of a group of chemicals produced in the brain that mediates transmission of nerve impulses across synapses between neurons. *See also* synapse.

neutral stimulus: (5) In learning, a stimulus that is neutral with respect to an unconditioned response. When first presented, the neutral stimulus elicits an attentive response; it becomes a conditioned stimulus after repeated pairing with the unconditioned stimulus.

night terror: (3) The apparent awakening of a sleeper, usually a child, in a state of great fear; distinguished from a nightmare by failure to remember the experience that caused the fright.

noise: (4) Unpatterned, meaningless sound.

nongonococcal urethritis (NGU): (8) Any inflammation of the urethra not caused by gonococcal bacteria.

norepinephrine: (3, 13) A neurotransmitter whose deficiency may induce depression and whose abundance may induce manic reactions; also believed to be involved in REM sleep.

norm: (11) A widely shared expectation about the appropriateness of behavior in a specific situation.

normal consciousness: (3) The most common state of mental alertness, characterized by an awareness of environmental events.

normal distribution: (A) An idealized, symmetrical, bell-shaped frequency distribution often assumed for statistical purposes to describe the values measured in psychological research.

nucleus: (3) In cell biology, the central part of a cell containing genetic material; a collection of identifiable neurons in the brain. *See also* ganglion.

null hypothesis: (A) The hypothesis that any pattern of research results is due to chance and not to a systematic influence; a statistical straw man that a researcher attempts to shoot down, using data as ammunition, in order to confirm the experimental hypothesis.

number: (11) In Bibb Latané's theory, the number of individuals exerting social pressure on a object of social impact.

nymphomaniac: (8) A woman with abnormal and uncontrollable sexual desires.

object-identity constancy: (9) The perception that an object remains the same despite changes in the angle from which it is viewed. *See also* shape constancy.

object permanence: (9) Understanding the world consists of objects that continue to exist when one is not perceiving them.

object reversal: (4) The alternating perception of objects in a drawing in which contours common to two different objects make the drawing ambiguous. *See also* figure–ground reversal.

objective self-awareness: (11) Self-consciousness; encourages evaluation of behavior in light of internal standards.

obsession: (13) A persistent, recurring thought.

Oedipus complex: (10) In psychoanalytic theory, the conflict experienced by young boys sexually attached to their mothers but fearful of their fathers; resolved by identifying with the father. *See also* Electra complex.

olfactory stimulus: (4, 8) A chemical that activates an organism's sense of smell.

one-way assistance: (10) A feature of Robert Selman's second stage of friendship formation, characteristic of the early school years, in which a friend is important because he or she does specific things that one wants done.

operant conditioning: (5) In learning, a form of instrumental conditioning that focuses on the number or frequency of responses emitted over time and on their pattern rather than on single responses, as in instrumental conditioning.

operation: (9) In Jean Piaget's theory, a reversible action, one that can be returned to its starting point.

operational definition: (1) A definition that specifies the operations or steps taken to measure or observe the term being defined.

optic nerve: (4) A bundle of nerves that carries information concerning the visual scene from the retina to the cortex.

optimal arousal theory: (7) The theory that the best physical and mental performance occurs at an intermediate (optimal) arousal level, with poorer performance occurring at lower or higher arousal levels. *See also* Yerkes-Dodson law.

oral character: (12) According to Sigmund Freud, the character type developed by people who fixate at the oral stage: either oral passive (excessively dependent on others, immature, and insecure) or oral aggressive (sarcastic, biting, and passively hostile.)

oral stage: (12) Sigmund Freud's first stage of psychosexual development, in which pleasure derives from the lips and mouth.

order: (2) In biology, a subdivision in the classification of animals. *See also* primate order.

organic mental disorder: (13) A disorder related to aging or to the ingestion of a toxic substance.

organismic self-regulation: (14) In Gestalt therapy, the sense of wholeness and responsibility necessary to relate fully to others and to behave spontaneously.

organization: (9) In Jean Piaget's theory, the continuous process of refining and integrating every level of thought from sensory-motor to formal-operational.

orgasm: (8) A neuromuscular release of pent-up sexual tension that peaks in the late plateau stage, producing an intense feeling of physical pleasure.

orienting response: An attentional reaction to any unexpected environmental change.

ossicles: (4) Three small bones in the middle ear that translate vibrations of the eardrum into wave motions of the cochlear fluid.

outer ear: (4) The fleshy flap that is the externally visible part of the ear.

oval window: (4) The thin, flexible membrane at the end of the cochlea connected to the ossicles.

overextension: (9) The young child's tendency to use a relatively specific word to refer to a wide class of referents (for example, using the word *dog* to refer to all animals).

overjustification effect: (11) In the presence of a large external reward or incentive, the tendency of individuals to infer that they do not want to engage in the rewarded behavior.

overregularization: (9) Children's misapplication of the grammatical rules governing regular past-tense endings and plurals to irregular forms (for example, applying the past-tense -*ed* to form words like *comed*).

ovulation: (8) In females, the shedding of an egg from the ovary; the stage of the menstrual cycle at which females become receptive to fertilization.

oxytocin: (3) A hormone produced by the hypothalamus, injections of which have been shown to impair performance on tasks requiring memory.

Pacinian corpuscle: (4) A pressure-sensitive receptor cell found in various parts of the body, particularly in deep layers of skin.

pair-bonding: (8) The formation of a social bond between two adults, usually occurring in monogamous species in which two parents are needed to care for offspring.

panic attack: (13) The sudden onset of intense and overwhelming terror and dread.

paralanguage: (2) Informative aspects of speech that do not involve meanings of words and sentences (for example: pitch, loudness, and tempo).

paraphilia: (13) A group of sexual disorders characterized by arousal in response to objects or situations that normally do not evoke arousal and that are inconsistent with mutually affectionate sexual activity.

paraprofessional: (14) One who has undergone special training in dealing with a particular problem and who is associated with a community agency such as a crisis intervention center or rape relief center.

parental investment: (8) In sociobiology, the behavior of a parent toward an offspring that enhances the offspring's reproductive success at a cost to the parent's investment in other offspring.

partial reinforcement effect: (5) In learning, the increased strength of learning—and therefore greater resistance to extinction—of a response reinforced intermittently rather than continuously.

partial reinforcement schedule: (5) In learning, a reinforcement schedule in which some but not all target responses are reinforced.

pedophilia: (8) A sexual deviation in which the object of sexual desire is a child.

perception of uniqueness: (11) The tendency for individuals to assume they are more unusual than they actually are.

perceptual world: (4) The coherent and meaningful environmental experience. *See also* physical world.

perennial monogamy: (8) A reproductive relationship in which one male pairs with one female for life. *See also* annual monogamy.

peripheral nervous system (PNS): (3) The sensory and motor nerves leading into and out of the central nervous system.

periphery: (12) The part of a personality that shows; the outer facade, including behavior.

permissive parenting: (10) A parenting style in which limits are not set, discipline rarely is used, and children are not constrained. *See also* authoritarian parenting, authoritative parenting.

personality: (12) The outer facades that people display and their inner, enduring qualities.

personality disorder: (13) The life-long behavioral patterns viewed as maladaptive by society but not maladaptive by the individual; sometimes called character disorder.

personality inventory: (12) A test used to assess personality that contains statements about attitudes, beliefs, opinions, feelings, and typical behaviors to which test takers respond, usually by indicating the extent to which the statements pertain to them.

personality type: (12) A cluster of associated personality traits. According to Hans Eysenck, there are four basic personality types: introverted, extraverted, stable, and unstable.

perspective: (4) A pictorial cue for distance in which parallel lines receding from the viewer appear to converge.

perspective-taking: (10) Understanding events from the viewpoint of another person.

phallic character: (12) In Freudian theory, the character developed by an adult who fixates at the phallic stage: vain, given to pride, self-assured, and reckless.

phallic stage: (12) Sigmund Freud's third stage of psychosexual development in which the penis becomes the young boy's primary source of pleasure. (Freud based his theory primarily on development in males.)

phenotype: (2) The external, observable characteristics of an organism. *See also* genotype.

pheromone: (8) A substance secreted by an animal that influences the behavior of other animals of the same species through their sense of smell.

phi phenomenon: (4) See apparent movement.

phobia: (13) An intense, persistent, irrational fear of —and desire to avoid—a particular object or situation.

phonology: (9) The rules of a language for combining sounds into words.

photon: (4) An energy particle whose motion creates light waves.

phylogenetic tree: (2) A schematic representation of the evolution of species.

physical world: (4) The objects, surfaces, and events that, through stimulation of the sensory systems, are translated into a perceptual world. *See also* perceptual world.

pictorial cue: (4) Information in a drawing or picture that specifies the depth or distance of the pictured objects and surfaces as if they were three-dimensional representations.

pitch: (4) The characteristic of sound determined by the frequency of the sound wave.

pituitary gland: (3) A gland attached to the base of the brain that secretes a number of hormones, including those that regulate skeletal growth.

place theory: (4) A theory of how sound-wave frequency is translated into perception of pitch; asserts that pitch varies with location of maximum wave action along the basilar membrane. *See also* frequency theory, volley principle.

placebo: (1) In drug studies, a pill that contains no active ingredient; used to determine the extent to which mere expectation of a particular outcome (such as feeling better) makes that outcome more likely to occur.

placing reflex: (9) A reflex response in human infants that occurs during the first few weeks after birth; lifting and placing feet on a flat surface when the infant is held in a vertical position.

plan: (9) In information processing theory, a strategy for responding to an environmental demand.

plasticity: (10) The ability to behave in a variety of ways in the same situation; mediated by learning and higher-level cognitive processes.

plateau phase: (8) An extension of the excitement phase in the sexual response cycle.

playmateship: (10) A feature of Robert Selman's first stage of friendship formation; characteristic of preschoolers.

pleasure principle: (12) In Freudian theory, reducing unpleasant tensions and maintaining a pleasurable state, notwithstanding circumstances and consequences.

polyandry: (8) A reproductive relationship in which one female mates with more than one male. *See also* monogamy, polygamy, polygyny.

polygamy: (8) A reproductive relationship in which a member of one sex mates with more than one member of the opposite sex. *See also* monogamy, polyandry, polygyny.

polygyny: (8) A reproductive relationship in which one male mates with more than one female. *See also* monogamy, polyandry, polygamy.

pons: (4) A structure in the brain's central core that connects to the cerebellum and comprises part of the reticular formation.

population: (1) All the individuals to whom an investigator wishes to generalize research results; the individuals from whom a sample is chosen for study.

position constancy: (4) The perceived stability of the visual world during voluntary eye movement.

positive reinforcer: (5) In learning, any event that increases the likelihood of a response being made again. *See also* negative reinforcer.

positron emission tomography (PET): (3) A method of forming an image of any part of the body based on the differential emission of particles (positrons) from specific bodily regions of varying activity levels.

postconventional level: (10) Lawrence Kohlberg's third level of moral development, including Stages 5 and 6, at which moral reasoning is based on universal principles of justice.

post-decision dissonance reduction: (11) The tendency of people who make a behavioral choice to adjust their attitudes to be consistent with that choice.

postsynaptic neuron: (3) A neuron activated by transmitter substances passing across the synaptic gap between it and a presynaptic neuron.

post-traumatic stress disorder: (13) A psychological disorder that occurs after such traumatic experiences as those induced by war, natural disasters, automobile and airplane crashes, rape, torture, and incarceration.

power assertion: (10) A disciplinary method that involves coercing children to comply by overpowering and intimidating them, typically through the threat or use of physical punishment.

power rape: (8) Rape in which the goal of the rapist is to humiliate, degrade, and hurt the victim.

PQ4R method: (6) A technique for studying material that maximizes the likelihood of later recall: preview; question; read, reflect, recite, and review.

pragmatics: (9) The practical rules for using language appropriately and effectively in social contexts.

preconscious: (12) In Sigmund Freud's psychoanalytic theory, the part of the mind not in awareness but accessible. *See also* unconscious.

preconventional level: (10) Lawrence Kohlberg's first level of moral development, including Stages 1 and 2, in which rules and social expectations are viewed as external to people, and in which individuals believe rules should be obeyed because they are imposed by authorities.

prefrontal lobotomy: (14) The first and best known psychosurgical procedure to sever the nerve tracts that connect the brain's frontal lobes to the structures responsible for emotions. It is no longer performed.

premarital sex: (8) Sexual relations before marriage.

premise: (6) In deductive reasoning, one of two or more propositions from which a conclusion is drawn.

preoperational stage: (9) In Jean Piaget's theory, the second stage of cognitive development — lasting from approximately the second year to six years of age — involving representational intelligence.

preparation: (6) The first of three typical problem-solving stages at which a representation of the problem is established and a plan of attack is developed. *See also* illumination, incubation, and verification.

preservation instincts: (12) According to Sigmund Freud, instincts that promote the survival of individuals and the species.

presynaptic neuron: (3) A nerve cell that generates a neural impulse by means of the passage of neurotransmitters across the synaptic gap separating it from a postsynaptic neuron.

primary affect: (7) A basic and elementary emotion; by most accounts: happiness, sadness, fear, anger, surprise, or disgust.

primary drive: (7) See primary motive.

primary mental ability: (12) L. L. Thurstone's term for one of the seven separate mental abilities that constitute intelligence.

primary motive: (7) The desire to satisfy a primary need.

primary need: (7) A state of physical tension caused by deprivation of such provisions as food, water, warmth, and sleep.

primary process thinking: (12) According to Sigmund Freud, a type of thinking that involves forming a mental image of an object that will satisfy a drive; not bound by realistic constraints.

primary reinforcer: (5) A stimulus that is innately reinforcing when satisfying a primary need such as hunger, thirst, sex, and the avoidance of or escape from pain. *See also* conditioned reinforcer.

primary retardation: (12) Genetically determined mental retardation. *See also* secondary retardation.

primate order: (2) A group of mammals that includes human beings and — in order of decreasing similarity to humans — the great apes (chimpanzees, gorillas, orangutans), gibbons, old world monkeys, new world monkeys, tree shrews, lemurs, and tarsiers.

prime: (7) Ross Buck's term for a biologically based primary motivational/emotional system that has evolved with the basic role of bodily adaptation and maintenance of homeostasis.

principle of conservation: (9) The understanding that basic properties of objects (for example: weight, volume, number, area) remain unchanged when the superficial appearance of objects is altered.

principle of proportionality: (9) In Jean Piaget's theory, a concept acquired during the formal operations stage involving an understanding of the logical relationship between two concepts (for example, weight and volume).

private self-awareness: (11) Consciousness of one's self that, when lost, may lead to deindividuation. *See also* public self-awareness.

problem in living: (13) In Thomas Szasz's theory, a type of inability to adapt to societal demands that is labeled mental disorder.

problem-solving: (6) The application of thought and action to the achievement of a specific goal.

process schizophrenia: (13) A type of schizophrenia distinguished from reactive schizophrenia on the basis of the length of time spent in the prodromal phase; behavior typically begins to deteriorate gradually, with the individual becoming increasingly ineffective.

prodromal stage: (13) The first phase in the development of schizophrenia — which may extend from a few weeks to several years — in which victims become increasingly withdrawn, eccentric, emotionally flat, bizarre, and ineffective.

projective test: (8, 12) A personality test — such as the Sentence Completion Test, the Thematic Apperception Test, and the Rorschach (ink blot) Test — that employs ambiguous stimuli and is believed to evoke projections of unconscious needs and desires.

promiscuity: (8) Frequent and indiscriminate sexual relations with different partners.

proof: (1) Argument that establishes a proposition as correct or true. *See also* confirmation.

propositional memory: (6) A proposed memory form in which information is stored in networks that link propositions, as distinct from images and verbal representations. *See also* dual code theory.

protozoa: (2) Single-cell animals. *See also* metazoa.

proxemics: (3) In nonverbal communication, such factors as the distance between sender and receiver.

proximity: (4) Gestalt principle of perceptual organization that describes the tendency to group elements on the basis of closeness in space.

psychiatric nurse: (14) A nurse who has undergone special training in the care of mental patients.

psychiatric social worker: (14) One who possesses a Master of Social Work degree and who typically attends to psychological problems related to the family and community.

psychiatrist: (14) A medical doctor who has undergone postgraduate training (called a residency) in the treatment of mental disorders.

psychoactive drug: (3, 14) A drug that affects the brain and mind.

psychoactive substance-use disorder: (13) A disorder defined by a dependence on drugs that seriously disrupts the victim's life.

psychoanalysis: (1, 14) Initially developed by Sigmund Freud, a theory of personality and technique of psychotherapy that involves recognition of unconscious thoughts, feeling, needs, and conflicts.

psychoanalyst: (14) A psychotherapist, usually a psychiatrist, who has undergone training at a psychoanalytic institute and has undergone psychoanalysis.

psychoanalytic model of psychological disorder: (13) Sigmund Freud's model of mental disorders that assumes they are caused by internal psychological factors usually associated with defenses against repressed wishes and desires.

psychoanalytic psychotherapy: (1) A method developed by Sigmund Freud for treating psychological disorders based on the technique of free association and dream analysis; the goal is to make the unconscious conscious.

psychodrama: (14) A form of group therapy in which members play the roles of important characters in members' lives, acting out significant interactions.

psychogenic amnesia: (13) A psychological disorder involving a partial or total relapse in memory for which no physical cause can be found; typically associated with extreme psychological stress.

psychological androgyny: (10) Possession of both feminine and masculine personality traits.

psychological representativeness: (1) The basis for subjective judgments on the probability that events will occur; insensitive to variation in sample size and includes a biased view of randomness.

psychology: (1) The scientific study of the mind and of behavior.

psychopharmacology: (3) The study of drugs that affect behavior and/or consciousness by altering the chemical functioning of the central nervous system.

psychosis: (13) In *DSM-II*, a severe mental disorder in which thinking and emotion are so impaired that there is a loss of contact with reality. *See also* neurosis.

psychosocial theory: (10) Erik Erikson's theory of personality development in which each of eight stages is marked by a major crisis or critical issue.

psychosurgery: (14) The destruction of brain tissues — not themselves necessarily diseased — with the intent of blunting severely disturbed thoughts, behaviors, or emotions.

psychotherapy: (14) The treatment of psychological problems with psychological techniques.

public self-awareness: (11) The sense that one is being observed and will be held accountable for one's actions. *See also* private self-awareness.

punishment: (5) In learning, an event that reduces the probability a response will reoccur.

pupil: (4) The opening formed by the iris through which light enters the eye.

Q-data: (12) Raymond Cattell's term for individual self-ratings.

Q-sort: (12) A set of cards (usually 100), each containing a description of a personality characteristic. Raters are required to organize the cards from least characteristic descriptions to those most characteristic of the person being assessed.

rape: (8) Forced sexual relations with an unwilling partner.

rape trauma syndrome: (8) The syndrome of a victim's reaction to rape, with acute and reorganization phases.

rapid eye movement (REM): (3) Closed-eye movement characteristic of a period of intense EEG activity and bodily immobility occurring during sleep. Vivid dreams are usually reported by a person wakened during REM sleep.

ratio schedule: (5) In learning, a reinforcement schedule based on the number of emitted responses. Reinforcement occurs only after a specified number of target responses have been emitted since the last reinforced response. *See also* interval schedule.

rational-emotive therapy: (14) Albert Ellis' therapy based on the idea that the primary source of psychological disorder lies in the ego, or rational processes, and involves fallacious assumptions about the self.

reactive schizophrenia: (13) A disorder that usually strikes relatively well-adjusted people in early adulthood; differs from process schizophrenia in that the prodromal phase is typically much shorter, as is the time to recovery.

reasoning by analogy: (6) A set of techniques for producing creative solutions to problems; based on the use of personal, direct, symbolic, or fantasy-related analogies that make the familiar strange.

receiver: (11) The intended object of a communication.

receptive field: (4) A property of a neuron in the visual system; the area of the retina that, when appropriately stimulated, leads to the firing of a neuron.

receptor: (4) A specialized neuron in a sensory system; translates stimulus energy into nerve impulses.

reciprocal altruism: (10) A system of interaction in which individuals who help others are thereby more likely to receive help in return.

reciprocity: (9) In Jean Piaget's theory, a form of reversibility that involves understanding that a change in one dimension is compensated by a change in another dimension.

reconstructed memory: (6) Recall that does not faithfully replicate the original information but is modified by assumptions about what the information should be.

reflection: (14) A technique employed in client-centered therapy, in which the therapist restates what the client has said or the emotional meanings behind the statements.

reflexive behavior: (9) An automatic, involuntary, specific response triggered by a specific stimulus.

refraction: (4) The bending of light waves as they pass from one medium to another medium of different density.

refractory period: (8) In sexual behavior, the time after ejaculation during which ejaculation cannot be repeated.

rehearsal: (6) Attending to items recently committed to memory; a common method for transferring information from short-term to long-term memory.

reinforcement: (5) In learning, the presence of a reinforcer following an appropriate response. *See also* negative reinforcer, positive reinforcer.

reinforcer: (5) In learning, a stimulus whose presentation (positive reinforcer) or termination (negative reinforcer) increases the likelihood a response will be made again.

reliability: (12) The extent to which a test produces the same results when given to the same people at different times or in different forms, or when scored by different people. *See also* validity.

representative sample: (1) A group of subjects who possess characteristics representative of all subjects like them (the population).

reproductive fitness: (8) A measure of evolutionary success assessed by the number of offspring an individual contributes to ensuing generations.

reproductive rate: (8) The rate at which a species reproduces.

residual phase: (13) The third phase in the development of schizophrenia, in which victims behave in much the same way as in the earlier prodromal phase; behavior is significantly less bizarre than in the active phase.

resistance: (14) According to Sigmund Freud, employing defenses to avoid dealing with threatening thoughts and feelings during psychotherapy.

resistance to extinction: (5) A measure of learning strength based on how long (how many trials) it takes to extinguish a learned response; the longer it takes, the higher the resistance to extinction and the stronger the original learning.

resolution phase: (8) The stage in the sexual response cycle that follows orgasm or ejaculation; during this phase the body returns to a relaxed state.

response bias: (12) A systematic tendency to make certain incorrect responses, such as the halo effect and yea-saying.

reticular formation: (3) A system of nuclei running through the core of the brain that controls arousal level.

retina: (4) A layer of light-sensitive cells lining the eye's interior surface. *See also* cone, rod.

retinal image: (4) The two-dimensional representation on the retina of the momentary scene viewed by the eye.

retrieval: (6) The process of transferring information from long-term memory to short-term memory.

rhodopsin: (4) The purple-colored pigment in retinal rod cells that is bleached in the photochemical process of responding to light and that is restored in the absence of light.

rigidity: (6, 11) In problem-solving, a block that occurs when the attempted solution is based on a strategy that was successful in the past with similar problems but does not work with the problem at hand; in group processes, a behavioral style characterized by inflexibility.

rod: (4) A receptor cell of the visual system primarily responsible for peripheral and dim-light vision. *See also* cone, retina.

rooting reflex: (9) An early reflex response of human infants evoked by touching their cheek; includes head turning and attempts at sucking.

Rorschach inkblot test: (12) Herman Rorschach's projective test in which people are shown ten inkblots and asked to describe what they see in them.

sadism: (8) Sexual gratification obtained through infliction of pain and subjugation of victim. *See also* masochism.

sadistic rapist: (8) A rapist who must hurt the victim in order to experience sexual excitement.

safety need: (7) The need to avoid pain and injury, balanced by the desire to seek excitement and stimulation.

sample survey: (1) A collection of information about the attitudes, opinions, beliefs, behaviors, or intentions of a sample of people that represents — and therefore enables one to predict these characteristics in — the population from which the sample was drawn.

saturation: (4) The degree of color purity. The broader the band of wavelengths represented in a light patch, the less saturated it appears.

scattergram: (A) A graphical representation of the association between two variables.

schema: (6) In cognition, organized structures of knowledge stored in memory that give meaning to new information and help individuals remember it.

scheme: (9) In Jean Piaget's theory, an organized pattern of behavior, or potential to behave in a specific way, repeated and applied to new objects and situations.

schizophrenia: (13) A group of mental disorders characterized by loss of contact with reality and abnormalities in attention, thinking, perception, emotional reactions, motor behavior, and social relations.

schizophrenogenic: (13) Causing schizophrenia.

schizotaxia: (13) Paul Meehl's term for an inherited disposition toward schizophrenia.

schizotypy: (13) Paul Meehl's term for a schizoid personality.

scholastic aptitude test (SAT): (12) A widely used aptitude test that assesses academic knowledge — especially vocabulary, mathematics, and general information.

sclera: (4) The tough white coat that covers most of the eyeball's surface.

secondary drive: (7) An aroused state caused by deprivation of a learned rather than a basic need.

secondary motive: (7) A learned rather than a primary motive that is capable of initiating goal-directed behavior.

secondary need: (7) See secondary motive.

secondary process thinking: (12) In Freudian theory, such intellectual abilities as perception, reasoning, and memory that people employ to satisfy their needs in effective and socially acceptable ways.

secondary reinforcer: (5) See conditioned reinforcer.

secondary retardation: (12) Retardation produced by brain injury. *See also* primary retardation.

secondary sexual characteristics: (8, 9) Physical characteristics appropriate to one's sex that appear in humans during puberty (for example: facial hair in males and breasts in women).

secular trend: (9) A systematic change in an attribute — such as age of onset of menstruation — characteristic of the population as a whole.

secure attachment: (10) A form of attachment in which the infant explores from the secure base of the caregiver and actively seeks contact or interaction upon reunion.

self-actualization: (7, 12) Striving to realize one's full inherent potential; considered by Abraham Maslow, Carl Rogers, and others as the ultimate goal of human development.

self-control program: (14) A program based on the principles of operant conditioning employed by troubled people to control their own reinforcement.

self-efficacy: (12, 14) Albert Bandura's term for the sense of control individuals feel over the outcomes in their lives.

self-fulfilling prophecy: (12) The expectation that a future event will occur that makes the event occur.

self-reinforcement: (12) Reinforcement experienced by rewarding and punishing oneself.

self-serving bias: (11) The tendency to attribute the unexpected successes of others to external factors such as luck, but to take credit for one's own successes; the tendency to attribute the failures of others to dispositional factors, but to attribute one's own failures to situational factors.

semantic generalization: (5) The type of stimulus generalization in which responses are made to events similar in meaning to a previously reinforced event.

semantics: (9) The representation of meaning in language.

semicircular canals: (4) Three fluid-filled tubes, aligned at right angles and located above the cochlea of the ear. Hair cells in the canals detect rotary motion of the head.

sensitive period: (2, 10) Generally, a period during development when the organism is particularly ready to acquire certain behaviors and optimally prepared to develop in particular ways that may be more difficult to learn at some other time during development. Also referred to as optimal period.

sensitization: (5) A primitive form of learning consisting of a stronger response or readiness to respond that occurs after an organism has encountered a biologically important stimulus.

sensory cortex: (3) The part of the cerebral cortex that receives and processes input from the sensory system. *See also* association cortex, motor cortex.

sensory deprivation: (7) A drastic reduction in overall levels of sensory stimulation — especially meaningful patterns of sensory input — that, if protracted, may lead to severe disorientation, emotional disturbances, and hallucinations.

sensory memory: (6) The information-processing stage at which unanalyzed representations of sensory input are stored for brief periods. *See also* echoic memory, iconic memory.

sensory-motor stage: (9) In Jean Piaget's theory, the period in which infants' knowledge of the world is based on their sensory experiences and physical interactions with the environment.

sensory preconditioning: (5) A form of learning in which, without reinforcement, animals associate two neutral (sensory) stimuli that regularly occur together.

sensory system: (4) A physiological mechanism that translates physical energy changes into nerve impulse patterns that form the basis of sensory and perceptual experiences.

sentence completion test: (12) A test consisting of several incomplete sentences that respondents are asked to complete with the first answer that comes to mind.

septal nuclei: (3) The part of the brain's limbic system in which electrical stimulation appears to induce intense pleasure.

seriate: (9) In Jean Piaget's theory, ordering objects serially along a dimension such as number or height.

serotonin: (3, 13) A neurotransmitter in the brain associated both with slow-wave sleep and with manic and depressive disorders.

sex education: (8) Formal instruction on sexual matters.

sex (gender) identity: (10) The sense that one is male or female (and all that such an identity entails).

sex role: (8, 10) The attitudes and behaviors a society considers appropriate for individuals of each sex.

sex-role stereotype: (10) A set of oversimplified assumptions about characteristics believed to differentiate males and females.

sex-typed identity: (10) *See* sex identity.

sex typing: (10) The process through which children learn they are male or female and how to behave in ways appropriate to their gender.

sexual deviation: (8) A sexual practice that deviates from cultural norms.

sexual disorder: (13) A disorder characterized by either arousal in response to sexual objects or situations not normally arousing, or by sexual inhibitions.

sexual dysfunction: (13) A sexual disorder characterized by sexual inhibitions and deficiencies in responses that normally occur during sexual arousal and intercourse (for example: impotence, frigidity, and premature ejaculation).

sexual guilt: (8) The expectation of self-induced punishment for approaching or thinking about sex.

sexual imagery: (8) The mental imagery of sexually arousing stimuli; sexual fantasies.

sexual recombination: (2) The combining of genetic material from two partners in sexual reproduction to produce genetically unique offspring. *See also* genetic transmission.

sexual reproduction: (8) Reproduction by union of male and female sex cells (gametes), wherein each individual transmits 50% of his or her genetic material to the offspring. *See also* asexual reproduction.

sexual script: (8) A sequence of acceptable behaviors in a familiar setting.

sexually transmitted disease: (8) A disease transmitted through sexual activity.

shading: (4) See shadow.

shadow: (4) A cue to depth in the visual scene based on blocking the sun's light. The corresponding cue in drawings is shading.

shape constancy: (4, 9) The tendency to see an object as having the same shape regardless of the point from which it is viewed. *See also* object-identity constancy.

shaping: (5, 14) In learning, the development of a novel response by reinforcing behaviors increasingly similar to the desired response.

shell shock: (13) A condition suffered by combat soldiers that involves a dazed or shock-like state.

short-term memory: (6) The information-processing

stage to which selected items from sensory memory are transferred; a limited capacity, short duration storage that accommodates the contents of conscious awareness.

similarity: (4) The Gestalt principle of perceptual organization that involves grouping elements of a visual pattern on the basis of their similarity.

simple phobia: (13) An irrational fear of specific objects or situations. *See also* complex phobia.

simultaneous conditioning: (5) In learning, a classical conditioning procedure in which the onset and offset of the conditioned and unconditioned stimuli occur simultaneously.

single-lens eye: (4) A type of mammalian eye in which a single lens focuses light onto the retina.

16PF: (12) Raymond Cattell's personality inventory consisting of 100 items (for example: "I like parties") inviting a *yes* or *no* response.

size constancy: (4, 9) The tendency to see an object as being the same size regardless of the distance from which it is viewed.

Skinner box: (5) B. F. Skinner's controlled environment equipped to record the effect of different reinforcement schedules on the bar-pressing responses of rats and pigeons.

slow-wave sleep: (3) Sleep stages 1 – 4 in which the brain waves are of large amplitude and low frequency, reflecting neural synchrony.

smell prism: (4) Hans Henning's early model of smell in which the odors of violet, hydrogen sulphide, lemon, nutmeg, tar, and balsam were represented by the six points of the prism.

social cognition: (11) A social psychology research area concerned with how individuals think about social issues and how they come to understand the complex social world in which they live.

social deviation model: (13) The model of psychological disorder that suggests the names we give to psychological disorders are labels for behaviors that violate society's social norms.

social facilitation: (11) A beneficial effect on performance caused by the presence of others. *See also* social inhibition.

social impact: (11) In Bibb Latané's theory, changes in physiological states, emotions, cognitions, values, and behavior that result from the real, implied, or imagined presence or actions of other individuals.

social influence: (11) Factors that lead to behavioral or attitudinal changes in an individual due to the presence of others (for example: bystander intervention, compliance, conformity, and obedience).

social inhibition: (11) A detrimental effect on performance caused by the presence of others. *See also* social facilitation.

social learning: (5) The acquisition of behaviors through social experiences, especially modeling.

social phobia: (13) A generalized fear of people.

socialization: (10) The process through which children internalize societal norms and values and learn to behave in accordance with them.

sociobiology: (2) An elaboration of the theory of evolution whose central construct is inclusive fitness.

somatic system: (3) The nervous system composed of neurons that carry information from receptors in the skin, tendons, and muscles to the central nervous system and that transmit instructions from the brain to skeletal muscles.

somatoform disorder: (13) A psychological disorder characterized by the belief that one has a physical ailment that, in fact, one does not have.

sound: (4) Auditory information.

sound localization: (4) The ability to determine the direction from which a sound originates.

sound wave: (4) Cyclic changes in pressure, caused by vibration of a solid object, that radiate through a surrounding medium (typically air).

source: (11) The individual conveying information, whose effectiveness depends on his/her power, attraction, and credibility.

source trait: (12) In Raymond Cattell's theory, one of 15 – 20 traits identified by factor-analyzing surface traits; considered the fundamental building block of personality.

specific mental capability: (12) Charles Spearman's term for specific abilities that cause people to perform better on some tasks than on others.

speech spectogram: (4) The distribution over time of the frequencies represented in sound waves generated by speech.

split-brain patient: (3) One who has had the corpus callosum of the brain surgically severed, creating two independently functioning cerebral hemispheres.

split-half reliability: (12) The comparability produced between two sets of scores when test performance is divided (for example, into odd-numbered and even-numbered items).

spontaneous recovery: (5, 14) In learning, reemergence following a rest period of a classically conditioned response that was previously extinguished. In abnormal psychology, recovery from a psychological disorder without psychotherapy.

stagnation: (10) In Erik Erikson's seventh stage of psychosocial development, feelings of self-indulgence, depression, and a sense that little matters any more.

standard deviation: (A) A descriptive statistic that measures the dispersion of a set or distribution of values.

standardize: (12) To obtain a representative sample of test scores so that an individual score can be compared to a norm.

Stanford-Binet intelligence scale: (12) The Binet-Simon intelligence test, as revised by Lewis Terman for use in North America.

state-dependent recall: (6) Recall in a physiological state (for example, sober or inebriated) similar to that in which a memory originally was established; typically superior to recall in a dissimilar state. *See also* context-dependent recall.

statistically significant: (A) The inference that a pattern of results is reliable and not due to chance or random error. *See also* level of significance.

stereogram: (4) A pair of pictures or drawings taken or rendered from slightly different viewpoints that, when fused, produce the impression of depth normally achieved when viewing the scene with two eyes. *See also* binocular disparity.

stereoscope: (4) A device that presents to each eye a picture or drawing of a scene that corresponds to the image that would have been received by an observer looking at the scene; thus introducing binocular disparity as a cue to depth in viewing two-dimensional representations of scenes.

stereotype: (12) An overgeneralized cognitive representation of the personality traits or physical attributes believed to be possessed by all members of a class or group of people.

stimulus control: (5) In learning, the control exerted by a specific stimulus in determining the occurrence of a learned response; typically measured by the total number of responses emitted during extinction in the presence of the stimulus. *See also* discriminative stimulus, stimulus generalization.

stimulus generalization: (5) In learning, the tendency to give the conditioned or target response in the presence of stimuli similar but not identical to the conditioned stimulus or the stimulus present during reinforcement. *See also* discriminative stimulus, stimulus control.

stimulus substitution: (5) In learning, the classical conditioning assumption that a bond or association is formed between the conditioned and unconditioned stimuli such that after conditioning occurs, the conditioned stimulus acts as a substitute for the unconditioned stimulus. *See also* expectancy.

strange situation: (10) Mary Ainsworth's technique in which a baby is exposed to a stranger in a series of eight increasingly direct ways.

strength: (11) In Bibb Latané's theory, increased effectiveness of social pressure due to an individual's ability to affect the fate of others; associated with social status, attractiveness, and personal power.

stroboscopic movement: (4) See apparent movement.

structuralism: (1) The first major school of psychology; advocated studying the immediate contents of the conscious mind through introspection.

subjective contour: (4) A contour not physically present in certain stimulus patterns that gives rise to perception of the shape outlined by the contour.

subjective probability: (6) An intuitive rather than objective estimate of the probability an event will occur.

subtractive color mixture: (4) The principle governing the mixing of paints; when paints of complementary color are mixed, the resultant paint is black. *See also* additive color mixture.

sucking reflex: (9) A reflex response in human infants that involves sucking on objects placed in the mouth.

surroundedness: (4) A primary determinant of the parts of a pattern seen as figure or ground; a figure is typically enclosed by a contour that separates it from the surrounding ground.

superego: (10, 12) In Sigmund Freud's division of the personality, the part of the psyche that corresponds to the conscience.

surface trait: (12) In Raymond Cattell's theory, one of

a cluster of 40 or so traits identified by determining the correlations among observable behaviors.

sweet, bitter, salty, sour: (4) The four pure tastes.

symbolic communication: (2) A means of communication, such as language, that employs symbols to represent objects, events, properties and relationships.

symptom substitution: (14) The appearance of other symptoms when particular symptoms are extinguished or suppressed.

synapse: (3) The minute gap between the axon endings of one neuron and the dendrite or cell body of an adjacent neuron. *See also* neurotransmitter.

synaptic gap: (3) *See* synapse.

syncretic cognition: (7) Ross Buck's speculative term for labeling nonlinear, holistic, nonverbal, unconscious, spontaneous, and indirect types of cognitive activity based in the right hemisphere. *See also* analytic cognition.

syndrome: (13) A reliable pattern of symptoms.

syntax: (9) The language rules for combining words to form acceptable and appropriate sentences.

syphilis: (8) A sexually transmitted disease caused by a spirochete, a spiral-shaped bacterium.

systematic desensitization: (14) The process of extinguishing a maladaptive response by substituting an adaptive response, usually relaxation, in the presence of the stimulus that elicits the maladaptive response.

systems approach: (14) A form of therapy that focuses on the family as a system—each member influencing the behavior of all other members—and on the mutually interacting and supporting roles that family members develop.

T-data: (12) Raymond Cattell's term for information derived from objective psychological tests.

T-group: (14) Kurt Lewin and his colleagues' name for *training groups,* an early type of self-analytic encounter group.

tactile stimulation: (8) Stimulation of an organism's sense of touch.

taste bud: (4) A bumpy receptor cell of the taste system clustered on the upper surface of the tongue.

tectorial membrane: (4) A tissue flap that rests on the tips of the hair cells in the cochlea.

telegraphic speech: (9) The manner in which children of approximately two years of age combine words

to convey meaning, omitting such nonessential, connecting words as articles and prepositions.

telephone hotline: (14) A phone-in service staffed by trained listeners for people experiencing an acute crisis.

temporary remission: (14) The transient improvement in an individual suffering from a disorder.

terminal drop: (9) The rapid decline in mental abilities a few months or years before death.

test–retest reliability: (12) The extent to which the same test produces the same pattern of scores when given to the same individuals on two different occasions.

testosterone: (8) A male hormone secreted by the testes.

texture gradient: (4) A depth cue in which nearby parts of a surface appear more coarsely textured than more distant parts.

thalamus: (3) A structure located in the brain's central core that relays information from the various sense organs (except the nose) to the cortex.

thematic apperception test (TAT): (12) A projective test in which the respondent is asked to create a story about all or some of 20 black-and-white pictures.

theory of self-perception: (11) Darryl Bem's theory that individuals infer their attitudes from their behavior.

theta rhythm: (3) Electrical brain activity of low frequency (4–7 cycles per second) arising from the vicinity of the hippocampus; prominent when memories are being established. *See also* alpha rhythm, beta rhythm.

third factor: (1) In correlational research, a variable whose changing value is responsible for the observed association between two other variables. *See also* confounding variable.

timbre: (4) The characteristic quality of complex tones produced by a musical instrument.

tip-of-the-tongue phenomenon: (6) The feeling that one knows but cannot immediately recall a piece of information.

tit-for-tat reciprocity: (10) The strategy of instigating an initial helping response, but continuing to help only those who help in return.

token economy: (14) An application of operant conditioning, used in such institutions as mental hospitals and reform schools, in which patients are given tokens that can be exchanged for privileges or desired goods when they behave in desirable ways.

trace conditioning: (5) In learning, a classical conditioning procedure in which the onset of the unconditioned stimulus occurs after the offset of the conditioned stimulus.

trait-rating approach: (12) The approach to personality assessment based on the direct rating of personality traits in self and others.

transactional analysis: (14) A technique derived from Freudian psychoanalysis that explains interpersonal conflicts in terms of three aspects of each individual's personality: the parent (superego), the adult (ego), and the child (id).

transference: (14) In psychoanalysis, unconsciously transferring emotions (especially love) felt for people in one's past (especially parents) to one's psychotherapist.

transitional period: (9) In Jean Piaget's theory, the period during which a child changes from one developmental stage to the next.

transmitter substance: (3) See neurotransmitter.

transsexuality: (8) Persistent discomfort and sense of inappropriateness with one's assigned sex.

transvestism: (8) A form of sexual deviance in which a man is aroused by wearing women's clothing.

trephining: (13) The early nonmedical procedure for cutting or drilling a large hole in the skull to release an evil spirit.

twin study: (2) A comparison of characteristics of children who are fraternal twins or identical twins, raised together or apart, designed to compare genetic and environmental influences on the measured characteristics. *See also* adoption study.

ultimate (distal) cause: (2) The evolutionary origin of a behavior, as distinct from the precipitating factor; more of interest to sociobiologists than psychologists. *See also* immediate (proximate) cause.

unconditional positive regard: (12, 14) Carl Rogers' term for support and love not dependent on conditions of worth.

unconditioned response (UR): (5) In learning, an innately determined response automatically elicited by an unconditioned stimulus.

unconditioned stimulus (US): (5) In learning, a stimulus that elicits an unconditioned response automatically, without prior learning.

unconscious: (12) In Sigmund Freud's psychoanalytic theory, the level of the mind that lies outside awareness and typically is inaccessible. *See also* preconscious.

unilateral respect: (10) As described by Jean Piaget, the moral orientation of young children characterized by awe of adults and obedience to authority.

validity: (12) The extent to which a test actually measures what it claims to measure. *See also* reliability.

variable schedule: (5) In learning, a reinforcement schedule in which reinforcement is delivered after either a variable interval or a variable number of responses since the last reinforced response. *See also* fixed schedule.

variance: (A) A descriptive statistic that represents the dispersion of a set or distribution of values; the square of the standard deviation.

vasocongestion: (8) An accumulation of blood in the blood vessels of a specific bodily region, especially the genitals; causes erection in males.

vasopressin: (3) A hormone produced by the hypothalamus to regulate the body's retention of water; also known to improve learning and retention in a wide variety of tasks.

verification: (6) Graham Wallas' fourth stage of the creative process, at which the created solution is checked. *See also* illumination, incubation, and preparation.

vertebrate: (2) An animal possessing a spinal column or backbone.

vestibular mechanism: (4) *See* semicircular canals.

vestibular sense: (4) The sensory system that detects changes in the position of the head and body.

vicarious reinforcement: (12) Reinforcement experienced by observing others being rewarded and punished.

visual cliff: (9) An apparatus used to determine whether human infants and young animals respond to visual cues signaling a drop-off.

visual threshold: (4) The least amount of light that can be detected; a measure of dark adaptation.

volley principle: (4) A modification of the frequency theory of pitch perception in which, for relatively low frequencies of sound waves, groups of neurons fire with every second, third (and so on) peak of a sound wave. *See also* frequency theory, place theory.

voyeurism: (8) Achieving sexual gratification from observing people who would be offended if they knew they were being watched.

walking reflex: (9) A reflex response in human infants that occurs during the first few weeks after birth; involves walking movements when the infant is held in a vertical position on a flat surface.

wavelength: (4) The distance between successive peaks of a light wave; determines the experience of color. *See also* frequency.

Wechsler adult intelligence scale (WAIS-R): (12) The most widely used adult intelligence test, consisting of twelve subtests of which half assess verbal abilities and half assess nonverbal abilities.

Wechsler intelligence scale for children (WISC-R): (12) Wechsler's intelligence test for children.

weighted averaging model: (12) An averaging model of impression formation in which certain traits exert a greater effect than others on overall impressions.

white light: (4) Light containing a mixture of wavelengths. Because no one wavelength predominates, the light has no hue or color.

Whorfian hypothesis: (9) The hypothesis that language determines thought: people cannot make distinctions for which they have no words.

yea-saying/nay-saying: (12) The tendency for people to agree (or to disagree) with whatever question they are asked.

Yerkes-Dodson law: (7) The principle proposed by two early psychologists that people are motivated to optimize mental and physical performance by keeping arousal at an intermediate level. *See also* optimal arousal theory.

REFERENCES

Abelson, R. P. (1972). Are attitudes necessary? In B. T. King & E. McGinnies (Eds.), *Attitudes, conflict and social change*. New York: Academic Press. **563**

Abramson, L. Y., Seligman, M. E. P., & Teasdale, J. D. (1978). Learned helplessness in humans: Critique and reformulation. *Journal of Abnormal Psychology, 87,* 49–74. **231, 701**

Abramson, P. R., & Handschumacher, I. W. (1978). The Mosher Sex Guilt Scale and the college population: A methodological note. *Journal of Personality Assessment, 42,* 635. **373**

Abramson, P. R., Michalak, P., & Alling, C. (1977). Perceptions of parental sex guilt and the sexual behavior and arousal of college students. *Perceptual and Motor Skills, 45,* 337–338. **372**

Ackerknecht, E. S. (1968). *History of psychology.* New York: Hafner. **663, 730**

Adams, H. E., Tollison, C. S., & Carson, T. P. (1981). Behavior therapy with sexual preventative medicine. In S. M. Turner, K. S. Calhoun & H. E. Adams (Eds.), *Handbook of clinical behavior therapy.* New York: Wiley. **754**

Adamson, J. D., Burdick, C., Corman, L., & Chebib, F. S. (1972). Physiological responses to sexual and unpleasant film stimuli. *Journal of Psychosomatic Research, 16,* 153–162. **385**

Adler, R. P., Lesser, G. S., Meringoff, L. K., Robertson, T. S., & Ward, S. (1980). *The effects of television advertising on children.* Lexington, MA: D. C. Heath. **559**

Agras, W. S. (1967). Behavior therapy in the management of chronic schizophrenia. *American Journal of Psychiatry, 124,* 240–243. **705**

Ainsworth, M. D. S. (1973). The development of infant-mother attachment. In B. M. Caldwell & H. N. Ricciuti (Eds.), *Review of child development research* (Vol. 3). Chicago: University of Chicago Press. **477**

Ainsworth, M. D. S., Blehar, M. C., Waters, E., & Wall, S. (1978). *Patterns of attachment.* Hillsdale, NJ: Lawrence Erlbaum Associates. **477, 478**

Ajzen, I., & Fishbein, M. (1972). Attitudinal and normative variables as predictors of specific behaviors. *Journal of Personality and Social Psychology, 27,* 1–9. **552**

Ajzen, I., & Fishbein, M. (1980). *Understanding attitudes and predicting social behaviors.* Englewood Cliffs, NJ: Prentice-Hall. **563**

Akerfeldt, S. (1957). Oxidation of N,N-Dimethyl-p-phenylenediamine by serum from patients with mental disease. *Science, 125,* 117–119. **37**

Akil, H., Watson, S. J., Young, E., Lewis, M. E., Khachaturian, H., & Walker, J. M. (1984). Endogenous opioids: Biology and function. *Annual Review of Neuroscience, 7,* 223–225. **165**

Akiskal, H. S. (1979). A biobehavioral model of depression. In R. A. Depue (Ed.), *The psychobiology of depressive disorders: Implications for the effects of stress.* New York: Academic Press. **703**

Alexander, B. K., & Hadaway, P. F. (1982). Opiate addiction: The case for an adaptive orientation. *Psychological Bulletin, 92,* 367–381. **215**

Alexander, C. N., Zucker, L. G., & Brody, C. L. (1970). Experimental expectations and autokinetic expectancies: Consistency theories and judgmental convergence. *Sociometry, 33,* 108–122. **539**

Alexander, R. D. (1985). A biological interpretation of moral systems. *Zygon, 20,* 3–18. **503, 504**

Allen, C. (1969). *A textbook of psychosexual disorders* (2nd ed.). London: Oxford University Press. **398**

Allen, M. G. (1976). Twin studies of affective illness. *Archives of General Psychiatry, 33,* 1476–1478. **700**

Allen, V. L., & Levine, J. M. (1968). Social support, dissent and conformity. *Sociometry, 31,* 138–149. **542**

Allgeier, A. R. (1981). Ideological barriers to contraception. In D. Byrne & W. A. Fisher (Eds.), *Adolescents, sex, and contraception.* New York: McGraw-Hill. **378**

Alliot, J., & Alexinsky, T. (1982). Effects of post-trial vasopressin injection on appetitively motivated learning in rats. *Physiology of Behavior, 28,* 525–530. **132**

Allison, T., & Van Twyver, H. (1970). Evolution. *Natural History, 79,* 56–65. **1, 39**

Allport, F. H. (1924). *Social psychology.* Cambridge, MA: Houghton Mifflin. **525, 529**

Allport, G. W. (1935). Attitudes. In C. Murchison (Ed.), *Handbook of social psychology.* Worcester, MA: Clark University Press. **552**

Allport, G. W. (1937). *Personality: A psychological interpretation.* New York: Holt. **594**

Allport, G. W. (1968). The historical background of modern social psychology. In G. Lindzey & E. Aronson (Eds.), *The handbook of social psychology* (Vol. 1). Reading, MA: Addison-Wesley. **552**

American Psychiatric Association. (1952). *Diagnostic and statistical manual of mental disorders.* Washington, DC: Author. **665**

American Psychiatric Association. (1968). *Diagnostic and statistical manual of mental disorders* (2nd ed.), (DSM-II). Washington, DC: Author. **666, 667, 704, 713, 721**

American Psychiatric Association. (1980). *Diagnostic and statistical manual of mental disorders* (3rd ed.), (DSM-III). Washington, DC: Author. **667, 670, 675, 691, 704, 708, 713, 719**

American Psychiatric Association. (1987). *Diagnostic and statistical manual of mental disorders* (3rd ed., revised), (DSM-III-R). Washington, DC: Author. **667, 670, 675, 678, 704, 713, 720, 721**

American Psychological Association. (1985). *Careers in psychology.* Washington, D.C.: Author. **26**

Ames, A. (1951). Visual perception and the rotating trapezoidal window. *Psychological Monographs, 65,* (Whole No. 324). **184**

Amir, Y. (1976). The role of intergroup contact in change of prejudice and ethnic relations. In P. A. Katz (Ed.), *Towards the elimination of racism.* New York: Pergamon Press. **556**

Amoore, J. E. (1970). *Molecular basis of odor.* Springfield, IL: Thomas. **168**

Anderson, B. F. (1971). *The psychology experiment* (2nd ed.). Belmont, CA: Wadsworth. **36**

Anderson, J. (1974, May 3). *Bystander intervention in an assault.* Paper presented at the meeting of the Southeastern Psychological Association, Hollywood, FL. **536**

Anderson, J. R. (1980). *Cognitive psychology and its implications.* New York: W. H. Freeman. **259–260**

Anderson, J. R. (1985). *Cognitive psychology and its implications* (2nd. ed.). New York: W. H. Freeman. **252, 259–260, 262**

Anderson, N. H. (1968). A simple model of information integration. In R. P. Abelson, E. Aronson, W. J. McGuire, T. M. Newcomb, M. J. Rosenberg, & P. H. Tannenbaum (Eds.), *Theories of cognitive consistency: A sourcebook.* Chicago: Rand McNally. **589**

Anderson, T. H. (1978). *Another look at the self-questioning study technique.* Technical Education Report, 6. Champaign: University of Illinois, Center for the Study of Reading. **271, 295**

Antelman, S. M., & Szechtman, H. (1975). Tail pinch induces eating in sated rats which appears to depend on nigrostriatal dopamine. *Science, 189,* 731–733. **305**

Appelbaum, P. S. (1982, March 21). Can mental patients say no to drugs? *New York Times Magazine,* p. 46. **742**

Apter, A., Galatzer, A., Beth-Halachmi, N., & Laron, Z. (1981). Self-image in adolescents with delayed puberty and growth retardation. *Journal of Youth and Adolescence, 10,* 501–505. **422**

Argyle, M., Furnham, A., & Graham, J. A. (1981). *Social situations.* New York: Cambridge University Press. **763**

Arieti, S. (1974). *Interpretation of schizophrenia.* New York: Basic Books. **686–688**

Aronfreed, J. (1976). Moral development from the standpoint of a general psychological theory. In T. Lickona (Ed.), *Moral development and behavior.* New York: Holt, Rinehart & Winston. **483, 505, 511**

Aronoff, M. S., & Lesse, S. (1983). Principles of psychotherapy. In B. Wolman (Ed.), *The therapist's handbook: Treatment methods of mental disorders.* New York: Van Nostrand Reinhold Co. **773, 774**

Aronson, E., & Mills, J. (1959). The effects of severity of initiation on liking for a group. *Journal of Abnormal and Social Psychology, 59,* 177–181. **567**

Asch, S. E. (1946). Forming impressions of personality. *Journal of Abnormal and Social Psychology, 41,* 258–290. **589**

Asch, S. E. (1951). Effects of group pressure upon the modification and distortion of judgments. In H. Guetzkow (Ed.), *Groups, leadership, and men.* Pittsburgh: Carnegie Press. **540, 542, 551**

Asch, S. E. (1955). Opinions and social pressure. *Scientific American, 193,* pp. 31–35. **542**

Asch, S. E. (1956). Studies of independence and conformity: A minority of one against a unanimous majority. *Psychological Monographs, 70,* 1–70. **542**

Askevold, F., & Heiberg, A. (1979). Anorexia nervosa: Two cases in discordant MZ twins. *Psychotherapy and Psychosomatics, 32,* 223–228. **671**

Assmus, G., Farley, J. U., & Lehmann, D. R. (1984). How advertising affects sales: Meta-analysis of econometric results. *Journal of Marketing Research, 21,* 65–74. **559**

Associated Press. (1983, March 12th). Leaks fought with lie tests. *Holland Sentinel,* 1. **329**

Averill, J. R. (1980). A constructivist view of emotion. In R. Plutchik & H. Kellerman (Eds.), Theories of emotion. New York: Academic Press. **341**

Axelrod, R., & Hamilton, W. D. (1981). The evolution of cooperation. *Science, 211,* 1390–1396. **59, 503**

Axelrod, S., & Apsche, J. (Eds.). (1983). *The effects of punishment on human behavior.* New York: Academic Press. **229**

Ayllon, T., & Azrin, N. H. (1968). *The token economy: A motivational system for therapy and rehabilitation.* New York: Appleton-Century-Crofts. **756**

Azrin, N. H. (1956). Some effects of two intermittent schedules of immediate and non-immediate punishment. *Journal of Experimental Psychology, 42,* 3–21. **229**

Baddeley, A. (1982). *Your memory: A user's guide.* New York: Macmillan. **266–267, 295**

Badia, P., & Defran, R. H. (1970). Orienting responses and GSR conditioning: A dilemma. *Psychological Review, 77,* 171–181. **204**

Ball, W., & Tronick, E. (1971). Infant responses to impending collision: Optical and real. *Science, 171,* 818–820. **430**

Bandura, A. (1969). *Principles of behavior modification.* New York: Holt, Rinehart & Winston. **759**

Bandura, A. (1977a). *Social learning theory.* Englewood Cliffs, NJ: Prentice-Hall. **242, 393, 441–442, 495, 505, 615, 709**

Bandura, A. (1977b). Self-efficacy: Toward a unifying theory of behavior change. *Psychological Review, 84,* 191–215. **763**

Bandura, A. (1986). *Social foundations of thought and action: A social-cognitive theory.* Englewood Cliffs, NJ: Prentice-Hall. **242**

Bandura, A., Adams, N. E., Hardy, A. B., & Howells, G. N. (1980). Tests of the generality of self-efficacy theory. *Cognitive Therapy and Research, 4,* 29–66. **763**

Bandura, A., Blanchard, E. G., & Ritter, R. (1969). The relative efficacy of desensitization and modeling approaches for inducing behavioral, affective, and attitudinal changes. *Journal of Personality and Social Psychology, 13,* 173–199. **762**

Bandura, A., Grusec, J. E., & Menlove, F. L. (1967). Vicarious extinction of avoidance behavior. *Journal of Personality and Social Psychology, 5,* 16–23. **489, 762**

Banks, M. S., & Salapatek, P. (1983). Infant visual perception. In M. M. Haith & J. J. Campos (Eds.), Infancy and developmental psychobiology, Vol. 2, in P. H. Mussen (Ed.), *Handbook of child psychology* (4th ed.). New York: Wiley. **428**

Barash, D. P. (1977). *Sociobiology and behavior.* New York: Elsevier North-Holland. **315**

Barash, D. P. (1982). *Sociobiology and behavior* (2nd ed.). New York: Elsevier. **55–58, 73, 75, 356, 358**

Bard, P. (1934). Central nervous system mechanisms for emotional behavior patterns in animals. *Research Publica-*

tions, *Association for Research into Nervous and Mental Disorders, 19,* 190–218. **327**

Barlow, D. H. (1977). Behavioral assessment in clinical settings: Developing issues. In J. D. Cone & R. P. Hawkins (Eds.), *Behavioral assessment: New directions in clinical psychology.* New York: Brunner/Mazel. **634**

Baron, R. A. (1977). *Human aggression.* New York: Plenum. **55**

Bartlett, F. C. (1958). *Thinking.* London: Allen & Unwin. **282**

Bastian, J. (1965). Primate signaling systems and human language. In I. DeVore (Ed.), *Primate behavior.* New York: Holt, Rinehart & Winston. **65**

Bates, E. (1979). *The emergence of symbols.* New York: Academic Press. **440**

Bates, E., Benigni, L. Bretherton, I., Camaloni, L., & Volterra, V. (1979). *Cognition and communication from 9–13 months: A correlational study program on cognitive and perceptual factors in human development* (Report No. 12). Boulder: University of Colorado, Institute for the Study of Intellectual Behavior. **434**

Bates, M. (1958). *Gluttons and libertines: Human problems of being natural.* New York: Vintage Books. **304, 306**

Bateson, G., Jackson, D., Haley, J., & Weakland, J. (1956). Toward a theory of schizophrenia. *Behavioral Science, 1,* 251–264. **693**

Batson, C. D., & Coke, J. S. (1981). Empathy: A source of altruistic motivation for helping? In J. P. Rushton & R. M. Sorrentino (Eds.), *Altruism and behavior: Social personality, and development perspectives.* Hillsdale, NJ: Lawrence Erlbaum Associates. **535**

Baumeister, R. F. (1985, April). The championship choke. *Psychology Today,* pp. 48–52. **302**

Baumrind, D. (1971). Current patterns of parental authority. *Developmental Psychology, 4,* 1–103. **483**

Baumrind, D. (1972). Socialization and instrumental competence in young children. In W. W. Hartup (Ed.), *The young child: Reviews of research, 2.* National Association for the Education of Young Children. **318**

Baumrind, D. (1973). The development of instrumental competence through socialization. In A. Pick (Ed.), *Minnesota symposium on child psychology* (Vol. 7). Minneapolis, MN: University of Minnesota Press. **483**

Baumrind, D. (1977). *Socialization determinants of personal agency.* Paper presented at the biennial meetings of the Society for Research in Child Development, New Orleans, LA. **483**

Bavelas, J. B. (1978). *Personality: Current theory and research.* Monterey, CA: Brooks/Cole. **618**

Bayley, N. (1970). Development of mental abilities. In P. H. Mussen (Ed.), *Carmichael's manual of child psychology* (Vol. 1). New York: Wiley. **650**

Beach, F. A. (Ed.). (1977). *Human sexuality in four perspectives.* Baltimore: Johns Hopkins University Press. **358, 402**

Beck, A. T. (1974). Depressive neurosis. In S. Arieti (Ed.), *Archives of general psychiatry* (2nd ed.). New York: Basic Books. **783**

Beck, A. T. (1976). *Cognitive therapy and emotional disorders.* New York: International Universities Press. **763, 764**

Beck, K. H. (1979). The effects of positive and negative arousal upon attitudes, belief acceptance, behavioral intention, and behavior. *Journal of Social Psychology, 107,* 239–251. **558**

Beck, S. B., Ward-Hull, C. I., & McLear, P. M. (1976). Variables related to women's somatic preferences of the male and female body. *Journal of Personality and Social Psychology, 34,* 1200–1210. **393**

Becker, B. J. (1986). Influence again: Another look at studies of gender differences in social influence. In J. S. Hyde & M. C. Linn (Eds.), *The psychology of gender: Advances through meta-analysis.* Baltimore, MD: Johns Hopkins University Press. **560**

Bednar, R. L., & Kaul, T. J. (1978). Experiential group research: Current perspectives. In S. L. Garfield & A. E. Bergin (Eds.), *Handbook of psychotherapy and behavior change* (2nd ed.). New York: Wiley. **768**

Beecher, H. K. (1959). *Measurement of subjective responses.* New York: Oxford University Press. **164**

Beilin, H. (1971). The training and acquisition of logical operations. In M. F. Rosskopf, L. P. Steffe, & S. Toback (Eds.), *Piagetian cognitive developmental research and mathematical education.* Washington, DC: National Council of Teachers of Mathematics. **456**

Bekesy, G. von. (1957). The ear. *Scientific American, 197,* pp. 66–78. **160**

Bell, A. P., & Weinberg, M. S. (1978). *Homosexualities: A study of diversity among men and women.* New York: Simon & Schuster. **401**

Bell, A. P., Weinberg, M. S., & Hammersmith, S. K. (1981). *Sexual preference: Its development in men and women.* Bloomingdale, IN: Indiana University Press. **404**

Bell, S. M., & Ainsworth, M. D. S. (1972). Infant crying and maternal responsiveness. *Child Development, 43,* 1171–1190. **479**

Bellack, A. S., Hersen, M., & Kazdin, A. E. (1982). *International handbook of behavior modification.* New York: Plenum. **233**

Bellack, A. S., Hersen, M., & Turner, S. M. (1976). Generalization effects of social skills training in chronic schizophrenics: An experimental analysis. *Behavior Research and Therapy, 14,* 391–398. **763**

Bem, D. J. (1965). An experimental analysis of self-persuasion. *Journal of Experimental Social Psychology, 1,* 199–218. **569**

Bem, D. J. (1967). Self-perception: An alternative interpretation of cognitive dissonance phenomena. *Psychological Review, 74,* 183–200. **569**

Bem, D. J. (1970). *Beliefs, attitudes and human affairs.* Monterey, CA: Brooks/Cole. **552**

Bem, D. J., & Allen, A. (1974). On predicting some of the people some of the time: The search for cross-situational consistency in behavior. *Psychological Review, 81,* 506–520. **613**

Bemis, K. M. (1978). Current approaches to the etiology and treatment of anorexia nervosa. *Psychological Bulletin, 85,* 593–617. **672**

Bennett, E. L. (1977). *Brain and behavior.* Monterey, CA: Brooks/Cole. **129**

Bennis, W. G., & Peabody, D. (1962). The conceptualization of two personality orientations and sociometric choice. *Journal of Social Psychology, 57,* 203–215. **561**

Benware, C., & Deci, E. (1975). Attitude change as a function of the inducement of exposing a proattitudinal communication. *Journal of Experimental Social Psychology, 11,* 271–278. **571**

Berge, O. G., Fasmer, O. B., Flatmark, T., & Hole, K. (1983). Time course of changes in nociception after 5, 6-dihydroxytryptamine lesions of descending 5-HT pathways. *Pharmacology and Biochemistry of Behavior, 18,* 637–643. **128**

Bergin, A. E. (1971). The evaluation of therapeutic outcomes. In A. E. Bergin & S. L. Garfield (Eds.), *Handbook of psychotherapy and behavior change: An empirical analysis.* New York: Wiley. **776**

Bergmann, G. (1956). The contribution of John B. Watson. *Psychological Review, 63,* 265–276. **12**

Berkowitz, L. (1974). Some determinants of impulsive aggression: Role of mediated association with reinforcement for aggression. *Psychological Review, 81,* 165–176. **562**

Berkowitz, W. R. (1969). Perceived height, personality, and friendship choice. *Psychological Reports, 24,* 373–374. **27**

Berlyne, D. E. (1960). *Conflict, arousal*

and curiosity. New York: McGraw-Hill. **319–320**

Berlyne, D. E. (1965). *Structure and direction in thinking.* New York: Wiley. **279**

Berndt, T. J. (1981). Relations between social cognition, nonsocial cognition, and social behavior: The case of friendship. In J. H. Flavell & L. D. Ross (Eds.), *Social cognitive development.* New York: Cambridge University Press. **489**

Berne, E. (1964). *Games people play.* New York: Grove. **749**

Bernstein, A. C. (1976). How children learn about sex and birth. *Psychology Today,* pp. 31–35. **414**

Berry, G. L., & Mitchell-Kernan, C. (Eds.). (1982). *Television and the socialization of the minority child.* New York: Academic Press. **501, 559**

Berscheid, E., & Walster, E. (1974). Physical attractiveness. In L. Berkowitz (Ed.), *Advances in experimental social psychology* (Vol. 7). New York: Academic Press. **588**

Berscheid, E., & Walster, E. (1978). *Interpersonal attraction* (2nd ed.). Reading, MA: Addison-Wesley. **28**

Bertelsen, A., Harvald, A., & Hauge, M. (1977). A Danish twin study of manic depressive disorders. *British Journal of Psychiatry, 130,* 330–351. **700**

Bessman, S. P., Williamson, M. L., & Koch, R. (1978). Diet, genetics, and mental retardation interaction between phenylketonuric heterozygous mother and fetus to produce nonspecific diminution of IQ: Evidence in support of the justification hypothesis. *Proceedings of the National Academy of Sciences, 78,* 1562–1566. **76**

Bever, T. G. (1970). The cognitive basis for linguistic structures. In J. R. Hayes (Ed.), *Cognition and the development of language.* New York: Wiley. **440**

Beyerstein, B. L. (1985). The myth of alpha consciousness. *Skeptical Inquirer, 10,* 42–59. **133**

Bieber, I., Dain, H., Dince, P., Drellich, M., Grand, H., Gundlach, R., Kremer, M., Rifkin, A., Wilbur, C., & Bieber, T. (1962). *Homosexuality.* New York: Vintage Books. **401–403**

Binet, A., & Simon, T. (1905). The development of intelligence in children. *L'Annee Psychologique, 11,* 163–191. [Reprinted in T. Shipley (Ed.) (1961), *Classics in psychology.* New York: Philosophical Library.] **637**

Birch, H. G. (1945). The relation of previous experience to insightful problem solving. *Journal of Comparative Psychology, 38,* 367–383. **239**

Blanchard, E. B., & Epstein, L. H. (1978). *A biofeedback primer.* Reading, MA: Addison-Wesley. **758**

Blasi, A. (1980). Bridging moral cognition and moral action: A critical review of the literature. *Psychological Bulletin, 88,* 1–44. **511, 717**

Bleuler, E. (1950). *Dementia praecox or the group of schizophrenias* (J. Zinken, Trans.). New York: International Universities Press. (Original work published in 1911.) **680**

Bleuler, M. (1978). *The schizophrenic disorders.* New Haven, CT: Yale University Press. **685**

Bliss, E. L. (1980). Multiple personalities: A report of 14 cases with implications for schizophrenia and hysteria. *Archives of General Psychiatry, 37,* 1388–1397. **713**

Bliss, T. V. P., & Lomo, T. (1973). Long-lasting potentiation of synaptic transmission in the dentate area of the anesthetized rabbit following stimulation of the perforant pathway. *Journal of Physiology, 232,* 331–356. **130**

Bloch, V. (1976). Brain activation and memory consolidation. In M. R. Rosenzweig & E. L. Bennett (Eds.), *Neural mechanisms of learning and memory.* Cambridge, MA: M.I.T. Press. **139**

Block, J. (1973). Conceptions of sex role: Some cross-cultural and longitudinal perspectives. *American Psychologist, 28,* 512–526. **495**

Block, J. (1978). Review of H. J. Eysenck & S. B. G. Eysenck, The Eysenck personality questionnaire. In O. Buros (Ed.), *The eighth mental measurement year book.* Highland Park, NJ: Gryphon. **498**

Block, J. (1981). The many faces of continuity. *Contemporary Psychology, 26,* 746–750. **519**

Block, J. H. (1976). Issues, problems and pitfalls in assessing sex differences: A critical review of "The psychology of sex differences." *Merrill-Palmer Quarterly, 22,* 283–308. **560**

Bloom, L., Hood, L., & Lightbown, P. (1974). Imitation in language development: If, when, and why. *Cognitive Psychology, 6,* 380–420. **442**

Blumberg, M. L. (1974). Psychopathology of the abusing parent. *American Journal of Psychotherapy, 28,* 21–29. **486**

Boden, M. (1977). *Artificial intelligence and natural man.* New York: Basic Books. **289**

Boe, E. E., & Church, R. M. (1967). Permanent effects of punishment during extinction. *Journal of Comparative and Physiological Psychology, 63,* 486–492. **229**

Bogen, J. (1979). The callosal syndrome. In K. M. Heilman & E. Valenstein, (Eds.), *Clinical neuropsychology.* New York: Oxford University Press. **120**

Bohus, B., Conti, L., Kovacs, G. L., & Versteeg,

D. H. G. (1982). Modulation of memory processes by neuropeptides: Interaction with neurotransmitter systems. In C. Ajmone-Marsan & H. Mathies (Eds.), *Neuronal plasticity and memory formation.* New York: Raven. **132**

Bond, C. F., Jr. (1982). Social facilitation: A self-presentational view. *Journal of Personality and Social Psychology, 42,* 1042–1050. **527**

Bond, C. F., Jr., & Titus, L. J. (1983). Social facilitation: A meta-analysis of 241 studies. *Psychological Bulletin, 94,* 265–292. **527**

Boring, E. G. (1923). Intelligence as the tests test it. *New Republic, 35,* 35–37. **636**

Boring, E. G. (1929). *A history of experimental psychology.* New York: Century. **15**

Boring, E. G. (1930). A new ambiguous figure. *American Journal of Psychology, 42,* 818–820. **183**

Boring, E. G. (1942). *Sensation and perception in the history of experimental psychology.* New York: Appleton-Century-Crofts. **9**

Boring, E. G. (1950). *A history of experimental psychology* (2nd ed.). New York: Appleton-Century-Crofts. **15**

Borysenko, J. Z. (1982). Behavioral-physiological factors in the development and management of cancer. *General Hospital Psychiatry, 4,* 69–74. **215**

Bourne, L. E., Dominowski, R. L., & Loftus, E. F. (1979). *Cognitive processes.* Englewood Cliffs, NJ: Prentice-Hall. **276–277, 284**

Bousfield, W. A. (1955). Lope de Vega on early conditioning. *American Psychologist, 10,* 828. **207**

Bower, G. H. (1972). Mental imagery and associative learning. In L. W. Gregg (Ed.), *Cognition in learning and memory.* New York: Wiley. **265**

Bower, G. H., & Clark, M. C. (1969). Narrative stories as mediators for serial learning. *Psychonomic Science, 14,* 181–182. **265**

Bower, G. H., Karlin, M. B., & Dueck A. (1975). Comprehension and memory for pictures. *Memory and Cognition, 3,* 216–220. **259–260**

Bower, T. G. R. (1964). Discrimination of depth in premotor infants. *Psychonomic Science, 1,* 368. **431**

Bower, T. G. R. (1965). The determinants of perceptual ability in infancy. *Psychonomic Science, 1,* 287–288. **431**

Bower, T. G. R. (1966). The visual world of infants. *Scientific American, 215,* pp. 80–92. **431**

Bower, T. G. R., Broughton, J. M., & Moore, M. K. (1970). Infant responses to approaching objects: An indicator of response to distal variables. *Perception and Psychophysics, 9,* 193–196. **430**

Bowers, K. S. (1973). Situationism in psychology: An analysis and a critique. *Psychological Review, 80,* 307–336. **613**

Bowlby, J. (1952). *Maternal care and mental health.* Geneva: World Health Organization. **472, 480**

Bowlby, J. (1969). Attachment and loss. In *Attachment* (Vol. 1). London: Hogarth Press. **87**

Bowlby, J. (1971). *Attachment and loss* (Vol. 1). Middlesex, England: Pelican Books. **472**

Bradshaw, J. L. (1969). The information conveyed by varying the dimensions of features in human outline faces. *Perception and Psychophysics, 6,* 5–9. **586**

Brady, J. F., Davison, G. C., Dewald, P. A., Egan, G., Fadiman, J., Frank, J. D., Gill, M. M., Hoffman, I., Kempler, W., Lazarus, A. A., Raimy, V., Rotter, J., & Strupp, H. H. (1980). Some views on effective principles of psychotherapy. *Cognitive Therapy and Research, 4,* 271–376. **774**

Brady, J. P. (1980). Behavior therapy. In H. I. Kaplan, A. M. Freeman, & B. J. Sadock (Eds.), *Comprehensive textbook of psychiatry* (Vol. III). Baltimore: Williams & Wilkins. **755**

Brady, J. V., Porter, R. W., Conrad, D. G., & Mason, J. W. (1958). Avoidance and the development of gastroduodenal ulcers. *Journal of the Experimental Analysis of Behavior, 11,* 69–73. **40**

Braine, M. D. S. (1976). Children's first word combinations. *Monographs of the Society for Research in Child Development, 41* (No. 266). **442**

Brainerd, C. J. (1973). Neo-Piagetian training experiments revisited: Is there any support for the cognitive-developmental stage hypothesis? *Cognition, 2,* 349–370. **456**

Brainerd, C. J. (1978). *Piaget's theory of intelligence.* Englewood Cliffs, NJ: Prentice-Hall. *458*

Brainerd, C. J., & Allen, T. (1971). Experimental inductions of the conservation of "first-order" quantitative invariants. Psychological Bulletin, 75, 128–144. **456**

Branch, C. H. H., & Eurman, L. K. (1980). Social attitudes toward patients with anorexia nervosa. *American Journal of Psychiatry, 137,* 623–633. **673**

Bransford, J. D., & Johnson, M. K. (1972). Contextual prerequisites for understanding: Some investigations of comprehension and recall. *Journal of Verbal Learning and Verbal Behavior, 11,* 717–722. **265**

Brantner, J. P., & Doherty, M. A. (1983). A review of timeout: A conceptual and methodological analysis. In S. Axelrod & J. Apsche (Eds.), *The effects of punish-*

ment on human behavior. New York: Academic Press. **231**

Bray, G. A. (Ed.). (1981). *Obesity in America* (DHEW Publication No. NIH 79–359). Washington, D.C.: U.S. Government Printing Office. **308**

Breland, K., & Breland, M. (1951). A field of applied animal psychology. *American Psychologist, 6,* 202–204. **235**

Breland, K., & Breland, M. (1961). The misbehavior of organisms. *American Psychologist, 16,* 681–684. *235*

Breuer, J., & Freud, S. (1895). *Studies in hysteria.* Boston, MA: Beacon Press. **14**

Briddell, D. W., & Wilson, G. T. (1976). Effects of alcohol and expectance set on male sexual arousal. *Journal of Abnormal Psychology, 85,* 225–234. **405**

Brody, S., & Axelrod, S. (1971). Maternal stimulation and the social responsiveness of infants. In H. R. Schaffer (Ed.), *The origins of human social relations.* New York: Academic Press. **92**

Broen, W. E., Jr., & Nakamura, C. Y. (1972). Reduced range of sensory sensitivity in chronic nonparanoid schizophrenics. *Journal of Abnormal Psychology, 79,* 106–111. **692**

Brogden, W. J. (1939). Sensory preconditioning. *Journal of Experimental Psychology, 25,* 323–332. **236**

Bronson, W. (1981). *Toddlers' behavior with agemates: Issues of interaction, cognition, and affect.* Norwood, NJ: Ablex Publishing. **485**

Brooks, J. (1985). Polygraph testing: Thoughts of a skeptical legislator. *American Psychologist, 40,* 348–354. **329**

Broude, G. J., & Green, S. J. (1976). Cross-cultural codes on twenty sexual attitudes and practices. *Ethology, 14,* 409–429. **400**

Broughton, R. J. (1982). Pathophysiology of enuresis nocturna, sleep terrors and sleepwalking: Current status and the Marseilles contribution. In R. J. Broughton (Ed.), Henri Gastaut and the Marseille school's contribution to the neurosciences. *Electroencephalography and Clinical Neurophysiology Supplement, 35,* 401–410. **136**

Broverman, I. K., Vogel, S. R., Broverman, D. M., Clark-Stewart, F. E., & Rosenkrantz, P. S. (1972). Sex role stereotypes: A current appraisal. *Journal of Social Issues, 28,* 59–78. **500**

Brown, J. J., & Hart, D. H. (1977). Correlates of females' sexual fantasies. *Perceptual and Motor Skills, 45,* 819–825. **394**

Brown, R. W. (1973). *A first language: The early stages.* Cambridge, MA: Harvard University Press. **438, 442**

Brown, R., Cazden, D., & Bellugi, U. (1969). The child's grammar from one to three. In J. P. Hill (Ed.), *Minnesota symposium on child psychology*

(Vol. 2). Minneapolis: University of Minnesota Press. **442**

Brown, R., & Kulik, J. (1977). Flashbulb memories. *Cognition, 5,* 73–99. **256–257**

Brown, R., & McNeill, D. (1966). The "tip of the tongue" phenomenon. *Journal of Verbal Learning and Verbal Behavior, 5,* 325–337. **266**

Brozek, J. (1978). Nutrition, malnutrition, and behavior. *Annual Review of Psychology, 29,* 157–177. **126**

Bruch, H. (1977). Psychological antecedents of anorexia nervosa. In R. A. Vigersky (Ed.), *Anorexia nervosa.* New York: Raven Press. **673**

Bruch, H. (1980). Preconditions for the development of anorexia nervosa. *American Journal of Psychoanalysis, 40,* 169–172. **671**

Bruner, J. S. (1974). The nature and uses of immaturity. In K. Connolly & J. Bruner (Eds), *The growth of competence.* New York: Academic Press. **477**

Bruner, J. S., Goodnow, J. J., & Austin, G. A. (1956). *A study of thinking.* New York: John Wiley. **665**

Bryan, J. H., & Walbek, N. H. (1970). The impact or words and deeds concerning altruism upon children. *Child Development, 41,* 747–757. **484**

Bryan, J. H., & Schwartz, T. H. (1970). The effects of film material upon children's behavior. *Psychological Bulletin, 75,* 50–59. **484**

Bucher, B., & Lovaas, O. I. (1968). Use of aversive stimulation in behavior modification. In M. R. Jones (Ed.), *Miami Symposium on the prediction of behavior, 1967: Aversive stimulation.* Coral Gables, FL: University of Miami Press. **230**

Buck, R. (1976). *Human motivation and emotion.* New York: John Wiley. **323, 325**

Buck, R. (1984). *The communication of emotion.* New York: Guilford Press. **342**

Buck, R. (1985). Prime theory: An integrated view of motivation and emotion. *Psychological Review, 92,* 389–413. **342–344**

Buck, R., & Duffy, R. (1980). Nonverbal communication of affect in brain-damaged patients. *Cortex, 16,* 351–362. **343**

Budinger, T. F., & Lauterbur, P. C. (1984). Nuclear magnetic resonance technology for medical science. *Science, 226,* 288–298. **106–107**

Budzynski, T. H., Stoyva, J. M., Adler, C. S., & Mullaney, D. J. (1973). EMG biofeedback and tension headaches. In N. E. Miller, T. Barber, L. V. D. Cara, J. Kamiya, D. Shapir, & J. Stoyva (Eds.), *Biofeedback and self-control.* Chicago: Aldine. **758**

Buell, S. J., & Coleman, P. D. (1979). Dendritic growth in the aged human brain and failure of growth in senile dementia. *Science, 206,* 854–856. **424**

Bugelski, B. R., Kidd, E., & Segmen, J. (1968). Image as a mediator in one-trial paired-associate learning. *Journal of Experimental Psychology, 76,* 69–73. **271**

Bugelski, R. (1938). Extinction with and without subgoal reinforcement. *Journal of Comparative Psychology, 26,* 121–133. **226**

Bugental, D. E., Love, L. R., & Gianetto, R. M. (1971). Perfidious feminine faces. *Journal of Personality and Social Psychology, 17,* 314–318. **335**

Bugental, J. (1967). *Challenges of humanistic psychology.* New York: McGraw-Hill. **16**

Bullough, V. L. (1979). *Homosexuality: A history.* New York: New American Library. **395, 400**

Burger, J. M. (1981). Motivational biases in the attribution of responsibility for an accident: A meta-analysis of the defensive-attribution hypothesis. *Psychological Bulletin, 90,* 296–512. **576, 579**

Burger, J. M., & Petty, R. E. (1981). The low-ball compliance technique: Task or person commitment? *Journal of Personality and Social Psychology, 40,* 492–500. **559**

Burgess, A. W., & Holmstrom, L. L. (1974). Rape trauma syndrome. *American Journal of Psychiatry, 131,* 981–986. **407**

Burgess, A. W., & Holmstrom, L. L. (1979). Rape: Sexual disruption and recovery. *American Journal of Orthopsychiatry, 49,* 648–657. **408**

Burt, M. R. (1980). Cultural myths and supports for rape. *Journal of Personality and Social Psychology, 38,* 217–230. **405**

Buss, D. M. (1985). Human mate selection. *American Scientist, 73,* 47–51. **360**

Buss, D. M. (1987). Sex differences in human mate selection criteria: An evolutionary perspective. In C. B. Crawford, M. F. Smith & D. L. Krebs (Eds.), *Sociobiology and psychology.* Hillsdale, NJ: Lawrence Erlbaum Associates. **360**

Butterfield, E. D., & Siperstein, G. N. (1974). Influence of contingent auditory stimulation upon non-nutritional suckle. In *Proceedings of the third symposium on oral sensation and perception: The mouth of the infant.* Springfield, IL: Charles C. Thomas. **435**

Byrne, D., & Lamberth, J. (1971). The effects of erotic stimuli on sex arousal, evaluative responses, and subsequent behavior. In *Technical report of the commission on obscenity and pornography* (Vol. 8). Washington: US Government Printing Office. **393**

Byrne, W. L., (and 22 others). (1966). Memory transfer. *Science, 153,* 658–659. **129**

Cain, W. S. (1978). The odiferous environment and the application of olfactory research. In E. C. Carterette & M. P. Friedman (Eds.), *Handbook of perception* (Vol. 7). New York: Academic Press. **169**

Caldwell, B., Wright, C., Honig, R., & Tannebaum, J. (1970). Infant day care and attachment. *American Journal of Orthopsychiatry, 40,* 397–412. **479**

Calvert-Boyanowsky, J., & Leventhal, H. (1975). The role of information in attenuating behavioral responses to stress: A reinterpretation of the misattribution phenomenon. *Journal of Personality and Social Psychology, 32,* 214–221. **341**

Campbell, D. T. (1960). Blind variation and selective retention in creative thought as in other knowledge processes. *Psychological Review, 67,* 380–400. **292**

Campos, J. J. (1976). Heart rate: A sensitive tool for the study of emotional development in the infant. In L. P. Lipsitt (Ed.), *Developmental psychobiology: The significance of infancy.* Hillsdale, NJ: Lawrence Erlbaum Associates. **431**

Campos, J. J., Hiatt, S., Ramsay, D., Henderson, C., & Svejda, M. (1978). The emergence of fear on the visual cliff. In M. Lewis & L. Rosenblum (Eds.), *The origins of affect.* New York: Wiley. **430**

Cannon, W. B. (1927). The James-Lange theory of emotions: A critical examination and an alternative theory. *American Journal of Psychology, 39,* 106–124. **327**

Cantor, J. R., Zillman, D., & Bryant, J. (1975). Enhancement of sexual arousal in response to erotic stimuli through misattribution of unrelated residual excitation. *Journal of Personality and Social Psychology, 32,* 69–75. **385**

Cantor, J. R., Bryant, J., & Zillman, D. (1974). Enhancement of humor appreciation by transferred excitement. *Journal of Personality and Social Psychology, 30,* 812–821. **322**

Cantwell, D. P., Baker, L., & Rutter, M. (1978). Family factors. In M. Rutter & E. Schopler (Eds.), Autism: *A reappraisal of concepts and treatment.* New York: Plenum Press. **675**

Cargan, L. (1981). Singles: An examination of two stereotypes. *Family Relations, 30,* 377–385. **368**

Carns, E. E. (1973). Talking about sex: Notes on first coitus and the double sexual standard. *Journal of Marriage and the Family, 35,* 677–688. **378**

Caron, A. J., Caron, R. F., & Carlson, V. R. (1979). Infant perception of the invariant shape of an object varying in slant. *Child Development, 50,* 716–721. **431**

Carpenter, G. C. (1973). Differential response to mother and stranger within the first month of life. *Bulletin of the British Psychological Society, 16,* 138. **429**

Cartwright, R. D. (1978). *Night life.* Englewood Cliffs, NJ: Prentice-Hall. **135**

Case, R. (1974). Structures and strictures: Some functional limitations on the course of cognitive growth. *Cognitive Psychology, 6,* 544–574. **459–461**

Cattell, R. B. (1971). *Abilities: Their structure, growth, and action.* Boston: Houghton Mifflin. **463**

Cattell, R. B. (1973, July). Personality pinned down. *Psychology Today,* pp. 40–46. **596**

Cautela, J. R. (1967). Covert sensitization. *Psychological Reports, 20,* 459–468. **754**

Cerletti, U., & Bini, L. (1938). L'Elettroshock. *Archivo di Psicologia, Neurologia, Psichiatria, & Psicoterapia, 19,* 266–267. **739**

Chaika, E. (1982). *Language, the social mirror.* Rowley, MA: Newbury House Publisher. **680**

Chaiken, S., & Baldwin, M. W. (1981). Affective-cognitive consistency and the effect of salient behavioral information on the self-perception of attitudes. *Journal of Personality and Social Psychology, 41,* 1–12. **570**

Chapanis, N., & Chapanis, A. (1964). Cognitive dissonance: Five years later. *Psychological Bulletin, 61,* 1–22. **569**

Chapman, L. J., & Chapman, J. P. (1973). *Disordered thought in schizophrenia.* New York: Appleton-Century-Crofts. **685**

Chase, W. G., & Ericsson, K. A. (1982). Skill and working memory. In G. H. Bower (Ed.), *The psychology of learning and motivation* (Vol. 16). New York: Academic Press. **254–255**

Cherry, S. H. (1976). *The menopause myth.* New York: Ballentine Books. **423**

Chomsky, N. (1968). *Language and mind.* New York: Harcourt, Brace & World. **434**

Chomsky, N. (1975). *Reflections on language.* New York: Pantheon Books. **441, 444**

Clark, H. H., & Clark, E. V. (1977). *Psychology and language: An introduction to psycholinguistics.* New York: Harcourt Brace Jovanovich. **439**

Clark, K. E., & Miller, G. A. (1970). *Psychology.* Englewood Cliffs, NJ: Prentice-Hall. **7**

Clark, R. D., III, & Word, L. E. (1974). Where is the apathetic bystander? Situational characteristics on the emergency.

Journal of Personality and Social Psychology, 29, 279–287. **536**

Clark, W., & Clark, S. (1980). Pain response in Nepalese porters. *Science, 209,* 410–412. **311**

Cleckley, J. (1976). *The mask of sanity* (5th ed.). St. Louis: Mosby. **716**

Colby, A., Kohlberg, L., Gibbs, J., & Lieberman, M. (1983). A longitudinal study of moral judgment. *Monographs of the society for research in child development* (Vol. 48). Chicago, IL: University of Chicago Press. **507, 511**

Coleman, E. (1978). Toward a new model of treatment of homosexuality: A review. *Journal of Homosexuality, 3,* 345–359. **393**

Coleman, E. (1982). Changing approaches to the treatment of homosexuality. In W. Paul, J. D. Weinrich, J. C. Gonsiorek, & M. E. Hotvedt (Eds.), *Homosexuality: Social, psychological and biological issues.* Beverly Hills, CA: Sage. **403**

Coleman, J. C., Butcher, J. N., & Carson, R. C. (1980). *Abnormal psychology and modern life* (6th ed.). Glenview, IL: Scott, Foresman & Company. **714**

Coleman, J. C., Butcher, J. N., & Carson, R. C. (1984). *Abnormal psychology and modern life* (7th ed.). Glenview, IL: Scott, Foresman & Company. **678, 690**

Colligan, R. C., Osborne, D., Swenson, W. M., & Offord, K. P. (1983). *The MMPI: A contemporary normative study.* New York: Praeger. **627**

Colombo, J. (1982). The critical period concept: Research, methodology, and theoretical issues. *Psychological Bulletin, 91,* 260–275. **89**

Colt, G. H. (1983, September-October). *Suicide.* Harvard Magazine, pp. 47–66. **698**

Comfort, A. A. (1976). *A good age.* New York: Crown. **518**

Conrad, R. (1964). Acoustic confusion in immediate memory. *British Journal of Psychology, 55,* 75–84. **253**

Cooper, J. E., Kendell, R. E., Gurland, B. J., Sharpe, L., Copeland, J. R. M., & Simon, R. (1972). *Psychiatric diagnosis in New York and London.* London: Oxford University Press. **721**

Coopersmith, S. (1967). *The antecedents of self-esteem.* San Francisco: W. H. Freeman. **317–318**

Coren, S., & Girgus, J. S. (1978). *Seeing is deceiving: The psychology of visual illusions.* Hillsdale, NJ: Lawrence Erlbaum Associates. **186**

Corsaro, W. A. (1981). Friendship in the nursery school: Social organization in a peer environment. In S. R. Asher & J. M. Gottman (Eds.), *The development of children's friendships.* New York: Cambridge University Press. **489**

Costa, P. T., Jr., & McCrae, R. R. (1980). Still stable after all these years: Personality as a key to some issues in adulthood and old age. In P. B. Baltes & O. G. Brin Jr. (Eds.), *Life-span development and behavior.* New York: Academic Press. **519**

Costrich, N., Feinstein, J., Kidder, L., Marecek, J., & Pascale, L. (1975). When stereotypes hurt: Three studies of penalties for sex-role reversals. *Journal of Experimental Social Psychology, 11,* 5200–5230. **502**

Cottrell, N. B. (1972). Social facilitation. In G. G. McClintock (Ed.), *Experimental social psychology.* New York: Holt, Rinehart & Winston. **526**

Cowan, T. M. (1973). Some variations of the twisted cord illusion and their analyses. *Perception and Psychophysics, 14,* 553–564. **186**

Craik, F. I. M., & Lockhart, R. S. (1972). Levels of processing: A framework for memory research. *Journal of Verbal Learning and Verbal Behavior, 11,* 671–684. **264**

Craik, F. I. M., & Tulving, E. (1975). Depth of processing and the retention of words in episodic memory. *Journal of Experimental Psychology: General, 104,* 268–294. **264**

Craik, F. I. M., & Watkins, M. J. (1973). The role of rehearsal in short-term memory. *Journal of Verbal Learning and Verbal Behavior, 12,* 599–607. **258**

Cratty, B. J. (1970). *Perceptual and motor development in infants and children.* New York: MacMillan. **88**

Crawford, C. B., Smith, M. F., & Krebs, D. L. (1987). *Sociobiology and psychology: Ideas, issues, and findings.* Hillsdale, NJ: Lawrence Erlbaum Associates. **57**

Crepault, C., & Couture, M. (1980). Men's erotic fantasies. *Archives of Sexual Behavior, 9,* 219–237. **405**

Crider, A. B., Goethals, G. R., Kavanaugh, R. D., & Solomon, P. R. (1986). *Psychology* (2nd ed.). Glenview, IL: Scott, Foresman. **201, 211**

Crisp, A. H. (1977). Diagnosis and outcome of anorexia nervosa. *Proceedings of the Royal Society of Medicine, 70,* 464–470. **672**

Crovitz, H. F. (1970). *Galton's walk: Methods for the analysis of thinking, intelligence, and creativity.* New York: Harper & Row. **271**

Crowder, R. G. (1976). *Principles of learning and memory.* Hillsdale, NJ: Lawrence Erlbaum Associates. **253**

Crowder, R. G. (1978). Sensory memory systems. In E. C. Carterette & M. P. Friedman (Eds.), *Handbook of perception* (Vol. 8). New York: Academic Press. **251**

Crowne, D., & Marlowe, D. (1964). *The approval motive: Studies in evaluative dependence.* New York: Wiley. **317**

Curtiss, S. (1977). *Genie: A psycholinguistic study of a modern-day "wild child."* New York: Academic Press. **444**

D'Andrade, R. G. (1966). Sex differences and cultural institutions. In E. E. Maccoby (Ed.), *The development of sex differences.* Stanford, CA: Stanford University Press. **500**

D'Andrea, V. J. (1977). Psychoactive drugs and transactional analysis. *Transactional Analysis Journal, 7,* 242–247. **743**

Daly, M., & Wilson, M. (1978). *Sex, evolution, and behavior.* Belmont, CA: Duxbury Press. **354, 360, 361, 389**

Darwin, C. (1858). Letter from Charles Darwin to C. Lyell. In F. Darwin (Ed.). (1888). *The life and letters of Charles Darwin* (2nd ed.). London: John Murray. **53**

Darwin, C. (1859). *The origin of species.* London: Murray. **53, 57**

Darwin, C. (1872). *The expression of the emotions in man and animals.* London: John Murray. **331**

Darwin, C. J., Turvey, M. T., & Crowder, R. G. (1972). An auditory analogue of the Sperling partial report procedure: Evidence for brief auditory storage. *Cognitive Psychology, 3,* 255–267. **251**

Davenport, W. H. (1977). Sex in cross-cultural perspective. In Beach, F. (Ed.), *Human sexuality in four perspectives.* Baltimore: Johns Hopkins University Press. **358, 362, 397**

Davis, H. (1849). *The works of Plato* (Vol. 2). London: Bohn. **50**

Davis, J. A. (1980). *General social surveys, 1972–1980: Cumulative data.* Chicago: National Opinion Research Center. New Haven, CT: Yale University, Roper Public Opinion Research Center. **367, 379**

Davis, J. H., Laughlin, P. R., & Komorita, S. S. (1976). The social psychology of small groups: Cooperative and mixed-motive interactions. *Psychological Review, 27,* 501–542. **29**

Davis, J. M. (1980). Antipsychotic drugs. In H. I. Kaplan, A. M. Freedman, & B. J. Sadock (Eds.), *Comprehensive textbook of psychiatry-III.* Baltimore: Williams & Wilkins. **743**

Davis, R. H., & Kubey, R. W. (1982). Growing old on television and with television. In D. Pearl, L. Bouthilet & J. Lazar (Eds.), *Television and behavior: Ten years of scientific progress and implications for the eighties* (Vol. 2). Technical reports. Washington, DC: U.S. Government Printing Office. **501, 559**

Davison, G. C., & Neale, J. M. (1986). *Abnormal psychology: An experimental clinical approach* (4th ed.). New York: Wiley. **633, 698, 699**

Davitz, J. R. (1969). *The language of emotion.* New York: Academic Press. **336**

Dawkins, R. (1976). *The selfish gene.* London: Granada. **358**

Day, R. H., & McKenzie, B. H. (1973). Perceptual shape constancy in early infancy. *Perception, 2,* 315–321. **431**

Deaux, K. (1972). Anticipatory attitude change: A direct test of the self-esteem hypothesis. *Journal of Experimental Social Psychology, 8,* 143–155. **561**

Deaux, K. (1985). Sex and gender. *Annual Review of Psychology, 36,* 49–81. **501**

Deci, E. L., & Ryan, R. M. (1980). The empirical exploration of intrinsic motivational processes. In L. Berkowitz (Ed.), *Advances in experimental social psychology* (Vol. 13). New York: Academic Press. **571**

de Groot, A. D. (1965). *Thought and choice in chess.* The Hague: Mouton. **287**

de Leeuw, L. (1978). Teaching problem solving: The effect of algorithmic and heuristic problem-solving training in relation to task complexity and relevant aptitudes. In A. M. Lesgold, J. W. Pellegrino, S. D. Fokema & R. Glaser (Eds.), *Cognitive psychology and instruction.* New York: Plenum. **286**

Delgado, J. M. R. (1969). *Physical control of the mind: Toward a psychocivilized society.* New York: Harper & Row. **323**

Delong, G. R. (1978). A neuropsychological interpretation of infantile autism. In M. Rutter & E. Schopler (Eds.), *Autism: A reappraisal of concept and treatment.* New York: Plenum Press. **675**

Dement, W. C. (1972). *Some must watch while some must sleep.* Stanford, CA: Stanford Alumni Association. **103**

Dennis, W. (1960). Causes of retardation among institutional children: Iran. *Journal of Genetic Psychology, 96,* 47–59. **419, 480**

Dennis, W., & Dennis, M. G. (1940). The effect of cradling practices upon the onset of walking in Hopi children. *Journal of Genetic Psychology, 56,* 77–86. **418**

Desmond, J. E., & Moore, J. W. (1982). A brain stem region essential for the classically conditioned but not unconditioned nictitating membrane response. *Physiology of Behavior, 28,* 1029–1033. **130**

Deutsch, J. A. (1973). Prolonged rewarding brain stimulation. In G. H. Bower (Ed.), *The psychology of learning and motivation* (Vol. VII). New York: Plenum. **302**

Deutsch, J. A., & Wang, M. L. (1977). The stomach as a site for rapid nutrient reinforcement sensors. *Science, 195,* 89–90. **304**

Deutsch, M., & Gerard, H. B. (1955). A study of normative and informative social influences upon individual judgment. *Journal of Abnormal and Social Psychology, 51,* 629–636. **542**

Diamond, M. C. (1978). The aging brain: Some enlightening and optimistic results. *American Scientist, 66,* 66–71. **423**

Diaz, R. M., & Berndt, T. J. (1982). Children's knowledge of a best friend: Fact or fancy? *Developmental Psychology, 18,* 787–794. **490**

Dibiase, W. J., & Hjelle, L. A. (1968). Body-image stereotypes and body type preferences among male college students. *Perceptual and Motor Skills, 27,* 1143–1146. **586**

Dickemann, W. (1979). Female infanticide, reproductive stratification: A preliminary model. In N. Chagnon & W. Irons (Eds.), *Evolutionary biology and human social behavior.* N. Scituate, MA: Duxbury. **58**

Diener, E. (1977). Deindividuation—causes and consequences. *Social Behavior and Personality, 5,* 143–155. **532**

Diener, E., Fraser, S. C., Beaman, A. L., & Kelsem, R. T. (1976). Effects of deindividuation variables on stealing among Halloween trick-or-treaters. *Journal of Personality and Social Psychology, 33,* 178–193. **531**

Diener, E., & Wallbom, M. (1976). Effects of self-awareness on antinormative behavior. *Journal of Research in Personality, 10,* 107–111. **532**

Dillehay, R. C. (1973). On the irrelevance of the classical negative evidence concerning the effects of attitudes on behavior. *American Psychologist, 28,* 887–891. **563**

Dion, K. K. (1972). Physical attractiveness and evaluations of children's transgression. *Journal of Personality and Social Psychology, 24,* 207–213. **588**

Dion, K. K., & Stein, S. (1978). Physical attractiveness and interpersonal influence. *Journal of Experimental Social Psychology, 14,* 97–108. **557**

Dixon, N. F. (1981). *Preconscious processing.* New York: Wiley. **252**

Doleys, D. M., Ciminero, A. R., Tollison, J. W., Williams, C. L., & Wells, K. C. (1977). Dry-bed training and retention control training: A comparison. *Behavior Therapy, 8,* 541–548. **215**

Donovan, J. M. (1975). Identity status and interpersonal style. *Journal of Youth and Adolescence, 4,* 37–55. **517**

Doppelt, J. E., & Wallace, W. L. (1955). Standardization of the Wechsler Adult Intelligence Scale for older persons. *Journal of Abnormal and Social Psychology, 51,* 312–330. **462**

Dornbusch, S., Hastorf, A. H., Richardson, S. A., Muzzy, R. E., & Vreeland, R. S. (1965). The perceiver and the perceived: Their relative influence on the categories of interpersonal cognition. *Journal of Personality and Social Psychology, 1,* 434–441. **592**

Douvan, E., & Adelson, J. (1966). *The adolescent experience.* New York: Wiley. **490**

Dove, A. (1968, July 15). Taking the chitling test. *Newsweek,* pp. 51–52. **647**

Downs, A. C. (1981). Sex-role stereotyping on prime-time television. *Journal of Genetic Psychology, 138,* 253–258. **501, 559**

Draguns, J. G., & Phillips, L. (1972). *Culture and psychopathology: The quest for a relationship.* Morristown, NJ: General Learning Press. **663**

Duncker, K. (1945). On problem solving. *Psychological Monographs, 58,* (No. 270). **284**

Dunnett, M. D., Campbell, J., & Jaastad, K. (1963). The effect of group participation on brainstorming effectiveness for two industrial samples. *Journal of Applied Psychology, 47,* 30–37. **29–30**

Dunnett, S. B., Bjorklund, A., Stenevi, U., & Iversen, S. D. (1981). Behavioral recovery following transplantation of substantia nigra in rats subjected to 6-OHDA lesions of the nigrostriatal pathway. II. Bilateral lesions. *Brain Research, 229,* 209–217. **129**

Durlach, I., & Colburn, H. S. (1978). Binaural phenomena. In E. C. Carterette & M. P. Friedman (Eds.), *Handbook of perception* (Vol. 4). New York: Academic Press. **161**

Dutton, D. G., & Aron, A. P. (1974). Some evidence for heightened sexual attraction under conditions of high anxiety. *Journal of Personality and Social Psychology, 30,* 510–517. **385**

Duval, S., & Wicklund, R. A. (1972). *A theory of objective self-awareness.* New York: Academic Press. **532**

Dworkin, R. H., Burke, B. W., & Maher, B. A. (1977). Genetic influences on the organization and development of personality. *Developmental Psychology, 13,* 162–163. **77**

Eagly, A. H. (1978). Sex differences in influenceability. *Psychological Bulletin, 85,* 86–116. **560**

Eagly, A. H., & Carli, L. L. (1981). Sex of researchers and sex-typed communications as determinants of sex differences in influenceability: A meta-analysis of social influence studies. *Psychological Bulletin, 90,* 1–20. **560**

Easterbrook, J. A. (1959). The effect of emotion on cue utilization and the organization of behavior. *Psychological Review, 66,* 183–201. **536**

Eckerman, C. O., Whatley, J. L., & Kutz, S. L. (1975). Growth of social play with peers during the second year of life. *Developmental Psychology, 11,* 42–49. **485**

Edelman, M. S., & Omark, D. R. (1973). Dominance hierarchies in young children. *Social Science Information, 12,* 1. **485**

Edwards, J. N., & Booth, A. (1976). The cessation of marital intercourse. *American Journal of Psychiatry, 133,* 1333–1336. **367**

Ehrhardt, A. A., & Baker, S. W. (1974). Fetal androgens, human central nervous system differentiation, and behavior sex differences. In R. C. Friedman, R. M. Richart, & R. L. Vande Wiele (Eds.), *Sex differences in behavior.* New York: Wiley. **84**

Eibl-Eibesfeldt, I. (1973). The expressive behavior of the deaf- and blind-born. In M. V. Cranach & I. Vino (Eds.), *Social communication and movement.* London: Academic Press. **334**

Eibl-Eibesfeldt, I. (1975). *Ethology: The biology of behavior* (2nd ed.). New York: Holt, Rinehart & Winston. **331**

Eich, J., Weingartner, H., Stillman, R. C., & Gillin, J. C. (1975). State-dependent accessibility of retrieval cues in the retention of a categorized list. *Journal of Verbal Learning and Verbal Behavior, 14,* 408–417. **267–268**

Eimas, P. D., & Tarter, V. C. (1979). On the development of speech perception: Mechanisms and analogies. In H. W. Reese & L. P. Lipsitt (Eds.), *Advances in child development and behavior* (Vol. 13). New York: Academic Press. **435**

Eisen, J. R. (1980). *Cognitive social psychology.* New York: McGraw-Hill. **566**

Ekman, P. (1972). Universals and cultural differences in facial expressions of emotion. In J. K. Cole (Ed.), *Nebraska Symposium on Motivation,* (Vol. 19). Lincoln: University of Nebraska Press. **335**

Ekman, P. (1973). Cross-cultural studies of facial expression. In P. Ekman (Ed.), *Darwin and facial expression: A century of research in review.* New York: Academic Press. **332–333**

Ekman, P., & Friesen, W. V. (1971). Constants across cultures in the face and emotion. *Journal of Personality and Social Psychology, 17,* 124–139. **334**

Ekman, P., & Friesen, W. V. (1975). *Unmasking the face.* Englewood Cliffs, N.J.: Prentice-Hall. **342**

Ekman, P., & Friesen, W. V. (1978). *Facial Action Coding system (FACS): A technique for the measurement of facial action.* Palo Alto, CA: Consulting Psychologists Press. **326**

Elder, G. (1969). Appearance and education in marriage mobility. *American Sociological Review, 34,* 519–533. **360**

Elias, J. E., & Gebhard, P. (1969). Sexuality and sexual learning in childhood. *Counseling Psychologist, 5,* 92–97. **371**

Elkind, D. (1967). Egocentrism in adolescence. *Child Development, 38,* 1025–1034. **516**

Elkind, D., & Weiner, I. B. (1978). *Development of the child.* New York: Wiley. **502**

Ellis, A. (1977). The basic clinical theory of rational-emotive therapy. In A. Ellis & R. Grieger (Eds.), *Handbook of rational-emotive therapy.* New York: Basic Books. **764**

Ellis, A. (1982). Self-direction in sport and life. *Rational Living, 17,* 27–33. **765**

Ellis, A. (1984). Rational-emotive therapy. In R. J. Corsini (Ed.), *Current psychotherapies* (3rd Ed.). Itasca, IL: Peacock Press. **764**

Ellison, C. R. (1980, Sept. 15). *Sexuality Today,* 3. **384**

Ellsworth, P. C., Carlsmith, J. M., & Henson, A. (1972). Staring as a stimulus to flight in human: A series of field studies. *Journal of Personality and Social Psychology, 21,* 302–311. **332**

Elson, B. D., Hauri, P., & Cunis, D. (1977). Physiological changes in yoga meditation. *Psychophysiology, 14,* 52–57. **133**

Emmerich, W. (1977). Structure and development of personal-social behaviors in economically disadvantaged preschool children. *Genetic Psychology Monographs, 95,* 191–245. **499**

Endler, N. S., & Magnusson, D. (1976). Toward an interactional psychology of personality. *Psychological Bulletin, 83,* 956–976. **613**

Entingh, D., Dunn, A., Glassman, E., Wilson, J., Hogan, E., & Damstra, T. (1975). Biochemical approaches to the biological basis of memory. In M. Gazzaniga & C. Blakemore, (Eds.), *Handbook of psychobiology.* New York: Academic Press. **131**

Epstein, A. N., & Teitelbaum, P. (1962b). The lateral hypothalamic syndrome: Recovery of feeding and drinking after lateral hypothalamic lesions. *Psychological Review, 69,* 74–90. **305**

Epstein, A. N., & Teitelbaum, P. (1962a). Regulation of food intake in the absence of taste, smell, and other oropharyngeal sensations. *Journal of Comparative and Physiological Psychology, 55,* 753–759. **304**

Epstein, C. J., & Golbus, M. S. (1977). Prenatal diagnoses of genetic diseases. *American Scientist, 65,* 703–711. **76**

Epstein, S. (1979). The stability of behavior: I. On predicting most people much of the time. *Journal of Personality and Social Psychology, 37,* 1097–1126. **613**

Erikson, E. H. (1968). *Identity: Youth and crisis.* New York: Norton. **515**

Ernst, G. W., & Newell, A. (1969). *GPS: A case study in generality and problem solving.* New York: Academic Press. **288**

Ervin-Tripp, S. (1964). Imitation and structural change in children's language. In Lenneberg, E. H. (Ed.), *New directions in the study of language.* Cambridge, MA: M.I.T. Press. **442**

Estes, W. K. (1944). An experimental study of punishment. *Psychological Monographs, 57, Whole No. 263.* **229**

Everett, G. M. (1975). Amyl nitrate (poppers) as an aphrodisiac. In M. Sandler & G. L. Gessa (Eds.), *Sexual behavior: Pharmacology and biochemistry.* New York: Raven. **390**

Eysenck, H. J. (1952). The effects of psychotherapy. *Journal of Consulting Psychiatry, 16,* 319–324. **775**

Eysenck, H. J. (1965). The effects of psychotherapy. *International Journal of Psychiatry, 1,* 97–142. **776**

Eysenck, H. J. (1967). *The biological basis of personality.* Springfield, IL: Charles C. Thomas. **708**

Eysenck, H. J. (1973). *Eysenck on extraversion.* New York: Wiley. **593, 594**

Eysenck, H. J. (1973). Personality and the maintenance of the smoking habit. In W. L. Dunn (Ed.), *Smoking behavior: Motives and incentives.* Washington D. C.: V. H. Winston. **313**

Eysenck, H. J., & Skinner, B. F. (1980, September). *Behavior modification, behavior therapy, and other matters: Invited dialogue.* Paper presented at the 88th Annual Convention of the American Psychological Association, Montreal, Canada. **752**

Fagot, B. I. (1978). The influence of sex of child on parental reactions to toddler children. *Child Development, 49,* 459–465. **495**

Fairburn, C. G., & Cooper, P. J. (1982). Self-induced vomiting and bulimia nervosa: An undetected problem. *British Medical Journal, 284,* 1153–1155. **671**

Fantz, R. L. (1966). Pattern discrimination and selective attention as determinants of perceptual development from birth. In A. H. Kidd & J. L. Rivoire (Eds.), *Perceptual development in children.* New York: International Universities Press. **428**

Farina, A., & Hagelauer, H. D. (1975). Sex and mental illness: The generosity of females. *Journal of Consulting and Clinical Psychology, 44,* 499. **722**

Farkas, G. M., Sine, L. F., & Evans, I. M. (1979). The effects of distraction, performance demand, stimulus explicitness and personality on objective and subjective measures of male sexual arousal. *Behavioral Research and Therapy, 17,* 25–32. **388**

Farley, J., & Alkon, D. L. (1985). Cellular mechanisms of learning, memory, and information storage. *Annual Review of Psychology, 36,* 419–494. **130**

Farley, J., Richards, W. G., Ling, L., Liman, E., & Alkon, D. L. (1983). Membrane changes in a single photoreceptor during acquisition cause associative learning in Hermissenda. *Science, 221,* 1201–1203. **214**

Faust, M. S. (1960). Developmental maturity as a determinant of prestige in adolescent girls. *Child Development, 31,* 173–184. **422**

Fazio, R. H., & Zanna, M. P. (1981). On the self-perception explanation of the overjustification effect: The role of the salience of initial attitude. *Journal of Experimental Social Psychology, 17,* 417–426. **565, 571**

Fazio, R. H., Zanna, M. P., & Cooper, J. (1977). Dissonance versus self-perception: An integrative view of each theory's proper domain of application. *Journal of Experimental Social Psychology, 13,* 464–479. **570**

Fechner, G. T. (1860). *Elemente der Psychphysik* (Vol. 1). Leipzig: Breitkopf & Harterl. (H. E. Adler, D. H. Howes, & E. G. Boring, Trans.). New York: Holt, Rinehart & Winston. **8**

Feigelman, W. (1977). Peeping: The pattern of voyeurism among construction workers. In C. D. Bryant (Ed.), *Sexual deviancy in social context.* New York: New Viewpoints. **398**

Feldman, M. P. (1966). Aversion therapy for sexual deviations: A critical review. *Psychological Bulletin, 65,* 65–79. **590**

Feldman, S. (1971). *The presentation of shortness in everyday life — Height and heightism in American society: Toward a sociology of stature.* Paper presented at the meeting of the American Sociological Association, Chicago, IL. **586**

Feldman-Summers, S., Gordon, P., & Meagher, J. R. (1979). The impact of rape on sexual satisfaction. *Journal of Abnormal Psychology, 88,* 101–105. **408**

Ferguson, N. B. L., & Keesey, R. E. (1975). Effect of a quinine adulterated diet upon body weight maintenance in male rats with ventromedial hypothalamic lesions. *Journal of Comparative Physiological Psychology, 89,* 478–488. **306**

Festinger, L. (1954). A theory of social comparison processes. *Human Relations, 7,* 117–140. **316**

Festinger, L. (1957). *A theory of cognitive dissonance.* Evanston, IL: Row, Peterson. **566**

Festinger, L., & Carlsmith, J. (1959). Cogni-

tive consequences of forced compliance. *Journal of Abnormal and Social Psychology, 58,* 203–210. **565**

Festinger, L., Pepitone, A., & Newcomb, T. M. (1952). Some consequences of deindividuation in a group. *Journal of Abnormal and Social Psychology, 47,* 382–389. **532**

Field, J., Muir, D., Pilon, R., Sinclair, M., & Dodwell, P. (1980). Infants' orientation to lateral sounds from birth to three months. *Child Development, 51,* 295–298. **429**

Fields, J. M., & Schuman, H. (1976). Public beliefs about the beliefs of the public. *Public Opinion Quarterly, 40,* 427–448. **578**

Firestone, I., Kaplan, J., & Russell, J. (1973). Anxiety, fear, and affiliation with similar-state and dissimilar-state others: Misery sometimes loves nonmiserable company. *Journal of Personality and Social Psychology, 26,* 409–414. **316**

Firkowska, A., Ostrowska, O., Sokolowska, M., Stein, Z., Susser, M., & Wald, I. (1978). Cognitive development and social policy. *Science, 200,* 1357–1362. **89**

Fischer, K. W. (1980). A theory of cognitive development: The control and construction of hierarchies of skills. *Psychological Review, 87,* 477–531. **459, 461**

Fischer, K. W. (1982). Human cognitive development in the first four years. *Behavioral and Brain Sciences, 5,* 282–283. **461**

Fishbein, M., & Ajzen, I. (1975). *Belief, attitude, intention and behavior: An introduction to theory and research.* Reading, MA: Addison-Wesley. **563**

Fisher, J. D., & Byrne, D. (1975). Too close for comfort: Sex differences in response to invasions of personal space. *Journal of Personality and Social Psychology, 32,* 15–21. **332**

Fiske, S. T., & Taylor, S. E. (1984). *Social cognition.* Reading, MA: Addison Wesley. 575–576, **592**

Fitzgerald, H. E., Strommen, E. A., & McKinney, J. P. (1977). *Developmental psychology.* Homewood, IL: Dorsey Press. **419**

Flaherty, C. F. (1985). *Animal learning and cognition.* New York: Alfred A. Knopf. **203, 231, 245**

Flavell, J. H. (1977). *Cognitive development.* Englewood Cliffs, NJ: Prentice-Hall. **459**

Flavell, J. H. (1980). Eulogy for Jean Piaget. *Society for Research in Child Development Newsletter,* p.1. **459**

Flavell, J. H. (1981). Cognitive monitoring. In W. P. Dickson (Ed.), *Children's oral communication skills.* New York: Academic Press. **461**

Fleischman, P. R. (1973). Psychiatric diag-

nosis. *Science, 180,* letters to the editor. **723**

Fling, S., & Manosevitz, M. (1972). Sex typing in nursery school children's play interests. *Developmental Psychology, 7,* 146–152. **501**

Floderus-Myrhed, B., Pedersen, N., & Ramuson, I. (1980). Assessment of heritability for personality, based on a short form of the Eysenck Personality Inventory: A study of 12,898 twin pairs. *Behavior Genetics, 10,* 153–162. **595**

Folstein, S., & Rutter, M. (1978). A twin study of individuals with infantile autism. In M. Rutter & E. Schopler (Eds.), *Autism: A reappraisal of concepts and treatment.* New York: Plenum Press. **674**

Footlick, J. K., & Lowell, J. (1978, December 18). The ten faces of Billy. *Newsweek,* p. 106. **713**

Ford, C. S., & Beach, F. A. (1951). *Patterns of sexual behavior.* New York: Harper & Row. **382, 392, 396**

Forsyth, D. R., Riess, M., & Schlenker, B. R. (1977). Impression management concerns governing reactions to a faulty decision. *Representative Research in Social Psychology, 18,* 12–22. **569**

Fox, S. (1984). *The mirror makers: A history of American advertising and its creators.* New York: Morrow. **559**

Fozard, J. L., & Popkin, S. J. (1978). Optimizing adult development: Ends and means of an applied psychology of aging. *American Psychologist, 33,* 975–989. **425**

Fraiberg, S. (1977). *Insights from the blind.* New York: Basic Books. **475**

Frank, J. D. (1973). *Persuasion and healing.* Baltimore: Johns Hopkins University Press. **730, 773**

Frank, J. D. (1982). Therapeutic components shared by all psychotherapies. In J. H. Harvey & M. M. Parks (Eds.), *Psychotherapy research and behavior change: The master lecture series* (Vol. 1). Washington, DC: American Psychological Association. **773, 774**

Frank, L. K. (1939). Projective methods for the study of personality. *Journal of Psychology, 8,* 389–413. **629**

Franken, R. E. (1982). *Human motivation.* Monterey, CA: Brooks Cole. **308–309, 330–331, 346**

Frase, L. T. (1975). Prose Processing. In G. H. Bower (Ed.), *The psychology of learning.* New York: McGraw-Hill. **271–272**

Frazier, A., & Lisonbee, L. K. (1950). Adolescent concerns with physique. *School Review, 58,* 397–405. **422**

Freedman, J. L. (1965). Long-term behavioral effects of cognitive dissonance. *Journal of Experimental Social Psychology, 1,* 145–155. **567**

Freeling, N. R., & Shemberg, K. M. (1970). The alleviation of test anxiety by systematic desensitization. *Behavior Research and Therapy, 8,* 293–299. **754**

Freud, S. (1960). *The ego and the id,* (J. Riviere & J. Strachey, Translators). New York: Norton. (Original work published 1920.) **487**

Freud, S. (1963). *Introductory lectures on psychoanalysis.* (J. Riviere & J. Strachey, Translators & Eds.). London: Hogarth. (Original work published 1917.) **504**

Freud, S. (1976). Some psychical consequences of the anatomical distinction between the sexes. In J. Strachey (Translator & Ed.), *The complete psychological works* (Vol. 19). New York: W. W. Norton. (Original work published 1925.) **504**

Freud, S. (1976). The interpretation of dreams. In J. Strachey (Translator and Ed.), *The complete psychological works* (Vols. 4–5). New York: Norton. (Original work published in 1900.) **746**

Frieder, B., & Allweis, C. (1982). Memory consolidation: Further evidence for the four-phase model from the time course of diethyldithiocarbamate and ethacrinic acid amnesias. *Physiology and Behavior, 29,* 1071–1075. **132**

Friedman, M. I., & Stricker, E. M. (1976). The physiological psychology of hunger: A physiological perspective. *Psychological Review, 83,* 409–431. **85**

Frieze, I. H., Parsons, J. E., Johnson, P. B., Ruble, D. N., & Zellman, G. L. (1978). *Women and sex roles: A social psychological perspective.* New York: Norton. **85**

Froming, W. J., Walker, G. T., & Lopyan, K. J. (1982). Public and private self-awareness: When personal attitudes conflict with societal expectations. *Journal of Experimental Social Psychology, 18,* 476–488. **532**

Fulcher, J. S. (1942). "Voluntary" facial expression in blind and seeing children. *Archives of Psychology, 272,* 5–49. **334**

Gallup, G. G. (1970). Chimpanzees: Self-recognition. *Science, 167,* 86–87. **493**

Gallup, G. H. (1978). The Gallup poll: Public opinion 1972–1977 (Vol. 4). Wilmington, DE: Scholarly Resources, Inc. **379**

Gallup G. H. (1981). *The Gallup Poll.* Wilmington, DE: Scholarly Resources, Inc. **558**

Galton, F. (1869). *Hereditary genius.* London: Macmillan. **10**

Galton, F. (1892). *Hereditary genius* (2nd ed.). London: Macmillan. **72**

Gamble, E. A. M. C. (1921). Review of Der Geruch by Hans Henning. *American Journal of Psychology, 32,* 290–295. **168**

Garber, H. L. (1984). On Sommer and Sommer. *American Psychologist, 39,* 1315. **88**

Garber, H., & Heber, R. (1973). *The Milwaukee Project: Early intervention as a technique to prevent mental retardation.* Unpublished technical paper. Storrs: University of Connecticut. **88**

Garcia, J., & Koelling, R. A. (1966). Relation of cue to consequence in avoidance learning. *Psychonomic Science, 4,* 123–124. **234**

Garcia, J., & Rusiniak, K. W. (1980). What the nose learns from the mouth. In D. Mueller Schwarze & B. M Silverstein (Eds.), *Chemical senses.* New York: Plenum. **313**

Garcia, J., Hankins, W. G., & Rusiniak, K. W. (1974). Behavioral regulation of the milieu interne in man and rat. *Science, 185,* 824–831. **312**

Gardner, B. T., & Gardner, R. A. (1975). Evidence for sentence constituents in the early utterances of child and chimpanzee. *Journal of Experimental Psychology: General, 104,* 244–267. **70**

Gardner, H. (1983). *Frames of the mind: The theory of multiple intelligences.* New York: Basic Books. **644**

Gardner, R. A., & Gardner, B. T. (1969). Teaching sign language to a chimpanzee. *Science, 65,* 664–672. **70**

Garfield, S. L. (1980). *Psychotherapy: An eclectic approach.* New York: Wiley. **778**

Garfield, S. L. (1983). Effectiveness of psychotherapy: The perennial controversy. *Professional psychology: Research and practice, 14,* 35–43. **777**

Garmezy, N. (1978). *New approaches to a developmental overview of schizophrenia.* Paper presented at the meeting of the American Psychological Association, Toronto. **670**

Garner, D. M., & Garfinkel, P. E. (1980). Social cultural factors in the development of anorexia nervosa. *Psychological Medicine, 10,* 647–656. **673**

Garner, D. M., Garfinkel, P. E., Schwartz, D., & Thompson, M. (1980). Cultural expectations of thinness in women. *Psychological Reports, 47,* 483–491. **673**

Gebhard, P. H., Gagnon, J. H., Pomeroy, W. B., & Christensen, C. V. (1965). *Sex offenders.* New York: Harper & Row. **393, 396, 397**

Geer, J. H., & Fuhr, R. (1976). Cognitive factors in sexual arousal: The role of distraction. *Journal of Consulting and Clinical Psychology, 44,* 238–243. **393**

Gelman, R. (1969). Conservation acquisition: A problem of learning to attend to relevant attributes. *Journal of Experimental Child Psychology, 7,* 167–187. **456**

Gelman, R. (1978). Counting in the preschooler: What does and does not develop. In R. S. Siegler (Ed.), *Children's thinking: What develops?* Hillsdale, NJ: Lawrence Erlbaum Associates. **459**

Gelman, R., & Baillargeon, R. (1983). A review of some Piagetian concepts. In J. H. Flavell & E. M. Markman (Eds.), Cognitive development, Vol. 3 in P. H. Mussen (Ed.), *Handbook of child psychology,* 4th edition. New York: John Wiley. **461**

Gerard, H. B., Wilhelmy, R. A., & Conolley, E. S. (1968). Conformity and group size. *Journal of Personality and Social Psychology, 8,* 79–82. **551**

Gerbner, G., Gross, L., Morgan, M., & Signorielli, N. (1980). The "mainstreaming" of America: Violence profile No. II. *Journal of Communication, 30*(3), 10–29. **501, 559**

Gergen, K. J., Gergen, M. M., & Barton, W. (1973, October). Deviance in the dark. *Psychology Today,* pp. 129–130. **532**

Geschwind, N. (1979). Specializations of the human brain. *Scientific American, 241,* pp. 180–199. **120**

Gesell, A., & Thompson, H. (1929). Learning and growth in identical twins: An experimental study by the method of co-twin control. *Genetic Psychology Monographs, 6,* 1–123. **419**

Giambra, L. M., & Arenberg, D. (1980). Problem solving, concept learning, and aging. In L. Poon (Ed.), *Aging in the 1980's.* Washington, DC: American Psychological Association. **425**

Giarrusso, R. P., Johnson, J., Goodchilds, J., & Zellman, G. (1979, April). *Adolescents' cues and signals: Sex and assault.* Paper presented at the Western Psychological Association Meeting. San Diego, CA. **405**

Gibbons, F. (1978). Sexual standards and reactions to pornography: Enhancing behavioral consistency through self-focused attention. *Journal of Personality and Social Psychology, 36,* 978–987. **372**

Gibson, E. J., & Walk, R. R. (1960). The "visual cliff." *Scientific American, 202,* pp. 2–9. **430**

Gibson, J. J. (1950). *The perception of the visual world.* Boston: Houghton Mifflin. **194**

Gibson, J. J. (1966). *The senses considered as perceptual systems.* Boston: Houghton Mifflin. **166, 194**

Gibson, J. J. (1979). *The ecological approach to visual perception.* Boston: Houghton Mifflin. **193–194, 197, 341**

Gilligan, C. (1977). In a different voice: Women's conceptions of the self and of morality. *Harvard Educational Review, 47*, 481–517. **512, 513**

Glass, A. L., & Holyoak, K. J. (1986). *Cognition* (2nd ed.). New York: Random House. **284–286, 295**

Glass, D. C., & Singer, J. E. (1972). *Urban stress.* New York: Academic Press. **204**

Glesener, R., & Tilman, D. (1978). Sexuality and the components of environmental uncertainty: Clues from geographic parthenogenesis in terrestrial animals. *American Naturalist, 122*, 659–673. **353**

Glickman, S. E. (1973). Adaptation and learning in evolutionary perspective. In P. Mussen & M. Rosenzweig (Eds.), *Psychology: An introduction.* Lexington, MA: D. C. Heath. **319**

Glickman, S. E., & Sroges, R. (1966). Curiosity in zoo animals. *Behavior, 26*, 151–188. **319**

Glickstein, M., Hardiman, M. J., & Yeo, C. H. (1983). The effects of cerebellar lesions on the conditioned nictitating membrane response of the rabbit. *Journal of Physiology, 341*, 30–31. **130**

Godden, D. R., & Baddeley, A. (1975). Context-dependent memory in two natural environments: On land and under water. *British Journal of Psychology, 66*, 325–331. **267**

Godden, D. R., & Baddeley, A. (1980). When does context influence recognition memory? *British Journal of Psychology, 71*, 99–104. **267**

Goldenberg, H. (1977). *Abnormal psychology.* Monterey, CA: Brooks/Cole. **719**

Goldenson, R. M. (1970). *The encyclopedia of human behavior; psychology, psychiatry, and mental health.* Garden City, NY: Doubleday. **298**

Goldin-Meadow, S., & Feldman, H. (1977). The development of language-like communication without a language model. *Science, 197*, 401–403. **444**

Goldstein, E. B. (1984). *Sensation and perception* (2nd ed.). Belmont, CA: Wadsworth. **157, 160, 197**

Goldstein, G. W., & Betz, A. L. (1986). The blood-brain barrier. *Scientific American, 255*, pp. 74–83. **124**

Goldstein, M. J., Baker, B. C. & Jamison, K. R. (1980). *Abnormal psychology: Experience, origins and interventions.* Boston, MA: Little, Brown. **696**

Goleman, D. (1978). Who's mentally ill? *Psychology Today, 11*(8), pp. 34–41. **669**

Gonzalez, A. E. J., & Cooper, J. (1975). *What to do with leftover dissonance: Blame it on the lights.* Unpublished manuscript, Princeton University. **570**

Goodman, M. J., Stewart, C. J., & Gilbert, F. (1977). A study of certain medical and physiological variables among Caucasian and Japanese women living in Hawaii.

Journal of Gerontology, 32, 291–298. **423**

Goodwin, D. W. (1979). Alcoholism and heredity: A review and hypothesis. *Archives of General Psychiatry, 36*, 57–61. **679**

Gordon, R. M. (1978). Emotion labelling and cognition. *Journal for the Theory of Social Behavior, 8*, 125–135. **339**

Gordon, W. J. (1961). *Synectics.* New York: Harper & Row. **292–293**

Gosselin, C., & Wilson, G. (1980). *Sexual variations: Fetishism, sadomasochism, and transvestism.* New York: Simon & Schuster. **399**

Gottesman, I. I. (1966). Genetic variance in adaptive personality traits. *Journal of Child Psychology and Psychiatry, 7*, 199–208. **77**

Gottesman, I., & Shields, J. (1972). *Schizophrenia and genetics: A twin study of vantage point.* New York: Academic Press. **688**

Gottman, J., Gonso, J., & Rasmussen, B. (1975). Social interaction, social competence and friendship in children. *Child Development, 46*, 709–718. **489**

Gough, H. G. (1965). *Adjective Check List.* Palo Alto, CA: Consulting Psychologists Press. **622**

Gough, H. G. (1975). *Californian Psychological Inventory.* Palo Alto, CA: Consulting Psychologists Press. **624**

Graham, S. (1848). *A lecture to young men on chastity, intended also for the serious consideration of parents and guardians* (10th ed.). Boston: C. H. Pierce. **368**

Gray, J. A. (1982). Precis of the neuropsychology of anxiety: An enquiry into the functions of the septo-hippocampal system. Oxford: Oxford University Press. In *Behavioral and Brain Sciences, 1982, 5*, 469–534 (includes commentaries). **330**

Green, R. (1980). Patterns of sexual identity in childhood: Relationship to subsequent sexual partner preference. In J. Marmor (Ed.), *Homosexual behavior.* New York: Basic Books. **403**

Green, R. (1982). Relationship between "feminine" and "masculine" behavior during boyhood and sexual orientation in manhood. In Z. Hoch & H. Lief (Eds.), *Sexology: Sexual biology, behavior, and theory.* New York: Excerpta Medica. **404**

Greenberg, B. S., Burgoon, M., Burgoon, J. K., & Korzenny, F. (1983). *Mexican Americans and the mass media.* Norwood, NJ: Ablex. **501, 559**

Greene, D., Sternberg, B., & Lepper, M. R. (1976). Overjustification in a token economy. *Journal of Personality and Social Psychology, 34*, 1219–1234. **571**

Gregory, R. (1968). Visual illusions. *Scientific American, 219*, pp. 66–76. **181, 183, 186**

Gregory, R. (1970). *The intelligent eye.* London: Weidenfeld & Nicolson. **183–186**

Gregory, R. (1977). *Eye and brain: The psychology of seeing* (3rd ed.). New York: McGraw-Hill. **151**

Gregory, R. L. (1977). *Eye and brain: The psychology of seeing* (3rd ed.). New York: McGraw-Hill. **126**

Gross, A. E. (1978). The male role and heterosexual behavior. *Journal of Social Issues, 34*, 87–107. **378**

Grossberg, S. (1982). Processing of expected and unexpected events during conditioning and attention: A psychophysiological theory. *Psychological Review, 89*, 529–572. **214**

Groth, A. N., & Burgess, A. (1977). Sexual disfunction during rape. *New England Journal of Medicine, 297*, 764–766. **406**

Groth, A. N., Burgess, A., & Holmstrom, L. L. (1977). Rape: Power, anger and sexuality. *American Journal of Psychiatry, 134*, 1230–1243. **406**

Gruendel, J. M. (1977). Referential overextension in early language development. *Child Development, 48*, 1567–1576. **436**

Grush, J. E., McKeough, K. L., & Ahlering, R. F. (1978). Extrapolating laboratory exposure research to actual political elections. *Journal of Personality and Social Psychology, 36*, 257–270. **554**

Guilford, J. P. (1967). *The nature of human intelligence.* New York: McGraw-Hill. **643**

Guilford, J. P., & Dallenbach, K. M. (1928). A study of the autokinetic sensation. *American Journal of Psychology, 40*, 83–91. **192**

Gustavson, C., Garcia, J., Hankins, W., & Rusiniak, K. W. (1974). Coyote predation control by aversive conditioning. *Science, 184*, 581–583. **163**

Guttman, N., & Kalish H. I. (1956). Discriminability and stimulus generalization. *Journal of Experimental Psychology, 51*, 79–88. **224–225**

Haan, N. (1978). Two moralities in action contexts: Relationship to thought, ego regulation, and development. *Journal of Personality and Social Psychology, 36*, 286–305. **511**

Haan, N., Smith, B., & Block, J. (1968). Moral reasoning of young adults. *Journal of Personality and Social Psychology, 10*, 183–201. **511**

Haber, R. N. (1978). Visual perception. *Annual Review of Psychology, 29*, 31–59. **194**

Haims, L. J. (1973). *Sex education and the*

public schools. Lexington, MA: Lexington Books. **379**

Hall, E. T. (1966). *The hidden dimension*. New York: Doubleday. **335–336**

Hall, E. T. (1974). *Handbook for proxemic research*. Washington, DC: Society for the Anthropology of Visual Communication, American Anthropological Association. **68**

Halmi, K. A., Powers, P., & Cunningham, S. (1975). Treatment of anorexia nervosa with behavior modification: Effectiveness of formula feeling and isolation. *Archives of General Psychiatry, 32*, 93–96. **757**

Hanson, R. D. (1980). Common sense attribution. *Journal of Personality and Social Psychology, 39*, 996–1009. **574**

Hardy, A. B. (1976). *Agoraphobia: Symptoms, causes, treatment*. Menlo Park, CA: Terrap. **705**

Hare, R. D. (1970). *Psychopathy: Theory and research*. New York: Wiley. **716, 717**

Hare, R. D. (1981). Psychopathy and violence. In J. Hays, T. Roberts, & K. Soloway (Eds.), *Violence and the violent individual*. New York: SP Books. **716**

Hariton, E. B., & Singer, J. L. (1974). Women's fantasies during sexual intercourse: Normative and theoretical explanations. *Journal of Consulting and Clinical Psychology, 42*, 313–322. **393**

Harlow, H. F. (1949). The formation of learning sets. *Psychological Review, 56*, 51–56. **238, 280**

Harlow, H. F. (1958). The nature of love. *American Psychologist, 13*, 673–685. **473**

Harlow, H. F. (1976). Monkeys, men, mice, motives and sex. In M. H. Siegal & H. P. Ziegler (Eds.), *Psychological research: The inside story*. New York: Harper & Row. **318**

Harlow, H. F., & Harlow, M. K. (1962). Social deprivation in monkeys. *Scientific American, 223*, pp. 137–146. **85**

Harlow, H. F., Harlow, M. K., Hansen, E. W., & Soumi, S. J. (1972). Infantile sexuality in monkeys. *Archives of Sexual Behavior, 2*, 1–7. **393**

Harlow, H. F., & Zimmerman, R. R. (1959). Affectional responses in the infant monkey. *Science, 130*, 421–423. **85, 473**

Harper, R. G., Wiens, A. N., & Matarazzo, J. D. (1978). *Nonverbal communication: The state of the art*. New York: John Wiley. **67**

Harrison, R. (1963). Functionalism and its historical significance. *Genetic Psychology Monographs, 68*, 387–423. **9**

Hartup, W. W. (1978). Children and their friends. In H. McGurk (Ed.), *Child social development*. London: Methuen. **489**

Hartup, W. W. (1983). Peer relations. In E. M. Hetherington (Ed.), Socialization, personality and social development, Vol. 4 in P. H. Mussen (Ed.), *Handbook of Child Psychology*, 4th edition. New York: Wiley. **489**

Hartup, W. W., & Coates, B. (1967). Imitation of a peer as a function of reinforcement from the peer group and rewardingness of the model. *Child Development, 38*, 1003–1010. **489**

Harvey, J. H., Wells, G. L., & Alvarez, M. D. (1978). Attribution in the context of conflict and separation in close relationships. In J. H. Harvey, W. Ickes & R. F. Kidd (Eds.), *New directions in attribution research* (Vol. 2). Hillsdale, NJ: Lawrence Erlbaum Associates. **578**

Hass, A. (1979). *Teenage sexuality: A survey of teenage sexual behavior*. New York: Macmillan. **378**

Hathaway, S. R., & McKinley, J. C. (1961). *The Minnesota Multiphasic Personality Inventory Manual* (rev. ed.). New York: Psychological Corporation. **625**

Heath, R. G. (1963). Electrical self-stimulation of the brain in man. *American Journal of Psychiatry, 120*, 571–577. **116**

Hebb, D. O. (1949). *Organization of behavior*. New York: Wiley. **99**

Hebb, D. O. (1955). Drives and the C.N.S. (conceptual nervous system). *Psychological Review, 62*, 243–254. **302**

Hebb, D. O. (1966). *A textbook of psychology* (2nd ed.). Philadelphia, PA: W. B. Saunders. **652**

Hebert, R., & Lehmann, D. (1977). Theta bursts: An EEG pattern in normal subjects practicing the transcendental meditation technique. *Electroencephalography and Clinical Neurophysiology, 42*, 397–405. **133**

Heider, F. (1958). *The psychology of interpersonal relations*. New York: Wiley. **525, 572, 574**

Heim, M. (1981). Sexual behavior of castrated sex offenders. *Archives of Sexual Behavior, 10*, 11–19. **389**

Heiman, J. R. (1975, December). Women's sexual arousal. *Psychology Today*, pp. 90–94. **388**

Henig, R. M. (1981, March 22). The child savers. *The New York Times*, section 6, pp. 34–36. **424**

Henning, H. (1916). *Der Geruch*. Leipzig: Barth. **168**

Henslin, J. M. (1967). Craps and magic. *American Journal of Sociology, 73*, 316–330. **575**

Heron, W. (1957, January). The pathology of boredom. *Scientific American, 196*, pp. 52–56. **300–301**

Herrnstein, R. J. (1973). *IQ in the meritocracy*. Boston, MA: Atlantic Monthly Press. **635**

Heston, L. L. (1966). Psychiatric disorders in foster home reared children of schizophrenic mothers. *British Journal of Psychiatry, 112*, 819–825. **687**

Heston, L. L. (1970). The genetics of schizophrenic and schizoid disease. *Science, 167*, 249–256. **688**

Heston, L. L., & Shields, J. (1968). Homosexuality in twins: A family study and a registry study. *Archives of General Psychiatry, 18*, 149–160. **402**

Hetherington, E. M. (1967). The effects of familial variables on sex-typing, on parent-child similarity, and on imitation in children. In J.P. Hill (Ed.), *Minnesota symposium on child psychology* (Vol. 1). Minneapolis, MN: University of Minnesota Press. **498**

Hetherington, E. M., & Morris, W. M. (1978). The family and primary groups. In W. H. Holtzman (Ed.), *Introductory psychology in depth: Developmental topics*. New York: Harpers College Press. **484**

Hetherington, E. M., & Parke, R. D. (1979). *Child psychology: A contemporary viewpoint*. New York: McGraw-Hill. **481, 482**

Higgins, R. L., & Marlatt, G. A. (1973). Effects of anxiety arousal on the consumption of alcohol by alcoholics and social drinkers. *Journal of Consulting and Clinical Psychology, 42*, 426–433. **679**

Hilgard, E. R. (1977). *Divided consciousness: Multiple controls in human thought and action*. New York: Wiley-Interscience. **136–137**

Hilgard, E. R. (1986). *Divided consciousness* (2nd ed.). New York: Wiley. **136–137**

Hilgard, E. R., Hilgard, J. R., Macdonald, H., Morgan, A. H., & Johnson, L. S. (1978). Covert pain in hypnotic analgesia: Its reality as tested by the real-simulator design. *Journal of Abnormal Psychology, 87*, 655–663. **134**

Hillyard, S. A., & Kutas, M. (1983). Electrophysiology of cognitive processing. *Annual Review of Psychology, 34*, 33–61. **104, 133**

Hinde R. A. (1962). Sensitive periods and the development of behavior. In S. A. Barnett (Ed.). *Lessons from animal behavior for the clinician*. London: National Spastics Society. **91**

Hirsch, H. V. B., & Jacobson, M. (1975). The perfectable brain. In M. Gazzaniga & C. Blakemore (Eds.). *Handbook of psychobiology*. New York: Academic Press. **125**

Hite, S. (1977). *The Hite report*. New York: Macmillan. **369**

Hodgson, R. J., & Rachman, S. J. (1972). The effects of contamination and washing on obsession patients. *Behavior Research and Therapy, 10*, 111–117. **707**

Hodkin, B. (1981). Language effects in assessment of class-inclusion ability. *Child Development, 52,* 470–478. **459**

Hoffer, A., & Osmond, H. (1968). Nicotinamide adenine dinucleotide in the treatment of chronic schizophrenic patients. *British Journal of Psychiatry, 114,* 915–917. **690**

Hoffman, M. L. (1970). Moral development. In P. H. Mussen (Ed.), *Carmichael's manual of child psychology* (Vol. 2). New York: Wiley. **495, 505**

Hofling, C., Brotzman, E., Dalrymple, S., Graves, N., & Pierce, C. (1966). An experimental study in nurse-physician relationships. *Journal of Nervous and Mental Diseases, 143,* 171–190. **549**

Hohmann, G. W. (1966). Some effects of spinal cord lesions on experienced emotional feelings. *Psychophysiology, 3,* 143–156. **329, 331**

Hollander, E. P. (1958). Conformity, status, and idiosyncrasy credit. *Psychological Review, 65,* 117–127. **543**

Holmberg, M. C. (1980). The development of social interchange patterns from 12 to 42 months. *Child Development, 51,* 448–456. **485**

Holmes, T. H., & Rahe, R. H. (1967). The social readjustment rating scale. *Journal of Psychosomatic Research, 11,* 213–218. **668**

Holstein, C. (1976). Development of moral judgment: A longitudinal study of males and females. *Child Development, 47,* 51–61. **512**

Honzik, M. P., Macfarland, J. W., & Allen, L. (1948). The stability of mental test performance between two and eighteen years. *Journal of Experimental Education, 17,* 39–334. **652**

Hooker, E. (1957). The adjustment of the male overt homosexual. *Journal of Projective Techniques, 21,* 18–31. **401**

Hoon, E. F., & Hoon, P. W. (1978). Styles of sexual expression in women: Clinical implications of multivariate analysis. *Archives of Sexual Behavior, 7,* 105–116. **388**

Hoon, E. F., Wincze, J. P., & Hoon, P. W. (1977). A test of reciprocal inhibition: Are anxiety and sexual arousal in women mutually inhibitory? *Journal of Abnormal Psychology, 86,* 65–74. **388**

Hoon, P. W., Bruce, K. E., & Kinchloe, B. (1982). Does the menstrual cycle play a role in sexual arousal? *Psychophysiology, 19,* 21–27. **389**

Hopkins, J. R. (1977). Sexual behavior in adolescence. In L. A. Peplau & C. L. Hammen (Eds.), *Journal of Social Issues, 33,* 67–85. **366**

Horn, J. L. (1975). Psychometric studies of aging and intelligence. In S. Gershon & A. Raskind (Eds.), *Aging: Vol. 2. Genesis and treatment of psychological disorders in the elderly*. New York: Raven. **463**

Horn, J. L., & Donaldson, G. (1976). On the myth of intellectual decline in adulthood. *American Psychologist, 31,* 701–719. **463**

Horner, M. (1972). Toward an understanding of achievement-related conflicts in women. *Journal of Social Issues, 28,* 157–174. **502**

Horos, C. B. (1974). *The private crime, a social horror*. New Canaan, CT: Tabey Publishing. **405**

Horowitz, M. J., & Solomon, G. F. (1975). A prediction of delayed stress response syndromes in Vietnam Veterans. *Journal of Social Issues, 31,* 67–80. **708**

Houston, L. N. (1981). Romanticism and eroticism among black and white college students. *Adolescence, 16,* 263–272. **378**

Howard, I. P. (1982). *Human visual orientation*. London: Wiley. **192**

Howarth, E., & Schokman-Gates, K.-L. (1981). Self-report multiple mood instruments. *British Journal of Psychology, 72,* 421–441. **326**

Hoyenga, K. B., & Hoyenga, K.T. (1979). *The question of sex differences*. Boston: Little-Brown. **494**

Hrdy, S. B. (1977). *The Langurs of Abu* Cambridge, MA: Harvard University Press. **486**

Hsu, G. L. K. (1983). The aetiology of anorexia nervosa. *Psychological Medicine, 13,* 231–238. **671–673**

Hubel, D. H. (1963). The visual cortex of the brain. *Scientific American, 209,* pp. 54–62. **156**

Huesmann, L. P., Eron, L. D., Klein, R., Brice, P., & Fischer, P. (1983). Mitigating the imitation of aggressive behaviors by changing children's attitudes about media violence. *Journal of Personality and Social Psychology, 44,* 899–910. **562**

Hull, C. L. (1943). Principles of behavior. New York: Appleton-Century Co. **300**

Hunt, D. E. (1951). *Studies in role concept repertory: Conceptual consistency*. Unpublished master's thesis, Ohio State University, Columbus, OH. **618**

Hunt, E. (1983). On the nature of intelligence. *Science, 219,* 141–146. **461**

Hunt, M. (1974). *Sexual behavior in the 1970's*. Chicago: Playboy Press. **363, 365–369, 397, 399, 400**

Huston, A. C. (1983). Sex-typing. In E. M. Hetherington (Ed.), *Socialization, personality and social development*, Vol. 4 in P. H. Mussen (Ed.), *Handbook of child psychology*, 4th edition. New York: Wiley. **495**

Hyden, H., & Lange, P. (1972). Protein changes in different brain areas as a function of intermittent training. *Proceedings of the National Academy of Sciences USA, 69,* 1980–1984. **131**

Ickes, W., Layden, M. A., & Barnes, R. D. (1978). Objective self-awareness and individuation: An empirical link. *Journal of Personality, 46,* 146–161. **532**

Ickes, W., Wicklund, R. A., & Ferris, C. B. (1973). Objective self-awareness and self-esteem. *Journal of Experimental Social Psychology, 9,* 202–219. **532**

Imperato-McGinley, J., Guerrero A., Gautier, T., & Peterson, R. E. (1974). Steroid 5-alpha reductase deficiency in man: An inherited form of male pseudohermaphroditism. *Science, 186,* 1213–1215. **84**

Insko, C. A., Drenan, S., & Soloman, M. R. (1983). Conformity as a function of the consistency of positive self-evaluation with being liked and being right. *Journal of Experimental Social Psychology, 19,* 341–358. **557**

Insko, C. A., Nacoste, R. W., & Moe, J. L. (1983). Belief congruence and racial discrimination: Review of the evidence and critical evaluation. *European Journal of Social Psychology, 13,* 153–174. **558**

Isaacson, R. L. (1970). When brains are damaged. *Psychology Today, 3,* pp. 38–42. **644**

Izard, C. E., Hembree, E. A., Dougherty, L. M., & Spizzirri, C. C. (1983). Changes in facial expressions of 2- to 19-month-old infants following acute pain. *Developmental Psychology, 19,* 418–426. **334**

Jacob, T. (1975). Interaction in disturbed and normal families. *Psychological Bulletin, 82,* 33–65. **693**

Jacobson, M. (1970). *Developmental neurobiology*. New York: Holt, Rinehart & Winston. **125**

James, W. (1884). What is an emotion? *Mind, 9,* 188–205. **327**

James, W. (1890). *The principles of psychology*. New York: Holt. **7, 19, 322, 427**

Janda, L. H., O'Grady, K., Nichelous, J., Harsher, D., Denny, C., & Denner, K. (1981). Effects of sex guilt on interpersonal pleasuring. *Journal of Personality and Social Psychology, 40,* 201–209. **367**

Jasnos, T. M., & Hakmiller, K. L. (1975). Some effects of lesion level and emotional cues on affective expression in spinal cord patients. *Psychological Reports, 37,* 859–870. **330**

Jastrow, J. (1900). Fact and fable in psychology. Boston: Houghton Mifflin. **183**

Jensen, A. R. (1963). Learning abilities in retarded, average, and gifted children. *Merrill Palmer Quarterly, 9,* 123–140. **650**

Jensen, A. R. (1964). The Rorschach technique: A re-evaluation. *Acta Psychologica, 22*, 60–77. **633**

Jensen, A. R. (1969). How much can we boost IQ and scholastic achievement? *Harvard Educational Review, 39*, 1–123. **80**

Jensen, A. R. (1978). The current status of the IQ controversy. *Australian Psychologist, 13*, 7–28. **80**

Jensen, A. R. (1981). Obstacles, problems, and pitfalls in differential psychology. In S. Scarr (Ed.), *Race, social class, and individual differences in IQ.* Hillsdale, NJ: Lawrence Erlbaum Associates. **80**

Jensen, G. D. (1973). Human sexual behavior in primate perspective. In Zubin, J. and Money, J. (Eds.), *Contemporary sexual behavior: Critical issues in the 1970s.* Baltimore: Johns Hopkins University Press. **65**

Johansson, G. (1977). Studies on visual perception of locomotion. *Perception, 6*, 365–376. **190**

Johansson, G. (1985). About visual event perception. In W. H. Warren & R. E. Shaw (Eds.), *Persistence and change.* Hillsdale, NJ: Lawrence Erlbaum Associates. **190**

Johansson, G., von Hofsten, C., & Jansson, G. (1980). Event perception. *Annual Review of Psychology, 31*, 26–63. **190**

Johnson, R. N. (1972). *Aggression in man and animals.* Philadelphia: Saunders. **330**

Johnson, R. D., & Downing, L. L. (1979). Deindividuation and valence of cues: Effects on prosocial and antisocial behavior. *Journal of Personality and Social Psychology, 37*, 1532–1538. **532**

Jones, E. E., & Davis, K. E. (1965). From acts to dispositions: The attribution process in person perception. In L. Berkowitz (Ed.), *Advances in experimental social psychology* (Vol. 2). New York: Academic Press. **572**

Jones, E. E., & Harris, V. A. (1967). The attribution of attitudes. *Journal of Experimental Social Psychology, 3*, 2–24. **574**

Jones, E. E., Gergen, K. J., & Jones, R. G. (1963). Tactics of ingratiation among leaders and subordinates in a status hierarchy. *Psychological Monographs, 77* (No. 566). **542**

Jones, M. C. (1925). A laboratory study of fear: The case of Peter. *Pedagogical Seminary, 31*, 308–315. **753**

Jones, M. C. (1957). The later careers of boys who were early or late maturing. *Child Development, 28*, 113–128. **422**

Jones, M. C., & Bayley, N. (1950). Physical maturing among boys as related to behavior. *Journal of Educational Psychology, 41*, 129–148. **422**

Jones, M. C., & Mussen, P. H. (1958). Self-conceptions, motivations, and interpersonal attitudes of early- and late-maturing girls. *Child Development, 29*, 491–501. **422**

Jouvet, M. (1975). The function of dreaming: A neurophysiologist's point of view. In M. Gazzaniga & C. Blakemore (Eds.). *Handbook of psychobiology.* New York: Academic Press. **140**

Jouvet, M. (1983). Hypnogenic indolamine-dependent factors and paradoxical sleep rebound. In M. Monnier & M. Meulders (Eds.), *Functions of the nervous system, Vol. 4: Psycho-neurobiology.* New York: Elsevier. **140**

Julesz, B. (1971). *Foundations of cyclopean perception.* Chicago: Chicago University Press. **176**

Jusczyk, P. W. Pisoni, D. B., Walley, A. C., & Murray, J. (1980). Discrimination of relative onset time of two-component tones by infants. *Journal of the Acoustical Society of America, 67*, 262–270. **435**

Kagan, J. (1973). A conversation with Jerome Kagan. *Saturday Review of Education, 1*, 41–43. **87**

Kagan, J., & Klein, R. E. (1973). Cross-cultural perspectives on early development. *American Psychologist, 28*, 947–961. **87**

Kahneman, D., & Tversky, A. (1972). Subjective probability: A judgement of representativeness. *Cognitive Psychology, 3*, 430–454. **276**

Kaij, L. (1960). *Alcoholism in twins: Studies on the etiology and sequels of abuse of alcohol.* Stockholm: Almquist and Wiksell. **679**

Kalinowsky, L. B. (1975). Electric and other convulsive treatments. In S. Arieti (Ed.), *American handbook of psychiatry* (2nd ed., vol. 5). New York: Basic Books. **740**

Kalish, R. A. (1975). *Late adulthood: Perspectives on human development.* Monterey, CA: Brooks/Cole. **425**

Kalish, R. A. (1976). Death and dying in a social context. In R. H. Binstock & E. Shanas (Eds.), *Handbook of aging and the social sciences.* New York: Van Nostrand Reinhold. **427**

Kalish, R. A. (1982). *Late adulthood: Perspectives on human development.* Monterey, CA: Brooks/Cole. **426**

Kalish, R. A., & Reynolds, D. K. (1976). *Death and ethnicity: A psycho-cultural study.* Los Angeles: University of Southern California Press. **427**

Kallmann, F. J. (1952). A comparative twin study on the genetic aspects of male homosexuality. *Journal of Nervous and Mental Disease, 115*, 283–298. **402**

Kamin, L. J. (1974). *The science and politics of IQ.* Potomac, MD: Lawrence Erlbaum Associates. **80**

Kandel, E. R. (1976). *Cellular basis of behavior: An introduction to behavioral neurobiology.* San Francisco: W. H. Freeman. **130**

Kanin, E. J. (1957). Male aggression in dating-courtship relations. *American Journal of Sociology, 63*, 197–204. **405**

Kanin, E. J. (1967). Reference groups and sex conduct norm violations. *Sociological Quarterly, 8*, 495–504. **405**

Kanizsa, A. (1976). Subjective contours. *Scientific American, 234*, pp. 48–52. **187–188**

Kanner, L. (1943). Autistic disturbances of affective contact. *Nervous Child, 2*, 217–250. **673**

Kanner, L., Rodriguez, A., & Alexander, B. (1972). How far can autistic children go in matters of social adjustment? *Journal of Autism and Childhood Schizophrenia, 2*, 9–33. **674**

Kaplan, B. J. (1972). Malnutrition and mental deficiency. *Psychological Bulletin, 78*, 321–337. **126**

Kaplan, H. S. (1974). *The new sex therapy.* New York: Brunner/Mazel. **388, 390**

Karakenick, S. A. (1983). Sex-relevance of content and influenceability: Sistrunk and McDavid revisited. *Personality and Social Psychology Bulletin, 9*, 243–252. **560**

Kasin, S. M. (1979). Consensus information, prediction, and causal attribution: A review of the literature and issues. *Journal of Personality and Social Psychology, 37*, 1966–1981. **575**

Kastenbaum, R. (1979). *Humans developing: A lifespan perspective.* Boston: Allyn & Bacon. **426**

Kastenbaum, R., & Weisman, A. D. (1972). The psychological autopsy as a research procedure in gerontology. In D. P. Kent, R. Kastenbaum & S. Sherwood (Eds.), *Research planning and action for the elderly.* New York: Behavioral Publications. **427**

Katchadourian, H. A., & Lunde, D. T. (1975). *Fundamentals of human sexuality.* New York: Holt, Rinehart & Winston. **389, 397**

Katchadourian, H. A., & Lunde, D. T. (1977). *Fundamentals of human sexuality* (2nd ed.). New York: Holt, Rinehart & Winston. **400**

Katkin, E. S. (1985). Polygraph testing, psychological research, and public policy: An introductory note. *American Psychologist, 40*, 346–348. **329**

Katona, G. (1940). *Organizing and memorizing.* New York: Columbia University Press. **278**

Kaufman, L., & Rock, I. (1962). The moon illusion. *Scientific American, 207*, pp. 120–130. **181**

Kellaway, P. (1946). The part played by electric fish in the early history of bioelectricity and electrotherapy. *Bulletin of the History of Medicine, 20,* 112–37. **739**

Keller, M. B., & Shapiro, R. W. (1981). Major depressive disorder: Initial results from a one-year prospective naturalistic follow-up study. *The Journal of Nervous and Mental Disease, 169,* 761–768. **696**

Kelley, H. H. (1967). Attribution theory in social psychology. In D. Levine (Ed.), *Nebraska Symposium on Motivation, 15,* 192–238. **572, 574**

Kelley, H. H. (1972). Causal schemata and the attribution process. In E. Jones, D. E. Kanouse, H. H. Kelley, R. E. Nisbett, S. Valins & B. Weiner (Eds.), *Attribution: Perceiving the causes of behavior.* Morristown, NJ: General Learning Press. **574**

Kelley, H. H., & Shapiro, M. M. (1954). An experiment on conformity to group norms where conformity is detrimental to group achievement. *American Sociological Review, 19,* 667–677. **542**

Kellogg, R., & Baron, R.F. (1975). Attribution theory, insomnia and the reverse placebo effect: The reversal of Storms and Nisbett's findings. *Journal of Personality and Social Psychology, 32,* 231–236. **341**

Kelly, D. D. (1985). Central representation of pain and analgesia. In E. R. Kandel & J. H. Schwartz (Eds.), *Principles of neural science* (2nd ed.). New York: Elsevier. **165**

Kelly, G. A. (1955). *The psychology of personal constructs* (Vol 1.). New York: Norton. **607–611**

Kelman, H. C. (1950). Effects of success and failure on "suggestibility" in the autokinetic effect. *Journal of Abnormal and Social Psychology, 45,* 267–285. **542**

Kempe, L. H. (1973). A practical approach to the protection of the abused child and rehabilitation of the abusing parent. *Pediatrics, 51,* 804–813. **486**

Kendell, R. E. (1975). *The role of diagnosis in psychiatry.* London: Blackwell. **673**

Kennedy, J. C. (1973). The high-risk maternal-infant acquaintance process. *Nursery Clinics of North America, 8,* 549–556. **479**

Kenshalo, D. R. (Ed.). (1979). *Sensory functions of the skin of humans.* New York: Plenum. **163**

Kerr, F. W. L. (1975). Structural and functional evidence of plasticity in the central nervous system. *Experimental Neurology, 48,* 16–31. **128**

Kesey, K. (1962). *One flew over the cuckoo's nest.* New York: Viking. **736**

Kessler, J. (1966). *Psychopathology of childhood.* Englewood Cliffs, NJ: Prentice-Hall. **673, 721**

Kety, S. S. (1959). Biochemical theories of schizophrenia: Part II. *Science, 129,* 1590–1596. **692**

Kety, S. S. (1980). Quoted in M. Scarf, *Unfinished business: Pressure points in the lives of women* (p. 240). New York: Doubleday. **700**

Kety, S. S., Rosenthal, D., Wender, P. H., & Schulsinger, F. (1968). The types and prevalence of mental illness in the biological and adoptive families of adopted schizophrenics. In D. Rosenthal & S. S. Kety (Eds.), *The transmission of schizophrenia.* Elmsford, NY: Pergamon Press. **688**

Kety, S. S., Rosenthal, D., Wender, P. H., Schulsinger, F., & Jacobson, B. (1975). Mental illness in the biological and adoptive families of adopted individuals who have become schizophrenic: A preliminary report based on psychiatric interviews. In R. R. Fieve, D. Rosenthal, & H. Brill (Eds.), *Genetic research in psychiatry.* Baltimore: Johns Hopkins University Press. **688**

Kiesler, C. A., & Pallak, M. S. (1976). Arousal properties of dissonance manipulations. *Psychological Bulletin, 83,* 1014–1025. **570**

Kihlstrom, J. F. (1985). Hypnosis. *Annual Review of Psychology, 36,* 385–418. **134**

Kimmel, D. C. (1980). *Adulthood and aging* (2nd ed.). New York: Wiley. **426**

Kinsey, A. C., Pomeroy, W. B., & Martin, C. C. (1948). *Sexual behavior in the human male.* Philadelphia: Saunders. **399, 400**

Kinsey, A. C., Pomeroy, W. B., Martin, C. C., & Gebhard, P. H. (1953). *Sexual behavior in the human female.* Philadelphia: Saunders. **352, 363–369, 395, 396**

Kintsch, W. (1974). *The representation of meaning in memory.* Hillsdale, NJ: Lawrence Erlbaum Associates. **259**

Kirkendall, L. A., & Whitehurst, R. N. (Eds.). (1971). *The new sexual revolution.* New York: D. W. Brown. **369**

Kirsch, M. A., & Glass, L. L. (1977). Psychiatric disturbances associated with Erhard Seminars Training: II. Additional cases and theoretical considerations. *American Journal of Psychiatry, 134,* 1254–1258. **768**

Kisker, G. W. (1964). *The disorganized personality.* New York: McGraw-Hill. **689**

Klahr, D., & Wallace, J. G. (1976). *Cognitive development: An information processing view.* Hillsdale, NJ: Lawrence Erlbaum Associates. **461**

Klaus, M., & Kennell, J. (1976). *Maternal-infant bonding.* St. Louis, MO: Mosby. **478**

Klebanoff, L. D. (1959). A comparison of parental attitudes of mothers of schizophrenics, brain injured, and normal children. *American Journal of Orthopsychiatry, 24,* 445–454. **693**

Klein, M., & Kandel, E. R. (1980). Mechanism of calcium current modulation underlying presynaptic facilitation and behavioral sensitization in Aplysia. *Proceedings of the National Academy of Sciences USA, 77,* 6912–6916. **130**

Kleine, C. L., & Staneski, R. A. (1980). First impressions of female bust size. *Journal of Social Psychology, 110,* 123–134. **393**

Kleinmuntz, B., & Szucko, J. J. (1984). A field study of the fallibility of polygraph lie detection. *Nature, 308,* 449–450. **329**

Kleitman, N. (1969). Basic rest-activity cycle in relation to sleep and wakefulness. In A. Kales (Ed.). *Sleep: Physiology and pathology.* Philadelphia: Lippincott. **137**

Kline, P. (1972). *Faculty and fantasy in Freudian theory* (1st ed.). London: Methuen. **618**

Knapp, M. L. (1972). *Nonverbal communication in human interaction* (2nd ed.). New York: Holt, Rinehart & Winston. **67**

Knox, R. E., & Inkster, J. A. (1968). Postdecision dissonance at posttime. *Journal of Personality and Social Psychology, 18,* 319–323. **568**

Koestler, A. (1964). *The act of creation.* New York: Macmillan. **285, 290, 295**

Koff, W. C. (1974). Marijuana and sexual activity. *Journal of Sex Research, 10,* 194–206. **390**

Koffka, K. (1935). *Principles of gestalt psychology.* New York: Harcourt Brace. **146**

Kohlberg, L. (1958). *The development of modes of moral thinking and choice in the years 10 to 16.* Unpublished doctoral dissertation, University of Chicago, Chicago, IL. **507**

Kohlberg, L. (1969). Stage and sequence: The cognitive-developmental approach to socialization. In D. A. Goslin (Ed.), *Handbook of socialization theory and research.* Chicago: Rand McNally. **505, 511**

Kohlberg, L. (1984). *Essays on moral development: The psychology of moral development* (Vol. 2). New York: Harper & Row. **513**

Kohlberg, L., & Candee, D. (1984). The relationship of moral judgment to moral action. In L. Kohlberg (Ed.), *The psychology of moral development.* New York: Harper & Row. **513**

Kohler, W. (1925). *The mentality of apes.* New York: Harcourt Brace. **239, 279**

Kolb, L. C. (1973). *Modern clinical psychiatry* (8th ed.). Philadelphia, PA: Saunders. **697**

Komarovsky, M. (1976). *Dilemmas of mas-*

culinity: A study of college youth. New York: W. W. Norton. **378**

Konishi, M. (1965). The role of auditory feedback in the control of vocalization in the white-crowned sparrow. *Zeitschrift fur Tierpsychologie, 22,* 770–783. **309**

Konner, M. (1977). Evolution of human behavior development and infancy among the Kalahari desert San. In P. H. Leiderman, S. R. Tulkin, & A. Rosenfeld (Eds.), *Culture and infancy.* New York: Academic Press. **486**

Kosterlitz, H. W., & Hughes, J. (1975). Some thoughts on the significance of enkephalin, the endogenous ligand. *Life Sciences, 17,* 91–96. **103**

Kramer, M. (1977). *Psychiatric services and the changing institutional scene, 1950–1985.* Washington, DC: National Institute of Mental Health. **680**

Krebs, D. L., & Adinolfi, A. A. (1975). Physical attractiveness, social relations, and personality style. *Journal of Personality and Social Psychology, 31,* 245–253. **588**

Krebs, D. L., & Miller, D. T. (1985). Altruism and aggression. In G. Lindzey & E. Aronson (Eds.), *Handbook of social psychology* (3rd ed., Vol. 2). New York: Random House. **57, 326, 489, 502, 608, 613**

Krebs, D. L., & Rosenwald, A. (1977). Moral judgment and moral behavior in conventional adults. *Merrill Palmer Quarterly, 23,* 77–87. **511**

Kubler-Ross, E. (1969). On death and dying. New York: Macmillan. **426**

Kuczaj, S. A., II. (1978). Why do children fail to overgeneralize the progressive inflection? *Journal of Child Language, 5,* 167–171. **439**

Kuhn, D. (1980). *On the development of developmental psychology.* Unpublished manuscript, Harvard University, Cambridge, MA. **459**

Kuhn, D., Langer, J., Kohlberg, L., & Haan, N. S. (1977). The development of formal operations in logical and moral judgment. *Genetic Psychology Monographs, 95,* 97–188. **459**

Kuhn, D., Nash, S. C., & Bruken, L. (1978). Sex role concepts of two- and three-year-olds. *Child Development, 49,* 445–451. **499**

Kulik, J. A. (1983). Confirmatory attribution and the perpetuation of social beliefs. *Journal of Personality and Social Psychology, 44,* 1171–1181. **575**

Kulik, J. A., & Taylor, S. E. (1980). Premature consensus on consensus? Effects of sample-based versus self-based consensus information. *Journal of Personality and Social Psychology, 38,* 871–878. **575**

Kurtines, W., & Greif, W. (1974). The development of moral thought: Review

and evaluation of Kohlberg's approach. *Psychological Bulletin, 81,* 453–470. **511**

Kurtz, P. (Ed.). *A skeptic's handbook of parapsychology.* Buffalo, NY: Prometheus Books. **168**

LaBarre, W. (1947). The cultural basis of emotions and gestures. *Journal of Personality, 16,* 49–68. **335**

Labouvie-Vief, G. (1980). Beyond formal operations: Uses and limits of pure logic in life-span development. *Human Development, 23,* 141–161. **459**

Lader, M. H. (1975). *The psychophysiology of mental illness.* London: Routledge & Paul. **708**

Lader, M. H., & Wing. L. (1966). *Physiological measures, sedative drugs, and morbid anxiety.* London: Oxford University Press. **708**

Laing, R. D. (1964). Is schizophrenia a disease? *International Journal of Social Psychiatry, 10,* 184–193. **694**

Lamb, M. E. (1977). Father-infant and mother-infant interaction in the first year of life. *Child Development, 48,* 167–181. **482**

Lamb, M. E. (1981). Fathers and child development: An integrative overview. In M. E. Lamb (Ed.), *The father's role in child development* (2nd ed.). New York: Wiley. **482**

Lamy, R. E. (1966). Social consequences of mental illness. *Journal of Consulting Psychology, 30,* 450–455. **722**

Landis, C., & Bolles, M. M. (1950). *Textbook of abnormal psychology.* New York: Macmillan. **661**

Lang, A. R., Searles, J., Lauerman, R., & Adesso, V. (1980). Expectancy, alcohol and sex guilt as determinants of interest in and reaction to sexual stimuli. *Journal of Abnormal Psychology, 89,* 644–653. **391**

Lange, R., & Fishbein, M. (1983). Effects of category differences on belief change and agreement with the source of a persuasive communication. *Journal of Personality and Social Psychology, 44,* 933–941. **559**

Langer, E. J., Rodin, J., Beck, P., Weinman, C., & Spitzer, L. (1979). Environmental determinants of memory improvement in late adulthood. *Journal of Personality and Social Psychology, 37,* 2003–2013. **425**

Langevin, R., Paitich, D., Anderson, C., Kamrad, J., Pope, S., Geller, G., Pearle, L., & Newman, S. (1979). Experimental studies of the etiology of genital exhibitionism. *Archives of Sexual Behavior, 8,* 307–331. **398**

Lansky, L. M. (1967). The family structure also affects the model: Sex-role attitudes

in parents of preschool children. *Merrill-Palmer Quarterly, 13,* 139–150. **501**

Lansky, L. M., Crandall, V. J., Kagan, J., & Baker, C. T. (1961). Sex differences in aggression and its correlates in middle class adolescents. *Child Development, 32,* 45–58. **498**

LaPiere, R. T. (1934). Attitudes vs. action. *Social Forces, 13,* 230–237. **562, 563**

Lashley, K. S. (1929). *Brain mechanisms and intelligence.* Chicago: University of Chicago Press. **129**

Lashley, K. (1950). In search of the engram. *Society for Experimental Biology: Symposium, 4,* 454–482. **129**

Last, C. G., Barlow, D. H., & O'Brian, G. T. (1984). Cognitive changes during in vivo exposure in an agoraphobic. *Behavior Modification, 8,* 93–113. **705**

Latane, B. (1981). The psychology of social impact. *American Psychologist, 36,* 343–356. **549, 550**

Latane, B., & Dabbs, J. M. (1975). Sex, group size and helping in three cities. *Sociometry, 38,* 180–194. **550**

Latane, B., & Darley, J. M. (1970). *The unresponsive bystander: Why doesn't he help?* New York: Appleton-Century-Crofts. **533**

Latane, B., & Darley, J. M. (1976). *Help in a crisis: Bystander response to an emergency.* Morristown, NJ: General Learning Press. **533, 534**

Latane, B., & Harkins, S. (1976). Cross-modality matches suggest anticipated stage fright as multiplicative function of audience size and status. *Perception and Psychophysics, 20,* 482–488. **550**

Latane, B., Nida, S. A., & Wilson, D. W. (1981). The effects of group size on helping behavior. In J. P. Rushton & R. M. Sorrentino (Eds.), *Altruism and helping behavior.* Hillsdale, NJ: Lawrence Erlbaum Associates. **533**

Latane, B., & Rodin, J. (1969). A lady in distress: Inhibitory effects of friends and strangers on bystander intervention. *Journal of Experimental Social Psychology, 5,* 189–202. **533**

Latane, B., Williams, K., and Harkins, S. (1979). Many hands make light the work: The causes and consequences of social loafing. *Journal of Personality and Social Psychology, 37,* 822–832. **527**

Lavie, P., & Kripke, D. F. (1981). Ultradian (circa 1 1/2 hour) rhythms: A multioscillatory system. *Life Sciences, 29,* 2445–2450. **137**

Lawson, E. D. (1971). *Change in communication nets and performance.* Paper presented at the meeting of the Eastern Psychological Association. **586**

Lazarus, R. S. (1982). Thoughts on the relations between emotion and cognition.

American Psychologist, 37, 1019–1024. **341**

Lazarus, R. S. (1984). On the primacy of cognition. *American Psychologist, 39,* 124–129. **341**

LeBon, G. (1968). *The crowd.* New York: Ballantine. (Original work published in 1895.) **529**

Leff, J. P. & Vaughn, C. (1985). *Expressed emotion in families: Its significance for mental illness.* New York: Guilford Press. **692**

Lefkowitz, M., Blake, R. P., & Mouton, J. (1955). Status factors in pedestrian violation of traffic signals. *Journal of Abnormal and Social Psychology, 51,* 704–705. **550**

Lehmann, H. E. (1975). Schizophrenia: Clinical features. In A. M. Freedman, H. I. Kaplan, & B. J. Sadock (Eds.), *Comprehensive textbook of psychiatry II.* Baltimore: Williams & Wilkins. **692**

Leiman, A. L., & Christian, C. (1973). Electrophysiological analysis of learning and memory. In J. A. Deutsch (Ed.), *The physiological basis of memory.* New York: Academic Press. **129–130**

Lele, P. P., & Weddell, G. (1956). The relationship between neurohistology and corneal sensitivity. *Brain, 79,* 119–154. **163**

Lenes, M. S., & Hart, E. J. (1975). The influence of pornography and violence on attitudes and guilt. *Journal of School Health, 45,* 447–451. **373**

Lenneberg, E. (1967). *Biological foundations of language.* New York: Wiley. **435, 441, 444**

Lepper, M. R., & Green, D. (Eds.) (1979). *The hidden costs of reward.* Hillsdale, NJ: Lawrence Erlbaum Associates. **571**

Leriche, R. (1939). *The surgery of pain.* Baltimore, MD: Williams & Wilkins. **164**

Lerner, M. J. (1965). Evaluation of performance as a function of performer's reward and attractiveness. *Journal of Personality and Social Psychology, 3,* 355–360. **576**

Lerner, M. J., & Simmons, C. H. (1966). Observer's reaction to the "innocent victim": Compassion or rejection? *Journal of Personality and Social Psychology, 4,* 203–210. **576**

Lerner, R. M., & Lerner, J. (1977). Effects of age, sex and physical attractiveness in child-peer relations, academic performance, and elementary school adjustment. *Developmental Psychology, 13,* 585–590. **489**

Leventhal, H., & Nerenz, D. (1983). Representations of threat and the control of stress. In D. Meichenbaum & M. Jarenko (Eds.), *Stress reduction and prevention: A cognitive behavioral approach.* New York: Plenum. **558**

Levine, C., Kohlberg, L., & Hewer, A. (1985). The current formulation of Kohlberg's theory and a response to critics. *Human Development, 28,* 94–100. **513**

Levine, J. M., & McBurney, D. H. (1983). The role of olfaction in social perception and behavior. In C. P. Herman, M. P. Zanna & E. T. Higgins (Eds.), *Physical appearance, stigma, and social behavior: The Ontario symposium* (Vol. 3). Hillsdale, NJ: Lawrence Erlbaum Associates. **169**

Levinson, D. J., Darrow, C. N., Klein, E. B., Levinson, M. H., & McKee, B. (1978). *The seasons of a man's life.* New York: Knopf. **518**

Levy, J. (1972). Autokinetic illusion: A systematic review of theories, measures and independent variables. *Psychological Review, 78,* 457–474. **192**

Lewinsohn, P., & Hoberman, H. (1982). Depression. In A. Bellack, M. Herson & A. Kazdin (Eds.), *International handbook of behavior modification and therapy.* New York: Plenum Press. **703**

Lewinsohn, P. M., Mischel, W., Chaplin, W., & Barton, R. (1980). Social competence and depression: The role of illusory self-perceptions. *Journal of Abnormal Psychology, 89,* 203–212. **700**

Lewis, M., & Brooks, J. (1975). Infants' social perception: A constructivist view. In L. B. Cohen & P. Salapatek (Eds.), *Infant perception: From sensation to cognition* (Vol. 2). New York: Academic Press. **492**

Lewis, S., Langan, C., & Hollander, E. P. (1972). Expectations of future interaction and the choice of less desirable alternatives in conformity. *Sociometry, 34,* 440–447. **542**

Li, S., & Owings, D. (1978). Sexual selection in the three-spined stickleback: II. Nest raiding during the courtship phase. *Behavior, 64,* 298–304. **356**

Lidz, T. (1973). *The origin and treatment of schizophrenic disorders.* New York: Basic Books. **692**

Lieberman, M. A. (1966). Observations on death and dying. *Gerontologist, 6,* 70–72. **426**

Lieberman, M. A., Yalom, I. D., & Miles, M. (1973). *Encounter groups: First facts.* New York: Basic Books. **768**

Lifton, R. J. (1963). Psychological effects of the atomic bomb in Hiroshima: The theme of death. *Daedalus, 92,* 462–497. **576**

Likert, R. (1932). A technique for the measurement of attitudes. *Archives of Psychology, 140,* 44–53. **554**

Lindsay, P. H., & Norman, D. A. (1977). *Human information processing* (2nd Ed.). New York: Academic Press. **282**

Lockard, J. S. (1980). Studies of human social signals: Theory, method and data. In J. S. Lockard (Ed.), *The evolution of human social behavior.* New York: Elsevier. **486**

Lockard, J. S., & Adams, R. M. (1980). Peripheral males: A primate model for a human subgroup. *Bulletin of the Psychonomic Society, 15,* 295–298. **486**

Loftus, E. F. (1979). *Eyewitness testimony.* Cambridge: Harvard University Press. **263**

Loftus, E. F., & Palmer, J. C. (1974). Reconstruction of automobile destruction: An example of the interaction between language and memory. *Journal of Verbal Learning and Verbal Behavior, 13,* 585–589. **263**

London, P. (1964). *The modes and morals of psychotherapy.* New York: Holt, Rinehart & Winston. **774**

Lorayne, J., & Lucas, J. (1974). *The memory book.* New York: Stein & Day. **265**

Lorenz, K. (1937). The companion in the bird's world. *Auk, 54,* 245–273. **90**

Lorenz, K. (1966). *On aggression.* New York: Harcourt, Brace & World. **54**

Lotter, V. (1978). Follow-up studies. In M. Rutter & E. Schopler (Eds.), *Autism: A reappraisal of concepts and treatment.* New York: Plenum Press. **673**

Lovaas, O. I., & Simmons, J. Q. (1969). Manipulation of self-destruction in three retarded children. *Journal of Applied Behavior Analysis, 2,* 143–157. **230**

Lovejoy, C. O. (1981). The origin of man. *Science, 211,* 341–350. **59, 358, 471, 494.**

Low, W. C., Lewis, P. R., Bunch, S. T., Dunnett, S. B., & Thomas, S. R. (1982). Function recovery following neural transplantation of embryonic septal in adult rats with septohippocampal lesions. *Nature, 300,* 260–262. **129**

Lubin, B., & Lubin, A. W. (1980). *An exhaustive bibliography of the group psychotherapy literature 1906–1978.* New York: Plenum. **767**

Luchins, A. S. (1942). Mechanization in problem solving. *Psychological Monographs, 54,* (No. 248). **280, 282**

Ludel, J. (1978). *Introduction to sensory processes.* San Francisco, CA: W. H. Freeman. **155, 160, 162, 167–168, 197**

Lumsden, C. J., & Wilson, E. O. (1983). *Promethean fire.* Cambridge, MA: Harvard University Press. **491**

Luria, A. R. (1968). *The mind of a mnemonist.* New York: Basic Books. **248**

Luria, A. R. (1972). *The man with the shattered world.* Chicago: Regney. **248**

Lykken, D. T. (1981). *A tremor in the blood: Uses and abuses of the lie detector.* New York: McGraw-Hill. **329, 347**

Lyman, B. E. (1984). An experiential theory of emotion: A partial outline with implications for research. *Journal of Mental Imagery, 4,* 77–86. **326**

Lynch, G., McGaugh, J. L., & Weinberger, N. (Eds.). (1984). *Neurobiology of learning and memory.* New York: Guilford Press. **130**

Lyons, R. D. (1984, November 13). Vietnam veterans turn to therapy. *The New York Times,* pp. C1, C6. **708**

Maccoby, E. E. (1980). *Social development: Psychological growth and the parent–child relationship.* New York: Harcourt Brace Jovanovich. **483**

Maccoby, E. E., & Jacklin, C. N. (1974). *The psychology of sex differences.* Stanford, CA: Stanford University Press. **496, 500, 560**

Maccoby, N., & Alexander, J. (1980). Use of media in lifestyle program. In P. O. Davidson & S. M. Davidson (Eds.), *Behavioral medicine: Changing health lifestyles.* New York: Brunner Mazel. **559**

Mack, S. (1981). Novel help for the handicapped. *Science, 212,* 26–27. **233**

Mackay, A. V. P., Iversen, L., Rossor, M., Spokes, E., Bird, A., Creese, I., & Snyder H. (1982). Increased brain dopamine and dopamine receptors in schizophrenia. *Archives of General Psychiatry, 39,* 991–997. **691**

Mackenzie, B. (1984). Explaining race differences in IQ. *American Psychologist, 39,* 1214–1233. **80–81**

Mackintosh, N. J. A. (1975). A theory of attention: Variation of the associability of stimuli with reinforcement. *Psychological Review, 82,* 276–298. **214**

MacLean, P. D. (1973). A triune concept of brain and behavior. In T. Boag & D. Campbell (Eds.), *The Hincks Memorial Lectures.* Toronto: University of Toronto Press. **110**

MacLean, P. D. (1982). On the origin and progressive evolution of the triune brain. In E. Armstrong & D. Falk (Eds.), *Primate brain evolution.* New York: Plenum Press. **110**

Maddi, S. R. (1976). *Personality theories: A comparative analysis.* Homewood, IL: Dorsey Press. **586**

Maher, B. A. (1966). *Principles of psychopathology: An experimental approach.* New York: McGraw-Hill. **692**

Mahoney, E. R. (1983). *Human sexuality.* New York: McGraw-Hill. **378, 379, 384**

Mahoney, M. J. (1980). *Abnormal psychology.* San Francisco: Harper & Row. **762**

Maier, N. R. F. (1945). Reasoning in humans III: The mechanisms of equivalent stimuli and of reasoning. *Journal of Experimental Psychology, 35,* 349–360. **280–281**

Malamuth, N. M., Heim, N., & Feshbach, S. (1980). Sexual responsiveness of college students to rape depictions: inhibi-

tory or disinhibitory effects? *Journal of Personality and Social Psychology, 38,* 399–408. **405**

Malan, D. H., Heath, E. S., Bacal, H. A., & Balfour, F. H. G. (1975). Psychodynamic changes in untreated neurotic patients. *Archives of General Psychiatry, 32,* 110–126. **776**

Maletzky, G. M., & Klotter, J. (1974). Smoking and alcoholism. *American Journal of Psychiatry, 131,* 445–447. **680**

Malmo, R. B. (1970). Emotions and muscle tension: The story of Anne. *Psychology Today, 3,* pp. 64–67. **710**

Malmo, R. B. (1975). *On emotions, needs and our archaic brain.* New York: Holt, Rinehart & Winston. **112**

Mandler, G. (1975). *Mind and emotion.* New York: Wiley. **132, 341**

Mandler, G., & Pearlstone, Z. (1966). Free and constrained concept learning and subsequent recall. *Journal of Verbal Learning and Verbal Behavior, 5,* 126–131. **265**

Mandler, J. M., & Ritchey, G. H. (1977). Long-term memory for pictures. *Journal of Experimental Psychology: Human Learning and Memory, 3,* 386–396. **260**

Mann, L. (1981). The baiting crowd in episodes of threatened suicide. *Journal of Personality and Social Psychology, 41,* 703–709. **532, 551**

Maratsos, M. P. (1983). Some current issues in the study of the acquisition of grammar. In J. H. Flavell & E. M. Markman (Eds.), Cognitive development, Vol. 3 in P. H. Mussen (Ed.), *Handbook of child psychology,* 4th edition. New York: Wiley. **445**

Maratsos, M. P., Fox, D. E. C., Becker, J., & Chaikley, M. A. (1984). *Semantic restrictions on children's early passives.* Unpublished manuscript, University of Minnesota, Minneapolis. **440**

Marcia, J. E. (1966). Development and validation of ego-identity status. *Journal of Personality and Social Psychology, 3,* 551–558. **516**

Marcia, J. E. (1976). Identity six years after: A follow-up study. *Journal of Youth and Adolescence, 5,* 145–160. **516**

Margulies, R., Kessler, R. C., & Kandel, D. B. (1977). A longitudinal study of onset of drinking among high-school students. *Journal of Studies on Alcohol, 38,* 897–912. **679**

Mark, V. H., & Ervin, F. R. (1970). *Violence and the brain.* New York: Harper & Row. **738**

Marks, D., & Kammann, R. (1980). *The psychology of the psychic.* Buffalo, NY: Prometheus Books. **168**

Marmor, J. (1976). Common operational factors in diverse approaches. In A. Burton (Ed.), *What makes behavior change*

possible. New York: Brunner Mazel. **774**

Marshall, G.D., & Zimbardo, P.G. (1979). Affective consequences of inadequately explained physiological arousal. *Journal of Personality and Social Psychology, 37,* 970–988. **341**

Marshall, J. F. (1984). Brain function: Neural adaptations and recovery from injury. *Annual Review of Psychology, 35,* 277–308. **128**

Martin, B. (1975). Parent-child relations. In F. D. Horowitz (Ed.), *Review of child development research* (Vol. 4). Chicago: University of Chicago Press. **483**

Martin, B. (1981). *Abnormal psychology* (2nd ed.). New York: Holt, Rinehart & Winston. **700, 711, 716, 774**

Martin, G., & Pear, J. (1983). *Behavior modification* (2nd ed.). Englewood Cliffs, NJ: Prentice-Hall. **233**

Maslow, A. (1954). *Motivation and personality.* New York: Harper. **15.**

Maslow, A. H. (1970). *Motivation and personality* (2nd ed.). New York: Harper & Row. **303, 519**

Masters, W. H., & Johnson, V. E. (1966). *Human sexual response.* Boston: Little, Brown. **382–385, 757**

Masters, W. H., & Johnson, V. E. (1970). *Human sexual inadequacy.* Boston: Little, Brown. **757**

Masters, W. H., & Johnson, V. E. (1979). *Homosexuality in perspective.* Boston: Little, Brown. **403**

Matheny, A. P., Wilson, R.S., & Dolan, A. B. (1976). Relations between twins' similarity of appearance and behavioral similarity: Testing an assumption. *Behavioral Genetics, 6,* 343–352. **77**

Mathes, E. W., & Edwards, L. I. (1978). Physical attractiveness as an input in social exchanges. *Journal of Psychology, 98,* 267–275. **392**

Mathes, E. W., & Guest, T. A. (1976). Anonymity and group antisocial behavior. *Journal of Social Psychology, 100,* 257–262. **533**

Matin, L., & Mackinnon, G. E. (1964). Autokinetic movement: Selective manipulation of directional components by image stabilization. *Science, 143,* 147–148. **192**

Matlin, M. (1983). *Cognition.* New York: Holt, Rinehart & Winston. **253, 277**

Matteson, D. R. (1975). *Adolescence today: Sex roles and the search for identity.* Homewood, IL: The Dorsey Press. **517**

Maurer, D., & Salapatek, P. (1976). Developmental changes in the scanning of faces by young infants. *Child Development, 47,* 523–527. **477**

Mawhinney, V. T., Bostow, D. E., Laws, D. R., Blumenfeld, G. J., & Hopkins, B. L. (1971). A comparison of students' studying-behavior produced by daily, weekly, and three-week testing schedules. *Journal of Applied Behavior Analysis, 4*, 257–264. **222**

Mayer, D. J. (1979). Endogenous analgesia systems: Neural and behavioral mechanisms. In J. J. Bonica (Ed.), *Advances in pain research and therapy,* (Vol. 3). New York: Raven. **165**

Mayer, R. E. (1977). *Thinking and problem solving.* Glenview, IL: Scott, Foresman. **289**

Mayr, E. (1977). The study of evolution, historically viewed. In C. E. Goulden (Ed.), *The changing scenes in natural sciences, 1776–1976.* Philadelphia: Academy of Natural Sciences, Special Pub. No. 12. **59**

Mazur, J. (1986). *Learning and behavior.* Englewood Cliffs, NJ: Prentice-Hall. **231, 235, 245**

McCaghy, C. (1968). Drinking and deviance disavowal: The case of child molesters. *Social Problems, 16*, 309–319. **396**

McCauley, C., & Swann, C. P. (1976). Male-female differences in sexual fantasy. *Journal of Research in Personality, 12*, 76–88. **394**

McCauley, C., & Swann, C. P. (1980). Sex differences in the frequency and functions of fantasies during sexual activity. *Journal of Research in Personality, 14*, 400–411. **393, 394**

McCauley, E., & Ehrhardt, A. A. (1976). Female sexual response: Hormonal and behavioral interactions. *Primary Care, 3*, 455. **389**

McConnell, J. V. (1962). Memory transfer through cannibalism in planarians. *Journal of Neuropsychiatry, 3*, 42–48. **129**

McCormick, N. B. (1979). Come ons and put offs: Unmarried students' strategies for having and avoiding sexual intercourse. *Psychology of Women Quarterly, 4*, 194–211. **379**

McCullogh, J. W., & Prins, H. A. (1978). *Signs of stress.* London: Collins. **704**

McGaugh, J. L. (1983). Hormonal influences on memory. *Annual Review of Psychology, 34*, 297–323. **132**

McGee, M. G. (1979). *Human spatial abilities: Sources of sex differences.* New York: Praeger. **494**

McGhie, A., & Chapman, J. S. (1961). Disorders of attention and perception in early schizophrenia. *British Journal of Medical Psychology, 34*, 103–116. **684**

McGinnies, E., & Ward, C. D. (1980). Better liked than right: Trustworthiness and expertise as factors in credibility. *Personality and Social Psychology Bulletin, 6*, 467–472. **558**

McGrath, M. J., & Cohen, D. B. (1978). REM sleep facilitation of adaptive waking be-havior: A review of the literature. *Psychological Bulletin, 85*, 24–57. **139**

McGraw, M. C. (1935). *Growth: A study of Johnny and Jimmy.* New York: Appleton. **419**

McGuire, W. J. (1964). Inducing resistance to persuasion. In L. Berkowitz (Ed.), *Advances in experimental social psychology* (Vol. 1). New York: Academic Press. **558, 562**

McGuire, W. J. (1985). Attitudes and attitude change. In G. Lindzey & E. Aronson (Eds.), *Handbook of social psychology* (3rd ed.). New York: Random House. **552, 553, 556, 561, 562**

McGuire, W. L. (1974). Communication persuasion models for drug education: Experimental findings. In M. Goodstadt (Ed.), *Research on methods and programs of drug education.* Toronto: Addiction Research Foundation. **721**

McKeachie, W., Lin, Y. G., Mulholland, J., & Isaacson, R. (1966). Student affiliation, motives, teacher warmth and academic achievement. *Journal of Personality and Social Psychology, 4*, 457–461. **316**

McKim, R. H. (1980). *Thinking visually: A strategy manual for problem solving.* Belmont, CA: Wadsworth. **285**

McLemore, C. W., & Benjamin, L. S. (1979). Whatever happened to interpersonal diagnosis? *American Psychologist, 34*, 17–34. **670**

McNamee, S. (1977). Moral behavior, moral development, and motivation. *Journal of Moral Education, 7*, 27–31. **511**

McNeill, D. (1966). Developmental psycholinguistics. In F. Smith & G. A. Miller (Eds.), *The genesis of language: A psycholinguistic approach.* Cambridge, MA: M.I.T. Press. **442**

Mednick, R. A. (1977). Gender-specific variances in sexual fantasy. *Journal of Personality Assessment, 41*, 248–254. **393, 394**

Meehl, P. E. (1962). Schizotaxia, schizotypy and schizophrenia. *American Psychologist, 17*, 827–838. **694**

Meichenbaum, D. (1977). *Cognitive behavior modification: An integrative approach.* New York: Plenum Press. **766**

Meichenbaum, D. H., & Goodman, J. (1969). Reflection-impulsivity and verbal control of motor behavior. *Child Development, 40*, 785–797. **692**

Meichenbaum, D. H., Henshaw, D., & Himmel, N. (1982). Coping with stress as a problem-solving process. In W. Krohne & L. Laux (Eds.), *Achievement, stress, and anxiety.* Washington, DC: Hemisphere. **766**

Melamed, B. G., Hawes, R. R., Heiby, E., & Glick, J. (1975). The use of filmed modeling to reduce uncooperative behavior of children during dental treatment. *Journal of Dental Research, 54*, 797–801. **489**

Melnick, B., & Hurley, J. (1969). Distinctive personality attributes of child-abusing mothers. *Journal of Consulting and Clinical Psychology, 33*, 746–749. **486**

Meltzoff, A. N., & Moore, M. K. (1983). Newborn infants imitate adult facial gestures. *Child Development, 54*, 702–709. **334**

Melzack, R. (1973). *The puzzle of pain.* New York: Basic Books. **163, 165, 311**

Melzack, R., & Scott, T. H. (1957). The effects of early experience on the response to pain. *Journal of Comparitive and Physiological Psychology, 50, 155.* **311**

Melzack, R., & Wall, P. D. (1965). Pain mechanisms: A new theory. *Science, 150*, 971–979. **163, 165**

Melzack, R., & Wall, P. D. (1982). *The challenge of pain.* New York: Penguin. **163, 165**

Mendel, G. J. (1866). Versuche ueber Pflanzenhybriden. Verhandlungen des Naturforschunden Vereines in Bruenn, 4, 3–47. (The Royal Horticultural Society of London, Trans.). Available in Dodson, E. O. (1956). *Genetics.* Philadelphia: W. B. Saunders. **55**

Mendelsohn, M. J., & Mosher, D. L. (1979). Effect of sex guilt and premarital sexual permissiveness on role-played sex education and moral attitudes. *Journal of Sex Research, 15*, 174–183. **378**

Mendinnus, B. R. (1966). Behavioral and cognitive measures of conscience development. *Journal of Genetic Psychology, 109*, 147–150. **511**

Meyer, A. (1982, June). Do lie detectors lie? *Science, 82*, 24–26. **329**

Meyer, K. K., Winick, M., & Harris, R. C. (1975). Malnutrition and environmental enrichment by early adoption. *Science, 190*, 1173–1175. **126**

Mialet, J. P., & Pichot, P. (1981). Eyetracking patterns in schizophrenia: An analysis based on the incidence of saccades. *Archives of General Psychiatry, 38*, 138–186. **692**

Michael, R. P., Bonsail, R. W., & Warner, P. (1974). Human vaginal secretions: Volatile fatty acid content. *Science, 8*, 101–120. **391**

Michaels, C. F., & Carello, C. (1981). Direct perception. Englewood Cliffs, NJ: Prentice-Hall. **194**

Miles, C. C., & Miles, W. R. (1932). The correlation of intelligence scores and chronological age from early to late maturity. *American Journal of Psychology, 44*, 44–78. **462**

Milgram, S. (1963). Behavioral study of obedience. *Journal of Abnormal and*

Social Psychology, 67, 371–378. **545–549**

Mill, J. S. (Ed.). (1869). *Analysis of the phenomena of the human mind* (2nd ed.). London: Longmans, Green, Reader, and Dyer. (Original edition by James Mill published in 1829; reprinted in 1967 by Augustus M. Kelley, Publishers, New York.) **50**

Miller, A. G. (1970). Role of physical attractiveness in impression formation. *Psychonomic Science, 19,* 241–243. **588**

Miller, D. T., & Ross, M. (1975). Self-serving biases in the attribution of causality: Fact or fiction? *Psychological Bulletin, 82,* 213–225. **578**

Miller, G. A. (1956). The magical number seven, plus or minus two: Some limits on our capacity for processing information. *Psychological Review, 63,* 81–97. **254**

Miller, G. A. (1978). The acquisition of word meaning. *Child Development, 49,* 999–1004. **436**

Miller, R. E., Caul, W. F., & Mirsky, I. A. (1967). Communication of affect between feral and socially isolated monkeys. *Journal of Personality and Social Psychology, 7,* 231–239. **334**

Miller, S. M. (1979). Controllability and human stress: Method, evidence and theory. *Behavior Research and Therapy, 17,* 287–304. **678**

Mims, F. H., & Swenson, M. (1980). *Sexuality: A nursing perspective.* New York: McGraw-Hill. **390**

Minuchin, P. (1965). Sex-role concepts and sex typing in childhood as a function of school and home environments. *Child Development, 36,* 1033–1048. **495**

Minuchin, S. (1974). *Families and family therapy.* Cambridge, MA: Harvard University Press. **769**

Mischel, W. (1968). *Personality and assessment.* New York: Oxford University Press. **495, 519**

Mischel, W. (1968). *Personality and assessment.* New York: Wiley. **612**

Mischel, W. (1981). *Introduction to personality* (3rd ed.). New York: Holt, Rinehart and Winston. **613**

Mischel, W., & Mischel, H. N. (1976). A cognitive social-learning approach to morality and self-regulation. In T. Lickona (Ed.), *Moral development and behavior.* New York: Holt, Rinehart & Winston. **511**

Mishkin, M. (1978). Memory in monkeys severely impaired by combined but not separate removal of amygdala and hippocampus. *Nature, 173,* 297–298. **132**

Mishkin, M., & Petri, H. L. (1984). Memories and habits: Some implications for the analysis of learning and retention. In L. R. Squire & N. Butters (Eds.), *Neuropsychology of memory.* New York: Guildford. **248**

Mita, T. H., Derner, M., & Knight, J. (1977). Reversed facial images and the mere-exposure hypothesis. *Journal of Personality and Social Psychology, 35,* 597–601. **554**

Mitchell, G., & Schroers, L. (1973). Birth order and prenatal experience in monkey and man. In H. W. Reese (Ed.), *Advances in child development and behavior* (Vol. 8). New York: Academic Press. **487**

Mitsos, S. B. (1958). Representative elements in role construct technique. *Journal of Consulting Psychology, 22,* 311–313. **618**

Moltz, H. (1973). Some implications of the critical period hypothesis. *Annals of the New York Academy of Sciences, 223,* 144–146. **91**

Moltz, H., Rosenblum, L., & Stettner, L. J. (1960). Some parameters of imprinting effectiveness. *Journal of Comparative and Physiological Psychology, 53,* 297–301. **92**

Money, J. (1971). Biological and behavioral aspects of sexual differentiation. In N. Kretchmer & D. N. Walcher (Eds.), *Environmental influences on genetic expression.* Washington, DC: Government Printing Office. **84**

Money, J. (1976). Human hermaphroditism. In F. Beach (Ed.), *Human sexuality in four perspectives.* Baltimore, MD: Johns Hopkins University Press. **84**

Money, J., & Ehrhardt, A. A. (1972). *Man and woman, boy and girl.* Baltimore, MD: Johns Hopkins University Press. **84, 496**

Monson, T. C., & Snyder, M. (1977). Actors, observers, and the attribution process: Toward a reconceptualization. *Journal of Experimental Social Psychology, 13,* 89–111. **580**

Montemayor, R., & Eisen, M. (1977). The development of self-conceptions from childhood to adolescence. *Developmental Psychology, 13,* 314–319. **499**

Montmollin, G. (1977). *L'Influence sociale: Phenomenes, facteures et theories.* Paris: Presses Universitaires de France. **539**

Montour, K. (1977). William James Sidis, the broken twig. *American Psychologist, 32,* 265–279. **90**

Mook, D. G. (1963). Oral and postingestional determinants of the intake of various solutions in rats with esophageal fistulas. *Journal of Comparative and Physiological Psychology, 56,* 645–659. **304**

Moreno, J. L. (1934). *Who shall survive?* New York: Nervous and Mental Disease Publishing Co. **766**

Morgan, C. D., & Murray, H. A. (1935). A method for investigating fantasies: The Thematic Apperception Test. *Archives*

of Neurology and Psychiatry, 34, 289–306. **631**

Morris, N. M., & Udry, J. R. (1978). Pheromonal influences on human sexual behavior: An experimental research. *Journal of Biosocial Science, 10,* 147–157. **391**

Morris, W. N., & Miller, R. S. (1975). The effects of consensus-breaking and consensus-preempting partners on reduction of conformity. *Journal of Experimental Social Psychology, 11,* 215–223. **542**

Morris, W. N., Miller, R. S., & Spangenberg, S. (1977). The effects of dissenter position and task difficulty on conformity and response conflict. *Journal of Personality, 45,* 251–266. **542**

Moruzzi, G. (1974). Neural mechanisms of the sleep-waking cycle. In O. Petre-Quadens & J. D. Schlag (Eds.), *Basic sleep mechanisms.* New York: Academic Press. **138**

Moscovici, S. (1985). Social influence and conformity. In G. Lindzey & E. Aronson (Eds.), *Handbook of social psychology* (3rd ed.). New York: Random House. **541, 543, 544**

Moscovici, S., & Lange, E. (1976). Studies in social influence III: Majority versus minority influence in a group. *European Journal of Social Psychology, 6,* 149–174. **544**

Moscovici, S., & Personnaz, B. (1980). Studies in social influence, V: Minority influence and conversion behavior in a perceptual task. *Journal of Social Experimental Psychology, 10,* 270–282. **544, 545**

Mosher, D. L. (1961). *The development and validation of a sentence completion measure of guilt.* Unpublished doctoral dissertation, Ohio State University, Columbus, OH. **372**

Mosher, D. L. (1968). Measurement of guilt in females by self-report inventories. *Journal of Consulting and Clinical Psychology, 32,* 690–695. **372**

Mosher, D. L. (1979). Sex guilt and sex myths in college men and women. *Journal of Sex Research, 15,* 224–234. **371**

Mosher, D. L., & Cross, H. J. (1971). Sex guilt and premarital sexual experiences of college students. *Journal of Consulting and Clinical Psychology, 36,* 27–32. **373**

Mosher, D. L., & White, B. B. (1980). Effects of committed or casual erotic guided imagery on females' subjective sexual arousal and emotional response. *Journal of Sex Research, 16,* 273–299. **372**

Moskowitz, D. S. (1982). Coherence and cross-situational generality in personality: A new analysis of old problems. *Journal of Personality and Social Psychology, 43,* 754–768. **613**

Mould, D. E. (1980). Neuromuscular

aspects of women's orgasms. *Journal of Sex Research, 16,* 197–201. **386**

Movshon, J. A., & Van Sluyters, R. C. (1981). Visual neural development. *Annual Review of Psychology, 32,* 477–522. **126**

Mowrer, O. H., & Mowrer, W. M. (1938). Enuresis: A method for its study and treatment. *American Journal of Orthopsychiatry, 8,* 436–459. **215**

Mowrer, O. H., & Viek, P. (1948). An experimental analogue of fear from a sense of helplessness. *Journal of Abnormal and Social Psychology, 43,* 193–200. **231**

Mueller, E. C., & Vandell, D. (1978). Infant-infant interaction. In J. D. Osofsky (Ed.), *Handbook of infancy.* New York: Wiley. **485**

Murdoch, B. B. (1961). The retention of individual items. *Journal of Experimental Psychology, 62,* 618–625. **255, 258**

Murdock, G. P. (1949). *Social structure.* New York: Macmillan. **362**

Murdock, G. P. (1965). *Culture and society.* Pittsburgh: University of Pittsburgh Press. **360**

Murphy, R. D. (1980). Consumer responses to cigarette health warnings. In L. A. Morris, M. B. Mazis, & I. Barofsky (Eds.), *Product labeling and health risks.* Cold Spring Harbor Laboratory Report, 6, 13–21. New York: Branbury. **559**

Myers, B. J. (1984). Mother-infant bonding: The status of the critical-period hypothesis. *Developmental Review, 4,* 240–274. **92**

Myers, D. G. (1983). *Social psychology.* New York: McGraw-Hill. **533, 571**

Myers, D. G. (1986). *Psychology.* New York: Worth. **329–330**

Nahas, G. G. (1975). *Marijuana— deceptive weed* (rev. ed.). New York: Raven Press. **103**

Nathan, P. E., & O'Brien, J. S. (1971). An experimental analysis of the behavior of alcoholics and nonalcoholics during prolonged experimental drinking: A necessary precursor of behavior therapy? *Behavior Therapy, 2,* 455–476. **679**

The National Commission for the Protection of Human Subjects of Biomedical and Behavioral Research. (1977). *Report and recommendations on psychosurgery* (DHEW Publication No. 77–0001). Washington, DC: U.S. Government Printing Office. **738**

National Institute of Law Enforcement and Criminal Justice. (1978). *Forcible rape: An analysis of legal issues.* Washington, DC: US Department of Justice. **404**

Necker, L. A. (1832). Observations on some remarkable phaenomena seen in Switzerland; and an optical phaenomenon which occurs on viewing of a crystal or geometrical solid. *Philosophical Magazine, 1,* pp. 329–337. **183**

Neilson, R. A. (1965). *Alcohol involvement in fatal motor accidents in 27 Californian counties in 1964.* San Francisco: California Traffic Safety Foundation. **792**

Neisser, U. (1963). The multiplicity of thought. *British Journal of Psychology, 54,* 1–4. **291**

Neisser, U. (1967). *Cognitive psychology.* New York: Appleton-Century-Crofts. **248, 250**

Nelson, K. (1973). Structure and strategy in learning to talk. *Monographs of the Society for Research in Child Development, 38*(149). **436**

Nelson, K., Rescorla, L., Gruendel, J., & Benedict, H. (1978). Early lexicons: What do they mean? *Child Development, 49,* 960–968. **436**

Nemeth, C., & Wachtler, J. (1973). Consistency and modification of judgment. *Journal of Experimental Social Psychology, 9,* 65–79. **544**

Neugarten, B. (1967). A new look at menopause. *Psychology Today,* pp. 42–45, 67–70. **423, 425**

Newell, A., & Simon, H. A. (1972). *Human problem solving.* Englewood Cliffs, NJ: Prentice-Hall. **288, 290, 461**

Nisbett, R. & Ross, L. (1980). *Human inference: Strategies and shortcomings of social judgment.* Englewood Cliffs, NJ: Prentice-Hall. **278, 575**

Nisbett, R. E., & Borgida, E. (1975). Attribution and the psychology of prediction. *Journal of Personality and Social Psychology, 32,* 932–943. **575**

Niven, R. G. (1979). Introduction to the drinking driver. In M. Galanter (Ed.), *Currents in alcoholism* (Vol. 6). New York: Grune & Stratton. **678**

Noonen, K. M. (1987). Evolution: A primer for psychologists. In Crawford, C. B., Smith, M., & Krebs, D. L., (Eds.), *Sociobiology and psychology: Ideas, issues, and findings.* Hillsdale, NJ: Lawrence Erlbaum Associates. **58**

Norris, J., & Feldman-Summers, S. (1981). Factors related to the psychological impacts of rape on the victim. *Journal of Abnormal Psychology, 90,* 562–567. **407**

Notman, M. (1979). Midlife concerns of women: Implications of the menopause. *American Journal of Psychiatry, 136,* 1270–1274. **423**

Novin, D., Wyrwicka, W., & Bray, G. A. (Eds.) (1976). *Hunger: Basic mechanisms and clinical implications.* New York: Raven Press. **305**

Nunnally, J. C. (1967). *Psychometric theory.* New York: McGraw-Hill. **633**

O'Connor, R. D. (1969). Modification of social withdrawal through symbolic modeling. *Journal of Applied Behavior Analysis, 2,* 15–22. **489**

Offir, C. W. (1982). *Human sexuality.* New York: Harcourt Brace Jovanovich. **389**

Olds, J., & Milner, P. (1954). Positive reinforcement produced by electrical stimulation of septal area and other regions of rat brain. *Journal of Comparative and Physiological Psychology, 47,* 419–427. **116**

Olweus, D. (1977). A critical analysis of the "modern" interactionist position. In D. Magnusson & N. S. Endler (Eds.), *Personality at the crossroads: Current issues in interactional psychology.* Hillsdale, NJ: Lawrence Erlbaum Associates. **613**

Omenn, G. S. (1978). Prenatal diagnosis of genetic disorders. *Science, 200,* 952–958. **76**

Orwell, G. (1949). *Nineteen eighty-four.* New York: Harcourt, Brace. **440**

Osborn, A. F. (1957). *Applied imagination* (rev. ed.). New York: Scribner. **27, 29**

Osofsky, J. D., & Danzger, B. (1974). Relationships between neonatal characteristics and mother-infant interaction. *Developmental Psychology, 10,* 124–130. **475**

Overmier, J. B., & Seligman, M. E. P. (1967). Effects of inescapable shock upon subsequent escape and avoidance responding. *Journal of Comparative and Physiological Psychology, 63,* 28–33. **231**

Owens, J., Bower, G. H., & Black, J. B. (1979). The "soap opera" effect in story recall. *Memory and Cognition, 7,* 185–191. **268–269**

Owens, J., Dafoe, J., & Bower, G. H. (1977). *Taking a point of view: Character identification and attributional processes in story comprehension and memory.* Paper presented at the convention of the American Psychological Association, San Francisco, California. **260**

Owens, W. A. (1966). Age and mental abilities: A second adult follow up. *Journal of Educational Psychology, 57,* 311–325. **462**

Page, E. B. (1975). Miracle in Milwaukee: Raising the IQ. In B. Z. Friedlander, G. M. Sterritt and G. E. Kirk (Eds.), *The exceptional infant.* New York: Brunner/Mazel. **89**

Paivio, A. (1971). *Imagery and verbal processes.* New York: Holt, Rinehart & Winston. **259**

Paivio, A. (1978). Comparison of mental clocks. *Journal of Experimental Psychology: Perception and Performance, 4,* 61–71. **259, 261**

Panksepp, J. (1981). Hypothalamic integration of behavior. *Hypothalamus* (Vol. 3, Part B). *Behavioral studies of the hypothalamus.* New York: Marcel Dekker. **330**

Panksepp, J. (1982). Toward a general psychobiological theory of emotions. *Be-*

bavioral and Brain Sciences, 5, 407–467. **330**

Papastamou, S. (1979). *Strategies d'influence minoritaires et majoritaires.* Unpublished doctoral dissertation. Paris: Ecole des Hautes Etudes en Sciences Sociales. **544**

Parke, R. D., & Collmer, C. W. (1975). Child abuse: An interdisciplinary analysis. In E. M. Hetherington (Ed.), *Review of child development research,* (Vol. 5). Chicago: University of Chicago Press. **486, 487**

Parker, E. S., Birnbaum, I. M., & Noble, E. P. (1976). Alcohol and memory: Storage and state dependency. *Journal of Verbal Learning and Verbal Behavior, 15,* 691–702. **267**

Parker, G. A., Baker, R. R., & Smith, V. G. F. (1972). The origin and evolution of gamete dimorphism and the male-female phenomenon. *Journal of Theoretical Biology, 36,* 529–533. **354**

Pascual-Leone, J. (1970). A mathematical model for the transition rule in Piaget's developmental stages. *Acta Psychologica, 63,* 301–345. **459**

Pascual-Leone, J. (1973). *A theory of constructive operators, a new-Piagetian model of conservation, and the problem of horizontal decalages.* Unpublished manuscript, York University. **459**

Pascual-Leone, J. (1980). Constructive problems for constructive theories: The current relevance of Piaget's work and a critique of information-processing simulation psychology. In R. H. Kluwe & H. Spads (Eds.), *Developmental models of thinking.* New York: Academic Press. **459**

Passons W. R. (1975). *Gestalt approaches to counseling.* New York: Holt, Rinehart & Winston. **751**

Paterson, C. A. (1979). Crystalline lens. In R. E. Records (Ed.), *Physiology of the human eye and visual system.* New York: Harper & Row. **152**

Patterson, F., & Linden, E. (1981). *The education of Koko.* NY: Holt, Rinehart & Winston. **71**

Patterson, T. E. (1980). *The mass media: How Americans choose their president.* New York: Praeger. **559**

Paupst, J. C. (1975). *The sleep book.* Toronto: Macmillan of Canada. **103**

Pavlov, I. (1927). *Conditioned reflexes: An investigation of the physiological activity of the cerebral cortex.* (G. V. Anrep., Trans.). London: Oxford University Press. **205**

Paykel, E. S. (1979). Recent life events in the development of the depressive disorders. In R. A. Depue (Ed.), *The psychobiology of the depressive disorders.* New York: Academic Press. **703**

Pearce, J. M., & Hall, G. (1980). A model for Pavlovian learning: Variations in the ef-

fectiveness of conditioned but not unconditioned stimuli. *Psychological Review, 87,* 532–552. **214**

Pearce, K. A., Schaver, A. H., Garfield, N. J., Chloe, C. D., & Patterson, T. W. (1985). A study of post-traumatic stress disorder in Vietnam Veterans. *Journal of Clinical Psychology, 41,* 9–14. **708**

Pedalino, E., & Gamboa, V. U. (1974). Behavior modification and absenteeism: Intervention in one industrial setting. *Journal of Applied Psychology, 59,* 694–698. **233**

Peller, L. E. (1954). Libidinal phases, ego development and play. *Psychoanalytic Study of the Child, 9,* 178–198. **487**

Penfield, W., & Boldrey, E. (1937). Somatic motor and sensory representation in the cerebral cortex of man as studied by electrical stimulation. *Brain, 60,* 389–443. **101, 104**

Peplau, L. A., & Hammen, C. L. (1977). Social psychological issues in sexual behavior: An overview. *Journal of Social Issues, 33,* 1–6. **352**

Perls, F. (1969). *Gestalt therapy verbatim.* Lafayette, CA: Real People Press. **751**

Perry, D. G., & Bussey, K. (1977). Self-reinforcement in high- and low-aggressive boys following acts of aggression. *Child Development, 48,* 653–657. **498**

Perry, W. G. (1968). *Forms of intellectual and ethical development in the college years.* New York: Holt, Rinehart & Winston. **6**

Peterson, C., Seligman, M. E. P. (1984). Causal explanations as a risk factor for depression: Theory and evidence. *Psychological Review, 91,* 347–374. **231**

Petras, J. W. (1973). *Sexuality and society.* Boston: Allyn & Bacon. **371**

Phelps, M. E., & Mazziotta, J. C. (1985). Positron emission tomography: Human brain function and biochemistry. *Science, 228,* 799–809. **106**

Phillips, J. R. (1973). Syntax and vocabulary of mother's speech to young children: Age and sex comparisons. *Child Development, 44,* 182–185. **444**

Phoenix, C. H. (1974). Prenatal testosterone in the nonhuman primate and its consequences for behavior. In R. C. Friedman, R. M. Richart & R. L. Vandewiele (Eds.), *Sex differences in behavior.* New York: Wiley. **496**

Piaget, J. (1932). *The moral judgment of the child.* New York: Harcourt, Brace. **488, 506**

Piaget, J. (1952). *The origins of intelligence in children.* New York: International Universities Press. **447, 448**

Piaget, J. (1954). *The construction of reality in the child* (M. Cook, Trans.). New York: Basic Books. **452, 493**

Piaget, J. (1977). The first year of life of the child. In H. E. Gruber & J. J. Voneche

(Translators & Eds.), *The essential Piaget.* New York: Basic Books. (Original work published 1927.) **492**

Piaget, J. (Ed.). (1967). Logique et connaissance scientifique. *Encyclopedie de la Pleide* (Vol. 22). Paris: Gallimard. **516**

Piaget, J., & Inhelder, B. (1969). *The psychology of the child,* (H. Weaver, Trans.). New York: Basic Books. **457**

Piggott, L. R. (1979). Overview of selected basic research in autism. *Journal of Autism and Developmental Disorders, 9,* 199–218. **674**

Piliavin, J. A., Dovidio, J. E., Gaertner, S. L., & Clark, R. D. III. (1981). *Emergency intervention.* New York: Academic Press. **534–536, 538, 551**

Pines, M. (1982, May 4). Movement grows to create guidelines for mental therapy. *New York Times,* C1, C6. **777**

Plomin, R., DeFries, J. C., & McClearn, G. E. (1980). *Behavioral genetics: A primer.* San Francisco: W. H. Freeman. **73–74**

Plutchik, R. (1980). *Emotion: A psychoevolutionary synthesis.* New York: Harper & Row. **331, 336–338, 347**

Plutchik, R. (Ed.). (1983). *Emotion: Theory, research and experience.* New York: Academic Press. **336**

Poincare, J. H. (1913). The value of science. In *The foundations of science* (G. B. Halstead, Trans.). New York: Science Press. **291**

Pola, J., & Matin, L. (1977). Eye movements following autokinesis. *Bulletin of the Psychonomic Society, 10,* 397–398. **192**

Pomeroy, W. B. (1975). The diagnosis and treatment of transvestites and transsexuals. *Journal of Sex and Marital Therapy, 1,* 215–224. **398, 399**

Poon, L. W., Fozard, J. L., & Walsh-Sweeney, L. (1980). Memory training for the elderly: Salient issues on the use of imagery mnemonics. In L. W. Poon, J. L. Fozard, L. S. Cermak, D. Arenberg & L. W. Thompson (Eds.), *New directions in memory and aging: Proceedings of the George A. Talland Memorial Conference.* Hillsdale, NJ: Lawrence Erlbaum Associates. **425**

Porter, I. H. (1977). Evolution of gentic counseling in America. In H. A. Lubs & F. de la Cruz (Eds.), *Genetic counseling: A monograph of the National Institute of Child Health and Human Development.* New York: Raven Press. **76**

Posner, M. I. (1973). *Cognition: An introduction.* Glenview, IL: Scott, Foresman. **291**

Posner, M. I., & Keele, S. W. (1967). Decay of information from a single letter. *Science, 158,* 137–139. **253**

Powley, T. L., Opsahl, C. A., Cox, J. E., & Weingarten, H. P. (1980). The role of the hypothalamus in energy homeostasis. In P. J. Morgane & J. Panksepp (Eds.), *Handbook of the hypothalamus* (Vol. 3). Behavioral studies on the hypothalamus. New York: Marcel Dekker. **305**

Premack, A. J., & Premack, D. (1972). Teaching language to an ape. *Scientific American, 227*, pp. 92–99. **70**

Premack, D. (1971). Language in chimpanzee? *Science, 172*, 808–822. **70**

Prentice-Dunn, S., & Rogers, R. W. (1983). Deindividuation in aggression. In R. G. Geen & E. I. Donnerstein (Eds.), *Aggression: Theoretical and empirical reviews* (Vol. 2). New York: Academic Press. **530**

Prince, V., & Bentler, P. M. (1972). Survey of 504 cases of transvestism. *Psychological Reports, 31*, 903–917. **399**

Proctor, F., Wagner, N., & Butler, V. (1974). The differentiation of male and female orgasm: An experimental study. In N. Wagner (Ed.), *Perspectives on Human Sexuality*. New York: Behavioral Publications. **387**

Pruyser, P. W. (1973). The beleaguered individual: Images of man in clinical practice. *Bulletin of the Menninger Clinic, 37*, 133–148. **768**

Puka, B. (1983). Altruism and moral development. In D. L. Bridgeman (Ed.), *The nature of prosocial development*. New York: Academic Press. **511**

Pyle, R. L., Mitchell, J. E., & Eckert, E. D. (1981). Bulimia: A report of 34 cases. *Journal of Clinical Psychiatry, 41*, 60–64. **671**

Rachman, S. (1966). Sexual fetishism: An experimental analogue. *Psychological Record, 16*, 293–296. **397**

Rachman, S. J., & Wilson, G. T. (1980). *The effects of psychological therapy* (2nd ed.). New York: Pergamon Press. **777**

Randell, J. (1969). Preoperative and postoperative status of male and female transsexuals. In R. Green & J. Money (Eds.), *Transsexualism and sex reassignment*. Baltimore: Johns Hopkins University Press. **399**

Randi, J. (1983a). The Project Alpha experiment: Part I. The first two years. *Skeptical Enquirer, 7*, 24–33. **168**

Randi, J. (1983b). The Project Alpha experiment: Part II: Beyond the laboratory. *Skeptical Enquirer, 8*, 36–45. **168**

Rao, T. V. (1978). Maternal age, parity, and twin pregnancies. In W. D. Nance (Ed.), *Twin research, Part B: Biology and epidemiology*. New York: Alan R. Liss. **75**

Raper, A. F. (1933). *The tragedy of lynching*. Durham: University of North Carolina Press. **528**

Rappaport, D. (1959). The structure of psychoanalytic theory: A systematizing attempt. In S. Koch (Ed.), *Psychology: A*

study of a science (Vol. 3). New York: McGraw-Hill. **618**

Razran, G. (1971). *Mind in evolution*. Boston: Houghton Mifflin. **204, 212, 235, 241, 245**

Rebelsky, F., & Hanks, C. (1972). Father's verbal interaction with infants in the first three months of life. *Child Development, 42*, 63–68. **481**

Reed, G. L., & Lederman, P. H. (1983). Is imprinting an appropriate model for human infant attachment? *International Journal of Behavioral Development, 6*, 51–69. **92**

Reed, J. A. (1974). *You are what you wear*. Human Behavior. **587**

Regan, D. T., & Fazio, R. (1977). On the consistency between attitudes and behavior: Look to the method of attitude formation. *Journal of Experimental Social Psychology, 13*, 28–45. **565**

Regan, D. T., & Totten, J. (1975). Empathy and attribution: Turning observers into actors. *Journal of Personality and Social Psychology, 32*, 850–856. **577**

Reh, T., & Kalil, K. (1982). Functional role of regrowing pyramidal tract fibres. *Journal of Comparative Neurology, 211*, 276–283. **128**

Reisenzein, R. (1983). The Schachter theory of emotion: Two decades later. *Psychological Bulletin, 94*, 239–264. **330, 339, 341**

Reiss, I. L. (1960). *Premarital sexual standards in America*. Glencoe, IL: The Free Press. **367**

Reiss, I. L. (1967). *The social context of premarital sexual permissiveness*. New York: Holt, Rhinehart & Winston. **351**

Reitman, W. (1964). Heuristic decision procedures, open constraints, and the structure of ill-defined problems. In M. W. Shelley & G. L. Bryan (Eds.), *Human judgement and optimality*. New York: Wiley. **287**

Rescorla, R. A., & Wagner, A. R. (1972). A theory of Pavlovian conditioning: Variations in the effectiveness of reinforcement and nonreinforcement. In A. H. Black & W. F. Prokasy (Eds.), *Classical conditioning II: Current research and theory*. New York: Appleton-Century-Crofts. **213**

Restak, R. M. (1984). *The brain*. New York: Bantam. **118, 132**

Rheingold, H. L. (1968). The social and socializing infant. In D. A. Goslin (Ed.), *Handbook of socialization theory and research*. New York: Rand McNally. **475, 482**

Rheingold, H. L., & Eckerman, C. (1973). Fear of the stranger: A critical examination. In H. Reese (Ed.), *Advances in child development and behavior* (Vol. 8). New York: Academic Press. **477**

Rice, B. (1973). The high cost of thinking the unthinkable. *Psychology Today, 7*, pp. 89–93. **636, 652**

Richards, J. E., & Rader, N. (1981). Crawling-onset age predicts visual cliff avoidance in infants. *Journal of Experimental Psychology, 7*, 382–387. **431**

Richardson, J. G., & Cranston, J. E. (1981). Social change, parental values, and the salience of sex education. *Journal of Marriage and the Family, 43*, 547–558. **379**

Ricks, D. F., Wanderman, A., & Popper, P. J. (1976). Humanism and behaviorism: Toward a new synthesis. In A. Wanderman (Ed.), *Humanism and behavior dialogue and growth*. New York: Pergamon. **735**

Riecken, H. W. (1952). Some problems of consensus and development. *Rural Sociology, 17*, 245–252. **539**

Riegel, K. F. (1976). The dialectics of human development. *American Psychologist, 31*, 689–700. **459**

Riegel, K. G., & Riegel, R. M. (1972). Development, drop, and death. *Developmental Psychology, 6*, 306–319. **426, 464**

Rimm, D. C. (1976). Behavior therapy: Some general comments and a review of selected papers. In R. L. Spitzer & D. F. Klein (Eds.), *Evaluation of psychological therapies*. Baltimore: Johns Hopkins University Press. **759**

Rimm, D. C., & Lefebvre, R. C. (1981). Phobic disorders. In S. M. Turner, K. S. Calhoun, & H. E. Adams (Eds.), *Handbook of clinical behavior therapy*. New York: Wiley. **754**

Rimm, D. C., & Masters, J. C. (1979). *Behavior therapy: Techniques and empirical findings* (2nd ed.). New York: Academic Press. **758, 763**

Rimm, L. D., & Somervill, J. W. (1977). *Abnormal psychology*. New York: Academic Press. **680**

Riordan, C. (1978). Equal-status interracial contact: A review and revision of the concept. *International Journal of Intercultural Relations, 2*, 161–185. **556**

Risley, T. R. (1968). The effects and side effects of punishing the autistic behaviors of a deviant child. *Journal of Applied Behavior Analysis, 1*, 21–34. **230**

Ristau, C. (1983). Symbols and indication in apes and other species? Comment on Savage-Rumbaugh et al. *Journal of Experimental Psychology: General, 122*, 498–507. **71**

Rizley, R. (1978). Depression and causal attribution. *Journal of Abnormal Psychology, 87*, 32–48. **701**

Robbins, L. N. (1978). Aetiological implications in studies of childhood histories relating to antisocial personality. In R. D. Hare & D. Schalling (Eds.), *Psychopathic behavior: Approaches to research.* New York: Wiley. **717**

Robbins, M., & Jensen, G. D. (1978). Multiple orgasm in males. *Journal of Sex Research, 14,* 21–26. **384**

Robertson, L. S., Kelley, A. B., O'Neill, B., Wixom, C. W., Elswirth, R. S., & Haddon, W., Jr. (1974). A controlled study of the effect of television messages on safety belt use. *American Journal of Public Health, 64,* 1071–1081. **559**

Robins, L. N., Helzer, J. E., Weissman, M. M., Orvashel, H., Gruenberg, E., Burke, J. D., & Regier, D. A. (1984). Lifetime prevalence of specific psychiatric disorders in three sites. *Archives of General Psychiatry, 41,* 949–958. **670**

Robinson, J. E., & Insko, C. A. (1969). Attributed belief similarity-dissimilarity versus race as determinants of prejudice: A further test of Rokeach's theory. *Journal of Experimental Research and Personality, 4,* 72–77. **558**

Robson, K. S., & Moss, H. A. (1970). Patterns and determinants of maternal attachment. *Journal of Pediatrics, 77,* 976–985. **475**

Rock, I. (1975). *An introduction to perception.* New York: Macmillan. **172, 178, 180, 188**

Rock, I. (1983). *The logic of perception.* Cambridge, MA: M.I.T. Press. **192, 197**

Rock, I. (1984). *Perception.* New York: W. H. Freeman. **188, 192**

Rodin, J. (1981). Current status of the internal-external hypothesis for obesity: What went wrong? *American Psychologist, 36*(4), 361–372. **308**

Rogers, C. R. (1951). *Client-centered therapy: Its current practice, implications, and theory.* Boston: Houghton Mifflin. **750**

Rogers, C. R. (1959). A theory of therapy, personality, and interpersonal relationships, as developed in the client-centered framework. In S. Koch (Ed.), *Psychology: A study of a science* (Vol. 3). New York: McGraw-Hill. **619**

Rogers, C. R. (1969). *Freedom to learn: A view of what education might become.* Columbus, Ohio: C. E. Merrill. **605**

Rogers, C. R. (1973). My philosophy of interpersonal relationships and how it grew. *Journal of Humanistic Psychology, 13,* 3–16. **607**

Rogers, T. B., Kuiper, N. A., & Kirker, W. S. (1977). Self-reference and the encoding of personal information. *Journal of Personality and Social Psychology, 35,* 677–688. **264–265**

Rokeach, M. (1964). *The three Christs of Ypsilanti.* New York: Vintage Books. **683**

Rokotova, N. A. (1954). Physiological mechanisms of temporary connection among "indifferent" stimuli. *Zhurnal*

Vysshey Nervnoy Deyatel'nosti imeni I. P. Pavlova, 4, 516–525. **236**

Rook, K. S., & Hammen, C. L. (1977). A cognitive perspective on the experience of sexual arousal. *Journal of Social Issues, 33,* 2. **385, 388**

Roper, G., Rachman, S., & Hodgson, R. (1973). An experiment on obsessional checking. *Behavior Research and Therapy, 11,* 171–277. **707**

Rose, R. M. (1975). Testosterone, aggression, and homosexuality: A review of the literature and implications for future research. In E. J. Sachar (Ed.), *Topics in psychoendocrinology.* New York: Grune & Stratton. **402**

Rosen, D. H. (1974). *Lesbianism: A study of female homosexuality.* Springfield, IL: Charles C. Thomas. **401**

Rosenberg, S., & Jones, R. A. (1972). A method for investigating and representing a person's implicit theory of personality: Theodore Dreiser's view of people. *Journal of Personality and Social Psychology, 22,* 372–386. **591, 592**

Rosenberg, S., Nelson, C., & Vivekananthan, P. S. (1968). A multidimensional approach to the structure of personality impression. *Journal of Personality and Social Psychology, 9,* 283–294. **591**

Rosenfeld, P., Giacalone, R. A., & Tedeschi, J. T. (1983). Cognitive dissonance vs. impression management. *Journal of Social Psychology, 120,* 203–211. **568**

Rosenhan, D. L. (1973). On being sane in insane places. *Science, 179,* 250–258. **722**

Rosenhan, D. L. & Seligman, M. E. (1984). *Abnormal psychology.* New York: W. W. Norton. **672**

Rosenthal, D. (1970). *Genetic theory and abnormal behavior.* New York: McGraw-Hill. **700**

Rosenthal, R. (1966). *Experimenter effects in behavioral research.* New York: Appleton-Century-Crofts. **773**

Rosenthal, T., & Bandura, A. (1978). Psychological modeling: Theory and practice. In S. L. Garfield & A. E. Bergin (Eds.), *Handbook of psychotherapy and behavior change: An empirical analysis* (2nd ed.). New York: Wiley. **776**

Rosenzweig, M. R. (1971). Effects of environment on development of brain and of behavior. In E. Tobach, E. L. Aronson, & E. Shaw (Eds.), *The biopsychology of development.* New York: Academic Press. **126**

Rosenzweig, M. R. (1984). Experience, memory, and the brain. *American Psychologist, 39,* 365–376. **126**

Rosenzweig, M. R., & Bennett, E. L. (1984). Basic processes and modulatory influences in the stages of memory formation. In G. Lynch, J. L. McGaugh & N. Weinberger (Eds.). *Neurobiology of*

learning and memory. New York: Guilford Press. **132**

Rosenzweig, M. R., Bennett, E. L., Alberti, M., Morimoto, H., & Renner, M. (1982). Effects of differential environments and hibernation on ground squirrel brain measures. *Society for Neuroscience Abstracts, 8,* 669. **127**

Rosenzweig, M. R., Bennett, E. L., & Diamond, M. C. (1972). Brain changes in response to experience. *Scientific American, 226,* pp. 22–29. **106, 127**

Ross, L. (1977). The intuitive psychologist and his shortcomings: Distortions in the attribution process. In L. Berkowitz (Ed.), *Advances in experimental social psychology* (Vol. 10). New York: Academic Press. **574**

Ross, L., Greene, D., & House, P. (1977). The "false consensus effect": An egocentric bias in social perception and attribution processes. *Journal of Experimental Social Psychology, 13,* 279–301. **578**

Ross, L., Rodin, J., & Zimbardo, P. G. (1969). Toward an attribution therapy: The reduction of fear through induced cognitive-emotional misattribution. *Journal of Personality and Social Psychology, 12,* 279–288. **340**

Ross, M. (1981). Egocentric biases in attributions of responsibility: Antecedents and consequences. In E. T. Higgins, C. P. Herman, & M. P. Zanna (Eds.), *Social cognition: The Ontario symposium* (Vol. 1). Hillsdale, NJ: Lawrence Erlbaum Associates. **578**

Ross, M., & Fletcher, G. J. O. (1985). Attribution and social perception. In G. Lindzey & E. Aronson (Eds.), *The handbook of social psychology* (3rd ed.). New York: Random House. **572**

Rossotti, H. (1985). *Colour.* Princeton, NJ: Princeton University Press. **148**

Rothkopf, E. Z. (1966). Learning from written instruction materials: An explanation of the control of inspection behavior by test-like events. *American Educational Research Journal, 3,* 241–249. **271, 273**

Roy, A. (1981). Role of past loss in depression. *Archives of General Psychiatry, 38,* 301–302. **703**

Roy, A. (1983). Early parental death and adult depression. *Psychological Medicine, 10,* 861–865. **743**

Rozin, P., & Kalat, J. (1971). Specific hungers and poison avoidance as adaptive specializations of learning. *Psychological Review, 78,* 459–486. **313**

Rubin, A. (1970). Measurement of romantic love. *Journal of Personality and Social Psychology, 16,* 265–273. **332**

Rubin, J. Z., Provenzano, F. J., & Luria, Z. (1974). The eye of the beholder: Parents' views on sex of newborns. *Ameri-*

can *Journal of Orthopsychiatry, 44,* 512–519. **82**

Rubin, Z. (1980). *Children's friendships.* Cambridge, MA: Harvard University Press. **489**

Ruble, D. N., Feldman, N. S., & Boggiano, A. K. (1976). Social comparison between young children in achievement situations. *Developmental Psychology, 12,* 192–197. **489**

Rumbaugh, D. M., & Gill, T. (1976). The mastery of language-type skills by the chimpanzee (Pan). In S. R. Harnad, H. O. Steklis & J. Lancaster (Eds.), *Origins and evolution of language and speech.* New York: New York Academy of Sciences. **70**

Rundus, D. (1971). Analysis of rehearsal processes in free recall. *Journal of Experimental Psychology, 89,* 63–77. **258**

Rushton, J. P. (1980). *Altruism, socialization, and society.* Englewood Cliffs, NJ: Prentice-Hall. **613**

Rushton, J. P. (1982). Moral cognition, behaviorism, and social learning theory. *Ethics, 92,* 459–467. **57**

Russek, M. (1971). Hepatic receptors and the neurophysiological mechanisms controlling feeding behavior. In S. Ehrenpreis & O. C. Solnitzky (Eds.). *Neurosciences research, 4.* New York: Academic Press. **305**

Russell, D. E. H. (1982). *Rape in marriage.* New York: Macmillan. **405**

Russell, G. F. M. (1977). The present status of anorexia nervosa. *Psychological Medicine, 7,* 353–367. **672**

Rutter, M. (1979). Maternal deprivation, 1972–1978: New findings, new concepts, new approaches. *Child Development, 50,* 283–305. **480**

Rutter, M. (1979). Attachment and the development of social relationships. In M. Rutter (Ed.), *Scientific foundations of developmental psychiatry.* London: Heinemann Medical. **92**

Rynearson, E. K. (1984). Bereavement after homicide: A descriptive study. *American Journal of Psychiatry, 141,* 1452–1454. **708**

Sach, J., & Johnson, M. (1976). Language development in hearing child of deaf parents. In W. Von Raffler Engel & Y. Le Brun (Eds.), *Baby talk and infant speech.* Neurolinguistic series (Vol. 5). Amsterdam: Swets & Zeitlinger. **444**

Sadock, B. J. (1980). Group psychotherapy, combined individual and group psychotherapy, and psychodrama. In H. I. Kaplan, A. M. Freedman, & B. Sadock (Eds.), *Comprehensive textbook of psychiatry* (Vol. 3). Baltimore: Williams & Wilkins. **766**

Salk, L. (1962). Mother's heartbeat as an imprinting stimulus. *Transactions of the New York Academy of Sciences, 24,* 753–763. **429**

Saltzberg, L., & Elkins, G. R. (1980). An examination of common concerns about rational-emotive therapy. *Professional Psychology, 11,* 324–330. **765**

Salzinger, K. (1980). Schizophrenia. In A. E. Kazdin, A. S. Bellack, & M. Hersen (Eds.), *New perspectives in abnormal psychology.* New York: Oxford University Press. **692**

Salzinger, K. (1981). Remedying schizophrenic behavior. In S. M. Turner, K. S. Calhoun, & H. E. Adams (Eds.), *Handbook of clinical behavior therapy.* New York: Wiley. **756**

Samuel, A. L. (1963). Some studies in machine learning using the game of checkers. In E. A. Feigenbaum & J. Feldman (Eds.), *Computers and thought.* New York: McGraw-Hill. **289**

Sanders, G. S. (1981). Driven by distraction: An integrative review of social facilitation theory and research. *Journal of Experimental Social Psychology, 17,* 227–251. **527**

Sanders, G. S., Baron, R. S., & Moore, D. L. (1978). Distraction and social comparison as mediators of social facilitation effects. *Journal of Experimental Social Psychology, 14,* 291–303. **527**

Santee, R. T., & Jackson, S. E. (1982). Identity implications of conformity: Sex differences in normative and attributional judgments. *Social Psychology Quarterly, 45,* 121–125. **560**

Sarnoff, I., & Zimbardo, P. (1961). Anxiety, fear and social affiliation. *Journal of Abnormal and Social Psychology, 62,* 356–363. **315**

Satir, V. (1967). *Conjoint family therapy.* Palo Alto, CA: Science and Behavior Books. **769**

Saugstad, P., & Raaheim, K. (1960). Problem solving, past experience and availability of functions. *British Journal of Psychology, 51,* 97–104. **282–283**

Savage-Rumbaugh, E. S., McDonald, K., Sevcik, R. A., Hopkins, D., & Rubert, E. (1986). Spontaneous symbol acquisition and communicative use by pygmy chimpanzees (Pan paniscus). *Journal of Experimental Psychology: General, 115,* 211–235. **71**

Savage-Rumbaugh, E. S., Romski, M. A., Sevcik, R., & Pate, J. L. (1983). Assessing symbol usage versus symbol competency. *Journal of Experimental Psychology: General, 112,* 508–512. **71**

Savage-Rumbaugh, E. S., Pate, J. L., Lawson, J., Smith, S. T., & Rosenbaum, S. (1983). Can a chimpanzee make a statement? *Journal of Experimental Psychology: General, 112,* 457–492. **71**

Savin-Williams, R. C. (1979). Dominance hierarchies in groups of early adolescents. *Child Development, 50,* 923–935. **485**

Saxe, L., Dougherty, D., Esty, K., & Fine, M. (1983). *Health technology case study 22: The effectiveness and costs of alcoholism treatment.* Washington, DC: Office of Technology Assessment. **678, 680**

Scarr, S. (1966). Social introversion-extroversion as a heritable response. *Child Development, 40,* 823–832. **708**

Scarr, S., & Carter-Saltzman, L. (1979). Twin method: Defense of a critical assumption. *Behavior Genetics, 9,* 527–542. **76**

Scarr, S., & Weinberg, R. A. (1978). The influence of "family background" on intellectual attainment. *American Sociological Review, 43,* 674–692. **78**

Scarr, S., & Weinberg, R. A. (1976). IQ test performance of black children adopted by white families. *American Psychologist, 31,* 726–739. **81**

Schachter, S. (1951). Deviation, rejection, and communication. *Journal of Abnormal and Social Psychology, 46,* 190–207. **543**

Schachter, S. (1959). *The psychology of affiliation.* Stanford: Stanford University Press. **315–316**

Schachter, S. (1971). Some extraordinary facts about obese humans and rats. *American Psychologist, 26,* 129–144. **309, 338**

Schachter, S., & Gross, L. P. (1968). Manipulated time and eating behavior. *Journal of Personality and Social Psychology, 10,* 98–106. **307**

Schachter, S., & Rodin, J. (1974). *Obese humans and rats.* Potomac, MD: Lawrence Erlbaum Associates. **306**

Schachter, S., & Singer, J. (1962). Cognitive, social and physiological determinants of emotional state. *Psychological Review, 69,* 379–399. **338–340**

Schaffer, H. R. (1971). *The growth of sociability.* Middlesex, England: Penguin Books. **474**

Schaffer, H. R., & Emerson, P. E. (1964). The development of social attachments in infancy. *Monographs of the Society for Research in Child Development, 29,* 1–77. **473, 477, 479**

Scheff, T. J. (1983). Toward integration in the social psychology of emotions. *Annual Review of Sociology, 9,* 333–354. **336**

Schein, E. H. (1968). Brainwashing. In W. G. Bennis, E. H. Schein, F. I. Steele, & D. E. Berlew (Eds.), *Interpersonal dynamics: Essays and readings on human interaction* (rev. ed.). Homewood, IL: Dorsey Press. **561**

Schiffman, H. R. (1976). *Sensation and*

perception: An integrated approach. New York: Wiley. **161, 167**

Schiffman, S. S. (1974). Physiochemical correlates of olfactory quality. *Science, 185,* 112–117. **169**

Schlesier-Stropp, B. (1984). Bulimia: A review of the literature. *Journal of Abnormal Psychology, 76,* 443–453. **671**

Schneider, G. E. (1967). Contrasting visuomotor functions of tectum and cortex in the golden hamster. *Psychologische Forschung, 31,* 52–62. **430**

Schofield, W. (1964). *Psychotherapy: The purchase of friendship.* Englewood Cliffs, NJ: Prentice-Hall. **766, 772**

Schoof-Tams, K., Schlaegel, J., & Walczak, L. (1976). Differentiation of sexual morality between 11 and 16 years. *Archives of Sexual Behavior, 5,* 239–248. **367**

Schreiber, F. (1974). *Sybil.* New York: Warner. **714**

Schultz, D. P., & Schultz, S. E. (1987). *A history of modern psychology* (4th ed.). New York: Academic Press. **10, 12**

Schulz, R. (1978). *The psychology of death, dying and bereavement.* Reading, MA: Addison-Wesley. **427**

Schuman, M. (1980). The psychophysiological model of meditation and altered states of consciousness: A critical review. In J. M. Davidson & R. J. Davidson (Eds.), *The psychobiology of consciousness.* New York: Plenum Press. **134**

Schwartz, B. (1984). *Psychology of learning and behavior* (2nd. ed.). New York: W. W. Norton. **230, 245**

Schwartz, G. E., Fair, P. L., Salt, P. S., Mandel, M. R., & Klerman, J. L. (1976). Facial muscle patterning to affective imagery in depressed and non-depressed subjects. *Science, 192,* 489–491. **323**

Schwartz, S. H., & Clausen, G. T. (1970). Responsibility, norms and helping in an emergency. *Journal of Personality and Social Psychology, 16,* 299–310. **550**

Scovern, A. W., & Kilmann, P. R. (1980). Status of electroconvulsive therapy: Review of the outcome literature. *Psychological Bulletin, 87,* 260–303. **740**

Scroggs, J. R. (1985). *Key ideas in personality theory.* St. Paul, MN: West Publishing. **596**

Sears, R. R. (1977). Sources of life satisfaction of the Terman gifted men. *American Psychologist, 32,* 119–128. **646**

Secord, P. F., Dukes, W. F., & Bevan, W. (1954). Personalities in faces: I. An experiment in social perceiving. *Genetics and Psychology Monograph, 49,* 231–279. **586**

Sekuler, R., & Blake, R. (1985). *Perception.* New York: Alfred A. Knopf. **156**

Seligman, M. E. P. (1975). *Helplessness: On depression, development and death.* San Francisco: Freeman. **40**

Seligman, M. E. P., & Maier, S. F. (1967). Failure to escape traumatic shock. *Journal of Experimental Psychology, 74,* 1–9. **701**

Seligman, M. E. P., Maier, S. F., & Geer, J. (1968). The alleviation of learned helplessness in the dog. *Journal of Abnormal and Social Psychology, 73,* 256–262. **231**

Selikof, W., Robitzek, E. H., & Ornstein, G. G. (1952). Toxicity of hydrazine derivatives of isonicotinic acid in the chemotherapy of human tuberculosis. *Quarterly Bulletin of Sea View Hospital, 13,* 17–26. **744**

Selman, R. (1981). The child as friendship philosopher. In S. R. Asher & J. M. Gottman (Eds.), *The development of children's friendships.* Cambridge, England: Cambridge University Press. **489**

Shaffer, D. R. (1985). *Developmental psychology.* Monterey, CA: Brooks/Cole. **459**

Shaffer, L. S. (1977). The golden fleece: Anti-intellectualism and social science. *American Psychologist, 32,* 814–823. **28**

Shapiro, D. A., & Shapiro, D. (1982). Meta-analysis of comparative therapy outcome studies: A replication and refinement. *Psychological Bulletin, 92,* 581–604. **777**

Shapiro, D. A., & Shapiro, D. (1983). Comparative therapy outcome research: Methodological implications of meta-analysis. *Journal of Consulting and Clinical Psychology, 51,* 42–53. **776**

Shaw, M. E., Rothschild, G. H., & Strickland, J. F. (1957). Decision processes in communication nets. *Journal of Abnormal and Social Psychology, 54,* 323–330. **542**

Shaw, R., & Bransford, J. (1977). *Perceiving, acting, and knowing: Toward an ecological psychology.* Hillsdale, NJ: Lawrence Erlbaum Associates. **194**

Sherif, M. (1936). *The psychology of social norms.* New York: Harper & Row. **538**

Sherman, A. D., Sacquitne, J. L., & Petty, F. (1982). Specificity of the learned helplessness model of depression. *Pharmacology, biochemistry, and behavior, 16,* 449–454. **231**

Shields, J. (1962). *Monozygotic twins, brought up apart and brought up together.* London: Oxford University Press. **77**

Shiffrin, R. M, & Schneider, W. (1977). Controlled and automatic human information processing: II. Perceptual learning, automatic attending, and a general theory. *Psychological Review, 84,* 127–190. **252**

Shock, N. W. (1977). Biological theories of aging. In J. E. Birren & K. W. Schaie (Eds.), *Handbook of the psychology of aging.* New York: Van Nostrand Reinhold. **423**

Shulman, H. G. (1972). Semantic confusion errors in short-term memory. *Journal of Verbal Learning and Verbal Behavior, 11,* 221–227. **253**

Siegel, R. K. (1984). Changing patterns of cocaine use: Longitudinal observations, consequences, and treatment. In J. Grabowski (Ed.), Cocaine: *Pharmacology, effects, and treatment of abuse* (National Institute of Drug Abuse Research Monograph 50). Washington, DC: U.S. Government Printing Office. **104**

Siegel, S. (1975). Evidence from rats that morphine tolerance is a learned response. *Journal of Comparative and Physiological Psychology, 89,* 498–506. **215**

Siegel, S., Hinson, R. E., Krank, M. D., & McCully, J. (1982). Heroin "overdose" death: The contribution of drug-associated environmental cues. *Science, 216,* 436–437. **215**

Siegler, R. S. (1978). The origins of scientific reasoning. In R. S. Siegler (Ed.), *Children's thinking: What develops?* Hillsdale, NJ: Lawrence Erlbaum Associates. **461**

Siegler, R. S., & Liebert, R. M. (1972). Effects of presenting relevant rules and complete feedback on the conservation of liquid quantity. *Developmental Psychology, 7,* 133–138. **456**

Simmons, J. V. (1981). *Project Seahunt: A report on prototype development and tests,* Technical Report 746. San Diego: Naval Oceans Systems Center. **232**

Simon, H. A. (1973). The structure of ill-structured problems. *Artificial Intelligence, 4,* 181–201. **287**

Simon, H. A., & Gilmartin, K. (1973). A simulation of memory for chess positions. *Cognitive Psychology, 5,* 29–46. **287**

Simons, A. D., Levine, J. L., Lustman, P. J., & Murphy, G. E. (1984). Patient attrition in a comparative outcome study of depression: A follow-up report. *Journal of Affective Disorders, 6,* 163–173. **703**

Simpson, E. L. (1974). Moral development research: A case of scientific cultural bias. *Human Development, 17,* 81–106. **511**

Singer, D. (1972). Piglet, Pooh, and Piaget. *Psychology Today, 1,* pp. 70–74, 96. **454**

Skeels, H. (1966). Adult status of children with contrasting early life experiences. *Monographs of the Society for Research in Child Development, 31,* 1–65. **87, 480**

Skinner, B. F. (1948). *Walden two.* New York: Macmillan. **12**

Skinner, B. F. (1951). How to teach animals. *Scientific American, 185,* pp. 26–29. **218**

Skinner, B. F. (1957). *Verbal behavior.* New York: Appleton-Century-Crofts. **441**

Skinner, B. F. (1960). Pigeons in a pelican. *American Psychologist, 15,* 28–37. **232**

Skinner, B. F. (1971). *Beyond freedom and dignity.* New York: Knopf. **12**

Skinner, B. F. (1974). *About behaviorism.* New York: Knopf. **612**

Sloan, R. B., Staples, F. R., Cristal, A. H., Yorkston, N. J., & Whipple, K. (1975). *Psychotherapy versus behavior therapy.* Cambridge, MA: Harvard University Press. **774, 776**

Slobin, D. I. (1979). *Psycholinguistics* (2nd ed.). Glenview IL: Scott, Foresman. **437**

Slovic, P., & Lichtenstein, S. (1971). Comparison of Bayesian and regression approaches to the study of information processing in judgement. *Journal of Organizational Behavior and Human Performance, 6,* 646–744. **276**

Smedslund, J. (1961). The acquisition of conservation of substance and weight in children. V. Practice in conflict situations without reinforcement. *Scandinavian Journal of Psychology, 2,* 156–160. **456**

Smith, C. L. (1979). Children's understanding of natural language hierarchies. *Journal of Experimental Child Psychology, 28,* 249–257. **424**

Smith, D. (1982). Trends in counseling psychotherapy. *American Psychologist, 37,* 802–809. **735**

Smith, M. L., Glass, G. V., & Miller, R. L. (1980). *The benefits of psychotherapy.* Baltimore: Johns Hopkins University Press. **776, 777**

Smith, P. K., & Daglish, L. (1977). Sex differences in parent and infant behavior in the home. *Child Development, 48,* 1250–1254. **498**

Smith, S. M. (1979). Remembering in and out of context. *Journal of Experimental Psychology: Human Learning and Memory, 5,* 460–471. **267**

Smith, W. L., & Kling, A. A. (Eds.). (1976). *Issues in brain-behavior control.* New York: Spectrum Publishers. **739**

Snow, C. E. (1972). Mothers' speech to children learning language. *Child Development, 43,* 549–567. **444**

Snow, C. E. (1983). Saying it again: The role of expanded and deferred imitations in language acquisition. In K. E. Nelson (Ed.), *Children's language* (Vol. 4). New York: Gardner Press. **442**

Snyder, C. R., Shenkel, R. J., & Lowery, C. R. (1977). Acceptance of personality interpretations: The "Barnum effect" and beyond. *Journal of Consulting and Clinical Psychology, 45,* 104–114. **634**

Snyder, M. (1979). Self-monitoring processes. In L. Berkowitz (Ed.), *Advances in experimental social psychology* (Vol. 12). New York: Academic Press. **565**

Snyder, M., & Ebbensen, E. B. (1972). Dissonance awareness: A test of dissonance theory vs. self-perception theory. *Journal of Experimental Social Psychology, 8,* 502–517. **570**

Snyder, M., & Kendzierski, D. (1982). Choosing social situations: Investigating the origins of correspondence between attitudes and behavior. *Journal of Personality and Social Psychology, 50,* 280–295. **613**

Snyder, M., & Uranowitz, S. (1978). Reconstructing the past: Some cognitive consequences of person perception. *Journal of Personality and Social Psychology, 36,* 941–950. **269**

Snyder, M., Mischel, W., & Lott, B. (1960). Value, information, and conformity behavior. *Journal of Personality, 28,* 333–342. **542**

Snyder, S. (1976). Dopamine and schizophrenia. *Psychiatric Annals, 6,* 23–31. **691**

Snyder, S. (1980). *Biological aspects of mental disorder.* New York: Oxford University Press. **691, 700**

Snyder, S. H. (1974). *Madness and the brain.* New York: McGraw-Hill. **102**

Snyder, S. H. (1984). Drug and neurotransmitter receptors in the brain. *Science, 224,* 22–31. **215**

Sokoll, G. R., & Mynatt, C. R. (1984). *Arousal and free throw shooting.* Paper presented at the meeting of the Midwestern Psychological Association, Chicago, IL. **302**

Sommer, R., & Sommer, B. A. (1983). Mystery in Milwaukee: Early intervention, IQ, and psychology textbooks. *American Psychologist, 38,* 982–985. **89**

Sorrentino, R. M., King, G., & Leo, G. (1980). The influence of the minority on perception: A note and a possible alternative explanation. *Journal of Experimental Social Psychology, 16,* 24–33. **545**

Spanier, G. B. (1977). Sources of sex information and premarital sexual behavior. *Journal of Sex Research, 13,* 659–674. **379**

Spence, J. T., Deaux, K., & Helmreich, R. L. (1985). Sex roles in contemporary American society. In G. Lindzey & E. Aronson (Eds.), *The handbook of social psychology* (3rd ed.). New York: Random House. **502**

Sperling, G. (1967). Successive approximations to a model for short-term memory. *Acta Psychologica, 27,* 285–292. **250**

Sperling, G. A. (1960). The information available in brief visual presentations. *Psychological Monographs, 74* (No. 498). **250–251**

Sperry, R. W. (1974). Lateral specialization in the surgically separated hemispheres. In F. O. Schmitt & F. G. Worden (Eds.), *The neurosciences: Third study program.* Cambridge, MA: M.I.T. Press. **119–120**

Spinetta, J. J., & Rigler, D. (1972). The child-abusing parent: A psychological review. *Psychological Bulletin, 77,* 296–304. **486**

Spitzer, R., Forman, J., & Nee, J. (1979). DSM-III field trials: Initial interrater diagnostic reliability. *American Journal of Psychiatry, 136,* 815–817. **721**

Springer, S. P., & Deutsch, G. (1985). *Left brain, right brain* (2nd ed.). San Francisco: W. H. Freeman. **120**

Stampfl, T. G., & Lewis, D. J. (1967). The essentials of implosive therapy: A learning-theory based psychodynamic behavioral therapy. *Journal of Abnormal Psychology, 72,* 496–503. **753**

Stang, D. J. (1972). Conformity, ability and self-esteem. *Representative Research in Social Psychology, 3,* 97–103. **542**

Stapp, J., & Fulcher R. (1983). The employment of APA members: 1982. *American Psychologist, 38,* 1298–1320. **24**

Staub, E. (1975). *The development of prosocial behavior in children.* New York: General Learning Press. **511**

Staub, E. (1979). Understanding and predicting social behavior – With emphasis on prosocial behavior. In E. Staub (Ed.), *Personality: Basic issues and current research.* Englewood Cliffs, NJ: Prentice-Hall. **483**

Staub, E., & Baer, R. S. (1974). Stimulus characteristics of a sufferer and difficulty of escape as determinants of helping. *Journal of Personality and Social Psychology, 30,* 279–284. **551**

Stein, Z., Susser, M., Saener, G., & Marolla, F. (1972). Nutrition and mental performance. *Science, 173,* 708–712. **499, 500**

Steiner, J. E. (1977). Facial expressions of the neonate infant indicating the hedonics of food-related chemical stimuli. In J. M. Weiffenbach (Ed.), *Taste and development: The genesis of sweet preference* (DHEW Publication No. NIH77-1068). Maryland: National Institutes of Health. **334**

Stephens, C. E., Pear, J. J., Wray, L. D., & Jackson, G. C. (1975). Some effects of reinforcement schedules in teaching picture names to retarded children. *Journal of Applied Behavior Analysis, 8,* 435–447. **221**

Sternbach, R., & Tursky, B. (1965). Ethnic differences among housewives in psychophysical and skin potential responses to electric shock. *Psychophysiology, 1,* 241. **311**

Sternbach, R. A. (1968). *Pain: A psycho-*

physiological analysis. New York: Academic Press. **163**

Sternberg, R. J., & Powell J. S. (1983). The development of intelligence. In J. H. Flavell & E. M. Markman (Eds.), Cognitive development, Vol. 3 in P. H. Mussen (Ed.), *Handbook of child psychology, 4th edition.* New York: Wiley. **461**

Stevens, J. E. (1971). *Awareness: Exploring, experimenting, experiencing.* Lafayette, CA: Real People Press. **772**

Stewart, B. J., & Smith, C. L. (1983). Prosocial behavior for and by older persons. In D. L. Bridgeman (Ed.), *The nature of prosocial development.* New York: Academic Press. **518**

Stoller, R. J. (1975). *Sex and gender, Vol. II: The development of masculinity and femininity.* New York: Jason Aronson. **399**

Storms, M. D. (1973). Videotape and the attribution process: Reversing actors' and observers' points of view. *Journal of Personality and Social Psychology, 27,* 165–175. **577**

Storms, M. D. (1980). Theories of sexual orientation. *Journal of Personality and Social Psychology, 38,* 383–392. **395**

Storms, M.D., & Nisbett, R.E. (1970). Insomnia and the attribution process. *Journal of Personality and Social Psychology, 16,* 319–338. **341**

Story, M. (1979). A longitudinal study of a university human sexuality course on sexual attitudes. *Journal of Sex Research, 15,* 184–204. **379**

Stratton, J. G., Parker, D. A., & Snibbe, J. R. (1984). Post-traumatic stress: A study of police officers involved in shootings. *Psychological Reports, 55,* 127–131. **708**

Strauss, J. S. (1979). Social and cultural influences on psychopathology. *Annual Review of Psychology, 30,* 397–415. **693**

Strayer, F. F. (1981). The nature and organization of altruistic behavior among preschool children. In J. P. Rushton & R. M. Sorrentino (Eds.), *Altruism and helping behavior.* Hillsdale, NJ: Lawrence Erlbaum Associates. **32**

Strayer, F. F., & Strayer, J. (1976). An ethological analysis of social agonism and dominance relations among preschool children. *Child Development, 47,* 980–989. **485**

Strupp, H. H. (1976). The nature of the therapeutic influence and its basic ingredients. In A. Burton (Ed.), *What makes behavior change possible.* New York: Brunner Mazel. **774**

Strupp, H. H., & Hadley, S. W. (1979). Specific vs. nonspecific factors in psychotherapy: A controlled study of outcome. *Archives of General Psychiatry, 36,* 1125–1136. **777**

Stuart, R. B., & Davis, B. (1972). *Slim chance in a fat world: Behavioral control of obesity.* Champaigne, IL: Research Press. **309**

Sturgis, E. T., & Meyer, V. (1981). Obsessive-compulsive disorders. In S. M. Turner, K. S. Calhoun, & H. E. Adams (Eds.), *Handbook of clinical behavior therapy.* New York: Wiley. **706**

Sue, D. (1979). Erotic fantasies of college students during coitus. *Journal of Sex Research, 15,* 299–305. **393, 394**

Sugarman, S. (1983). Why talk? Comment on Savage-Rumbaugh et al. *Journal of Experimental Psychology: General, 112,* 493–497. **71**

Sulzer-Azaroff, B., & Mayer, G. R. (1977). *Applying behavior-analysis procedures with children and youth.* New York: Holt, Rinehart & Winston. **228**

Suomi, S. J., & Harlow, H. F. (1978). Early experience and social development in rhesus monkeys. In M. E. Lamb (Ed.), *Social and personality development.* New York: Holt, Rinehart & Winston. **86**

Sweet, W. H., Ervin, F., & Mark V. H. (1969). The relationship of violent behavior to focal cerebral disease. In S. Garattini & E. B. Sigg (Eds.), *Aggressive behavior.* New York: Wiley. **331**

Szasz, T. S. (1961). *The myth of mental illness.* New York: Harper & Row. **662**

Szasz, T. S. (1970). *The manufacture of madness.* New York: Harper & Row. **662**

Tanford, S., & Penrod, S. (1984). Social influence model: A formal integration of research on majority and minority influence processes. *Psychological Bulletin, 95,* 189–225. **543**

Taylor, J. (1980). Dimensionalizations of racialism and the black experience: The Pittsburgh project. In R. L. Jones (Ed.), *Black psychology* (2nd ed.). New York: Harper & Row. **575**

Taylor, J., & Deaux, K. (1975). Equity and perceived sex differences: Role behavior as defined by the task, the mode, and the actor. *Journal of Personality and Social Psychology, 32,* 381–390. **502**

Television Audience Assessment (1983). *Methodology report.* Boston: Author. **559**

Teller, D. Y., & Bornstein, M. H. (1984). Infant color vision. In P. Salapatek & L. Cohen (Eds.), *Handbook of infant perception.* New York: Academic Press. **428**

Terman, L. M. (1916). *The measurement of intelligence.* Boston: Houghton Mifflin. **638**

Terman, L. M., & Merrill, M. A. (1959). *Genetic studies of genius. V. The gifted group at mid-life.* Stanford, CA: Stanford University Press. **646**

Terr, L. C. (1983). Time sense following psychic trauma: A clinical study of ten adults and twenty children. *American Journal of Orthopsychiatry, 53,* 244–261. **708**

Terr, L. C. (1983). Chowchella revisited: The effects of psychic trauma four years after a school bus kidnapping. *American Journal of Psychiatry, 140,* 1543–1550. **708**

Terrace, H. S., Pettito, L. A., Sanders, R. J., & Bever, T. C. (1979). Can an ape create a sentence? *Science, 206,* 891–900. **71**

Tetlock, P. E. (1983). Accountability and complexity of thought. *Journal of Personality and Social Psychology, 45,* 74–83. **559**

Tetlock, P. E., & Levi, A. (1982). Attribution bias: On the inconclusiveness of the cognition-motivation debate. *Journal of Experimental Social Psychology, 18,* 68–88. **579**

Thigpen, C. H., & Cleckley, H. (1954). *The three faces of Eve.* Kingsport, TN: Kingsport Press. **714**

Thomas, E. L., & Robinson, H. A. (1972). *Improving reading in every class: A sourcebook for teachers.* Boston: Allyn & Bacon. **272**

Thompson, J. (1941). Development of facial expression of emotion in blind and seeing children. *Archives of Psychology, 264,* 5–47. **334**

Thompson, S. K. (1975). Gender labels and early sex-role development. *Child Development, 46,* 339–347. **499**

Thorndike, E. L. (1898). Animal intelligence: An experimental study of the associative processes in animals. *Psychological Review Monograph Supplement, 2.* **216**

Thorndike, E. L. (1911). *Animal intelligence.* New York: Macmillan. **278**

Thorndike, E. L. (1911). *Animal intelligence: Experimental studies.* New York: Macmillan. **216**

Thurstone, L. L. (1928). Attitudes can be measured. *American Journal of Sociology, 33,* 529–554. **552**

Thurstone, L. L. (1938). Primary mental abilities. *Psychometrika Monographs, 1.* **643**

Tiernari, P. (1963). Psychiatric illnesses in identical twins. *Acta Psychiatrica Scandinavia, 39,* 1–195. **708**

Timiras, P. (1972). *Developmental physiology and aging.* New York: Macmillan. **424**

Tinbergen, N. (1965). *Social behavior in animals* (2nd ed.). New York: Wiley. **63**

Tolman, E. C. (1948). Cognitive maps in rats and men. *Psychological Review, 55,* 189–208. **214**

Tolman, E. C., & Honzik, C. H. (1930). Introduction and removal of reward and maze performance in rats. *University of California Publications in Psychology, 4,* 257–275. **236, 237**

Tomaszewski, R. J., Strickler, D. P., & Maxwell, W. A. (1980). Influence of social setting and social drinking stimuli on drinking behavior. *Addictive Behaviors, 5,* 235–240. **679**

Trabasso, T. (1977). The role of memory as a system in making transitive inferences. In R. V. Kail & J. W. Hagen (Eds.), *Perspectives on the development of memory and cognition.* Hillsdale, NJ: Lawrence Erlbaum Associates. **462**

Trager, G. (1958). Paralanguage: A first approximation. *Studies in Linguistics, 13,* 1–12. **68**

Trieschmann, R. B. (1980). *Spinal cord injuries.* New York: Pergamon Press. **330**

Triplett, N. (1898). The dynamogenic factors in pace making and competition. *American Journal of Psychology, 9,* 509–533. **524**

Trivers, R. L. (1971). The evolution of reciprocal altruism. *Quarterly Review of Biology, 46,* 33–57. **503**

Trivers, R. L. (1983). The evolution of cooperation. In D. L. Bridgeman (Ed.), *The nature of prosocial behavior.* New York: Academic Press. **503, 504**

Trivers, R. L. (1985). *Social evolution.* Menlo Park, CA: Benjamin/Cummings. **58**

Truax, C. B. (1966). Reinforcement and nonreinforcement in Rogerian psychotherapy. *Journal of Abnormal Psychology, 71,* 1–9. **774**

Tucker, D. M. (1981). Lateral brain function, emotion and conceptualization. *Psychological Bulletin, 89,* 19–46. **343**

Tucker, J. A., Vuchinich, R. E., Sobell, M. B., & Maisto, S. A. (1980). Normal drinkers alcohol consumption as a function of conflicting motives induced by intellectual stress. *Addictive Behaviors, 5,* 171–178. **679**

Turvey, M. T. (1977). Contrasting orientations to a theory of visual information processing. *Psychological Review, 84,* 67–88. **194**

Tversky, A., & Kahneman, D. (1973). Availability: A heuristic for judging frequency and probability. *Cognitive Psychology, 5,* 207–232. **278**

Ugerer, J. C., Harford, R. J., Brown, F. L., & Kieger, H. D. (1976). Sex guilt and preferences for illegal drugs among drug abusers. *Journal of Clinical Psychology, 32,* 891–895. **390**

Ullman, L. P., & Krasner, L. (1969). *A psychological approach to abnormal behavior.* Englewood Cliffs, NJ: Prentice-Hall. **692**

Ullman, S. (1980). Against direct perception. *The Behavioral and Brain Sciences, 3,* 373–415. **194**

Ulrich, R. E., Stachnik, T. J., & Stainton, N. R. (1963). Student acceptance of generalized personality interpretations. *Psychological Reports, 13,* 831–834. **634**

Updike, J. (1974). *A month of sundays.* Greenwich, CT: Fawcett Publications. **514**

Valenstein, E. S. (1973). *Brain control.* New York: Wiley. **323, 330, 738**

Valenstein, E. S. (1976). The interpretation of behavior evoked by brain stimulation. In A. Wauquier & E. T. Rolls (Eds.), *Brain stimulation reward.* Amsterdam: North Holland. **739**

Valenstein, E. S. (1980). A prospective study of cingulatomy. In E. S. Valenstein (Ed.), *The psychosurgery debate: Scientific, legal, and ethical perspectives.* San Francisco: Freeman. **736, 739**

Valle, F. P. (1975). *Motivation: Theories and issues.* Monterey, CA: Brooks/Cole. **319–320**

Van Houten, R. (1983). Punishment: From the animal laboratory to the applied setting. In S. Axelrod & J. Apsche (Eds.), *The effects of punishment on human behavior.* New York: Academic Press. **226**

Van Houten, R., & Doleys, D. M. (1983). Are social reprimands effective? In S. Axelrod & J. Apsche (Eds.), *The effects of punishment on human behavior.* New York: Academic Press. **231**

Van Parys, M. M. (1983). *The relation of use and understanding of sex and age categories in preschool children.* Doctoral dissertation, University of Denver, 1983. Dissertation Abstracts International, 45, 11938A. **499**

Vaughan, E. (1977). Misconceptions about psychology among introductory psychology students. *Teaching of Psychology, 4,* 138–141. **30–31**

Verhave, T. (1966). *The experimental analysis of behavior.* New York: Appleton. **232**

Vernon, P. E. (1965). Ability factors and environmental influences. *American Psychologist, 20,* 723–733. **652**

Vilensky, J. A., Van Hoesen, G. W., & Damasio, A. R. (1982). The limbic system and human evolution. *Journal of Human Evolution, 11,* 447–460. **111**

Von Frisch, K. (1974). Decoding the language of the bee. *Science, 185,* 663–668. **66**

Vygotsky, L. S. (1962). *Thought and language.* Cambridge, MA: M.I.T. Press. **70, 440**

Vygotsky, L. S. (1976). Play and its role in the mental development of the child. In J. Bruner, A. Jolly, & K. Sylva (Eds.), *Play: Its role in development and evolution.* New York: Basic Books. **489**

Walk, R. D. (1966). The development of depth perception in animals and human infants. In H. W. Stevenson (Ed.), Concept of development. *Monographs of the society for research in child development, 31*(107). **430**

Walker, I. (1972). Habituation to disturbance in the fiddler crab (Uca annulipes) in its natural environment. *Animal Behavior, 20,* 139–146. **204**

Walker, L. (1986). Cognitive processes in moral development. In G. L. Sapp (Ed.), *Handbook of moral development: Models, processes, techniques, and research.* Birmingham, AL: Religious Education Press. **513**

Wallace, P. (1974). Complex environments: Effects on brain development. *Science, 185,* 1035–1037. **87**

Wallas, G. (1926). *The art of thought.* New York: Harcourt Brace. **291**

Wallin, J. A., & Johnson, R. D. (1976). The positive reinforcement approach to controlling employee absenteeism. *Personnel Journal, 55,* 390–392. **233**

Walls, G. L. (1963). *The vertebrate eye and its adaptive radiation.* New York: Hafner. **158**

Walsh, R. H., & Leonard, W. M. (1974). Usage of terms for sexual intercourse by men and women. *Archives of Sexual Behavior, 3,* 127–142. **378**

Walster, E. (1966). The assignment of responsibility for an accident. *Journal of Personality and Social Psychology, 5,* 508–516. **575**

Walster, E. (1971). Passionate love. In B. I. Murstein (Ed.), *Theories of attraction and love.* New York: Springer. **340**

Wanner, H. E. (1968). On remembering, forgetting and understanding sentences. A study of the deep structure hypothesis. Unpublished doctoral dissertation, Harvard University, Cambridge, MA. **259**

Washburn, S. L. (1978). The evolution of man. *Scientific American, 239,* pp. 194–208. **59, 62**

Washburn, S. L., & Lancaster, C. S. (1968). The evolution of hunting. In R. B. Lee & I. DeVore (Eds.). *Man the hunter.* Chicago: Aldine. **59**

Watson, J. B. (1913). Psychology as the behaviourist views it. *Psychological Review, 20,* 158–177. **11**

Watson, J. B. (1919). *Psychology from the standpoint of a behaviorist.* Philadelphia, PA: Lippincott. **7**

Watson, J. B. (1930). *Behaviorism* (rev. ed.). New York: Norton. **11**

Watson, J. B. (1936). Autobiography. In C. Murchison (Ed.), *A history of psychology in autobiography* (Vol. 3). Worcester, MA: Clark University Press. **11**

Watson, J. B., & Rayner, R. (1920). Conditioned emotional reactions. *Journal of Experimental Psychology, 3,* 1–14. **207**

Watson, R. I., Jr. (1973). Investigation into deindividuation using a cross-cultural survey technique. *Journal of Personality and Social Psychology, 25,* 342–345. **531**

Weary, G. (1980). Examination of affect and egotism as mediators of bias in causal attributions. *Journal of Personality and Social Psychology, 38,* 348–357. **579**

Weaver, K. F. (1985). The search for our ancestors. *National Geographic, 168,* pp. 560–623. **60**

Wechsler, D. (1958). *The measurement and appraisal of adult intelligence* (4th ed.). Baltimore, MD: Williams and Wilkins. **643**

Wechsler, D. (1974). *Wechsler Intelligence Scale for Children* (rev. ed). New York: Psychological Corporation. **638**

Wechsler, D. (1975). Intelligence defined and undefined. *American Psychologist, 30,* 135–139. **651**

Wechsler, D. (1981). *Wechsler Adult Intelligence Scale* (rev. ed.). New York: Psychological Corporation. **638, 640**

Weddell, G., Gutmann, L., & Gutmann, E. (1941). The local extension of nerve fibers into denervated areas of skin. *Journal of Neurological Psychiatry, 4,* 206–225. **128**

Weinberg, H., Stroink, G., & Katila, T. (Eds.). (1985). *Biomagnetism: applications and theory.* New York: Pergamon Press. **105**

Weinberger, N. M., Gold, P. E., & Sternberg, D. B. (1984). Epinephrine enables Pavlovian fear conditioning under anesthesia. *Science, 223,* 605–607. **214**

Weiner, B. (1980). *Human motivation.* N.Y: Holt, Rinehart & Winston. **320–321**

Weinmann, G. (1982). Dealing with bureaucracy: The effectiveness of different persuasive appeals. *Social Psychology Quarterly, 45,* 136–144. **558**

Weinstein, N. D. (1980). Unrealistic optimism about future life events. *Journal of Personality and Social Psychology, 39,* 806–820. **578**

Weisberg, M., & Jefferson, T. (1981). Note on female ejaculation. *Journal of Sex Research, 17,* 90–91. **386, 387**

Weisberg, P., & Waldrop, P. B. (1972). Fixed-interval work habits of Congress. *Journal of Applied Behavior Analysis, 5,* 93–97. **222–223**

Weisberg, R. W. (1986). *Creativity.* New York: W. H. Freeman. **291, 295**

Weisberg, R. W., & Alba, J. W. (1981). An examination of the alleged role of "fixation" in the solution of several "insight" problems. *Journal of Experimental Psychology: General, 110,* 169–192. **284**

Weisenberg, M. (1977). Pain and pain control. *Psychological Bulletin, 84*(5), 1008–1044. **311**

Weiss, J. M. (1968). Effects of coping responses on stress. *Journal of Comparative and Physiological Psychology, 65,* 251–260. **40**

Weiss, R. L., & Cerreto, M. C. (1980). The marital status inventory: Development of a measure of dissolution potential. *American Journal of Family Therapy, 8,* 80–85. **703**

Weisz, D. J., Solomon, P. R., & Thompson, R. F. (1980). The hippocampus appears necessary for trace conditioning. *Bulletin of the Psychonomic Society Abstracts, 193,* 244. **130**

Wells, G. L., & Harvey, J. H. (1977). Do people use consensus information in making causal attributions? *Journal of Personality and Social Psychology, 35,* 279–293. **575**

Wells, W. J., & Wells, J. (1971). Conditioning and sensitization in snails. *Animal Behavior, 19,* 305–312. **205**

Wertheimer, M. (1978). Humanistic psychology and the humane but tough-minded psychologist. *American Psychologist, 23,* 739–745. **303, 321**

Wever, E. G. (1970). *Theory of hearing.* New York: Wiley. **160**

White, B. (1971). *Human infants: Experience and psychological development.* Englewood Cliffs, NJ: Prentice-Hall. **88**

Whiting, B. B. (1983). The genesis of prosocial behavior. In D. L. Bridgeman (Ed.), *The nature of prosocial behavior.* New York: Academic Press. **496**

Whorf, B. L. (1956). *Language, thought, and reality.* New York: Wiley. **440**

Wickelgren, W. A. (1974). *How to solve problems.* San Francisco: W. H. Freeman. **292–293**

Wickelgren, W. A. (1979). *Cognitive psychology.* Englewood Cliffs, NJ: Prentice-Hall. **291–293**

Wicker, A. W. (1969). Attitudes versus actions: The relationship of verbal and overt behavior responses to attitude objects. *Journal of Social Issues, 25,* 41–78. **563**

Wicklund, R. A., & Brehm, J. W. (1976). *Perspectives on cognitive dissonance.* Hillsdale, NJ: Lawrence Erlbaum Associates. **569**

Wiggins, J. S., Wiggins, N., & Conger, J. C. (1968). Correlates of heterosexual somatic preference. *Journal of Personality and Social Psychology, 10,* 82–92. **393**

Wilcoxon, H. C., Dragoin, W. B., & Kral, P. A. (1971). Illness-induced aversions in rat and quail: Related salience of visual and gustatory cues. *Science, 171,* 826–828. **234**

Wilder, D. A. (1977). Perception in groups, size of opposition, and social influence. *Journal of Experimental Social Psychology, 13,* 253–268. **542**

Wilder, D. A., & Allen, V. L. (1977). Veridi-

cal social support, extreme social support, and conformity. *Representative Research in Social Psychology, 8,* 33–41. **542**

Wildman, R. W., Wildman, R. W., II, Brown, A., & Trice, C. (1976). Note on males' and females' preference for opposite sex body parts, bust sizes, and bust revealing clothing. *Psychological Reports, 38,* 485–486. **393**

Wilkinson, A. (1976). Counting strategies and semantic analysis as applied to class inclusion. *Cognitive Psychology, 8,* 64–85. **462**

Wilsnack, S. C. (1974). The effects of social drinking on women's fantasy. *Journal of Personality, 42,* 43–61. **391**

Wilson, E. O. (1975). *Sociobiology: The new synthesis.* Cambridge, MA: Harvard University Press. **57**

Wilson, G. T., & Lawson, D. M. (1976). Expectancies, alcohol, and sexual arousal in male social drinkers. *Journal of Abnormal and Social Psychology, 85,* 587–594. **391**

Wilson, G. T., & Lawson, D. M. (1978). Expectancies, alcohol and sexual arousal in women. *Journal of Abnormal Psychology, 87,* 358–367. **388, 391**

Wilson, P. R. (1968). Perceptual distortion of height as a function of ascribed academic status. *Journal of Social Psychology, 74,* 97–102. **587**

Winick, M., & Rosso, P. (1969). Head circumference and cellular growth of the brain in normal and marasmic children. *Journal of Pediatrics, 74,* 774–778. **126**

Witkin, H. A., Dyk, R. B., Paterson, H. F., Goodenough, D. R., & Karp, S. A. (1962). *Psychological differentiation.* New York: Wiley. **460**

Wohlwill, J. F., & Lowe, R. C. (1962). An experimental analysis of the development of conservation of number. *Child Development, 33,* 153–167. **456**

Wolberg, L. R. (1977). *The technique of psychotherapy* (3rd ed.). New York: Grune & Stratton. **748**

Wolchik, S. A., Beggs, V. E., Wincze, J. P., Sakheim, D. K., Barlow, D. H., & Mavissakalian, M. (1980). The effect of emotional arousal on subsequent sexual arousal in men. *Journal of Abnormal Psychology, 89,* 595–598. **388**

Wolf, M. M., Risley, T., & Mees, H. L. (1964). Applications of operant conditioning procedures to the behavior problems of an autistic child. *Behavior Research and Therapy, 1,* 305–312. **756**

Wolfe, J. B. (1936). Effectiveness of token-rewards for chimpanzees. *Comparative Psychology Monographs, 12* (Whole No. 60). **227, 300**

Wolff, C. (1971). *Love between women.* New York: Harper & Row. **403**

Wolman, B. B. (1977). *Handbook of para-*

psychology. New York: Van Nostrand Reinhold. **168**

Wolpe, J. (1973). *The practice of behavior therapy* (2nd ed.). New York: Pergamon. **634, 760**

Wolpe, J., & Rachman, S. J. (1960). Psychoanalytic "evidence": a critique based on Freud's case of Little Hans. *Journal of Nervous and Mental Diseases, 131,* 135–147. **34**

Woods, P. J. (1976). (Ed.). *Career opportunities for psychologists: Expanding and emerging areas.* Washington, DC: American Psychological Association. **26**

Woolfolk, R. L. (1975). Psychophysiological correlates of meditation. *Archives of General Psychiatry, 32,* 1326–1333. **133**

World Health Organization. (1948). *Manual of the International Statistical Classification of Diseases, Injuries, and Causes of Death* (6th rev.). Geneva: Author. **665**

Wurtman, R. J. (1982). Nutrients that modify brain function. *Scientific American,* pp. 50–59. **132**

Wurtman, R. J., & Fernstrom, J. D. (1974). Nutrition and the brain. In F. O. Schmitt & F. G. Worden (Eds.) *The Neurosciences: Third study program.* Cambridge, MA: M.I.T. Press. **126**

Wyer, R. S. (1966). Effects of incentive to perform well, group attraction and group acceptance on conformity in a judgmental task. *Journal of Personality and Social Psychology, 4,* 21–27. **542**

Wylie, R. C. (1974, 1979). *The self-concept* (Vols. 1 & 2). Lincoln: University of Nebraska Press. **561**

Yarrow, L. J. (1964). Separation from parents during early childhood. In M. L. Hoffman & L. W. Hoffman (Eds.), *Review of child development research* (Vol. 1). New York: Russell Sage Foundation. **480**

Yerkes, R. M., & Learned, B. W. (1925). *Chimpanzee intelligence and its vocal expression.* Baltimore, MD: Williams & Wilkins. **70**

Yonas, A., Cleaves, W., & Pettersen, L. (1978). Development of sensitivity to pictorial depth. *Science, 200,* 77–79. **430**

Young, L. (1964). *Wednesday's children: A study of child neglect and abuse.* New York: McGraw-Hill. **486**

Yussen, S. R., & Santrock, J. W. (1982). *Child development* (2nd ed.). Dubuque, IA: Wm. C. Brown. **458**

Zajonc, R. B. (1965). Social facilitation. *Science, 149,* 269–274. **525**

Zajonc, R. B. (1968). Attitudinal effects of mere exposure. *Journal of Personality and Social Psychology Monogram Supplement, 9*(2, Part 2), 2–27. **554**

Zajonc, R. B. (1976). Family configuration and intelligence. *Science, 192,* 227–236. **642**

Zajonc, R. B. (1980). Cognition and social cognition: A historical perspective. In L. Festinger (Ed.), *Retrospections on social psychology.* New York: Oxford University Press. **526**

Zajonc, R. B. (1980). Feeling and thinking: Preferences need no inferences. *American Psychologist, 35,* 151–175. **341**

Zajonc, R. B. (1984). On the primacy of affect. *American Psychologist, 39,* 117–123. **341–342**

Zajonc, R. B. (1986). The decline and rise of scholastic aptitude scores: A prediction derived from the confluence model. *American Psychologist, 41,* 862–867. **643**

Zajonc, R. B., Heigartner, A., & Herman, E. M. (1969). Social enhancement and impairment of performance in the cockroach. *Journal of Personality and Social Psychology, 13,* 83–92. **526**

Zeiss, R. A., & Zeiss, A. M. (1979, April). *The role of sexual behavior in the post-divorce adjustment process.* Paper presented at the annual meeting of the Western Psychological Association, San Diego, CA. **368**

Zelazo, P. R., Zelazo, N. A., & Kolb, S. (1972). "Walking" in the newborn. *Science, 176,* 314–415. **419**

Zelnik, M. (1979). Sex education and knowledge of pregnancy risk among U.S. teenage women. *Family Planning Perspectives, 11,* 355–357. **379**

Zigler, E., & Butterfield, E. C. (1968). Motivational aspects of changes in IQ test performance of culturally deprived nursery school children. *Child Development, 39,* 1–14. **651**

Zigler, E. F., & Phillips, L. (1961). Psychiatric diagnosis and symptomatology. *Journal of Abnormal and Social Psychology, 63,* 69–75. **720, 721**

Zillman, D. (1971). Excitation transfer in communication-mediated aggressive behavior. *Journal of Experimental Social Psychology, 7,* 419–434. **385**

Zimbardo, P. G. (1970). The human choice: Individuation, reason and order versus deindividuation, impulse and chaos. In W. J. Arnold & D. Levine (Eds.), *Nebraska symposium on motivation.* Lincoln: University of Nebraska Press. **530, 532**

Zimbardo, P. G., Ebbensen, E. B., & Maslach, C. (1977). *Influencing attitudes and changing behavior.* Reading, MA: Addison-Wesley. **561**

Zimbardo, P. G., Hane, C., Banks, W. C., & Jaffe, D. A. (1973, April 8). Pirandellian prison: The mind is a formidable jailer. *The New York Times Magazine,* pp. 38–60. **547**

Zubek, J. P. (Ed.). (1969). *Sensory deprivation.* New York: Appleton-Century-Crofts. **301**

Zucker, S. H., & Altman, R. (1973). An on-the-job training program for adolescent trainable retardates. *Training School Bulletin, 70,* 106–110. **646**

Zuckerman, M. (1978). The search for high sensation. *Psychology Today,* pp. 30–46, 96–99. **312**

Copyrights and Acknowledgments

and Illustration Credits

TABLES, BOXES, AND TEXT

Chapter 1

Table 1-1 Adapted from Endler, N. S., Rushton, J. P., and Roediger, H. L., III (1978). Productivity and scholarly impact (citations) of British, Canadian, and U.S. departments of psychology (1975). *American Psychologist*, Table 2, p. 1064. Copyright by the American Psychological Association. Reprinted by permission of the publisher. **Box 1-7** *American Psychologist*, Vol. 36, 1981. Copyright by the American Psychological Association. Reprinted by permission of the publisher.

Chapter 2

Table 2-5 After Plomin, R., and DeFries, J. C. (1980). Genetics and intelligence: Recent data. *Intelligence, 4*, 15-24.

Chapter 4

Table 4-2 Goldstein, E. B. (1984). *Sensation and perception* (2nd ed., p. 52, Table 2.1). Belmont, CA: Wadsworth. Reprinted by permission.

Chapter 5

Table 5-1 Ellis, H. C. (1978). *Fundamentals of human learning, memory and cognition* (2nd ed., p. 19). Dubuque, IA: Wm. C. Brown. Reprinted by permission.

Chapter 6

Table 6-3 Based on material reported in Brown, R., and McNeill, D. (1966). The "tip of the tongue" phenomenon. *Journal of Verbal Learning and Verbal Behavior, 5*, 325-37. Reprinted by permission of Academic Press and the authors. **Table 6-4** Baddeley, A. (1982). *Memory: A user's guide* (p. 96). New York: Macmillan. **Box 6-5** Doyle, C. A. (1953). The Sign of Four. In *The Complete Sherlock Holmes*. New York: Doubleday. Copyright 1953. **Table 6-8** Based on material reported in Luchins, A. (1942). Mechanization in problem solving. *Psychological Monographs, 54* (Whole No. 248). Copyright by the American Psychological Association. Reprinted by permission of the publisher. **Table 6-9** Bourne, L. E., Dominowski, R. L., and Loftus, E. F. (1979). *Cognitive processes*. Englewood Cliffs, NJ: Prentice-Hall. Reprinted by permission.

Chapter 7

Table 7-2 Adapted from Franken, R. E. (1982). *Human motivation* (pp. 136-41). Belmont, CA: Brooks/Cole. Reprinted by permission. **Table 7-3** Adapted from Plutchik, R. (1980). *Emotion: A psycho-evolutionary synthesis*. New York: Harper & Row.

Chapter 8

Table 8-1 Mahoney, M. J. (1980). *Abnormal psychology: Perspectives on human variance*. Abridged from Table 15-3, Some Common Myths about Sexuality (pp. 406-40). Copyright © 1980 by Michael J. Mahoney. Reprinted by permission of Harper & Row, Publishers, Inc. **Table 8-3** Adapted from Barash, D. P. *Sociobiology and behavior* (2nd ed.). Reprinted by permission of the publisher from Table 12.1, p. 274. Copyright 1982 by Elsevier Science Publishing, Co., Inc. **Box 8-3** Sex-orgasm questionnaire from *Perspectives in Human Sexuality* by Proctor, Wagner, and Butler. Copyright 1974 by Human Sciences Press, Inc. Re-

Seraut: *Invitation to The Sideshow/La Parade*, The Metropolitan Museum of Art, bequest of Stephen C. Clark, 1960. **Color Plate X**: (top) Jasper Johns, *Target*, published by Universal Limited Art Editions, Inc. (bottom) from *Sensation and perception*, Second Edition, by Stanley Coren, et al. Copyright © 1984 by Harcourt Brace Jovanovich, Inc. Reprinted by permission of the publisher. **Color Plate XI**: (top) from *Interaction of color* by Josef Albers, plate VI-3. Copyright © by Yale University Press. Transparency courtesy of The Josef Albers Foundation. (bottom) from *An Introduction to Color* by R. M. Evans, 1948, New York, John Wiley & Sons, Inc. Reprinted by permission of the publisher. **Color Plate XII**: Courtesy of the North Carolina Travel and Tourism Division.

FIGURES

Chapter 1

1-2 Copyright 1985 by the American Psychological Association. Reprinted by permission of the publisher. **1-3** Copyright 1985 by the American Psychological Association. Adapted by permission of the publisher and the authors. **1-4** (bottom) © M. C. Escher Heirs, c/o Cordon Art BV, Baarn, Holland. **1-5** Rorschach, H.: *Psychodiagnostics.* © 1921 by Verlag Hans Huber, Bern (renewed 1948).

Chapter 2

2-2 From *Biology: The study of life* by Ruth Bernstein and Stephen Bernstein, copyright © 1982 by Harcourt Brace Jovanovich, Inc. Reproduced by permission of the publisher. **2-3** © Patricia Caulfield. **2-4** Reprinted by permission of the publisher from *Sociobiology and behavior*, 2/e, by D. P. Barash, p. 149. Copyright 1982 by Elsevier Science Publishing Co. **2-5** From "The Evolution of Man" by Sherwood L. Washburn. Copyright © 1978 by Scientific American, Inc. All rights reserved. **2-6** Adapted from N. Tinbergen, *The study of instinct*, 1951, Oxford University Press and from *Biology: The study of life* by Ruth Bernstein and Stephen Bernstein, copyright © 1982 by Harcourt Brace Jovanovich, Inc. Reprinted by permission of the publisher. **2-7** (left) Courtesy of Baron H. van La-

wick. (right) AP/Wide World Photos. **2-9** Reprinted by permission of the publisher from *Sociobiology and behavior*, 2/e, by D. P. Barash, p. 30. Copyright 1982 by Elsevier Science Publishing Co., Inc.

Chapter 3

3-1 From W. Penfield, *The excitable cortex in conscious man*, 1958. Courtesy of Charles C Thomas, Publisher, Springfield, Illinois. **3-3** © 1984 Martin M. Rotker/Taurus Photos. **3-4** © Copyright 1984 by the American Association for the Advancement of Science. **3-5a** Adapted from Stanley L. Weinberg, *Biology: An inquiry into the nature of life.* © Copyright 1974 by Allyn and Bacon, Inc. Used with permission. And from *Biology: The study of life* by Ruth Bernstein and Stephen Bernstein, copyright © 1982 by Harcourt Brace Jovanovich, Inc. Reprinted by permission of the publisher. **3-5b** Adapted from *Elements of biological science*, Second Edition, by William Keeton, by permission of W. W. Norton and Company, Inc., © Copyright 1973, 1972, 1969, 1967 by W .W. Norton and Company, Inc. and from *Biology: The study of life* by Ruth Bernstein and Stephen Bernstein, copyright © 1982 by Harcourt Brace Jovanovich, Inc. Reprinted by permission of the publisher. **3-5c** Adapted from R. E. Snodgrass: *Anatomy of the honey bee.* Copyright © 1956 by Cornell University. Used by permission of the publisher, Cornell University Press, and from *Biology: The study of life* by Ruth Bernstein and Stephen Bernstein, copyright © 1982 by Harcourt Brace Jovanovich, Inc. Reprinted by permission of the publisher. **3-5d** Adapted from A. J. Vander, et al., *Human physiology: The mechanisms of body functions*, 1970, Second Edition, Fig. 16-32, p. 524, McGraw-Hill. Reproduced with permission of McGraw-Hill Book Co., and from *Biology: The study of life* by Ruth Bernstein and Stephen Bernstein, copyright © 1982 by Harcourt Brace Jovanovich, Inc. Reprinted by permission of the publisher. **3-8** Adapted from *Life: An introduction to biology,* Second Edition, by George Gaylond Simpson and William S. Beck, copyright © 1965 by Harcourt Brace Jovanovich, Inc. Reproduced by permission of the publisher, and from *Biology: The study*

of life by Ruth Bernstein and Stephen Bernstein, copyright © 1982 by Harcourt Brace Jovanovich, Inc. Reproduced by permission of the publisher. **3-9** From "Casts of fossil hominid brains" by Ralph L. Holloway. Copyright © July 1974 by Scientific American, Inc. All rights reserved, and from *Biology: The study of life* by Ruth Bernstein and Stephen Bernstein, copyright © 1982 by Harcourt Brace Jovanovich, Inc. Reprinted by permission of the publisher. **3-10** From "The development of the brain" by W. M. Cowan. Copyright © 1979 by Scientific American, Inc. All rights reserved. **3-11** Adapted from Stephens and North, *Biology.* Copyright © 1974 by John Wiley & Sons, Inc. Reprinted by permission of John Wiley & Sons, Inc., and from *Biology: The study of life* by Ruth Bernstein and Stephen Bernstein, copyright © 1982 by Harcourt Brace Jovanovich, Inc. Reprinted by permission of the publisher. **3-13** From "Brain function and blood flow" by Nick A. Lassen, David H. Ingvar and Erik Shinhoj. Copyright © 1978 by Scientific American, Inc. All rights reserved. From *Biology: The study of life* by Ruth Bernstein and Stephen Bernstein, copyright © 1982 by Harcourt Brace Jovanovich, Inc. Reprinted by permission of the publisher. **3-14** Adapted with permission of Macmillan Publishing Company from *The cerebral cortex of man* by Wilder Penfield and Theodore Rasmussen. Copyright 1950 by Macmillan Publishing Company, renewed 1978 by Theodore Rasmussen, and from *Biology: The study of life* by Ruth Bernstein and Stephen Bernstein, copyright © 1982 by Harcourt Brace Jovanovich, Inc. Reprinted by permission of the publisher. **3-15** Figure 204 from *Biology*, Second Edition, by Richard A. Goldsby. Copyright © 1979 by Harper & Row, Publishers, Inc. Reprinted by permission of Harper & Row, Publishers, Inc., and from *Biology: The study of life* by Ruth Bernstein and Stephen Bernstein, copyright © 1982 by Harcourt Brace Jovanovich, Inc. Reprinted by permission of the publishers. **3-16** From "Brain changes in response to experience" by Mark R. Rosenweig, Edward L. Bennett, and Marian C. Diamond. Copyright © 1972 by Scientific American, Inc. All rights reserved. **3-17** Alan R. Liss, Inc., Publisher and copyright holder. **3-18** From "Nerve cells and behavior" by Eric R. Kandel. Copyright © 1970 by Scientific American, Inc. All rights reserved. **3-19** Adapted from *Psychology: An introduction*, Brief Edition by P. Mussen and M. Rosenweig. Copyright © 1979 by D. C. Health and Company. Reprinted by permission of the publisher. From *Biology: The study of life* by Ruth Bernstein and Stephen Bernstein, copyright © 1982 by Harcourt Brace Jovanovich, Inc. Reprinted by permission of the publisher.

Chapter 4

4-1 Adapted from Neil R. Carlson, *Physiology of behavior*, Third Edition. Copyright © 1986 by Allyn and Bacon, Inc. Used with permission. From *Biology: The study of life* by Ruth Bernstein and Stephen Bernstein, copyright © 1982 by Harcourt Brace Jovanovich, Inc. Reprinted by permission of the publisher. **4-2** From *Fundamentals of hearing: An introduction*, 2/e, by William A. Yost and Donald W. Nielsen. Copyright © 1985 by CBS College Publishing. Reprinted by permission of CBS College Publishing. **4-3** Adapted by permission of the publisher, University of Illinois Press. **4-4** Figure 20-11 from *Biology*, Second Edition, by Richard A. Goldsby. Copyright © 1979 by Harper & Row, Publishers, Inc., Reprinted by permission of Harper & Row, Publishers, Inc. And from *Biology: The study of life* by Ruth Bernstein and Stephen Bernstein, Copyright © 1982 by Harcourt Brace Jovanovich, Inc. Reprinted by permission of the publisher. **4-5** Reprinted from *Human factors in undersea warfare*, 1949, with permission of the National Academy of Sciences, Washington, D.C. **4-7** Adapted from *Health*, Second Edition, by Benjamin A. Kogan, copyright © 1974 by Harcourt Brace Jovanovich, Inc. Reprinted by permission of the publisher. From *Biology: The study of life* by Ruth Bernstein and Stephen Bernstein, copyright © 1982 by Harcourt Brace Jovanovich, Inc. Reprinted by permission of the publisher. **4-8a** Adapted from *Elements of biological science*, 2nd Edition, by William T. Keeton and Carol Hardy McFadden. Illustrated by Paula de Santo Bensadoun. Copyright © 1973 by W. W. Norton and Company, Inc., and from *Biology: The study of life* by Ruth Bernstein and Stephen Bernstein, copyright © 1982 by Harcourt Brace Jovanovich, Inc. Reprinted by permission of the publisher. **4-8b** Adapted from A. J. Vander, et al., 1970, *Human physiology*, McGraw-Hill, and from *Biology: The study of life* by Ruth Bernstein and Stephen Bernstein, copyright © 1982 by Harcourt Brace Jovanovich, Inc. Reprinted by permission of the publisher. **4-10** Adapted from *Sensation and perception: An integrated approach*, by R. H. Schiffmann. Copyright © 1976 by John Wiley & Sons, Inc. Reprinted by permission of John Wiley & Sons, Inc. **4-18**, **4-19**, **4-21**, **4-23**, **4-24**, **4-34** Adapted with permission of Macmillan Publishing Company from *An introduction to perception* by Irwin Rock. Copyright © 1975 by Irwin Rock. **4-20** Courtesy of KC Publications. **4-26** Kaiser Porcelain Ltd., London, England. **4-32** J. A. Fraser, 1908, "A new visual illusion of direction," *British Journal of Psychology, 2*, 307–320. **4-35**, **4-36** From "Subjective contours" by Gaetano Kaniza. Copyright © 1976 by Scientific American, Inc. All rights reserved. **4-38** Gregory, R. L., 1971, *The intelligent eye*, London, Weidenfeld and Nicolson, 57.

Chapter 5

5-1 V. G. Dethier/Eliot Stellar, *Animal behavior*, 3/e, © 1970, p. 91. Adapted by permission of Prentice-Hall, Inc., Englewood Cliffs, New Jersey. **5-2** © Barbara Rios/Photo Researchers. **5-3** The Bettmann Archive, Inc. **5-9** From *Psychology*, 2nd Edition, by A. B. Crider, et al. Copyright © 1986 by Scott, Foresman and Company. Reprinted by permission. **5-16** Reprinted by permission from *Psychology: Science and application* by M. G. McGee and D. W. Wilson. Copyright © 1984 by West Publishing Company. All rights reserved. **5-17** Reprinted with permission from Howard, S. R., Figlerski, R. W. and O'Brien, R. M., 1982, "The performance of major league baseball pitchers on long-term guarantee contracts," in R. M. O'Brien, A. M. Dickinson and M. P. Rosow (eds.) *Industrial behavior modification: A management handbook*, Elmsford, NY: Pergamon Press, Ltd. **5-18** Copyright 1971 by the Society for the Experimental Analysis of Behavior, Inc. **5-19** Copyright 1972 by the Society for the Experimental Analysis of Behavior, Inc. **5-26** © Jim Pozarik/Gamma-Liaison.

Chapter 6

6-1 From "The control of short-term memory" by Richard C. Atkinson and Richard M. Shiffrin. Copyright © 1971 by Scientific American, Inc. All rights reserved. **6-5** Copyright 1961 by the American Psychological Association. Adapted by permission of the author. **6-8** From *Cognitive psychology and its implications* by John R. Anderson. Copyright © 1980 W. H. Freeman and Company. Reprinted by permission. **6-9** Copyright 1977 by the American Psychological Association. Adapted by permission of the authors. **6-12** Copyright 1945 by the American Psychological Association. Adapted by permission of the author.

Chapter 7

7-1 From "The pathology of boredom" by W. Heron. Copyright © 1957 by Scientific American, Inc. All rights reserved. **7-3** Data for diagram based on Hierarchy of Needs in *Motivation and personality*, 2nd Edition, by Abraham H. Maslow. Copyright © 1970 by Abraham H. Maslow. Reprinted by permission of Harper & Row, Publishers, Inc. **7-4** Photo from Neal E. Miller. **7-5a** Copyright 1968 by the American Psychological Association. Adapted by permission of the author. **7-5b** Copyright 1968 by the American Psychological Association. Adapted by permission of the author. **7-6** Copyright © American Journal of Clinical Nutrition, American Society for Clinical Nutrition. **7-7** Copyright 1966 by the American Psychological Association. Adapted by permission of the author. **7-8** (top) © Robin Risque (bottom) Harlow Primate Laboratory, University of Wisconsin. **7-11** Adapted from Kimball, *Biology*, © 1974, Addison-Wesley, Reading, MA, Figure 27.17. Reprinted with permission. **7-13** Copyright © 1962, The Society for Psychophysiological Research. Reprinted with permission of the author and the publishers from Hohman, G. W., 1962, "Some effects of spinal cord lesions on experienced emotional feelings," *Psychophysiology, 3*, 143–156. **7-14** Photos © Ed Gallob; experimental data courtesy of Dr. Silvan Tomkins and P. Ekman, *Darwin and facial* *expression*, Academic Press, 1973. **7-15** Fig. 11.3 (p. 157) in *Emotion: A psychoevolutionary synthesis* by Robert Plutchik. Copyright © 1980 by Individual Dynamics, Inc. Reprinted by permission of Harper & Row, Publishers, Inc. **7-16** Fig. 11.5 (p. 164) in *Emotion: A psychoevolutionary synthesis* by Robert Plutchik. Copyright © 1980 by Individual Dynamics, Inc. Reprinted by permission of Harper & Row, Publishers, Inc. **7-17** Reprinted from *Psychology Today* magazine. Copyright © 1980 American Psychological Association. **7-19** Copyright 1985 by the American Psychological Association. Adapted by permission of the author. **7-20** Copyright 1985 by the American Psychological Association. Adapted by permission of the author.

Chapter 8

8-1 From *Biology: The study of life* by Ruth Bernstein and Stephen Bernstein, copyright © 1982 by Harcourt Brace Jovanovich, Inc. Reprinted by permission of the publisher. **8-4, 8-5** Reprinted from *Ethnographic atlas* by George Peter Murdock by permission of the University of Pittsburgh Press. © 1967 by the University of Pittsburgh Press. **8-6, 8-7, 8-8, 8-9, 8-10** Reprinted by permission of the Kinsey Institute for Research in Sex, Gender and Reproduction, Inc. **8-11** Reproduced by Special Permission of *Playboy* magazine: "Sexual Behavior in the 1970's, Part V: Masturbation," by Morton Hunt. Copyright © 1974 by PLAYBOY; From *Sexual behavior in the human male* by A. C. Kinsey, W. B. Pomeroy and C. E. Martin, Saunders, 1948, 141 and *Sexual behavior in the human female* by A. C. Kinsey, C. E. Martin and P. H. Gebhard, Saunders, 1953, 502. Reprinted by permission of the Kinsey Institute for Research in Sex, Gender and Reproduction, Inc. **8-12** Reprinted from *Psychology Today* magazine, Copyright © 1983 American Psychological Association. **8-13** Reprinted by permission of *The Journal of Sex Research*, a publication of the Society for the Scientific Study of Sex. **8-15** From *Biology: The study of life* by Ruth Bernstein and Stephen Bernstein, copyright © 1982 by Harcourt Brace Jovanovich, Inc. Reprinted by permission of the publisher. **8-20** Reprinted by permission of *The Journal of Sex Research*, a

publication of the Society for the Scientific Study of Sex. **8-21** Reprinted by permission of the Kinsey Institute for Research in Sex, Gender and Reproduction, Inc. **8-22** Copyright 1980 by the American Psychological Association. Adapted by permission of the author. **8-23** © *Rape in marriage* by Diana E. H. Russell, New York, Macmillan, 1982. Reprinted by permission.

Chapter 9

9-1 From *Human development* by Kurt W. Fischer and Arlyne Lazerson. Copyright © 1984. Reprinted by permission of W. H. Freeman and Company. **9-2** From "External human fertilization" by C. Grobstein. Copyright © 1979 by Scientific American, Inc. All rights reserved. **9-3** Fig. 12-2 from *The psychology of being human*, Third Edition, by Zick Rubin and Elton B. McNeil. Copyright © 1981 by Zick Rubin. Reprinted by permission of Harper & Row, Publishers, Inc. **9-4** Copyright 1972 by the American Association for the Advancement of Science. **9-5** From *Human development* by Kurt W. Fischer and Arlyne Lazerson. Copyright © 1984. Reprinted by permission of W. H. Freeman and Company. **9-6** E. P. Sarafino and J. W. Armstrong, 1980, *Child and adolescent development*, Glenview, IL: Scott, Foresman and Company. Copyright © E. P. Sarafino. **9-7** From "Getting old" by Alexander Leaf. Copyright © 1973 by Scientific American, Inc. All rights reserved. From *Biology: The study of life* by Ruth Bernstein and Stephen Bernstein, copyright © 1982 by Harcourt Brace Jovanovich, Inc. Reprinted by permission of the publisher. **9-8** Copyright 1984, *U.S. News and World Report*. Reprinted from issue of July 2, 1984. **9-9** From "The origin of form perception" by R. L. Fantz. Copyright 1961 by Scientific American, Inc. All rights reserved. Drawing adapted from photo by David Linton. R. L. Fantz, "Pattern vision in newborn infants," *Science, 140*, 296–97, 19 April 1963. Copyright 1963 by American Association for the Advancement of Science. **9-10** Copyright 1974 and 1977 by the American Psychological Association. Adapted by permission of the author. **9-11** From *The psychology of visual perception*, 2/e, by R. M. Heber and M. Hershenson. Copyright © 1980

by Holt, Rinehart and Winston, Inc. Reprinted by permission of CBS College Publishing. **9-12** Adapted from photo by William Vandivert, *Scientific American*, 1960, 202(4), 80–92. **9-14** From *Child development* by A. Clarke-Stewart, S. Friedman and J. Koch. Copyright © 1985 by John Wiley & Sons, Inc. Reprinted by permission of John Wiley & Sons, Inc. **9-15** From Howard Gardner, *Developmental psychology: An introduction*, 4.6. Copyright © 1978 by Little, Brown and Company, Inc.. Adapted by permission. **9-16** From *Human development* by Kurt W. Fischer and Arlyne Lazerson. Copyright © 1984. Reprinted by permission of W. H. Freeman and Company. **9-18** From *Theories of development* by Jonas Langer. Copyright © 1969 by Holt, Rinehart and Winston, Inc. Reprinted by permission of CBS College Publishing. **9-19** From *Human development* by Kurt W. Fischer and Arlyne Lazerson. Copyright © 1984. Reprinted by permission of W. H. Freeman and Company. **9-20** From *Psychology* by David Hothersall. Copyright © 1985 by Scott, Foresman and Company. Reprinted by permission.

Chapter 10

10-1 J. Garbarino, "Sociocultural risk: Dangers to competence." In Kipp and Krakow, *The child*, © 1982, Addison-Wesley Publishing Company, Inc. Reading, MA, p. 648, Fig. 12.1. Reprinted with permission. **10-2** Copyright 1959 by the American Association for the Advancement of Science. **10-3** From C. Tomlinson-Keasey, *Child development*, Homewood, IL: The Dorsey Press, copyright © 1985. **10-4** Fig. 4-7 from *Essentials of child development and personality* by Paul Henry Mussen, John Janeway Conger, Jerome Kagan. Copyright © 1980 by Paul Henry Mussen, John Janeway Conger, Jerome Kagan. Reprinted by permission of Harper & Row, Publishers, Inc. **10-6** Copyright 1975 by the American Psychological Association. Adapted by permission of the authors. **10-9** © The Society for Research in Child Development, Inc. **10-10** From *Exploring child behavior*, 2/e, by Donald B. Helms and Jeffrey S. Turner. Copyright © 1976 by W. B. Saunders Company. Copyright © 1981 by CBS College Publishing. Reprinted by permission of CBS

PICTURES

Page 3 George Segal, *Bus riders*, Hirshhorn Museum and Sculpture Garden, Smithsonian Institution. Gift of Joseph H. Hirshhorn, 1966. **4** (left) New York Post photo by Robert Kalfus. (right) UPI/Bettmann News Photos. **14** The Bettmann Archive, Inc. **15** Photo by Ted Polumbaum. **17** The Bettmann Archive, Inc. **26** Copyright 1985 by the American Psychological Association. Adapted by permission of the publisher and authors. **27** Photograph by Edmund Engelman (Copyright: Edmund Engelman, New York). **39** © Mimi Forsyth/Monkmeyer. **41** © 1986 by Sidney Harris. **49** © Michele Ballard/EKM Nepenthe. **66-67** From *Biology: The study of life* by Ruth A. Bernstein and Stephen Bernstein, copyright © 1982 by Harcourt Brace Jovanovich, Inc. Reproduced by permission of the publisher. **71** (left) © Irven DeVore/Anthro-Photo. (right) Nina Leen, **LIFE** Magazine, © Time, Inc. **79** AP/Wide World Photos. **82** Dr. J. H. Tijo, National Institutes of Health. **86** © Jean-Pierre Laffont/Sygma. **91** Courtesy of the Harvard University Archives. **92** Thomas McAvoy, **LIFE** Magazine, © 1955, Time, Inc. **97** © Martin M. Rotker/Taurus Photos **119** © 1986 by Sidney Harris. **120** a) Reprinted with permission from *Neuropsychologia 9*, by R. D. Nebs and C. Sperry. Copyright 1971 Pergamon Press, Ltd. b) Illustration adapted from *The brain: The last frontier* by Richard Restak. Copyright © 1979 by Richard M. Restak, M.D. Reprinted by permission of Doubleday & Co., Inc. a) & b) From *Biology: The study of life* by Ruth Bernstein and Stephen Bernstein, copyright © 1982 by Harcourt Brace Jovanovich, Inc. Reprinted by permission of the publisher. **139** Copyright 1966 by the American Association for the Advance-

ment of Science. **145** Josef Albers, *Reverse and Obverse*, photo courtesy of Sidney Janis Gallery. **176** Adapted with permission of Macmillan Publishing from *An introduction to perception* by Irwin Rock. Copyright © 1975 by Irwin Rock. **177** (top) © Mike Chikiris. (bottom) From *Formation of cyclopean perception* by Bela Julesz, © 1971, University of Chicago Press. **185** Gregory, R. L., 1973, *Eye and brain*, 2/e, New York: McGraw-Hill, 55. **199** © Peter Menzel/Stock, Boston. **213** Vito Modigliani. **224** © Elizabeth Crews/Stock, Boston. **227** © J. R. Holland/Stock, Boston. **242** © Peter Vandermark/Stock, Boston. **247** © R. D. Ullmann/Taurus Photos. **249** © Robert Burroughs. **257** UPI/Bettmann News Photos. **287** Courtesy of Fidelity Electronics. **288** Courtesy of Hayden Software. **292** © 1985 Sam Gross. **297** © Paul Conklin. **308** © David Strickler/Monkmeyer. **314** © Jerry Irwin/Black Star. **321** (left) Albert Einstein College of Medicine of Yeshiva University. (right) The Bettmann Archive, Inc. **328** © Sybil Shelton/Monkmeyer; line drawing adapted from David C. Raskin, University of Utah. **332** © Z. Leszczynski/Animals, Animals. **349** © Mike Yamashta/Woodfin Camp. **356** Courtesy of R. D. Nadler, Yerkes Regional Primate Research Center of Emory University. **359** © Melanie Kaestner/Zephyr Pictures. **377** © Alon Reininger/Contact Stock Images. **399** (left) Derek Bayes, **LIFE** Magazine, © Time, Inc. (right) Henry Grossman/People Weekly, © 1974 Time, Inc. **403** © Rick Kopstein/Monkmeyer. **413** © Nancy Durell McKenna/Photo Researchers. **414** (top) *Discover* Magazine, December 1984. (bottom) Black Star. **420** © Melanie Kaestner/Zephyr Pictures. **425** © Ken Karp. **446** © Yves De Braine/Black Star. **469** © Shirley Zeiberg/Taurus

Photos. **481** © Laimute E. Drukis/Taurus Photos. **482** © Mimi Forsyth/Monkmeyer. **488** Stock, Boston. **491** © Melanie Kaestner/Zephyr Pictures. **492** © George Zimbel/Monkmeyer. **502** © Shirley Zeiberg/Taurus Photos. **523** © Paul Conklin/Monkmeyer. **530** © Owen Franklin/Sygma. **548** Adapted from Figure 6, *Obedience to authority: An experimental view* by Stanley Milgram. Copyright © 1974 by Stanley Milgram. Reprinted by permission of Harper & Row Publishers, Inc. **579** © 1975 Reprinted by permission of *Better Homes and Gardens* and Henry R. Martin. **585** © Robert V. Eckert/EKM-Nepenthe. **631** Henry A. Murray, *Thematic Apperception Test*, Cambridge, Harvard University Press. Copyright 1943 by the President and Fellows of Harvard College. Copyright 1971 by Henry A. Murray. Reprinted by permission. **637** © Mimi Forsyth/Monkmeyer. **639** © Judith R. Sedwick/The Picture Cube. **655** © David M. Grossman/Photo Researchers. **657** (top) Neg # 31593 (Photo by J. O. Wheelock), Courtesy, Department of Library Services, American Museum of Natural History. (bottom) National Library of Medicine. **678** Derek Bayes, **LIFE** Magazine, © Time, Inc. **682** © Elinor S. Beckwith/Taurus Photos. **688** Courtesy of Edna A. Morlock and Sarah C. Morlock. **703** (bottom) Adapted from drawing by Jim Sharpe reproduced in *Psychology Today*, May 1986, 29. **710** UPI/Bettmann News Photos. **711** AP/Wide World Photos. **729** © Bohdan Hrynewych/Stock, Boston. **731** The Bettmann Archive/BBC Hulton. **735** Cartoon by James Thurber, *The art in cartooning*, edited by E. Fischer, M. Gerberg and R. Wolin for The Cartoonists Guild. Copyright 1975 Cartoonists Guild Inc. **740** © Will McIntyre/Photo Researchers. **780** © Jonathan Perry/Photo Reseachers.

NAME INDEX

Emmerich, W. 499
Empedocles, 665
Endler, N. S. 12, 613
Entingh, D. 131
Epstein, A. N. 304, 305
Epstein, C. J. 76
Epstein, L. H. 758
Epstein, S. 613
Ericsson, K. A. 254, 255
Erikson, E. H. 12, 450, 515–18, 520, 521, 586, 602–604, 615, 619, 620, 652
Ernst, G. W. 288
Ervin, F. R. 738, 739
Ervin-Tripp, S. 442
Estes, W. K. 229
Eurman, L. K. 673
Everett, G. M. 390
Eysenck, H. J. 12, 27, 313, 314, 586, 592–95, 597, 652, 654, 708, 752, 775, 776

F

Fagot, B. I. 495
Fairburn, C. G. 671
Fantz, R. L. 428
Farina, A. 722
Farkas, G. M. 388, 391
Farley, J. 130, 214
Faust, M. S. 422
Fazio, R. H. 565, 570, 571
Fechner, G. T. 8
Feigelman, W. 398
Feldman, H. 444
Feldman, M. P. 590
Feldman, N. S. 489
Feldman, S. 586
Feldman-Summers, S. 407, 408
Ferguson, N. B. L. 306
Fernstrom, J. D. 126
Ferris, C. B. 532
Festinger, L. 316, 524, 532, 565, 566, 569, 570, 572
Field, J. 429
Fields, J. M. 578
Figlerski, R. W. 221
Firestone, I. 316
Firkowska, A. 89
Fischer, K. W. 416, 443, 453, 459, 461
Fishbein, M. 552, 559, 563–65
Fisher, J. D. 332, 392
Fisher, L. J. 143
Fisher, S. 654
Fiske, S. T. 575, 576, 583, 592
Fitzgerald, H. E. 419
Flaherty, C. F. 203, 231, 245
Flavell, J. H. 459, 461, 467
Fleischman, P. R. 722, 723
Fleming, A. 661
Fletcher, G. J. O. 572
Fling, S. 501
Floderus-Myrhed, B. 595
Folstein, S. 674
Footlick, J. K. 713
Ford, C. S. 382, 392, 396, 411
Forsyth, D. R. 569

Fox, S. 559
Fozard, J. L. 425
Fraiberg, S. 475
Frank, J. D. 730, 773, 774
Frank, L. 629
Franken, R. E. 308, 309, 330
Frase, L. T. 271, 272
Frazier, A. 422
Freedman, J. L. 567
Freeling, N. R. 754
Freud, A. 25
Freud, S. 12, 14–16, 23, 25, 27, 33, 34, 134, 351, 352, 384, 450, 487, 492, 494, 495, 504, 505, 515, 529, 535, 586, 597–600, 602, 603, 605, 606, 608, 615, 617–20, 629, 633, 635, 652, 654, 655, 661, 662, 680, 704, 710, 717, 744–47, 749, 751, 764, 770, 782
Frieder, B. 132
Friedman, M. I. 305
Friedman, S. 433, 435
Friesen, W. V. 324, 326, 327, 334, 342
Frieze, I. H. 85
Fritsch, C. 101
Froming, W. J. 532
Fromm-Reichman, F. 692
Fuhr, R. 393
Fulcher, J. S. 334
Fulcher, R. 24
Furnham, A. 763

G

Gaertner, S. L. 534–36, 582
Gagne, R. M. 245
Gagnon, J. H. 393
Galen, 99, 374
Galleys, G. G. 493
Gallup, G. H. 379, 558
Galton, F. 10, 19, 72, 93, 620, 637
Gamble, E. A. M. C. 168
Gamboa, V. U. 233
Gandhi, 505, 510
Garbanno, J. 470
Garber, H. 88, 643
Garcia, J. 201, 234, 311–13
Gardner, B. T. 70
Gardner, H. 644, 653
Gardner, R. A. 70
Garfield, S. L. 777, 778, 784
Garfinkel, P. E. 673
Garmezy, N. 670
Garner, D. M. 673
Garske, J. P. 346
Gebhard, P. H. 363, 364, 371, 393, 396, 397
Geen, R. G. 531
Geer, J. 231
Geer, J. H. 393
Gelman, R. 456, 459, 461
Gerard, H. B. 542, 551
Gerbner, G. 501, 559
Gergen, K. J. 532, 542
Gergen, M. M. 532
Gerson, S. 734
Geschwind, N. 120

Gesell, A. 419
Gewirtz, J. C. 514
Giacalone, R. A. 568
Giambra, L. M. 425
Gianetto, R. M. 335
Giarrusso, R. P. 404, 405
Gibbons, F. 372
Gibbs, J. 507, 510, 511
Gibson, E. J. 430
Gibson, J. J. 166, 193–95, 197, 341
Gilbert, F. 423
Gill, T. 70
Gilligan, C. 512, 513
Gillin, J. C. 268
Gilmartin, K. 287
Ginsberg, H. 467
Girgus, J. S. 186
Glass, A. L. 284, 286
Glass, D. C. 204
Glass, G. V. 776, 777
Glass, L. L. 768
Glesener, R. 353
Glick, J. 489
Glickman, S. E. 319
Glickstein, M. 130
Godden, D. R. 267
Godow, A. G. 373
Goethals, G. R. 201, 211
Goffman, E. 12
Gogol, N. 658, 664
Golbus, M. S. 76
Gold, P. E. 214
Goldberg, L. R. 577
Goldenberg, H. 719
Goldenson, R. M. 298
Goldin-Meadow, S. 444
Goldsby, R. A. 121, 151
Goldschmid, M. L. 449
Goldstein, E. B. 157, 160, 197
Goldstein, G. W. 124
Goldstein, M. J. 696
Goleman, D. 669
Gonso, J. 489
Gonzalez, A. E. J. 570
Goodchilds, J. 404, 405
Goodman, J. 692
Goodman, M. J. 423
Goodnow, J. J. 665
Goodwin, D. W. 679
Gordon, R. M. 339
Gordon, W. J. 292, 293
Gosselin, C. 399
Gottesman, I. I. 74, 77, 688, 691
Gottman, J. M. 489, 490
Gough, H. G. 622, 624, 626
Gould, S. J. 655
Graham, J. A. 763
Graham, S. 368
Gray, J. A. 330
Green, R. 403, 404
Green, S. J. 361, 362, 400
Greenberg, B. S. 501, 559
Greenberg, R. P. 654
Greene, D. 571, 578
Gregory, R. L. 126, 151, 181, 183–86
Grey, W. 511

SUBJECT INDEX